Ray Wiggins

Visual C++® 6 Bible

Visual C++® 6 Bible

Richard C. Leinecker and Tom Archer
with
Kevin Smith
Lars Klander
Derrel Blain
Garrett Pease

IDG Books Worldwide, Inc.
An International Data Group Company

Foster City, CA ✦ Chicago, IL ✦ Indianapolis, IN ✦ New York, NY

Visual C++® 6 Bible

Published by
IDG Books Worldwide, Inc.
An International Data Group Company
919 E. Hillsdale Blvd., Suite 400
Foster City, CA 94404
www.idgbooks.com (IDG Books Worldwide Web site)

Library of Congress Catalog Card Number: 98-71862

ISBN: 0-7645-3228-6

Printed in the United States of America

10 9 8 7 6 5 4 3 2 1

1B/SR/QZ/ZY/FC

Distributed in the United States by IDG Books Worldwide, Inc.

Distributed by Macmillan Canada for Canada; by Transworld Publishers Limited in the United Kingdom; by IDG Norge Books for Norway; by IDG Sweden Books for Sweden; by Woodslane Pty. Ltd. for Australia; by Woodslane (NZ) Ltd. for New Zealand; by Addison Wesley Longman Singapore Pte Ltd. for Singapore, Malaysia, Thailand, Indonesia, and Korea; by Norma Comunicaciones S.A. for Colombia; by Intersoft for South Africa; by International Thomson Publishing for Germany, Austria, and Switzerland; by Toppan Company Ltd. for Japan; by Distribuidora Cuspide for Argentina; by Livraria Cultura for Brazil; by Ediciencia S.A. for Ecuador; by Ediciones ZETA S.C.R. Ltda. for Peru; by WS Computer Publishing Corporation, Inc., for the Philippines; by Unalis Corporation for Taiwan; by Contemporanea de Ediciones for Venezuela; by Computer Book & Magazine Store for Puerto Rico; by Express Computer Distributors for the Caribbean and West Indies. Authorized Sales Agent: Anthony Rudkin Associates for the Middle East and North Africa.

For general information on IDG Books Worldwide's books in the U.S., please call our Consumer Customer Service department at 800-762-2974. For reseller information, including discounts and premium sales, please call our Reseller Customer Service department at 800-434-3422.

For information on where to purchase IDG Books Worldwide's books outside the U.S., please contact our International Sales department at 650-655-3200 or fax 650-655-3297.

For information on foreign language translations, please contact our Foreign & Subsidiary Rights department at 650-655-3021 or fax 650-655-3281.

For sales inquiries and special prices for bulk quantities, please contact our Sales department at 650-655-3200 or write to the address above.

For information on using IDG Books Worldwide's books in the classroom or for ordering examination copies, please contact our Educational Sales department at 800-434-2086 or fax 317-596-5499.

For press review copies, author interviews, or other publicity information, please contact our Public Relations department at 650-655-3000 or fax 650-655-3299.

ABOUT IDG BOOKS WORLDWIDE

Welcome to the world of IDG Books Worldwide.

IDG Books Worldwide, Inc., is a subsidiary of International Data Group, the world's largest publisher of computer-related information and the leading global provider of information services on information technology. IDG was founded more than 25 years ago and now employs more than 8,500 people worldwide. IDG publishes more than 275 computer publications in over 75 countries (see listing below). More than 90 million people read one or more IDG publications each month.

Launched in 1990, IDG Books Worldwide is today the #1 publisher of best-selling computer books in the United States. We are proud to have received eight awards from the Computer Press Association in recognition of editorial excellence and three from *Computer Currents'* First Annual Readers' Choice Awards. Our best-selling *...For Dummies®* series has more than 50 million copies in print with translations in 38 languages. IDG Books Worldwide, through a joint venture with IDG's Hi-Tech Beijing, became the first U.S. publisher to publish a computer book in the People's Republic of China. In record time, IDG Books Worldwide has become the first choice for millions of readers around the world who want to learn how to better manage their businesses.

Our mission is simple: Every one of our books is designed to bring extra value and skill-building instructions to the reader. Our books are written by experts who understand and care about our readers. The knowledge base of our editorial staff comes from years of experience in publishing, education, and journalism — experience we use to produce books for the '90s. In short, we care about books, so we attract the best people. We devote special attention to details such as audience, interior design, use of icons, and illustrations. And because we use an efficient process of authoring, editing, and desktop publishing our books electronically, we can spend more time ensuring superior content and spend less time on the technicalities of making books.

You can count on our commitment to deliver high-quality books at competitive prices on topics you want to read about. At IDG Books Worldwide, we continue in the IDG tradition of delivering quality for more than 25 years. You'll find no better book on a subject than one from IDG Books Worldwide.

John Kilcullen
CEO
IDG Books Worldwide, Inc.

Steven Berkowitz
President and Publisher
IDG Books Worldwide, Inc.

Eighth Annual Computer Press Awards ≥1992

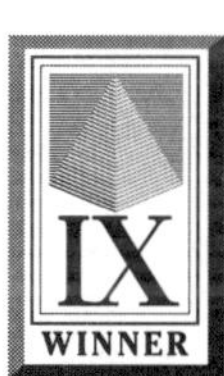

Ninth Annual Computer Press Awards ≥1993

Tenth Annual Computer Press Awards ≥1994

Eleventh Annual Computer Press Awards ≥1995

IDG Books Worldwide, Inc., is a subsidiary of International Data Group, the world's largest publisher of computer-related information and the leading global provider of information services on information technology. International Data Group publishes over 275 computer publications in over 75 countries. More than 90 million people read one or more International Data Group publications each month. International Data Group's publications include: **ARGENTINA:** Buyer's Guide, Computerworld Argentina, PC World Argentina; **AUSTRALIA:** Australian Macworld, Australian PC World, Australian Reseller News, Computerworld, IT Casebook, Network World, Publish, Webmaster; **AUSTRIA:** Computerwelt Österreich, Networks Austria, PC Tip Austria; **BANGLADESH:** PC World Bangladesh; **BELARUS:** PC World Belarus; **BELGIUM:** Data News; **BRAZIL:** Annuário de Informática, Computerworld, Connections, Macworld, PC Player, PC World, Publish, Reseller News, Supergamepower; **BULGARIA:** Computerworld Bulgaria, Network World Bulgaria, PC & MacWorld Bulgaria; **CANADA:** CIO Canada, Client/Server World, ComputerWorld Canada, InfoWorld Canada, NetworkWorld Canada, WebWorld; **CHILE:** Computerworld Chile, PC World Chile; **COLOMBIA:** Computerworld Colombia, PC World Colombia; **COSTA RICA:** PC World Centro America; **THE CZECH AND SLOVAK REPUBLICS:** Computerworld Czechoslovakia, Macworld Czech Republic, PC World Czechoslovakia; **DENMARK:** Communications World Danmark, Computerworld Danmark, Macworld Danmark, PC World Danmark, Techworld Denmark; **DOMINICAN REPUBLIC:** PC World Republica Dominicana; **ECUADOR:** PC World Ecuador; **EGYPT:** Computerworld Middle East, PC World Middle East; **EL SALVADOR:** PC World Centro America; **FINLAND:** MikroPC, Tietoverkko, Tietoviikko; **FRANCE:** Distributique, Hebdo, Info PC, Le Monde Informatique, Macworld, Reseaux & Telecoms, WebMaster France; **GERMANY:** Computer Partner, Computerwoche, Computerwoche Extra, Computerwoche FOCUS, Global Online, Macwelt, PC Welt; **GREECE:** Amiga Computing, GamePro Greece, Multimedia World; **GUATEMALA:** PC World Centro America; **HONDURAS:** PC World Centro America; **HONG KONG:** Computerworld Hong Kong, PC World Hong Kong, Publish in Asia; **HUNGARY:** ABCD CD-ROM, Computerworld Szamitastechnika, Internetto online Magazine, PC World Hungary, PC-X Magazin Hungary; **ICELAND:** Tolvuheimur PC World Island; **INDIA:** Information Communications World, Information Systems Computerworld, PC World India, Publish in Asia; **INDONESIA:** InfoKomputer PC World, Komputek Computerworld, Publish in Asia; **IRELAND:** ComputerScope, PC Live!; **ISRAEL:** Macworld Israel, People & Computers/Computerworld; **ITALY:** Computerworld Italia, Macworld Italia, Networking Italia, PC World Italia; **JAPAN:** DTP World, Macworld Japan, Nikkei Personal Computing, OS/2 World Japan, SunWorld Japan, Windows NT World, Windows World Japan; **KENYA:** PC World East African; **KOREA:** Hi-Tech Information, Macworld Korea, PC World Korea; **MACEDONIA:** PC World Macedonia; **MALAYSIA:** Computerworld Malaysia, PC World Malaysia, Publish in Asia; **MALTA:** PC World Malta; **MEXICO:** Computerworld Mexico, PC World Mexico; **MYANMAR:** PC World Myanmar; **NETHERLANDS:** Computer! Totaal, LAN Internetworking Magazine, LAN World Buyers Guide, Macworld Netherlands, Net, WebWereld; **NEW ZEALAND:** Absolute Beginners Guide and Plain & Simple Series, Computer Buyer, Computer Industry Directory, Computerworld New Zealand, MTB, Network World, PC World New Zealand; **NICARAGUA:** PC World Centro America; **NORWAY:** Computerworld Norge, CW Rapport, Datamagasinet, Financial Rapport, Kursguide Norge, Macworld Norge, Multimediaworld Norge, PC World Ekspress Norge, PC World Nettverk, PC World Norge, PC World ProduktGuide Norge; **PAKISTAN:** Computerworld Pakistan; **PANAMA:** PC World Panama; **PEOPLE'S REPUBLIC OF CHINA:** China Computer Users, China Computerworld, China InfoWorld, China Telecom World Weekly, Computer & Communication, Electronic Design China, Electronics Today, Electronics Weekly, Game Software, PC World China, Popular Computer Week, Software Weekly, Software World, Telecom World; **PERU:** Computerworld Peru, PC World Profesional Peru, PC World SoHo Peru; **PHILIPPINES:** Click!, Computerworld Philippines, PC World Philippines, Publish in Asia; **POLAND:** Computerworld Poland, Computerworld Special Report Poland, Cyber, Macworld Poland, Networld Poland, PC World Komputer; **PORTUGAL:** Cerebro/PC World, Computerworld/Correio Informático, Dealer World Portugal, Mac*In/PC*In Portugal, Multimedia World; **PUERTO RICO:** PC World Puerto Rico; **ROMANIA:** Computerworld Romania, PC World Romania, Telecom Romania; **RUSSIA:** Computerworld Russia, Mir PK, Publish, Seti; **SINGAPORE:** Computerworld Singapore, PC World Singapore, Publish in Asia; **SLOVENIA:** Monitor; **SOUTH AFRICA:** Computing SA, Network World SA, Software World SA; **SPAIN:** Communicaciones World España, Computerworld España, Dealer World España, Macworld España, PC World España; **SRI LANKA:** Infolink PC World; **SWEDEN:** CAP&Design, Computer Sweden, Corporate Computing Sweden, Internetworld Sweden, it.branschen, Macworld Sweden, MaxiData Sweden, MikroDatorn, Nätverk & Kommunikation, PC World Sweden, PCaktiv, Windows World Sweden; **SWITZERLAND:** Computerworld Schweiz, Macworld Schweiz, PCtip; **TAIWAN:** Computerworld Taiwan, Macworld Taiwan, NEW ViSiON/Publish, PC World Taiwan, Windows World Taiwan; **THAILAND:** Publish in Asia, Thai Computerworld; **TURKEY:** Computerworld Turkiye, Macworld Turkiye, Network World Turkiye, PC World Turkiye; **UKRAINE:** Computerworld Kiev, Multimedia World Ukraine, PC World Ukraine; **UNITED KINGDOM:** Acorn User UK, Amiga Action UK, Amiga Computing UK, Apple Talk UK, Computing, Macworld, Parents and Computers UK, PC Advisor, PC Home, PSX Pro, The WEB; **UNITED STATES:** Cable in the Classroom, CIO Magazine, Computerworld, DOS World, Federal Computer Week, GamePro Magazine, InfoWorld, I-Way, Macworld, Network World, PC Games, PC World, Publish, Video Event, THE WEB Magazine, and WebMaster; online webzines: JavaWorld, NetscapeWorld, and SunWorld Online; **URUGUAY:** InfoWorld Uruguay; **VENEZUELA:** Computerworld Venezuela, PC World Venezuela; and **VIETNAM:** PC World Vietnam. 5/7/98

Credits

Acquisitions Editor
John Osborn

Development Editors
Terry O'Donnell
Matthew E. Lusher

Technical Editor
Allen Wyatt

Copy Editors
Nancy Crumpton
Eric Hahn
Anne Friedman
Colleen Dowling

Project Coordinator
Tom Debolski

Quality Control Specialists
Mick Arellano
Mark Schumann

Graphics and Production Specialists
Mario Amador
Linda Marousek
Hector Mendoza
Mark Yim

Proofreader
Mary C. Barnack

Indexer
Liz Cunningham

Cover Design
Murder By Design

Cover Illustration
MDB, Design & Photography/ San Francisco

Cover Coordinator
Annie Romanowitz

About the Authors

Richard C. Leinecker is a professional software developer. He holds the position of Software Engineer with Landmark Community Interests, where he writes imaging software. His previous positions include Senior Programmer at MCI's Digital Imaging division, Director of Technology at IntraCorp, Inc., and Manager of Programming and Online Services at COMPUTE publications. He has had many of his software titles published, including Championship Chess, BridgeMaster, and Miami Vice.

Rick also wrote a regular column and dozens of feature articles and reviews for *COMPUTE* magazine. Many of *COMPUTE*'s software disk offerings were the result of his programming labors. He also brought *COMPUTE* and *OMNI* magazines online, creating two of the first online magazines. He is the author of *Visual J++ Bible* (IDG Books Worldwide, Inc.), *Visual C++ 5 Bible* (IDG Books Worldwide, Inc.), *Visual C++ 5 Power Toolkit* , and *Visual C++ Programmer's Reference.*

When Rick isn't writing books or software, he's playing with his three girls or roller-blading with his wife. He enjoys the position of musical director for the Rockingham County Theater Guild, and singing in a contemporary Christian group named Gentle Healer.

Tom Archer has almost 15 years of experience programming in several operating systems as well as with a multitude of languages. He has also worked on the development of two successful software products, Peachtree Software's Office Accounting, and IBM/World Book's Multimedia Encyclopedia. In addition to being a senior level Windows NT/VC++ consultant, Tom also writes books. He has co-authored two books on Visual C++ and one on Visual J++. Tom is currently working on a book on Windows NT system-level programming, which will be published in early 1999.

Kevin Smith has been involved in software development for over five years. His past projects include network automation, problem management systems, as well as the development of Internet-enabled applications. His current projects include finding new ways to extend Microsoft's Internet Information Server and designing database connectivity middleware for Java. Kevin resides in Greensboro, North Carolina, with his wife and two ferrets. When he isn't being a geek, Kevin enjoys cycling and racquetball.

Lars Klander is the author of numerous best selling books, including *Hacker Proof: The Ultimate Guide to Network Security* and *1001 Visual Basic Programmer's Tips.* A professional software developer, he lives in Las Vegas with his wife and their dogs and cats. He currently spends his days writing programs for the Nevada Power Company.

Derrel Blain has spent more than ten years programming and writing about computers.

To Jane, Judy, and Beth: three wonderful children. —Rick Leinecker

To my two wonderful sons, Peter and Christopher. You're the best kids a dad could wish for!—Tom Archer

To my parents, who taught me to love books and gave me my first computer. —Kevin Smith

To Chuck and Tracy Axelrod: Thanks for everything. I love you both very much. —Lars Klander

To my wife September for her continuing support. —Derrel Blain

Preface

The authors could be Visual C++ evangelists. We love the language and use it almost daily. Microsoft does a fantastic job of advancing the technology, and the Visual C++ community does an admirable job helping each other reach higher and higher goals.

To say that things have come a long way from the days of 16-bit Windows programming, when everyone used Visual C++ 1.5, would be a great understatement. Visual C++ 6 is an awesome tool; you can program and deploy some powerful applications without even trying.

What's in This Book

This book teaches you how to write killer Windows applications. It takes you from the basics of menus and mouse input, to advanced topics such as Internet programming and database connectivity. Each chapter teaches a subject, shows you how to use the techniques described, and then follows up with at least one demonstration program.

There's a CD-ROM included with the book that's worth its weight in gold. You won't have to type anything to try the techniques presented in the book. Just open the files on the CD-ROM, look at the code, and make any changes you want. Many third-party demo programs and libraries are also included. You'll have the chance to try some of the best add-ons available for Windows program development.

Whom This Book Is For

This book is for anyone who needs to learn about Windows programming. If you're new to Visual C++, or even new to Windows programming, you can learn the basics and master Windows programming fundamentals in no time.

Some programmers, even seasoned veterans, might feel they need a comprehensive manual on Visual C++ programming that covers all bases. While you may find plenty of programming books, you won't find many that cover the variety of topics discussed in this book. We've made an effort to give you in-depth coverage of valuable areas such as Internet programming and database connectivity — subjects that other books shy away from or deal with on a superficial level.

Others might be looking for help on a very specific topic. For instance, you might be responsible for writing a program that sends and receives files to and from an FTP server. If you don't know how to do this, just turn to Chapter 34 and learn all about it. You won't have to spend days poring through the online help and scouring the Internet for help on the subject. We teach you how to send and receive files via FTP in such a way that you learn to do it in less than an hour.

In short, almost everyone can benefit from this book. It's a comprehensive guide to writing Windows applications with Visual C++ that you won't want to miss.

How Things Are Organized

This book is divided into eight main parts:

- Part I is entitled "Visual C++ Fundamentals" and covers the basics of programming using Visual C++.
- Part II is called "Windows Programming Fundamentals" and talks about subjects such as windows, mouse handling, menus, and dialogs.
- Part III is entitled "Architecture" and teaches topics such as document/view architecture and printing.
- Part IV is called "Database Programming" and covers the all-important topic of database connectivity.
- Part V is named "Extending Applications" and talks about topics such as writing and using DLLs.
- Part VI is "Component Object Model Programming," which covers the relatively new subject of ActiveX controls.
- Part VII "Internet Programming" is where you learn how to write applications that communicate over the Internet.
- Part VIII is entitled "Advanced Visual Studio Use."

Almost every chapter follows the same basic format. A topic is presented along with some short code examples. In addition to the explanation of the subject, we give expert tips. These expert tips are the result of countless hours of struggle—hours we hope to save you. Summaries of many techniques are given for your convenience in what we call the Nutshell sections.

Most of the chapters have at least one demonstration program. The demo programs take the concepts presented in the chapter and tie them together so you can see how to use them in a real application. The entire program's source code is never included in the text—this would be a waste of paper. Instead, we pull out those portions of the program that best illustrate what's going on. The full demo programs are included on the CD-ROM.

Icons Used in This Book

Several icons are used throughout the book. They're intended to make it easier for you to identify key sections within the text. Familiarity with these icons can greatly enhance your ability to quickly find the information you need.

Nutshell

This icon identifies a short section in which a topic is summarized into a nutshell. Typically, these sections enumerate a procedure in a step-by-step manner.

Try This

This icon identifies a section in which it's recommended that you learn by creating a project similar to the one that's being described.

Expert Tip

This icon identifies a short section that contains an expert's advice on a particular programming issue. These tips are those that can't be found in the normal documentation. They're the result of experienced programmers who've run across difficult problems and found solutions. You benefit immeasurably from these expert tips.

Demo Program

This icon identifies a demonstration program. These programs are found throughout the book, and they illustrate the salient points of the current topic by showing you a complete program using the principles that have just been presented.

Class Wizard Addition

This icon identifies an element that was added with the ClassWizard. Below the icon you are shown the message (or virtual function) name, followed by the function that's created, and in which source code module it's placed.

Class Library

This icon identifies a section of the chapter that documents one of the classes we've included with the book to make it easier to program with certain technologies. The section lists the functions of the class and describes their uses.

Note

This icon identifies an interesting point you'll find worth remembering.

Tip

This icon points out a helpful hint or technique you'll find useful in your programming.

Contacting the Authors

All of the authors welcome your comments and feedback. We all carry a heavy load with full-time jobs and writing in the evenings, so it sometimes takes us a few days to respond. If we're on vacation, it might even be a couple of weeks before you get an answer from us! But in any case, we're eager to hear from you.

You can contact Richard C. Leinecker at `ivt-rcl@interpath`. His Web page addresses are `http://www.interpath.com/~phaedrus` and `http://www.infinitevision.net`. Tom Archer can be emailed at `tarcher@mindspring.com`. His Web page is `http://www.mindspring.com/~tarcher`.

Acknowledgments

Rick Leinecker: I would like to thank Matt Lusher above all others. He's the best development editor this side of the galaxy. I hope I can work with him on the rest of the books I write. I'd also like to thank John Osborn for help and support. Yes, those acquisitions editors make valuable contributions, even after the contract is signed.

Tom Archer: I wish to thank Rick Leinecker, who gave me my first shot at professional writing. Thanks Rick!

Kevin Smith: I'd like to thank, first and foremost, Rick Leinecker for inviting me to be a part of this book. Writing this book has been a wonderful learning experience. I'd also like to thank everyone at IDG Books for providing a prodding when needed and turning my prose into something fit for human consumption. Last, but certainly not least, I'd like to thank my wife for supporting me during the months it took to put this book together.

Lars Klander: Thanks to Matt Lusher, Allan Wyatt, and Terry O'Donnell, without whom my contribution to this book would be slightly harder to read and probably not make quite as much sense. Thanks also to Rick Leinecker, who is always a gentleman and has been a great pleasure to work with.

Derrel Blain: All programmers everywhere get a lot done using tools and concepts that others developed, then gave away. Thanks to all of you.

Contents at a Glance

Preface ix
Acknowledgments xiii

Part I: Visual C++ Fundamentals 1

Chapter 1 : Getting Started....3
Chapter 2: Taking Advantage of the Visual Studio IDE....17
Chapter 3: Debugging: When Your Applications Don't Work 29
Chapter 4: Improving Your Application's Performance 53
Chapter 5: Miscellaneous Tools....81

Part II: Windows Programming Fundamentals....91

Chapter 6: Overview of MFC Programming 93
Chapter 7: Menus....107
Chapter 8: Mouse and Keyboard....131
Chapter 9: Graphics....161
Chapter 10: Bitmaps, Palettes, DIBs, and Double Buffering 203
Chapter 11: MFC Exception Handling....245
Chapter 12: Controls 277
Chapter 13: Modal and Modeless Dialogs 311
Chapter 14: Property Sheets and Property Pages....349
Chapter 15: Data I/O 375
Chapter 16: Sound 423
Chapter 17: Timers and OnIdle Loop Processing 449

Part III: Architecture 467

Chapter 18: Memory Management 469
Chapter 19: Documents, Views, and SDI....513
Chapter 20: The Layout of an MDI Application....553
Chapter 21: Printing and Print Preview 597
Chapter 22: The MFC for Advanced Windows User Interfaces....633
Chapter 23: Status Bars and Toolbars 663
Chapter 24: Tree View and List View Controls 679
Chapter 25: Threads 705

Part IV: Database Programming....727

Chapter 26: ODBC 729
Chapter 27: MFC Database Classes....761
Chapter 28: DAO Database Programming 801

Part V: Extending Applications 837

Chapter 29: Working with DLLs 839
Chapter 30: Adding Imaging to Your Programs 871

Part VI: Component Object Modeling Programming..............................903

Chapter 31: Introduction to ActiveX and ActiveX Control Design 905
Chapter 32: Creating ActiveX Automation Servers Using MFC 953
Chapter 33: Active Template Library 999

Part VII: Internet and HTML Programmzing 1017

Chapter 34: Internet Programming 1019
Chapter 35: The CHtmlView Class..1063
Chapter 36: Dynamic HTML 1081

Part VIII: Advanced Visual Studio Use 1107

Chapter 37: Visual Studio Scripting 1109
Chapter 38: Writing a Custom AppWizard 1139

Appendix: What's on the CD-ROM..1165
Index 1187
End-User License Agreement 1234
CD-ROM Installation Instructions 1238

Contents

Preface ix

Acknowledgments xiii

Part I: Visual C++ Fundamentals 1

Chapter 1: Getting Started 3

What's New in Visual C++ 6.0 4
The HelloWorld1 Program 5
The HelloWorld2 Program 9
The HelloWorld3 ATL Control 11
Summary 15

Chapter 2: Taking Advantage of the Visual Studio IDE 17

Using Visual Studio's IDE 17
Creating Your First Project 19
Customizing the IDE 23
  Viewing the current shortcuts 23
  Adding, editing, or deleting shortcuts 24
Using Toolbars 26
  Displaying and hiding toolbars 26
  Customizing toolbars 27
Summary 28

Chapter 3: Debugging: When Your Applications Don't Work 29

What Every Debugger Should Have 30
The Visual Studio Integrated Debugger 31
  Preparing an application for debugging 31
  Using the debugger when you run an application 34
  Debug windows 35
  Using breakpoints and single-stepping when debugging 39
  Using the DataTips information and the QuickWatch window 43
  Using the Threads and the Exceptions dialog boxes when debugging 44
Simple Debugging Techniques 45
  Using message boxes to speed debugging 45
  Debugging output 45
  Using assertions 46
  Object dumping 47
  Detecting memory leaks and the CMemoryState class 47

Using MFC tracing 48
Remote Debugging 48
Just-In-Time Debugging 51
Edit and Continue debugging 51
Debugging Windows NT services 52
Summary 52

Chapter 4: Improving Your Application's Performance 53

Optimizing Your Code 54
Introduction to Profiling 57
Understanding the application profiling basics 58
Understanding the Profiler's operation 59
Types of profiling 60
Setting advanced Profiler settings 60
Enabling Profiling within Visual C++ 6.0 61
Controlling profiling from the development environment 62
Selecting a function to profile 63
Understanding the PREP program 63
Profiling for function timing 66
Profiling for function coverage 67
Line profiling options 67
Line coverage profiling 68
Merging Profiler output 69
Exporting data from the Profiler 69
Analyzing Profiler data 69
Understanding global information records 71
Local information records 72
Analyzing Profiler statistics 72
Processing Profiler output with Microsoft Excel 74
Profiling dynamic link libraries 74
Profiling an ActiveX component or ActiveX control 74
Profiling inlined code 76
Profiling multithreaded applications 76
Profiling your application's performance 77
Using the CAP Tool to Eliminate
Duplicated Calls 77
Profiling Windows NT services 79
Summary 80

Chapter 5: Miscellaneous Tools 81

Spy++ 81
Customizing the Tools Menu 85
Miscellaneous Tools Operations 86
Browsing Classes 87
Browse the MFC Source Code 89
Summary 90

Part II: Windows Programming Fundamentals

Chapter 6: Overview of MFC Programming 93

What Is MFC? 94
Design Philosophy of MFC 95
Advantages of Using MFC 95
  Features, features, features 97
  Extensible architecture 98
  MFC Hierarchy Design 98
  File services 99
  Windows 99
  Graphics 103
  Database support 103
You Don't Use MFC? 105
Summary 106

Chapter 7: Menus 107

Creating and Editing Menus 108
  Creating menus 109
  Menu messages in MFC 111
Accelerator Keys 113
  Examining keyboard input 113
  Defining accelerator keys 114
  Selecting appropriate accelerator keys 116
  Multiple accelerator tables 118
Dynamically Changing Menus 121
  Menu command ranges 121
  Changing menus at runtime 122
  Changing an existing pop-up menu 123
  Permanent and temporary handle maps 126
Context Menus 128
Summary 130

Chapter 8: Mouse and Keyboard 131

Input Basics and System State 131
Mouse Input 132
  Creating mouse message handlers 133
  Converting between screen and window coordinates 135
Creating an MFC Program That Handles Mouse Events 136
  Nonclient mouse events 142
  Changing the mouse cursor 143
Creating an MFC Demo Program that Changes Mouse Cursors 144
  Capturing the mouse 147
  Limiting mouse movement 148

Keyboard Input 149
The physical keyboard 149
Echoing keyboard focus 153
Summary 160

Chapter 9: Graphics 161

Introducing the Graphics Device Interface 161
Types of graphics 162
Types of GDI devices 164
The Device Context 165
DC drawing attributes 165
The WM_PAINT message 169
Drawing coordinates 170
Triggering WM_PAINT 170
Drawing outside WM_PAINT 172
Manipulating Text 173
GDI color support 173
Text color 175
Aligning text 176
Justifying text 178
About Fonts 178
What is a font? 178
Selecting devices into DCs 179
Selecting stock fonts 179
Selecting nonstock fonts 180
Pens and Brushes 185
Pens 185
Brushes 187
Mapping Modes 189
Raster Operations 191
Text drawing functions 192
Text coordinate calculations 194
Clipping Regions 200
Summary 201

Chapter 10: Bitmaps, Palettes, DIBs, and Double Buffering 203

Bitmap Memory and Video Memory 203
Creating CBitmap Objects 206
Loading and Setting Bitmap Content 208
Drawing CBitmaps to the Screen 209
Raster Operations 212
The BlitDemo Program 215
Palettes and Color 222
Logical palettes 225
Palette events 228
The SetSystemPaletteUse() function 229

Device-Independent Bitmaps 229
The anatomy of a DIB file 230
The CDib class 232
The ShowDIB Demo program 238
Double Buffering 241
Summary 244

Chapter 11: MFC Exception Handling 245

Structured Exception Handling 246
Exception-Handling Syntax 246
Throwing the exception 246
Catching the exception 247
Comparing Error-Handling Techniques 248
Dealing with error codes 248
Handling errors in the correct context 249
Improving code readability 251
Throwing exceptions from constructors 253
The CException Class 253
Creating and deleting CException objects 254
Retrieving error information from a CException object 255
Catching multiple exception types 256
Defining CException-Derived Classes 257
Discovering the CFileException class 258
A CFileException demo program 260
Defining your own CException-derived classes 263
Advanced Exception-Handling Techniques 267
Deciding what function should catch an exception 267
Deciding what code to put in a try block 269
Deciding what code to put in a catch block 270
Throwing exceptions from virtual functions 271
Summary 275

Chapter 12: Controls 277

Background 277
Creating Controls 278
Using the CButton class 281
Using the CListBox class 283
Using the CEdit class 287
Using the CStatic class 290
Using the CScrollBar class 294
Using the CComboBox class 298
The Mini Editor Program 302
Advanced Control Programming 302
Adding a keyboard interface 302
Modifying control behavior 303
Bitmap buttons 304
Changing a control's color 307
Summary 309

Chapter 13: Modal and Modeless Dialogs....................311

Using the Dialog Editor 312
  Dialog templates....................312
  Creating a new dialog template....................313
  Editing a dialog template 314
  Testing the dialog....................319
The CDialog Class 319
  Modal versus modeless dialogs 319
  Creating CDialog-derived classes with ClassWizard 321
Dialog Data Exchange and Validation....................322
  Creating DDX variables....................323
  DoDataExchange and UpdateData 323
The AddressBook Demo 326
  Editing the demo dialog 326
  The CContact class 327
  Overriding OnInitDialog 328
  Handling the WM_DESTROY message....................330
  Displaying data 331
  Handling button notifications....................332
  Building and testing the demo 332
Derived Control Classes in Dialogs 332
  Creating control classes 333
  AddressBook demo: CAutoCompleteComboBox....................337
Serialization 339
  Making each class serializable 340
  Implementing the Serialize() virtual function 340
  Reading data from disk....................341
  Saving data to disk....................341
  Adding serialization to the AddressBook demo 341
Summary 348

Chapter 14: Property Sheets and Property Pages 349

CPropertySheet and CPropertyPage 350
  Creating property page resources 350
  Creating the CPropertyPage class....................351
  Creating and displaying a modal CPropertySheet 352
  Creating and displaying a modeless CPropertySheet....................352
  Creating and displaying a property sheet within an existing dialog......354
A Modal Property Sheet Demo....................354
Property Sheet and Property Page Tips and Techniques 357
  Removing standard buttons 357
  Repositioning standard buttons....................359
  Changing the standard button's caption 360
  Disabling tabs 361
  Re-enabling property pages 365
  Dynamically setting CPropertyPage tab captions 367
  Changing a tab's font 370

Using mnemonics with CPropertyPage tabs 370
Summary 373

Chapter 15: Data I/O 375

The CString Class 375
Creating strings 376
Accessing string data....377
Comparison 378
Extraction 380
Searching 380
The StringDemo Program 381
The CFile Class 388
The FileDemo Program....392
The CCompressedFile Class 399
The CompressDemo Program 400
Data Compression....402
Huffman 403
LZSS....404
LZW 404
CCompressedFile class functions 405
Behind CompressDemo 407
The CSerial Class for Serial Communications....410
Serial communications 410
The CSerial class 411
The CRegistry Class....413
Registry values 413
Predefined Registry keys....414
Commonly used Registry keys 414
The CRegistry class in action....415
Using the Clipboard....417
Summary 422

Chapter 16: Sound 423

Playing Recorded Sounds 423
The CWave class in brief....424
Playing wave files using the Windows API....424
The CWave class functions 426
The WaveDemo Program 428
Playing MIDI Files....431
What Is MIDI?....432
The CMidi class in brief 432
The CMidi class functions....432
The MIDIDemo Program....433
CD Audio 437
The CCDAudio class library in brief....438
The Media Control Interface....439
CCDAudio class functions....440

The CDPlayer Program....441
Summary....447

Chapter 17: Timers and OnIdle Loop Processing....449

Timers....450
Setting a timer using WM_TIMER....450
Setting a timer with a callback procedure....452
The Clock Program....454
Using CWinApp's OnIdle Capability....461
The OnIdleDemo Program....463
Summary....466

Part III: Architecture

Chapter 18: Memory Management....469

System Memory Management....469
Intel-86 32-bit paged addressing mode....472
Windows 98 per-process address space....474
System memory cleanup....478
Process Private Memory....481
Allocating pages....482
Compiler memory allocation....486
Win32 private heaps....492
Shared Memory....499
Memory-mapped file I/O....501
Dynamically allocating shared pages....507
Statically allocating shared pages....510
Summary....512

Chapter 19: Documents, Views, and SDI....513

Document/view designs....513
The CDocument Class....515
Declaring a document class in your application....515
CDocument's member functions....517
Understanding documents and message processing....519
Overriding virtual document functions....520
Working with complex document data....521
Understanding the benefits of CCmdTarget and CDocItem....524
The Importance of the InitInstance Function to Documents....526
How your applications manage documents and views....527
Focusing on the CSingleDocTemplate class....528
Working briefly with frame windows....529
Document template resources....529
How the string resource affects the document template....530
Breaking apart the string resource....531
Looking at the stock view resources....532

Considering the document template life cycle 533
Advanced work with templates....534
Working with multiple templates....534
Destroying documents added with the AddDoc Template() member function....537
Understanding and Using the CView Class 537
Declaring a view class 537
Analyzing the CView member functions....539
Working with views and messages 541
MFC-derived variants of the CView class 541
Evaluating CForm view versus dialog-based applications 543
Returning to frame windows 543
Understanding the role of AfxGetMainWnd() 544
The HexView SDI Application....545
Summary 551

Chapter 20: The Layout of an MDI Application 553

Revisiting the Document/View Model: A Brief Refresher....554
Reviewing the CDocument Class 556
Managing More Complex Combinations of Documents, Views, and Frame Windows....557
Working with multiple document types....557
Using multiple views with documents 558
Understanding the CMDIFrameWnd class....560
Understanding the CMDIChildWnd class....562
Understanding the CMultiDocTemplate class....564
Reviewing the overhead of using the CDocument classes....564
Further considering MDI applications 565
The PaintObj Program....566
Understanding Splitter Windows....574
Differentiating between splitter windows....575
Understanding specifics of the CSplitterWnd class 575
More on dynamic splitters....577
Using different views in dynamic panes 579
Using a CRuntimeClass object....580
Using splitters with views associated with more than one document 581
Using static splitters....582
Creating a static splitter....583
Understanding shared scroll bars 584
Determining actual and ideal sizes....585
Understanding performance issues with splitters 585
The Dynsplit Program 586
Subclassing Child Windows....591
Using MFC to subclass windows....592
Alternatives to the document/view architecture....594
Summary 595

Chapter 21: Printing and Print Preview 597

Windows API Printer Support 597
  Printer information 601
  Understanding the importance of text characteristics....................602
The PortLand Program..603
Printing with MFC 605
  Understanding your role and the framework's role in printing............606
  Understanding the MFC printing sequence....................................606
  Further insight into MFC default printing....................................610
  The printing protocol 611
  Overriding view class functions and pagination 611
  Understanding the CPrintInfo class..613
  Understanding printer pages versus document pages......................613
  Implementing pagination 614
  Adding the helper functions..617
  Print-time pagination 620
  Revisiting the printing of headers and footers 620
  Allocating GDI resources for printing..621
  Enlarging the printed image 622
Understanding the Print Preview Architecture 622
  The print preview process..623
  Modifying print preview..623
  Enhancing an application's print preview 624
  Understanding the CPrintDialog class 626
The HexViewMDI Program..627
Summary 631

Chapter 22: The MFC for Advanced Windows User Interfaces............633

Sometimes You Need More Control 633
Understanding the Modal Loop 635
RunModalLoop() Internals 635
Modal Loop Parameters..638
Ending the Modal Loop..639
Generating the Modal Application 640
Creating and Closing the Modal Window 640
  Adding handlers 641
  Simple modal application..644
Pushing the Modal Window Further 645
Drawing a Transparent Bitmap on a Transparent Client Area 649
  Painting the bitmap..650
  Determining where to paste the bitmap 654
  Compatible device contexts 655
  The BITMAP structure..656
  Blitting all the pieces together 658
  Making sure they noticed..661
Summary 662

Chapter 23: Status Bars and Toolbars....663

Creating and Using Status Bars....663
Creating a status bar....664
Customizing status bars....665
Creating and Controlling Toolbars....669
MFC control bars....670
Creating and initializing a toolbar....671
Using the ReBar Control....677
Summary....678

Chapter 24: Tree View and List View Controls....679

CTreeCtrl....681
Tree view control basics....681
CTreeCtrl....683
CTreeCtrl Demo....692
CListCtrl....697
List view basics....697
CListCtrl....698
Summary....704

Chapter 25: Threads....705

Threads....706
Creating a worker thread....707
The thread function....708
Creating a user interface thread....709
Suspending and resuming threads....710
Putting threads to sleep....711
Terminating a thread....711
Terminating a thread from another thread....712
Threads, processes, and priorities....715
Process priority classes....716
Sharing MFC objects among threads....717
Using C Runtime Functions in Multithreaded Applications....720
ThreadDemo1 Program....721
Summary....725

Part IV: Database Programming

Chapter 26: ODBC....729

Definitions of ODBC and Database Terms....730
ODBC — The Need for a Standard....732
The ODBC standard....732
ODBC API conformance levels....734
ODBC SQL conformance levels....735

ODBC—Implementation 735
Configuring ODBC 735
Connecting to a data source 737
Querying the data and the data source 739
Preparing and executing SQL requests 739
Retrieving data 740
Disconnecting from a data source 742
Using ODBC to Fetch Data 742
Adding ODBC support to a Visual C++ project 743
Modifying the ODBCDemo dialog 744
Adding the initialization and database code 745
Using ODBC to Dynamically Query a Data Source 751
Looking at the CODBCDynamic class declaration 752
How the CODBCDynamic class works 753
Using the CODBCDynamic class 759
Summary 760

Chapter 27: MFC Database Classes 761

CDatabase 762
CRecordset 766
Constructing a recordset 771
Opening a recordset 771
Reading and writing data using RFX 772
Filtering records 772
Sorting records returned with a recordset 775
Moving through the result set 776
Saving records 776
Deleting records 777
Using the MFC Database Classes 777
Adding support for the MFC database classes 778
Creating the UI for the demo 778
Adding a utility class to encapsulate the user's data 779
Creating a CRecordset class for the UserMaster table 780
Modifying the dialog's header file 780
Modifying the dialog's implementation file 780
Parameterized Recordsets and Queries 788
Creating the UI for the demo 789
Creating the UserMaster recordset 790
Modifying the CRecordset class to accept parameters 790
Adding search capability to the application 791
Building the application 793
Creating parameterized queries 793
The demo database 793
Creating the permissions recordset 795
Summary 799

Chapter 28: DAO Database Programming 801

DAO Overview 802

The history of DAO 802
The DAO hierarchy 804
The many (inter)faces of DAO....808
Using the MFC DAO Classes 809
CDaoDatabase 810
CDaoWorkspace....813
CDaoRecordset 814
MFC DAO demo 824
Summary 836

Part V: Extending Applications

Chapter 29: Working with DLLs 839

DLL Overview 840
Dynamic and static libraries....840
Loading DLLs 840
Visual C++ Regular DLLs 842
Understanding the regular DLL internals 843
Dynamically loading DLLs....845
Examples of when to dynamically load a DLL 845
Windows hooks 847
Global C++ objects with DLLs....854
MFC Extension DLLs....862
Understanding the internals of the MFC extension DLLs 862
Exporting classes via MFC extension DLLs 863
More on the AFX_EXT_CLASS 864
Using nested MFC extension DLLs....864
Exporting resources....865
Writing a demo that encapsulates documents and views in a DLL 865
Summary 870

Chapter 30: Adding Imaging to Your Programs 871

Third-Party Libraries....871
The ImageObject Library in Brief....875
The BMP file format....876
The GIF file format 877
The JPEG file format 877
The PCX file format....878
The TGA file format 878
The TIF file format....878
Loading Images 878
Displaying Images 880
The Display Program....882
Scaling, Cropping, and Changing Color Depth....885
Creating an Image from a Device Context 888
Creating an Image from the Clipboard....889
Saving Images 890

Image Processing 891
The ProcessImage Program....894
Summary 902

Part VI: Component Object Modeling Programming

Chapter 31: Introduction to ActiveX and ActiveX Control Design......905

Understanding the Origins and Uses of ActiveX 906
Understanding Various ActiveX Technologies....907
- Understanding automation servers....908
- Understanding automation controllers....908
- Defining ActiveX controls....908
- Understanding component object model (COM) objects 909
- Understanding ActiveX documents....909
- Understanding ActiveX containers....910

Understanding What ActiveX Can Do for You 911
Determining What Type of ActiveX Component You Need....912
- Using automation servers and controllers....912
- Using ActiveX controls 913
- Using COM objects....914
- Using Microsoft Foundation Classes to create ActiveX components 915
- Using the ActiveX Template Library to create ActiveX components.....916
- Using the BaseControl framework to create ActiveX components 916
- Create your own framework....918

Basic ActiveX Component Architecture 918
- ActiveX automation servers 918
- ActiveX controls....920

Support Tools Required to Build ActiveX Components....920
- MIDL compiler 921
- Mktyplib....921
- GUIDGEN....921
- RegEdit....921
- Registration Server 922
- Ole2View....922
- Adding the tools to the Visual C++ development environment............922

Using MFC to Create a Basic ActiveX Control....923
- Creating the basic control project....923
- Control registration 927
- Creating methods....928
- Properties....934
- Creating property sheets 939
- Adding events 943
- Persistence....945

Drawing the Control 947
Standard Drawing....947
Summary 950

Chapter 32: Creating ActiveX Automation Servers Using MFC 953

Creating the Basic Project 953
- Adding an automation interface to the application 955
- Registering the server 959
- Writing support code for the sample server 961
- Adding methods 964
- Adding properties to the server 969

Generating OLE Exceptions 971
- Understanding dual-interface servers 977
- Generating dual-interface OLE exceptions 986

Server Instantiation Using C++ 992
- Common problems when instantiating OLE servers using C++ 993
- Creating shareable servers 994
- Single instance servers 997

Summary 998

Chapter 33: Active Template Library 999

A Brief Look at ATL 999
Creating an ATL Control 1001
Adding a COM Object to the Project 1002
Modifying the CDoublePend Include File 1004
Implementing the Interface Functions 1005
Using the Control from C++ 1010
Data Types 1013
- Converting to and from BSTRs 1013
- Comparing BSTRs 1014
- Viewing the contents of a BSTR in the debugger 1015

Embedding an ActiveX Control in a Web Page 1015
Summary 1016

Part VII: Internet and HTML Programming

Chapter 34: Internet Programming 1019

The CInternetSession Class 1019
The CFtpConnection Class 1021
- Retrieving a file from an FTP server 1024
- Sending a file to an FTP server 1028
- Other FTP functions 1028
- The CInternetFile class 1029
- The CFtpFileFind class 1031

The FTP Program 1031
Sockets and the CSocket Class 1040
- Creating sockets 1040
- Connecting to a socket 1041
- Listening for a connection 1043
- Reading and writing data 1044

The Sockets Program 1045
The SendEmail Program 1052
Retrieving an HTTP File 1057
The AutoDialer Program 1058
Summary 1061

Chapter 35: The CHtmlView Class 1063

Creating a CHtmlView Project 1064
Converting Projects to Use CHtmlView 1065
Navigating CHtmlViews 1066
The SimpleBrowser Program 1068
The MultiBrowser Program 1071
Direct Use of the Web Browser Control 1075
Writing a Browser that Logs Navigation 1077
Writing a Browser That Blocks Sites 1078
Summary 1079

Chapter 36: Dynamic HTML 1081

HTML Fundamentals 1081
Cascading Style Sheets 1085
  Global style sheets 1087
  Style sheet syntax 1088
Simple File Viewer 1090
Event and Object Models 1091
Scripting 1093
Scripting for Elements 1095
Changing Things Other Than Text Elements 1099
Running a Script As the Document Is Loaded 1100
Scripting Dialogs 1104
Summary 1106

Part VIII: Advanced Visual Studio Use

Chapter 37: Visual Studio Scripting 1109

Visual Studio Macros 1109
  Quick Macros 1110
Creating VBScript Macros 1112
  Understanding a VBScript macro 1114
  Editing a VBScript macro 1115
  Creating an empty macro 1116
Using VBScript Macros 1118
  Loading macro files 1118
  Running VBScript macros 1119
  Assigning macros to toolbars 1120
  Assigning macros to keystrokes 1121

Understanding VBScript 1122
Programming VBScript 1123
Using variables 1123
Using constants 1123
Using functions and procedures 1124
Using the Developer Studio Object Model 1124
Accessing the object model 1124
Using the Application object 1125
Using Sample Applications 1129
Running the sample macro 1129
Understanding the sample macro 1130
Summary 1138

Chapter 38: Writing a Custom AppWizard 1139

The Internal Workings of the AppWizard 1140
The AppWizard manager 1140
The CCustomAppWiz class and the Dictionary 1141
Creating a Custom AppWizard 1145
A Demo to Preset a Project's Default Settings 1146
Creating the SDIAutomationWiz demo project 1146
Defining the CCustomAppWiz class 1146
Working with macro dictionaries 1148
A More Advanced Custom AppWizard 1149
Adding a customized dialog 1149
Creating your own templates 1151
Changing the newproj.Inf file 1154
Changing the ClassWizard files 1155
Changing the AppWizard templates 1156
Changing the CONFIRM.INF file 1160
Using the Registry for persistent macros 1160
Modifying the CAboutWizAppWiz class to use the Registry 1161
Summary 1164

Appendix: What's on the CD-ROM 1165

Index 1187

End-User License Agreement 1234

CD-ROM Installation Instructions 1238

P A R T

I

Visual C++ Fundamentals

The first five chapters get you started with Visual C++. You learn how to create, edit, and compile projects. You learn the ins and outs of Visual C++ tools such as the debugger and the profiler.

The topics include creating and compiling projects, the integrated development environment, the debugger, the profiler, and other Visual C++ tools. You learn the basics of how to use these tools and tips that help you get the most out of them in your development work.

These five chapters give you the skills you need to use the Visual C++ tools when developing your programs.

✦ ✦ ✦ ✦

In This Part

Chapter 1:
Getting Started

Chapter 2:
Taking Advantage of the Visual Studio IDE

Chapter 3:
Debugging: When Your Applications Don't Work

Chapter 4:
Improving Your Application's Performance

Chapter 5:
Miscellaneous Tools

✦ ✦ ✦ ✦

Getting Started

It has been said by many motivational speakers, “What the mind can conceive and believe, it can achieve.” It might be easier than you think to achieve your dreams. That’s because Windows 95, Windows 98, and Windows NT are fantastic operating systems that give you power as a developer, and great features and robustness as a user.

Add to those Microsoft operating systems Visual Studio 6, and you have a one-two punch that’s going to knock your socks off. The possibilities are endless. I get excited just thinking about them. “Yeah, right,” some of you are thinking — a sentiment I may have shared some time ago. But over and over again, I’ve seen developers create the most astounding solutions in short time using the Microsoft tools, and thus my skepticism has faded.

What kind of solutions? For starters, when I attended the Microsoft Visual C++ Insiders Summit in Redmond, Christian Beaumont created a Web browser in five minutes using Visual C++ 6.0. At the same conference, I watched Mike Blaszczak create applications using new controls that blew me away. As I watched, I painfully recalled the long hours I’ve spent performing similar feats before Visual C++ 6.0 came along.

One of the things we do at my office is to create eCommerce solutions for small- to mid-sized vendors. These vendors don’t have the money to pay for custom Web site development. In several months, we created a wizard-based system with which we can automate the creation and administration of eCommerce stores. This reduces our development costs and makes it possible for us to provide a solution at a much lower cost than previously possible. Without the suite of tools in Visual Studio 6, the development cycle would have taken years. And in the suite of Visual Studio 6 tools, Visual C++ 6.0 ranked up at the top for our development efforts.

In This Chapter

What’s new in Visual C++ version 6.0

The HelloWorld1 program

The HelloWorld2 program

The HelloWorld3 ATL control

What's New in Visual C++ 6.0

The major purpose of Visual C++ is to support the newest Microsoft platforms and technologies, such as the new Active Desktop in Internet Explorer 4.0. With Visual C++ 6.0 you can develop for Internet Explorer 4.0 by accessing the power and flexibility of Dynamic HTML and the new Common Controls. Internet Explorer 4.0 support enables you to integrate the Web directly into your Microsoft Foundation Class (MFC) applications.

You can now easily create Web-based front ends for your MFC applications. Simply use the new `CHtmlView` class in MFC to create a view in your MFC application that hosts Dynamic HTML. This view has all the power and browsing capabilities of Internet Explorer 4.0.

You can build browser-based front ends that leverage all your existing work. The new Dynamic HTML support means your ActiveX controls can use Dynamic HTML to interact "on the fly" with data you have downloaded to the browser. Dynamic HTML support also enables you to reduce server round-trips by manipulating data and performing calculations right on the Web page, without going back to the server.

You can give your user interfaces the compelling "look and feel" of Internet Explorer 4.0—with support for all the new Internet Explorer 4.0 Common Controls in MFC. This control support is complete, including MFC, wizards, and Resource Editor support for the new controls, styles, messages, and system headers. These new controls include the Internet Explorer 4.0-style toolbars, the IP Address control, the Date Picker and Month Calendar controls, and the Extended Combo Box control. In addition, Visual C++ 6.0 makes it easy to use the enhancements to the Slider, Toolbar, Tab, Status Bar, Image List, Hot Key, Progress Bar, and Tool Tip controls.

Visual C++ has supported writing ActiveX documents for some time. Now it supports writing ActiveX document containers, including support for printing, saving, and loading. You can seamlessly get all the functionality of programs such as Excel or Word (or Internet Explorer 4.0, of course) in your MFC applications with DocObject Containment. You can easily put full-featured charts, graphs, or even Web browsers right in your MFC applications, with full menu merge.

Visual C++ 6.0 also supports the Microsoft Universal Data Access strategy with enhanced support for OLE DB. OLE DB provides high-performance access to any data source—relational and nonrelational, e-mail and file systems, text and graphics, custom business objects, and more. New OLE DB Consumer and Provider templates make it easier to implement the OLE DB data access interfaces. You can take advantage of the speed and reach of new OLE DB—get at all the data types OLE DB supports with this special preview of the new OLE DB templates.

OLE DB Consumer templates enable you to go directly to OLE DB to provide high-speed data access from your applications and controls. OLE DB Consumer templates provide exacting control and significantly reduce your code size. The OLE DB Consumer templates are designed to work with C++, MFC, and Active Template Library (ATL) applications.

You can use the new OLE DB Provider templates to build access to any database with OLE DB. OLE DB Provider templates with wizard support make it easier to implement the OLE DB data access interfaces, significantly reducing your development time. The OLE DB Provider templates are built around ATL to provide high performance and small code size. OLE DB Provider templates provide C/C++, OLE Automation, Java, and scripting access to your data.

The remainder of this chapter gives a tour of Visual C++ 6.0 by creating some applications, a control, and a DLL. The section on each project includes a discussion of the tools with which the project was created and shows you the highlights of the tool. This overview will prepare you for the rest of the book in which we get into the nitty gritty of Visual C++ 6.0 programming.

The HelloWorld1 Program

The first program we created for this chapter is a variation of the traditional "Hello World" program that all C and C++ programmers start with. The program was created with the MFC AppWizard. Only one of the default settings throughout the AppWizard process was changed to make the application a single-document interface program. Most of the same project types are included in Visual C++ 6.0. Figure 1-1 shows the selections that are available.

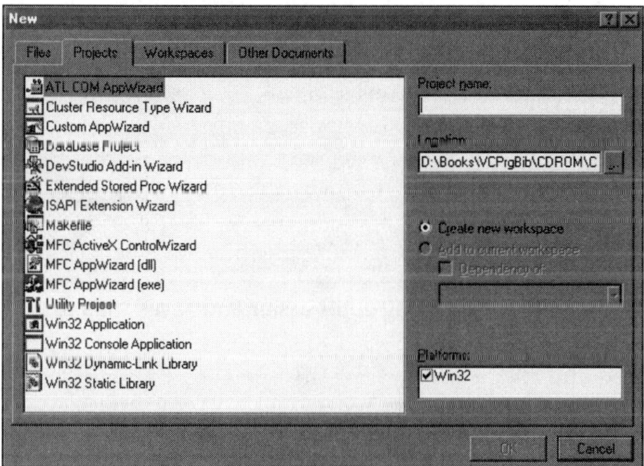

Figure 1-1: The project types in Visual C++ 6.0 are about the same as they were for Visual C++ 5.0.

One important thing to note is that you can now create programs with AppWizard that don't have document/view architecture support. For me this is a tremendously valuable option. I can't tell you how many times I've created document/view programs that simply display graphics or images and totally ignore all of the document features. Every time this happened, I'd look at the files in the project and deep down long to delete the document source code files. (Good thing I never did; the project wouldn't compile if I had.)

When I went to add the code to the view class' `OnDraw()` function, I was surprised when the IntelliSense feature took over and tried to make my job easier. IntelliSense is a system in which the editor gives you a list of functions and function arguments based on the context of what you're typing. For instance, if I type `TextO`, a list with `TextOut` is displayed. If I hit Enter or Tab, the function name is completed, and I have to type fewer characters. It also provides a list of arguments for the function, which reduces greatly the number of trips to online help you'll have to make. Figure 1-2 shows the IntelliSense feature as it appeared when the HelloWorld1 program was created.

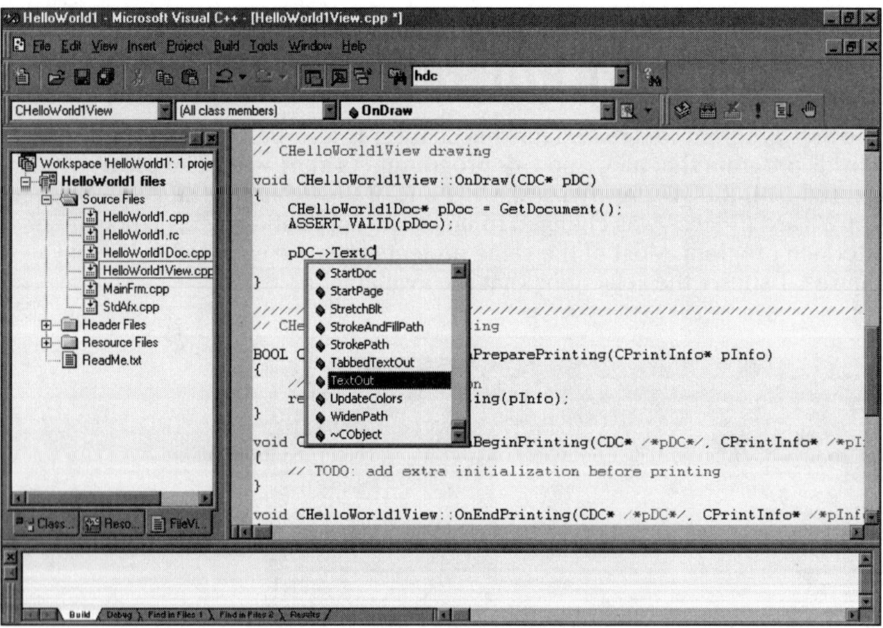

Figure 1-2: IntelliSense makes the job of writing code easier and saves trips to online help.

One additional new item in the AppWizard is the capability to create Explorer-style programs in which a treeview control displays objects. Figure 1-3 shows a program that uses an Explorer-style look. The source code for the program can be seen in Listing 1-1.

Figure 1-3: You can easily create Explorer-style applications.

HelloWorld1

CD-ROM Location: **Chap1\HelloWorld1**

Program Name: **HelloWorld1.exe**

Source Code Modules in Text: `HelloWorld1View.cpp`

◆ ◆ ◆ ◆ ◆

Listing 1-1: **Highlights of the HelloWorld1 Program's View Class**

```
// HelloWorld1View.cpp : implementation of the
// CHelloWorld1View class
//

#include "stdafx.h"
#include "HelloWorld1.h"

#include "HelloWorld1Doc.h"
#include "HelloWorld1View.h"
```

(continued)

Listing 1-1 *(continued)*

```
/////////////////////////////////////////////////////////
// CHelloWorld1View

IMPLEMENT_DYNCREATE(CHelloWorld1View, CView)

BEGIN_MESSAGE_MAP(CHelloWorld1View, CView)
  //{{AFX_MSG_MAP(CHelloWorld1View)
  //}}AFX_MSG_MAP
  // Standard printing commands
  ON_COMMAND(ID_FILE_PRINT, CView::OnFilePrint)
  ON_COMMAND(ID_FILE_PRINT_DIRECT, CView::OnFilePrint)
  ON_COMMAND(ID_FILE_PRINT_PREVIEW, CView::OnFilePrintPreview)
END_MESSAGE_MAP()

/////////////////////////////////////////////////////////
// CHelloWorld1View construction/destruction

CHelloWorld1View::CHelloWorld1View()
{
}

CHelloWorld1View::~CHelloWorld1View()
{
}

BOOL CHelloWorld1View::PreCreateWindow(CREATESTRUCT& cs)
{
  return CView::PreCreateWindow(cs);
}

/////////////////////////////////////////////////////////
// CHelloWorld1View drawing

void CHelloWorld1View::OnDraw(CDC* pDC)
{
  CHelloWorld1Doc* pDoc = GetDocument();
  ASSERT_VALID(pDoc);

  pDC->TextOut( 20,20, "Hello Visual C++ World!" );

}

/////////////////////////////////////////////////////////
// CHelloWorld1View printing

BOOL CHelloWorld1View::OnPreparePrinting(
  CPrintInfo* pInfo)
{
  // default preparation
  return DoPreparePrinting(pInfo);
}
```

```
void CHelloWorld1View::OnBeginPrinting(CDC* /*pDC*/,
  CPrintInfo* /*pInfo*/)
{
}

void CHelloWorld1View::OnEndPrinting(CDC* /*pDC*/,
  CPrintInfo* /*pInfo*/)
{
}
```

When the HelloWorld1 program runs, you'll see a familiar Single Document Interface (SDI) application. The text string "Hello Visual C++ World!" appears in the view window, as you can see in Figure 1-4.

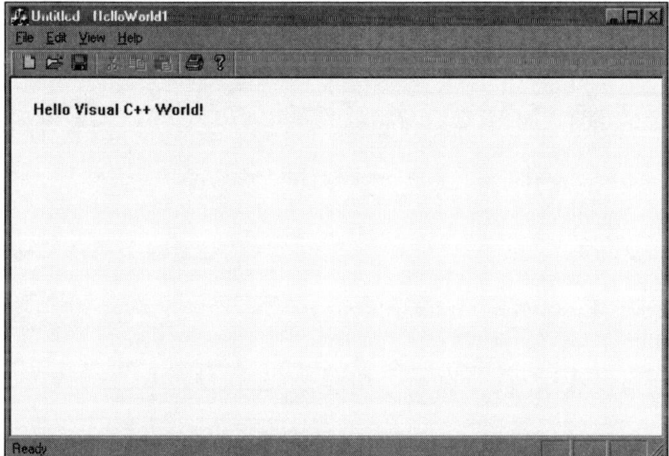

Figure 1-4: The AppWizard still creates the familiar SDI application.

The HelloWorld2 Program

I never thought there was a place for Win32 console applications until two things happened. The first was that I started teaching C++ at Rockingham Community College. The very first application I started teaching was creating AppWizard-based Windows applications. It took me only about 15 minutes before I realized how lost everyone was, and then I quickly learned about Win32 console applications. With these gems I was able to teach C++ concepts without students getting lost in the myriad of project and MFC classes.

Once I made this startling revelation, I began to realize the Win32 console applications are handy for utilities that don't need a user interface. With almost no effort, I can create programs that do useful things such as move and rename files, convert binary files to source code, and other tasks software developers such as myself need. I don't yearn for the old days when I could whip up a DOS application in five minutes to automate some programming tasks. And I (usually) don't even have to worry about segmented pointers or running out of memory.

This second program is a Win32 console application that displays "Hello Visual C++ Console World!". When you create a Win32 console application, one of the choices, believe it or not, is a "Hello World" application. The source code for the HelloWorld2 program is shown in Listing 1-2.

HelloWorld2

CD-ROM Location: **Chap1\HelloWorld2**
Program Name: **HelloWorld2.exe**
Source Code Modules in Text: `HelloWorld2.cpp`

◆ ◆ ◆ ◆ ◆

Listing 1-2: The Entire Source Code for the HelloWorld2 Program

```
// HelloWorld2.cpp : Defines the entry point
// for the console application.
//

#include "stdafx.h"

int main(int argc, char* argv[])
{
  printf("Hello Visual C++ Console World!\n");
  return 0;
}
```

When the program runs, a console window is displayed. This console window contains the message "Hello Visual C++ Console World!" as shown in Figure 1-5.

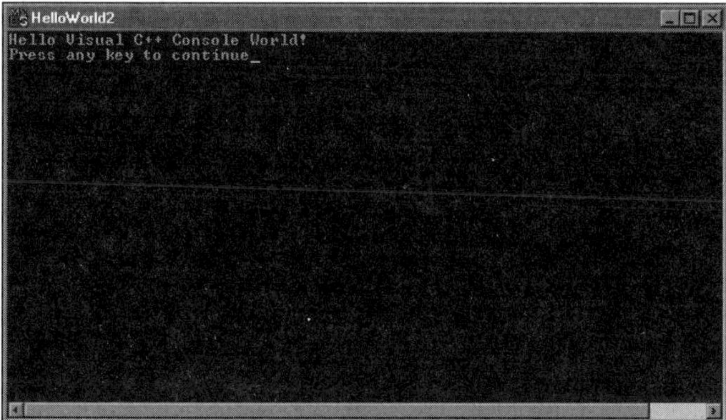

Figure 1-5: You may find yourself in need of a Win32 console application.

The HelloWorld3 ATL Control

It won't be long in your programming career, especially with the direction in which Microsoft is pushing, before you'll need to create ActiveX controls. For most situations, the best way to do this is with the Active Template Library (ATL) wizard. It creates the startup code for an ATL project and saves the time and drudgery of doing it yourself.

In spite of the ease with which you can create an ATL control, the footprint turns out to be relatively small. A full control with minimal code that's added (such as the HelloWorld3 control) ends up at about 37K. ATL controls have a lot of options, one being the capability to use MFC. If you want to use MFC, be prepared for another 80 to 100K to be added to the footprint. The source code for the HelloWorld3 control can be seen in Listing 1-3.

HelloWorld3
CD-ROM Location: **Chap1\HelloWorld3**
Program Name: **HelloWorld3.dll**
Source Code Modules in Text: `Full.h`

✦ ✦ ✦ ✦ ✦

Listing 1-3: The Source Code for the ATL Wizard-Created CFull Class in Which the Text Is Displayed

```
// Full.h : Declaration of the CFull class

#ifndef __FULL_H_
#define __FULL_H_

#include "resource.h"       // main symbols
#include <atlctl.h>

/////////////////////////////////////////////////////////////
// CFull
class ATL_NO_VTABLE CFull :
  public CComObjectRootEx<CComSingleThreadModel>,
  public IDispatchImpl<IFull, &IID_IFull,
    &LIBID_HELLOWORLD3Lib>,
  public CComControl<CFull>,
  public IPersistStreamInitImpl<CFull>,
  public IOleControlImpl<CFull>,
  public IOleObjectImpl<CFull>,
  public IOleInPlaceActiveObjectImpl<CFull>,
  public IViewObjectExImpl<CFull>,
  public IOleInPlaceObjectWindowlessImpl<CFull>,
  public IPersistStorageImpl<CFull>,
  public ISpecifyPropertyPagesImpl<CFull>,
  public IQuickActivateImpl<CFull>,
  public IDataObjectImpl<CFull>,
  public IProvideClassInfo2Impl<&CLSID_Full, NULL,
    &LIBID_HELLOWORLD3Lib>,
  public CComCoClass<CFull, &CLSID_Full>
{
public:
  CFull()
  {
  }

DECLARE_REGISTRY_RESOURCEID(IDR_FULL)

BEGIN_COM_MAP(CFull)
  COM_INTERFACE_ENTRY(IFull)
  COM_INTERFACE_ENTRY(IDispatch)
  COM_INTERFACE_ENTRY(IViewObjectEx)
  COM_INTERFACE_ENTRY(IViewObject2)
  COM_INTERFACE_ENTRY(IViewObject)
  COM_INTERFACE_ENTRY(IOleInPlaceObjectWindowless)
  COM_INTERFACE_ENTRY(IOleInPlaceObject)
  COM_INTERFACE_ENTRY2(IOleWindow,
    IOleInPlaceObjectWindowless)
  COM_INTERFACE_ENTRY(IOleInPlaceActiveObject)
  COM_INTERFACE_ENTRY(IOleControl)
  COM_INTERFACE_ENTRY(IOleObject)
  COM_INTERFACE_ENTRY(IPersistStreamInit)
  COM_INTERFACE_ENTRY2(IPersist, IPersistStreamInit)
```

```
  COM_INTERFACE_ENTRY(ISpecifyPropertyPages)
  COM_INTERFACE_ENTRY(IQuickActivate)
  COM_INTERFACE_ENTRY(IPersistStorage)
  COM_INTERFACE_ENTRY(IDataObject)
  COM_INTERFACE_ENTRY(IProvideClassInfo)
  COM_INTERFACE_ENTRY(IProvideClassInfo2)
END_COM_MAP()

BEGIN_PROP_MAP(CFull)
  PROP_DATA_ENTRY("_cx", m_sizeExtent.cx, VT_UI4)
  PROP_DATA_ENTRY("_cy", m_sizeExtent.cy, VT_UI4)
  // Example entries
  // PROP_ENTRY("Property Description", dispid, clsid)
  // PROP_PAGE(CLSID_StockColorPage)
END_PROP_MAP()

BEGIN_MSG_MAP(CFull)
  CHAIN_MSG_MAP(CComControl<CFull>)
  DEFAULT_REFLECTION_HANDLER()
END_MSG_MAP()
// Handler prototypes:
//  LRESULT MessageHandler(UINT uMsg, WPARAM wParam,
//    LPARAM lParam, BOOL& bHandled);
//  LRESULT CommandHandler(WORD wNotifyCode, WORD wID,
//    HWND hWndCtl, BOOL& bHandled);
//  LRESULT NotifyHandler(int idCtrl, LPNMHDR pnmh,
//    BOOL& bHandled);

// IViewObjectEx
  DECLARE_VIEW_STATUS(VIEWSTATUS_SOLIDBKGND |
    VIEWSTATUS_OPAQUE)

// IFull
public:

  HRESULT OnDraw(ATL_DRAWINFO& di)
  {
    RECT& rc = *(RECT*)di.prcBounds;
    Rectangle(di.hdcDraw, rc.left, rc.top,
      rc.right, rc.bottom);

    SetTextAlign(di.hdcDraw, TA_CENTER|TA_BASELINE);
    LPCTSTR pszText = _T("Hello Visual C++ ATL World!");
    TextOut(di.hdcDraw,
      (rc.left + rc.right) / 2,
      (rc.top + rc.bottom) / 2,
      pszText,
      lstrlen(pszText));

    return S_OK;
  }
};

#endif //__FULL_H_
```

The first thing you have to realize about this project is that you can't just execute it. You need some sort of container to load it into. And even before you do that, you have to register it. To register the control so that applications can use it, run Regsvr32 (in the `Windows\System` directory or `Winnt\System32` directory) with a parameter of the control you want to register. For instance `C:\Winnt\System32\Regsvr32 HelloWorld3.dll`.

If you compile the project, Visual C++ registers the control for you. This makes it easy to test controls when you develop them. Once a control is registered, though, it's always expected to be in the directory in which it was registered. If you change it to a different directory, you must reregister it.

Visual C++ provides a container program into which you can load controls. This saves you from having to write your own container just to test a control. To run the test container program, simply select ActiveX Control Test Container from the Tools menu. Figure 1-6 shows the HelloWorld3 control loaded into the test container.

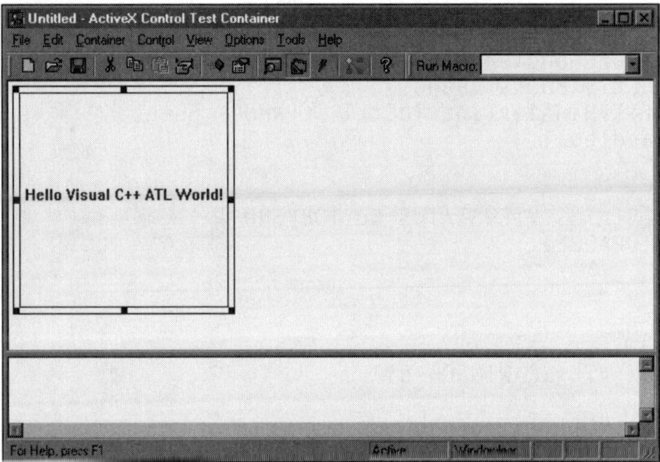

Figure 1-6: The HelloWorld3 control must be loaded into a control container. Here it's loaded into the ActiveX Control Test Container tool that comes with Visual C++.

Summary

As a software developer, you have some of the most unbelievable opportunities in front of you. I remember the days of 256K machines with CGA graphics. We had to squeeze to get anything to work well, and getting something to look good was a challenge. The Microsoft operating systems bring a solid, stable, and feature-filled platform to the equation. They're operating systems that make development a pleasure. My all-time vote for what's been the greatest single contribution to software is preemptive multitasking. It's a blessing.

Visual C++ 6.0 complements the Microsoft operating systems in ways I'm discovering every day. It's a well-rounded, robust, and flexible tool that'll enable you to achieve your wildest software dreams.

✦ ✦ ✦

Taking Advantage of the Visual Studio IDE

✦ ✦ ✦ ✦

In This Chapter

The major areas of the Visual Studio IDE

Creating a project

Customizing the behavior and look of the IDE

Using the IDE to manage programming projects

Using the IDE toolbars

✦ ✦ ✦ ✦

Using Visual Studio's IDE

The Visual C++ Integrated Development Environment, or IDE for short, is organized into four distinct areas: menu and toolbars, Project View window, code editor, and debug window. Figure 2-1 illustrates these areas. The menu items enable you to access different options not only for the IDE but also for your overall project. Using different menu options, you can control everything from the compiler's behavior to the font formatting behavior of the code editor. All the toolbars are fully dockable. This means that they can be docked to any of the four sides of the IDE's main window. You can also "float" the toolbars anywhere on your desktop.

The debug window displays important information during the project building process and while your project is executing within the Visual Studio debugger. Typically, the debug window will display error messages that occur when you compile, or build, your project. You can also write messages directly to the debug window from within your project by using the `TRACE` macro.

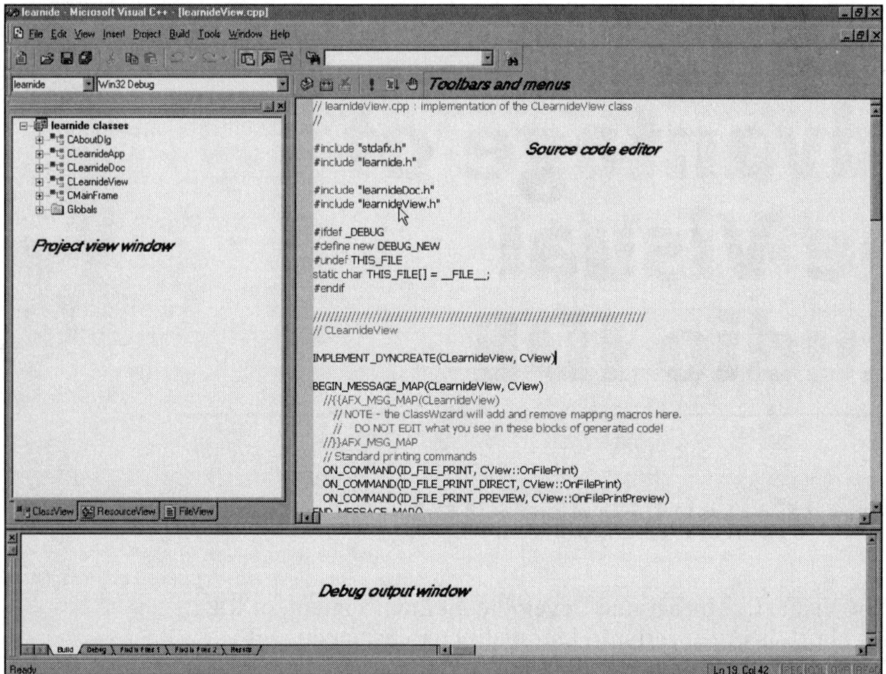

Figure 2-1: The four main areas of the Visual Studio IDE

The Project View window displays the different aspects of your project. The Project View is really the gateway to your project. You can display different classes for editing, work with different project resources such as dialogs or icons, and toggle between the Class View and the File View of your project. Outside of the code editor, most of the interaction with your project will occur within the Project View window using either File View or Class View.

File View displays a file-oriented view of your project. Every file included in the project is displayed in a hierarchical tree format. To edit a file, simply double-click it in the Project View window, and it will be loaded into the code editor. File View loads the entire file into the editor and displays it from beginning to end. Editing multiple files is also a snap. Each file is loaded into its own editor window. These windows can be tiled using the Window menu. You can then cut and paste between windows or display windows next to each other for easier line-by-line comparisons.

Class View is a class-oriented view of your project. The Class View combines each class's `.h` and `.cpp` file into one logical class entity. Every class in the project is displayed in a hierarchical tree format. This logical grouping of classes can make programming easier, especially in large projects that have many classes. Double-clicking a class name displays that class's implementation code in the editor, starting at the beginning of the class. Expanding a class's tree node displays that class's list of member functions, member variables, and message handler functions. Private functions or variables are denoted by a padlock icon displayed next to their name.

Any changes made in File View will not be shown or available in Class View until the project is rebuilt or saved.

◆ ◆ ◆ ◆ ◆

Creating Your First Project

Now that you have an overview of the IDE, let's get our hands dirty and use the IDE to develop a basic Visual C++ project. This exercise will walk you through creating a new program that opens a window and displays a single line of text. Let's get started!

Step 1: Use the AppWizard to generate a basic single document project.

Select New from the File menu, making sure the Projects tab is selected, as shown in Figure 2-2.

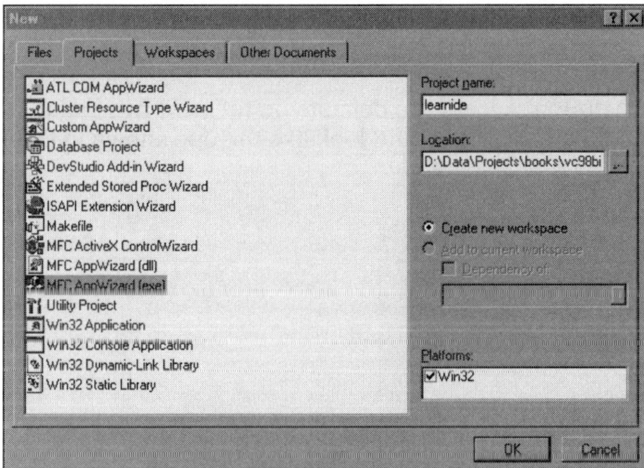

Figure 2-2: New Projects dialog box

Make sure that MFC AppWizard (exe) is selected. Type **c:\vcbib98** in the Location box. You can use another directory and/or drive letter if you want. Just make sure to substitute this information throughout the rest of the exercise. Type **learnide** in the Project Name box. Notice how Visual Studio uses the Project Name and Location information to create the directory that will store your project. Click the OK button.

The AppWizard displays a series of dialog boxes that will create the basic framework for a Windows C++ application. The first window is displayed in Figure 2-3.

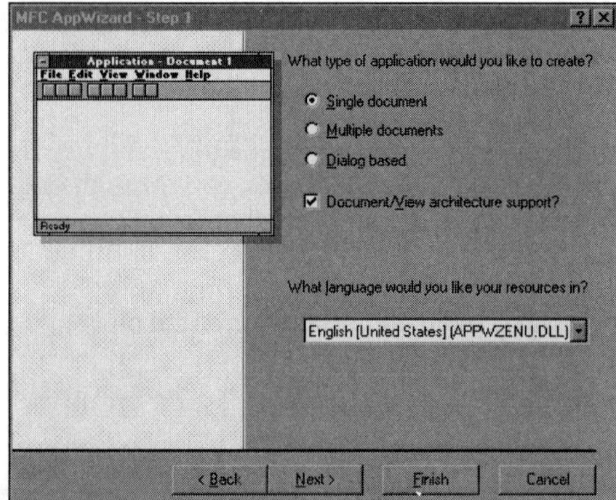

Figure 2-3: Selecting the type of application

Select the Single document option. Accept the defaults on the next five dialog boxes that are displayed. Your summary dialog should look like the one shown in Figure 2-4.

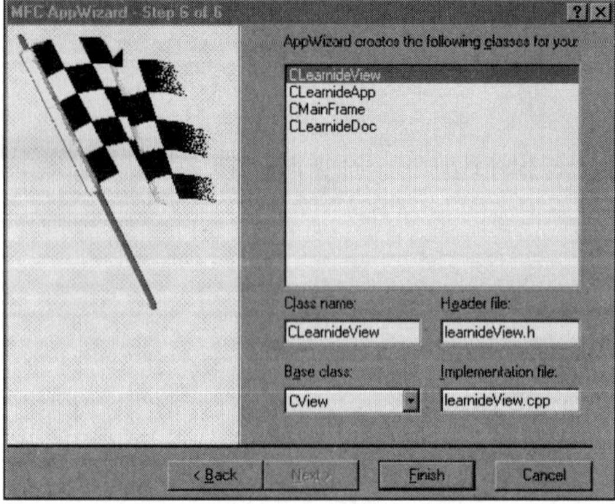

Figure 2-4: AppWizard summary dialog

Notice how the AppWizard uses your project name to create class names. To finish creating the project, click the OK button.

Step 2: Edit the project.

The AppWizard-generated code contains basic Windows functionality. If you compiled and ran the project now, the application would open a single window with a title bar, a menu bar, and an empty client area. Let's add something interesting to the program.

Click the Class View tab of the Project View window. Expand the learnide node, and then expand the node named CLearnideView by clicking the plus sign (+) next to the class name. All the names displayed beneath the class are functions that belong to that class.

Double-click the `OnDraw()` member function. This displays the code for this function in the code editor window. Edit the function so it looks like this:

```
void CLearnide::OnDraw(CDC* pDC)
{
CLearnideDoc* pDoc = GetDocument();
ASSERT_VALID(pDoc);

TRACE("This was printed during debugging\n";

pDC->TextOut(0,0,"I'm a little Visual C++ app short and
stout.");
}
```

Notice when you type the line `pDC->TextOut(...)`, a combo box appears with several functions listed. This is a new feature of Visual Studio 6 called IntelliSense. IntelliSense displays a list of possible functions that could be used from within your code. Holding up the "Intelli" part of IntelliSense is that this feature only shows you the functions that would be legal at your current position.

Using our exercise as an example, because `CLearnide` is derived from `CView`, which is in turn derived from `CWnd`, the IntelliSense combo box only displays the functions available from each of these classes. IntelliSense uses each keystroke you type to narrow the field of possible functions. Once it has found a match, all you need do is hit the spacebar or the Enter key for IntelliSense to complete the function name for you. IntelliSense will display the types and numbers of arguments a specific function requires as well.

Step 3: Debug the project.

You can build the project by selecting "Build learnide.exe" from the Build menu or hitting the F7 key or by clicking the Build button from the Build toolbar.

As the compiler and linker build your project into an executable file, they will post messages to the debug window. At the end of the build process, you should see only one error message:

```
learnideView.cpp(61) : error C2143: syntax error :

 missing ')' before ';'
```

Double-clicking the error message displays the offending line of code in the code editor window. The offending line of code is located in the `OnDraw()` member function of `CLearnideView`. Locate the line that begins with the `TRACE` command. If you entered the line as described, it should be missing a closing parenthesis. Add the parenthesis, as shown in bold in the following code:

```
TRACE("This was printed during debugging\n");
```

Now rebuild your project again. It should compile error free.

Step 4: Run the application.

Now that you have built an executable file, let's run it. Select "Execute learnide.exe" from the Build menu, or press Ctrl+F5. The application should look like the window in Figure 2-5.

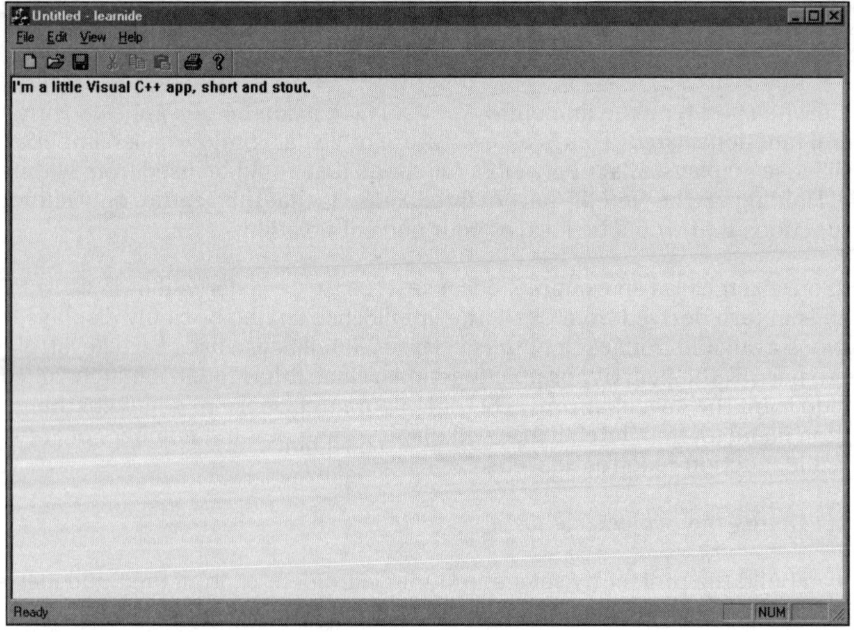

Figure 2-5: Your first MFC application

Take a few minutes to explore your new application. Notice that the AppWizard includes dockable toolbars and print preview menu options without any programming required from you. These are all benefits of an application framework called the Microsoft Foundation Classes (MFC). In later chapters we will explore MFC in much more detail.

Select Exit from the application's File menu. Now run the application using Visual Studio's debugger. You can do this by selecting Start Debug ➪ Go from the Build menu. Now the application is running from within Visual Studio's debugger. Exit the application again.

Look at the messages displayed in the IDE's debugger window. Most of these messages are not important and can be disregarded for now. You should see one line that looks like this:

```
This was printed during debugging.
```

Remember the `TRACE` statement that you debugged in Step 3? This is the result of that statement. `TRACE` is a Visual C++ macro that writes information to the debugger window. You will learn more about debugging and the `TRACE` statement in the next chapter.

Customizing the IDE

One of the strengths of the IDE is its flexibility. Many aspects of Visual Studio are easily customizable. In this section we will learn how to view the current list of keyboard shortcuts and add, edit, or delete the existing shortcuts.

Viewing the current shortcuts

You can easily view the current list of keyboard shortcuts from the Help submenu on the main IDE toolbar. Select the Keyboard Map to display a list of keyboard shortcuts. One the first things you'll notice is that it is a very long list. Custom shortcuts along with all of the default shortcuts are listed. The default keyboard map is shown in Figure 2-6.

Any shortcut that is listed in the window can be customized. While this gives you an enormous amount of flexibility, it can also be a hindrance. As you make changes to the shortcuts, especially the default ones, make sure that you aren't deleting some of the standard ones such as F5, which starts a program inside the debugger.

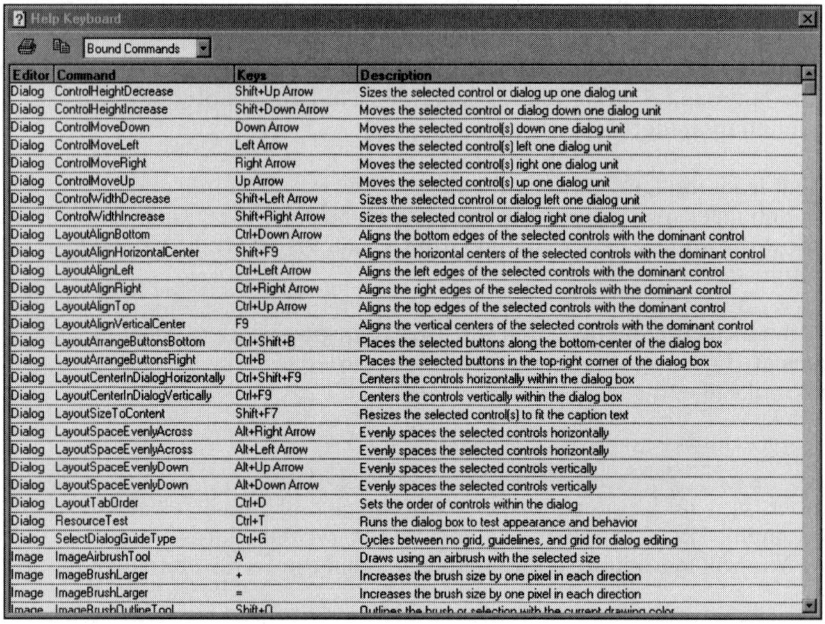

Help Keyboard

Bound Commands

Editor	Command	Keys	Description
Dialog	ControlHeightDecrease	Shift+Up Arrow	Sizes the selected control or dialog up one dialog unit
Dialog	ControlHeightIncrease	Shift+Down Arrow	Moves the selected control or dialog down one dialog unit
Dialog	ControlMoveDown	Down Arrow	Moves the selected control(s) down one dialog unit
Dialog	ControlMoveLeft	Left Arrow	Moves the selected control(s) left one dialog unit
Dialog	ControlMoveRight	Right Arrow	Moves the selected control(s) right one dialog unit
Dialog	ControlMoveUp	Up Arrow	Moves the selected control(s) up one dialog unit
Dialog	ControlWidthDecrease	Shift+Left Arrow	Sizes the selected control or dialog left one dialog unit
Dialog	ControlWidthIncrease	Shift+Right Arrow	Sizes the selected control or dialog right one dialog unit
Dialog	LayoutAlignBottom	Ctrl+Down Arrow	Aligns the bottom edges of the selected controls with the dominant control
Dialog	LayoutAlignHorizontalCenter	Shift+F9	Aligns the horizontal centers of the selected controls with the dominant control
Dialog	LayoutAlignLeft	Ctrl+Left Arrow	Aligns the left edges of the selected controls with the dominant control
Dialog	LayoutAlignRight	Ctrl+Right Arrow	Aligns the right edges of the selected controls with the dominant control
Dialog	LayoutAlignTop	Ctrl+Up Arrow	Aligns the top edges of the selected controls with the dominant control
Dialog	LayoutAlignVerticalCenter	F9	Aligns the vertical centers of the selected controls with the dominant control
Dialog	LayoutArrangeButtonsBottom	Ctrl+Shift+B	Places the selected buttons along the bottom-center of the dialog box
Dialog	LayoutArrangeButtonsRight	Ctrl+B	Places the selected buttons in the top-right corner of the dialog box
Dialog	LayoutCenterInDialogHorizontally	Ctrl+Shift+F9	Centers the controls horizontally within the dialog box
Dialog	LayoutCenterInDialogVertically	Ctrl+F9	Centers the controls vertically within the dialog box
Dialog	LayoutSizeToContent	Shift+F7	Resizes the selected control(s) to fit the caption text
Dialog	LayoutSpaceEvenlyAcross	Alt+Right Arrow	Evenly spaces the selected controls horizontally
Dialog	LayoutSpaceEvenlyAcross	Alt+Left Arrow	Evenly spaces the selected controls horizontally
Dialog	LayoutSpaceEvenlyDown	Alt+Up Arrow	Evenly spaces the selected controls vertically
Dialog	LayoutSpaceEvenlyDown	Alt+Down Arrow	Evenly spaces the selected controls vertically
Dialog	LayoutTabOrder	Ctrl+D	Sets the order of controls within the dialog
Dialog	ResourceTest	Ctrl+T	Runs the dialog box to test appearance and behavior
Dialog	SelectDialogGuideType	Ctrl+G	Cycles between no grid, guidelines, and grid for dialog editing
Image	ImageAirbrushTool	A	Draws using an airbrush with the selected size
Image	ImageBrushLarger	+	Increases the brush size by one pixel in each direction
Image	ImageBrushLarger	=	Increases the brush size by one pixel in each direction
Image	ImageBrushOutlineTool	Shift+O	Outlines the brush or selection with the current drawing color

Figure 2-6: Default keyboard map

Open the combo box at the top of the window. You can use this combo box to selectively filter your view of the shortcuts. If you select File, the window displays all the commands associated with working with files as well as any bound keyboard shortcuts. At the top of the keyboard shortcut table are several column headings. Try selecting another filtered view from the combo box. Notice how the headings change. Each time a different view is selected, the headings change to match the view.

These column headings are also clickable. Clicking a column heading once sorts the display by that column. This is especially handy if the All Commands view is displayed. Clicking the Keys heading sorts the display by bound keystrokes. Now you can see which keystroke combinations are bound to which commands.

Adding, editing, or deleting shortcuts

Changing or deleting existing shortcuts is just as easy as viewing them. Select the Tools menu, and then select Customize. When the Customize dialog opens, select the Keyboard tab. From here you can edit or delete existing keyboard shortcuts.

This dialog includes two combo boxes: category and editor. You can use these boxes to specifically assign shortcuts to one area of Visual Studio. As an exercise, follow these steps:

1. Select File from the Category combo box.
2. Select Text from the Editor combo box.
3. In the Commands list box, select FileSaveAll.
4. Put the cursor in the Press new shortcut key edit box.
5. Type **Ctrl-S**. Notice that this shortcut's current assignment is displayed beneath the edit box. This lets you know when you have selected a keystroke combination that is already in use.
6. Erase the Ctrl-S shortcut from the edit box. Now type **Ctrl-Shift-S**. This combination should not be assigned to anything.
7. Click the Assign button to bind the keystroke combination to the command.

Congratulations! You have just created your first keyboard shortcut. Deleting shortcuts is as simple. With the Customize dialog box opened follow these steps:

1. Select the command whose keyboard shortcut you wish to delete.
2. Click that command to display the shortcut.
3. Delete the keystroke combination from the edit box.
4. Click the Assign button to save your changes.

You can also use this dialog box to assign shortcuts to Visual Studio commands that don't have a default keystroke combination. In fact, many of the Visual Studio commands that you'll use every day have no direct keyboard equivalent. As you become more proficient in using Visual C++, you will save time if you can use shortcuts to basic commands.

Even though Visual Studio is an incredibly good application, it seems like the designers left out one useful feature. One of the most common things done in Visual Studio, aside from compiling, is to change between Debug and Release build settings. However, Microsoft doesn't provide any keyboard shortcuts to speed the operation along. Here's a recipe you can use to automate this function:

1. Open the Customize dialog from the Tools submenu, and select the Keyboard tab.
2. Select Build from the Category combo box.
3. Select BuildConfigurations from the Command list box.

4. Select Ctrl-Shift-C for the shortcut combination.
5. Click Assign to save the shortcut.

When you complete these steps, Ctrl+Shift+C should open the Build Configurations dialog when you are working with a project. Using these same steps, you can assign shortcuts to any command available in Visual Studio.

✦ ✦ ✦ ✦ ✦

Using Toolbars

Using toolbars, you can group commonly used commands in Visual Studio so you can find and use them quickly. Toolbars can be easily customized in almost any way you desire. You can add and delete menus and buttons, create your own custom toolbars, hide and display toolbars, and dock toolbars to different parts of the IDE. By the end of this section, you will be comfortable performing any of these tasks.

Displaying and hiding toolbars

The current toolbar settings are accessed from the Tools ➪ Customize dialog we used in the last section. Click the Toolbars tab to display the current toolbar settings. All Visual Studio toolbars, even custom ones, are listed in this dialog. Any toolbars that have a check next to them are displayed. To hide a toolbar, simply click the check box next to its name. This will deselect the toolbar and hide it immediately. Displaying toolbars is done in the same way. Check a hidden toolbar, and it will immediately pop onto the screen. The toolbar dialog is shown in Figure 2-7.

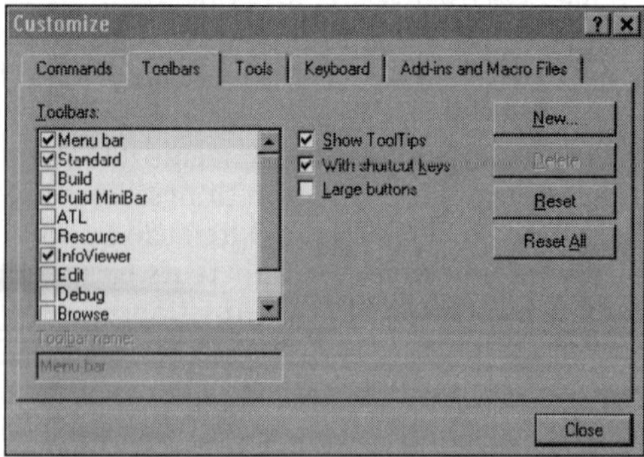

Figure 2-7: Toolbar tab of the Customize dialog box

One toolbar included in the list is a special case that cannot be hidden from this dialog. The menu bar is always displayed. You can dock it to another portion of the IDE by clicking the toolbar and dragging it to the bottom, right, or left sides of the main IDE window. Optionally, the menu bar can be made to float over any other windows by simply dragging it out of the toolbar area and leaving it over a window.

You can cause the code editor window to take up the entire screen if you really want to hide the menu bar. From the View submenu, select the Full Screen option. This will cause the editor to expand and fill the entire screen, hiding not only the menu bar but any other available toolbars as well.

Customizing toolbars

Creating custom toolbars or customizing existing toolbars is as easy as a drag-and-drop. Visual Studio gives you the ability to customize existing toolbars and also create new toolbars for functions you use all the time. The dialog box that enables you to create a toolbar is shown in Figure 2-8.

Figure 2-8: Adding a new toolbar

To create your own toolbar, simply select the Toolbars tab on the Customize dialog box. Click the New button, and enter the name of your toolbar. This creates and displays a blank toolbar, which is ready for you to add new buttons and menus. Leave the toolbar displayed for the next steps.

To add a button or menu

1. Select the Commands tab on the Customize dialog.
2. Select the category of button you want from the Categories combo box.
3. The dialog displays all the buttons associated with the selected category in a group box. Click the desired button or pull-down menu and drag it to your new toolbar.

If the item does not have a default button, the Custom Button dialog box opens. Select an image for the button from the Buttons area, or you can create your own button image with your favorite graphics program. You can also create a plain-Jane button with a text label.

Notice that while the Customize dialog is open and your custom toolbar is displayed, you can drag and drop *any* items from any IDE menu or toolbar to your new toolbar. This is a handy way to create one or two toolbars that encompass most every command you'll use on a regular basis.

Summary

In this chapter, you were introduced to the Visual Studio IDE. You saw each of the main areas of the IDE and how they interact. You also compiled a simple C++ project and used the debugger to find errors in the program code.

You also learned how to customize the IDE to the way you work. You should now know how to create new keyboard shortcuts, as well as completely new toolbars.

✦ ✦ ✦

Debugging: When Your Applications Don't Work

✦ ✦ ✦ ✦

In This Chapter

Understanding debugging

Necessary capabilities of a debugger

Using the Visual Studio Integrated Debugger

Using the Debugging Windows to gather information

Using breakpoints and single-stepping to track errors

Managing multithreaded application debugging

Using some simple debugging techniques

Using MFC tracing

Using remote debugging

✦ ✦ ✦ ✦

When you write programs in any language, it is virtually certain that you will make mistakes during the initial programming. You will make two basic types of errors when you write programs: syntax errors and logic errors. Syntax errors tend to be much simpler than logic errors and are generally easier to locate. In fact, when you compile programs that you write within Visual C++, the compiler will advise you of the existence of syntax errors within your program code. In some cases, the compiler will not compile executable code for your program because it cannot interpret the syntax errors.

Logic errors, on the other hand, are not so easy for you to track down and solve. A logic error may be relatively simple to locate, or it may be very difficult. For example, the following logic error is relatively straightforward:

```
cout << "This is line one." << "This is line
two.";
```

The code will print both lines of text on the same line. Solving a logic error of this simplicity is relatively easy. However, solving a logic error similar to the following can be substantially more difficult:

```
if (a!=c)
  cout << "A is not equal to C";
  cout << "Make A equal to C!";
```

When the program code executes, the program always displays the text

```
Make A Equal to C!
```

The logic error is in the lack of brackets around the two output statements. Even this second error, however, is simple, compared to the logic errors that you can make within a complex Windows program. Luckily, Visual C++ includes an excellent, integrated symbolic debugger. The Visual C++ debugger includes many powerful and useful features, such as Just-In-Time debugging (the capability to debug programs that crash while launched outside the development environment) and remote debugging. The debugger is also fully integrated with other features of the Visual Studio, such as the Source Browser and source editors.

When you are faced with the task of having to identify performance bottlenecks — a very specific type of logic error — you will use another tool, the Source Profiler, to identify the location of the performance bottlenecks. You will learn about the Source Profiler in the next chapter.

What Every Debugger Should Have

Clearly, debugging applications can be a complex and difficult process. As applications have become more complex and larger, the need for powerful debugging tools has increased. As a rule, a debugger should have at least four capabilities:

- ✦ Tracing
- ✦ Breakpoints
- ✦ Watching variables
- ✦ Changing values

Probably the most important facility a debugger can offer is a *trace* utility. A trace utility enables you to watch exactly where the execution pointer is in your actual source code while you run an application. In Visual C++, you have several different means of tracing program execution, from stepping through each line of code individually to executing entire programs until the program reaches a certain point.

As you can imagine, simply tracing through a program, line by line, can be tedious — particularly when you know that some code in the program works correctly. Even a small program (say, a thousand lines) could take a long time to step through, looking for one particular area of concern in the program. For larger programs, the prospect of stepping through thousands of lines of code — taking hours — just to reach a single routine that is not executing correctly is daunting. Because of the size of many program files, an efficient means of stopping the program's execution at some predetermined point in the source code or when some specific condition happens is a second important tool in any debugger. Most debuggers handle stopping program execution through the use of *breakpoints*.

Clearly, watching an application step through a series of instructions, and understanding what execution path leads to a certain error, is a useful debugging technique. However, you will generally find that understanding *why* an error occurs is as valuable, if not more valuable, than understanding *what* happened before the error. A good debugging tool should enable you to view the current values or contents of all program variables having scope or context at the current point of execution within the program file.

Once you understand how the contents of a variable can negatively impact program performance (oversize values, undefined values, and so on) or cause an exception, it often will be helpful to be able to change that variable's contents on the fly—to ensure that values within the correct range do not also cause an error. The fourth valuable feature of a debugging tool, then, is that it enables your changing the values or contents of variables during program execution—giving you the capability of checking your program's reaction to a broad spectrum of variable values without your needing to rerun the program for each value set.

As you will learn through the rest of this chapter, the Visual Studio integrated debugger provides all of the capabilities, and many others, already identified as necessary for a good debugging tool.

The Visual Studio Integrated Debugger

Visual C++ and the Visual Studio shell launch the integrated debugger whenever you run an application in debug mode. As you will learn later in this chapter, the shell also launches the integrated debugger whenever you select the Debug button on an Illegal Operation dialog box. To launch an application in debug mode within Visual C++, you can select the Go, Step Into, or Run to Cursor commands from the Start Debug submenu of the Build menu. However, before you can start the debugger, you must ensure that Visual C++ has compiled the application that you intend to debug with debugging information.

Preparing an application for debugging

As the previous section indicates, for the symbolic debugger to function currently and for you to be able to use debugging information with your Visual C++ projects, you must instruct the compiler to compile the application with debugging information. If the application you want to debug is an MFC application that you originally created through AppWizard, chances are that you do not have to do anything: the AppWizard already created a debug configuration for your project and made it the default configuration.

However, if you created the project from scratch or it is not an MFC application and you must create a debug configuration yourself, you can do so in the Project Settings dialog box. You must set the appropriate compiler and linker options within this dialog box. After you do so, the Visual C++ IDE enables you to debug the application.

To set the compiler options, select the Settings option from the Build menu. Visual C++ will display the Project Settings dialog box. Within the Project Settings dialog box, select the C/C++ tab. Visual C++ will change the display on the dialog box to the reflect the C/C++ project settings. On the left side of the dialog box, select the Win32 Debug option within the combo box. Within the Category combo box, select the General category. To enable debugging for your project, you must alter two settings. First, in the Debug info combo box, select the Program Database for Edit and Continue option. Second, in the Optimizations combo box, select the Disable (Debug) option. Figure 3-1 shows the Project Settings dialog box after you enable debugging.

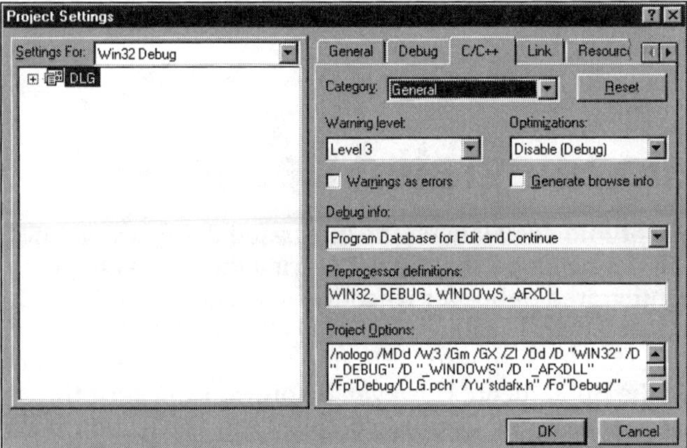

Figure 3-1: The Project Settings dialog box as it appears after you set the debug options.

If you wish to use Visual Studio's Source Browser features, you may also set the Generate browse info check box. Visual C++ automatically turns off the "Generate browse info" switch to save compiler time when it generates a new application through the AppWizard.

If you are using the compiler from the command line or from within a custom makefile, you may have to set the debugging options manually. To turn off optimization, use the `/Od` compiler option. To turn on the generation of debugging information, specify the `/ZI` option. You can learn more about command-line compiler directives in the Visual C++ help file.

Another setting that is important to keep in mind when setting debugging options is the option that enables you to specify that your project should be linked with the debug version of the C runtime library during compilation. To instruct the compiler to use the debug library, change the selection within the Category combo box to the Code Generation option. Next, select the debug library option that is correct for your application within the "Use run-time library" combo box. Figure 3-2 shows the Project Settings dialog box and the possible selections for runtime library choices.

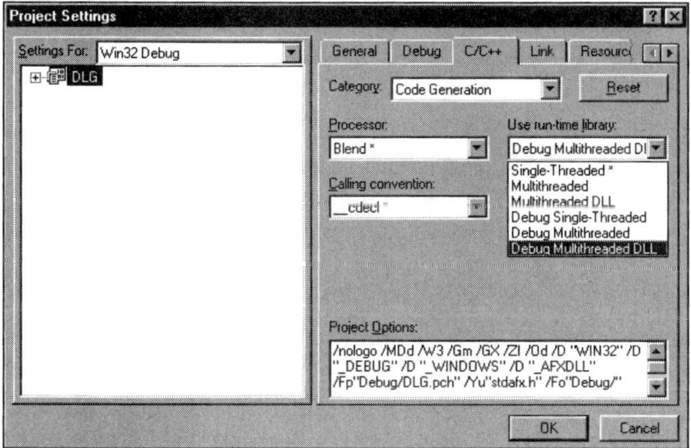

Figure 3-2: The Project Settings dialog box during the selection of the debugging runtime library linking.

Again, to set the correct option from the command line, you would use the `/M` compiler switch. To select the Debug DLL option, select the `/MDd` command-line option. To select the Debug Single-Threaded library option, select the `/MLd` command-line option. Finally, to select the Debug Multithreaded library option, select the `/MTd` command-line option.

When you create a project for debugging, you must also modify the linker settings for the project to compile and link correctly. You can also set the linker settings from within the Project Settings dialog box. Select the Link tab and the General option with the Category combo box. To turn on the generation of debugging information, set the "Generate debug info" check box. Figure 3-3 shows the Project Settings dialog box after you set the Linker for debugging.

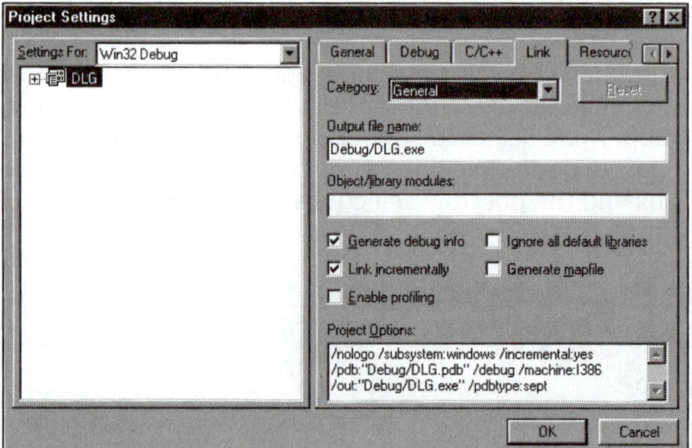

Figure 3-3: The Link tab after you set the linker for debugging.

Just as you can set the debug options from the compiler command line, you can set the debug options in the linker from the linker command line. To do, specify the `/debug` switch on the linker command line.

Using the debugger when you run an application

After you recompile your application with the debug settings, you can run the application in debug mode by using any of the commands (except the Attach to Process command) on the Start Debug submenu on the Build menu.

You can also control how the debugger runs the application through the Project Settings dialog box. On the Debug tab of the Project Settings dialog box, you can control certain factors about how the program executes within the debugger. One of the fields of special interest on the Debug tab is the Executable for debug session field. You can use this field to debug dynamic link library (DLL) projects. Instead of specifying the name of the DLL, however, you should specify the name of a program that loads and accesses the DLL. For example, to debug an ActiveX control (which is a special type of DLL), you can use the Visual C++ utility `tstcon32.exe` as the debug session executable. Figure 3-4 shows the Project Settings dialog box after you select `tstcon32.exe`.

When you begin a debug session, depending on your Visual Studio settings, any one of a variety of debug windows may appear within the Visual Studio window. Other windows (such as the Project Workspace window) that are normally present may disappear. The Visual Studio menu bar also changes — the Debug menu replaces the Build menu.

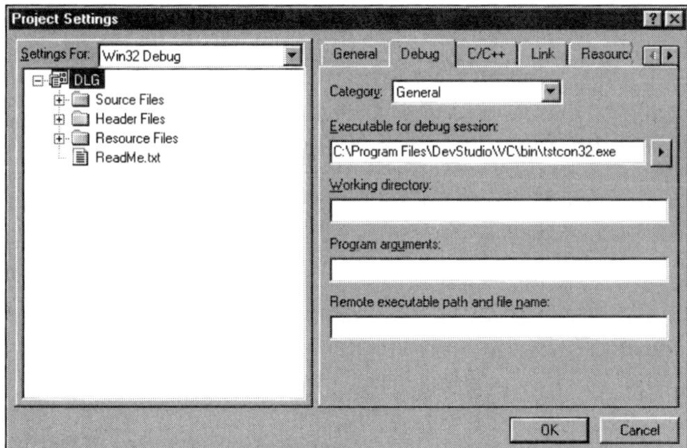

Figure 3-4: Setting the Debugger to debug an ActiveX control within a control container.

The application that you select for debugging starts executing and continues to execute until either the debugger reaches a breakpoint or you select the Break option from the Debug menu and interrupt the application's execution.

Debug windows

During a debugging session, Visual Studio presents debugging information in a series of debug windows. If Visual Studio is not currently displaying any or all of these windows, you can use the Visual Studio View menu to instruct the IDE to display each or all of the windows. You can display all of the debugging windows that you will learn about in this section as either normal windows or docking windows. If you set the windows to display as docking windows, the windows also appear in the toolbar pop-up menu — the menu that Visual Studio displays when you right-click an empty toolbar area.

Source windows are regular source editor windows. However, during a debugging session, special debugging functions are also available through the pop-up menu that you invoke by right-clicking inside a source window. You can set, clear, enable, and disable breakpoints from the source window pop-up menu. You can also execute single-stepping commands (that is, execute a single line of program at a time). You can also invoke the Disassembly window and the QuickWatch dialog from the source window pop-up menu.

The Variables window presents a look at variables that have definition within the current function. The window has three tabs: the Auto tab, the Locals tab, and the `this` tab. The Auto tab displays variables that the program uses within the current line and on the previous line. The Locals tab shows all variables that have local definition within the current function, including both locally defined variables and function parameters. The `this` tab, as you might expect, shows the object that the `this` pointer currently points to. Figure 3-5 shows the Variables window with the Auto tab selected.

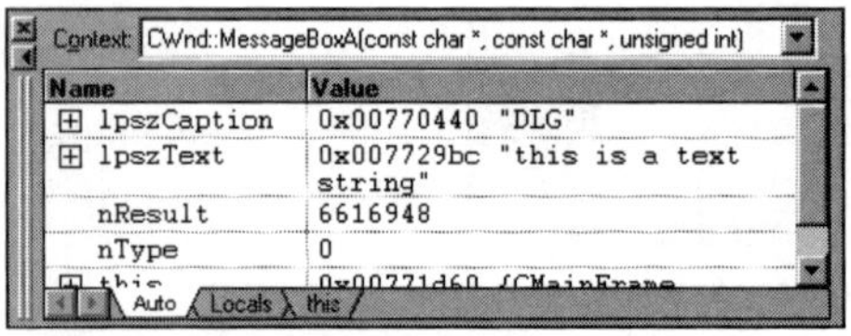

Figure 3-5: The Variables window shows the Name and Value of variables having definition in the current function.

You can also use the Variables window to view variables in the scope of functions that called the currently executing function. In addition, as you single-step through your code within the currently executing function, the Variables window displays all changed variables in a different color.

You can also use the Variables window to modify the values of data items that are of a simple type (such as `int`, `double`, or pointer types). To modify a value, double-click the value in the Variables window. If the debugger lets you modify the value, the IDE displays a text cursor within the window.

During a debugging session, you can use the Watch window to monitor the values of expressions. You can use the keyboard to enter an expression within the Name field in the Watch window, or you can drag the expression or paste it from a source window. Figure 3-6 shows the Watch window.

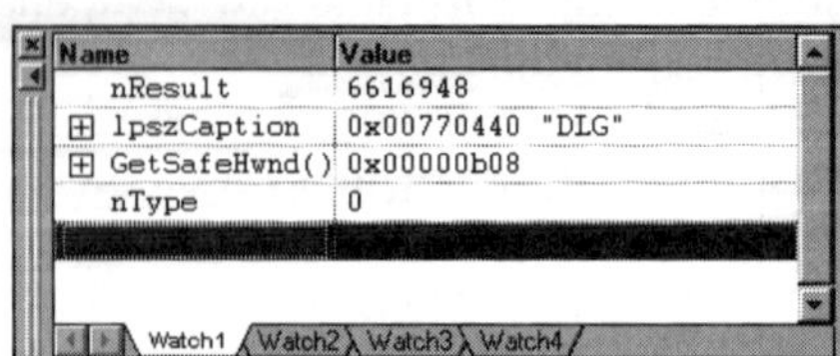

Figure 3-6: The Watch window displays information about expressions' current values.

As you can see, the Watch window has four tabs. During a debugging session, you can use these tabs to maintain four different sets of watch expressions. As your programs become more complex and you use custom classes and objects, being able to watch different expression sets will become more valuable.

Like the Variables window, the Watch window uses a different color to mark expressions whose values change as you single-step through your code. In addition, you can use the Watch window to modify the values of data items of a simple type just as you would the Variables window.

The Registers window shows the current values of the registers in the computer's processor, including its floating-point registers (if you should decide to include them). Just as with the Variables window and the Watch window, the Registers window changes the color of values that change during single-stepping. Figure 3-7 shows the Registers window.

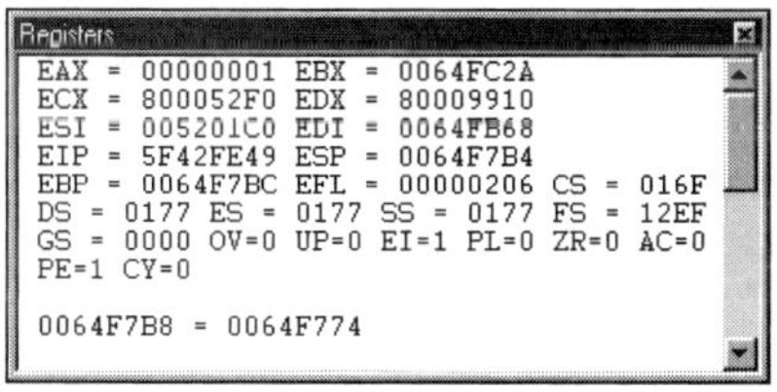

```
Registers
EAX = 00000001 EBX = 0064FC2A
ECX = 800052F0 EDX = 80009910
ESI = 005201C0 EDI = 0064FB68
EIP = 5F42FE49 ESP = 0064F7B4
EBP = 0064F7BC EFL = 00000206 CS = 016F
DS = 0177 ES = 0177 SS = 0177 FS = 12EF
GS = 0000 OV=0 UP=0 EI=1 PL=0 ZR=0 AC=0
PE=1 CY=0

0064F7B8 = 0064F774
```

Figure 3-7: The Registers window shows the current values within the processor registers.

The Memory window enables you to view memory contents in the address space of the process (application, DLL, or other program) that you are debugging. The Memory window can display memory contents in byte format, word (short hex) format, and double word (long hex) format. If you choose byte format, the Memory window also displays the ASCII characters that the bytes you are viewing represent along the window's right side. You can use the Memory window pop-up menu to select the format that the Memory window uses to display values. To invoke the pop-up menu, right-click anywhere within the Memory window. Figure 3-8 shows the Memory window starting at the `hInstance` variable's location in memory.

```
Memory
Address: hInstance
0064FDA0  00 00 40 00 00 00 00   ..@....
0064FDA7  00 46 E1 73 81 01 00   .Fás...
0064FDAE  00 00 00 00 00 00 5C   ......\
0064FDB5  8B 77 81 00 00 54 00   ▮w...T.
0064FDBC  01 00 00 00 00 00 00   .......
0064FDC3  00 46 E1 73 81 A0 04   .Fás...
0064FDCA  77 00 00 00 00 00 39   w.....9
0064FDD1  85 11 40 F0 0B 77 00   ▮.@ð.w.
0064FDD8  01 00 00 00 44 00 00   ....D..
0064FDDF  00 00 00 00 00 00 00   .......
0064FDE6  00 00 00 00 00 00 00   .......
0064FDED  00 00 00 00 00 00 00   .......
0064FDF4  00 00 00 00 00 00 00   .......
0064FDFB  00 00 00 00 00 00 00   .......
```

Figure 3-8: The Memory window displays values within process memory.

To display memory at a specific location, type an expression in the Address field of the Memory window's toolbar. Note that the Memory window may display memory locations that precede the specified address. Because the window might display both preceding and trailing values, it may be difficult for you to interpret the Memory window's contents if you specify the address to display as a symbolic expression (such as a variable name). However, the window automatically positions the text cursor at the location that corresponds to the beginning of that expression's memory location, so you can use the cursor's position as a guide to where the block of memory you want to analyze begins. Like the other debug windows you have learned about, the Memory window displays changed memory contents in a different color as you single-step through a project.

The Call Stack window lists the hierarchy of function calls that led to the current function the application is executing. If you double-click a function within the Call Stack window, the debugger updates source windows and other debug windows to reflect the context of the function you select. Selecting a function in the Call Stack window (by single-clicking) and pressing the F7 key executes code until the program reaches the specified function. Figure 3-9 shows the Call Stack window.

```
Call Stack
CWnd::MessageBoxA(const char * 0x007729bc, const char * 0x00770440, unsigned in
CMainFrame::OnViewDialog() line 118
_AfxDispatchCmdMsg(CCmdTarget * 0x00771d60 {CMainFrame}, unsigned int 32771, in
CCmdTarget::OnCmdMsg(unsigned int 32771, int 0, void * 0x00000000, AFX_CMDHANDL
CFrameWnd::OnCmdMsg(unsigned int 32771, int 0, void * 0x00000000, AFX_CMDHANDLE
CWnd::OnCommand(unsigned int 32771, long 0) line 2087
CFrameWnd::OnCommand(unsigned int 32771, long 0) line 317
CWnd::OnWndMsg(unsigned int 273, unsigned int 32771, long 0, long * 0x0064fb04)
CWnd::WindowProc(unsigned int 273, unsigned int 32771, long 0) line 1584 + 30 b
AfxCallWndProc(CWnd * 0x00771d60 {CMainFrame hWnd=???}, HWND__ * 0x00000b08, un
AfxWndProc(HWND__ * 0x00000b08, unsigned int 273, unsigned int 32771, long 0) l
AfxWndProcBase(HWND__ * 0x00000b08, unsigned int 273, unsigned int 32771, long
KERNEL32! bff735d9()
KERNEL32! bff9222f()
```

Figure 3-9: The Call Stack window displays the function call series that led to the currently executing function.

When you debug your programs, you can use the Call Stack window as an effective tool in determining the call series that caused a specific bug.

The Disassembly window provides a view of the assembly language code that the compiler generates when it compiles your application. While the Disassembly window has the focus (that is, it is the currently selected window), you can use the single-stepping functions of the debugger to step through the assembly language code (rather than the actual program code) one instruction at a time. Stepping through assembly language code may help you determine what part of an expression is causing an error. Figure 3-10 shows the Disassembly window.

```
Disassembly
5F42FE49   mov          dword ptr [nResult],eax
2249:      return nResult;
5F42FE4C   mov          eax,dword ptr [nResult]
2250:  }
5F42FE4F   mov          esp,ebp
5F42FE51   pop          ebp
5F42FE52   ret          0Ch
2251:
2252: CWnd* PASCAL CWnd::GetDescendantWindow(HWND hWnd, int nID, BOOL bOnlyPerm)
2253: {
5F42FE55   push         ebp
5F42FE56   mov          ebp,esp
5F42FE58   sub          esp,8
2254:      // GetDlgItem recursive (return first found)
2255:      // breadth-first for 1 level, then depth-first for next level
2256:
2257:      // use GetDlgItem since it is a fast USER function
```

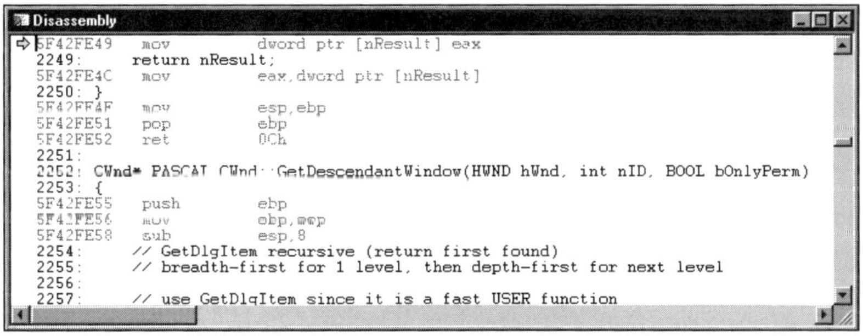

Figure 3-10: The Disassembly window shows the actual assembly language code for your program.

You can access a special feature of the Disassembly window through the pop-up menu that Visual Studio displays each time you right-click within the window. The Set Next Statement option enables you to alter the processor's instruction pointer. With the Set Next Statement option, you can set the next instruction for the processor to perform to whatever instruction is under the text cursor. For example, you can use this feature to skip portions of your program code. However, you should use this feature with extreme care. If you set the statement to be one in the body of another function or if you fail to maintain the stack correctly, the results will be unpredictable, and the application you are debugging will probably crash.

Using breakpoints and single-stepping when debugging

The two most fundamental features of any debugger, and two of the most powerful features of the integrated debugger that comes with Visual C++, are the capability to insert breakpoints into program code and the capability to execute program code step by step (a single instruction at a time).

The simplest way to place a breakpoint into your code is to move the text cursor in the source window to the specific location where you want to set a break. After placing the text cursor, press the F9 key to set the breakpoint. Visual Studio will place a large red dot to the left of the line to indicate the breakpoint. Figure 3-11 shows a source window with two breakpoints set within it.

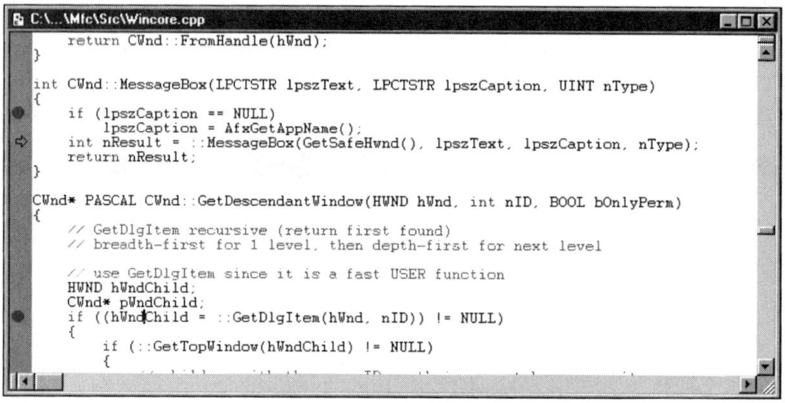

Figure 3-11: Two breakpoints are set in this source window.

There are two important things to note about simple breakpoints before you learn about more complex breakpoints. First, you can set a breakpoint at any location within a source file—on a comment line, on a bracket, and so on. However, when you compile the program, Visual C++ disables the program and won't commence execution. Second, Visual Studio enables you to set breakpoints within the Disassembly window.

You can achieve much finer control over breakpoint settings through the Breakpoints option on the Edit menu. When you select the Breakpoints option, Visual Studio displays the Breakpoints dialog, where you can set three different kinds of breakpoints.

Location breakpoints are breakpoints that interrupt program execution at a specific location. Location breakpoints are the breakpoints that you use the F9 key to set within your source code. You can also add a conditional check to a location breakpoint. If you add a conditional check, the breakpoint only interrupts execution if the specific condition evaluates as true.

Data breakpoints interrupt program execution when a specific expression's value changes. For both data and location breakpoints, you can click the triangular button next to the breakpoint identifier to invoke the Advanced Breakpoint dialog box. Within the Advanced Breakpoint dialog box, you can specify the context of the breakpoint, including the function within which the breakpoint applies, the source file that contains the breakpoint, and the executable file in which the breakpoint is located. Figure 3-12 shows the Advanced Breakpoint dialog box.

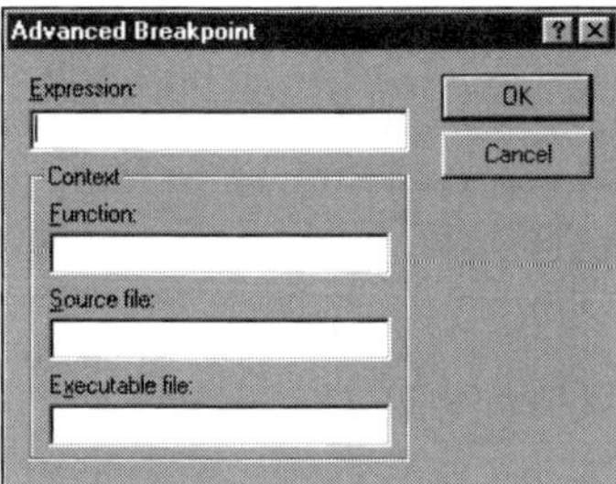

Figure 3-12: The Advanced Breakpoint dialog box enables you to specify the context of a breakpoint.

The third type of breakpoint that you can set within your program is called a *message breakpoint*. A message breakpoint interrupts your program's execution whenever one of your program's window procedures receives a specific message. (Windows receive messages from the operating system all the time—each time the user presses a key while the window is active, for example.) Setting message breakpoints enables you to stop program execution only when a certain action (such as an OLE drag-and-drop action or the user's pressing of a key combination such as Alt+F10) occurs, and ensures that the window in question processes the action correctly. Figure 3-13 shows the Breakpoints dialog box during the setting of a message breakpoint.

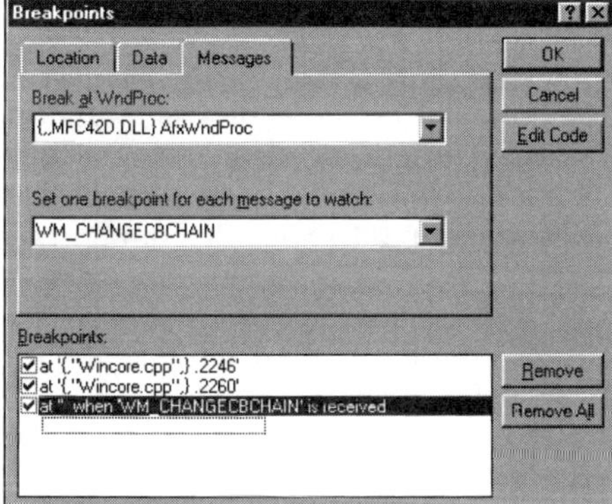

Figure 3-13: Use the Breakpoints dialog box for setting a message breakpoint to halt execution when the window receives the CHANGECBCHAIN message.

A breakpoint can be either active or disabled. When a breakpoint of any type is active and your application is executing in Debug mode, the Breakpoints dialog box displays a check mark next to the breakpoint. If you click the check mark next to a breakpoint, the breakpoint becomes inactive. Visual Studio displays inactive breakpoints as hollow red circles in the source window.

In addition to using breakpoints, you can use the Break option on the Debug menu to interrupt program execution at any time. However, such an interruption is asynchronous by nature and often interrupts the program deep inside a series of nested system function calls. In such cases, you can use the Step Out option on the Debug menu to step out of such system functions until you reach a recognizable location in your code.

The Step Out option on the Debug menu is one of several single-stepping commands that you can use to execute your program one step at a time. The most basic single-stepping command is the Step Into command, which executes the next line in the program's source file or the next instruction in the Disassembly window (depending on what window has the focus). If the next line in the program or instruction in the Disassembly window is a function call (or a `JMP` statement), the program steps into the body of the function on the next Step Into command.

The Step Over command is similar to the Step Into command, except the Step Over command does not step into the body of a function. Rather, the debugger executes all the code within the function (and any other functions it calls) and resumes step-by-step execution at the first statement following the function call in the original (calling) function.

The Run to Cursor command, effectively, places a one-shot breakpoint at the cursor's current location in a source window or the Disassembly window. The debugger continues executing the program code until it reaches the cursor position or until the debugger encounters another breakpoint.

You can use the Step Into Specific Function command to control which function the program's execution enters in the case of nested function calls in a single source line. If the debugger's execution pointer is not currently on a line that calls nested function calls, the Visual Studio IDE disables the Step Into Specific Function option.

Many of the Debug menu's step commands have keyboard shortcuts. As you will learn, stepping through a program is generally simpler if you use the keyboard shortcuts. Table 3-1 lists the keyboard shortcuts for the Step commands on the Debug menu.

Table 3-1
Keyboard Shortcuts for Single-Stepping Commands

Command	*Function Key*
Step Over	F10
Run to Cursor	Ctrl+F10
Step Into	F11
Step Out	Shift+F11

While the program is halted within the debugger, you can specify the instruction at which the program's execution should continue. To do so, you should use the Set Next Statement command in either a source window or the Disassembly window. As you have learned, you must be careful when you use the Set Next Statement command — placing it in another function or in a way that corrupts the stack can cause serious errors.

Using the DataTips information and the QuickWatch window

Despite the power that the debug windows put at your fingertips to help you debug program code, at times you will require information about a specific symbol within an executing program that does not appear in either the Variables or Watch windows. The Visual C++ integrated debugger provides two additional tools you can use for just such a purpose: the DataTips information and the QuickWatch window.

DataTips are similar to the tooltips that you are probably familiar with, which show hints for a button or other user interface object when the cursor rests over the object for a brief period of time. If during a debugging session you position the mouse cursor over the name of a symbol that can be evaluated, the IDE displays the symbol's value in a tooltip-like window. Figure 3-14 shows a DataTip display.

```
        }
    }
    LeaveCriticalSection(&m_sect);
}

/////////////////////////////////////////////////////////////////////////////
// CThreadLocalObject

CNoTrackObject* CThreadLocalObject::GetData(
    CNoTrackObject* (AFXAPI* pfnCreateObject)())
{
    if (m_nSlot == 0)
    {
        if (_afxThreadData == NULL)
        {
            _afxThreadData = new(__afxThreadData) CThreadSlotData;
            ASSERT(_afxThreadData != NULL);
        }
        m_nSlot = _afxThreadData->AllocSlot();
        ASSERT(m_nSlot != 0);
    }
    CNoTrackObject* pValue =
        (CNoTrackObject*)_afxThreadData->GetThreadValue(m_nSlot);
    if (pValue == NULL)        _afxThreadData = 0x5f4ce148 unsigned char * __afxThreadData
    {
        // allocate zero-init object
        pValue = (*pfnCreateObject)();

        // set tls data to newly created object
        _afxThreadData->SetValue(m_nSlot, pValue);
```

Figure 3-14: A DataTip displays information about the AfxThreadData object.

The function and appearance of the QuickWatch window is similar to that for the Watch window. You can alter the values of simple types within the QuickWatch window, just as with the Watch window. However, as the previous paragraph indicates, you can also choose specific symbols to add to the QuickWatch window. Figure 3-15 shows the QuickWatch window.

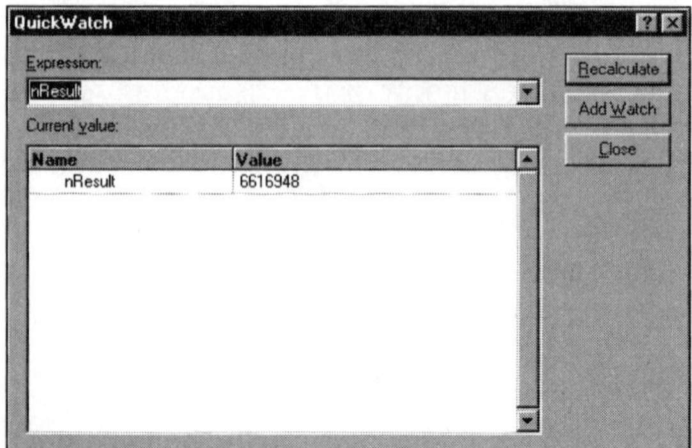

Figure 3-15: This QuickWatch window is displaying a single expression.

Using the Threads and the Exceptions dialog boxes when debugging

As you know, the Windows 32-bit programming environment is a multithreaded environment. Debugging multithreaded applications creates additional difficulties that can make effective debugging even harder. The Visual C++ debugger includes the Threads dialog box, which you can use to set the focus to a specific thread within a multithreaded application when you are debugging that application. You invoke the Threads dialog box through the Threads option on the Debug menu. Figure 3-16 shows the Threads dialog box.

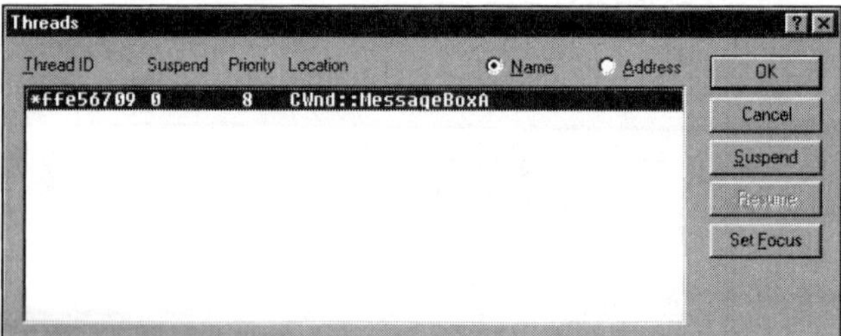

Figure 3-16: This Threads dialog box displays with the current thread highlighted.

Visual C++ provides the Exceptions dialog box, in addition to the Threads dialog box. You can use the Exceptions dialog box to specify how your program responds to exceptions during a debug session. You can select a standard exception or a user-defined exception. Within the dialog box, specify the action the debugger should take when the program notifies the debugger of a specific exception. By default, the debugger sets most exception types to Stop if not handled. Figure 3-17 shows the Exceptions dialog box.

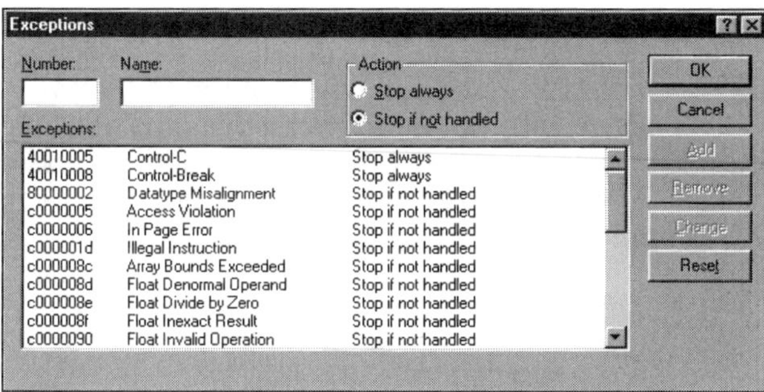

Figure 3-17: The Exceptions dialog box lists exceptions.

Simple Debugging Techniques

The Visual C++ integrated debugger and the various debugging features that Microsoft built into the Microsoft Foundation Classes provide a variety of debugging techniques. The following sections detail some of the more common debugging techniques that you can use when debugging your programs.

Using message boxes to speed debugging

Although the integrated debugger provides great power and usability, sometimes it is not convenient for you to use the debugger when debugging your programs. For example, the debugger window's presence might interfere with your program's execution, or perhaps the bug you are trying to eliminate appears only in the release version of your program. In such cases, a message box may be all you need to effectively catch the bug. For example, if you determine that a two-parameter function called `ErrFunc` misbehaves, you can easily verify that the function is receiving the correct parameters by adding a call to `AfxMessageBox`, as shown in the following code:

```
char temparr[100];
wsprintf(temparr, "Calling ErrFunc(x = %d, y = %d)", x, y);
AfxMessageBox(temparr);
ErrFunc(x, y);
```

The message box will display the string before the function call — which might enable you to break the execution sequence, change the values of `x` and `y`, or simply verify that the error is internal to `ErrFunc` and not in the calling values.

Debugging output

One of the features that Microsoft built into the Microsoft Foundation Classes is that most MFC functions automatically generate debugging output. You can also use the TRACE or the TRACE0, TRACE1, TRACE2, and TRACE3 macros to generate debugging output within your own program code. The debugger sends debugging output to the afxDump object, which is a predefined object of the MFC class CDumpContext. Visual Studio usually sends output from the afxDump object to the Output window. To see the output, select the Debug tab in the Output window. For example, to examine the values the calling program passes to the ErrFunc() function, you would write code similar to the following:

```
TRACE2("Calling ErrFunc(x = %d, y = %d)", x, y);
ErrFunc(x, y);
```

You will be able to view the output only from TRACE2 if you have compiled your application for debugging. In addition, you must launch the application from the debugger, even if you do not want to use the other debugging features the debugger offers.

You should generally use the TRACE0, TRACE1, TRACE2, and TRACE3 macros when doing so is appropriate because each of these macros requires less memory than TRACE does. The TRACE0 macro takes a format string (Only) and can be used for simple text messages that the application dumps to afxDump. The TRACE1 macro processes a format string plus one argument (one variable that the macro dumps to afxDump). The TRACE2 macro takes a format string plus two arguments (two variables that the macro dumps to afxDump). The TRACE3 macro, as you might expect, takes a format string plus three arguments (three variables that the macro dumps to afxDump). You can use the TRACE*n* macros when you know how many variables you intend to dump. Also, the TRACE*n* macros are also useful in Unicode builds because you must use the _T formatting character with TRACE in a Unicode build, but you do not need to with the TRACE*n* macros.

Furthermore, you cannot use any member of the TRACE family if you do not build the program for debugging—release compilations ignore TRACE macros altogether.

Using assertions

One of the most commonly used, and most powerful, tools in the debugger's arsenal is the ASSERT macro. You can use the ASSERT macro to interrupt the execution of your application when a specific condition evaluates as false. You can use the ASSERT macro within debug versions of your application to verify, for example, that a function receives the proper parameters. Again using the ErrFunc() example, you might place the ASSERT macro at the function's very beginning, as shown here:

```
void ErrFunc(int x, int y)
 {
   ASSERT (x >= 0 && y < 100);
```

You can also use the ASSERT_VALID macro to verify that a pointer points to a valid CObject class-derived object. For example, when you have a function within your application called GetDocument() that returns a pointer to an object of type

CSampleDoc, you may verify that the pointer is valid with the ASSERT_VALID macro. You might use code similar to the following to do so:

```
CSampleDoc *pDoc;
pDoc = GetDocument();
ASSERT_VALID(pDoc);
```

Both ASSERT and ASSERT_VALID display a message box that indicates the line number within the program at which the assertion failed. The debugger interrupts program execution and leaves the execution pointer at the line containing the ASSERT macro. Like the TRACE macro, neither ASSERT macro has any effect if you do not build the application with debugging support.

Object dumping

The CObject class has a member function, Dump(), that dumps the contents of an object to the debugging Output window (through the afxDump object). If you intend to dump the contents of objects you derive from the CObject class, you should implement the Dump() member function for those objects. For example, if you derive a custom document class from the MFC CDocument class that you call CSampleDoc, and that class includes two member variables, m_xPos and m_yPos, your CSampleDoc::Dump() implementation might look similar to the following code:

```
#ifdef _DEBUG          // check that it is a debug build
void CSampleDoc::Dump(CDumpContext& dc) const
 {
   CDocument::Dump(dc);
   dc << "m_xPos = " << m_xPos << endl;
   dc << "m_yPos = " << m_yPos << endl;
 }
#endif                 // _DEBUG
```

Detecting memory leaks and the CMemoryState class

You can use the CMemoryState class to detect memory leaks that occur due to a program's inappropriate use of the C++ new or delete operators for memory allocation and retrieval. To take a snapshot of memory allocation at any point, you can create a CMemoryState object and call its Checkpoint member function. Later, you can call the DumpAllObjectsSince() member function to dump the contents of all objects the program allocated space to since the last time the program called the Checkpoint() member function. For example, to dump any objects that the SloppyFunc() function allocates and then fails to deallocate, you could use code similar to the following:

```
CMemoryState memState;
memState.Checkpoint();
SloppyFunc(x,y);
memState.DumpAllObjectsSince();
```

If you do not require a complete dump of all objects allocated between `Checkpoint()` invocations, you can also use the `DumpStatistics()` member function. You can call `DumpStatistics()` after your program evaluates the difference between two memory states with the `Difference()` member function. To use `DumpStatistics()`, you must create, in total, three `CMemoryState()` objects. You will use the first two to take snapshots of the state of memory, and the third to evaluate the differences between the two. You might use code similar to the following to check the state of memory:

```
CMemoryState msBeforeCall, msAfterCall, msDiffBA;
// other code here
msBeforeCall.Checkpoint();
SloppyFunc(x,y);
msAfterCall.Checkpoint();
if (msDiffBA.Difference(msBeforeCall, msAfterCall))
   msDiffBA.DumpStatistics();
```

You cannot use `CMemoryState` objects to detect memory leaks that result from incorrect program calls to `malloc/free`, `GlobalAlloc/GlobalFree` or `LocalAlloc/LocalFree`.

✦ ✦ ✦ ✦ ✦

Using MFC tracing

As you learned earlier in this chapter, the debug version of the MFC Library sends a variety of trace messages to the Debug tab in the Output window. You can use the MFCTracer application, `tracer.exe`, to enable or disable some or all of the MFC trace messages. You can use the Tools menu to invoke the MFCTracer application. The MFCTracer application displays a simple dialog box interface in which you can specify the MFC trace messages you want to enable or disable. Figure 3-18 shows the MFC Trace Options dialog box in which you specify when MFC should generate trace messages.

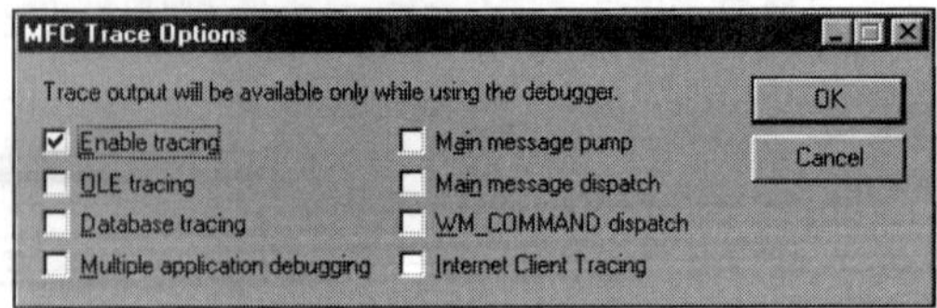

Figure 3-18: The MFCTracer application displays this MFC Trace Options dialog box.

Remote Debugging

You may often work on or help debug programs that reside on another user's machine. *Remote debugging* enables you to debug program code that is running on another machine that your machine is connected to. The local and the remote machines must be connected either through a serial connection or a local area network. The local machine must run Visual C++ and the integrated debugger, while the remote machine runs the application that you wish to debug and the Visual C++ Debug Monitor. Figure 3-19 shows the communications process between the local machine and the remote machine during remote debugging.

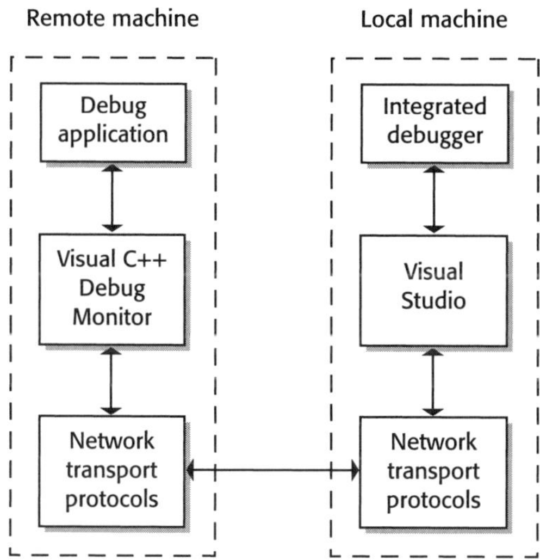

Figure 3-19: The communications path between the local, debugging machine and the remote application

As the previous paragraph indicates, the remote machine must run the Visual C++ Debug Monitor application, `Msvcmon.exe`, for the machine to support remote debugging of the application. In order for the `Msvcmon.exe` application to run properly, you must also install the following DLLs on the remote computer: `Msvcrt.dll`, `Tln0t.dll`, `Dm.dll`, `Msvcp60.dll`, and `Msdis100.dll`. You must copy all the files into a directory that is on the system path — preferably the Windows system directory.

Visual Studio installs all the files automatically onto any computer on which you install Visual Studio. Default installation places the `Msvcmon.exe` application into the Visual Studio directory's `Common\MSDev98\Bin` subdirectory.

✦ ✦ ✦ ✦ ✦

To use remote debugging, you must run the Debug Monitor on the remote computer before you run the program itself. When you execute the Debug Monitor, the program displays a dialog box within which you must specify the program settings. You will most often use remote debugging over a TCP/IP network connection. After you select the connection, you can click the Settings button to specify the details of the connection — the target machine's name or address and an access password, if any. Figure 3-20 shows the Debug Monitor dialog box.

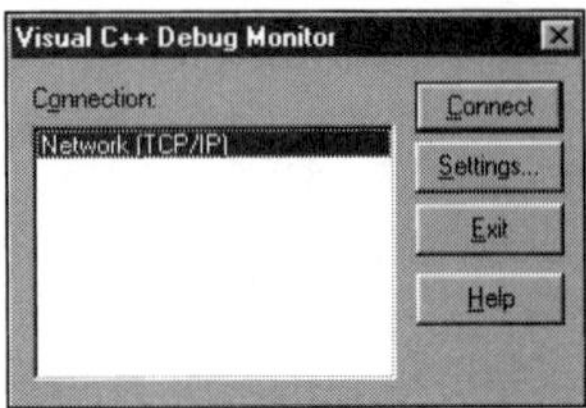

Figure 3-20: You can specify the details of the connection in the Visual C++ Debug Monitor dialog box.

After you select the target machine, click the Connect button. The Debug Monitor then waits for an incoming connection. To configure the local computer to request the connection, you must first run Visual Studio on the local machine.

After you have run Visual Studio, select the Remote Connection command from the Tools menu. Visual Studio will display the Remote Connection dialog box. Within this dialog box, you should specify the type of connection (in this case, a Network TCP/IP connection) and then set the parameters for the connection. Click the Settings button to set connection parameters. Figure 3-21 shows the Remote Connection dialog box.

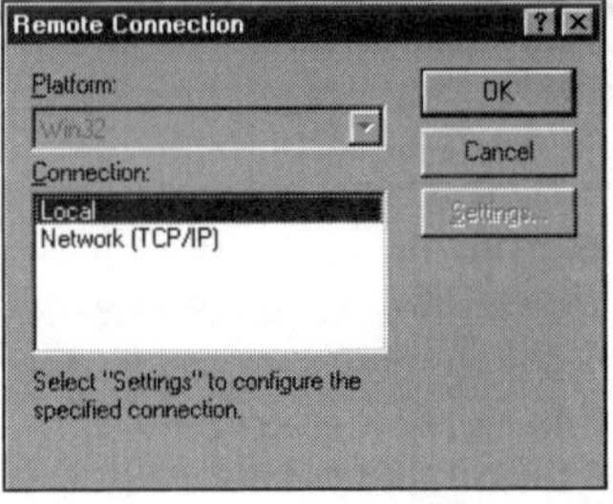

Figure 3-21: You specify the type of connection in the Remote Connection dialog box.

When you set a network connection, both the Debug Monitor and the Remote Connection ask you to supply a password for the connection. Make sure that both passwords are the same; otherwise, the two computers won't be unable to communicate properly.

✦ ✦ ✦ ✦ ✦

The major advantage of remote debugging is that the application runs on a machine unaffected by the presence of the debugger. Remote debugging is ideal, then, for debugging applications that take over the Windows display, keyboard, sound drivers, and so on — such as full-screen game applications. Remote debugging is also ideal for debugging applications that work properly when you compile them as Win32 debug applications but don't work correctly when you compile them as Win32 release applications.

Just-In-Time Debugging

Just-In-Time debugging represents the Visual C++ compiler's capability to attach itself to a running program that just halted because of an unhandled exception. Just-In-Time debugging is useful for debugging applications that were not originally launched from within the integrated debugger or that were not built with debugging information.

You can turn on Just-In-Time debugging from the Option command on the Tools menu inside Visual Studio. In the Options dialog, select the Debug tag, and set the Just-In-Time debugging check box.

Visual Studio automatically enables Just-In-Time debugging when you install it onto your computer.

✦ ✦ ✦ ✦ ✦

Edit and Continue debugging

As Rapid Application Development (RAD) tools such as Visual Basic have become more popular, many of their characteristics have carried over into the Visual Studio interface (in fact, Microsoft is currently trying to design a single, unified interface for Visual Basic, Visual C++, Visual FoxPro, Visual J++, and some supporting programs). One of the Visual Basic compiler's most-commonly used features is the Edit and Continue feature, which enables you to makes changes to an application that you are debugging while the application executes, and use those changes to resolve application errors.

With Visual C++ 6.0, you can actually use Edit and Continue with debug builds of your Visual C++ applications. Unlike Visual Basic, however, the Visual C++ debugger has one major limitation on its use within programs. When you use the Edit and Continue feature of the debugger, you must ensure that you replace the exact same number of bytes with your change as the application had when you built it originally. For example, you could replace a number with another number — but you could not replace a string constant (such as 'A') with a string variable (such as "A") because the replacement is one byte longer than the original (because of the trailing 0 character that C++ appends to strings). If you make a change that Edit and Continue cannot support directly, Visual Studio alerts you and asks you to recompile the project or cancel the change.

Visual Studio Edit and Continue debugging works only if the debugger successfully compiles the application — meaning you can use it only to capture logic errors, not syntax errors. The compiler catches syntax errors before you ever start to debug.

✦ ✦ ✦ ✦ ✦

Debugging Windows NT services

As you have learned, the integrated debugger enables you to debug any application that you can design in Visual Studio — not just standard executable applications. An excellent example of another application type that you can debug if it fails during execution is a Windows NT service.

The easiest way to begin debugging a service of Windows NT Server is to artificially run it as a console application — in other words, at a command prompt . Doing so enables you to step through the service's code from the first instruction, provides more complete access to the Visual Studio debugger, and supplies a window for viewing MAPI messages.

To set up your service as a console application, you must handle the return codes from the Windows NT service control manager and then take the appropriate code path in your startup code. In other words, when an application runs as a service on Windows NT Server, the operating system usually calls the service control manager to find the application's main function. If the process is artificially running as a console application, calls to the service control manager fail. When calls to the service control manager fail, you should branch within the debugger and call your main function explicitly.

To run your application as a console application, you must include the `Winwrap.Lib` library in your makefile (or your application's external dependency). Doing so handles the service control manager calls. If you do not include this library, look at the library's source code, and make the necessary changes to your application's main function.

Summary

In this chapter, you have learned about the Visual C++ integrated debugger and the benefits that it provides for debugging and testing your programs. The debug windows provide more information about a program, in many cases, than you could ever need. The `ASSERT` macros, breakpoints, DataTips, and more provide instant feedback about your application's performance.

However, all the debugging in the world is no substitute for good, solid programming. The more solid your code is when you initially write it, the less time you will spend working with the debugger, and the less time another programmer will spend with the debugger whenever he or she makes additions or changes to your programs. The integrated debugger helps you solve many logic errors — but you should make every effort to learn from those errors, so that you don't repeat them in other programs in the future.

✦ ✦ ✦

Improving Your Application's Performance

In This Chapter

Profiling techniques to improve your code

Using the Visual Studio Profiler to review code and analyze problems

Controlling profiling from the development environment

Profiling ActiveX servers and controls

Profiling Windows NT services

When developing a new application, developers must overcome various hurdles. You have to get your application to compile and to run without blowing up, and you have to be sure that it does what you want it to do. On some projects, there is time to determine if your application can run faster, use less memory, or have a smaller executable file. The performance improvement techniques discussed in this chapter can make the difference between a program that sells and keeps customers satisfied and a program that results in constant calls to your help desk or, worse yet, does not sell to customers at all. These improvements are not just final tweaks on a finished product.

As you learned in Chapter 3, you should get in the habit of adding important information to your code as you write and of using the debugging capabilities provided by Developer Studio to be sure of what's going on in your program. If you save all your testing to the end, both the testing and the bug fixing will be more difficult than if you had been testing all along. However, after you finish making sure that the application runs correctly, it then becomes necessary for you to make sure the application is as efficient and as fast as you can make it. To do so, you use the Visual Studio profiling tool. You can also produce faster or smaller code today, simply by asking the compiler to optimize it for you. Learn what options are available and how to make your decision. Too many programmers sweat bullets trying to speed up code that is rarely called, while ignoring slow code that is causing a bottleneck. Profiling shows you where to spend your energy.

Optimizing Your Code

There was a time, not so long ago, when programmers were expected to optimize their code themselves. Many a night was spent arguing about the order in which to test conditions or which variables should be register variables and which automatic storage variables. These days, most compilers (including Visual C++ 6.0) come with optimizers that can speed execution or shrink program size far beyond what a typical programmer can accomplish by hand.

Here's a simple example of how optimizers work. Imagine you have written a piece of code similar to the following:

```
for (i=0; i<10; i++)
 {
   y=2;
   x[i]=5;
 }

for (i=0; i<10; i++)
 {
   total += x[i];
 }
```

Your code will run faster, with no impact on the final results, if the `y=2` is moved before the first loop. In addition, you can easily combine the two loops into a single loop. If you do that, it's faster to add 5 to `total` each time than it is to calculate the address of `x[i]` each time through the second loop to retrieve the value just stored into it. Really bright optimizers may even realize that `total` can be calculated outside the loop as well. The revised code may look like this:

```
y=2;
for (i=0;i<10;i++)
 {
   x[i]=5;
 }
total += 50;
```

Optimizers do far more than this, of course, but this example gives you an idea of what's going on behind the scenes. It's up to you whether the optimizer focuses on speed, occasionally at the expense of memory usage, or tries to minimize memory usage, perhaps at a slightly lower speed.

To set the optimization options for your project, select the Project menu's Settings option. Visual Studio displays the Project Settings property sheet. Click the C/C++ tab, make sure you are looking at the Release settings, and then select Optimizations in the Category box. Optimization should be turned off for debug builds, because the code in your source files and the code being executed won't match line for line, which will confuse you and the debugger. You should turn on some kind of optimization for release builds. Choose the appropriate optimization for your project from the drop-down list box, as shown in Figure 4-1.

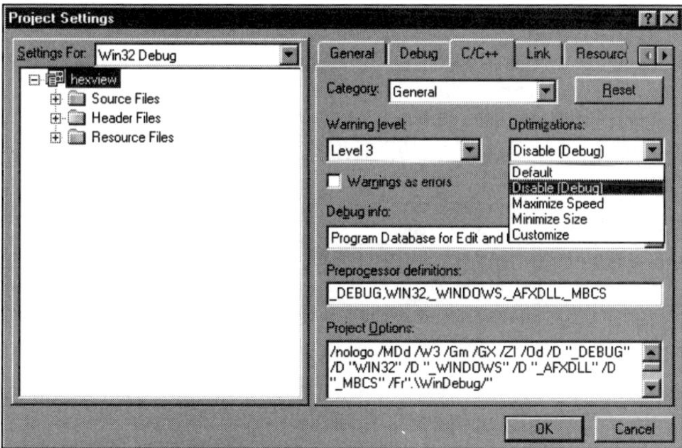

Figure 4-1: Select the type of optimization you want.

If you select the Customize option in the Optimizations box, you can select from the list of individual optimizations, including Assume No Aliasing, Global Optimizations, Favor Fast Code, Generate Intrinsic Functions, Frame-Pointer Omission, and more. However, as you can tell from the names of these optimizations, you have to have a pretty good idea of what you are trying to accomplish before you set up a custom optimization scheme. Until you become more comfortable with what each of the customized options means, accept the predefined optimization methods that Visual Studio provides. Table 4-1 lists the individual optimization options and a brief explanation of what each does.

Table 4-1
Individual Optimization Options Available to You and the Effects They May Have on Your Program Code

Project Settings	*Description*
Minimize Size	Creates the smallest code in the majority of cases.
Maximize Speed	Creates the fastest code in the majority of cases.
Assume No Aliasing	Tells the compiler that your program does not use aliasing. An alias is a name that refers to a memory location that is already referred to by a different name. Using this option enables the compiler to apply optimizations it couldn't otherwise use, such as storing variables in registers and performing loop optimizations.

(continued)

Table 4-1 *(continued)*

Project Settings	***Description***
Assume Aliasing Across Function Calls	Tells the compiler that no aliasing occurs within function bodies but might occur across function calls. After each function call, pointer variables must be reloaded from memory.
Inline Function Expansion	Controls which functions become expanded. Expanding a function inline makes the program faster because it does not incur the overhead of calling the function.
Global Optimizations	Provides local and global optimizations, automatic-register allocation, and loop optimization.
Disable (Debug)	Turns off all optimizations in the program and speeds compilation. This option simplifies debugging because it suppresses code movement.
Generate Intrinsic Functions	Replaces some function calls with intrinsic or otherwise special forms of the function that help your application run faster. Programs that use intrinsic functions are faster because they do not have the overhead of function calls, but may be larger because of the additional code created.
Improve Float Consistency	Improves the consistency of floating-point tests for equality and inequality by disabling optimizations that could change the precision of floating-point calculations.
Favor Small Code	Minimizes the size of .EXE files or DLLs by instructing the compiler to favor size over speed. The compiler can reduce many C and C++ constructs to functionally similar sequences of machine code. Occasionally these differences offer trade-offs of size versus speed. If you do not select this option, code may be larger and may be faster.
Favor Fast Code; Default	Maximizes the speed of .EXE files and DLLs by instructing the compiler to favor speed over size. The compiler can reduce many C and C++ constructs to functionally similar sequences of machine code. Occasionally these differences offer trade-offs of size versus speed.
Full Optimization	Combines optimizing options to produce the fastest possible program.

Project Settings	*Description*
Frame-Pointer Omission	Suppresses creation of frame pointers on the call stack. This option speeds function calls, because no frame pointers need have to be set up and removed. It also frees one more register for storing frequently used variables and sub-expressions.

Introduction to Profiling

Profiling an application enables you to discover bottlenecks — pieces of code that are slowing your application's execution and deserve special attention. In other words, it is a pointless exercise to hand-optimize a routine if you do not know that the routine is called often enough for its speed to matter.

Another use of a profiler is to see whether the test cases you have put together result in every one of your functions being called, or in each line of your code being executed. You may think you have selected test inputs that guarantee this; however, the profiler can confirm it.

Visual C++ includes a profiler integrated with the IDE — Microsoft provides you with the tool, like the debugger, built-in to the development environment. In turn, your sole obligation is to use the profiler to speed and optimize your applications. First, adjust your project settings to include profiler information. Bring up the Project Settings property sheet as you did in the preceding section, and click the Link tab. Check the Enable Profiling check box. Click the OK button, and rebuild your project. Links are slower now, because you cannot do an incremental link when you are planning to profile, but you can go back to your old settings once you've learned a little about the way your program runs. After you finish rebuilding the project, choose the Profile option from the Build menu. Visual Studio displays the Profile dialog box as shown in Figure 4-2.

If you are not sure what any of the radio buttons in this dialog box mean, click the question mark (?) in the upper-right corner of the dialog box, and then click the radio button you don't understand. You will receive a short explanation of the option.

You do not profile as a way to catch bugs, but it can help to validate your bug testing (by proving that your application is faster after testing than it was before) or show you the parts of your application that need work, which makes it a vital part of the developer's toolbox. Get in the habit of profiling all of your applications at least once in the development cycle — preferably toward the end of the cycle

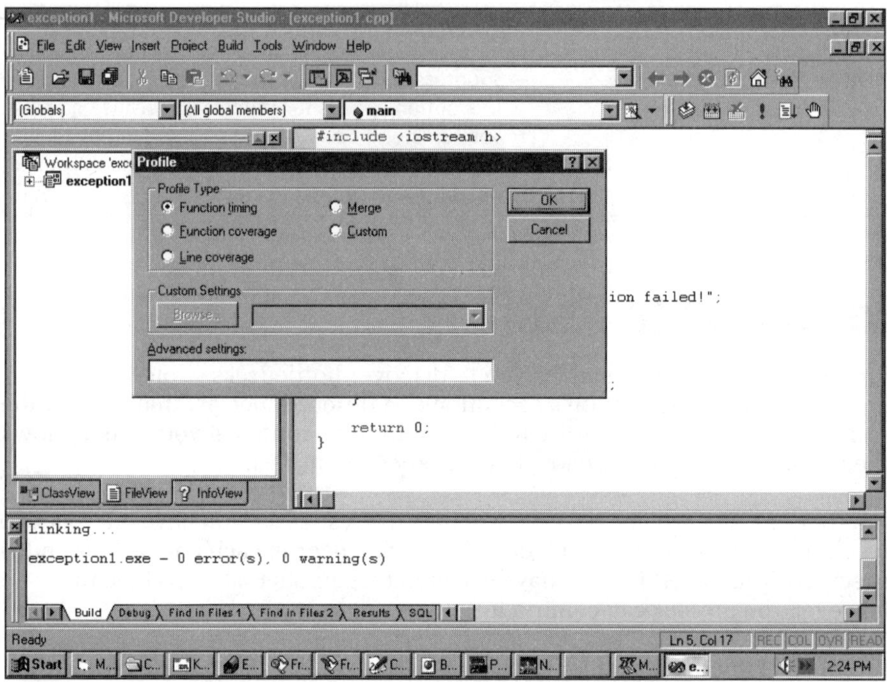

Figure 4-2: The Profile dialog box within Visual Studio is displayed when you select the Profile option on the Build menu.

It usually doesn't make much sense to profile an entire program, because in most applications for Windows, the majority of the application's time is spent waiting for messages. Often, only one section of a program, such as repagination, might be performing poorly. Narrowing the region of code being profiled can speed the execution of profiler sessions. For maximum profiler accuracy, close as many other applications as possible during profiling. In particular, do not run programs such as electronic mail that execute at random intervals. If you have a network connection, you might want to disconnect it as well, because networks can cause differences in profile results.

Understanding the application profiling basics

The Visual C++ Profiler is a performance analysis tool that collects reliable statistics on the number of times certain elements of your code are executed and the amount of elapsed time spent executing them. The Profiler can be used from within the Developer Studio or from the command line.

If you installed Visual C++ with default settings, the Profiler may not be installed on your system. In this case, profiling features may not be available. To install the Profiler, rerun the Visual C++ installation program.

✦ ✦ ✦ ✦ ✦

You can use the Profiler for *function profiling* and for *line profiling*. Function profiling analyzes the way functions in your program are executed, while line profiling analyzes the way your program executes on a per-line basis. For line profiling to work, you must compile your code with debugging information. If you do function profiling, the Profiler ignores debugging information.

Understanding the Profiler's operation

Because the Profiler is such a crucial part of good application development, understanding how the Profiler works is valuable. The Profiler actually consists of not one, but three tools that can be executed from the command line. These are the PREP, PROFILE, and PLIST tools. Figure 4-3 shows a simplified view of how these tools operate.

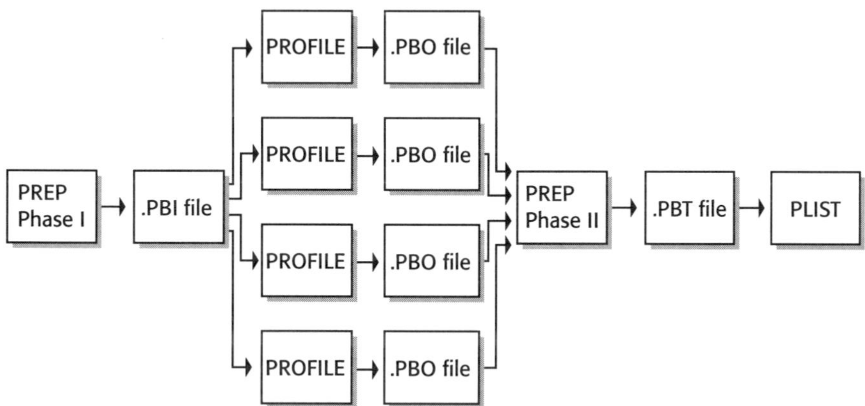

Figure 4-3: The interaction between the Profiler's three components demonstrates how they operate.

The PREP tool is run twice during profiling. First, it reads the application's executable file and produces a .PBI and a .PBT file. The .PBI file serves as the input to the PROFILE tool, which actually executes and profiles the application. The PROFILE tool, in turn, writes its results to a .PBO file. The .PBO file and the .PBT file serve as the input when the PREP tool is run for the second time, this time generating a new .PBT file. Finally, the PLIST tool generates human-readable results.

The Profiler is typically run from batch files that invoke PREP, PROFILE, and PLIST as appropriate (which batch files the IDE invokes and manages for you occurs automatically in most cases if you use the IDE to profile rather than the command line). The output of PLIST is a readable (natural language) summary of profiling results.

If you have remote debugging enabled, you may not be able to invoke the Profile command from the Tools menu. To disable remote debugging, use the Remote Connection command in the Tools menu, and select Local as the connection type in the Remote Connection dialog box.

◆ ◆ ◆ ◆ ◆

Types of profiling

The Profiler can be used to perform a variety of different types of profiling operations. Some of these can be invoked from the Profile dialog box; others require the use of batch files that are typically found in your `Common\Msdev98\bin` directory.

✦ **Function timing** evaluates the amount of time your application spends executing specific functions. By default, the Profiler generates timing statistics for all functions. You can invoke this type of profiling by selecting Function timing in the Profile dialog box.

✦ **Function coverage** records whether specific functions have been called. You can use this capability, for example, to verify whether certain portions of your code are executed. Function coverage can also be invoked from the Profile dialog box.

✦ **Function counting** evaluates the number of times the application calls specific functions. To invoke function counting from the Profile dialog box, select the Custom profile type, and specify the `fcount.bat` batch file (usually located in `Common\Msdev98\bin`) in the Custom Settings field.

✦ **Line counting** evaluates the number of times your application executes specific lines in your code. To invoke line counting, select Custom in the Profile dialog box, and specify `lcount.bat` (usually located in `Common\Msdev98\bin`) in the Custom Settings field.

✦ **Line coverage** evaluates whether or not specific lines in your code have been executed. Note that line coverage is much faster than line counting, because after a line has been executed once, the Profiler can remove its breakpoint from that line. You can directly invoke line coverage from the Profile dialog box by selecting the Line coverage option.

In addition to these Profiler options, the Profile dialog box also provides a Merge option. This option enables you to combine Profiler statistics from several sessions (with identical settings).

Setting advanced Profiler settings

Profiling your entire application rarely makes sense. By identifying specific sections of your code for profiling analysis, you can also greatly speed up program execution during a profiling session.

There are three ways to fine-tune the Profiler. You can either modify your `tools.ini` and `profiler.ini` files; you can specify advanced settings in the Profile dialog box in Developer Studio; or you can write custom batch files.

The `tools.ini` and `profiler.ini` files contain Profiler-related settings in the `[profiler]` section. In the `[profiler]` section, you can specify library (.LIB) and object (.OBJ) files that the Profiler should exclude from profiling. For example, your `tools.ini` file may contain the following lines to exclude the `user32.lib` and `gdi32.lib` files:

```
[profiler]
exclude:user32.lib
exclude:gdi32.lib
```

When reading `tools.ini` and `profiler.ini`, the Profiler reads settings from both files and merges them. Note that the location of `tools.ini` is defined by the `INIT` environment variable. In contrast, you will almost always find `profiler.ini` in the `Common\Msdev98\bin` directory.

If you select the Function timing, Function coverage, or Line coverage options in the Profile dialog box, you can specify additional parameters that are passed to the PREP tool in its Phase I invocation. For example, if you wish to invoke the profile to analyze only a specific range of source lines in the file `SampleApp.cpp`, you could specify the following in the Advanced settings field:

```
/EXCALL /INC SampleApp.cpp(30-67)
```

Finally, you can develop your own custom profiling batch files. Use the batch files that are installed in your `Common\Msdev98\bin` directory (`fcount.bat`, `fcover.bat`, `ftime.bat`, `lcount.bat`, and `lcover.bat`) as examples for developing Profiler batch files.

Enabling Profiling within Visual C++ 6.0

Profiling is available only in the Professional and Enterprise Editions of Visual C++. Before using the profiler, you must build the current project with profiling enabled (equivalent to the command-line setting LINK /PROFILE). If you want to perform function profiling only in the current project, you need to enable profiling only for the linker. If you want to do line profiling, you also need to include debugging information. To build your project for function profiling, do the following:

1. On the Build menu, click Settings to display the Project Settings dialog box.
2. Click the Link tab.
3. In the Category drop-down list box, click General.
4. Select the Enable Profiling check box.

5. Click OK.

   On the Build menu, click "Build projectname.exe."

Selecting the Enable Profiling check box turns off incremental linking. To re-enable incremental linking, clear the Enable Profiling option.

✦ ✦ ✦ ✦ ✦

To build your project for line profiling:

1. Perform the procedure to enable function profiling described earlier in this section.
2. Select the Generate Debug Info check box.
3. Click the C/C++ tab.
4. In the Category drop-down list box, click General.
5. In the Debug Info drop-down list box, click Program Database or Line Numbers Only.
6. Click OK.
7. On the Build menu, click "Build projectname.exe."

When the build is complete, the project is ready to be profiled.

If you haven't built your current project with profiling enabled, an error message informs you that you need to rebuild your project.

✦ ✦ ✦ ✦ ✦

Controlling profiling from the development environment

If you are specifying function timing, function coverage, or line coverage from within the Profile dialog box, you can exclude object files or libraries from profiling by using `/EXC`, which is available in PREP Phase I and the Advanced settings box. For example, following is a line that you might type into the Advanced settings box that excludes two object files, `file1.obj` and `file2.obj`, from profiling:

```
/EXC file1.obj /EXC file2.obj
```

You can also use `/EXCALL` to exclude all object files and libraries and then use the `/INC` option to specify which object files and libraries to profile. For example, following is a line from a sample batch file that first excludes all object files and libraries and then includes `file1.obj` and `file2.obj`:

```
/EXCALL /INC file1.obj /INC file2.obj
```

Selecting a function to profile

With the /SF option (PREP Phase I) you can profile a selected function and the functions it calls, so you can easily isolate a routine and its children for analysis. To profile only SampleFunc and the functions it calls, you might use the following line for Phase I PREP in a batch file or at the command line:

```
PREP /SF ?SampleFunc@@YAXPAH@@ /FC %1
```

Or if you are in the development environment, you might type the following in the Advanced settings textbox of the Profile dialog box:

```
SF ?SampleFunc@@YAXPAH@@
```

Using function selection can give you more useful results than function exclusion/inclusion, but function selection can be slower.

When you specify a C++ function name to the Profiler, you must provide its decorated name. The easiest way to get the decorated name is to look it up in the project's .MAP file.

◆ ◆ ◆ ◆ ◆

Understanding the PREP program

As you learned earlier in this chapter, the PREP program runs twice during a normal profiling operation. In Phase I, it reads an executable (.EXE) file and then creates .PBI and .PBT files. In Phase II, it reads .PBT and .PBO files and then writes a new .PBT file for PLIST. From the command line, you can invoke PREP as shown here:

```
PREP [options] [programname1] [programname2...programname8]
```

PREP reads the command line from left to right, so the rightmost options override contradictory options to the left. None of the options are case sensitive. You must prefix options with a forward slash (/) or a dash (-), and options must be separated by spaces. Table 4-2 lists parameters for the PREP executable.

PREP Phase I options can be issued either from the Profiler dialog box or from the command line. PREP Phase II options can be issued only at the command line. Table 4-3 lists the options you can use with the PREP program. An "X" in the I or II column indicates that a PREP command-line option applies to a particular phase.

The /INC and /EXC options specify individual library (.LIB), object (.OBJ), and application source (.C, .CPP, or .CXX) files. For line counting and line coverage, you can specify line numbers with source files, as shown here:

```
/EXCALL /INC test.cpp(3-41,50-67)
```

Table 4-2
Parameters for the PREP Executable

Parameter	*Description*
Options	See Table 4-3.
Programname1	Filename of primary program to profile (.DBG, .EXE, or .DLL). PROFILE adds the .EXE extension if no extension is given. This parameter must be specified for PREP Phase I, but not for Phase II.
Programname2...programname8	Additional programs to profile. These parameters can be specified for PREP Phase I only.

Table 4-3
Options for the PREP Executable

Option	*I*	*II*	*Description*
/AT			Collects attribution data for function timing and function counting. Function attribution reports which function called another function. See the /STACK switch later in this list.
/CB	X		Used with function timing; enables you to set the calibrated overhead of Profiler calls in the event that your function timing calls have varied because of varied calibrated overhead values. The calibrated overhead is displayed in default (non-tab-delimited) PLIST output.
/EXC	X		Excludes a specified module from the profile. You can also exclude part of a module; for example, /EXC test.cpp(9-18).
/EXCALL	X		Excludes all modules from the profile. Used with /INC.
/FC	X		Selects function count profiling.
/FT	X		Selects function timing profiling. This option causes the Profiler to generate count information as well. This is the default setting from the command line.
/FV	X		Selects function coverage profiling.
/INC	X		Includes in profile. Used in conjunction with /EXCALL.
/H[ELP]	X	X	Provides a short summary of PREP options.

Option	***I***	***II***	***Description***
`/IO filename`		X	Merges an existing .PBO file (PROFILE output). Up to eight .PBO files can be merged at a time. The default extension is .PBO.
`/IT filename`		X	Merges an existing .PBT file (PREP Phase I output). Up to eight .PBT files can be merged at a time. You cannot merge .PBT files from different profiling methods. The default extension is .PBT.
`/LC`	X		Selects line count profiling. May take a long time.
`/LV`	X		Selects line coverage profiling.
`/M filename`	X		Substitutes for the `/IT`, `/IO`, and `/OT` options.
`/NOLOGO`	X	X	Suppresses the PREP copyright message.
`/OI filename`	X		Creates a .PBI file. The default extension is .PBI. If `/OI` is not specified, the output .PBI file is programname1.PBI.
`/OM`	X		Creates a self-profiling file with an ._XE or ._LL extension for function timing, function counting, and function coverage. Without this option, the executable code is stored in the .PBI file. This option speeds up profiling.
`/OT filename`	X	X	Specifies the output .PBT file. The default extension is .PBT. If `/OT` is not specified, the output .PBT file is programname1.PBT.
`/SF function`	X		Starts profiling with function. The function name must correspond to an entry in the .MAP file.
`/STACK` *dpt*	X		When using the `/AT` switch, you can also set the stack depth (dpt) to which the functions that will have their attribution data recorded.
`/?`	X	X	Provides a short summary of PREP options.

This example includes only lines 3 through 41 and lines 50 through 67 from the source file `TEST.CPP`. Note the absence of spaces in the source specification. To specify all source lines in a particular module, specify the .OBJ file as shown here:

```
/EXCALL /INC test.obj
```

or by using the source filename with zero line numbers like this:

```
/EXCALL /INC test.cpp(0-0)
```

The following statement profiles from line 50 to the end of the file:

```
/EXCALL /INC test.cpp(50-0)
```

Profiling for function timing

The Function timing option in the Profile dialog box profiles the current project, recording how many times each function was called (hit count) as well as how much time was spent in each function and called functions. The following listing is a sample of the data provided by function timing:

```
Func Time    %    Func+Child Time    %    Hit Count    Function
----------------------------------------------------------------
2.606      48.1    2.606            48.1     2            _SetCursor@4
```

The `Func Time` column reports how much time it took for the function to run in seconds. The next column shows what percent of the total profile time is represented by the function time. `Func+Child Time` refers to the total time profiled for the function as well as any functions called by that function. The next column shows what percent of the total profile time is represented by the `Func+Child Time`. The `Hit Count` column reports the number of times that the function was called. The `Function` column displays the decorated name of the function. Function attribution is also available with function timing.

As you have learned, the `Function` column of the Profiler report displays the decorated name of the function it is profiling. A decorated name for a C++ function contains the following information:

- The function name.
- The class that the function is a member of, if it is a member function. This may include the class that encloses the function's class, and so on.
- The namespace the function belongs to (if it is part of a namespace).
- The types of the function's parameters.
- The calling convention.
- The function's return type.

The function and class names are encoded in the decorated name. The rest of the decorated name is a code that has internal meaning only for the compiler and the linker. Table 4-4 lists two examples of undecorated and decorated C++ names.

✦ ✦ ✦ ✦ ✦

Table 4-4
Examples of Undecorated and Decorated C++ Names

Undecorated Name	*Decorated Name*
`int a(char){int i=3;return i;};`	`?a@@YAHD@Z`
`void __stdcall b::c(float){};`	`?c@b@@AAGXM@Z`

Profiling for function coverage

The Function coverage option in the Profile dialog box profiles the current project, recording whether a function was called. Function coverage profiling is useful for determining which sections of your code are not being executed. The Profiler lists all profiled functions, with an asterisk (*) marking those that were executed. The profiling overhead for function coverage matches the overhead for function counting. Here is a sample function coverage report:

```
Covered  Function
----------------------------------------------------------------
   .     _InitInstance (generic.obj)
   .     _LoadAcceleratorsA@8 (user32.def)
   *     _LoadCursorA@8 (user32.def)
   .     _LoadIconA@8 (user32.def)
   .     _SendMessageA@16 (user32.def)
   *     _SetCursor@4 (user32.def)
   .     _SetDlgItemTextA@12 (user32.def)
```

Line profiling options

With the Profiler's two line profiling options, you can see which source lines are being executed.

- ✦ Line counting shows you how many times each line was executed.
- ✦ Line coverage shows you which lines were executed at least once.

Line profiling uses debugging information in your .EXE file to trigger the Profiler, so it does not need a .MAP file. The Line counting option in the Profile dialog box records how many times each line was called (also known as the *hit count*). To start a line count profile, use a custom batch file that specifies the source module and the lines to profile. Here is a sample of the output of a line counting profile run:

```
          Hit
  Line    count   %     Source Line
----------------------------------------------------------------
    1:                  // test.cpp
    2:
    3:                  #include <windows.h>
```

```
 4:
 5:                void WasteTime(HANDLE hInstance,
                      HWND hWnd)
 6:      1     0.0    {
 7:                     LONG lCount, lX;
 8:                     HCURSOR hOldCursor;
 9:      1     0.0      hOldCursor = SetCursor(
                            LoadCursor(NULL, IDC_WAIT));
10:      1     0.0      for (lCount = 0; lCount < 1000L;
                            lCount++) {
11:   1000    49.9          lX = 57L;
12:   1000    49.9        }
13:      1     0.0      SetCursor(hOldCursor);
14:      1     0.0    }
```

The report prints all included source lines, even if the application does not execute the source line.

◆ ◆ ◆ ◆ ◆

Line counting profiling is very slow because the Profiler inserts a debugging breakpoint for every source code line, and these breakpoints remain for the duration of the profile session. To speed up profiling, reduce the number of lines that you select for profiling.

Line coverage profiling

The Line coverage option in the Profile dialog box profiles the current project, recording whether the application executed a given line. Line coverage profiling is useful for determining which sections of your code are not being executed. The Profiler lists all profiled lines, marking with an asterisk (*) those lines that the application executed. The profiling overhead for line coverage is lower than it is for line counting, because the Profiler needs to stop at a line only once (the first time the application executes the line). Here is a sample line coverage report:

```
  Line Covered  Source
---------------------------------------------------------------
   1:           // waste.cpp
   2:
   3:           #include <windows.h>
   4:
   5:           void WasteTime(HANDLE hInstance, HWND hWnd)
   6:     *      {
   7:              LONG lCount, lX;
   8:              HCURSOR hOldCursor;
   9:     *        hOldCursor = SetCursor(LoadCursor(NULL,
                        IDC_WAIT));
  10:     *        for(lCount=0; lCount<1000L; lCount++) {
  11:     *           lX = 57L;
  12:     *         }
  13:     *        if (lCount == 0) {
  14:     .           lCount = 1; // should never execute
```

```
                }
      *           SetCursor(hOldCursor);
      *         }
```

Like the line counting report, the line coverage report prints all included source lines, even if the application does not execute the source line.

✦ ✦ ✦ ✦ ✦

Line coverage profiling is much faster than line counting profiling because the Profiler can remove the inserted breakpoints when those lines are first executed.

Merging Profiler output

With the Profiler's modular design, you can make several profiling runs without having to run PREP each time. After PREP has created .PBI and .PBT files, you can reuse these files with PROFILE to create multiple .PBO files. You can then merge the .PBO files using the PREP `/IO` command-line option with multiple .PBO files. The Visual C++ Profile dialog box contains a Merge option button that automates this process.

If you profile and merge with different data, you can see if all functions or lines are being tested. If you are doing function timing, the times that you will see are cumulative times for the first profile run and all subsequent merge runs. To determine the average time, divide all times by the number of Profiler runs.

Exporting data from the Profiler

The PLIST `/T` command-line option causes PLIST to export the contents of a .PBT file into a tab-delimited format suitable for import into a spreadsheet or database. This format can also be used by user-written programs. For example, to create a tab-delimited file called `MYPROG.TXT` from `MYPROG.PBT`, enter the following command-line sequence:

```
PLIST /T MYPROG > MYPROG.TXT
```

Or if you are using tokens in a batch file, you might use:

```
PLIST /T %1 > MYPROG.TXT
```

The ASCII tab-delimited format was designed to be read by other programs; it is not intended for general reporting.

✦ ✦ ✦ ✦ ✦

Analyzing Profiler data

The PLIST tool ordinarily provides Profiler output in a human-readable form. However, it is also possible to generate output in an exportable tab-delimited format (using the `/T` linker switch). The tab-delimited output can be read by other applications. For example, you can import it into a Microsoft Excel spreadsheet. Provided with your Visual C++ installation is a Microsoft Excel 4 macro file, `profiler.xlm`, that provides some profile analysis tools (if you load the file into a more recent version of Excel, it updates automatically).

Every piece of data stored by the Profiler is available through the tab-delimited file. Because not all aspects of the database are recorded by every profiling method, unused fields within a record may be zero. For example, the total time of the program will be zero if the program is profiled for counts only. In addition, all included functions are listed for function counting and timing profiles, even if those functions were not executed.

The tab-delimited format is arranged with one record per line and two to eight fields per record. Figure 4-4 shows how a database looks when it is loaded into Microsoft Excel. This database was produced using the PLIST `/T` command-line option.

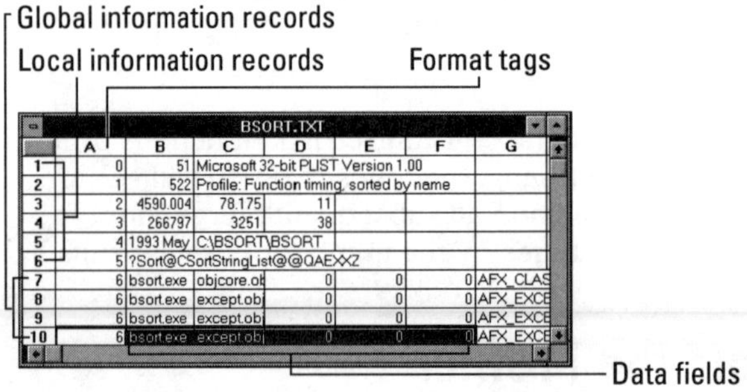

Global information records
Local information records
Format tags

BSORT.TXT

	A	B	C	D	E	F	G
1	0	51	Microsoft 32-bit PLIST Version 1.00				
2	1	522	Profile: Function timing, sorted by name				
3	2	4590.004	78.175	11			
4	3	266797	3251	38			
5	4	1993 May	C:\BSORT\BSORT				
6	5	?Sort@CSortStringList@@QAEXXZ					
7	6	bsort.exe	objcore.ob	0	0	0	AFX_CLAS
8	6	bsort.exe	except.obj	0	0	0	AFX_EXCE
9	6	bsort.exe	except.obj	0	0	0	AFX_EXCE
10	6	bsort.exe	except.obj	0	0	0	AFX_EXCE

Data fields

Figure 4-4: The Profiler data for HexView.
cpp appears this way within Microsoft Excel.

The first item in each record is a format tag number. These tags range from 0 through 7 and indicate the kind of data given in the other fields of the record. The fields in each record are described in either a global information record or a local information record. You will learn more about information records in the next section.

Tab-delimited files are created with global information records first, organized in numerical order by format tag. The local information records, containing information about specific lines or functions, are created last. Local information records are organized by line number.

If the .PBT file contains information from more than one .EXE or .DLL file, the global information records will cover them all. Local information records include the Exe field, which specifies the name of the executable file that each record pertains to.

Understanding global information records

The global information records contain information about the entire .EXE file. The format tag numbers for global information records are 0 through 5. The record formats are as shown in Table 4-5.

Table 4-5
Record Formats

Field	*Explanation*
0	Format tag number Version: PLIST version number Banner: PLIST banner Profiling Method Line Format Method: Description
1	Format tag number Method: Numeric value that indicates the profiling type Description: ASCII description of the profiling type given by the Method field, as shown in Table 4-3
2	Format tag number Total time: Total amount of time used by the program being profiled. This field is zero for counting and coverage profiles. Outside time: Amount of time spent before the first profiled function (with function profiling) or line (with line profiling) was executed. This field is zero for counting and coverage profiles. Call depth: Maximum number of nested functions found while profiling. Only profiled functions are counted. This field is zero for line profiling.
3	Format tag number Total hits: Total number of times the Profiler detected a profiled line or function being executed Lines/funcs: Total number of lines or functions marked for profiling Lines/funcs hit: Number of marked lines or functions executed at least once while profiling
4	Format tag number Date: Date and time that the profile was run (ASCII format) Command line: PLIST command-line arguments
5	Format tag number Starting function name: Decorated name of the starting function identified by the PREP /SF parameter

Table 4-6 lists the different profiling types that the Profiler indicates within field 1 of the record.

Table 4-6
Profiling Types Listed in the Global Information Record

Method	*Description*
321	Profile: Line counting, sorted by line
324	Profile: Line coverage, sorted by line
521	Profile: Function counting, sorted by function name
522	Profile: Function timing, sorted by function name
524	Profile: Function coverage, sorted by function name

Local information records

The local information records contain information about specific functions or lines that were profiled. The format tag numbers for local information records are 6 and 7. A file can have only one type of local information record. The line formats are as shown in Table 4-7.

Analyzing Profiler statistics

Clearly, depending on what type of profiling you are doing and the number of lines within the application that you intend to profile, the Profiler tab-delimited file format can contain a considerable amount of information. You can process this data in a spreadsheet, database, or user-written program. When you plan to analyze Profiler statistics, you will want to perform (at a minimum) the following four steps:

Table 4-7
Format Tag Numbers for Local Information Records

Field	*Explanation*
6	Format tag number. Exe: ASCII name of the executable file that contains the function. Source: ASCII name of the object module (including the .OBJ extension) that contains the function. Count: Number of times the function has been executed. Time: Amount of time spent executing the function in milliseconds. This field is zero for counting or coverage profiles. Child: Amount of time spent executing the function and any child functions it calls. This field is zero for counting or coverage profiles. Func: ASCII name of the function.
7	Format tag number. Exe: ASCII name of the executable file that contains the first line of this function. Source: ASCII name of the source file that contains the first line of this function. Line: Line number. Count: Number of times the line has been executed. For coverage profiles, this field is 1 if the line has been executed and 0 otherwise.
8	Format tag number Number of stacks: Number of stacks for each function call
9	Format tag number Stack size: Stack size for each function call Hit count: Hit count for this stack Stack time: This stack's self-time Child time: This stack's child-time
10	Format tag number. Function name: Each function's name on the stack. The number of names that appear here will be equal to the stack size field in the Profiling Stack Hits and Timing Line Format.

1. Collect the cumulative data from the global information records. These lines begin with the numbers 0 through 5. Each of these lines appears only once and always in ascending order.
2. Determine the type of database by finding the value of the Method field. This field is the second field of the first record in the tab-delimited file. If the value in the Method field is greater than 400, the file comes from function profiling.

If it is less than 400, the file comes from line profiling. The type of information in the local information records given later is directly related to this value. In any one file, the local information records are always of the same type, either line information or function information.

3. Process data from the local information records. For example, to calculate the percentage of hits on a given function, divide the value of the Count field in the sixth record in the file by the total number of hits from the Total Hits field in the third record.

4. Send the results to a file or stdout.

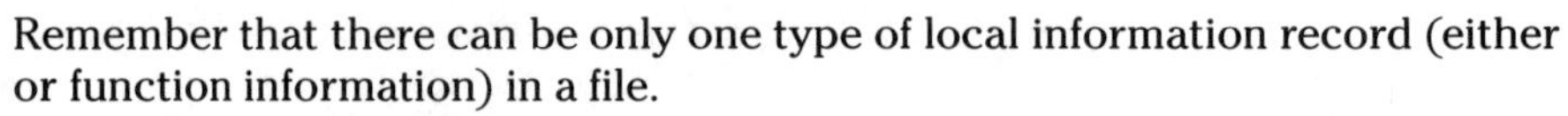
Remember that there can be only one type of local information record (either line or function information) in a file.

✦ ✦ ✦ ✦ ✦

Processing Profiler output with Microsoft Excel

As you learned earlier in this chapter, `profiler.xlm` is a sample Microsoft Excel version 4.0 macro that processes the tab-delimited file and graphs the results. The macro is in the `\Program Files\DevStudio98\VC98\bin` directory.

The `profiler.xlm` macro is composed of four submacros. The first two macros, in columns A and B, are helper macros that copy and preprocess the data for use by the second pair of macros, in columns C and D. The macro in column C, labeled `CreateColumnChart()`, creates a graph showing the number of times that each function or line was executed. The macro in column D is `CreateColumnTimeChart()`; it works like `CreateColumnChart()` but operates on timing information.

Profiling dynamic link libraries

Profiling a dynamic link library (DLL) is similar to profiling an .EXE file. When you profile a DLL, you follow the same steps and use the same commands that you would for an .EXE file. The same profiling rules that apply to .EXE files (such as the need to include debugging information and to supply a .MAP file) apply to DLLs.

Profiling an ActiveX component or ActiveX control

Because an ActiveX component (formerly OLE server) is basically an .EXE or a DLL and an ActiveX control (formerly OLE control) is a DLL even though it has an extension of .OCX, profiling them is similar to profiling an .EXE or a DLL. When you profile an ActiveX component or ActiveX control, you follow the same steps and use the same commands that you would for an .EXE or a DLL. The same profiling rules that apply to .EXEs and DLLs (such as the need to include debugging information and to supply a .MAP file) apply to ActiveX components and ActiveX controls.

You may need to register the mini ActiveX component, the in-process Automation server, or the ActiveX control explicitly. You can do one of the following steps to register them:

✦ For a DLL (and thus for an ActiveX control), run REGSVR32 from the command prompt. Alternatively, you can open the corresponding project in the development environment and select the Register Control option from the Tools menu.

✦ For an .EXE, simply run the executable file. You may not be able to run it or you may get a message saying, "This server can only be run from a container application," but click OK. It will have been registered.

To run the Profiler, you may need to copy the `\Program Files\DevStudio98\VC98\bin\PROFILE.DLL` file to the directory containing the file that you are profiling, or to one of the system directories.

The following four examples illustrate the steps required to profile a full ActiveX component, a mini ActiveX component, an in-process Automation server (formerly OLE Automation server), and an ActiveX control. Each step in the following examples is a command at the command prompt. Alternatively, you could create a batch file with these commands. To profile a full ActiveX component or an Automation server, enter the following command sequence, where `FullSrvr.exe` is the file corresponding to a full ActiveX component or Automation server:

```
PREP /OM /FT FullSrvr
PROFILE FullSrvr
PREP /M FullSrvr
PLIST FullSrvr > FullSrvr.txt
```

To profile a mini ActiveX component, enter the following command sequence, where `MiniSrvr` is the file corresponding to a mini ActiveX component and `Container` is a container application that runs the `MiniSrvr`:

```
COPY MiniSrvr.exe MiniSrvr.sav
PREP /OM /FT MiniSrvr
COPY MiniSrvr._xe MiniSrvr.exe
PROFILE /I MiniSrvr /O MiniSrvr Container
PREP /M MiniSrvr
PLIST MiniSrvr > MiniSrvr.txt
COPY MiniSrvr.sav MiniSrvr.exe
```

To profile an in-process Automation server (the steps are similar to those when profiling a mini ActiveX component except that you have a .DLL extension instead of .EXE), enter the following command sequence, where `InProc` is the file corresponding to an in-process Automation server and `Client` is an Automation client application that drives the `InProc.dll`:

```
COPY InProc.dll InProc.sav
PREP /OM /FT InProc.dll
COPY InProc._ll InProc.dll
```

```
PROFILE /I InProc /O InProc Client
PREP /M InProc
PLIST InProc > InProc.txt
COPY InProc.sav InProc.dll
```

To profile an ActiveX control with an .OCX extension (the steps are similar again except that you have an .OCX extension), enter the following command sequence, where `Control` is the ActiveX control and `ControlContainer` is an ActiveX control container application:

```
COPY Control.ocx Control.sav
PREP /OM /FT Control.ocx
COPY Control._cx Control.ocx
PROFILE /I Control /O Control ControlContainer
PREP /M Control
PLIST Control > Control.txt
COPY Control.sav Control.ocx
```

Profiling inlined code

When specified, the Visual C++ compiler performs inlining, which replaces a function call with an actual copy of the code. Profiling inlined code requires special attention. Because inlined functions do not generate .MAP file entries or CALL instructions, the Profiler cannot tell when the computer is executing one of these functions. The time, hit, and coverage data is attributed to the "calling" function.

In many cases, there are .MAP file entries for "inlined" functions because the functions are not necessarily inlined everywhere in the application. Take this into account when you analyze Profiler results.

✦ ✦ ✦ ✦ ✦

The Profiler can provide line-level hit count and coverage information for inlined functions. Be sure to include the source lines in the Phase I PREP command-line options, just as you would include source lines in the calling program.

Profiling multithreaded applications

For multithreaded applications, the Profiler's behavior depends on the profiling method. For line counting and line coverage, the Profiler does not discriminate among threads. The hit counts encompass all the program's threads.

For function timing, function counting, and function coverage, profiling is thread dependent. You can profile an individual thread by

- ✦ Declaring the thread's main function as the starting function (PREP `/SF` option)
- ✦ Including all functions in the program (do not use the PREP `/EXC` option)

The profile results are difficult to interpret if you do not specify a starting function, if you specify a starting function that is called from multiple threads, or if you do not include all functions.

Profiling your application's performance

If you suspect that CPU usage may be causing performance bottlenecks, use the Call Attributed Profiler (CAP) tool, which is part of the Windows NT Server Resource Kit. This tool requires a special build of applications but performs a detailed trace of every function call and how much time that call requires. It identifies frequently called functions that are slow and need to be optimized or called less often. You can also use the CAP tool to parse the data into a Microsoft Excel readable format and to identify calling functions and called functions.

Using the CAP Tool to Eliminate Duplicated Calls

A Microsoft Exchange Client application often opens multiple folders, but its performance is slow and you can see it redraw every message in the folder. This performance bottleneck can be identified by CAP profiling.

In case of the Exchange Client's slow performance, CAP profiling results might indicate, for example, that the application is asking for time zone information on every call. Because time zone information does not often change, this information can be requested once, and then saved for the entire session. This reduces the time spent making multiple calls, reduces CPU time, and improves performance significantly. To use CAP profiling, perform the following steps:

1. Copy `CAP.DLL` from the Windows NT Server Resource Kit to your system directory.
2. Compile your application for profiling (as you have learned to do throughout this chapter).

   Make any necessary changes to the `CAP.INI` file. See Optimizing Windows NT or cap.txt of the Windows NT Server Resource Kit for general information on preparing cap.ini. Use the information Table 4-6 contains to customize your copy of *cap.ini*.

For more information, see CAP FLAGS in the Windows NT Server cap.ini file. Table 4-8 explains the sections in cap.ini and a brief explanation of the commands to insert within the sections.

Table 4-8
Sections and Usage of the Cap.Ini File

Section in CAP.INI	*Usage Notes*
[EXES]	List the CAP-ready .EXE files to profile. The Profiler automatically starts when you launch one of these .EXE files.
[PATCH CALLERS]	List the DLLs called by the file names (not compiled for CAP) into `%SystemRoot%\SYMBOLS\DLL`. For example, if you put `KERNEL32.DLL` in this section, copy `KERNEL32.DBG` to `%SystemRoot%\SYMBOLS\DLL`. List DLLs built for profiling if you want to profile internal calls. Note that all exported functions in this DLL are listed twice.
[OUTPUT FILE]	CAP output is directed to the file specified in the following line: `FILENAME=C:\CAP.END` If you set the profile flag to off, profiling defaults to OFF (otherwise the default is ON). In this case, profiling starts manually only when you use `CAPDUMP.EXE`. If you do not need to profile immediately after startup, set profile to OFF. As a result, the .EXE file starts much faster. Note that the *perthreadmem* parameter is required. It represents the amount of memory CAP allocates per thread to collect data. This parameter is expressed in bytes (for example, 8 MB). If you experience problems such as running out of memory, try changing this value.

After you set up the correct information for the cap program, you must execute your files in a certain order to profile them correctly with the CAP tool. To profile your executables, perform the following steps:

1. Start your .EXE files.
2. Run `CAPDUMP.EXE`. For more information, see the Windows NT Server Resource Kit.
3. In CAPDUMP, choose Clear and Restart, and then choose OK to begin profiling.
4. Run your test.
5. In CAPDUMP, choose Stop, and then choose OK.

   In CAPDUMP, choose Dump and Stop, and then choose OK. CAP will start writing to disk.

Refer to the Windows NT Server Resource Kit for more information on CAP data analysis tools.

Profiling Windows NT services

As developers spend more and more time writing to the Windows NT platform, writing Windows NT services has become a significantly more important task for many professionals. As with other programs, you can profile Windows NT services. To do so, perform the following steps:

1. Set necessary environment variables using the System control panel. You may find that necessary system environment variables include `ComSpec`, `windir`, and `Path`.
2. Add two new environment variables, as shown here:

   ```
   __ProfilePBI=<full path of your PBI file>
   __ProfilePBO=<full path of your PBO file>
   ```

   Note the exact spelling and two leading underscores. If these are not correctly set, profile.dll warns you that these settings cannot be found. For example, if your compiler is on your D drive, these variables might be similar to the following:

   ```
   __ProfilePBI=d:\idg\vcbib\service\simpsrv.pbi
   __ProfilePBO=d:\idg\vcbib\service\simpsrv.pbo
   ```

   Copy the Profiler DLL, *profile.dll*, from the `\VC98\BIN` subdirectory to either the directory where the service .EXE resides or to one of the directories listed in the `PATH` environment variable.

4. Build the service (in this example case, simpsrv.exe). Instruct the linker to create a .MAP file.
5. Run PREP to create SIMPLE._XE, which has been modified for profiling:

   ```
   prep /om /ft /sf _worker_thread simple.exe
   ```

   The PREP command also sets up the code to follow the call stack from the `worker_thread()` routine. By default, the Profiler profiles calls from the main thread, so servicing requests from a secondary thread without specifying the `/sf` option will produce incomplete results. If your service uses a second thread to service requests (which most services do), it will likely create the second thread by calling `CreateThread( )`. If the main thread was servicing the requests, you wouldn't need to use the `/sf` option.
6. Copy SIMPLE._XE to `SIMPLE.EXE`. This overwrites the original executable file with the modified version, which has the profile hooks added to the code.
7. Start the service by using the Services program in the Control Panel, and run the client application. Stop the service using the Control Panel. You can get the timing information by executing the following commands from the command prompt:

   ```
   prep /m simple
   plist simple
   ```

Summary

Visual Studio and the Windows operating systems provide valuable tools to ensure that your applications are running as efficiently as possible. From code optimization during compilation to profiling of service performance, both Visual Studio and the operating system assist you in writing the fastest applications.

Within the Integrated Development Environment, you can use the Profiler to profile application performance. Make sure to enable profiling within the Project Settings dialog box Link tab.

Several different types of profiling are available, and the Profiler types generally fall into the categories of function profiling and line profiling. With function profiling you can determine how often an application executes a function or if the application executes the function at all. With line profiling you can perform similar processing on a line-by-line basis.

You typically will not profile an entire application — only the parts of the application that you are concerned may be performance bottlenecks. However, function profiling may help determine which functions the application calls most frequently, which may save you the time of closely analyzing functions that the application does not execute regularly. Saving one second of performance time in a function that the application calls only once is not as useful as saving one-half a second of performance time in a function that the application may call hundreds or even thousands of times during the application's lifetime.

Windows NT also provides the CAP tool, which you can use to profile applications outside the Visual Studio IDE, as well as to profile application performance "in the real world," such as service application performance.

As with the debugger that you learned about in Chapter 3, using the Profiler in your development cycle is a crucial step in creating applications that are speedy, efficient, and have a minimal memory footprint.

✦ ✦ ✦

CHAPTER 5

Miscellaneous Tools

A number of tools come with Visual C++ 6.0 that make your job as a developer easier. This chapter describes these tools and shows you how to use them effectively.

Spy++

The Windows system delivers messages to individual windows, notifying them of user activity. As such, understanding the available types of messages is clearly important to your success in Windows programming. But with more than 200 messages in the system, it's sometimes hard to figure out which messages you should pay attention to. Microsoft's Spy++ utility shows you every message that gets sent to a window. It's also handy for sleuthing through the system to figure out which windows, threads, and processes are present in a particular application. To start Spy++, select Spy++ from the Tools menu.

When Spy++ first comes up, it displays a list of windows running in the system, as shown in Figure 5-1. You can open other windows in Spy++ to learn about the processes and threads currently running in the system. These lists are tightly interconnected, because processes own threads, and threads own windows. And starting in the window list, you can get a more precise idea of the parent-child relationships that exist between various windows.

In This Chapter

Using the Spy++ utility

Customizing the Tools menu

Browsing classes

Browsing the MFC source code

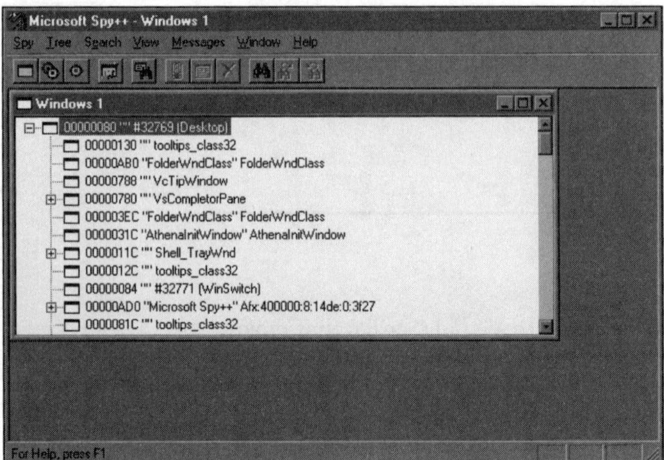

Figure 5-1: Spy++ starts by displaying a list of the windows that are running in the system.

To give you an idea of how Spy++ is typically used, Figure 5-2 shows Spy++ displaying three lists: a process list, a thread list, and a window list. Although Spy++ can tell you about any Windows program that's running in the system, in our example Spy++ is actually spying on itself. In Figure 5-2, the window list shows that the main window has four child windows. Some of these windows also have their own child windows. In other words, one of the things that Spy++ helps you learn is how an application might organize its windows in the creation of a user interface.

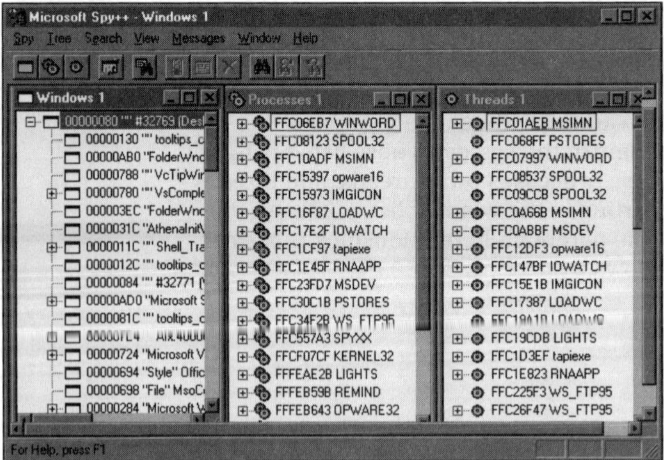

Figure 5-2: To get more details about processes, threads, or windows, click an item in any Spy++ window.

In general, you'll find that developers typically prefer to create fewer rather than more windows. Consider a spreadsheet program: should individual cells each be a window, or should a group of cells be a window? If you run Spy++ with any commercially available spreadsheet program, you learn that groups of cells are windows. This design decision was made because of the relatively high overhead of a window. You'll want to follow this strategy in designing the windowing for your own applications.

During the development of a Windows program, a bug might prevent your program from terminating properly. Although all of the windows in your program might be hidden, the process itself is still running in the system. Using the details that you can see in the Process window in Spy++, you could quickly ascertain whether or not your program has shut down properly. You open the Process window in Spy++ by selecting Spy from the Processes menu. The Process window shows all of the processes that are currently running in the system. Nested in the hierarchy under each process is a list of the threads that are owned by that process. (Remember that threads are the unit of scheduling in Windows 95, Windows 98, and in Windows NT.) Any windows that are owned by a thread are listed in the hierarchy under that thread.

Similarly, when you are adding new threads to a program, you aren't always sure that secondary threads are created and destroyed at the proper time. The Threads window in Spy++ enables you to know exactly how many threads are currently running in your program. To open the Threads window in Spy++, you choose the Spy item from the Threads menu. This window lists all of the threads in the system, sorted by thread ID. The items in the Threads window also serve as the top of a hierarchy, this time for the windows that are connected to threads. A quick glance at this listing shows that more threads are windowless than have windows. Such threads have no user interface; instead, they provide services to the threads that do have windows.

To get more details about processes, threads, or windows, click an item in any Spy++ window.

The hierarchies shown by Spy++ suggest the hierarchy of system objects — for example, processes own threads and threads own windows. You can't have a process without a thread, because it wouldn't be able to accomplish any work. But you can have a thread that has no windows. Threads that have windows get a priority boost when one of their windows receives a message. This mechanism makes the user interfaces of Windows 95, Windows 98, and Windows NT highly responsive to user input.

To see the messages that are being sent to a window, you open a Messages window in Spy++. There are several ways to select a window for spying, but using the Finder tool is preferred. Select the Spy item from the Find Windows menu, which opens a dialog box containing the Finder tool. After clicking the Show Messages button, click and drag the Finder tool onto the window that interests you.

As shown in Figure 5-3, the Messages window shows all the messages being delivered to a window, with one or two lines per message. The leftmost column lists the handle — or ID — of the window that is receiving a message. For each message, the second column contains either P, S, or R. You'll learn more about that column in a moment. The third column lists the message received and the decoded values of two 4-byte parameters that were passed along with the message.

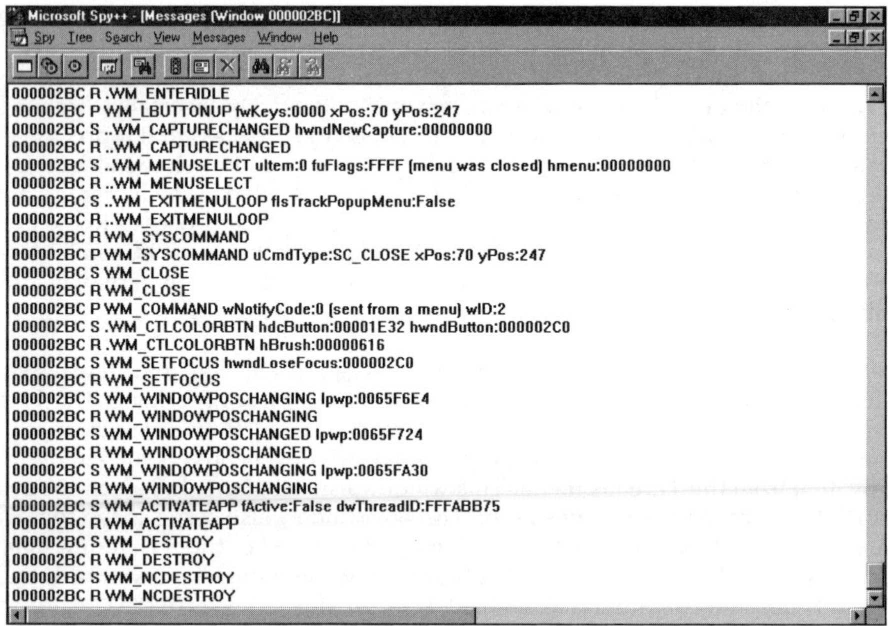

Figure 5-3: The Spy++ window shows message received by a window.

Even without understanding the meaning of individual messages, you can see with Spy++ that a lot of message traffic is associated with even the smallest user interface actions. When viewing the Messages window, you can learn more about a particular message by selecting the message (click the message with the right mouse button), and then selecting the Help item from the menu that is displayed.

The second column in Spy++ indicates whether a message was Posted (P) to a window. The difference between posting and sending has to do with whether the sender of the message wanted to wait for a reply. Posted messages wait in a message queue until the recipient asks for a new message. Such messages notify the recipient that something has occurred, but no reply is necessary.

Sent messages don't wait in a message queue; instead, the sender of a message waits for a reply. A sent message behaves like a function call; the message sender waits until the recipient processes the message and provides a return value. Spy++ flags the reply to a sent message with an R in the second column of the Messages window.

Figure 5-3 shows the messages that are generated when the user closes a window. The first message displayed in the window, WM_SYSCOMMAND, starts the window-closing process. It's the only queued message in the entire data stream. The other messages each indicate an additional step in the window shutdown and closing process. The process continues until the window has been completely destroyed, which is represented in Figure 5-3 by the WM_DESTROY and WM_NCDESTROY messages.

It is strongly recommended that you take the time to learn how to use Spy++ so you can take advantage of all the great things Spy++ shows you about the system. You'll find this program quite useful as you begin building your Windows application software.

Customizing the Tools Menu

You can add up to 16 commands to the Tools menu. These commands can be associated with any program that runs on your operating system. You can also specify arguments for any command that you add to the Tools menu.

Adding a Command to the Tools Menu

As an example, the following procedure demonstrates how to add the Windows Notepad accessory to the Tools menu:

1. On the Tools menu, click Customize, and then click the Tools tab.
2. To add a tool, scroll to the bottom of the list in the Menu Contents box, double-click the blank line (indicated by an empty rectangle), type the name of the tool as you want it to appear on the Tools menu, and press Enter. For example, if you want to add a command for the Windows Notepad accessory, you might type **Notepad**.
3. In the Menu Contents box, highlight the name of the tool you just entered.
4. In the Command box, browse or type the path and name of the program — for example, C:\WINDOWS\NOTEPAD.EXE.
5. In the Arguments textbox, browse or type any arguments to be passed to the program. You can use the drop-down arrow next to the Arguments textbox to display a menu of arguments. Select an argument from the list to insert argument syntax into the Arguments textbox. Visual C++ provides the argument macros shown in the Argument Macros table.
6. In the Initial Directory box, type the file directory where the command is located, and click OK.
7. You can use the drop-down arrow next to the Initial Directory textbox to display a menu of directories. Select a directory from the list to insert directory syntax into the Initial Directory textbox. Once the command appears on the Tools menu, choose it from the menu to run the program.

8. You can change the default menu name of the newly added tool by editing the Menu Text box. You can also add arguments to be passed to the program by typing them in the Arguments textbox, or set the initial directory for your program by typing it in the Initial Directory textbox.

✦ ✦ ✦ ✦ ✦

Editing a Command on the Tools Menu

You can edit the commands that are placed on the Tools menu. This section shows you how.

1. On the Tools menu, click Customize, and then click the Tools tab.
2. In the Menu Contents box, select the command that you want to edit.
3. Perform one or more of the following actions: to move the command up one position in the menu, choose the Move Up button. To move the command down one position in the menu, choose the Move Down button. To change the menu text, command line (tool path and filename), command-line arguments, or the initial directory, type the new information in the appropriate textbox. To specify a letter in the menu title as an access key, precede that letter in the Menu Contents box with an ampersand.
4. The first letter in the title is the keyboard access key by default.
5. To specify that a console application's output is displayed in the Output window rather than in the console window, click Use Output Window.
6. To specify that the window associated with the tool close when you close the tool, select Close Window on Exiting.
7. To be prompted for command-line arguments each time you run the tool, select Prompt For Arguments.

✦ ✦ ✦ ✦ ✦

Miscellaneous Tools Operations

Here's how to delete a tool on the Tools menu. Click Customize on the Tools menu, and then click the Tools tab. In the Menu Contents box, select the command you want to delete, and press the Delete button.

To specify arguments for tools on the Tools menu: click Customize on the Tools menu, and then click the Tools tab. In the Menu Contents box, select the command for which you want to specify arguments. In the Arguments textbox, type the arguments that you want or press the drop-down arrow to the right of the Arguments textbox to display a list of arguments. Visual C++ provides the argument macros shown in the Argument Macros table.

Browsing Classes

Browse windows display information about the symbols (classes, functions, data, macros, and types) in your program. If you have browse information turned on when you build a project, the compiler creates .SBR files with information about each program file in your project. The BSCMAKE utility (`BSCMAKE.EXE`) assembles these .SBR files into a single browse file. This browse file has the project's base name and the extension .BSC.

To create a browse file, open the Settings dialog box from the Project menu. In the Browse Info tab, select the "Build browse info file" option. Then go to the C/C++ tab; in the General category, select Generate browse info. Then rebuild your application.

You view browse information in browse windows, which have different appearances and different controls depending on the type of information displayed. Using browse commands, you can look at information about all the symbols in any source file.

Using Browse Files

Whenever you open a project, the browse file for the project is opened if it exists. If you close the browse file, the file is reopened when you do a query. To query the current information file about a symbol, do the following:

1. On the Tools menu, click Source Browser. The Browse dialog box appears.
2. In the Identifier textbox, type the name of the symbol you want to query for. You can use the asterisk as a wildcard to match any string.
3. In the Select Query list box, select the type of query you want.
4. If necessary, click the Case Sensitive Queries option.
5. Choose OK. A browse window specific to the query type appears. The query results for the symbol you selected are displayed. If you select a symbol in a source file, the symbol appears in the Identifier box when you open the Browse dialog box. This eliminates Step 2 in this procedure.

When the browse information file is open, you can use it to find where a symbol used in a source file is defined or first referenced.

◆ ◆ ◆ ◆ ◆

To find the definition of a symbol, select the symbol in a source file or the standard toolbar Find box. Then click Go To on the Edit menu. The Go To dialog box is displayed. In the "Go to what:" list, click Definition. Finally, click the Go To button.

To find the first reference to a symbol, start by selecting the symbol in a source file or the standard toolbar Find box. Click Go To on the Edit menu. The Go To dialog box is displayed. In the "Go to what:" list, select Reference. Now click the Go To button.

The browse file is based on the state of the source files at the time of the last build. If you edit source files and then go to a definition or a reference, the location in the browse file may no longer be accurate. If the browse file has not been built, a dialog box provides the option of building the browse file.

You can jump to the previous or next definition or reference by choosing one of the navigation buttons, Previous or Next, on the Go To dialog box.

Displaying a Symbol Definition or Reference

Using the Browse toolbar, you can quickly display the definition or reference of a symbol. The development environment opens the source file containing the first definition or reference and highlights the symbol. To see the next definition or reference, click the Next Definition/Reference button on the toolbar. To display the definition or reference of a symbol using the Browse toolbar, do the following:

1. Select the symbol in a source file or the standard toolbar Find box. You can use the asterisk as a wildcard to match any string.
2. On the Browse toolbar, click either the Go To Definition or Go To Reference button.
3. If the symbol is a member of more than one class, the Resolve Ambiguity dialog box is displayed. Select the symbol that you want from the list.

✦ ✦ ✦ ✦ ✦

To display the definition or reference of a symbol using the right mouse button, point to the symbol in a source file (either a text editor window or the pane containing ClassView), and click the right mouse button. On the pop-up menu, click either Go To Definition or Go To Reference.

To display the definition or reference of a symbol using the Go To dialog box on the Edit menu, click Go To. In the "Go to what:" list box, click either Definition or Reference. Enter the additional selection criteria. Click one of the navigation buttons: Go To, Previous, or Next.

To display the definition or reference of a symbol using the Definitions And References window, select the symbol in a source file or the standard toolbar Find box. You can use the asterisk as a wildcard to match any string. On the Tools menu, click Source Browser. In the Select Query list box, click Definitions And References. Click OK. If the symbol is a member of more than one class, the Resolve Ambiguity dialog box is displayed. Select the symbol that you want from the list. In the Definitions And References window, double-click the definition or reference you want to see. The Definitions And References window is displayed, with the selected symbol at the top of the left pane.

Displaying a Call Graph

To display the graph of all functions that a selected function calls, follow these steps:

1. Select the function name in a source file or the standard toolbar Find box.
2. On the Tools menu, click Source Browser.
3. In the Select Query list box, click Call Graph.
4. Click OK.
5. If the function is an overloaded function or a member function of more than one class, the Resolve Ambiguity dialog box is displayed. Select the function that you want from the list. The Call Graph window is displayed, with the selected function at the top of the left pane.

◆ ◆ ◆ ◆ ◆

Displaying a Graph of Calling Functions

A callers graph displays all the functions that call a selected function. To display the graph of all functions that call a selected function, do the following:

1. Select the function name in a source file or the standard toolbar Find box.
2. On the Tools menu, click Source Browser.
3. In the Select Query list box, click Callers Graph.
4. Click OK.
5. If the function is an overloaded function or a member function of more than one class, the Resolve Ambiguity dialog box is displayed. Select the function that you want from the list. The Callers Graph window is displayed, with the selected function at the top of the left pane.

◆ ◆ ◆ ◆ ◆

Browse the MFC Source Code

`MFC.Bsc` is the browse information file for the Microsoft Foundation Class Library. Use it to quickly look through the MFC source code for debugging purposes or to get a better idea of what's going on behind the scenes.

Not all MFC classes and symbols are included in the browse info file. For example, the Internet Server Application Programming Interface (ISAPI) classes are not included because they are in a separate library. If you want to take a look at symbols that are not in the browse file, the Find In Files command on the File menu is another good way of locating items.

MFC.BSC is not installed by the setup program but can be copied manually from the distribution disk. From the root CD directory, the path is `\Program Files\Microsoft Visual Studio\VC98\MFC\Src\MFC.Bsc`. Copy this file to the same directory on your hard disk where Visual C++ is installed. Once installed, the file can be opened and used the same as any other browse information file.

Summary

The Visual C++ tools can help in your application development. Especially useful is Spy++, which you can use to peer into the inner workings of applications.

✦ ✦ ✦

P A R T

Windows Programming Fundamentals

These twelve chapters teach you the basics of Windows programming. After working through this part, you'll probably be able to write Windows programs easily. The topics covered in this part range from menus and mouse-and-keyboard input to using GDI and bitmaps to draw to the screen. You learn how to create and use dialog boxes as well as how to handle errors by catching exceptions. These twelve chapters provide a solid foundation for the more advanced topics included in the remainder of the book.

✦ ✦ ✦ ✦

In This Part

Chapter 6: Overview of MFC Programming

Chapter 7: Menus

Chapter 8: Mouse and Keyboard

Chapter 9: Graphics

Chapter 10: Bitmaps, Palettes, DIBs, and Double Buffering

Chapter 11: MFC Exception Handling

Chapter 12: Controls

Chapter 13: Modal and Modeless Dialogs

Chapter 14: Property Sheets and Property Pages

Chapter 15: Data I/O

Chapter 16: Sound

Chapter 17: Timers and OnIdle Loop Processing

✦ ✦ ✦ ✦

CHAPTER 6

Overview of MFC Programming

✦ ✦ ✦ ✦

In This Chapter

Becoming familiar with the overall design of the Microsoft Foundation Classes

The design goals behind MFC

Exploring the most commonly used MFC classes

The MFC hierarchy design

When and when not to use MFC

✦ ✦ ✦ ✦

This chapter is a little different from the remaining chapters in this book in that it doesn't contain any demo programs and very few code samples. This doesn't mean that you should skip this chapter and move on to the other "meatier" ones, however. The topics covered in this chapter are key to your understanding of the Microsoft Foundation Classes (MFC) and effectively using this framework to create 32-bit Windows programs.

MFC is arguably the biggest thing to happen to Windows application development in quite some time. Before MFC, applications programmers had to use the Windows API exclusively. If you've done any API-only development, you'll understand what an onerous task this is. Imagine writing switch statements whose source code runs several pages long or hand-coding window creation. Back then Windows C/C++ development was regarded as even more of a black art than it is considered now. During this time two competing application development frameworks emerged, MFC and Borland's Object Window Library (OWL). While both frameworks had their strong and weak points, MFC emerged as the dominant development framework for Windows development.

This chapter will give you a tour of the design of MFC and a peek at the guiding philosophy and principles that shape the architecture. We'll also take a look at the hierarchy of objects within the framework and then end with a short analysis of when to use MFC and when to use the raw Windows API.

What Is MFC?

MFC is the abbreviation for a collection of C++ classes produced by Microsoft that are called the Microsoft Foundation Classes. MFC provides an object-oriented framework that application developers can use to create Windows applications. MFC is organized as a hierarchy of C++ classes. Several high-level classes provide general functionality while the low-level classes implement more specific behaviors. Each of the low-level classes is derived from a high-level class and, thus, inherits the behaviors of the high-level class.

For example, the class `CWnd` is a high-level class that implements most of the functionality common to all windows. The class has functions to print text, draw graphics, and track the movement of the mouse pointer among others. The class `CSplitterWnd` is derived from `CWnd` and inherits all `CWnd`'s functions. The `CSplitterWnd` implements a special kind of window, one called a splitter window. A splitter window is a window that is separated into at least two sections. The border between the two sections can be moved by the user. Windows Explorer uses a splitter window to display information about the computer. `CSplitterWnd` is a low-level class that is derived from the high-level class `CWnd`.

MFC provides other benefits as well. MFC handles many common Windows-related tasks, such as message handling and routing, in the background. Instead of having to write the same message handling loop in every Windows application you develop, MFC implements the message loop for you and provides easy to understand and use member functions, like `OnPaint()`, which enables you to insert code to handle the window message.

In addition to the class hierarchy, MFC also provides an application development model. This model is called the *document/view model*. Document/view, or doc/view for short, is a method of designing an application so that the application's data is separated from the user interface elements. This allows the two parts of the application to stand on their own, enabling the programmer to make changes to one without having to make drastic changes to the other.

The Power of MFC

The flexibility and strength of the document view model cannot be emphasized enough. This model can be used in the great majority of all applications.

✦ ✦ ✦ ✦ ✦

For example, consider a word processor or spreadsheet application. The data contained in the application is the document in document/view. The presentation of the data is the view. The document class has member functions that let the view class work with the application data. As long as these functions themselves do not change, the user interface does not need to change. In fact, the document doesn't even have to be a word processed document or a spreadsheet. It can be records from a database or graphic images. As long as the member functions don't change, it doesn't matter what type of information is used. Details of the document/view architecture are presented in Chapter 19.

Design Philosophy of MFC

An application development framework, such as MFC, is a collection of libraries, which provide a set of services to the application developer to aid in the development process. Normally, an application development framework is designed to streamline the development process as much as possible, as well as to simplify difficult or tedious programming tasks. In particular, MFC is designed to simplify the use of large parts of the Windows API. MFC takes some of the functionalities of the API, such as window management, graphics output, or message routing, and wraps them in more programmer-friendly C++ classes, which are easier to use. In many cases, MFC performs some sophisticated operations behind the scenes, which presents a simpler programming interface to the developer and hides some of the ugliness of the Windows API.

One overriding concern of the MFC team was to provide a usable framework while at the same time incurring as little overhead as possible. MFC would be of limited use if applications incurred a 30 percent performance hit just by using the framework. The MFC developers have tried to reduce the "footprint" of the framework wherever possible. Their efforts have resulted in a fairly lean architecture that incurs a minimal performance hit while at the same time easing the load placed on the poor old Windows developer.

The robustness of a framework's design can be seen in the framework's extensibility. Any framework worth its salt should be able to be easily extended. Many C++ frameworks rely on the language's object-oriented features to achieve this extensibility. Merely relying on traits of the language is not enough. The internal structure of the framework must also be well constructed and coherent in order for the framework to be truly extensible.

MFC is made up of many C++ classes. Some, such as `CWnd` or `CwinThread`, provide the basis for a large percentage of the entire framework. These base classes encapsulate basic functionality, such as opening a window that is required of most Windows applications. Other more specialized classes, such as `CsplitterWnd`, are derived from the base classes. Derived classes inherit all the features of their parent, or base, classes and also add some functionality of their own. As a Windows developer, you can take advantage of the extensibility of MFC's class hierarchy and create custom classes, which perform specialized tasks. We'll look at MFC's class hierarchy a little bit later in the section "MFC Hierarchy Design."

Advantages of Using MFC

MFC object-oriented design groups together related areas of the Windows API into C++ classes, or objects. For example, the `CWnd` class encapsulates most of the API's windowing functionality. As the applications programmer, you don't have to memorize a lot of API function calls. All you have to do is instantiate a new instance of the `CWnd` class and call a few member functions. Listings 6-1 and 6-2 illustrate the difference MFC makes for the task of creating a simple window.

Listing 6-1: Creating a Window without MFC

```
int WINAPI WinMain (HINSTANCE hInstance,
     HINSTANCE hPrevInstance, PSTR szCmdLine,
     int iCmdShow)

static char szAppName[] = "NonMFC";
HWND                        hwnd;
MSG                         msg;
WNDCLASSEX                  wndclass;

// Fill in wndclass structure with required information
// These settings create a simple window with
// no menu, scroll or status bars

wndclass.cbSize = sizeof(wndclass);
wndclass.Style = CS_HREDRAW | CSVREDRAW;
wndclass.lpfnWndProc = WndProc;
wndclass.cbClsExtra = 0;
wndclass.cbWndExtra = 0;
wndclass.hInstance = hInstance;
wndclass.hIcon = LoadIcon(NULL, IDI_APPLICATION);
wndclass.hCursor = LoadCursor(NULL, IDC_ARROW);
wndclass.hbrBackground = (HBRUSH) GetStockObject
     (WHITE_BRUSH);

wndclass.lpszMenuName = NULL;
wndclass.lpszClassName = szAppName;
wndclass.hIconSm = LoadIcon(NULL, IDI_APPLICATION);

RegisterClassEx (&wndclass);
hwnd=CreateWindow  ( szAppName,
                    "Non-MFC App,
                     WS_OVERLAPPEDWINDOW,
                     CW_USEDEFAULT,
                     CW_USEDEFAULT,
                     CW_USEDEFAULT,
                     CW_USEDEFAULT,
                     NULL,
                     NULL,
                     hInstance,
                     NULL );

// At this point the window class has been
// registered with the operating system
// and an instance of the class has been created
// but is not visible.

// Let's make the window visible and update it

ShowWindow (hwnd, iCmdShow);
UpdateWindow (hwnd);
```

Programming at the raw API level requires working with several different data structures as well as four different function calls. In larger projects, the non-object "orientedness" of the API makes it difficult for you to manage your code. Compare Listing 6-1 with Listing 6-2.

Listing 6-2: Creating a Window with MFC

```
CMyApp myApp;

BOOL CMyApp::InitInstance()
{
    m_pMainWnd = new CMainWindow;
    m_pMainWnd->ShowWindow(m_nCmdShow);
    m_pMainWnd->UpdateWindow();
    return TRUE;
}

CMainWindow::CMainWindow()
{
    Create (NULL, "MFC App");
}
```

In Listing 6-2, the class `CMainWindow` is derived from the base class `CWnd`. `CMainWindow` inherits all the functionality of `CWnd` that includes `CWnd`'s implementation of the window creation process. You can be assured that somewhere deep in the inner workings of the framework, MFC is executing code similar to Listing 6-1. Because the framework does all the dirty work, you don't have to.

Now then, which would you rather write? If you take into consideration that opening a window is a common task that you'll perform quite a bit during your programming career, the benefits of MFC become apparent.

Features, features, features

MFC provides an incredible number of features. The major supported features of MFC follow:

- ✦ Document/view architecture
- ✦ Multiple document interface (MDI)
- ✦ Print and print preview support
- ✦ Using and creating ActiveX controls
- ✦ ODBC and Access database support

✦ Internet (TCP/IP) programming support

✦ Windows 95/Windows 98/Windows NT common control support

✦ Multithreaded support

Extensible architecture

Because MFC is written in C++, you can take advantage of the language's features to derive your own custom classes from the framework's classes. This can save enormous amounts of time and energy. Rather than implement your own Windows objects from scratch, you can rely on the time-tested codebase of MFC and add just the functionality that you require.

MFC's hierarchical design enables you to easily extend the framework for your own purposes. Several specialized types of windows are already included, such as `CSplitterWnd`, which implements the split window style used in Explorer. MFC also includes classes for user interface elements, such as buttons and drop-down lists, and operating system elements, such as threads and semaphores.

Need a class to represent a special-purpose window for your application? No problem, just derive your custom class from MFC's `CWnd`. Want to implement a new style of user interface button? Go ahead, just derive your button class from `CButton`. Do you need to use a separate thread of execution for a function in your application? Use the MFC function `AfxBeginThread()`. In all of these examples, you are able to take advantage of the work already done by the framework and add only what you need.

MFC Hierarchy Design

Now that we have a high-level understanding of MFC, let's drop down a bit and examine the framework's object hierarchy. MFC's object hierarchy closely resembles the organization of a directory structure. MFC has a root object, `CObject`, and most all other objects are derived from it. Within the hierarchy, objects of similar type can be grouped together into categories. MFC includes well over 100 different classes.

Reading information about all of the MFC classes can be a bit overwhelming. Rather than provide a listing of all the MFC classes, in this section we'll look at some of the most commonly used classes and group them into easy-to-understand categories. Information about any of these classes or others, such as `CString` or `CException`, can be found in the Developer Studio online help.

File services

This family of MFC classes provides general file support and is derived directly from `CObject`. In this context, the term *file* doesn't refer only to a file that resides on a disk, but is extended to cover Web page requests, memory-mapped files, and TCP/IP sockets. Table 6-1 lists the classes included in this category.

Table 6-1
File Services Classes

Class Name	*Description*
`CFile`	Provides unbuffered, binary disk I/O services.
`CRecentFileList`	Provides control of the most recently used (MRU) file list.
`CMemFile`	Provides access to memory-mapped files.
`COleStreamFile`	Represents a stream of data in an OLE structured storage compound file.
`CSocketFile`	Used to send and receive data over a TCP/IP network connection.
`CStdioFile`	Provides buffered disk I/O services similar to a C runtime file stream.
`CSharedFile`	Supports shared memory files.
`CMonikerFile`	Represents a stream of data in a compound file in the same way that a pathname identifies a regular disk file.
`CAsyncMonikerFile`	Supports the capability of ActiveX controls to load data from a data stream asynchronously.
`CDataPathProperty`	Allows an ActiveX control to load control property data asynchronously.
`CCachedDataPathProperty`	Allows an ActiveX control to load control property data asynchronously and cache the data in RAM.
`CGopherFile`	Encapsulates transferring data from a Gopher server.
`CHttpFile`	Encapsulates transferring data from a Web server.

Windows

Sometimes it seems that everything in Windows is a window. Every user interface element, from a simple button to combo boxes to toolbars, has a window handle associated with it. And if that wasn't enough, MFC also introduces the programming concept of the document/view architecture.

Keeping pace with all the different types of windows, MFC also provides quite a few different window classes. These window classes can be broken out into four broad categories: frame windows, view windows, dialog boxes, and controls. Each of these classes provides different types of functionality. The one thing that they all have in common is that they all represent one type of window or another and are all derived from the CWnd class.

Frame windows provide a container for document/view-based applications. The frame window contains the view window that in turn contains the document. Table 6-2 lists the different frame window classes, and Table 6-3 lists the different view window classes.

Table 6-2
Frame Window Classes

Class Name	*Description*
CFrameWnd	SDI frame window
CMDIChildWnd	MDI child window
CMDIFrameWnd	MDI frame window
COleIPFrameWnd	TODO
CSplitterWnd	Explorer-style split window

Table 6-3
View Window Classes

Class Name	*Description*
CView	Encapsulates a basic view in a document/view application.
CCtrlView	Applies the document/view architecture to the Windows common controls. Serves as a base class for the following four classes.
CEditView	Applies the document/view architecture to the Windows common edit control.
CListView	Applies the document/view architecture to the Windows common list control.
CRichEditView	Applies the document/view architecture to the Windows common rich edit control.
CTreeView	Applies the document/view architecture to the Windows common tree control.

Class Name	*Description*
`CScrollView`	Provides a `CView` with built-in scrolling capabilities.
`CFormView`	Base class for views containing controls, such as dialog boxes. The layout of the form is based on a dialog resource included in the application at compile time.
`CDaoRecordView`	A type of `CView` that displays Jet database recordset information in controls
`CRecordView`	A type of `CView` that displays ODBC database recordset information in controls

Also included in the windows family of classes are dialog boxes. As any user of Windows knows, myriad different dialog boxes are available such as file selection dialogs, error message dialogs, and font selection dialogs. Each of these has a corresponding MFC class. These classes are listed in Table 6-4.

Table 6-4
Dialog Box Classes

Class Name	*Description*
`CDialog`	Base class used for displaying dialog boxes
`CCommonDialog`	Encapsulates the base functionality of the Windows common dialogs and serves as a base class for the following five classes.
`CColorDialog`	Encapsulates the Windows common color selection dialog.
`CFileDialog`	Encapsulates the Windows common file selection dialog.
`CFindReplaceDialog`	Encapsulates the Windows common find and replace dialog.
`CFontDialog`	Encapsulates the Windows common font selection dialog.
`CPrintDialog`	Encapsulates the Windows common print dialog. Provides an easy way to implement Print and Print Setup dialog boxes.
`CPropertyPage`	Represents a single page of a property sheet.

The windows family of MFC classes includes all Windows objects that have a windows handle associated with them. This also includes all the Windows controls such as buttons and combo boxes. These control classes are listed in Table 6-5.

Table 6-5
Control Classes

Class Name	*Description*
CButton	Normal push button
CBitmapButton	A push button that is labeled with a bitmap rather than text
CComboBox	An edit box with an associated pull-down list
CEdit	A text box
CHeaderCtrl	A window that is positioned above columns of text and that contains the column titles. Encapsulates the Windows common header control.
CHotKeyCtrl	Encapsulates the Windows common hot key control
CListBox	A control that contains a list of choices
CCheckListBox	A control that displays a box that can be checked or unchecked
CDragListBox	Encapsulates the standard list box, and enables the user to rearrange list items by dragging them to a new position.
CListCtrl	Encapsulates the functionality of a list view control. A list view provides several ways of viewing list data. Windows Explorer uses list views.
COleControl	Base class used to develop ActiveX controls
CProgressCtrl	Encapsulates the Windows common progress bar control and provides member functions to manipulate the display.
CRichEditCtrl	Encapsulates the Windows common rich edit control. The rich edit control enables a user to enter, edit, and format text.
CScrollBar	Provides the functionality of a scroll bar.
CSliderCtrl	Encapsulates the Windows common slider control. Provides member functions to manipulate the size, scale, and frequency of tic marks.
CSpinButtonCtrl	Encapsulates the Windows common spin button control. The spin button "attaches" to a buddy window. Clicking the up button on the spin control increases the value of the buddy window.
CStatic	Encapsulates a static control. A Windows static control can display a text string, box, rectangle, icon, bitmap, or cursor.
CStatusBarCtrl	Encapsulates the Windows common status bar control. A status bar is a small window that is usually displayed at the bottom of a parent window. The status bar is used to display various kinds of application status data.

Class Name	Description
CTabCtrl	Encapsulates the Windows common tab control. A tab is used to delineate multiple pages for the same window or dialog box. It appears as a divider tab, such as the ones used in notebooks.
CToolBarCtrl	Encapsulates the Windows common toolbar control. A toolbar is a floating bar containing buttons and edit, list, or combo box controls.
CToolTipCtrl	Encapsulates the Windows common tooltip control. A tooltip is a small window that appears when the mouse pointer hovers over a tool for approximately one-half second.
CTreeCtrl	Encapsulates the Windows common tree control. A tree control displays application data in a hierarchical format. Windows Explorer as well as the older File Manager both use tree controls to display directory and file information.

Graphics

Another important family of MFC classes is the graphics family. Within this category, the classes can be further broken down into two subcategories: *device contexts* and *graphics devices*. A device context represents a graphics container, such as a window or a file, where graphics or text can be drawn. All device context classes are derived from the `CDC` class that is in turn derived from `CObject`. A graphics device is an object used for the drawing operation. All of the graphics device classes are derived from the `CGdiObject` class, which is derived from `CObject`. The graphics device classes sound like their real-life counterparts such as `CPen` for drawing lines or `CBrush` for painting the screen. Table 6-6 lists each of the MFC graphics classes.

Database support

The MFC framework supports two types of databases: ODBC and Microsoft Jet (the latter is otherwise known as Microsoft Access). Using these classes you can access almost any type of database available today. The ODBC classes provide access to many client-server database platforms such as Oracle, Sybase, Informix, or Microsoft's own SQL Server.

The Jet database classes enable you to use the object model, referred to as Data Access Objects, built in to every Access- or Jet-based database. Data Access Objects (DAO) provides its own rich model hierarchy suitable for manipulating database tables and queries as well as managing user and group security. Table 6-7 lists the available database classes.

Table 6-6
Graphics Classes

Class Name	*Description*
CDC	Encapsulates a device context and provides member functions to manipulate the context.
CClientDC	Constructs a device context that is associated with the client area of a window.
CMetaFileDC	Constructs a device context that is associated with a Windows metafile.
CPaintDC	Constructs a device context that can only be used when responding to WM_PAINT messages.
CBitmap	Encapsulates a Windows bitmap and provides member functions to manipulate the image.
CBrush	Encapsulates a Windows GDI brush.
CFont	Encapsulates a Windows GDI font.
CPalette	Encapsulates a Windows GDI color palette.
CPen	Encapsulates a Windows GDI pen.
CRgn	Encapsulates a Windows GDI region.

Table 6-7
Database Classes

Class Name	*Database Type*	*Description*
CDatabase	ODBC	Represents a connection to an ODBC database.
CRecordset	ODBC	Represents an ODBC-based recordset.
CLongBinary	ODBC	Encapsulates manipulating large binary objects, such as images, within an ODBC database.
CDaoDatabase	DAO	Represents a connection to a Microsoft Jet (Access) database.
CDaoQueryDef	DAO	Represents a Jet query definition.
CDaoRecordset	DAO	Represents a Jet recordset.
CDaoTableDef	DAO	Represents a Jet table definition.
CDaoWorkspace	DAO	Represents a Jet workspace.

This concludes our tour of the MFC framework. While we have covered the most commonly used classes, we've only touched on a few of the many classes available within the framework. Throughout the remainder of this book, we'll be working with not only the classes introduced in this chapter, but also several others that are outside the scope of a simple overview.

You Don't Use MFC?

Even though MFC provides a great many benefits for the applications programmer, there are times when you might not want to use MFC in your development efforts. The developers of MFC have worked to minimize the size and number of files required. In a traditional application, these supporting files are not generally a problem. They are installed alongside the main application files.

The rise in popularity of the Internet has caused a reevaluation of MFC. The Internet has changed the traditional programming model. In days past, it was accepted that an application was installed part and parcel on each machine. The application was freestanding and self-contained. This is referred to as a *monolithic application*. MFC provided all the functionality required by a monolithic application. Because all the code executed on a single machine, MFC is a good fit for this programming model.

As client-server programming arrived on the scene, some parts of the application were moved to the server. However, the user interface and some lightweight application tasks were left on the client machine. Because user interface development is something at which MFC excels, it was still appropriate to continue to use MFC.

With the increased influence of the Internet, programming requirements have changed again. In many cases, an application is fully distributed, with a database server providing data access, a Web server providing application services, and the Web browser providing the user interface. Given the distributed nature of this programming model, MFC is not always appropriate.

Current Web technology enables ActiveX controls to be embedded into a Web page. When a client browser downloads the page, the browser also downloads the control and executes it. Because the majority of users continue to access the Internet via slow modems, reducing the amount of data that must be downloaded is extremely important.

MFC requires several sizable support DLLs, most of them in excess of 100K. If a browser has to download not only the page and the control but also several hundred kilobytes of supporting files, this clearly makes for a very long download. In an attempt to rectify this shortcoming, Microsoft has introduced another framework called the Active Template Library (ATL). ATL enables the creation of lightweight controls that are small in size and easily downloadable. ATL is discussed in Chapter 33.

Summary

So here ends our introduction to the Microsoft Foundation Classes. Hopefully, you now have a better understanding of what MFC is and why an application framework such as MFC eases the developer's burden. You should also have a feel for the organization of MFC and feel familiar with some of the more common classes.

✦ ✦ ✦

C H A P T E R 7

Menus

✦ ✦ ✦ ✦

In This Chapter

Creating menus and editing menu resources

Writing menu handlers

Defining and using accelerator resources

Performing on-the-fly menu reconfiguration

Generating context menus

✦ ✦ ✦ ✦

One of the most important user interface objects is menus because menus are one of the primary ways that users interact with your application. The emphasis that Microsoft places on menus as a key user interface element is evidenced by the number of menu support functions available in the Win32 API.

In this chapter, we'll cover menus and their close companion, accelerator keys. Menus and accelerator keys are among the most commonly used input mechanisms, so it's important that you have a good understanding of how to work with them. Well-constructed menus serve as the informal documentation for the features and commands of your application.

An accelerator key is a keystroke or set of keystrokes, such as Ctrl+C, that a program interprets as a command. From your application's point of view, the events generated by either an accelerator key or a menu selection are the same. In many cases, you'll see menu commands and their corresponding accelerator key displayed in the menu. Application programmers do this to indicate which accelerator keys are bound to which commands.

For example, you'll often see Ctrl+V next to the Paste command in an Edit menu. Interestingly, even though accelerator keys and menu items generate the same messages and events within Windows and MFC, they are separate types of resources that are defined differently. Specifically, menus are defined using menu resources, and accelerators are defined with accelerator resources.

By the end of this discussion, you should have a good grasp of the fundamentals of basic menu and accelerator resource creation and handling. You'll also become familiar with more advanced topics such as generating context menus and dynamically changing a menu's configuration.

Creating and Editing Menus

A menu resource lives in a resource script (.RC) file, along with an application's other resources. To access the resource file, click the Resources tab on the bottom of the Project View window. This displays a resource summary in the form of a tree control.

The resource summary list shows all the types of resources available in your application including bitmaps, dialogs, icons, menus, a string table, and a version resource. When you open the Menu node, a list of menu resources is displayed. To start editing a particular menu resource, double-click its name in this list. The selected menu resource is displayed in the menu editor. If you use MFC and the AppWizard to start a new project, you have at least one menu resource. This is the default menu MFC provides, and its name is `IDR_MAINFRAME`.

Using the menu editor, you can open the Menu Item Properties dialog box. This dialog box lists all the details of individual menu items. It also enables you to change any detail of a menu. As you work with the resource editor, you'll find yourself moving between several windows. To make sure that the Menu Item Properties doesn't go into hiding, click the thumbtack button, which "pins" the dialog and keeps it from moving.

A menu item has three key fields: ID, Caption, and Prompt. The ID field is a numeric constant that uniquely identifies the menu item. As you'll see later on when menu messages are discussed, making sure each menu item has a unique ID is critically important. The Caption field contains the text that is actually displayed on the menu. When users see a menu selection, they are seeing the Caption field. The Prompt field is any text that you'd like to display in the status bar at the bottom of the window when the user "browses" the menu item. The Prompt field also contains the ToolTip for the menu item. A user can browse a menu item by using either the keyboard to highlight the item or the mouse to hover over the item. The point is that a menu item is browsed when it is highlighted but not selected.

When you are creating a new menu item, you start with one of two fields in the Menu Item Properties dialog box: the ID or the Caption. You start with the ID when creating a menu item using one of MFC's predefined identifier values. You use a predefined value for commands that the MFC framework may handle for you. For example, the ID for New in the File menu is `ID_FILE_NEW`, the ID for Cut in the Edit menu is `ID_EDIT_CUT`, and the ID for New in the Window menu is `ID_WINDOW_NEW`. For a complete list of these predefined identifier values, see `afxres.h`, the MFC include file in which all of its default resource IDs are defined.

To create a brand new menu item of your own, start by selecting the blank menu item and entering a menu item name in the Caption field. As you start typing the caption, the menu editor instantly modifies the menu to show the results of your changes. You can see the effect of text length on the menu as you type. If you define the caption first, the menu editor defines an ID value for you. If you want to view the automatically created ID, click another menu item, and then click back. If you don't like the name of the ID that the menu editor supplies, you can always define your own name by typing over the supplied name.

When filling in the Caption field, give some thought to a menu item's keyboard mnemonic. A keyboard mnemonic defines the keyboard interface to a menu item. The mnemonic comes into play when the user activates a menu by holding the Alt key while pressing the underlined letter, or mnemonic, for that menu. Take care that you don't duplicate mnemonics. For example, because of keyboard mnemonics, Open from the File menu can be selected with the Alt+F-O key combination — that is, by holding down the Alt key and pressing F and then O.

From your user's point of view, keyboard mnemonics are the same as accelerator keystrokes. From a programming perspective, however, they differ in that mnemonic support comes from the menu system. Accelerators, as you'll see later, are defined in an accelerator table. To define a mnemonic, insert an ampersand (&) before the letter that is to be underlined. To insert an ampersand in your menu text, insert two ampersands (&&) in the Caption field.

The third field you should always define for a menu item is the Prompt field. As mentioned earlier, the Prompt field contains the text that is displayed in the status bar when the user browses a menu item. Even though you fill in this field in the menu editor, the string itself isn't stored as part of the menu resource. Instead, an entry is made in the string table resource, with the string ID set to the same value as the menu item command ID. This is yet another benefit of using the resource editor to define menu resources.

The Prompt field has two parts: the status bar string and the ToolTip string. You already know about the status bar string. A ToolTip is a small box that pops up when a user browses a toolbar button with the mouse. As shown in the following example (which shows the prompt value that MFC creates for the Print command), you separate the two parts with a newline character (`\n`):

```
Print the active document\nPrint
```

Creating menus

You can create a menu using several different methods. The most common way to create a menu is to predefine the menu as a menu resource while you are coding the application. During application runtime, MFC uses the frame window class to create several user interface elements from the application's resources. Accelerator keys and menus are created at this time. MFC loads the resources via a call to `CFrameWnd::LoadFrame()` and passes the function the resource IDs for each of the interface elements.

Each menu item has two essential elements: a string name (such as "Copy") and a numeric constant ID (3, for example). In a menu resource, each menu item requires a unique command ID. By generating unique IDs for your menu items, the Visual C++ resource editor ensures that this requirement is met. It also creates a symbolic constant by combining the pop-up menu name with the menu item name.

After you've created a menu resource, the next step is to run ClassWizard to create code for each menu item. As you'll soon see, ClassWizard treats each menu item as a separate user interface element with a C++ class representing it. For each menu item, you have to decide which class should handle that item. Then you have to decide whether you want code for the COMMAND menu message, the UPDATE_COMMAND_UI menu message, or both.

A WM_COMMAND message means that a user has selected a menu item, an accelerator key, or a toolbar button. This message is a request from the user for action, and a response is expected. As such, you must provide a WM_COMMAND message handler for each menu item in your menus. If MFC cannot find a WM_COMMAND handler for a given menu item, that menu item is disabled and made unavailable to the user. Here's an example of an empty WM_COMMAND handler function created by ClassWizard:

```
void CMainFrame::OnMenuEnable()
{
  // TODO: Add your command handler code here
}
```

In the context of a menu, the WM_COMMAND message informs you that the user has selected a menu item and is waiting for something to happen. You must provide a message handler function that is ready to carry out the action requested.

On the other hand, handling the CN_UPDATE_COMMAND_UI message is completely optional. This message is a request from MFC to update the appearance of individual menu items. For example, you might place a check mark next to a menu item, gray out a menu item, or enable a menu item. Here's an example of a CN_UPDATE_COMMAND_UI message handler that does it all:

```
void CMainFrame::OnUpdateCheckedMenuItem(CCmdUI* pCmdUI)
{
  // Set check mark if g_bMenuChecked is TRUE,
  // Otherwise clear check mark.
  pCmdUI->SetCheck( g_bMenuChecked );

  // Enable if g_bMenuEnable is TRUE,
  // Otherwise gray out.
  pCmdUI->Enable( g_bMenuEnable );
}
```

As shown in this code snippet, you are passed a pointer to a CCmdUI object. You control the menu item state by calling CCmdUI member functions. The message WM_COMMAND signals that the user has selected a menu item and is now waiting for a response from the application. This is where your menu-specific message handler jumps into action. To understand how your message handler is called, it's necessary to understand how MFC routes messages — specifically, menu messages.

Menu messages in MFC

Most of the messages that you handle in an MFC program are directed at one object type: a window. This follows the model used by the Windows API, and — given the types of messages — it seems to make sense. After all, windowing messages such as WM_CREATE, WM_MOVE, and WM_SIZE notify you that a window has been created, moved, or sized. In the Windows API and in MFC, only a window object is interested in such events. In addition, nonwindowing messages — for example, mouse and keyboard messages — direct data to a particular window, and therefore cannot be rerouted without creating confusion.

MFC departs from the Windows API in its handling of the two menuing messages. When an application creates a menu command, the frame window holding a menu doesn't have to process every menu message. Instead, the work can be delegated to message handlers (such as your WM_COMMAND handler) within objects that own the resources to which the command applies. Among the candidates for handling menu messages are CCmdTarget-derived classes, which include windows (such as view windows) and application (CWinApp-derived) objects. In a document/view application, document objects and view objects (which are windows) are also candidates for handling menu messages.

Although any CCmdTarget-derived class *can* receive menu messages, in fact, menu messages take a specific path when they are routed. Table 7-1 lists the order that MFC uses to check the message maps when delivering command messages for non-doc/view applications, single document doc/view applications, and multiple-document doc/view applications.

If MFC's command message routing isn't to your liking, you can define your own priorities and send command messages to any object. However, you will have to override the OnCmdMsg() command message routing functions in several classes. Before doing this, you'll want to spend some time reviewing the MFC source files to make sure that your changes are in sync with the base classes. In particular, look for the default OnCmdMsg() handlers in the following classes: CView, CDocument, CFrameWnd, and CMDIFrameWnd. (You could also override PreTranslateMessage() to get the same result.)

Table 7-1
Message Processing Sequences for Command Messages

Application Type	*Base Class*	*Message Processing Sequence*
Non-Document/ View	`CFrameWnd`	The frame window has first chance to process message.
	`WinApp`	The application object is handled second.
Single Document (SDI)	`CView`	The active view has the first shot at messages.
	`CDocument`	Then the active document is next in message priority after the active view.
	`CSingleDocTemplate`	Then the document template of the active view follows the active document in processing messages
	`CFrameWnd`	The frame window is next.
	`CWinApp`	The application object has the last shot at any messages.
Multiple Document (MDI)	`CView`	The active view is checked first.
	`CDocument`	Document of the active view comes next.
	`CMultiDocTemplate`	Then the template for the active view is checked.
	`CMDIChildFrame`	The child frame comes next.
	`CMDIFrameWnd`	The parent window follows after `CMDIChildFrame`.
	`CWinApp`	Application object is last.

You should now have a good grounding in the basics of menu programming. This section has defined what a menu resource is, learned how to create a menu resource, and examined the in's and out's of basic menu programming. In order to provide a solid usable menu interface, you'll need to understand accelerator keys, so that's the next subject.

Accelerator Keys

An accelerator key, otherwise referred to as a *keyboard shortcut*, enables a user to send a command using the keyboard. The Win32 API provides the accelerator table resource where the accelerator key definitions for your application reside. The AppWizard provides a default table when it generates a document/view application. In addition, if you initialize a frame window by a call to `CFrameWnd::LoadFrame()`, the table is automatically loaded and connected to the frame window.

Our exploration of accelerator keys starts with a general examination of keyboard input. To help you determine which keys to use and which ones to avoid, this section provides guidelines for appropriate accelerator key assignment. Next, you'll learn how to create accelerator resources by using the accelerator table editor. Then you'll examine the Windows API mechanisms behind accelerators and learn how to dynamically install an accelerator table.

Examining keyboard input

There are four defined categories of keyboard input: text keys, access keys, mode keys, and shortcut keys. The term *shortcut keys* refers to accelerator keys. Let's take a look at each of these four types of keyboard input, paying special attention to the relationship between accelerator keys and one other category of keys.

The term *text keys* refers to printable characters — that is, uppercase and lowercase letters, numbers, punctuation marks, and other symbols. Nothing in MFC or the Windows API prevents you from using text keys for command keys. If you've spent much time in a character-based, mainframe world, you have probably encountered this type of command key. Coming from that background, simple text commands seem natural. But this practice is inconsistent with the user interface style that has evolved for Windows and can be frustrating for your users. Put simply, users expect that letter and number keys will generate printable letters and numbers.

The second category of keyboard input is access keys. An access key (which, as mentioned earlier, is sometimes called a *mnemonic*) is an alphanumeric key that, when pressed in combination with the Alt key, accesses a pop-up menu, a menu item, or a dialog box control. Adding an access key to a menu or a dialog box control isn't difficult; a simple ampersand (&) identifies the access key to the system, and Windows just makes them work. You need to make sure that your accelerator keys don't conflict with access keys. The simplest solution is to avoid defining accelerator keys that take the form of the Alt key plus a letter or number key.

Mode keys, the third type of keyboard input, have a significant effect on possible accelerator key combinations. Mode keys change the actions of other keys (or other input devices). There are two subcategories of mode keys: toggle keys and modifier keys. Toggle keys are somewhat of an artifact from the IBM PC family of computers. A standard Windows-compatible keyboard has three toggle keys: Caps Lock, Num Lock, and Scroll Lock.

The second type of mode keys — modifier keys — is even more important. Although there are a few single-key accelerators (function keys, for example), the presence of modifier keys multiplies the number of key combinations that are available for defining accelerator keys. The standard 101-key keyboard defines three modifier keys: Shift, Ctrl, and Alt. Microsoft has defined a specification for a new, 104-key keyboard in which the basic 101-key layout is enhanced with three new keys: two Windows keys (sporting the Windows logo) and an Applications key. The Windows key is an additional modifier key. Its use is reserved for the operating system.

The final category is the shortcut keys, or accelerators. Any keys that are not included in the other categories are available for use as single-key accelerators. This group includes the function keys (F1, F2, and so on) and the cursor (insertion point) movement keys (Home, the Up arrow key, and so on). With these keys and the modifier-plus key combinations, you have a wide range of choices for creating accelerator keys. Let's look at the mechanics of defining an accelerator key assignment.

Defining accelerator keys

Defining an accelerator key involves two basic steps. First, you must create an accelerator table resource. The accelerator table resource defines the key codes and the command ID that are the result when a user presses the accelerator key. Then you advertise the availability of the key combination to the user. For key combinations that match menu item selections, you do this by modifying the menu item text. Let's look at what's involved in each of these steps.

Creating an accelerator table resource

The Visual C++ IDE has a built-in accelerator table editor. Just like the menu editor, the accelerator table editor provides access to a properties dialog box in which you can edit individual items. To open the Accel Properties dialog box, double-click any accelerator. To make this dialog box stick around, click the Thumbtack icon.

By clicking the Help button in the Accel Properties dialog box, you can obtain details about each control. The accelerator table itself has three columns: ID, Key, and Type. You'll probably need only a little experimentation to feel comfortable with creating and editing accelerator entries. To fill in some of the gaps, though, let's look at each set of accelerator properties, starting with the command ID.

The command ID identifies the command code that is passed — via a `WM_COMMAND` message — when a user presses an accelerator key. The command list is filled with values from your program's `resource.he` file, along with a set of MFC's predefined values from `afxres.h`. When you define an accelerator, be sure that its command ID matches the command ID for the corresponding menu item. By doing so, you have to provide only a single command handler function that works for both menu input and accelerator input.

The Key field identifies the keyboard key for the accelerator. For alphanumeric characters, you simply type the number or letter. For nonprintable characters, you use virtual key codes. As you scroll through the combo box that's connected to this field, you'll see that it contains 86 virtual key codes, each with a `VK_` prefix. For example, `VK_F1` is the virtual key code for the F1 function key, and `VK_DOWN` is the virtual key code for the Down arrow key.

If you're not sure which virtual key code to use, the simplest solution is to click the Next Key Typed button. You can then press a modifier-key combination that you want to use for your accelerator, and the accelerator editor will automatically fill in the correct entries for the Key, Modifiers, and Type fields in the Accel Properties dialog box.

You choose the modifier key for your accelerator by clicking one of the check boxes in the Modifiers field. It's recommended that you use the Ctrl key as a modifier before the others. In addition, you should avoid using the Alt key with an alphanumeric accelerator because it might conflict with a menu access key. Even if you find Alt-alphanumeric-key combinations that don't conflict with your menu access keys, the access keys in internationalized versions often differ.

The Type field gives you a choice between ASCII and VirtKey. Almost every accelerator key should be a virtual key, because these transcend the different types of keyboards used around the world. However, you'll occasionally have to define an ASCII accelerator, most notably for using symbol characters (for example, <, >, or /) as commands. Selecting the ASCII option in the Type field enables you to define character—instead of keyboard key—commands. The ASCII Type enables you to differentiate between uppercase and lowercase letters. However, even though it's possible, for example, to have an *A* command that differs from an *a* command, you should avoid this practice. After all, users expect case-insensitive commands.

Creating accelerator menu hints

To let users know about your accelerator keys, you'll want to advertise them. The best place for doing this is next to the corresponding menu item. Following the menu item name within a menu resource, you simply insert a tab character (\t) and the accelerator key name. For example, the standard accelerator for the Paste menu item is Ctrl+V. The following menu resource entry shows how the hint for this accelerator is included in the Paste menu item:

```
&Paste\tCtrl+V
```

In some cases, your accelerator keys don't correspond to menu item selections. To make sure that your users can take advantage of these accelerator keys, you should add a help database entry.

You know how to create accelerator keys and how to add hints within menus, but you still need to figure out which keys to use for keyboard commands. This subject is covered in the following section.

Selecting appropriate accelerator keys

When you define accelerator keys, be sure to use standard accelerator key combinations that are consistent with other Windows applications. Table 7-2 summarizes the standard Windows keyboard commands. Two of the five categories in this table are implemented by the operating system (system commands) or by an MFC class (`CMDIFrameWnd` implements the MDI accelerator keys). The rest are up to you to implement in your own accelerator table. You'll want to be aware of all of them, however, to avoid defining an accelerator that conflicts with standard Windows keyboard commands.

Table 7-2
Standard Windows Keyboard Commands

Category	*Key Combination*	*Description*
System Commands	Ctrl+Alt+Del	Causes a reboot in Windows 3.1 and Window 95, and logon/logoff in Windows NT.
	Alt+Tab	Brings the next active application into the foreground.
	Alt+Esc	Brings the next active application into the foreground.
	Ctrl+Esc	Displays the task list in Windows 3.1 Displays the Start menu in Window 95/NT.
	Alt+spacebar	Displays the window's system menu.
	PrintScrn	Takes a snapshot of the screen and places it on the Clipboard.
	Alt+PrintScrn	Takes a snapshot of the active window, and places it on the Clipboard
	Alt	Toggles the application menu bar.
	Alt+Enter	Toggles a DOS window in and out of full-screen mode.
Application Commands	Esc	Cancels the current mode or operation.
	Tab	Moves the input focus to the next control.
	Alt+F4	Closes the top-level window (not the desktop).

Category	Key Combination	Description
	Shift+F10	Displays a context menu.
	F1	Summons a help menu.
	Shift+F1	Summons context help.
File Commands	Ctrl+N	Opens a new document.
	Ctrl+O	Summons the Open… dialog box.
	Ctrl+P	Summons the Print… dialog box.
	Ctrl+S	Saves the document.
Clipboard Commands	Ctrl-Z	Undoes the last action.
	Alt+Backspace	Undoes the last action (backwards compatible with Windows 3.*x*).
	Ctrl+X	Cuts selected items.
	Shift+Del	Cuts selected items (backwards compatible with Windows 3.*x*).
	Ctrl+C	Copies selected items to the Clipboard.
	Ctrl+Ins	Copies selected items to the Clipboard (backwards-compatible with Windows 3.*x*).
	Ctrl+V	Pastes items from Clipboard at the insertion point.
	Shift+Ins	Pastes items from Clipboard at the insertion point (backwards compatible with Windows 3.*x*).
Multiple Document (MDI)	Ctrl+F4	Closes the currently active document window.
	Ctrl+F6	Activates the next document window.
	Shift+Ctrl+F6	Activates the previous document window.

Here are suggestions to help you pick a reasonable set of accelerator keys:

✦ Assign single keys where possible because these keystrokes are the easiest for the user to perform.

✦ Make modifier+letter key combinations case insensitive.

- ✦ Use Shift+key combinations for actions that extend or complement the actions of the key or key combination used without the Shift key. For example, Alt+Tab switches windows in a top-to-bottom order. Shift+Alt+Tab switches windows in reverse order. However, avoid Shift+text keys because the effect of the Shift key may differ for some international keyboards.
- ✦ Use Ctrl+key combinations for actions that represent a larger scale effect. For example, in text editing contexts, Home moves to the beginning of a line, Ctrl+Home moves to the beginning of the text. Use Ctrl+key combinations for access to commands where a letter key is used—for example, Ctrl+B for bold. Remember that such assignments might be meaningful only for English-speaking users.
- ✦ Avoid Alt+key combinations because they may conflict with the standard keyboard access for menus and controls. The Alt+key combinations—Alt+Tab, Alt+Esc, and Alt+spacebar—are reserved for system use. Alt+numeric-key combinations enter special characters.
- ✦ Avoid assigning shortcut keys that are commonly used for other operations in your software. For example, if Ctrl+C is the shortcut for the Copy command and your application supports the standard copy operation, don't assign Ctrl+C to another operation.
- ✦ Provide support, when possible, for enabling the user to change the shortcut key assignments in your software.
- ✦ Use the Esc key to terminate a function in process or to cancel a direct manipulation operation. It is also usually interpreted as the shortcut key for a Cancel button.

Once you've selected the accelerator keys for your application, you have to decide whether to put them all in a single accelerator table or spread them out between multiple accelerator tables. For small- to medium-sized applications, a single accelerator table is sufficient. For larger, more complex applications working with several different types of data, you might find that you require several accelerator tables. The following section explains the issues involved in using multiple accelerator tables in an MFC application.

Multiple accelerator tables

The use of multiple accelerator tables enables you to divide the work that's to be done and gives you greater flexibility in enabling different keyboard command sets. MFC's Doc/View classes take advantage of this capability to support multiple accelerator tables. But avoiding Doc/View for now, let's see how you use multiple accelerator tables in a non-Doc/View application. (Incidentally, Doc/View is being avoided so that the MFC fundamentals can be focused on, not because there's anything wrong with it. Once you grasp MFC fundamentals, Doc/View is simpler to understand and use.) To help you understand what's required, let's start with a review of how the native Windows API provides accelerator support.

Native Windows API accelerator support

For all that accelerators do for you, the Win32 API has only six accelerator functions. (The scarcity of native API functions is one reason why you *don't* find a CAccelerators class in MFC.) The most important features are provided by two of these accelerator functions: LoadAccelerators() and TranslateAccelerator(). LoadAccelerators() creates a RAM-resident accelerator table from an accelerator resource. The second function, TranslateAccelerator(), tests whether a particular keyboard message corresponds to an accelerator table command entry.

In a Windows program written in C, you call the load function to create the accelerator table and then call the translate function from your program's message loop. As we describe in Chapter 9, MFC provides the message loop that every MFC-based program uses. The message loop in the thread class' CWinThread::Run() function calls CWinThread::PumpMessage(), which does the following:

```
::GetMessage(&m_msgCur, NULL, NULL, NULL);
if (!PreTranslateMessage(&m_msgCur))
{
  ::TranslateMessage(&m_msgCur);
  ::DispatchMessage(&m_msgCur);
}
```

In this code fragment, the three functions with the global scope operators (: :) are native Windows API functions. The fourth function, PreTranslateMessage(), is the name of an overloaded function that appears in several MFC classes. These functions exist for one primary reason — to check for accelerator keys. To experienced Windows API programmers, this is a familiar message loop, with the exception that Translate Accelerator() is usually called instead of PreTranslateMessage().

By the way, the function's name comes from the fact it is called before ::TranslateMessage(). This latter function takes raw keyboard (virtual key) messages and turns them into cooked ASCII character input. For accelerator keys to be handled properly, they must be raw. In addition, if a particular message is associated with an accelerator, the function returns TRUE, and no further processing is required. Otherwise, the normal message loop functions are called.

Although many MFC classes have PreTranslateMessage() functions, not all can support an accelerator table. In some cases — such as with CWinApp and CWinThread — the base member function simply calls the corresponding member in the window classes. This implies that accelerator tables can be used only by window classes. However, this limitation is not a design feature of MFC; it is a trait that MFC inherits from the native Windows API.

The basic flow of messages is from the innermost data window to the outermost container window. The command is handled by whichever window first claims it. In a single-document doc/view application, the view window gets the first chance to handle an accelerator, followed by the frame window. In a multiple document doc/view application, the sequence progresses from the view window to the child frame, and then to the parent frame. In our doc/view-free world, our BASEMENU sample program has only one window — a frame window — which alone among the MFC objects can receive accelerator key commands.

Let's take a closer look at the mechanics of providing accelerator tables to MFC's window classes.

Connecting a new accelerator table to a window class

Because an accelerator table by itself doesn't do anything, some way of connecting an accelerator table to a window is necessary. To connect an accelerator table to a window class, you start by loading the accelerator table into memory. You'll do this sometime during the initialization of your window — `PreCreateWindow()` is generally a good choice. You load an accelerator table into memory by calling `::LoadAccelerators()`, which is defined as follows:

```
HACCEL LoadAccelerators(
  HINSTANCE hinst,    // EXE file instance handle
  LPCTSTR lpTableName); // Accelerator table name
```

The first parameter, the instance handle, identifies who you are in this system. This is passed to your program's `WinMain()` entry point. The second parameter is the accelerator table name, which you specified in the resource file. The following code fragment loads an accelerator table named `IDR_VIEW_COMMMANDS`:

```
HINSTANCE hInst = AfxGetResourceHandle();
LPCTSTR lpID = MAKEINTRESOURCE(IDR_VIEW_COMMMANDS);
HACCEL g_hAccel = LoadAccelerators( hInst, lpID );
```

The `AfxGetResourceHandle()` function helps make sure that you get the correct instance handle — for code in an application as well as in a dynamic link library. The `MAKEINTRESOURCE()` macro converts the accelerator table's integer ID into a character string, which is the type required by the function. The return value, `g_hAccel`, is a Windows system handle that gives our program access to the accelerator table in memory.

Once an accelerator table is loaded into memory, the next step is to make sure it is called at the right time. This is a simple matter of overloading the `PreTranslateMessage()` function in a `CWnd`-derived class. Here's a sample implementation that does just that:

```
BOOL CWindowingClass::PreTranslateMessage(MSG * pMsg)
{
  if( g_hAccel == NULL )
   return FALSE; // we didn't process

  return ::TranslateAccelerator(m_hWnd, g_hAccel, pMsg);
}
```

The next two sections explore a couple of more advanced programming topics: dynamically created menus and context menus. You'll be introduced to the theory behind each concept and then review practical implementations. Understanding these topics will enable you to add a professional polish to your applications, so let's get started!

Dynamically Changing Menus

In general, any change you can make to a menu in the menu editor can also be made dynamically at runtime. For example, you can create menus from scratch, add menu items, or remove menu items. Certain menu features — for example, owner-drawn menu items and custom bitmap check marks — are accessible *only* at runtime. (An owner-drawn menu item contains a graphic image — such as a bitmap or geometric figure drawn using calls to GDI — instead of a text string.)

Menu command ranges

If you dynamically create menu items, you must provide command handlers. Although you could use ClassWizard to "dummy up" a set, you don't always know how many command handlers you should create. For such situations, MFC enables you to handle a range of command IDs with a single command handler. Because ClassWizard can't deal with a range of command IDs, you must write the code by hand that ClassWizard would otherwise create for you.

Your first concern is picking a range of command IDs that doesn't interfere with existing command IDs. Table 7-3 summarizes how the available command ranges are used by ClassWizard, in particular, and the MFC framework, in general. As shown in this table, what's left for your use is a range of IDs from 0x9000 (36864) to 0xDFFF (57343).

Table 7-3
Available Command Ranges

Range	*Description*
0x8000–0x8FFF	ClassWizard uses this range for application-defined menus.
0x9000–0xDFFF	This range of command IDs is available for your use.
0xE000–0xFFFF	MFC uses this range for its own purposes.

Next, you need to add a function to the class declaration. ClassWizard creates three pieces of code for every message: an include file declaration, a message map definition, and a function definition. Here's an example of a function declaration for a message-handling function that can handle a range of command IDs:

```
class CMainFrame : public DFrame
{  ...
  void OnCommandRange (UINT id);
  ...
};
```

The next piece is the message map entry, which MFC's message-handling mechanism must have to be able to find your function. To create this message map entry, you add an `ON_COMMAND_RANGE()` message map macro between the boundaries of a `BEGIN_MESSAGE_MAP()` and `END_MESSAGE_MAP()` pair. This message map macro takes three parameters: start of range, end of range, and function:

```
ON_COMMAND_RANGE(ID_MIN, ID_MAX, OnCommandRange);
```

The final piece is the function definition itself. It takes a single parameter, which is the command ID for a selected menu item. Here's an example:

```
void CMainFrame::OnCommandRange (UINT id)
{
  switch (id)
  {
    case ID_DYNA_COMMAND_1: ...
    case ID_DYNA_COMMAND_2: ...
    ...
  }
}
```

Changing menus at runtime

By adding menu items on the fly, your programs can be responsive to changes in the user's environment. Dynamic menu items are commonly used to update the lists of most recently used files, which often appear in File menus. Sometimes, you know only at runtime how many dynamic menu items you're going to create. To simplify the receipt of command notifications for such items, MFC enables you to create command handlers for a range of command IDs. Unfortunately, ClassWizard doesn't (yet) support this feature. The following section shows you how it's done manually.

Although MFC provides a menu class (`CMenu`), AppWizard's code doesn't use this class to create a menu. Instead, the Windows API supports the simultaneous creation of a window with a menu. When creating a Windows window, MFC's `CFrameWnd` class requests the creation of a menu. In the process, it also creates a bit of an object-oriented design paradox. Although a `CFrameWnd` *logically* contains a `CMenu`, it *physically* contains no `CMenu` data type.

Although you won't use CMenu to create the menu that is attached to your program's frame window, you'll use it extensively for dynamic menu operations. To get a CMenu pointer to the menu that is connected to a window, you call CWnd::GetMenu():

```
// Fetch pointer to main menu.
CMenu * pmenu = GetMenu();
```

You might notice another twist to this paradox. This line of code fetches a pointer to an object that was never created. What's happening? The short answer, which will soon be elaborated upon, is that MFC creates a CMenu while adding it to a temporary object storage list.

For now, let's examine some of the issues involved in making dynamic modifications to menus, starting with the most common task you'll probably need: modifying the contents of an existing pop-up menu.

Changing an existing pop-up menu

Using a CMenu pointer from CWnd::GetMenu(), you can do such things as inserting a new pop-up menu between the File menu and the Help menu. That's a subject that's explored a bit later in this chapter.

For now, a more common operation — adding menu items to and removing menu items from an existing pop-up menu — are of interest. For this, you need another CMenu * pointer — in this case, to one of the submenus. As shown in the following lines of code, you use CMenu::GetSubMenu() to get a submenu pointer:

```
CMenu * pmenu = GetMenu();
CMenu * pmSub = pmenu->GetSubMenu(1);
CMenu::GetSubMenu() is defined as follows:
CMenu* GetSubMenu( int nPos)
```

The sole parameter, nPos, is a zero-based index to the submenu that you want to access. Table 7-1 summarizes common CMenu functions for modifying (or simply querying) the contents of a menu.

For example, using the pmSub submenu pointer from the previous example, you can append a new menu item to an existing submenu like this:

```
pmSub->AppendMenu (MF_STRING,      // Menu flag
         ID_MENU_ADDMENUITEM, // Command id.
         "Add Menu &Item");  // Menu string.
```

Table 7-4
Common CMenu Functions

Function	*Description*
`AppendMenu()`	Adds a new menu item to the end of an existing menu or to a new pop-up menu.
`CheckMenuItem()`	Sets or clears the menu check mark. (Rarely used). In place of this function, you should provide an `UPDATE_COMMAND_UI` handler.
`GetMenuItemID()`	Queries a menu item's command ID.
`GetMenuString()`	Queries a menu item's text label.
`EnableMenuItem()`	Enables and disables menu items (works only if `CFrameWnd::m_bAutoMenuEnable = FALSE`). In place of this function, you should provide an `UPDATE_COMMAND_UI` handler.
`InsertMenu()`	Inserts a new menu item at a specified offset within an existing menu.
`RemoveMenu()`	Deletes a specific menu item.

Although the MFC help database describes the parameters, let's take a closer look at the declaration for `CMenu::AppendMenu()`:

```
BOOL AppendMenu( UINT nFlags,
        UINT nIDNewItem = 0,
        LPCTSTR lpszNewItem = NULL);
```

The first parameter, `nFlags`, is a flag field for specifying the state of the menu item you create. Many menu modification functions use these flags. They're summarized in Table 7-5.

The meaning of the second parameter, `nIDNewItem`, depends on whether you're inserting a new menu item or a new pop-up menu (indicated by `MF_POPUP` in `nFlags`). If you're inserting a menu item, this parameter holds an integer command ID for the menu item. If you're inserting a new pop-up menu, this field is the menu handle of the menu to be inserted. (As you'll see, you use the value of `CMenu::m_hMenu` for this field.)

The meaning of the last parameter, `lpszNewItem`, depends on what type of item you're inserting. It's either a pointer to a character string for an `MF_STRING` item or a unique item identifier for an `MF_OWNERDRAW` item.

Table 7-5
Menu Modification Flags

Menu Flag	*Description*
MF_BITMAP	Signifies a menu item with an image rather than a string
MF_OWNERDRAW	Signifies an application-drawn menu item — more flexible than MF_BITMAP
MF_POP-UP	Indicates a pop-up menu
MF_SEPARATOR	Indicates a visual divider for menu item groups
MF_STRING	Signifies a menu item, either regular menu or pop-up menu, with a string
MF_CHECKED	Displays a check mark on a menu item.
MF_UNCHECKED	Unchecks a checked menu item.
MF_ENABLED	Makes a menu selection available to a user.
M_GRAYED	Makes a menu item unavailable to the user; the item is displayed "grayed" out.
MF_MENUBREAK	Changes the way the menu item is displayed. At a menu item with this flag, the menu will changes direction. For example, a menu bar item, whose text normally is displayed horizontally, will wrap to a new line.
MF_MENUBARBREAK	Same as above previous item except that in pop-up menus, a line is used to separate columns.
MF_BYCOMMAND	Sets the program to pick menu items with the command ID.
MF_BYPOSITION	Sets the program to pick menu items based on their zero-based position.

You should note that when you dynamically create menu items, MFC doesn't know how to display help strings in the status window. (Recall that MFC does this automatically for static menu resources, using strings that you enter in the menu editor's Prompt field.) To enable this feature for dynamically created menu items, override `CFrameWnd::GetMessageString()` with your own version of `GetMessageString()`. For dynamically created menu items, you supply the required strings. For statically created menu items, call the default handler that reads in the correct string from the string table.

Although the menu modification techniques that have been described certainly work as advertised, an important issue has been glossed over. Even though it was stated that an MFC program doesn't create a `CMenu` object for its menu, a `CMenu` object is clearly being used to change the menu. Where did this object come from? And who will delete the object when it's no longer needed? The answer to these questions lies in structures MFC manages called *handle maps*. Let's take a short detour, and explore how these maps affect menu programming.

Permanent and temporary handle maps

To bridge the gap between MFC objects and Windows API objects, MFC maintains a set of look-up tables, called *handle maps*. In simplest terms, Windows uses handles to identify objects, and MFC uses pointers. The origin of pointer semantics was primarily for maintaining a one-to-one ratio between Windows system objects (windows and menus, for example) and C++/MFC objects (such as `CWnd` and `CMenu` objects). And while we identify a C++ object with a pointer, a Windows system object is always identified by a *handle*.

Remember, a handle is a number that uniquely identifies a particular object. The meaning of the number is known only to the part of the system that's issued the handle. Internal to the operating system, a handle might be a pointer or an index, but to the outside world it's just a number.

MFC uses handle maps to identify the C++ object that corresponds to a given Windows object handle. After all, when MFC calls Windows API functions, it cannot use the C++ object; MFC must use a handle. And when the Windows system libraries communicate back to MFC, they also use handles. Although MFC can easily figure out the handle from a C++ object (after all, it's usually one of the first data members), a little extra work is required for MFC to convert a system handle to a C++ pointer. To assist in this task, MFC creates handle maps.

MFC creates handle maps for two user interface objects (windows and menus) and for seven graphic output objects (bitmaps, brushes, device contexts, fonts, palettes, pens, and regions). The creation of handle maps and handle map entries is handled transparently most of the time by individual MFC objects as needed.

In a few cases, such as when merging existing Windows API code into an MFC application, you'll find that you have to convert system handles to MFC object pointers. Each of the MFC classes that wrap Windows API objects has member functions that can help with this task. For example, `CWnd::Attach()` connects a `CWnd` object to an existing system window and creates the proper handle map entry. `CWnd::Detach()` deletes a window handle entry from the MFC handle maps.

MFC creates two types of handle maps: permanent and temporary. A *permanent handle map* exists for Windows API objects that are created via an MFC class. For example, when you initialize a `CFrameWnd` object by calling `CFrameWnd::Create()` or `CFrameWnd::LoadFrame()`, an entry is made in the permanent handle table. When you delete an MFC object that has a permanent handle table entry, the object knows that it can also destroy the corresponding Windows API object.

Programmers who are experienced with SDK-style programming might wonder why an alternative mechanism wasn't chosen. In particular, why does MFC use handle tables for windows instead of window extra bytes? (Window extra bytes are a fixed number of extra bytes allocated by Windows on a per-window basis.) The reason is that predefined window types — such as dialog box controls — already use window extra bytes. Microsoft designed MFC to be able to wrap around preexisting classes. If MFC tried using window extra bytes with a window that already used window extra bytes, a conflict would occur.

MFC's automatic destruction of Windows system objects can cause you untold grief if you don't understand some of the subtler implications. In particular, you should avoid creating `CObject`-derived objects as local variables. At the end of the function — when the local objects go out of scope — the destructor is called, which destroys the Windows API object. The following code fragment taught this lesson to one of the authors:

```
// DON'T DO THIS!!!-When local variable goes out
// of scope, Windows API object is destroyed.
CMenu cm;
cm.LoadMenu(IDR_POP-UP_MENU);

// The append operation will be short-lived...
CMenu * pmenu = GetMenu();
pmenu->AppendMenu(MF_POP-UP, (UINT)cm.m_hMenu, "Pop-up");
```

With one important change, this code fragment could work properly. The only reason the object is destroyed is because `CMenu::~CMenu()` finds the object in the permanent handle map. By calling `CMenu::Detach()`, you disconnect the handle map entry and avoid this particular headache.

On the other hand, for objects that are not created via an MFC class, MFC has a *temporary handle map*. MFC creates an entry in the temporary handle map for objects that it must create on the fly to wrap Windows system objects. Such objects are very short lived, though, because all entries to the temporary handle map are deleted during idle time processing. For this reason, you'll always reference temporary objects using pointers that are created as local variables. This way, you avoid the problem of having a pointer to an object that has been automatically deleted.

Every MFC function that wraps Windows API objects has the two functions described: `Attach()` and `Detach()`. There's also a third function, `FromHandle()`, which is a universal "get pointer from handle" function. This function first searches a permanent handle map and then the temporary handle map. If no entry is found in either map, an object is created, and an entry is made in the temporary handle map.

Here's an example that clarifies when an entry is made in the temporary handle map. The menu function that's been discussed, `CWnd::GetMenu()`, calls `CMenu::FromHandle()`. When you call this function in an AppWizard-generated program—which loads a menu from a resource—MFC automatically creates a `CMenu` for you. To ensure that you have complete access to this object, MFC adds an entry to the temporary handle map. Your access to the object lasts at least until your program fetches its next message, because cleanup is handled at idle time.

So how does MFC determine when things are idle? Idle time occurs only when you're not in the middle of handling a message. Idle time is a Windows API artifact that was first created long ago to provide printer spooling support. Idle time occurs whenever the user pauses a moment and allows all message queues to empty. Even the busiest worker on the slowest machine must pause sometime, whether it's to answer a phone, talk to a friend, or just think. A blink is all it takes for an idle moment to occur, at which time MFC frees the C++ objects (but *not* the Windows API objects) that are referenced in temporary handle maps.

Context Menus

Since the debut of Windows 95, Microsoft has promoted the creation of *context menus*. A context menu—sometimes called a *pop-up menu*—is not connected to the menu bar. Instead, it is displayed when the user selects an object and then clicks with the secondary (usually the right) mouse button. (It's also possible to simultaneously select an object and summon a context menu with just a single click of the secondary mouse button.) The Visual C++ IDE already makes extensive use of this type of menu, as do many other commercially available applications. Starting with Windows 95, the operating system itself uses context menus for handling numerous routine operations. To fit your applications into this environment, you should consider adding context menus to them as well.

Besides clicking the right mouse button, a user can summon a context menu using a keystroke. The Applications key appears on newer 104-key keyboards, such as the Microsoft Natural keyboard. On keyboards that are so equipped, users can open a context menu by pressing the Applications key. To accommodate users whose keyboards are not equipped with this key, applications should define the Shift+F10 accelerator for summoning context menus.

Like most other MFC objects that wrap Windows API objects, two steps are required for creating a fully functioning object. First, you allocate a C++ object, and then you initialize the object. These lines of code show one way to create and initialize a `CMenu` object:

```
// Allocate CMenu for context menu.
g_pmenuContext = new CMenu();
if (!g_pmenuContext) return -1;

// Initialize CMenu (connect menu to MFC menu object).
BOOL bSuccess = g_pmenuContext->LoadMenu(IDR_CONTEXT);
if (!bSuccess) return -1;
```

This code fragment is from a function that expects a return value of -1 on failure (the handler function for the WM_CREATE message). Allocation involves the new operator. Initialization involves a call to CMenu::LoadMenu(), which takes as its only parameter a menu resource identifier.

Once it's created and initialized, the context menu is ready to appear whenever you want to see it. From the user's perspective, this menu should display when the user clicks the right mouse button. The following WM_RBUTTONDOWN message handler displays the context menu:

```
void CMainFrame::OnRButtonDown(UINT nFlags, CPoint point)
{
  // Convert client coordinate to screen coordinates.
  ClientToScreen(&point);

  // Display context menu at mouse location.
  CMenu * psubmenu = g_pmenuContext->GetSubMenu(0);
  psubmenu->TrackPopupMenu(TPM_LEFTALIGN | // Flags
                TPM_RIGHTBUTTON,
                point.x,     // x-coordinate
                point.y,     // y-coordinate
                this);       // "this" window

  CFrameWnd::OnRButtonDown(nFlags, point);
}
```

The second of the two parameters to OnRButtonDown() gives the location of the mouse in client-area coordinates. But TrackPopupMenu() expects screen coordinates, so you call CWnd::ClientToScreen(). This function converts from client-area coordinates (the origin in the top-left corner of the client area) to screen coordinates (the origin in the top left corner of the screen).

Most of the parameters to CMenu::TrackPopupMenu() are reasonably straightforward. However, the last parameter is worth discussing. When the context menu appears, a stream of messages is generated that must be sent to some window or another. The pointer *this*, in the context of a CFrameWnd-derived class, identifies the window that should receive the menu messages.

The final step that you'll need to consider is how to clean up a context menu when you're finished with it. The example simply deletes the CMenu object when you're done using it. Like all other entries in the permanent handle map table, when the object is destroyed, the system object is destroyed, and the handle map entry is erased. Although you might delete the menu object in any of several different places, you could do it in the destructor for the window frame object:

```
CMainFrame::~CMainFrame()
{
  if (g_pmenuContext)
    g_pmenuContext->DestroyMenu();
}
```

As part of the Windows user interface standard, Microsoft recommends using the right mouse button for context menus. Users expect this feature, and you put yourself at a disadvantage if you don't make use of it.

Summary

This chapter has explored two mechanisms for getting command input from the user: accelerator keys and menus. In both cases, the same command message, WM_COMMAND, is sent when the user requests an action in the form of a command. Menus and acclerator keys also send CN_UPDATE_COMMAND_UI messages to determine the state of commands and menu items. As seen, most of the work involved in using these mechanisms is in setting them up.

The next chapter looks at the two most common ways a user interacts with applications: through the keyboard and mouse. Without keyboard and mouse support, your application, and Windows in general, wouldn't do very much.

✦ ✦ ✦

CHAPTER 8

Mouse and Keyboard

✦ ✦ ✦ ✦

In This Chapter

Input basics and system state

Understanding mouse input

Creating mouse event handlers

Handling screen and window coordinate systems

Nonclient mouse messages

Changing mouse cursors

Understanding keyboard input

✦ ✦ ✦ ✦

In this chapter, we'll learn to handle mouse and keyboard input. In the first section, we'll examine the overall system used by Windows to manage input state. We'll also take a look at a concept called *local input state* that made its first debut in Windows NT and is used in both Windows 95 and Windows 98.

Next, we'll look at mouse input specifically. Thanks to the Microsoft Foundation Classes (MFC), the days of writing low-level mouse handling code are over (unless you have a lot of free time). In this section we'll examine the methods MFC provides to manage and manipulate the mouse. We'll consider such issues as the shape of the mouse pointer (cursor), the capture of mouse input, and the clipping of the mouse pointer to a specific clipping rectangle.

Lastly, we'll look at the various ways that a program can use keyboard input. Using user interface elements such as the edit control, we can allow Windows and MFC to manage the keyboard for us. Many times, however, we might need tighter control over the keyboard. As part of this discussion, we will consider the keyboard focus, the keyboard cursor (insertion point), the selection state, and other user interface constructs that are related to keyboard input.

Input Basics and System State

Many seasoned non-Windows programmers have trouble with the event-driven nature of Windows programming when they first start writing applications. In the context of user input processing, event driven means that rather than polling the system for a key press or a mouse click from the user, Windows sends our application a *windows message* whenever the user hits a key or clicks the mouse.

MFC maps these windows messages to C++ functions called *message handlers*. (For a more complete explanation of MFC, take a look at Chapter 6.) The input handling logic of our application will reside in these message handling functions. Later in this chapter, we'll talk more about message handlers. For now, you should remember that message handlers are C++ functions that handle windows messages.

The challenge to properly handling mouse and keyboard input in Windows is understanding and managing the context in which input occurs. The input itself is rather simple; you get several types of windows messages for both mouse and keyboard events. When you write code for keyboard input, you decide between two keyboard messages. The most critical mouse input is communicated by two or three mouse messages.

Creating the input message handling functions is quite easy. In fact, Visual C++ provides a wizard that creates the skeleton of the function for you. However, its not enough to have a basic input message handler. We must write our code in such a way that it understands the context of the input message so that the application behaves appropriately. Nothing is more confusing and irritating to a user than to try to use an application that has input processing bugs. To avoid this, we must understand the context of input messages—the not so obvious but critical ways that input interacts with application state, as viewed by both a user and Windows itself. Let's start by looking at the input state of first the mouse and then the keyboard.

Mouse Input

As was mentioned previously, Windows sends input to a program's windows as messages that get stored in a hardware input queue. Table 8-1 lists the main Windows mouse messages to which you'll respond when handling user input.

Table 8-1
Windows Mouse Input Messages

Message	*Message Trigger*
WM_LBUTTONDOWN	The left mouse button has been clicked down while the mouse pointer was over the window's client area.
WM_LBUTTONUP	The left mouse button was released.
WM_RBUTTONDOWN	The right mouse button has been clicked down while the mouse pointer was over the window's client area.
WM_RBUTTONUP	The right mouse button was released.
WM_MBUTTONDOWN	The middle mouse button has been clicked down while the mouse pointer was over the window's client area.
WM_MBUTTONUP	The middle mouse button was released.
WM_MOUSEMOVE	The mouse pointer was moved over the window's client area.

Creating mouse message handlers

It's easy to create handler functions for the mouse messages in Table 8-1. Start by bringing up the ClassWizard. An easy way to do this is to right-click the class, and select Add Windows Message Handler as shown in Figure 8-1.

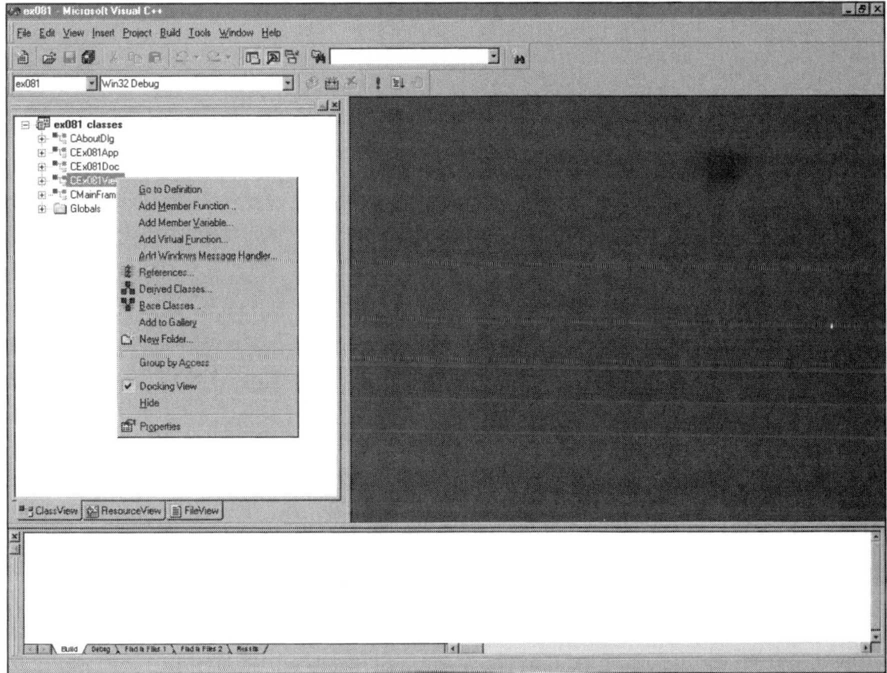

Figure 8-1: You can add message handlers to a class by right-clicking the class.

If you scroll down through the messages list box, you'll see `WM_LBUTTONDOWN`, `WM_MOUSEMOVE`, and other mouse messages listed in Table 8-1. Figure 8-2 shows the list box of messages.

To create a message handler for the mouse, double-click the message for which you want to create a handler function. A function will be created and automatically added to the Member Functions list box. The message appears in bold text in the messages list box indicating that there's a message handler function for the message in the selected class.

Adding Mouse Event Handlers

Here's how you add a mouse event handler to your program:

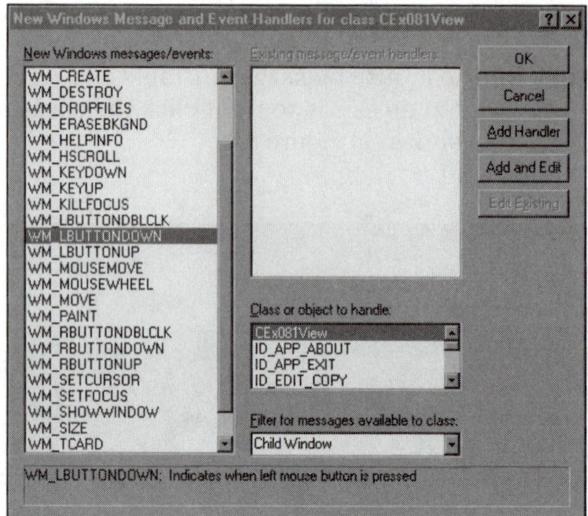

Figure 8-2: The list of messages appears in the list box.

1. Right-click the target class.
2. Find the message for which you'll be creating a handler in the messages list box, and double-click it.

The handler is added to the Member Functions list box.

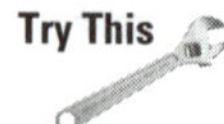

Creating Handler Functions

Now that you've learned how to create handler functions for mouse messages, you should take a minute and create one. This will ensure that you understand everything that's been discussed to this point.

1. Create a single-document interface application named MouseHandler.
2. Right-click the `CMouseHandlerView` class, and select Add Windows Message Handler.
3. Find the `WM_MOUSEMOVE` message in the messages list box, and double-click it.
4. Click the `OnMouseMove` function in the Member Functions list box, and then click the Edit Code button.
5. Add the following code to the `OnMouseMove()` function:

```
CClientDC ClientDC( this );
CString strInfo;
strInfo.Format( "X:%d Y:%d      ",
  point.x, point.y );
ClientDC.TextOut(10,10, strInfo, strInfo.GetLength() );
```

6. Compile and run the program. As you move the mouse in the client window, you'll see the mouse position coordinates as they're drawn in the window.

✦ ✦ ✦ ✦ ✦

Converting between screen and window coordinates

In the `OnMouseMove()` handler you just created, MFC passes the coordinates of the mouse pointer to the handler function using an MFC class called `CPoint`. An object of type `CPoint` is typically used to describe a point on the screen. The `CPoint` object's *x* and *y* members, accessed as `CPoint::x` and `CPoint::y`, respectively, contain the *x* and *y* coordinates for the physical point it represents.

The coordinates that are sent to the `OnMouseMove()` function are in terms of the view window's client area. The lowest value you'll get for both *x* and *y* is zero. The greatest value for the *x* and *y* values will be equal to the width and height of the view window, respectively. The *x* and *y* values may vary depending on the window's mapping mode. For instance, the values when in `MM_TEXT` mapping mode will be pixels, and the values when in `MM_TWIPS` will be TWIPS.

On occasion you might want to know what the mouse coordinates are in terms of the entire screen. A convenient conversion member function named `ClientToScreen()` has been provided. It takes as an argument a `CPoint` class and converts the values in the class from client window values to screen values.

For instance, a window might be placed on the screen at 50, 75. The mouse coordinates returned to `OnMouseMove()` will be in reference to the coordinate pair of 50, 75. If the user is pointing to a location inside of the window that's 15 pixels to the right of the window's top left corner and 25 pixels down from the window's top left corner, the coordinates sent to `OnMouseMove()` will be 15, 25. By using the `ClientToScreen()` function, those values are converted to literal screen values by adding the offset into the window to the screen position of the window. In this case, the screen coordinates will be 65, 100. The following code fragment illustrates the use of this function:

```
void CMyClassView::OnMouseMove(UINT nFlags, CPoint point)
{
  CPoint pt;
  pt = point;
  ClientToScreen( pt );
  CString strInfo;
  strInfo( "Scrn X:%d ScrnY:%d   ",
    pt.x, pt.y );
  CClientDC ClientDC( this );
  ClientDC.TextOut(10,10, strInfo, strInfo.GetLength() );
  CScrollView::OnMouseMove(nFlags, point);
}
```

Another option is to convert from screen coordinates to client coordinates. This is helpful when you get mouse coordinates from the Windows API function `GetCursorPos()`. This function returns coordinate values in terms of the entire screen. Following is an example in which the mouse position is obtained and then converted to client window coordinates:

```
void CMyClassView::TestFunction()
{
  POINT point;
  ::GetCursorPos( &point );
  CPoint pt( point );
  ScreenToClient( pt );
  CString strInfo;
  strInfo( "Scrn X:%d ScrnY:%d ClntX:%d ClntY:%d",
    point.x, point.y, pt.x, pt.y );
  AfxMessageBox( strInfo );
  CScrollView::OnMouseMove(nFlags, point);
}
```

Creating an MFC Program That Handles Mouse Events

We've created a simple demo program that shows you how to respond to the main mouse events. It handles mouse movement events, mouse button down events, and mouse button up events. It does not handle middle mouse button events.

MouseDemo1

CD-ROM Location: **Chap08\MouseDemo1**

Program Name: `MouseDemo1.EXE`

Source Code Modules in Text: `MouseDemo1View.cpp`

✦ ✦ ✦ ✦ ✦

Listing 8-1: MouseDemo1View.cpp Source Code File Highlights

```
// MouseDemo1View.cpp : implementation of the
// CMouseDemo1View class
//

/////////////////////////////////////////////////////////////
// CMouseDemo1View construction/destruction

CMouseDemo1View::CMouseDemo1View()
{

  // Start in the mode that shows mouse
  // info, not the grid of rectangles.
  m_nInfoMode = MOUSE_SHOWINFO;
```

```
  // Clear the two dimensional grid array.
  for( int y=0; y<10; y++ )
    for( int x=0; x<10; x++ )
      m_nGrid[x][y] = 0;

}

CMouseDemo1View::~CMouseDemo1View()
{
}

/////////////////////////////////////////////////////////////////
// CMouseDemo1View drawing

void CMouseDemo1View::OnDraw(CDC* pDC)
{
  CMouseDemo1Doc* pDoc = GetDocument();
  ASSERT_VALID(pDoc);

  // We only perform a redraw when we're
  // set to MOUSE_SHOWGRID mode.
  if( m_nInfoMode == MOUSE_SHOWGRID ){

    // Use the client rectangle
    // in order to draw the grid
    // rectangles in a size proportional
    // to the client rectangle.
    RECT Rect;
    GetClientRect( &Rect );

    // Create red, white and blue brushes.
    CBrush RedBrush( RGB( 255, 0, 0 ) );
    CBrush BlueBrush( RGB( 0, 0, 255 ) );
    CBrush WhiteBrush( RGB( 255, 255, 255 ) );
    CBrush *pUseBrush;

    // The grid has ten horizontal and ten
    // vertical components.
    for( int y=0; y<10; y++ ){
      for( int x=0; x<10; x++ ){

        // Assign DrawRect by calculating
        // one tenth of the client
        // rectangle.
        RECT DrawRect;
        DrawRect.left =
          ( x * Rect.right ) / 10;
        DrawRect.top =
```

(continued)

Listing 8-1 *(continued)*

```
        ( y * Rect.bottom ) / 10;
      DrawRect.right =
        DrawRect.left + ( Rect.right / 10 ) + 1;
      DrawRect.bottom =
        DrawRect.top + ( Rect.bottom / 10 );

      // Select the brush for drawing
      // based on whether the grid
      // is empty, set to left, or
      // set to right.
      pUseBrush = &WhiteBrush;
      if( m_nGrid[x][y] == 1 )
        pUseBrush = &BlueBrush;
      else if( m_nGrid[x][y] == 2 )
        pUseBrush = &RedBrush;

      // Draw the filled rectangle.
      pDC->FillRect( &DrawRect, pUseBrush );
      }
    }
  }

}

/////////////////////////////////////////////////////////////
// CMouseDemo1View message handlers

void CMouseDemo1View::OnLButtonDown(UINT nFlags,
  CPoint point)
{

  // Call the function that displays the mouse
  // information.
  ShowMouseInfo( "LButtonDown", point, 1 );

  // Call the default OnLButtonDown() function.
  CView::OnLButtonDown(nFlags, point);
}

void CMouseDemo1View::OnLButtonUp(UINT nFlags,
  CPoint point)
{

  // Call the function that displays the mouse
  // information.
  ShowMouseInfo( "LButtonUp", point );

  // Call the default OnLButtonUp() function.
  CView::OnLButtonUp(nFlags, point);
}
```

```
void CMouseDemo1View::OnLButtonDblClk(UINT nFlags,
  CPoint point)
{

  // Call the function that displays the mouse
  // information.
  ShowMouseInfo( "LButtonDblClk", point );

  // Call the default OnLButtonDblClk() function.
  CView::OnLButtonDblClk(nFlags, point);
}

void CMouseDemo1View::OnRButtonDown(UINT nFlags,
  CPoint point)
{

  // Call the function that displays the mouse
  // information.
  ShowMouseInfo( "RButtonDown", point, 2 );

  // Call the default OnRButtonDown() function.
  CView::OnRButtonDown(nFlags, point);
}

void CMouseDemo1View::OnRButtonUp(UINT nFlags,
  CPoint point)
{

  // Call the function that displays the mouse
  // information.
  ShowMouseInfo( "RButtonUp", point );

  // Call the default OnRButtonUp() function.
  CView::OnRButtonUp(nFlags, point);
}

void CMouseDemo1View::OnRButtonDblClk(UINT nFlags,
  CPoint point)
{

  // Call the function that displays the mouse
  // information.
  ShowMouseInfo( "RButtonDblClk", point );

  // Call the default OnRButtonDblClk() function.
  CView::OnRButtonDblClk(nFlags, point);
}

void CMouseDemo1View::OnMouseMove(UINT nFlags,
  CPoint point)
{
```

(continued)

Listing 8-1 *(continued)*

```
  // Only show the mouse position if
  // we're set to MOUSE_SHOWINFO
  if( m_nInfoMode == MOUSE_SHOWINFO ){
    CClientDC ClientDC( this );

    CString strInfo;

    // Copy the CPoint class so
    // that we can convert it to
    // screen coordinates.
    CPoint pt = point;

    // Convert to screen coordinates.
    ClientToScreen( &pt );

    // Format the information.
    strInfo.Format(
      "X:%d Y:%d ScnX:%d ScnY:%d              ",
      point.x, point.y,
      pt.x, pt.y );

    // Draw the information string to
    // the window.
    ClientDC.TextOut( 0, 0,
      strInfo, strInfo.GetLength() );
    }

  // Call the default OnMouseMove() function.
  CView::OnMouseMove(nFlags, point);
}

void CMouseDemo1View::ShowMouseInfo(
  const char *lpszText, CPoint point, int nFlag )
{

  // Perform the following code if
  // we're set to MOUSE_SHOWGRID.
  if( m_nInfoMode == MOUSE_SHOWGRID ){
    if( nFlag != -1 ){

      // Get the client rectangle
      // so that we can calculate which
      // x and y index the current
      // click position.
      RECT Rect;
      GetClientRect( &Rect );

      // Use the client rectangle
      // and divide by ten to calculate
      // the x and y grid indexes.
      int x = ( point.x * 10 ) / Rect.right;
```

```
      int y = ( point.y * 10 ) / Rect.bottom;

      // Either set the grid to left or right
      // button states, or clear them so that
      // the grid array is empty.
      if( m_nGrid[x][y] == nFlag )
        m_nGrid[x][y] = 0;
      else
        m_nGrid[x][y] = nFlag;

      // Cause the window to redraw.
      InvalidateRect( NULL, FALSE );
      UpdateWindow();
      }
    return;
    }

  // Get a DC to the client window.
  CClientDC ClientDC( this );

  CString strInfo;

  // Format the output string.
  strInfo.Format(
    "X:%d Y:%d %s          ",
    point.x, point.y, lpszText );

  // Draw the output string to the
  // window.
  ClientDC.TextOut( point.x, point.y,
    strInfo, strInfo.GetLength() );

}

void CMouseDemo1View::OnFileMouseGriddisplay()
{

  // Set to MOUSE_SHOWGRID mode.
  if( m_nInfoMode != MOUSE_SHOWGRID ){
    m_nInfoMode = MOUSE_SHOWGRID;
    InvalidateRect( NULL, TRUE );
    UpdateWindow();
    }

}

void CMouseDemo1View::OnUpdateFileMouseGriddisplay(
  CCmdUI* pCmdUI)
{

  // Set the menu check if we're
  // in MOUSE_SHOWGRID mode.
```

(continued)

Listing 8-1 *(continued)*

```
  pCmdUI->SetCheck( m_nInfoMode == MOUSE_SHOWGRID );

}

void CMouseDemo1View::OnFileMousePositioninformation()
{

  // Set to MOUSE_SHOWINFO mode.
  if( m_nInfoMode != MOUSE_SHOWINFO ){
    m_nInfoMode = MOUSE_SHOWINFO;
    InvalidateRect( NULL, TRUE );
    UpdateWindow();
    }

}

void CMouseDemo1View::OnUpdateFileMousePositioninformation(
  CCmdUI* pCmdUI)
{

  // Set the menu check if we're
  // in MOUSE_SHOWINFO mode.
  pCmdUI->SetCheck( m_nInfoMode == MOUSE_SHOWINFO );

}
```

Nonclient mouse events

At this point you might be asking yourself where the nonclient areas of a window are. The easiest answer is also the most accurate. That is, the nonclient areas are all the areas of the window that surround the client area. As an illustration, open the WordPad application. The client area is the large white area where you can type text. The nonclient areas include all the parts of the window that surround this area. This includes the caption bar, menu bar, scroll bars, and so on.

Windows uses about half of the defined input messages for nonclient area objects. The mouse messages with names that contain the letters *NC* are messages that Windows handles for the nonclient area components of a window. For example, Windows receives a `WM_NCLBUTTONDOWN` message when a user selects a menu command, resizes a window frame, or minimizes a window. The differences between these actions depend on the mouse location when the mouse button is clicked.

The nonsystem mouse messages are for application use — that is, they are for your use. With the help of ClassWizard, creating and responding to the basic set of messages is fairly straightforward. Table 8-2 lists the nonclient mouse messages that Windows manages.

Table 8-2
Nonclient Mouse Messages

Message	*Description*
WM_NCLBUTTONDOWN	The left mouse button has been clicked down while the mouse pointer is on a nonclient area.
WM_NCLBUTTONUP	The left mouse button has been released while the mouse pointer is on a nonclient area.
WM_NCRBUTTONDOWN	The right mouse button has been clicked down while the mouse pointer is on a nonclient area.
WM_NCRBUTTONUP	The right mouse button has been released while the mouse pointer is on a nonclient area.
WM_NCMBUTTONDOWN	The middle mouse button has been clicked down while the mouse pointer is on a nonclient area.
WM_NCMBUTTONUP	The middle mouse button has been released while the mouse pointer is on a nonclient area.
WM_NCMOUSEMOVE	The mouse pointer has moved over a nonclient area of a window.
WM_NCHITTEST	A query message that asks, "Where in the window is the mouse pointer?" The NC in this query message doesn't mean that it's only for the nonclient area, although that is the system's primary interest. Instead, this message returns a hit-test code that identifies the pointer position in the window – for example, over a border, over a menu, or over the client area.

Changing the mouse cursor

One of the most common ways to give feedback to the end user is to change the shape of the mouse pointer. The commonly used hour glass pointer is the simplest to display because MFC provides two functions to accomplish this. `BeginWaitCursor()` displays the hour glass cursor, while `EndWaitCursor()` returns the pointer to its normal shape. These functions are most commonly used during any application task that may take a long time to complete.

We should also note that this is not the only way to display an hour glass pointer. You could also display one by handling the `WM_SETCURSOR` message. If a program needs to interact with the user — that is, retrieve any type of message — while still displaying the hour glass pointer, you *must* respond to the `WM_SETCURSOR` message. Windows sends a constant stream of these messages to each window, causing a continual updating of each window's pointer. Take a few minutes now, and run Spy++ to observe this.

The function call for displaying pointers is the Windows API function SetCursor(). For example, here is a line of code that displays the right-arrow pointer:

```
::SetCursor( ::LoadCursor( AfxGetInstanceHandle(),
   IDC_ARROW ) );
```

Creating an MFC Demo Program that Changes Mouse Cursors

To demonstrate how to change mouse cursors within an application, we've written a special program named MouseDemo2. The program loads in 16 cursors and sets the cursor depending on the mouse position.

The application looks at the location inside of the view window where the mouse currently is. Dividing the view window into 16 rectangular regions allows the program to decide which of 16 mouse cursors to use. When you run the program and move the mouse around inside of the view window, you'll see the mouse cursor change. The name of the mouse cursor is also displayed.

MouseDemo2

CD-ROM Location: **Chap08\MouseDemo2**

Program Name: MouseDemo2.EXE

Source Code Modules in Text: MouseDemo2View.cpp

✦ ✦ ✦ ✦ ✦

Listing 8-2: MouseDemo2View.cpp Source Code File Highlights

```
// MouseDemo2View.cpp : implementation of
// the CMouseDemo2View class
//

/////////////////////////////////////////////////////////////
// CMouseDemo2View construction/destruction

CMouseDemo2View::CMouseDemo2View()
{

  // Keep a list of the cursor IDs that
  // we'll load in.
  static char *szCursor[] = {
    IDC_ARROW, IDC_IBEAM, IDC_WAIT,
    IDC_CROSS, IDC_UPARROW, IDC_SIZENWSE,
    IDC_SIZENESW, IDC_SIZEWE, IDC_SIZENS,
    IDC_SIZEALL, IDC_NO, IDC_APPSTARTING,
```

```
    IDC_HELP, IDC_ARROW, IDC_ARROW, IDC_ARROW };

  // Load the cursors.
  for( int i=0; i<16; i++ )
    m_hCursor[i] =
      ::LoadCursor( NULL, szCursor[i] );

}

CMouseDemo2View::~CMouseDemo2View()
{
}

/////////////////////////////////////////////////////////////
// CMouseDemo2View message handlers

BOOL CMouseDemo2View::OnSetCursor(CWnd* pWnd, UINT nHitTest,
  UINT message)
{

  // See if this is a HTCLIENT
  // hit test.
  if( nHitTest == HTCLIENT ){

    // Get the mouse position. This
    // will be in terms of the
    // entire screen.
    POINT pt;
    GetCursorPos( &pt );

    // Convert the coordinates to
    // client rectangle coordinates.
    ScreenToClient( &pt );

    // Call the function that we created
    // which gets the cursor region.
    int nCursor = GetCursorRegion( &pt );

    // Set the window cursor.
    ::SetCursor( m_hCursor[nCursor] );

    // Return indicating that we responded
    // to this message.
    return( TRUE );
    }

  // Call the default OnSetCursor() function.
  return CView::OnSetCursor(pWnd, nHitTest, message);
}

int CMouseDemo2View::GetCursorRegion( POINT *lpPt )
{
```

(continued)

Listing 8-2 *(continued)*

```
  // We'll need the client
  // rectangle so that we can
  // calculate the cursor region.
  // It'll be an x value from 0-3
  // and a y value from 0-3.
  RECT Rect;
  GetClientRect( &Rect );

  // Divide the client rectangle width
  // by four to obtain the x region
  // index.
  int x =
    ( lpPt->x * 4 ) / Rect.right;
  if( x > 3 ) x = 3;


  // Divide the client rectangle height
  // by four to obtain the y region
  // index.
  int y =
    ( lpPt->y * 4 ) / Rect.bottom;
  if( y > 3 ) y = 3;

  // Return the index. It'll be a value
  // from 0-15.
  return( y * 4 + x );

}

void CMouseDemo2View::OnMouseMove(UINT nFlags, CPoint point)
{

  // Keep a list of the cursor names
  // so that we can display them
  // in the client window.
  static CString strCursor[] = {
    "IDC_ARROW", "IDC_IBEAM", "IDC_WAIT",
    "IDC_CROSS", "IDC_UPARROW", "IDC_SIZENWSE",
    "IDC_SIZENESW", "IDC_SIZEWE", "IDC_SIZENS",
    "IDC_SIZEALL", "IDC_NO", "IDC_APPSTARTING",
    "IDC_HELP", "IDC_ARROW", "IDC_ARROW",
    "IDC_ARROW" };

  // Get the cursor region. This
  // will be a value from 0-15 and
  // will correspond to the 16
  // cursors we loaded.
  int nCursor =
    GetCursorRegion( &point );
```

```
    // Get a DC to the client window
    // so that we can draw.
    CClientDC ClientDC( this );

    CString strInfo;

    // Format a string.
    strInfo = "Cursor:" +
      strCursor[nCursor] +
      "           ";

    // Draw the string to the client window.
    ClientDC.TextOut( 0, 0,
      strInfo, strInfo.GetLength() );

    // Call the default OnMouseMove() function.
    CView::OnMouseMove(nFlags, point);
}
```

Capturing the mouse

As you become more experienced with Windows programming, you will need to trap all mouse messages and send them to a particular window. This is called *capturing the mouse*. The most common use of this technique is to trap a matching pair of button down/button up messages. Very weird and hard-to-debug problems can arise if you don't capture the mouse.

For example, say we have implemented a message handler for the WM_LBUTTONDOWN. Inside this message handler, we use a Boolean (true/false) variable to track the state of the left mouse button m_bClicked. If the left mouse button is down, that is, if we receive a WM_LBUTTONDOWN message, we set this variable equal to TRUE. If the left mouse button is not clicked, this variable is set equal to FALSE.

Now imagine that the user has clicked the mouse button and then moves the mouse pointer out of the window before he or she releases the button. If we don't capture the mouse during the WM_LBUTTONDOWN message handler, our application will not receive the WM_LBUTTONUP message. The m_bClicked variable will still set to TRUE even though the button has been released. Our application will be out of synch with the state of the mouse, and all kinds of confusing things can happen.

To understand mouse capture, it helps to see it in action. Run almost any application, and open the File Open dialog box. The mouse can be captured by two dialog box controls: list boxes and edit controls. Mouse capture takes place when you click to select an item in a list box or text in the edit control. After clicking in such controls, when you drag the mouse outside the border, you'll see the control scroll its contents. The scrolling is caused by mouse capture.

Another place you can see mouse capture at work is within most text editing windows (including the Visual C++ editor). These windows scroll when you click in a window filled with text and drag beyond the window border. These windows are only able to continue receiving mouse input — in the form of WM_MOUSEMOVE messages — because the mouse has been captured.

Now that you've seen it at work, you probably want to know how you can capture the mouse yourself. It's easy; you just call CWnd::SetCapture(). As we mentioned, you typically do this in response to a mouse down message. To *release* the capture — something you must be sure to do — call CWnd::ReleaseCapture(). A good time to release the mouse capture is in response to a button up message (WM_LBUTTONUP).

Here's some ClassWizard-generated code that shows a typical scenario for mouse capture and release. The mouse is captured when the left mouse button is clicked (in reply to the WM_LBUTTONDOWN message), and it is released when the left mouse button comes up (in reply to the WM_LBUTTONUP message):

```
void CMainFrame::OnLButtonDown(UINT nFlags, CPoint point)
{
  // Grab the mouse.
  SetCapture();

  CFrameWnd::OnLButtonDown(nFlags, point);
}

void CMainFrame::OnLButtonUp(UINT nFlags, CPoint point)
{
  // Release the mouse.
  ReleaseCapture();

  CFrameWnd::OnLButtonUp(nFlags, point);
}
```

Incidentally, when you capture the mouse, Windows doesn't send you any hit-test (WM_NCHITTEST) or pointer-setting (WM_SETCURSOR) messages. The assumption is that you already have complete control of the mouse and that you will change the pointer when you need to. If you want to change the pointer during mouse capture, you would probably do so in response to WM_MOUSEMOVE, the only mouse message you get when the mouse is captured.

Limiting mouse movement

Another facility that Windows lets you control is *mouse pointer clipping*. It's not something you'll do very often, but to complete our discussion of mouse state, we must at least mention it. Mouse pointer clipping involves the definition of a clipping rectangle boundary. The mouse pointer can move only within its defined pointer clipping rectangle.

One example of pointer clipping is obvious when using Windows. Windows itself clips the pointer to the display screen. If it didn't, a user might accidentally send the pointer over the edge of the screen and into oblivion. We've seen some display drivers that have an option that enables the pointer to wrap around the left edge onto the right, and over the top of the screen onto the bottom. Although that's not our preference in mouse pointer, some users undoubtedly appreciate being able to do this.

So why should a program clip the pointer? Obviously, it's necessary to prevent the user from moving the pointer outside a given area. For example, a security program might let the user move the pointer only around the password dialog box. It's tough to come up with good examples of when to use pointer clipping because the few places where it's done, it's disconcerting. For example, the Paintbrush program in Windows 3.1 clips the pointer when you're drawing shapes such as bézier curves. We find it more annoying than useful.

Microsoft's MFC developers apparently agree with our assessment that this isn't a general purpose function. They don't include the Windows API function that controls pointer clipping — `::ClipCursor()` — in any MFC class. What's interesting, though, is that although MFC doesn't wrap this function in any of its own classes, it *does* clip the pointer in one specific circumstance. When resizing an OLE toolbar, the pointer is clipped to the parent window's client area. This is one use that makes sense because the size of a child window should be limited by the size of the parent window.

Keyboard Input

Handling keyboard input is fairly simple and straightforward. Once you know which messages to handle, it's merely a matter of creating handlers for each of the desired messages. When working with keyboard input, you can choose to handle one or more of three possible messages. Windows sends three messages for each key press. The first is `WM_KEYDOWN`, which signals that a key has been pressed. The next message sent is `WM_CHAR`, along with the virtual keycode of the character pressed. The last message sent is `WM_KEYUP`, which is sent when the key is released. With all of these messages available, we can take complete control of keyboard input.

We're also going to cover some of the less obvious aspects of keyboard input. We'll start with a look at how the keyboard hardware's scan codes are translated into visible character codes. Then we'll discuss general user interface issues that relate to keyboard input; namely, what to do when a window gets the keyboard focus.

The physical keyboard

Getting keyboard input to an MS-DOS program often involves an intimate knowledge of how a low-level keyboard code, known as a *scan code*, is generated. Although C-runtime functions translate keyboard input for you, MS-DOS programmers who opt for high performance will grab keyboard scan codes directly. Scan codes are not related to any character set; instead, they are a set of 8-bit codes that indicate which key has been pressed. For example, the key that generates a *Y* on a U.S.-English keyboard has a scan code of 15 hex. It doesn't take too much imagination — or code — to build a table for converting scan code data to ASCII characters. That's what many MS-DOS programmers must do.

Intimate knowledge of the keyboard was required because MS-DOS programmers have to ignore about half of the scan codes that are generated. Each key on the keyboard actually has *two* scan codes. One indicates that a key has been pressed, and the other indicates that the key has been released. The difference between the two scan codes is 80 hex. For example, the *Y* key that we discussed a moment ago sends a scan code of 15 hex when pressed and 95 hex when released. Of these two, the down transition is more interesting. When reading scan codes, the up transition — which has the sign bit set — is usually ignored.

One problem with scan codes is that they are a very hardware-dependent, low-level type of input. To properly perform scan code conversion, you must take into account the keyboard that is currently installed on the system. Most types of keyboards are distinguished on the basis of language or, in some cases, country.

One example, the Swiss-German keyboard, takes into account both language and country. On that keyboard, the *Z* key and the *Y* key are reversed from what they are on the U.S.-English keyboard. As a result, an MS-DOS program that relies on scan code conversions according to the U.S.-English keyboard layout won't work correctly in Switzerland without modification.

When we say that keyboard scan codes are hardware dependent, we really mean that they are dependent on the different way keys are laid out to follow various cultural conventions. For a scan code-dependent program that could work worldwide, approximately two dozen different translation tables are required. And that's only taking into account the keyboards that use the Roman alphabet. For other keyboards, such as Russian Cyrillic, and Arabic, and the various Asian keyboards, a whole new set of problems arise.

In addition to being hardware dependent, scan codes are so low level that they don't take into account keyboard state, such as the Shift key or the Caps Lock key. As a result, considerable effort is required to simply detect the difference between an upper- and a lowercase letter. For example, a scan code-dependent program can't tell the difference between *Y* and *y* without a lot of extra work. Scan codes aren't case sensitive because keyboards aren't case sensitive.

Windows has different solutions for each of these two problems. To avoid relying on country-specific keyboard layouts, Windows keyboard drivers convert scan codes into a standard set of *virtual key codes*. This set of keys make up what is sometimes called the *Windows logical keyboard*. To solve the problem of keyboard state, Windows provides a helper function to convert virtual key codes into printable characters. This latter conversion creates the distinction between upper- and lowercase that we rely on when reading text.

The Windows logical keyboard

The logical keyboard is an abstraction that serves to hide differences between keyboards in countries that use Roman characters. You won't see a keyboard layout for the logical keyboard anywhere in the Windows documentation. What you will see, however, are the definitions for virtual key (VK_) codes. It's the job of the keyboard device driver to convert hardware-specific scan codes into virtual key codes.

In particular, Windows calls the keyboard driver to convert raw hardware scan codes into virtual key codes. These virtual key codes are sent to applications as messages. Because there are two scan codes per keyboard key — that is, a key pressed code and a key released code — there are also two messages per key. The WM_KEYDOWN message indicates that a keyboard key has been pressed, and the WM_KEYUP message indicates that a key has been released.

Although virtual key messages solve one problem with scan codes, they don't solve the other problem. The problem they solve is that you don't have to worry about different keyboards. The device driver does whatever translation is necessary to produce a uniform set of keycodes.

The problem that still exists, however, is that virtual key codes are fairly low level. In particular, you have to do a lot of work to decide whether letters are upper- or lowercase. And virtual key codes aren't influenced by changes to shift key states, which include the Shift, Ctrl, and Alt keys. Virtual key codes also ignore the state of the Caps Lock, Num Lock, and Scroll Lock keys.

Although they don't provide enough information to get character input, virtual key codes are suitable for use as accelerator key codes. There are two types of accelerators: VIRTKEY and ASCII. We recommend that you always use VIRTKEY, which — as the name suggests — corresponds to virtual keys. The other type of accelerator, ASCII, is created from the other type of keyboard message, which we're going to discuss next.

An accelerator is a keystroke that a program interprets as a command. From your program's perspective, the results of a menu selection and an accelerator keystroke are identical because Windows generates identical messages for both. You can connect the two in the mind of a user by displaying the accelerator name in the menu, next to the equivalent menu item. For example, you'll often see Ctrl+V next to the Paste command in an Edit menu. Although both types of commands are connected in the user's mind, from a programming perspective the two are defined separately. Specifically, menus are defined using menu resources, and accelerators are defined with accelerator resources.

Printable character messages

The Windows API contains a function for converting between virtual key code messages and WM_CHAR messages. We call these the *printable character messages* because most are uppercase letters, lowercase letters, numbers, or punctuation marks. That is, they correspond to characters that you can see on the display screen and send to the printer.

The ::TranslateMessage() function is the Windows API function that converts virtual key messages into WM_CHAR messages. Unless you've written Windows SDK programs, you've probably never seen this function. And because MFC calls this function for you in its message loop, you don't ever have to worry about it.

What's important is that this function adds WM_CHAR messages to your application's message queue. Every WM_CHAR message that you receive will be preceded by a WM_KEYDOWN message and followed by a WM_KEYUP message. You get printable character input from the WM_CHAR message, and you can safely ignore the associated virtual key messages.

If you ignore WM_KEYDOWN messages, why does Windows bother sending them to you? This message is for all the keys that *don't* have a corresponding printable character. We should mention that such keystrokes seem more like commands than data, and the easiest way to handle keyboard commands is with an accelerator table. However, you can't always use an accelerator table. In particular, it's something of a convention that only one accelerator table is active at any point in time. That accelerator table would be the one for an application's frame window. All other windows must process low-level keyboard input directly, without the benefits that accelerator tables provide.

Table 8-3 lists the virtual key codes for keys that don't create printable characters. When you can't create accelerator table entries, you'll rely on the WM_KEYDOWN message to detect when these keys have been pressed.

To summarize, keyboard input starts as scan codes. A Windows keyboard driver converts these codes to a hardware-independent form: virtual key codes. Typically, Windows applications then send the virtual key code messages to a Windows API function that generates WM_CHAR character messages when printable characters are typed. For nonprintable characters — such as function keys and navigation keys — you must rely on the WM_KEYDOWN virtual key message.

Table 8-3
Virtual Key Codes for Nonprintable Keys

Virtual Key Code	*Key*
VK_MENU	Menu (Windows 95/98 keyboards only)
VK_APPS	Application (Windows 95/98 keyboards only)
VK_CONTROL	Control
VK_DELETE	Delete
VK_DOWN	Down arrow
VK_END	End
VK_F1 through VK_F12	F1 through F12

VK_HOME	Home
VK_INSERT	Insert
VK_LEFT	Left arrow
VK_PAUSE	Pause
VK_NEXT	Page Down
VK_PRIOR	Page Up
VK_SNAPSHOT	Print Screen
VK_RIGHT	Right arrow
VK_SHIFT	Shift
VK_UP	Up arrow

Now that you understand the types of keyboard input messages that Windows will send you, it's time to address input issues related to application state. Toward that end, the following section describes how an application lets the user know that a window has the keyboard focus. This can be done using several techniques, which we call *echoing the keyboard focus*.

Echoing keyboard focus

When you build support for keyboard input into a window, you must provide a visual cue that lets the user know when that support is enabled. Because a window gets keyboard input when it has the focus, the proper time for displaying those visual cues is when the window gets the focus. It follows, then, that you should disable the visible signs of the focus when the window loses the focus.

To help you build windows that display the proper visual cues, the following sections describe three ways that a window can advertise its ownership of the focus. We'll start with a look at creating insertion points, which are Windows' keyboard pointers. Then, we'll talk about focus rectangles, something you'll see in dialog box controls but can also be displayed in other types of windows. Finally, we'll talk about the relationship between a window's selection state and the keyboard focus.

Creating and maintaining keyboard cursors

A keyboard cursor or insertion point is a blinking bitmap that lets the user know where keyboard input will have an effect.

Table 8-4 lists the eight `CWnd` member functions that create and manage keyboard cursors. This group of functions is fairly small and easy to understand. The challenge with keyboard cursors revolves around timing issues, such as when to create, show, hide, and destroy the cursors.

Table 8-4
CWnd Member Functions for Creating and Managing Keyboard Cursors

Function	*Description*
CreateCaret()	Creates a keyboard cursor using a bitmap that you provide.
CreateGrayCaret()	Creates a solid gray cursor using the size you specify.
CreateSolidCaret()	Creates a solid black cursor using the size you specify.
GetCaretPos()	Returns the location of the cursor. Because of local input state in Windows 95, Windows 98, and Windows NT, you can find the location of a cursor only if it's contained within a window that's created by the calling thread.
DestroyCaret()	Destroys a cursor. To avoid putting your application in an unknown state, destroy the cursor when you lose the keyboard focus (and create a cursor when you gain the keyboard focus).
HideCaret()	Makes a cursor invisible.
SetCaretPos()	Moves a cursor to a position in a window. When a window containing a cursor is scrolled, the cursor gets scrolled with the window data.
ShowCaret()	Makes a cursor visible.

You create a keyboard cursor when a window gets the keyboard focus. Although you might be tempted to create it earlier, you should resist the temptation. After all, you only need a cursor to echo the results of keyboard input. And without the focus, you don't have any keyboard input. In addition to creating the cursor, you need to position it within your window and make it visible. Here's a fragment of code that does the right thing in response to a WM_SETFOCUS message:

```
void CMainFrame::OnSetFocus(CWnd* pOldWnd)
{
  // First call default handler.
  CFrameWnd::OnSetFocus(pOldWnd);

  // Create, position, and make caret appear.
  CreateSolidCaret(0, d_cyLineHeight );
  SetCaretPos( d_ptCaretLocation );
  ShowCaret();
}
```

Just as you create a keyboard cursor when you get the focus, the logical time to destroy the cursor is when you lose the focus. In response to the WM_KILLFOCUS message, you'll first hide the cursor and then destroy it. Here's a code fragment that shows how this is done:

```
void CMainFrame::OnKillFocus(CWnd* pNewWnd)
{
  CFrameWnd::OnKillFocus(pNewWnd);

  // Query and save current caret position.
  d_ptCaretLocation = GetCaretPos();

  // Eliminate caret.
  HideCaret();
  DestroyCaret();
}
```

The only other keyboard cursor issue involves drawing outside of normal WM_PAINT drawing. If a cursor is in a window, you must hide the cursor before any non-WM_PAINT drawing. Otherwise, you might overwrite the cursor. When the non-WM_PAINT drawing is done, you can restore the cursor. Here's a code fragment that shows what we mean:

```
void CMainFrame::OnChar(UINT nChar, UINT nRepCnt,
  UINT nFlags)
{
  CSize sizeTextBox;

  // Fetch caret position.
  CPoint pt = GetCaretPos();

  // Hide caret before fetching DC.
  HideCaret();

  // Drawing in non-WM_PAINT message.
  // Bracket required to force DC to disappear.
  {
    CClientDC ClientDC( this );
    ClientDC.TextOut(pt.x, pt.y, (LPCTSTR)&nChar, 1);
    sizeTextBox =
      ClientDC.GetTextExtent( (LPCTSTR)&nChar, 1 );
  }

  // Advance caret position.
  pt.x += sizeTextBox.cx;
  SetCaretPos( pt );

  // Display caret.
  ShowCaret();
}
```

This code fragment actually does more than just hide the keyboard cursor. It shows how you respond to the WM_CHAR message to both draw the character that's typed and advance the cursor. Such drawn objects won't be a permanent part of a window's contents unless they are also drawn in response to the WM_PAINT message. Because our code makes no provision for saving the text anywhere, this isn't done. (When you understand why this code fragment is "broken," you truly understand the meaning of the WM_PAINT message.)

To test your cursor-creation code, be sure to force the focus to switch away from your program. Do this by activating the Task Manager (Ctrl+Esc), or by activating any other application that's currently running. When you switch away, the cursor should disappear without a trace. When you switch back, the cursor should be in the same place it was before you switched focus.

The keyboard cursor is called the "insertion point" because it shows users the exact point in a window at which keyboard input will have an effect. Users expect to be able to navigate insertion points around a window through the use of the arrow keys. Another way to echo the keyboard focus is with a focus rectangle, which we discuss next.

Focus rectangles

A focus rectangle provides an alternative to a cursor for signaling the keyboard focus location. Unlike cursors, focus rectangles don't blink. Instead, they provide subtle highlighting that draws a user's eye to a particular part of a window. Whether you use a focus rectangle or a cursor depends on what you are trying to highlight. The most common examples of focus rectangles occur in dialog boxes. For all nonedit controls, focus rectangles are drawn as the user moves the focus—via the Tab key or the mouse—to the different controls in the dialog.

Focus rectangles aren't solely for dialog box controls, although this is the most obvious and most common use. You can use them anywhere a cursor just doesn't seem right. One difference between focus rectangles and cursors is that cursors are always solid rectangles. Focus rectangles, on the other hand, are hollow, and they wrap around other objects. If you need to echo the focus in a way that is solid or blinking, you want a cursor. For a subtler, hollow pointer, try a focus rectangle instead.

Drawing a focus rectangle is extremely easy. You simply call MFC's `CDC::DrawFocusRect()` function. The following example shows how to draw a focus rectangle around a block of text:

```
void CMainFrame::OnLButtonDown(UINT nFlags, CPoint point)
{
  CClientDC ClientDC( this );

  // Draw a line of text at mouse cursor location.
  CString str;
  str.Format("Focus rectangle around this text");
  ClientDC.TextOut(point.x, point.y, str);

  // Calculate width and height of text.
  CSize sizeText =
    ClietnDC.GetTextExtent( str, str.GetLength() );

  // Calculate a margin around the focus rectangle.
  int cxMargin = GetSystemMetrics( SM_CXBORDER ) * 4;
  int cyMargin = GetSystemMetrics( SM_CYBORDER ) * 1;
```

```
    // Calculate size of focus rectangle.
    CRect rTextBox;
    rTextBox.left = point.x - cxMargin;
    rTextBox.top = point.y - cyMargin;
    rTextBox.right = point.x + sizeText.cx + cxMargin;
    rTextBox.bottom = point.y + sizeText.cy + cyMargin;

    // Draw a focus rectangle around a block of text.
    ClientDC.DrawFocusRect( &rTextBox );

    CFrameWnd::OnLButtonDown(nFlags, point);
}
```

This code fragment draws a focus rectangle in response to a `WM_LBUTTONDOWN` message. We show this simply as an example of *how* to call `CDC::DrawFocusRect()`. But the truth of the matter is that button messages aren't the events that typically trigger the drawing of focus rectangles.

You're more likely to draw the focus rectangle when a window gets the focus. The reason should be obvious: that's when you are certain that your window has the focus. And, as you may recall from our earlier discussion, this means that you draw a focus rectangle in response to a `WM_SETFOCUS` message. Here's a fragment of code taken from an MFC program that shows how to do this:

```
void CMainFrame::OnSetFocus(CWnd* pOldWnd)
{
    CFrameWnd::OnSetFocus(pOldWnd);

    CClientDC ClientDC( this );

    // Draw focus rectangle when we get the focus.
    CRect rFocus;
    rFocus.left = d_ptFocusRect.x;
    rFocus.top = d_ptFocusRect.y;
    rFocus.right = d_ptFocusRect.x + d_cxIcon;
    rFocus.bottom = d_ptFocusRect.y + d_cyIcon;
    ClientDC.DrawFocusRect( &rFocus );
}
```

If you draw a focus rectangle, you must be sure to erase it. Because a focus rectangle exists just to show focus ownership, the logical time to erase a focus rectangle is when the window loses the focus. Interestingly enough, a focus rectangle is erased by calling the exact same function that drew it in the first place: `CDC::DrawFocusRect()`. The following code fragment erases the focus rectangle we drew a moment ago. This is done in response to — what else? — the `WM_KILLFOCUS` message:

```
void CMainFrame::OnKillFocus(CWnd* pNewWnd)
{
    CFrameWnd::OnKillFocus(pNewWnd);

    CClientDC ClientDC( this );
```

```
    // Hide focus rectangle when we lose the focus.
    CRect rFocus;
    rFocus.left = d_ptFocusRect.x;
    rFocus.top = d_ptFocusRect.y;
    rFocus.right = d_ptFocusRect.x + d_cxIcon;
    rFocus.bottom = d_ptFocusRect.y + d_cyIcon;
    ClientDC.DrawFocusRect(&rFocus);
  }
```

You might find it a bit puzzling that the same code can erase *and* draw a focus rectangle. To explain how this is possible, we need to describe how `CDC::DrawFocusRect()` works. This function uses Boolean arithmetic to invert a set of pixels. To draw a focus rectangle, pixels are inverted. To erase the same focus rectangle, the same pixels are inverted again, which completely and effectively erases the focus rectangle. This is often referred to as a Boolean operation, and it makes use of GDI's Boolean *raster operations* (or *ROP codes*).

So far, we've described how you make a focus rectangle appear when you get a `WM_SETFOCUS` message, and how you make it disappear in response to a `WM_KILLFOCUS` message. But there's one more message that can affect the health and well-being of a focus rectangle. To provide complete support for a focus rectangle, you must redraw the focus rectangle in response to the `WM_PAINT` message.

You need to draw a focus rectangle when handling a `WM_PAINT` message for the same reason that you draw any other object in a window's client area. You can't determine ahead of time when some outside event will damage the contents of a window's client area. It might be as simple as a screen saver that automatically starts after 10 minutes of idle time. Whatever the reason, you draw a focus rectangle with the same function we described earlier, `CDC::DrawFocusRect()`. With `WM_PAINT`, however, you must first determine whether the window has the focus. If it doesn't, you don't draw the focus rectangle. Only if it has the focus do you draw the focus rectangle. Here's a `WM_PAINT` handler that first checks for the presence of the focus before drawing a focus rectangle:

```
  void CMainFrame::OnPaint()
  {
    CPaintDC PaintDC( this ); // DC for painting

    // Only draw focus rectangle if our window has focus.
    if( GetFocus() == this ){
      // Calculate coordinate
      CRect rFocus;
      rFocus.left = d_ptFocusRect.x;
      rFocus.top = d_ptFocusRect.y;
      rFocus.right = d_ptFocusRect.x + d_cxIcon;
      rFocus.bottom = d_ptFocusRect.y + d_cyIcon;

      // Draw actual focus rectangle.
      PaintDC.DrawFocusRect(&rFocus);
      }
  }
```

Both types of focus-echoing mechanisms — keyboard cursors and focus rectangles — are relatively easy to create and use. But a third issue — the selection state — is closely related to the keyboard focus. By *selection state*, we mean the display of objects selected by a user in a window. To support Windows' standards for user interface activity, selection state must be visible only when a window has focus. At all other times, the selection state of objects must be hidden.

Selection state and keyboard focus

With Windows applications, a common mode of operation involves *noun-verb* operations. This means that the user first selects an object, and then chooses the action to take on that object. For example, to change the formatting of a word in a word processing program, the user first selects the word and then chooses the format command. Although this mode of operation is obvious to experienced Windows users, the opposite — that is, verb-noun operation — is quite common in character-based environments.

Objects can be selected using either the mouse or the keyboard. Regardless of how it's done, Windows programs change the color of selected objects to help users distinguish them from other objects. We talk about selecting text colors in Chapter 6. But for now, suffice it to say that you fetch the colors to use by calling `::GetSysColor()` with the appropriate color indices. Then you perform a bitwise exclusive OR to determine the color of selected text. This is summarized in the following lines of code:

```
COLORREF d_crForeground = GetSysColor(COLOR_WINDOWTEXT);
COLORREF d_crBackground = GetSysColor( COLOR_WINDOW );
COLORREF d_crSelectFore = d_crForeground ^ 0x00ffffff;
COLORREF d_crSelectBack = d_crBackground ^ 0x00ffffff;
```

In general, when a window loses the keyboard focus, it should hide its selection. When focus is restored, the window should again show the selection. We say "in general" because in a few situations a window will still show its selection state even though it has lost the focus. In particular, two windows might need to simultaneously display the selected state.

To get a sense for when to show selection state and when to hide it, run some of the popular Windows applications. If you watch closely, you'll see that numerous small visual cues indicate changes in activation and focus. Some of these — for example, the change in title bar color — are handled by Windows. Other state changes — such as the three we've discussed here — must be handled by your application. But rather than dictate hard-and-fast rules, we should point out that the most important criterion is what works for your users.

Summary

In marked contrast to the abstraction layer that MFC provides in many other aspects of Windows programming, handling mouse and keyboard input requires some rather low-level coding. Windows sends you notifications for not only mouse button clicks and movements of the mouse pointer but as many as three separate messages for each key press!

Of course, along with the added complexity also comes greater flexibility. You should be comfortable with the concepts and techniques we covered in this chapter. Because interacting with the user is what almost all applications are about, you'll get plenty of practice using this information.

✦ ✦ ✦

Graphics

Operating systems have come a long way since the early 1980s. Back then it was common to see text-based menu systems with function keys that sent application commands. Computers such as Atari, Amiga, and the Mac enjoyed the luxury of graphical user interfaces. With the success of the IBM PC platform and the Windows operating system, everything is graphical.

Programmers don't have to worry about the low-level details involved in drawing a window, displaying a dialog box, or creating a button (most of the time). Programming in a graphical environment does bring about a different set of concerns, especially when your application displays data graphically such as graphs, charts, and diagrams.

That's what this whole chapter is about: graphical programming under Windows 98. We'll explore the basic graphical architecture, called GDI, and see how each part works to provide the programmer with some tremendous flexibility and power. We'll explore the different GDI classes and learn about GDI-related constructs such as brushes, pens, and fonts.

In This Chapter

The architecture of the GDI

How the GDI abstracts the graphics hardware

The different types of GDI graphics

The device context

How to draw on the display with text and vector graphics

Manipulating text

Fonts

Pens and brushes

Raster operations

Clipping regions

Introducing the Graphics Device Interface

The graphics device interface, or GDI for short, forms part of the core of the Windows operating system. The GDI manages all graphics output from a Windows program. This means that no matter if a window is displayed on the screen or a screen saver displays some dazzling graphics or if an application prints a document, the GDI is involved in making it happen.

Windows itself uses the GDI to draw user interface elements such as windows, menus, and dialog boxes. Windows even uses the GDI to display the mouse pointer even though it appears to "float" over other screen objects.

Microsoft created the GDI to decouple rendering graphics from the underlying hardware. The GDI provides high-level drawing functions that produce generally the same results regardless of the underlying hardware. Decoupling the graphics functions from the hardware enables you to produce interesting graphics with very little effort or concern for the supporting hardware.

Types of graphics

GDI functions come in three flavors: text, raster, and vector graphics. Although each of these categories might seem arbitrary, they exist for good reason. At the device driver level, each type has its own set of entry points and ways of operating. At the higher-level programming interface, a program controls the appearance of each type by using slightly different sets of drawing attributes. Understanding each of these types is the first step on your way to GDI mastery. Because you want to become a graphics guru, let's examine each of the different types of graphics.

Text

An irony of Windows programming is that even though the GDI simplifies graphical rendering, it adds complexity to creating textual output. With the added complexity also comes added flexibility. Because text is treated as graphics, you can control more aspects than you could ever dream of back in the text-based world. Want to create 18-point, red, Helvetica text? No problem. How about 12-point, shadowed, Arial text? No problem at all. You'd have to resort to some pretty intricate programming to get the same effects in a text-based environment. You can do all of this in Windows with a few GDI calls.

Raster graphics

The second type of GDI graphic output is raster graphics. Raster-type graphics are the most commonly used type of graphics within the Windows environment. A raster graphics function operates on data stored in arrays called *bitmaps*. A standard VGA monitor's 640 × 480 image is simply a bitmap that the display adapter makes visible on the screen. Part of Windows' support for raster graphics is the capability to create off-screen bitmap images. You can render these images off screen very quickly and then transfer them to the screen. This makes your images appear to display quickly.

Other examples of raster graphics include icons and cursors that are added to your application by editing the resource file (.RC). Moving windows around the screen is another example of the use of raster graphics. When a window is moved from one part of the screen to another, a raster graphics function picks up the pixels that make up the window and moves them to the destination location on the screen.

Because the data on the display screen is stored in arrays, bitmaps are useful for caching complex graphical objects for quick on-screen rendering. You can create complex objects ahead of time, either during compile time or during runtime, and then quickly copy them to the screen. The only problem with bitmaps is the space that they require. One bitmap with 640 × 480 pixels and 8-bit color depth requires approximately 300K of storage space. Obviously, as the image size or color depth increases, the storage requirement increases as well.

Vector graphics

Within the GDI, the term *vector graphics* refers to the drawing functions that create lines and filled figures. The GDI features an entire set of functions that draw straight lines, curves, pie wedges, and polygons. You can mix and match these function calls with the raster functions in any way.

Normally, people think of geometric shapes when they think about vector graphics. However, Windows uses very few of the GDI vector function calls when it draws the user interface. Most applications don't really make much use of GDI vector graphics, except for drawing programs. There's nothing inherently wrong with these functions. Business applications are mostly text oriented, and programs that need complex images depend on bitmaps and the raster functions.

GDI devices

In order for a physical graphics device, such as a printer or display adapter, to be a GDI device it doesn't need to support all three graphics types. This is the beauty of the GDI. Based on the installed device drivers, the GDI can adapt itself to the hardware installed to provide reasonable graphics results across a wide variety of hardware. In fact, most devices don't have nearly this level of built-in support.

The only requirement for being a GDI device is the capability to turn on a pixel. That's it. For all operations beyond this simple requirement, the GDI can decompose the drawing requests into a simpler form that the hardware can understand. But it's up to the device driver to tell the GDI exactly what features it supports. The driver communicates this to GDI by passing a set of capability bits that the GDI uses to "tune" its own drawing requests.

On basic devices with limited capability, the GDI adapts and performs most of the work itself. The GDI can internally convert all text and vector graphics calls into raster data that the device can understand. As we've already seen, even though raster graphics require more storage space, this is offset by the capability of rendering even highly complex graphics on bargain basement hardware.

If a device informs the GDI that it supports more advanced capabilities, the GDI does less of the work. If a hardware device can directly service a drawing request, the GDI passes this request off to the device. This results in overall higher performance in two ways. First, the GDI has less work to do internally and puts less strain on the CPU. Second, higher-level drawing requests take up less memory and disk space than if the same request was broken down into its lower-level components. Less information to store means less strain on the overall system, which translates into higher performance as well.

This capability to work on a wide range of devices is one reason why the GDI is described as a device-independent graphics interface. If a device does not support a drawing operation itself, the GDI can step in and simulate the request in software. On the other hand, if the device provides native support for the request, the GDI passes the request off to the device and reaps higher system performance.

Types of GDI devices

The types of devices that GDI supports can be divided into two categories: physical devices and pseudodevices. It's a useful distinction because it helps clarify the device-independent nature of the GDI. We'll now turn our attention to understanding the differences between these different types of devices.

Physical devices

From a programmatic point of view, there are only two basic physical devices: display screens and printers. When an application draws to the screen, it always draws inside a window. The window manager makes sure that one unruly window doesn't overstep its bounds and draw inside another window.

The GDI polices these boundaries by using a technique known as *clipping*. Clipping is the act of drawing boundaries. The most obvious and common boundaries are the borders of windows that the window manager oversees for you. You can create your own clipping regions as well. You might want to use this capability to fill in areas between drawings created by separate parts of an application without incurring the overhead of creating additional windows.

Spooling is another GDI technique that is used to enforce boundaries between drawings produced on the printer. Print jobs are stored, or spooled, until the printer is ready to receive them. Without spooling, the printer would intermingle pages of different print jobs.

When writing output to a printer, you must make special considerations. These include the size of the paper, the page orientation, and available fonts. You'll still use the same GDI functions to draw on the printer and the display screen.

Pseudodevices

Pseudodevices provide different ways of storing pictures. GDI has two types of pseudodevices: bitmaps and metafiles. When a pseudodevice is referred to, the fact that the operating system gives the same respect to these devices as it does to physical devices is what's being referred to. Outside of the RAM or disk space used to store them, bitmaps and metafiles have no associated hardware. That is to say, they are software simulations of logical devices.

Metafiles are lists of drawing calls. Bitmaps store the results of drawing calls while metafiles capture the drawing calls before any pixels are rendered. Think of a metafile as a recording of your program as it draws an image. Metafiles can also be "played back" to the screen to draw the image it stores.

As you've seen before, a bitmap is an array of data that represents a picture. In the same way you can use GDI functions to draw on the screen or to the printer, you can use GDI functions to draw on a bitmap. Even though a bitmap simulates a raster drawing, you aren't limited to using only the raster graphics calls. You can make any text, raster, or vector call to draw on a bitmap.

In this section you've been introduced to the vocabulary of the GDI. You should now understand how the GDI abstracts graphics operations, and how this simplifies Windows programming. The different types of drawing functions have been described and the two categories of devices were investigated. Before you're ready to draw images in Windows, you'll need to understand one more concept: the device context. That's the subject of the next section.

The Device Context

A device context — also known as a DC — is a data structure that the GDI creates to represent a device connection. For example, to draw on the display screen, a Windows program must have a DC for the display. And to create output on a printer, yet another DC is required — this one created specifically for the printer. If the same program also wants to create output in a metafile and a bitmap, a third and a fourth DC are required. The role of a DC, then, is to provide a connection between a program and either a physical device or a pseudodevice.

In addition to providing a device connection, a DC holds a collection of drawing attribute settings. For example, one drawing attribute in the DC is the text color. When a text drawing function is called, the function refers to the text color attribute to determine the correct color for the text.

You can change any drawing attribute at any time by calling specific GDI functions. For example, the `SetTextColor()` function sets the text color. For every attribute-setting function is a comparable attribute query function. For example, to find out the current text color settings, you call `GetTextColor()`.

DC drawing attributes

Table 9-1 summarizes the 25 attributes that the GDI stores in a DC. The table indicates which drawing attributes affect each of the three types of graphic objects. The Comments column provides details about default settings and how to change each attribute. The functions that are mentioned in Table 9-1 are member functions of `CDC`, the MFC class that wraps the GDI device context.

Table 9-1
Attributes of the GDI DC

Attribute	*Text*	*Raster*	*Vector*	*Comments*
Arc direction			X	Default is counterclockwise. Can be set with the function SetArcDirection() and constants AD_CLOCKWISE or AD_COUNTERCLOCKWISE.
Background color	X	X	X	Default is white. Used for the background of normal text, color to monochrome conversions, and for the background of styled pens and hatched brushes.
Background mode	X	X	X	Default is OPAQUE. Turns background color on (OPAQUE) or off (TRANSPARENT). Set by calling SetBkColor().
Bounds rectangle	X	X	X	Default is disabled. When enabled it tells GDI to keep track of the drawing area. Set by calling SetBoundsRect().
Brush		X	X	Default is white. Defines the interior color of closed figures.
Brush origin			X	Default is 0,0. Sets the point in device space to align a brush. Necessary for hatched and dithered brushes, because they can have misalignments.
Clipping region	X	X	X	Default is entire drawing surface. Defines drawing boundaries.
Color adjustment		X		Default is no adjustment. Defines the changes to bitmaps stretched by the functions StretchBlt() and StretchDIBits(). Set by calling SetColorAdjustments().
Current position	X		X	Default is 0,0. An *x,y* pair originally created to assist in line drawing. Enable for text by calling SetTextAlign() with the TA_UPDATECP flag. Set attribute by calling SetCurrentPosition().

Attribute	*Text*	*Raster*	*Vector*	*Comments*
Drawing mode			X	Default is `R2_COPYPEN`. Determines how Boolean operators are used when vector graphics are drawn. Set by calling `SetROP2()`.
Font	X			Default is system font. Determines which set of graphic figures are used for drawing text.
Graphics mode	X	X	X	Default is `GM_COMPATIBLE`. Determines whether GDI ignores world transform and other Win32 enhancements. Set by calling `SetGraphicsMode()`.
Mapping mode	X	X	X	Default is `MM_TEXT`. Controls much of coordinate mapping. In the default mode, one logical unit equals one device unit. Set by calling `SetMapMode()`.
Miter limit			X	Default is 10.0. Controls the "pointiness" in a join of a geometric line before capping off the corner.
Palette	X	X	X	Default is system palette. Supported only by certain devices, it gives applications control over how the physical color table, palette, is set.
Pen			X	Default is black pen. Used by vector graphics functions to draw the borders of geometric figures.
Polygon filling mode			X	Default is Alternate. Determines how the interior spaces of complex, overlapping polygons are to be filled.
`StretchBlt()` mode		X		Default is `BLACKONWHITE`. Determines how pixels are removed when a bitmap is shrunk using `StretchBlt()`. Set by calling `SetStretchBltMode()`.
Text alignment	X			Default is `TA_LEFT | TA_TOP`. Determines the alignment between text drawing coordinates and the resulting textbox. Set by calling `SetTextAlign()`.

(continued)

Table 9-1 (continued)

Attribute	*Text*	*Raster*	*Vector*	*Comments*
Text color	X			Default is black. Set by calling `SetTextColor()`.
Text extra spacing	X			Default is 0. Determines how many pixels are to be padded into each character cell in string. Set by calling `SetTextCharacterExtra()`.
Text justification	X			Default is 0,0. Determines how many pixels to pad into break characters, spaces, to pad a line of text to fill out a margin. Set by calling `SetTextJustification()`.
Viewport extent	X	X	X	Default is 1,1. Used with a mapping mode of `MM_ISOTROPIC` or `MM_ANISOTROPIC`. Helps scale a drawing by modifying the device coordinate side of the scaling ratio. Set by calling `SetViewportExt()`.
Viewport origin	X	X	X	Default is 0,0. Moves the origin around the device space. Set by calling `SetViewportOrg()`.
Window extent	X	X	X	Default is 1,1. Used with a mapping mode of `MM_ISOTROPIC` and `MM_ANISOTROPIC`. Scales a drawing by modifying the world side of the scaling ratio. Set by calling `SetWorldExt()`.
Window origin	X	X	X	Default is 0,0. Moves the origin around the world coordinate space. Set by calling `SetWindowOrg()`.

When you create a single or multiple document AppWizard program, you'll find a function in the view class named `OnDraw()`. This function is automatically created by the AppWizard. It receives a message every time your view window gets a `WM_PAINT` message (more about this message in the next section). A `CDC` class pointer is passed to the `OnDraw()` function. The `CDC` pointer can be used to draw to the view window. Listing 9-1 shows a simple `OnDraw()` function that draws a rectangle to the view window.

Listing 9-1: An OnDraw() Function Drawing a Rectangle

```
void CMyView::OnDraw(CDC* pDC)
{
  CMyDoc* pDoc = GetDocument();
  ASSERT_VALID(pDoc);

  // Here is where the code we add
  // to draw a rectangle begins.
  RECT Rect;
  Rect.left = Rect.top = 10;
  Rect.right = Rect.bottom = 100;

  // Create a red brush.
  // The RGB macro lets you specify
  // the R, G, and B color components
  // respectively. Their values range
  // from 0 to 255.
  CBrush Brush( RGB( 255, 0, 0 ) );

 // Draw to the window using the GDI
 // FillRect() function.
 pDC->FillRect( &Rect, &Brush );

}
```

The default DC settings provide a good starting place for drawing. The best way to learn about GDI drawing is by writing small programs that draw a few simple objects. As you begin to experiment with new drawing functions, you won't have to make many changes to DC attributes to get reasonable results. Once you have a clearer understanding of how various drawing functions work, you can begin to explore the role of individual drawing attributes.

The WM_PAINT message

For drawing in a window, the most important message is WM_PAINT. In simplest terms, this message asks a window to redraw its contents. You might get this message for many reasons. For example, another window might open on top of your window and overwrite its contents. Or a user might decide to unminimize a previously minimized window. Or you might get this message simply because your program is just starting up.

Whatever the reason for a window getting a WM_PAINT message, the system can't re-create the contents of a window's client area. The original Windows development team considered various ways that the system might be able to store window data. One possibility was to take a snapshot of a window before it was covered by other windows. The sheer amount of memory required for this approach made it an unworkable solution.

In the character-based world, a screen full of data can be stored in a tiny, 2K buffer. In the graphics world of Windows, however, a 256-color, 640 × 480 window needs 300K. With several applications running, a megabyte or more would be quickly eaten up. This was too high a price to pay for the first version of Windows, when system memory totaled only one megabyte! With Windows 98 targeted to run in 16 megabytes, a megabyte of window snapshots is still too much memory for too little benefit.

Even if memory wasn't a problem, however, another problem remains. If the system stores window snapshots and any part of a window's data changed, the cache would be worthless. In such a situation, the application would have to redraw the contents of the window anyway. As a result, all of the memory and all of the processor time spent saving the snapshot would be wasted.

The `WM_PAINT` message is the solution to the problem of keeping the state of a window up to date. Windows makes every application entirely responsible for maintaining the contents of its windows. The `WM_PAINT` message provides the mechanism by which the system tells you that it's time to refresh a window. All you have to do is make sure that your program retains whatever state information it needs for accomplishing this task.

Drawing coordinates

When a DC is first created, its default coordinates are pixel—or device—units. As needed, you can modify the entire coordinate system to use inches, centimeters, or printer point units. You can also arbitrarily scale your drawings using rubber sheet graphics. But the default units, which are used in this chapter, are device units. In DC attribute terms, this is known as the `MM_TEXT` mapping mode.

The default origin—that is, coordinate (0,0)—is located in the upper-left corner of the drawing surface. On the display screen, this means the upper-left corner of the window's client area. On the printed page, it means the upper-left corner of whatever would be the top of the page. Just as you can change the coordinate system, you can also change the location of the origin. For the examples in this chapter, though, the default origin is used.

The default direction of movement along the x and y axes is a little different from the Cartesian coordinate system you may have studied in school. In a window, the default coordinate system is called *client-area coordinates*. Because the same coordinates are used for mouse input, client-area coordinates make it easy to match mouse clicks to objects you've drawn in your window.

Triggering WM_PAINT

When we introduced the `WM_PAINT` message, it was described as the most important drawing message. We also noted that you can never know the cause of the message; your window might have changed size, or it might have been previously covered by another window. However, you don't really need to worry about the cause. You simply need to redraw whatever is in your window.

In some cases, however, the cause of a paint message isn't an external factor such as the user changing a window size. Instead, it's an internal factor that only you can recognize. For example, the user might have entered some additional text in a text input window. Or the user might have added or removed a column of data from a spreadsheet window. Whatever the internal cause, when the data represented in the window changes, you need to generate a paint message.

To generate a paint message, you declare that the contents of the window are invalid. You can do this by calling a few different `CWnd` member functions. Of these, `Invalidate()` is the simplest because it takes only a single parameter, a Boolean value that specifies whether to erase the background before drawing. This function declares the entire client area to be invalid:

```
// Force redraw of entire window-first erase contents.
Invalidate( TRUE );
```

Another function that generates paint messages is `InvalidateRect()`. This function enables you to identify the specific rectangle to be redrawn. On slower hardware, this helps minimize screen flicker. On any hardware, you'll want to be conservative when you request a redraw, because too much screen flicker can annoy users. From an ergonomic point of view, such flicker causes fatigue—which not only annoys users but forces them to take more frequent breaks than might otherwise be necessary when using your software. Here's how to request a paint message for a rectangle that's bounded by the coordinates 10, 10, and 100:

```
// Define invalid rectangle and request paint message.
CRect Rect( 10, 10, 100, 100 );
InvalidateRect( &Rect, TRUE );
```

Compared to other messages—for example, those that are associated with mouse or keyboard input—paint messages have a very low priority. After all, if more data comes in, additional paint messages might be necessary. When you declare a window to be invalid, the window might receive other messages before getting the `WM_PAINT` message.

In some cases, you need to raise the priority of a `WM_PAINT` message. To force an immediate paint message, you call `UpdateWindow()`. For example, you might need to do this if you've already called `Invalidate()` to request a redraw, but you also want to immediately draw on the updated window. It's not uncommon to declare part of a window invalid and then immediately force a paint message, as in:

```
InvalidateRect( &Rect, TRUE );
UpdateWindow();
```

To summarize, when you want the image in a window to be changed, you invalidate the area in which the change will be seen. This area will be drawn during a subsequent WM_PAINT message. The UpdateWindow() call does not declare part of a window to be invalid. It simply accelerates repainting for invalidated areas. If no area is invalid, calls to UpdateWindow() have no effect on the contents of a window. Windows' conservative paint policy limits the drawing — via clip rectangles — to only the part of a window that is invalid.

As mentioned previously, calling UpdateWindow() forces an immediate repaint so that you can draw over a valid window. However, this makes sense only if you're drawing in response to some other message besides WM_PAINT. Let's talk about how you'd do this, and explore some of the issues you must address.

Drawing outside WM_PAINT

In some cases, you need to draw in response to messages other than WM_PAINT. One school of thought suggests that you draw only when you get a paint message. This centralizes your drawing code, which helps to make it more robust. This is a worthwhile goal.

However, to enhance a program's performance or its interactivity for the user, you might need to draw in response to other messages. For example, consider a text-editing window. If such a program generated a paint message for every character typed, it would run very slowly (which would be particularly noticeable on slower systems). The overhead associated with continually creating paint messages would use too much processing time.

Or consider a drawing program that enables a user to pick up a graphic object and move it around a window. As the object is moved, it must be redrawn to show the user its new, tentative location. Once again, creating a paint message for each new location would create too much overhead. For both of these cases, you'll want to draw in response to other messages besides the paint message.

However, a word of caution is needed here. If you draw and erase a temporary object — for example, a stretchable rubber rectangle — there's no problem. But if you draw more permanent objects, your painting code has to know about those objects. After all, you don't know when a user will force a redraw of a window. All the user needs to do to make this happen is to minimize and then maximize your window. The same result occurs when another application's window is maximized over your window. When your application becomes the active application, you'll have to handle a paint message for your entire window. Any lack of synchronization between your paint and nonpaint drawing code will become painfully obvious to your users.

Setting aside these caveats and concerns, it's relatively easy to draw in response to other messages. Instead of using the CDC class, you use a CClientDC object. The clipping for a CClientDC is set to the entire client area of a window. For example, Listing 9-2 shows how to say "Hello Windows 98," which is centered under the cursor, when the user clicks the left mouse button.

Listing 9-2: Saying "Hello Windows 98" with the CClientDC Object

```
void CMyView::OnLButtonDown(UINT nFlags, CPoint point)
{
  // Create a CClientDC class.
  CClientDC ClientDC( this );

  // Create a CString object with the text.
  CString strText = "Hello Windows 98";

  // Get the size of this text string in terms of
  //this DC.
  CSize size =
  ClientDC.GetTextExtent(strText, strText.GetLength());

  // Calculate the coordinates to which we need to draw
  // in order to center the text about the mouse point.
  int xCentered = point.x - ( size.cx / 2 );
  int yCentered = point.y - ( size.cy / 2 );

  // Draw the text to the window.
  ClientDC.TextOut( xCentered, yCentered, strText );
}
```

So what have you learned so far? You've seen how to get a device context (DC) and draw a line of basic text to the display using the default DC attributes. While the DC defaults are reasonable and produce good results, you'll eventually want to control the attributes that affect the appearance of text. That's what is covered next.

Manipulating Text

To change the appearance of text, you change one of the DC attributes that affect text. As summarized in Table 9-1, eight attributes affect the appearance or the positioning of text. The most effective way to understand the changes that a DC attribute controls is to see the text change in a real program. If your computer is handy, you might consider generating a tiny SDI AppWizard program so that you can experiment with each attribute, as it is discussed.

GDI color support

Before you can change the color of text, you need to understand how to specify color in GDI. The basic Windows data type for holding color values is `COLORREF`. The easiest way to define colors is by using the `RGB()` macro, which takes three parameters that define the red, green, and blue color components. For each color component, you specify a value in the range 0–255. For example, here are three color values — one each for red, green, and blue:

```
COLORREF crRed   = RGB( 255, 0, 0 );
COLORREF crGreen = RGB( 0,255, 0 );
COLORREF crBlue  = RGB( 0, 0,255 );
```

Although this might seem fairly straightforward, a number of factors make this more complex than it first appears. In GDI, these types of color references are called *logical colors*. In this context, logical doesn't mean Boolean. Instead, this term is used to differentiate between logical colors and physical colors, which are the colors that a physical hardware device can actually display. A high-resolution, 16-million color device shouldn't have a problem displaying various combinations of red, green, and blue. But it's a different story for a black-and-white printer. How are these differences handled?

You should think about logical colors in terms of requests. If you request red and the device can produce red, you get what you asked for. If you request red and the device can't give you what you want, the device provides the closest possible match. That might mean black! To solve the problem of the black-and-white printer, you start by not asking for colors that aren't available. To find out the number of available colors, you call `CDC::GetDeviceCaps()`, as in:

```
int nColors = pDC->GetDeviceCaps( NUMCOLORS );
```

On color display screens, the system creates a default palette with 20 colors. For devices that support only 16 colors, only the first 16 of these 20 colors are used (the rest turn into white or gray). On devices that support more than 16 colors, these 20 form the default set that are available to applications. Listing 9-3 lists the standard RGB values for fetching these colors.

Listing 9-3: **Colors for Common Shades**

```
// 16-color device support
const COLORREF g_crBlack     = RGB( 0, 0, 0);
const COLORREF g_crYellow    = RGB(255,255, 0);
const COLORREF g_crDkYellow  = RGB(128,128, 0);
const COLORREF g_crRed       = RGB(255, 0, 0);
const COLORREF g_crDkRed     = RGB(128, 0, 0);
const COLORREF g_crMagenta   = RGB(255, 0,255);
const COLORREF g_crDkMagenta = RGB(128, 0,128);
const COLORREF g_crBlue      = RGB( 0, 0,255);
const COLORREF g_crDkBlue    = RGB( 0, 0,128);
const COLORREF g_crCyan      = RGB( 0,255,255);
const COLORREF g_crDkCyan    = RGB( 0,128,128);
const COLORREF g_crGreen     = RGB( 0,255, 0);
const COLORREF g_crDkGreen   = RGB( 0,128, 0);
const COLORREF g_crGray      = RGB(192,192,192);
const COLORREF g_crDkGray    = RGB(128,128,128);
const COLORREF g_crWhite     = RGB(255,255,255);
```

```
// Additional four colors for displays with more than
// 16 colors.
const COLORREF g_crLtYellow  = RGB(255,251,240);
const COLORREF g_crLtGreen   = RGB(192,220,192);
const COLORREF g_crLtBlue    = RGB(166,202,240);
const COLORREF g_crMedGray   = RGB(160,160,164);
```

On displays that support more than 16 colors, you can always define your own custom palette. When selected into a DC, this gives you access to a much wider range of colors. However, the use of alternate palettes is an advanced topic that is beyond the scope of this book. The default palette serves nicely for all but the most demanding applications.

Text color

Now that you know how to use the RGB macros to pick colors, let's look at the three DC attributes that affect text color. These attributes are: text color, background color, and background mode. When you first get a DC, it contains the following default settings for these three values as shown in Table 9-2.

Table 9-2
Default DC Settings

Text Color Attributes	*Default Setting*
Text color	`RGB (0,0,0)`: black text
Background color	`RGB(255,255,255)`: white background
Background mode	`OPAQUE`

To set the color that is to be used for drawing the foreground pixels of text, you call `CDC::SetTextColor()`. This function is defined as follows:

```
COLORREF SetTextColor( COLORREF crColor );
```

This function takes a color value as input and returns the previous text color setting. For example, here's how to get red text:

```
pDC->SetTextColor(RGB( 255, 0, 0 ) );
pDC->TextOut ( x, y, "This is red text" );
```

To set the color for background text pixels, call `CDC::SetBkColor()`. This function is defined as follows:

```
COLORREF SetBkColor( COLORREF crColor );
```

As you may have surmised, the background pixels are those that are inside the text box but not part of letter strokes. Here's how you set the background color to black:

```
pDC->SetBkColor(RGB( 0, 0, 0));
pDC->TextOut (x, y, "This text has a black
   background", 32);
```

The final DC attribute that affects the color of text is the background mode. It's basically an on/off toggle for the background mode. The default setting, `OPAQUE`, tells the GDI to use the background color. The alternate setting, `TRANSPARENT`, tells the GDI not to use the background color in drawing text. You set the background mode by calling `CDC::SetBkMode()`, which is defined as follows:

```
int SetBkMode( int nBkMode );
```

If you're interested in letting your users set the foreground or background colors, you'll probably want to use the Color Selector dialog. This is one of the common dialogs that is included as part of Windows 98. With just a few lines of code, you get a fully functioning dialog as follows:

```
CColorDialog ColorDialog;
if( ColorDialog.DoModal() == IDOK ){

  COLORREF Color = ColorDialog.GetColor();

  CString strText;
  strText.Format( "The selected color was RGB( %d, %d,
    %d )", GetRValue( Color ), GetGValue( Color ),
       GetBValue( Color ) );

  AfxMessageBox( strText );
  }
```

Aligning text

Text alignment describes the relationship between the (x,y) text coordinates and the textbox. The default setting aligns the text below and to the right of the text coordinate. To set the text alignment, you call `CDC::SetTextAlign()`. This function takes a single parameter, a combination of the flags listed in Table 9-1. The flags in each column are mutually exclusive — that is, you take one flag from each column. The first row of Table 9-3 lists the default settings, which are in **bold**.

Table 9-3
Text Alignment Constants

Y-Axis Alignment	*X-Axis Alignment*	*Update Current Position*
TA_LEFT	**TA_TOP**	**TA_NOUPDATECP**
TA_CENTER	TA_BASELINE	TA_UPDATECP
TA_RIGHT	TA_BOTTOM	

You might want to change the default settings if you're going to mix text of different sizes (or even the same size and different fonts) on the same line. The y-axis default alignment, TA_TOP, would yield strange results if you didn't adjust the y-axis values yourself. Here's how you set the text alignment to accommodate multifont drawing:

```
pDC->SetTextAlign( TA_LEFT | TA_BASELINE );
```

It's also convenient to change the text alignment when you are trying to align the right side of text with another graphic object. Although you could tinker with the x-axis value, it's easier to set the alignment as follows:

```
pDC->SetTextAlign( TA_RIGHT | TA_TOP );
```

Another situation in which you might want to change the text alignment is when you want to use the DC's current position value for text. The current position is a (x,y) coordinate pair that's typically used for vector graphics. However, you can use it for text when you set the `TA_UPDATECP` flag:

```
pDC->SetTextAlign( TA_UPDATECP );
```

With this setting, the only coordinates used for text drawing are at the current position. As each line of text is drawn, the position is updated so it's ready for the next text. You set the current position by calling `CDC::MoveTo()`. Because it uses the `TA_UPDATECP` flag, the following code draws its text at 12,92 instead of at the coordinates specified in the `TextOut()` call:

```
// Request that text drawing use current position.
pDC->SetTextAlign( TA_UPDATECP );

// Set current value of current position.
pDC->MoveTo( 12, 92 );

// Even though coordinates are specified here, they are
// ignored.
pDC->TextOut( 100, 200, "This text is not drawn at
 100,200", 33 );
```

Justifying text

There are two final text attributes in the basic set: text justification and text extra spacing. Each of these helps you pad out lines of text. You'll pad out text lines to produce WYSIWYG (what-you-see-is-what-you-get) output. For the most part, this means that you tweak the display screen output to mimic the printed output.

To adjust the settings of these two attributes, you call `CDC::SetTextJustification()` and `CDC::SetTextCharacterExtra()`, respectively. `SetTextJustification()` enables you to specify the number of pixels to add to each space character. This setting represents additional room beyond what the font would normally use for spaces. If even more padding is needed, you call `SetTextCharacterExtra()` instead of `SetTextJustification()`. `SetTextCharacterExtra()` adds extra pixels to every character (not just the space characters).

We should mention that these two drawing attributes date back to the very first version of Windows and that other techniques for accomplishing the same results have since been added to Windows. For example, the `ExtTextOut()` function gives you complete control over the width of individual character cells. If you can take the time for the extra work it requires, it's well worth the results. The addition of TrueType fonts to Windows has also cut down on the differences between display screen fonts and printer fonts. An application that exclusively uses TrueType fonts can get reasonably close to WYSIWYG output with little or no character cell padding.

All the basic text attributes were covered first because they are the simplest. The following section directs your attention to the text attribute that has the greatest effect on the appearance of text — the font.

About Fonts

This section covers the basics for creating and using fonts. The easiest approach for working with fonts is to use the GDI's stock fonts. But to access a broader range of fonts that are installed in a typical Windows system, you'll need to create a `CFont` object.

What is a font?

A font is a collection of complex graphical images, of a single size and design, that are used to represent character data. Fonts are commonly identified by point size and by name, such as Arial or Times Roman, and perhaps also by style. To refer to specific fonts, such terms as 18-point Times Roman or 8-point bold Arial are used.

If you've never been exposed to the world of fonts, it can be quite a shock to learn that literally thousands of different fonts are available. Windows 98 ships with a basic set of fonts, but numerous font packs are sold to add to this set. And it's not at all uncommon for Windows applications to include even more fonts. For example, Corel Corporation's CorelDraw application ships with more than 800 fonts.

Before delving into customizing different display fonts, you need to understand how different graphic objects are used within a device context. This process is called *selecting* an object into (or out of) a DC.

Selecting devices into DCs

Any time you select a nonstock object in a DC, it's a good idea to remember what object was previously selected into the DC. You always get a pointer to the object when you use the `SelectObject()` function. For instance, if you use the `SelectObject()` function to select a newly created font into the DC, a pointer to a `CFont` object is returned. You can record the font that was selected into the DC before you selected your nonstock font in the following way:

```
CFont *pOldFont;
pOldFont = pDC->SelectObject( &NewFont );
```

After you're done using the nonstock font (or any other GDI object for that matter), you must select the old object back into the DC. If your newly created GDI object is still selected into the DC when you try to delete it (or the object's destructor tries to delete it), the deletion fails, and the memory that the GDI object occupies is locked until your application quits. Following is the final line that you should add once you're done drawing with the nonstock GDI object:

```
pDC->SelectObject( pOldFont );
```

Selecting stock fonts

To select a font, you start by getting your hands on one. In an MFC program, this means having a properly initialized `CFont` object. The simplest way to get a font is to use one of the predefined stock fonts that Windows provides. The following example shows how to get one of the stock fonts:

```
CFont fontStock;
fontStock.CreateStockObject( ANSI_FIXED_FONT );
```

Like every other drawing attribute, a font must be connected to a DC before it affects the appearance of any output. To connect a font to a DC, you call `CDC::SelectObject()`. For example, this code fragment connects the font that we just created to a DC:

```
pDC->SelectObject( &fontStock );
```

Until we select a different font into the DC, all text that we draw is formatted in this font.

Fonts differ from other drawing attributes in an important way. Most attributes are simply numbers that are stored in the DC. Within the system, however, a font is its own object, and it has its own life separate from the DC. For every font object that you create, you need to make sure that you destroy the object when you're done using it. Otherwise, space is wasted somewhere.

In practical terms, this means simply making sure that you destroy every `CFont` object that you create. The destructor to this class helps you make sure that no system memory is wasted. But how do you catch those `CFont` objects that you forget to delete? Fortunately, the Visual C++ tools can help you catch them. Just run the debug build of your program in the debugger that's built into the Visual C++ development environment. When the program shuts down, you'll see a laundry list of objects that haven't been properly cleaned up.

Stock fonts aren't actually cleaned up even when you delete their `CFont` wrapper. The reason is that the system created those fonts for everyone to use.

Selecting nonstock fonts

To select a font other than a stock font, you have to submit a font request to the GDI. One way to represent a font request is with the `LOGFONT`—logical font—data structure. To submit a font request to the GDI, you fill in this data structure and pass it to a `CFont` initialization function, `CFont::CreateFontIndirect()`. The term "Indirect" in this function name refers to the fact that the function takes a pointer parameter. Another initialization function, `CFont::CreateFont()`, takes a series of parameters that, when taken together, match `LOGFONT`.

A logical font is a lot like the logical color described earlier in this chapter when setting text color was discussed. A logical font represents a logical request that the GDI and the device driver use to figure out which specific physical font to use. In the same way that you can ask for red and get black, you might ask for 24-point Times New Roman and get 12-point Courier.

The simplest solution would be to always use the device default. A font that you can create using a stock font always provides the device default. It is generally a 10- or 12-point device font. Or limit your choices to the dozen or so fonts that are built into Windows 98. This is the same general solution that we applied to the red-black color mismatch: don't ask for something that the system doesn't have. Listing 9-4 shows you how to create and use a font in a program's `OnDraw()` function.

Listing 9-4: Using the OnDraw() Function to Create and Use a Font

```
void CFrameView::OnDraw(CDC* pDC)
{
  CFrameDoc* pDoc = GetDocument();
  ASSERT_VALID(pDoc);

  // Create a CFont object, then create the
  // font with the CreateFont() function.
  CFont NewFont;
  NewFont.CreateFont( 45, 45,
    0, 0, FW_DONTCARE,
    FALSE, FALSE, FALSE,
    DEFAULT_CHARSET,
    OUT_CHARACTER_PRECIS, CLIP_CHARACTER_PRECIS,
    DEFAULT_QUALITY, DEFAULT_PITCH | FF_DONTCARE,
    "Times New Roman" );

  // Select the newly created font into the
  // DC and remember the old font so that
  // we can restore it later.
  CFont *pOldFont;
  pOldFont = pDC->SelectObject( &NewFont );

  // Draw the text.
  pDC->TextOut( 10, 10, "Hello Fonts!" );

  // Select the old font back into the DC.
  pDC->SelectObject( pOldFont );

}
```

The `CreateFont()` function expects a lot of parameters. An explanation of the `CreateFont()` parameters follows.

The first parameter is the height. It specifies the desired height (in logical units) of the font. The font height can be specified as a value greater than 0, in which case the height is transformed into device units and matched against the cell height of the available fonts. It can be equal to 0, in which case a reasonable (or average) default size is used. Otherwise, it can be less than 0, in which case the height is transformed into device units and the absolute value is matched against the character height of the available fonts. The absolute value of `nHeight` must not exceed 16,384 device units after it is converted. For all height comparisons, the font mapper looks for the largest font that does not exceed the requested size or the smallest font if all the fonts exceed the requested size.

The second parameter is the width. It specifies the average width (in logical units) of characters in the font. If the width is 0, the aspect ratio of the device is matched against the digitization aspect ratio of the available fonts to find the closest match, which is determined by the absolute value of the difference.

The third parameter is the font's escapement. It specifies the angle (in 0.1-degree units) between the escapement vector and the *x* axis of the display surface. The escapement vector is the line through the origins of the first and last characters on a line. The angle is measured counterclockwise from the *x* axis.

The fourth parameter is the font's orientation. It specifies the angle (in 0.1-degree units) between the baseline of a character and the *x* axis. The angle is measured counterclockwise from the *x* axis for coordinate systems in which the *y* direction is down, and clockwise from the *x* axis for coordinate systems in which the *y* direction is up.

The fifth parameter is the font's weight. It specifies the font weight (in inked pixels per 1,000). Although `nWeight` can be any integer value from 0 to 1,000, the common constants can be as follows:

```
FW_DONTCARE
FW_THIN
FW_EXTRALIGHT
FW_ULTRALIGHT
FW_LIGHT
FW_NORMAL
FW_REGULAR
FW_MEDIUM
FW_SEMIBOLD
FW_DEMIBOLD
FW_BOLD
FW_EXTRABOLD
FW_ULTRABOLD
FW_BLACK
FW_HEAVY
```

These values are approximate; the actual appearance depends on the typeface. Some fonts have only `FW_NORMAL`, `FW_REGULAR`, and `FW_BOLD` weights. If `FW_DONTCARE` is specified, a default weight is used.

The sixth parameter is a Boolean value that specifies whether the font is italic, the seventh parameter is a Boolean value that specifies whether the font is underlined, and the eighth parameter is a Boolean value that specifies whether characters in the font are struck out.

The ninth parameter specifies the font's character set. The predefined constants that can be used are:

```
ANSI_CHARSET
DEFAULT_CHARSET
SYMBOL_CHARSET
SHIFTJIS_CHARSET
OEM_CHARSET
```

The OEM character set is system dependent. Fonts with other character sets may exist in the system. An application that uses a font with an unknown character set must not attempt to translate or interpret strings that are to be rendered with that font. Instead, the strings should be passed directly to the output device driver. The font mapper does not use the `DEFAULT_CHARSET` value. An application can use this value to enable the name and size of a font to fully describe the logical font. If a font with the specified name does not exist, a font from any character set can be substituted for the specified font. To avoid unexpected results, applications should use the `DEFAULT_CHARSET` value sparingly.

The tenth parameter specifies the desired output precision. The output precision defines how closely the output must match the requested font's height, width, character orientation, escapement, and pitch. The values it can be are as follows:

```
OUT_CHARACTER_PRECIS
OUT_STRING_PRECIS
OUT_DEFAULT_PRECIS
OUT_STROKE_PRECIS
OUT_DEVICE_PRECIS
OUT_TT_PRECIS
OUT_RASTER_PRECIS
```

Applications can use the `OUT_DEVICE_PRECIS`, `OUT_RASTER_PRECIS`, and `OUT_TT_PRECIS` values to control how the font mapper chooses a font when the system contains more than one font with a given name. For example, if a system contains a font named Symbol in raster and TrueType form, specifying `OUT_TT_PRECIS` forces the font mapper to choose the TrueType version. (Specifying `OUT_TT_PRECIS` forces the font mapper to choose a TrueType font whenever the specified font name matches a device or raster font, even when there is no TrueType font of the same name.)

The eleventh parameter specifies the desired clipping precision. The clipping precision defines how to clip characters that are partially outside the clipping region. The values it can be are as follows:

CLIP_CHARACTER_PRECIS

CLIP_MASK

CLIP_DEFAULT_PRECIS

CLIP_STROKE_PRECIS

CLIP_ENCAPSULATE

CLIP_TT_ALWAYS

CLIP_LH_ANGLES

To use an embedded read-only font, an application must specify CLIP_ENCAPSULATE. To achieve consistent rotation of device, TrueType, and vector fonts, an application can use the OR operator to combine the CLIP_LH_ANGLES value with any of the other clip precision values. If the CLIP_LH_ANGLES bit is set, the rotation for all fonts depends on whether the orientation of the coordinate system is left-handed or right-handed. For more information about the orientation of coordinate systems, see the description of the orientation parameter. If CLIP_LH_ANGLES is not set, device fonts always rotate counterclockwise, but the rotation of other fonts is dependent on the orientation of the coordinate system.

The twelfth parameter specifies the font's output quality, which defines how carefully the GDI must attempt to match the logical font attributes to those of an actual physical font. The values it can be are DEFAULT_QUALITY, DRAFT_QUALITY, and PROOF_QUALITY.

The thirteenth parameter specifies the pitch and family of the font. The two low-order bits specify the pitch of the font and can be a combination of either DEFAULT_PITCH, VARIABLE_PITCH, or FIXED_PITCH and FF_DECORATIVE, FF_DONTCARE, FF_MODERN, FF_ROMAN, FF_SCRIPT, or FF_SWISS. An application can specify a value for the pitch and family by using the Boolean OR operator to join a pitch constant with a family constant. Font families describe the look of a font in a general way. They are intended for specifying fonts when the exact typeface desired is not available.

The fourteenth and final parameter is a pointer to a null-terminated string that specifies the typeface name of the font. The length of this string must not exceed 30 characters. The Windows EnumFontFamilies() function can be used to enumerate all currently available fonts. If this parameter is NULL, the GDI uses a device-independent typeface.

Pens and Brushes

GDI provides a number of API functions an application can call to create custom pens and brushes, including `CreatePen()`, `CreateSolidBrush()`, `CreateHatchBrush()`, and `CreatePatternBrush()`. MFC wraps these functions in the `CPen` and `CBrush` classes so pens and brushes can be dealt with as objects rather than through the raw handles that GDI provides.

Pens

MFC represents pens with objects of the class `CPen`. The simplest way to create a GDI pen is to construct a `CPen` object and pass it the parameters that define the pen as follows:

```
CPen Pen( PS_SOLID, 1, RGB( 255, 0, 0 ) );
```

A second way to create a GDI pen is to construct an uninitialized `CPen` object and call `CPen::CreatePen()` as follows:

```
CPen Pen;
Pen.CreatePen( PS_SOLID, 1, RGB( 255, 0, 0 ) );
```

A third method is to construct an uninitialized `CPen` object, fill in a `LOGPEN` structure describing the pen, and then call `CPen::CreatePenIndirect()` to create the pen as follows:

```
CPen Pen;
LOGPEN LogPen;
LogPen.lopnStype = PS_SOLID;
LogPen.lopnWidth = 1;
LogPen.lpenColor = RGB( 255, 0, 0 );
Pen.CreatePenIndirect( &LogPen );
```

`CreatePen()` and `CreatePenIndirect()` return `TRUE` if a pen is successfully created, `FALSE` if it is not. If you enable the object's constructor to create the pen, an exception of type `CResourceException` is thrown if the pen can't be created. This should happen only if the system is critically low on memory.

A pen has three defining characteristics: style, width, and color. All three of these examples create a pen whose style is `PS_SOLID`, whose width is 1 logical unit, and whose color is bright red. The first of the three parameters passed to the `CPen` constructor, `CreatePen()` or `CreatePenIndirect()`, specifies the pen style, which defines the type of line the pen draws. `PS_SOLID` creates a pen that draws solid, unbroken lines. The other pen styles are listed in Table 9-4.

Table 9-4
Pen Styles

Style	*Description*
PS_SOLID	Solid pen
PS_DASH	Creates a dashed pen. This style is only valid with pen widths of 1 device unit or less.
PS_DOT	Creates a dotted pen. This style is valid only with pen widths of 1 device unit or less.
PS_DASHDOT	Creates a pen with alternating dashes and dots. Valid only with pen widths of 1 device unit or less.
PS_DASHDOTDOT	Creates a pen with an alternating pattern of one dash and two dots. Valid only with pen widths of 1 device unit or less.
PS_NULL	NULL pen
PS_INSIDEFRAME	Creates a pen that draws a line inside the frame of closed shapes created by GDI functions that specify a bounding rectangle.

The NULL pen draws nothing. Why would you ever want to create a NULL pen? Believe it or not, a NULL pen comes in handy at times. Suppose you want to draw a solid red circle with no border. If you draw the circle with MFC's CDC::Ellipse() function, Windows automatically borders the circle with the pen currently selected into the device context. You can't tell the Ellipse() function you don't want a border, but you can select a NULL pen into the device context so that the circle does not have a visible border. NULL brushes are used in a similar way. If you wanted the circle to have a border but wanted the interior of the circle to be transparent, you could select a NULL brush into the device context before doing your drawing.

The second parameter passed into CPen's pen-create functions specifies the pen width — the width of the lines the pen will draw. Pen widths are specified in logical units whose physical meanings depend on the mapping mode. You can create PS_SOLID, PS_NULL, and PS_INSIDEFRAME pens of any logical width. But the other pen styles must be one logical unit in width. Specifying a pen width of zero in any style creates a pen that is one pixel in width, no matter what the mapping mode.

The third and final parameter specified when a pen is created is the pen's color. This is a 24-bit RGB color in which each possible color is defined by red, green, and blue color values ranging from 0 to 255.

Windows predefines three special solid, 1-pixel-wide pens you can use without explicitly creating a pen object. Called *stock pens*, these pens belong to a group of GDI objects know as *stock objects* and are created with the CreateStockObject().

The stock pens that are available are defined as WHITE_PEN, BLACK_PEN, and NULL_PEN. The following code creates a stock white pen:

```
CPen Pen;
Pen.CreateStockObject( WHITE_PEN );
```

The following code creates an identical white pen that's not a stock object:

```
CPen Pen;
Pen.CreatePen( PS_SOLID, 1, RGB( 255, 255, 255 ) );
```

In case none of the basic pen styles fits your needs, the CPen class provides a separate constructor for cosmetic and geometric pens that support a wide variety of styling options. You can create a geometric pen, for example, that draws a pattern described by a bitmap image, and you can exercise precise control over endpoints and joins by specifying the end cap style (flat, round, or square) and join style (beveled, mitered, or rounded). The following code creates a geometric pen 16 units wide and draws green solid lines with flat ends. Where two lines meet, the adjoining ends are rounded to form a smooth intersection:

```
LOGBRUSH LogBrush;
LogBrush.lbStyle = BS_SOLID;
LogBrush.lbColor = RGB( 0, 255, 0 );
CPen Pen( PS_GEOMETRIC | PS_SOLID | PS_ENDCAP_FLAT |
  PS_JOIN_ROUND,16, &LogBrush );
```

Windows 98 places several restrictions on the use of cosmetic and geometric pens, not the least of which is that for the endpoint and join styles to work, figures must first be drawn to paths and then rendered with the CDC::StrokePath() function. You define a path by enclosing drawing commands between calls to CDC::BeginPath() and CDC:EndPath() functions as follows:

```
pDC->BeginPath();
pDC->MoveTo( 0, 0 );
pDC->LineTo( 200, 0 );
pDC->LineTo( 200, 200 );
pDC->LineTo( 0, 200 );
pDC->CloseFigure();
pDC->EndPath();
pDC->StrokePath();
```

Brushes

MFC's CBrush class encapsulates GDI brushes. Brushes come in three basic varieties: solid brushes, hatch brushes, and pattern brushes. Solid brushes paint with solid colors. If your display hardware won't enable a particular solid brush color to be displayed directly, Windows simulates the color by dithering colors that can be displayed. A hatch brush paints with one of six predefined hatch styles modeled after hatching patterns used in engineering and architectural drawings. A pattern brush paints with a bitmap. The CBrush class provides a constructor for each different brush style. You can create a solid brush in one step by passing a COLORRREF value to the CBrush constructor as follows:

```
CBrush Brush( RGB( 255, 0, 0 ) );
```

Or you can create a solid brush in two steps by creating an uninitialized CBrush object and calling CBrush::CreateSolidBrush() as follows:

```
CBrush Brush;
Brush.CreateSolidBrush( RGB( 255, 0, 0 ) );
```

Both examples create a solid brush that paints bright red. You can also create a brush by initializing a LOGBRUSH structure and calling CBrush::CreateBrushIndirect(). As with CPen constructors, all CBrush constructors that create a brush throw a resource exception if GDI is critically low on memory and a brush can't be created.

Hatch brushes are created by passing CBrush's constructor both a hatch index and a COLORREF value or by calling Cbrush::CreateHatchBrushIndirect(). Following is an example that creates a hatch brush with perpendicular crosshatch lines that are oriented at 45 degree angles:

```
CBrush Brush( HS_DIAGCROSS, RGB( 255, 0, 0 ) );
```

The next example creates the same hatch brush in two steps:

```
CBrush Brush;
Brush.CreateHatchBrush( HS_DIAGCROSS, RGB( 255, 0, 0 ) );
```

HS_DIAGCROSS is one of six hatch styles you can choose from. Table 9-5 lists all six hatch styles that are available.

Table 9-5
Hatch Styles

Hatch Style	*Description*
HS_BDIAGONAL	Downward hatch (left to right) at 45 degrees
HS_CROSS	Horizontal and vertical crosshatch
HS_DIAGCROSS	Crosshatch as 45 degrees
HS_FDIAGONAL	Update hatch (left to right) at 45 degrees
HS_HORIZONTAL	Horizontal hatch
HS_VERTICAL	Vertical hatch

When painting with a hatch brush, Windows fills the space between hatch lines with the default background color unless you change the device context's current background color with `CDC::SetBkColor()`, or turn off background fills by changing the background mode from `OPAQUE` to `TRANSPARENT` with `CDC::SetBkMode()`. The following example draws a rectangle 100 units square and fills it with white crosshatch lines drawn against a light gray background:

```
CBrush Brush( HS_DIAGCROSS, RGB( 255, 255, 255 ) );
CBrush *pOldBrush;
pOldBrush = pDC->SelectObject( &Brush );
pDC->SetBkColor( RGB( 192, 192, 192 ) );
pDC->Rectangle( 0, 0, 100, 100 );
pDC->SelectObject( pOldBrush );
```

The next example draws a black crosshatched rectangle against the existing background. The background color mode also determines how Windows fills the gaps in lines drawn with stylized pens and fills between the characters in text strings:

```
CBrush Brush( HS_DIAGCROSS, RGB( 0, 0, 0 ) );
CBrush *pOldBrush
pOldBrush = pDC->SelectObject( &Brush );
pDC->SetBkMode( TRANSPARENT );
pDC->Rectangle( 0, 0, 100, 100 );
pDC->SelectObject( pOldBrush );
```

Windows makes seven stock brushes available:

```
BLACK_BRUSH
DKGRAY_BRUSH
GRAY_BRUSH
LTGRAY_BRUSH
HOLLOW_BRUSH
NULL_BRUSH
WHITE_BRUSH
```

All are solid brushes, and in each case, the identifier is an accurate indicator of the brush's color. `HOLLOW_BRUSH` and `NULL_BRUSH` are two different ways of referring to the same thing: a brush that paints nothing.

Mapping Modes

When an application draws a line from point A to point B, the coordinates passed to `MoveTo()` and `LineTo()` don't specify physical locations on the screen. Instead, they specify coordinates within a logical coordinate system whose properties are defined by the device context. The GDI translates logical coordinates into physical coordinates on the screen, or device coordinates, using equations that factor in the current mapping mode as well as other attributes of the device context.

In the device coordinate system, the point (0, 0) corresponds to the upper-left corner of the device context's display surface, values of *x* and *y* increase as you move to the right and down, and one device unit equals one pixel. In a logical coordinate system, the point (0, 0) defaults to the upper-left corner of the display surface but can be moved, and the orientation of the *x* and *y* axes and the physical distance that corresponds to one unit in the *x* or *y* direction are governed by the mapping mode. You can change the mapping mode with the `CDC::SetMapMode()` function, and you can move the origin of a logical coordinate system with the `CDC:SetViewportOrg()` and `CDC::SetWindowOrg()` functions. Windows supports eight different mapping modes. They are summarized in Table 9-6.

Table 9-6
Mapping Modes

Mapping Mode	*Description*
`MM_ISOTROPIC`	Logical units are converted to arbitrary units with equally scaled axes; that is, 1 unit along the *x*-axis is equal to 1 unit along the *y*-axis. Use the `SetWindowExt` and `SetViewportExt` member functions to specify the desired units and the orientation of the axes. The GDI makes adjustments as necessary to ensure that the *x* and *y* units remain the same size.
`MM_ANISOTROPIC`	Logical units are converted to arbitrary units with arbitrarily scaled axes. Setting the mapping mode to `MM_ANISOTROPIC` does not change the current window or viewport settings. To change the units, orientation, and scaling, call the `SetWindowExt` and `SetViewportExt` member functions.
`MM_HIENGLISH`	Each logical unit is converted to 0.001 inch. Positive *x* is to the right; positive *y* is up.
`MM_LOENGLISH`	Each logical unit is converted to 0.01 inch. Positive *x* is to the right; positive *y* is up.
`MM_HIMETRIC`	Each logical unit is converted to 0.01 millimeter. Positive *x* is to the right; positive *y* is up.
`MM_LOMETRIC`	Each logical unit is converted to 0.1 millimeter. Positive *x* is to the right; positive *y* is up.
`MM_TEXT`	Each logical unit is converted to 1 device pixel. Positive *x* is to the right; positive *y* is down.
`MM_TWIPS`	Each logical unit is converted to 1/20 of a point. (Because a point is 1/72 inch, a twip is 1/1440 inch; however, compare "Font point size" under "Raster Operations" below.) Positive *x* is to the right; positive *y* is up.

The default MM_TEXT mapping mode is the easiest of all the mapping modes to understand because in that mode, logical coordinates translate directly to device coordinates: one logical unit in the *x* or *y* direction equals one pixel on the screen, and values of *x* and *y* increase as you move right and down. In MM_TEXT, as in all of the other mapping modes, the origin of the logical coordinate system coincides with the origin of the device coordinate system unless it is moved with CDC::SetWindowOrg() or CDC::SetViewportOrg(). For a client-area device context, this means that the pixel in the upper-left corner of the window's client area initially has the logical coordinates (0, 0).

If you'd prefer that the origin of the coordinate system be in the center of the display surface rather than in the upper-left corner, you can move it with CDCLSetWindowOrg() or CDC::SetViewportOrg(). This option applies to all mapping modes, not just MM_TEXT. If you use CWnd::GetClientRect() to initialize a CRect object named Rect with the device coordinates of a window's client area and the DC represents a client-area device context, the following example moves the origin of the coordinate system to the center of the client area:

```
CRect Rect;
GetClientRect( Rect );
pDC->SetViewportOrg( Rect.Width() / 2,
  Rect.Height() / 2 );
```

Raster Operations

One thing you can do is change how the draw color combines with the destination. Most of the time, though, drawing to the screen so it appears exactly as you'd expect is what you'll want. For instance, if you draw a red circle, 99 percent of the time you'll want a red circle to be drawn. At other times, a simple draw operation won't do.

You might want to use another raster operation, for example, in some animations. A common technique for moving figures around on the screen is to XOR them before moving them to a new location. That is, you'd set to an XOR operation, then draw the figure where it currently is. XORing one figure over itself completely removes it. That's because when you first draw the figure to the screen using an XOR raster operation, the image source combines with the destination. Anywhere the source has a bit that's set toggles the corresponding bit in the destination to its opposite value. For instance, if the source bit is set (a one) and the destination bit is not set (a zero), the result is a one. If the animation must be moved, XORing the same figure in the same location toggles those same bits, once again restoring them to their original state. The bitmap can then be drawn in a new location using an XOR raster operation. The raster operation codes are defined in Table 9-7.

Table 9-7
Raster Operation Codes

Raster Operation	*Description*
R2_WHITE	Pixel is always white.
R2_BLACK	Pixel is always black.
R2_NOP	Pixel remains unchanged.
R2_NOT	Pixel is the inverse of the screen color.
R2_COPYPEN	Pixel is the pen color.
R2_NOTCOPYPEN	Pixel is the inverse of the pen color.
R2_MERGEPENNOT	Pixel is a combination of the pen color and the inverse of the screen color (final pixel = (NOT screen pixel) OR pen).
R2_MASKPENNOT	Pixel is a combination of the colors common to both the pen and the inverse of the screen (final pixel = (NOT screen pixel) AND pen).
R2_MERGENOTPEN	Pixel is a combination of the screen color and the inverse of the pen color (final pixel = (NOT pen) OR screen pixel).
R2_MASKNOTPEN	Pixel is a combination of the colors common to both the screen and the inverse of the pen (final pixel = (NOT pen) AND screen pixel).
R2_MERGEPEN	Pixel is a combination of the pen color and the screen color (final pixel = pen OR screen pixel).
R2_NOTMERGEPEN	Pixel is the inverse of the R2_MERGEPEN color (final pixel = NOT(pen OR screen pixel)).
R2_MASKPEN	Pixel is a combination of the colors common to both the pen and the screen (final pixel = pen AND screen pixel).
R2_NOTMASKPEN	Pixel is the inverse of the R2_MASKPEN color (final pixel = NOT(pen AND screen pixel)).
R2_XORPEN	Pixel is a combination of the colors that are in the pen or in the screen, but not in both (final pixel = pen XOR screen pixel).
R2_NOTXORPEN	Pixel is the inverse of the R2_XORPEN color (final pixel = NOT(pen XOR screen pixel)).

Text drawing functions

As summarized in Table 9-8, the GDI provides five text-drawing functions.

Table 9-8
GDI Text Drawing Functions

Function	*Description*
DrawText()	Provides some text formatting while text is drawn. Among the 14 flags that set draw options, some control text alignment (for example, left, right, center, top). Another flag requests that tab characters be expanded to tab stops, and the DT_WORDBREAK flag requests enabling of word wrapping to produce multiple lines of text output.
ExtTextOut()	Draws a single line of text with three added features. First, you can specify a clipping rectangle to limit text to an arbitrary rectangle. Second, you can specify an opaque rectangle, which involves filling in a rectangle with the background text color. And third, you can control the spacing of characters by providing an array of character cell width values.
GrayString()	Creates mottled text, like that used in menus to show a disabled menu item.
TabbedTextOut()	Draws a line of text, just like TextOut(). The only difference is that you can define an array of tab stop positions for the support of tab characters.
TextOut()	Draws a single line of text.

To draw a single line of text, the easiest function to call is CDC::TextOut(). This function is defined in two different ways:

```
BOOL TextOut( int x, int y, LPCTSTR lpszString,
  int nCount);
```

and

```
BOOL TextOut( int x, int y, const CString& strText );
```

For the TextOut() function, *x* and *y* are coordinates for positioning the text string. By default, text hangs below and to the right of this point. The lpszString parameter is a pointer to a character string. The fourth parameter, nCount, is the count of characters in the string. strText is a CString, which therefore contains both character string and string length information about the text that is to be drawn. Here's an example of a WM_PAINT handling function that calls TextOut() to display the text "Hello Windows 98" at location (100,100):

```
void CMyView::OnFunction ()
{
  CClientDC ClientCD( this );
  LPCTSTR lpszText = "Hello Windows 98";
  ClientDC.TextOut( 100, 100, lpszText, strlen( lpszText ) );
}
```

Here's the same function, rewritten for the second form of `TextOut()`:

```
void CMyView::OnFunction()
{
 CClientDC ClientDC( this );
 CString strText = "Hello Windows 98";
 ClientDC.TextOut( 100, 100, strText );
}
```

When specifying drawing coordinates in GDI drawing functions such as `TextOut()`, remember that Windows 98 recognizes only 16 bits of significance. Even though you might pass a 32-bit integer value, the GDI under Windows 98 operates in only 16 bits (just like the GDI did under Windows 3.*x*). Under Windows NT, however, all 32 bits of precision are recognized and supported. Unless you want your programs to run only on Windows NT, limit the range of your drawing coordinates to those that fit in 16-bit integers.

`CDC::TextOut()` draws a single line of text. In many cases, however, you want to draw multiple lines of text, which requires several calls to `TextOut()` with different coordinates for each call. Unlike text drawing in a character-oriented environment, drawing coordinates in the GDI are something other than character cells (for now, pixels). To properly space the text that's drawn by different calls, you need to do some text coordinate calculation. This subject is explored in the following section.

♦ ♦ ♦ ♦ ♦

Text coordinate calculations

The GDI provides several functions that are useful in the calculation of text coordinates. You need to use this set of functions because the spacing of text strings depends not only on the font specified by the user, but on the resolution of the target device. Before drawing any text, you need to ask the GDI for the required text coordinate values.

Table 9-9 lists some of the GDI's more useful text measurement functions. To help you understand these functions, let's take a look at some of their more common uses. The discussion starts with how to calculate point size, a common concern when working with text. Then how to get to the next string—whether it's on the same line as the current string, or the next line—is described. The last text coordinate topic is centering a line of text around a point.

Table 9-9
Font Measurement Functions

Function	*Description*
`GetCharWidth()`	Gets a copy of the default character width values for a range of letters in the font currently selected in a DC.
`GetDeviceCaps()`	Gets various bits of device-specific data. In the context of text, `LOGPIXELSY` provides the number of pixels in a logical vertical inch. This is useful for calculating font point size.
`GetTextExtent()`	Gets the width and height that a given string would occupy when drawn with the font currently selected in a DC.
`GetTabbedTextExtent()`	Like `GetTextExtent()`, this function gets the width and height that a character string would occupy when drawn with the font selected in a DC. This also takes into account tab settings.
`GetTextMetrics()`	Gets a copy of the `TEXTMETRIC` data for the font currently selected in a DC. This data structure contains basic font measurement information

Font point size

Even a casual user of word processing programs knows that text is measured in *points*. One point is approximately 1/72.54 inches, which makes a point small, but not too small to be seen by the unaided eye. Windows uses a value of 1/72 inch for a point — a reasonable approximation for most uses. Common sizes for regular text range between 8 points and 12 points. Headlines can be anywhere from 14 points up to 24 or 36 points, or even larger. Text is usually measured by its height and not by its width, although in Windows you can request a font using either or both attributes.

As mentioned earlier, the focus here is on device units, which are the simplest to deal with. The basic formula for converting between device units and point size is as follows:

```
PointSize = ( 72 * DeviceUnits ) / LogicalInch
```

Going the other way, here's the formula for converting points to device units:

```
DeviceUnits = ( PointSize * LogicalInch ) / 72
```

Incidentally, you'll probably want to use Windows' `MulDiv()` helper function rather than letting the compiler do the math. This function eliminates rounding and overflow errors that sometimes occur with plain integer arithmetic. Here's the previous formula written to use this function:

```
DeviceUnits = ::MulDiv( PointSize, LogicalInch, 72 );
```

An explanation of a few points about these formulas is required. First, the term *logical inch* refers to the number of pixels in an inch. It's called *logical* because of the way this measurement is defined for display screens. On display screens, a logical inch is usually larger than a physical inch. This helps ensure that 8-point fonts — which are typically the smallest size used — are readable. On printers, logical inches and physical inches are the same.

To obtain the logical inch for a particular device, you call `CDC::GetDeviceCaps()`, the device capabilities function. `GetDeviceCaps()` takes a single parameter, an index of the capability to query. Two indices return logical inch values: `LOGPIXELSX` for movement in the *x* direction, and `LOGPIXELSY` for movement in the *y* direction. Because point size refers to the height of text — that is, its size along the *y* axis — you use `LOGPIXELSY` to determine the logical inches for a given device:

```
LogicalInch = dc.GetDeviceCaps( LOGPIXELSY );
```

Another point worth mentioning is that our formulas use a ratio of 1:72 instead of the more accurate 1:72.54 ratio of points to inches. This rounding down is done because the GDI in particular — and Windows, in general — doesn't use any floating-point arithmetic. The reason is performance. Intel x86 processors prior to the 80486 lacked hardware support for floating-point arithmetic. Because floating-point arithmetic in software can be very slow, Windows uses integer arithmetic, which provides faster operation and a reasonable degree of accuracy. Although this may change in future versions, for now Windows relies solely on integer arithmetic.

Next string, same line

You must sometimes split a single line of text between multiple text-drawing calls — that is, multiple calls to `TextOut()`. This can be necessary for any number of reasons. It might simply be more convenient, given the way your data is stored. Or you might want to display a line of text in which parts of the text use different drawing attributes. For example, displaying red text next to blue text requires two calls to `TextOut()`. Using two fonts in the same line of text also requires two text-drawing calls.

To calculate the position for the next string, you call `CDC::GetTextExtent()`. This function tells you both the width and height of a character string for the currently selected font. This function is defined as follows:

```
CSize GetTextExtent( LPCTSTR lpszString, int nCount )
  const;
```

Where:

lpszString is a pointer to the character string, and *nCount* is the number of characters to include.

The return value, CSize, is a structure with two members: *cx* is the width of the character string, and *cy* is the height. For example, here's how you write "Hello Windows 98" on the same line using two calls to TextOut():

```
int x, y;
x = 100;
y = 100;
LPCTSTR lpszHello = "Hello ";
LPCTSTR lpszWin95 = "Windows 98";

// Draw the first string.
ClientDC.TextOut( x, y, lpszHello, strlen( lpszHello ) );

// Calculate size of first string.
CSize sizeString =
 ClientDC.GetTextExtent(lpszHello, strlen( lpszHello ));

// Adjust x-coordinate.
x += sizeString.cx;

// Draw second string.
ClientDC.TextOut( x, y, lpszWin95, strlen( lpszWin95 ) );
```

To preserve the space between the strings, the first string—"Hello"—ends with a space.

Next string, next line

Another common text calculation involves determining how much space to put between two lines of text. As a shortcut, you could use the return value from the function looked at a moment ago, GetTextExtent(). After all, this function provides both the width and the height of a character string. Here's how to use this function to calculate the spacing between two lines of text:

```
// Draw first string.
ClientDC.TextOut( x, y, lpszHello, strlen( lpszHello ) );

// Calculate size of first string.
CSize sizeString =
  ClientDC.GetTextExtent(lpszHello, strlen( lpszHello ));

// Adjust y-coordinate.
y += sizeString.cy;

// Draw second string.
ClientDC.TextOut( x, y, lpszWin95, strlen( lpszWin95 ) );
```

Although this is workable for many situations, it's not the most accurate calculation. It takes into account the character cell height, but the font designer might have decided that more space is needed between lines of text. And if the font designer went to the trouble of defining additional pixels for interline spacing, it's worthwhile to use that spacing.

The term that font designers use for the space between lines of text is *external leading*. With its origins in the days when type was set by hand as tiny pieces of metal, the term *leading* refers to flat bars of metal that were placed between lines of text. It is considered external leading because it's not included—that is, it's outside of—the character cell height. Another term, *internal leading*, refers to intercharacter spacing that's been built into each character cell.

Both the internal and external leading values are stored in a `TEXTMETRIC` data structure. To get a copy of this data structure for a given font, you call `CDC::GetTextMetrics()`. This function provides text metric data for the font that's currently selected in the DC. Here's an example of calling this function:

```
TEXTMETRIC TmSys;
ClientDC.GetTextMetrics( &TmSys );
```

Expert Tip

Note that the data structure—`TEXTMETRIC`—is singular, while the function call—`GetTextMetrics()`—is plural. This annoying inconsistency has bubbled up from the native Windows API.

◆ ◆ ◆ ◆ ◆

To calculate the space between lines of text, you need to use two `TEXTMETRIC` members: character cell height and external leading size. For the text metric structure just filled, here's how you calculate the value that must be added to the *y* coordinate before drawing the next line:

```
int cyLineHeight = TmSys.tmHeight +
  TmSys.tmExternalLeading;
```

In the earlier example, this would have been added to the *y* coordinate before drawing the second line of text:

```
// Adjust y-coordinate.
y += cyLineHeight;

// Draw second string.
ClientDC.TextOut( x, y, lpszWin95, strlen( lpszWin95 ) );
```

Two ways to get the height of a character cell have been shown, and you might be wondering how this value relates to a font's point size. Watch out, they are probably not the same—*probably* because it's possible that they are the same. But to be absolutely sure, you must check another text metric value, the internal leading.

Eternal vs. Internal Leading

As discussed, *leading* is a typesetting word for interline spacing. External leading is the space not included in the character cell height. Internal leading, on the other hand, is the space that is included in the character cell height. Dennis Adler, a font guru at Microsoft, pointed out this distinction to one of the authors. To calculate the point size of a font, you subtract the value of the internal leading from the font height. In code terms, that means:

```
int DeviceUnits = TmSys.tmHeight -
  TmSys.tmInternalLeading;
```

✦ ✦ ✦ ✦ ✦

The result of this calculation is the height of the character cells in device units. To convert this value to points, you must take into account the device's logical inch. Using the size from the previous formula, here's how you get the font size in points:

```
int LogicalInch = ClientDC.GetDeviceCaps( LOGPIXELSY );
int PointSize = ::MulDiv( 72, DeviceUnits, LogicalInch );
```

Centering text

It's often useful to center a string of text over a particular point. For example, you might want to center a text label over a column of text. Or you might want to center a label within another graphic object. Whatever the reason, when you need to solve problems like this, it's helpful to think of text as a graphic object. Like a birthday present, text comes in a box—which we sometimes call a *textbox*.

By default, a character string hangs below and to the right of the text coordinate. As a result, the centering of text requires figuring out how to shift the control point up and to the left. The size of the shift is equal to one-half the size of the textbox—that is, we shift the text up by one-half of the textbox height, and to the left by one-half of the textbox width. To show you what is meant by this, here's a code fragment that centers a text string over a given (*x*,*y*) point:

```
// The string.
CString strText = "Centered Line of Text";

// Calculate the shift up and to the left.
CSize size =
  ClientDC.GetTextExtent(strText, strText.GetLength());
int xCentered = x - ( size.cx / 2 );
int yCentered = y - ( size.cy / 2 );

// Draw line of centered text
ClientDC.TextOut( xCentered, yCentered, strText );
```

Clipping Regions

On many occasions you must limit your draw operations to a specific region and prevent anything from being drawn outside of this region. The `SelectClipRgn()` function takes care of this by limiting draw operations in a particular device context.

The `SelectClipRgn()` function selects the given region as the current clipping region for the device context. Only a copy of the selected region is used. The region itself can be selected for any number of other device contexts, or it can be deleted. The function assumes that the coordinates for the given region are specified in device units.

The `CRgn` class encapsulates a Windows GDI region. A region is an elliptical or polygonal area within a window. To use regions, you use the member functions of class `CRgn` with the clipping functions defined as members of class `CDC`. The following example shows how to create a simple rectangular region bounded by the coordinates (10, 10) and (100, 100):

```
CRgn Rgn;
Rgn.CreateRectRgn( 10, 10, 100, 100 );
```

With a region created, you can then limit the device context's drawing to only the region that's been created as follows:

```
pDC->SelectClipRgn( &Rgn );
```

A more advanced version of `SelectClipRgn()`enables you to choose between five different modes. These modes affect the way the clipping region is combined with regions that are already selected into the device context, and how the region is to be used. The five modes are listed in Table 9-10.

Table 9-10
Clipping Modes

Mode	*Description*
RGN_AND	The new clipping region combines the overlapping areas of the current clipping region and the region identified by pRgn.
RGN_COPY	The new clipping region is a copy of the region identified by pRgn. This functionality is identical to the first version of SelectClipRgn. If the region identified by pRgn is NULL, the new clipping region becomes the default clipping region (a NULL region).
RGN_DIFF	The new clipping region combines the areas of the current clipping region with those areas excluded from the region identified by pRgn.
RGN_OR	The new clipping region combines the current clipping region and the region identified by pRgn.
RGN_XOR	The new clipping region combines the current clipping region and the region identified by pRgn but excludes any overlapping areas.

Summary

This chapter has covered the basics of creating text output in a window. Most of what was covered also applies to other types of GDI devices, all of which you'll someday want to use for graphic output. The chapter has presented the basics that are required for the more commonly needed operations.

The next chapter explores mouse and keyboard input. Although each type of input has its own uses, what they have in common is the fact that Windows handles the low-level details of catching the input from each type of hardware and placing it in a queue. When your program is ready to receive the input, Windows sends it to your program in the form of — what else? — messages.

✦ ✦ ✦

Bitmaps, Palettes, DIBs, and Double Buffering

In This Chapter

Bitmap memory and video memory

CBitmap objects

Loading bitmap data from the resource file

Drawing with CBitmap objects

Raster operations for CBitmap objects

Using the BlitDemo program

Palettes and color

Loading, displaying, and saving DIBs

Reducing screen flicker by double buffering

This chapter shows you how to use bitmaps of several varieties in your applications. You'll be able to display images in many places and in ways that you might have avoided because you thought they were too difficult. This chapter solves your problems. It'll have you displaying images in no time flat.

Bitmap Memory and Video Memory

At the heart of your computer's video system is memory. This memory contains data that represent the patterns that appear on the monitor. Every time the mouse pointer moves, a small amount of data in memory changes. You then see the mouse pointer move across the screen. Each and every graphics operation affects video memory as the GDI makes its calculations and alters video memory in an appropriate way.

Bitmaps represent regions of RAM similar to video memory. They're similar because each one represents a memory address that holds data. The difference is that the bitmap memory isn't seen while the video memory is. The RAM that a bitmap allocates represents a rectangular region. In terms of the Windows API, this handle to the allocated memory is known as an `HBITMAP`. In this memory resides data that, if moved into video memory, would cause a pattern to appear on the monitor. For example, consider a desktop icon. Icons are loaded from disk into memory. This memory is then moved into video memory at the appropriate addresses so that when video memory is rendered on the screen by the video hardware, the icons become visible.

Bitmaps add graphical objects to the screen in a different way than drawn objects such as lines and ellipses. Lines and ellipses are mathematically calculated, and then the pixels in video memory are set in such a way that the object appears. Bitmap data isn't calculated. The pattern already exists in bitmap memory. It's simply a matter of copying a block of memory from the bitmap to video memory. Because of this, using bitmaps is preferable to using a series of draw operations when the end result is a complex graphics image. Imagine how many separate operations it would take to draw your photograph on the screen — it may take thousands. By using a bitmap, the complex photographic image can reside in bitmap memory. Then, with a single operation, the bitmap memory can be quickly copied to a region of video memory.

This chapter discusses two types of bitmap objects. One is wrapped in the MFC `CBitmap` class. Bitmaps of this type are referred to as *device-dependant bitmaps*. They can be drawn successfully only on a video system that matches their own configuration. For instance, a device-dependent bitmap that has a color depth of 24 bits per pixel will draw only to a video system that's 24 bits per pixel. The only exception to this rule is monochrome bitmaps of one bit plane with a color depth of one bit per pixel. These can be drawn to video memory of any configuration.

Before starting the discussion, a few words on terminology are in order. In this chapter, the Windows GDI object known as an `HBITMAP` is referred to as a bitmap. The MFC class that wraps a bitmap is called a *CBitmap class* (sometimes referred to as a *CBitmap object*). A logical palette is a Windows GDI object, and in this chapter they're called *palettes*. The MFC class that wraps a palette is known as a *CPalette object*. A device-independent bitmap such as the kind that make up BMP files are referred to as *DIBs*. DIBs can't be found anywhere in the Windows API or MFC as separate items. Instead, this chapter's code loads them into `HGLOBAL` memory objects. They're still referred to as DIBs, though, so you know what's in the memory. There's a class that's built later on in the chapter that wraps a DIB. It'll be referred to as a *CDib object*.

No discussion of bitmaps would be complete without including palettes. This chapter uses MFC's `CPalette` object to perform all of the palette operations. For video adapters with pixel depths (or bit-depths) of 8 bits or less, effective use of palettes is essential for optimizing the appearance of bitmaps.

Bit planes, bits per pixel, and color depth3

Back when CGA video was the standard, there were four colors to choose from: black, cyan, magenta, and white. (A seldom-used variation produced black, yellow, green, and red.) CGA video memory stores data for each pixel in two contiguous bits. Each byte of video memory contains enough data for four screen pixels. Oddly enough, the data is stored in two banks of memory. The first bank contains data for the odd scanlines, and the second contains data for the even scanlines.

With the advent of EGA and VGA monitors, the number of possible colors expanded. In EGA/VGA, there are four variables to contend with: the red, blue, and green color bits and the high/low intensity bit. By combining these four bits, you can create 16 colors (high-intensity green, low-intensity green, high-intensity blue and red, and so on). The four variables became known as *bit planes*. It's interesting to note for EGA/VGA video memory that the bits for each of the four color variables reside in different banks of memory. For instance, all of the red memory for an EGA setting of 320 × 200 resides in a bank of memory of 8,000 bytes.

MCGA systems introduced eight bits of information for each pixel. Because the concept of a color plane doesn't describe the capabilities of this type of system, the eight bits of information for each color have become known as the *bits-per-pixel value*. MCGA video memory contains a single byte for each screen pixel. To get the RGB value (RGB is explained later in this chapter) with which the video system will render the pixel, a lookup into a palette is used. MCGA palettes have only 256 entries, so MCGA video can display only 256 simultaneous colors.

All video cards support older modes such as CGA and EGA, but most of them support newer modes in which the actual RGB values are stored in video memory. The most common is 24-bit truecolor video. In this mode, each screen pixel is represented by three consecutive bytes. Each of these bytes has an RGB value for red, green, and blue. Two other common modes in which literal RGB values reside in video memory use 16- and 32-bits of data to represent the RGB color.

To determine the actual bit-depth (the number of bits that make up a pixel) of a given video system, you must check both the bits-per-pixel value and the number of bit planes. You can call the `GetDeviceCaps()` API function with the `BITSPIXEL` constant to determine the bits-per-pixel value. To determine the number of color planes, you can call the same API function with the `PLANES` constant.

A simple way to calculate the true bit-depth is to retrieve both of these values and multiply them. This calculation is valid because an EGA/VGA system returns one for the bits-per-pixel value, and a truecolor/highcolor system returns one for the color planes value.

As mentioned previously, the second type of bitmap covered in this chapter is a device-independent bitmap (DIB). These bitmaps are not wrapped in an MFC class of any kind. Toward the end of this chapter, a class similar to `CBitmap` will be created that will make it easier to work with DIBs. The advantage that DIBs have over device-dependent bitmaps is that the DIB's configuration doesn't have to match the video configuration for a draw operation to be successful. The bitmap is drawn to the screen taking the configurations of the bitmap and the video into account. For instance, a 24-bit DIB draws successfully to a video system of 8-, 16-, 24-, and 32-bits per pixel. When a color depth mismatch occurs, a color-matching algorithm is used to achieve the best possible match. For instance, a 24-bit DIB that's drawn to an 8-bit video system has to reduce to the 256 colors that are available in the video system. When the DIB is drawn to the screen, the color downsizing is performed during the draw operation. This doesn't affect the DIB data that's in memory. The drawback to this is that performance is greatly reduced. For this reason, if performance is an issue, DIBs should not be used. Instead, device-dependent bitmaps are recommended.

The last thing you'll learn in this chapter is how to use `CBitmap` objects to reduce or eliminate screen flicker during screen redraws.

Creating CBitmap Objects

`CBitmap` objects are empty when they're first instantiated. The bitmap that the class wraps must eventually be created for the object to be useful. There are several ways to create bitmaps within a `CBitmap` class. The first uses the `CreateBitmap()` function and has the following syntax:

```
CBitmap::CreateBitmap( int nWidth, int nHeight,
  int nPlanes, int nBits, const *void lpBits );
```

The `nWidth` and `nHeight` parameters specify the size of the bitmap in pixels. The `nPlanes` argument specifies the number of bit planes that the bitmap will be—this is almost always one. The `nBits` argument specifies the number of bits for each pixel. The last argument, `lpBits`, enables you to initialize the bitmap with a bit pattern. The bit pattern is copied into the bitmap memory, but it's still the caller's responsibility to maintain and dispose of the original bit pattern memory. Normally a bit pattern isn't specified when creating a bitmap, and in this case, the `lpBits` parameter is `NULL`. Without initializing the bitmap pattern, it will contain meaningless data and look like a jumbled mess. The following example creates a bitmap with a width of 50, a height of 60, 1 bit plane, 24 bits per pixel, and no initial bit pattern:

```
CBitmap Bitmap;
Bitmap.CreateBitmap( 50, 60, 1, 24, NULL );
```

Many times, it's important to find out the configuration of a bitmap that's already been created. To do this, you must use the `GetObject()` function to have a `BITMAP` structure filled in with information about the bitmap. When retrieving information about the `CBitmap` object, the `bmBits` member will be `NULL` because you can't get a direct pointer to bitmap memory. However, if you use `CBitmap`'s `CreateBitmapIndirect()` function, `bmBits` will be used to initialize the bitmap data if the structure member is not `NULL`. The `bmType` member will always be zero. The following `BITMAP` structure definition is followed by an example of using `GetObject()` to fill in a `BITMAP` structure:

```
typedef struct tagBITMAP{
  int bmType;
  int bmWidth;
  int bmHeight;
  int bmWidthBytes;
```

```
    BYTE bmPlanes;
    BYTE bmBitsPixel;
    void *bmBits;
  } BITMAP;

  // Bitmap is a CBitmap object.
  BITMAP bm;
  Bitmap.GetObject( sizeof( BITMAP ), &bm );
```

Another way to create a bitmap is with the `CreateBitmapIndirect()` function. To do this, a `BITMAP` structure must first be filled in with the values for the bitmap that's to be created. A call to `CreateBitmapIndirect()` then uses the members of the structure to create the bitmap. An example that uses the `CreateBitmapIndirect()` function to create a bitmap with a width of 100, a height of 200, 1 bit plane, and 16 bits of color depth follows:

```
BITMAP bm;
bm.bmType = 0;
bm.bmWidth = 100;
bm.bmHeight = 200;
bm.bmWidthBytes = 200;
bm.bmPlanes = 1;
bm.bmBitsPixel = 16;
bm.bmBits = NULL;

CBitmap Bitmap;
Bitmap.CreateBitmapIndirect( &bm );
```

Even though the term *RGB* is commonly used, the order of the RGB triplets in video memory is the reverse of RGB. In other words, if each pixel is represented by three bytes in video memory, the first byte is for blue, the second for green, and the third for red.

◆ ◆ ◆ ◆ ◆

Many times you simply want to create a bitmap that's compatible with the video system. You can do this without having to specify the bit planes or bits per pixel by using the `CreateCompatibleBitmap()` function. This function takes a pointer to a device context and uses the device context to figure out how many bit planes and how many bits per pixel the bitmap must be. Following is an example of using this from the `OnDraw()` function:

```
void CBitmapView::OnDraw(CDC* pDC)
{
 CBitmapDoc* pDoc = GetDocument();
 ASSERT_VALID(pDoc);

 CBitmap Bitmap;
 Bitmap.CreateCompatibleBitmap( pDC );
}
```

Loading and Setting Bitmap Content

Before using a bitmap, you'll want to set its contents with meaningful data. When bitmaps are first created, their memory contains unpredictable data. If you display a bitmap on the screen before setting the data, what you'll see resembles a television that's not set to a station and is just producing random patterns. There are two different ways to set the contents of a bitmap. One uses the `SetBitmapBits()` function, and the other uses the `LoadBitmap()` function.

The `SetBitmapBits()` function copies the contents of a memory buffer into the bitmap memory. The source memory must be created and subsequently managed and deleted by the calling code. There are two reasons you'd want to set bitmap contents from a memory buffer. One is because you want to algorithmically create a pattern in memory and move it into the bitmap. Another is because you want to load bitmap data from disk and then move it into bitmap memory. The following example creates a 24-bit bitmap, creates a memory buffer that'll produce a red rectangle when copied to memory, and then sets the contents of the bitmap to the red pattern:

```
// Instantiate CBitmap and create the bitmap
CBitmap Bitmap;
Bitmap.CreateBitmap( 50, 50, 1, 24, NULL );

// Get the bitmap dimensions and allocation a buffer
// large enough for its contents.
BITMAP bm;
Bitmap.GetObject( sizeof( BITMAP ), &bm );
unsigned char pData =
    new unsigned char [bm.bmHeight*bm.bmWidthBytes];
// Loop through and set the buffer values so
// that the pattern will be solid red.
for( int y=0; y<bm.bmHeight; y++ ){
 for( int x=0; x<bm.bmWidth; x++ ){
  pData[x*3+y*bm.bmWidthBytes] = 0;
  pData[x*3+1+y*bm.bmWidthBytes] = 0;
  pData[x*3+2+y*bm.bmWidthBytes] = 255;
  }
 }

// Set the bitmap with the red data.
Bitmap.SetBitmapBits( bm.bmHeight * bm.bmWidthBytes,
 pData );

// Delete the data buffer.
delete [] pData;
```

For bitmaps that are 16 colors (four bits per pixel), there's another alternative. You can put the bitmap into your program as a resource and then use the `LoadBitmap()` function to transfer the data into a bitmap. A bonus of using `LoadBitmap()` is that you don't have to use `CreateBitmap()` or any of the other bitmap creation functions; it's done by `LoadBitmap()`. Another nice thing is that

LoadBitmap() will create a bitmap that's compatible with the current video system, regardless of the format of the resource bitmap. Following is an example of loading a bitmap with a resource ID of IDB_BITMAP1 into a CBitmap object:

```
CBitmap Bitmap;
Bitmap.LoadBitmap( IDB_BITMAP1 );
```

One other function that you might find useful is LoadMappedBitmap(). It takes the same argument that LoadBitmap() takes but converts various colors in the bitmap according to how the user's system colors are set. For instance, it converts black pixels to the color of button text and dark gray to the color of button shadows.

Drawing CBitmaps to the Screen

Once you have a CBitmap object that contains a valid bitmap, you're ready to draw it to the screen. Most of the time, you'll rely on the BitBlt() function. This function is fast. The BitBlt() function is hard to beat when it comes to data transfer between memory and video. It's evident that Microsoft placed a high priority on fast algorithms for blitting operations — and considering the importance of these in such a graphically intensive environment, it's a wise decision. *Blitting* is a generic term that refers to the operation of copying bitmap data to a destination (whether visible video memory or other bitmap data in RAM).

The first thing you must understand is that BitBlt() technically copies data from one device context to another. That means a device context must be created for a bitmap before operations to and from it are carried out. In addition, the bitmap must be selected into the device context before performing operations. The BitBlt() function is a member of the CDC class and has the following syntax:

```
CDC:BitBlt( int x, int y, int nWidth, int nHeight,
    CDC *pSrcDC, int xSrc, int ySrc, DWORD dwROP );
```

The x and y parameters are the destination coordinates to which the bitmap will be drawn. The nWidth and nHeight parameters are the width and height of the destination rectangle and must match the source bitmap. The pSrcDC parameter is a pointer to the source device context — the source bitmap must have been selected previously into this device context for the operation to work correctly. The xSrc and ySrc parameters are the upper-left corner of the source bitmap that's to be copied. By changing the xSrc and ySrc and nWidth and nHeight parameters, you can draw partial bitmaps to the screen. The dwROP parameter specifies the raster operation that's to be performed. A more detailed discussion of raster codes appears later in the chapter in the section "Raster Operations."

The following example loads a bitmap with the LoadBitmap() function in an application's view class constructor. The example then shows how to draw the bitmap to the screen using the OnDraw() function. One important item to note: when selecting the bitmap into the newly created device context, you obtain a pointer to the old bitmap. This enables you to select the old bitmap back into the device context after the bitmap is drawn.

```
CmyView::CmyView()
{

 m_Bitmap.LoadBitmap( IDC_BITMAP1 );

}

CmyView::OnDraw(CDC *pDC)
{
 CBitmapDoc* pDoc = GetDocument();
 ASSERT_VALID(pDoc);

 CDC MemDC;
 MemDC.CreateCompatibleDC( pDC );
 CBitmap *pOldBitmap = MemDC.SelectObject( &m_Bitmap );
 BITMAP bm;
 m_Bitmap.GetObject( sizeof( BITMAP ), &bm );
 pDC->BitBlt( 10, 10, bm.bmWidth, bm.bmHeight, &MemDC,
  0, 0, SRCCOPY );
 MemDC.SelectObject( pOldBitmap );

}
```

Drawing Bitmaps

These steps describe the process necessary to display a `CBitmap` object:

1. Create a device context for the bitmap that's compatible with the video device context.
2. Select the `CBitmap` object into the newly created device context, and save a pointer to the old bitmap.
3. Fill in a `BITMAP` structure using `GetObject()` so that you know what the bitmap's dimensions are. (Skip this step if you already know the dimensions.)
4. Perform the `BitBlt()` function.
5. Select the old bitmap back into the newly created device context.

✦ ✦ ✦ ✦ ✦

The examples you've seen so far don't take into account mapping mode (look at Chapter 9 for a complete explanation of mapping modes) and the difference between device and logical coordinates. Most applications you write won't change the mapping mode, and most applications have device and logical coordinates that are the same. If you're not sure, though, of the situation in which you'll find yourself, you must add some extra code (and additional overhead). An example using the `DrawBitmap()` function follows in which these additional factors are accounted for:

```
void DrawBitmap( int x, int y, CDC *pDC, CBitmap *pBitmap )
{
 BITMAP bm;
 pBitmap->GetObject( sizeof( BITMAP ), &bm );

 CPoint size( bm.bmWidth, bm.bmHeight );
 pDC->DPtoLP( &size );

 CPoint org( 0, 0 );
 pDC->DPtoLP( &org );

 CDC MemDC;
 MemDC.CreateCompatibleDC( pDC );
 CBitmap *pOldBitmap = MemDC.SelectObject( pBitmap );
 MemDC.SetMapMode( pDC->GetMapMode() );
 pDC->BitBlt( x, y, size.x, size.y, &MemDC,
  org.x, org.y, SRCCOPY );
 MemDC.SelectObject( pOldBitmap );
}
```

Try This

Creating and Displaying Bitmaps

By creating this application, you'll learn how to create and display bitmaps. Only three of the seven bitmaps will successfully draw to the screen. The other four won't draw because they don't match your video's configuration. The monochrome (1-bit) bitmap displays in all video configurations.

1. Create a single document application.
2. Declare an array of `CBitmap` objects in the view class.
3. Import a bitmap as a resource object, and give it an ID of `IDB_BITMAP1`.
4. Initialize the seven bitmaps in the view class constructor as follows:

```
static int nBits[] = { 1, 4, 8, 16, 24, 32 };
 for( int i=0; i<6; i++ )
 m_Bitmap[i].CreateBitmap( 40, 40, 1, nBits[i], NULL );
 m_Bitmap[6].LoadBitmap( IDB_BITMAP1 );
```

5. Draw the bitmaps in the `OnDraw()` function as follows:

```
for( int i=0; i<7; i++ ){
 CDC MemDC;
 CBitmap *pOldBitmap;
 MemDC.CreateCompatibleDC( pDC );
 pOldBitmap = MemDC.SelectObject( &m_Bitmap[i] );
 pDC->BitBlt( 20 + i * 50, 30, 40, 40, &MemDC,
  0, 0, SRCCOPY );
 MemDC.SelectObject( pOldBitmap );
 }
```

✦ ✦ ✦ ✦ ✦

At times it's necessary to copy video memory into a bitmap. Because `BitBlt()` doesn't care what the source and destination are as long as it gets two valid device contexts, it couldn't be easier. All you have to do in order to copy from the screen to a bitmap is reverse the roles of the two device contexts.

For instance, the previous examples all used the pDC device context pointer as the destination, and the function call was structured as pDC->BitBlt(). In order to specify the second device context, the address of MemDC was passed in as a function argument to BitBlt(). The destination is MemDC and the function call is structured MemDC.BitBlt(). The pDC pointer is passed in as an argument to BitBlt() so that it knows what the second device context is from which the source will be obtained. An example follows that uses a function named GetImage() that copies from the screen into a bitmap:

```
void GetImage( int x, int y, CDC *pDC, CBitmap *pBitmap )
{

  BITMAP bm;
  pBitmap->GetObject( sizeof( BITMAP ), &bm );

  CDC MemDC;
  MemDC.CreateCompatibleDC( pDC );

  CBitmap *pOldBitmap = MemDC.SelectObject( pBitmap );
  MemDC.BitBlt( 0, 0, bm.bmWidth, bm.bmHeight, pDC,
   x, y, SRCCOPY );
  MemDC.SelectObject( pOldBitmap );

}
```

Raster Operations

The last argument in the BitBlt() function determines how the source combines with the destination. Most of the time, though, copying a bitmap to the screen to have it appear exactly as it does in the bitmap data is what you want. At other times, a simple data copy won't do. One example of this is when you want to draw a bitmap to the screen allowing a transparent color to be masked out. The transparent color, when it appeared in the source bitmap, would be rejected. Whatever color was in the destination at any pixel location in which the source contained the transparent color would remain unchanged.

This masking technique must be carried out with two separate BitBlt() calls. The first part of the process creates a mask based on the source bitmap. It finds the transparent pixels and is created based on them. It then masks the destination in such a way as to eliminate all destination pixels into which the nontransparent source pixels will be drawn. The same mask is then used to mask the source and remove the unwanted transparent-color pixels. The source is then ORed (or XORed) into the destination. The original bitmap must then be restored to its original state; otherwise, the transparent color will no longer exist, and the pair of transparent operations won't work correctly.

A faster way to accomplish this double-masking process is to create a mask ahead of time. That way it doesn't have to be created every time you want to go through the process. If execution time is important, seriously consider this option. The BlitDemo program uses such preformed masks when it draws the fly images. Taking a good look at this demo program will give you a good idea of how it's done.

Another example in which you might want to use another raster operation is in animations. A common technique for moving bitmaps around on the screen is to XOR them before moving them to a new location. XORing one image over itself completely removes it. That's because when you first draw the image to the screen using an XOR raster operation, the image source combines with the destination. Anywhere the source has a bit that's set, XOR toggles the corresponding bit in the destination to its opposite value. For instance, if the source bit is set (a one) and the destination bit is not set (a zero), the result is a one. If the animation must be moved, XORing the same bitmap in the same location toggles those same bits to their previous values, once again restoring them to their original state. The bitmap can then be drawn in a new location using an XOR raster operation. Table 10-1 defines the raster operation codes.

Table 10-1
Raster Operations and Their Definitions

Raster Operation Codes	*Definition*
`BLACKNESS`	Turns all output black.
`DSTINVERT`	Inverts the destination bitmap.
`MERGECOPY`	Combines the pattern and the source bitmap using the Boolean AND operator.
`MERGEPAINT`	Combines the inverted source bitmap with the destination bitmap using the Boolean OR operator.
`NOTSRCCOPY`	Copies the inverted source bitmap to the destination.
`NOTSRCERASE`	Inverts the result of combining the destination and source bitmaps using the Boolean OR operator.
`PATCOPY`	Copies the pattern to the destination bitmap.
`PATINVERT`	Combines the destination bitmap with the pattern using the Boolean XOR operator.
`PATPAINT`	Combines the inverted source bitmap with the pattern using the Boolean OR operator. Combines the result of this operation with the destination bitmap using the Boolean OR operator.
`SRCAND`	Combines pixels of the destination and source bitmaps using the Boolean AND operator.

(continued)

Table 10-1 (continued)

Raster Operation Codes	*Definition*
SRCCOPY	Copies the source bitmap to the destination bitmap.
SRCERASE	Inverts the destination bitmap and combines the result with the source bitmap using the Boolean AND operator.
SRCINVERT	Combines pixels of the destination and source bitmaps using the Boolean XOR operator.
SRCPAINT	Combines pixels of the destination and source bitmaps using the Boolean OR operator.
WHITENESS	Turns all output white.

If you need a function that draws a bitmap to the screen and masks a single transparent color, the `DrawTransparent()` function shown in Listing 10-1 will come in handy. You can add it to your program or, better yet, derive a class from `CBitmap` that you can always use.

Source code for the `DrawTransparent()` function can be found in `Transparent.c` in the `Chap10` directory of the CD-ROM accompanying this book.

✦ ✦ ✦ ✦ ✦

Listing 10-1: **The DrawTransparent() Function**

```
void DrawTransparent( int x, int y, CDC *pDC,
 CBitmap *pBitmap, COLORREF Color )
{
 BITMAP bm;
 pBitmap->GetObject( sizeof( BITMAP ), &bm );

 CDC ImageDC;
 ImageDC.CreateCompatibleDC( pDC );
 CBitmap *pOldImageBitmap =
   ImageDC.SelectObject( pBitmap );

 CDC MaskDC;
 MaskDC.CreateCompatibleDC( pDC );

 CBitmap MaskBitmap;
 MaskBitmap.CreateBitmap( bm.bmWidth, bm.bmHeight,
   1, 1, NULL );
 CBitmap *pOldMaskBitmap =
   MaskDC.SelectObject( &MaskBitmap );
```

```
    ImageDC.SetBkColor( Color );
    MaskDC.BitBlt( 0, 0, bm.bmWidth, bm.bmHeight,
      &ImageDC, 0, 0, SRCCOPY );

    CDC OrDC;
    OrDC.CreateCompatibleDC( pDC );

    CBitmap OrBitmap;
    OrBitmap.CreateCompatibleBitmap( &ImageDC,
      bm.bmWidth, bm.bmHeight );
    CBitmap *pOldOrBitmap = OrDC.SelectObject( &OrBitmap );

    OrDC.BitBlt( 0, 0, bm.bmWidth, bm.bmHeight,
      &ImageDC, 0, 0, SRCCOPY );
    OrDC.BitBlt( 0, 0, bm.bmWidth, bm.bmHeight,
      &MaskDC, 0, 0, 0x220326 );

    CDC TempDC;
    TempDC.CreateCompatibleDC( pDC );

    CBitmap TempBitmap;
    TempBitmap.CreateCompatibleBitmap( &ImageDC,
      bm.bmWidth, bm.bmHeight );
    CBitmap *pOldTempBitmap =
      TempDC.SelectObject( &TempBitmap );

    TempDC.BitBlt( 0, 0, bm.bmWidth, bm.bmHeight,
      pDC, x, y, SRCCOPY );
    TempDC.BitBlt( 0, 0, bm.bmWidth, bm.bmHeight,
      &MaskDC, 0, 0, SRCAND );
    TempDC.BitBlt( 0, 0, bm.bmWidth, bm.bmHeight,
      &OrDC, 0, 0, SRCPAINT );

    pDC->BitBlt( x, y, bm.bmWidth, bm.bmHeight,
      &TempDC, 0, 0, SRCCOPY );

    TempDC.SelectObject( pOldTempBitmap );
    OrDC.SelectObject( pOldOrBitmap );
    MaskDC.SelectObject( pOldMaskBitmap );
    ImageDC.SelectObject( pOldImageBitmap );

}
```

The BlitDemo Program

The BlitDemo program that's included on the CD-ROM shows you how to perform common operations using `CBitmap` objects. The actual bitmaps are contained as resource objects and are loaded using the `LoadBitmap()` member function.

The program begins by displaying one of three rising bubble images as shown in Figure 10-1. Clicking the left mouse button with the mouse pointer in the client window displays the next image in the sequence. After the third image has been displayed, the initial image is drawn.

You can use the Operations menu to select one of four different image sequences. The second is a set of four images that show a man on an old-fashioned railroad trolley. The third and fourth use a set of flies. When the left mouse button is clicked, the fly moves vertically on the screen as if it's flying.

The flies are drawn in two different ways according to your menu selection. The third menu selection causes the flies to be drawn with a combination of an AND operation and an OR operation. There's a mask image for each fly that's loaded at the start of the program. These are used for the AND operation.

Figure 10-1: The BlitDemo program begins by showing the first of three in a sequence of rising bubbles.

The fourth menu selection causes the flies to move across the screen with an XOR operation. You'll notice that the resultant color of the fly depends on the color of the client window. Highlights of the `BlitDemoView.cpp` program are provided in Listing 10-2.

BlitDemo
CD-ROM Location: **Chap10\BlitDemo**
Program Name: **BlitDemo.EXE**
Source Code Modules in Text: `BlitDemoView.cpp`

◆ ◆ ◆ ◆ ◆

Listing 10-2: Highlights of the BlitDemoView.cpp Source Code

```
// BlitDemoView.cpp:implementation of CBlitDemoView class
//
////////////////////////////////////////////////////////////
// CBlitDemoView construction/destruction

CBlitDemoView::CBlitDemoView()
{

 // Start the program showing bubbles.
 m_nOperation = OPERATION_BUBBLES;

 // Initialize our indexes to the fly,
 // bubble, and trolley.
 m_nCurrentFly = 2;
 m_nCurrentBubble = 0;
 m_nCurrentTrolley = 0;

 // Set the fly's position.
 m_nFlyX = 20;
 m_nFlyY = 10;

 static int nBubble[] = {
 IDB_BUBBLE1, IDB_BUBBLE2, IDB_BUBBLE3 };

 static int nFly[] = {
 IDB_FLY1, IDB_FLY2, IDB_FLY3, IDB_FLY4 };

 static int nFlyMask[] = {
 IDB_FLYMASK1, IDB_FLYMASK2,
 IDB_FLYMASK3, IDB_FLYMASK4 };

 static int nTrolley[] = {
 IDB_TROLLEY1, IDB_TROLLEY2,
 IDB_TROLLEY3, IDB_TROLLEY4 };

 // Load in the bitmaps using LoadBitmap().
 for( int i=0; i<4; i++ ){
  if( i < 3 )
   m_Bubble[i].LoadBitmap( nBubble[i] ),
  m_Fly[i].LoadBitmap( nFly[i] );
  m_FlyMask[i].LoadBitmap( nFlyMask[i] );
  m_Trolley[i].LoadBitmap( nTrolley[i] );
  }

}

CBlitDemoView::~CBlitDemoView()
{
}
```

(continued)

Listing 10-2 *(continued)*

```
//////////////////////////////////////////////////////////
// CBlitDemoView drawing

void CBlitDemoView::OnDraw(CDC* pDC)
{
 CBlitDemoDoc* pDoc = GetDocument();
 ASSERT_VALID(pDoc);

 // When a redraw message comes, just
 // call DrawBitmaps()
 DrawBitmaps( pDC );

}

void CBlitDemoView::DrawBitmaps( CDC *pDC )
{

 // Create a DC into which the bitmap
 // will be selected.
 CDC MemDC;
 MemDC.CreateCompatibleDC( pDC );
 CBitmap *pOldBitmap;

 BITMAP bm;

 switch( m_nOperation ){
  case OPERATION_BUBBLES:
   // Select the appropriate bitmap into
   // the DC.
   pOldBitmap =
    (CBitmap *) MemDC.SelectObject(
     &m_Bubble[m_nCurrentBubble] );
   // We need the width and height of the
   // bitmap for the BitBlt() function.
   m_Bubble[m_nCurrentBubble].GetObject(
    sizeof( BITMAP ), &bm );
   // Perform the BitBlt() function to the destination
   // coordinates 0, 0.
   pDC->BitBlt( 0, 0, bm.bmWidth, bm.bmHeight, &MemDC,
    0, 0, SRCCOPY );
   break;
  case OPERATION_TROLLEY:
   // Select the appropriate bitmap into
   // the DC.
   pOldBitmap =
    (CBitmap *) MemDC.SelectObject(
     &m_Trolley[m_nCurrentTrolley] );
   // We need the width and height of the
   // bitmap for the BitBlt() function.
   m_Trolley[m_nCurrentTrolley].GetObject(
    sizeof( BITMAP ), &bm );
```

```
      // Perform the BitBlt() function to the destination
      // coordinates 0, 0.
      pDC->BitBlt( 0, 0, bm.bmWidth, bm.bmHeight, &MemDC,
        0, 0, SRCCOPY );
      break;
    case OPERATION_XORFLY:
      // Select the appropriate bitmap into
      // the DC.
      pOldBitmap =
        (CBitmap *) MemDC.SelectObject(
          &m_Fly[m_nCurrentFly] );
      // We need the width and height of the
      // bitmap for the BitBlt() function.
      m_Fly[m_nCurrentFly].GetObject(
        sizeof( BITMAP ), &bm );
      // Perform the BitBlt() function to the destination
      // coordinates calculated by using m_nFlyX and m_nFlyY
      // as the center of the object. The width and height
      // of the bitmap are then used to draw the object
      // centered on m_nFlyX and m_nFlyY.
      pDC->BitBlt( m_nFlyX - ( bm.bmWidth / 2 ), m_nFlyY,
        bm.bmWidth, bm.bmHeight, &MemDC,
        0, 0, SRCINVERT );
      break;
    case OPERATION_MASKFLY:
      // Select the appropriate bitmap into
      // the DC.
      pOldBitmap =
        (CBitmap *) MemDC.SelectObject(
          &m_FlyMask[m_nCurrentFly] );
      // We need the width and height of the
      // bitmap for the BitBlt() function.
      m_FlyMask[m_nCurrentFly].GetObject(
        sizeof( BITMAP ), &bm );
      pDC->BitBlt( m_nFlyX - ( bm.bmWidth / 2 ), m_nFlyY,
        bm.bmWidth, bm.bmHeight, &MemDC,
        0, 0, SRCAND );
      MemDC.SelectObject( &m_Fly[m_nCurrentFly] );
      // Perform the BitBlt() function to the destination
      // coordinates calculated by using m_nFlyX and m_nFlyY
      // as the center of the object. The width and height
      // of the bitmap are then used to draw the object
      // centered on m_nFlyX and m_nFlyY.
      pDC->BitBlt( m_nFlyX - ( bm.bmWidth / 2 ), m_nFlyY,
        bm.bmWidth, bm.bmHeight, &MemDC,
        0, 0, SRCINVERT );
      break;
    }

  // Select the old bitmap back
  // into the DC.
  MemDC.SelectObject( pOldBitmap );
```

(continued)

Listing 10-2 *(continued)*

```
}

////////////////////////////////////////////////////////////
// CBlitDemoView message handlers

void CBlitDemoView::OnLButtonDown(UINT nFlags,
 CPoint point)
{

 CClientDC ClientDC( this );

 switch( m_nOperation ){
  case OPERATION_BUBBLES:
   // Increment to next bubble.
   m_nCurrentBubble++;
   // Make sure the bubble value is in range.
   if( m_nCurrentBubble >= 3 )
    m_nCurrentBubble = 0;
   break;
  case OPERATION_TROLLEY:
   // Increment to next trolley.
   m_nCurrentTrolley++;
   // Make sure the trolley value is in range.
   if( m_nCurrentTrolley >= 4 )
    m_nCurrentTrolley = 0;
   break;
  case OPERATION_XORFLY:
   // XORFLY uses the same movement calculations
   // as MASKFLY. The only difference is that
   // to erase the previous image, XORFLY
   // calls DrawBitmaps() and MASKFLY draws
   // a rectangle.
   DrawBitmaps( &ClientDC );
  case OPERATION_MASKFLY:
   if( m_nOperation == OPERATION_MASKFLY ){
    // Get the bitmap size so that we
    // can calculate the rectangle that
    // we must draw to erase the fly.
    BITMAP bm;
    m_FlyMask[m_nCurrentFly].GetObject(
     sizeof( BITMAP ), &bm );
    RECT Rect;
    Rect.left = m_nFlyX - ( bm.bmWidth / 2 );
    Rect.top = m_nFlyY;
    Rect.right = Rect.left + bm.bmWidth;
    Rect.bottom = Rect.top + bm.bmHeight;
    // Create a brush that's the same as the
    // window color and then draw a rectangle.
    CBrush Brush( GetSysColor( COLOR_WINDOW ) );
    ClientDC.FillRect( &Rect, &Brush );
    }
```

```
    // We're toggling between 2 and 3 going down
    // and 0 and 1 going up. We can use ^ 1 to
    // accomplish this. If the fly moves past a
    // threshold point, we reverse the direction.
    m_nCurrentFly ^= 1;
    if( m_nCurrentFly >= 2 ){
     m_nFlyY += 10;
     if( m_nFlyY > 300 )
      m_nCurrentFly -= 2;
     }
    else{
     m_nFlyY -= 10;
     if( m_nFlyY <= 10 )
      m_nCurrentFly += 2;
     }
    break;
   }
 DrawBitmaps( &ClientDC );

 CView::OnLButtonDown(nFlags, point);
}

void CBlitDemoView::OnOperationsMaskfly()
{

 // Set the operation to OPERATION_MASKFLY.
 m_nOperation = OPERATION_MASKFLY;
 // Invalidate the client window and force
 // an immediate redraw.
 InvalidateRect( NULL, TRUE );
 UpdateWindow();

}

void CBlitDemoView::OnOperationsShowbubbles()
{

 // Set the operation to OPERATION_BUBBLES.
 m_nOperation = OPERATION_BUBBLES;
 // Invalidate the client window and force
 // an immediate redraw.
 InvalidateRect( NULL, TRUE );
 UpdateWindow();

}

void CBlitDemoView::OnOperationsShowtrolley()
{

 // Set the operation to OPERATION_TROLLEY.
 m_nOperation = OPERATION_TROLLEY;
 // Invalidate the client window and force
 // an immediate redraw.
```

(continued)

Listing 10-2 *(continued)*

```
 InvalidateRect( NULL, TRUE );
 UpdateWindow();

}

void CBlitDemoView::OnOperationsXorfly()
{

 // Set the operation to OPERATION_XORFLY.
 m_nOperation = OPERATION_XORFLY;
 // Invalidate the client window and force
 // an immediate redraw.
 InvalidateRect( NULL, TRUE );
 UpdateWindow();

}
```

Palettes and Color

The color on IBM-compatible video systems is represented using RGB triplets. Each of the RGB triplets contains a value for the red, green, and blue components of a color. The combination of the three component values determines the color that's seen on the screen.

RGB is a common color space (or color definition). The colors red, green, and blue are considered fundamental and undecomposible. Color systems can be separated into two categories: additive color systems and subtractive color systems. Colors in additive systems, such as the RGB system, are created by adding colors to black to create new colors. The more color that's added, the more the resulting color tends towards white. The presence of all the primary colors in sufficient amounts creates pure white, while the absence of all the primary colors leaves pure black.

We use the common RGB macro in this section to describe RGB triplets. The RGB macro converts three byte values ranging from 0 to 255 into a COLORREF value. The macro's first argument is the red value, the second green, and the third blue. Values range from 0 to 255. For instance, an RGB value with a red component of 244, a green component of 142, and a blue component of 34 can be notated as RGB(244, 142, 34). Table 10-2 lists some of the common colors found in the default Windows palette.

Table 10-2
RGB Colors in the Default Windows Palette

RGB Values	*Color*
RGB(0, 0, 0)	Black
RGB(255, 255, 255)	White
RGB(255, 0, 0)	Red
RGB(0, 255, 0)	Green
RGB(0, 0, 255)	Blue
RGB(255, 255, 0)	Yellow
RGB(255, 0, 255)	Magenta
RGB(0, 255, 255)	Cyan
RGB(128, 128, 128)	Dark Gray
RGB(192, 192, 192)	Light Gray

Two additional color spaces that you may encounter

CMY Color Space

CMY (cyan, magenta, and yellow) is a subtractive color system used by printers and photographers for the rendering of colors with an emulsion of ink, normally on a white surface. It is used by most hard copy devices that deposit color pigments on white paper, such as laser and ink jet printers. When illuminated, each of the three colors absorbs its complementary light color. Cyan absorbs red, magenta absorbs green, and yellow absorbs blue. By increasing the amount of yellow ink, for instance, the amount of blue in the image is decreased.

The CMY system colors, as in all subtractive systems, are subtracted from white light by pigments to create new colors. The new colors are the wavelengths of light reflected, rather than absorbed, by the CMY pigments. For example, when cyan and magenta are absorbed, the resulting color is yellow. The yellow pigment is said to subtract the cyan and magenta components from the reflected light. When all of the CMY components are subtracted, or absorbed, the resulting color is black.

It is, however, difficult to achieve a good black color in CMY space. A variant of CMY, known as CMYK, has been spawned. CMYK color has a separate component for the color black.

You can calculate a CMY value from an RGB value. To calculate cyan, subtract the RGB red value from 255; for magenta, subtract the RGB green value from 255; and for yellow, subtract the RGB blue from 255. For instance, RGB(240, 12, 135) have equivalent CMY values of 15, 243, and 120.

(continued)

(continued)

HSV

HSV is one of many color systems that vary the degree of properties of colors to create new colors, rather than using a mixture of the colors themselves. Hue specifies color in the common use of the term, such as red, orange, blue, and so on. Saturation (also called *chroma*) refers to the amount of white in a hue: a fully saturated hue contains no white and appears pure. By extension, a partly saturated hue appears lighter in color due to the admixture of white. Red hue with 50 percent saturation appears pink, for instance. Value (also called *brightness*) is the degree of self-luminescence of a color—that is, how much light it emits. A hue with high intensity is very bright, while a hue with low intensity is dark.

HSV most closely resembles the color system used by painters and other artists who create colors by adding white, black, and gray to pure pigments to create tints, shades, and tones. A tint is a pure, fully saturated color combined with white, and a shade is a fully saturated color combined with black. A tone is a fully saturated color with both black and white added to it. Relating HSV to this color mixing, saturation is the amount of white, value is the amount of black, and hue is the color that the black and white are added to.

You can convert a color from RGB space to HSV space with the following function, which can be found in a file named `HSV.c` in the `Chap10` directory on the CD-ROM:

```
#define mid( a, b, c ) \
  ( a >= b && a <= c ? \
   a : ( b >= a && b <= c ? b : c ) )

void RGB2HSV( int nRed, int nGreen, int nBlue,
  int *nH, int *nS, int *nV )
{
  int nLow, nMid, nHigh;

  if( nRed == nGreen &&
    nGreen == nBlue ){
    *nH = 0;
    *nS = 0;
    *nV = nRed;
    return;
  }

  nLow = min( nRed, min( nGreen, nBlue ) );
  nHigh = max( nRed, max( nGreen, nBlue ) );
  nMid = mid( nRed, nGreen, nBlue );

  *nV = ( nLow + nHigh ) / 2;
  *nS = nHigh - nLow;

  int nCommon = (int)
    ( 60.0 * (double) ( nMid - nLow ) /
```

```
    (double) ( nHigh - nLow ) );

  if( nRed == nLow && nBlue == nHigh )
    *nH = 240 - nCommon;
  else if( nRed == nLow && nGreen == nHigh )
    *nH = 120 + nCommon;
  else if( nGreen == nLow && nRed == nHigh )
    *nH = 360 - nCommon;
  else if( nGreen == nLow && nBlue == nHigh )
    *nH = 240 - nCommon;
  else if( nBlue == nLow && nGreen == nHigh )
    *nH = 120 - nCommon;
  else if( nBlue == nLow && nRed == nHigh )
    *nH = nCommon;
}
```

Logical palettes

Video systems that are set for 16-, 24-, and 32-bit display determine how individual pixels appear on the screen by storing RGB values into video memory. Video systems that are set for 8-bit display and less operate in a more indirect way, and many times are referred to as *palettized devices*. Images that contain data of depths that are 8 bits or less are referred to as *palettized images*.

Palettized video memory doesn't contain the actual RGB data with which a pixel is rendered. Instead, it contains an index into a table of 256 RGB values. This table resides in a section of video memory know as the Digital Adapter Color (DAC). You can't directly set the DAC table yourself from Windows because it's a shared resource. Instead, you must use GDI to set the hardware palette stored in the DAC.

The GDI palette manager performs many roles as arbitrator of the hardware palette. One important thing it does is maintain 20 colors (known as *static colors*) with which Windows draws common items such as dialog objects and icons. You can force GDI to override the 20 static colors, but it's not a good idea. More about this subject is provided later in this chapter.

The palette manager prevents duplicate entries from getting into the hardware palette. Duplicate palette entries would diminish the effectiveness of your application if it had to display images in an optimal way. This feature is very valuable for palettized display systems. As with the palette manager's enforcement of the 20 static colors, the rule against duplicate colors can be overridden. This chapter describes how this can be done later.

A logical palette is created with a `LOGPALETTE` structure. Within the `LOGPALETTE` structure is a list of `PALETTEENTRY` structures. The `PALETTEENTRY` list contains the RGB values with which Windows can set the hardware palette. The number of

PALETTEENTRY structures that can be in the list ranges from 1 to 256. If your video system supports more than 256 palette entries, your logical palette can be more. The real limit to the size of palette entries is the size of your hardware's palette. Most of the time this will be 256. The LOGPALETTE structure definition follows:

```
typedef struct tagLOGPALETTE{
 WORD palVersion;
 WORD palNumEntries;
 PALETTEENTRY palPalEntry[1];
} LOGPALETTE;
```

The palVersion member specifies the LOGPALETTE version. In all current releases of Windows, this value should be 0x300. The palNumEntries member contains the number of palette entries that can be found in the PALETTEENTRY list. The PALETTEENTRY structure definition is as follows:

```
typedef struct tagPALETTEENTRY{
 BYTE peRed;
 BYTE peGreen;
 BYTE peBlue;
 BYTE peFlags;
} PALETTEENTRY;
```

The peRed, peGreen, and peBlue members contain the RGB values. The peFlags member contains a value of one or more flags describing the type of palette entry. Table 10-3 shows these flags.

Table 10-3
Palette Entry Flags

Flag	*Description*
PC_EXPLICIT	Creates a palette entry that specifies an index into the system palette rather than an RGB color. Used by programs that display the contents of a system palette.
PC_NOCOLLAPSE	Creates a palette entry that's mapped to an unused entry in the system palette even if an entry for that color already exists. Used to ensure the uniqueness of palette colors when two entries map to the same color.
PC_RESERVED	Creates a palette entry that's private to this application. When a PC_RESERVED entry is added to the system palette, it isn't mapped to colors in other logical palettes even if the colors match. Used by programs that perform palette animation.

Here's how you'd create a logical palette with 16 colors in which the RGB colors are calculated based on the loop counter:

```
LOGPALETTE *pLogPal;
pLogPal = (LOGPALETTE *)
 new char [sizeof(LOGPALETTE)+16*sizeof(PALETTEENTRY)];

pLogPal->palVersion = 0x300;
pLogPal->palNumEntries = 16;

for( int i=0; i<16; i++ ){
 pLogPal->palPalEntry[i].peRed =
  (unsigned char) ( i * 16 );
 pLogPal->palPalEntry[i].peGreen =
  (unsigned char) ( i * 12 );
 pLogPal->palPalEntry[i].peBlue =
  (unsigned char) ( i * 8 );
 pLogPal->palPalEntry[i].peFlags = 0;
}
```

You can use a LOGPALETTE in conjunction with Windows API functions to set the palette. It's better, though, to use the MFC CPalette class. This class makes it more convenient to perform palette operations because the CDC class that wraps the GDI API expects a CPalette object. If you don't use a CPalette class, the CDC class won't be of any use when you set the palette.

Once you have a LOGPALETTE, creating a CPalette object couldn't be easier. The following code takes the LOGPALETTE (named pLogPal) created in the last code fragment and creates a CPalette object with it. Once the CPalette object is created, the LOGPALETTE memory can be deleted.

```
CPalette Palette;
Palette.CreatePalette( pLogPal );
delete [] pLogPal;
```

Once you've created a CPalette object, you must select the palette into the device context and then realize it. Realizing a palette occurs when Windows actually copies the palette into the hardware registers. As with most GDI objects, the old object must be selected back into the device context after you're done. Following is code in an OnDraw() function that takes the CPalette object created in the last code fragment and uses it to set the Windows palette:

```
CPalette *pOldPalette;
pOldPalette = pDC->SelectPalette( &Palette, FALSE );
pDC->RealizePalette();
pDC->SelectPalette( pOldPalette, FALSE );
```

You can create a CPalette object that contains a generic and fairly uniform distribution of colors. These palettes are known as *halftone palettes* and can be created with the CreateHalftonePalette() function. Following is an example of creating such a CPalette object:

```
CPalette Palette;
Palette.CreateHalftonePalette( pDC );
```

If you pass an argument of NULL to the CreateHalftonePalette() function, a 256-color halftone palette is created that's independent of the output device.

Palette events

When you write an application that sets the palette, be aware that other applications may receive the focus and set the palette differently. If this happens, your graphics may not look like what you expect when your application gets the focus back. For this reason, you'll have to add some event handlers so that you can restore the palette when it's appropriate.

The WM_QUERYNEWPALETTE message is sent to an application's top-level window (usually a CMainFrame object for AppWizard-created applications) when a palette realization causes a change in the system palette. Palette realization causes Windows to send the palette data that resides in the selected palette to the video hardware effecting a change. The WM_PALETTECHANGED message is sent to the top-level window when it receives the focus. For multiple document interface applications that maintain different palettes, each child window should look for a WM_GETFOCUS message so that the child window can set its own palette.

The following example assumes that a CPalette object named m_Palette has already been created. It shows how a WM_QUERYNEWPALETTE message should be handled.

Handling a WM_QUERYNEWPALETTE message

Message: WM_QUERYNEWPALETTE

Function Created: OnQueryNewPalette()

Source Code Module: **MainFrm.cpp**

```
BOOL CMainFrame::OnQueryNewPalette()
{

 CClientDC ClientDC( this );
 CPalette *pOldPalette =
  ClientDC.SelectPalette( &m_Palette, FALSE );

 if( ClientDC.RealizePalette() > 0 )
  Invalidate();

 ClientDC.SelectPalette( pOldPalette, FALSE );

}
```

✦ ✦ ✦ ✦ ✦

Handling a WM_PALETTECHANGED message

Message: WM_PALETTECHANGED

Function Created: OnPaletteChanged()

Source Code Module: MainFrm.cpp

```
BOOL CMainFrame::OnPaletteChanged(CWnd *pFocusWnd)
{

 if( pFocusWnd != this ){

  CClientDC ClientDC( this );
  CPalette *pOldPalette =
   ClientDC.SelectPalette( &m_Palette, FALSE );

  if( ClientDC.RealizePalette() > 0 )
   Invalidate();

  ClientDC.SelectPalette( pOldPalette, FALSE );
 }

}
```

✦ ✦ ✦ ✦ ✦

The SetSystemPaletteUse() function

At times you may want access to the entire system palette, including the 20 static colors. If you find yourself in this situation, you can use the SetSystemPaletteUse() function to change the number of static colors Windows reserves for itself. The following code reduces the number of static colors to two: one for white and one for black.

```
CClientDC ClientDC( this );
SetSystemPalette( ClientDC.m_hDC, SYSPAL_NOSTATIC );
```

Device-Independent Bitmaps

One of the biggest drawbacks to device-dependent bitmaps is the inability to draw to device contexts with different pixel depths. This problem can be overcome by using a DIB. Unfortunately, DIBs aren't wrapped by any MFC classes. This creates extra work for developers because they must write load, save, draw, manipulation, and support code into their application.

To overcome the lack of a DIB class, this section creates a class named CDib that conveniently wraps a DIB. A demo program that uses the class comes next and shows how easy it is to load and display DIBs in programs using the CDib class.

The anatomy of a DIB file

Files containing DIBs always start with a BITMAPFILEHEADER data structure. This structure doesn't contain much useful information except the size of the file and the offset of the actual DIB data within the file. The offset refers to the number of bytes from the beginning of the file at which the actual image data (as opposed to header information) is located. The first two bytes contain a signature of "BM" that can be useful for an initial validity check. (The "BM" signature must be referred to as "MB" because of the way Intel processors swap bytes.) The BITMAPFILEHEADER structure follows:

```
typedef struct tagBITMAPFILEHEADER {
  WORD bfType;
  DWORD bfSize;
  WORD bfReserved1;
  WORD bfReserved2;
  DWORD bfOffBits;
} BITMAPFILEHEADER;
```

The bfType member is always set to "BM" to indicate that it's a bitmap file. The bfSize member contains a value equal to the file size. The reserved members aren't used and should be zero. The bfOffBits member contains the offset from the beginning of the file to the actual image date.

The next thing that comes in a DIB file is a BITMAPINFOHEADER data structure. In this structure resides essential information about the DIB. It contains such things as width, height, and color depth. The BITMAPINFOHEADER structure follows:

```
typedef struct tagBITMAPINFOHEADER{
  DWORD biSize;
  LONG biWidth;
  LONG biHeight;
  WORD biPlanes;
  WORD biBitCount
  DWORD biCompression;
  DWORD biSizeImage;
  LONG biXPelsPerMeter;
  LONG biYPelsPerMeter;
  DWORD biClrUsed;
  DWORD biClrImportant;
} BITMAPINFOHEADER;
```

The biSize field is simply the size of the BITMAPINFOHEADER structure. The biWidth and biHeight members refer to the image width and height. The biPlanes and biBitCount members describe the image color depth. The biCompression member is almost always zero but in rare cases may be a value that represents some sort of compression. The biSizeImage member contains the size of the image in bytes. The next two members, biXPelsPerMeter and biYPelsPerMeter, refer to the image resolution and are rarely used. The biClrUsed member is usually zero — the only exception is when the number of colors used is actually less than the maximum number of colors for the specified color depth. The biClrImportant member indicates how many of the colors are important — zero, which is typically used, means they're all important.

The last information in the file before the actual DIB data is the palette information. For DIBs with bit-depths greater than 8, there is no palette data. For DIBs of 8 bits or less, the number of palette entries can be calculated by the following formula:

```
int nNumPaletteEntries =
 1 << BitmapInfoHeader.biBitCount;
```

DIBs can contain fewer palette entries than the maximum allowable. For instance, an 8-bit DIB has a maximum of 256 colors allowed. Applications that save DIBs may choose to save fewer than 256 palette entries in the disk file.

The BITMAPINFOHEADER member biClrUsed can be used to determine if a DIB has been saved with an explicit number of palette entries. If biClrUsed is zero, the DIB file contains the maximum number of palette entries for the DIB's color depth. If it's nonzero, the DIB file contains exactly the number of palette entries in biClrUsed. Palette entries are stored in an RGBQUAD structure. The format of the RGBQUAD structure follows:

```
typedef struct tagRGBQUAD {
 BYTE rgbBlue;
 BYTE rgbGreen;
 BYTE rgbRed;
 BYTE rgbReserved;
} RGBQUAD;
```

Finally, after the BITMAPFILEHEADER, the BITMAPINFOHEADER, and any palette entries comes the DIB data. For 8-bit DIBs, each byte represents a pixel; for 16-bit DIBs, every two bytes represents a pixel; for 24-bit DIBs, every three bytes represents a pixel; and for 32-bit DIBs, every four bytes represents a pixel.

Calculating a DIB's Bytes Per Line

If you find yourself needing to calculate an offset into DIB data, heed this warning. To find the number of bytes of each line of a DIB, most programs would multiply the pixel width by the number of bytes per pixel. This may not give you accurate results because the number of bytes for each DIB line must be an even multiple of four. The following code calculates the byte width of a DIB:

```
int nWidthBytes = BitmapInfoHeader.biWidth;
if( BitmapInfoHeader.biBitCount == 16 )
 nWidthBytes *= 2;
else if( BitmapInfoHeader.biBitCount == 24 )
 nWidthBytes *= 3;
else if( BitmapInfoHeader.biBitCount == 32 )
 nWidthBytes *= 4;
while( ( nWidthBytes & 3 ) != 0 )
 nWidthBytes++;
```

✦ ✦ ✦ ✦ ✦

The CDib class

The CDib class can save you time and help keep your program tidy. In this section, the class is described one function at a time.

CDib::Load

The Load() function takes a single argument of a char pointer, which points to a NULL-terminated ASCII string of the filename. If the function is successful, it returns TRUE. If for some reason it fails, it returns FALSE. If a DIB has already been loaded, the Load() function deletes the old DIB if the new one is successfully loaded. Source code for the Load() function is in Listing 10-3.

Listing 10-3: Source Code for the CDib::Load() Function

```
BOOL CDib::Load( const char *pszFilename )
{

  CFile cf;

  // Attempt to open the Dib file for reading.
  if( !cf.Open( pszFilename, CFile::modeRead ) )
    return( FALSE );

  // Get the size of the file and store
  // in a local variable. Subtract the
  // size of the BITMAPFILEHEADER structure
  // since we won't keep that in memory.
  DWORD dwDibSize;
  dwDibSize =
    cf.GetLength() - sizeof( BITMAPFILEHEADER );

  // Attempt to allocate the Dib memory.
  unsigned char *pDib;
  pDib = new unsigned char [dwDibSize];
  if( pDib == NULL )
    return( FALSE );

  BITMAPFILEHEADER BFH;

  // Read in the Dib header and data.
  try{

    // Did we read in the entire BITMAPFILEHEADER?
    if( cf.Read( &BFH, sizeof( BITMAPFILEHEADER ) )
      != sizeof( BITMAPFILEHEADER ) ||

      // Is the type 'MB'?
      BFH.bfType != 'MB' ||

      // Did we read in the remaining data?
```

```
    cf.Read( pDib, dwDibSize ) != dwDibSize ){

    // Delete the memory if we had any
    // errors and return FALSE.
    delete [] pDib;
    return( FALSE );
    }
  }

// If we catch an exception, delete the
// exception, the temporary Dib memory,
// and return FALSE.
catch( CFileException *e ){
  e->Delete();
  delete [] pDib;
  return( FALSE );
  }

// If we got to this point, the Dib has been
// loaded. If a Dib was already loaded into
// this class, we must now delete it.
if( m_pDib != NULL )
  delete m_pDib;

// Store the local Dib data pointer and
// Dib size variables in the class member
// variables.
m_pDib = pDib;
m_dwDibSize = dwDibSize;

// Pointer our BITMAPINFOHEADER and RGBQUAD
// variables to the correct place in the Dib data.
m_pBIH = (BITMAPINFOHEADER *) m_pDib;
m_pPalette =
 (RGBQUAD *) &m_pDib[sizeof(BITMAPINFOHEADER)];

// Calculate the number of palette entries.
m_nPaletteEntries = 1 << m_pBIH->biBitCount;
if( m_pBIH->biBitCount > 8 )
  m_nPaletteEntries = 0;
else if( m_pBIH->biClrUsed != 0 )
  m_nPaletteEntries = m_pBIH->biClrUsed;

// Point m_pDibBits to the actual Dib bits data.
m_pDibBits =
  &m_pDib[sizeof(BITMAPINFOHEADER)+
    m_nPaletteEntries*sizeof(RGBQUAD)];

// If we have a valid palette, delete it.
if( m_Palette.GetSafeHandle() != NULL )
  m_Palette.DeleteObject();
```

(continued)

Listing 10-3 *(continued)*

```
  // If there are palette entries, we'll need
  // to create a LOGPALETTE then create the
  // CPalette palette.
  if( m_nPaletteEntries != 0 ){

    // Allocate the LOGPALETTE structure.
    LOGPALETTE *pLogPal = (LOGPALETTE *) new char
        [sizeof(LOGPALETTE)+
        m_nPaletteEntries*sizeof(PALETTEENTRY)];

    if( pLogPal != NULL ){

      // Set the LOGPALETTE to version 0x300
      // and store the number of palette
      // entries.
      pLogPal->palVersion = 0x300;
      pLogPal->palNumEntries = m_nPaletteEntries;

      // Store the RGB values into each
      // PALETTEENTRY element.
      for( int i=0; i<m_nPaletteEntries; i++ ){
        pLogPal->palPalEntry[i].peRed =
          m_pPalette[i].rgbRed;
        pLogPal->palPalEntry[i].peGreen =
          m_pPalette[i].rgbGreen;
        pLogPal->palPalEntry[i].peBlue =
          m_pPalette[i].rgbBlue;
        }

      // Create the CPalette object and
      // delete the LOGPALETTE memory.
      m_Palette.CreatePalette( pLogPal );
      delete [] pLogPal;
      }
    }

  return( TRUE );

}
```

To use the `Load()` function, just call it with a valid filename. If the function successfully loads a valid .BMP file, the function returns `TRUE`. If for some reason the function fails, it returns `FALSE`. An example of using the `Load()` function follows:

```
CDib Dib;
BOOL bRet;
bRet = Dib.Load( "C:\\Windows\\Clouds.bmp" );
```

```
if( bRet )
 AfxMessageBox( "The Load() function succeeded." );
else
 AfxMessageBox( "The Load() function failed." );
```

CDib::Save

You may find it necessary to save a DIB. This situation arises when you modify the DIB data and want to save it back to disk. The `Save()` function takes the DIB data that's in the `CDib` memory and saves it to disk. The only argument it takes is a pointer to a filename. It returns `TRUE` if the save operation was successful, `FALSE` if it wasn't. The source code for the `CDib::Save()` function is in Listing 10-4.

Listing 10-4: Source Code for the CDib::Save() Function

```
BOOL CDib::Save( const char *pszFilename )
{

 // If we have no data, we can't save.
 if( m_pDib == NULL )
  return( FALSE );

 CFile cf;

 // Attempt to create the file.
 if( !cf.Open( pszFilename,
  CFile::modeCreate | CFile::modeWrite ) )
  return( FALSE );

 // Write the data.
 try{

  // First, create a BITMAPFILEHEADER
  // with the correct data.
  BITMAPFILEHEADER BFH;
  memset( &BFH, 0, sizeof( BITMAPFILEHEADER ) );
  BFH.bfType = 'MB';
  BFH.bfSize = sizeof( BITMAPFILEHEADER ) + m_dwDibSize;
  BFH.bfOffBits = sizeof( BITMAPFILEHEADER ) +
   sizeof( BITMAPINFOHEADER ) +
   m_nPaletteEntries * sizeof( RGBQUAD );

  // Write the BITMAPFILEHEADER and the
  // Dib data.
  cf.Write( &BFH, sizeof( BITMAPFILEHEADER ) );
  cf.Write( m_pDib, m_dwDibSize );
  }
```

(continued)

Listing 10-4 *(continued)*

```
  // If we get an exception, delete the exception and
  // return FALSE.
  catch( CFileException *e ){
   e->Delete();
   return( FALSE );
   }

  return( TRUE );

}
```

To use the `Save()` function, just call it with a valid filename. A word of caution is in order. If a file exists with the same name as the one that's specified as an argument, that file will be overwritten by the newly created file. It might be a good idea to check for the existence of the file before saving. If the function successfully saves the .BMP file, the function returns `TRUE`. If for some reason the function fails, it returns `FALSE`. An example of using the `Save()` function follows:

```
CDib Dib;
BOOL bRet;
bRet = Dib.Save( "C:\\Windows\\NewClouds.bmp" );
if( bRet )
 AfxMessageBox( "The Save() function succeeded." );
else
 AfxMessageBox( "The Save() function failed." );
```

CDib::Draw

Of course, a `CDib` class isn't much good if you can't draw the DIB to the screen. An essential function for the class is one that draws the DIB to a device context. The `Draw()` function does just this. It has one required parameter, a `CDC` pointer. The next two arguments, `nX` and `nY` (the *x* and *y* coordinates), are optional. If you don't specify the *x* and *y* coordinates, the DIB is drawn to 0, 0. The fourth and fifth arguments, `nWidth` and `nHeight`, are also optional. If you don't specify either of them, they default to the width and/or height of the DIB itself. Otherwise, the function takes the DIB data and stretches (or shrinks or both) the data so that it exactly fits the width and height that are specified. Source code for the `CDib::Draw()` function is in Listing 10-5.

Listing 10-5: Source Code for the CDib::Draw() Function

```
BOOL CDib::Draw( CDC *pDC, int nX, int nY, int nWidth,
 int nHeight )
{

 // If we have not data we can't draw.
 if( m_pDib == NULL )
  return( FALSE );

 // Check for the default values of -1
 // in the width and height arguments. If
 // we find -1 in either, we'll set them
 // to the value that's in the BITMAPINFOHEADER.
 if( nWidth == -1 )
  nWidth = m_pBIH->biWidth;
 if( nHeight == -1 )
  nHeight = m_pBIH->biHeight;

 // Use StretchDIBits to draw the Dib.
 StretchDIBits( pDC->m_hDC, nX, nY,
  nWidth, nHeight,
  0, 0,
  m_pBIH->biWidth, m_pBIH->biHeight,
  m_pDibBits,
  (BITMAPINFO *) m_pBIH,
  BI_RGB, SRCCOPY );

 return( TRUE );

}
```

To use the `Draw()` function in its simplest form, just pass in a `CDC` pointer. The function returns `TRUE` if it was successful and `FALSE` if it was not. Following are three examples of using the `CDib::Draw()` function. The first just passes a `CDC` pointer. The second passes a `CDC` pointer and *x* and *y* coordinates. The third passes a `CDC` pointer, *x* and *y* coordinates, and width and height values.

```
CDib Dib;
Dib.Load( C:\\Windows\\Clouds.bmp" );
```

Using a CDC Only:

```
Dib.Draw( pDC );
```

Using a CDC and Screen Coordinates:

```
Dib.Draw( pDC, 10, 25 );
```

Using a CDC, Screen Coordinates, and Width and Height:

```
Dib.Draw( pDC, 10, 25, 100, 150 );
```

CDib::SetPalette

The last function you'll need in order to correctly draw the DIBs to the screen is one that sets the palette. For DIBs with pixel depths greater than 8, this function does nothing. For DIBs with pixel depths of 8 bits or less, the palette that was obtained from the DIB data became part of the `CDib` class' `Cpalette` member. Source code for the `SetPalette()` function is in Listing 10-6.

Listing 10-6: Source Code for the SetPalette() Function

```
BOOL CDib::SetPalette( CDC *pDC )
{

 // If we have not data we
 // won't want to set the palette.
 if( m_pDib == NULL )
  return( FALSE );

 // Check to see if we have a palette
 // handle. For Dibs greater than 8 bits,
 // this will be NULL.
 if( m_Palette.GetSafeHandle() == NULL )
  return( TRUE );

 // Select the palette, realize the palette,
 // then finally restore the old palette.
 CPalette *pOldPalette;
 pOldPalette = pDC->SelectPalette( &m_Palette, FALSE );
 pDC->RealizePalette();
 pDC->SelectPalette( pOldPalette, FALSE );

 return( TRUE );

}
```

The ShowDIB Demo program

A demo program that shows you how to use the `CDib` class is included on this book's CD-ROM. It's called `ShowDIB`, and it loads, displays, and saves DIBs. Because the `CDib` class does most of the work, the source code for the program is limited to the `ShowDIBView.cpp` source code file and is minimal. Figure 10-2 shows the program running with a DIB loaded. The source code for the ShowDIB program can be found in Listing 10-7.

Figure 10-2: The ShowDIB program enables you to load DIBs from a disk file and display them in the view window.

ShowDib

CD-ROM Location: **Chap10\ShowDIB**

Program Name: **ShowDIB.EXE**

Source Code Modules in Text: `ShowDIBView.cpp`

✦ ✦ ✦ ✦ ✦

Listing 10-7: **Highlights of the ShowDib Program**

```
// ShowDIBView.cpp:implementation of CShowDIBView class
//

#include "stdafx.h"
#include "ShowDIB.h"

#include "ShowDIBDoc.h"
#include "ShowDIBView.h"

#ifdef _DEBUG
#define new DEBUG_NEW
#undef THIS_FILE
static char THIS_FILE[] = __FILE__;
#endif

////////////////////////////////////////////////////////////////
// CShowDIBView
```

(continued)

Listing 10-7 *(continued)*

```
IMPLEMENT_DYNCREATE(CShowDIBView, CView)

BEGIN_MESSAGE_MAP(CShowDIBView, CView)
 //{{AFX_MSG_MAP(CShowDIBView)
 ON_COMMAND(ID_FILE_OPEN, OnFileOpen)
 //}}AFX_MSG_MAP
END_MESSAGE_MAP()

/////////////////////////////////////////////////////////////////////
// CShowDIBView construction/destruction

CShowDIBView::CShowDIBView()
{
}

CShowDIBView::~CShowDIBView()
{
}

BOOL CShowDIBView::PreCreateWindow(CREATESTRUCT& cs)
{
 return CView::PreCreateWindow(cs);
}

/////////////////////////////////////////////////////////////////////
// CShowDIBView drawing

void CShowDIBView::OnDraw(CDC* pDC)
{
 CShowDIBDoc* pDoc = GetDocument();
 ASSERT_VALID(pDoc);

 RECT Rect;
 GetClientRect( &Rect );
 m_Dib.SetPalette( pDC );
 m_Dib.Draw( pDC, 0, 0,
  Rect.right, Rect.bottom );

}

/////////////////////////////////////////////////////////////////////
// CShowDIBView diagnostics

#ifdef _DEBUG
void CShowDIBView::AssertValid() const
{
 CView::AssertValid();
}

void CShowDIBView::Dump(CDumpContext& dc) const
{
 CView::Dump(dc);
}
```

```
CShowDIBDoc* CShowDIBView::GetDocument()
 // non-debug version is inline
{
 ASSERT(
  m_pDocument->IsKindOf(RUNTIME_CLASS(CShowDIBDoc)));
 return (CShowDIBDoc*)m_pDocument;
}
#endif //_DEBUG

/////////////////////////////////////////////////////////////
// CShowDIBView message handlers

void CShowDIBView::OnFileOpen()
{
 static char szFilter[] = "BMP Files(*.BMP)|*.BMP||";

 CFileDialog FileDlg( TRUE, NULL, NULL,
  OFN_HIDEREADONLY, szFilter );

 if( FileDlg.DoModal() == IDOK &&
  m_Dib.Load( FileDlg.GetPathName() ) ){
  InvalidateRect( NULL, TRUE );
  UpdateWindow();
  }

}
```

Double Buffering

When your applications draw to the window with a large number of GDI calls, this often causes noticeable flicker as the window clears and is then drawn. There's an easy way to eliminate this flicker using the CBitmap class. You simply create a CBitmap object and a device context, select the bitmap into the device context, draw to the newly created device context, then draw the bitmap to the window. It's a way to draw to memory with the GDI, then move the entire memory object to the visible window with one single, fast BitBlt() function call. In almost every case this eliminates the redraw flicker that's so annoying.

Create an Application with Flicker

By creating this application, you'll see a great example of screen flicker. This program will be modified later to eliminate the screen flicker by using a CBitmap. It's best if you create this project from scratch — you'll learn more. If you would rather not though, a complete project for this program can be found on the CD-ROM in the Chap10\Flicker directory.

1. Create a single document application.
2. Set a timer to go off every second.

3. Use the `InvalidateRect( NULL, TRUE )` and `UpdateWindow()` functions in the timer to cause the view window to redraw.

4. Add the following code to the `OnDraw()` function:

```
RECT Rect;
GetClientRect( &Rect );

static BOOL bColor = FALSE;
if( bColor )
 pDC->SelectStockObject( WHITE_PEN );
else
 pDC->SelectStockObject( BLACK_PEN );
bColor = !bColor;

for( int i=0; i<Rect.right; i++ ){
 pDC->MoveTo( i, 0 );
 pDC->LineTo( i, Rect.bottom );
 }
```

5. Run the program, and maximize it.

✦ ✦ ✦ ✦ ✦

When the program is running, you'll see the window flicker every second. That's because there's a delay between the time that the line drawing begins and the time it ends. Because the lines are drawn in alternating colors (white and black), you can easily see the delay and the resulting flicker.

Here's how to get rid of the screen flicker in the Flicker program that you just created. In the `OnDraw()` function before the lines are drawn, use `CreateCompatibleDC()` and `CreateCompatibleBitmap()` to create in-memory device context and bitmap objects to which you'll do your drawing. Perform all draw operations. Finally, use `BitBlt()` to move the entire memory bitmap to the visible window. A replacement `OnDraw()` function follows in Listing 10-8.

Listing 10-8: Moving the Entire Memory Bitmap to the Visible Window

```
RECT Rect;
GetClientRect( &Rect );

static BOOL bColor = FALSE;

CDC MemDC;
MemDC.CreateCompatibleDC( pDC );
```

```
CBitmap MemBitmap;
MemBitmap.CreateCompatibleBitmap( pDC,
 Rect.right, Rect.bottom );

CBitmap *pOldBitmap = MemDC.SelectObject( &MemBitmap );

if( bColor )
 MemDC.SelectStockObject( WHITE_PEN );
else
 MemDC.SelectStockObject( BLACK_PEN );
bColor = !bColor;

for( int i=0; i<Rect.right; i++ ){
 MemDC.MoveTo( i, 0 );
 MemDC.LineTo( i, Rect.bottom );
 }

pDC->BitBlt( 0, 0, Rect.right, Rect.bottom,
 &MemDC, 0, 0, SRCCOPY );

MemDC.SelectObject( pOldBitmap );
```

Double Buffering

These steps summarize the process for double buffering a series of draw operations:

Create a compatible device context using a `CDC` object.

Create a compatible bitmap using a `CBitmap` object.

Select the `CBitmap` object into the `CDC` object, and store the old bitmap so that it can be restored when you're done.

Perform all draw operations to the newly created `CDC` object.

Use the `BitBlt()` function to quickly move the newly created `CBitmap` object to the window's device context.

Restore the old bitmap in the newly created `CDC` object.

The `CDC` and `CBitmap` objects will be cleaned up by their destructors.

◆ ◆ ◆ ◆ ◆

Summary

In this chapter you've learned how to create and use device-dependent bitmaps with the `CBitmap` class. You've also learned about `Palettes` and the `CPalette` class, and their importance for images of 8-bit pixel depth. You've also seen how to make DIB manipulation easier by creating a `CDib` class and how to optimize performance with double buffering.

Bitmaps and DIBs are powerful and flexible tools in your arsenal. In an age of visual applications, it would be difficult to overstate their importance. Now that you've read this chapter, it's a good time to roll up your sleeves and do your own experimentation.

✦ ✦ ✦

MFC Exception Handling

In This Chapter

Exceptions and exception handling

Discovering the CException class

Examining how MFC defines CException-derived classes

Discovering the CSimpleException and CUserException classes

Developing your own exception classes

Advanced exception-handling techniques

Exceptions are error conditions that arise when the normal flow of a program is impractical. Both hardware and software can generate exceptions. Hardware exceptions include dividing by zero and the overflow of a numeric type. Software exceptions include the inability of an application to allocate memory or open a disk file. An example of a software exception can be seen with the `CFile` class. If the `CFile` class is used to open a disk file and the file cannot be opened, an exception of type `CFileException` is *thrown*, and the `CFileException` object contains the specific information as to why the opening of the file failed. The function that called the `CFile::Open` function is then responsible for deciding what to do based on the information contained within the exception object. Therefore, exception handling is the handling of these scenarios in an orderly and controlled manner. Because the Microsoft Visual C++ compiler implements the C++ exception-handling model based on ISO WG21/ANSI X3J16, the term "exception handling" in this chapter should be understood as referring to C++ exception handling.

One important thing to note here is that exception handling should not be used to handle "normal" or "expected" errors that the application should be able to recover from quite easily. Because functions exist to test for the existence of a file before attempting to open it, the programmer in the example mentioned previously would naturally have expected to be able to open the specified file. The fact that the file could not be opened represents an unexpected or abnormal condition, and in all likelihood, the function that attempted to open the file in the first place would not be able to continue with its task. Therefore, exception handling should be used in this case. Software exceptions and C++ exception handling within the context of a Visual C++ application are the topic of this chapter.

After learning the syntax of exception handling, exception handling will be compared to the more standard method of using return codes to signal error conditions. Once you have seen the benefits that exception handling has over other error-handling techniques, the `CException` class is introduced as well as a demo illustrating how to handle exceptions returned from the `CFileException` class. Because some functions can throw many exception types, the subject of how to define and implement a single exception class is fully covered with several examples. The chapter then finishes by presenting several advanced exception-handling issues and techniques.

Structured Exception Handling

All 32-bit versions of Windows support a form of exception handling at the operating system level called *SEH* (structured exception handling). SEH provides exception handling for almost any programming language even when the language itself does not directly support it. However, in the documentation concerning exception handling that is provided on MSDN, Microsoft states the following with regards to C++ exception handling versus SEH:

> Although structured exception handling can also be used with C++, the new C++ exception handling method should be used for C++ programs.

For more information on structured exception handling, you can refer to the "Adding Program Functionality" section of the *Visual C++ Programmer's Guide*. This guide can be found in the library edition of the MSDN.

Exception-Handling Syntax

Exception-handling syntax consists of only three keywords: `try`, `catch`, and `throw`. In exception handling, there are two participants: a server function that is *throwing* the exception and a client function that is *catching* the exception.

Throwing the exception

When a function reports the fact that an exception has occurred, it throws an exception using the following syntax:

```
throw assignment-expression
```

The manner in which the `throw` statement is called is similar to the C/C++ `return` statement. In C++, the preceding "assignment-expression" can be any type. For example, a function can throw a `char` pointer as follows:

```
void GetBuffer(char** ppBuffer, unsigned int uiSize)
{
 *ppBuffer = NULL;
 *ppBuffer = new char(uiSize);
 if (NULL == *ppBuffer)
 {
  throw "Memory Error: Could not allocate memory";
 }
}
```

However, because MFC provides a base class called `CException`, this chapter will concentrate on throwing and catching exceptions of type `CException` as well as classes that are derived from `CException`. Using the `CException` class and developing your own `CException`-derived classes will be covered shortly.

Catching the exception

Because a called function can throw an exception, the calling function must be able to respond to this event. This is done via the catch statement. In order to catch an exception, you need to bracket your code in a `try` block and specify which types of exceptions the code within that `try` block is capable of handling. All of the statements in the `try` block will be processed in order as usual unless an exception is thrown by one of the functions being called. If that happens, control is passed to the first line of the appropriate `catch` block. Using the previous example, this is how a calling function might appear:

```
#include <iostream.h>

int main()
{
 char* pBuffer;
 try
 {
  GetBuffer(&pBuffer, 512);
  cout << pBuffer;
 }
 catch(char* szException)
 {
  cout << szException;
 }

 return 0;
}
```

As you are aware of, if your function attempted to call the `cout` function with an invalid `char` pointer, your application would probably receive some type of Access Validation error. However, in the preceding example, if the string buffer could not be allocated by the `GetBuffer` function, an exception would have been thrown by `GetBuffer` and caught in main's `catch` block. Therefore, in the event that the memory could not be allocated, the `cout` function would not be executed.

So what happens if a called function throws an exception, and it is not caught by the calling function? This depends on the design of the application. When an exception is thrown, control is passed back up the call stack until a function is located that has a `catch` block for the type of exception being thrown. If a function with the appropriate `catch` block is not located, the application aborts. Therefore, if you write a function that calls another function that can throw an exception and your function doesn't catch that exception, you must be sure that some function in the call stack does handle the exception.

Another important point about catching exceptions is how to catch multiple types of exceptions. Simply adding a `catch` block for every exception type that will be caught accomplishes this. Another way to handle catching multiple exceptions types in C++ is to define a `catch` block for the base class of all the exceptions that can be thrown and use C++ RTTI (runtime type information) to figure out which exception was thrown. That way, your function needs to contain only a single `catch` block. Because the MFC exception classes have special support for the runtime checking of MFC class types, this topic is covered in more detail in the section entitled "The CException Class," later in this chapter.

Now that you know how easy it is to syntactically implement exception handling, let's take a look at why you would want to use exception handling as opposed to the more familiar approach of returning error codes to signal error conditions.

Comparing Error-Handling Techniques

The standard approach to error handling typically has been to return an error code to the calling function. The calling function is then left with the responsibility of deciphering the returned value and acting accordingly. The return value can be as simple as a basic C/C++ type or a pointer to a C++ class. More elaborately designed error-handling techniques involve the called function returning a simple value that signifies that an error has occurred. These systems then also incorporate a global function to retrieve the error information about the error. However, the concept is still the same: the calling function in some way calls a function and must inspect a returned value to verify the success or failure of the function that was called. This approach is severely flawed in a number of important ways. What follows are a few of the areas where exception handling provides tremendous benefits over using return codes.

Dealing with error codes

When using return codes, the called function returns an error code, and the error condition is handled by the calling function. Because the error handling occurs outside the scope of the called function, there is no guarantee that the caller will check the returned error code. As an example, let's say that you write a class called `CCommaDelimitedFile` that wraps the functionality of reading and writing comma-delimited files. Among other things, your class would have to expose functions to open the file and read data from the file. Using the older return code method of reporting errors, these functions would return some variable type that would have to be checked by the caller in order to verify the success of the function call. If the user of your class called the `CCommaDelimitedFile::Open()` function and then attempted to call the `CCommaDelimitedFile::Read()` function without checking whether or not the open succeeded, this could lead to undesired results. However, if the class' open function threw an exception, the caller would be forced to deal with the fact that the open failed. This is because anytime a function throws an exception, control is passed back up the call stack until it is caught. Here's an example of what that code might look like:

```
try
{
 CCommaDelimitedFile file;
 file.Open("c:\\test.csv");

 CString strFirstLine;
 file.Read(strFirstLine);
}
catch(CException* pe)
{
 AfxMessageBox("Exception caught");
}
```

As you can see, if either the `CCommaDelimitedFile::Open()` or the `CCommaDelimitedFile::Read()` function throws an exception, the calling function is forced to deal with it. If this function does not catch the exception and no other function in the current code path attempts to catch an exception of this type, the application aborts. Pay particular attention to the fact that because both the `Open()` and `Read()` functions were placed in the same `try` block, an invalid read would not be attempted if an exception was thrown. This is because programmatic control is passed from the `Open()` call `try` block to the first line of the `catch` block. Therefore, exception handling ensures that a failure in a called function cannot be ignored.

Handling errors in the correct context

The calling function often does not have enough information to handle the error. This is perhaps the biggest advantage to using exception handling. If Function A calls Function B to carry out a very simple task, it is easy to deal with an error code. However, what if Function B calls Function C, which then calls Function D and Function E? How can Function A deal with the fact that an error occurred several function layers down? Let's take a look at an example that better illustrates the problem.

In this example, a class (`CAccessDb`) is used to generate and manipulate Microsoft Access databases. Let's say this class has a static function called `GenerateDb()`. Because the `GenerateDb()` function would be used to create new Microsoft Access databases, it would have to perform several tasks to create the database. For example, it would have to create the physical database file, the specified tables (including any rows and columns), and define any necessary indexes and relations. The `GenerateDb` function may even have to create some default users and permissions. Figure 11-1 illustrates the number of function levels that would be traversed in this example.

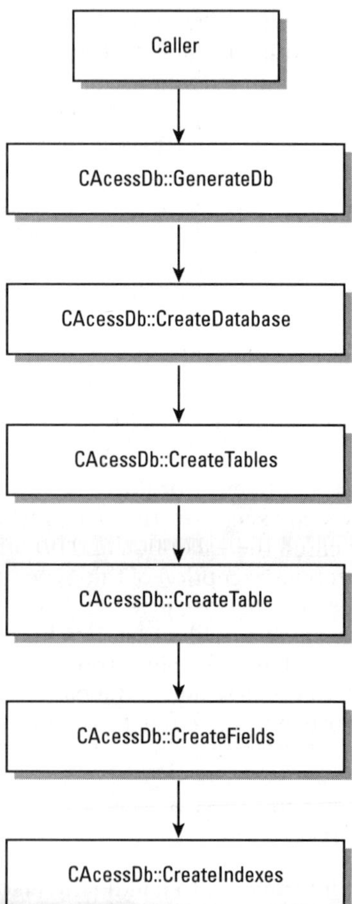

Figure 11-1: Without exception handling, long code paths make it extremely difficult for the calling function to handle returned errors.

The programmatic design problem is that if an error were to occur in the `CreateIndexes` function, which function would handle it and how? Obviously at some point, the function that originally called the `GenerateDb` function would have to handle the error, but how could it? It would have no idea how to handle an error that occurred several function calls deep in the code path. The calling function would not be in the correct "context" to handle the error. In other words, the only function that could logically create any meaningful error information about the error is the function that failed. Having said that, if return codes were used in this example, each function in the code path would have to check for every single error code that every single function below it could return. One obvious problem with this is that the calling function would have to handle a ridiculously large number of error codes. In addition, maintenance would be extremely difficult because every time an error condition is added to any of the functions in the code path, every other instance in the application where a function calls it would have to be updated to handle the new error code.

Exception handling resolves all of these issues by enabling the calling function to trap for a given type of exception. In this example, if a class called `CAccessDbException` was derived from `CException`, it could be used for any types of errors that occur within any of the `CAccessDb` member functions. (The `CException` class will be covered shortly.) Then if the `CreateIndexes()` function failed, it would construct and throw an exception of type `CAccessDbException`. The calling function would catch that exception and be able to inspect the exception object in order to decipher what exactly went wrong. Therefore, instead of handling every possible type of return code that the `GenerateDb()` and any of its called functions could return, the calling function would be assured that if *any* of the functions in that code path failed, the proper error information would be returned. An additional bonus is that because the error information is contained with a class, new error conditions can be added, and the calling function would remain unchanged.

Improving code readability

When using exception-handling code, code readability is greatly improved. This directly relates to reduced costs in terms of code maintenance. The reason for this is the way in which return codes are handled versus the exception-handling syntax. Using return codes with the `CAccessDb::GenerateDb()` function mentioned previously, code similar to the following would be required in order to handle error conditions:

```
void CCallingClass::CallingFunction()
{
 if (CAccessDb::GenerateDb())
 {
  ...
 }
 else
 {
   // somehow figure out which function in the
   // failed and why
 }
}

RETURN_CODE CAccessDb::GenerateDb()
{
 if (CreatePhysicalDb())
 {
  if (CreateTables())
  {
```

```
      if (CreateIndexes())
      {
       return SUCCESS;
      }
      else
      {
       // handle error
      }
     }
     else
     {
      // handle error
     }
    }
    else
    {
     // handle error
    }
   }
```

Add a few pointer validations to the preceding code, and you have a tremendous amount of error validation code mixed in with the rest of the code. If you have your editor set to display tabs instead of spaces and the tab value is set to 4 (the Visual Studio default), the first character of a line of code will start around column 20 at times! While none of this is disastrous for your code, it does make the code more difficult to maintain. Code that is difficult to maintain is code that invites bugs. Let's look at how this same example would look if exception handling was used:

```
void CCallingClass::CallingFunction()
{
 try
 {
  CAccessDb::GenerateDb();
  ...
 }
 catch(CAccessDbException* pe)
 {
  pe->DisplayError();
  pe->Delete();
 }
}

void CAccessDb::GenerateDb() // throws CAccessDbException
{
 CreatePhysicalDb();
 CreateTables();
 CreateIndexes();
}
```

Notice how much cleaner and elegant the second solution is. This is because error detection and recovery code are no longer mixed with the logic of the calling code itself. As you can see, because exception handling has made this code much more straightforward, maintaining this code has been made easier.

Throwing exceptions from constructors

Because constructors can not return values, exceptions are a great way of signaling that an error has occurred during the construction of an object. Therefore, if you know that the class you are attempting to instantiate throws an exception, you must bracket its construction in a `try` block. This includes scenarios in which you are constructing the object on the stack. Here are two examples of catching exceptions that are thrown during object construction. The first example shows an attempt to construct an object on the heap, and the second example shows an attempt to construct an object on the stack:

```
// example of handling exception when constructing
// an object on the heap
try
{
 CTest pTest = new CTest;
}
catch(someexceptiontype)
{
 // handle exception
}

// example of handling exception when constructing
// an object on the stack frame
try
{
 CTest Test;
}
catch(someexceptiontype)
{
 // handle exception
}
```

The CException Class

As mentioned earlier, C++ exception handling enables you to catch exceptions of almost any type. However, using C++ classes gives you the benefit of catching an object that includes the information necessary to describe the error condition as well as functions to retrieve that information. MFC provides a set of classes for just this purpose. The base class for all MFC exception classes is called `CException`. The base `CException` class is not very complex at all. In fact, aside from the constructor, the class includes just three functions: `GetErrorMessage()`, `ReportError()`, and `Delete()`.

Creating and deleting CException objects

While the CException class does define functions for *retrieving* information about a specific exception, it does *not* contain any member variables for *defining* that information. This is because you would normally never instantiate a CException object directly. You should use instead one of the MFC CException-derived classes, or derive your own exception classes from CException and implement the GetErrorMessage() and ReportError() virtual member functions.

The CException constructor takes as its only argument a BOOL value (m_bAutoDelete) that represents whether the exception object should automatically be deleted. Setting this value to TRUE specifies that the exception object was created on the heap. This causes the exception object to be deleted when the Delete() member function is called. The only time you should set m_bAutoDelete to FALSE is when the exception object was created on the stack or when the exception object is a global object. In all but a very few cases, you will set this value to TRUE.

As mentioned previously, the CException class provides a member function called Delete() for deleting an exception object. Calling this function is very straightforward; however, here are a couple of guidelines to follow when deleting an exception object:

- ✦ Never delete an exception object directly using the C++ delete operator. Instead use the CException::Delete() function.
- ✦ If an exception is caught and will be thrown or somehow still used outside the scope of the current catch block, do not delete it.
- ✦ If an exception is caught and will not be used outside the current catch block, it should be deleted (using the Delete() function). This includes scenarios in which an exception of one type is caught and an exception of another type is being thrown. The caught exception should still be deleted if it will no longer be referenced.

Exception Cleanup the Old-Fashioned Way

If you are new to the C++ try/catch mechanism and are familiar instead with the MFC TRY/CATCH macros, you are probably wondering why you have to delete the exceptions that your function catches. Actually, you have always had to delete any caught exceptions that were not rethrown. The MFC macros deleted the exception for you "under the hood." However, if you are going to use the C++ try/catch mechanism, you are now responsible for this cleanup.

✦ ✦ ✦ ✦ ✦

Retrieving error information from a CException object

The CException class has two functions for retrieving information as to the cause of the exception: ReportError() and GetErrorMessage(). The ReportError() function displays a message box indicating the cause of the exception. Because most applications have to format any messages that are displayed to the end user, the ReportError() function is normally only used when debugging the application. Here's an example of the ReportError() function in use:

```
CStdioFile file;
CFileException fe;

try
{
 file.Open("IKnowThisFileDoesNotExist.txt",
  CFile::typeText | CFile::modeReadWrite,
  &fe);
 file.Close();
}
catch(CFileException* pe)
{
 pe->ReportError();
}
```

In the preceding example, the CFileException class was used. The CFileException class is used for exceptions when dealing with the CFile class and any of its derived classes. This class is covered in more detail shortly. Also notice that the exception was not deleted. That is because the exception object was constructed on the stack. Therefore, the exception object will be destructed automatically when it goes out of scope.

While the ReportError() function displays the exception's description, the GetErrorMessage() function returns a textual description of the error that occurred. When calling this function, the application needs to supply an LPTSTR for the description's buffer and a maximum length for the description that will be returned. When the function returns, the description can then be used to do such things as formatting an error message for display or logging the error condition to a file. Using the previous example, here's how you might format a CFileException description and display the result to the user:

```
CStdioFile file;
CFileException fe;

try
{
 file.Open("IKnowThisFileDoesNotExist.txt",
  CFile::typeText | CFile::modeReadWrite,
  &fe);
 file.Close();
}
catch(CFileException* pe)
```

```
{
 TCHAR szErrorMessage [CHAR_MAX];
 if (pe->GetErrorMessage(szErrorMessage,
  _countof(szErrorMessage)))
 {
  CString strErrorMessage;
  strErrorMessage.Format("File error encountered: %s",
   szErrorMessage);
  AfxMessageBox(strErrorMessage);
 }
}
```

Catching multiple exception types

The functions in a `try` block at times have to catch exceptions that are different from one another. For example, let's say that you create a class called `CValidatePtr` that validates pointers. If this class throws an exception, the calling function has to catch it. However, what if in the same `try` block another function is being called that can throw an exception that is not an exception of type `CValidatePtrException`? This scenario can be handled in two ways. The first method, shown in Listing 11-1, is to declare multiple `catch` blocks where each `catch` block exists for the exception type that it is prepared to handle.

Listing 11-1: Declaring Multiple Catch Blocks

```
CTestDlg::OnOk()
{
 try
 {
  CValidatePtrException::ValidatePtr(m_pTestPtr,
   RUNTIME_CLASS(CTestPtr));

  m_pTestPtr->DoSomeThing();
 }
 catch(CValidatePtrException* pe)
 {
  // do something with this type of exception
  pe->Delete();
 }
 catch(CTestPtrException* pe)
 {
  // do something else with this exception
  pe->Delete();
 }
```

A second method used to catch multiple exception types from the same try block is to use the IsKindOf function. Because the CException class specifies the DECLARE_DYNAMIC and IMPLEMENT_DYNAMIC macros, the CObject::IsKindOf() function can be used to determine what type of exception was thrown. Listing 11-2 is an example of how the IsKindOf() function would be implemented.

Listing 11-2: Implementing the IsKindOf function

```
CTestDlg::OnOk()
{
 try
 {
  CValidatePtrException::ValidatePtr(m_pTestPtr,
   RUNTIME_CLASS(CTestPtr));

  m_pTestPtr->DoSomeThing();
 }
 catch(CException* pe)
 {
  if (pe->IsKindOf(RUNTIME_CLASS(CValidatePtrException)))
  {
   // do something with this type of exception
   pe->Delete();
  }
   else if (pe->IsKindOf(CTestPtrException))
  {
   // do something else with this exception
   pe->Delete();
  }
 }
}
```

Defining CException-Derived Classes

As explained earlier, because the CException class does not expose a method of defining the cause of the exception, you must derive a class from CException. The following list shows the MFC-provided exception classes that are derived from CException:

CSimpleException

CArchiveException

CFileException

CDaoException

CDBException

COleException

COleDispatchException

CInternetException

Although defining your own CException class is by no means difficult, one of the greatest benefits of using MFC is that you have the MFC source code readily available. And who better to take tips from insofar as deriving a class from an MFC base class than an MFC-derived class! Therefore, before taking a look at how to derive your own class from CException, let's look at how MFC did the same thing with the CFileException class.

Discovering the CFileException class

The CFileException class is used when dealing with the errors in association with the CFile class or any of its derived classes. A CFileException can be thrown as a result of several different error conditions. Among those are conditions such as the specified file not being found, an invalid directory path, and a sharing violation when attempting to access a file.

The CFileException class has to associate a string value for each exception for use in the CFileException::Dump and AfxThrowFileException functions. However, the designers of the CFileException class wanted to enable the function instantiating the CFileException to be able to specify a numeric value that would represent the cause of the exception. These numeric values are defined in an enum within the CFileException class itself. Because each enum automatically has a number associated with it, a static string array is defined for the CFileException class. That way the textual description of any given CFileException can be found by using the enum value as an index into this static string array. Because this is a good technique for using in your own CException-derived classes, the enum structure and the static string array are found in Listing 11-3.

Listing 11-3: The enum Structure and the Static String Array

```
enum {
 none,
 generic,
 fileNotFound,
 badPath,
 tooManyOpenFiles,
 accessDenied,
 invalidFile,
 removeCurrentDir,
 directoryFull,
 badSeek,
 hardIO,
 sharingViolation,
 lockViolation,
```

```
 diskFull,
 endOfFile
};

static const LPCSTR rgszCFileExceptionCause[] =
{
 "none",
 "generic",
 "fileNotFound",
 "badPath",
 "tooManyOpenFiles",
 "accessDenied",
 "invalidFile",
 "removeCurrentDir",
 "directoryFull",
 "badSeek",
 "hardIO",
 "sharingViolation",
 "lockViolation",
 "diskFull",
 "endOfFile",
};
```

As you can see, each `enum` value matches a specific textual description in the `rgszCFileExceptionCause` static string array. Therefore, when a `CFileException` object is constructed and thrown, it can be done in the following manner:

```
throw new CFileException(CFileException::fileNotFound);
```

This is a very good example of how to implement specific error types with your exception classes. Actually, however, there is an even better way to deal with situations in which you have to associate a text value with an exception. One point you might have missed in the preceding definition of the static string array was that it is defined only for debug builds. In other words, the `rgszCFileExceptionCause` array is defined only within an #ifdef `_DEBUG`/#endif block. So where does the `CFileException` class get its error descriptions, and how are they associated with the `int` value that is passed to its constructor? The answer is the resource file. Due to having to localize all messages that the user will see, the `CFileException` class stores its error descriptions in the resource file. If you take a peek at how the `CFileException::GetErrorMessage()` function is defined, you will see the following:

```
BOOL CFileException::GetErrorMessage(LPTSTR lpszError,
UINT nMaxError, PUINT pnHelpContext)
{
 ASSERT(lpszError != NULL
 && AfxIsValidString(lpszError, nMaxError));
```

```
   if (pnHelpContext != NULL)
    *pnHelpContext = m_cause + AFX_IDP_FILE_NONE;

   CString strMessage;
   CString strFileName = m_strFileName;
   if (strFileName.IsEmpty())
    strFileName.LoadString(AFX_IDS_UNNAMED_FILE);
   AfxFormatString1(strMessage,
    m_cause + AFX_IDP_FILE_NONE, strFileName);
   lstrcpyn(lpszError, strMessage, nMaxError);

   return TRUE;
  }
```

The first couple of lines validate the `lpszError` argument's address and set the help context. Next the filename that was specified when the `CFileException` was constructed is retrieved. If a filename was not passed to the constructor, a string value of "unnamed file" is loaded from the resource file

Notice the line that calls `AfxFormatString1`. This function formats a `CString` using a string resource identified by the resource ID in the second argument. As you can see, a value identified as `AFX_IDP_FILE_NONE` is used. Actually what is happening here in a release build is much like what happens in a debug build. The only difference is that when you build a debug version of your application, the `enum` value is used as an index into a static string array. In the release build of your application, however, the `enum` value is added to the `AFX_IDP_FILE_NONE` value and used as a string resource ID. That way all of the `CFileException` error descriptions are kept in the MFC DLL for release builds that use the MFC in a shared DLL. For release builds that statically link MFC into their applications, the same resources are compiled into the application.

Viewing the Resources of Binary Files

If you want to view the resources of a DLL or .EXE, you can do so in Visual Studio. For example, if you want to view the string resources previously specified in the `MFC42.DLL` files, simply click the File Open toolbar icon, locate the files in your Windows `System32` folder and select the Resources entry in the Open As combo box.

✦ ✦ ✦ ✦ ✦

A CFileException demo program

Here is a demo application that shows the `CFileException` class in action. This demo can be located on the companion CD in the `\Chap11\FileExceptionTest` folder. Because you have seen how the `CFileException` class is defined, the purpose of this demo is to illustrate how easy it is to throw and catch exceptions of this type.

1. Start by using AppWizard to create a dialog-based application called FileExceptionTest. Once the project files have been created, modify the `IDD_FILEEXCEPTIONTEST_DIALOG` dialog so that when you are finished it looks like the dialog in Figure 11-2.

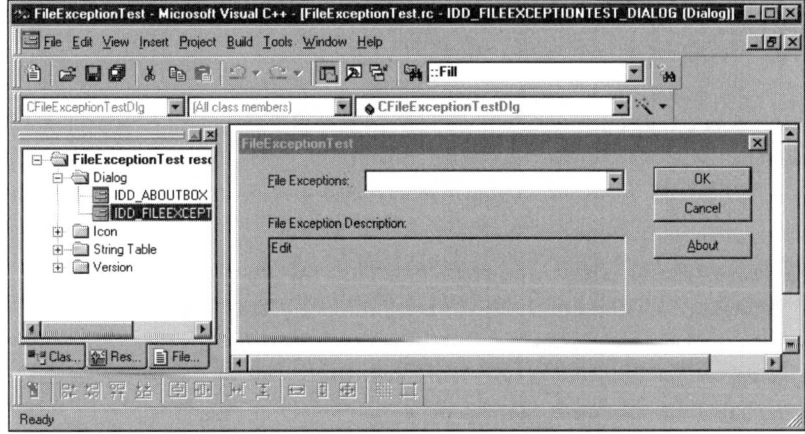

Figure 11-2: The FileExceptionTest dialog box after the new controls have been added

2. After creating the controls on the application's dialog, use ClassWizard to create a `CString` variable named `m_strFileExceptionDescription` for the File Exception Description edit control. Then create a `CComboBox` variable named `m_cboFileExceptions` for the File Exceptions combo box.

3. Open the `FileExceptionTestDlg.cpp` file, and add the code to the end of the `OnInitDialog` function right before the `return` statement.

```
static struct
{
int iException;
char szException[25];
} FILE_EXCEPTIONS[] = {
CFileException::none, "None",
CFileException::generic, "Generic",
CFileException::fileNotFound, "File Not Found",
CFileException::badPath, "Bad Path",
CFileException::tooManyOpenFiles, "Too many open files",
CFileException::accessDenied, "Access denied",
CFileException::invalidFile, "Invalid File",
CFileException::removeCurrentDir, "Remove Current Dir",
CFileException::directoryFull, "Directory Full",
CFileException::badSeek, "Bad Seek",
CFileException::hardIO, "Hard I/O",
CFileException::sharingViolation, "Sharing Violation",
```

```
CFileException::lockViolation, "Lock Violation",
CFileException::diskFull, "Disk Full",
CFileException::endOfFile, "End of File",
};

int iIndex;
for (int i = 0; i < sizeof FILE_EXCEPTIONS /
 sizeof FILE_EXCEPTIONS[0]; i++)
{
 iIndex = m_cboFileExceptions.AddString(
  FILE_EXCEPTIONS[i].szException);
 m_cboFileExceptions.SetItemData(iIndex,
  (DWORD)FILE_EXCEPTIONS[i].iException);
}
```

4. Next, use ClassWizard to add a handler for the `CBN_SELCHANGE` notification message for the combo box (`IDC_COMBO1`). This function calls the `DisplayFileException` function every time a file exception cause is selected from the combo box.

```
void CFileExceptionTestDlg::OnSelchangeCombo1()
{
 try
 {
  DisplayFileException();
  AfxMessageBox("We should never get here!");
 }
 catch(CFileException* pe)
 {
  char sz[255];
  pe->GetErrorMessage(sz, 255);

  m_strFileExceptionDescription = sz;
  UpdateData(FALSE);

  pe->Delete();
 }
}
```

5. Now implement the `DisplayFileException()` function as follows. As you can see, this function simply uses the selected combo box entry's item data (set in the `OnInitDialog()` function) to determine which type of exception should be thrown.

```
void CFileExceptionTestDlg::DisplayFileException()
{
 int iIndex;
 if (CB_ERR != (iIndex =
  m_cboFileExceptions.GetCurSel()))
 {
```

```
  int iFileException =
   m_cboFileExceptions.GetItemData(iIndex);
  throw new CFileException(iFileException);
  }
}
```

6. Building and running the demo application at this point should show results similar to what you see in Figure 11-3.

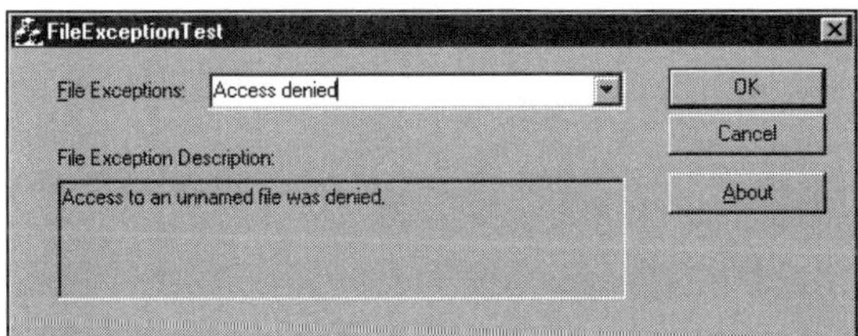

Figure 11-3: The FileExceptionTest demo application demonstrates throwing and catching exceptions of type CFileException.

Defining your own CException-derived classes

Now that you know how `CFileException` is designed, it's time to see how to derive your own exception classes from `CException`. Let's begin by imagining a real-life scenario in which you would use exceptions. Let's say you are developing a distribution system that has a few maintenance dialogs such as a dialog for maintaining customers. According to the principles of effective object-oriented design, the customer maintenance dialog would contain a pointer to the customer being created or edited on the dialog. When the user chooses to save the customer, the dialog would call `UpdateData(TRUE)` and then call the `Ccustomer::Save()` function.

In keeping with the MFC technique of having a `CFileException` class that is used for all exceptions that occur with `CFile` objects, let's create an exception class called `CCustomerException` (derived from `CException`) that is used in conjunction with the `CCustomer` class (see Listing 11-4).

Notice the `const int CUSTOMER_EXCEPTION_STRING_RESOURCE` definition. This would be used just like the `AFX_IDP_FILE_NONE` value is used in the `CFileException::GetErrorMessage()` function. In other words, the `m_iCause` member variable would be added to this value, and the result would be used as the string resource ID in order to retrieve the exception description at runtime.

Listing 11-4: The CCustomerException Exception Class

```
const int CUSTOMER_EXCEPTION_STRING_RESOURCE = 1000;

class CCustomerException : public CException
{
DECLARE_DYNAMIC(CCustomerException)

public:
 CCustomerException(int iCause);
protected:
 int m_iCause;

public:
 enum
 {
  causeDuplicateCustomer = 0,
  causeInvalidTermsCode,
  causeInvalidSupplierCode
 }
public:
 virtual BOOL GetErrorMessage(LPTSTR lpszError,
   UINT nMaxError, PUINT pnHelpContext = NULL);
};
```

Functions that use the `CCustomer` class can now simply catch exceptions of type `CCustomerException` and call its member functions in order to display or retrieve the cause of the error.

```
CCustomerMaintenanceDlg::OnOK()
{
 try
 {
  if (UpdateData(TRUE))
  {
   m_pCustomer->Save();
   CDialog::OnOK();
  }
 }
 catch(CCustomerException* pe)
 {
  TCHAR szErrorMessage[CHAR_MAX];
  if (pe->GetErrorMessage(szErrorMessage,
   _countof(szErrorMessage)))
  {
   AfxMessageBox(strErrorMessage);
  }

  pe->Delete();
 }
}
```

But now a couple of problems with this approach arise. First, you would need to create a new exception class for every class in the system that would have to signal an exception. In a very large system, this could be a ridiculously large number of classes and files to maintain. The second problem is that if a different class were created for every exception with the only difference in their class declarations being the values of an `enum` structure, this would definitely not be following effective object-oriented design techniques. In other words, you should declare a new class type only when a class does not exist that exhibits the same behavior that is needed. Therefore, there must be a better way of defining exceptions for the entire system without having an exception class for each one. Actually, there is a very simple way to do this.

Start by examining a class that is itself derived from `CException`: the `CSimpleException` class. This class is said to be a "resource critical" exception because it is based on string resources. Actually, yet another level of abstraction has to be traversed. While the `CSimpleException` class does declare a member variable to hold a string resource ID, it does not declare a function to set that resource ID. However, the `CUserException` class (derived from `CSimpleException`) does provide a constructor that takes as one of its arguments the string resource ID. That way, when the `GetErrorMessage()` function (inherited from the `CSimpleException` base class) is called, the appropriate string resource that represents the cause of the exception is loaded. Listing 11-5 shows how the `CSimpleException::GetErrorMessage()` function is implemented.

Listing 11-5: Implementing the CSimpleException::GetErrorMessage Function

```
BOOL CSimpleException::GetErrorMessage(LPTSTR lpszError,
  UINT nMaxError, PUINT pnHelpContext)
{
 ASSERT(lpszError != NULL
 && AfxIsValidString(lpszError, nMaxError));

 if (pnHelpContext != NULL)
  *pnHelpContext = 0;

 // if we didn't load our string (eg, we're a
 // console app) return a null string and FALSE

 if (!m_bInitialized)
  InitString();

 if (m_bLoaded)
  lstrcpyn(lpszError, m_szMessage, nMaxError);
 else
  lpszError[0] = '\0';
```

(continued)

Listing 11-5 *(continued)*

```
 return m_bLoaded;
}

void CSimpleException::InitString()
{
 m_bInitialized = TRUE;
 m_bLoaded = (AfxLoadString(m_nResourceID,
 m_szMessage, _countof(m_szMessage)) != 0);
}
```

Now instead of creating a new exception class for every class that needs to throw an exception, your application can construct a `CUserException` object with the correct string resource ID and `throw` it. To see just how easy this is to implement, let's take a look at some code that illustrates two example classes that can throw exceptions: `CCustomer` and `CSupplier`. Because the `CUserException` does most of the work, all you have to do is define the exception causes in the `CCustomer` and `CSupplier` class declarations. The code would like this:

```
class CCustomer : public CObject
{
...
public:
 enum
 {
  causeDuplicateCustomer = 1000,
  causeInvalidTermsCode = 1001,
  causeInvalidSupplierCode = 1002
...
};

class CSupplier : public CObject
{
enum
 {
  causeDuplicateSupplier = 2000,
  causeInvalidDiscountRate = 2001
};
```

Using this approach, you would have to catch only one exception class for all of the error conditions in your application. At this point, you only have to create the string resources with the IDs that you specify in the different class' `enum` structures. The `CCustomerMaintenanceDlg::OnOK()` function from the preceding code would now look as follows:

```
CCustomerMaintenanceDlg::OnOK()
{
 try
```

```
{
 if (UpdateData(TRUE))
 {
  m_pCustomer->Save();
  CDialog::OnOK();
 }
}
catch(CUserException* pe)
{
 TCHAR szErrorMessage[CHAR_MAX];
 if (pe->GetErrorMessage(szErrorMessage,
  _countof(szErrorMessage)))
 {
  AfxMessageBox(szErrorMessage);
 }

 pe->Delete();
}
}
```

Advanced Exception-Handling Techniques

So far the basic concepts of using exception handling and the semantics related to throwing and catching exceptions have been covered, and a few of the MFC classes that make doing all of this very easy were discovered. However, now that the basics are understood, some very important questions still remain.

Let's say that Function A calls Function B, which in turn calls Function C. If Function C can advertise the fact that it can throw a particular kind of exception, does Function B have to catch it even though it won't, or can't, do anything with it? How should code be split with regards to the `try` and `catch` blocks? Are there special considerations for throwing exceptions from virtual functions? Now that the basics of implementing MFC exception handling have been covered, let's take a look at these issues while delving a little more deeply into how to make exception handling work and deliver on its promise of making your code tighter.

Deciding what function should catch an exception

Now you know how to catch an exception that a called function may throw, and you know that control passes up the call stack until an appropriate `catch` block is found. So the question is should a `try` block catch every possible exception that a function within it may throw? The answer to that is no. As mentioned earlier, two of the biggest benefits of using exception handling in your application is reduced coding and lower maintenance cost. Listing 11-6 provides an example to illustrate the point.

Listing 11-6: The Benefits of Exception Handling

```
#include <iostream.h>

int main()
{
 try
 {
  PerformWork()
  cout << "Program terminated without any problems";
 }
 catch(char* szException)
 {
  cout << szException;
 }

 return 0;
}
void PerformWork()
{
 try
 {
  char* pBuffer;
  GetBuffer(&pBuffer, 512);
  cout << pBuffer;
 }
 catch(char* szException)
 {
  throw szException;
 }
}

void GetBuffer(char** ppBuffer, unsigned int uiSize)
{
 *ppBuffer = NULL;
 *ppBuffer = new char(uiSize);
 if (NULL == *ppBuffer)
 {
  throw "Memory Error: Could not allocate memory";
 }
}
```

As you can see in Listing 11-6, the `PerformWork` function catches the exception that `GetBuffer` might throw even though it doesn't do anything with the exception except rethrow it. The `main` function then catches the rethrown exception and truly handles it by doing something (in this case displaying an error message). Following are a few reasons why functions that simply rethrow an exception shouldn't catch the exception to begin with:

✦ Because the function doesn't do anything with the exception, you would be left with a `catch` block in the function that is at best superfluous. Obviously, it's never a good idea to have code in a function simply for the sake of its existence.

✦ If the exception type being throw by the `GetBuffer` function changed, you would have to go back and change both the `main` function and the `PerformWork` function. This results in an increased maintenance cost for the system.

✦ Doing this enough times in a large application can degrade your system performance. This is because during the process of an exception being handled every function in the stack would be returned to in order for it to simply rethrow the exception back up the call stack.

Because C++ automatically continues up the call stack until a function catches the exception, intermediate functions can ignore the exceptions that it cannot process. Recall that if a function with the appropriate `catch` block is not located, the application aborts.

Deciding what code to put in a try block

Determining what code to put in a `try` block is often really a stylistic issue. Normally you would only put code in a `try` block whose operation could result in an exception being thrown. However, many programmers tend to put almost the entire function in a `try` block for reasons of readability. Therefore, you will routinely see code like the following:

```
void SomeClass::SomeFunction(CWnd* pWnd)
{
 try
 {
  CString strWindowText;
  pWnd->GetWindowText(strWindowText);

  m_pRecord->Save(strWindowText);

  ...
 }
 catch(CException* pe)
 {
  pe->ReportError();
  pe->Delete();
 }
}
```

As you can see in the `SomeClass::SomeFunction()` function, the first two lines of code to define a `CString` object and to retrieve text from a window don't have anything to do with the possibility of the `Save` function throwing an exception. Therefore, these two lines of code could have been placed before the `try` block like this:

```
void SomeClass::SomeFunction(CWnd* pWnd)
{
 CString strWindowText;
 pWnd->GetWindowText(strWindowText);

 try
 {
  m_pRecord->Save(strWindowText);

  ...
 }
 catch(CException* pe)
 {
  pe->ReportError();
  pe->Delete();
 }
}
```

As mentioned earlier, this really comes down to a stylist choice. Although placing all of the code in the `try` block can make it more readable, both techniques are perfectly valid.

Deciding what code to put in a catch block

The only code that should ever appear in a `catch` block is code that will at least partially process the exception. For example, at times a function will catch an exception, do what it can to process the exception, and then rethrow the exception so that further exception handling can be done. Listing 11-7 provides a scenario that illustrates this.

Listing 11-7: Processing an Exception

```
CMyDialog::OnOk()
{
 try
 {
  m_pDoc->SaveInvoice(*m_pInvoice);
  CDialog::OnOK();
 }
 catch(CException* pe)
 {
  pe->ReportError();
  pe->Delete();
 }
}

CMyDoc::Save(CInvoice const& rInvoice)
{
 try
 {
```

```
    m_pDB->Commit();

    m_pDB->SaveInvoiceHdr(rInvoice->GetHeader());
    m_pDB->SaveInvoiceDtl(rInvoice->GetDetail());

    m_pDB->Commit();

    SetModifiedFlag(TRUE);
  }
  catch(CDBException* pe)
  {
    m_pDB->Rollback();

    throw pe;
  }
}
```

In Listing 11-7, a dialog called CMyDialog is used to enter invoices. Upon handling the OnOK function, the dialog attempts to use its embedded document object (m_pDoc) to save the invoice. If the SaveInvoice() function throws an exception, CMyDialog::OnOK() catches it and displays an error message. Otherwise, the dialog is dismissed (as the invoice has been saved).

You've already seen this type of "call and catch" done several times in this chapter. However, take a look at the CMyDoc::Save() function. This function calls the Commit() function, saves the data, and then calls the Commit() function again before exiting. Now look at its catch block. Before this function rethrows the exception, it calls the Rollback() function to undo any uncompleted changes from the database. This is an example of a function that catches an exception, performs some internal cleanup, and then rethrows the exception it caught.

Throwing exceptions from virtual functions

Throwing exceptions from virtual functions can definitely be tricky. As is always the case with overriding a virtual function, you should never do anything that previously written code cannot handle. In other words, let's say you have the class declaration shown in Listing 11-8.

In Listing 11-8, an exception has been derived from the CException base class. This class adds the functionality of logging an exception to a file when the LogException() function is called. Therefore, CSomeClass::SomeFunction() places the DoSomething() function call in a try block in order to catch the CTestException exception if it is thrown.

Listing 11-8: Throwing an Exception from a Virtual Function

```
class CTest
{
 ...

public:
virtual void DoSomething(); // throws CTestException

 ...
};

class CTestException : public CException
{
 ...

public:
 void LogException ();

...
};

CSomeClass::SomeFunction(CTest* pTest)
{
...
 try
 {
  pTest->DoSomething();
 }
 catch(CTestException* pe)
 {
  pe->LogException();
  pe->Delete();
 }
...
}
```

What happens now if another programmer derives a new class from `CTest`, overrides its `DoSomething()` virtual member function, and wants to throw a different type of exception? The answer is simple. If the exception is derived from a class that the `SomeFunction()` function is documented as throwing, there is no problem. In other words, all previous code continues to work as before. However, if the new class' implementation of the `DoSomething()` function throws an exception that was not documented when code was developed using the `DoSomething()` function, you will have to go back and modify all of the existing code that calls the `DoSomething()` function. Otherwise, you run the risk of breaking existing code if exceptions of the new type are thrown. Listing 11-9 shows an example of how that would fail.

Listing 11-9: Throwing an Undocumented Exception

```
class CNewTest : public CTest
{
 ...

public:
 // throws CNewTestException
 virtual void DoSomething();
 ...
};

CSomeClass::SomeFunction(CTest* pTest)
{
 try
 {
  pTest->DoSomething();
 }
 catch(CTestException* pe)
 {
  pe->LogException();
  pe->Delete();
 }
}
```

Now if the `CSomeClass::SomeFunction()` function is called with a pointer to a `CNewTest` object and the `DoSomething()` function throws an exception, it will not be caught. One of the biggest selling points of C++ is the capability to add new code to a system without having to rewrite existing code. In this case, however, existing code has been broken. The reason is that the `DoSomething()` function was documented as throwing an exception of one type and then an overridden version of this function threw an exception of another type. Luckily there are two ways to solve this problem.

If you override a function documented as throwing a specific type of exception and you need to throw a different type of exception, throw an exception derived from the originally documented exception type. In Listing 11-9, that means because the `DoSomething()` function was originally documented as throwing an exception of type `CTestException`, the `CNewTest::DoSomething()` override should only throw exceptions of that type or a class that is derived from that type.

Another way to solve this problem is for the calling function to generically catch an exception type that represents the base class to all of the exception types in the system. Then the calling function can use the `IsKindOf` function to check for specific exception types. This type of approach should definitely be used when you are designing a class that has functions that you know will be overridden. Listing 11-10 shows a better way of handling the example shown in Listing 11-9.

Listing 11-10: Catching an Exception that Represents a Base Class to All Exception Types

```
class CTest
{
 ...

 // Upon failure, DoSomething() throws
 // CTestException (derived from CException)
 virtual void DoSomething(); // throws CException

 ...
};

class CTestException : public CException
{
 ...

public:
 void LogException ();

 ...
};

class CNewTest : public CTest
{
 ...

 // Upon failure, DoSomething() throws
 // CNewTestException (NOT derived from CException)
 virtual void DoSomething();

 ...
}

CSomeClass::SomeFunction(CTest* pTest)
{
 try
 {
  pTest->DoSomething();
 }
 catch(CTestException* pe)
 {
  pe->LogException();
  pe->Delete();
 }
 catch(CException* pe)
 {
  TCHAR szErroMessage[512];
  if (pe->GetErrorMessage(szErrorMessage,
   _countof(szErrorMessage)))
  {
```

```
      // call global logging function
      // passing szErrorMessage so that
      // all exceptions get logged
    }

    pe->Delete();
  }
}
```

Summary

As you've seen throughout this chapter, exception-handling syntax is simple, the MFC exception classes are straightforward, and implementing exception handling in your application is as easy as designing your functions ahead of time. What makes exception handling so powerful is not obtuse syntax or a complex lattice of C++ classes. It is the overall use of exceptions in your application and the benefits derived therein that make exception handling an important tool to developing dependable applications with robust and complete error checking.

✦ ✦ ✦

C H A P T E R 12

Controls

◆ ◆ ◆ ◆

In This Chapter

The history of Windows controls

The anatomy of a control

How to program with commonly used controls

Owner-drawn controls

Using the CButton class

Using the CListBox class

Using the CEdit class

Using the CStatic class

Using the CScrollBar class

Using the CComboBox class

Customizing controls

Adding keyboard interaction

◆ ◆ ◆ ◆

In this chapter, we look closely at Windows controls and the MFC classes that encapsulate them. By the end of the chapter, you should be an expert in using these controls, and you should be able to take what you have learned and apply it to new controls.

Background

The 32-bit versions of Windows currently ship with over 20 readily available controls. Six of these have been included in Windows since the very first version. These controls reside in `user.exe`. The remaining controls are referred to as *common controls*. These controls reside in `comctl32.dll`. While the original six are available in every released version of Windows, the common controls are available only in 32-bit environments.

Controls appear as child windows that are clipped to their parent window. When the parent window is moved, the child window is moved with it. When the parent window is destroyed, the child windows are automatically destroyed as well. Controls and their functionality are encapsulated in MFC by various control classes. A listbox control is encapsulated by `CListBox`, an edit control is encapsulated by `CEdit`, and so on. Each of the six original controls, their corresponding MFC class names, and their actual window classes are listed in Table 12-1.

Because controls are specialized windows, MFC derives the control classes from a base class of `CWnd`. One advantage of deriving the control classes from `CWnd` is that, in many cases, the same functionality for different controls is accessed through the same member function. Thus `ctl➪ SetWindowText ((char*) "Hello")` sets the text displayed on a button control to "Hello" and also inserts the string "Hello" into an edit control.

Table 12-1
Windows Control Classes

Control	*MFC Class*	*Window Class (WNDCLASS)*
Button	CButton	BUTTON
List Box	CListBox	LISTBOX
Combo Box	CComboBox	COMBOBOX
Edit Control	CEdit	EDIT
Static Control	CStatic	STATIC
Scroll Bar	CScrollBar	SCROLLBAR

Creating Controls

You can create a control using one of two methods. One is to include the control inside a dialog resource. When the dialog resource is loaded, Windows automatically creates the included controls. The built-in DevStudio wizards make this almost trivial. Once you have finished creating your dialog, you can run the ClassWizard that generates all the code you need to make your controls work. ClassWizard also enables you to point and click your way to setting up the controls' message handlers.

The other method is to explicitly call the control's `create` member function. If you were creating a list box control, the function call would look like this:

```
m_ListBox.Create(WS_CHILD | WS_VISIBLE | WS_VSCROLL,
    ctlRect, this, IDC_CUSTS)
```

The first group of parameters, `WS_CHILD`, `WS_VISIBLE`, and `WS_VSCROLL` are style flags that are combined to create an overall style for the control. In this case, these flags specify that the list box should be created as a visible child window with a vertical scroll bar. The next parameter, `ctlRect`, is a `CRect` object that specifies the location and size of the list box. The next parameter, `this`, is a pointer to the parent window. This is how MFC establishes the child-parent relationship. The last parameter, `IDC_CUSTS`, is an unsigned integer that represents the control's resource ID.

When you explicitly create a control using `Create`, you must manually position the control within the parent window. A bounding box described by a `CRect` object governs the positioning and size of the control. When you are setting the `CRect` that will be used to create the control, always take into account the height and width of the current font. Otherwise, your control may mangle text and not be correctly positioned in the window. Also, the positioning coordinates of a control within a window are always relative to the window's client area, as shown in Listing 12-1.

Listing 12-1: **Positioning a Control**

```
CClientDC dc (this);
CFont TempFont;
TEXTMETRIC metric;
CRect TempRect;
CEdit TempEdit;
int CharHeight,CharX,CharY;

// Get output device size and convert it to points
CharHeight=-((dc.GetDeviceCaps(LOGPIXELSY)*8/72));
// Create the font
TempFont.CreateFont(CharHeight, 0, 0, 0, FW_NORMAL, 0, 0,
   0, DEFAULT_CHARSET, OUT_CHARACTER_PRECIS,
   CLIP_CHARACTER_PRECIS, DEFAULT_QUALITY, DEFAULT_PITCH
   | FF_DONTCARE, "Arial");

// Select the font into the client area device context //and
save the existing font setting
CFont* pOldFont=dc.SelectObject(&TempFont);

// Retrieve the new font's metrics
dc.GetTextMetrics (&metric);
CharX=metric.tmAveCharWidth;
CharY=metric.tmHeight+metric.tmExternalLeading;

// Set bounding box coordinates in TempRect
TempRect.SetRect(CharX*2,CharY*2,CharX*20,CharY*2);

//Create the control
TempEdit.Create(WS_CHILD | WS_VISIBLE, TempRect, this,
  IDC_EDIT1);
```

This snippet of code illustrates how to change a window's client-area font to Arial and then use the font and client-area information to position a control. First, we obtain the size of the window's client area and convert it from pixels per logical inch to points. Because computer monitors vary in size, Windows measures the screen in something called *logical* inches. A logical inch is a unit of measurement that stays the same no matter what size image is used. Logical inches are used quite a bit in window-positioning code because they let the programmer specify different positions on the screen without having to worry about the actual size of the image. In order to apply this measurement to our font operations, we must convert it to a unit of measure we can use — in this case, points.

Once we have the character height computed, we use it to create an instance of the Arial font using a `CFont` object. After the font is created, we must select it into the current device context. The call to `CDC::SelectObject` selects the new font into the window's client device context. Now that we have the font in a device context, we can get the average width and height information of the font by using `CDC::GetTextMetric` and storing the result in a `TEXTMETRIC` structure. We then use the member variables `tmAveCharWidth`, `tmHeight`, and `tmExternalLeading`, to calculate the width and height of one character.

After all this work, we're almost done. Now that we know how wide and tall one character is, we can use it to size a `CRect` and position the control. Using a call to `CRect::SetRect()`, we define a rectangle that has an upper coordinate of 2,2 and a lower-right coordinate of 20,2. When we use this to create the edit control, it positions the control's upper-left corner two characters over and two characters down from the top of the client area. The bottom right corner is positioned twenty characters over and two characters down from the top.

When controls are constructed in this manner, an interesting "feature" of Windows rears its ugly head. If a control is included as part of a dialog resource, it is drawn as if the control were sculpted into the face of the dialog box. This is referred to as a *3D border*. Controls that are manually created lack this 3D effect. They are drawn with a flat 2D border. The 3D border is controlled by the `WS_EX_CLIENTEDGE` style flag. As the WS_EX prefix indicates, this is an extended window style. The standard Create function we have analyzed to this point does not accept extended style flags.

What is the resolution to this sticky problem? The `CWnd` class, from which the six basic controls inherit, provides another member function called `CreateEx()` that does accept extended style flags. Instantiating the edit control in Listing 12-1 with `CreateEx()` would look like this:

```
TempEdit.CreateEx(WS_EX_CLIENTEDGE, "EDIT", NULL,
   WS_CHILD | WS_VISIBLE, TempRect, this, IDC_EDIT1);
```

As you can see, the syntax of `CreateEx()` differs a bit from `Create()`. The first argument specifies any extended window styles, such as `WS_EX_CLIENTEDGE`. The second argument specifies the window class (`WNDCLASS`) of the control, which is, in this case, `EDIT`. The fourth argument specifies the window name. For control-creation purposes, you should pass in `NULL`. The fifth, sixth, seventh, and eighth arguments specify the standard style flags, the control's bounding box in a `CRect` object, a pointer to the parent window, and the control's resource ID, respectively.

So far we have covered the fundamentals of creating controls. We have examined using controls within dialogs as well as manually creating our own controls in parent windows. You may be wondering how you access the information contained in the control. If the control is part of a dialog resource, access to the control's data is governed by a mechanism called Dialog Data Exchange (DDX). We will cover DDX in more detail in Chapter 14. However, if the control is part of a regular window, you'll need the control's member function to access its data. In the next section, we will look at the details of programming each of the six basic controls.

Using the CButton class

The `CButton` class can create four different button styles: check boxes, radio buttons, group boxes, and the ever-popular push button. The type of button that you create is controlled by a style flag. Table 12-2 lists the relevant style flags and a short description of the button type they represent.

Table 12-2
CButton Style Flags

Style	*Description*
`BS_PUSHBUTTON`	Garden-variety push button control.
`BS_DEFPUSHBUTTON`	A push button with a thick border, this is used in dialog boxes to denote the default button.
`BS_RADIOBUTTON`	A radio button control.
`BS_AUTORADIOBUTTON`	A radio button that when clicked deselects all other radio buttons in a group.
`BS_GROUPBOX`	A group box.
`BS_CHECKBOX`	A standard check box.
`BS_AUTOCHECKBOX`	A check box that checks and unchecks itself when clicked.
`BS_3STATE`	A check box that has three states: checked, unchecked, and indeterminate.
`BS_AUTO3STATE`	Same as `BS_3STATE` except that it automatically cycles through the three states when it is clicked.

Creating push buttons

A push button (Figure 12-1) is created by specifying either `BS_PUSHBUTTON` or `BS_DEFPUSHBUTTON` in the call to `CButton::Create`. `BS_DEFPUSHBUTTON` is normally only used for buttons that represent the default action for a dialog or a window. A button created with `BS_DEFPUSHBUTTON` is clicked when the user hits the Enter key while the window or dialog has focus.

Figure 12-1: A typical push button

Handling button messages

All button types send a `WM_COMMAND` message to their parent window when they are clicked. The corresponding MFC message handler name is *OnButtonName* where

ButtonName corresponds to the resource ID of the button. If you need to trap the click event of the button, add code to this message handler.

Creating radio buttons

You can create a radio button (Figure 12-2) with a call to `CButton::Create`, specifying either `BS_RADIOBUTTON` or `BS_AUTORADIOBUTTON`. Because radio buttons are normally used to represent a group of options where only one option can be selected, the easiest style to use is `BS_AUTORADIOBUTTON`.

Figure 12-2: A typical radio button

Setting and interrogating radio buttons

If you decide to create radio buttons without the `BS_AUTORADIOBUTTON` style, you must manually maintain the correct settings for all the radio buttons in a group. To maintain the correct state for all radio buttons in a group, follow these steps in each of the buttons' `BN_CLICKED` handler:

1. Set the radio button's state to `BST_CHECKED` via a call to `CButton::SetCheck`.
2. Set the other radio buttons to `BST_UNCHECKED`.

The following code sample demonstrates these steps:

```
void CMainWindow::OnRadioButton1()
{
    // Check this button since it was clicked
    m_ctlRadioButton1.SetCheck (BST_CHECKED);

// Uncheck this button since m_ctlRadioButton1 was
// clicked
    m_ctlRadioButton2.SetCheck (BST_UNCHECKED);
}
```

A much simpler approach is to use the `BS_AUTORADIOBUTTON` style. Because this style operates on groups of controls, you must help Windows figure out which radio buttons are part of a group. To create a group of radio buttons that will automatically maintain mutual exclusivity, follow these steps:

1. Create the radio buttons in your code in sequence. Make sure that you don't create other controls in this sequence.
2. Use the `WS_GROUP` style to mark the beginning of a group. Assign this style to the first button in the group.

3. If you have multiple groups of radio buttons, assign WS_GROUP to the first radio button in each group. Windows uses WS_GROUP to find the boundaries between groups.
4. Always use SetCheck to ensure that one radio button in each group is checked when the group is created.
5. CButton::GetCheck returns the radio button's current state. Radio buttons return either BST_CHECKED or BST_UNCHECKED.

Creating check boxes

Check boxes (Figure 12-3) are buttons that are created with one of the following style flags: BS_CHECKBOX, BS_AUTOCHECKBOX, BS_3STATE, or BS_AUTO3STATE. Check boxes that are created with one of the "AUTO" styles automatically change their states when they are clicked. As we just saw with radio buttons, if you choose to create a check box using one of the non-"AUTO" styles, you will have to manually change the check box's state in response to click events.

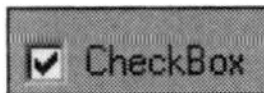

Figure 12-3: A typical check button

Setting and interrogating check boxes

Interrogating check boxes is done through a call to CButton::GetCheck(). Check boxes return either BST_CHECKED or BST_UNCHECKED.

You can manually set a check box's state through a call to CButton::SetCheck. SetCheck accepts BST_CHECKED or BST_UNCHECKED for two- or three-state check boxes.

Using the CListBox class

The MFC CListBox class encapsulates the List Box window class. List boxes display lists of strings that are referred to as *items*. List boxes are useful for displaying information that is organized in a flat manner, such as lists of states or zip codes. In fact, a list box can display anything that can be represented by a string.

List boxes come in several flavors. The default list box presents data in a single vertical column and only allows one list item to be selected at a time. Using the style flags listed in Table 12-3, you can create several variations on the standard list box. Each of the style flags used by CListBox are listed in Table 12-3.

Table 12-3
CListBox Style Flags

Style	*Description*
LBS_STANDARD	Default list box that has a border and vertical scroll bar, sorts items alphabetically, and sends notification messages to the parent window when a selection changes or an item is double-clicked.
LBS_SORT	Sorts items alphabetically. List boxes lacking this style display items in the order that they were added.
LBS_NOSEL	Allows items to be viewed but not selected.
LBS_MULTIPLESEL	Allows multiple selections.
LBS_EXTENDEDSEL	Allows the user to use the Ctrl and Shift keys to make selections. Normally paired with LBS_MULTIPLESEL.
LBS_NOTIFY	Notifies the parent window when the selection changes or an item is double-clicked.
LBS_DISABLENOSCROLL	Displays a vertical scroll bar at all times. If the list box does not have enough items to scroll, the scroll bar is disabled. Default list boxes hide the scroll bar when not needed.
LBS_MULTICOLUMN	Enables multiple column display.
LBS_USETABSTOPS	Expands tab stops contained in item strings. Tab stops are set using CListBox::SetTabStops().
LBS_NOREDRAW	Does not automatically redraw when an item is added or removed. Can be selectively enabled and disabled using the WM_SETREDRAW message.
LBS_HASSTRINGS	Remembers the items added to it. LBS_STANDARD includes this feature.
LBS_WANTKEYBOARDINPUT	Sends the parent window a WM_VKEYTOITEM or WM_CHARTOITEM message when a key is pressed and the list box has input focus.
LBS_NOINTEGRALHEIGHT	List box height does not have to be a multiple of the item height.

Creating list boxes

List boxes (Figure 12-4) can be created using either CListBox::Create or CListBox::CreateEx. If you want to construct a standard list box with a 3D border and alphabetically sorted items, the function call would look like this:

```
m_ListStates.CreateEx(WS_EX_CLIENTEDGE,
    "LISTBOX", NULL, WS_CHILD | WS_VISIBLE |
    LBS_STANDARD, TempRect, this, IDC_STATES);
```

The style LBS_STANDARD is kind of an "all in one" style for list boxes. It includes alphabetic sorting, a vertical scroll bar when necessary, and sends both BN_CLICKED and BN_DOUBLECLICKED notifications to its parent window.

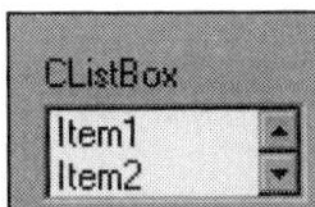

Figure 12-4: A typical list button

Adding and deleting items

Adding items to a list box is accomplished through the AddString() member function:

```
m_ListBox1.AddItem(NewItem);
```

This function accepts either a null-terminated string or a CString object. If the list box was created with either LBS_STANDARD or LBS_SORT, the items are alphabetically sorted as they are added. Items added to list boxes lacking these styles are appended to the end of the list. You can override the sorting behavior of LBS_STANDARD and LBS_SORT list boxes by using the InsertString() member function:

```
m_ListBox1.InsertString(8, NewItem);
```

InsertString() inserts an item to the list at a location based on the list box's zero-based index. This example inserts NewItem in position eight. Both AddString() and InsertString() return the position of the newly added or inserted item.

Strings are deleted from a list box with the member function DeleteString(). DeleteString() expects a single argument, the index of the item to be removed. If you want to delete all the strings in a list box, use the ResetContent() function

Selecting items and searching

CListBox has several functions that enable you to get information about and manipulate the current selection. For single selection list boxes, use GetCurSel(). This function returns the zero-based index of the currently selected item. GetCurSel() returns the value LB_ERR when nothing is selected.

Conversely, setting a list box's selection is done by passing the function SetCurSel() the index of the item to be selected. To clear all selections in a list box, pass SetCurSel() with the value –1. You can also set the selection based on a string using the function SelectString():

```
m_ListBox1.SelectString(1,"CA");
```

SelectString() expects two arguments. The first argument tells SelectString() where to start its search. Use the value –1 to specify the beginning of the list. SelectString() wraps around to the beginning of the list if it receives a value other than –1. The second argument specifies the starting text of the item. The first item SelectString() finds that matches the search criteria is selected so it is important to be as specific as possible.

To search a list box for a string without selecting any items, use either FindString() or FindStringExact(). FindString() uses the same starting text search as SelectString(), while FindStringExac()t searches for the exact text specified. Both functions return the index of the item found or LB_ERR if no items are located.

Multiple selection list boxes work a bit differently. Items can be selected with SetSel(), for a single selection, or SelItemRange(). These functions can be combined to create multiple selections:

```
m_ListBox1.SetSel(5);
m_ListBox1.SelItemRange(TRUE,7,12);
m_ListBox1.SelItemRange(FALSE,1,4);
```

This code selects items 5 and 7 through 12 and deselects items 1 through 4.

Handling button messages

As we've seen before, list box controls send notifications to their parent windows via WM_COMMAND messages. MFC message macros map these messages to ON_LBN map entries. Table 12-4 lists the notification types, the associated macro, and special comments.

Table 12-4
CListBox Messages

Notification	*Trigger*	*Associated Macro*
LBN_SELCHANGE	Current selection changes *(not programmatically)*.	ON_LBN_SELCHANGE
LBN_SELCANCEL	Selection is canceled.	ON_LBN_SELCANCEL
LBN_SETFOCUS	Control receives input focus.	ON_LBN_SETFOCUS
LBN_KILLFOCUS	Control loses input focus.	ON_LBN_KILLFOCUS
LBN_DBLCLK	Item is double-clicked.	ON_LBN_DBLCLK
LBN_ERRSPACE	Operation failed due to lack of memory.	ON_LBN_ERRSPACE

Using the CEdit class

The CEdit MFC class encapsulates the Edit window class. The CEdit control is a single- or multi-line box that can contain text. The MFC class provides additional functionality in the form of cut, paste, and undo support, text insertion, and basic text formatting.

Creating edit controls

CEdit objects (Figure 12-5) are created by calling CEdit::Create.

Figure 12-5: CEdit objects

CEdit recognizes the flags listed in Table 12-5.

Table 12-5
CEdit Style Flags

Style	*Description*
ES_LEFT	Causes text contained in the control to be left justified.
ES_RIGHT	Causes text contained in the control to be right justified.
ES_CENTER	Causes text contained in the control to be center justified.
ES_LOWERCASE	Displays all text as lowercase.
ES_UPPERCASE	Displays all text as uppercase.
ES_WANTRETURN	Causes the Enter key to break lines while the control has input focus instead of activating the parent window's default button.
ES_AUTOVSCROLL	Control automatically scrolls vertically.
ES_AUTOHSCROLL	Control automatically scrolls horizontally.
ES_OEMCONVERT	Performs ANSI-to-OEM-to-ANSI conversion on all characters.
ES_NOHIDESEL	Control does not hide the current selection if it loses focus.
WS_VSCROLL	Causes the control to display a vertical scroll bar. *Must be used with ES_AUTOVSCROLL.*
WS_HSCROLL	Causes the control to display a horizontal scroll bar. *Must be used with ES_AUTOHSCROLL.*

Controlling a CEdit control

You can programmatically limit the number of characters that a CEdit control will accept by calling CEdit::SetLimitText:

```
m_Edit1.SetLimitText(40);
```

In any case, CEdit has a maximum upper limit of approximately 60K of text. This makes CEdit suited to smaller text entry tasks. If you need to manipulate more text than 60K, use CRichEditCtrl.

The member function SetTabStops() is used to set the tab stops on a newly created edit control. CEdit::SetTabStops() measures distance in *dialog units*. A dialog unit is approximately equal to one-quarter the average width of the system font. The default distance between tab stops in CEdit is 32 dialog units. With CEdit::SetTabStops() you can set the distance between tab stops or set each tab stop individually with an absolute position. This example demonstrates both of these concepts:

```
m_Edit1.SetTabStops(16);
//Sets the tab stops to 16 dialog units

int nTabStops[]={5,10,30,45,52 };
m_Edit1.SetTabStops(5,nTabStops);
//Sets variable distance tab stops at 5,10,30,45,52
```

Adding and deleting text

When it comes to inserting and retrieving text from CEdit, you have two basic choices. CEdit::SetWindowText() and CEdit::GetWindowText() affect all the text contained within a CEdit control. This means that SetWindowText() replaces any text that is currently in the control with whatever string you pass to it. CEdit::GetWindowText() returns all the control's text to you.

If you only want to work with part of the existing text in the control, then you'll have to use a different set of functions. CEdit::GetLine() returns one line of text. A call to GetLine looks like this:

```
m_Edit1.GetLine(5, pBuf, sizeof(pBuf));
```

GetLine expects three parameters: the zero-based index of the line position you want to retrieve, a pointer to a string buffer that the control uses to store the text, and the maximum size of the buffer. You can use CEdit::LineLength() to determine how much space to allocate in your buffer. When GetLine() copies text to the buffer, it does not have a null terminator. In order to use the buffer once GetLine() fills it, you must have some way of determining where in the buffer the string ends. GetLine returns the size of the buffer it used to copy text. You can then use this information to find the end of the string.

If you need to know the total number of lines in a CEdit control, use CEdit::GetLineCount(). GetLineCount() returns the current line count for the target control. However, `GetLineCount()` returns a line count of 1 even if the control is empty. This detail is overlooked by many beginning Windows C++ programmers.

Cut, copy, paste, and undo (oh my!)

`CEdit` provides straightforward member functions that enable you to programmatically cut, copy, and paste text, as well as undo editing changes. The statement

```
m_Edit1.Cut();
```

cuts the currently selected text from the control and places it on the Clipboard. The statement

```
m_Edit1.Copy();
```

copies the currently selected text from the control and places it on the Clipboard as well.

If the target control has no current selection, then `Cut()` and `Copy()` do nothing.

If you need to manually select text from your program, use `CEdit::SetSel`:

```
m_Edit1.SetSel(25,100);
```

This example selects 75 characters starting with the twenty-fifth character in the control. If the selection spans multiple lines within the control, `CEdit` automatically scrolls the text as it makes the selection. If you need to disable this scrolling behavior, pass `SetSel` a third Boolean parameter `FALSE`:

```
m_Edit1.SetSel(25,100,FALSE);
```

Now the same 75 characters will be selected but without any annoying text scrolling.

What if you need to select some text, but you know only the line index? `CEdit` provides a handy member function `CEdit::LineIndex`. `LineIndex` accepts a zero-based line index value for the control and returns the character index for the first character in the line. From this you can locate the beginning of your selection. Finding the end is a little more work. The following code snippet demonstrates how to locate the beginning and end of a selection based on line index values. For the purposes of this example, let's assume that the selection begins on line 5 and ends on line 12:

```
int SelStart;
int SelEnd=0;
int t;

SelStart=m_Edit1.LineIndex(5);
```

```
    //Retrieves the first character index for line 5

SelEnd=SelStart;

//Iterate through each line and add the line lengths together

for (t=5,t<13,t++) {
        SelEnd=SelEnd + m_Edit1.LineLength(t);
    }

m_Edit1.SetSel(SelStart,SelEnd,FALSE);
    // Now lines 5 thru 12 are selected
```

`CEdit::Paste()` pastes the contents of the Clipboard into the control. If text is selected within the control, `Paste()` overwrites the selection with the Clipboard's contents. If the control doesn't have a selection, then `Paste()` inserts text at the current caret position. If the Clipboard is empty, then `Paste()` does nothing. You can determine if the Clipboard contains text by calling the Win32 API function `::IsClipboardFormatAvailable()` and passing in the constant `CF_TEXT`. The function returns a Boolean value indicating whether or not the Clipboard is empty:

```
m_bHasText=::IsClipboardFormatAvailable(CF_TEXT);
```

Editing changes can be rolled back by `CEdit::Undo`.

Making Use of Undo

`CEdit::Undo()` can rollback multiple times as long as there are no intervening edit changes. This means that you can make changes to the contents of a `CEdit` control and call `CEdit::Undo()` to rollback your changes. As long as you do not type anything else in the `CEdit` control, `CEdit::Undo()` continues to rollback changes. Editing text after a call to `CEdit::Undo()` reset the control's undo buffer to contain only your most current change.

◆ ◆ ◆ ◆ ◆

Handling CEdit messages

`CEdit` controls send notifications to their parent windows via EN_ messages. MFC message macros map these messages to `ON_EN` macros. Table 12-6 lists the notification types, the associated macro, and special comments.

Using the CStatic class

The `CStatic` MFC class encapsulates the `STATIC` window class. The `CStatic` control is a rectangle that can either describe a rectangular area, display text, or display an image. Depending on the style flags used during creation, `CStatic` can also send event messages to its parent window.

Table 12-6
CEdit Messages

Notification	*Trigger*	*Associated Macro*
`EN_UPDATE`	The control's text is about to be changed.	`ON_EN_UPDATE`
`EN_CHANGE`	The control's text has been changed.	`ON_EN_CHANGE`
`EN_HSCROLL`	The text is scrolled horizontally using a scroll bar.	`ON_EN_HSCROLL`
`EN_VSCROLL`	The text is scrolled vertically using a scroll bar.	`ON_EN_VSCROLL`
`EN_SETFOCUS`	The control receives input focus.	`ON_EN_SETFOCUS`
`EN_KILLFOCUS`	The control loses input focus.	`ON_EN_KILLFOCUS`
`EN_MAXTEXT`	The maximum amount of text has been entered, or the caret is at the bottom right corner of the formatting rectangle.	`ON_EN_MAXTEXT`
`EN_ERRSPACE`	Insufficient memory to complete operation.	`ON_EN_ERRSPACE`

Creating CStatic controls

`CStatic` objects (Figure 12-6) are created by calling `CStatic::Create()`.

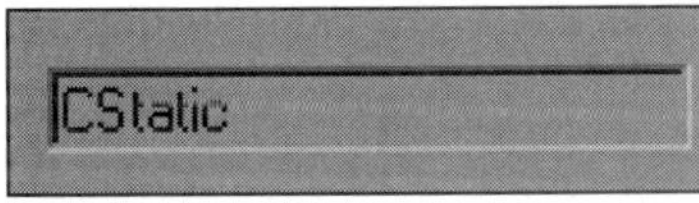

Figure 12-6: CStatic object

`CStatic` recognizes the style flags listed in Table 12-7.

Because there are three different types of `CStatic` controls, each require slightly different steps for their creation. The text type of `CStatic` is the easiest to create. Simply make the standard call to `Create`, and `OR` together the other necessary parameters and whatever style flags you desire:

```
m_Static1.Create("Names",WS_CHILD | WS_VISIBLE | SS_LEFT
  | SS_SUNKEN, TempRect, this, IDC_STATIC1);
```

Table 12-7
CStatic Style Flags

Style	*Control Type*	*Description*
SS_LEFT	Text	Left-aligns the control's text, and wraps text if it won't fit on one line.
SS_CENTER	Text	Same as SS_LEFT, except this style center-aligns text.
SS_RIGHT	Text	Same as SS_LEFT, except this style right-aligns text.
SS_LEFTNOWORDWRAP	Text	Left-aligns the control's text, but clips any text that doesn't fit on one line.
SS_CENTERNOWORDWRAP	Text	Same as SS_LEFTNOWORDWRAP, but center-aligns text.
SS_RIGHTNOWORDWRAP	Text	Same as SS_LEFTNOWORDWRAP, but right-aligns text.
SS_SIMPLE	Text	Creates a CStatic object whose text can not be changed after creation.
SS_CENTERIMAGE	Text	Centers text in control both horizontally and vertically.
SS_NOPREFIX	Text	Suppresses the default behavior of showing ampersands as shortcuts.
SS_SUNKEN	Text	Causes a sunken border to be displayed around the control.
SS_BLACKRECT	Rectangle	Draws a solid rectangle in the system COLOR_WINDOWFRAME color.
SS_WHITERECT	Rectangle	Draws a solid rectangle in the system COLOR_WINDOW color.
SS_GRAYRECT	Rectangle	Draws a solid rectangle in the system COLOR_BACKGROUND color.
SS_BLACKFRAME	Rectangle	Draws a hollow rectangle (outline) in the system COLOR_WINDOWFRAME color.
SS_WHITEFRAME	Rectangle	Draws a hollow rectangle (outline) in the system COLOR_WINDOW color.
SS_GRAYFRAME	Rectangle	Draws a hollow rectangle (outline) in the system COLOR_BACKGROUND color.
SS_ETCHEDFRAME	Rectangle	Draws a hollow rectangle (outline) with an etched border.
SS_ETCHEDHORZ	Rectangle	Draws a hollow rectangle (outline) with etched top and bottom borders.

Style	Control Type	Description
SS_ETCHEDVERT	Rectangle	Draws a hollow rectangle (outline) with etched left and right borders.
SS_BITMAP	Image	Creates a static control that displays a bitmap.
SS_ENHMETAFILE	Image	Creates a static control that displays a metafile.
SS_REALSIZEIMAGE	Image	Prevents the control from being automatically resized to match the displayed image.
SS_ICON	Image	Creates a static control that displays an icon.
SS_NOTIFY	Text, Rectangle, Image	Causes the control to send event messages to its parent window.

A call to SetWindowText sets the control's text, while GetWindowText() retrieves the currently displayed text. Creating rectangle CStatic controls is just as straightforward:

```
m_Static1.Create("", WS_CHILD | WS_VISIBLE |
  SS_BLACKFRAME, TempRect, this, IDC_Static1);
```

Creating and displaying an image in a CStatic control requires a few more steps, but it's still very easy. Control creation follows the same form as outlined previously. Each type of image file requires a different member function to load it into the control. The following example creates a CStatic object and displays a bitmap where hImage is a handle to a bitmap:

```
m_Static1.Create("",WS_CHILD | WS_VISIBLE | SS_ICON,
TempRect, this, IDC_STATIC1);

m_Static1.SetIcon(hImage);
```

while this code loads an enhanced metafile where hImage is a handle to a metafile image:

```
m_Static1.Create("",WS_CHILD | WS_VISIBLE |
   SS_ENHMETAFILE, TempRect, this, IDC_STATIC1);

m_Static1.SetEnhMetaFile(hImage);
```

and this code loads a bitmap where hImage is a handle to a bitmap image:

```
m_Static1.Create("",WS_CHILD | WS_VISIBLE | SS_BITMAP,
   TempRect, this, IDC_STATIC1);

m_Static1.SetBitmap(hImage);
```

You can also retrieve a handle to the image the control is displaying by calling either GetIcon(), GetEnhMetaFile(), or GetBitmap.

Handling CStatic messages

By default, CStatic controls do not send event notification messages to their parent window. If a CStatic control is created with the SS_NOTIFY style flag, it sends event messages to its parent window. These messages are summarized in Table 12-8.

Table 12-8
CStatic Messages

Notification	*Trigger*	*Associated Macro*
STN_ENABLE	The control is enabled.	ON_STN_ENABLE
STN_DISABLE	The control is disabled.	ON_STN_DISABLE
STN_CLICKED	The control was clicked.	ON_STN_CLICKED
STN_DBLCLK	The control was double-clicked.	ON_STN_DBLCLK

Creating CStatic objects with SS_NOTIFY enables you to create some interesting effects within your application. You can create transparent "hot spots" within windows that respond to mouse events, clickable image maps, or even images that look like sunken buttons that respond to mouse events.

Using the CScrollBar class

CScrollBar is MFC's representation and encapsulation of the window class SCROLLBAR. The scroll bars created with CScrollBar are generally the same as the scroll bars you're used to seeing with a few key differences. Window scroll bars are aligned to the side or bottom of their parent window's client area and run the entire width or height of their parent window. In addition, window scroll bars are generally created for you. CScrollBar controls can appear anywhere in a window's client area, can be of any length and height, and must be explicitly created.

Creating CScrollBar controls

Let's take a look at what is required to create a `CScrollBar` control (Figure 12-7).

Figure 12-7: CScrollBar control

`CScrollBar` accepts the style flags listed in Table 12-9.

Table 12-9
CScrollBar Style Flags

Style	*Description*
SBS_BOTTOMALIGN	Used with the SBS_HORZ style. The bottom edge of the scroll bar is aligned with the bottom edge of the rectangle specified in the Create member function. The scroll bar has the default height for system scroll bars.
SBS_HORZ	Designates a horizontal scroll bar. If neither the SBS_BOTTOMALIGN nor SBS_TOPALIGN style is specified, the scroll bar has the height, width, and position given in the Create member function.
SBS_LEFTALIGN	Used with the SBS_VERT style. The left edge of the scroll bar is aligned with the left edge of the rectangle specified in the Create member function. The scroll bar has the default width for system scroll bars.
SBS_RIGHTALIGN	Used with the SBS_VERT style. The right edge of the scroll bar is aligned with the right edge of the rectangle specified in the Create member function. The scroll bar has the default width for system scroll bars.
SBS_SIZEBOX	Designates a size box. If neither the SBS_SIZEBOXBOTTOMRIGHTALIGN nor SBS_SIZEBOXTOPLEFTALIGN style is specified, the size box has the height, width, and position given in the Create member function.
SBS_SIZEBOXBOTTOM RIGHTALIGN	Used with the SBS_SIZEBOX style. The lower-right corner of the size box is aligned with the lower-right corner of the rectangle specified in the Create member function. The size box has the default size for system size boxes.

(continued)

Table 12-9 *(continued)*

Style	*Description*
SBS_SIZEBOXTOPLEFTALIGN	Used with the SBS_SIZEBOX style. The upper-left corner of the size box is aligned with the upper-left corner of the rectangle specified in the Create member function. The size box has the default size for system size boxes.
SBS_TOPALIGN	Used with the SBS_HORZ style. The top edge of the scroll bar is aligned with the top edge of the rectangle specified in the Create member function. The scroll bar has the default height for system scroll bars.
SBS_VERT	Designates a vertical scroll bar. If neither the SBS_RIGHTALIGN nor SBS_LEFTALIGN style is specified, the scroll bar has the height, width, and position given in the Create member function.

The function call to Create() looks like this:

```
m_VertScrollBar.Create(WS_CHILD | WS_VISIBLE | SBS_VERT |
  SBS_RIGHTALIGN, TempRect, this, IDC_SBVERT);
```

First, we specify all of our desired style flags. In this case, we are specifying a visible child window that is a vertical scroll bar and is aligned with the right edge of the rectangle described by TempRect. As indicated in Table 12-9, because SBS_RIGHTALIGN was used, CScrollBar uses TempRect only to establish the end points of the scroll bar. The width of TempRect does not influence the width of the scroll bar. The new scroll bar width will be the system default scroll bar width.

Next is TempRect, the bounding box (or rectangle) we've seen before that describes the size of our control. If we hadn't used SBS_RIGHTALIGN, the scroll bar would've been the same width as TempRect. The last two parameters are also ones that we've seen before: a pointer to the parent window and the resource ID for the control.

Controlling CScrollBar

CScrollBar provides several member functions you can use to query the scroll bar for its current position, set the current position, and limit the total scrolling range for the scroll bar. CScrollBar::SetScrollPos() and CScrollBar::GetScrollPos() set and get the position of the scroll bar's thumb (the sliding box that rides on the scroll bar), respectively. ScrollBar::SetScrollRange() and CScrollBar::GetScrollRange() set and get the absolute scrolling range for the scroll bar.

While you can use these functions to control the scroll bar, you can get and set the thumb position as well as the scrolling range in one step if you are programming for a 32-bit environment. The two member functions `CScrollBar::SetScrollInfo()` and `CScrollBar::GetScrollInfo()` enable you to do this. These two functions accept a `SCROLLINFO` structure:

```
typedef struct tagSCROLLINFO {  // si
    UINT cbSize;
    UINT fMask;
    int  nMin;
    int  nMax;
    UINT nPage;
    int  nPos;
    int  nTrackPos;
}   SCROLLINFO;
typedef SCROLLINFO FAR *LPSCROLLINFO
```

that specifies just about everything you'd ever need in a scroll bar. The first parameter `cbSize` is the total size of the structure. `fMask` is a bit mask that describes the scroll bar parameters requested. You can set `fMask` to the constants listed in Table 12-10.

Table 12-10
CScrollBar Attribute Constants

Constant	*Description*
`SIF_DISABLENOSCROLL`	Disables the scroll if it is not needed. This constant is only used during `CScrollBar::SetScrollInfo`.
`SIF_PAGE`	`nPage` member of `SCROLLINFO` contains page information for a proportional scroll bar.
`SIF_POS`	`nPos` contains the current position of the scroll bar's thumb.
`SIF_RANGE`	`nMin` and `nMax` contain the lower and upper limits of the scroll bar's range.
`SIF_ALL`	Combination of all other constants.

The member `nTrackPos` specifies the immediate position of a scroll box that the user is dragging. An application can retrieve this value while processing the `SB_THUMBTRACK` notification message. You can't set the immediate scroll position; `CScrollBar::SetScrollInfo()` function ignores this member. Now that we are familiar with `CScrollBar`'s member functions, let's look at the code snippet in Listing 12-2 that creates and controls a scroll bar.

Listing 12-2: Creating and Controlling a Scroll Bar

```
CScrollBar  VertBar;
SCROLLINFO  si;
CRect TempRect;
int nCurrentPos;
LPINT nMin;
LPINT nMax;

TempRect.SetRect(100,10,100,150)
VertBar.Create(WS_CHILD | WS_VISIBLE | SBS_VERT |
  SBS_SIZEBOXTOPLEFTALIGN, TempRect, this, IDC_SCVERT1);
.
.
.
.
VertBar.GetRange(nMin, nMax);
//Now nMin and nMax hold the scrolling range
//limits

si.fMask=SIF_ALL;
VertBar.GetScrollInfo(si);
//Now the si structure holds all the information about
//the scroll bar

si.nMin=10;
si.nMax=90;
VertBar.SetScrollInfo(si);
//Scrolling range was changed in one call
```

Handling CScrollBar messages

CScrollBar doesn't send WM_COMMAND messages to its parent window like the other controls that we've studied. Scroll bars send WM_VSCROLL or WM_HSCROLL messages that contain the new scroll bar position and the ID of the scroll bar sending the message. The control ID is important because MFC maps these messages to OnVScroll and OnHScroll message handlers. A window can have only one of each message handler and must have some way of determining which scroll bar sent the message. That's where the control ID comes in. When MFC maps the message to the message handler function, these different parts of the scroll bar's messages are presented as function arguments. You can then easily determine which scroll bar is scrolling and take appropriate action. We will look more closely at scrolling in general in Chapter 20.

Using the CComboBox class

The CComboBox MFC class encapsulates the window class Combo Box. A combo box provides all the functionality of a CEdit control combined with a CListBox control. Because CComboBox has many functions in common with CEdit and CListBox, we will focus just on what is unique to CComboBox.

Creating a CComboBox control

The standard call to Create is used to instantiate a CComboBox control. View the CComboBox in Figure 12-8.

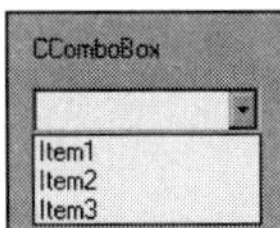

Figure 12-8: The CComboBox control

CComboBox::Create() accepts the flags listed in Table 12-11.

Table 12-11
CComboBox Style Flags

Style	*Description*
CBS_AUTOHSCROLL	Edit control portion of the combo box scrolls horizontally.
CBS_DISABLENOSCROLL	Vertical scroll bar is displayed in a disabled state when there are not enough items to scroll. The default is to hide the scroll bar when it isn't needed.
CBS_DROPDOWN	Specifies a drop-down combo box.
CBS_DROPDOWNLIST	Specifies a combo box with a drop-down list.
CBS_LOWERCASE	Converts all strings to lowercase.
CBS_UPPERCASE	Converts all strings to uppercase.
CBS_OWNERDRAWFIXED	Specifies an owner-drawn combo box whose items are all the same height.
CBS_OWNERDRAWVARIABLE	Specifies an owner-drawn combo box whose items are of varying heights.
CBS_SIMPLE	A simple combo box.
CBS_SORT	Automatically sorts entries as they are added.
CBS_HASSTRINGS	Causes the combo box to retain the strings that are added to it. Normal combo boxes have this style by default. Owner-drawn combo boxes do not.
CBS_OEMCONVERT	Performs an ANSI-to-OEM-to-ANSI conversion. See CListBox.

CComboBox::Create() accepts the standard parameters we have seen in other controls:

```
m_Combo1.Create(WS_CHILD | WS_VISIBLE | CBS_DROPDOWNLIST
  | CBS_SORT | WS_BORDER | WS_VSCROLL, TempRect, this,
  IDC_SSN);
```

It is important to remember that TempRect describes not only the length of the edit control portion of the combo box, but also the length of the drop-down list. Make sure that you size your CRect appropriately.

Controlling CComboBox

There really aren't many new functions that you'll use to control a CComboBox control. CComboBox::GetWindowText() and CComboBox::SetWindowText() get and set the text within the edit box portion of the control. CComboBox::AddString(), CComboBox::DeleteString(), and CComboBox::InsertString() manipulate the drop-down list portion of a combo box in the same way you'd use a CListBox object.

The functions that are unique to CComboBox include CComboBox::ShowDropDown(), which displays or hides the drop-down list; CComboBox::GetDroppedState(), which queries the state of the drop-down list; CComboBox::GetLBText() retrieves a list entry given a zero-based index value; and CComboBox::GetLBTextLen() gets the length of a specified entry given a zero-based index value.

One important CComboBox function is SetExtendedUI(). This enables the extended user interface for the drop-down portion of the combo box. By default, the drop-down list is displayed whenever the combo box is clicked, regardless of combo box type. If the extended user interface is enabled, the drop-down list is displayed only for combo boxes created with the CBS_DROPDOWNLIST style. In addition, normal settings cause Alt+F4 to display the drop-down list when the control has focus. The down arrow is then used to scroll through the list. If the extended user interface is enabled, only the down arrow is needed to display and scroll through the drop-down list. Most users expect combo boxes to exhibit this extended behavior. Use SetExtendedUI() wherever possible.

Handling CComboBox messages

CComboBox controls can emit several different messages. However, only certain types of combo boxes can emit specific messages. Table 12-12 summarizes this information.

Table 12-12
CComboBox Messages

Message	*CComboBox Style*	*Trigger*	*Associated Macro*
CBN_DBLCLK	CBS_SIMPLEN	Item in list box is double-clicked.	ON_CBN_DBLCLK
CBN_SELCHANGE	ALL	Selection is changed.	ON_CBN_SELCHANGE
CBN_SELENDOK	ALL	Selection is made.	ON_CBN_SELENDOK
CBN_SELEND CANCEL	CBS_DROPDOWN CBS_DROPDOWN LIST	Selection is canceled.	ON_CBN_ SELENDCANCEL
CBN_EDITUPDATE	CBS_SIMPLE, CBS_DROPDOWN	Immediately before text in the edit control is about to change.	ON_CBN_EDITUPDATE
CBN_EDITCHANGE	CBS_SIMPLE, CBS_DROPDOWN	Immediately after text in the edit control has changed.	ON_CBN_EDITCHANGE
CBN_DROPDOWN	CBS_DROPDOWN, CBS_DROP DOWNLIST	When the drop-down list is displayed.	ON_CBN_DROPDOWN
CBN_CLOSEUP	CBS_DROPDOWN, CBS_DROP DOWNLIST	When the drop-down list is closed.	ON_CBN_CLOSEUP
CBN_KILLFOCUS	ALL	When the control loses input focus.	ON_CBN_KILLFOCUS
CBN_SETFOCUS	ALL	When the control receives input focus.	ON_CBN_SETFOCUS
CBN_ERRSPACE	ALL	When an operation fails due to lack of memory.	ON_CBN_ERRSPACE

Wow! We've covered a lot in the last section. We've looked at the basic control-creation process, how to create a control on your own, as well as the in's and out's of working with each of the six basic controls. Before we dive headlong into the next section, let's try some example code that should help pull together all we've learned so far.

The Mini Editor Program

A demonstration program is on the CD to show you how to use many of the controls we've discussed. The Mini Editor is a minimal text file editor. It only understands files with the extension .mne. Using this application, you can search directories for files. You can open, display, edit, and save these files as well as create new ones. The Mini Editor was implemented using Visual Studio's AppWizard to create a dialog-based application.

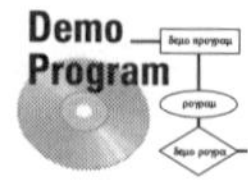

Mini Editor
CD-ROM Location: **Chap12\MiniEdit**
Program Name: `MiniEdit.exe`

✦ ✦ ✦ ✦ ✦

Advanced Control Programming

Up to this point, we have looked at basic control programming functions such as control creation and positioning and handling the different control messages. In many situations, the stock features that a control provides may be sufficient for your needs. In other cases you might need to modify the behavior of a control or perhaps change its on-screen appearance. In this section we will cover:

- ✦ Adding a keyboard interface to controls
- ✦ Extending the stock behavior of a control
- ✦ How to create custom buttons
- ✦ How to change a control's color

Adding a keyboard interface

We have already seen one of the benefits of using dialog boxes with controls. It saves you from having to manually muck with control creation and placement. One of the other big advantages of using dialog boxes is the inherent keyboard interface a dialog box adds to all controls. When a dialog contains several controls, you can use the Tab key to move the input focus from one control to another. The dialog box takes care of moving the focus from control to control.

A normal window does not have this feature. This means that you'll have to take care of manually moving the input focus at each Tab key press. This isn't as difficult as it sounds, but it does require that you understand how Windows uses messages and the order that MFC processes those messages. Deep in the darkest recesses of the application framework is a segment of code referred to as the *message pump*. The message pump constantly checks the message queue for new messages. When it receives a message, it translates it into the MFC messages we are used to seeing, such as `ON_DBLCLICK`, and then dispatches that message to the appropriate control or child window.

`::IsDialogMessage()` is a Win32 API function that checks for keyboard messages and converts them into selection commands for the corresponding dialog box, or in our case, window. For example, the Tab key, when pressed, selects the next control or group of controls, and the down arrow key, when pressed, selects the next control in a group.

In order for `::IsDialogMessage()` to work its magic, we need to call it before MFC can translate the message. This is where it's important to understand the order of events when MFC processes a message. When a window receives a message, it calls `TranslateMessage()` to translate any keyboard-based messages into virtual keycodes. MFC then calls `DispatchMessage()` to send the message to the appropriate control or child window. Fortunately, MFC provides a function, `PreTranslateMessage()`, we can use to override the default window behavior.

Whether or not a window translates a message is determined by the return value from `PreTranslateMessage()`. If it returns 0, the message is sent on to `TranslateMessage()`. If `PreTranslateMessage()` returns a non-zero value, MFC assumes that the message has been processed and moves on to the next message. When `PreTranslateMessage()` returns a non-zero value, `TranslateMessage()` is never called.

This is where we insert the call to `::IsDialogMessage()`. When `::IsDialogMessage()` receives a message that it can process, it returns the Boolean value `TRUE`. Because `TRUE` is a non-zero value by definition, we can conveniently use the return value of `::IsDialogMessage()` as the return value of `PreTranslateMessage()`:

```
BOOL CMainWin::PreTranslateMessage(MSG* pMsg)
{
    return ::IsDialogMessage(m_hWnd, pMsg);
}
```

`::IsDialogMessage()` expects two parameters. The first is a handle to the window that is receiving the message. This is easily accessible from `CWnd`'s member variable `m_hWnd`. The second parameter it expects is a pointer to an MSG structure.

`::IsDialogMessage()` uses the window handle and the information in the MSG structure to determine if the message contains a "dialog box" type message such as the Tab key or down arrow. It then sends the appropriate selection message to move the input focus to the next control.

Modifying control behavior

As you work more with Visual C++ and MFC, you may find yourself wishing that you could change the behavior of some controls. For example, assume that you are writing an application that is data entry intensive. Quite a bit of your code would be spent doing data validation and error checking. Wouldn't it be nice if you could create your own versions of controls that encapsulated the application's data entry rules? Thanks to MFC's message mapping and C++ inheritance, rolling your own control is very straightforward.

For the purposes of this demonstration, let's assume that you are writing a human resources application. One of the fields is a CEdit control that is a Social Security number field. This field can only contain hyphens or numbers. The following code implements this behavior:

```
Class CSsnEdit : public CEdit
{
    protected:
        afx_msg void OnChar(UINT, UINT, UINT);
        DECLARE_MESSAGE_MAP()
};

BEGIN_MESSAGE_MAP (CSsnEdit, CEdit)
    ON_WM_CHAR()
END_MESSAGE_MAP()

void CSsnEdit::OnChar(UINT nChar, UINT nRepCnt, UINT
  nFlags)
{
    if (((nChar>='0') && (nChar<='9')) || (nChar=='-'))
        CEdit::OnChar(nChar,nRepCnt,nFlags);
}
```

The line `afx_msg void OnChar(UINT, UINT, UINT)` and its corresponding message map entry `ON_WM_CHAR()` intercept any key presses and route them to the specialized message handler. Within the `OnChar()` message handler, we determine if the character typed was between zero and nine or if it was a hyphen. If it was, we call `Edit::OnChar()` to add the character to the control. If the message does not meet this criteria, the message is ignored, and no characters are added to the control.

In order to derive your customized control, you should follow these steps. First, derive a custom class from a control that most closely matches the functionality you need. Second, create an entry in the classes message map, and declare a message handler function for the message you wish to process. Because most control classes are derived themselves from CWnd, refer to the Visual C++ online documentation for a complete list of CWnd messages. Next, insert code into the message handler to customize the control's behavior.

Bitmap buttons

In addition to customizing a control's behavior, you can also change how the control appears on the screen. In these next two sections, we will address how to change the appearance of push buttons and how to change the control of a control.

MFC and Windows 95/NT provide two different ways to create push buttons with customized appearances. MFC provides the CBitmapButton class, which is derived from CButton. Windows 95/NT includes two new button styles BS_BITMAP and BS_ICON. Either of these methods let you create push buttons with customized faces.

Creating a custom button using CBitmapButton is simple. You must have at least two bitmap images of the customized button. These images represent the button when it is up and when it is down (when it is clicked). You can also provide two other bitmaps that represent the button when it has the input focus and when it has been disabled. While there are no restrictions for your button's appearance, it is a commonly accepted practice that your buttons approximate the look of ordinary buttons. This means that a disabled button should appeared "grayed" or washed out, a button with the input focus should have a dotted rectangle, and buttons that are clicked should appear to be depressed. The bitmaps should also include the button's edges. Once you have created your custom bitmaps, they can be added to your application's resource file:

```
SENDU  BITMAP    sendu.bmp
SENDD  BITMAP    sendd.bmp
SENDF  BITMAP    sendf.bmp
SENDX  BITMAP    sendx.bmp
```

The last step is to actually create the button and load the button bitmap resources:

```
m_Send.Create("", WS_VISIBLE | WS_CHILD | BS_PUSHBUTTON
  | BS_OWNERDRAW, TempRect, this, IDC_SEND);
m_Send.LoadBitmaps("SENDU","SENDD","SENDF","SENDX");
```

Notice the use of the BS_OWNERDRAW style during the call to Create(). You must use this style in order for the custom bitmaps to display. It is this style flag that tells Windows you will be providing the button bitmaps. In addition, the bounding box you specify should match the size of the button's bitmaps.

If you are writing an application that will run strictly in a 32-bit environment, you may want to use one of the new button style flags, BS_ICON and BS_BITMAP. Either one of these style flags reduces the amount of work necessary to create a custom bitmap button. The trade-off is that these style flags are only available in Windows 95/NT.

BS_BITMAP

Using BS_BITMAP is even easier than using CBitmapButton. You need only provide one button bitmap. Windows will draw the up, down, focus, and disabled states on its own. Creating a button using BS_BITMAP looks like this:

```
hBmp=::LoadBitmap(AfxGetInstanceHandle(),"SEND");

m_Send.Create("",WS_VISIBLE | WS_CHILD | BS_PUSHBUTTON |
  BS_BITMAP, TempRect, this, IDC_SEND);

m_Send.SetBitmap(hBmp);
```

The bitmap does not include the borders of the button. This is another advantage of using this style. If button borders change in future releases of Windows, your custom buttons will continue to look correct. Because they include borders, buttons created with CBitmapButton will have to have new bitmaps created. By default the bitmap will be centered on the face of the button. You can use the styles listed in Table 12-13 to change the positioning of the bitmap.

Table 12-13
Bitmap Positioning Constants

Style	*Description*
BS_TOP	Aligns the bitmap with the top of the button.
BS_BOTTOM	Aligns the bitmap with the bottom edge of the button.
BS_CENTER	Centers the bitmap horizontally.
BS_VCENTER	Centers the bitmap vertically.
BS_LEFT	Aligns the bitmap with the left edge of the button.
BS_RIGHT	Aligns the bitmap with the right edge of the button.

CBitmapButton destroys the button's bitmaps when it is destroyed. When you use BS_BITMAP, you must explicitly destroy the bitmap yourself:

```
::DeleteObject(hBmp);
```

BS_ICON

Using the BS_ICON style is similar to BS_BITMAP. The only difference between the two is that BS_ICON uses an icon resource. The following code snippet illustrates how to create a button that uses the BS_ICON style:

```
m_Send.Create("",WS_CHILD | WS_VISIBLE | BS_ICON, TempRect,
this, IDC_SEND);

m_Send.SetIcon(AfxGetApp()->LoadIcon("SEND");
```

The only drawback to using BS_ICON is that the button is limited to the maximum size of an icon, 48 × 48 pixels. However, buttons created with BS_ICON do have one interesting feature that BS_BITMAP buttons lack. They understand the concept of transparent colors. This means that BS_ICON buttons can easily adapt to changes in system colors. CBitmapButtons, on the other hand, can display ugly color boxes when the system colors are changed.

Changing a control's color

One of the most obvious omissions in the design of controls is the lack of a member function that changes the color of the control. You can change a control's font with SetFont(), but there is not an equivalent member function to change colors such as SetColor().

Using MFC, there are two ways to change a control's color. Both take advantage of the fact that controls send a WM_CTLCOLOR message to the parent window before they paint themselves. This message contains a handle to the device context used to paint the control. Because we have access to the device context, we can call member functions such as CDC::SetTextColor() or CDC::SetBkColor() to change the colors on the control. With this knowledge, you can write a message handler to select different colors. The message handler must return a brush handler (HBRUSH) that the control will use to paint its background. The prototype of the message handler looks like this:

```
afx_msg HBRUSH OnCtlColor(CDC* pDC, CWnd* pWnd, UINT nCtlColor)
```

MFC passes this handler three values. The first, pDC, is a pointer to the control's device context. pWnd is a pointer to the control itself, and nCtlColor describes the type of WM_CTLCOLOR message that triggered the message handler. These message types are summarized in Table 12-14.

The following code sample illustrates a basic message handler for WM_CTLCOLOR. Assume that m_Name is an edit control and m_brGrnBrush is a CBrush object.

Table 12-14
WM_CTLCOLOR Message Types

nCtlColor Value	*Type of Control*
CTLCOLOR_STATIC	Static text control, all button styles except push buttons, read-only or disabled edit controls, and the edit portion of a disabled combo box.
CTLCOLOR_EDIT	Edit control and the edit portion of a combo box.
CTLCOLOR_LISTBOX	List box and the list box portion of a combo box.
CTLCOLOR_BTN	Push button – processing this message has no effect in Windows 95.
CTLCOLOR_SCROLLBAR	Scroll bar.
CTLCOLOR_DLG	Dialog box.
CTLCOLOR_MSGBOX	Message box.

```
HBRUSH CMainWin::OnCtlColor(CDC* pDC, CWnd* pWnd, UINT
  nCtlColor)
{
    if (m_Name.m_hWnd==pWnd->m_hWnd)
    {
        pDC->SetTextColor(RGB(255,255,255));
        pDC->SetBkColor(RGB(255,0,0));
        return (HBRUSH) m_brGrnBrush;
    }
    CFrameWnd::OnCtlColor(pDC, pWnd, nCtlColor);
}
```

This code changes the color of m_Name to white with a red background. This is one way to change a control's color. The only disadvantage of using this technique is that the parent window is responsible for changing each control's color. It would be better if we could encapsulate this behavior inside each control. This way, each control becomes a separate entity that can be reused. Because the controls send messages to their parent windows before they paint themselves, we need some way of "reflecting" these messages back to the child window, or control, that originated the message.

MFC provides such a mechanism. By using the ON_WM_CTLCOLOR_REFLECT message map macro, we can cause the parent window to send all unprocessed WM_CTLCOLOR messages back to the child window that originated the message. Now we can write customized controls that change their colors without relying on their parent window. The following code sample describes a custom control that changes its background, text, and text background:

```
class CMyStatic : public CStatic
{
public:
    CMyStatic();
protected:
    CBrush m_Brush;
afx_msg HBRUSH CtrlColr(CDC*, UINT);
    DECLARE_MESSAGE_MAP()
};

BEGIN_MESSAGE_MAP(CMyStatic, CStatic)
    ON_WM_CTLCOLOR_REFLECT()
END_MESSAGE_MAP()

CMyStatic::CMyStatic()
{
    m_Brush.CreateSolidBrush (RGB(255,255,255));
}

HBRUSH CMyStatic::CtlColor (CDC* pDC, UINT nCtlColor)
{
    pDC->SetTextColor(RGB(nRed,nGreen,nBlue));
    pDC->SetBkColor(RGB(255,0,0);
    return (HBRUSH) m_Brush;
}
```

Summary

In this chapter you have learned how to use the basic controls that are a part of the Windows operating system. We have examined the control-creation process and learned the differences between placing controls in a dialog box and placing them on a window. Next, you investigated the different types of controls and how each of them are used. You were introduced to the unique style flags each control used and how you could use the flags to create variations of the controls. Finally, we looked at some advanced control programming topics and learned how to customize controls for almost any situation.

You should now be comfortable using controls in your programming projects. As you learn more about programming the different types of windows — dialog and document/view — you'll be able to apply more of your knowledge of controls to your programming tasks.

The Windows "common" controls have not been covered in this chapter. They will be covered in detail in Chapter 24.

✦ ✦ ✦

CHAPTER 13

Modal and Modeless Dialogs

✦ ✦ ✦ ✦

In This Chapter

Creating a dialog template resource

Using the dialog editor

Discovering the CDialog class

Using modal and modeless dialogs

Understanding how to use DDX and DDV

Creating derived custom controls

Serializing data from a dialog-based application

✦ ✦ ✦ ✦

Dialogs are used to display information as well as receive input from the user. Dialogs perform this task by utilizing Windows controls such as edit controls, list boxes, combo boxes, and buttons. These controls are sometimes referred to as *child controls* because they are usually created as children of a dialog. MFC provides an object-oriented programming approach to working with dialogs and controls via several classes that encapsulate the dialog (`CDialog`) and the different controls (covered in Chapter 12) that can be placed on a dialog.

As with anything else in programming, the quickest way to learn is by doing. Therefore, a simple address and phone book application will be built and modified throughout this chapter in order to illustrate the different aspects of programming dialogs. The first few sections of this chapter will illustrate the basics of working with dialogs. Included in these sections are such topics as learning how to use the dialog editor to create dialog templates, how to use the `CDialog` class, and how to use dialog data exchange (DDX) and dialog data validation (DDV). Once these topics have been covered, the address and phone book demo application will be introduced and built.

As with the other chapters in this book, programming the demos is not entirely necessary to learn the skills used in the chapter. However, to reinforce the concepts being taught, it is recommended that you work your way through the demos. After creating the demo application, the following sections of the chapter will introduce more advanced topics such as creating and working with derived control classes, using "extra DDX," managing modeless dialogs, and serializing data from a dialog-based application. As you finish each section, you will update the demo application to include the newly learned functionality.

Using the Dialog Editor

Visual Studio includes several resource editors that can be used to create the different resources for a Windows application. One of these editors, the dialog editor, is used to create and edit dialog templates from which dialog boxes are created when the application is run. Using the dialog editor, you can do any of the following:

- ✦ Create new dialog templates
- ✦ Edit dialog template properties
- ✦ Add or remove controls from the dialog
- ✦ Arrange and size a dialog's controls
- ✦ Edit the properties of a dialog's controls
- ✦ Set the tab order of a dialog's controls
- ✦ Test a dialog

Dialog templates

At this point, use AppWizard to create a dialog-based project called AddressBook. Once you have created the AddressBook project, you should see results similar to those illustrated in Figure 13-1. Notice the Resource View tab, the Controls toolbar, and the Dialog toolbar; these are the principal means of creating and editing dialog templates with the dialog editor. How to use each of these will be covered shortly.

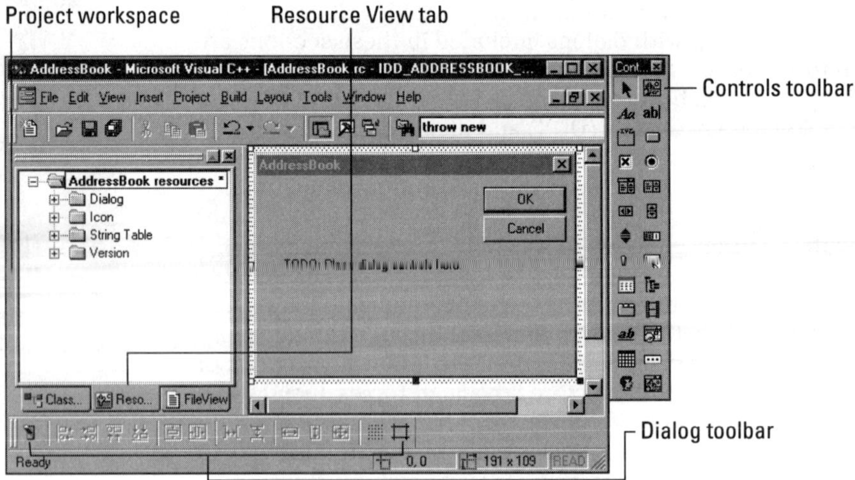

Figure 13-1: The Visual Studio dialog editor is used to create and modify dialog template resources.

The Project workspace docked to the left side of Visual Studio contains three tabs. The tab of interest at this point is the Resource View tab. This tab lists all of the resources that have been created for this project. As you can see in Figure 13-1, when you use AppWizard to create a dialog-based application, two dialogs are automatically created (`IDD_ABOUTBOX` and `IDD_ADDRESSBOOK_DIALOG`). Actually, two *dialog templates* are created. A dialog template is a resource type that describes the dialog, its height width, styles, and the controls it contains. As with any resource, a dialog template is associated with a resource ID. This resource ID is used when creating the dialog at runtime. Therefore, the Dialog entry in the Resource View tab contains all of the dialog templates defined for the current project.

Creating a new dialog template

Creating a new dialog template with the dialog editor is easy. Simply select the Resources option from the Insert menu (or press Ctrl+R) to display the Insert Resource dialog. This dialog, shown in Figure 13-2, can be used to create a resource of almost any type. The different types of resources that can be created are listed in the Resource type list box.

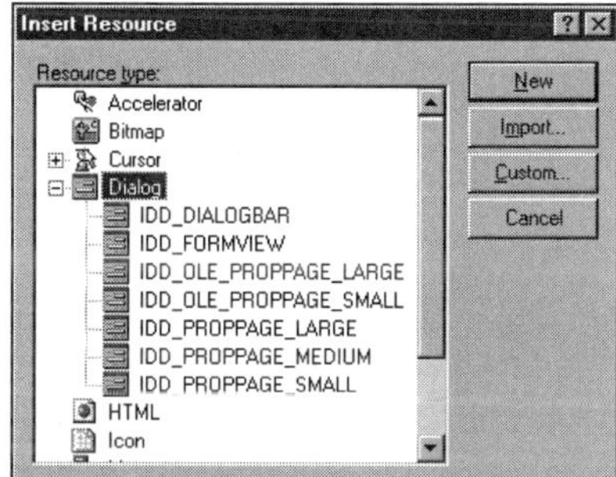

Figure 13-2: The Insert Resource dialog shows the different types of resources that can be created with the Visual Studio resource editor.

As you can see from Figure 13-2, several types of dialog templates can be created. Actually, there is only one type of dialog template. What you are seeing is a list of dialog templates with different default settings for the different dialog properties. For example, to create a form view, you must first create a dialog template and set certain properties (which are covered in Chapter 19). Because creating a form view is something that developers do quite often, Visual Studio has added it to the Resource type list box. In the case of a plain-vanilla dialog, simply double-click the Dialog entry, or select it and click the New button. Once you have done this, a default dialog template is created, and its resource ID is added to the Resource View tab of the Project workspace. At this point, the dialogs for the demo application are available, but a new dialog template will be created later in the chapter.

Editing a dialog template

To edit a dialog template, simply locate the desired template in the Resource View tab, and double-click it. At this point you can resize the dialog template, change any of its properties, and add or remove controls. Once you have finished adding controls to the dialog, you can even set the tab order of the dialog's controls and test the dialog.

Setting a dialog template's properties

A dialog's properties are changed via the Dialog Properties dialog. The Dialog Properties dialog can be displayed by clicking the dialog template and pressing the Alt+Enter key combination. Alternatively, you can display this dialog by right-clicking the dialog template and selecting the Properties menu option. Figure 13-3 shows the properties dialog for the `IDD_ADDRESSBOOK_DIALOG` dialog template.

Figure 13-3: The Dialog Properties dialog is used to set properties such as the dialog template ID, caption, and menu resource ID.

As you can see, four tabs of properties are associated with a dialog template. The tab shown in Figure 13-3 is the General tab and contains two of the most important properties for a dialog template: the resource ID and the Caption. The resource ID is used when the dialog is created at runtime, while the Caption is the text that appears in the dialog's title bar. Notice also that you can specify a menu resource for a dialog. If you specify a menu resource for a dialog, working with that menu is the same as it is with any other type of application (for example, SDI or MDI). Menus are covered in detail in Chapter 7.

It's not necessary to go through all of the dialog template properties; however, another set of properties that you will change quite often is on the Styles tab (shown in Figure 13-4).

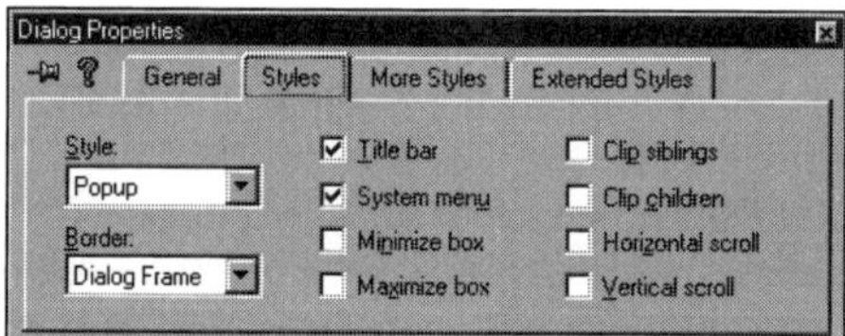

Figure 13-4: The Dialog Properties dialog is also used to set the many styles associated with dialogs.

The dialog template properties shown on the Styles tab enable you to do such things as add or remove the minimize and maximize buttons as well as the system menu and title bar. In addition, notice the Style type and the Border type. These two properties are used quite often to specify a certain type of dialog. For example, to create a form view (covered in Chapter 19), you must specify the resource ID of a dialog template whose Style type is set to Child and whose Border type is set to None. For a normal dialog, these properties should be set to Popup and Dialog Frame, respectively. Note that in order to have a dialog that can be resized at runtime, you must set the Border type to Resizing.

Adding controls to a dialog template

To add controls to a dialog the controls toolbar is used. Let's add a few controls to the demo application at this point. If the controls toolbar is not visible, right-click the Visual Studio menu. A menu should be displayed that contains all of the toolbars that can be used within Visual Studio. Clicking the Controls option should cause the controls toolbar to be displayed (see Figure 13-5). To add one of these controls to a dialog template, simply click the desired control, and drag it to the dialog template.

✦ ✦ ✦ ✦ ✦

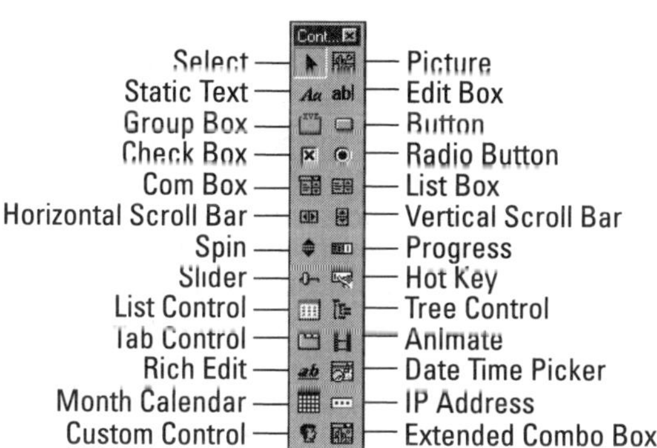

Figure 13-5: The controls toolbar is used to add controls to a dialog template.

Setting a control's properties

Setting a control's properties is accomplished via a properties dialog specific to the type of the currently selected control or group of controls. The properties dialog is displayed by selecting one or more controls and pressing the Alt+Enter key combination. While each control has its own specific tabs, the properties dialog looks very much like the Dialog Properties dialog shown in Figure 13-4. To view the properties that are specific to each type of control, refer to Chapter 12.

Selecting a group of controls

It is often more efficient to work with groups of controls than with one control at a time. For example, let's say you want to move several controls on a dialog template. By moving the controls as a group, you save time by not having to move each control one at a time. In addition, moving the controls in unison enables you to keep the controls in the same visual arrangement relative to one another.

Another example of when it would be useful to group controls is when setting properties. If you wanted to set a property for a group of controls, you could select the desired controls, display the Multiple Select Properties dialog (by pressing Alt+Enter), and set the properties that are available for that group of controls. Note that only the properties that are applicable for *every control in the group* can be changed this way. For example, you cannot change the controls' resource ID this way because each control has its own resource ID.

There are a couple of ways to select a group of controls. The fastest way is a method called *rubber banding*. To rubber band a group of controls, position the mouse pointer above and to the left of the group of controls you want to select. Then click and hold down the left mouse button. While continuing to hold down the left mouse button, move the mouse pointer to a point below and to the right of the group. When you release the left mouse button, the controls are selected.

One problem with rubber banding is that every control within the "drawn" (using the mouse) rectangle is selected. What if within a given rectangle you have ten controls and only want five of them selected? Another way to select multiple controls is by using the keyboard and mouse together. You've probably already noticed that when you click one control, it becomes selected, and then, if you click another control, the first control is deselected. To select multiple controls, hold down the Ctrl key while clicking the controls. Notice that the last control you click in this manner has a different look to it. Its *sizing handles* are dark, while all of the other controls have lighter-color sizing handles. This indicates that the last selected control is the *dominant control*. Dominant controls are used when sizing or arranging multiple controls. That will be covered shortly.

Now that you've seen how to select multiple controls, there's only one problem. How do you deselect a control? Holding down the Ctrl button while clicking a selected control simply makes that control the dominant control in a group of selected controls. It does not enable you to deselect a control. For this, you must hold down the Shift key and click the unwanted control. Upon doing that, the control you click is no longer selected, yet the other controls you have selected continue to be selected.

Sizing and arranging multiple controls

Once a control or set of controls is on the dialog template, they can be independently arranged or moved. However, because working with groups of controls is often more efficient, Visual Studio includes a special toolbar (the dialog toolbar) specifically for this purpose. Figure 13-6 shows this toolbar.

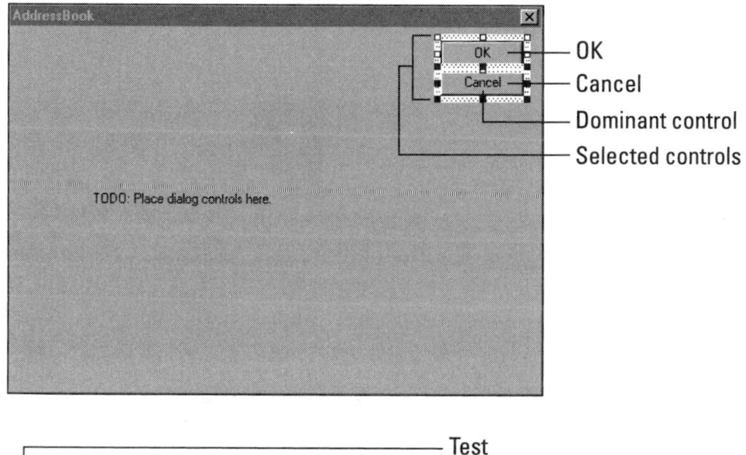

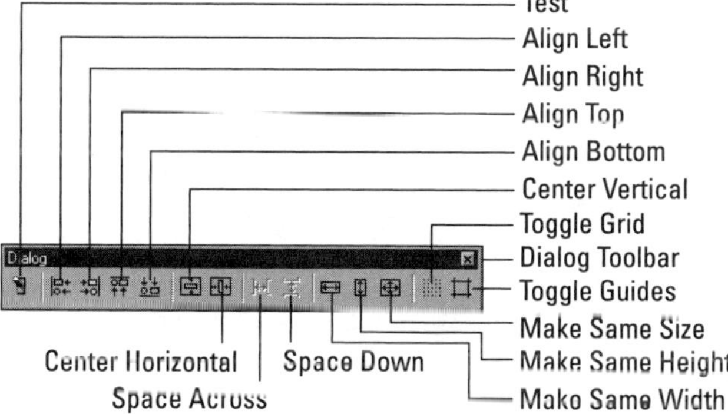

Figure 13-6: The dialog toolbar is used to add controls to a dialog template.

Most of the buttons on this toolbar are used when dealing with groups of controls and make use of the dominant control mentioned earlier. As an example, let's look at the Make Same Width button. The Make Same Width button is used when you want to make a group of controls all the same width as another control on the dialog template. First, select all of the controls (see the previous section, "Selecting a group of controls") whose width you want to change. Then, hold down the Ctrl key while clicking the control whose width will be used as the width for the other controls. This is the dominant control. Now, when you click the Make Same Width button, all of the controls are made the same width as the dominant control.

This technique of selecting multiple controls, selecting a dominant control, and clicking a dialog toolbar button works for the following buttons:

- Align Left
- Align Right
- Align Top
- Align Bottom
- Make Same Width
- Make Same Height
- Make Same Size

Setting the tab order

Once you have added the controls to the dialog template, you must set the tab order for these controls. This can be done by pressing Ctrl+D. What you will see is similar to Figure 13-7.

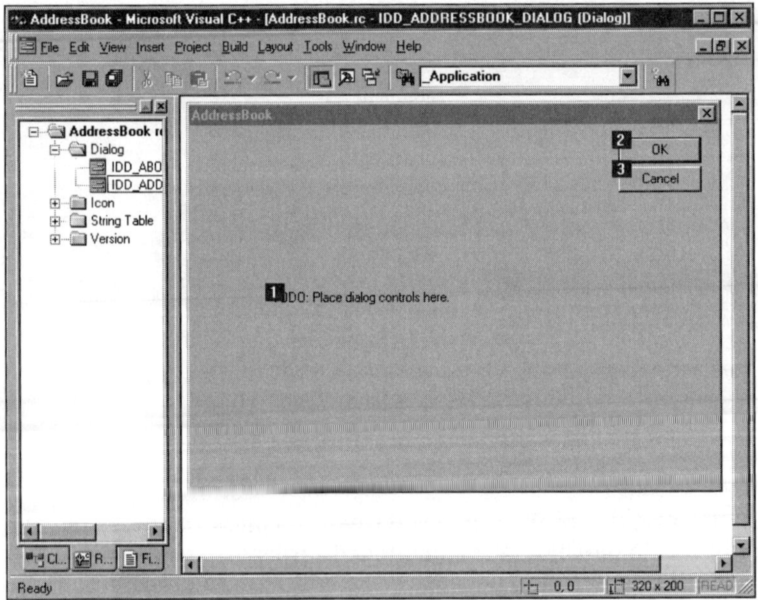

Figure 13-7: The dialog editor enables you to visually set the tab order of a dialog template's controls.

When setting the tab order of a dialog template's controls, blocks appear in the upper-left corner of each control. Within each block is the number that represents each control's place in the tab order relative to the other controls. The first control you click becomes the first control in the tab order, the second control becomes the second control in the tab order, and so on.

Tab Order Tip

Setting the tab order for a dialog template's controls requires that you sequentially click each control whose sequence you want to set. However, what happens if in the middle of setting the tab order for a large number of controls, you click the wrong control? Luckily, you can correct this without starting over. Simply hold down the Ctrl key, and click the last control whose tab order value is correct. The next control you click then begins with the next tab order value.

◆ ◆ ◆ ◆ ◆

Testing the dialog

Once you have added, arranged, and set the properties of a dialog template's controls and then set the tab order for the controls, you may want to visually test the dialog. This can be done to a very limited extent using the Ctrl+T key combination. The main advantages to the dialog editor having this feature is that you can test the dialog template's tab order and quickly see how the dialog will appear at runtime without having the guidelines and grid turned on.

The CDialog Class

Once you have created a dialog template resource, the next step is to learn how to programmatically create a dialog based on that template and manage that dialog at runtime. In the past, this meant coding a Windows SDK application that defined a dialog procedure, called the `DialogBox` SDK function, and handling the desired Windows messages with a huge `switch` statement from within the dialog procedure. However, using the MFC `CDialog` class, this process is much easier. You can now derive a class from the `CDialog` class, instantiate an object of that class, and let MFC do all the dirty work.

Modal versus modeless dialogs

The `CDialog` class encapsulates the functionality of two types of dialogs: modal and modeless. When a modal dialog is displayed, Windows disables user input to the dialog's parent window. Conversely, when a modeless dialog is displayed, Windows enables user input to the dialog's parent window. In this case, the modeless window is usually relegated to the background while the parent window, which is receiving the input, is in the foreground. A `CDialog` object can be constructed and displayed in one of two ways depending on whether the dialog will be modal or modeless.

Creating a modal dialog with CDialog

If a modal dialog is being created, one of the following CDialog constructors must be used. With both of these constructors, the resource ID is specified as the first argument, and the parent window is specified in the second argument. If you do not specify a parent window (or if you specify NULL), the court will appoint a parent window for you. Actually, in that case, MFC automatically uses the application's top-level window as the dialog's parent:

```
CDialog(LPCTSTR lpszTemplateName,
 CWnd* pParentWnd = NULL);

CDialog(UINT nIDTemplate, CWnd* pParentWnd = NULL);
```

After constructing the CDialog object, the application need only call the CDialog::DoModal() function. This causes the dialog to be displayed, and as mentioned previously, the parent window will not be permitted to receive user input until the dialog has been dismissed:

```
virtual int DoModal();
```

Notice that the DoModal() function returns an int. This value usually responds to IDOK or IDCANCEL. However, you can override this behavior in your CDialog-derived class by calling the CDialog::EndDialog() member function and specifying the value that should be returned to the caller of the DoModal() function:

```
void EndDialog(int nResult);
```

Let's look at a simple example of constructing and displaying a modal dialog using the CDialog class. Assuming that you had created an AppWizard-generated project and had a dialog template with a resource ID of IDD_ABOUTBOX, the code would look like the following:

```
CDialog dlg(IDD_ABOUTBOX);
int nResult = dlg.DoModal();
CString str;
if (IDOK == nResult)
{
 str = _T("OK");
}
else if (IDCANCEL == nResult)
{
 str = _T("Cancel");
}
else
{
 str = _T("Unknown value");
}
AfxMessageBox(str);
```

Notice that you would very rarely instantiate a CDialog object directly. This is due to the fact that to add your own processing logic to a dialog, you must derive your own class from CDialog and instantiate it. Using ClassWizard to create a CDialog-derived class will be covered shortly.

Creating a modeless dialog with CDialog

If a modeless dialog is being created, the CDialog constructor without any arguments is used. Once the CDialog object has been instantiated, one of the two CDialog::Create() functions must be called to display the dialog:

```
BOOL Create(LPCTSTR lpszTemplateName,
 CWnd* pParentWnd = NULL);

BOOL Create(UINT nIDTemplate,
 CWnd* pParentWnd = NULL);
```

Notice how these two Create() functions have identical argument lists to the two CDialog constructors that are used to construct modal dialogs. This is due to a very logical reason. When an application constructs and displays a modal dialog, the calling function is *blocked* until the DoModal() function returns. Therefore, the construction and displaying of the dialog can occur within the same function. However, the displaying of a modeless dialog is asynchronous. When the calling function calls the Create() function and the modeless dialog is displayed, the Create() function returns immediately after displaying the dialog. This means that the calling function will almost certainly terminate while the dialog is still visible. The problem is that if the CDialog object had been created on the stack, it would go out of scope and destruct. The result would be a dialog that, after being displayed for mere milliseconds, would disappear due to the destructor's having destroyed it. Therefore, it is common to see applications create a CDialog-derived object in one function, store a pointer to that dialog object, and call the Create() in another function. You will see how to do this in one of the demos presented later in the chapter.

It was stated previously that to display a modeless dialog, you must call its Create() function. Actually, for the Create() function to display the dialog, the dialog template's Visible style must be turned on. If the dialog template's Visible style is turned off, the application must also call the ShowWindow() function:

```
ShowWindow(SW_NORMAL);
```

Creating CDialog-derived classes with ClassWizard

At this point, you should know how to create a dialog template and instantiate a CDialog object (both modal and modeless) based on that template's resource ID. The next logical step is to learn how to create your own CDialog-derived classes. Luckily, ClassWizard makes this a snap. Creating new classes via ClassWizard is done with the New Class dialog (shown in Figure 13-8).

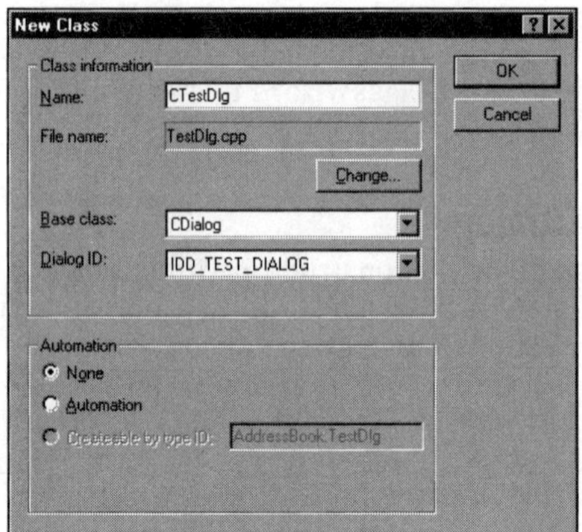

Figure 13-8: ClassWizard's New Class dialog is used to create new C++ classes that are based on MFC classes.

The New Class dialog can be displayed in a couple of ways. The first and most obvious way is to display the ClassWizard (Ctrl+W) and click the Add Class button (available on each of the ClassWizard tabs). Once you do that, a menu is displayed. Selecting the New entry in that menu causes the New Class dialog to be displayed. Using this method, you must fill in the fields on the dialog specifying the new class' name, its base class, and resource ID. Another way to display the New Class dialog is via the dialog editor. Once you have created a new dialog template, holding down the Ctrl key while double-clicking the dialog template with the left mouse button displays the New Class dialog. The advantage to the second method is that the values for the base class and resource ID will be defaulted for you based on the dialog template currently being displayed in the dialog editor. Once you have created your `CDialog`-derived class, you start modifying it to suit the needs of your specific application.

Dialog Data Exchange and Validation

Once you create the dialog template and use ClassWizard to create a `CDialog`-based class, the next step is knowing how to get data from the dialog to your application's variables and vice versa. Dialog Data Exchange (DDX) enables you to create member variables in your `CDialog`-derived class that are associated with the controls on the dialog template. There are two categories of DDX variables: control and value.

DDX control variables enable you to associate the MFC control classes you learned about in Chapter 12 with the appropriate controls on a dialog template. For example, using DDX, you can associate a member variable of type `CEdit` with an edit control on the dialog template. Doing this enables you to manage the edit control by calling the appropriate `CEdit` member functions.

DDX value variables are member variables that contain the *value* of a specific control. The specific C++ type that can be used to declare the member variable is dependent on the type of control. For example, when creating a DDX value variable for an edit control, the built-in valid variable types are `CString`, `int`, `UINT`, `long`, `DWORD`, `float`, `double`, `BYTE`, `short`, `BOOL`, `COleDateTime`, and `COleCurrency`. However, when creating a DDX value variable for a check box control, the only built-in valid variable type is `BOOL`. You should also understand that while a DDX control variable can be created for any control, you cannot create a DDX value variable for all controls. A button control is an example of one such case because it doesn't hold any type of value.

Creating DDX variables

DDX variables (both control and value) are created through ClassWizard's Add Member Variable dialog (shown in Figure 13-9).

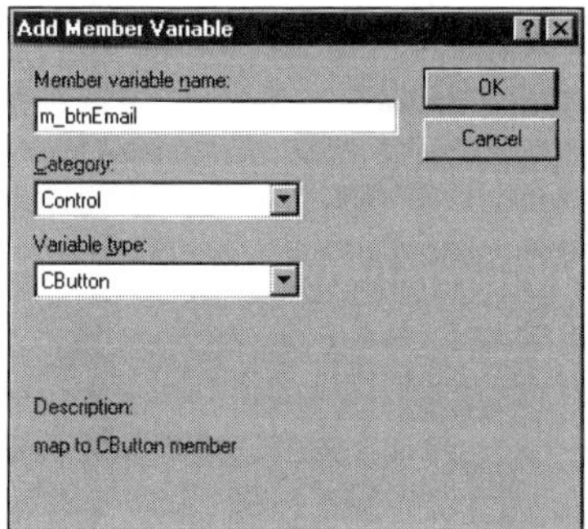

Figure 13-9: ClassWizard's Add Member Variable dialog is used to create DDX control and value variables.

You can display the Add Member Variable dialog in a couple of ways. One method is via the ClassWizard Member Variables tab. To do this, display ClassWizard, and select the Member Variable tab. From there, select the desired `CDialog`-derived class from the Class name combo box, and select the desired control's resource ID. Once you have done that, click the Add Variable button to see the dialog shown in Figure 13-9. A much quicker method is to display the dialog in the dialog editor, and while holding down the Ctrl key, double-click the desired control.

DoDataExchange and UpdateData

The key element in linking the controls that you see on a dialog with the DDX member variables of your `CDialog`-derived class is the `CWnd::DoDataExchange()` function. If you create DDX member variables using one of the techniques described previously, the `DoDataExchange()` function will be created and maintained automatically by ClassWizard. However, understanding how DDX works "under the covers" is imperative to effectively using DDX with your dialogs.

Here's a simple example of a DoDataExchange() function where a single edit control has both a DDX control variable and a DDX value variable defined:

```
void CTestDlg::DoDataExchange(CDataExchange* pDX)
{
 CDialog::DoDataExchange(pDX);

 //{{AFX_DATA_MAP(CTestDlg)
 DDX_Control(pDX, IDC_EDIT1, m_edtMyEdit);
 DDX_Text(pDX, IDC_EDIT1, m_strMyEdit);
 //}}AFX_DATA_MAP
}
```

Let's take a look at the DDX_Control() function call. The DDX_Control() function is used to associate a CWnd-derived object with a control so that the control can be manipulated by calling member functions of the CWnd-derived object. The first argument to the DDX_Control function is a pointer to a CDataExchange object that was passed from the framework to the DoDataExchange() function. You will almost never use this pointer as it used by the framework to carry out the work necessary to making DDX work. The second argument is used to specify the resource ID of a control on the dialog, while the third argument is used to pass a reference to a CWnd-derived object. Because the preceding example refers to an edit control, m_edtMyEdit is a reference to a member variable of type CEdit. Once this function has been called, the m_edtMyEdit member variable can be used to access and control the edit control IDC_EDIT1.

The DDX_Text() function is used to transfer the value of a control to a member variable and vice versa. Actually, because several C++ types can be used to hold the control's value, there are several overloaded versions of the DDX_Text() function. In the preceding case, the edit control (IDC_EDIT1) is being associated with a CString named m_strMyEdit.

The DoDataExchange() function is called by the framework as a result of the CWnd::UpdateData() function being called. This function takes a single argument that dictates whether the control is being updated or if the member variable is being updated:

```
BOOL UpdateData(BOOL bSaveAndValidate);
```

If the value of bSaveAndValidate is TRUE (the default if no value is passed), then the DDX value member variables associated with the controls are updated with the text that is in the controls on the dialog. Therefore, if the edit control in the preceding example had a value of "Test" and UpdateData(TRUE) was called, then the m_strMyEdit would also contain the value "Test." However, if the application needed to update the control with a different value, it would set the m_strMyEdit member variable to the desired value and call UpdateData(FALSE). This would update the control with the value of the m_strMyEdit member variable.

It is important to realize that the UpdateData() function is automatically called twice by the framework. The first time UpdateData() is called is by the CDialog::OnInitDialog() virtual function that is invoked when the dialog is initialized and before it is displayed. In this case, UpdateData() is called with a value of FALSE so that the controls on the dialog are updated. Therefore, if your dialog wants to initialize a DDX value member variable before the dialog is displayed, it needs to do so before the CDialog::OnInitDialog() function is called. Following is an example of a dialog called CTestDialog that has overridden the virtual OnInitDialog() function to initialize a member variable. Notice that the member variable is set *before* the call to the base class' implementation of OnInitDialog():

```
BOOL CTestDlg::OnInitDialog()
{
 m_strMyEdit = _T("My Initial Value");
 CDialog::OnInitDialog();

 // TODO: Add extra initialization here

 return TRUE;
}
```

If, however, your application needs to update the member variables after the call to OnInitDialog(), you must then call the UpdateData() function yourself:

```
BOOL CTestDlg::OnInitDialog()
{
 CDialog::OnInitDialog();

 // TODO: Add extra initialization here
 m_strMyEdit = _T("My Initial Value");
 UpdateData(); // updates the dialog's controls

 return TRUE;
}
```

The second time the UpdateData() function is called automatically by the framework is in the CDialog::OnOK() virtual function. This is done so that if a dialog has member variables that will be accessible to the function that displayed the dialog, once the dialog has ended (assuming that the CDialog::OnOK() function was called), the calling function can access the updated versions of the member variables. Here is an example of a function that constructs and displays a modal dialog and then accesses one of its member variables after the DoModal() function has returned. This example also illustrates why ClassWizard creates all DDX variables as public:

```
CTestDlg dlg;
if (IDOK == dlg.DoModal())
{
 // use m_strMyEdit
}
```

The AddressBook Demo

Up to this point, this chapter has covered creating dialog templates, adding controls to a dialog template, and using DDX. It's finally time to start putting some of this to practice by writing a simple address and phone book application. Begin by using AppWizard to create a dialog-based application called AddressBook.

The complete source for this project can be found on the accompanying CD in the `Chap13\AddressBook` folder.

◆ ◆ ◆ ◆ ◆

Editing the demo dialog

Once AppWizard has created the project's files, you must update the application's main dialog template. Because this application was created as a dialog-based application, the main dialog template has been created automatically. If you named the project AddressBook, this dialog template will be named `IDD_ADDRESSBOOK_DIALOG`. Using what you learned in the previous section "Using the Dialog Editor," modify the dialog template so that when finished the dialog looks like that shown in Figure 13-10. Note that the Address group box surrounds five edit controls that are positioned right up against one another. In addition, the Notes edit control has its `Multiline` style turned on.

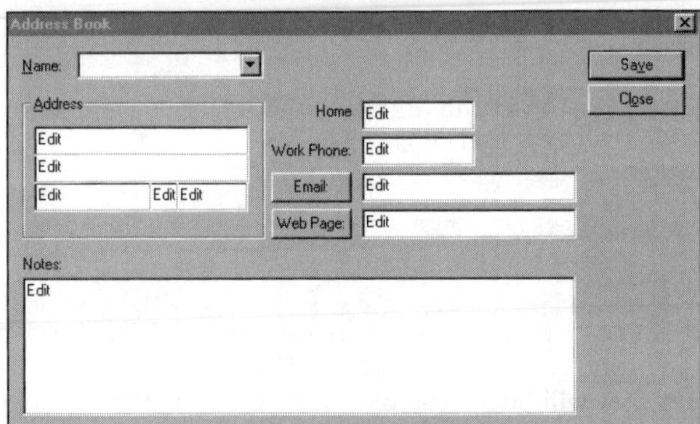

Figure 13-10: After modifying the AddressBook main dialog, it should look like this.

Once you have added and positioned the dialog template's controls, you use ClassWizard to create the variables necessary for transferring data to and from the dialog. Table 13-1 lists the values you will need to use in the Add Member Variable dialog described previously. In addition, make sure that the combo box Type style is set to Dropdown.

Table 13-1
Add Member Variable Values

Control	*Category*	*Variable Type*	*Variable Name*
Name combo box	Control	CComboBox	m_cboNames
First Address Line	Value	CString	m_strAddress1
Second Address Line	Value	CString	m_strAddress2
City	Value	CString	m_strCity
State	Value	CString	m_strState
Zip Ccode	Value	CString	m_strZip
Home Phone	Value	CString	m_strHomePhone
Work Phone	Value	CString	m_strWorkPhone
Email button	Control	CButton	m_btnEmail
Email edit	Value	CString	m_strEmail
Web Page button	Control	CButton	m_btnWebPage
Web Page edit	Value	CString	m_strWebPage
Notes	Value	CString	m_strNotes

The CContact class

Now that you have a functioning dialog, you need data! Because the dialog's controls consist of contact information, the logical thing would be to create a CContact class. To do that, create a new file called Contact.h, and verify that it looks like the code shown in Listing 13-1. Because the dialog will have multiple contacts, a templatized map (CContactCollection) is also declared.

Listing 13-1: Create a New Contact.h File

```
#pragma once
#include "afxtempl.h"

class CContact
{
public:
 CString m_strName;
 CString    m_strAddress1;
 CString    m_strAddress2;
 CString    m_strCity;
```

(continued)

Listing 13-1 *(continued)*

```
    CString     m_strState;
    CString     m_strZip;
    CString     m_strNotes;
    CString     m_strHomePhone;
    CString     m_strWorkPhone;
    CString     m_strEmail;
    CString     m_strWebPage;
};

typedef CTypedPtrMap<CMapStringToPtr,
 CString /* Name */,
 CContact*>CContactCollection;
```

Next, open the AddressBookDlg.h file, and place the following #include directive directly above the declaration of the CAddressBookDlg class:

```
#include "Contact.h"
```

Now, add the following member variable to the CAddressBookDlg class. This is the map that will hold all of the contacts:

```
protected:
 CContactCollection m_Contacts;
```

Overriding OnInitDialog

Because database connectivity won't be covered until Chapter 26, you will have to dummy up some data for this application. As you learned earlier, the OnInitDialog() function is where initialization code for the dialog is usually placed. The code shown in Listing 13-2 should be inserted into the CAddressBookDlg::OnInitDialog() function just before the return statement.

Notice that as the for loop iterates through the following static struct, a CContact object is created for each entry in the structure. The strName member of each structure entry is then added to the m_cboNames combo box. The combo box control can have a DWORD associated with each of its entries. This value is called *item data*, and it is usually used in situations where the application needs to associate a value or object with each entry in the combo box. Therefore, after each contact's name is added to the combo box, that combo box entry's item data is set to the pointer of the associated CContact object. That way, when the user selects a name from the combo box, its data (stored in the CContact object) can be retrieved and displayed.

Listing 13-2: Insert This Code before the return Statement in the CAddressBookDlg::OnInitDialog() Function

```
static struct
{
 LPTSTR strName;
 LPTSTR strAddress1;
 LPTSTR    strAddress2;
 LPTSTR    strCity;
 LPTSTR    strState;
 LPTSTR    strZip;
 LPTSTR    strNotes;
 LPTSTR    strHomePhone;
 LPTSTR    strWorkPhone;
 LPTSTR    strEmail;
 LPTSTR    strWebPage;
} contacts [] = {
 "Tom Archer", "", "", "Atlanta", "GA", "30047",
 "Notes for Tom", "911", "work?!",
 "tma-books@mindspring.com",
 "http://tarcher.home.mindspring.com",

 "Rick Leinecker", "", "", "", "NC", "",
 "Notes for Rick", "411", "", "ivt-rcl@interpath.com",
 "http://mercury.interpath.com/~phaedrus"
};

CContact* pContact;
int iIndex;
for (int i = 0;
 i < sizeof contacts / sizeof contacts[0];
 i++)
{
 pContact = new CContact;
 pContact->m_strName = contacts[i].strName;
 pContact->m_strAddress1 = contacts[i].strAddress1;
 pContact->m_strAddress2 = contacts[i].strAddress2;
 pContact->m_strCity = contacts[i].strCity;
 pContact->m_strState = contacts[i].strState;
 pContact->m_strZip = contacts[i].strZip;
 pContact->m_strNotes = contacts[i].strNotes;
 pContact->m_strHomePhone = contacts[i].strHomePhone;
 pContact->m_strWorkPhone = contacts[i].strWorkPhone;
 pContact->m_strEmail = contacts[i].strEmail;
 pContact->m_strWebPage = contacts[i].strWebPage;

 m_Contacts.SetAt(contacts[i].strName, pContact);

 if (CB_ERR !=
  (iIndex =
```

(continued)

Listing 13-2 *(continued)*

```
    m_cboNames.AddString(contacts[i].strName)))
  {
   m_cboNames.SetItemData(iIndex, (DWORD)pContact);
  }
 }
```

Handling the WM_DESTROY message

Using what you learned earlier about using ClassWizard to create message handlers for `CDialog`-derived classes, create a handler for the `WM_DESTROY` message, and code it as shown in Listing 13-3. Windows sends the `WM_DESTROY` to a window that is about to be destroyed so that it can do some last-minute cleanup. The following code snippet will iterate through the `m_Contacts` collection and free up the memory for each of the `CContact` objects that was allocated in the `OnInitDialog()` function.

Listing 13-3: Create This Handler for the WM_DESTROY Message

```
void CAddressBookDlg::OnDestroy()
{
 CDialog::OnDestroy();

 POSITION pos;
 CString strKey;
 CContact* pContact;

 pos = m_Contacts.GetStartPosition();
 while(NULL != pos)
 {
  m_Contacts.GetNextAssoc(pos, strKey, pContact);
  if (pContact)
  {
   m_Contacts.RemoveKey(strKey);
   delete pContact;
  }
 }
 ASSERT(NULL == m_Contacts.GetCount());
}
```

Displaying data

Now that you have data, it's time to see how easy the CDialog class and DDX makes displaying that data. As you saw earlier, each entry in the m_cboNames combo box has a CContact object pointer set as its item data. Therefore, when the user selects a different entry in the combo box, you will want the dialog to retrieve that entry's item data (CContact) and display the correct information on the dialog.

The combo box sends a CBN_SELCHANGE message to its parent (the dialog) to inform the parent that the user has changed the current selection in the combo box. This is where you will want to place your code to retrieve the new CContact. Therefore, use ClassWizard to implement a message handler for the CBN_SELCHANGE notification message (see Listing 13-4). In the handler for this function, you need only retrieve the index of the current combo box selection and retrieve that entry's item data, which is CContact. After that, you simply set the DDX member variables and call UpdateData(FALSE).

Listing 13-4: Use ClassWizard to Implement a Message Handler

```
void CAddressBookDlg::OnSelchangeCboNames()
{
 int iIndex = m_cboNames.GetCurSel();
 if (CB_ERR != iIndex)
 {
  CContact* pContact =
  (CContact*)m_cboNames.GetItemData(iIndex);

  ASSERT(pContact);
  if (pContact)
  {
   m_strAddress1 = pContact->m_strAddress1;
   m_strAddress2 = pContact->m_strAddress2;
   m_strCity = pContact->m_strCity;
   m_strState = pContact->m_strState;
   m_strZip = pContact->m_strZip;
   m_strNotes = pContact->m_strNotes;
   m_strHomePhone = pContact->m_strHomePhone;
   m_strWorkPhone = pContact->m_strWorkPhone;
   m_strEmail = pContact->m_strEmail;
   m_strWebPage = pContact->m_strWebPage;

   UpdateData(FALSE);
  }
 }
}
```

Handling button notifications

As you learned earlier, child controls send notification messages to their parents when certain events occur. The button, not being a very exciting control, has only two such messages: BN_CLICKED and BN_DOUBLECLICKED. These two messages are sent when the *left* mouse button is clicked or double-clicked with the mouse pointer pointing at a button. While the button control may very well be a simple control, it is the one control that you will most likely use on the majority of your dialogs. Therefore, the last thing you'll do with this demo is handle the user clicking the contact's Web Page button. To do this, use ClassWizard to add a message handler for the BN_CLICKED notification message, and add the following code to enable the user to surf to the contact's Web page:

```
void CAddressBookDlg::OnBtnWebPage()
{
 if (UpdateData(TRUE))
 {
  if (!m_strWebPage.IsEmpty())
  {
   if (32 >= (int)ShellExecute(NULL, "open",
    m_strWebPage, NULL, NULL, SW_SHOWNORMAL))
   {
    AfxMessageBox("::ShellExecute failed "
    "to open this link!");
   }
  }
  else
  {
   AfxMessageBox("You must first specify a URL");
  }
 }
}
```

Building and testing the demo

Building and testing the demo application is as easy as selecting the Rebuild All option from the Visual Studio Build menu. Once the application has been built, press Ctrl+F5 to run it, and you should see results similar to the dialog in Figure 13-11.

Derived Control Classes in Dialogs

In the first version of the AddressBook demo, you learned how to add controls to a dialog and use DDX to move data from the dialog to your application's variables and vice versa. The controls used were static controls, edit controls, buttons, and combo boxes. However, what happens if you write your own cool little widget and want to use it on a dialog instead of one of the standard Windows controls? Using derived control classes in a dialog is the subject of this section.

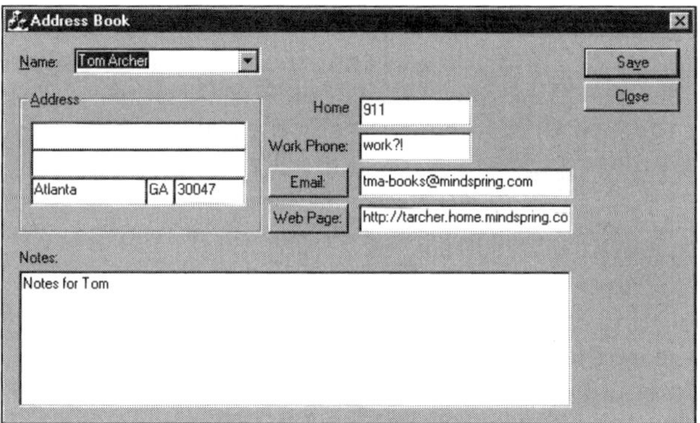

Figure 13-11: The first variation of the AddressBook demo illustrates how using some simple DDX techniques and message handlers can create a fairly useful address book in no time.

Creating control classes

Being able to derive your own classes from the MFC control classes is one of the many things that makes MFC both a robust and powerful programming platform. Let's say for example that you wanted to have an edit control that accepted the input only of numbers. You obviously wouldn't want to code an entire edit control class just to add this extra bit of functionality. Instead, you would derive your own specialized version of the edit control from the MFC `CEdit` class. That way, you maintain all of the `CEdit` class' functionality while adding your own specialized class' functionality. This part is obvious. However, the main question is how do you associate your new class with the edit control on the dialog? The answer is DDX.

Using DDX with Derived Control Classes

In the first demo, DDX was used to associate a `CComboBox` member variable with the combo box on the dialog box. Therefore, to write your own derived control class, you simply have to do the following:

1. Use ClassWizard to create the derived control class.
2. Implement the necessary member functions.
3. If the class was not created with ClassWizard, insert the appropriate ExtraDDX lines (explained subsequently) into the project's .CLW file.
4. Use ClassWizard to create member variables of the new type for the desired controls. If you used ClassWizard to create the control class, it will show up in the Add Member Variable dialog along with the MFC control classes.

◆ ◆ ◆ ◆ ◆

Using ClassWizard to create the class

Let's take the previous example of a numeric edit control. Let's call the control CNumericEdit. To create the new class, simply use the ClassWizard New Class dialog (shown earlier). On the New Class dialog, specify the Name as CNumericEdit and the base class as CEdit.

Implementing the necessary functions

In a simple case such as a numeric edit control, you just have to handle the WM_CHAR message and reject any characters that are not numeric. Because ClassWizard was used to create the CNumericEdit class, a handler for the WM_CHAR message can be added through ClassWizard as well. Simply start ClassWizard, click the Message Maps tab, select the CNumericEdit from the Class name combo box, and double-click the WM_CHAR entry in the Messages list box. This automatically creates a member function for the CNumericEdit class called OnChar(). Double-click the OnChar() function in the Member functions list box to edit the function. When finished, your function should look like the following:

```
void CNumericEdit::OnChar(UINT nChar,
 UINT nRepCnt, UINT nFlags)
{
 if (0 <= nChar && 9 >= nChar)
 {
  CEdit::OnChar(nChar, nRepCnt, nFlags);
 }
}
```

Creating an ExtraDDX entry

This step is optional and depends on how you created the derived control class. Earlier in the chapter, you learned how to create DDX control variables using the ClassWizard Add Member Variable dialog. This dialog included a Category combo box that listed the appropriate MFC class for the currently selected control. This works fine if you want an MFC control class, but what if you have a derived control class? If you created the control class with Visual C++ 6.0's ClassWizard, the derived control class automatically shows up on the list, and the rest of this section may not pertain to you. However, if your derived control class was not created with the new ClassWizard and you want the class to be displayed on the ClassWizard Add Member Variable dialog, there are a few options.

In earlier versions of Visual C++, when you had a derived control class, there were three ways to create the DDX control member variable for your control. One way was to manually add the member variable's declaration to the dialog's header file and then add a DDX_Control function call (or your class' specific DDX_ function) to the dialog's DoDataExchange() function. The second way was to use ClassWizard to create a member variable of the derived control's base class. Then you would manually change the member variable type in the dialog's header file and, if necessary, change the DoDataExchange() function to call your class' specific DDX function. Therefore, using the CNumericEdit control shown previously, you would have ClassWizard create a CEdit member variable and then manually open the dialog's header file and change the member variable type from CEdit to CNumericEdit. However, none of these methods enables you to create a member variable of the type of your derived control class with the Add Member Variable dialog. For that, you need to use ExtraDDX.

ExtraDDX enables you to add your own derived control classes to the ClassWizard Add Member Variable combo box. In order to implement ExtraDDX for a control and class, simply add the following two lines to the project's CLW (ClassWizard) file. Note that the ExtraDDX1 line has to be on one line in your .CLW file:

```
ExtraDDXCount=1
ExtraDDX1=E;;Control;CNumericEdit;;Control;
 This is my cool Numeric Edit class!
```

The ExtraDDXCount value represents the number of ExtraDDX lines in the file. The ExtraDDX? line represents a new DDX type and is documented as follows. (When entered into your .CLW file, each DDX type definition must exist on one physical line.) Note that the delimiter for DDX type values is a semicolon:

```
ExtraDDX?=<keys>;<vb-keys>; <prompt>; <type>;
 <initValue>; <DDX_Proc> [;<DDV_Proc>; <prompt1>;
 <arg1>; [<prompt2>; <fmt2>]]
```

- *?*—This value is a number that specifies which DDX type is being defined. The total number of DDX types is specified with ExtraDDXCount. In the previous example, this value was set to 1.
- *keys*—This value represents the type of control for which this DDX type is valid. In the previous example, this value was set to *E* because the new control was only valid for edit controls. The valid entries for this value are as follows:

  ```
  E = edit
  C = two-state check box
  c = tri-state check box
  R = first radio button in a group
  L = non-sorted list box
  l = sorted list box
  M = combo box (with edit item)
  N = non-sorted drop list
  n = sorted drop list
  1 = if the DDX insert should be added to head of list
  (default is add to tail). This is generally used for
  DDX routines that transfer the 'Control' property.
  ```

- *vb-keys*—This value is used to support VBX controls. Because VBX controls are supported only in the 16-bit versions of Visual C++, this value is not valid for any of the 32-bit versions of Visual C++ (including Visual C++ 6.0). Therefore, this value should be left blank.

✦ *prompt*—The text you enter for this value is used in the Category combo box. You do not need to place quotes around the text. In the previous example, this value was set to `Control`.

✦ *type*—This value represents the class name of your derived control class. When the member variable is declared, it will be declared as this type. In the previous example, this value was set to `CNumericEdit`.

✦ *initValue*—This value is the initial value that you want the member variable set to when the dialog is displayed. If you leave this value blank, no initialization line is written to the dialog's constructor. All of the DDX initialization lines can be found after the `//{{AFX_DATA_INIT` comment. If the `type` argument is a C++ class, the `initValue` argument is usually left blank. This is the case in the example above where the `type` argument was set to `CNumericEdit`.

✦ *DDX_Proc*—This value represents the name of the `DDX_` function if you are providing one. The name of the function in your source code must start with `DDX_` but don't include the `DDX_` for this value. For example, if you have a function called `DDX_MYCONTROL`, you would specify this value as being `MY_CONTROL`. In the previous example, this value was set to Control so that the MFC-provided `DDX_Control()` function would be used in the dialog's `DoDataExchange()`.

✦ *DDV_Proc*—This value is optional and is used for the DDV function that will be used in the dialog's `DoDataExchange()` function. As with the `DDX_Proc` value, you do not have to specify the DDV_ prefix to the function name. This value is optionally followed by one or two DDV arguments. In the previous example, this value was left blank because a customized `DDV_Proc` was not needed.

✦ *comment*—This value is used to display a comment at the bottom of the Add Member Variable dialog when this DDX type is selected. This value can contain spaces, but you do not need to use quotes.

Looking through the laundry list of arguments for DDX types can be a bit overwhelming. Therefore, it might be easier to simply take the `CNumericEdit` example, use it as a template, and just look up the necessary arguments for your DDX type.

Using ClassWizard to create the member variable

Once you have created the derived control class, you must add a member variable to the dialog for the desired control. If the control class was created via ClassWizard or implemented a new DDX type via ExtraDDX, this can be done in the Add Member Variable dialog as shown earlier in the chapter.

The previous `CNumericEdit` example was not very realistic because the edit control has a style that specifies that it only accept numeric values. However, let's take a look at a more realistic scenario in which a derived control class would improve the usability of the AddressBook application.

AddressBook demo: CAutoCompleteComboBox

One of the useful features of Microsoft Explorer is that the Address combo box not only contains the last several addresses typed in, but it also supports something called "auto complete." What this means is that while you type into the combo box's edit control, the combo box is busy finding the nearest match in its list of entries. For example, let's say that the combo box has the following entries:

```
c:\mycode\docviewtest
c:\mycode\editcontroltest
```

Suppose you want to search for the `c:\mycode\editcontroltest`. When you type the letter *c*, the first entry that matches what you typed, c:\mycode\docviewtest, is selected into the combo box. Actually, what you see is the letter you typed and the rest of the entry using the selected text color, so that you can distinguish what you've typed from the rest of the text. As you continue typing, the entry doesn't change until you type the letter *e* of "editcontroltest" (because both entries contain the "\mycode\" text). At this point, the combo box automatically selects the second entry into the combo box. For a combo box with just a couple of entries, that may not seem like such a big deal. However, when users have hundreds of entries, you are not going to be very popular with your users if they have to manually scroll through the entire list while searching for a specific entry.

Actually, the curious thing is that the regular Windows combo box does support this auto-complete function somewhat. However, the biggest difference is that with the Windows combo box control, there is no way of distinguishing between what you've typed versus what was filled in by the combo box. Using the previous example, as you type the string "c:\mycode\", there is no change in what you see in the combo box. The combo box changes only when another match is found. Unfortunately, with the combo box providing no feedback that it is searching for a match with each keystroke, the user typically abandons the idea of typing the entry and resorts to dropping down the list and manually searching for the desired entry. Therefore, let's create a `CComboBox`-derived class called `CAutoCompleteComboBox` and add it to the AddressBook main dialog.

CAutoCompleteComboBox source code

Implementing the `CAutoCompleteComboBox` is straightforward. Use ClassWizard to create a `CComboBox`-derived class called `CAutoCompleteComboBox`. Once ClassWizard has generated the source code, open the `AutoCompleteComboBox.h` file, and add a declaration of a BOOL member variable called `m_bFindNearestMatch` (its purpose will be explained shortly). After that, use ClassWizard to implement a handler for the `CBN_EDITUPDATE` notification message and an override of the `PreTranslateMessage()` virtual function.

The first thing the `OnEditUpdate()` (the `CBN_EDITUPDATE` handler) function does is to check a member variable called `m_bFindNearestMatch` to see if you still want to keep searching for matches (this flag will be explained shortly). The text that has been typed in the combo box's edit control is used as an argument to the `CComboBox::FindString()` member function. This is basically a function that enables you to perform a case-independent search of a combo box for a string. If the search is successful, the index of the corresponding entry is returned. If an index is returned, it is used to set the current selection of the combo box (via a call to `CComboBox::SetCurSel()`). The length of the original string that the user typed is then used to determine the starting position for the `CComboBox::SetEditSel()` function. Using this value, you can be sure that the only characters that appear as selected text are the characters that have not been typed in, but are a result of the `FindString()` function.

```
void CAutoCompleteComboBox::OnEditupdate()
{
 if (m_bFindNearestMatch)
 {
  char szEntry[CHAR_MAX];
  int nLen = GetWindowText(szEntry,
   CHAR_MAX);

  int iIndex;
  if (CB_ERR != (iIndex = FindString(-1,
   szEntry)))
  {
   SetCurSel(iIndex);
   SetEditSel(nLen, -1);
  }
 }
}
```

The only other thing that must be done is to use ClassWizard to implement an override of the `PreTranslateMessage()` function, which is done so that if the user presses the Del or the Backspace key, a match to the text typed in so far is no longer searched for. If the user presses one of those keys, a member variable called `m_bFindNearestMatch` is set. This variable is used by the `OnEditUpdate()` function to decide if it should continue searching the combo box while the user types.

```
BOOL CAutoCompleteComboBox::PreTranslateMessage(
 MSG* pMsg)
{
 if (WM_KEYDOWN == pMsg->message)
 {
  if ((VK_BACK == pMsg->wParam)
  || (VK_DELETE == pMsg->wParam))
  {
   m_bFindNearestMatch = FALSE;
  }
  else
  {
   m_bFindNearestMatch = TRUE;
  }
 }

 return CComboBox::PreTranslateMessage(pMsg);
}
```

Adding the CAutoCompleteComboBox to the demo

Once you have finished coding the `CAutoCompleteComboBox` class, you can implement it with the AddressBook demo. Display ClassWizard, and click the Member Variables tab. Delete the existing `m_cboNames` member variable, and click the Add Variable button to display the Add Member Variable dialog. Type **m_cboNames** as the Name of the class, and select Control from the Category combo box. Now when you drop down the Variable type combo box, in addition to the standard `CComboBox` type, you should also see your new `CAutoCompleteComboBox`. Selecting it creates a member variable of its type for the dialog. Because you are selecting a non-MFC-provided control class, ClassWizard displays a message box reminding you to add the `#include` directive for the derived control class. At this point, open the `AddressBookDlg.h` file, and add the following `#include` directive before the declaration of the `CAddressBookDlg` class:

```
#include "AutoCompleteComboBox.h"
```

Because the `CAutoCompleteComboBox` works with combo boxes that a user can type into, you must open the dialog in the dialog editor and change the Names combo box Type style to Dropdown. Building and running the demo should now cause results similar to the dialog shown in Figure 13-12.

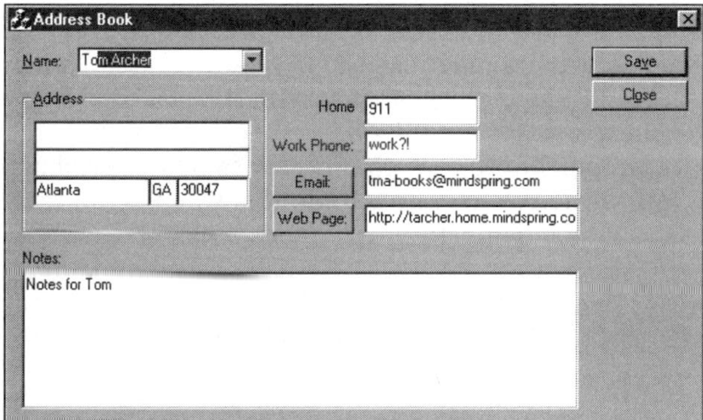

Figure 13-12: Creating your own derived control class can assist in creating much more attractive and usable applications.

Serialization

Object persistence is the process of reading and writing objects to and from disk. MFC implements object persistence via a mechanism called *serialization*. With serialization, the capability to save data can easily and quickly be incorporated into an MFC application without the need or cost of a more traditional DBMS. Because serialization is typically used from document-based (SDI or MDI) applications, it is covered in more detail in Chapter 19. Therefore, it is assumed, as a prerequisite for this section, that the reader has either read Chapter 19 or already has a firm grip on the basics of serialization. This section is, therefore, devoted to illustrating what is needed to implement serialization with a dialog-based application. Having said that, the only difference between serializing data from a document-based application and a dialog-based application is that in the latter case, the programmer is responsible for creating the `CArchive` object (and its underlying `CFile` object) that will be used to serialize the data to and from disk. Here are the steps involved in adding serialization to a dialog-based application. Each step is discussed in more detail subsequently.

Implementing Serialization in a Dialog-Based Application

Follow these steps to implment serialization in a dialog-based application:

1. Make each class that is to be written and read to and from disk serializable.
2. Implement the dialog class' `Serialize()` virtual member function.
3. Add code to the dialog object to read the objects from disk.
4. Add code to the dialog object to save the objects from disk.

◆ ◆ ◆ ◆ ◆

Making each class serializable

In order to make a class serializable, you must use the `DECLARE_SERIAL` macro in the class' declaration and the `IMPLEMENT_SERIAL` macro in the class' implementation file. Both of these macros are fully described in the online documentation. However, it is important to note that the class being serialized *must* be derived from `CObject`. You will see exactly how to do this when serialization is implemented in the AddressBook demo shortly.

Implementing the Serialize() virtual function

After adding the `DECLARE_SERIAL` and `IMPLEMENT_SERIAL` macros to the classes that you want serializable, you need to override the `Serialize` virtual member function for each class that will be serialized. The `Serialize()` function takes as its only argument a reference to a `CArchive` object. The `CArchive` object is based on a `CFile` object, which in turn is based on a physical disk file. In order to serialize an object to disk, the `CArchive` `<<` operator function is used. Conversely, to restore an object from disk, the `>>` operator function is used. The `CArchive` object has several overridden versions of the `operator>>` and `operator<<` member functions so that almost any C/C++ type can be serialized with a single line of code. Here's an example of a class (`CEmployee`) that needs to serialize three fields (`m_strName`, `m_iAge`, and `m_dtBirthdate`). Notice the `CArchive` `IsStoring` member function. This function is used to determine if the data is being written to disk (stored) or read from disk (loaded).

```
void CEmployee::Serialize(CArchive& ar)
{
 if (ar.IsStoring())
 { // storing code
  ar << m_strName;
  ar << m_iAge;
  ar << m_dtBirthdate;
 }
 else
 { // loading code
  ar > m_strName;
  ar > m_iAge;
  ar > m_dtBirthdate;
 }
}
```

Reading data from disk

Because dialog-based applications are the current focus, the most logical place to place the code necessary for reading objects from disk is in the OnInitDialog member function. Here you would add code to check for the existence of the data file and, if that data file existed, create a CFile object. The newly created CFile object would then be used to create a CArchive object that would be passed to the dialog's Serialize() function.

Saving data to disk

While the reading of objects from disk would logically be done in the OnInitDialog() function, deciding from what function to save the data is application specific. For example, you might have a button on your dialog called Commit that, upon being pressed, saves all the work done up to that point to disk. On the other hand, your application might simply save the data only when the user exits the application (the demo will take this approach). In order to save the object to disk, the application would need to check for the existence of the data file and create the file if it didn't already exist. Once the file existed, a CFile object would be instantiated and used to construct a CArchive object that would then be passed to the dialog's Serialize() function.

Adding serialization to the AddressBook demo

Now that you know the basic steps required to implement serialization for a dialog-based application, let's update the AddressBook demo to save and write the CContact objects to and from disk.

Let's start by opening the contact.h file and changing the CContact class to be derived from CObject. For any class to be serializable, it must be derived from CObject:

```
class CContact : public CObject
```

Next, add the following DECLARE_SERIAL macro to the CContact class declaration:

```
DECLARE_SERIAL(CContact)
```

Add the declaration of the Serialize member function:

```
virtual void Serialize(CArchive& ar);
```

Remove the CContactCollection templatized collection.

Declare the following CMapStringToOb-derived class:

```
class CContactCollection : public CMapStringToOb
{
public:
 CContactCollection(int nBlockSize = 10)
 : CMapStringToOb(nBlockSize) {};
};
```

Define the following templatized collection:

```
typedef CTypedPtrMap<CContactCollection,
 CString /* Name */,
 CContact*>TContactCollection;
```

When you have finished with the CContact and CContactCollection declarations, you must create a file called Contact.cpp, and add it to the AddressBook project. This file's main purpose is to implement the Serialize() function for the CContact class. When you have finished, the file should look like Listing 13-5.

Listing 13-5: Implementing the Serialize Function in Contact.cpp

```
#include "stdafx.h"
#include "Contact.h"

IMPLEMENT_SERIAL(CContact, CObject, 1)
void CContact::Serialize(CArchive& ar)
{
 if (ar.IsLoading())
 {
  ar >> m_strName;
  ar >> m_strAddress1;
  ar >> m_strAddress2;
  ar >> m_strCity;
  ar >> m_strState;
```

```
      ar >> m_strZip;
      ar >> m_strNotes;
      ar >> m_strHomePhone;
      ar >> m_strWorkPhone;
      ar >> m_strEmail;
      ar >> m_strWebPage;
    }
    else
    {
      ar << m_strName;
      ar << m_strAddress1;
      ar << m_strAddress2;
      ar << m_strCity;
      ar << m_strState;
      ar << m_strZip;
      ar << m_strNotes;
      ar << m_strHomePhone;
      ar << m_strWorkPhone;
      ar << m_strEmail;
      ar << m_strWebPage;
    }
  }
```

Due to the preceding changes to the CContact and CContactCollection classes, open the AddressBookDlg.h file, and change the m_Contacts type to TContactCollection.

Now that the CContact class is serializable, the CAddressBookDlg class must be made serializable as well. Using ClassWizard, override the Serialize() function for the CAddressBookDlg class, and modify it so that when finished, it appears like the following. Notice that in order to save all of the contacts, you need to call only the collection's (m_Contacts) Serialize() function. This is because the m_Contacts member variable is a templatized collection of type CContactCollection, which is derived from CMapStringToOb. The CMapStringToOb class implements the Serialize() function and calls Serialize() on each of its objects (in this case, CContact objects). This is why you have to call only the collection's Serialize() instead of having to iterate through the collection yourself:

```
void CAddressBookDlg::Serialize(CArchive& ar)
{
  m_Contacts.Serialize(ar);
  if (ar.IsStoring())
  {     // storing code
  }
  else
  {     // loading code
  }
}
```

At this point, all of the necessary classes (CContact, CContactCollection, and CAddressBookDlg) are serializable. You now must add the code to call the dialog's Serialize function. Before you can do that, however, you must add a simple helper function to see if the data file exists and if it can be accessed for reading and writing.

```
BOOL CAddressBookDlg::CanSerialize()
{
 return (0 == _access(DATA_FILE, 6));
}
```

In order for the CanSerialize function to compile, you need to add an #include directive for the io.h file (for the _access function) and the following #define directive:

```
#define DATA_FILE _T("AddressBook.dat")
```

Add the following member function to the CAddressBookDlg class. The LoadRecords function is used to serialize the objects from disk. After verifying that the file exists and can be opened for reading, the first thing this function does is to create a CFile object based on the data file (address.dat). The newly instantiated CFile object is then used to construct a CArchive object. Notice the second argument to the CArchive constructor. This value is used by the Serialize() function to determine whether data is being read in or written out.

```
void CAddressBookDlg::LoadRecords()
{
 if (CanSerialize())
 {
  CFile file;
  CFileException fe;

  if (file.Open(DATA_FILE,
  CFile::typeBinary | CFile::modeRead, &fe))
  {
   CArchive ar(&file, CArchive::load);
   Serialize(ar);
  }
 }
}
```

Because the LoadRecords() function is used to fill the m_Contact collection with all previously saved contacts, you need a function to load the combo box with those values. For that, implement the member function in Listing 13-6 in the CAddressBookDlg class.

Listing 13-6: Implementing the Member Function in the CAddressBookDlg Class

```
void CAddressBookDlg::FillContactsComboBox()
{
 POSITION pos;
 CString strKey;
 CContact* pContact;

 int iIndex;

 pos = m_Contacts.GetStartPosition();
 while(NULL != pos)
 {
  m_Contacts.GetNextAssoc(pos, strKey, pContact);
  if (pContact)
  {
   if (CB_ERR != (iIndex =
   m_cboNames.AddString(pContact->m_strName)))
   {
    m_cboNames.SetItemData(iIndex, (DWORD)pContact);
   }
  }
 }
}
```

At this point, modify the `CAddressBookDlg OnInitDialog()` function so that the only code between the call to the second `SetIcon` function and the `return` statement is the following:

```
LoadRecords();
FillContactsComboBox();
```

Now that the application can read objects from disk, you only need to update the demo so that when the user clicks the Close button, all of the contacts are saved before the application terminates. Add the `SaveRecords()` function in Listing 13-7 to the `CAddressBookDlg` class. This code is just a bit more involved than the `LoadRecords()` function because it must create the file if it does not already exist. Other than that, the only other major difference is that the `CArchive` object is created with the `CArchive::store` flag so that the `Serialize()` function knows that data is being saved when it is called with this `CArchive` object.

Listing 13-7: Adding the SaveRecords Function to the CAddressBookDlg Class

```
void CAddressBookDlg::SaveRecords()
{
 BOOL bCanSave = FALSE;

 UINT nFlags = CFile::typeBinary | CFile::modeWrite;

 // file doesn't exist, so create it
 if (_access(DATA_FILE, 0))
 {
  nFlags |= CFile::modeCreate;
  bCanSave = TRUE;
 }
 else
 {
  bCanSave = CanSerialize();
 }

 if (bCanSave)
 {
  CFile file;
  CFileException fe;

  // file exists with read & write permissions
  if (file.Open(DATA_FILE, nFlags, &fe))
  {
   CArchive ar(&file, CArchive::store);
   Serialize(ar);
  }
 }
}
```

Next, use ClassWizard to implement a message handler for the Save button's `BN_CLICKED` notification message, as demonstrated in Listing 13-8. This function will be used to create a `CContact` object from the information on the dialog and save it into `CContactCollection`. Remember, however, that the data won't be saved to disk until the user ends the application.

Listing 13-8: Implementing a Message Handler for the BN_CLICKED Notification Message

```
void CAddressBookDlg::OnBtnSave()
{
 if (UpdateData(TRUE))
 {
  CContact* pContact = NULL;

  CString strName;
  m_cboNames.GetWindowText(strName);
  if (0 != strName.GetLength())
  {
   if (!m_Contacts.Lookup(strName, (CContact*)pContact))
   {
    pContact = new CContact;
    int iIndex = m_cboNames.AddString(strName);
    if (CB_ERR != iIndex)
    {
     m_cboNames.SetItemData(iIndex, (DWORD)pContact);
     m_Contacts.SetAt(strName, pContact);
    }
   }

   if (pContact)
   {
    pContact->m_strName = strName;
    pContact->m_strAddress1 = m_strAddress1;
    pContact->m_strAddress2 = m_strAddress2;
    pContact->m_strCity = m_strCity;
    pContact->m_strState = m_strState;
    pContact->m_strZip = m_strZip;
    pContact->m_strNotes = m_strNotes;
    pContact->m_strHomePhone = m_strHomePhone;
    pContact->m_strWorkPhone = m_strWorkPhone;
    pContact->m_strEmail = m_strEmail;
    pContact->m_strWebPage = m_strWebPage;
   }
  }
  InitializeDialog();
 }
}
```

Add the following function that will initialize the controls to blanks when the Save button is clicked:

```
void CAddressBookDlg::InitializeDialog()
{
 m_cboNames.SetCurSel(CB_ERR);
 m_strAddress1 = _T("");
 m_strAddress2 = _T("");
 m_strCity = _T("");
 m_strState = _T("");
 m_strZip = _T("");
 m_strHomePhone = _T("");
 m_strWorkPhone = _T("");
 m_strEmail = _T("");
 m_strWebPage = _T("");
 m_strNotes = _T("");

 UpdateData(FALSE);
}
```

Finally, use ClassWizard to implement the following message handler for the Save button's `BN_CLICKED` notification message:

```
void CAddressBookDlg::OnBtnClose()
{
 SaveRecords();
 OnOK();
}
```

At this point, building and running the application should result in a simple little address book in which the entries are made persistent via the use of MFC's serialization.

Summary

In this chapter, you learned a lot about the power and flexibility of the `CDialog` class. In addition, you learned about DDX, implementing message handlers for control notification messages, coding both modal and modeless dialogs, and creating derived custom controls. As you've seen, knowing about each of these things individually is helpful, but fully understanding how to incorporate all of them into an application will make you a much more productive programmer.

✦ ✦ ✦

Property Sheets and Property Pages

In This Chapter

Discovering the CPropertySheet and CPropertyPage classes

Working with modal and modeless property sheets

Removing the standard CPropertySheet buttons

Repositioning the standard CPropertySheet buttons

Enabling and disabling CPropertyPage tabs

Changing a tab's caption and font

Utilizing mnemonics with CPropertyPage tabs

Tab dialogs are certainly no strangers to anyone who has used any of the 32-bit Windows operating systems. In fact, it is difficult to use Windows without running into these dialogs. Tab dialogs are found not only within operating system applications, but within popular applications such as Word for Windows, Excel, and even Visual Studio. Tab dialogs consist of a dialog with one or more tab indices. They are usually implemented in situations in which the application must display such a large number of options that a single dialog would not be practical. Using tab dialogs, however, the application can group the different options by function and place each group on its own tab. Figure 14-1 shows an example of a tab dialog in Visual Studio.

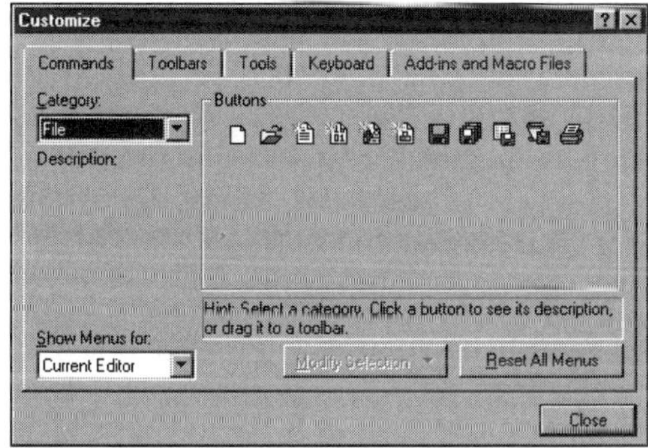

Figure 14-1: Visual Studio's Customize Tools dialog provides an example of a tab dialog.

This dialog is a perfect example of why tab dialogs exist. Instead of wading through several different dialogs in order to customize the different features of Visual Studio, the programmer needs to view only one dialog for all of Visual

Studio's customization options. Each tab is then defined to contain a given set of logically related options.

When MFC 3.0 (Visual C++ 2.0) shipped, support for creating tab dialogs was among the most notable additions to the framework. However, in MFC parlance, the name was changed from *tab dialogs* to *property sheets* and *property pages*. Property sheets represent the actual dialog, and property pages represent the individual tabs. Property sheets and property pages are implemented by the `CPropertySheet` and `CPropertyPage` classes, respectively, and are the focus of this chapter.

In this chapter, you will learn about these two MFC classes and how to implement them in both a modal and modeless environment. Once you have learned the different options and ways in which to implement these classes, a demo with several variations will be presented. While working your way through the demo, you will learn how to do many tasks that are frequently asked for with regards to property sheets and property pages. These tasks include property sheet level functions such as removing, renaming, and repositioning the standard property sheet buttons. In addition, property page level topics such as changing the tabs' caption and font as well as implementing mnemonics on tabs are covered.

CPropertySheet and CPropertyPage

As already mentioned, `CPropertySheet` objects represent property sheets, or tab dialogs. However, surprisingly, the `CPropertySheet` class is not derived from `CDialog`, but instead is derived directly from `CWnd`. Even though the `CPropertySheet` class is not derived from `CDialog`, the functions used to manage `CPropertySheet` objects are very similar to the functions used to manage `CDialog` objects. For example, construction of both a `CPropertySheet` and `CDialog` object is done in a two-part process. Modal property sheets and dialogs are both displayed by first constructing the object and then calling its `DoModal()` member function. Modeless property sheets and dialogs are both displayed by first constructing the object and then calling the object's `Create()` function.

However, aside from their similarities in appearance and the functions used to display them, property sheets and dialogs are different from an MFC standpoint. For example, the dialog object maintains the data viewed on a dialog. By contrast, the data viewed on a property sheet is usually maintained in the different property pages. Because the separate property pages are used to represent each tab and usually maintain the data that is displayed on that page, it is the `CPropertyPage` class that is derived from `CDialog`.

Creating property page resources

Creating property pages in the resource editor is similar to creating dialog resource templates. In both cases, the resource editor is used to create a dialog template resource upon which controls are positioned and sized. However, the property page settings differ from those of a dialog with regards to the following:

✦ The value of the `Caption` property appears on the tab instead of on the dialog's title bar.

✦ The `Style` property of a property page must be set to `Child`.

✦ The `Border` property of a property page must be set to `Thin`.

✦ The `Disabled` check box of a property page must be checked.

Luckily, you needn't remember these different styles every time you create a property page. This is because the Insert Resource dialog has three different options for creating property pages. Pressing Ctrl+R displays the Insert Resource dialog shown in Figure 14-2. As you can see, the only difference between the different default property pages is the initial size of the property sheet. When a property sheet is created from the Insert Resource dialog, the settings previously listed are preset automatically.

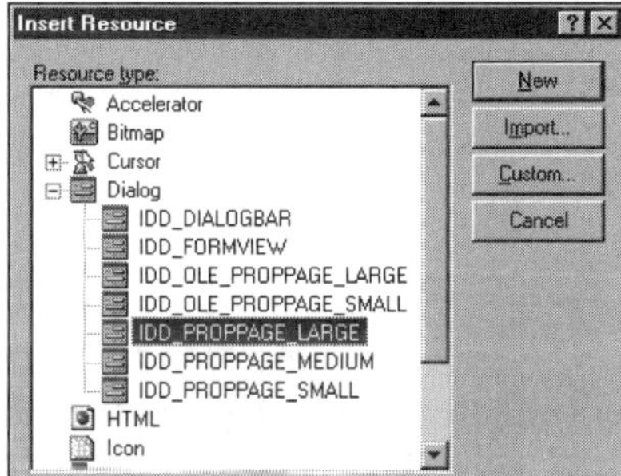

Figure 14-2: The Insert Resource dialog can be used to create the dialog template resources for property pages.

Creating the CPropertyPage class

Once a property page has been designed in the resource editor, a `CPropertyPage`-derived class can be created via ClassWizard. Once again, this is done much the same way as creating a `CDialog`-derived class. The only difference is that instead of selecting `CDialog` as the base class, you should select `CPropertyPage`. Be careful about the last part. If you invoke the ClassWizard to create a new class of a dialog template resource, ClassWizard always defaults the base class to `CDialog`. Unfortunately, ClassWizard doesn't look at the styles to determine that a `CPropertyPage` is probably the correct way to go in some cases.

Creating and displaying a modal CPropertySheet

As mentioned earlier, the CPropertySheet class is not derived from CDialog although CPropertySheet objects are constructed and displayed in the same manner that CDialog objects are constructed and displayed. For example, to create and display a modal property sheet, you would normally declare a CPropertySheet object on the stack and call its DoModal() function (just as you'd do with a CDialog object). However, in the case of a property page, you need to add the relevant property pages to the property sheet before calling the property sheet's DoModal() function.

Following is an example of how to do this. As you can see, CPropertyPage objects are added to a CPropertySheet object via the CPropertySheet::AddPage() function:

```
void ShowModalPropertySheet()
{
 CPropertySheet sheet;
 CMyPropertyPage1 pageMyPage1;
 CMyPropertyPage2 pageMyPage2;

 sheet.AddPage(&pageMyPage1);
 sheet.AddPage(&pageMyPage2);
 sheet.DoModal();
}
```

Creating and displaying a modeless CPropertySheet

Displaying a modeless property sheet is almost identical to displaying a modal property sheet. The main difference is instead of using the DoModal() function to display the property sheet, the CPropertySheet::Create() function is used. In addition, you should take a couple of important points into account when dealing with modeless property sheets and property pages.

Modal property sheets are displayed in a synchronous manner. This means that when a function calls the property sheet's DoModal() function, control does not return to the calling function until the property sheet has been dismissed. Therefore, the property sheet and property page objects can be allocated on the stack within the function that called the property sheet's DoModal() function.

Modeless property sheets, however, are displayed in an asynchronous manner because the call to display the property sheet does return while the property sheet is still visible. Great care must be taken insofar as how and when to allocate the property sheet and property page objects when dealing with modeless property sheets. Because of this fact, the property sheet and property page objects are normally allocated on the heap so that if the function displaying the property sheet ends before the property sheet is dismissed, the objects will not go out of scope and destruct while the property sheet is still displayed. Following is an example of creating and displaying a modeless property sheet and its property pages:

```
void CMyView::DisplayPropertySheet()
{
 m_pPropertySheet = new CMyPropertySheet();

 CMyPropertyPage1* ppageMyPage1 =
  new CMyPropertyPage1();
 CMyPropertyPage2* ppageMyPage2 =
  new CMyPropertyPage2();

 m_pPropertySheet->AddPage(ppageMyPage1);
 m_pPropertySheet->AddPage(ppageMyPage2);
 m_pPropertySheet->Create();
}
```

But how do the property pages objects get destructed? This is usually done by deriving a class from `CPropertySheet` and overriding the `PostNcDestroy()` virtual function. That way, when the property sheet is destroyed, the property sheet's list of property pages can be iterated and each page deleted. Here's an example of how that might look. As you can see, the `GetPageCount()` function returns the total number of pages added to the `CPropertySheet` object. Because `CPropertyPage` objects are stored in an array in the `CPropertySheet` object, the `GetPage()` function returns a pointer to a `CPropertyPage` object using the passed integer value as an index into that array.

```
CMyPropertySheet::PostNcDestroy()
{
 for (int i = 0; i < GetPageCount(); i++)
 {
  CPropertyPage* pPage = GetPage(i);
  ASSERT(pPage);
  if (pPage)
  {
   delete pPage;
  }
 }

 CPropertySheet::PostNcDestroy();
}
```

Another difference between modal and modeless property sheets is that unlike modal property sheets, modeless property sheets are not automatically displayed with an OK and Cancel button; your program has to create these buttons manually. You will see how to do this in the next section as `CPropertySheet` is delved into a little further.

Creating and displaying a property sheet within an existing dialog

So far, you've seen how to create and display both modal and modeless property sheets. However, at times you will need to display a property sheet within another dialog. If you are in need of this rather advanced user interface functionality, it can be accomplished by following a couple of easy steps.

First, declare the `CPropertySheet` and `CPropertyPage` objects as member variables of the dialog class.

```
class CYourDialog : public CDialog
{
 ...
protected:
 CPropertySheet m_sheet;
 CMyPropertyPage1 m_pageMyPage1;
 CMyPropertyPage2 m_pageMyPage2;
 ...
```

Then, in the dialog's `OnInitDialog()` function, call the `CPropertySheet::AddPage()` function to add the `CPropertyPage` objects. After that, create the property sheet (specifying that the property sheet is a child of the dialog with the `WS_CHILD` flag). Once the `CPropertySheet` object has been created, you need to modify a couple of styles that deal with tabbing. The final step is to position the property sheet on the dialog via a call to the `SetWindowPos()` function. Here's how your `OnInitDialog()` might look:

```
void CYourDialog::OnInitDialog()
{
 ...
 m_sheet.Create(this, WS_CHILD | WS_VISIBLE, 0);
 m_sheet.ModifyStyleEx (0, WS_EX_CONTROLPARENT);
 m_sheet.ModifyStyle( 0, WS_TABSTOP );
 CRect rect;
 GetDlgItem(IDC_PROPSHEET)->GetWindowRect(&rect);
 ScreenToClient(&rect);
 m_sheet.SetWindowPos(NULL, rect.left-7, rect.top-7,
  0, 0, SWP_NOZORDER | SWP_NOSIZE | SWP_NOACTIVATE);
 ...
```

A Modal Property Sheet Demo

This demo (ModalDemo) teaches many aspects of using modal property sheets by writing a Find dialog. The Find dialog is like many in other applications with one exception: Once a search has been completed, the results are displayed on a second tab. This handles scenarios in which a search results in more than one hit.

The complete source for the ModalDemo project can be found on the accompanying CD in the `Chap14\ModalDemo` folder.

✦ ✦ ✦ ✦ ✦

This demo will enable you to deal with many realistic scenarios concerning programming property sheets. For example, in a Find dialog, you wouldn't want the Results tab enabled unless matches are found. Therefore, after you get the basic property sheet up and running, you will learn to enable and disable tabs. In addition, it's a nice touch for the end user to see the number of matches on the Results tab. To accomplish that task, you will learn to dynamically change a tab's caption. The full source for this demo can be found on the accompanying CD in the `\Chap14\ModalDemo` folder.

The main objective of this demo is to teach the different aspects of the `CPropertySheet` and `CPropertyPage` classes. Therefore, many aspects of this demo will be "faked" so that the demo doesn't go on a five-page tangent on how to deal with issues that have nothing to do with property sheets or property pages. Here's how to create the demo application:

1. Use AppWizard to create a new MFC SDI application named ModalDemo.
2. Create a property page resource called `IDP_FINDBOOK_FIND`, and add the necessary controls to make it look like the property page in Figure 14-3. You may need to resize the dialog so your controls look the way you want. In addition, make sure to disable the Author and Publisher edit controls.

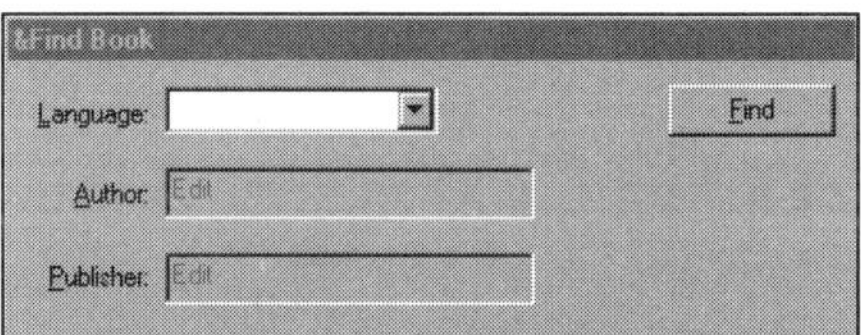

Figure 14-3: After modifying the Find Book property page, it should look like this.

3. Once the controls have been placed on the `IDP_FINDBOOK_FIND` dialog, use the ClassWizard to create a `CPropertyPage` class called `CFindPage`.
4. Next create DDX control member variables for the Language combo box and the Find button. Name them `m_cboLanguages` and `m_btnFind`, respectively.
5. After the Find property page is complete, create a second property page called `IDP_FINDBOOK_RESULTS`, and modify it so that when finished, it looks like the property sheet in Figure 14-4.

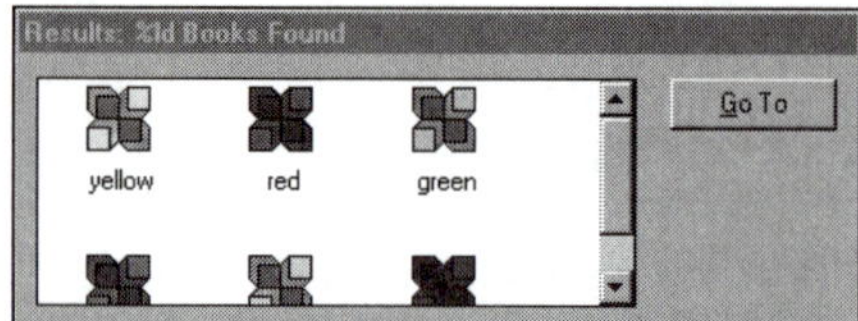

Figure 14-4: The Results property page after the controls have been added

6. Once again, use ClassWizard to create a `CPropertyPage`-derived class called `CResultsPage`.
7. After ClassWizard creates the `CResultsPage` class, create two DDX control member variables for the list control and the button. Name them `m_lstResults` and `m_btnGoto`, respectively.
8. Add a string resource with the ID of `IDS_FIND`. The value for this string should be "Find Book". This string resource will be passed to the `CPropertySheet` constructor.
9. After you create the two property pages, locate the `IDR_MAINFRAME` menu resource, and add a new menu item labeled "Find Book" to the Edit menu.
10. Create a menu handler via ClassWizard for your new menu entry in the `CMainFrame` class. The code should look like the following when you are done:

```
void CMainFrame::OnEditFindbook()
{
 CPropertySheet sheet(IDS_FIND);
 CFindPage pageFind;
 CResultsPage pageResults;

 sheet.AddPage(&pageFind);
 sheet.AddPage(&pageResults);
 sheet.DoModal();
}
```

In the preceding code, a `CPropertySheet` is created on the stack using the constructor that takes as its only argument a string resource ID. Next, two `CPropertyPage` objects are instantiated. After the property pages are created, they are both added to the `CPropertySheet` via the `CPropertySheet::AddPage()` function, and the `CPropertySheet::DoModal()` function is called to display the property sheet.

11. The last thing to do before running the demo is to add the following two `#include` directives to the beginning of the `mainfrm.cpp` file for the two `CPropertyPage`-derived classes:

```
#include "FindPage.h"
#include "ResultsPage.h"
```

12. At this point, build and run the application. Once you select the Find Book option from the Edit menu, your modal property sheet should look like that shown in Figure 14-5.

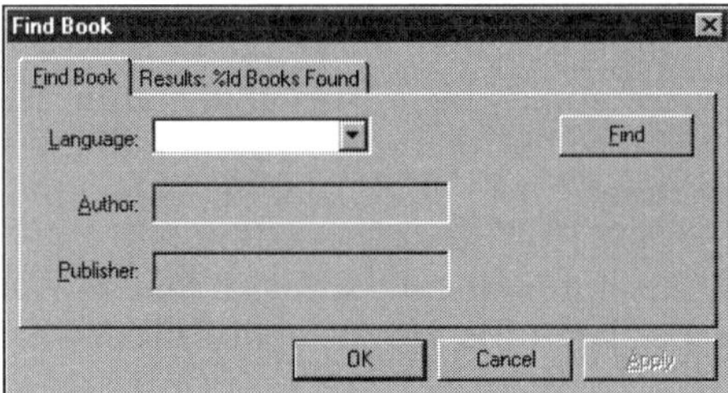

Figure 14-5: Using the MFC CPropertySheet and CPropertyPage classes, dialogs like this can be created in minutes.

Property Sheet and Property Page Tips and Techniques

As you have seen, it is very easy to create and display both modal and modeless property sheets. Unfortunately, this is the point where the Visual C++ online documentation and most books leave off. However, you aren't reading this chapter to learn something that can be covered in just a few pages. So roll up your sleeves, and let's start doing some real work with property sheets and property pages.

Note that this section involves making changes to the modal property sheet demo (ModalDemo). Unless otherwise noted, all the tips and techniques presented in this section are valid for both modal and modeless property sheets.

Removing standard buttons

As you have seen, when a modal `CPropertySheet` is displayed, several buttons are automatically created. However, there may be situations where your application doesn't have a need for all of these standard buttons. For example, the Apply button is certainly not applicable for every application. So the question is, "If the buttons are displayed automatically, how does the programmer specify that they are not needed?" Actually, as you are about to see, removing any or all of the standard buttons from a `CPropertySheet` is not difficult.

Let's say you want to remove the Cancel and Apply buttons. Users select the Cancel button when they have changed their minds and want to back out of the dialog without affecting any changes. The Apply button gives users the capability to apply the changes while remaining on the property sheet. In other words, when using a dialog, it is customary to expect that changes will only be made once the dialog has been dismissed. However, with property sheets, you can use the Apply button to enable users to view their changes while the property sheet remains displayed. This enables users to continue making changes and, depending on the application, see the effects as they work their way through the property sheet's pages.

However, this demo is about a Find Book property sheet and because no data will be changed, neither of these buttons is applicable to this application. The question now becomes, "How do you remove these buttons when you don't have the dialog template resource for the property sheet?"

Because MFC is creating these buttons automatically for you, they are all created with static, nonchanging resource IDs. Their IDs are listed in Table 14-1.

Table 14-1
Resource IDs for Buttons

Button	*Resource ID*
OK	`IDOK`
Cancel	`IDCANCEL`
Help	`IDHELP`
Apply	`ID_APPLY_NOW`

In order to remove the standard buttons, you only need to do the following for each control (where `id` is one of the IDs listed in Table 14-1):

```
CWnd* pWnd = GetDlgItem(id);
if (pWnd)
{
 pWnd->ShowWindow(FALSE);
}
```

Therefore, to remove the Cancel and Apply buttons from the demo's property sheet, you need to make only the following modifications to the demo:

1. Using ClassWizard, create a `CPropertySheet`-derived class called `CFindSheet`.
2. Place an `#include` directive for the `FileSheet.h` file in the `mainfrm.cpp` file.
3. Modify the `CMainFrame:: OnEditFindbook()` function to instantiate this new `CFindSheet` class (instead of the standard `CPropertySheet`).
4. Using ClassWizard, override the `CFindSheet::OnInitDialog()` function to hide the unwanted buttons (`IDCANCEL` and `ID_APPLY_NOW`).

```
BOOL CFindSheet::OnInitDialog()
{
 BOOL bResult = CPropertySheet::OnInitDialog();

 int ids[] = {ID_APPLY_NOW, IDCANCEL};
 for (int i = 0; i < sizeof ids / sizeof ids[0]; i++)
 {
  CWnd* pWnd = GetDlgItem(ids[i]);
  ASSERT(pWnd);
  if (pWnd) pWnd->ShowWindow(FALSE);
 }

 return bResult;
}
```

When you run the application, you still have one problem concerning the standard buttons. The only remaining button (IDOK) appears as if it has been marooned in the middle of the dialog. The next section shows how to move that button or any other of the standard buttons.

Repositioning standard buttons

At this point, the property sheet looks a little strange because it only has one button and that button is horizontally positioned almost in the middle of the dialog. In addition, both property pages have buttons that are aligned along the right side of the property page. Therefore, it would certainly look a lot more appealing if the OK button were also aligned along the right side of the property sheet. Unfortunately, there is no single member function along the lines of AlignButtons(). Therefore, you will have to do this the old-fashioned way: using the MoveWindow() function. The code shown in Listing 14-1 should be added to the OnInitDialog() function.

Here's a brief explanation of the code. First, a CWnd object (pbtnOK) is associated with the OK button. Then, the property sheet is shortened by the height of a button and widened by the width of a button. After the property sheet is properly sized, the screen position of the first property page is used to properly align the OK button with the property page.

Listing 14-1: Moving Buttons in a Property Sheet

```
CWnd* pbtnOk = GetDlgItem(IDOK);
ASSERT(pbtnOk);

CRect rectSheet;
GetWindowRect(rectSheet);
```

(continued)

Listing 14-1 *(continued)*

```
// get size of ok button
CRect rectOkBtn;
pbtnOk->GetWindowRect(rectOkBtn);

// get border space between btn bottom and sheet bottom
int iBorder = rectSheet.bottom - rectOkBtn.bottom;

// resize sheet
rectSheet.right += rectOkBtn.Width() + iBorder;
rectSheet.bottom = rectOkBtn.top;
MoveWindow(rectSheet);

// find first page
CPropertyPage* pPage = GetPage(0);
ASSERT(pPage);
CRect rectPage;
pPage->GetWindowRect(rectPage);

// save width and height
int cxOk = rectOkBtn.Width();
int cyOk = rectOkBtn.Height();

// move ok button
rectOkBtn.top = rectPage.top;
rectOkBtn.bottom = rectOkBtn.top + cyOk;
rectOkBtn.left = rectSheet.right -
 (cxOk + iBorder);
rectOkBtn.right = rectOkBtn.left + cxOk;
ScreenToClient(rectOkBtn);
pbtnOk->MoveWindow(rectOkBtn);
```

After you have inserted the code in Listing 14-1 in the `CFindSheet OnInitDialog()` member function, build the project and run it. You should see results similar to Figure 14-6.

Changing the standard button's caption

A button's caption should reflect what will happen if the button is clicked. If someone is using this Find Book dialog and sees an OK button, he or she would naturally be confused as to what will happen once that button is clicked. Will the pressing of an OK button on a Find Book dialog close the dialog or perform the search? Therefore, the next task will be to illustrate how to change the text of a property sheet button.

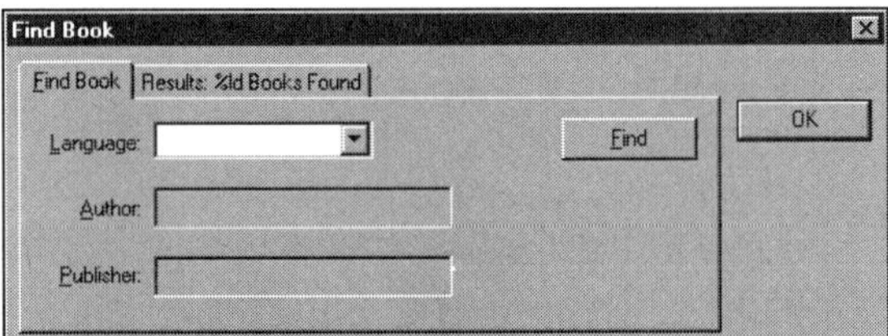

Figure 14-6: Moving a property sheet's buttons and resizing the property sheet accordingly can be easily accomplished via the GetWindowRect() and MoveWindow() functions.

Because the `CPropertySheet` and its standard buttons are created dynamically, changing a standard button's caption will have to be done in your application code. The following is all that is needed to change the OK button's caption (including setting a mnemonic). Once again, any of the property sheet's standard button IDs could be used (as listed previously), as well as any IDs for controls that you have added to the property sheet.

```
CWnd* pWnd = GetDlgItem(IDOK);
pWnd->SetWindowText(_T("Cl&ose"));
```

Disabling tabs

You might need to disable a given tab within a property sheet at times. Let's say, for example, that the application needs certain fields on one page to be entered before it can display another page. Unfortunately, at the time of this writing, no elegant means of disabling a tab existed. Therefore, in lieu of a `CPropertySheet` member function, here's an outline of the steps required to disable a property page. After the numbered steps, each step is expanded so that you can see exactly what is required to implement this functionality in code.

1. Create a member variable to store the current tab index.
2. Create an array member variable to hold all of the index values for the currently disabled tabs.
3. Handle the `TCN_SELCHANGING` notification message to set the current tab index.
4. Handle the `TCN_SELCHANGED` notification message to decide if you want to enable the tab to be activated. If you don't, you must post a `PSM_SETCURSEL` message. In this message, the last active tab index is specified.

Creating a member variable to store the current tab index

Add a member variable to the `CFindSheet` class to hold the current tab index. When a user attempts to access a disabled tab, this index value represents the tab that will be activated. Actually, it happens so fast that the user will only perceive not being able to switch to the disabled tab.

```
protected:
 int m_iLastActivePage;
```

Creating a member variable to hold currently disabled tabs

The next step is to add a member variable of type CUIntArray to the CFindSheet class. This array will hold all of the indexes to the currently disabled tabs on the property sheet:

```
CUIntArray m_arrDisabledPages;
```

Adding member functions to disable specified tabs

Next, add the function declaration to the CFindSheet class to enable the disabling of property pages (see Listing 14-2). The property pages that need to be disabled are specified in a variable argument list that is terminated with the standard value of –1. This function adds the specified tab indexes to the m_arrDisabledPages array. After that, the SetDisabledText() function is called to append the " – Disabled" text to the tab's caption.

In addition to having to do all of this work to simply disable a tab, there is also no way to change the font for a specific tab. In other words, you cannot "gray out" the text of the specific tab so that the user can intuitively see that the tab is not accessible. Therefore, Microsoft recommends that you simply append the text "– Disabled" to the tab's caption. Bogus? Absolutely. Unfortunately, at this time, it's all there is.

Listing 14-2: Adding the Function Declaration to the CFindSheet Class

```
void CFindSheet::DisablePage(int iFirstPage, ...)
{
 int iPage = iFirstPage;

 va_list marker;
 va_start (marker, iFirstPage);
 int nArgs = 0;

 while (iPage != -1)
 {
  // add page to disabled page index array
  m_arrDisabledPages.Add(iPage);

  SetDisabledText(iPage);

  // Get next page index
```

```
    iPage = va_arg(marker, UINT);

    // the list MUST end with a -1!!!
    ASSERT(nArgs++ < 100);
  }
}
```

Adding member functions to set captions of disabled tabs

Once you have added the `DisablePage()` function, add the following `#define` directive and `SetDiabledText()` function. This function appends the `DISABLED_TEXT` value to the tab's caption so that the user knows that the tab cannot be activated.

```
#define DISABLED_TEXT " - Disabled"

void CFindSheet::SetDisabledText(int iPage)
{
 CTabCtrl* pTab = GetTabControl();
 ASSERT(pTab);
 TC_ITEM ti;
 char szText[100];
 ti.mask = TCIF_TEXT;
 ti.pszText = szText;
 ti.cchTextMax = 100;
 VERIFY(pTab->GetItem(iPage, &ti));
 strcat(szText, DISABLED_TEXT);
 VERIFY(pTab->SetItem(iPage, &ti));
}
```

Handling tab notification messages for disabled tabs

Now that you have everything in place to know if a tab should be disabled or not, you need to add the function that actually disables user activation of a disabled tab. Use ClassWizard to implement the `OnNotify()` virtual function, and edit it to look like Listing 14-3.

As mentioned earlier, any time the user attempts to activate a property page, this function checks to see if the desired property page is disabled. If it is, the `OnNotify()` function resets the current property page to the last active property page by posting a `PSM_SETCURSEL` message to the object's underlying property sheet.

Listing 14-3: Implementing the OnNotify() Virtual Function

```
BOOL CFindSheet::OnNotify(WPARAM wParam,
 LPARAM lParam, LRESULT* pResult)
{
 NMHDR* pnmh = (NMHDR*)lParam;
 ASSERT(pnmh);
 if (TCN_SELCHANGING == pnmh->code)
 {
  m_iLastActivePage = GetActiveIndex();
 }
 else if (TCN_SELCHANGE == pnmh->code)
 {
  int iCurrPage = GetActiveIndex();
  if (IsPageDisabled(iCurrPage))
  {
   PostMessage(PSM_SETCURSEL, m_iLastActivePage);
  }
 }

 return CPropertySheet::OnNotify(wParam,
  lParam, pResult);
}
```

Adding a function that verifies if a tab is disabled

Add the function shown in Listing 14-4 to verify if a specified property page is disabled. This function simply iterates through the `m_arrDisabledPages` array to see if the specified property page has been disabled and returns a `BOOL` value indicating if it is disabled or not.

Listing 14-4: Verifying If a Property Page Is Disabled

```
BOOL CFindSheet::IsPageDisabled(int iPage)
{
 BOOL bFoundEntry = FALSE;
 int iSize = m_arrDisabledPages.GetSize();

 int i = 0;
 while (i < iSize && !bFoundEntry)
 {
  if (m_arrDisabledPages.GetAt(i) == (UINT)iPage)
  {
   bFoundEntry = TRUE;
  }
  else
  {
   i++;
```

```
        }
      }

      return bFoundEntry;
    }
```

Testing the capability to disable tabs

The Find Book property sheet has a property page for the search criteria and a property page for the search results. Therefore, it would be logical to assume that the Results property page would be disabled until the user has initiated a search that successfully found books that matched the criteria specified on the Find Books property page.

Therefore, locate the `CFindSheet OnInitDialog()` function, and place the following line of code just before the `return` statement. Notice that with any function that takes a variable argument list, you must send a value that is recognized as the terminating value to the list. In this case, the standard value of –1 is being used. Testing and running the application at this point should produce a property sheet in which the Results property page is not accessible. Because you want to re-enable this tab once the user initiates a search, the next section will show how to re-enable tabs.

```
DisablePage(1, -1);
```

Re-enabling property pages

Now that you disabled the property page(s), you need to be able to re-enable it. To accomplish this, simply add the following functions to both enable a given property page and to remove the " – Disabled" text from the tab's caption.

Understanding the EnablePage function

Because the code is in place to add a property page to an array (`m_arrDisabledPages`) when it is disabled, the `EnablePage()` function simply needs to search the `m_arrDisabledPages` array for the specified page (see Listing 14-5). If the page is found, it is removed from the array, and the `SetEnabledText()` function is called.

Listing 14-5: Searching the m_arrDisabledPages Array for a Specified Page

```
void CFindSheet::EnablePage(int iPage)
{
 BOOL bFoundEntry = FALSE;
 int iSize = m_arrDisabledPages.GetSize();

 int i = 0;
 while (i < iSize && !bFoundEntry)
 {
  if (m_arrDisabledPages.GetAt(i) == (UINT)iPage)
  {
   bFoundEntry = TRUE;
  }
  else
  {
   i++;
  }
 }

 if (bFoundEntry)
 {
  m_arrDisabledPages.RemoveAt(i);
  SetEnabledText(iPage);
 }
}
```

Examining the SetEnabledText function

Once a page has been re-enabled, this function must be called to strip the " – Disabled" string from the end of the tab's caption. The `EnableTab()` function calls this function when it has removed a property page from the `m_arrDisabledPages` array:

```
void CFindSheet::SetEnabledText(int iPage)
{
 CTabCtrl* pTab = GetTabControl();
 ASSERT(pTab);
 TC_ITEM ti;
 char szText[100];
 ti.mask = TCIF_TEXT;
 ti.pszText = szText;
 ti.cchTextMax = 100;
 VERIFY(pTab->GetItem(iPage, &ti));
 char* pFound = strstr(szText, DISABLED_TEXT);
 if (pFound)
 {
  *pFound = '\0';
  VERIFY(pTab->SetItem(iPage, &ti));
 }
}
```

Testing the EnableTab function

To test the capability to re-enable a tab, use the ClassWizard to add a message handler for the Find button on the `CFindPage` property page. This function gets a pointer to the property page's parent window (the property sheet) and calls the `CFindSheet::EnablePage()` function. You will have to add an `#include` directive for the `FindSheet.h` file at the top of the `FindPage.Cpp` file for this function to compile. In addition, you need to ensure that the `CFindSheet::EnablePage()` is a public member function.

```
void CFindPage::OnBtnFind()
{
 CFindSheet* pParentSheet = (CFindSheet*)GetParent();

 ASSERT(pParentSheet-IsKindOf(
  RUNTIME_CLASS(CFindSheet)));

 pParentSheet->EnablePage(1);
}
```

Building and testing the application at this point should result in a property sheet in which the Find Book property page is enabled and the Results property page is disabled. Upon clicking the Find button, however, the Results property page should become enabled.

Dynamically setting CPropertyPage tab captions

When you created the dialog template resources for the two property pages, you specified a Caption property. However, what happens when you want to change a tab's caption at runtime? This demo provides an example of when you would want to do so. Because the Results property page contains a list of the items found, it would be helpful for the user if the tab also indicated the number of items found.

Using the SetItem function to set a tab's caption

To set a tab's caption, you get a pointer to the tab control (`CTabCtrl`) object, retrieve the current text (`CTabCtrl::GetItem()`), and then set the text with the `CTabCtrl::SetItem()` function call. At its simplest, this can be performed as follows:

```
CTabCtrl* pTab = GetTabControl();
ASSERT(pTab);
TC_ITEM ti;
char szText[100];
ti.mask = TCIF_TEXT;
ti.pszText = szText;
ti.cchTextMax = 100;
VERIFY(pTab->GetItem(iIndexOfDesiredTab, &ti));

strcpy(szText, "Your new tab Caption");
VERIFY(pTab->SetItem(iIndexOfDesiredTab, &ti));
```

Testing the SetItem function to set a tab's caption

The preceding example is simple. But what if you want to format the caption? For example, what if you needed to show the caption as "Results: 5 books found"? Let's see the changes that would be necessary with the demo application to make that happen.

Add these `#defines` directives to the top of the `FindSheet.cpp` file:

```
#define RESULTS_TAB_INDEX 1
#define RESULTS_TAB_CAPTION "Results: %ld books found"
```

After the `#defines` are in place, add the following functions to the `CFindSheet` class. As you can see, the `SetResults` function simply calls a function to alter the Results tab's caption and then enables or disables the tab based on the value of `nHits`. After all, why enable the property page if the search turned up nothing? Because `CFindPage` will be calling the `SetResults()` function, declare the `SetResults()` function as being `public`:

```
void CFindSheet::SetResults(int nHits)
{
 SetResultsTabCaption(nHits);
 if (0 == nHits)
 {
  DisablePage(1, -1);
 }
 else
 {
  EnablePage(1);
 }
}
```

After retrieving the tab's caption via the `CTabCtrl::GetItem()` function call, the `RESULTS_TAB_CAPTION` is used to format the new caption:

```
void CFindSheet::SetResultsTabCaption(int nHits)
{
 CTabCtrl* pTab = GetTabControl();
 ASSERT(pTab);
 TC_ITEM ti;
 char szText[100];
 ti.mask = TCIF_TEXT;
 ti.pszText = szText;
 ti.cchTextMax = 100;
 VERIFY(pTab->GetItem(RESULTS_TAB_INDEX, &ti));

 sprintf(szText, RESULTS_TAB_CAPTION, nHits);
 VERIFY(pTab->SetItem(RESULTS_TAB_INDEX, &ti));
}
```

Once these two functions are defined, you just need to update the `CFileSheet::OnInitDialog()` by removing the call to `DisablePage()` and replacing it with a call to the SetResults() function. You no longer have to disable the tab because the SetResults() function does that automatically if a value of 0 (indicating no hits) is passed to it:

```
SetResults(0);
```

To test our search logic, let's hard-code a couple of entries in the Languages combo box of the Find Books property page. Use ClassWizard to add the OnInitDialog() function to the CFindPage class, and update it as follows:

```
BOOL CFindPage::OnInitDialog()
{
 CPropertyPage::OnInitDialog();

 m_cboLanguages.AddString(_T("Visual C++"));
 m_cboLanguages.AddString(_T("Visual J++"));
 m_cboLanguages.SetCurSel(0);

 return TRUE;
}
```

Finally, update the CFindPage::OnBtnFind() function to "find" two books if the "Visual C++" combo box entry is selected and to "find" zero books if the "Visual J++" combo box entry is chosen. Obviously, this is being hard-coded so that you can concentrate on simply testing the code that implements dynamically changing a tab's caption.

```
void CFindPage::OnBtnFind()
{
 CFindSheet* pParentSheet = (CFindSheet*)GetParent();
 ASSERT(pParentSheet->IsKindOf(
  RUNTIME_CLASS(CFindSheet)));

 int iIndex;
 if (0 == (iIndex = m_cboLanguages.GetCurSel()))
 {
  pParentSheet->SetResults(2);
 }
 else
 {
  pParentSheet->SetResults(0);
 }
}
```

If you build and test this demo application at this point, you will see that if you select the "Visual C++" entry and then click the Find button, not only does the Results tab's caption change, but it also becomes enabled so that you can activate it. Conversely, if you select the "Visual J++" entry and click the "Find" button, the Results tab's caption indicates that no books could be located, and the Results property page will be disabled as a result.

Changing a tab's font

You may recall that a specific tab's font cannot be changed. However, you can change the font for all tabs contained within a property sheet. If you take a close look at the different tabs you added to the demo application, one thing that is obvious is that the tab captions don't stand out. In other words, they fade into the background. If you ever want to change the tab caption's font, here is how you do it:

1. Create the desired font.
2. Acquire a pointer to the `CTabCtrl` object.
3. Call the `CTabCtrl::SetFont()` function.

Actually, this demo was going to change the font for the "active" tab, but unfortunately, this doesn't appear to be possible. In other words, all of the tab's captions are displayed with the same font, and that font is changed with the `CTabCtrl::SetFont()` function. To change the font in the demo application, declare a member variable of type `CFont` in the `CFindSheet` class called `m_fontTab`. Then, add the following lines of code to the end of the `CFindSheet::OnInitDialog()` function:

```
m_fontTab.CreateFont(-8, 0, 0, 0, FW_BOLD, 0, 0,
 0, 1, 0, 0, 0, 0, _T("MS Sans Serif"));
CTabCtrl* pTab = GetTabControl();
ASSERT(pTab);
if (pTab)
{
 pTab->SetFont(&m_fontTab);
}
```

Using mnemonics with CPropertyPage tabs

One advantage the Windows interface has over other operating systems is its sense of user interface consistency. Take the example of a mnemonic. Whenever you see static text on the screen with one of the letters underlined, the underlined letter is known as a *mnemonic*. Holding down the Alt key and pressing the mnemonic usually results in that field getting focus. Actually, as you learned in Chapter 13, if the control is read-only, the next input-capable control in the tab order receives focus.

However, just when you get comfortable with the concept of putting mnemonics in all of your dialogs, along comes the `CPropertyPage` class, which completely ignores them. If, for example, you set a `CPropertyPage`'s tab caption to "&Result", and press Alt+R, nothing happens. To get around this glaring shortcoming of the `CPropertyPage` class, you have to override the `CPropertySheet::PreTranslateMessage()`. Every single keystroke is filtered through this function for every property page owned by the property sheet.

At this point, use ClassWizard to create the `PreTranslateMessage()` function. The demo's implementation of this function is shown in Listing 14-6. As you can see, `WM_SYSKEYDOWN` messages are the only concern because that is the message that is sent when the user is holding down the Alt key. The `pMsg->wParam` value is then evaluated to make sure that the key that was pressed is a number or a letter. After that, the function simply iterates through the property sheet's property pages and compares the mnemonic that was typed to the mnemonic (if any) for each property page. If a matching property page is found, the `SetActivePage()` function is called only if the page is not disabled. Figure 14-7 shows the demo after having implemented the changes outlined in this section.

Listing 14-6: Implementation of CFindSheet::PreTranslateMessage()

```
BOOL CFindSheet::PreTranslateMessage(MSG* pMsg)
{
 BOOL bHandledMsg = FALSE;

 switch(pMsg->message)
 {
  case WM_SYSKEYDOWN:
  {
   // we only want 0-9 and letters
   if ((0x2f < pMsg->wParam)
     && (0x5b > pMsg->wParam))
   {
    CTabCtrl *pTab = GetTabControl();
    ASSERT(pTab);

    TC_ITEM ti;
    char szText[100];
    ti.mask = TCIF_TEXT;
    ti.pszText = szText;

    char szMnemonic[3];
    sprintf(szMnemonic, "&%c", pMsg->wParam);

    BOOL bFoundMatchingPage = FALSE;
    int iCurrPage = 0;
    while ((iCurrPage < pTab->GetItemCount())
      && (!bFoundMatchingPage))
    {
     ti.cchTextMax = 99;
     pTab->GetItem(iCurrPage, &ti);

     CString strText = szText;
     strText.MakeUpper();
     if (-1 != strText.Find(szMnemonic))
```

(continued)

Listing 14-6 *(continued)*

```
        {
         bFoundMatchingPage = TRUE;
         if (!IsPageDisabled(iCurrPage))
         {
          SetActivePage(iCurrPage);
          bHandledMsg = TRUE;
         }
        }
        else
        {
         iCurrPage++;
        }
       }
      }
     }
     break;

     default: break;
    }

    return (TRUE == bHandledMsg ?
     TRUE : CPropertySheet::PreTranslateMessage(pMsg));
   }
```

Figure 14-7: While the CPropertySheet class does offer a good deal of functionality, performing tasks such as removing standard buttons, repositioning buttons, and implementing mnemonics on the tabs has to be done manually.

Summary

In this chapter, you learned about the `CPropertySheet` and `CPropertyPage` classes and how to use them in both modal and modeless environments. You also learned that while these classes are good at encapsulating their intended functionality, they fall somewhat short of expectations when it comes to providing basic functions. However, you also learned how to circumvent these classes' shortcomings and to provide your own support for the enabling and disabling of property pages, property page navigation through keyboard mnemonics, and setting a specific property page tab's font and caption. Hopefully, the code in this chapter will make these and other related tasks easier than they might have otherwise been.

✦ ✦ ✦

Data I/O

CHAPTER 15

✦ ✦ ✦ ✦

In This Chapter

CString class

String manipulation with CString

CFile class

Working with files

CCompressedFile class

Working with compressed files

CSerial class

Working with serial communications

CRegistry class

Working with the system Registry

The Clipboard

Working with the Clipboard

✦ ✦ ✦ ✦

Most programs have some sort of data that they use, create, and transfer while doing their job. Word processors maintain the document as data and perform operations on the data such as loading, saving, and spell checking. Spreadsheets not only load and save data, but they also make calculations on the data. Even games such as Solitaire (which comes with Windows) keep track of the cards and treat this information as a data set.

MFC gives you plenty of tools to deal with data. This chapter covers `CString`, `CFile`, and the Clipboard support in `CWnd`. It also gives you some non-MFC classes that make it easier to deal with other types of data. One class is intended to give you easy access to the serial port. With our `CSerial` class you can communicate with other computers through your modem. Another thing that MFC left out was easy access to the Registry. This is the accepted way of storing configuration information for applications, and as an application developer, you'll have to go to the Registry often.

The CString Class

If you've used C-style character arrays to store strings and the C string functions to manipulate them, you'll eventually be grateful for the introduction of the `CString` class — eventually, not immediately. When I first started using Visual C++ Version 1.5, I was a seasoned C programmer. It took me at least a year before I preferred using `CStrings` to the tried and true C-style character strings and functions. If you started off in Visual C++, you're lucky — you didn't have to unlearn any of the things I had to unlearn.

So what does this be-all, end-all class do for you? Two things. It stores your data and provides functions to perform all of the operations previously done with C functions such as `strcpy()` and `strcmp()`. You don't have to declare a character array (or allocate one), and then copy a string into it worrying about whether there's enough room in the array. You can concatenate additional data to the string without regard for the size of the array—the CString class makes sure there's enough storage space for every operation you perform.

Creating strings

The easiest way to assign string data to a CString class is with the = operator. You can assign it from a character string or a CString object. The following two examples show you how to assign a string to CString objects:

Example 1, assigning with a character string using the = operator:

```
strText = "This is text";
```

Example 2, assigning with a CString object using the = operator:

```
CString strCopy = strText;
```

Another easy way to assign data to a CString object is in the CString constructor. Simply pass a string or CString to the CString constructor, and the data will be copied to the newly created string. Two examples follow:

Example 1, assigning with a character string in the CString constructor:

```
CString strText1( "This is the first text" );
```

Example 2, assigning with a CString object in the CString constructor:

```
CString strText2( strText1 );
```

In some cases you may want to ensure support for unicode strings. To do this, just use the _T macro. The following example assigns a unicode-aware string to a CString object:

```
CString strText =
  _T( "This is a unicode-aware string." );
```

Several support functions relate to the CString contents. They are the GetLength(), IsEmpty(), and Empty() functions. The GetLength() function returns the length of the string. For a string such as "This is a test", it returns an integer value of 14. The IsEmpty() function returns TRUE if a CString object has either no data buffer or an empty data buffer. If a CString object contains a string such as "This is a test", the IsEmpty() function returns FALSE. And the Empty() function clears the CString data so that nothing remains. Immediately after calling the Empty() function, the IsEmpty() function always returns TRUE.

Accessing string data

You can get a pointer to the data contained in a CString object with the GetBuffer() function. This function takes an integer argument specifying the minimum size of the character buffer in characters. The recommended practice is to call ReleaseBuffer() after you've called GetBuffer() and are done with the pointer. The following code gets a pointer to the data in a CString object, examines it, and then releases it:

```
CString strText = "This is a test";
char *lpText = strText.GetBuffer( 10 );
if( lpText[3] == 's' )
  AfxMessageBox( "This is the correct data." );
else
  AfxMessageBox(
  "This pointer doesn't point to the correct data.");
strText.ReleaseBuffer();
```

You can also access the string data with the GetAt() and SetAt() functions. The GetAt() function takes a single argument to the string index you want to retrieve and returns the character that's found at that index. The SetAt() function takes arguments for the string index you want to set, and the character that you want to store at that location. The following example shows how to get and set characters in a CString object:

```
CString strText = "This is another test";
strText.SetAt( 16, 'b' );
// The string is now "This is another best";
if( strText.GetAt( [3] ) == 's' )
  AfxMessageBox( "Sure enough, the character is 's'.");
else
  AfxMessageBox( "There was some sort of error!" );
```

A shortcut to using the GetAt() function is to use the [] operator, which is really just an alias for the GetAt() function. The following example uses the [] operator to examine a character in a CString object:

```
CString strText = "This is yet another test";
if( strText[3] == 's' )
  AfxMessageBox( "Sure enough, the character is 's'.");
else
  AfxMessageBox( "There was some sort of error!" );
```

Let's say you're calling a function that expects a char pointer and you're working with a CString object. You might instinctively think that you have to use GetBuffer() and obtain a pointer to the CString data, and then pass the pointer to the function. If the function prototype is a const char *, then the CString operator LPCTSTR does the work for you. All you have to do is pass the CString object to the function, and the operator takes care of the details. The following example shows a function that expects a const char * as an argument, and after the function it shows how to properly call the function:

```
void ShowText( const char *lpszText )
{

  AfxMessageBox( lpszText );

}

void UseShowText( void )
{
  CString strText = "This is another test";

  ShowText( strText );

}
```

While dealing with the contents of `CString` objects, you'll find two more operators especially useful. They are the + and += operators. Two examples follow that show how to use them both:

Example 1, using the + operator:

```
CString strOne = "This is ";
CString strTwo = "a test";
CString strThree = strOne + strTwo;
// strThree now contains "This is a test"
```

Example 2, using the += operator:

```
CString strOne = "This is ";
strOne += "a test";
//strOne now contains "This is a test"
```

Comparison

It's very easy to compare two `CString` objects. Six operators, <, <=, >, >=, ==, and !=, make it easy. These six operators return a Boolean value of `TRUE` or `FALSE` if the comparison is true or false. The following three examples show how to use these operators:

Example 1, using the `CString` == operator:

```
CString strOne = "This is One';
CString strTwo = "This is Two";
BOOL bResult;
bResult = ( strOne == strTwo );
// bResult will now be FALSE
```

Example 2, using the CString != operator:

```
CString strOne = "This is One';
CString strTwo = "This is Two";
BOOL bResult;
bResult = ( strOne != strTwo );
// bResult will now be TRUE
```

Example 3, using the CString >= operator:

```
CString strOne = "This is One';
CString strTwo = "This is Two";
BOOL bResult;
bResult = ( strOne == strTwo );

// bResult will now be FALSE
```

At times your program will need more than a Boolean return value. This is true, for instance, in a sorting routine. In order to sort, you need to obtain a value that's less than zero (indicating the first string is less than the second string), a value that equals zero (indicating that both strings are the same), and a value that's greater than zero (indicating the first string is greater than the second). The `Compare()` member function is what you'll need to use. The `Compare()` function performs a case-sensitive comparison of two strings. Three examples follow:

Example 1, a comparison string that's greater than the CString object:

```
CString strText( "abc" );
int nResult = strText.Compare( "abd" );
// nResult now is less than 0
```

Example 2, a comparison string that's less than the CString object:

```
CString strText( "abc" );
int nResult = strText.Compare( "abb" );
// nResult now is greater than 0
```

Example 3, a comparison CString that's equal to the CString object:

```
CString strOne( "abc" );
CString strTwo( "abc" );
int nResult = strOne.Compare( strTwo );
// nResult now is equal to 0
```

If you want to do a noncase-sensitive comparison, you'll need to use the `CompareNoCase()` function. It works the same way that `Compare()` works except that the results it returns are without regard to case.

Extraction

Many situations can arise in which you'll need to extract a substring of a CString object. For instance, a long string is contained in a CString object, but you only want the first ten characters. Three functions make extraction of substrings easy. They are Left(), Mid(), and Right().

The Left() function extracts a CString object containing a copy of the specified range of characters. The following example shows how to extract a substring that's the first ten characters of another string:

```
CString strText = "This is a test text string";
CString strPart = strText.Left( 10 );
// strPart now contains "This is a ";
```

The Right() function extracts a CString object containing a copy of the specified range of characters. The difference between the Right() and Left() function is that the Right() function obtains the specified number of characters beginning at the end of the string (or the right). The following example shows how to extract a substring that's the last ten characters of another string:

```
CString strText = "This is a test text string";
CString strPart = strText.Right( 10 );
// strPart now contains "ext string";
```

The Mid() function, as you might guess, extracts a string of a specified number of characters from the middle of a string. The Mid() function comes in two flavors. The first takes a single integer argument specifying the starting character of the substring to extract. The end character that's extracted is the last character in the string. The second flavor takes two integer arguments specifying the starting character of the substring to extract and the number of characters to extract. The following two examples show both of these varieties of the Mid() function in action:

Example 1, the single-argument version of Mid():

```
CString strText = "This is a test text string";
CString strPart = strText.Mid( 10 );
// strPart now contains "test text string";
```

Example 2, the two-argument version of Mid():

```
CString strText = "This is a test text string";
CString strPart = strText.Mid( 10, 6 );
// strPart now contains "test t";
```

Searching

Somewhere in your programming career, you're going to have to search for a string that's contained inside of another string. Three functions are provided that make this possible: Find(), ReverseFind(), and FindOneOf(). The Find() function searches for the occurrence of a string inside of a CString object. If it finds the given string, it returns a value indicating the index in the string at which the search string was found. If the search string isn't found in a CString object, the value of -1 is returned. For instance, a CString object might contain "My name is Thomas Jefferson", and you might want to search for the string "name". If you use the Find() function on the text string "My name is Thomas Jefferson", the value returned when you search for "name" will be 3. If you search the same string for "bonnie", the value returned will be -1 because "bonnie" isn't in the "My name is Thomas Jefferson" string. An example of using the Find() function follows:

```
CString strText = "My name is Thomas Jefferson";
int nIndex = strText( "name" );
// nIndex now has the value of 3.
nIndex = strText( "bonnie" );
// nIndex now has the value of -1.
```

The ReverseFind() function works exactly like the Find() function except that it starts searching from the end (or right) of the string. The following example illustrates the difference between Find() and ReverseFind():

```
CString strText = "This is my name and not your name, right?";
int nIndex = strText.Find( "name" );
// nIndex now has the value of 11.
nIndex = strText.ReverseFind( "name" );
// nIndex now has the value of 29.
```

The FindOneOf() function is used to search a string for the first character that matches any character contained in a string that's passed in. For instance, if a CString object contains the text "To be or not to be, that is the question." and you search using the FindOneOf() function with a string of "qz", a value of 32 will be returned. That's because the first character found in the "qz" string is a "q"' at index 32.

The StringDemo Program

The following demo program named StringDemo (Listing 15-1) shows you how to use the basic CString functions. The application loads a file named AESOP.txt when it first runs. This text file contains many fables from Aesop's Fables.

You can search the text for any string, as shown in Figure 15 1. You can choose to do a case-sensitive search or a noncase-sensitive search. You can also perform a search and replace operation on the file. Once the search and replace operation is done, you'll be able to see the altered text inside of WordPad. (When you see it in WordPad, though, make sure WordPad is set for text wrapping.)

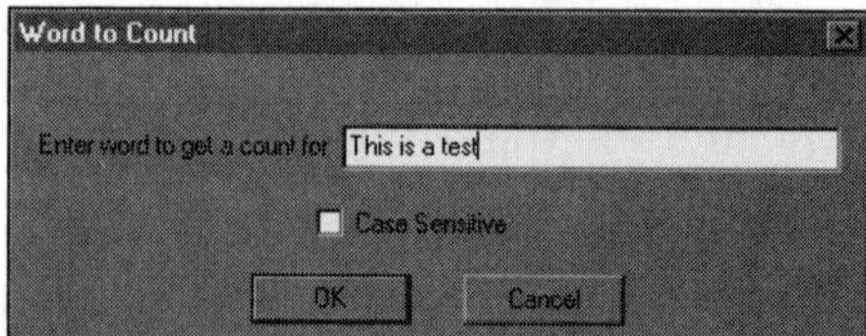

Figure 15-1: You can search through the Aesop.txt file for any word or phrase.

StringDemo
CD-ROM Location: **Chap15\StringDemo**
Program Name: **StringDemo.exe**
Source Code Modules in Text: `StringDemoView.cpp`

◆ ◆ ◆ ◆ ◆

Listing 15-1: **StringDemo**

```
// StringDemoView.cpp : implementation of
// the CStringDemoView class
//

//////////////////////////////////////////////////////////////////
// CStringDemoView construction/destruction

CStringDemoView::CStringDemoView()
{

  // Attempt to open the data file.
  CFile cf;
  if( cf.Open( "AESOP.txt", CFile::modeRead ) ){

    // Get the file length.
    int nFileLength = cf.GetLength();

    // Allocate a temporary buffer.
    char *lpBuffer = new char [nFileLength+1];

    try{
      // Read the data.
      cf.Read( lpBuffer, nFileLength );
      }

    // Catch a Read exception if it's
    // thrown.
    catch( CFileException *e ){
      e->Delete();
      delete [] lpBuffer;
      return;
      }
```

```
        // NULL terminate the string.
        lpBuffer[nFileLength] = 0;

        // Set the m_strOriginalText and
        // m_strAlteredText CString objects.
        m_strOriginalText = lpBuffer;
        m_strAlteredText = m_strOriginalText;

        // Free the temporary buffer.
        delete [] lpBuffer;
        }

}

CStringDemoView::~CStringDemoView()
{
}

/////////////////////////////////////////////////////////////////////////////
// CStringDemoView drawing

void CStringDemoView::OnDraw(CDC* pDC)
{
  CStringDemoDoc* pDoc = GetDocument();
  ASSERT_VALID(pDoc);

  // Let users know if the file was
  // loaded or not.
  if( m_strOriginalText.GetLength() > 0 )
    pDC->TextOut( 10, 10, "AESOP.txt loaded." );
  else
    pDC->TextOut( 10, 10, "AESOP.txt not loaded." );

}

/////////////////////////////////////////////////////////////////////////////
// CStringDemoView message handlers

void CStringDemoView::OnFilePerformwordcount()
{
  CGetWord GetWord,
  // Get the word in a dialog box.
  if( GetWord.DoModal() == IDOK ){

    // Set the count to 0.
    int nCount = 0;
    int nIndex;
    CString strTempString;

    // Set a temporary CString object
    // to contain the altered text.
    strTempString = m_strAlteredText;
```

(continued)

Listing 15-1 *(continued)*

```
// Set a temporary string to
// contain the word for which
// we're searching.
CString strTempWord =
  GetWord.m_strWordToCount;

// If we're not making a case sensitive
// search, make both strings upper case.
if( !GetWord.m_bCaseSensitive ){
  strTempWord.MakeUpper();
  strTempString.MakeUpper();
  }

do{
  // Attempt to find the word.
  nIndex =
    strTempString.Find( strTempWord );

  // If nIndex != -1, we found the word.
  if( nIndex != -1 ){

    // Make sure the character before the
    // word is not an alphanumeric character.
    // If it is, the word we found is
    // embedded in something else.
    if( nIndex == 0 ||
      !isalnum( strTempString.GetAt( nIndex - 1 ) )){

      // Make sure the character after the
      // word is not an alphanumeric character.
      // If it is, the word we found is
      // embedded in something else.
      if( !isalnum( strTempString.GetAt(
        nIndex + strTempWord.GetLength() ) ) )

        // Increment the count.
        nCount++;
      }

    // Shorten the string containing the
    // body of data
    strTempString =
      strTempString.Right(
        strTempString.GetLength() -
        strTempWord.GetLength() -
        nIndex );
    }
  } while( nIndex != -1 );

// Format a string and tell users
// how many matches were found.
```

```
    CString strInfo;
    strInfo.Format( "The count was %d.", nCount );
    AfxMessageBox( strInfo );

    }

}

void CStringDemoView::OnFileRestoreoriginalfiledata()
{

  // Restore the working text string
  // with the original text string.
  m_strAlteredText = m_strOriginalText;

}

void CStringDemoView::OnFileSearchandreplace()
{
  CSearchReplace SearchReplace;

  // Get the search and replace word.
  if( SearchReplace.DoModal() == IDOK ){

    // See if both strings are identical.
    if( SearchReplace.m_strWordToFind ==
      SearchReplace.m_strWordToReplace ){
      AfxMessageBox("Those two strings are identical!");
      return;
      }

    // Set the count to 0.
    int nCount = 0;
    int nIndex;
    CString strTempString;

    // Set a temporary CString object
    // to contain the altered text.
    strTempString = m_strAlteredText;

    // Set a temporary string to
    // contain the word for which
    // we're searching.
    CString strTempWord =
      SearchReplace.m_strWordToFind ;

    // If we're not making a case sensitive
    // search, make both strings upper case.
    if( !SearchReplace.m_bCaseSensitive ){
      strTempWord.MakeUpper();
      strTempString.MakeUpper();
      }
```

(continued)

Listing 15-1 *(continued)*

```
do{
  BOOL bReplaced = FALSE;

  // Attempt to find the word.
  nIndex =
    strTempString.Find( strTempWord );

  // If nIndex != -1, we found the word.
  if( nIndex != -1 ){

    // Make sure the character before the
    // word is not an alphanumeric character.
    // If it is, the word we found is
    // embedded in something else.
    if( nIndex == 0 ||
      !isalnum( strTempString.GetAt( nIndex - 1 ) )){

      // Make sure the character after the
      // word is not an alphanumeric character.
      // If it is, the word we found is
      // embedded in something else.
      if( !isalnum( strTempString.GetAt(
        nIndex + strTempWord.GetLength() ) ) ){

        // Increment the count.
        nCount++;

        // Calculate the number of
        // characters to the right
        // of the word that was found.
        int nRightLength =
          strTempString.GetLength() -
          nIndex -
          strTempWord.GetLength();
        // Calculate the number of
        // characters to the left
        // of the word that was found.
        int nLeftLength =
          m_strAlteredText.GetLength() -
          nRightLength -
          strTempWord.GetLength();

        // Form a left and right string.
        CString strLeft, strRight;
        strLeft =
          m_strAlteredText.Left( nLeftLength );
        strRight =
          m_strAlteredText.Right( nRightLength );

        // Put the altered text string
        // together.
```

```
          m_strAlteredText = strLeft +
            SearchReplace.m_strWordToReplace +
            strRight;

          }
        }

      // Shorten the temporary string.
      strTempString =
        strTempString.Right(
          strTempString.GetLength() -
          strTempWord.GetLength() -
          nIndex );

      }

    } while( nIndex != -1 );

  // Format a string and tell users
  // how many replacements were made.
  CString strInfo;
  strInfo.Format( "%d replacements made.", nCount );
  AfxMessageBox( strInfo );

  }

}

void CStringDemoView::OnFileViewalterationsinnotepad()
{
  CFile Out;

  // Attempt to create a temporary file
  // which will be loaded into wordpad.
  if( Out.Open( "StringDemoTempFile.txt",
    CFile::modeCreate | CFile::modeWrite ) ){
    try{
      // Write the data.
      Out.Write( m_strAlteredText,
        m_strAlteredText.GetLength() );
      }

    // Catch a write exception if it's thrown.
    catch( CFileException *e ){
      e->Delete();
      return;
      }

    // Close the file so that wordpad
    // won't get a sharing violation.
    Out.Close();
```

(continued)

Listing 15-1 *(continued)*

```
        // Use WinExec() to bring up wordpad.
        WinExec( "WRITE.EXE StringDemoTempFile.txt",
          SW_NORMAL );
        }

  }
```

The CFile Class

Loading information from and saving information to disk files is important for almost every application that's written. The data that's saved can range from binary image data to a body of text to specialized data files. At the heart of MFC's support for file operations is the `CFile` class. This section shows you how to use its member functions to do file I/O.

The first thing you must do is create a `CFile` object. Most of the time, you'll use the `CFile` constructor that takes no arguments. You might find two additional `CFile` constructors useful. The first takes a single argument — an `HFILE` handle of a file that's already open. The second takes two arguments — a filename and an integer value that holds the file open flags. This is the equivalent of creating a `CFile` object with no arguments to the constructor and then calling the `Open()` function.

The `Open()` function must be used after constructing a `CFile` class to open a file. Of course, if you used one of the `CFile` constructors that opens a file or takes the handle to a file that's already opened, you won't have to use the `Open()` function. The `Open()` function takes two arguments — a filename and an integer value that holds the file open flags. The `Open()` function returns a Boolean value indicating success or failure. It doesn't throw an exception as many of the other `CFile` functions do.

The flags for file opening can be any combination of the values in Table 15-1. Flags specify the action to take when opening the file. You can combine options by using the `bitwise-OR ( | )` operator. One access permission and one share option are required; the `modeCreate` and `modeNoInherit` modes are optional.

Table 15-1
File Open Flags

Flag	*Description*
`CFile::modeCreate`	Directs the constructor to create a new file. If the file exists already, it is truncated to 0 length.
`CFile::modeNoTruncate`	Combine this value with `modeCreate`. If the file being created already exists, it is not truncated to 0 length. Thus the file is guaranteed to open, either as a newly created file or as an existing file. This might be useful, for example, when opening a settings file that may or may not exist already. This option applies to `CStdioFile` as well.
`CFile::modeRead`	Opens the file for reading only.
`CFile::modeReadWrite`	Opens the file for reading and writing.
`CFile::modeWrite`	Opens the file for writing only.
`CFile::modeNoInherit`	Prevents the file from being inherited by child processes.
`CFile::shareDenyNone`	Opens the file without denying other processes read or write access to the file. Create fails if the file has been opened in compatibility mode by any other process.
`CFile::shareDenyRead`	Opens the file and denies other processes read access to the file. Create fails if the file has been opened in compatibility mode or for read access by any other process.
`CFile::shareDenyWrite`	Opens the file and denies other processes write access to the file. Create fails if the file has been opened in compatibility mode or for write access by any other process.
`CFile::shareExclusive`	Opens the file with exclusive mode, denying other processes both read and write access to the file. Construction fails if the file has been opened in any other mode for read or write access, even by the current process.
`CFile::shareCompat`	This flag is not available in 32-bit MFC. This flag maps to `CFile::shareExclusive` when used in `CFile::Open`.
`CFile::typeText`	Sets text mode with special processing for carriage return/linefeed pairs (used in derived classes only).
`CFile::typeBinary`	Sets binary mode (used in derived classes only).

The following three examples show how to open a file for reading:

Example 1, using a `CFile` constructor with no arguments:

```
CFile cf;
if( cf.Open( "Filename", CFile::modeRead ) )
  AfxMessageBox( "File open successful." );
else
  AfxMessageBox( "File open unsuccessful." );
```

Example 2, using a `CFile` constructor that takes a file handle:

```
HFILE hFile = _lopen( "Filename", OF_READ );
if( hFile != HFILE_ERROR ){
  // The file was successfully opened.
  CFile cf( hFile );
  }
```

Example 3, using a `CFile` constructor that takes a filename and file open flags:

```
try{
  CFile cf( "Filename", CFile::modeRead );
  // Do file operations here.
  }
catch( CFileException *e ){
  // Alert user to the error.
  CString strError;
  strError.Format( "Error number %d",
    e->m_cause );
  e->Delete();
  AfxMessageBox( strError );
  }
```

Once you open a file for reading, you're going to read data from the file. To do this, use the `Read()` function. It takes two arguments. The first is a pointer to a buffer into which the data will be read. The second is the number of bytes to read. The `Read()` function returns the number of bytes that have been read. An example of reading data follows:

```
CFile cf;
if( cf.Open( "Filename", CFile::modeRead ) ){
  char cbBuffer[1000];
  try{
    // Read data into the buffer.
    int nBytesRead =
      cf.Read( cbBuffer, sizeof( cbBuffer ) );
    }
  catch( CFileException *e ){
    // Notify user of error.
    e->Delete();
    }
```

If you open a file with the write attribute as part of the open flags (CFile::modeWrite by itself or combined with other flags) you can write data to the file. The Write() function, as with the read function, takes two arguments. The first is the data buffer from which the data will be written to disk. The second argument is the number of bytes to write to disk. The Write() function does not return anything. The absence of a value indicating how many bytes were written to disk is sometimes handicapping to programmers. The following example shows how to write data to an open disk file:

```
CFile cf;
if( cf.Open( "Filename", CFile::modeWrite ) ){
  char szData[] = "This is a test";
  try{
    // Move to the end of the file so
    // that we don't overwrite what's already there.
    cf.SeekToEnd();
    cf.Write( szData, strlen( szData ) );
    }
  catch( CFileException *e ){
    // Alert user to error.
    e->Delete();
    }
```

In the previous example, you'll notice that the SeekToEnd() function was used to move to the end of the file. This is done so that the data at the beginning of the file isn't overwritten each time additional data is written to the file. Other navigation functions that are useful are the Seek() and SeekToBegin() functions. The Seek() function takes two arguments. The first is the number of bytes to move, the second is a value indicating how to move. Table 15-2 shows the options available for the Seek() function.

Table 15-2
Seek() Function Pointer Movement Modes

Mode	*Description*
CFile::begin	Move the file pointer the specified number of bytes forward from the beginning of the file.
CFile::current	Move the file pointer the specified number of bytes from the current position in the file.
CFile::end	Move the file pointer the specified number of bytes from the end of the file. Note that the number of bytes must be negative to seek into the existing file; positive values will seek past the end of the file.

One of the most common things that my programs need with regard to file operations is a function that copies a file. I've written a function that copies a file, and I use it often in my programs. The function is called `CopyFile()`, and it takes three arguments. The first is the source filename, the second is the destination filename, and the third argument is the size of the buffer that the copy operation will use. The larger the buffer, the faster the copy operation. If the buffer specified is too large, though, the allocation may fail. I recommend 50KB or so. The function returns a Boolean value indicating whether or not it was successful.

The `CopyFile()` function catches all file exceptions and displays an error message if an exception is caught. The `CopyFile()` function can be found by itself on the CD in the `Chap15\CopyFile` directory in the `CopyFile.cpp` file. It's also part of the FileDemo program that is provided in the next section.

◆ ◆ ◆ ◆ ◆

The FileDemo Program

You'll often use the `CFile` class to load and save buffers of data. For that reason, a program named FileDemo was written that does just that. It lets you create a list of files and then saves all of the files to one large file. You can also copy a single file from one source to a destination. To do this, just select Copy First File. The program then copies the first file in the list to a destination file you select. The source code highlights are in Listing 15-2.

Here are some things to note in the `CopyFile()` function. The first is the use of the `GetStatus()` and `SetStatus()` functions. `GetStatus()` is used to obtain the status of a file. Especially important in this case is the time and date of the source file. This information is then used to set the time/date stamp of the destination file so that it matches that of the source file.

Another thing to note is the use of the `GetLength()` function to obtain the file size of the source file. This lets us know how many bytes in total need to be copied. Use a local buffer to copy `nBufferSize` bytes at a time until the entire file has been copied. You could increase the performance of the `CopyFile()` function by increasing the size of the buffer.

FileDemo

CD-ROM Location: **Chap15\FileDemo**

Program Name: **FileDemo.exe**

Source Code Modules in Text: `FileDemoView.cpp`

◆ ◆ ◆ ◆ ◆

Listing 15-2: **FileDemo**

```
// FileDemoView.cpp : implementation of
// the CFileDemoView class
//

////////////////////////////////////////////////////////////
// CFileDemoView drawing

void CFileDemoView::OnDraw(CDC* pDC)
{
  CFileDemoDoc* pDoc = GetDocument();
  ASSERT_VALID(pDoc);

  // Draw the list of files in the list.
  int y = 0;
  for( int i=0; i<m_Filename.GetSize(); i++ ){
    // Get the string at this index.
    CString strText = m_Filename.GetAt( i );
    // Draw it to the DC.
    pDC->TextOut( 0, y, strText );
    // Get the size so we can increment
    // the y coordinate.
    CSize size =
      pDC->GetTextExtent( strText, 1 );
    // Increment the y coordinate by
    // the text height.
    y += size.cy;
    }

}

////////////////////////////////////////////////////////////
// CFileDemoView message handlers

char szFilter[] = "All Files(*.*)|*.*||";

void CFileDemoView::OnFileAddtolist()
{

  // Common dialog box.
  CFileDialog FileDlg( TRUE, NULL, NULL,
    OFN_HIDEREADONLY, szFilter );

  if( FileDlg.DoModal() == IDOK ){
    // Add the full path and file name
    // to the m_Pathname list.
    m_Pathname.Add( FileDlg.GetPathName() );
    // Add the file name to the m_Filename
    // list.
    m_Filename.Add( FileDlg.GetFileName() );
```

(continued)

Listing 15-2 *(continued)*

```
    // Cause a window redraw.
    InvalidateRect( NULL, TRUE );
    UpdateWindow();
    }

}

void CFileDemoView::OnFileSavefilesinlist()
{

  // Check to make sure we have some
  // files in the list.
  if( m_Pathname.GetSize() == 0 ){
    AfxMessageBox( "There are no files in the list." );
    return;
    }

  // Common dialog box.
  CFileDialog FileDlg( FALSE, NULL, NULL,
    OFN_HIDEREADONLY, szFilter );

  if( FileDlg.DoModal() == IDOK ){

    // Attempt to open the output file.
    CFile Out;
    if( Out.Open( FileDlg.GetPathName(),
      CFile::modeWrite | CFile::modeCreate ) ){

      // Loop through each file.
      for( int i=0; i<m_Pathname.GetSize(); i++ ){

        // Attempt to create the input
        // file.
        CFile In;
        if( In.Open( m_Pathname.GetAt( i ),
          CFile::modeRead ) ){

          // Temporary buffer.
          char cbBuffer[4000];

          // Get the input file size so we
          // know when we're done writing.
          int nFilesize = In.GetLength();

          while( nFilesize > 0 ){

            // Start off by assuming
            // we'll read in enough bytes
            // to fill the buffer.
            int nSize = sizeof( cbBuffer );
```

```
// If the number of bytes remaining
// isn't enough to fill the
// buffer, adjust the size.
if( nSize > nFilesize )
  nSize = nFilesize;

// Read in the bytes and make
// sure we catch any exceptions
// that are thrown.
try{
  In.Read( cbBuffer, nSize );
  }
catch( CFileException *e ){

  // Format a message from
  // the system.
  char *lpMsgBuf;
  if( FormatMessage(
    FORMAT_MESSAGE_ALLOCATE_BUFFER |
    FORMAT_MESSAGE_FROM_SYSTEM,
    NULL, e->m_lOsError,
    MAKELANGID( LANG_NEUTRAL,
      SUBLANG_DEFAULT ),
    (LPSTR) &lpMsgBuf, 0, NULL ) > 0 ){
    AfxMessageBox( lpMsgBuf );
    LocalFree( lpMsgBuf );
    }

  // Free the exception and
  // return.
  e->Delete();
  return;
  }
// Write out the bytes and make
// sure we catch any exceptions
// that are thrown.
try{
  Out.Write( cbBuffer, nSize );
  }
catch( CFileException *e ){

  // Format a message from
  // the system.
  char *lpMsgBuf;
  if( FormatMessage(
    FORMAT MESSAGE ALLOCATE BUFFER |
    FORMAT_MESSAGE_FROM_SYSTEM,
    NULL, e->m_lOsError,
    MAKELANGID( LANG_NEUTRAL,
      SUBLANG_DEFAULT ),
    (LPSTR) &lpMsgBuf, 0, NULL ) > 0 ){
    AfxMessageBox( lpMsgBuf );
```

(continued)

Listing 15-2 *(continued)*

```
                  LocalFree( lpMsgBuf );
                  }

                // Free the exception and
                // return.
                e->Delete();
                return;
                }
              nFilesize -= nSize;
              }
            }

          // Alert user to problem.
          else
            AfxMessageBox( "Could not open "
              + m_Pathname.GetAt( i ) );
          }
        }

      // Alert user to problem.
      else
       AfxMessageBox("Could not create the output file.");
      }

}

void CFileDemoView::EmptyStringArrays( void )
{

  // Empty the arrays which contain
  // the full path and file name,
  // and just the file name.
  m_Pathname.RemoveAll();
  m_Filename.RemoveAll();

}

void CFileDemoView::OnFileEmptylist()
{

  // Empty everything and then
  // cause a screen redraw.
  EmptyStringArrays();
  InvalidateRect( NULL, TRUE );
  UpdateWindow();

}

BOOL CFileDemoView::CopyFile( const char *lpSrcFilename,
  const char *lpDestFilename, int nBuffersize )
{
```

```
CFile Out, In;
int nFilesize;
char *lpBuffer;

// Attempt to open the input file.
if( !In.Open( lpSrcFilename, CFile::modeRead ) ){
  AfxMessageBox( "Could not open the input file." );
  return( FALSE );
  }

// Attempt to create the output file.
if( !Out.Open( lpDestFilename,
  CFile::modeWrite | CFile::modeCreate ) ){
  AfxMessageBox( "Could not open the output file." );
  return( FALSE );
  }

// Create the copy buffer.
lpBuffer = new char [nBuffersize];
if( lpBuffer == NULL ){
 AfxMessageBox("Could not allocate the copy buffer.");
  return( FALSE );
  }

// Get the input file status so that
// we can set the output file's status
// to the same. This will preserve
// things such as time and date.
CFileStatus rStatus;
In.GetStatus( lpSrcFilename, rStatus );

// Get file file size so that we know
// when we're done copying.
nFilesize = In.GetLength();

while( nFilesize > 0 ){

  // Start off by assuming
  // we'll read in enough bytes
  // to fill the buffer.
  int nSize = nBuffersize;

  // If the number of bytes remaining
  // isn't enough to fill the
  // buffer, adjust the size.
  if( nSize > nFilesize )
    nSize = nFilesize;
  // Read in the bytes and make
  // sure we catch any exceptions
  // that are thrown.
  try{
```

(continued)

Listing 15-2 *(continued)*

```
    In.Read( lpBuffer, nSize );
    }
  catch( CFileException *e ){

    // Format a message from
    // the system.
    char *lpMsgBuf;
    if( FormatMessage(
      FORMAT_MESSAGE_ALLOCATE_BUFFER |
      FORMAT_MESSAGE_FROM_SYSTEM,
      NULL, e->m_lOsError,
      MAKELANGID( LANG_NEUTRAL,
        SUBLANG_DEFAULT ),
      (LPSTR) &lpMsgBuf, 0, NULL ) > 0 ){
      AfxMessageBox( lpMsgBuf );
      LocalFree( lpMsgBuf );
      }

    // Free the exception and
    // return.
    e->Delete();
    return( FALSE );
    }

  // Write out the bytes and make
  // sure we catch any exceptions
  // that are thrown.
  try{
    Out.Write( lpBuffer, nSize );
    }

  catch( CFileException *e ){

    // Format a message from
    // the system.
    char *lpMsgBuf;
    if( FormatMessage(
      FORMAT_MESSAGE_ALLOCATE_BUFFER |
      FORMAT_MESSAGE_FROM_SYSTEM,
      NULL, e->m_lOsError,
      MAKELANGID( LANG_NEUTRAL,
        SUBLANG_DEFAULT ),
      (LPSTR) &lpMsgBuf, 0, NULL ) > 0 ){
      AfxMessageBox( lpMsgBuf );
      LocalFree( lpMsgBuf );
      }
```

```
            // Free the exception and
            // return.
            e->Delete();
            return( FALSE );
            }

          nFilesize -= nSize;

          }

        // Close the output file so that the
        // SetStatus() function won't fail.
        Out.Close();
        CFile::SetStatus( lpDestFilename, rStatus );

        // Delete the buffer.
        delete [] lpBuffer;

        return( TRUE );

      }


      void CFileDemoView::OnFileCopyfirstfile()
      {


        // Check to make sure we have some
        // files in the list.
        if( m_Pathname.GetSize() == 0 ){
          AfxMessageBox( "There are no files in the list." );
          return;
          }

        // Common dialog box.
        CFileDialog FileDlg( FALSE, NULL, NULL,
          OFN_HIDEREADONLY, szFilter );

        // If the selected OK, do the copy.
        if( FileDlg.DoModal() == IDOK )
          CopyFile( m_Pathname.GetAt( 0 ),
            FileDlg.GetPathName() );

      }
```

The CCompressedFile Class

Today computers have average hard drives 100 to 200 times larger than the average hard drive of ten years ago. That's good news for consumers who want more hard drive space to fit more applications on their systems. Applications developers, though, have risen to the challenge by creating programs that do their best to consume as much hard drive space as possible. Therefore, the net gain for most computer users is minimized.

In addition, developers have stopped compressing data. Most of them figure that hard drives are big, so they don't have to fool with compressing data. The worst offenders are graphics and sound files. Windows' native graphical format is the BMP file, which is completely uncompressed. A full-screen BMP in 640 × 480 with 256 colors is 300K. Windows' native sound format is the WAV file, which is also completely uncompressed. These files can easily be several hundred kilobytes.

In the early 1980s, when most applications came on a single floppy disk, developers went to great lengths to cram it all in. There was no question about whether to compress data — the only question was which method to use. Time passed and current applications are now very sophisticated. But large applications with lots of data are no excuse for consuming more hard drive space than is necessary. Developers need to start compressing data on a regular basis and stop cutting that corner just because hard drives have gotten larger. This class library gives you the tools you need to compress and decompress data. It's easy, so you won't have any excuses. Go ahead and crunch things down!

The `CCompressedFile` data compression class can be added to any Visual C++ project. Besides being part of the CompressDemo program, there's a separate directory on the CD-ROM in which all of the compression files are stored. It's the `Chap15\CompressedFile` directory.

◆ ◆ ◆ ◆ ◆

The CompressDemo Program

The following simple demonstration program shows what the class library can do. When it first runs, all you'll see is an empty application window as shown in Figure 15-2.

The program can be found in the `Chap15\CompressDemo` directory on the CD-ROM. Using File Manager or Program Manager, run the program named `CompressDemo.exe`. It's a multiple-document program.

◆ ◆ ◆ ◆ ◆

Figure 15-2: The empty application window you'll see when the data compression demo first runs

The first thing you'll need to do is load a file. Any file or file type will do, but text, BMP, and WAV files compress well so you might want to try one of those file types. To load a file, select Open from the File menu, and then use the standard Windows file selector to select a file. The file will load, and a window will appear with some relevant information about the file. Unless the file you load has been compressed with the data compression library, it will be labeled as "no compression" in the window, because it wasn't compressed with the data compression libraries that come on the CD-ROM. Figure 15-3 shows the window with a file loaded.

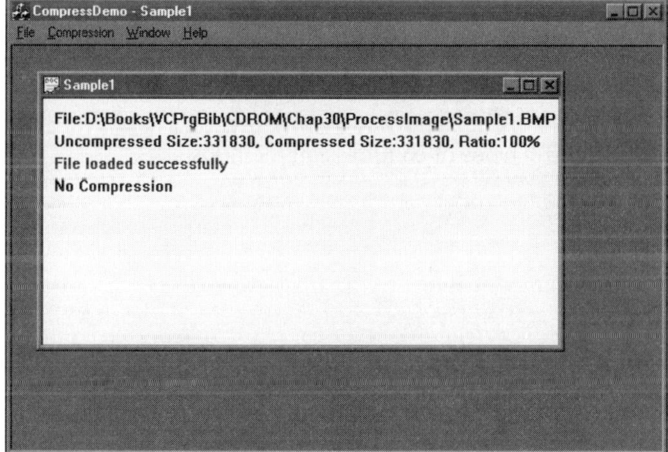

Figure 15-3: When a file is loaded, a window displays information about the file.

The next thing to do to test the program is select a compression type from the Compression menu. The choices offered are Huffman, LZSS, LZW, and None. LZW is the default choice and usually produces the best results. Leave this choice selected for now as shown in Figure 15-4.

To save the file with the chosen compression method, select Save As from the File menu. A standard Windows file selector will appear. Type a filename, and click the OK button. This example saves your file as `TEST.CMP` using LZW compression. After the file is saved, the information in the window is updated to reflect the saved file size and the compression type (see Figure 15-5).

Data Compression

An explanation of the three different compression methods supported by the compression library will help you understand the rest of the chapter. This section gives a short presentation on each one.

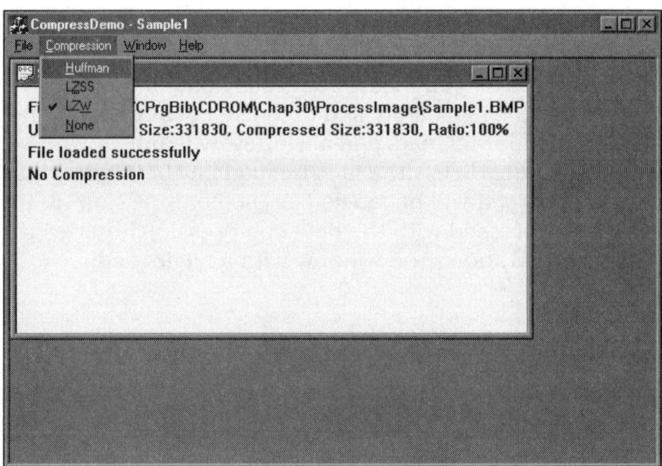

Figure 15-4: You can select several types of compression methods.

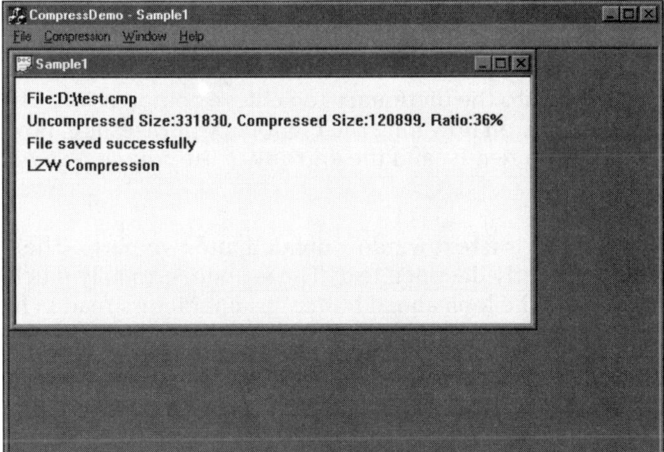

Figure 15-5: The window is updated with new information after the file is saved.

Huffman

Huffman coding takes a probabilistic approach to data compression. It depends on knowing the probability of each symbol's appearance in a message. Given the probabilities, a table of codes is constructed with different codes having a different number of bits. The codes with the greater probability have the least number of bits, and the codes with the lesser probability have the most number of bits.

The Huffman compression algorithm starts off by looking at a list of characters and developing a corresponding list of probabilities (or frequency counts). This way the frequency of occurrence is known for each character. The list is sorted by frequency count so that the most probable characters are at the top of the list and the least probable at the bottom. A binary tree is developed with which the binary token for each character can be accessed.

The individual symbols in the tree are laid out as a string of leaf nodes that are going to be connected by a binary tree. Each node has a weight, which is simply the frequency or probability of the symbol's appearance.

The two free nodes with the lowest weights are located. A parent node for these two nodes is created, and it is assigned a weight equal to the sum of the two child nodes. The parent node is added to the list of free nodes, and the two child nodes are removed from the list. One of the child nodes is designated as the path taken from the parent node when decoding a 0 bit. The other is arbitrarily set to the 1 bit. These steps are repeated until only one free node is left. This free node is designated as the root of the tree.

LZSS

LZSS compression uses previously seen text as a dictionary. It replaces phrases in the input text with pointers into the dictionary to achieve compression. The amount of compression depends on how long the dictionary phrases are, how large the window into previously seen text is, and the entropy of the source text with respect to the LZSS model.

The main data structure in LZSS is a text window divided into two parts. The first consists of a large block of recently decoded text. The second, normally much smaller, is a look-ahead buffer. The look-ahead buffer has characters read in from the input stream but not yet encoded.

The normal size of the text window is several thousand characters. The look-ahead buffer is generally much smaller, maybe 10 to 100 characters. The algorithm tries to match the contents of the look-ahead buffer to a string in the dictionary.

The code that implements this compression algorithm is fairly simple. It merely has to look through the entire text window for the longest match, encode it, and then shift.

The decompression algorithm is even simpler because it doesn't have to do comparisons. It reads in a token, outputs the indicated phrase, outputs the following character, shifts, and repeats. It maintains the window, but it does not work with string comparisons.

LZW

LZW is a dictionary-based compression scheme. It stores phrases in a potentially unlimited dictionary. It is different than LZSS in that it abandons the concept of a text window. LZW does output a series of tokens similar to LZSS. Each LZW token has two components: a phrase location and a character that follows the phrase. Each token consists of a code that selects a given phrase and a single character that follows the phrase. The phrase length is already known by the decoder and doesn't have to be part of the token.

When using the LZW algorithm, both the encoder and decoder start off with a very small dictionary consisting of 256 phrases, each a single character. As each character is read in, it is added to the current string. As long as the current string matches some phrase in the dictionary, this process continues.

But eventually the string will no longer have a corresponding phrase in the dictionary. This is when LZW outputs a token and a character. Remember that the string did have a match in the dictionary until the last character was read in. The current string, therefore, is defined as that last match with one new character added on.

The compression algorithm outputs the index for the previous match, and the character that broke the match. It then takes an additional step. The new phrase, consisting of the dictionary match and the new character, is added to the dictionary. The next time the phrase appears, it can be used to build an even longer phrase.

LZW can arbitrarily set the size of the phrase dictionary. This may cause two effects that must be dealt with. First, you have to consider the number of bits allocated in the output token for the phrase code. Second, and more importantly, you have to consider how much CPU time managing the dictionary will take.

CCompressedFile class functions

This section is provided as a reference to the public function calls the data compression library offers. Because the library was designed with simplicity as a major goal, there aren't many calls. That's good because using data compression is easy — it just takes a few lines of code.

You may want to skip over this section and read the section entitled "Behind CompressDemo," which shows how the calls are used. (For some people, it's better to look at the usage of function calls before actually studying their syntax.)

✦ `CCompressedFile::MakeNewFile()` — This is the static function that creates `CompressedFile` classes. The first argument is the existing filename that's to be opened. The second argument that can be given determines the data compression type that will be used. If you don't give the constructor an argument for the compression type, it defaults to LZW compression. This is important: If you give the function a filename, the object created carries the compression type of that file, regardless of the compression type that's given in the second argument. Following is an example of creating a `CCompressedFile` object for LZW compression:

```
CCompressedFile *pFile = MakeNewFile( NULL, LZW );
```

✦ `CCompressedFile::Open()` — This function is almost exactly like the `CFile::Open()` function. It opens a file for reading or writing. At the same time, it initializes all arrays and variables for the data compression or decompression. Following is an example of opening a file for reading:

```
CCompressedFile *pFile = MakeNewFile( "Filename" );
if( pFile->Open( "Filename", CFile::modeRead ) )
  AfxMessageBox( "File open success." );
else
  AfxMessageBox( "File open failure." );
delete pFile;
```

✦ `CCompressedFile::Close()` — This function closes the file and flushes all buffers.

✦ `CCompressedFile::GetPosition()`—This function returns the position to which the file pointer points. If 500 bytes have been written to a newly created file, the value returned will be 500. If 2,048 bytes have been read from a newly opened file, the value returned will be 2048. Following is an example that reads 500 bytes and then displays the position in a message box:

```
CCompressedFile *pFile = MakeNewFile( "Filename" );
if( pFile->Open( "Filename", CFile::modeRead ) ){
  char cbBuffer[500];
  pFile->Read( cbBuffer, 500 );
  CString strText;
  strText.Format( "The current position is %ld",
    pFile->GetPosition() );
  AfxMessageBox( strText );
  }
else
  AfxMessageBox( "File open failure." );
delete pFile;
```

✦ `CCompressedFile::GetLength()`—This function returns the byte length of the file.

✦ `CCompressedFile::FindFileInArchive()`—Compressed archive files that are created with the `CompressedFile` class library can have more than one file stored in each archive file. Before this function is called, the compressed file must be opened with the `Open()` function. The `FindFileInArchive()` function then searches the file list up to the file specified by `nIndex`. If five files are in the archive and an argument of 2 is passed in, the file at index 2 is sought. This is the third file in the archive, and that's the one that will be decompressed. Following is an example that opens a file with multiple files stored inside, finds the second file (index 1), and reads 500 bytes:

```
CCompressedFile *pFile = MakeNewFile( "Filename" );
if( pFile->Open( "Filename", CFile::modeRead ) ){
  if( pFile->FindFileInArchive( 1 ) ){
    char cbBuffer[500];
    pFile->Read( cbBuffer, 500 );
    AfxMessageBox( "FindFileInArchive() successful." );
    }
  else
    AfxMessageBox( "FindFileInArchive() failed." );
  }
else
  AfxMessageBox( "File open failure." );
delete pFile;
```

✦ `CCompressedFile::ReadByte()`—This function reads a single byte from an opened file. Following is an example:

```
CCompressedFile *pFile = MakeNewFile( "Filename" );
if( pFile->Open( "Filename", CFile::modeRead ) ){
  int nData = pFile->ReadByte();
  if( nData == -1 ){
```

```
    // There was a read error.
    }
  }
delete pFile;
```

✦ `CCompressedFile::WriteByte()` — This function writes a single byte to an opened file. Following is an example:

```
CCompressedFile *pFile = MakeNewFile( NULL, HUFFMAN );
if( pFile->Open( "Filename",
  CFile::modeWrite | CFile::modeCreate ) ){
  pFile->WriteByte( 'C' );
  }
delete pFile;
```

✦ `CCompressedFile::Read()` — This function reads a specified number of bytes into a buffer. It returns the number of bytes actually read. This functions almost exactly like the `CFile::Read()` function. Following is an example:

```
CCompressedFile *pFile = MakeNewFile( "Filename" );
if( pFile->Open( "Filename", CFile::modeRead ) ){
  char cbBuffer[500];
  pFile->Read( cbBuffer, 500 );
  }
delete pFile;
```

✦ `CCompressedFile::Write()` — This function writes a specified number of bytes that are in a buffer to the file. This functions almost exactly like the `CFile::Write()` function. An example follows:

```
CCompressedFile *pFile = MakeNewFile( NULL, HUFFMAN );
if( pFile->Open( "Filename",
  CFile::modeWrite | CFile::modeCreate ) ){
  static char szString[] = "This is a test";
  pFile->Write( szString, strlen( szString ) );
  }
delete pFile;
```

✦ ✦ ✦ ✦ ✦

Behind CompressDemo

This section explores the ways in which the `CCompressedFile` class member functions are used by showing them in a sample application: CompressDemo.

Complete source code for CompressDemo can be found in the `Chap15\CompressDemo` directory of the CD.

✦ ✦ ✦ ✦ ✦

Opening a file

The code that loads a file from disk into memory can be found in the CCompressDemoView class. The function in which it's placed is the OnDraw() function. Every time a file is opened, a new MDI window is opened and drawn. The file can then be loaded the first time the OnDraw() function is called.

Once the file is loaded, information about it is drawn to the child window. That way the user can see the details about the file, its compression method, its size, and its compression ratio. The first thing that happens in the OnDraw() function is to see whether or not the file has been loaded. The Boolean variable m_bLoaded is FALSE if the file hasn't been loaded, or TRUE if it has been loaded.

Obtaining the filename from the document class, a CCompressedFile class object is created with the MakeNewFile() static function. When the file is loaded, a determination is made whether or not the file has been compressed with the CCompressedFile compression class. This is transparent to the programmer, but it's nice to know that you don't have to worry about it.

A buffer is allocated for the data that will be read. The size that's needed for the uncompressed data can be obtained by examining the CCompressedFile member variable named m_dwUncompressedSize. Once the buffer is allocated, a single call to the Read() function is made. The Read() function looks exactly like the Read() function of the CFile class. It takes two arguments: a pointer to a buffer and the size to read.

The compressed and uncompressed sizes are stored into the view class from the CCompressedFile class. This is just so that the information can be displayed in the view window after the CCompressedFile object is deleted. The file is closed, and then deleted. No further CCompressedFile read operations are performed in the application.

Information about the file is displayed at the end of the OnDraw() function. The filename, compression type, compressed and uncompressed sizes, the compression ratio, and the status of the read operation are all drawn.

Saving files

Saving files is done in the CCompressDemoView class, in the OnFileSaveAs() function. The first things that happen in the OnSaveAs() function are checks to make sure there is an allocated buffer, and that the size of the data is not zero. Either one of these situations creates an unsuccessful write operation.

The next thing the code does is create a CCompressedFile object with the static MakeNewFile() function. This function takes as its second argument the compression type for the file.

The Open() function is then called. It is called in the same way as the Open() function of the CFile class. It takes a filename as its first argument and the file attributes as its second argument. It returns TRUE if successful or FALSE if unsuccessful.

A single call to the Write() function is made. Doing this causes the CCompressedFile to write all of the data to disk. This Write() function is called exactly as the Write() function of the CFile class. It takes a buffer pointer as its first argument and an integer value representing the number of bytes to write to disk. The display variables are all updated so that any change in file status, size, or compression type is reflected in the view window.

Opening a Compressed File

Follow these steps to open a compressed file:

1. Start off by creating a CCompressedFile object by calling the static MakeNewFile() function. The first parameter is not necessary. It's the filename of the file, but you'll usually give the filename when you open the file. The second argument is the compression type. This can be either HUFF, LZSS, LZW, or UNCOMP. The second argument defaults to LZW if you don't pass it a value:

   ```
   CCompressedFile *pFile = MakeNewFile( "TEST.TXT" );
   ```

2. Next you have to open the file. Here's the code to open a file named TEST.TXT:

   ```
   pFile->Open( "TEST.TXT", Cfile::modeRead );
   ```

   If you're dynamically allocating a buffer into which the data will be read, use the pFile➪m_dwUncompressedSize variable to obtain the size of the buffer. The following code allocates a buffer for reading:

   ```
   char *pBuffer = new char[pFile->m_dwUncompressedSize];
   ```

3. Now you can read the data with a call to the Read() function. The code to do this follows:

   ```
   pFile->Read( pBuffer, pFile->m_dwUncompressedSize );
   ```

4. Finally, you must close the file. Here's the code for that:

   ```
   pFile->Close();
   ```

✦ ✦ ✦ ✦ ✦

Saving a Compressed File

Follow these steps to save a compressed file:

1. Once again, start off by creating a CCompressedFile object by calling the static MakeNewFile() function:

   ```
   CCompressedFile *pFile = MakeNewFile( NULL, LZW );
   ```

2. Next you have to open the file. Here's the code to open a file named `TEST.CMP`:

```
pFile->Open( "TEST.CMP",
  Cfile::modeWrite | Cfile::modeCreate);
```

3. Now you can write the data with a call to the `Write()` function. The code to do this follows:

```
char szBuffer[] =
  "This is a test of this compression class.";
pFile->Write( szBuffer, strlen( szBuffer ) );
```

4. Finally, you must close the file. Here's the code for that:

```
pFile->Close();
```

✦ ✦ ✦ ✦ ✦

The CSerial Class for Serial Communications

Common uses of remote communications are business applications that link different sites in order to keep tabs on inventories and transactions. For example, I once wrote a large drug-dispensing program in which many clinic sites automatically received new orders and updated pharmacy information each evening from a central host location. The central host gets inventory levels and transaction information from each site during evening hours. A large part of my time was spent constructing telecommunications routines that sent and received information packets. If I had had the class library that's included on the CD-ROM that comes with this book, my development time would have been reduced significantly.

The next section describes a class for performing serial communications through the PC COM ports. This class can empower your programs with all of the computer-accessible information in the world.

Serial communications

The PC communications port uses asynchronous communication, or asynch for short. Each byte of data is potentially a separate unit. The PC sending data can pause between any two bytes of a message. The receiver, however, may have to catch the data as quickly as it arrives.

To accomplish this trick, asynch data requires on extra bit's worth of time to announce the beginning of a new byte (the "start" bit) and one extra bit's worth of time at the end (the "stop" bit). A 9600 baud modem can transfer only 9600 bytes of data per second because each byte requires a minimum of 10 bits to be transferred.

Modern high-speed modems do not actually transmit the start and stop bits. They are squeezed out as part of the general data compression. However, the start and stop bits will be generated on the wire that connects a COM port to an external modem (the RS-232 interface). Because of this and the general availability of data compression, the modern COM port is usually configured to use a higher speed (between the COM port and the modem) than the actual data transmission will support (between the two modems over the phone line). As an example, modems may operate at 14,400 bits per second, but the COM port will be configured for 38,400 bits per second.

This is just an example of older conventions adapted to new requirements. The standards for asynchronous communications go back to the days before computers. The first modems were used by teletype machines to send cablegrams. When the first computers were developed, the existing population of teletype machines provided convenient terminals.

The standards made sense up to the point where it became possible to put computer chips inside the modems. "Smart" modems can dial the phone, send a fax, compress data, and correct transmission errors. None of these functions were even imagined when standards such as RS-232 were originally developed. Although the rules have been adapted to accommodate modern technology, some of the old junk still pops up.

The CSerial class

This section describes the member functions for the `CSerial` class. Most function descriptions include examples showing how to use them.

✦ `CSerial::CSerial` — This is the `CSerial` class constructor, and it takes no arguments. It initializes all of the class member variables.

✦ `CSerial::Open` — This member function opens the communications port. It takes two integer arguments. The first argument contains the port number through which you'll communicate. Valid values normally range from 1 to 4. The second argument is the baud rate. Valid values for the baud rate are 300, 1200, 2400, 4800, 9600, 19200, 38400, and 76800. The function returns a Boolean value indicating success or failure. You'll get a `TRUE` if everything worked okay or a `FALSE` if the port didn't open. Following is an example of opening communications port 2 at 9600 baud:

```
CSerial Serial;
if( Serial.Open( 2, 9600 ) )
  AfxMessageBox( "The port opened OK." );
else
  AfxMessageBox( "The port didn't open." );
```

✦ `CSerial::Close` — This function closes the communications port. The `CSerial` destructor calls this function, so you don't have to call this explicitly unless you have a reason to close the port before you destroy the class. The following two functions both create a `CSerial` class. The first example explicitly closes the port and the second example allows the class destructor to close the port:

```
void FunctionOne( void )
{
  CSerial Serial;
  if( Serial.Open( 2, 9600 ) )
    Serial.Close();  // Explicit closing of port.
}

void FunctionTwo( void )
{
  CSerial Serial;
  Serial.Open( 2, 9600 );
  // Implicit closing of port, the CSerial
  // destructor takes care of it.
}
```

✦ `CSerial::SendData`—This function writes data from a buffer to the serial port. The first argument it takes is to a `const char *` buffer that contains the data that's to be sent. The second argument is the number of bytes that are to be sent. The function returns the actual number of bytes that have been written to the port. Following is an example in which the communications port is opened and a text string is sent to the port:

```
void Function( void )
{
  CSerial Serial;
  if( Serial.Open( 2, 9600 ) ){
   static char *szMessage[] = "This is a test message";
    int nBytesSent;
    nBytesSent = Serial.SendData( szMessage,
      strlen( szMessage ) );
  }
}
```

✦ `CSerial::ReadDataWaiting`—This function returns the number of incoming bytes that are waiting in the communications port's buffer. It takes no arguments.

✦ `CSerial::ReadData`—This function reads data from the port's incoming buffer. The first argument that it takes is a `void *` to a buffer into which the data will be placed. The second argument is an integer value that gives the size of the buffer. For instance, if the buffer passed in is allocated at 500 bytes, this value will be 500. This prevents buffers from becoming overrun. The `ReadData()` function returns an integer value for the actual number of bytes that were read. Following is an example in which a serial port is opened and waiting serial data is read into an allocated buffer:

```
void Function( void )
{
  CSerial Serial;
  if( Serial.Open( 2, 9600 ) ){
    char *lpBuffer = new [500];
    int nBytesRead;
    nBytesRead = Serial.ReadData( lpBuffer, 500 );
   delete [] lpBuffer;
  }
}
```

You can find the .cpp and the .h files for the `CSerial` class in the `Chap15\Serial` directory. To use them, copy the files into your project's directory and add them to the project.

The CRegistry Class

This mysterious object appeared with the introduction of OLE under Windows 3.1. No matter how hard programmers try to ignore it, it's here to stay; in fact, while you were looking the other way, it quietly took over the role of initialization, or INI files, among other things.

The Registry is a hierarchically organized store of information. Each entry in this tree-like information structure is called a *key*. A key may contain any number of subkeys; it can also contain data entries called *values*. In this form, the Registry stores information about the system, its configuration, hardware devices, and software applications. It also assumes the role of the ubiquitous INI files by providing a place where application-specific settings can be stored. A Registry key is identified by its name. Keynames consist of printable ASCII characters except the backslash (\), space, and wildcard (* or ?) characters. The use of keynames that begin with a period (.) is reserved. Keynames are not case sensitive.

Registry values

A value in the Registry is identified by its name. Value names consist of the same characters as keynames. The value itself can be a string, binary data, or a 32-bit unsigned value.

Generally, storing items larger than a kilobyte or two in the Registry is not recommended. For larger items, use a separate file, and use the Registry for storing the filename. Under Windows 95/98, Registry values are limited to 64K. Another consideration when using the Registry is that storing a key generally requires substantially more storage space than storing a value. Whenever possible, organize values under a common key rather than using several keys for the same purpose.

Predefined Registry keys

The Registry contains several predefined keys:

- `HKEY_LOCAL_MACHINE` contains entries that describe the computer and its configuration. This includes information about the processor, system board, memory, and installed hardware and software.
- `HKEY_CLASSES_ROOT` is the rear key for information relating to document types and OLE/COM. This key is a subordinate key to `HKEY_LOCAL_MACHINE`. (It is equivalent to `HKEY LOCAL MACHINE\SOFTWARE\Classes`.) Information that is stored here is used by shell applications such as Program Manager, File Manager, or the Explorer, and by OLE/ActiveX applications.
- `HKEY_USERS` serves as the key for the default user preference settings as well as individual user preferences.
- `HKEY_CLASSES_USER` is the root key for information relating to the preferences of the current (logged in) user. Under Windows 95, there are two additional predefined keys.
- `HKEY_CURRENT_CONFIG` contains information about the current system configuration settings.
- `HKEY_DYN_DATA` provides access to dynamic status information, such as information about plug-and-play devices.

Commonly used Registry keys

Information about Registry keys is often difficult to find. For this reason, I decided to collect information on some frequently used Registry keys that are of interest to the programmer and provide it here.

A number of subkeys are in `HKEY_LOCAL_MACHINE`. Keys in `HKEY_LOCAL_MACHINE` contain information about the computer's software and hardware configuration. Of these, the `Config` and `Enum` subkeys are specific to Windows 95/98 and its plug-and-play capabilities. The `Config` subkey is where Windows stores various hardware configurations; the `Enum` subkey contains Windows 95/98 bus enumerators that build the tree of hardware devices.

Windows maintains the `System` subkey under `HKEY_LOCAL_MACHINE`. The `System\CurrentControlSet` subkey contains configuration information for services and device drivers. Other subkeys in `HKEY_LOCAL_MACHINE` include Software and Classes.

The `Software` subkey is where information about installed software packages can be found. The `Classes` subkey is where `HKEY_CLASSES_ROOT` points to. The `Software` subkey is of particular interest to application programmers. This is where you should store configuration and installation information specific to your application. Microsoft recommends that you build a series of subkeys under

HKEY_LOCAL_MACHINE\Software. These subkeys should represent your company name, the name of your product, and the product's version.

What you store under such a key is entirely application dependent. You should not store anything here that is user specific; user-specific information pertinent to your application should be organized under a subkey of HKEY_CURRENT_USER.

Of particular interest is the key HKEY_LOCAL_MACHINE\SofWare\Microsoft\Windows\CurrrentVersion, which describes the current Windows configuration.

Subkeys in HKEY_CLASSES_ROOT

The HKEY CLASSES_ROOT key contains two types of subkeys: subkeys that correspond to filename extensions and class definition subways. A filename extension subkey has a name that corresponds to the filename extension (such as .doc). The key typically contains one unnamed value, which holds the name of the class definition subkey. A class definition subkey describes the behavior of a document class. The information stored here includes data on shell and OLE-related properties. A subkey under HKEY CLASSES ROOT is CLSID. This is the place where COM class identifiers are stored. When you create an MFC application using the Visual C++ AppWizard, a series of subkeys that are to be installed under HKEY_CLASSES ROOT are also created. These identify the document type and filename extension of your new application and also its OLE properties such as the OLE class identifier.

Subkeys in HKEY_USERS

The key HKEY_USERS contains a subkey named Default and zero or more subkeys corresponding to users on the system. The Default subkey corresponds to the default user profile. Other entries correspond to profiles of existing users.

Subkeys in HKEY_CURRENT_USER

The HKEY_CURRENT_USER key corresponds to the profile of the currently logged in user. Application configuration information specific to the current user should be stored under the subkey Software. Information should be organized by keys corresponding to company name, product name, and product version number.

The CRegistry class in action

This section documents the functions available in the CRegistry class.

To make it easier to access the Registry, a special class named CRegistry is included on the CD-ROM in the Chap15\Registry directory. To use it, just copy the two files into your project's directory, and add them to your project. Descriptions of the class functions along with examples follow.

✦ ✦ ✦ ✦ ✦

✦ **CRegistry::CRegistry**—There are two forms of the CRegistry constructor. One creates a CRegistry object and takes no arguments, and the other creates a CRegistry object and tries to open the Registry key that was passed in as a pair of arguments. Two examples follow:

```
CRegistry Registry;
// Create a CRegistry object that's not opened.

OR
CRegistry Registry( HKEY_LOCAL_MACHINE,
  "SOFTWARE\\GreatSoftware" );
// Create a CRegistry object that
// attempts to open SOFTWARE\GreatSoftware.
```

✦ **CRegistry::Open**—This function opens a Registry key. It takes two arguments: a subkey keyname and a keyname of the subkey that you wish to open. The function returns TRUE if the Registry key opened successfully and FALSE if it did not. Following is an example:

```
CRegistry Registry;
  if( Registry.Open( HKEY_LOCAL_MACHINE,
   "SOFTWARE\\GreatSoftware" ) )
    AfxMessageBox( "The registry key opened OK." );
else
  AfxMessageBox( "The registry key didn't open." );
```

✦ **CRegistry::Close**—This function closes the Registry key that was opened. You don't need to explicitly call this because the CRegistry destructor closes the key.

✦ **CRegistry::IsOpen**—This function returns TRUE if the Registry key is currently open, FALSE if it is not.

✦ **CRegistry::ReadDWORD**—This function reads a DWORD value from an open Registry key. The first argument the function takes is the value name. The second argument is a pointer to a DWORD, which accepts the value that's read in. A third optional argument is a pointer to a DWORD, which accepts an error code if this third argument is given. The function returns TRUE if successful, FALSE if not. An example that opens a Registry key and reads a DWORD value follows:

```
CRegistry Registry;
DWORD dwValue;
if( Registry.Open( HKEY_LOCAL_MACHINE,
  "SOFTWARE\\GreatSoftware" ) )
  Registry.ReadDWORD( "WindowColor", &dwValue );
```

✦ **CRegistry::ReadString**—This function reads a character string from an open Registry key. The first argument the function takes is the value name. The second argument is a pointer to a character buffer, which accepts the string that's read in. The third argument is the size of the buffer to which the data will be copied. A fourth optional argument is a pointer to a DWORD, which accepts an error code if this fourth argument is given. The function returns TRUE if successful, FALSE if not. An example that opens a Registry key and reads a string follows:

```
CRegistry Registry;
char cbBuffer[250];
if( Registry.Open( HKEY_LOCAL_MACHINE,
  "SOFTWARE\\GreatSoftware" ) )
  Registry.ReadString( "UserName", cbBuffer, 250 );
```

✦ **CRegistry::WriteDWORD**—This function writes a DWORD value to an open Registry key. The first argument the function takes is the value name. The second argument is a DWORD value that's to be written. A third optional argument is a pointer to a DWORD, which accepts an error code if this third argument is given. The function returns TRUE if successful, FALSE if not. An example that opens a Registry key and writes a DWORD value follows:

```
CRegistry Registry;
if( Registry.Open( HKEY_LOCAL_MACHINE,
  "SOFTWARE\\GreatSoftware" ) )
  Registry.WriteDWORD( "WindowColor", 50 );
```

✦ **CRegistry::WriteString**—This function writes a character string to an open Registry key. The first argument the function takes is the value name. The second argument is a pointer to a character buffer, which contains the string data that's to be written. A third optional argument is a pointer to a DWORD, which accepts an error code if this third argument is given. An example that opens a Registry key and writes a string follows:

```
CRegistry Registry;
if( Registry.Open( HKEY_LOCAL_MACHINE,
  "SOFTWARE\\GreatSoftware" ) )
  Registry.WriteString( "UserName", "John Doe" );
```

✦ ✦ ✦ ✦ ✦

Using the Clipboard

The Clipboard is a standard Windows method of transferring data between two processes. A process can put a chunk of data into the Clipboard in one of the predefined formats (listed in Table 15-3), or register a custom format. Another process can look at the Clipboard and decide to retrieve a chunk of data that has been placed in the Clipboard. It's an easy way to send data to another process.

Table 15-3
Predefined Clipboard Formats

Define	*Description*
CF_BITMAP	A handle to a bitmap (HBITMAP).
CF_DIB	A memory object containing a BITMAPINFO structure followed by the bitmap bits.
CF_DIF	Software Arts' Data Interchange Format.
CF_DSPBITMAP	Bitmap display format associated with a private format. The hMem parameter must be a handle of data that can be displayed in bitmap format in lieu of the privately formatted data.
CF_DSPENHMETAFILE	Enhanced metafile display format associated with a private format. The hMem parameter must be a handle of data that can be displayed in enhanced metafile format in lieu of the privately formatted data.
CF_DSPMETAFILEPICT	Metafile-picture display format associated with a private format. The hMem parameter must be a handle of data that can be displayed in metafile-picture format in lieu of the privately formatted data.
CF_DSPTEXT	Text display format associated with a private format. The hMem parameter must be a handle of data that can be displayed in text format in lieu of the privately formatted data.
CF_ENHMETAFILE	A handle of an enhanced metafile (HENHMETAFILE).
CF_GDIOBJFIRST through CF_GDIOBJLAST	Range of integer values for application-defined GDI object Clipboard formats. Handles associated with Clipboard formats in this range are not automatically deleted using the GlobalFree function when the Clipboard is emptied. Also, when using values in this range, the hMem parameter is not a handle to a GDI object, but is a handle allocated by the GlobalAlloc function with the GMEM_DDESHARE and GMEM_MOVEABLE flags.
CF_HDROP	A handle of type HDROP that identifies a list of files. An application can retrieve information about the files by passing the handle to the DragQueryFile() functions.

Define	Description
CF_LOCALE	The data is a handle to the locale identifier associated with text in the Clipboard. When you close the Clipboard, if it contains CF_TEXT data but no CF_LOCALE data, the system automatically sets the CF_LOCALE format to the current input locale. You can use the CF_LOCALE format to associate a different locale with the Clipboard text. An application that pastes text from the Clipboard can retrieve this format to determine which character set was used to generate the text.
CF_METAFILEPICT	Handle of a metafile picture format as defined by the METAFILEPICT structure. When passing a CF_METAFILEPICT handle by means of dynamic data exchange (DDE), the application responsible for deleting hMem should also free the metafile referred to by the CF_METAFILEPICT handle.
CF_OEMTEXT	Text format containing characters in the OEM character set. Each line ends with a carriage return/linefeed (CR-LF) combination. A null character signals the end of the data.
CF_OWNERDISPLAY	Owner-display format. The Clipboard owner must display and update the Clipboard viewer window, and receive the WM_ASKCBFORMATNAME, WM_HSCROLLCLIPBOARD, WM_PAINTCLIPBOARD, WM_SIZECLIPBOARD, and WM_VSCROLLCLIPBOARD messages. The hMem parameter must be NULL.
CF_PALETTE	Handle of a color palette. Whenever an application places data in the Clipboard that depends on or assumes a color palette, it should place the palette on the Clipboard as well. If the Clipboard contains data in the CF_PALETTE (logical color palette) format, the application should use the SelectPalette and RealizePalette functions to realize (compare) any other data in the Clipboard against that logical palette. When displaying Clipboard data, the Windows Clipboard always uses as its current palette any object on the Clipboard that is in the CF_PALETTE format.
CF_PENDATA	Data for the pen extensions to the Microsoft Windows for Pen Computing.

(continued)

Table 15-3 (continued)

Define	*Description*
CF_PRIVATEFIRST through CF_PRIVATELAST	Range of integer values for private Clipboard formats. Handles associated with private Clipboard formats are not freed automatically; the Clipboard owner must free such handles, typically in response to the WM_DESTROYCLIPBOARD message.
CF_RIFF	Represents audio data more complex than can be represented in a CF_WAVE standard wave format.
CF_SYLK	Microsoft Symbolic Link (SYLK) format.
CF_TEXT	Text format. Each line ends with a carriage return/linefeed (CR-LF) combination. A null character signals the end of the data. Use this format for ANSI text.
CF_WAVE	Represents audio data in one of the standard wave formats, such as 11 kHz or 22 kHz pulse code modulation (PCM).
CF_TIFF	Tagged-image file format.
CF_UNICODETEXT	Windows NT only: Unicode text format. Each line ends with a carriage return/linefeed (CR-LF) combination. A null character signals the end of the data.

A member function of the CWnd class named OpenClipboard() must be used before you put data into or get data from the Clipboard. The following example shows how to open the Clipboard using the CWnd member function and get text data from it:

```
if( OpenClipboard() ){
  HGLOBAL hMem = GetClipboardData( CF_TEXT );
  if( hMem != NULL ){
    char *lpText = (char *) GlobalLock( hMem );
    if( lpText != NULL ){
      // Work with the text...
      }
    // Don't free memory handle, the clipboard owns it
    }
  else
    AfxMessageBox("Couldn't get text from clipboard.");

  // Close the clipboard.
  CloseClipboard();
  }
```

Putting data into the Clipboard is almost as easy as getting it out. The important difference is that after you call the OpenClipboard() function, you must call the EmptyClipboard() function. You also must allocate a global memory handle into which you'll copy the data (unless the data is already contained in a global memory handle). Once the global memory handle has been placed in the Clipboard, it should not be freed. The following example places text into the Clipboard:

```
if( OpenClipboard() ){
  static char szMessage[] = "This is a test";

  // Allocate enough space for the message string
  // and the NULL terminator.
  HGLOBAL hMem = GlobalAlloc( GMEM_MOVEABLE,
    strlen( szMessage ) + 1 );

  // Lock the allocated memory, copy the text
  // into it, and then unlock it.
  char *lpDest = (char *) GlobalLock( hMem );
  strcpy( lpDest, szMessage );
  GlobalUnlock( hMcm );

  // Empty the clipboard and store the text data in it.
  EmptyClipboard();
  SetClipboardData( CF_TEXT, hMem );

  // Don't free hMem since the clipboard now owns it.

  // Close the clipboard.
  CloseClipboard();
  }
```

Summary

In this chapter you've learned how to manage data in many forms, including string data, file data, serial data, system Registry data, and Clipboard data. All of these techniques give you powerful tools for application development.

You should easily be able now to write programs that manipulate and search through strings. The `CString` class makes this easy as shown earlier in this chapter. You've seen how easy it is to perform file I/O with the `CFile` class. A bonus class named `CSerial` gives you an easy way to perform serial communications. And the `CRegistry` class gives you an easy way to save and load user preferences.

✦ ✦ ✦

CHAPTER 16

Sound

✦ ✦ ✦ ✦

In This Chapter

Playing recorded sounds

Playing MIDI files

CD audio

✦ ✦ ✦ ✦

Back in the age of the dinosaurs, when the 80286 was king, the most sound a program was able to make was a feeble beep or boop through the small and tinny PC speaker. But time and progress march on, and today PCs are equipped with wavetable sound cards and powered speaker systems that can produce extremely realistic sound. Why be satisfied with mere beeps when your application can *thunder* majestically?

This chapter shows you how to play music from a MIDI file, replay recorded sounds from WAV files, and play CD audio from CD tracks. We will take a different approach to covering this material. Rather than muck through all the details of using the Win32 API to record and play different sound formats, we will instead provide three classes that will enable you to easily play waveform, MIDI, and CD-based sounds. In each section we will introduce and describe each of the classes.

Playing Recorded Sounds

Adding sound to your application can really set your application above other products. By appealing to another of your users' senses, you are involving them on another level and are bringing them closer to the world that you are trying to create. Sound is also a great way to give feedback to the user. Good use of sound can also make a user feel that they are really interacting with your application. If you use your imagination, the possibilities for sound are endless.

We will cover the basics of playing waveform audio (WAV files) in addition to recording, saving, and playing multiple sounds at the same time. Multiple sound support is provided by DirectSound, which is, in turn, part of Microsoft's DirectX API. DirectX is a gaming API that provides support for 3D graphics, fast screen rendering, and force-feedback game controls. We will also examine how the functions behind the class library work, although you can still easily use the classes presented here to add sound to your programs without learning this functionality.

Visual C++ does include support for playing waveform audio. In this chapter, we will expand on that support and provide a class library that makes it much easier to add sound to your Windows applications. The Wave class library that comes with this book, along with the Windows multimedia library `winmm.lib` that is provided with Visual C++, provide a quick and easy method for adding sound effects to any Windows 95, Windows 98, or Windows NT application. We have also created a class library that takes advantage of the DirectSound technology that is built into Visual C++ to play multiple wave files at the same time.

The CWave class in brief

The `CWave` class can be added to any Visual C++ project (you must also link `winmm.lib`). Now, you are ready to add sound to your own applications. You don't necessarily have to know what's happening within the class; it will do all the work for you.

The class offers more than just the capability of playing wave files. The class has a big advantage over the Windows sound routines in that it loads the sound data into memory and can repeatedly play the sounds without a delay for loading the sound. The library also provides the capability of recording and saving your own wave files. If you want to examine the class library in detail or make changes to the member functions, the source code is part of the WaveDemo program and can be found in the Sound library source code.

You can open a wave file by two different methods with the `CWave` class. You can load a file from disk or from the resource file. To open a wave from an application's resource file, the application must be compiled with the wave files in the resource segment.

Playing wave files using the Windows API

The Microsoft API provides three different ways for applications to work with wave files:

1. The `PlaySound()` function is a powerful function that allows playback of waveform audio with one line of code. We will use this as the basis for the `CWave` class but enhance it by preloading the sound data into memory.
2. The Media Control Interface (MCI) is similar to the method we use to play MIDI files. The `CWave` class uses this method for the recording and saving of wave files.
3. Low-level waveform audio services are used by applications that require complete control over the waveform data.

The PlaySound() function

The Windows API includes a function called `PlaySound()` that is used to play waveform audio. The function has two minor limitations: The entire sound must fit into available physical memory and the sound must be in a data format supported by one of the installed audio drivers. A good rule of thumb is to use PlaySound() for files under 100KB and MCI for files larger than that.

The PlaySound() function offers the programmer a lot of flexibility for digitized sound playback. It plays disk-based wave files, wave resources, or specific system event sounds. It can loop sounds, play them asynchronously, and play them from memory. The CWave class uses this function extensively. One of the main advantages of the class library is that it loads the waveform data into memory and then uses the PlaySound() function to play the sound. This allows the application to load the sound only once and eliminates any delay at the start of sound playback. The prototype for PlaySound() looks like this:

```
BOOL PlaySound( LPCSTR pszSound, HMODULE hmod,
    DWORD fdwSound );
```

The first parameter, pszSound, specifies the filename, resource identifier, or system event. If this parameter is NULL, playback is stopped. The second parameter, hmod, is the handle of the resource. The third parameter, fdwSound, specifies flags for the command. Table 16-1 lists these flags.

Table 16-1
Sound Flags

Flag	*Description*
SND_ASYNC	Play the sound asynchronously.
SND_SYNC	Play the sound synchronously (default).
SND_NODEFAULT	Don't use the default sound.
SND_MEMORY	First parameter points to a memory file.
SND_LOOP	Loop sound until next call to PlaySound().
SND_NOSTOP	Don't stop any currently playing sound.

The Media Control Interface

The Media Control Interface (MCI) enables the control of the Windows waveform audio devices. The CWave class uses the MCI to record and save wave files. The MCI can be implemented with one of two functions: mciSendCommand() or mciSendString(). Although they serve the same purpose and produce the same result, they have different syntax. One uses a command-based interface, and the other uses a string-based interface. We will use only mciSendCommand() because the command-based interface should seem more logical to those programmers accustomed to the Windows command-based API.

The mciSendCommand() function is used to communicate with the MCI device by sending command messages such as MCI_OPEN and MCI_PLAY. The MCI command-based messaging interface allows for a lot of flexibility through the use of MCI parameter blocks. The parameter blocks are structures defined in MMSYSTEM.H that allow large amounts of information to be passed to and returned from the mciSendCommand() function. The prototype for mciSendCommand() looks like this:

```
DWORD mciSendCommand( UINT wDeviceID, UINT wMessage,
    dwParam1, DWORD dwParam2 );
```

The first parameter, wDeviceID, is the device that receives the message. The second parameter, wMessage, is the MCI command message. The third parameter, dwParam1, specifies flags for the command. The last parameter, dwParam2, specifies a pointer to the parameter block to be used.

The MCI device ID identifies which device has been opened. This value is returned in the parameter block when you send the MCI_OPEN command and should be saved for later use. The ID is used to identify this device when sending subsequent commands. The information in Table 16-2 is a brief overview of the MCI commands that we use and are relevant to waveform audio.

Table 16-2
MCI Commands for Waveform Audio (WAV)

Command	*Description*
MCI_OPEN	Opens the device.
MCI_CLOSE	Closes the device.
MCI_PLAY	Starts file playback.
MCI_STOP	Stops file playback.
MCI_SEEK	Seeks to a specific position within the file.
MCI_RECORD	Begins recording of waveform audio.
MCI_SAVE	Saves audio to disk.

The CWave class functions

This section is provided as a reference to the public function calls of the CWave class. The calls should be easy to use and easy to implement in your own programs.

CWave Class Functions

✦ **CWave::CWave** — This is the CWave class constructor. It simply creates a CWave object and initializes its internal variables.

✦ `CWave::GetDevices`— Most of the time, you'll want to make sure the computer on which your program is running is capable of playing wave files. The `GetDevices()` function returns an integer value indicating the number of devices installed on the system that support wave audio output. This function takes no parameters.

✦ `CWave::LoadFromDisk`— You'll want to use the `LoadFromDisk()` function if you're trying to load a .wav sound directly from a .wav file. This function is not to be used when you want to load a sound from the resource file. This function opens the file and reads the waveform data into memory. It remains in memory until another sound is loaded into the `CWave` class, or the `CWave` class is destroyed. The function takes a `CString` object as a parameter. It returns `TRUE` for success or `FALSE` for failure. An example follows:

```
CWave Wave;
CString strFilename;
strFilename = "Sound.wav";
BOOL bSuccess = Wave.LoadFromDisk( strFilename );
```

✦ `CWave::LoadFromRes`—You'll want to use the `LoadFromRes()` function if you're trying to load a .wav sound as a resource. This function is not to be used when you want to load a sound directly from a disk file. This function loads waveform data into memory. It remains in memory until another sound is loaded into the `CWave` class, or the `CWave` class is destroyed. The function takes a `CString` object, and an `HINSTANCE` handle as parameters. It returns `TRUE` for success, `FALSE` for failure. An example follows:

```
CWave Wave;
CString strResname;
strResname = "IDR_SOUND1";
BOOL bSuccess = Wave.LoadFromRes( strResname,
    AfxGetInstanceHandle() );
```

✦ `CWave::Close`—This function stops the file from playing and releases memory that is storing the waveform data. You should not need to call this function because it automatically is called by the destructor. You can call it if you want to free up memory sooner. The `Close()` function takes no arguments and returns `TRUE` for success or `FALSE` for failure.

✦ `CWave::Play`—This function plays the sound that's in memory. It first checks to see if a sound has been loaded. If no sound is loaded, it returns `FALSE`. Then, any sound that's currently playing is stopped. Finally, the sound that's currently loaded is begun. This function takes one `Boolean` parameter that enables you to specify whether the sound will loop repeatedly. It returns `TRUE` for success or `FALSE` for failure.

✦ `CWave::Stop`—This function stops the current sound from playing if it's currently playing. This function takes no arguments and returns nothing.

✦ `CWave::Record`—At times you'll want to record a sound. You'll be able to do this as long as users have a microphone plugged into the back of their sound cards. This function records new waveform data. Recording continues until the `Stop()` function is called. The `Record()` function takes no parameters. It returns `TRUE` for success or `FALSE` for failure.

✦ `CWave::Save` — Most of the time you'll be loading sounds for playback. But if you've recorded a sound, you might want to save it to disk. This function enables you to save the sound that's in the class' memory to disk. It takes a single argument, a `CString` object, that contains the filename to which the data will be saved.

✦ `CWave::PlayFromDisk` — This static function synchronously plays a sound from disk. It takes a single argument, a `CString` object, that contains the filename from which the sound data is played. It returns `TRUE` for success or `FALSE` for failure.

✦ `CWave::PlayFromRes` — This static function synchronously plays a sound from disk. It takes two arguments: a `CString` object that contains the resource name from which the sound data is played, and an `HINSTANCE` handle for the application. It returns `TRUE` for success or `FALSE` for failure.

◆ ◆ ◆ ◆ ◆

The WaveDemo Program

The first demo program in this chapter plays six different prerecorded sounds. Three of the sounds are saved to disk as .wav files. The other three are part of the program's resource file. Users can select any of the six sounds and play them. The sounds can be played directly from disk or the resource file, or they can be loaded and then played at a later time. You can see what the program looks like in Figure 16-1; highlights of the program are given in Listing 16-1.

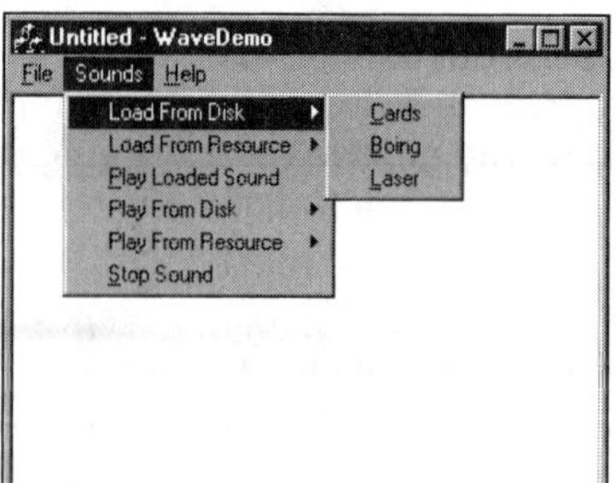

Figure 16-1: The WaveDemo program is simple but shows you how to use the CWave class.

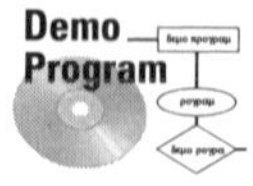

WaveDemo
CD-ROM Location: **Chap16\WaveDemo**
Program Name: **WaveDemo.EXE**
Source Code Modules in Text: `WaveDemoView.cpp`

◆ ◆ ◆ ◆ ◆

Listing 16-1: Highlights of WaveDemoView.cpp Source Code

```
// WaveDemoView.cpp : implementation of
// the CWaveDemoView class
//

/////////////////////////////////////////////////////////////
// CWaveDemoView message handlers

void CWaveDemoView::OnSoundsLoadfromdisk()
{
  // Get the menu ID for this message.
  WORD wID = GetCurrentMessage()->wParam;

  // Have the CWave object load the .wav
  // file from disk for the sound that's
  // been selected.
  if( wID == ID_SOUNDS_LOADFROMDISK_CARDS )
    m_Wave.Load( "Sample1.wav" );
  else if( wID == ID_SOUNDS_LOADFROMDISK_BOING )
    m_Wave.Load( "Sample2.wav" );
  else
    m_Wave.Load( "Sample3.wav" );

}

void CWaveDemoView::OnSoundsLoadfromresource()
{
  // Get the menu ID for this message.
  WORD wID = GetCurrentMessage()->wParam;
  // Have the CWave object load the wave
  // resource for the sound that's been
  // selected.
  if( wID == ID_SOUNDS_LOADFROMRESOURCE_BARK )
    m_Wave.Load( IDR_WAVE3,
      AfxGetInstanceHandle() );
  else if( wID == ID_SOUNDS_LOADFROMRESOURCE_SHOCK )
    m_Wave.Load( IDR_WAVE2,
      AfxGetInstanceHandle() );
  else
    m_Wave.Load( IDR_WAVE1,
      AfxGetInstanceHandle() );

}

void CWaveDemoView::OnSoundsPlayfromdisk()
{
  // Get the menu ID for this message.
  WORD wID = GetCurrentMessage()->wParam;

  // Let them know when we start
```

(continued)

Listing 16-1 *(continued)*

```
    // by changing the mouse cursor
    // to the hourglass.
    BeginWaitCursor();

    // Have the CWave object play the .wav
    // file from disk for the sound that's
    // been selected.
    if( wID == ID_SOUNDS_PLAYFROMDISK_CARDS )
      m_Wave.PlayFromDisk( "Sample1.wav" );
    else if( wID == ID_SOUNDS_PLAYFROMDISK_BOING )
      m_Wave.PlayFromDisk( "Sample2.wav" );
    else
      m_Wave.PlayFromDisk( "Sample3.wav" );

    // Change the mouse cursor back to
    // it's original state before
    // the call to BeginWaitCursor().
    EndWaitCursor();

}

void CWaveDemoView::OnSoundsPlayfromresource()
{
    // Get the menu ID for this message.
    WORD wID = GetCurrentMessage()->wParam;

    // Let them know when we start
    // by changing the mouse cursor
    // to the hourglass.
    BeginWaitCursor();

    // Have the CWave object play the wave
    // resource for the sound that's been
    // selected.
    if( wID == ID_SOUNDS_PLAYFROMRESOURCE_BARK )
      m_Wave.PlayFromRes( IDR_WAVE3,
        AfxGetInstanceHandle() );
    else if( wID == ID_SOUNDS_PLAYFROMRESOURCE_SHOCK )
      m_Wave.PlayFromRes( IDR_WAVE2,
        AfxGetInstanceHandle() );
    else
      m_Wave.PlayFromRes( IDR_WAVE1,
        AfxGetInstanceHandle() );

    // Change the mouse cursor back to
    // it's original state before
    // the call to BeginWaitCursor().
    EndWaitCursor();

}
```

```
void CWaveDemoView::OnSoundsPlayloadedsound()
{

  // Let them know when we start
  // by changing the mouse cursor
  // to the hourglass.
  BeginWaitCursor();

  // Play the loaded sound.
  m_Wave.Play();

  // Change the mouse cursor back to
  // it's original state before
  // the call to BeginWaitCursor().
  EndWaitCursor();

}

void CWaveDemoView::OnUpdateSoundsPlayloadedsound(
  CCmdUI* pCmdUI)
{

  // Enable the menu item if a sound has
  // been loaded.
  pCmdUI->Enable( m_Wave.IsLoaded() );

}

void CWaveDemoView::OnSoundsStopsound()
{

  // Stop the sound that's playing.
  m_Wave.Stop();

}
```

Playing MIDI Files

Music is one of the easiest ways to enhance your multimedia applications. Nearly every popular game or multimedia title features some sort of background music, either Musical Instrument Digital Interface (MIDI) or CD audio. Music is very effective for putting the user in a specific mood or evoking certain feelings. The right music at the right time can work wonders for you and your Visual C++ programs.

You may wonder why you would want to use MIDI when you could skip to the `CCDAudio` class and add CD audio to your applications. Although CD audio is the current trend and is of a much higher quality, MIDI music does still have its advantages. Of course, your applications may not be CD-based, or you're not requiring your user to have a CD-ROM drive. MIDI is cheaper to produce than CD audio, and a huge library of MIDI music is available on the Internet and through freeware and shareware. Finally, if you are producing a high-end CD-ROM product, every time your program accesses the disk you would have to pause CD audio, while you can continue to play MIDI music when a program accesses the disk.

Believe it or not, you don't need to know anything about music or MIDI to add music to your Visual C++ applications. We will cover the basics of MIDI and the Windows MIDI interface in this chapter, but you could still easily use the classes presented here to add music to your programs without this background.

What is MIDI?

MIDI is a protocol originally developed within the music industry by several large companies involved in the production of electronic music synthesizers. It has since been adopted by the computer industry and is the standard format for multimedia music files. A MIDI file is a set of commands for storing and transmitting information about music. A MIDI file doesn't contain any actual music but does contain the commands necessary for a device to play back the music stored in the files. In more simple terms, a MIDI file is the electronic equivalent of sheet music.

Windows supports the General MIDI Specification, which is the industry standard on how MIDI is developed and used. This standard defines the particular sounds and instruments that are supported, as well as the commands that control them. Microsoft and most MIDI sound card manufacturers support this standard.

The CMidi class in brief

The `CMidi` class can be linked with any Visual C++ project (you must also link `winmm.lib`). Before you know it, you will be playing MIDI files in your own applications. You don't need to know what's going on behind the scenes, the class will do all the work for you.

The library offers much more than just the capability of playing MIDI files. You can pause the playback, skip around to different positions within the file, and even change the tempo of the playback. Of course, if you want to examine the class library in detail or make changes to the member functions, the source code is part of the MIDIDemo program and is also included in the Sound library project.

The CMidi class functions

This section serves as a reference for the functions found in the `CMidi` class. Use it when you study the MIDIDemo program, and create your own programs that use the `CMidi` class.

CMidi Class Functions

- `CMidi::CMidi`—This is the `CMidi` class constructor. It simply creates a `CMidi` object and initializes its internal variables.
- `CMidi::DeviceCount`—This function returns the number of MCI devices that are capable of playing MIDI tracks. It takes no arguments and returns an integer value containing the number of MIDI-capable devices.
- `CMidi::Open`—The `Open()` function opens the MCI for playing MIDI files. It issues the necessary `mciSendCommand()` functions to set up everything. The `CMidi` class retains a handle to the open MCI device for its own internal use. The function takes one argument, a character pointer to a string containing the filename of the MIDI file that's to be loaded. It returns `TRUE` if successful, `FALSE` if it fails.
- `CMidi::Close`—This function stops a MIDI track if it's currently playing and closes the MCI device. It sets all internal flags to indicate that everything is closed down properly. This function is called anytime a `CMidi` class is destroyed so that things are cleaned up. The `Close()` function takes no arguments and returns `TRUE` if successful or `FALSE` if it fails.
- `CMidi::Play`—The `Play()` function begins the playback of the MIDI file that's been loaded into memory. If the `CMidi` class hasn't been opened, this function returns `FALSE`. The `Play()` function takes no arguments and returns `TRUE` if successful or `FALSE` if it fails.
- `CMidi::Stop`— The `Stop()` function causes the MIDI track that's currently playing to stop.The `Stop()` function takes no arguments and returns `TRUE` if successful or `FALSE` if it fails.
- `CMidi::IsPlaying`— This function returns a `Boolean` value indicating whether the MIDI track is currently playing. It returns `TRUE` if the MIDI track is playing or `FALSE` if it isn't. `IsPlaying()` takes no parameters.
- `CMidi::Pause`—This function pauses the playback of the MIDI track that's currently being played. The `Pause()` function takes no arguments and returns `TRUE` if successful or `FALSE` if it fails.

◆ ◆ ◆ ◆ ◆

The MIDIDemo Program

The MIDIDemo program shows you how to play and manage MIDI files. Four MIDI files are in the `MIDIDemo` directory, and any one of them can be loaded and played. The program uses the `CMidi` class for performing MIDI operations. It will make playing MIDI files very easy. The MIDIDemo program can be seen in Figure 16-2; highlights of the code are given in Listing 16-2.

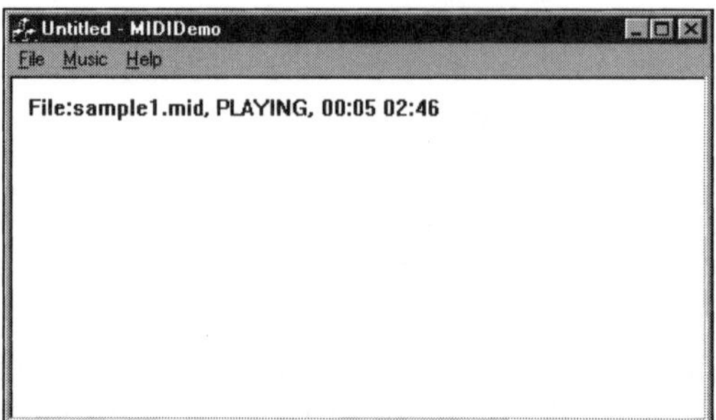

Figure 16-2: By studying the MIDIDemo program, you'll learn how to use the CMidi class.

MIDIDemo
CD-ROM Location: **Chap16\MIDIDemo**
Program Name: **MIDIDemo.EXE**
Source Code Modules in Text: `MIDIDemoView.cpp`

✦ ✦ ✦ ✦ ✦

Listing 16-2: **Highlights of MDIDemoView.cpp Source Code**

```
// MIDIDemoView.cpp : implementation of
// the CMIDIDemoView class
//

//////////////////////////////////////////////////////////
// CMIDIDemoView construction/destruction

static char *szFilename[] = {
  "sample1.mid", "sample2.mid",
  "sample3.mid", "sample4.mid" };

CMIDIDemoView::CMIDIDemoView()
{

  // Set the initial song to 0
  // and the initial file to sample1.mid.
  m_nSong = 0;
  m_Midi.Open( szFilename[0] );

}

CMIDIDemoView::~CMIDIDemoView()
{
}

//////////////////////////////////////////////////////////
// CMIDIDemoView message handlers
```

```
void CMIDIDemoView::OnMusicSelectsong()
{
  // Remember if the file is playing.
  BOOL bIsPlaying = m_Midi.IsPlaying();

  // Close the midi file.
  m_Midi.Close();

  // Get the menu message ID.
  WORD wID = GetCurrentMessage()->wParam;

  // Set the song number to 0, 1, 2, or 3
  // depending on the menu ID.
  if( wID == ID_MUSIC_SELECTSONG_JUNGLE )
    m_nSong = 0;
  else if( wID == ID_MUSIC_SELECTSONG_WINTER )
    m_nSong = 1;
  else if( wID == ID_MUSIC_SELECTSONG_CANDYLAND )
    m_nSong = 2;
  else
    m_nSong = 3;
  // Open the CMidi object with the selected
  // song's filename.
  m_Midi.Open( szFilename[m_nSong] );

  // If we were playing when we came into
  // this function, start the audio.
  if( bIsPlaying )
    m_Midi.Play();

}

void CMIDIDemoView::OnUpdateMusicSelectsong(
  CCmdUI* pCmdUI)
{

  // Set the check for the currently
  // selected song.
  pCmdUI->SetCheck( m_nSong ==
    (int) pCmdUI->m_nIndex );

}

void CMIDIDemoView::OnMusicStop()
{

  // Stop the playing.
  m_Midi.Stop();

}
```

(continued)

Listing 16-2 *(continued)*

```
void CMIDIDemoView::OnUpdateMusicStop(CCmdUI* pCmdUI)
{

  // Enable the 'stop' menu selection
  // if the file is currently playing.
  pCmdUI->Enable( m_Midi.IsPlaying() );

}

void CMIDIDemoView::OnMusicPlay()
{

  // Play the midi file.
  m_Midi.Play();

}

void CMIDIDemoView::OnUpdateMusicPlay(CCmdUI* pCmdUI)
{

  // Enable the 'play' menu selection
  // if the file is not currently playing.
  pCmdUI->Enable( !m_Midi.IsPlaying() );

}

int CMIDIDemoView::OnCreate(
  LPCREATESTRUCT lpCreateStruct)
{
  if (CView::OnCreate(lpCreateStruct) == -1)
    return -1;

  // Kick off the timer.
  SetTimer( 1, 500, NULL );

  return 0;
}

void CMIDIDemoView::OnTimer(UINT nIDEvent)
{

  // Get a DC to the window.
  CClientDC ClientDC( this );

  // We'll need a CString object
  // to form the information text.
  CString strInfo;

  // Use the GetMinutes() and GetSeconds()
  // functions to obtain the current minutes
  // and seconds. We'll get negative values
```

```
    // if the midi file isn't opened, so check
    // for this.
    int nMinutes = m_Midi.GetMinutes();
    if( nMinutes < 0 )
      nMinutes = 0;
    int nSeconds = m_Midi.GetSeconds();
    if( nSeconds < 0 )
      nSeconds = 0;

    // Use the GetLength() function to obtain
    // the total midi file length. We'll get
    // negative values if the midi file isn't
    // opened, so check for this.
    int nTotalMinutes, nTotalSeconds;
    m_Midi.GetLength( &nTotalMinutes, &nTotalSeconds );
    if( nTotalMinutes < 0 )
      nTotalMinutes = 0;
    if( nTotalSeconds < 0 )
      nTotalSeconds = 0;

    // Format the information string so that we can display
    // it to the window.
    strInfo.Format( "File:%s, %s, %02d:%02d %02d:%02d    ",
      szFilename[m_nSong],
      m_Midi.IsPlaying() ? "PLAYING" : "!PLAYING",
      nMinutes, nSeconds,
      nTotalMinutes, nTotalSeconds );

    // Write the information string to the
    // window.
    ClientDC.TextOut( 10, 10, strInfo );

    CView::OnTimer(nIDEvent);
}
```

CD Audio

CD audio is one of the best sound sources that you can use in your applications. Two characteristics set CD audio apart from most other sound sources. One is how CD audio tracks are organized on a disk. The format is one that is immediately familiar to most people and easy to work with. You can also access tracks randomly. This means that your application can skip to different positions within a track or can skip to a different track altogether.

The other, and more important, characteristic of CD audio is its sound quality. CD audio has the unique advantage of sounding exactly the way the composer designed it and the musicians produced it. While a MIDI file playing on one person's computer could sound completely different than on another, CD audio always sounds exactly the same. Along with this improved sound quality comes the ability to completely immerse the user in the musical experience. You might be surprised at the effects high-quality audio can have on a user.

Are there disadvantages to CD audio? Unfortunately, CD audio, like everything else, is not perfect. The main disadvantage involves disk access. You can't play CD audio while you are accessing the CD for other purposes. So when your application accesses the CD to read data, you must pause the CD audio until the process is complete. In addition, unless you happen to run your own music studio, CD-quality audio may be expensive and hard to produce.

When making the decision to use CD audio in your applications, you must take all of these factors into account. But if you have the resources and the know-how to use CD audio, no other one feature can add more to the user experience. The `CCDAudio` class that comes on the CD-ROM, along with the Windows multimedia library (`winmm.lib`) provided with Visual C++, can provide a quick and easy method for adding CD audio to any Windows 95, Windows 98, or Windows NT application. You can now make your programs sound like the ones the pros offer.

The CCDAudio class library in brief

If you link in the `CCDAudio` class, you can have all the features of a CD player in your own program with just a few additions to your application. You don't have to learn the programming required to play CD audio. The class library will do all the work for you.

We've built a class that encapsulates all of the MCI commands necessary to play CD audio. The `CCDAudio` class is linked in to the CDAudio program as a .cpp file. For your convenience, a .lib file named `Sound.lib` and a .h file named `Sound.h` are provided that contain the `CWave`, `CMidi`, and `CCDAudio` classes. These two files, along with the entire project, can be found in the `Chap16\Library` directory on the CD-ROM.

◆ ◆ ◆ ◆ ◆

We've also provided a set of functions that enable you to do much more than just play audio: skip around on the CD, get information on different tracks, and even open and close the CD drive. All of this is handled in a way that's transparent to the program. Of course, if you want to examine the class library in detail or make changes to the member functions, you can.

The Media Control Interface

The brains behind the `CCDAudio` class is the Media Control Interface. This is how Microsoft Windows talks to such devices as VCRs, videodisc players, and of course, CD audio.

The MCI can be implemented with one of two functions: `mciSendCommand()` or `mciSendString()`. Although they serve the same purpose and produce the same result, they have different syntax. One uses a command-based interface, and the other uses a string-based interface. We use only the `mciSendCommand()` function because the command-based interface usually seems more logical to programmers accustomed to the Windows command-based API.

The `mciSendCommand()` function is used to communicate with the MCI device, either to send command messages (`MCI_OPEN` and `MCI_PLAY`) or to query for information (`MCI_STATUS`) on the device. The MCI command-based messaging interface allows a lot of flexibility through the use of MCI parameter blocks. The parameter blocks are structures defined in `MMSYSTEM.H` that allow larger amounts of information to be passed to a return from the `mciSendCommand()` function. The values for the MCI commands relevant to CD audio can be seen in Table 16-3; the MCI command flags can be seen in Table 16-4.

Table 16-3
MCI Commands for CD Audio

Command	*Description*
`MCI_OPEN`	Opens the device.
`MCI_CLOSE`	Closes the device.
`MCI_PLAY`	Starts audio playback.
`MCI_STOP`	Stops audio playback.
`MCI_PAUSE`	Pauses audio playback.
`MCI_SEEK`	Seeks to a specific position on the CD
`MCI_SET`	Used with the MCI flags.
`MCI_STATUS`	Used with the MCI flags.

Table 16-4
MCI Command Flags for CD Audio

Flag	*Type*	*Description*
MCI_SET_TIME_FORMAT	Set	Changes the time format.
MCI_SET_DOOR_OPEN	Set	Opens the CD drive.
MCI_SET_DOOR_CLOSED	Set	Closes the CD drive.
MCI_STATUS_CURRENT_TRACK	Status	Gets the current track.
MCI_STATUS_LENGTH	Status	Gets the length of the CD or a specific track.
MCI_STATUS_MODE	Status	Gets the current status of the drive.
MCI_STATUS_NUMBER_OF_TRACKS	Status	Gets the number of tracks on the CD.
MCI_STATUS_POSITION	Status	Gets the current position in the current time.
MCI_STATUS_READY	Status	Checks to see if the device is ready.
MCI_STATUS_CDA_TYPE_TRACK	Status	Checks to make sure the track is an audio track.
MCI_STATUS_TIME_FORMAT	Status	Gets the current time format.
MCI_STATUS_MEDIA_PRESENT	Status	Checks to make sure a CD is in the drive.

CCDAudio class functions

This section serves as a reference for the functions found in the `CCDAudio` class. Use it when you study the CDPlayer program, and create your own programs that use the `CCDAudio` class.

CCDAudio Class Functions

- ✦ `CCDAudio:: CCDAudio`—This is the `CCDAudio` class constructor. It simply creates a `CCDAudio` object and initializes its internal variables.
- ✦ `CCDAudio::Open`—The `Open()` function opens the MCI for playing CD audio tracks. It issues the necessary `mciSendCommand()` functions to set up everything. The `CCDAudio` class retains a handle to the open MCI device for its own internal use. The `Open()` function takes no arguments. It returns `TRUE` if successful or `FALSE` if it fails.
- ✦ `CCDAudio::Close`—This function stops a CD audio track if it's currently playing and closes the MCI device. It sets all internal flags to indicate that

everything is closed down properly. This function is called anytime a CCDAudio class is destroyed so that things are cleaned up. The Close() function takes no arguments and returns nothing.

✦ CCDAudio::Play — The Play() function causes the currently selected track to begin playing. If the audio device isn't opened, this function returns FALSE. The Play() function takes no arguments. It returns TRUE if successful or FALSE if it fails.

✦ CCDAudio::Stop — This function stops the playback of the current track. If the track isn't playing or the CD device isn't opened, this function returns FALSE. The Stop() function takes no arguments. It returns TRUE if successful or FALSE if it fails.

✦ CCDAudio::Pause — This function pauses the playback of the current track. If the track isn't playing or the CD device isn't opened, this function returns FALSE. The Pause() function takes no arguments. It returns TRUE if successful or FALSE if it fails.

✦ ✦ ✦ ✦ ✦

The CDPlayer Program

Very few programs play CD audio music. Most programs load and play MIDI files. This program plays the high-quality sound data that's found on audio CDs. It does so with the CCDAudio class.

Because the CD that comes with the book doesn't have any CD audio tracks, you'll have to put one of your own in the CD drive. After you've done this, you'll be able to play any of the tracks on the CD. This program also lets you pause playback and move around inside of each track. You can see the CDPlayer application pictured in Figure 16-3; the dialog shown is produced by the code given in Listing 16-3.

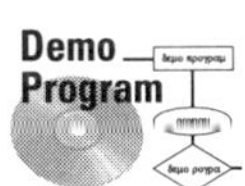

CDPlayer

CD-ROM Location: **Chap16\CDPlayer**

Program Name: **CDPlayer.EXE**

Source Code Modules in Text: CDPlayerDlg.cpp

✦ ✦ ✦ ✦ ✦

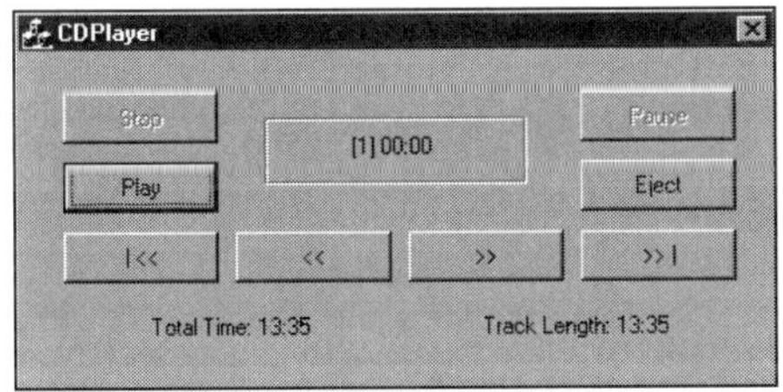

Figure 16-3: The CDPlayer application is dialog-based.

Listing 16-3: Highlights of the CDPlayerDlg.cpp Source Code

```
// CDPlayerDlg.cpp : implementation file
//


/////////////////////////////////////////////////////////////
// CCDPlayerDlg dialog

CCDPlayerDlg::CCDPlayerDlg(CWnd* pParent /*=NULL*/)
  : CDialog(CCDPlayerDlg::IDD, pParent)
{
  //{{AFX_DATA_INIT(CCDPlayerDlg)
    // NOTE: the ClassWizard will add member
// initialization here
  //}}AFX_DATA_INIT
  m_hIcon = AfxGetApp()->LoadIcon(IDR_MAINFRAME);

  // Open the CD device.
  m_CDAudio.Open();

}

/////////////////////////////////////////////////////////////
// CCDPlayerDlg message handlers

int CCDPlayerDlg::OnCreate(LPCREATESTRUCT lpCreateStruct)
{
  if (CDialog::OnCreate(lpCreateStruct) == -1)
    return -1;

  // Kick off the timer.
  SetTimer( 1, 1000, NULL );

  return 0;
}

void CCDPlayerDlg::OnTimer(UINT nIDEvent)
{

  BOOL bDriveReady = TRUE;

  // Format an information string. We'll use
  // it to display the track and current time
  // within the track.
  CString strStatus;
  strStatus.Format( "[%d] %02d:%02d",
    m_CDAudio.GetCurrentTrack(),
    m_CDAudio.GetMinutes(),
    m_CDAudio.GetSeconds() );

  // If the current track is -1, that means
  // we have no audio CD. Update the information
```

```
  // string to reflect this condition.
  if( m_CDAudio.GetCurrentTrack() == -1 ){
    strStatus = "No CD Audio";
    bDriveReady = FALSE;
    }
  SetDlgItemText( IDC_TRACKINFO, strStatus );

  // The next information string will contain the total
  // time for this CD. We'll use the GetTotalLength()
  // function to obtain the minutes and seconds.
  CString strLength;
  int nMinutes, nSeconds;
  m_CDAudio.GetTotalLength( &nMinutes,
    &nSeconds );
  strLength.Format( "Total Time: %02d:%02d",
  nMinutes, nSeconds );
  if( nMinutes == -1 )
    strLength = "Total Time: 00:00";
  SetDlgItemText( IDC_TOTALTIME, strLength );

  // The next information string will contain the total
// time for this track. We'll use the GetTrackLength()
// function to obtain the minutes and seconds.
  m_CDAudio.GetTrackLength(
    m_CDAudio.GetCurrentTrack(),
    &nMinutes, &nSeconds );
  strLength.Format( "Track Length: %02d:%02d",
nMinutes, nSeconds );
  if( nMinutes == -1 )
    strLength = "Total Time: 00:00";
  SetDlgItemText( IDC_TRACKTIME, strLength );

  // We'll use the boolean flags we've already
  // gotten in this function to update the
  // dialog buttons.
  CWnd *pWnd;
  pWnd = GetDlgItem( IDC_BACK );
  pWnd->EnableWindow( bDriveReady );
  pWnd = GetDlgItem( IDC_FORWARD );
  pWnd->EnableWindow( bDriveReady );
  pWnd = GetDlgItem( IDC_SKIPBACK );
  pWnd->EnableWindow( bDriveReady );
  pWnd = GetDlgItem( IDC_SKIPFORWARD );
  pWnd->EnableWindow( bDriveReady );

  // Update the approriate buttons
  // that depend on whether the CD is playing.
  BOOL bPaused;
  if( m_CDAudio.IsPlaying( &bPaused ) ){
    pWnd = GetDlgItem( IDC_PLAY );
    pWnd->EnableWindow( bPaused );
    pWnd = GetDlgItem( IDC_STOP );
```

(continued)

Listing 16-3 *(continued)*

```
    pWnd->EnableWindow( bDriveReady );
    pWnd = GetDlgItem( IDC_PAUSE );
    pWnd->EnableWindow( bDriveReady && !bPaused );
    }
  else{
    pWnd = GetDlgItem( IDC_PLAY );
    pWnd->EnableWindow( bDriveReady );
    pWnd = GetDlgItem( IDC_STOP );
    pWnd->EnableWindow( FALSE );
    pWnd = GetDlgItem( IDC_PAUSE );
    pWnd->EnableWindow( FALSE );
    }

  CDialog::OnTimer(nIDEvent);
}

void CCDPlayerDlg::OnPlay()
{

  // If the drive is ready, begin the
  // audio playback.
  if( m_CDAudio.IsDriveReady() )
    m_CDAudio.Play();

}

void CCDPlayerDlg::OnStop()
{

  // Stop the playback.
  m_CDAudio.Stop();

}

void CCDPlayerDlg::OnPause()
{

  // Pause the playback.
  m_CDAudio.Pause();

}

void CCDPlayerDlg::OnEject()
{

  // If the drive is read, close it.
  // Otherwise, attempt to open the drive.
  if( !m_CDAudio.IsDriveReady() )
    m_CDAudio.CloseDrive();
  else m_CDAudio.OpenDrive();
```

```
}

void CCDPlayerDlg::OnForward()
{

  // Get the current minutes, seconds
  // and track.
  int nMinutes = m_CDAudio.GetMinutes();
  int nSeconds = m_CDAudio.GetSeconds();
  int nTrack = m_CDAudio.GetCurrentTrack();

  // If minutes == -1, then the
  // CD device didn't open or there's
  // some other problem.
  if( nMinutes == -1 )
    return;

  // Go forward five seconds. Make
  // sure that the seconds haven't gone
  // out of range.
  nSeconds +- 5;
  if( nSeconds > 59 ){
    nMinutes++;
    nSeconds -= 60;
    }

  // Get the length of this track so
  // that we can check to make sure
  // we haven't gone past the end
  // of the track.
  int nTrackMinutes, nTrackSeconds;
  m_CDAudio.GetTrackLength( nTrack,
    &nTrackMinutes, &nTrackSeconds );

  // Check that the new values will be
  // in range, not past the end of the
  // track.
  if( nMinutes * 60 + nSeconds >
    nTrackMinutes * 60 + nTrackSeconds ){
    nMinutes = nTrackMinutes;
    nSeconds = nTrackSeconds;
    }

  // Seek to the new location in this track.
  m_CDAudio.SeekTo( nTrack,
    nMinutes, nSeconds, 0 );

}

void CCDPlayerDlg::OnBack()
{
```

(continued)

Listing 16-3 *(continued)*

```
  // Get the current minutes, seconds
  // and track.
  int nMinutes = m_CDAudio.GetMinutes();
  int nSeconds = m_CDAudio.GetSeconds();
  int nTrack = m_CDAudio.GetCurrentTrack();

  // If minutes == -1, then the
  // CD device didn't open or there's
  // some other problem.
  if( nMinutes == -1 )
    return;

  // Back up five seconds. Make sure
  // we haven't gone out of range.
  nSeconds -= 5;
  if( nSeconds < 0 ){
    nMinutes—;
    nSeconds += 60;
    if( nMinutes < 0 )
      nMinutes = 0;
    }

  // Seek to the new location in this track.
  m_CDAudio.SeekTo( nTrack,
    nMinutes, nSeconds, 0 );

}

void CCDPlayerDlg::OnSkipback()
{

  // Get the current track and deccrement.
  int nTrack = m_CDAudio.GetCurrentTrack() - 1;

  // If we're below the lowest allowable
  //track, go up to the highest track.
  if( nTrack < 1 )
    nTrack = m_CDAudio.GetTotalTracks();

  // Seek to the beginninig of the
  // previous track.
  m_CDAudio.SeekTo( nTrack, 0, 0, 0 );

}

void CCDPlayerDlg::OnSkipforward()
{

  // Get the current track and increment.
  int nTrack = m_CDAudio.GetCurrentTrack() + 1;
```

```
    // Get the total number of tracks and
    // make sure nTrack hasn't exceeded it.
    if( nTrack > m_CDAudio.GetTotalTracks() )
      nTrack = 1;

    // Seek to the beginning of the next track.
    m_CDAudio.SeekTo( nTrack, 0, 0, 0 );

  }
```

For convenience, use the Sound.lib and Sound.h files found in the Chap16\Library directory of the CD-ROM. This will make it easier to add sounds to any of your applications because you won't have to link in any source code.

◆ ◆ ◆ ◆ ◆

Summary

In this chapter we covered the basics of making some noise in Windows. We examined the basic concepts behind multimedia sound and discussed three classes that encapsulate the Windows sound API calls: CWave, CMidi, and CCDAudio. The three demonstration programs showed you how to take advantage of their functionality. You now have the tools and knowledge to add some interesting sounds to your applications.

✦ ✦ ✦

CHAPTER 17

Timers and OnIdle Loop Processing

✦ ✦ ✦ ✦

In This Chapter

Setting a timer using WM_TIMER

Setting a timer with a callback procedure

The Clock program

Using CWinApp's OnIdle capability

The OnIdleDemo program

✦ ✦ ✦ ✦

We will now turn our attention to the topics of timers and OnIdle loop processing. Up to now, we have concerned ourselves with programming topics that are easily seen by the end user of your application. However, as you continue in your programming career, you will find many instances where it is useful to perform some task in the background where it is not easily noticed. As an example, think of the autosave feature included in many of today's applications. If the application stopped responding whenever it was time for an automatic save to occur, using the application would quickly become a frustrating experience. It is better if the autosave can occur as a background task where it does not detract from the overall usability of the application.

We'll explore two mechanisms Windows provides that enable you to create these background tasks. In the first half of this chapter, we'll look at timers, which can be programmed for intervals as low as 55 milliseconds. You can incorporate timers into a wide range of applications such as clocks, disk backup programs, or any other type of application that needs to "wake up" at a certain time.

In the second half of the chapter, we'll leave timers behind and move on to idle processing. A few of the many uses for the framework's OnIdle mechanism include background print spooling and garbage collection. Some chores that were ideal candidates for idle processing in 16-bit Windows are better done in background threads in Windows 98, but OnIdle still has its uses. We'll look at one example of how idle calls can be put to work in a 32-bit application in the second of this chapter's two sample programs.

Timers

You need to know about only two functions to use timers: CWnd::SetTimer() programs a timer to fire at specified intervals, and CWnd::KillTimer() stops a running timer. Depending on the parameters passed to SetTimer(), a timer notifies an application that a timer interval has elapsed in two ways: by sending a WM_TIMER message and by calling an application-defined callback function.

The WM_TIMER method is the simpler of the two, but the callback method is sometimes preferable when multiple timers are used. Both types of timer notifications receive low priority when they are sent to an application. They're processed only when the message queue is devoid of other messages.

Timer notifications are never allowed to stack up in the message queue, which is a very good thing. Think about what could happen if a timer was set to fire every 250 milliseconds, but the code executing as a result of the WM_TIMER message took longer to run. If the messages were allowed to stack up in the queue, a race condition would result. Messages would queue up faster than your application could service them. Your code would never empty the queue and so would continue to run all the time.

Because Windows doesn't allow messages to stack up, this potential problem is solved. In this example, once the loop of code finishes executing, it receives another message at the end of the next 250-millisecond cycle.

Still, a Windows application should never spend an excessive amount of time processing a message unless processing has been delegated to a secondary thread. Responsiveness suffers if the primary thread goes too long without checking the message queue.

Setting a timer using WM_TIMER

The easiest way to set a timer is to call SetTimer() with nothing more than a timer ID and a timeout value and then map WM_TIMER messages to an OnTimer() function in your application's window class. A timer ID is a non-zero value that identifies the timer. When OnTimer() is activated in response to a WM_TIMER message, the timer ID is passed as an argument. If you use only one timer, the ID value probably won't interest you because all WM_TIMER messages come from the same timer. An application that uses two or more timers can use the timer ID to determine which timer a message has come from.

The timeout value passed to SetTimer() specifies the interval between WM_TIMER messages in thousandths of a second. Value values range from 1 through the highest number a 32-bit integer can hold: 2^{32}–1 milliseconds, which equals slightly more than 49.5 days. The following code allocates a timer, assigns it the ID of 1, and programs it to send a WM_TIMER message every 500 milliseconds to the window whose `SetTimer()` function was called. The `NULL` third parameter configures the timer to send `WM_TIMER` messages rather than use a callback function:

```
SetTimer( 1, 500, NULL );
```

Although the programmed interval is 500 milliseconds, the window will actually receive a `WM_TIMER` message about once every 550 milliseconds because the hardware timer upon which timers are based ticks once every 54.9 milliseconds. In effect, Windows rounds the value you pass to `SetTimer()` up to the next multiple of 55 milliseconds. Thus, the following two lines of code both program a timer to send a `WM_TIMER` message roughly every 55 milliseconds:

```
SetTimer( 1, 1, NULL );
SetTimer( 1, 50, NULL );
```

If you change the timer to an interval of 60 as in the following line, `WM_TIMER` messages arrive every 110 milliseconds:

```
SetTimer( 1, 60, NULL );
```

Timers can't be relied upon for stopwatch-like accuracy. If you write a clock application that programs a timer for 1,000-millisecond intervals and updates the display each time a `WM_TIMER` message arrives, you shouldn't assume that 60 `WM_TIMER` messages means that one minute has passed. Instead, you should check the current time whenever a message arrives and update the clock accordingly. Then, if the flow of timer messages is interrupted, the clock's accuracy will be maintained.

Multimedia Timers

If you write an application that demands precision timing, you can use Windows multimedia timers in lieu of conventional timers and program them for intervals of 1 millisecond or less. Multimedia timers offer superior precision and are ideal for specialized applications such as MIDI sequencers, but they also incur more overhead and can adversely impact other programs running on the system.

◆ ◆ ◆ ◆ ◆

The value returned by `SetTimer()` is the timer ID if the function succeeded or 0 if it failed. In versions of Windows before Windows 95, timers were a shared global resource of which a limited number were available. Beginning with Windows 95, the number of timers the system can dole out is limited only by available memory. Failures should be rare, but it's still prudent to check the return value just in case the system is critically low on resources. The timer ID returned by `SetTimer()` equals the timer ID you specified in the function's first parameter unless you specify 0, in which case `SetTimer()` returns a timer ID of 1. `SetTimer()` won't fail if you assign two or more timers the same ID. Rather, it will assign duplicate IDs as requested.

`SetTimer()` can also be used to change a previously assigned timeout value. If timer 1 already exists, the following statement reprograms it for intervals of 1,000 milliseconds:

```
SetTimer( 1, 1000, NULL );
```

Reprogramming a timer also resets its internal clock so that the next notification won't arrive until the specified time period has elapsed.

Creating Timers

The following procedure summarizes the steps involved in creating and using a Windows timer:

1. In the Messages list box, find the `WM_CREATE` and `WM_TIMER` messages, and add handlers for them.
2. In the `OnCreate()` function, kick off the timer:

   ```
   SetTimer( 1, 1000, NULL );
   ```

3. In the `OnTimer()` message handler, insert your timer-driven code.
4. Compile and run the program.

◆ ◆ ◆ ◆ ◆

An important point to understand is that `WM_TIMER` messages are not processed asynchronously with other messages. That is to say, one `WM_TIMER` message never interrupts another `WM_TIMER` message in the same thread of execution, nor does the timer message interrupt another nontimer message. As we saw before, `WM_TIMER` messages are assigned a very low priority.

`WM_TIMER` messages wait their turn in the message queue just as other messages do and are not processed until they are retrieved and dispatched by the message loop. This low priority even extends to the execution of the `OnTimer()` message handler. For example, if two functions modify the same member variable, Windows guarantees that the code in the `OnTimer()` handler will not modify the variable before the other function completes. Of course, this guarantee doesn't hold true if the functions exist in separate threads.

Setting a timer with a callback procedure

Timers don't have to generate `WM_TIMER` messages. If you prefer, you can configure a timer to call a callback function inside your application rather than post a `WM_TIMER` message to the message queue. This method is often used in applications that use multiple timers so that each timer can be handled independently with minimum fuss.

A common misconception among Windows programmers is that timer callbacks are processed more expediently than timer messages because callbacks are sent directly to the application's window procedure, whereas `WM_TIMER` messages are posted to the message queue. In reality, callbacks and messages are handled identically up to the point at which `DispatchMessage()` is called.

When a timer fires, Windows sets a flag in the message queue to indicate that a timer message or callback is awaiting processing. If GetMessage() finds that the message queue is empty and no windows need repainting, it checks the timer flag. If the flag is set, GetMessage() builds a WM_TIMER message that is subsequently dispatched by DispatchMessage().

However, if the timer that generated the message is of the WM_TIMER variety, the message is dispatched to the window procedure. But if a callback function is registered instead, DispatchMessage() calls the callback function. Therefore, callback timers enjoy virtually no performance advantage over message timers. Slightly less overhead is involved when a timer callback is invoked because no sorting of message IDs has to be done in the message map or the window procedure, but the difference is all but immeasurable. In practice, you'll find that WM_TIMER-type timers and callback timers work with the same regularity.

To set a timer that uses a callback function, specify the name of the callback function in the third parameter as follows:

```
SetTimer( 1, 100, TimerProc );
```

The callback procedure, which is named TimerProc(), is prototyped as follows:

```
void CALLBACK TimerProc( HWND hWNd, UINT nMsg,
  UINT nTimerId, DWORD dwTime );
```

The hWnd parameter to TimerProc() contains the window handle, nMsg contains the message ID, WM_TIMER, nTimerID holds the timer ID, and dwTime specifies the number of milliseconds that have elapsed since Windows was started. The callback function should be declared as a static member function of the window class, or other measures should be taken to prevent this pointer from being passed on the stack.

One obstacle you'll run into when you're using a static member function as a timer callback is that the timer procedure doesn't receive a user-defined lParam value as some Windows callback functions do. In a timer procedure, you have to manufacture that window pointer yourself if you want to access nonstatic function and data members. Fortunately, you can get a pointer to your application's main window with MFC's AfxGetMainWnd() function as follows:

```
CmainWindow *pMainWd = (CmainWindow *) AfxGetMainWnd();
```

Casting the return value to a CMainWindow pointer is necessary if you want to access the CMainWindow function and data members because the pointer returned by AfxGetMainWnd() is a generic CWnd pointer. Once pMainWnd is initialized in this way, a TimerProc() function that is also a member of CMainWindow can access nonstatic CMainWindow functions and data members as if it, too, were a nonstatic member function.

The opposite of `CWnd::SetTimer()` is `CWnd::KillTimer()`, which stops a timer and stops the flow of `WM_TIMER` messages of callbacks. The following statement releases the timer whose ID is 1:

```
KillTimer( 1 );
```

A good place to kill a timer created using `OnCreate()` is in the window's `OnClose()` or `OnDestroy()` handler. If an application fails to free a timer before it terminates, Windows cleans up after it when the process ends.

The Clock Program

The first demo program shows you how to create a clock application using a timer. The `SetTimer()` function passes a `NULL` as its third parameter and therefore causes a `WM_TIMER` message to be posted to the window.

This program enables you to view either an analog clock or a digital clock. To change the display, simply change the setting in the Type menu. The program is shown in Figure 17-1; highlights of the code are given in Listing 17-1.

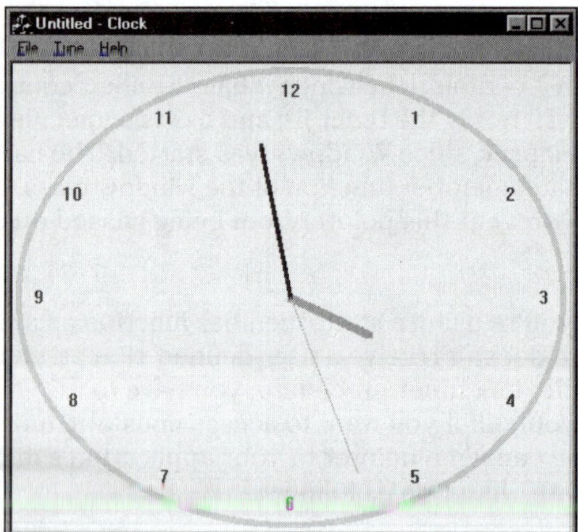

Figure 17-1: The Clock program enables you to view the time with an analog or a digital display.

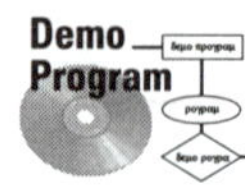

Clock
CD-ROM Location: **Chap17\Clock**
Program Name: **Clock.EXE**
Source Code Modules in Text: `ClockView.cpp`

◆ ◆ ◆ ◆ ◆

Listing 17-1: Implementing the CClockView Class

```
// ClockView.cpp : implementation of
// the CClockView class
//

//////////////////////////////////////////////////////////
// CClockView construction/destruction

CClockView::CClockView()
{

  // Set the initial clock type
  // to analog.
  m_nClockType = CLOCK_ANALOG;

}

CClockView::~CClockView()
{
}

//////////////////////////////////////////////////////////
// CClockView drawing

void CClockView::OnDraw(CDC* pDC)
{
  CClockDoc* pDoc = GetDocument();
  ASSERT_VALID(pDoc);

  // Get the client rectangle so that we
  // can dynamically fit the clock to
  // the window.
  RECT Rect;
  GetClientRect( &Rect );

  // For easier calculations, get the
  // x and y coordinates of the
  // window center.
  int nCenterX = Rect.right / 2;
  int nCenterY = Rect.bottom / 2;

  // Get the current time.
  CTime Time = CTime::GetCurrentTime();

  CString strDigits;
  int i, x, y;
  CSize size;

  switch( m_nClockType ){
    case CLOCK_ANALOG:
```

(continued)

Listing 17-1 *(continued)*

```
{
// Create a yellow pen with which we'll
// draw the ellipse.
CPen Pen( PS_SOLID, 5, RGB( 255, 255, 0 ) );

// Select the new pen into the DC and
// remember the pen that was selected out.
CPen *pOldPen = pDC->SelectObject( &Pen );

// Draw the clock face border with
// the Ellipse function.
pDC->Ellipse( 5, 5, Rect.right - 5,
  Rect.bottom - 5 );

double Radians;

// Out text color will be red.
pDC->SetTextColor( RGB( 255, 0, 0 ) );

for( i=1; i<=12; i++ ){

  // Format the digit CString object
  // for the current clock number.
  strDigits.Format( "%d", i );

  // Get the text extent of the
  // text so that we can center
  // it about a point.
  size =
    pDC->GetTextExtent( strDigits,
    strDigits.GetLength() );

  // Calculate the number of radians
  // for the current clock number.
  Radians = (double) i * 6.28 / 12.0;

  // Calculate the x coordinate. We
  // use the text extent to center
  // the text about a point.
  x = nCenterX -
    ( size.cx / 2 ) +
    (int) ( (double) ( nCenterX - 20 ) *
           sin( Radians ) );

  // Calculate the y coordinate. We
  // use the text extent to center
  // the text about a point.
  y = nCenterY -
    ( size.cy / 2 ) -
    (int) ( (double) ( nCenterY - 20 ) *
          cos( Radians ) );
```

```
    // Draw the text.
    pDC->TextOut( x, y, strDigits );

    }

  // Calculate the radians for the hour hand.
  Radians = (double) Time.GetHour() +
    (double) Time.GetMinute() / 60.0 +
    (double) Time.GetSecond() / 3600.0;
  Radians *= 6.28 / 12.0;

  // Create a pen for the hour hand that's five
  // pixels wide with a green color.
  CPen HourPen( PS_SOLID, 5, RGB( 0, 255, 0 ) );

  // Select the newly-created CPen object
  // into the DC.
  pDC->SelectObject( &HourPen );

  // Move to the center of the clock, then
  // draw the hour hand line.
  pDC->MoveTo( nCenterX, nCenterY );
  pDC->LineTo(
    nCenterX + (int) ( (double) ( nCenterX / 3 ) *
        sin( Radians ) ),
    nCenterY - (int) ( (double) ( nCenterY / 3 ) *
        cos( Radians ) ) );

  // Calculate the radians for the minute hand.
  Radians = (double) Time.GetMinute() +
    (double) Time.GetSecond() / 60.0;
  Radians *= 6.28 / 60.0;

  // Create a pen for the minute hand that's three
  // pixels wide with a blue color.
  CPen MinutePen( PS_SOLID, 3, RGB( 0, 0, 255 ) );

  // Select the newly-created CPen object
  // into the DC.
  pDC->SelectObject( &MinutePen );

  // Move the to center of the clock, then
  // draw the minute hand line.
  pDC->MoveTo( nCenterX, nCenterY );
  pDC->LineTo(
    nCenterX + (int) ( (double) (
        ( nCenterX * 2 ) / 3 ) * sin( Radians ) ),
    nCenterY - (int) ( (double) (
        ( nCenterY * 2 ) / 3 ) * cos( Radians ) ) );

  // Calculate the radians for the second hand.
  Radians = (double) Time.GetSecond();
```

(continued)

Listing 17-1 *(continued)*

```
    Radians *= 6.28 / 60.0;

    // Create a pen for the second hand that's one
    // pixels wide with a cyan color.
    CPen SecondPen( PS_SOLID, 1, RGB( 0, 255, 255 ) );

    // Select the newly-created CPen object
    // into the DC.
    pDC->SelectObject( &SecondPen );

    // Move the to center of the clock, then
    // draw the second hand line.
    pDC->MoveTo( nCenterX, nCenterY );
    pDC->LineTo(
      nCenterX + (int) ( (double) (
          ( nCenterX * 4 ) / 5 ) * sin( Radians ) ),
      nCenterY - (int) ( (double) (
          ( nCenterY * 4 ) / 5 ) * cos( Radians ) ) );

    // Select the old CPen object back into
    // the DC.
    pDC->SelectObject( pOldPen );
    }
    break;
  case CLOCK_DIGITAL:
    {

    // Begin by creating the text string
    // that represents the digital time.
    strDigits.Format( "%d:%02d:%02d",
      Time.GetHour(),
      Time.GetMinute(),
      Time.GetSecond() );

    CFont Font, *pOldFont;
    int nWidth = 100;
    int nHeight = 140;

    do{

      // We may have already created
      // a font in the CFont object. Here
      // we make sure it's deleted.
      if( Font.GetSafeHandle() != NULL )
        Font.DeleteObject();

      // Create the font with mostly default
      // values. Use a Times New Roman font.
      Font.CreateFont( nHeight, nWidth, 0, 0,
        FW_DONTCARE, 0, 0, 0, ANSI_CHARSET,
        OUT_CHARACTER_PRECIS, CLIP_CHARACTER_PRECIS,
```

```
          DEFAULT_QUALITY, DEFAULT_PITCH | FF_DONTCARE,
          "Times New Roman" );

        // Select the newly-created CFont object into
        // the DC and remember the CFont object that
        // was selected out.
        pOldFont = pDC->SelectObject( &Font );

        // Get the text extent so we can decide if
        // this font is too large.
        size =
          pDC->GetTextExtent( strDigits,
            strDigits.GetLength() );

        // Select the old font back into the DC.
        pDC->SelectObject( pOldFont );

        // If the text extent is too wide,
        // reduce the font width.
        if( size.cx > Rect.right )
          nWidth -= 5;

        // If the text extent is too high,
        // reduce the font height.
        if( size.cy > Rect.bottom )
          nHeight -= 5;

        } while( size.cx > Rect.right ||
          size.cy > Rect.bottom );

      // Select the final font into the
      // DC and remember the CFont object
      // that's selected out.
      pOldFont = pDC->SelectObject( &Font );

      // Draw the text.
      pDC->TextOut( nCenterX - ( size.cx / 2 ),
        nCenterY - ( size.cy / 2 ),
        strDigits );

      // Select the old font back into the DC.
      pDC->SelectObject( pOldFont );
      }
      break;
    }

}

int CClockView::OnCreate(LPCREATESTRUCT lpCreateStruct)
{
  if (CView::OnCreate(lpCreateStruct) == -1)
    return -1;
```

(continued)

Listing 17-1 *(continued)*

```
  // Kick off the timer.
  SetTimer( 1, 1000, NULL );

  return 0;
}

void CClockView::OnTimer(UINT nIDEvent)
{

  // The timer just causes a redraw to occur.
  // In the OnDraw() function the current
  // time is obtained.
  InvalidateRect( NULL, TRUE );
  UpdateWindow();

  CView::OnTimer(nIDEvent);
}

void CClockView::OnTypeAnalog()
{

  // Set to an analog clock and
  // cause a window redraw.
  m_nClockType = CLOCK_ANALOG;
  InvalidateRect( NULL, TRUE );
  UpdateWindow();

}

void CClockView::OnUpdateTypeAnalog(CCmdUI* pCmdUI)
{

  // Set the check if we have an analog clock.
  pCmdUI->SetCheck( m_nClockType == CLOCK_ANALOG );

}

void CClockView::OnTypeDigital()
{

  // Set to an digital clock and
  // cause a window redraw.
  m_nClockType = CLOCK_DIGITAL;
  InvalidateRect( NULL, TRUE );
  UpdateWindow();

}

void CClockView::OnUpdateTypeDigital(CCmdUI* pCmdUI)
{
```

```
    // Set the check if we have an digital clock.
    pCmdUI->SetCheck( m_nClockType == CLOCK_DIGITAL );

}
```

Using CWinApp's OnIdle Capability

Setting timers aside for a moment, you can use another mechanism to perform low priority tasks. MFC provides something called the OnIdle loop. The OnIdle loop is entered whenever the message queue is empty. This is where MFC performs general housekeeping and where you can insert code that runs during the idle moments of your application.

If you could log the calls to an application's `OnIdle()` function without slowing it down, you'd find that `OnIdle()` is called 100 or more times per second when the message queue is empty. Even with so much apparent idle time, there are trade-offs, as with everything else in life. As we'll see, code that executes in the OnIdle loop affects an application's capability to service the message queue. This means that the code must execute quickly to avoid the appearance of a sluggish application.

An application can perform idle processing of its own by overriding the application object's virtual `OnIdle()` function. `OnIdle()` is prototyped as follows:

```
virtual BOOL OnIdle( LONG lCount );
```

The `lCount` parameter is a 32-bit value that specifies the number of times `OnIdle()` has been called since the last message was processed. The count continually increases until the message loop in `CWinThread::Run` calls `PumpMessage()` to retrieve and dispatch another message. The count is then reset to 0 and starts again. Mouse messages, `WM_PAINT` messages, and `WM_SYSTIMER` messages don't cause `lCount` to be reset. `lCount` can be used as a rough measure of the time elapsed since the last message or of the length of time the application has been idle.

If you have two background tasks you'd like to perform during idle time, one that's high priority and another that's low, you can use `lCount` to determine when to execute each task. For example, the high priority task might be executed when `lCount` reaches 10, and the low priority task might be deferred until `lCount` is 100 or even 1,000.

A high priority task that begins when `lCount` reaches 10 would be executed much more often because the count frequently reaches or exceeds 10 even when the message loop is relatively busy. Idle processing should be carried out as quickly as possible because message traffic is blocked until the `OnIdle()` function returns.

The value returned by `OnIdle()` determines whether `OnIdle()` will be called again. If `OnIdle()` returns a non-zero value, it is called again if the message queue is still empty. If `OnIdle()` returns 0, however, further calls to `OnIdle()` are suspended until another message finds its way into the message queue, and the idle state is reentered after the message is dispatched.

The mechanism that makes this work is the `bIdle` flag in `CWinThread::Run`, which is initially set to `TRUE` but is set to `FALSE` if `OnIdle()` returns `FALSE`. The while loop that calls `OnIdle()` tests the value of `bIdle` at the beginning of each iteration and fails through if `bIdle` is `FALSE`. `bIdle` is set to `TRUE` again when a message shows up in the message queue and `PumpMessage()` is called to retrieve and dispatch it.

From a practical standpoint, you can save a few CPU cycles by returning `FALSE` from your `OnIdle()` override if background processing is complete for the moment and you don't want `OnIdle()` to be called again until the flow of messages resumes. Be careful, however, not to return `FALSE` before the framework has finished its most recent spate of idle processing chores and thus deprive it of the idle time it needs. There's an easy way to avoid this trap that we'll cover in just a moment.

The cardinal rule in using `OnIdle()` is to call the base class version of `OnIdle()` from the overridden version. The following `OnIdle()` override demonstrates the proper technique. The base class' `OnIdle()` function is called first, and after the call returns, the application performs its own idle processing.

```
BOOL CMyApp::OnIdle( LONG lCount )
{
  CwinApp::OnIdle( lCount );
  DoIdleWork(); // Do idle processing
  return( TRUE );
}
```

An even better approach is to accord higher priority to the framework's `OnIdle()` handler by delaying the start of your own idle processing until `lCount` reaches a value of 2 or higher as follows:

```
BOOL CMyApp::OnIdle( LONG lCount )
{
  CwinApp::OnIdle( lCount );
  if( lCount > 2 )
    DoIdleWork(); // Do idle processing
  return( TRUE );
}
```

The framework does its processing when `lCount` is 0 and 1. You can find out exactly what's done and when by looking at the source code for `CWinThread::OnIdle()` in `Thrdcore.cpp` and `CWinApp::OnIdle` in `Appcore.cpp`.

Because the version of `OnIdle()` shown in the preceding example always returns `TRUE`, an application will continue receiving `OnIdle()` calls even if both it and the framework are finished doing idle chores for the time being. The following

OnIdle() override minimizes wasted clock cycles by returning FALSE when the application's own idle processing is complete:

```
BOOL CMyApp::OnIdle( LONG lCount )
{
  CwinApp::OnIdle( lCount );
  BOOL bContinue = TRUE;
  if( lCount > 2 ){
    DoIdleWork(); // Do idle processing
    BContinue = FALSE;
    }
  return( bContinue );
}
```

The fact that application-specific idle processing isn't started until lCount equals 2 means that the framework won't be deprived of the idle time it needs if the application's OnIdle() function returns FALSE.

It's very important to remember that any code that executes inside the OnIdle loop affects the application's capability to dispatch messages. Any code that runs inside the idle loop should run very quickly. If necessary, break up large OnIdle() tasks into smaller, more manageable pieces, and process one piece at a time in successive calls to OnIdle(). The following OnIdle() function begins its work when lCount reaches 2 and continues responding to OnIdle() calls until DoIdleWork() returns FALSE, indicating that no further idle time is required:

```
BOOL CMyApp::OnIdle( LONG lCount )
{
  CwinApp::OnIdle( lCount );
  BOOL bContinue = TRUE;
  if( lCount > 2 )
    bContinue = DoIdleWork(); // Do idle processing
  return( bContinue );
}
```

The OnIdleDemo Program

The OnIdleDemo program, highlights of which are given in Listing 17-2, shows you how to override and use the OnIdle() function. It shows numeric values for the OnIdle lCount value and the elapsed time since lCount was reset. The OnIdleDemo program is shown in Figure 17-2.

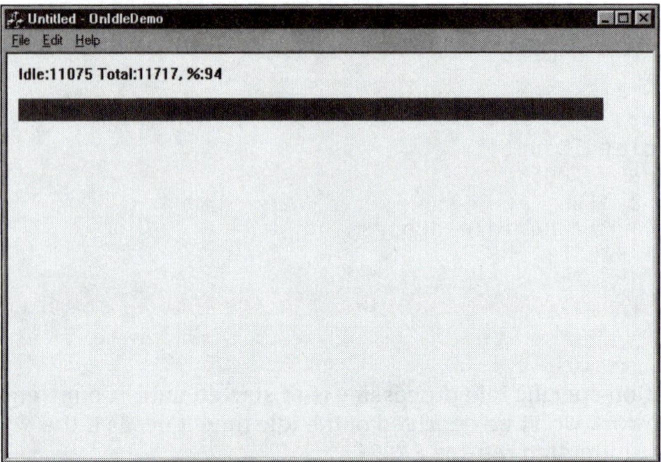

Figure 17-2: The OnIdleDemo program shows a bar graph with the relative amount of time given to the program's OnIdle() function.

The program also draws a bar graph to provide a graphical indication of the relative amount of idle processing that the application has made available to the `OnIdle()` function. If you move the mouse around or perform window operations such as resizing, the graph will decrease. That's because all of the messages that Windows services reduce the amount of processing time that's available to the `OnIdle()` function.

OnIdleDemo

CD-ROM Location: **Chap17\OnIdleDemo**

Program Name: **OnIdleDemo.EXE**

Source Code Modules in Text: `OnIdleDemo.cpp`

✦ ✦ ✦ ✦ ✦

Listing 17-2: Defining the Class Behaviors for OnIdleDemo

```
// OnIdleDemo.cpp : Defines the class behaviors
// for the application
//

/////////////////////////////////////////////////////////////
// COnIdleDemoApp commands

DWORD dwTotal = 0, dwIdle = 0, dwFirst, dwLast;

BOOL COnIdleDemoApp::OnIdle(LONG lCount)
{
  CWinApp::OnIdle(lCount);
```

```
// If dwTotal == 0, this is the first time through
// and we need to record dwFirst.
if( dwTotal == 0 )
  dwFirst = GetTickCount();

// Get the current clock tick.
DWORD dwTemp = GetTickCount();

// Calculate dwTotal—this is the total tick count
// since the first time into OnIdle(). We add one
// because the very first time through, dwTotal
// will be 0 and cause a divide by zero error. This
// extra '1' won't affect the percentage significantly
// since the values get so large.
dwTotal = dwTemp - dwFirst + 1;

// If lCount != 0, then we haven't had a skip in the
// OnIdle processing. That means we need to add to
// dwIdle the elapsed time since we came through last
// time. If lCount == 0 that means the application
// processed some messages and didn't come through
// OnIdle(). For this reason, we don't add the elapsed
// time in this case since it was chewed up while
// processing messages.
if( lCount != 0 )
  dwIdle += ( dwTemp - dwLast );

// Record the current time in dwLast since all of
// our calculations have been made.
dwLast = dwTemp;

// We need a DC so we'll get the CMainFrame class and
// then the COnIdleDemoView class. From this, we
// create a CClientDC object for painting.
CMainFrame *pFrame =
  (CMainFrame *) AfxGetMainWnd();
COnIdleDemoView *pView =
  (COnIdleDemoView *) pFrame->GetActiveView();
CClientDC ClientDC( pView );

// Calculate the percentage and store in a local
// variable since we need the value twice.
int nPercent = dwIdle * 100 / dwTotal;

// Format a CString object, and draw it to the window.
CString strInfo;
strInfo.Format( "Idle:%ld Total:%ld, %%:%d       ",
  dwIdle, dwTotal, nPercent );
ClientDC.TextOut( 10, 10, strInfo );

// Get the client RECT for the view window DC.
```

(continued)

```
    // We'll scale the bar graph to fit nicely in the
    // window, regardless of its size.
    RECT Rect;
    pView->GetClientRect( &Rect );

    // Indent the bar graph from the left, top, bottom
    // so it doesn't go to the edge of the window and
    // it's below the text we just drew. Calculate the
    // length of the bar based on the percentage of
    // OnIdle time we've gotten.
    Rect.left += 10;
    Rect.top += 40;
    int nRight = Rect.right - 10;
    Rect.bottom = Rect.top + 20;
    int nWidth = nRight - Rect.left;
    nWidth = nWidth * nPercent / 100;
    Rect.right = Rect.left + nWidth;

    // Draw the blue rectangle to indicate
    // the relative amount of OnIdle time
    // we've gotten.
    CBrush BlueBrush( RGB( 0, 0, 255 ) );
    ClientDC.FillRect( &Rect, &BlueBrush );

    // Draw a white rectangle to the right
    // of the blue bar so that any blue
    // from an old value will be erased.
    Rect.left = Rect.right;
    Rect.right = nRight;
    CBrush WhiteBrush( RGB( 255, 255, 255 ) );
    ClientDC.FillRect( &Rect, &WhiteBrush );

    return( TRUE );
}
```

Summary

We have covered two very useful Windows mechanisms: timers and OnIdle processing. With them you can create applications that are very responsive but also perform a great deal of work in the background. These mechanisms are so common, in fact, that you'll find yourself using at least one of them in almost every program you write.

✦ ✦ ✦

P A R T

Architecture

This part on application architecture shows you how to take advantage of Microsoft's application architecture scheme. The Microsoft Foundation Classes (MFC) promote an application architecture commonly referred to as document/view architecture. It provides a practical way to organize applications. Documents and data are separated into a document class that is engineered to make storage and retrieval easy. The many support functions built into MFC assist in this process. The visual representation of data within applications is handled by a View class, engineered to make display easy. A special window update function is provided as standard startup code so developers can easily draw to the screen.

✦ ✦ ✦ ✦

In This Part

Chapter 18:
Memory Management

Chapter 19:
Documents, Views, and SDI

Chapter 20:
The Layout of an MDI Application

Chapter 21:
Printing and Print Preview

Chapter 22:
The MFC for Advanced Windows User Interfaces

Chapter 23:
Status Bars and Toolbars

Chapter 24:
Tree View and List View Controls

Chapter 25:
Threads

✦ ✦ ✦ ✦

CHAPTER 18

Memory Management

✦ ✦ ✦ ✦

In This Chapter

Types of memory available

Examining operating system memory management

Defining process memory similarities and differences between Windows 98 and Windows NT

Dynamic private memory allocation

Sharing memory between processes

✦ ✦ ✦ ✦

Memory is the currency of software. Without sufficient memory, software runs sluggishly or not at all. With sufficient memory, software operates properly and can do its assigned work. However, determining what is sufficient for a particular program depends on how the program spends the available memory. Although memory prices continue to fall, memory isn't free. Developers must decide on a realistic memory budget for their software and then build software that can live within its means.

This chapter covers every type of memory available to an MFC/Win32 program running on Windows 98. Just as there are many types of currency — for example, U.S. dollars, Swiss francs, and Japanese yen — there are many types of memory. In addition to cataloging what's available, this chapter describes when and why particular types of memory are useful in a typical MFC program. One thing is clear: Even simple programs can require a world traveler's portfolio of different types of memory. Table 18-1 summarizes the types of memory available to an MFC/Win32 program.

System Memory Management

Perhaps the most important improvement that Windows 98 offers over earlier versions of Windows is its flat 32-bit addressing. A Win16 program running on Windows 3.x had to be chopped up into segments, blocks of memory ranging in size from 16 bytes to 64K. When building a Win16 program, developers must wrestle with the proper use of compiler keywords such as `_near` and `_far` to establish the proper framework for addressing. Developers writing to the Win32 API don't have to worry about these issues. Few developers leaving the Win16 API for a life of Win32 programming will miss the segmented addressing headaches they leave behind.

Table 18-1
Types of Memory Available to MFC/Win32 Programs Running on Windows 98

Category	*Type*	*Description*
Compiler	Automatic	Local variables or local objects. Created on entry to a function using stack space, and freed on exit.
	Static	Global variables and global objects defined outside the scope of any function. Static data also includes string constants. Variables and objects defined using the static keyword also add to the store of static data. The lifetime of such data is the duration that its executable file is resident in memory.
	Class	Class member data refers to variables and objects allocated in an object due to the member data defined for a class. This data lives as long as the object in which it is contained. The data in local (stack) objects is allocated on entry to a function and cleaned up on exit. Data in global (static) objects exists while the executable file is in memory.
	Dynamically Allocated	Memory allocated with calls to `malloc()` or operator `new()`. For proper memory management, applications should call `free()` or operator `delete()` on all allocated data areas and objects.
Win16	Global Heap	Memory allocated with calls to `GlobalAlloc()`. In Win16, this corresponds to an allocated segment. In Win32, such objects are allocated in a Win32 process heap [(just like `LocalAlloc()`-allocated memory)].
	Local Heap	Memory allocated with calls to `LocalAlloc()`. In Win16, this corresponds to a subsegment allocation. In Win32, such memory—like `GlobalAlloc()`-allocated memory—resides in a Win32 private heap.
	Resources	Read-only data defined in resource (.RC) files. Predefined types include menus, dialog boxes, and string tables. A program can also create custom resource types, using techniques that we'll describe later in this chapter.

Category	*Type*	*Description*
	Atoms	Strings stored in memory tables and accessed using a unique integer ID. Both the Win16 and the Win32 APIs include AddAtom(), FindAtom(), and DeleteAtom(). Internally, Windows uses atoms for registered clipboard formats and registered messages. Applications use the global atom table for dynamic data exchange (DDE) support. Global atom routines include GlobalAddAtom() and GlobalFindAtom().
	Window Extra Bytes	Windows creates instance data for each window created. Window extra bytes are private bytes in addition to what the system itself stores. Access these bytes using various Win16/Win32 APIs that we describe in this chapter.
	Class Extra Bytes	Windows creates instance data for each defined window class (different from the C++/MFC window class). Class extra bytes are private bytes in addition to what the system stores in class data. Access these bytes using various Win16/Win32 APIs that we describe in this chapter.
	Properties	Attributes dynamically connected to windows. For example, you could create a COLOR attribute and attach a color index. Access by calling Win16/Win32 routines, SetProp(), GetProp(), and RemoveProp().
Win32	Private Pages	Allocates memory in page increments (4K in Windows 98, possibly larger in Windows NT) by calling Virtual-Alloc(). This Win32 function also reserves ranges of addresses when called with the MEM_RESERVE flag.
	Private Heap	Memory allocated with calls to HeapAlloc(). Multiple heaps can be created in a Win32 process by calling HeapCreate(). Get a handle to the process default heap by calling GetProcessHeap().
	Thread Local Storage	Memory allocated on a per-thread basis. There are two types: dynamic thread local storage is allocated by calls to TlsAlloc(), and static thread local storage is allocated by the compiler.

(continued)

Table 18-1 *(continued)*

Category	*Type*	*Description*
	Shared Pages	Memory allocated with calls to `MapViewOfFile()`, which can also create a view into a memory mapped file depending on the file handle parameter. An invalid file handle value (–1) creates shared pages, and a valid file handle creates a memory mapped file.
	Shared Sections	Static (global) variables declared with `__declspec(thread)` define a shared section in an executable image. When loaded into memory, such variables are shared between processes in both Windows 98 and Windows NT programs.
	Memory Mapped Files	Shared pages connected to a process address space with calls to `MapViewOfFile()`. Note that this is the same API used to create shared pages.
	Executable Image	Executable (.EXE) file or dynamic link library (.DLL) file in memory.

Windows 98 runs many types of programs, including MS-DOS programs, Win16 programs, and of course Win32 programs. For a complete picture of how the Intel-86 processors are able to do this, you must understand Intel's four addressing modes for its 32-bit x86 processors. These modes are: teal mode, 16-bit protected mode, 32-bit paged mode, and 16-bit virtual 8086 mode. Because Win32 programs run in 32-bit paged mode, our discussion focuses on this mode.

Intel-86 32-bit paged addressing mode

The Win32 API was designed for processors that could support two memory features: 32-bit addressing and paged memory. Within the Intel-86 family of processors, only Intel 80386 and later CPUs meet these requirements. Earlier processors — including the 8088 and the 80286 — don't meet the memory feature requirements of Win32 and therefore cannot run Windows 98.

Later members of this processor family — including the 80386, the i486, and the Pentium — meet both requirements. All of these processors support a single page size: 4K. As such, Win32 programs running under Windows 98 must work with this page size.

But don't assume that every Win32 implementation will have 4K pages. For example Digital's Alpha processor, a platform that runs Windows NT, has 8K pages. And

Win32 was designed to accommodate other page sizes, including 16K pages and even 32K pages. If you create Win32 software that somehow relies on a 4K page size, you may create incompatibilities when running on a non-4K page processor.

The addressing scheme that's described is basically hard wired into the Intel processors. Because it represents a reasonable scheme for paged, virtual memory, this same approach is also used by Windows NT — even when running on non-Intel processors.

The three parts of a virtual address

Intel's 32-bit paged addressing works by dividing a 32-bit address into three parts. A 32-bit address has one 12-bit portion and two 10-bit portions. To help you understand how this works, the low-order 12 bits are described first.

The low-order 12 bits are described first because they are the simplest to understand. They describe an offset into a single page of memory. As mentioned earlier, a page is 4K, which makes sense given that 2^{12} is 4K (4,096). Individual pages are little more than arrays of bytes with 4K entries. Of course, a 12-bit address can't buy what it used to. To store any useful amount of data, multiple pages are needed.

You can access more pages by making use of the middle 10 bits in your 32-bit virtual address. Those 10 bits are used as an offset into a special memory page called a *page table*. A page table resides in a 4K memory page and can refer to 1,024 other pages that each hold application code or data. Taken together, the 22 address bits can address 4MB of RAM. Although 4MB used to be a lot of memory, it isn't much anymore. To gain access to the full address space of the processor, you have to use the final 10 bits from the virtual address.

The high-order 10 bits of a 32-bit address are used as an index into yet another page table. But this page table is special because it points to other page tables, rather than code or data pages. For this reason, it has a special name: a page directory. Like other page tables, page directories contain arrays of 32-bit values. In all, up to 1,024 page tables can be addressed from a given page directory. If you do the math, you'll see that a single page directory can reference up to 4GB of memory. As you may know, that is the size of the address space for 32-bit Intel-86 CPUs.

One question that may still concern you is how the addressing mechanism knows how to get started. That is, how does it know which page holds the page directory? The page directory is referenced in a special CPU register: the CR3 register. (There are also CR0, CR1, and CR2 registers, but their use is beyond the scope of this discussion.) The CPU relies on operating system software to manage the contents of this register. That is why different operating systems with different memory schemes can all run on Intel-86 processors. Among the operating systems that run on Intel processors are MS-DOS, 16-bit Windows 3.x, Windows NT, UNIX, OS/2, and iRMX (an Intel operating system).

The translation lookaside buffer

Before getting into Windows 98-specific memory management issues, one more point about paged addressing should be made. It might seem as though each access to an individual memory location requires access to two other memory locations: a page directory and a page table. That would make paged memory three times as costly to access as nonpaged memory.

This would be true, except that the processors maintain a cache — called the *translation lookaside buffer* (TLB) — that stores the most recently used page table entries. The size of the cache varies by individual processor but is generally quite small. For example, a TLB on a 486 can cache up to 32 page table entries. In turn, these entries reference 128K of code or data.

This small number of cache entries proves to be sufficient in most cases because most software exhibits a trait called *locality of reference*. In other words — speaking metaphorically, of course — most software chases its own tail, running in circles while working on a tiny dataset that tends to be close together. Cache hit rates of 95 percent and higher make performance problems related to memory addressing fairly rare, but not impossible.

Although most software tends to work in a way that the TLB can accommodate, there's no guarantee that every program will do so. From our description of how memory is addressed, it should be easy to write software that renders the TLB useless. For example, allocate 33 pages of RAM, and then circulate among them in a round-robin style. A program based on such a memory access scheme would run noticeably slower than a program that respected the role of the TLB. Keep this in mind when designing the way your software arranges and accesses its memory.

Windows 98 per-process address space

So how does Windows 98 create a private, per-process address space? At first blush, you might think that it updates the CPU's CR3 register on a context switch. Although Windows NT and other operating systems work that way, Windows 98 doesn't. Instead, Windows 98 sets up the CR3 register once — during system initialization — and leaves it alone during normal system operation. A private, per-process address space on Windows 98 isn't set up by using the processor's CR3 register. Instead, Windows 98 plays some tricks during a context switch, setting up a memory context.

Windows 98 memory contexts

Windows 98 is less generous than Windows NT, which provides each process with a private address space. As mentioned elsewhere, part of the reason is that Windows 98 itself doesn't have a generous budget. Giving each process a private address space would cost a 4K page directory plus several 4K page tables per process.

Instead, Windows 98 creates a single set of page tables. During a context switch between a thread in one process and a thread in another process, Windows 98 updates the page tables. The view that each process sees is called a *memory context*. Part of the address space consists of system dynamic link libraries (DLLs), which are shared by all processes. The page table entries that refer to this part of the address space — from 2GB to 4GB — don't ever have to change. Instead, during a context switch, the only page entries that have to change are those associated with private, per-process pages — that is, from 4MB to 2GB. As might be expected, the changes made by Windows 98 to the page tables appear to each process as the magic of the operating system. Each sees private data in one range of addresses, and shared memory in another.

Whatever tricks are played by the operating system, the processor's addressing mechanism stays the same. It's up to the operating system's memory manager to decide what memory should be made visible to which process. A particular code or data page can be mapped in the address space of a single process or into the address spaces of multiple processes. Windows 98 does both of these, thanks to the flexibility of the Intel processors.

For compatibility with Windows 3.x, Win16 programs on Windows 98 don't have a private address space. Instead, they run in a common address space. This enables the type of memory sharing that Win16 programs are used to: free access to memory pointers, object handles, and memory handles. When converting Win16 programs to the Win32 API, any Win16-style memory sharing must be updated to support Win32-compatible sharing techniques.

Windows 98 and Windows NT share a common executable file format for Win32 programs. This is significant because executable files in both operating systems are loaded as memory mapped files. As will be discussed later in this chapter, this mechanism relies on the virtual memory manager to connect a disk-based file with a range of memory addresses. Pages are read from disk only when the corresponding memory addresses are accessed.

The file format of a Win32 executable is called the *portable executable format*. It is one of several executable file formats created for various Microsoft operating systems. Table 18-2 summarizes the executable file formats used for other Microsoft operating systems. The Signature column identifies a two-letter code in the file header that identifies the specific type of an executable file.

Table 18-2
Executable File Formats Used by Various Microsoft Operating Systems

Executable File Type	*Signature*	*Description*
MS-DOS program	MZ	Mark Zbikowski's relocatable executable file format. Mark created the MS-DOS 2.0 executable file format, and made himself immortal by using his initials for the executable file signature.
Win16	NE	New executable files are segment-oriented Win16 programs. OS/2 1.x used the same file format for its 16-bit programs.
Win32	PE	Portable executable files are Win32 programs. This file format is used for Win32 programs built for Windows 98 and Windows NT.
Windows virtual	LE	Linear executable files are 32-bit device drivers, sometimes called VxDs, introduced with Windows 3.0 and still used by Windows 98.

From the perspective of process address space, Windows 98 and Windows NT share another common trait: use of a no-man's-land address range. These are invalid addresses that exist to help catch various types of pointer errors, in particular the use of NULL pointers. On Windows NT, there are two such areas, each of which is 64K. One is at the base of the address space (address 0 to 10000h). The other is at the top of the application's address space (from 7FFF0000 to 7FFFFFFF).

The Windows 98 no-man's-land, on the other hand, is a single 4MB area at the bottom of the address space. Any attempt to access memory in this range causes a processor exception (as it also does on Windows NT). Both operating systems terminate any process with an unhandled exception. Hidden in the Windows 98 no-man's-land are parts of real-mode MS-DOS, as well as an area reserved for use by Win16 programs.

It's interesting to note that the no-man's-land for Win16 programs is only 64K. This exists to help catch pointers that access segment 0. Other than this similarity, the memory view of Win16 programs is quite different from that seen by Win32 programs. For backward compatibility, a Win16 program running on Windows 98 has almost the same memory view as it does when running on Windows 3.1.

Another trait shared by Windows 98 and Windows NT is the way in which DLLs are mapped into the address space of a process. With both systems, application-specific DLLs get mapped into the range of addresses set aside for application-specific uses — that is, below 2GB.

The only exception on Windows 98 are system DLLs, which provide all of the functions that make up the Win32 API. These are loaded into the shared memory area between 2GB and 3GB. By their very nature, these DLLs are shared by all Win32 applications. As such, it makes sense that they reside in the part of the address space that's shared by all processes.

As you can see, there are some similarities between the way Windows 98 and Windows NT provide memory access to a Win32 process. Now, let's look at some of the differences.

Process memory differences between Windows 98 and Windows NT

The chief differences between Windows 98 and Windows NT involve security. Windows NT erects rigid barriers between processes. On the other hand, Windows 98 is more trusting, continuing the tradition started by MS-DOS and the various 16-bit versions of Windows. Although Windows 98 provides each process with a private address space, everything within the shared memory area is fully accessible.

The chief benefit that Windows 98 derives from this open, trusting approach is that it requires fewer resources than Windows NT. In the same way that a sophisticated building security system requires more resources — wiring, electricity, security guards, and cameras — so does a more secure operating system. Windows 98 was built to run on an 80486 processor with 8MB of RAM (although 16MB is probably more realistic). To support its silicon fortress, Windows NT needs at least a Pentium and 32MB of RAM. (Although once again more RAM — say 48MB to 64MB — makes a difference in overall performance.)

Windows NT requires more processor resources because the bulk of its GUI system is implemented outside the address space of a Win32 process. For example, each call to create a window or draw graphics issues requests that are implemented in a separate process and a separate address space from the calling process. The name of this process is the *Win32 Subsystem*. Running in a separate address space, core operating system components are safe from both accidental and deliberate tampering. The cost of this security is in performance — that is, more resources are required to get the same performance as on more open systems such as Windows 98.

Windows 98 places all system libraries within its 2GB to 3GB shared memory area. For better or worse, all of the system libraries are within easy reach of every Win32 (and Win16) program. When your Win32 program is running on Windows 98, it never takes more than a simple function call (plus perhaps a jump instruction) to reach the actual system functions. On Windows NT, there's typically a context switch between a function call and the code that actually does the work. (However, simple query functions on Windows NT are as fast as they are on Windows 98.)

Because it was designed with security in mind, Windows NT doesn't share memory lightly. For example, there is no common, shared memory area as in Windows 98. Instead, nothing gets shared that isn't explicitly assigned to be shared. This enhanced security also makes Windows NT more robust than Windows 98. You can have a higher degree of confidence that shared data isn't being viewed by someone who shouldn't see it.

On Windows 98, on the other hand, shared memory is allocated in the shared memory area, where it is immediately accessible to every process in the system. If security is an issue for you, this might be a problem. Except for knowing the address, nothing special is needed for a process to read or write data stored in the shared area. (And it's not hard to write a brute force routine that scans shared addresses for interesting tidbits.)

Setting aside security concerns, the different memory sharing approaches can create programming problems. (Security concerns are certainly important, but security isn't our focus here.) At issue is how to share memory between two Win32 programs that will run on both Windows 98 and Windows NT. You'll use the same APIs to access shared memory. So what is different?

The differences arise from the fact that a shared object in Windows NT can be mapped to different addresses in different processes. Consider a 64K shared buffer. When made available to three different processes on Windows NT, it might get mapped to address 800000h in one process, to 850000h in a second process, and to 900000h in a third. Although you can try to map a shared object to a particular address, it's difficult and — depending on the size of the object and the contents of each address space — may be impossible. A single memory object can get mapped to different locations in different Win32 processes on Windows NT because each process address space is independent of every other process address space.

On Windows 98, a shared object created by one process is visible to every process, at the same address. As mentioned earlier, that address is always between 2GB and 3GB. When 2 — or even 200 — other Win32 processes access the shared memory, it is always at the same address on Windows 98.

At issue here is how you write a single Win32 program that will share memory properly on both operating systems. The short answer is to avoid passing addresses directly between Win32 programs, and to make sure to use the proper memory sharing APIs. In addition, when writing memory sharing programs, be sure to test them on Windows NT. It is, after all, the fussier of the two operating systems. When memory sharing is discussed in more detail, tricks for writing memory sharing code compatible on all Win32 platforms will also be provided.

An important improvement over Windows 3.1 that both Windows 98 and Windows NT provide to Windows programmers involves cleanup of system memory. That's the next topic discussed.

System memory cleanup

A problem shared by every 16-bit version of Windows — from Version 1.01, released in 1985, to 3.11, released in 1993 — is the inability to clean up all allocated system memory. This problem arises from what was, in retrospect, a bad design decision.

Windows required applications to manage the creation and cleanup of objects allocated in system memory. When Win16 applications forget to delete objects, system memory is lost. On systems that operate continually for weeks or months without being rebooted, the behavior of such applications causes one of the various system heaps to become exhausted. The inevitable result is a system crash of one form or another.

To understand how Windows 98 and Windows NT solve this problem, it helps to understand why the problem occurred in the first place. The primary reason why Windows 3.1 (and earlier versions) didn't remove system objects from memory was to enable sharing of GDI drawing objects between programs. To solve the problem, the Win32 specification differs from Win16 in this one point: Win32 doesn't recognize the sharing of GDI objects between processes.

In 16-bit Windows, all GDI objects are designed to be freely shareable between programs. Shareable objects include bitmaps, brushes, DCs, fonts, metafiles, palettes, pens, and regions. Ironically, the reason for object sharing was to save memory; several cooperating programs could pool their GDI drawing objects, thereby reducing the load on the GDI's heap. After all, six red pens consume more memory than a single red pen. To enable this sharing, Windows 3.1 leaves all leftover GDI drawing objects in memory. Other types of objects — including windows, menus, cursors, and icons — automatically get cleaned up at application termination time. Leftover GDI objects that aren't actually being shared represent memory forever lost in Windows (at least until Windows is restarted).

When running Win16 programs, Windows 98 and Windows NT continue to respect the rights of Win16 programs to share objects. This can cause a problem on these systems, because a buggy Win16 program can consume system resources and potentially harm the operation of Win32 programs. These operating systems defend themselves against wasteful Win16 programs in several ways.

Windows 98 and Windows NT delete leftover GDI objects from Win16 programs, but only when no Win16 programs are running. In this way, Windows 98 and Windows NT respect the sharing rights of Win16 programs. But when all Win16 programs have terminated, GDI objects created by 16-bit programs can be removed from memory. The effect of buggy, wasteful Win16 programs will diminish over time, as they are replaced by newer Win32 programs.

Windows 98 has a second defense, which seems like something Windows probably should have been doing all along. When either a Win16 program or a Win32 program attempts to create a GDI object, Windows 98 doesn't blindly create a new one, as was done in previous versions. Instead, it determines whether an object of that type already exists. If so, the previously created object is reused. A reference count ensures that objects aren't deleted prematurely. For example, if a program asks GDI to create a red pen and no red pen exists in the system, GDI creates one and returns a handle to that object. But if a red pen already exists, GDI increments the reference count to the existing red pen and lets the caller have a handle to the existing pen. Neither the original creator nor the new user need know that GDI is enabling objects to be shared.

Incidentally, the implicit sharing of GDI objects between programs on Windows 98 can cause spurious assertion messages with older versions of MFC. When an MFC program creates a GDI object — wrapped in an MFC `CBitmap`, `CBrush`, or `CPen`, for example — MFC debug builds verify that handle values are unique. For example, if a program creates two red pens, Windows 98 provides the same handle for both pens. This behavior isn't expected by versions of MFC prior to version 3.1. In fact, these older versions of MFC check to make sure that handle tables contain no duplicate values. When duplicates are found, MFC displays an assertion — in the form of a large, ugly message box. You can ignore such messages (or upgrade to a version of MFC that is Windows 98-aware).

For programmers experienced with Win16 programming, the automatic cleanup provided for Win32 programs on Windows 98 and Windows NT is a welcome relief. No longer do you need to worry about system crashes caused by exhausted system heaps. All objects exist on a per-process basis, and when a process terminates, its leftover objects are deleted.

Automatic cleanup of system objects comes at a slight cost: Win32 GDI objects can't be freely shared between processes in the way they could in Win16. If two programs each need to use a red pen, each program must create its own. Note that Clipboard sharing of GDI objects — a set that includes metafiles and bitmaps — is fully supported in Win32 just as it was in Win16. Only the internal implementation has changed, which shouldn't affect normal Clipboard use.

Automatic cleanup of leftover objects isn't an excuse for sloppy coding. All objects that you create should be accounted for. You have several means for checking your code to ensure that objects are cleaned up properly. One is built into MFC and the IDE debugger. Debug builds of MFC programs keep a list of all objects that have been allocated and destroyed. At program termination time, a list of all leftover objects gets displayed — what MFC calls memory leaks — that includes system objects as well as all dynamically allocated chunks of memory. To see this list, you must run your program in a debugger, such as the IDE debugger, which can display the MFC's debugging messages. Another tool that detects leftover system objects — but not internally allocated data — is Nu-Mega's Bounds Checker.

One minor hitch in automatic cleanup involves global atoms. An atom is a unique integer ID that can be used to access a variable-length character string. The system libraries in both Windows NT and Windows 98 create atoms in the global atom table for registered system messages and registered clipboard formats. Because such values are shared between processes, they must reside in a shared memory area. Although both operating systems could clean up the global atom table, they don't. The good news is that the number of available atom values is large: about 1K atoms on Windows 98 and 16K atoms on Windows NT. And because duplicate strings create the same atom, you won't exhaust a heap by repeatedly running a program that registers the same string in the atom table but forgets to clean it up. Nonetheless, you'll want to keep in mind that this is one resource that the system doesn't manage perfectly.

One possible hitch for the global atom table is caused by applications that use Windows' dynamic data exchange (DDE). As you may know, this is a data sharing mechanism that involves messages (such as `WM_DDE_DATA`) sent between windows. DDE doesn't use atoms for the data being shared, but rather for human-readable data identifiers. (For example, a range of spreadsheet cells might be identified by the string "A12:C52".) If you're creating Windows programs that use low-level DDE to share data, make sure you destroy all atoms that you create. (Alternatively, use Windows' DDE-Management Library—DDEML—which properly handles the cleanup of the global atom table.)

Process Private Memory

Although you might be tempted to stick with `new` as your memory allocator, it's not always the best choice. With large objects, for example, you get more control by using the native Win32 memory allocators. For performance-critical or hard real-time applications, you might decide to create per-class allocators. Bjarne Stroustrup recommends this for frequently used classes in Chapter 10 of his book, *The Design and Evolution of C++*.

Even if operator `new` is your primary allocator, you might want to store the resulting pointer somewhere other than in a regular variable. In particular, the Win32 API provides memory wallets—window extra bytes and thread local storage—to tuck away data associated with operating system objects. Such nooks and crannies can help simplify the relationship between a program's data and operating system objects. Even if you never use these memory cubbyholes, learning about them will help you understand the operation of various user interface objects. For example, dialog box controls—including edits, list boxes, combo boxes, and buttons—use window extra bytes to store control-specific data.

The following sections describe every available place to store data that is private to a process. The focus in this section is private memory; shared memory types are covered later in this chapter.

This layered approach has the hardware on the bottom, and the connection to the application on the top. Although many types of memory are available, all ultimately rely on private pages that have been allocated in the process address space. In addition to providing per-process pages, Win32 enables the creation of per-thread data. Finally, there is a set of APIs for heap allocation. Visual C++ provides its own default heap allocator that it builds on top of raw pages. In addition, the Win32 heap allocator provides basic heap support, and—for backward compatibility—supports both types of Win16 heap allocation functions.

Microsoft operating systems always seem to provide memory allocation APIs in pairs. For example, the 16-bit OS/2 API provides `DosAllocSeg()` to allocate segments and `DosSubAlloc()` to allocate subsegments. (Yes, Microsoft did create this portion of the OS/2 API.) Win16 provides a comparable pair of allocation routines, with `GlobalAlloc()` for allocating segments and `LocalAlloc()` for subdividing segments into smaller, subsegment-sized chunks.

Win32 continues the tradition, providing `VirtualAlloc()` to allocate pages and `HeapAlloc()` for subpage allocation. These are the first two types of memory discussed. (Dual sets of allocators are sometimes referred to as "biggie" and "teeny allocators," because this captures the key difference between sets of allocators: granularity of allocated memory.)

Allocating pages

In the paged memory environment of Windows 98 (and Windows NT), all memory available to a Win32 process resides in paged memory, meaning it resides in one page or another. Several subpage allocators are supported. Only two Win32 functions add new pages to the address space of a process. One function, `VirtualAlloc()`, allocates private pages. The other function, `MapViewOfFile()`, allocates shared pages. Every other allocator relies on these two — directly or indirectly — to provide memory pages.

The Win32 private page allocator is `VirtualAlloc()`. In addition to allocating private-process pages, it has another role. It reserves memory address ranges without actually causing the consumption of any physical space — either in RAM-based pages or in disk-based page-file pages. This enables a program to reserve large address ranges, with no cost in terms of pages consumed. As needed, sets of memory pages can be mapped to the reserved address range. For example, tiny incremental portions of a large chunk of data from a gigabyte-sized database can be loaded into "real" memory as needed. To allocate a new page in a range of reserved addresses, a program calls this same function — `VirtualAlloc()` — to commit memory.

To allocate shared pages, a Win32 process calls `MapViewOfFile()`. The name of this function is quite strange, but it reflects the function's dual role. On the one hand, `MapViewOfFile()` creates a view into a memory-mapped file. On the other hand, it allocates shared pages, which is another way to describe a memory-mapped file that also happens to be the system's paging file. The allocation of shared pages is discussed later in this chapter.

For now, the focus is process-specific page allocation, beginning with a look at how `VirtualAlloc()` lets you reserve address space. Then, the allocation of pages is discussed. Finally, stack allocation in a Win32 program is covered.

Reserving address space

Win32 enables you to manage your process address space. Most programmers don't think of the address space as a resource to be managed. After all, with billions of addresses, why be choosy? But direct control of the address space can be helpful in some situations.

For example, it's helpful to manage the address space when you need to dynamically allocate a block of memory for a data object that might grow. Although it's not always necessary, keeping all of the parts of the object in contiguous memory simplifies data handling. To enable a block to grow in contiguous memory, however, most operating systems require you to preallocate memory beyond what you actually need.

Allocating more memory than you need is wasteful, but it's sometimes the easiest way to get what you need. Otherwise, when an object outgrows one piece of memory, it may need to be moved to a larger space. Moving large objects is expensive, in terms of processor time, and can fragment the address space. Of course, there are alternatives to preallocating too much space. You can move objects when they grow, and you can use linked lists to logically connect different data blocks. But that creates other problems such as list management overhead and bugs due to the complexity of data handling.

The Win32 API provides a much more elegant solution to this problem. Instead of wasting memory by overallocating what you need, you can allocate the exact number of pages for a given block of data. (On average, the wasted memory will be one-half page, or 2,048 bytes.) But that is the second half of the solution.

Before allocating any pages for an object that might grow, you need to reserve a range of addresses that can accommodate the maximum expected size. Once addresses have been reserved, you allocate memory by committing memory pages from the range of reserved addresses. At first, you only allocate for the initial memory needed. As memory needs increase, you commit incremental pages. This makes efficient use of memory by avoiding the wasteful practice of overallocating. In addition, new pages added to the existing set are accessible in a range of addresses that are contiguous with previously allocated pages.

An example will help clarify this. Suppose you need to read a file into memory that occupies 100K, and you anticipate that this object will never grow larger than 500K. Using the Win32 virtual memory APIs, you first reserve a 500K range of memory addresses. Within the range of reserved addresses, you commit 100K to "real" memory so that you can read the file into memory. As needed, you extend the size of the committed pages to accommodate the growth in your object.

It's important to understand when memory actually gets consumed. In particular, no pages of physical memory are consumed by reserving addresses (aside from a small amount on the virtual memory manager's address list). As proof, try to access memory in a range of reserved (but not committed) addresses. You'll get an error — a general protection fault — that, if unhandled, causes your program to terminate.

Although reserving addresses doesn't give you access to physical memory, it's a necessary first step to plan for the object's growth. Otherwise, another part of your application — or a DLL used by your application — might use addresses just beyond the end of your allocated area. If that happens, you're back to the problem of having to move the entire data object when you need the object to grow.

To reserve a range of addresses, call VirtualAlloc() and pass the MEM_RESERVE flag. This is one of three flags defined for VirtualAlloc()'s third parameter. The function itself is defined as follows:

```
LPVOID VirtualAlloc( LPVOID lpvAddress, DWORD dwSize,
  DWORD dwAction, DWORD dwAccess);
```

The lpvAddress parameter is a memory address. When reserving a range of addresses, set this to NULL for the system to pick a starting address, or to a non-NULL value if you have a desired starting address. When committing a previously reserved address to memory pages, this is rounded down to a page (4K) boundary. When reserving a range of addresses, this is rounded down to a region (64K) boundary.

The dwSize argument is the number of bytes to reserve or commit. This number is rounded up to the nearest page (4K) boundary when committing and to the nearest region (64K) boundary when reserving.

The dwAction parameter is MEM_RESERVE to reserve a range of addresses, MEM_COMMIT to commit previously reserved addresses to memory pages, or a combination of MEM_RESERVE|MEM_COMMIT to reserve and commit the memory. (MEM_COMMIT by itself does the same thing.)

The dwAccess argument is a flag field for specifying the page access status. Among the defined flags are PAGE_READWRITE for full access and PAGE_NOACCESS to make pages off limits. (Windows 98 doesn't support PAGE_GUARD.)

The return value to VirtualAlloc() is either the base address of the memory region, or NULL to indicate failure. A set of reserved addresses is referred to as a *region*. The granularity of regions — for both Windows 98 and Windows NT — is 64K. In other words, if you reserve a one-byte range of addresses, at least 64K addresses are included in the region. To put it another way, the entire 4GB virtual address space could hold 64K regions if each were 64K.

Allocating memory pages

You can allocate memory pages with VirtualAlloc() in either two steps or one step. The two-step approach involves first reserving the memory and then committing the memory to pages. Here's an example of the two-step approach:

```
// Reserve a 64K range of addresses.
LPVOID p = VirtualAlloc( 0, 0x10000, MEM_RESERVE,
  PAGE_READWRITE );
if( p == NULL ){
  /* Error. */
 }
```

```
// Commit a 4K range of addresses.
LPVOID pTemp = VirtualAlloc( p, 0x1000, MEM_COMMIT,
  PAGE_READWRITE );
if( pTemp == NULL ){
  /* Error. */
  }
```

The first call to `VirtualAlloc()` reserves a 64K region of addresses, located at a site chosen by the operating system. The second call commits 4K of the reserved addresses to a memory page. Notice how this code fragment stores the return value from each call separately. Because of the different granularity of pages and regions, as well as the possibility of failure of either call, you need to think of each type of call as a separate, independent memory allocation action.

The one-step approach involves a call to `VirtualAlloc()` with the `MEM_COMMIT` flag. In other words, you don't reserve addresses before you get pages; instead, you combine a reserve and a commit request into a single call:

```
// Commit a 4K range of addresses.
LPVOID pTemp = VirtualAlloc( 0, 0x1000, MEM_COMMIT,
  PAGE_READWRITE);

if( pTemp == NULL ){
  /* Error. *
  }
```

To decommit previously committed pages, or to unreserve a range of previously reserved addresses, you call `VirtualFree()`. When called with the `MEM_DECOMMIT` flag, pages are decommitted (but the address range stays reserved). To release a range of reserved messages, you call `VirtualFree()` and specify `MEM_RELEASE`.

The complete set of Win32 virtual memory functions is summarized in Table 18-3. Most are straightforward and require no further explanation other than to direct your attention to the Win32 function name in the Win32 help database or documentation. The final set of private pages that are directly allocated for a Win32 process are the pages for the stack, which are covered next.

Table 18-3
Functions That Control Process Page Allocation

Function	***Description***
`VirtualAlloc()`	Reserves a range of addresses and/or allocates pages of memory.
`VirtualFree()`	Decommits a reserved range of addresses and/or frees pages of allocated memory.

(continued)

Table 18-3 *(continued)*	
Function	***Description***
`VirtualLock()`	Adds a set of pages to the core working set of a process. Although the pages can be written to the page file, they will be read back into memory whenever threads in the process are scheduled to run.
`VirtualProtect()`	Changes the access protection on a set of committed pages in the current process.
`VirtualProtectEx()`	Changes the access protection on a set of committed pages in any process in the system for which the caller has sufficient access.
`VirtualQuery()`	Returns virtual memory details about a specific address in the current process.
`VirtualQueryEx()`	Returns virtual memory details about a specific address in any process in the system for which the caller has sufficient access.
`VirtualUnlock()`	Removes a set of pages from the core working set of a process so it doesn't have to be in memory when threads in the process are executing.

Allocating stack space

A *stack* is a temporary memory area used by the compiler for short-term memory needs. The stack holds four types of data: a function's local variables, parameters passed when a function is called, register values, and return addresses. Use of the stack is quite dynamic, rising and falling like the tides.

Perhaps the most important issue regarding stacks is the stack size. The default stack size for Win32 threads on both Windows 98 and Windows NT is 1MB. For Win32 programs running on Win32s, a slightly smaller stack is available: only 128K. If you write a Win32 program that either uses a lot of local variables or does a lot of recursion, you should test your application on Win32s to make sure that you don't overflow available stack space.

Compiler memory allocation

Although understanding page allocation enhances your knowledge of the Win32 API, most MFC programmers will probably rely on the default Visual C++ allocator to get dynamically allocated memory. For that reason alone, the compiler memory allocator has earned the right to be described prior to the native Win32 heap allocators.

An important characteristic of the compiler's allocator is that individual heaps are created on a per-module basis. (In Microsoft-speak, the term *module* doesn't refer to a program source file, but to an executable image such as an .EXE program or a .DLL dynamic link library.) This is an important factor when building dynamic link libraries, because an application can use any memory object that its dynamic link libraries create for it (because all exist in a single address space). However, if a DLL exits from memory, the C-runtime library destroys the heaps that the compiler created for that DLL.

When deciding which allocator to use, an important issue is cost in terms of memory consumed per allocated object. The discussion of `VirtualAlloc()` didn't address this issue because page allocation overhead is small relative to page size. But because heap allocators are often used to allocate relatively small chunks of memory, issues such as per-allocation overhead and granularity can become important.

MFC uses a custom allocator instead of using the native Win32 allocator. (By *native allocator*, we mean `HeapAlloc()` and associated API functions.) The reasons are mostly historical. The Win32 heap allocator on Windows NT 3.1 was inefficient. With a granularity of 32 bytes and an overhead of 16 bytes per object, it proved too costly when allocating large numbers of tiny objects. As will be discussed, heap support is significantly improved in Windows NT and even better on Windows 98. At some point, Microsoft may modify MFC to rely on the operating system allocator instead of its own. To give you an idea of what might motivate such a change, the default Visual C++ heap allocator will be discussed next.

MFC's default memory allocator

The MFC default allocator is an old friend with a new face. The friend — familiar to C programmers — is `malloc()`. Its new face is a Win32-specific implementation that relies on `VirtualAlloc()` to allocate pages for its heap.

The cost of allocation for each heap object is 12 bytes. Those 12 bytes are consumed in the following way: Each heap block has a 4-byte header plus an 8-byte node on a linked list of block descriptors. As a result, allocating a 24 byte buffer costs 36 bytes. Here's an example:

```
//   Data bytes:       24
// + Header bytes:      4
// + Block descriptor: 8
//                   -------
//   Total Cost:       36 bytes
void *pData = malloc( 24 );
```

Another allocation issue involves allocation granularity. *Allocation granularity* is the rounding factor or multiple when a particular size is requested. The default allocator has a granularity of 4 bytes. The average waste due to rounding up in a large number of objects is approximately 2 bytes — a relatively small amount to waste.

The Visual C++ default allocator is a straightforward, general-purpose allocator. When searching through the heap to satisfy allocation requests, it uses a first-fit algorithm. As it searches, it coalesces adjacent free blocks. As needed, it adds more pages to its free store in 64K increments. Each region can grow to 1MB, and the allocator itself can accommodate 64 regions, for a total 64MB heap.

When building a release version of an MFC program, calls to operator `new()` — for both `CObject`-derived and non-`CObject`-derived classes — cause calls to `malloc()`. The characteristic of release programs that is of interest here is that the _DEBUG preprocessor symbol is not defined. Also, half of MFC's link libraries are reserved for release builds, which don't include the diagnostic assertions of the debug version.

Memory allocation gets interesting with a debug version of an MFC program. Debug builds cause the _DEBUG preprocessor symbol to become defined. Among other things, the definition of _DEBUG triggers the availability of the MFC diagnostic allocator. (It also triggers use of the debug link libraries.) The source code to the diagnostic allocator appears in `AFXMEM.CPP`. The diagnostic allocator is not a substitute for the Visual C++ allocator. Instead, it's a layer that does some extra work to help trap certain common memory problems. Ultimately, the debug allocator itself calls `malloc()`. The following section will describe how the diagnostic allocator works and suggest some ways you can take advantage of it.

The MFC diagnostic allocator

Here's a loaded question that your manager may have already asked — or perhaps should ask: How do you find a bug that involves writing past the end of a memory buffer? Some developers rely on luck and hard work to avoid writing such code. Given the dynamic nature of code, however, managing that approach quickly becomes too complicated. Other developers use memory wrapper functions that are built to automatically detect such problems. When a problem is detected, a notification alerts the developer. MFC provides this type of memory wrapper function to make certain types of bug detection almost automatic.

The MFC diagnostic allocator defines its own global operator `new()` and its own `CObject::operator new()`. Both eventually call `malloc()`, but not before adding a few features to help catch common memory errors.

Among the types of problems that MFC's diagnostic allocator helps locate are memory leaks (allocated objects not freed), buffer underflow and overflow (writing prior to the start or after the end of a buffer), use of uninitialized buffers, and use of a buffer after it has been freed. Although the diagnostic allocator can't always diagnose the exact cause of these problems, it can get you started in the right direction. If there's a problem with a particular memory block, for example, the diagnostic allocator can identify the source file and the line of code that allocated that memory.

To do that, the diagnostic allocator has to store additional information, which it does by adding 36 bytes to every allocation using operator `new()`. Every object so allocated has a 28-byte header that stores key values for allocated memory blocks.

Eight extra bytes are also allocated as a no-man's-land: four before and four after the object. These bytes help locate writes beyond the boundaries of an allocated memory block. (By the way, this is different from the address space no-man's-land that a Win32 process sees when running on Windows 98 and Windows NT.) Here's the structure for the diagnostic allocator's memory block header, as defined in AFXMEM.CPP:

```
struct CBlockHeader
{
  struct CBlockHeader* pBlockHeaderNext;
  struct CBlockHeader* pBlockHeaderPrev;
  LPCSTR               lpszFileName;
  int                  nLine;
  size_t               nDataSize;
  enum CMemoryState::blockUsage use;
  LONG                 lRequest;
  BYTE                 gap[nNoMansLandSize];
  // followed by:
  //  BYTE             data[nDataSize];
  //  BYTE             anotherGap[nNoMansLandSize];
  BYTE* pbData()
 { return (BYTE*) (this + 1); }
};
```

Although 36 bytes are a lot to add to every object allocated, keep in mind that this is just development scaffolding. After you've found and removed all of your memory handling problems, you can create a release build of your program. As the name suggests, that's the build that gets released to the users of your software. Although the presence of some extra diagnostic bytes will consume more memory and cause your program to run slower, it's well worth the cost. After all, software developers often have the fastest, highest capacity systems. You may scarcely notice the performance hit caused by a debug release.

In addition to allocating a memory block header, the diagnostic allocator fills memory with known, non-zero values. This helps detect various pointer problems, including buffer overflow and underflow and access to objects that have already been freed. Even allocated areas are filled with a known value: 0xCD. Knowing this can help you determine whether a function has written any data to a buffer. If so, you see the data. If not, the debugger shows an array of 0xCD values instead of whatever you expected to be written to the buffer. (As an aside, the 32-bit OLE libraries fill empty memory with the value 0x0BADF00D, which a Microsoft developer suggests was prompted by a visit to a company cafeteria.)

In the diagnostic heap, sentinels — what MFC calls *no-man's-land areas* — are set up at the start and the end of allocated objects to catch buffer overflow and underflow problems. In production code, writing beyond either the beginning or the end of a buffer can cause program crashes, data loss, and endless user frustration. In a debug build, however, overwritten objects are more easily identified, helping you find the source of a problem.

Incidentally, although the granularity of malloc() is 4 bytes, the granularity of the default allocator is only 1 byte. The location of the no-man's-land is immediately after the end of the requested data area. If you overwrite by just 1 byte, you trigger an assertion. This makes the debug version allocator much stricter than the allocator used for release versions. Off-by-one overwrite errors that might not be detected in the release version will set off alarms in the debug version.

Here are the three values that the debug allocator uses to fill memory, as defined in AFXMEM.CPP:

```
#define bNoMansLandFill 0xFD // fill no-man's land with this
#define bDeadLandFill 0xDD // fill free objects with this
#define bCleanLandFill 0xCD // fill new objects with this
```

A comment block that appears in the same source file just before these values explains why these particular values were chosen. These comments can be summarized as follows:

- ✦ The use of non-zero fill values makes memory overwrites more obvious, because the most common memory fill operation results in zero-filled data.
- ✦ Constant values make memory filling deterministic, which helps make bugs reproducible. Depending on how this data gets used, however, the use of a non-zero value can occasionally mask a bug.
- ✦ Mathematically odd numbers are helpful for finding bugs assuming a cleared lower bit, and for trapping on the Macintosh.
- ✦ Large numbers (byte values at least) are less typical and are useful for finding bad addresses.
- ✦ Atypical values (that is, values that are not often used) are useful because they typically cause early detection in code.
- ✦ For the case of no-man's-land and free blocks, if you store to any of these locations, the memory integrity checker will detect it.

In a debug build of MFC, several global variables enable you to control the operation of the diagnostic allocator. One of these is a flag field that is stored in a global variable, afxMemDF. This integer variable is defined as follows in the MFC source file APPDATA.CPP:

```
int afxMemDF = allocMemDF;
```

This default setting turns on the debugging allocator. Other values for this flag, as defined in AFX.H, are shown in Table 18-4.

You can also set a counter, _afxBreakAlloc, to break into the debugger after a certain number of allocations. When the debug allocator is enabled, it keeps count of the number of times it has been called, and it tags each allocated object in sequence. When a leak is detected, the diagnostic allocator reports the lost block's sequence number. When you're using the IDE debugger, this feature enables you to catch your program in the act of allocating a block that doesn't get freed, presumably to help you figure out the cause of a memory leak. The `_afxBreakAlloc` counter is defined in its disabled state as follows in `AFXMEM.H`:

Table 18-4
Debug Memory Flags

Flag	*Value*	*Description*
n/a	0	Turn off the debugging allocator.
`allocMemDF`	0x01	Turn on the debugging allocator to add a header and no-man's land for each allocated object.
`delayFreeMemDF`	0x02	Delay freeing memory to test out-of-memory handling. This also helps make sure that freed pointers don't get referenced.
`checkAlwaysMemDF`	0x04	Check heap integrity on every call to allocator (both new and delete) as well as during idle-time processing. When this flag is set, `AfxCheckMemory()` gets called to validate the heap. You can also call this function yourself at any time to verify heap validity.

```
// for debugging memory leaks
static LONG _afxBreakAlloc = -1;
```

But it's a simple matter to set this value to indicate how many allocations should pass before breaking into the debugger. Incidentally, you'll probably want to define this value within a conditionally compiled block of code such as the following, because this variable is not defined for the release version:

```
#ifdef _DEBUG
_afxBreakAlloc = 1000;
#endif
```

Another feature that the diagnostic allocator provides to help you test your software is an allocation hook function. Right before it allocates an object, the allocator calls into the chain of hook functions to ask whether an artificial allocation failure should be created. By simulating a low-memory situation, this tests whether error handling is doing the right thing. For details, see the function `AfxSetAllocHook()` in `AFXMEM.CPP`.

To catch pointer errors that overwrite the heap, you can request heap validation, which you can do in two ways. You can simply call `AfxCheckMemory()`, which validates the heap. Or you can set the `afxMemDF` diagnostic flag to the value checkAlwaysMemDF. That causes AfxCheckMemory() to be called whenever memory is allocated or freed. It even causes the heap to get checked during idle time (from within CWinThread::OnIdle(), which is located in THRDCODE.CPP).

The diagnostic allocator also detects memory leaks, which are objects allocated but not freed. In a debug build, the AfxDumpMemoryLeaks() function is automatically called when an MFC program terminates. Any objects still on the heap are displayed in the debugger's Output window. To get this output, you must run your program while the IDE debugger is running. That is, you can't just have the IDE running; you must have started your MFC program by selecting Go from the Debug menu (or equivalent). The detection of memory leaks can be a great help in plugging those leaks so your program uses memory efficiently.

Win32 private heaps

The Win32 API provides a set of functions for creating and allocating memory in multiple, private heaps. Although the Win32 page allocator should be used to allocate large objects — in multiples of 4K pages on Windows 98 — the private heap allocator provides memory allocation for subpage-sized data items.

We refer to Win32 heap support as a private heap allocator because Win32 doesn't provide any mechanism for sharing heaps between processes (although two threads in the same process can easily share a single heap). Because they are private to a process, heaps are created within the memory pages visible only to a single process. When sharing memory between Win32 processes, Win32 unfortunately doesn't organize the memory for you. You must do that yourself.

Win32 provides the capability to create multiple heaps, so you can separate your data any way that suits you. For example, a large application might create multiple heaps and put the data for different subsystems in different heaps. Problems created by memory leaks or bad pointers in one subsystem have a lower probability of harming the operation of other subsystems.

Another reason for creating multiple heaps is to segregate objects of different sizes. For general-purpose allocators, fragmentation occurs when many different objects of widely varying sizes get allocated and freed. For example, by creating a heap that is private to a particular class, you cut down on heap fragmentation and the resulting wasted memory.

Background on heap implementation

Table 18-5 summarizes some operating characteristics of the heap allocation routines in two Win32 implementations, Windows 98 and Windows NT. You might find it surprising that these two operating systems provide the same API so differently. But it's not terribly surprising when you consider that each was created by a different development group at Microsoft, with different goals and different constraints.

Table 18-5
Operating Characteristics of Heap Allocation Routines

Memory Allocation Issue	*Windows 98*	*Windows NT*
Minimum object size	12 bytes	8 bytes
Overhead per object	4 bytes	8 bytes
Allocation granularity	4 bytes	8 bytes

Perhaps a word or two on Table 18-5 would be appropriate. The minimum object size should be self-explanatory. When allocating small objects, that value identifies the minimum amount of memory that's allocated. For both Windows 98 and Windows NT—if you add up the overhead per object—each allocation takes a minimum of 16 bytes.

The overhead-per-object value is the size of the header for each heap object. In both systems, the header is stored just below the address of the start of the allocated data area. Although you don't typically think about this overhead when allocating from a heap, it's a real cost that you may want to take into account when evaluating a program's memory use.

The granularity on the Windows 98 heap allocator is 4 bytes. For example, when the heap allocator is asked for 15 bytes, it supplies a 16-byte area. Add in the 4-byte header, and your 15-byte request ends up costing 20 bytes of actual memory space consumed.

As shown in Table 18-5, Windows 98 has lower allocation overhead and lower allocation granularity than Windows NT. The reason is that the target machine for Windows 98 is a lowly 80486-based system with 8MB of RAM. Windows NT, on the other hand, was built for systems with more RAM and more powerful processors. The "skinnier" heap allocator in Windows 98 helps that operating system run leaner overall.

When comparing memory allocators, you need some way to measure the differences. One way is to calculate the memory tax that the allocator charges for the size of objects that you allocate. In the example—in which a 15-byte request consumes a 19-byte area—the tax is $^5/_{15}$ or 33 percent. Although 5 bytes doesn't seem very expensive, a 33 percent tax puts the relative cost into perspective. (In human terms, a 33 percent sales tax would be outrageous; yet a 33 percent marginal income tax somehow seems more reasonable.) On Windows NT, the same 15-byte object would consume 24 bytes a 60 percent surcharge on the actual bytes you plan to store.

If some part of your Win32/MFC programs use the private heap functions, you must test extensively on both platforms. Otherwise, you risk missing subtle bugs that appear on one platform but not the other. For example, a bug that overwrites 6 bytes past the end of an allocated object might not be noticed on Windows NT. But on Windows 98, such a bug would overwrite other objects.

On Windows 98, a heap always resides within the per-process, private memory ranges — that is, between 4MB and 2GB. Although the location of a heap in a Windows NT process won't tell you whether it's private or shared, heaps are, in fact, always private on Windows NT. To convince yourself that this is the case, you can call `VirtualQuery()` on a heap address. It reports that heap memory pages are private (`MEM_PRIVATE`) pages.

Although some of the operating characteristics differ, the allocation of private heaps from private pages is similar on Windows 98 and Windows NT. The Win32 API that creates a heap is `HeapCreate()`, which in turn calls `VirtualAlloc()` twice. The first call to `VirtualAlloc()` reserves a range of memory addresses to anticipate heap growth. The second call commits memory pages at the start of this address range.

The Win32 heap API

Table 18-6 summarizes Win32's heap management functions. Most are relatively straightforward. For details on calling these functions, refer to the Win32 documentation or the online help database. Some basic design and implementation details are worth discussing. Chief among these is the fact that every Win32 process gets a heap. Most Win32 heap functions take a heap handle as a parameter. To get a handle to the system-provided heap, call `GetProcessHeap()`. With the returned handle, you can allocate within a heap to your heart's content.

Another important issue with Win32 heaps is serialization. Almost every heap function has a heap allocation flag parameter, and one possible flag is `HEAP_NO_SERIALIZE`. This flag disables the heap's default operation, which is to serialize — or synchronize — access to the heap by multiple threads. Note that this use of the term *serialize* has nothing to do with C++ serialization. In other words, in this context serialization isn't related to moving data between memory and disk. When enabled, the heap serialization support forces two threads to wait in line if both want to modify the heap — that is, add or remove a data object — at the same time.

Threads are a Win32 feature that allow the creation of multiple, independently scheduled entities in a Win32 process. The Win32 heap functions enable multiple threads to access heaps at the same time. By default, the Win32 heap functions avoid having two threads modify the heap at the same time. The type of operating system object used to perform this task is a critical section.

Table 18-6
The Win32 Private Heap Support Functions

Function	*Description*
`GetProcessHeap()`	Retrieves a handle to the default process heap.
`GetProcessHeaps()`	Retrieves a list of heap handles for all available heaps in the current process.
`HeapAlloc()`	Allocates memory from the heap identified by a heap handle. All objects are fixed, unlike Win16 objects, which can be allocated as moveable or discardable. More on that later in this chapter.
`HeapCompact()`	Performs some cleaning of the heap by coalescing free areas and, when possible, releasing unneeded pages.
`HeapCreate()`	Creates a new heap in the process address space. Calls `Virtual Alloc()` twice: first to reserve a range of addresses and then again to commit the requested minimum memory for the heap.
`HeapDestroy()`	Destroys a heap created with `HeapCreate()`.
`HeapFree()`	Frees a heap object allocated with a call to `HeapAlloc()` or `HeapReAlloc()`.
`HeapLock()`	Acquires the heap's critical section. This is required only when two or more threads will be accessing a heap. You should call `HeapUnlock()` as soon as possible.
`HeapReAlloc()`	Resizes an object allocated with a call to `HeapAlloc()` or a previous call to `HeapReAlloc()`.
`HeapSize()`	Returns the size of an object. On Windows 98, this is the size of the allocated area (rounds to next 4-byte boundary) instead of the requested size. On Windows NT, `HeapSize()` returns the size requested in the call to `HeapAlloc()` or `HeapReAlloc()`.
`HeapUnlock()`	Releases ownership of the heap's critical section. See `HeapLock()`.
`HeapValidate()`	Checks the integrity of an entire heap or an object within the heap.
`HeapWalk()`	Enumerates all of the objects allocated in the heap.

Use the `HEAP_NO_SERIALIZE` flag when you have only one thread in your application. It helps the heap allocation functions run a little faster, because serialization does take a tiny bit of processor time. Not to imply that it's sluggish or poorly implemented, but when allocating a very large number of objects, tiny savings such as this can add up.

The `HeapValidate()` function checks the integrity of a particular heap. This can be useful when you suspect a bad pointer or a buffer overflow is causing a problem. Even if you've coded defensively—as detailed in Steve Maguire's *Writing Solid Code*—you may find that memory sometimes gets overwritten. Strategic placement of calls to this function can help pinpoint the exact cause of such problems.

Another potentially useful function is `HeapWalk()`. Win16 programmers may recall Microsoft's HeapWalker utility program. Called Luke HeapWalker (after Luke SkyWalker, the character in the *Star Wars* movies), the Win16 HeapWalker utility displays the contents of the various heaps. This function lets you programmatically examine all of the data objects that are allocated on a heap. To help you build your own memory testers and diagnostic routines, this function will let you know almost everything about a Win32 heap.

Thread local storage

Thread local storage provides the capability to connect data to a thread. Win32 supports two types of thread local storage: dynamic and static. Although dynamic thread local storage is the most cumbersome to use, it also provides the greatest flexibility. (That is, it can be used in a dynamically loaded dynamic link library—a DLL loaded with a call to `LoadLibrary()`.) Static thread local storage is much easier to use—so easy, in fact, that it is almost indistinguishable from regular global variables. Unfortunately, there is a limitation on when static thread local storage can be used. Operating system quirks disable this feature in dynamically loaded DLLs.

As mentioned earlier, threads are the unit of scheduling in a Win32 program. When a Win32 process on Windows 98 or Windows NT starts running, Windows starts a thread. (Threads are not supported in Win32s.) After that, the only way to get new threads is by calling a Win32 function, `CreateThread()`. The C-runtime library provides a wrapper function, `_beginthread()` that calls `CreateThread()`, which sets up the C-runtime library to be "thread aware." MFC calls this function when it needs to create new threads (actually, it calls `_beginthreadex()`, which is a slight variation on `_beginthread()`).

To keep track of thread-specific data, operating systems such as Windows 98 and Windows NT allocate memory to hold thread instance data. On Windows NT, this memory area is called the *thread environment block* (TEB). And on Windows 98—as reported by Andrew Schulman—it's the *thread control block* (THCB). Whatever the name, these memory blocks hold operating system instance data that Windows maintains on a per thread basis. Among the types of data held as thread instance data are the state of processor registers when a thread is not running, a pointer to the thread's stack, and a pointer to the exception data that is stored on the stack.

Dynamic thread local storage—like window extra bytes—is nothing more than application data that's stored in an operating system's data structure. When a thread is created under Windows NT or Windows 98, a TEB or THCB structure gets allocated. In addition to the memory that each operating system allocates for its own use, an array of DWORD (unsigned long) values is set aside for application use.

Any part of an application's code — whether it is EXE code or DLL code — can reserve an array entry by making an API call, which applies to every thread in a given process. For example, if a process has three threads, a successful call to reserve dynamic thread local storage provides access to three DWORD entries, with one for each thread. When a given block of code is running, it automatically reads thread local storage values for the current thread in which it is executing.

How might EXE code or DLL code use dynamic thread local storage? The 4 bytes in a DWORD easily accommodate any 32-bit pointer to, for example, dynamically allocated data. If a program created threads for background tasks (such as printing, data sorting, or database integrity checks), thread-specific data could hold a queue of tasks to be accomplished. The Win32 API functions that maintain dynamic thread local storage are described in Table 18-7.

Table 18-7
Dynamic Thread Local Storage

Function	*Description*
`TlsAlloc()`	For all threads in the current process, request an element into the arrays of application-specific storage set aside by Windows in the thread instance data structure of each thread.
`TlsFree()`	Relinquish an index in the current process to the thread instance data structures.
`TlsGetValue()`	For the current thread, query the contents of a specific element in thread instance data.
`TlsSetValue()`	For the current thread, set the contents of a specific element in thread instance data.

When a thread local storage area is allocated (with a call to `TlsAlloc()`), an index into the arrays of thread data is returned. That index must be stored in a shared memory area, which probably means in a global variable. Per-thread data could then be allocated dynamically, and a pointer to that data stored as thread local storage.

The second type of per-thread data is static thread local storage. This is the easiest to use because — once declared — it looks just like global variables. In reality, the compiler and loader work together to automatically allocate a new set for every thread that is created within a process. And if you examine the assembly language code that the compiler generates to access this data, you see that some additional instructions add an extra level of indirection to that normally used to access data. The beauty of static thread local storage is that it looks like a global variable but acts like per-thread data.

The key to static thread local data is a pair of keywords specific to the Microsoft C compiler: __declspec and thread. Here is how to define an integer value on a per-thread basis:

```
__declspec (thread) int i = 0;
```

All compiler keywords that start with an underscore (_) represent non-ANSI-standard C/C++ keywords. In the past, Microsoft freely added new declarators to its compiler: _pascal, _cdecl, _near, _far, _stdcall, and so on. But a problem might arise if such declarators clash with new keywords that become part of standard C++.

To control the proliferation of new declarator specifications, Microsoft created one more general, all-purpose declarator: __declspec. This is supposed to be the master declarator. All new compiler extensions — like static thread local storage — will be accessed using modifiers to the master declarator. At present, we know of only three other declarator specifications: dllimport, dllexport, and naked. More will be created to extend the compiler as needed. To make the declaration of static thread local storage somewhat more readable, create a preprocessor symbol:

```
#define THREADDATA __declspec (thread)
```

The previous per-thread integer can then be rewritten in a slightly more readable form:

```
THREADDATA int i = 0;
```

Per-thread data must be initialized. The preceding example sets the integer variable to zero. Although it's a tiny difference to the application programmer, it makes a big difference to the compiler, which treats initialized data differently from uninitialized data. The current compiler implementation does not support per-thread uninitialized data, but it does support initialized per-thread data. A small difference helps ensure that you get the data support you need. (In our discussion of shared data later in this chapter, you'll see that you must also initialize global data to be shared between processes.)

As we've mentioned, the chief advantage of this type of per-thread data is that it looks just like a regular global variable. Once it's defined, you don't need to fuss with API calls to access data: It just appears when you need it. If you look at the machine code that the compiler creates, you will notice that access to this type of per-thread data does involve some additional instructions. But when you need per-thread data, it's a small price to pay.

Another advantage to this type of per-thread data is that you can allocate as much of it as you need. Although this example shows the allocation of a single variable, it's no problem to allocate thousands or even tens of thousands of bytes. Variables allocated on a per-thread basis are placed in their own section in the executable file. So, like other code and data sections, such data can span multiple megabytes as needed.

However, static thread local storage has one limitation. It cannot be used in dynamic link libraries that are dynamically loaded into memory. If a program calls

`LoadLibrary()` to explicitly load a DLL into memory, static thread local storage cannot be used. An example of DLLs loaded into memory this way are printer device drivers. For statically loaded DLLs, static thread local storage works fine. These are DLLs that are brought into memory when the calling executable file is started. Aside from this limitation, however, static thread local storage provides a great way to connect application data to system threads.

This concludes our look at the different types of private, per-process memory. We now turn our attention to all the types of memory that exist for sharing memory between processes.

Shared Memory

The rest of this chapter will focus on the part of the Win32 API used to allocate shared memory — that is, memory shareable between two or more processes. So far this chapter has focused on private memory allocation. Private data is arguably more important than shared because most process data is private data. Perhaps for this reason, Win32 provides more private data routines than shared memory routines. An important benefit of private process memory is that it enhances system stability. Because it lessens the risk that one application will overwrite the memory areas of another application, this is the default type of memory allocated for a process. To share memory, an application must explicitly override this default.

To an application developer, the distinction between private and shared memory may seem arbitrary. After all, data that's private one moment can be shared the next. To an operating system, however, the difference between private and shared memory is fundamental and important. As mentioned earlier in this chapter, the Win32 API exposes this difference by providing two routines to create address space: `VirtualAlloc()` for private address space and `MapViewOfFile()` for shared. Before a process allocates pages — on either Windows 98 or Windows NT — it must decide whether sharing is to be allowed. Let's look at some of the subtle ways in which each operating system handles the distinction between shared and private memory.

Windows 98 puts private pages in one part of the address space and shared pages in another. Private pages reside between 4MB and 2GB. As described earlier in this chapter, when a context switch occurs from one Win32 process to another, one set of pages is mapped out and another set is mapped into this address range, which is done by updating the CPU's page tables. Shared pages, on the other hand, reside between 2GB and 3GB. During a context switch, the Windows 98 memory manager doesn't touch the page tables for pages mapped into this area. By leaving the shared pages alone, the Windows 98 memory manager makes it quick and easy to share memory between processes.

The way in which Windows 98 places the image of executable files in a process address space presents an apparent contradiction. Because executable files are shareable entities, you might think that Windows 98 would place them in the shared address range. Although one type of DLL — system DLLs — gets loaded to the shared address range, that's not where private executables reside. Windows 98 maps private executable (.EXE) files and private dynamic link libraries (.DLL) to the private address range. By placing them in the private range, Windows 98 can pick and choose how to handle private executables. For efficient use of private DLLs and private EXE files, for example, Windows 98 maps a single set of physical pages into the address space of several processes.

Windows NT also differentiates between shared and private pages, though in a way that's subtler than Windows 98's use of different address ranges. The difference has to do with how Windows NT sets up processor page tables. Private pages on Windows NT simply use the Intel-86 paged memory addressing scheme described at the beginning of this chapter. Each process has its own page directory and page tables, and on a context switch the CPU's CR3 register is updated for a new address space.

Windows NT differentiates shared pages from private pages in a subtler manner than Windows 98. Access to a memory location in a shared page causes a page fault. In many operating systems, a page fault means that either a page resides in the page file or a memory addressing error — such as a NULL pointer reference — has occurred. Windows NT recognizes these two traditional uses of a page fault but adds some others as a way to reveal shared memory to a process. When a fault occurs on a range of shared pages, Windows NT responds to the page fault to cause shared pages to magically appear to a process. Such fault-on-access pages are specially coded in the page table in a format called a *prototype page table entry*. The prototype page table entry contains a reference to a set of system page tables — an additional level of page tables that's not required for private pages — that indicates the location of the shared page. Just as on Windows 98, the decision to share a page or make it private has a profound impact on how Windows NT shoehorns a page into the address space of a process.

Incidentally, the differences between Windows 98 and Windows NT are described in order to promote a deeper understanding of how each operates. By no means should you write code that, for example, tests for shared memory by looking for pointer values between 2GB and 3GB on Windows 98. (This implementation-specific characteristic might change in a future version. To check for shared pages, call `VirtualQuery()`.) Nor should you worry that Windows NT somehow runs slower because of the overhead required to handle page faults on shared memory access; the processor time required for handling these page faults is much less than the time taken to draw a single line in a window border!

A common element unites all shared pages. In one form or another, all memory sharing in Win32 relies on Win32's memory-mapped file I/O support. A memory-mapped file uses shared memory to provide a common image of file-based data to two or more processes.

What's not so obvious about memory-mapped file I/O is that it provides memory sharing. To turn Schulman's definition around, sharing memory in a Win32 process uses a portion of the operating system's virtual memory page file like a memory-mapped file. Although the emphasis is on sharing memory, the data in the memory pages could end up on disk. But rather than ending up in a permanent, named file, shared pages reside in the system's page file.

The following sections explore four ways to share memory between processes, starting with memory-mapped files because they are the backbone for other types of sharing. Next is a look at sharing memory pages that are not in a specifically named memory-mapped file. Then a look at both types of shared pages: dynamically allocated and statically allocated.

Memory-mapped file I/O

Memory-mapped file I/O refers to a feature of the Win32 API that simplifies the movement of data between a disk-based file and a range of memory addresses. When a file is mapped into a region of memory, the reading of bytes in the mapped memory produces the same results as the reading of bytes from the file, except that the virtual memory manager handles data buffering. Writing to mapped memory produces the same results as writing to the disk file, except that, once again, the virtual memory manager handles data buffering.

Memory-mapped file I/O is highly efficient. Using what we call *creative procrastination*, the virtual memory manager doesn't do any work that isn't needed. When a view into a memory-mapped file is first created, a range of addresses is set aside, but no data is actually read. You first encountered the idea of reserving memory ranges in the discussion of reserving private address ranges with `VirtualAlloc()`. With a memory-mapped file, access to a memory location reserved for memory-mapped pages causes a page fault, to which the virtual memory manager responds by reading pages from disk and restarting the faulting instruction. Modified pages are written back to disk only when the virtual memory manager needs more pages (or when an application wants to force a write by calling the Win32 `FlushFileBuffers()` API). This lazy approach keeps memory and processor use to a minimum.

Memory-mapped file I/O enables two (or more) processes to share file-based data. Each process involved in the sharing has direct access to a common set of pages. Because the sharing occurs with a minimum of overhead, sharing with memory-mapped file I/O can be quite useful when a large amount of data must be shared. And because each process has direct access to the data, high bandwidth sharing is handled very efficiently.

You don't have to share memory to take advantage of memory-mapped file I/O. There is clearly a difference between memory that is shareable and memory actually shared between two or more processes. The pages that are set up as memory-mapped file pages are shareable — that is, you can share them — but sharing isn't required if it doesn't suit your purposes. There's nothing wrong with using memory-mapped file I/O to simplify access to disk-based data with no intent to share. The capability to share is just an added feature that can be used when you need it.

Three Windows KERNEL objects are required for memory-mapped file support: a file object, a file mapping object, and a view object. (MFC provides no wrappers for these objects.) To map a file to memory, the file is first opened, which causes a file object to be created. Next, a file object must be connected to a memory-mapped file object, which provides a logical connection to a disk-based file for synchronizing data between different processes. However, the presence of a memory-mapped file object doesn't provide a pointer to data. For that, a view object is required. A view object provides a pointer to some block of data from the file. Multiple views can be created from a single memory-mapped file object, which enables a process to pick and choose the specific parts of a file to access.

Creating a file object

Two functions can be used to open files: one from the Win16 API and one from the Win32 API. We'll discuss the Win32 function first, though the Win16 function is easier to use. The Win32 function for opening files is `CreateFile()`, which gets its name from the fact that it creates an operating system file object. This function can create files, open files, and open other operating system objects such as communications ports and named pipes. The Win16 function to open files is `OpenFile()`. We prefer this function because it takes fewer parameters and has the added feature that it can be used to delete files. It isn't as capable as `CreateFile()`, which can open other types of operating system objects as well as set file and security attributes. To open normal disk-based files, use `OpenFile()`—which more or less simply wraps around a call to `CreateFile()`. For details on an important difference in error handling between these functions and the rest of the Windows API, see the accompanying sidebar. To open a file, `OpenFile()` function, which is defined as follows, is preferred:

```
HFILE WINAPI OpenFile(
    LPCSTR lpFileName,
    LPOFSTRUCT lpReOpenBuff,
    UINT uStyle);
```

The `lpFileName` parameter is a text string that describes the path of the file to open. The `lpReOpenBuff` argument is a pointer to a structure of type `OFSTRUCT`. This structure was created to support a style of file I/O required when accessing files on floppy disk, which requires that the files be kept closed most of the time. Otherwise, if a user changes disks, the entire file system of a floppy disk can be damaged. In fact, the only usable field in this structure is `fFixedDisk`, which indicates whether a floppy disk has been opened. (Despite its name, it doesn't detect CD ROM drives, which appear as network drives.) The `OFSTRUCT` is defined in the Windows include files as follows:

```
typedef struct _OFSTRUCT {
    BYTE cBytes;
    BYTE fFixedDisk;
    WORD nErrCode;
    WORD Reserved1;
    WORD Reserved2;
    CHAR szPathName[OFS_MAXPATHNAME];
```

```
} OFSTRUCT, *LPOFSTRUCT, *POFSTRUCT;
```

The `uStyle` parameter contains file-opening flags. Various flags indicate how the memory is to be accessed (`OF_READ`, `OF_WRITE`, `OF_READWRITE`), how the file is to be shared with other processes (`OF_SHARE_EXCLUSIVE`, `OF_SHARE_DENY_WRITE`, and so on), and the action to be taken (`OF_CREATE`, `OF_DELETE`, `OF_EXIST`, and so on). For a complete set of flags, see the Win32 documentation. Here is an example of calling this function to open a file:

```
HFILE hfile;
OFSTRUCT of;
hfile = OpenFile( "FILE.DAT", &of,
  OF_READ | OF_SHARE_EXCLUSIVE );
if( hfile == (HFILE) -1 )
{
    // Error opening file.
}
```

Windows file handle error handling

While on the subject of files, an inconsistency between files and other types of Windows objects should be mentioned. The way you detect errors when opening files is different from the way you detect errors when creating other Win32 objects. For other types of objects, a handle value of `NULL` (zero) indicates failure. When a file-opening failure occurs, the file-opening functions return a handle value of –1. This value is represented by `INVALID_HANDLE_VALUE`, a long-winded but descriptive preprocessor symbol. Some developers prefer this symbol to hard-coding a test for a –1 return value.

For programmers new to Windows programming, the symbol `INVALID_HANDLE_VALUE` is twice confusing. First, its name suggests that it is generic to all types of handles when in fact it applies only to file handles. Second, there isn't a symbol for other types of invalid handles. Don't check for this value when testing for failure in the creation of windows, menus, dialog boxes, cursors, and icons; for GDI objects such as pens, brushes, fonts, DCs, bitmaps, and regions; or for `KERNEL` objects such as processes, threads, or semaphores. (As a form of protest against this inconsistency, one might test for file-opening failure with a hard-coded –1.)

You might wonder why a failure to open a file in a Win32 program results in a handle value of –1 instead of 0. The reasons are historical. The Win32 API supports this feature to be backward compatible with the Win16 API. But you might wonder why Win16 works this way, given that `NULL` is also an invalid handle value in Win16? The answer is that Win16 programs (under Windows 3.x and earlier) rely on MS-DOS for file I/O, so Win16 programs must deal with what MS-DOS provides—which is a return value of -1 for file-opening failure. The saga continues if you consider that MS-DOS itself was built as a CP/M clone by Tim Patterson at Seattle Computer, and CP/M itself uses –1 (actually 0xff) for an invalid handle value. The end result is that Win32 running on Windows 98—and on Windows NT!—provides a file failure return value based on an operating system built in the mid-1970s.

Here's a comparable call to `CreateFile()`:

```
HFILE hfile;
hfile = CreateFile(achFile,                // Filename.
                   GENERIC_READ,           // Access mode.
                   0,                      // Share
                   0,                      // Security.
                   OPEN_EXISTING,          // Create flags.
                   FILE_ATTRIBUTE_NORMAL,// File
                                           // attributes.
                   0 );                    // File emulate.

if( hfile == (HFILE) -1 )
{
    // Error opening file.
}
```

On success, the `OpenFile()` function — and its `CreateFile()` cousin — returns a valid `HFILE` file handle. To close the file, call `CloseHandle()`. You'll use this same function to close several different types of `KERNEL` objects, including file mapping objects, which are discussed next. However, it cannot be used to close user interface objects (such as windows, menus, cursors, and icons) or GDI drawing objects (such as DCs, pens, brushes, and fonts). It is unfortunate that the very generic name of this function suggests a widespread usability that does not exist for the Win32 API.

Creating a file mapping object

Once a file has been opened, the second step for memory-mapped file support involves creating a file mapping object. This is done with a call to `CreateFileMapping()`, a function that accepts a file handle as its first parameter. Although you might expect that this function would fail if you accidentally passed an invalid (–1) file handle, that's not what happens. As will be discussed shortly, an invalid file handle for the first parameter creates shared memory instead of shared file access. The `CreateFileMapping()` function is defined as follows:

```
HANDLE WINAPI CreateFileMapping (
  HANDLE hFile,
  LPSECURITY_ATTRIBUTES lpsa,
  DWORD dwProtect,
  DWORD dwMaxSizeHigh,
  DWORD dwMaxSizeLow,
  LPCTSTR lpszMapName )
```

The `hFile` parameter is a file handle returned from a call to `OpenFile()` or `CreateFile()`. The `lpsa` argument points to a `SECURITY_ATTRIBUTES` structure that defines the security attributes of the file mapping object on Windows NT. A value of `NULL` provides default security.

The dwProtect parameter is a flag field for page protection flags, such as PAGE_READONLY, PAGE_READWRITE, and PAGE_WRITECOPY. These must be consistent with the access flags specified when opening the file.

The dwMaxSizeHigh argument is the high-order 32 bits for the maximum file size. (In anticipation of file systems that support files larger than 4GB, Win32 uses 64-bit file offsets.) The dwMaxSizeLow parameter is the low-order 32 bits for the maximum file size.

The lpszMapName argument is an optional string name that identifies the file mapping object. Provide NULL for none, or a character string that uniquely names the file mapping object. Here's an example of calling this function to create an unnamed file mapping object:

```
// Create file mapping object.
HANDLE hfm
hfm = CreateFileMapping(hfile,         // File handle.
                        0,             // Security Ptr.
                        PAGE_READONLY,// Pg protection
                        0,             // Size-Hi 32-bits
                        dwFileSize,    // Size-Low 32-bits
                        0 );           // Mapping Name.
```

When you create a file mapping object, you can give it a unique name if you'd like (in the lpszMapName field), such as "RICK_SHARED." Make sure that the name is unique, though, because an unexpected name collision with an unknown process will cause sharing in an unexpected and unwanted manner.

For two or more processes to share a single file, a single file mapping object must be created and shared between them. Once a file mapping object has been created with a call to CreateFileMapping(), three different functions enable interprocess sharing: CreateFileMapping(), OpenFileMapping(), and DuplicateHandle().

One way to share a single file mapping object is to give the file mapping object a name. Then, when two or more processes call CreateFileMapping() with the same name, a single file mapping object can be shared. The first process actually creates the file mapping object, and subsequent processes simply attach to the existing object. It might seem odd that only a single file mapping object is created even though several different processes might call this function, but the nature of sharing is that it isn't always easy to determine which process will get started first. To identify when a call to this function has not created a new and unique file mapping object, call GetLastError(), and check for the ERROR_ALREADY_EXISTS return value.

A second function for interprocess sharing of a memory-mapped file is OpenFileMapping(), which takes as one of its parameters the name of the file mapping object. This function assumes that a file mapping object was already created with a call to CreateFileMapping(). If the object named doesn't exist, this function returns a NULL file mapping handle. (Remember that a handle value of –1 only indicates file-opening errors.)

A third function for connecting to an existing file mapping object is `DuplicateHandle()`, which creates a `KERNEL` handle that another process can use. `KERNEL` handles are for the private use of a single process, but this function lets you freely create new handles from an existing handle for other processes. Notice that this function can only be used to map certain types of handles (a complete list is given in the Win32 documentation). In general, this function cannot duplicate user interface object handles or GDI drawing object handles. It can, however, be used to duplicate `KERNEL` objects — which on Windows NT are more properly called *Executive objects* — including handles for files, file mapping objects, processes, threads, semaphores, mutexes, and events.

Creating a view object

Once a file object and a file mapping object have been created, the third step in accessing a memory-mapped file is to create one or more views of the data file. When a view is created, address space is reserved to enable access to portions of the memory-mapped file. On access to this range of addresses, memory pages are allocated, and data is read from disk. Multiple views can be created into a single file, to enable selective access to different portions of the memory-mapped file. For example, views might be created to the beginning of a file to access header information; to the end, where a duplicate header might be stored; and to areas in the middle, where various pieces of data reside. To create a view into a memory-mapped file, call `MapViewOfFile()`. This function is defined as follows:

```
LPVOID
WINAPI
MapViewOfFile(
  HANDLE hFileMappingObject,
  DWORD dwDesiredAccess,
  DWORD dwFileOffsetHigh,
  DWORD dwFileOffsetLow,
  DWORD dwNumberOfBytesToMap);
```

The `hFileMappingObject` parameter is a handle to a file mapping object. The `dwDesiredAccess` argument is the access desired to the file mapping data. For example, it could be `FILE_MAP_READ` for read-only access, or `FILE_MAP_READ | FILE_MAP_WRITE` for read-write access.

The `dwFileOffsetHigh` parameter is the high order 32 bits of the offset in the file of the beginning of the area to map to memory. The `dwFileOffsetLow` argument is the low-order 32 bits of the offset in the file of the beginning of the area to map to memory. The `dwNumberOfBytesToMap` parameter is the number of bytes to map. This will be rounded up to the nearest page boundary (4K on Intel). If zero, the entire file is mapped.

Here's an example of how this function might be called to create a view that references the first 4,096 bytes in a file:

```
// Create view of file mapping object.
LPVOID lpData;
```

```
lpData = MapViewOfFile( hFileMapping,
            FILE_MAP_READ,   // Page protection.
            0,               // File Offset - Hi 32-bits
            0,               // File Offset - Low 32-bits
            4096 );          // Size of view
```

A slight variation on the routines that share access to a memory-mapped file also enables sharing of pages between processes. A discussion of what this involves follows.

Dynamically allocating shared pages

The second technique for memory sharing involves dynamically allocating shared pages. Although the Windows 98 and Windows NT implementations differ, when you use them, you want the same results: getting access to the same physical memory pages between two or more processes. For complete compatibility between Windows 98 and Windows NT, you should be aware of some of the implementation differences.

Windows 98 and Windows NT sharing differences

The key difference between the implementation of memory sharing on Windows 98 and Windows NT involves memory addresses. On Windows 98, a shared page is visible to all Win32 processes at the same address — guaranteed. That's because shared pages are mapped into the window of shared addresses between 2GB and 3GB. On Windows NT, on the other hand, the address of shared pages can be different within the address space of different processes. And they can be the same, depending on which objects are already mapped into a process address space. To properly share pages on both operating systems, a Win32 process must be prepared for the worst case — that is, for the way in which Windows NT shares pages.

Tempting shortcuts on Windows 98 will break in Windows NT. For example, if you merely share the address between two processes — which always works on Windows 98 — you are guaranteed to crash on Windows NT. This shortcut may be particularly attractive to developers who are porting Win16 programs from Windows 3.1 to the Win32 API for operation on Windows 98. Because Win16 programs on Windows 3.1 can share memory by just passing pointers, a quick fix to get running on Windows 98 would be to again share a pointer to a shared block. But don't do it; instead, make the calls to the necessary functions to ensure that you run on Windows NT and on future Win32 implementations.

There is an important difference between the way that Windows 98 and Windows 3.1 share data. To allocate a shared object in Windows 3.1, programmers called `GlobalAlloc()` and passed the `GMEM_SHARE` (or `GMEM_DDESHARE`) flag. That flag overrides some of the automatic memory cleanup that Windows 3.1 otherwise imposes on a dynamically allocated segment. In Win32, this flag has no effect. As described earlier in this chapter, all `GlobalAlloc()`-allocated memory is placed within the range of addresses for process-private memory. This memory sharing mechanism has no support under the Win32 API.

Win32 functions for sharing pages

The functions you call to share memory pages are the same ones you call to share memory-mapped files. You first create a file mapping object by calling `CreateFileMapping()`. When called with a file handle of `(HFILE)-1`, the file mapping object connects itself to a system page file. To access specific shared bytes, you call `MapViewOfFile()`. Both functions were discussed in the previous section. The following code fragment creates a shared memory object with the name "RICK_DATA":

```
DWORD   dwSize; // Desired size of file mapping object.
HANDLE  hfm;    // Handle to file mapping object.
LPVOID  lpData; // Pointer to shared data.

// Create file mapping object.
hfm = CreateFileMapping( (HANDLE)0xffffffff, // Handle.
                         0,                 // Ptr to Security.
                         PAGE_READWRITE,    // Page protection
                         0,                 // File Size - Hi-bits
                         dwSize,            // File Size - Low-bits
                         "RICK_DATA" );     // Mapping Name.

if( hfm == 0 )
{
  AfxMessageBox("Unable to Create File Mapping Object");,
  return( FALSE );
}

// Exit if named object already exists.
if( GetLastError() == ERROR_ALREADY_EXISTS )
{
  AfxMessageBox( "File Mapping Object Already Exists." );
  CloseHandle( hfm );
  return( FALSE );
}

// Create view of file mapping object.
lpData = MapViewOfFile( hfm,
                   FILE_MAP_WRITE, // Protection.
                   0,              // File Offset - Hi 32-bits
                   0,              // File Offset - Low 32-bits
                   0 );            // Size is whole object.

if( lpData == 0 )
{
  AfxMessageBox( "Can't Create View of Mapping Object" );
  CloseHandle( hfm );
  return( FALSE );
}
```

Notice in this code fragment that the file handle provided in the call to `CreateFileMapping()` is 0xffffffff — or –1. We could as easily have provided `INVALID_HANDLE_VALUE`, which might make this code more understandable.

The size of the shared area is set in the call to `CreateFileMapping()`—`dwSize` in this example. The assumption here is that 4GB of shared data is the limit. The call to `MapViewOfFile()` in this example passes a view size of zero, which sets the view size equal to include all of the shared pages.

When creating shared memory areas, the protection attributes of the file mapping object limit what can be set in view objects. For example, a read-only (`PAGE_READONLY`) setting on a file mapping object can't be mapped by a writable (`FILE_MAP_WRITE`) view. The file mapping object sets the maximum allowable protection, which is enforced for individual views.

As mentioned earlier, a given shared page in Windows NT can be mapped to a different address in different processes. When designing a memory sharing strategy, you must be careful to avoid relying on the Windows 98 implementation, which guarantees that shared pages are at the same address for different processes. The Microsoft Visual C++ compiler supports the creation of based pointers—a feature that helps simplify access to shared data with a minimum of programming hassles.

Sharing pointers between processes using based pointers

Data containing absolute pointers cannot be easily shared between Win32 processes. By absolute pointers, we simply mean absolute memory addresses within the 4GB address space of a Win32 process. Because pointers are so useful and efficient in connecting data structures, the Visual C++ compiler supports a feature called *based pointers* that enables you to create relative pointers. At the cost of a tiny bit of hidden pointer arithmetic, based pointers provide all the advantages of pointers within the constraints of Win32-shared memory.

Absolute pointers are only a problem when sharing memory between Win32 processes on Windows NT. Under Win32s, in which all processes run in a common address space, absolute pointers create no problems. And on Windows 98, as has been discussed, a common shared memory area between 2GB and 3GB helps simplify memory sharing both for the operating system—which can run fast and lean—and for Win32 processes that all share a common view of objects in this address range. On Windows NT, all Win32 processes have a private address space between 0 and 2GB. Although it's possible for memory to be mapped to the same address in different address spaces, there's no guarantee. For that reason, if you want a Win32 program to share memory properly on Windows NT, you must assume that the shared memory will appear at a different address in each process that accesses the memory. Within the shared memory object, only relative pointers can be used.

A relative pointer is an offset—something familiar to programmers who have written Win16 programs, which rely on Intel's segmented addressing. Although you could do your own pointer arithmetic, the compiler's support for based pointers makes pointer arithmetic automatic. Microsoft first introduced support for based pointers for efficient access of segmented memory in a 16-bit program. Under

Win32, this same feature is employed in the creation and use of relative pointers in shared memory.

To support based pointers, Microsoft added a new keyword to its compiler: `__based`, which takes as an operand a base address. Given a base address of `pData` —which is perhaps a char * —here is how to define a based pointer named `pBasedPointer`:

```
char __based(pData) * pBasedPointer;
```

Once declared, a based pointer can be used the same way as a regular pointer:

```
char * pData;
char __based(pData) * pBasedPointer;

pData = (char *) MapViewOfFile( ... );
pBasedPointer = pData;
strcpy( pBasedPointer, "Relative (based) pointer" );
strcpy( pData, "Absolute pointer" );
```

Based pointers are useful when you need to store a pointer within a shared memory block. You don't need to use relative pointers to access shared memory itself—for that, absolute pointers work quite nicely. If you're counting processor cycles—a practice that is becoming less important as processors get faster—absolute pointers are a bit faster than based pointers. But when you need to store an actual pointer inside the shared memory block, you should use a based pointer. This enables different processes to freely use the pointer without worrying about whether the shared block itself is at the same address in the address space of different processes.

Statically allocating shared pages

The Microsoft Visual C++ compiler provides the capability to share global variables between different processes. This feature relies on the compiler and the linker allocating shared pages within an executable file. At runtime, the loader enables such pages to get mapped into the address space of several processes at the same time. As with shared pages that are dynamically allocated, a single set of physical pages gets magically mapped into the address space of multiple processes.

Three requirements must be met for shared global variables to be available. First, the global variables must be initialized. Second, the shared global variables should be declared in their own section. And third, the shared attribute must be assigned to the executable file's section in which variables to be shared are contained. This is done by making an entry in the module definition (.DEF) file. Let's look at these requirements, one at a time.

Shared global variables must be initialized because the compiler, linker, and loader treat uninitialized data different from initialized data. A copy of the initialized data actually appears in the executable file. On the other hand, there isn't a need for uninitialized data to take up space on disk in executable files, so the loader can handle allocating memory for uninitialized data without reading data from the executable file. An added benefit of initializing the data is that it begins life in a known state without any process worrying about it.

The second requirement, that shared global variables should be declared in their own section, is not strictly necessary. For example, an executable file could share all of its global variables. After all, Win16 dynamic link libraries have a single data segment that is shared by all processes. But because this tends to cause more problems than it solves, you'll probably want both shared and private global variables.

To declare global variables in their own section, you sandwich the declaration between a pair of `data_seg pragma` statements. As you probably suspect, the `seg` part of this name is a holdover from the segmented addressing of 16-bit MS-DOS and Windows. Here's an example of a character array that is placed into a section named ".shared":

```
// Put shared data into section named ".shared".
#pragma data_seg (".shared")
char achPublic[BUFSIZE] = "";
// Set name of data section back to default _DATA
#pragma data_seg ()
```

The `#pragma` keyword looks like a preprocessor statement, but it's not. It's an instruction to the compiler to provide some special service. In this case, the `data_seg` keyword requests a change in the name of the segment in which data is stored. When no name is specified, as appears in the second `#pragma data_seg` statement, the default name of `_DATA` is used. Incidentally, the name used for the shared memory section does not make it shared, so an arbitrary name such as "DanielBoone" could have been provided. Sharing only happens when a section is marked as shared in the module definition file, which happens in the third step.

The third step in sharing global variables between processes is to mark as shared the section that contains the variable(s) to be shared. To do this, you make an entry in the module definition file. This is a file that essentially contains a set of linker switches. When building dynamic link libraries, for example, a list of functions to make available to the outside world is listed under the `EXPORTS` keyword. To set the memory attributes for a section of an executable file, the `SECTIONS` keyword is required. The following example is the entire module definition file from a dynamic link library that contains shared global variables. The entry under the SECTIONS keyword enables the section named ".shared" to be shared between different processes:

```
LIBRARY DATASTOR

DESCRIPTION 'Sample Win32 DLL'

SECTIONS
    .shared READ WRITE SHARED

EXPORTS
    GetPrivateData
    SetPrivateData
    GetPublicData
    SetPublicData
```

Summary

From the subjects covered in this chapter, you can see that the Win32 API provides many types of memory. Although the C-runtime `malloc()` function and the C++ `new` operator provide basic memory allocation, they are intended for general purpose use. Special purposes may require more specialized allocation mechanisms that provide better control, better performance, or greater fine-tuning of memory operations.

✦ ✦ ✦

CHAPTER 19

Documents, Views, and SDI

✦ ✦ ✦ ✦

In This Chapter

The Document object

The View object

The CDocument class

Understanding the role InitInstance plays

The Frame Window object

The CView class

Dynamic object creation

The SDI document template

Registering document types with the operating system

Creating a real document/view application

✦ ✦ ✦ ✦

At the core of an MFC application is the concept of a *document object* and a corresponding *view window*. The document object usually represents a file the application has opened, while the view window provides a visual presentation of the document's data and accepts user interaction. The relationship between documents and views is a one-to-many relationship. In other words, a document can have many views, but you can associate a view with only one document.

Within your applications, you represent document objects within classes that you derive from the MFC `CDocument` base class. You derive your view window classes from the MFC `CView` class. In this chapter, you will learn about `CDocument` and `CView` and how you will use them with simple, single document interface (SDI) applications. You will learn about more complex manipulations of the documents and views in Chapter 20.

Document/view designs

Any AppWizard-produced MFC applications that support SDI or the Multiple Document Interface (MDI) use the document/view architecture. AppWizard designs the application in such a way that an instance of the application's document class is created for each file that the application loads. The application then uses an instance of a view class to let the user interact with the application and the data in the document.

Your applications may associate more than one instance of a particular view with a given document, and you may even associate instances of different views with the same document.

◆ ◆ ◆ ◆ ◆

The built-in power of the document/view architecture, therefore, is that as users work with the application, they create and destroy instances of the file and user interface management code (and data) that define their very perception of the data with which they work.

A user-friendly application gives views to the application's data that make more sense to the user. For example, for most readers, it is probably difficult to imagine how cold it will be in South Dakota based on tabular temperature data for the entire U.S. However, the common "blue is cold, orange is hot" weather graphs that appear in newspapers make it easy to guess what range of temperatures a traveler might expect with a quick glance at the right part of the map. The tabular data still has value, though. It's an easy way to enter the data in the first place, and it's the only way you might ever find out what the weather is like in South Dakota if you weren't completely sure where it was.

Single document interface applications that you use AppWizard to produce only use one document and one view type and only instantiate one of each of these classes. However, this is only true of the AppWizard-generated code — after the AppWizard creates your application, you are free to change the composition of your project as much as you desire, if you decide that it's convenient to use multiple instances of each different view or document.

MDI applications make use of at least one document/view pair, but they may make use of additional documents and views in different combinations to enable the user to work with other files or to represent their data in many different ways. As noted previously, you will learn more about multiple document interface applications in Chapter 20. Figure 19-1 shows which classes may support a simple SDI application that you implement using MFC objects.

In AppWizard-generated SDI applications, the `CMainFrame` class implements the frame window itself. In such cases, AppWizard defines the `CMainFrame` class for you in the `MainFrm.h` header file and implements the class in the `MainFrm.cpp` source file. The `CMainFrame` class derives most of its functionality from the `CFrameWnd` class, which is the MFC wrapper class for a simple window. The `CFrameWnd` class does not do much in the single document interface application. The notable exceptions are, if you have added a status bar or dockable toolbars to the application, the `CMainFrame` class handles the creation and initialization of those objects.

Conventional Windows applications written in C (and using the Windows API) would modify the way that Windows' own classes work. Within the application's body, your program code then would paint, draw, or store something as a direction to input messages (or combinations of input messages) to your application's windows. Fortunately, by using MFC, you are able to focus more closely on working with classes, rather than working with a series of system function calls. These MFC classes also support the capability to intercept those basic Windows messages and, when appropriate, do work at a much lower level.

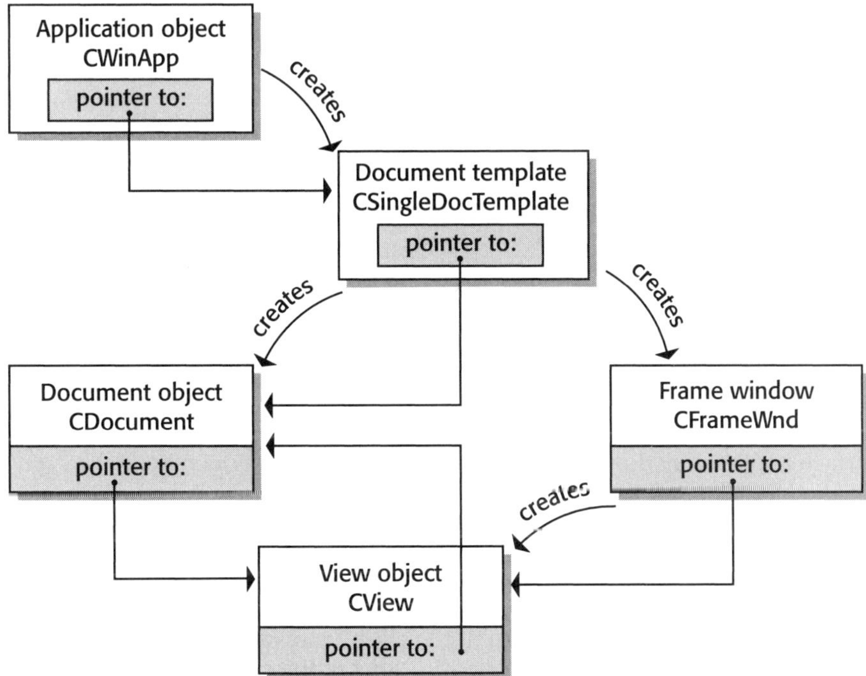

Figure 19-1: The model of the relationship between the five base classes for an SDI application.

The CDocument Class

The MFC-provided `CDocument` class provides the basic functionality for your application's document objects. The `CDocument` class' basic functionality includes the capability to create new documents, serialize document data, provide basic cooperation between a document object and a view window, and more. MFC also provides a series of `CDocument`-derived classes that implement functionality specific to certain application types. For example, MFC provides the `CRecordset` and `CDAORecordset` types to simplify the creation of database views. The relationship between documents and views is shown in Figure 19-2.

Declaring a document class in your application

When you use the AppWizard to create your applications, you often do not need to worry about declaring your base document class — the AppWizard does it for you. However, it is still useful for you to understand the behavior of the `CDocument` class — because more complex programs might very possibly require multiple instances of multiple derivations from `CDocument`. In addition, understanding the behavior of `CDocument` enables you to easily enhance the AppWizard-generated application skeleton.

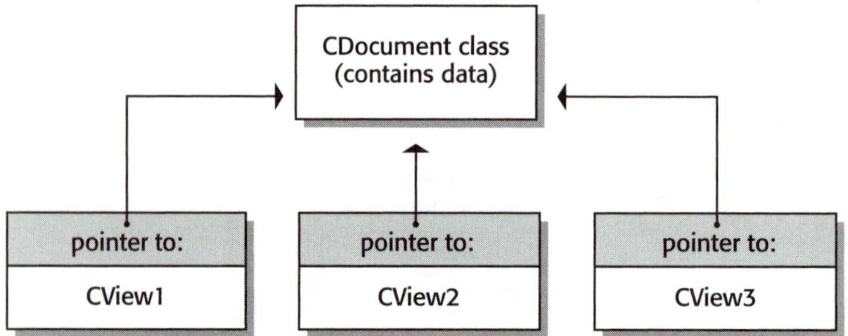

Figure 19-2: The one-to-many relationship between a document and its views.

Whether you create a single document interface application or a multiple document interface application, the AppWizard derives only a single document class for you from the MFC `CDocument` base class.

◆ ◆ ◆ ◆ ◆

When you build a simple MFC application, it is often enough for you to make relatively minor modifications to your AppWizard-supplied document class. You often will not need to do much more to the class than add some member variables and some member functions that other portions of the program can use to access those member variables.

For example, the document object for a simple communications program (such as a terminal emulator) might contain member variables for modem settings. Those member variables would probably store information such as telephone number, speed, parity, number of bits in each transmission segment, and so on. You could easily represent the communications settings with a set of simple member variables in the derived document class, as shown in the following code listing:

```
class CSimpleTermDoc : public CDocument
 {
 protected:
    CSimpleTermDoc();
    DECLARE_DYNCREATE(CSimpleTermDoc)
 public:
    CString m_sPhoneNum;
    DWORD m_dwTransSpeed;
    WORD m_nTransParity;
    WORD m_nTransBits;
    DWORD m_dwConnectTime;
```

After you declare the member variables, you must ensure that the program initializes the variables to some default values in the `CSimpleTermDoc` class' `OnNewDocument()` member function. In addition, you must place code in the `Serialize` function to ensure that the program properly serializes the variables. The code for the `OnNewDocument()` and `Serialize()` member functions would probably look similar to Listing 19-1.

Listing 19-1: Standard Code for the OnNewDocument() and Serialize() Member Functions

```
BOOL CSimpleTermDoc::OnNewDocument
 {
   if (!CDocument::OnNewDocument())
     return FALSE;
   m_sPhoneNum = _T("555-1212");
   m_dwTransSpeed = 28800;
   m_nTransParity = 0;
   m_nTransBits = 8;
   m_dwConnectTime = 0;
   return TRUE;
 }

void CSimpleTermDoc::Serialize(Carchive &ar)
 {
   if (ar.IsStoring())
    {
       ar << m_sPhoneNum;
       ar << m_dwTransSpeed;
       ar << m_nTransParity;
       ar << m_nTransBits;
       ar << m_dwConnectTime;
    }
   else
    {
       ar >> m_sPhoneNum;
       ar >> m_dwTransSpeed;
       ar >> m_nTransParity;
       ar >> m_nTransBits;
       ar >> m_dwConnectTime;
    }
 }
```

For your simpler applications, you really need do nothing beyond the initialization and serialization of your member variables to have a complete, fully functioning document class.

CDocument's member functions

The `CDocument` class has several member functions, in addition to the serialization and initialization member functions that your applications will frequently use. The first set of member functions provides access to the associated view objects. Every document object that you use within your applications will have a list of view objects that you associate with it. You can call the `GetFirstViewPosition()` member function for the document object to obtain an iterator to this list. The iterator will be of type `POSITION`.

You will use values of type POSITION throughout the MFC, primarily with collection classes. When your applications must traverse a list, you will typically request an iterator that the collection class associates with the first object on the list, and then use an iterator function to access the actual elements the list contains, one-by-one. CDocument, in this context, is a collection class: it maintains information about the collection of views associated with the class. Therefore, after you obtain the iterator to the first view in the class with the GetFirstViewPosition() member function, you can repeatedly call the GetNextView() member function to work through the remaining views in the collection.

In other words, to process all the views that your program has associated with a given document object, your program code will generally look similar to the following:

```
POSITION posView = GetFirstViewPosition();
while (posView != NULL)
 {
   CView *pView = GetNextView(posView);
   // Do something with the pointer to the view
 }
```

However, if all your program code is trying to accomplish is to notify all the views for the document that information within the document has changed, you can update the views without using an iterator and an iteration loop. Instead, you can call the document object's UpdateAllViews() member function. Furthermore, you can also specify application-specific data that instructs the views to selectively update only portions of the view windows when you call the UpdateAllViews() function. You will learn more about selective updates later in this chapter, when you work with the CView::OnUpdate member function.

Some other view-related member functions for the document object that you will use much less frequently include the AddView() and RemoveView() functions. As their names indicate, the functions let you manually add and remove views from a document's list of views. You generally will use the functions only rarely, as most developers simply use the default MFC implementation with little or no modification.

Whenever the document's data changes (through either a user's action or internal program processing), your program should call the SetModifiedFlag() member function. Consistent use of SetModifiedFlag()ensures that the MFC framework prompts the user before letting the user destroy an unsaved, changed document. Should you decide to override the framework, you can call the IsModified() member function to obtain the status of the flag.

You can use the SetTitle() member function to set the document object's title. The application, in turn, displays the title you set in the frame window (the main frame window in an SDI application, and the child frame window for the object in an MDI application).

You can also set the fully qualified pathname for the document with the `SetPathName()` function and obtain the pathname with the `GetPathName()` function. Finally, you can obtain the document template that the program associated with the document at the document's creation through a call to `GetDocTemplate()`.

Understanding documents and message processing

One of the most important features of a document, which you may have inferred from earlier paragraphs in this chapter, is that a `CDocument` object is not directly associated with a window. However, a `CDocument` object is a command-target object—which means the object can receive messages from the operating system. The view objects that you associate with a `CDocument` object are responsible for routing messages from the operating system to the document.

Because the view objects you associate with the document and the frame window that holds the document receive messages before passing them through to the document, you have a great deal of control over which messages the frame window, views, and document process. However, some common sense rules of thumb (as well as some simplicity issues) can provide a good starting point for how to process incoming messages.

When you consider messages, or for that matter any time that you are working with the document/view architecture, you should always keep in mind that a document is an abstract representation of your data—a representation, that is, which is independent of the visual representation of the data that the view window provides. Just as important, a document may have one, many, or no views attached to it—so documents should only respond to messages that are global in nature. That is, a document should only respond to messages that have an immediate effect on the document's data; the effect of such messages should then be reflected by all the views attached to the document. On the other hand, views should respond to messages that are specific to that window's view only.

In practical terms, the division of responsibilities between documents and views generally makes it easier to determine how to process a given command. For example, if your application has a Save command, which the user would select to save the *data* in the object, the document should handle that command—because the command is concerned with the data, not how the user sees the data.

On the other hand, if your application supports a Copy command, which the user would generally select to copy data the user has selected within the display, you would probably want to handle the command in the view. In fact, if a document supports multiple views, the data selected in each view might vary making it even more clear that you should generally process the Copy command separately for each view attached to a document.

Both the cases you have considered already are relatively clean cut—you are saving the data in the first example, and you are copying a representation of the data from within one view to another view in the second example. However, there are some borderline cases. A common one is the Paste command. Determining whether the document class or the view class should handle it is slightly more complex. The Paste command impacts the entire document (you are inserting data into the document), not just a single view. On the other hand, the current view may have significant importance when pasting information into a document. For example, the Paste action may actually replace existing, selected text within the view. In other words, the decision you must make about whether the document object or the view object should handle actions of this type is dependent on your application's design, and is generally something you should think through carefully.

Just to keep it interesting, you should not handle certain commands in either the document class or the view class, but rather in the frame window's code. Excellent examples of commands that you should handle within the frame window include commands to hide and display toolbars. The presence or absence of the toolbar is not particularly material to a document or its views. Rather, it is a configuration issue with effects global to the entire application.

Overriding virtual document functions

As you learned earlier in this chapter (when working with `OnNewDocument()` and `Serialize()`), many of the member functions the `CDocument` class defines are virtual functions, meaning that you can override them in your own class declarations. The virtual functions in the `CDocument` class provide default processing that is sufficient for most needs. However, you will find that your programs must also perform specific processing for a certain document that the default processing does not provide.

For example, the `CDocument` class and its derivatives call the `OnNewDocument()` member function whenever the program initializes a new document object (or when the program reuses an existing document object in an SDI application). Your applications typically call the `OnNewDocument()` function when handling a File New command. Similarly, your `CDocument` calls the `OnCloseDocument()` member function when the application is about to close a document. You should override this function within your own document classes if your application must perform any cleanup operations before destroying the document object.

Your document classes will call the `OnOpenDocument()` and `OnSaveDocument()` functions to read a document from disk or to write a document to disk, respectively. You should override these functions only if the default implementation (which calls the `Serialize()` member function) is not sufficient. An excellent example of a situation where you would override `OnOpenDocument()` and `OnSaveDocument()` is when you are encrypting data before you write it to the disk and decrypting it when you reload it from the disk.

The default implementations of both `OnOpenDocument()` and `OnCloseDocument()` call the `DeleteContents()` member function. The `DeleteContents()` member function deletes the document's contents without actually destroying the document object itself. Using DeleteContents() when opening a new document is more efficient (in terms of both memory usage and application speed) than actually closing and destroying the original document object and creating a new document object.

The OnFileSendMail() member function sends the document object as an attachment to a mail message. It first calls OnSaveDocument() to save a copy of the document to a temporary disk file (in the directory set by your TEMP environment variable). Next, the program code within the member function attaches the temporary file to a Messaging API (MAPI) message. The member function uses the OnUpdateFileSendMail() member function to enable the command that you identify with the constant ID_FILE_SEND_MAIL in the applications menu or remove it altogether if MAPI support is not available to the program. Both OnFileSendMail() and OnUpdateFileSendMail() are overridable functions, which enables you to (relatively easily) implement customized messaging behavior within your applications.

Working with complex document data

Earlier in this chapter you learned how to derive simple document classes from CDocument, within which you can store the document's data in a series of simple member variables. However, creating applications that you can use in the real world tends to be more demanding. Most applications you will develop will require significantly more advanced data than what you could ever possibly represent with a few variables of simple data types.

You can use many different approaches to manage complex data types within a document object; however, arguably the best approach is to use a set of classes that you derive from the CObject class. Each derived class, then, stores the complex data objects. The document, in turn, uses a standard or custom-created collection class to embed the objects within the document class. For example, you might create data definitions similar to the following for an application:

```
class CAppObject : public CObject
 {
   // definitions
 }
class CAppSubObject1 : public CObject
 {
   // definitions
 }
class CAppSubObject2 : public CObject
 {
   // definitions
 }
```

Then, within the declaration of the document class, you would include a CObList member. The CObList class supports ordered lists of non-unique CObject pointers accessible sequentially or by pointer value. CObList lists behave like doubly linked lists. Your document declaration, therefore, would look similar to the following:

```
class CSampleDoc : public CDocument
 {
   // code here
 public:
   CObList m_DataObList;
   // code here
 }
```

In a complex situation such as the one just outlined, it is often not sufficient to simply declare member variables. Your document class is also likely to require member functions that provide methods to let views and other objects that must access the document's data do so. For example, you may not want to let other classes (such as a view class) directly manipulate the `m_DataObList` variable. Instead, you should generally provide a member function that the view class can access to iterate through the `m_DataObList` object as it needs to.

Such member functions should also ensure that, each time the document's data changes, the application properly updates all the document's views. The member functions should also call the document's `SetModifed` member function to indicate to the document that an accessing function or class has changed the document's data. If your application will support an undo-type capability, you should also place your application's buffered undo data into its correct storage location while inside the member function. To better understand this, consider the following member function, `AddNewObj`, which adds a new object to the document's object list:

```
BOOL CSampleDoc : AddNewObj(CAppObject *pObject)
 {
   try
    {
       m_DataObList.AddTail((CObject *)pObject);
       SetModifiedFlag(TRUE);
       UpdateAllViews(NULL, UPDATE_OBJECT, pObject;
       return TRUE;
    }
   catch(CMemoryException *e)
    {
       TRACE("Doc-AddNewObj memory allocation error.\n");
       e->Delete();
       return FALSE;
    }
 }
```

Understanding the importance of the `AddNewObj()` member function is easier when you consider the relationship between the document and its views and how the program will pass control back and forth between the two.

First, the user will interact with the view, which might result in a new object being added, an existing object being modified or deleted, or some other action. For now, presume that the user's actions result in the need to add a new object to the document. To add a new object, the view object calls the `AddNewObj()` member function. After the member function adds the new object successfully, the document object calls the UpdateAllViews() member function, which, in turn, calls the OnUpdate() member function of each view that you have previously associated with the document. The AddNewObj() member function passes a hint to the UpdateAllViews() member function through the use of the application-defined UPDATE_OBJECT constant and a pointer to a CObject. The hint assists all the views in most efficiently updating their component windows by instructing the views to repaint only those regions of the view directly and indirectly affected by the addition of the new object. Figure 19-3 shows the control-passing mechanism that the views and the document will use.

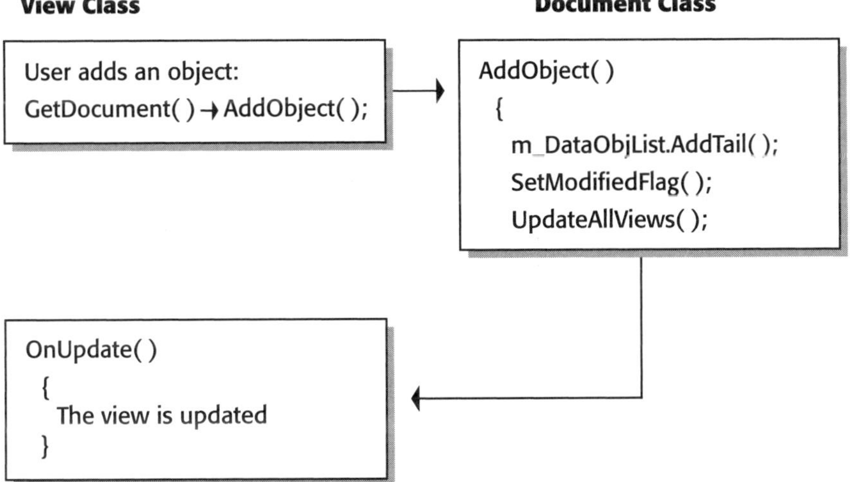

Figure 19-3: Control passes from the view class to the document class and back.

Another advantage of using MFC collection classes within your application is that collection classes support serialization. For example, to load and save your document's data that is stored in CObject objects and referenced through a CObList object, all your need to do is to construct the document's Serialize() member function as shown here:

```
void CSampleDoc::Serialize(CArchive &ar)
 {
   if (ar.IsStoring())
    {
       // serialize any non-collection class data here
    }
   else
    {
       // serialize any non-collection class data here
    }
   m_DataObList.Serialize(ar);
 }
```

You should be aware, however, that for this technique to work, you must implement the `Serialize()` member function for all your object classes. A `CObject`-derived class does not serialize itself. If you decide to use one of the general purpose collection templates, serialization is an issue that you must pay close attention to. The collection `CArray`, `CList`, and `CMap` rely on the `SerializeElements()` member function to serialize the objects within the collection. MFC declares this function as shown here:

```
template <class TYPE> void AFXAPI
    SerializeElements(CArchive &ar, TYPE *pElements,
    int nCount);
```

Because the collection class templates do not require that you derive `TYPE` from `CObject`, they do not call the `Serialize()` member function for each element (because the `Serialize()` member function is not guaranteed to exist). Instead, the default implementation of `SerializeElements()` performs a *bitwise* read or write action. However, as you can imagine, in most cases, a bitwise read or write is not what you will want to perform. Rather, you should implement your own `SerializeElements()` function for your objects. You might implement such a function as shown here:

```
void SerializeElements(CArchive &ar, CAppObject **pObs,
    int nCount);
 {
   for (int i = 0; i < nCount; i++; pObs++)
     (*pObs)->Serialize(ar);
 }
```

Understanding the benefits of CCmdTarget and CDocItem

As you learned in the previous section of this chapter, you can use objects that you derive from the `CObject` class to store data within your documents. Unfortunately, if you wish your documents and applications to support OLE automation, the `CObject` class is insufficient. Instead, you must declare your objects as *command targets*. If you wish to support OLE automation, you may prefer to derive your data from the MFC `CCmdTarget` base class.

Alternatively, and generally better, you may want to derive your data objects from the MFC `CDocItem` class. You can either create a collection of `CDocItem` objects yourself or rely on MFC's `COleDocument` class to create the collection. In other words, rather than deriving your document class from `CDocument`, derive it from `COleDocument`. You can use `COleDocument` in OLE applications where either the `COleDocument` class or a class previously derived from `COleDocument` is the base class for the OLE application's document class. Like `CDocument`, `COleDocument` is a collection class. `COleDocument` supports a collection of `CDocItem` objects, which are derived in turn either from `COleServerItem` or `COleClientItem`. However, `COleDocument` supports `CDocItem` generically (that is, it doesn't care whether the item is a server or client item). COleDocument's generic implementation means that you can add your own CDocItem-derived objects to the collection without fear that doing so will interfere with normal OLE operations and behavior.

One nice thing about working with COleDocument is that it automatically adds CDocItem members for you. In other words, if you use AddItem(), RemoveItem(), GetStartPosition(), and GetNextItem(), you can add, remove, and retrieve document items without further processing. The underlying MFC code handles your other needs (such as serialization) without further programming on your part.

However, working with COleDocument is not without its pitfalls. Because of how you derive your document items and the OLE COleClientItem and COleServerItem objects, you may need to perform certain special programming actions to add certain functions to a given object. For example, suppose that you declare your object items as shown here:

```
class CSampleDocItem : public CDocItem
 {
   //  more code here
   CRect m_Rect;
 };
```

In addition, suppose that you also support the m_Rect member variable within your OLE client items, as shown here:

```
class CSampleClientItem : public COleClientItem
 {
   //  more code here
   CRect m_Rect;
 };
```

Given these two declarations, you might suppose that you can create a function that takes an item from your document and manipulates its m_Rect member as shown here:

```
void sampFunc(CDocItem *pItem)
 {
   samp2Func(pItem->m_Rect);       // Error!
 }
```

Because the CDocItem class, by itself, does not contain an m_Rect member variable, the compiler halts the program's compilation with an error at the function declaration. Unfortunately, using a pointer to your own CDocItem-derived class doesn't really solve the problem either:

```
void sampFunc(CSampleDocItem *pItem)
 {
   samp2Func(pItem->m_Rect);
 }
```

While declaring the function in this manner supports your derived class, it won't support OLE client items of type `CDocItem`—a significant issue. An obvious solution is to simply create two overridden versions of `sampFunc`, but maintaining two separate, identical versions of the same function is not only lacking in elegance, it makes maintenance all that much more difficult. The best solution is to instead create a wrapper function that takes a pointer to a `CDocItem` object and uses MFC runtime-type information to obtain the member variable, as shown here:

```
CRect GetRect(CDocItem *pDocItem)
 {
   if (pDocItem->IsKindOf(RUNTIME_CLASS(CSampleDocItem)))
     return ((CSampleDocItem *)pDocItem)->m_Rect;
   else if
       (pDocItem->IsKindOf(RUNTIME_CLASS(CSampleClientItem)))
     return  ((CSampleClientItem *)pDocItem)->m_Rect;
   ASSERT(FALSE);
   return CRect(0, 0, 0, 0);
 }

sampFunc(CDocItem *pItem)
 {
    samp2Func(GetRect(pItem));
 }
```

This solution, however, does require that you declare and implement both the `CSampleDocItem` and the `CSampleClientItem` classes with the `DECLARE_DYNAMIC` and `IMPLEMENT_DYNAMIC` macros. However, that generally should not be an issue because your document objects will typically support serialization. When you declare and implement a class with the `DECLARE_SERIAL` and `IMPLEMENT_SERIAL` macros, the `DECLARE_DYNAMIC` and `IMPLEMENT_DYNAMIC` macros are implied.

The Importance of the InitInstance Function to Documents

Throughout this chapter, you have learned about deriving document classes for use within your applications. In the next section, you will learn about view classes and how to use them to access the data the document contains. However, before you continue on to views, it is valuable to understand how your SDI-based MFC applications access the starting document for the application.

When you use AppWizard to create a new application, AppWizard implements the `InitInstance()` overridable function according to the options you select within the AppWizard screen. For example, if you select the single document interface (SDI) option, AppWizard creates the following code:

```
BOOL CMyApp::InitInstance()
 {
   // Standard initialization
   SetDialogBkColor(); // Set dialog background color to gray
   LoadStdProfileSettings(); // Load standard INI file options
   // Register the application's document templates.
   // Document templates serve as the connection between
   // documents, frame windows and views.
   CSingleDocTemplate* pDocTemplate;
   pDocTemplate = new CSingleDocTemplate(IDR_MAINFRAME,
       RUNTIME_CLASS(CMyDoc),
       RUNTIME_CLASS(CMainFrame), // main SDI frame window
       RUNTIME_CLASS(CMyView));
   AddDocTemplate(pDocTemplate);
   OnFileNew();                   // create an empty document
   if (m_lpCmdLine[0] != '\0')
    {
      // TODO: add command line processing here
    }
   return TRUE;
 }
```

The `InitInstance()` function that the AppWizard creates first sets the background color of the dialog to gray. Next, it loads any standard INI file options that may be set. After taking care of this basic housekeeping, the code creates a pointer to a document template, which serves as the connection between the `CDocument` class, the frame window class, and any views you create for the document. In this case, AppWizard registered the document class as `CMyDoc`, the frame window as `CMainFrame`, and the view class as `CMyView`. The program code then adds the newly created document template to the collection of document templates with the `AddDocTemplate` member function, and calls the `CMyDoc` class' `OnFileNew()` member function to create an empty document for the program's startup. The last lines in the function enable you to add stubs within the program to process command-line options (for example, a filename to open within the program).

In Chapter 20 you will learn how the `InitInstance()` member function differs within a multiple document interface (MDI) program from within an SDI program. For now, it is sufficient to see how MFC uses the `CSingleDocTemplate` class to combine a document, view, and window frame class within your programs.

How your applications manage documents and views

Now that you have learned about documents and been briefly introduced to document templates, it is important to understand how MFC keeps track of the documents and views that comprise the application, and which documents and views are related to one another. The runtime class information that you have learned about in previous chapters helps you understand when you consider these relationships.

Because the document/view architecture is the cornerstone of any document-based application (as you learned earlier, dialog-based applications perform differently than document/view applications), MFC must be able to create and destroy objects from the document/view implementation classes. Because your application may handle more than one type of document/view relationship, MFC must have some way of knowing which document, view, and display classes you implement, what the relationships are between the classes, and how to create the implementations of the classes at runtime. After all, while one document might support many different types of views, associating other views with that same document might be nonsensical.

Focusing on the CSingleDocTemplate class

To learn how MFC describes and maintains these associations, use the AppWizard to create a simple single document application, or look at the HexView application that you will create later in this chapter. In either case, you will find source code that looks like the following (which is identical to the code you saw in the earlier section about the `InitInstance()` member function):

```
CSingleDocTemplate* pDocTemplate;
pDocTemplate = new CSingleDocTemplate(
   IDR_MAINFRAME,
   RUNTIME_CLASS(CSIMPLEDoc),
   RUNTIME_CLASS(CMainFrame),      // main SDI frame window
   RUNTIME_CLASS(CSIMPLEView));
AddDocTemplate(pDocTemplate);
```

The code dynamically allocates a new `CSingleDocTemplate` object. The constructor for `CSingleDocTemplate` takes four parameters. The first parameter is a resource ID. You will learn the significance of the resource ID later in this chapter. The second, third, and fourth parameters associated with the `CSingleDocTemplate()` constructor are pointers to runtime class information. The `RUNTIME_CLASS()` macro generates a pointer to the runtime class information for the application's document, main frame, and view classes. These pointers are all passed to the `CSingleDocTemplate` constructor, which keeps the pointers so that it can create instances of the objects as needed to put together a complete document/view team.

The `CSingleDocTemplate` object lives as long as the application continues to execute. MFC uses the object internally and destroys any added document templates as the application's `CWinApp` object is destroyed. You can find the code that allocates `CSingleDocTemplates` to your application in its `CWinApp::InitInstance()` function, but you will never write code that deletes the document template objects if you use `AddDocTemplate()` to add the template, because the `CWinApp` destructor function will automatically clean up that document template allocation.

Working briefly with frame windows

Throughout this chapter you have learned about documents and frames — and you will continue to do so throughout the remainder of the chapter. However, as you have probably gathered already, understanding the importance of frames in a document/view application is also important — even though you will not work with the frame class(es) anywhere near as frequently as you will work with the document and view classes.

In fact, the view your application implements is a window but not a pop-up or frame window. Instead, it is a borderless child window that doesn't have a menu of its own, so it must be contained by some sort of frame window. MFC places the view window you create into the client area of the frame window identified in the document template constructor. In an SDI application, the frame window is always the main window for the application. As you will see in Chapter 20, the frame window for views within a multiple document interface application is an MDI child window.

When developing a Windows application, most programmers do not take the extra step of separating the client area of their application from the frame window. Instead, you would typically create a `WS_OVERLAPPED`-style window and paint right in its client area. To make MFC a little more modular, Microsoft implemented it so that it distinguishes the two types of frame windows that you might use. That is, MFC makes both an internal and an external distinction between a single document interface frame window and a Multiple Document Interface frame window. You will learn more about frame windows later, but for now, it's enough to understand that the frame window is the one that receives all of the menu and window frame messages.

Window frame messages are messages that only windows with frames receive. Such messages include messages about resizing the window, maximizing the window, minimizing the window, and so on. The frame window also receives many nonclient area messages because the frame window is responsible for implementing the nonclient area of your application.

Document template resources

As you learned in the section entitled "Focusing on the CSingleDocTemplate class," the first parameter to the `CSingleDocTemplate` constructor is a resource ID. The first parameter tells the frame that the template will use what kind of resources the frame must have available to complete the link. This ID identifies the resources used to supply the frame with an accelerator table, menu, and icon. The frame window that your application uses should have the same resource ID for each resource type it wishes to use.

If you examine `HexView.rc`, you will find an accelerator table, a menu, and an icon, each with the ID of `IDR_MAINFRAME` — that corresponds to the ID the application passes to the `CSingleDocTemplate` constructor. Having exactly the same frame window resource IDs is far more convenient than requiring the constructor for `CSingleDocTemplate` to take six or seven parameters.

The resource ID is also the ID of an entry in your application's string table. The identified string has a very special format: it's really seven strings in one, each separated by a newline (\n) character.

How the string resource affects the document template

As the previous section explains, the `IDR_MAINFRAME` resource ID actually refers to several resources within your application. One of the resources is a string resource, which contains seven substrings. The substrings within the string resource identify seven things about your application and, specifically, about the document your application implements. The first substring provides a window title for the application's main window when the document type you will be registering is active. The second substring is a basis for the name of the default document—MFC appends a number to this substring for each document the user opens. For example, the third document opened against a given document template would be named `HexDoc3` if the second string contained `HexDoc`. You may see this substring referred to as a *document name* in other books you read on Visual C++. If the second string is blank, your application always uses `Untitled` as the document name.

The third substring is the name of the document type. If your application supports more than one document type, when the user selects the New command in the File menu, they are provided a list of document types to choose from. If you specify an empty string for the third substring entry, the document type that you are registering is not exposed in the New dialog box. You can use this as a technique to hide document types that you don't want the user to be able to directly create.

The fourth string provides a description of the document type and a wildcard filename filter that the application uses to match document files of the type you are registering. The string is added to the List Files Of Type: combo box in the File Open dialog box for your application. You might want to set the string to Pole Maps (*.plm), for instance, if you have a document that maps telephone poles and has the file extension .plm. The text in this string is used only for the benefit of the user—in other words, it doesn't actually determine the wildcards used to find files in the File Open dialog box.

Instead, the fifth string specifies the extension for any files stored by the document type in question. If you don't specify an extension here, the window defaults to the first in the list of filters. Your extension name should include a leading period, but not an asterisk (*). For instance, `.xyz` is correct, while `xyz` and `*.xyz` are not.

The sixth string element identifies the document type for the registration database. This string is used by Windows Explorer, the Registry, and OLE to register your document type. It is not shown to users unless they examine the File Associations dialog box in Windows Explorer or search the Registry itself.

The seventh and final string element is the name of the document as stored in the Windows Registry. Assuming that you are implementing OLE support, this string is used in the Registry (and therefore by OLE itself) to identify the type of document your application implements. For example, both Excel and Word show this string to users when they use the Object option available from the Insert menu to embed an object serviced by your application in the host application's document. You should make this string as short and as meaningful as possible, in order to keep the information from confusing the user.

Breaking apart the string resource

Since the string resource is the cornerstone of the document registration process and you can alter many of your application's subtle features using the string resource that your application registers, you should carefully check what you place in the string. The default string produced by the AppWizard for the HexView example looks like this:

```
"HexView\n\nHexView\n\n\nHexView.Document\nHexView Document"
```

The default string gives the application a window title of `HexView`, a File menu New option type name of `HexView`, an OLE internal name of `HexView.Document`, and an external name of `HexView Document`.

The `CDocTemplate` class from which MFC derives the `CSingleDocTemplate` and `CMultiDocTemplate` classes includes the `GetDocString()` member function. `GetDocString()`, which accepts a reference to a `CString` object and an index, enables you to query the values of the registered string resource. `CDocTemplate` implements the `GetDocString()` member function as shown here:

```
virtual BOOL GetDocString( CString& rString,
    enum DocStringIndex index ) const;
```

The second parameter, `index`, is expressed as a private enum of the `CDocTemplate` class. Valid values are shown in Table 19-1.

Table 19-1
Valid Values for the Index Parameter

Value	*Description*
CDocTemplate::windowTitle	Text for the application window's title bar, important only for SDI applications
CDocTemplate::docName	Root for the default document name
CDocTemplate::fileNewName	Name of the document for the file New box
CDocTemplate::filterName	Text for the File/Open dialog's File Type drop-down list box
CDocTemplate::filterExt	Wildcard filename filter matching files for this document type
CDocTemplate::regFileTypeId	Registry database internal name, used by OLE and the File Manager
CDocTemplate::regFileTypeName	Registry database document name, used by all OLE applications and exposed to the user

There's no corresponding `CDocTemplate::SetDocString()` function. You cannot change the attributes of a document template after you create it.

As you have learned, the string resource dictates many subtle aspects of your application, and the default string resource the AppWizard produces gives your application a healthy but basic user interface. You can also change many of the values within the string resource in the Document Template Strings tab of AppWizard's Advanced Options window. All the fields in this tab of the dialog box correspond directly to substrings in the document template string resource. If you know what your application will look like when you finish developing it, you can change the appropriate strings in the Advanced Options dialog box and avoid editing the string resource directly.

However, as you add features, you will certainly have to make adjustments to the string resource. To perform these adjustments, you must edit the string resource directly, using the string table editor. If you make a mistake, MFC will either blindly put the wrong string in the wrong part of your user interface or generate an Assert Failed error message at runtime. When you change the document template resource string, you should generally test your application immediately to make sure that you have not accidentally disabled or invalidated any other features of your application.

Looking at the stock view resources

Many other resources in your application are identified by the resource ID in your document template. All these resources are associated with the document type that your application is currently editing. For the SDI AppWizard application, the ID that is used for the default document template string resource and all of the other resources associated with the template is called `IDR_MAINFRAME`.

The AppWizard gives your application's main frame a menu that is also identified by `IDR_MAINFRAME`. In single document interface applications, this means that your menu depends on what kind of document is active. For Multiple Document Interface applications, it means that each individual document type has its own type of menu. If you want all your document types to share a common menu, you can simply change each template type to point at the same menu resource.

The frame also has an icon with the same identifier as the other resources, which indicates that the icon should be used to represent that SDI application. For example, the operating system displays the named icon when the user minimizes the application. For Multiple Document Interface applications, the icon is the icon for minimized MDI child windows. The icon used for the application comes from another source, which you will learn about later in Chapter 20.

Your application may also feature a dialog named after that same template resource ID. Such applications are rare — they are generally applications that have a dialog as the core interface for the view of their document. You will learn later in this chapter about views that use a dialog as the core of their interface, and you will use this technique in Chapters 26, 27, and 28, when you work with databases.

The application uses the bitmap resource the AppWizard provides to build the default toolbar for the frame window. While the toolbar seems to be composed of several buttons, the buttons are actually sections of a single bitmap. You will learn more about the `CToolbar` class, used to make toolbars in MFC, in Chapter 23.

Since the frame implements a window with a menu, it may also provide an accelerator table. This table provides translations between keystrokes and `WM_COMMAND` messages, which the application should send when the operating system detects the keystroke. The framework takes care of searching for the accelerator table and translating and dispatching the messages the operating system generates when the user presses the appropriate key. The default accelerator table that the AppWizard produces has accelerators for the standard user interface elements in the menu.

You should feel free to modify any of these resources to suit the needs of your application. However, you may need to change more than the resource to keep things working. Make sure you read up on the classes that make use of the resources before you change them so that your application stays healthy.

Considering the document template life cycle

As you might imagine, `CSingleDocTemplate` is a lightweight class — that is, it takes very little memory. You shouldn't worry about keeping document template classes lying about, even if you have dozens of them.

CSingleDocTemplate (and CMultiDocTemplate, which you will learn about in Chapter 20) is used heavily by the application frameworks. After setting them up and getting them started, your application depends on the templates to manage the document, view, and frame windows objects — but you no longer need to manipulate the templates directly. As you saw earlier in this chapter, your application should register all of the document templates that it will use during its CWinApp::InitInstance() member function. By making them public members of your application object, you can access them later on when you need to juggle documents and views.

When you think about and manipulate document templates, probably the best single perspective to maintain is to let MFC do the work. In other words, you should ask MFC's code in the document template object to create the view and document you need and hook up all of the associations. In a well-designed application, you should almost never have to directly create your own views, documents, and frames. The best applications let the document template do the work.

Advanced work with templates

Now that you understand the basics of templates, it is important to think about them from the perspective of application design. The way your application works really depends on your point of view. If your users have to do a lot of work to get to a view of the data they are interested in, they'll quickly get frustrated. Worse yet, if the views your application offers do not represent information in the way your users perceive as intuitive, your application will be perceived as awkward, because the users will have to spend too much time thinking about how things should work instead of actually getting work done.

Out-of-the-box application frameworks that the AppWizard produces are too good not to use for most of your applications. Even after some modification, MFC reacts to your changes in ways that are generally preceived by the user as intuitive and consistent with the interfaces they are used to.

If you register several different document templates, you get the extra dialog box to enable the users to choose their document type after selecting the New option from the File menu. And once you have taken advantage of this simple opportunity, you will soon find that there are several other instances where you might want your application to differ slightly from the mainstream.

Working with multiple templates

You can always use more than one template when you are running an MFC document/view application. Your application will generally create any necessary templates as it handles CWinApp::InitInstance(). If your application initially came from the AppWizard, you will find that the function has been coded to create and register a template for the document/view pair that your application uses by default.

If you ever need to use documents or views in any other combination, you should add code to create a template for those particular document/view pairs. Doing so makes it much easier to create instances of the pairs at the user's request. The CDocTemplate-derived object you create is just that — an object — and as such, you need to maintain a pointer to it after you use new to create it. You generally should keep these pointers to document templates as instance data in your application's CWinApp-derived class. If you do, you can reference them at almost any time during the application's execution.

Each template you register with the frameworks using CWinApp::AddDocTemplate() is kept in a linked list. MFC uses this list to find templates when the user asks to create a new document or a new view, or performs any operation that requires that the application find an appropriate document template. For example, if more than one document template exists when CWinApp::OnFileNew() is called, the framework presents a list box that lets the user select the template for the type of document they wish to create.

The Undocumented CDocManager Class

The list is managed by an internal instance of an MFC collection class called CDocManager. This class is an undocumented implementation feature of MFC. Understanding how it works, though, can be quite useful. The CWinApp-derived object in your application creates an instance of the class. CWinApp holds a pointer to the CDocManager object. It destroys the object just before your application exits, in CWinApp's destructor function. CWinApp stores this pointer in the m_pDocManager member variable. In fact, you can use this pointer at any time to gain access to the document manager.

The document manager's main importance derives from its management of that linked list of template objects. The document manager stores the list in its public m_TemplateList member. You can walk the list using code similar to the following:

```
void CSampleWinApp::IterateEveryTemplate()
{
   CDocManager* pManager = AfxGetApp()->m_pDocManager;
   if (pManager == NULL)
      return;
   POSITION pos = pManager->GetFirstDocTemplatePosition();
   while (pos != NULL)
   {
      // get the next template
      CDocTemplate* pTemplate =
          pManager->GetNextDocTemplate(pos);
      // you can now do work with each pointer
      DoSomething(pTemplate);
  }
}
```

One of the most interesting things you can do with the list of templates is to derive a list of all active documents. This involves a nested loop; so for each template you find, you can loop through the documents that the template has created. To do this, you might use some code similar to the following:

```
void CSampleWinApp::IterateEveryDocument()
 {
   CDocManager* pManager = AfxGetApp()->m_pDocManager;
   if (pManager == NULL)
      return;
   POSITION posTemplate =
       pManager->GetFirstDocTemplatePosition();
   while (posTemplate != NULL)
    {
      // get the next template
      CDocTemplate* pTemplate =
          pManager->GetNextDocTemplate(posTemplate);
      POSITION posDoc = pTemplate->GetFirstDocPosition();
      while (posDoc != NULL)
       {
         CYourDocument* pThisOne =
            (CSampleDocument*) GetNextDoc(posDoc);
         // do some work with each document
         pThisOne->SomeFunctionCall();
       }
    }
 }
```

In both of these code fragments, you retrieve a pointer to the manager by first getting a pointer to the application object with a call to AfxGetApp(). Next, you examine the m_pDocManager member for the pointer to the template manager. This is, actually, more than a little duplicative because the code fragments are member functions in CSampleWinApp; so they're presumably members of the very object that you are obtaining with the call to AfxGetApp(). Instead, you could have accessed the m_pDocManager member directly. However, the inefficiency lets you see the use of AfxGetApp() to retrieve information about the running application object. More importantly, you have learned how to implement the code in any function of any object in your application — because the code does not presume that it is running within the CWinApp-derived object.

The code fragments make use of the CDocManager member functions GetFirstDocTemplatePosition() and GetNextDocTemplate(), which should look familiar to you because they perform similar processing to the GetFirstViewPosition() and GetNextView() member functions of the CDocument class that you learned about earlier in this chapter. GetNextDocTemplate() is the one that does the real work — it gets a pointer of type POSITION to the next document. As you can see, some runtime casting is also in the code fragments because the second program fragment must promote the pointers to plain CDocument objects to pointers to the CSampleDocument class. It would be good programming to do IsKindOf() tests here, or use MFC's DYNAMIC_DOWNCAST() macro to make sure you get what you really wanted, but the code does not do so for simplicity's sake.

✦ ✦ ✦ ✦ ✦

Destroying documents added with the AddDocTemplate() member function

If you use `AddDocTemplate()` to add your new template to the list that MFC manages for you, you needn't worry about deleting the template when your application closes. However, in some circumstances, you may wish to have the template hidden from the user, and it is then that you need to make sure your template is deleted. Deleting the template object during the program's execution of the destructor function of your application's `CWinApp` object is too good an opportunity to miss.

When designing your applications, don't worry about keeping templates around as long as you need them — as you learned earlier in this chapter, templates are very lightweight. As with any other object, reasonableness guidelines apply. A thousand templates are probably a little much (and a coding nightmare), but adding ten or twenty templates to an application should not be burdensome, provided you need the additional templates.

Understanding and Using the CView Class

As you have learned, for every `CDocument`-derived class that presents a visual interface to the user is a `CView`-derived class that provides the interface. The `CView`-derived class provides the visual presentation of the document's data and handles user interaction through the view window.

The view window, in turn, is a child of a frame window. In an SDI application, the view window is a child of the main frame window. In MDI applications, the view window is a child of an MDI child window. In addition, the frame window can be the in-place frame window during OLE in-place editing, if your application supports OLE in-place editing. A frame window, in turn, may contain several view windows (for example, through the use of splitter windows, which you will learn about in Chapter 20).

Declaring a view class

As earlier sections of this chapter have explained in detail, you should declare all data that is part of a document as part of the document's class. With that overriding precept in mind, however, it is important to recognize that many data elements in your applications will probably pertain to a specific view. More importantly, most of those data elements will be nonpersistent — meaning you will not save them as part of the document.

Suppose, for example, that you create an application that is capable of presenting the data within the document at different zoom factors. The zoom factor is specific to each individual view — meaning that different views may use different zoom factors even when the views are presenting information from the same document.

Given these considerations, you are probably best served to declare the zoom factor as a member variable of the view class, as shown here, rather than as a variable in the document class:

```
class CZoomView : public CView
 {
 protected:
   CZoomView();
   DECLARE_DYNCREATE(CZoomView)
 public:
   CZoomableDoc* GetDocument();
   WORD m_wZoomPercent;
 }
```

However, much more important than any member variables representing a setting is a member variable that represents the *current selection*. The current selection is the collection of objects within the document that the user has selected for manipulation. The nature and type of manipulation that the user might perform is entirely application dependent, but it may include such operations as Clipboard cutting and copying or OLE drag-and-drop placement support.

Arguably, the easiest way to implement a current selection is to use a collection class, just as you would in the document class. For example, you might declare the collection that represents the current selection as shown here:

```
class CSelectableView : public CView
 {
   //  more code here
   CList <CDocItem *, CDocItem *> m_SelectList;
   //
 }
```

In addition to modifying the view class declaration, you must write one or more member functions so that your view class can respond to selection activities — filling and emptying the list, and so on. However, you must also always override the `OnDraw()` member function. The default implementation of `OnDraw()` performs no processing — you absolutely have to write code that displays your document's data items (even if the view class doesn't contain member variables of its own).

For example, if you derive your document class from `COleDocument` and use `CDocItems` to maintain the document's data, your `OnDraw()` member function for your class will probably look similar to the following:

```
void COleCapView::OnDraw(CDC *pDC)
 {
   COLECapDoc *pDoc = GetDocument();
   ASSERT_VALID(pDoc);
   POSITION posDoc = pDoc->GetStartPosition();
   while (posDoc != NULL)
    {
```

```
        CDocItem *pObject = pDoc->GetNextItem(posDoc);
        if (pObject->IsKindOf(RUNTIME_CLASS(CNormDocItem)))
        {
          ((CNormDocItem *)pObject)->Draw(pDc);
        }
        else if (pObject->IsKindOf(RUNTIME_CLASS(COleDocItem)))
        {
          ((COleDocItem *)pObject)->Draw(pDc);
        }
        else
          ASSERT(FALSE);
    }
```

Analyzing the CView member functions

Like the CDocument class, the CView class offers a wide variety of member functions that you can use in their default form or override to provide specific functionality within your applications.

Among the most commonly used member functions in the CView class is the GetDocument() member function, which returns a pointer to the document object that you have previously associated with the view. Another commonly used member function is DoPreparePrinting(). The DoPreparePrinting() function displays the Print dialog and creates a printer device context based on the user's selections within the dialog. You will learn more about the DoPreparePrinting() function in Chapter 21.

GetDocument() and DoPreparePrinting() are the only CView member functions that are not overridable. You can override any of the remaining CView member functions. These member functions supplement the large number of overridable functions that the CWnd class (which is the base class for the CView class) provides. In addition, the member functions handle the vast majority of user interface events. Trying to list all the member functions here is a relatively futile exercise because there are far too many of them to make it worthwhile. However, among the member functions are functions to handle keyboard, mouse, timer, system, and other messages, Clipboard and MDI events, and initialization and termination messages. Your application should override the view class member functions as it needs to. For example, if your application enables the user to place an object in a document by clicking and dragging the mouse, you should override the CWnd::OnLButtonDown member function to support that functionality. In general, you can use the ClassWizard to create the override function and simply add the appropriate code in the section the ClassWizard marks as TODO.

Most applications will override some important functions whenever you work with a CView class. You already learned about the first one — overriding OnDraw() is necessary for any CView-derived object to display information at all. In addition, for any application you create that supports OLE (which, in today's development environment, is virtually any application), you must override the IsSelected() member function. The IsSelected() member function returns TRUE if the object that its argument points to is part of the view's current selection. If you implemented your current selection using the CList template collection as a list of CDocItem objects (as you learned to earlier in this chapter), you would implement IsSelected() in a form similar to that shown here:

```
BOOL CSampView::IsSelected(const CObject* pDocItem) const
 {
   return (m_SelectList.Find((CDocItem *)pDocItem) != NULL);
 }
```

Another important member function that most applications override is the OnUpdate() member function. As you learned earlier in this chapter, the document class' UpdateAllViews() member function calls the OnUpdate() member function for each view associated with a document each time you invoke it. The default implementation of OnUpdate() simply invalidates the entire client area of the view window (which, in turn, results in redrawing the entire client area). To improve your application's performance, you may wish to override OnUpdate() and invalidate only the areas of the view window that the application must update. For example, you might implement OnUpdate() as shown here:

```
void CSampView::OnUpdate(CView *pView,
     LPARAM lHint, CObject *pObj)
 {
   if (lHint==UPDATE_OBJECT)      // app-defined constant
     InvalidateRect((CAppObject *)pObj)->m_Rect);
   else
     Invalidate();
 }
```

You ordinarily should not do any drawing in the OnUpdate() member function. Instead, you should do any drawing in the view's OnDraw() member function.

◆ ◆ ◆ ◆ ◆

If your application supports nonstandard mapping modes such as zooming or rotating, the CView class OnPrepareDC() member function acquires special significance. In this function, you will set the view window's mapping mode before the application actually draws anything onto the window. You should always be sure, in the event that you create a device context for your view window, that your application calls OnPrepareDC() to ensure that the application applies the proper settings to the device context.

Similarly, your applications may often need to create a device context for the sole purpose of retrieving the current mapping of the view window. For example, you might need to convert the position of a mouse click from physical to logical coordinates within the view's `OnLButtonDown()` member function, as shown here:

```
void CSampView::OnLButtonDown(UITN nFlags, Cpoint point)
 {
   CClientDC dc(this);
   OnPrepareDC(&dc);
   dc.DPtoLP(&point);
   // further processing
 }
```

Working with views and messages

In addition to those messages for which MFC provides default handlers in either `CView` or its parent class, `CWnd`, a typical view class processes many other system messages. Other messages typically include command messages that represent the user's selection of a menu item, toolbar button, or other user interface object.

As you learned earlier in this chapter, whether it is the view or the document (or in some cases, the frame) that should handle a particular message is a decision entirely left up to you. Remember, however, that the most important criteria in making the decision is the scope and the effect of the message or command on the application's processing. If the command affects the entire document or the data stored within it, you should generally handle the command in the document class (except when the command's effect is *through* a specific view, as it might be in some implementations of a Cut or Paste command). If the command affects only a particular view (such as setting a zoom or rotation factor), the view object affected should handle the command.

MFC-derived variants of the CView class

In addition to the basic `CView` class, MFC provides several derived classes that serve specific purposes and that are intended to simplify handling of complex tasks. Table 19-2 summarizes the MFC-derived `CView` classes.

Table 19-2
MFC-Derived Variations of the CView Class

Class Name	*Description*
CCtrlView	Supports views that are directly based on a control (such as a tree control or edit control).
CDaoRecordView	Uses dialog controls to display database records. You will learn more about the CDaoRecordView class in Chapter 27.
CEditView	Uses an edit control to provide a multi-line text editor.
CFormView	Displays dialog box controls. You must base CFormView objects on dialog templates.
CHtmlView	Provides a window in which the user can browse sites on the World Wide Web, as well as folders on the local file system and on a network. You will learn more about CHtmlView in Chapter 36.
CListView	Displays a list control.
COleDBRecordView	Displays database records using dialog controls. You will learn more about the COleDBRecordView class in Chapter 28.
CRecordView	Displays database records using dialog controls. You will learn more about the CRecordView class in Chapter 26.
CRichEditView	Displays a rich-text edit control.
CScrollView	Enables the use of scroll bars for the user to move through the logical data in the document.
CTreeView	Displays a tree control.

Another, rarely overriden variant of the CView class is the CPreviewView class. The MFC framework uses CPreviewView to provide print preview support to your applications. You will learn more about CPreviewView in Chapter 21.

All the CView-derived classes provide member functions that are specific to the class' goal. Member functions of view classes that derive from CCtrlView encapsulate Windows messages specific to the control class they represent.

CFormView and the classes that MFC derives from it (including CDataRecordView, COleDBRecordView, and CRecordView) support Dialog Data Exchange (DDE). You can use all four of these classes in a fashion similar to how you would use CDialog-derived classed (you learned about CDialog-derived classes in Chapter 13).

Evaluating CForm view versus dialog-based applications

As you have learned, dialog-based applications represent an exception from the standard MFC document/view model. If you create a dialog-based application using the AppWizard, the resulting program does not have a document or a view class (nor a frame window class, for that matter). Instead, the application implements all its functionality in a single dialog class derived from `CDialog`.

Although deriving a single dialog class may be sufficient for many simple applications, in doing so you sacrifice support for many MFC features that you can include within a document/view application. A dialog-based application does not have a menu, toolbar, or status bar (all of which reside in the frame window), it will not support OLE or MAPI, and it will not have printing capabilities (at least not without significant additional programming effort on your part).

If you need a dialog-style interface but still want the benefits of the document/view architecture, you can build your application with the `CFormView` class as the base class for your view window and use the SDI application model. Doing so enables you to retain all the advantages of a full-featured MFC application while still presenting the same dialog-based appearance, using a dialog box template to define the view and take advantage of Dynamic Data Exchange.

Returning to frame windows

So far in this chapter, you have learned what documents, document templates, and views are all about, and you have learned (if only briefly) that a view almost always lives in a frame window. This concept is often overlooked but is an important key to your management of different views within your application.

The only time your applications do not create a view within a real frame window is when the view is active as an embedded OLE object. The view still has a frame in such situations — but the frame is a very different one from the standard frame windows you have learned about.

As this chapter explains, an SDI application usually creates a `CFrameWnd` instance, while an MDI application typically creates a `CMDIFrameWnd` instance. Of course, if you've written a dialog-based application, the dialog is the main window, and your application doesn't have any frame window.

Due to the way command dispatching works, you will find that the frame window often acts as a catch-all for choices in your command window. In other words, any command from a menu that isn't handled by your view is offered to your frame window for it to handle.

You should implement handlers, ready for any frame message, no matter which view the user is currently working with. If you have menu choices that should react in different ways for different views, you can implement handlers in both the frame and the view classes. The view handler is executed when the view object is active; otherwise, the frame's handler is called.

Understanding the role of AfxGetMainWnd()

Frames act as the main window for the thread that controls your process. If you call `AfxGetMainWnd()` at any point in your program, you can retrieve a pointer to the `CWnd` class that your application uses as its main window. You need to cast that pointer to the appropriate type if you want to access any `CFrameWnd`- or `CMDIFrameWnd`-specific members.

A frame window is responsible for more than just making sure your application has a menu and a sizable frame. It also serves as an anchor for your window's toolbar and status bar. As yet, you haven't learned about these classes, but because they are so often paired with a frame window, it's valuable to understand what they do.

If your application has a status bar or toolbar, you will find code in your main frame window that creates instances of `CStatusBar` or `CToolBar`. As you might guess, `CStatusBar` creates a status bar, and `CToolBar` handles a toolbar. In most applications, the creation of these windows is handled in the `OnCreate()` member of the application's frame window. You will learn more about both these classes in Chapter 23.

Note

This code creates the actual window. Because the C++ objects are members of the frame window, your application creates them at the same time as it creates the frame window object.

✦ ✦ ✦ ✦ ✦

When you are working with an AppWizard-produced application, the status bar in your application is called `m_wndStatusBar`, and your first toolbar is called `m_wndToolBar`. Note it is your "first'" toolbar that receives this name. Your frame is completely capable of handling more than one toolbar — in fact, MFC lays out as many toolbars as you would like.

By the way, `CStatusBar` and `CToolBar` classes are dependent on a frame window. Using them in other types of windows (such as dialogs) is beyond the scope of this book and is not generally something that most programmers would have a need to do. Suffice it to say that these classes are not really dependent on the document/view architecture, but they do rely on the frame window associated with the document and view classes in order to lay themselves out in your application's user interface, and they keep the view informed of the area it has available to draw in.

The HexView SDI Application

You can find a demonstration program on the CD-ROM in the Chap19\HexView directory. The demonstration program uses a single document interface with a class derived from the `CScrollView` base class and shows the user a hexadecimal representation of a file's contents. You can rebuild the program by loading the `HexView.dsw` project file or simply run the HexView.exe program with the Windows Explorer. When you first run the program, it displays a blank view. You can then load a file using the Open option from the File menu or by clicking your mouse on the File Open icon. Figure 19-4 shows the HexView program with the `HexView.cpp` file loaded.

◆ ◆ ◆ ◆ ◆

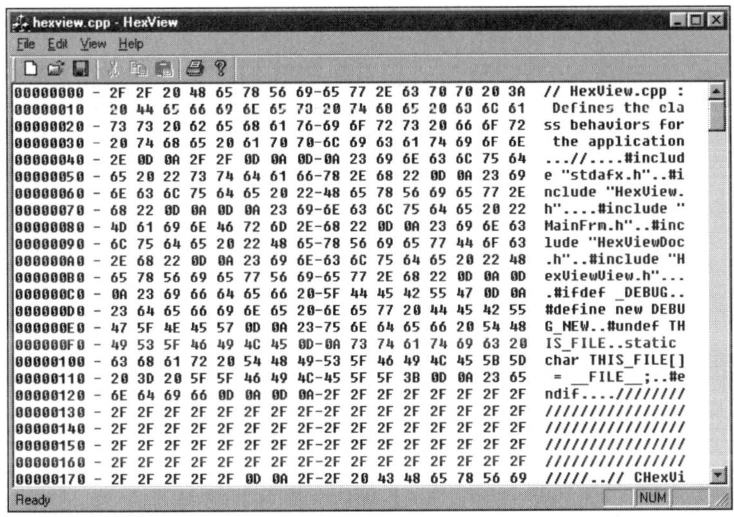

Figure 19-4: The HexView program with the HexView.cpp file loaded.

HexView

Project Name: **HexView**

CD-ROM Location: **Chap19\HexView**Prebuilt Program: **Chap19\HexView\HexView.exe**

Source Code Highlights in Text: `HexViewDoc.cpp`, `HexViewView.cpp`

◆ ◆ ◆ ◆ ◆

Listing 19-2: Highlights of HexViewDoc.cpp and HexViewView.cpp

```
// HexViewView.cpp : implementation of the CHexViewView class
//
/////////////////////////////////////////////////////////////////////////////
// CHexViewView construction/destruction

CHexViewView::CHexViewView()
{
   memset(&m_logfont, 0, sizeof(m_logfont));
    m_nPointSize = 120;
    _tcscpy(m_logfont.lfFaceName, _T("Fixedsys"));
   // start out with a system font
   CWindowDC dc(NULL);
   m_logfont.lfHeight =::MulDiv(m_nPointSize,
       dc.GetDeviceCaps(LOGPIXELSY), 720);
   m_logfont.lfPitchAndFamily = FIXED_PITCH;
   m_pFont = new CFont;
   m_pFont->CreateFontIndirect(&m_logfont);
   m_pPrintFont = NULL;
   m_bPrinting = FALSE;
}

CHexViewView::~CHexViewView()
{
   if (m_pFont != NULL)
      delete m_pFont;
   if (m_pPrintFont != NULL)
      delete m_pPrintFont;
}
/////////////////////////////////////////////////////////////////////////////
// CHexViewView drawing

void CHexViewView::OnDraw(CDC* pDC)
{
   CHexViewDoc* pDoc = GetDocument();
   ASSERT_VALID(pDoc);

   CString strRender;
   CFont*   pOldFont;
   CSize   ScrolledSize;
   int      nStartLine;
   int      nHeight;
   CRect   ScrollRect;
   CPoint   ScrolledPos = GetScrollPosition();

   if (m_bPrinting)
   {
      // find the first line for this page
      ScrolledSize = CSize(m_nPageWidth, m_nPageHeight);
      ScrollRect = CRect(0, ScrolledPos.y,
```

```
            ScrolledSize.cx,
            ScrolledSize.cy + ScrolledPos.y);
         pOldFont = pDC->SelectObject(m_pPrintFont);
         nStartLine = m_nPrintLine;
      }
      else
      {
         CRect   rectClient;
         GetClientRect(&rectClient);
         // figure out how high each line is
         pOldFont = pDC->SelectObject(m_pFont);
         nHeight = MeasureFontHeight(m_pFont, pDC);
         // find a starting line based on scrolling
         ScrolledSize =
             CSize(rectClient.Width(), rectClient.Height());
         ScrollRect = CRect(rectClient.left, ScrolledPos.y,
            rectClient.right,
            ScrolledSize.cy + ScrolledPos.y);
         nStartLine = ScrolledPos.y/16;
         // make sure we are drawing where we should
         ScrollRect.top = nStartLine*nHeight;
      }
      if (pDoc->m_pFile != NULL)
      {
         int nLine;
         for (nLine = nStartLine;
              ScrollRect.top < ScrollRect.bottom;
              nLine++)
         {
            if (!pDoc->ReadLine(strRender, 16, nLine*16))
               break;
            nHeight = pDC->DrawText(strRender, -1,
               &ScrollRect,
               DT_TOP | DT_NOPREFIX | DT_SINGLELINE);
            ScrollRect.top += nHeight;
         }
      }
      pDC->SelectObject(pOldFont);
   }

   /////////////////////////////////////////////////////////////////////////////
   // CHexViewView printing

   BOOL CHexViewView::OnPreparePrinting(CPrintInfo* pInfo)
   {
      BOOL bResult;
      CWinApp* pApp = AfxGetApp();

      // ask our app what the default printer is
      // if there isn't any, have MFC generate an error

      if (!pApp->
```

(continued)

Listing 19-2 *(continued)*

```
        GetPrinterDeviceDefaults(&pInfo->m_pPD->m_pd) ||
        pInfo->m_pPD->m_pd.hDevMode == NULL)
      return DoPreparePrinting(pInfo);

   HGLOBAL   hDevMode = pInfo->m_pPD->m_pd.hDevMode;
   HGLOBAL hDevNames = pInfo->m_pPD->m_pd.hDevNames;

   DEVMODE* pDevMode = (DEVMODE*) ::GlobalLock(hDevMode);
   DEVNAMES* pDevNames = (DEVNAMES*)
        ::GlobalLock(hDevNames);

   LPCSTR pstrDriverName = ((LPCSTR)
        pDevNames)+pDevNames->wDriverOffset;
   LPCSTR pstrDeviceName = ((LPCSTR)
        pDevNames)+pDevNames->wDeviceOffset;
   LPCSTR pstrOutputPort = ((LPCSTR)
        pDevNames)+pDevNames->wOutputOffset;

   CDC dcPrinter;
   if (dcPrinter.CreateDC(pstrDriverName, pstrDeviceName,
      pstrOutputPort, NULL))
   {
      CalcPageCount(&dcPrinter, pInfo);
      dcPrinter.DeleteDC();
      bResult = DoPreparePrinting(pInfo);
   }
   else
   {
      MessageBox("Could not create printer DC");
      bResult = FALSE;
   }
   ::GlobalUnlock(hDevMode);
   ::GlobalUnlock(hDevNames);
   return bResult;
}

/////////////////////////////////////////////////////////////////////////////
// CHexViewView message handlers

void CHexViewView::OnInitialUpdate()
{
   CHexViewDoc* pDoc = GetDocument();
   ASSERT_VALID(pDoc);

   // hook up our initial size
   CSize sizeTotal(0, pDoc->m_lFileSize);
   SetScrollSizes(MM_TEXT, sizeTotal);
   CScrollView::OnInitialUpdate();
}

void CHexViewView::OnViewFont()
```

```
{
   // let the user change their mind about the font
   LOGFONT   lfCopy;
   memcpy(&lfCopy, &m_logfont, sizeof(lfCopy));

   // pop up the existing font in the dialog
   CFontDialog dlg(&lfCopy);
   dlg.m_cf.Flags |= CF_FORCEFONTEXIST |
       CF_FIXEDPITCHONLY;

   // if they say so, create the font and put it in a
   // member variable for use later
   if (dlg.DoModal() == IDOK)
   {
      CFont*   pFontCopy = new CFont;
      if (pFontCopy->CreateFontIndirect(&lfCopy))
      {
         m_nPointSize = dlg.GetSize();
         if (m_pFont != NULL)
            delete m_pFont;
         m_pFont = pFontCopy;
         memcpy(&m_logfont, &lfCopy, sizeof(lfCopy));
           Invalidate();
      }
      else
      {
         delete pFontCopy;
         MessageBox(_T("Could not create new font!"));
      }
   }
}

/////////////////////////////////////////////////////////////////
// HexViewDoc.cpp : implementation of the CHexViewDoc class
/////////////////////////////////////////////////////////////////

/////////////////////////////////////////////////////////////////
// CHexViewDoc commands

BOOL CHexViewDoc::OnOpenDocument(LPCTSTR lpszPathName)
{
   if (!CDocument::OnOpenDocument(lpszPathName))
      return FALSE;
   if (m_pFile != NULL)
   {
      m pFile->Close();
      delete m_pFile;
   }
   try
   {
      m_pFile =
         new CFile(lpszPathName, CFile::modeRead |
```

(continued)

Listing 19-2 (continued)

```
            CFile::typeBinary);
   }
   catch (CFileException* e)
   {
      CString strError;

      strError.Format(_T("Couldn't open file: %d"),
         _sys_errlist[e->m_lOsError]);
      AfxMessageBox(strError);
      return FALSE;
   }
   m_lFileSize = m_pFile->GetLength();
   return TRUE;
}

/////////////////////////////////////////////////////////////////////
// CHexViewDoc implementation

BOOL CHexViewDoc::ReadLine(CString& strLine, int nLength,
    LONG lOffset = -1L)
{
   LONG lPosition;

   if (lOffset != -1L)
      lPosition = m_pFile->Seek(lOffset, CFile::begin);
   else
      lPosition = m_pFile->GetPosition();

   if (lPosition == -1L)
   {
      TRACE2("::ReadLine is FALSE Seek(%8.8lX, %8.8lX)\n",
         lOffset, lPosition);
      return FALSE;
   }

   BYTE* pszBuffer = new BYTE[nLength];
   int nReturned = m_pFile->Read(pszBuffer, nLength);

   if (nReturned <= 0)
   {
      TRACE2("::ReadLine returns FALSE Read(%d, %d)\n",
         nLength, nReturned);
      delete pszBuffer;
      return FALSE;
   }

   CString strTemp;
   CString strCharsIn;

   strTemp.Format(_T("%8.8lX - "), lPosition);
   strLine = strTemp;
```

```
    for (int nIndex = 0; nIndex < nReturned; nIndex++)
    {
       if (nIndex == 0)
          strTemp.Format(_T("%2.2X"), pszBuffer[nIndex]);
       else if (nIndex % 16 == 0)
          strTemp.Format(_T("=%2.2X"), pszBuffer[nIndex]);
       else if (nIndex % 8 == 0)
          strTemp.Format(_T("-%2.2X"), pszBuffer[nIndex]);
       else
          strTemp.Format(_T(" %2.2X"), pszBuffer[nIndex]);

       if (_istprint(pszBuffer[nIndex]))
          strCharsIn += pszBuffer[nIndex];
       else
          strCharsIn += _T('.');
       strLine += strTemp;
    }

    if (nReturned < nLength)
    {
       CString strPadding(_T(' '), 3*(nLength-nReturned));
       strLine += strPadding;
    }
    strLine += _T("  ");
    strLine += strCharsIn;

    delete pszBuffer;
    return TRUE;
}
```

Summary

Most MFC applications are based on the *document/view model*. The document, an abstract object, represents the application's data and typically corresponds to the contents of a file. The view, in turn, provides a presentation of the data and accepts user interface events. The relationship between documents and views is one-to-many: a document may (and generally does) support several associated views, but a view is always associated with exactly one document.

Your applications will derive their document classes from the MFC-provided `CDocument` class. The `CDocument` class encapsulates much of the basic functionality of a document object. In the simplest case, applications need add only member variables that represent application-specific data and provide overrides for the `OnNewDocument()` (for initialization) and `Serialize()` (for saving and loading data) member functions to obtain a fully functional document class.

More sophisticated applications generally rely on collection classes to implement the set of objects that comprise a document. In particular, applications can use the `COleDocument` class and rely on its capability to manage a list of `CDocItem` objects that MFC does not restrict to OLE client and server objects.

You will derive view classes from the MFC `CView` base class. View windows that `CView` objects represent are child windows. In an SDI project, the parent window is the main frame window; in an MDI project, the parent window is the controlling MDI child window.

A view object, in addition to containing member variables that represent view-specific settings (such as zoom and rotation settings), often implements a current selection. The current selection is the set of document objects that the user has designated or selected within the current view for further manipulation. As with documents, most complex applications use collection classes to manage the current selection.

While a view class may, and generally does, override many member functions of the `CView` class from which it derives, every view class must override the `OnDraw()` member function. For OLE applications, you must also override the `IsSelected()` member function. In addition, you generally override `OnUpdate()` and `OnPrepareDC()` within your applications.

Beyond `CView` implementations that you may derive, MFC provides several derivatives of the `CView` class that you may use within your applications to handle scrolling views, views based on dialogs, controls, and views representing database records. When you design your application, you should be sure to select the class most appropriate to your application as the base class for your view class.

Finally, document, views, and frame windows all handle messages. Your decision about which of the three classes should handle a particular message is based upon that message's effects. If the message affects the entire document, the document class should handle the message, unless the effect takes place through a specific view. In that case, or in the case where the effect is specific to a view, the view class should handle the message. Lastly, the frame window class should handle messages that have a global effect on the application but do not affect a document's data directly (such as toolbar display or hide messages).

✦ ✦ ✦

The Layout of an MDI Application

CHAPTER 20

In This Chapter

A review of the document/view model

A review of the CDocument class

Managing complex document, view, and frame combinations

The PaintObj program

Dynamic splitter windows

Linking views with documents

Creating static splitter windows

The Dynsplit program

Subclassing child windows

In Chapter 19, you learned about MFC's document/view model. You then used the document/view model to build a single document interface (SDI) application. While designing the SDI application is a useful exercise, SDI is generally only acceptable when you create small, simple applications. With most applications that you design for actual use, whether public use or within your own organization, you will require the capability of using multiple views, and generally multiple documents, to organize information. When you use multiple documents within a single application, you will use the multiple document interface (MDI) model for the document/view structure. The layout of a multiple document interface application is a little more complicated than the layout of a single document interface application. Figure 20-1 shows the basic layout of the MDI application structure.

As you can see from the figure, multiple document applications still use a main frame that holds the menu, toolbar, and status bars. However, in the MDI application, the `CMainFrame` class derives from MFC's `CMDIFrameWnd` class, instead of the `CFrameWnd` class. `CMDIFrameWnd` has the same visual characteristics as `CFrameWnd`, but it also implements the MDI frame protocol that Windows expects in an MDI application.

The child windows that the figure depicts are also frame windows, but the child windows are instances of the MFC class `CMDIChildWnd`. This MFC class provides the child window that Windows MDI applications use in their client area to hold each instance of the MDI application's views. The frameworks create one `CMDIChildWnd` to contain each view the application needs, just like the `CMainFrame` object wrapped the single view in the SDI application. The wrapped view may be of any type and can refer to any open document that the application is currently managing.

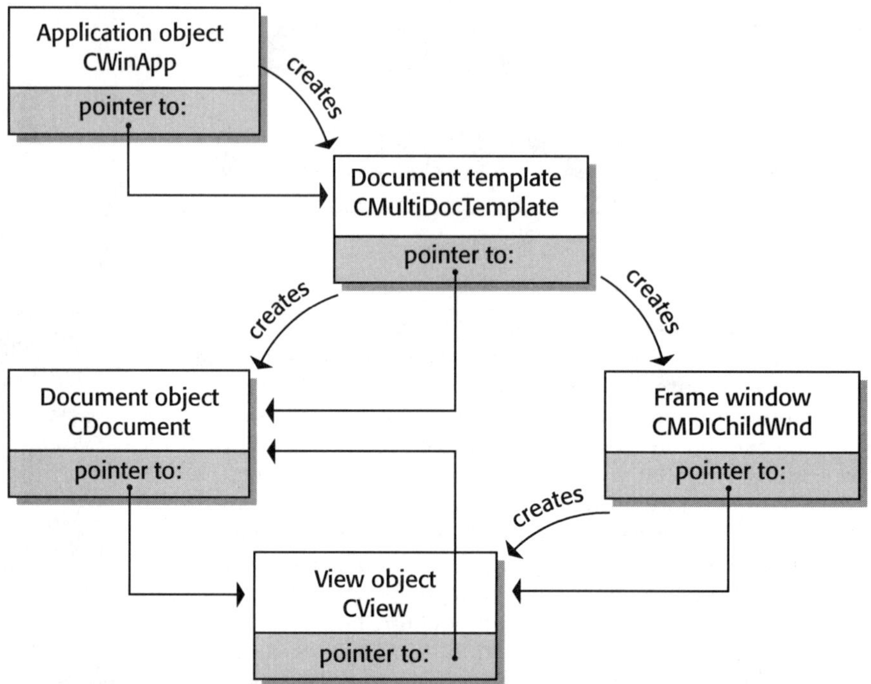

Figure 20-1: This is the basic layout of the object structure of an MDI application.

As a developer of MFC applications, it is your responsibility to decide exactly what kind of documents and views you will implement and how they'll interact with the basic framework provided by MFC's implementation of the single document or multiple document interfaces. Your code alters and enhances the way the generic documents and views interact and behave. By tuning things to work the way you want them to, you will eventually develop the skeleton MFC provides into an application that does exactly what you need. Over the course of this chapter, you will learn more about the components of the MDI application, and you will use a simple MDI application so that you can better decide what structure your applications require.

Revisiting the Document/View Model: A Brief Refresher

As you learned in Chapter 19, MFC applications use, by default, a programming model that separates a program's data from the display of that data and from most user interaction with the data. (You will avoid the document/view model within your applications only if you instruct the AppWizard to create the application as a dialog-based application or if you are creating a nonstandard project, such as an ActiveX automation server.) In the document/view model, an MFC document object reads and writes data to persistent storage. The document may also provide an interface to the data wherever the data itself resides (such as in a database). A separate view object manages data display — from rendering the data in a window to user selection and editing of data. The view obtains display data from the document and communicates back to the document any data changes.

While you can easily override or ignore the document/view separation, there are compelling reasons to follow the model in most cases. One of the best is when you need multiple views of the same document, such as both a spreadsheet and a chart view. In the document/view model, a separate view object represents each view of the data, while code common to all views (such as a calculation engine) can reside in the document. The document also takes on the task of updating all views whenever the data changes.

MFC's document/view architecture makes it easy to design applications that support multiple views, multiple document types, splitter windows, and other valuable user interface features. You have learned already how to support multiple views within your application; in this chapter, you will learn how to support multiple document types and splitter windows within your application. At the heart of the document/view architecture are four key classes, all of which you learned about in Chapter 19 and which are restated here:

✦ `CDocument` (or the even more powerful `COleDocument` derivative), an object that your application will use to store or control the application's data, and that provides the data to the views that you associated with the document class.

✦ `CView` (or one of its many derived classes, such as `CScrollView`, `CEditView`, and so on), an object that your application will use to display a document's data and manage user interaction with the data — both viewing the data and modifying and changing the data.

✦ `CFrameWnd` (or one of its variations, such a `CMDIChildWnd`), an object that provides the frame window around one or more views of a document. With an MDI application, your application includes a minimum of two frame windows — one that encloses the application (and that does not have a document class associated with it), and one or more that display the application data stored within one or more document classes.

✦ `CDocTemplate` (or one of its derived classes, such as `CSingleDocTemplate` or `CMultiDocTemplate`), an object that coordinates one or more existing documents of a given type and manages the underlying tasks that the framework must perform to create the correct document, view, and frame window objects for that type.

Reviewing the CDocument Class

As you have learned, the `CDocument` class provides the basic functionality for user-defined document classes. A document represents the unit of data that the user typically opens with the Open option on the File menu and saves with the Save option on the File menu. The `CDocument` class supports standard operations such as creating a document, loading data into the document, and saving data the document contains. The framework manipulates documents using the interface defined by `CDocument`.

An application can support more than one type of document. For example, an application might support both spreadsheets and text documents (although, in most applications that you would design today, the application would support text documents as its native document type and support spreadsheets through Object Linking and Embedding (OLE)). Each type of document has an associated document template that you create in the application's `InitInstance()` member function. The document template specifies what resources (for example, menu, dialog, icon, or accelerator table) that type of document uses. Each document contains a pointer to its associated `CDocTemplate` object. In Chapter 19, you used a `CSingleDocTemplate` object derived from `CDocTemplate` to design your single document interface program. When you design MDI applications, you will use a `CMultiDocTemplate` object.

Users interact with a document through the `CView` objects that the program associates with the document. A view renders an image of the document in a frame window and interprets user input as operations on the document. You can associate multiple views with a document. When the user opens a window on a document, the framework creates a view and attaches it to the document. The document template specifies what type of view and frame window the application uses to display each type of document.

A document receives commands that the active view for that document forwards to it. If the document doesn't handle a given command, it forwards the command to the document template that manages the document (which, in turn, may forward the command to the document's frame window, and then the application's frame window, and so on).

When the user modifies a document's data, each of the document's views must reflect those modifications. `CDocument` provides the `UpdateAllViews()` member function that you use to notify the document's views of such changes, so the views can repaint themselves as necessary. The framework also prompts the user to save a modified file before closing it. To implement documents in a typical application, you must do the following:

- ✦ Derive a class from `CDocument` (or `COleDocument`) for each type of document that your application will use.

✦ Add member variables to the document to store each document's data (either simple variables for simple applications or more complex variables such as `CCmdTarget` objects for more complex applications, such as those that support OLE).

✦ Implement member functions for reading and modifying the document's data. The document's views are the most important users of these member functions. You will implement different document views based on the number of different ways that users must access the data the document contains.

✦ Override the `CObject::Serialize()` member function in your document class to write and read the document's data to and from disk. Note that you should read information back from the disk in the same order that you wrote the information to the disk in a first-in first-out (FIFO) order.

The `COLEDocument` class, which also derives from `CDocument`, enables support of OLE drag-and-drop and embedding and linking operations within your document classes.

◆ ◆ ◆ ◆ ◆

Managing More Complex Combinations of Documents, Views, and Frame Windows

As you have learned, the standard relationship among a document, its view(s), and its frame window(s) is described in a relatively straightforward manner: a one-to-many relationship between documents and views, and a one-to-one relationship between each view and a frame window. Many applications need to support only a single document type (but possibly enable the user to open multiple documents of that type) with a single view on the document and only one frame window per document. But some applications may need to alter one or more of those defaults — creating multiple views on a single document type, single views on multiple document types, or multiple views on multiple document types. It is worthwhile to consider the different situations that you may encounter when working with documents and views and how you should design your applications to respond appropriately.

Working with multiple document types

Whether you create an SDI or an MDI application, AppWizard creates only a single document class for you. In some cases, though, you may need to support more than one document type. For example, your application may need both worksheet and chart documents. Your application will probably represent each document type with its own document class and typically by its own view class or classes as well. When the user chooses the New option from the File menu, the framework displays a dialog box that lists the application's supported document types. After the user chooses a document type, the application creates a document of that type. The application then manages each document type with its own document-template object.

To create extra document classes within your own applications, use the Add Class button in the ClassWizard dialog box. Choose CDocument (or COLEDocument) as the Class Type to derive from and supply the requested document information. Then implement the new class' data structures.

To inform the framework about your extra document class, you must then add a second call to AddDocTemplate() in your application class' InitInstance() member function. For example, an application with two documents would include code within its InitInstance() member function similar to the following:

```
CMultiDocTemplate* pDocTemplate;
pDocTemplate = new CMultiDocTemplate(
  IDR_OPAINTTYPE,
  RUNTIME_CLASS(CSample1Doc),
  RUNTIME_CLASS(CMDIChildWnd),  // standard MDI child frame
  RUNTIME_CLASS(CSample1View));
AddDocTemplate(pDocTemplate);
pDocTemplate = new CMultiDocTemplate(
  IDR_OPAINTTYPE,
  RUNTIME_CLASS(CSample2Doc),
  RUNTIME_CLASS(CMDIChildWnd),  // standard MDI child frame
  RUNTIME_CLASS(CSample2View));
AddDocTemplate(pDocTemplate);
```

Using multiple views with documents

As you have learned, many documents require only a single view. However, you also learned that the MFC document/view model enables your applications to support more than one view of a single document — in fact, you can support as many different views on a single document as your application might require. To help you implement multiple views, a document object keeps a list of its views, provides member functions for adding and removing views, and supplies the UpdateAllViews() member function for letting multiple views know when the document's data has changed. MFC supports three common user interfaces that you might design within your applications that implement interfaces requiring multiple views on the same document. These three models are described in the following list:

✦ Your application might enable the user to view objects of the same class, each in a separate MDI document frame window (an MDI child window, to be specific). The user would use the New Window option on the Window menu (that the AppWizard supplies automatically within the IDR_MAINFRAME menu resource) to open a second frame with a view of the same document. Then the user could use the two frames to view different portions of the document simultaneously. MFC's default implementation of the New Window option duplicates the initial frame window and view attached to the document (that is, the frame window and view that you attach to the document through its CDocumentTemplate object). Figure 20-2 shows the multiple frame window on a document model.

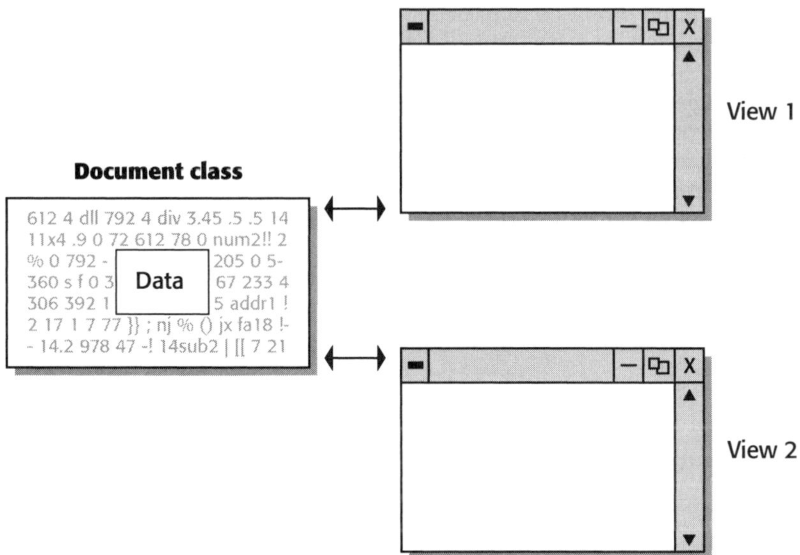

Figure 20-2: The multiple views on the same document model.

✦ Your application might enable the user to view objects of the same class in the same document frame window. The application would then use splitter windows (which you will learn more about later in this chapter) to split the view space of a single document window into multiple separate views of the document. The framework, in conjunction with the splitter window, creates multiple view objects from the same view class. You will learn more about the process that splitter windows use to create multiple views and how to implement the `CSplitterWnd` class later in this chapter. Figure 20-3 shows the splitter windows model that implements only a single view.

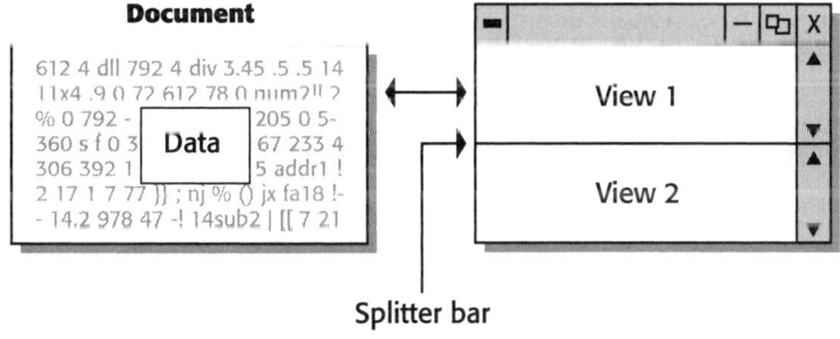

Figure 20-3: The splitter windows document model.

✦ Your application might enable the user to view objects of different classes in a single frame window. In this third model (which is a common variation of the splitter window model), the application's multiple views of the document share a single frame window. The application and the framework construct the views from different classes (all of which you derive from `CView` or one of its derivatives). In this model, each view that you construct provides the user with a different way to view the same document. For example, one view might show a spreadsheet in normal mode while the other view shows the spreadsheet with all the formulas displayed. You would then use a splitter control (which you create with `CSplitterWnd`) to enable the user to adjust the relative sizes of the views. Figure 20-4 shows the splitter windows model variation that uses multiple views.

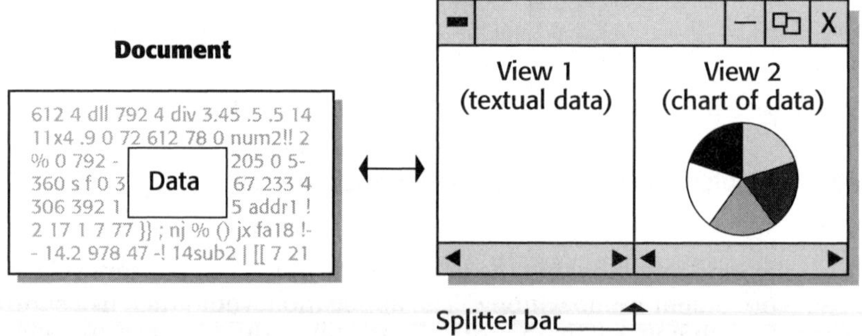

Figure 20-4: The splitter windows model variation.

The framework provides the three models to use within your application through the New Window option on the Window menu for the first model and, for the second two models, the `CSplitterWnd` class. You will learn more about splitter windows later in this chapter. Clearly, the three models that this section describes are the simplest possible implementations of the model that you can do; using the principles that these three models define, you can implement other models using these three models as your starting point.

Understanding the CMDIFrameWnd class

The `CMDIFrameWnd` class provides the functionality of a Windows multiple document interface (MDI) frame window, along with member functions that you will use within your applications to manage the window. To create a useful MDI frame window for your multiple document interface application, you must derive a class for the main frame window from `CMDIFrameWnd`. After you derive the class, you add member variables to the derived class to store data specific to your application (but not data specific to an individual document). In addition, you must implement message handler member functions and a message map in the derived class to specify what happens when messages are directed to the window, either by the operating system or by the document template.

You can construct an MDI frame window in two ways — by calling either the `Create()` member function or the `LoadFrame()` member function of `CFrameWnd()`. However, before you call `Create()` or `LoadFrame()`, you must use the C++ `new` operator to construct the frame window object on the heap. Before calling the `Create()` member function, you can also use the `AfxRegisterWndClass()` global function to register the window class and set the icon and class styles for the frame. You should use the `Create()` member function to pass the frame's creation parameters as immediate arguments.

On the other hand, the `LoadFrame()` member function requires fewer arguments than the `Create()` member function and instead retrieves most of its default values from resources that you create within the project, including the frame's caption, icon, accelerator table, and menu. To be accessed by `LoadFrame()` (and loaded into the definition for the new window), all these resources must have the same resource ID (for example, the MFC default resource ID `IDR_MAINFRAME` or any other resource ID such as `IDR_PARENTFRAME`).

The `CMDIFrameWnd` class inherits much of its default implementation from `CFrameWnd`. The `CMDIFrameWnd` class has the following additional features that it does not inherit from `CFrameWnd`:

- An MDI frame window manages the child windows within the application, repositioning the child window in conjunction with the user's actions on the child window's control bars and the application window's scroll bars. The MDI client window is the direct parent of every MDI child frame window within the application. The `WS_HSCROLL` and `WS_VSCROLL` window styles specified on a `CMDIFrameWnd` apply to the MDI client window rather than the main frame window so the user can scroll the MDI client area (in other words, the scroll bars will move the child windows within the MDI client area, and not the child windows' client areas themselves).
- An MDI frame window owns a default menu that it uses as the menu bar when no MDI child window is active. When an MDI child window is active, the MFC framework automatically replaces the MDI frame window's menu bar with the MDI child window's menu bar.
- An MDI frame window works in conjunction with the currently active MDI child window, if there is one. For instance, the currently active MDI child window receives command messages before the MDI frame window.
- An MDI frame window has a default implementation of `ID_WINDOW_NEW`, which creates a new frame and view on the current document. An application can override these default command implementations to customize MDI window handling.

Do not use the C++ `delete` operator to destroy a `CMDIFrameWnd` window object — if you do, it may result in bad reference counts or memory leaks within your application. Instead, you should use the `CWnd::DestroyWindow()` member function. The `CFrameWnd` implementation of the `PostNcDestroy()` member function deletes the C++ object when the application destroys the window. When the user closes the CMDIFrameWnd window object, the default OnClose() handler function calls the DestroyWindow() member function (which, in turn, calls the DestroyWindow() member function for each of the currently open CMDIChildWnd window objects).

Although MFC derives the CMDIFrameWnd class from the CFrameWnd class, you do not need to use the DECLARE_DYNCREATE macro when you declare a frame window class that you derive from CMDIFrameWnd.

◆ ◆ ◆ ◆ ◆

Understanding the CMDIChildWnd class

The CMDIChildWnd class provides the functionality of a Windows multiple document interface (MDI) child window, along with members for managing the window. An MDI child window looks much like a typical frame window, except that the MDI child window appears inside an MDI frame window rather than on the desktop. An MDI child window does not have a menu bar of its own but instead shares the menu of the MDI frame window. The framework automatically changes the MDI frame window's menu bar to represent the currently active MDI child window's menu bar.

To create a useful MDI child window for your application, you must derive a class from CMDIChildWnd (or, if you do not intend to customize the window's actions, you can simply use the default CMDIChildWnd class). You then add member variables to the derived class to store data specific to the document that the child window will be associated with within the application. Furthermore, you must implement message handler member functions and a message map in the derived class to specify what happens when messages are directed to the window. (Otherwise, MFC will use the CMDIChildWnd class's default handlers to respond to messages the window receives.) There are three ways to construct an MDI child window:

- ✦ Directly, using the Create() member function
- ✦ Directly, using the LoadFrame() member function
- ✦ Indirectly, through a document template

Just as with the CMDIFrameWnd class, before you call the Create() or LoadFrame() member functions to create a CMDIChildWnd object, you must use the C++ new operator to construct the frame window object on the heap. Before you call the Create() member function, you can also use the AfxRegisterWndClass() global function to register the window class and set the icon and class styles for the frame. As with the CMDIFrameWnd class, you should use the Create() member function to pass the frame's creation parameters as immediate arguments.

Also similar to the CMDIFrameWnd class, the LoadFrame() member function requires fewer arguments than the Create() member function does and instead retrieves most of its default values from resources, including the frame's caption, icon, accelerator table, and menu. To be accessible by LoadFrame(), all these resources must have the same resource ID (such as IDR_CHILDWND).

When a CMDIChildWnd object contains views and documents, they are created indirectly by the framework instead of directly by the programmer. The CDocTemplate object orchestrates the creation of the frame, the creation of the containing views, and the connection of the views to the appropriate document. The parameters of the CDocTemplate constructor specify the CRuntimeClass of the three classes involved (document, frame, and view). A CRuntimeClass object is used by the framework to dynamically create new frames when specified by the user (for example, by using the New option from the File menu or the MDI frame's New option from the Window menu).

The CMDIChildWnd class inherits much of its default implementation from CFrameWnd. However, the CMDIChildWnd class has the following additional features beyond those it derives from CFrameWnd:

- ✦ In conjunction with the CMultiDocTemplate class, multiple CMDIChildWnd objects from the same document template share the same menu, saving Windows system resources.
- ✦ As you learned in the previous section, the currently active MDI child window menu bar entirely replaces the MDI frame window's menu bar, and the caption of the currently active MDI child window is added to the MDI frame window's caption.

Do not use the C++ delete operator to destroy a CMDIChildWnd window object. Doing so may cause reference counter errors. Instead, you should use the CWnd::DestroyWindow() member function. The CFrameWnd implementation of the PostNcDestroy() member function deletes the C++ object when the application destroys the window. When the user closes the child window, the default OnClose() handler function calls the DestroyWindow() member function.

Unlike a frame window class that you derive from the CMDIFrameWnd class, a frame window class that you derive from CMDIChildWnd must be declared with the DECLARE_DYNCREATE macro for the RUNTIME_CLASS creation mechanism to work correctly.

✦ ✦ ✦ ✦ ✦

Understanding the CMultiDocTemplate class

Much as the `CSingleDocTemplate` class defines a document template that implements the single document interface, the `CMultiDocTemplate` class defines a document template that implements the multiple document interface (MDI). An MDI application uses the main frame window as a workspace in which the user can open zero or more document frame windows, each of which displays a document. As you learned in Chapter 19, a document template defines the relationships among three types of classes:

- ✦ A document class, which you derive from `CDocument` or `COleDocument`.
- ✦ A view class, which displays data from the document class that you associate with the template. You can derive this class from `CView`, `CScrollView`, `CFormView`, `CEditView`, or one of the other `CView`-based classes. You can also use `CEditView` directly.
- ✦ A frame window class, which contains the view. For an MDI document template, you can derive this class from `CMDIChildWnd`, or if you do not need to customize the behavior of the document frame windows, you can use `CMDIChildWnd` directly without deriving your own class.

An MDI application can support more than one type of document, and documents of different types can be open at the same time. Your application has one document template for each document type that it supports. For example, if your MDI application supports both spreadsheets and text documents, the application will have two `CMultiDocTemplate` objects.

The application uses the document templates when the user creates a new document. If the application supports more than one type of document, then the framework gets the names of the supported document types from the document templates and displays them in a list in the File New dialog box. Once the user has selected a document type, the application creates a document class object, a frame window object, and a view object and attaches them to each other.

You do not need to call any member functions of `CMultiDocTemplate` except the constructor. The MFC framework handles `CMultiDocTemplate` objects internally.

◆ ◆ ◆ ◆ ◆

Reviewing the overhead of using the CDocument classes

As you have learned, you will generally use the document/view architecture when you design your applications. In most applications, in fact, you will use some combination of documents and dialogs to design the application interface. One of the most significant benefits of using the document/view architecture is that the `CDocument` class (and its derivatives) is so naturally thin. A single `CDocument` object incurs only a small amount of overhead by itself, plus the small overhead of CDocument's base classes. Both of CDocument's base classes are small.

In fact, the CDocument class, without allowance for your own custom data that you will place within each document object, contains only seven members that the MFC framework always places within the class. The CDocument class contains the following framework-defined members (all of which the framework uses internally):

✦ Two CString objects

✦ Three BOOL variables

✦ One CDocTemplate pointer

✦ One CPtrList object, which contains a list of the document's views

In addition, during execution, the document requires the amount of time (which, on today's faster computers, is almost negligible) to create the document object, its view objects, a frame window, and a document template object.

Further considering MDI applications

Now that you have reviewed the MDI application's components, and noted their differences from the SDI application's components, you should be able to tell that working with an MDI application is essentially the same as working with an SDI application as you did in Chapter 19. In fact, the only significant differences between the two application types are in the differences in frame windows, the need to define additional resources for each of the child windows, and the greater power and flexibility that MDI applications provide. Managing the various documents and views, however, remains fundamentally the same as it was when you were working with only a single document and view. For example, to save the data in a given document, you still use the Serialize() member function, just as you did in the SDI application, similar to the following:

```
void CSampleObjDoc::Serialize(CArchive& ar)
 {
   m_Objects.Serialize(ar);
   if (ar.IsStoring())
    {
      ar << m_size;
    }
   else
    {
      ar > m_size;
    }
 }
```

The difference, of course, is that you have a separate Serialize() member function for each document you create, and each Serialize() member function stores and retrieves the data specific to that document.

The PaintObj Program

A demonstration program can be found on the CD-ROM in the `Chap20\PaintObj` directory. The sample program is built to use a single document class, `CPaintobjDoc`, but uses a `CMultiDocTemplate` and a `CMDIChildWnd` to create an MDI application that enables the user to perform simple painting within multiple windows.

You can rebuild the program by loading the `CPaintobjDoc` project file, or just run the `Paintobj.exe` program using Explorer. Figure 20-5 shows the program during execution. Listing 20-1 provides highlights of the program code within the `Paintobj.cpp` and `Paintvw.cpp` source files.

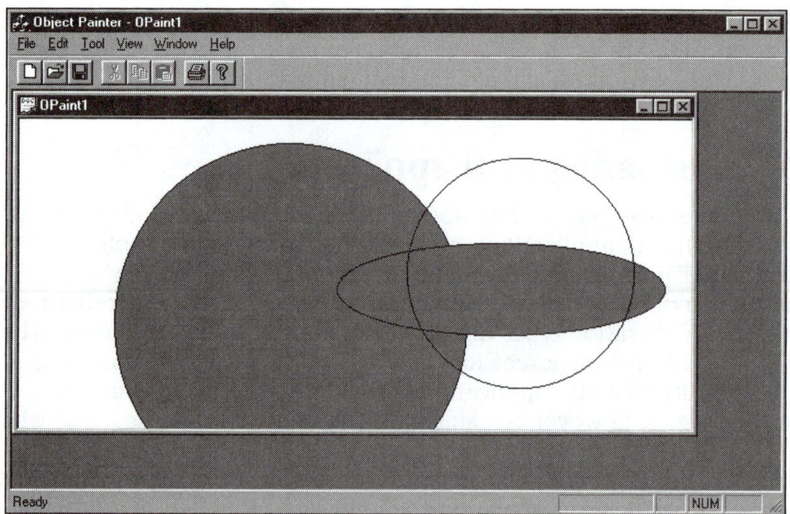

Figure 20-5: The Paintobj.exe program during execution.

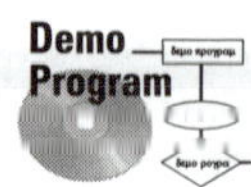

PaintObj
Project Name: **PaintObj**
CD-ROM Location: **Chap20\Paintobj**
Prebuilt Program: **Chap20\Paintobj\Paintobj.exe**
Source Code Highlights in Text: `Paintobj.cpp` **and** `Paintvw.cpp`

◆ ◆ ◆ ◆ ◆

Listing 20-1: Highlights of the Paintobj.cpp and Paintvw.cpp Source Code for the Paintobj.exe Program

```
// paintobj.cpp : Defines the class behaviors
// for the application.
//
// CPaintobjApp initialization

BOOL CPaintobjApp::InitInstance()
 {
   // Standard initialization
   Enable3dControls();
   LoadStdProfileSettings();  // Load standard INI file
                              // options

   // Register the application's document templates, which
   // serve as the connection between documents,
   // frame windows and views.
   CMultiDocTemplate* pDocTemplate;
   pDocTemplate = new CMultiDocTemplate(
      IDR_OPAINTTYPE,
      RUNTIME_CLASS(CPaintobjDoc),
      RUNTIME_CLASS(CMDIChildWnd),  // MDI child frame
      RUNTIME_CLASS(CPaintobjView));
   AddDocTemplate(pDocTemplate);

   // create main MDI Frame window
   CMainFrame* pMainFrame = new CMainFrame;
   if (!pMainFrame->LoadFrame(IDR_MAINFRAME))
      return FALSE;
   m_pMainWnd = pMainFrame;

   // Enable DDE Execute open
   EnableShellOpen();
   RegisterShellFileTypes();

   // simple command line parsing
   if (m_lpCmdLine[0] == '\0')
    {
      // create a new (empty) document
      OnFileNew();
    }
   else
    {
      // open an existing document
      OpenDocumentFile(m_lpCmdLine);
    }

   // Enable drag/drop open
   m_pMainWnd->DragAcceptFiles();
```

(continued)

Listing 20-1 *(continued)*

```
    // The main window has been initialized,
    // so show and update it.
    pMainFrame->ShowWindow(m_nCmdShow);
    pMainFrame->UpdateWindow();

    return TRUE;
 }

////////////////////////////////////////////////////////////
// paintvw.cpp : implementation of the CPaintobjView class
//

#include "stdafx.h"
#include "paintobj.h"
#include "mainfrm.h"

#include "paintdoc.h"
#include "paintvw.h"

#ifdef _DEBUG
#undef THIS_FILE
static char BASED_CODE THIS_FILE[] = __FILE__;
#endif

////////////////////////////////////////////////////////////
// CPaintobjView

IMPLEMENT_DYNCREATE(CPaintobjView, CScrollView)

BEGIN_MESSAGE_MAP(CPaintobjView, CScrollView)
   //{{AFX_MSG_MAP(CPaintobjView)
   ON_WM_LBUTTONDOWN()
   ON_WM_LBUTTONUP()
   ON_WM_MOUSEMOVE()
   ON_COMMAND(ID_VIEW_SCROLL, OnViewScroll)
   ON_UPDATE_COMMAND_UI(ID_VIEW_SCROLL, OnUpdateViewScroll)
   ON_UPDATE_COMMAND_UI(ID_VIEW_ZOOMFIT, OnUpdateViewZoomfit)
   ON_COMMAND(ID_VIEW_ZOOMFIT, OnViewZoomfit)
   ON_UPDATE_COMMAND_UI(ID_EDIT_COPY, OnUpdateEditCopy)
   ON_UPDATE_COMMAND_UI(ID_EDIT_CUT, OnUpdateEditCut)
   ON_COMMAND(ID_EDIT_CUT, OnEditCut)
   //}}AFX_MSG_MAP
   // Standard printing commands
   ON_COMMAND(ID_FILE_PRINT, CScrollView::OnFilePrint)
   ON_COMMAND(ID_FILE_PRINT_PREVIEW,
CScrollView::OnFilePrintPreview)
END_MESSAGE_MAP()

////////////////////////////////////////////////////////////
// CPaintobjView construction/destruction
```

```
CPaintobjView::CPaintobjView()
{
   CWinApp* pApp = AfxGetApp();

   m_bZoomMode = FALSE;
   m_bTracking = FALSE;
   m_hcurArrow = pApp->LoadStandardCursor(IDC_ARROW);
   m_hcurCross = pApp->LoadStandardCursor(IDC_CROSS);
   m_pActive = NULL;

   ASSERT(m_hcurArrow != NULL);
   ASSERT(m_hcurCross != NULL);

   // Win95 has IDC_SIZEALL, WinNT 3.51/4.0 has IDC_SIZE
   m_hcurSize = pApp->LoadStandardCursor(IDC_SIZEALL);
   if (m_hcurSize == NULL)
      pApp->LoadStandardCursor(IDC_SIZE);
   ASSERT(m_hcurSize != NULL);
}

CPaintobjView::~CPaintobjView()
{
}

/////////////////////////////////////////////////////////////
// CPaintobjView drawing

void CPaintobjView::OnDraw(CDC* pDC)
{
   CPaintobjDoc* pDoc = GetDocument();
   ASSERT_VALID(pDoc);

   POSITION pos;
   pos = pDoc->m_Objects.GetHeadPosition();
   while (pos != NULL)
   {
      CPainted* pPainter =
           (CPainted*) pDoc->m_Objects.GetNext(pos);
      ASSERT(pPainter->IsKindOf(RUNTIME_CLASS(CPainted)));

      if (m_pActive != pPainter)
         pPainter->Draw(pDC);
      else
         pPainter->DrawSelected(pDC);
   }
}

/////////////////////////////////////////////////////////////
// CPaintobjView diagnostics

#ifdef _DEBUG
```

(continued)

Listing 20-1 *(continued)*

```
void CPaintobjView::AssertValid() const
 {
   CScrollView::AssertValid();
 }

void CPaintobjView::Dump(CDumpContext& dc) const
 {
   CScrollView::Dump(dc);
 }

CPaintobjDoc* CPaintobjView::GetDocument()
// non-debug version is inline
 {
   ASSERT(m_pDocument->IsKindOf(RUNTIME_CLASS(CPaintobjDoc)));
   return (CPaintobjDoc*)m_pDocument;
 }
#endif //_DEBUG

/////////////////////////////////////////////////////////////////
// CPaintobjView message handlers

void CPaintobjView::OnLButtonDown(UINT nFlags, CPoint point)
 {
   CPaintobjDoc* pDoc = (CPaintobjDoc*) GetDocument();

   CClientDC ClientDC(this);
   OnPrepareDC(&ClientDC);
   ClientDC.DPtoLP(&point);

   if (pDoc->m_pSelectedTool == NULL)
    {
      POSITION    pos;
      CPainted*   pPainted;
      CPainted*   pHit;
      pos = pDoc->m_Objects.GetHeadPosition();

      pHit = NULL;
      while (pos != NULL)
       {
         pPainted = (CPainted*) pDoc->m_Objects.GetNext(pos);
         if (pPainted->IsHit(point))
          {
            pHit = pPainted;
            break;
          }
       }
      if (pHit != NULL)
       {
         if (m_pActive != NULL)
          {
            CRect rectInvalid;
```

```
            m_pActive->GetBoundingRect(&rectInvalid);
            rectInvalid.InflateRect(1, 1);
            InvalidateRect(&rectInvalid);
          }
        m_pActive = pHit;
        m_pActive->DrawSelected(&ClientDC);
      }
    return;
   }
  SetCapture();
  m_bTracking = TRUE;
  pDoc->m_pSelectedTool->OnDown(point);
  CScrollView::OnLButtonDown(nFlags, point);
}

void CPaintobjView::OnLButtonUp(UINT nFlags, CPoint point)
{
  CPaintobjDoc* pDoc = (CPaintobjDoc*) GetDocument();
  ASSERT(pDoc != NULL);

  if (m_bTracking)
   {
    ASSERT(pDoc->m_pSelectedTool != NULL);
    pDoc->m_pSelectedTool->OnUp(point, this);

    CRect rect;
    pDoc->m_pSelectedTool->GetBoundingRect(&rect);
    pDoc->ExpandBounds(&rect);
    pDoc->m_Objects.AddTail(pDoc->m_pSelectedTool);
    pDoc->m_pSelectedTool = NULL;
    pDoc->m_nSelectedTool = ID_TOOL_SELECTOR;
    m_bTracking = FALSE;
    ReleaseCapture();
    CMainFrame* pMain =
        (CMainFrame*) AfxGetApp()->m_pMainWnd;
    pMain->ClearPositionText();
   }

  CScrollView::OnLButtonUp(nFlags, point);
}

void CPaintobjView::OnMouseMove(UINT nFlags, CPoint point)
{
  CClientDC ClientDC(this);
  OnPrepareDC(&ClientDC);
  ClientDC.DPtoLP(&point);

  CPaintobjDoc* pDoc = (CPaintobjDoc*) GetDocument();
  ASSERT(pDoc != NULL);
  if (pDoc->m_pSelectedTool == NULL)
   {
```

(continued)

Listing 20-1 *(continued)*

```
         ::SetCursor(m_hcurArrow);
         return;
      }
      ::SetCursor(m_hcurCross);
      if (!m_bTracking)
         return;

      CMainFrame* pMain = (CMainFrame*) AfxGetApp()->m_pMainWnd;
      pMain->SetPositionText(point);
      pDoc->m_pSelectedTool->DragDraw(&ClientDC, point);
      CScrollView::OnMouseMove(nFlags, point);
   }

void CPaintobjView::OnInitialUpdate()
   {
      CScrollView::OnInitialUpdate();

      CPaintobjDoc* pDoc = GetDocument();
      ASSERT_VALID(pDoc);
      CSize siz;
      pDoc->GetBounds(&siz);

      m_bZoomMode = FALSE;
      SetScrollSizes(MM_TEXT, siz);
      SetScrollSizes(MM_TEXT, siz);
   }

void CPaintobjView::OnViewScroll()
   {
      CPaintobjDoc* pDoc = GetDocument();
      ASSERT_VALID(pDoc);

      CSize siz;
      pDoc->GetBounds(&siz);
      m_bZoomMode = FALSE;
      SetScrollSizes(MM_TEXT, siz);
   }

void CPaintobjView::OnUpdateViewScroll(CCmdUI* pCmdUI)
   {
      pCmdUI->SetCheck(!m_bZoomMode);
   }

void CPaintobjView::OnUpdateViewZoomfit(CCmdUI* pCmdUI)
   {
      CPaintobjDoc* pDoc = GetDocument();
      ASSERT_VALID(pDoc);

      POSITION pos;
      pos = pDoc->m_Objects.GetHeadPosition();
      pCmdUI->SetCheck(m_bZoomMode);
```

```
    pCmdUI->Enable(pos != NULL);
  }

void CPaintobjView::OnViewZoomfit()
  {
    CPaintobjDoc* pDoc = GetDocument();
    ASSERT_VALID(pDoc);

    CSize siz;
    pDoc->GetBounds(&siz);
    m_bZoomMode = TRUE;
    SetScaleToFitSize(siz);
  }

void CPaintobjView::OnUpdateEditCopy(CCmdUI* pCmdUI)
  {
    pCmdUI->Enable(m_pActive != NULL);
  }

void CPaintobjView::OnUpdateEditCut(CCmdUI* pCmdUI)
  {
    pCmdUI->Enable(m_pActive != NULL);
  }

void CPaintobjView::OnEditCut()
  {
    ASSERT(m_pActive != NULL);

    CPaintobjDoc* pDoc = GetDocument();
    ASSERT_VALID(pDoc);
    POSITION    pos;
    CRect       rectUpdate;
    CPainted*   pPainted;
    BOOL        bFoundIt = FALSE;
    pos = pDoc->m_Objects.GetHeadPosition();

    while (pos != NULL)
      {
        pPainted = (CPainted*) pDoc->m_Objects.GetAt(pos);
        if (pPainted == m_pActive)
          {
            bFoundIt = TRUE;
            break;
          }
        pDoc->m_Objects.GetNext(pos);
      }
    ASSERT(bFoundIt == TRUE);
    if (bFoundIt == TRUE)
      {
        pDoc->m_Objects.RemoveAt(pos);
        m_pActive->GetBoundingRect(&rectUpdate);
        rectUpdate.InflateRect(1, 1);
```

(continued)

Listing 20-1 (continued)

```
        delete m_pActive;
        m_pActive = NULL;
        InvalidateRect(&rectUpdate);
      }
    pDoc->RecalcBoundary();

    if (m_bZoomMode)
        OnViewZoomfit();
    else
        OnViewScroll();
    return;
}
```

Understanding Splitter Windows

In a splitter window, the window is, or can be, split into two or more scrollable panes. A splitter control (or *split box*) in the window frame next to the scroll bars enables the user to adjust the relative sizes of the window panes. Each pane is a view on the same document. In dynamic splitter windows, the views are generally of the same class. In static splitter windows, the views are more often of different classes. You implement splitter windows of both kinds with the `CSplitterWnd` class.

Dynamic splitter windows enable the user to split a window into multiple panes at will and then scroll different panes to see different parts of the document. The user can also unsplit the window to remove the additional views.

Static splitter windows start with the window split into multiple panes, each with a different purpose. For example, in the Visual C++ bitmap editor, the image window shows two panes side by side. The left pane displays an actual size image of the bitmap. The right pane displays a zoomed or magnified image of the same bitmap. The panes are separated by a "splitter bar" that the user can drag to change the relative sizes of the panes.

Until now, you've learned about applications that present only one main window for their user interface. For some applications, it's interesting or valuable to have two related sections of the application's document visible in the application. Applications that can potentially render wide ranges of information to the user are common candidates for this sort of user interface. Microsoft Excel, for example, enables you to split your view of a spreadsheet and independently scroll over each pane of the window (or over an entirely different portion of the sheet in each window).

Many of the applications that you will design, such as the PaintObj project just presented, could easily present more information than could possibly fit on one screen. Even though the application enables the user to scroll within the window, the user might be interested in seeing two sections of the window simultaneously that are too far apart to ever show in a single window on a screen. By enabling the user to split their view of the window, you can pack more information onto the screen in the same amount of space.

Unfortunately, painting this kind of window without MFC support is tiresome, to say the least. You have to run the paint code twice, essentially fooling it into believing that the window is smaller than it really is — transposing the coordinates painted into each half of the split. Thankfully, MFC provides a simple solution — the `CSplitterWnd` class. `CSplitterWnd` is a special window class provided by MFC to live inside your application's frame window. Before you learn how to incorporate a splitter window into the design of your application, it's valuable to briefly review the different types of splitter windows that are available.

Differentiating between splitter windows

Programmers generally call the `CSplitterWnd` class, and the windows it represents, splitters, so you should be aware of the different terms. Before you implement the `CSplitterWnd` class, it's worthwhile to take some time to think a little about the way a `CSplitterWnd` is used within your application and the semantic rules that must be true for the class to make any sense and work properly.

When users split a window, they might decide to add another pane in the window either horizontally or vertically. In other words, the splitter will have to request that another view be created to fill the area to the right or below the divider. A user can also further divide a window, requiring three new views to be created immediately. This fills the area to the right, beneath, and to the bottom right of the existing window, illustrating the quartering effect.

The `CSplitterWnd` class is capable of doing all of this work, because it records contextual information about the document template during its own creation. This enables the splitter to know what document and which view class will be referenced by the new view windows. You can develop code to have the splitter generate different views for each pane in the window, or, alternatively, you can enable it to generate a new instance of the same view type used in the original window. You should first decide how you'd like the user to approach the splitter window in your application. As you learned earlier in this chapter, you have two general choices for your splitter windows: a dynamic splitter or a static splitter.

Understanding specifics of the CSplitterWnd class

As you have learned, you use the `CSplitterWnd` class within your MFC applications to provide users with the functionality of a splitter window, a window that contains multiple panes. A pane is usually an application-specific object that you derive from `CView`, but it can be any `CWnd` object that has the appropriate child window ID.

You usually embed a `CSplitterWnd` object in a parent `CFrameWnd` or `CMDIChildWnd` object. Create a `CSplitterWnd` object using the following steps:

1. Embed a `CSplitterWnd` member variable in the parent frame.
2. Override the parent frame's `CFrameWnd::OnCreateClient()` member function.
3. From within the overridden `OnCreateClient()` member function, call the `Create()` or `CreateStatic()` member function of `CSplitterWnd` (depending on the splitter window type you intend to create).

Call the `Create()` member function to create a dynamic splitter window. A dynamic splitter window typically is used to create and scroll a number of individual panes, or views, of the same document. The framework automatically creates an initial pane for the splitter; then the framework creates, resizes, and disposes of additional panes as the user operates the splitter window's controls. When you call `Create()`, you specify a minimum row height and column width that determine when the panes are too small to be fully displayed. After you call `Create()`, you can adjust these minimums by calling the `SetColumnInfo()` and `SetRowInfo()` member functions.

In addition, you can use the `SetColumnInfo()` and `SetRowInfo()` member functions to set an "ideal" width for a column and "ideal" height for a row. When the framework displays a splitter window, it first displays the parent frame and then the splitter window. The framework then lays out the panes in columns and rows according to their ideal dimensions, working from the upper-left to the lower-right corner of the splitter window's client area.

To create a static splitter window, use the `CreateStatic()` member function. The user can change only the size of the panes, not their number or order, in a static splitter window. You must specifically create all the static splitter's panes when you create the static splitter. Make sure you create all the panes before the parent frame's `OnCreateClient()` member function returns, or the framework won't display the window correctly.

The `CreateStatic()` member function automatically initializes a static splitter with a minimum row height and column width of 0. After you call `Create()`, adjust these minimums (just as you would with a dynamic splitter) by calling the `SetColumnInfo()` and `SetRowInfo()` member functions.

The individual panes of a static splitter often belong to different classes. A splitter window supports special scroll bars (apart from the scroll bars that panes may have). These scroll bars are children of the `CSplitterWnd` object and are shared between the two panes. You create these special scroll bars when you create the splitter window. For example, a `CSplitterWnd` that has one row, two columns, and the `WS_VSCROLL` style displays a vertical scroll bar that is shared by the two panes. When the user moves the scroll bar, `WM_VSCROLL` messages are sent to both panes. When the panes set the scroll bar position, the shared scroll bar is set.

When creating either kind of splitter window, you must specify the maximum number of rows and columns that the splitter will manage. For a static splitter, panes must be created to fill all the rows and columns. For a dynamic splitter, the framework automatically creates the first pane when the application creates the `CSplitterWnd` object.

The maximum number of panes you can specify for static splitters is 16 rows by 16 columns. However, splitting a window into more than two panes generally is confusing to the user, and you are typically better served to create multiple views within multiple frame windows, which the user switches back and forth between. Microsoft's recommended configurations and usage for static splitters are as follows:

✦ 1 row × 2 columns for displaying two dissimilar panes side by side (each pane is longer than it is wide)

✦ 2 rows × 1 column for displaying two dissimilar panes, one on top of the other (each pane is wider than it is long)

✦ 2 rows × 2 columns for displaying similar panes, usually in four side-by-side squares (best for displaying graphical data)

The maximum number of panes you can specify for dynamic splitters is 2 rows by 2 columns. Microsoft's recommended configurations for dynamic splitters are as follows:

✦ 1 row × 2 columns for displaying columnar data

✦ 2 rows × 1 column for displaying textual or other data

✦ 2 rows × 2 columns for displaying grid or table-oriented data

More on dynamic splitters

As you learned earlier in this chapter, dynamic splitters enable users to split the window at their leisure. An application with dynamic splitters has small boxes, one above the vertical scroll bar and one to the left of the horizontal scroll bar. These can be dragged to split the window in one direction or the other: Figure 20-6 shows an application with a dynamic splitter, after the user has split the display into four window panes.

After dragging the box above the vertical bar down a little, the window splits and automatically creates another view. To set up this kind of splitter, you must declare an instance of `CSplitterWnd` in your application's frame window. For SDI applications, this would be the `CMainFrame` class, while for MDI applications, it would be within the `CMDIChildWnd` class for each view that implements dynamic splitter windows.

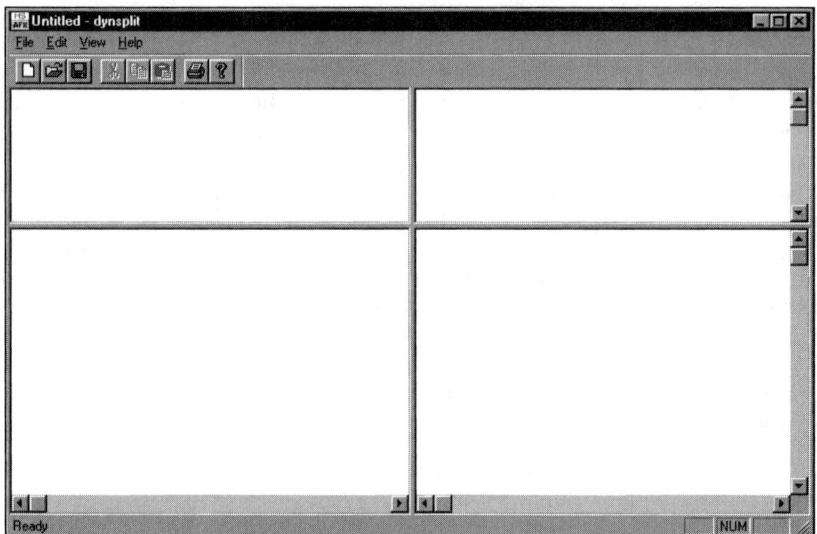

Figure 20-6: This application with dynamic splitter windows shows four user-split panes.

To initialize a dynamic splitter window, create the splitter window when the frame wants to create a client area of the frame window. Normally, the frame window simply creates the view and inserts it into the client area of the frame, but you can have the splitter create and insert itself into the frame. The splitter initializes a single view to populate itself and creates more views when the user splits the window's content.

To get your frame to create the splitter, install an override of the `OnCreateClient()` function. For a dynamic splitter in an SDI application, the function just needs code similar to the following:

```
BOOL CMainFrame::OnCreateClient(LPCREATESTRUCT lpcs,
     CCreateContext* pContext)
  {
    return m_wndSplitter.Create(this, 2, 2,
        CSize(1,1), pContext);
  }
```

The `CSplitterWnd::Create()` function accepts a few parameters. The first parameter is a pointer to the parent window of the splitter, which must be the frame. Your next two parameters are the maximum number of rows and columns that the splitter supports. You can force it to disallow horizontal splits by passing 1 for the maximum number of rows or to avoid vertical splits by passing 1 for the maximum number of columns. Such a splitter window won't have a split box on the appropriate side of the window.

Dynamic splitters in MFC are unable to support more than two rows and two columns. If you try to pass numbers larger than 2 to the `Create()` function, MFC will `ASSERT()` your debug build and not compile the application.

✦ ✦ ✦ ✦ ✦

The value of `CSize()` that you pass to the function causes the splitter to enforce lower size limits for the panes it creates. A size of one-by-one, as the previous code fragment uses, effectively makes the splitter allow any window size. If, because of its content, your view has problems painting in very small windows, you may want to enforce a lower limit on your splitter by passing a larger `CSize()` to the creation function.

MFC won't enable your user to create a pane smaller than your passed `CSize()` values. It snaps the pane shut when the user releases the mouse while dragging a new size. Debug builds of MFC display an appropriate warning within the debug window, such as the following:

```
Warning: split too small to create new pane.
```

Given the way all this works, with the splitter creating all of the views, there clearly must be a way for the splitter to know what view to create—and for the splitter to hook up the view to the right document. A `pContext` parameter gets passed about, from the `OnCreateClient()` parameter to the `Create()` function in `CSplitterWnd`. The `pContext` parameter points at the contextual information that tells the `CSplitterWnd` code who should handle the creation of the new view and its subsequent attachment to a document.

Using different views in dynamic panes

The code snippet from `CChildFrame::OnCreateClient()` shown in the previous section results in a splitter that contains two instances of `CView`, registered in the document template that created the frame. You can use a different view in the extra panes of your splitter that enables you to convey information in a different manner —side by side with information from the same document in a different view or even a different document in a different view.

When the user creates new panes in a dynamic splitter window, MFC calls the `CreateView()` member function of the `CSplitterWnd` class to perform the creation. Normally, `CreateView()`simply creates the required view, based on the context information you pass to it through the `pContext` parameter. If `pContext` is `NULL`, the function determines what view is the currently active view and tries to create the same one.

You must derive your own class from CSplitterWnd if you want to have different views in the panes of your application's dynamic splitter window. You will have to override the CreateView() function, creating the view of your choice. Fortunately, the overriding code is simple — all you must do is pass the call along to CSplitterWnd::CreateView(), naming the RUNTIME_CLASS of the view class you wish to create for the splitter, as shown in the following code:

```
BOOL CMySplitterWnd::CreateView(int row, int col,
   CRuntimeClass* pViewClass, SIZE sizeInit,
   CCreateContext* pContext)
 {
   if (row == 0 && col == 0)
    {
      return CSplitterWnd::CreateView(row, col,
          pViewClass, sizeInit, pContext);
    }
   else
    {
      return CSplitterWnd::CreateView(row, col,
        RUNTIME_CLASS(CSecondView), sizeInit, pContext);
    }
 }
```

The code first checks to determine if the view is being created at row 0, column 0 in the splitter. If this is the case, the splitter is just now being initialized, and you must create a view object of the class requested. If the code is indeed creating the first view for the splitter, it creates whatever view type the splitter originally wanted. But if the view is being created at a position other than the very first, the code returns the RUNTIME_CLASS() of the CSecondView class.

Using a CRuntimeClass object

What the code in the previous section is doing is not necessarily obvious because the calls to CreateView() supply a pointer to a CRuntimeClass object. A CRuntimeClass object describes the runtime type information for a class. Given this pointer, the code inside of CreateView() can accomplish the construction of whatever object the runtime type information describes.

If you set a breakpoint on the CMySplitterWnd::CreateView() function and check the execution stream of an application that uses the code in the previous section, you will learn some important facts about the splitter window class. Most notably, you will find out that the splitter destroys views that are no longer visible and re-creates them later. This effectively means that the life cycle of a splitter and its views might be represented as shown in Table 20-1.

Table 20-1
Phases in the Life Cycle of a Splitter and Its Views

User Action	*Splitter Response*
Start the application (`CframeWnd` creates the `CSplitterWnd` within it).	Create a view at 0, 0.
Drag the horizontal splitter box down.	Create a view at 1, 0.
Drag the vertical splitter box over.	Create a view at 0, 1. Also create a view at 1, 1, because there are four panes now.
Drag the horizontal splitter box up, erasing the split.	Destroy the panes at 0, 0 and 1, 0.
Drag the horizontal splitter down again, re-creating the split.	Create a view at 1, 0 again, and then create the view at 1, 1, because we have four panes again.

If you try this out with an application that uses dynamic splitters as you have implemented them so far, you will end up with four views of the second view class. You can fix this by ensuring that only row or column 1 is ever deleted. You can see that the splitter window does a lot of work to juggle the logical row and column position of the views in the splitter. Behind the scenes, it's also doing a bunch of math to correctly lay out each view window in the client area of the splitter.

Using splitters with views associated with more than one document

The whole process that the previous section details works fine in situations where your new view references the same document as the existing views. However, if you want the second view to open another document, you have to handle the splitter's creation a bit differently. You have to actually create the splitter and give it a different creation context. You must inform it that it must instantiate new documents and views, as well as move the view window to the correct coordinates, so that it fits with the rest of the window. Believe it or not, this last part is the most difficult portion of the process.

You can avoid doing all of this work by eliminating the call to `CSplitterWnd::CreateView()`. Instead, develop your own creation context to pass along to the `CreateView()` function, which lets it know exactly what it needs to do.

The pContext parameter is a pointer to a CCreateContext object. The CCreateContext object records which frame, object, and document should be used for the newly created document/view pair. The following code fragment builds its own CCreateContext object called ctxSample1. The object is initialized to have the view, document, and template information that the application should create in the new splitter panel:

```
BOOL CYourSplitterWnd::CreateView(int row, int col,
    CRun timeClass* pViewClass, SIZE sizeInit,
    CCreateContext* pContext)
{
   CCreateContext ctxSample1;
   // if there is no active view, ASSERT
   CView* pOldView = (CView*)GetActivePane();
   ASSERT(pOldView == NULL);
   // you should test pOldView here and do something
   // reasonable with it.
   // in this fragment, simply find out where the old view is
   ctxSample1.m_pLastView = pOldView;
   ctxSample1.m_pCurrentDoc = pOldView->GetDocument();
   ctxSample1.m_pNewDocTemplate =
       m_pCurrentDoc->GetDocTemplate();
   // pass call along
   return CSplitterWnd::CreateView(row, col,
       pOldView->GetRun timeClass(),
       sizeInit, &ctxSample1);
}
```

Using static splitters

Static splitters are used in applications where dynamic splitters are inadequate or inappropriate. Static splitters can be used when your application needs to show more than two split rows or two split columns. If you are interested in having your window split (no matter what column or row count) but refuse to enable the user to select how and where the splits should occur, you should use a static splitter instead of a dynamic splitter, because it's easier to code what you need using static splitters than it is to write code to negate the actions of MFC.

Static splitters still use the CSplitterWnd class but require a slightly different creation mechanism. You will still put a CCreateWnd instance in the CFrameWnd or CMDIChildWnd derivative of your application, but your override of the OnCreateClient() function will contain quite different code.

Creating a static splitter

To begin with, you should call CSplitterWnd::CreateStatic() instead of CSplitterWnd::Create(). The CreateStatic() function still creates and wires up the splitter, but you will have to create the content for the individual panes yourself. If you do not, MFC will ASSERT the application and stop its execution immediately. To create the pane, call CreateView() on the CSplitterWnd object you are using. You have to make one CSplitterWnd call for each splitter pane you add. For example, code to create a static splitter with five rows and three columns would look similar to the following:

```
BOOL CMainFrame::OnCreateClient(LPCREATESTRUCT /*lpcs*/,
    CCreateContext* pContext)
 {
   BOOL bRet;
   int nRow;
   int nCol;

   if(!m_wndSplitter.CreateStatic(this, 5, 3))
      return FALSE;
   for (nRow = 0; nRow < 5; nRow++)
      for (nCol = 0; nCol < 3; nCol++)
       {
         bRet = m_wndSplitter.CreateView(nRow, nCol,
             RUN TIME_CLASS(CStaticSplitView),
             CSize(50, 30), pContext);
         if (bRet ==  FALSE)
             return FALSE;
       }
   return TRUE;
 }
```

If you wanted to have different views in each pane, you would write the function's code to pass different RUNTIME_CLASS() information for each CreateView() call.

This chapter outlines ways to manually add a splitter window to your application mainly because a splitter window is most often an afterthought. If you are starting from scratch, you can check the Use Splitter Window check box in your application's MDI Child Frame or Frame Window page. You can reach this check box (shown in Figure 20-7) by pressing the Advanced button in step four of the AppWizard request for information.

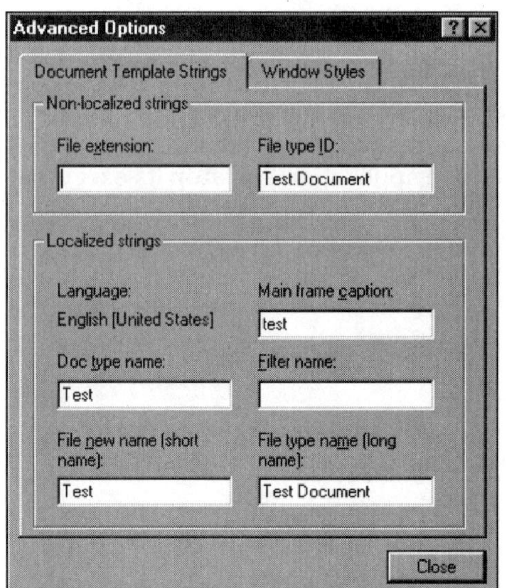

Figure 20-7: You can create splitter windows within the AppWizard.

Understanding shared scroll bars

As you learned earlier in this chapter, the `CSplitterWnd` class also supports shared scroll bars. These scroll bar controls are children of the `CSplitterWnd` and are shared with the different panes in the splitter. For example, in a 1 row × 2 column window, you can specify `WS_VSCROLL` when creating the `CSplitterWnd`. A special scroll bar control will be created that is shared between the two panes, as shown in Figure 20-8.

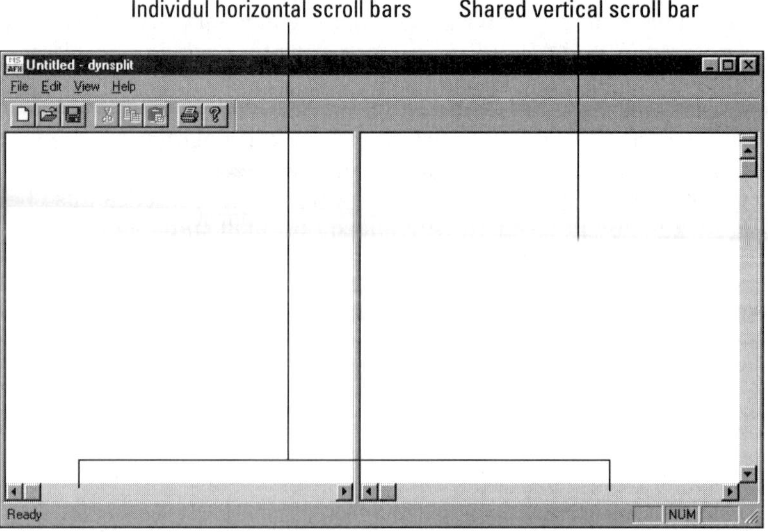

Figure 20-8: The splitter windows share a single scroll bar.

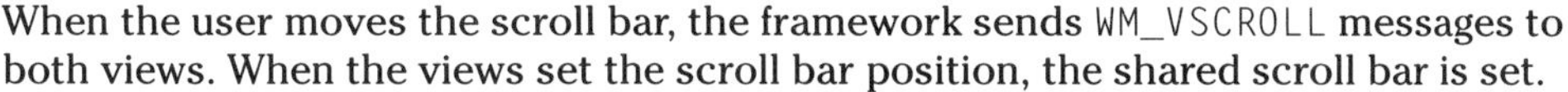

When the user moves the scroll bar, the framework sends WM_VSCROLL messages to both views. When the views set the scroll bar position, the shared scroll bar is set.

Shared scroll bars are most useful with dynamic or static splits that display two view objects of the same class within their different panes. If you mix views of different types in a splitter, you may have to write special code to coordinate their scroll positions. Any CView-derived class that uses the CWnd scroll bar APIs delegates to the shared scroll bar if it exists. The CScrollView implementation is one example of a CView class that supports shared scroll bars. Non-CView-derived classes, classes that rely on noncontrol scroll bars, or classes that use standard Windows implementations (for example, CEditView), won't work with the shared scroll bar feature of CSplitterWnd.

◆ ◆ ◆ ◆ ◆

Determining actual and ideal sizes

The layout of the panes in the splitter window depends on the size of the containing frame window (which in turn resizes the CSplitterWnd). CSplitterWnd repositions and resizes the panes within the containing frame so that they fit as ideally as possible.

The row height and column width sizes set by the user, or that the application sets through the CSplitterWnd API calls, represent the ideal size. The actual size can be smaller than the ideal size (if room is insufficient to make that pane the ideal size) or larger than the ideal size (if that pane must be made larger to fill the leftover space on the right or bottom of the splitter window).

Understanding performance issues with splitters

Splitters make it easy to divide the client area of your frame or MDI children to make the frame hold more than one view. However, this means that your view's painting code will be called many more times than before the split. Your view window will necessarily be smaller than it was before you adopted a splitter window, so you must make sure your view does not do any drawing that is not absolutely necessary. Specifically, your view should not do any drawing beyond the bounds of the window. Limiting your drawing in such a manner helps ensure the greatest possible performance for your application.

Limiting the amount of redrawing that views must do is by far the most important consideration for applications that paint their views repeatedly in the different panes of a splitter window.

The likelihood that one view will change when another visible view must update its content for the same document is increased when you are working with splitter windows. You should think about the different views in your application and make sure that your UpdateAllViews() or UpdateView() calls pass enough information to the updating view, thus ensuring that it can the do the smallest amount of repainting required.

The Dynsplit Program

The Dynsplit sample program is built around a single document class, `CDynsplitDoc`, and uses a `CSingleDocTemplate` and a `CSplitterWnd` class to create dynamic splitter windows within the application.

A demonstration program can be found on the CD-ROM in the `Chap20\Dynsplit` directory. You can rebuild the program by loading the `CDynsplitDoc` project file or just run the `Dynsplit.exe` program using Explorer.

◆ ◆ ◆ ◆ ◆

Listing 20-2 shows code highlights from the `Dynsplit.cpp` and `dynspvw.cpp` source code for the `Dynsplit.exe` program.

Dynsplit
Project Name: **Dynsplit**
CD-ROM Location: **Chap20\Dynsplit**
Prebuilt Program: **Chap20\Dynsplit\Dynsplit.exe**
Source Code Highlights in Text: `Dynsplit.cpp` **and** `Paintvw.cpp`

◆ ◆ ◆ ◆ ◆

Listing 20-2: Highlights of the Dynsplit.cpp and dynspvw.cpp Source Code for the Dynsplit.exe Program

```
// dynsplit.cpp :
// Defines the class behaviors for the application.
//

#include "stdafx.h"
#include "dynsplit.h"

#include "mainfrm.h"
#include "dynspdoc.h"
#include "dynspvw.h"

#ifdef _DEBUG
#undef THIS_FILE
static char BASED_CODE THIS_FILE[] = __FILE__;
#endif

/////////////////////////////////////////////////////////////
// CDynamicSplitApp

BEGIN_MESSAGE_MAP(CDynamicSplitApp, CWinApp)
   //{{AFX_MSG_MAP(CDynamicSplitApp)
```

```
    ON_COMMAND(ID_APP_ABOUT, OnAppAbout)
       // NOTE-ClassWizard adds and removes mapping
       // macros here.
       // DO NOT EDIT these blocks of generated code!
    //}}AFX_MSG_MAP
    // Standard file based document commands
    ON_COMMAND(ID_FILE_NEW, CWinApp::OnFileNew)
    ON_COMMAND(ID_FILE_OPEN, CWinApp::OnFileOpen)
    // Standard print setup command
    ON_COMMAND(ID_FILE_PRINT_SETUP, CWinApp::OnFilePrintSetup)
END_MESSAGE_MAP()

////////////////////////////////////////////////////////////
// CDynamicSplitApp construction

CDynamicSplitApp::CDynamicSplitApp()
 {
    // TODO: add construction code here,
    // Place all significant initialization in InitInstance
 }

//////////////////////////////////////////////////////////////
// The one and only CDynamicSplitApp object

CDynamicSplitApp theApp;

/////////////////////////////////////////////////////////////
// CDynamicSplitApp initialization

BOOL CDynamicSplitApp::InitInstance()
 {
    // Standard initialization

    Enable3dControls();
    LoadStdProfileSettings();  // Load standard INI file
                               // options
                               //  (including MRU)

    // Register the application's document templates.
    //  Document templates serve as the connection between
    // documents, frame windows and views.

    CSingleDocTemplate* pDocTemplate;
    pDocTemplate = new CSingleDocTemplate(
       IDR_MAINFRAME,
       RUNTIME_CLASS(CDynamicSplitDoc),
       RUNTIME_CLASS(CMainFrame),    // main SDI frame window
       RUNTIME_CLASS(CDynamicSplitView));
    AddDocTemplate(pDocTemplate);

    // create a new (empty) document
    OnFileNew();
```

(continued)

Listing 20-2 (continued)

```
   if (m_lpCmdLine[0] != '\0')
    {
      // TODO: add command line processing here
    }
   return TRUE;
 }

/////////////////////////////////////////////////////////////////////////////
// CAboutDlg dialog used for App About

class CAboutDlg : public CDialog
{
public:
   CAboutDlg();

// Dialog Data
   //{{AFX_DATA(CAboutDlg)
   enum { IDD = IDD_ABOUTBOX };
   //}}AFX_DATA

// Implementation
protected:
   virtual void DoDataExchange(CDataExchange* pDX);
   //{{AFX_MSG(CAboutDlg)
      // No message handlers
   //}}AFX_MSG
   DECLARE_MESSAGE_MAP()
};

CAboutDlg::CAboutDlg() : CDialog(CAboutDlg::IDD)
 {
   //{{AFX_DATA_INIT(CAboutDlg)
   //}}AFX_DATA_INIT
 }

void CAboutDlg::DoDataExchange(CDataExchange* pDX)
 {
   CDialog::DoDataExchange(pDX);
   //{{AFX_DATA_MAP(CAboutDlg)
   //}}AFX_DATA_MAP
 }

BEGIN_MESSAGE_MAP(CAboutDlg, CDialog)
   //{{AFX_MSG_MAP(CAboutDlg)
      // No message handlers
   //}}AFX_MSG_MAP
END_MESSAGE_MAP()

// App command to run the dialog
void CDynamicSplitApp::OnAppAbout()
 {
```

```
    CAboutDlg aboutDlg;
    aboutDlg.DoModal();
 }

/////////////////////////////////////////////////////////////
// dynspvw.cpp : implementation of the CDynamicSplitView class
//

#include "stdafx.h"
#include "dynsplit.h"

#include "dynspdoc.h"
#include "dynspvw.h"

#ifdef _DEBUG
#undef THIS_FILE
static char BASED_CODE THIS_FILE[] = __FILE__;
#endif

/////////////////////////////////////////////////////////////
// CDynamicSplitView

IMPLEMENT_DYNCREATE(CDynamicSplitView, CView)

BEGIN_MESSAGE_MAP(CDynamicSplitView, CView)
   //{{AFX_MSG_MAP(CDynamicSplitView)
      // NOTE- ClassWizard adds and removes mapping
      // macros here.
      // DO NOT EDIT these blocks of generated code!
   //}}AFX_MSG_MAP
   // Standard printing commands
   ON_COMMAND(ID_FILE_PRINT, CView::OnFilePrint)
   ON_COMMAND(ID_FILE_PRINT_PREVIEW, CView::OnFilePrintPreview)
END_MESSAGE_MAP()

/////////////////////////////////////////////////////////////
// CDynamicSplitView construction/destruction

CDynamicSplitView::CDynamicSplitView()
 {
   // TODO: add construction code here

 }

CDynamicSplitView::~CDynamicSplitView()
 {
 }

/////////////////////////////////////////////////////////////
// CDynamicSplitView drawing

void CDynamicSplitView::OnDraw(CDC* pDC)
```

(continued)

Listing 20-2 *(continued)*

```
{
   CDynamicSplitDoc* pDoc = GetDocument();
   ASSERT_VALID(pDoc);

   // TODO: add draw code for native data here
 }

/////////////////////////////////////////////////////////////
// CDynamicSplitView printing

BOOL CDynamicSplitView::OnPreparePrinting(CPrintInfo* pInfo)
 {
   // default preparation
   return DoPreparePrinting(pInfo);
 }

void CDynamicSplitView::OnBeginPrinting(CDC* /*pDC*/,
    CPrintInfo* /*pInfo*/)
 {
   // TODO: add extra initialization before printing
 }

void CDynamicSplitView::OnEndPrinting(CDC* /*pDC*/,
    CPrintInfo* /*pInfo*/)
 {
   // TODO: add cleanup after printing
 }

/////////////////////////////////////////////////////////////
// CDynamicSplitView diagnostics

#ifdef _DEBUG
void CDynamicSplitView::AssertValid() const
 {
   CView::AssertValid();
 }

void CDynamicSplitView::Dump(CDumpContext& dc) const
 {
   CView::Dump(dc);
 }

CDynamicSplitDoc* CDynamicSplitView::GetDocument()
   // non-debug version is inline
 {
   ASSERT(m_pDocument-
>IsKindOf(RUNTIME_CLASS(CDynamicSplitDoc)));
   return (CDynamicSplitDoc*)m_pDocument;
 }
#endif //_DEBUG
```

Subclassing Child Windows

To subclass an instance of a window using the Windows API, you must call the `SetWindowLong()` API function and specify the handle of the window to subclass the `GWL_WNDPROC` flag and a pointer to the subclass procedure. `SetWindowLong()` returns a pointer to the original window procedure; use this pointer to pass messages to the original procedure. The subclass window procedure must then use the `CallWindowProc()` function to call the original window procedure.

Listing 20-3 shows how to subclass an instance of an edit control in a dialog box. The subclass window procedure enables the edit control to receive all keyboard input, including the Enter and Tab keys, whenever the control has the input focus. Listing 20-3 shows how you would perform subclassing when using only the Windows API to program.

Listing 20-3: A Window Procedure That Uses Only the Windows API to Perform Subclassing

```
WNDPROC wpOrigEditProc;

LRESULT APIENTRY EditBoxProc(HWND hwndDlg, UINT uMsg,
    WPARAM wParam, LPARAM lParam)
 {
    HWND hwndEdit;

    switch(uMsg)
     {
        case WM_INITDIALOG:
            // Retrieve the handle of the edit control.
            hwndEdit = GetDlgItem(hwndDlg, ID_EDIT);

            // Subclass the edit control.
            wpOrigEditProc =
                (WNDPROC) SetWindowLong(hwndEdit,
                GWL_WNDPROC, (LONG) EditSubclassProc);

            // Continue the initialization procedure.
            return TRUE;

        case WM_DESTROY:
            // Remove the subclass from the edit control.
            SetWindowLong(hwndEdit, GWL_WNDPROC,
                (LONG) wpOrigEditProc);

            // Continue the cleanup procedure.
            //
            break;
```

(continued)

Listing 20-3 *(continued)*

```
        }
    return FALSE;
        UNREFERENCED_PARAMETER(lParam);
}

// Subclass procedure
LRESULT APIENTRY EditSubclassProc(HWND hwnd, UINT uMsg,
    WPARAM wParam, LPARAM lParam)
{
    if (uMsg == WM_GETDLGCODE)
        return DLGC_WANTALLKEYS;

    return CallWindowProc(wpOrigEditProc, hwnd, uMsg,
        wParam, lParam);
}
```

Using MFC to subclass windows

As you might expect, MFC provides an easier way to subclass any window that you derive from a CWnd-derived object. Rather than making the call to SetWindowLong(), you can simply invoke the SubclassWindow() member function. Much as you would use SetWindowLong() with an API-created window, you call the SubclassWindow() member function to dynamically subclass a window and attach it to the CWnd object calling the member function. You must pass the window handle (HWND) of the window to subclass to the SubclassWindow() member function, which, in turn, returns a BOOL value that represents whether the subclassing was successful. When you dynamically subclass a window, Windows messages route through the CWnd's message map and call message handlers in the CWnd's class first. Messages that are passed to the base class are passed to the default message handler in the window.

On the side of the window being subclassed, the SubclassWindow() member function attaches the Windows control or window to a CWnd object and replaces the subclassed window's WndProc() and AfxWndProc() functions. The function stores the old WndProc() function in the location returned by the GetSuperWndProcAddr() member function. You must override the GetSuperWndProcAddr() member function for every unique window class to provide a place to store the old WndProc() function. You might subclass an existing edit control in a dialog box with code similar to that shown in Listing 20-4.

Listing 20-4: Using MFC to Subclass an Existing Edit Control in a Dialog Box

```
BOOL CSubbedDlg::OnInitDialog()
 {
... Other initialization stuff

   // grab a pointer to the edit control
   CWnd* pEdit;
   pEdit = GetDlgItem(IDC_SSN);
   ASSERT(pEdit != NULL);

   // make the control use the system fixed-width font
   // because with numbers and dashes, it will look nicer

   HFONT hFont = (HFONT) ::GetStockObject(SYSTEM_FIXED_FONT);
   CFont* pFont = CFont::FromHandle(hFont);
   pEdit->SetFont(pFont);


   // subclass the edit control so it is connected to the
   // custom CSubbedEdit class.
   m_Subbed.SubclassWindow(pEdit->m_hWnd);
   return TRUE;  // return TRUE unless you
                 // set the focus to a control
 }
```

From the point when this code is executed, the messages sent to the IDC_SSN control are offered first to the m_Subbed object, an instance of the CSubbedEdit class. CSubbedEdit is a class that subclasses (in the C++ way) from the MFC CEdit class. Because, after the SubclassWindow() call, the CSubbedEdit class is now an actual MFC window, it will start to receive messages via the CCmdTarget instance inside the CEdit class. You can perform the edits using ClassWizard to create message map entries for WM_CHAR and WM_KEYUP and to code whatever validation you need in response to those messages.

You can see that the CSubbedEdit class is a member of the application's dialog class. When the dialog initializes, the SubclassWindow() call is made against the social security number (IDC_SSN). The program code never does anything to undo the subclassing because the functionality is disconnected when the dialog window is closed.

One additional possibility is to use a local instance of the `CSubbedEdit` class, and call `SubclassWindow()` on that. This usually isn't acceptable because the `CSubbedEdit` instance has to outlive the control that it subclasses. Locally declaring a subclassing MFC class to a function is almost worthless because very few functions continue to run while messages are being dispatched. The subclassing code would never be installed while messages were being received.

When you want to return the subclassed window to its original state, you should call the `CWnd::UnsubclassWindow()` member function to unsubclass the window. The `UnsubclassWindow()` member function returns a window handle to the newly detached window.

Alternatives to the document/view architecture

While the document/view model is a good default that's useful in many applications, some applications have to bypass it. The point of the document/view architecture is to separate data from viewing. In most cases, this simplifies your application and reduces redundant code. This is not the case, for example, when porting an application written in C for Windows. If your original code already mixes data management with data viewing, moving the code to the document/view model is harder because you must separate the two. You might prefer to leave the code as it is. There are many approaches to bypassing the document/view architecture, of which the following are only several:

- ✦ Treat the document as an unused appendage, and implement your data management code in the view class. Overhead for the document is relatively low, as described in the text that follows.
- ✦ Treat both document and view as unused appendages. Put your data management and drawing code in the frame window rather than the view. This is close to the C-language programming model.
- ✦ Override the parts of the MFC framework that create the document and view to eliminate creating them at all. As you have learned, the document creation process begins with a call to `CWinApp::AddDocTemplate()`. Eliminate that call from your application class' `InitInstance()` member function, and instead, create a frame window in `InitInstance()` yourself. Put your data management code in your frame window class. This is more work and requires a deeper understanding of the framework, but it frees you entirely of the document/view overhead.

Summary

In this chapter you have covered a lot of additional material about the document/view interface. You have learned how to create and use the multiple document interface, not only to create multiple views of the same document, but also to create multiple views of multiple documents and present them all to the user. You used the information that you learned about the multiple document interface within the PaintObj demonstration program, which enables you to create and draw as many windows as memory will allow.

You've also learned about splitter windows, a powerful tool for effectively using the limited "real estate" that users will grant your applications on their desktops. Effective splitter window use enables you to increase and manage not only how much information that you can present to your users within your application, but how you present the information itself. As people become more and more accustomed to the power that computers provide, designing applications that enable the user to view the data as text in one window pane and as a graph in a second window pane without forcing the user to exit the application or run another application will only become more important for application design.

Finally, you learned about subclassing windows, which enables you to instruct the operating system and your application what windows should process messages and how to respond when the user clicks certain windows. You learned that subclassing windows, while relatively simple from the Windows API, is very easy within MFC, and that the `CWnd` class from which you will derive most windows includes the `SubclassWindow()` and `UnsubclassWindow()` member functions.

In the next chapter, you will go one step further with your documents and views and learn how to add printing support to your applications, how to manage the MFC printing process, and how to generate attractive output from within your applications.

✦ ✦ ✦

21

CHAPTER

Printing and Print Preview

✦ ✦ ✦ ✦

In This Chapter

The Windows print architecture

The MFC print architecture

Print previewing

Creating the print preview MFC demo program

Printing to the printer

Creating the basic printing MFC demo program

Debugging print applications

Pagination support

Enumerating printers

✦ ✦ ✦ ✦

As you develop applications, you will find that most require some type of physical output — a permanent record of what the user has done. Generating and managing printing in your applications is a relatively simple process. Much of what you have already learned about graphics device interface (GDI) management applies to printing — printers are merely a different type of device than a screen. In other words, sending output to a printer in a Windows program is almost the same as sending output to the screen. The same functions that work with screen output also work with printer output, except that the applications use a printer device context instead of a screen device context.

Windows API Printer Support

Before Win32, Windows used printer driver messages known as *escape sequences* and the `Escape()` API function to communicate with the printer. For the most part, in the Win32 API, the `Escape()` function is obsolete. Microsoft, instead, replaced it with more specific functions, such as `StartDoc()`, `EndDoc()`, `StartPage()`, `EndPage()`, and so on.

As you might expect, an application must create a device context for a printer using the `CreateDC()` function before the application can print to the printer. After the application acquires a device context for a printer, the application can start the printing process by calling the `StartDoc()` function. The `StartDoc()` function requires as its parameter a `DOCINFO` structure that describes the document that the application is about to print. After you start to print, your application must call the `StartPage()` function to begin each page and the `EndPage()` function to end each page. You can think of a page as a drawing screen. The application must complete all the drawing for each page it prints before the application begins to draw on the next page. When the application finishes printing the entire document, the application should call the `EndDoc()` function. Listing 21-1, the `Print2Page()` function, shows a simple implementation of the steps necessary to print text information to a printer.

Listing 21-1: Print2Page() Prints Simple Text Information to a Printer

```
void Print2Page()
{
  HDC hDC;
  DOCINFO di;

  // create a device context for the printer
  hDC = CreateDC("WINSPOOL", "HP Laser Printer", NULL, NUL);

  // set up DOCINFO
  memset(&di, sizof(DOCINFO));
  di.cbSize = sizof(DOCINFO);
  di.lpszDocName = "Sample Document";

  // start the printing
  if(StartDoc(hDC,&di) != SP_ERROR)
   {
     // Print Page 1
     StartPage(hDC);
     TextOut(hDC, 10, 10, "This is on Page 1.", 18);
     EndPage(hDC);

     // Print Page 2
     StartPage(hDC);
     TextOut(hDC, 10, 10, "This is on Page 2.", 18);
     EndPage(hDC);

     // End Printing
     EndDoc(hDC);
   }
  DolotoDC(hDC);
}
```

Clearly, this type of simple implementation is suitable only for very small print jobs. For example, an application with larger print jobs should provide a way for the user to stop a print job currently in progress. You might display a dialog box with a

Cancel button to alert users to the ongoing print job and give them the opportunity to interrupt the job. You could also use threads within your application to provide background printing on your print jobs so that users can continue working without waiting for the printing process to finish. You will learn more about creating and managing threads in Chapter 25.

If an application does not use threads, you can instead use an *abort procedure*— an application-defined function that processes messages while the application is printing. To set the abort procedure within your applications, call the `SetAbortProc()` API function, and pass the address of the abort procedure to the function prior to starting the print job. Windows, in turn, periodically sends messages to the abort procedure during the printing process. Using the abort procedure gives the application a chance to stop printing whenever it processes a specific message or set of messages. Typically, your application should watch for the activity in question, and then call the `AbortDoc()` API function to stop printing. You might implement the code for a dialog box with a Cancel button as shown in Listing 21-2.

Listing 21-2: Dialog Box Code to Display a Cancel Button During a Printing Operation

```
BOOL bAbort     = FALSE;
HWND hAbortDlg = NULL;

LRESULT CALLBACK AbortDlg(HWND hWnd, UINT message,
    WPARAM wParam, LPARAM lParam)
  {
    switch(message)
     {
       case WM_INITDIALOG :
            ShowWindow(hWnd, SW_NORMAL);
            SetFocus(hWnd);
            UpdateWindow(hWnd);
            return(TRUE);

       case WM_COMMAND     :
             // The cancel button was pressed, abort the doc.
             if (LOWORD(wParam) == IDCANCEL)
              {
                bAbort = TRUE;
                DestroyWindow(hWnd);
                return(TRUE);
              }
             break;
     }
    return(FALSE);
  }
```

(continued)

Listing 21-2 (continued)

```
int CALLBACK Abort(HDC hdcPrinter, int Code)
 {
   MSG msg;

   while (!bAbort &&
       PeekMessage(&msg, NULL, 0, 0, PM_REMOVE))
    {
      if (!IsDialogMessage(hAbortDlg, &msg))
       {
         TranslateMessage(&msg);
         DispatchMessage(&msg);
       }
    }

   // The bAbort argument is TRUE (return is FALSE)
   // if the user has canceled the print operation.

   return (!bAbort);
 }

LRESULT CALLBACK WndProc(HWND hWnd, UINT uMsg,
    WPARAM wParam, LPARAM lParam)
 {
   switch(uMsg)
    {
      case WM_COMMAND :
          switch(LOWORD(wParam))
           {
             case IDM_PRINT:
                   {
                     HDC     hDC;
                     bAbort = FALSE;

                     // Create a device context for the printer
                     // to which the app is going to print.
                     hDC = CreateDC("WINSPOOL", "My Printer",
                         NULL, NULL);

                     // Create the abort dialog.
                     hAbortDlg = CreateDialog(hInst, "ABORTDLG",
                         hWnd, (DLGPROC)AbortDlg);

                     // Disable the main application window.
                     EnableWindow(hWnd, FALSE);

                     // Set the abort procedure to handle
                     // messages for the abort dialog.
                     SetAbortProc(hDC, (ABORTPROC)Abort);

                     /*
                       Send output to the printer here.
```

```
                */

                // If the user aborted the print job,
                // abort the document;
                // otherwise destroy the abort dialog.
                if (bAbort)
                  AbortDoc(hDC);
                else
                  DestroyWindow(hAbortDlg);
                EnableWindow(hWnd, TRUE);
                SetFocus(hWnd);
                DeleteDC(hDC);
              }
            break;

      case WM_DESTROY:
          PostQuitMessage(0);
          break;

      default:
          return(DefWindowProc(hWnd, uMsg, wParam, lParam));
   }

   return(0L);
}
```

Printer information

Although Windows shields the application from direct dealings with the printer hardware, a few situations require it to retrieve hardware-specific information. For example, an application may need to determine the size of the paper, the number of paper bins, the graphic capabilities of a printer, and so on.

Windows has two functions, `DeviceCapabilities()` and `GetDeviceCaps()`, that provide the information that your application might need about a printer. The `GetDeviceCaps()` function is a general function that provides information about displays, printers, plotters, and other output devices. The function retrieves information that is common to all types of devices, such as graphics capability, resolution, number of colors, and so on. The `DeviceCapabilities()` function, on the other hand, retrieves information that is specific to printers, such as information about paper bins, duplexing capabilities, paper size, and so forth. In versions of Windows previous to the Win32 implementations, `DeviceCapabilities()` was not directly supported by the operating system, but rather was part of the printer driver. Win32 moved the function into the operating system to simplify its use during application development. Listing 21-3 shows a simple implementation within the `WndProc()` window procedure that checks an attached printer to see if it supports font substitution.

Listing 21-3: Program Code to Check a Printer's Capabilities for Font Substitution Support

```
LRESULT CALLBACK WndProc(HWND hWnd, UINT uMsg, WPARAM wParam,
    LPARAM lParam)
 {
   switch(uMsg)
   {
     case WM_COMMAND :
         switch(LOWORD(wParam))
          {
            case IDM_TEST :
                 {
                   DWORD dwResult;

                   dwResult = DeviceCapabilities(
                       "HP Laserjet 4M",
                       NULL, DC_TRUETYPE, NULL, NULL);
                   if (dwResult & DCTT_SUBDEV)
                    {
                      MessageBox(hWnd,
                          "Font substitution supported.",
                          "Message",
                          MB_OK | MB_ICONINFORMATION);
                    }
                 }
               break;

   // more code here
   return(0L);
 }
```

Understanding the importance of text characteristics

When an application outputs text, the application can control several characteristics of the text with the functions the Win32 API provides, including text placement, distance between characters, text color, the background color behind the text, and so on.

Each font has different sizing characteristics that you can determine with the `GetTextMetrics()` API function. TrueType fonts also contain information about characteristics such as *kerning pairs*. Kerning pairs are pairs of characters that, when placed together in a string, have the spacing between them adjusted to get the best appearance. You can retrieve these character combinations with the `GetKerningPairs()` function. TrueType fonts also have other characteristics that are not applicable to other fonts. You can retrieve those characteristics with the `GetOutlineTextMetrics()` function.

When you scale and use fonts in an application, it is important that you understand the system of measurements that printers use to describe a character. Figure 21-1 shows two sample characters and the names of the measurements printers use to describe the characters.

✦ ✦ ✦ ✦ ✦

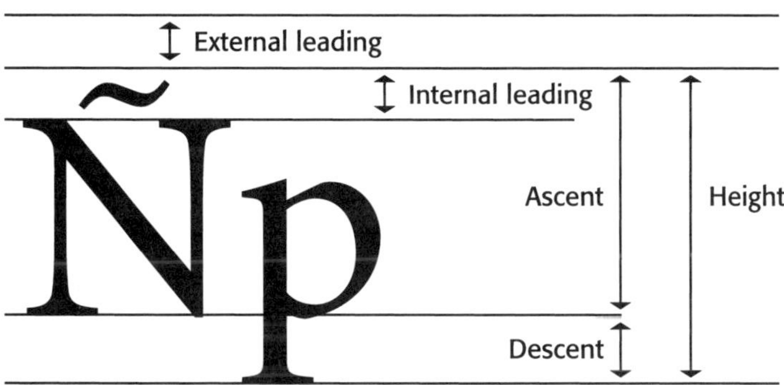

Figure 21-1: These are the measurements and metrics that apply to text characters.

The PortLand Program

The PortLand demonstration program uses the Windows API to print two pages— the first in portrait mode, the second in landscape mode. Highlights of the source code are shown in Listing 21-4.

A demonstration program that shows how to use some of the API functions to print pages can be found on the CD-ROM in the `Chap21\PortLand` directory. You can rebuild the program by loading the `PortLand.dsw` project file, or just run the `PortLand.exe` program using Explorer.

Because the PortLand program uses an SDI interface, you can use the program only to print the two pages previously noted. Select the Test menu item to print the pages.

PortLand

Project Name: **PortLand**
CD-ROM Location: **Chap21\PortLand**
Pre-Built Program: **Chap21\PortLand\PortLand.exe**
Source Code Highlights in Text: `PortLand.cpp`

Listing 21-4: Highlights of the PortLand.cpp Source Code for the PortLand Program

```
LRESULT CALLBACK WndProc(HWND hWnd, UINT uMsg, WPARAM wParam,
    LPARAM lParam)
 {
   switch(uMsg)
   {
      case WM_COMMAND :
          switch(LOWORD(wParam))
           {
             case IDM_TEST:
                    {
                      HDC hDC;
                      DOCINFO di;
                      DEVMODE dm;

                      // Create a device context for the
                      // printer to which text will be output.

                      hDC = CreateDC("WINSPOOL",
                          "HP Laserjet 4",NULL, NULL);

                      // Set up DEVMODE structure.
                      memset(&dm, 0, sizeof(dm));
                      dm.dmSpecVersion = DM_SPECVERSION;
                      dm.dmSize = sizeof(DEVMODE);
                      dm.dmFields = DM_ORIENTATION;

                      // Set up the DOCINFO structure.
                      memset(&di, 0, sizeof(DOCINFO));
                      di.cbSize = sizeof(DOCINFO);
                      di.lpszDocName = "Test Document";

                      // Start the printing.
                      if (StartDoc(hDC, &di) != SP_ERROR)
                       {
                         // Print page 1 portrait.
                         dm.dmOrientation = DMORIENT_PORTRAIT;
                         hDC = ResetDC(hDC, &dm);
                         StartPage(hDC);
                         TextOut(hDC, 10, 10,
                             "This is print portrait.",23);
                         EndPage(hDC);

                         // Print page 2 landscape.
                         dm.dmOrientation = DMORIENT_LANDSCAPE;
                         hDC = ResetDC(hDC, &dm);
                         StartPage(hDC);
```

```
                    TextOut(hDC, 10, 10,
                        "This is print landscape.",24);
                    EndPage(hDC);

                    // End printing.
                    EndDoc(hDC);
                  }

                DeleteDC(hDC);
               }
             break;

         case IDM_ABOUT :
             DialogBox(hInst, "AboutBox", hWnd,
                 (DLGPROC)About);
             break;

         case IDM_EXIT :
             DestroyWindow(hWnd);
             break;
       }
      break;

   case WM_DESTROY :
       PostQuitMessage(0);
       break;

   default :
       return(DefWindowProc(hWnd, uMsg, wParam, lParam));
  }

  return(0L);
}
```

Printing with MFC

After everything you have learned thus far, it should not be surprising that Visual C++ 6.0 provides a set of MFC wrappers that you can use within your programs to support printing and device output. As you know, Microsoft Windows implements device-independent display. In MFC, this means that the same drawing calls, in the `OnDraw()` member function of your view class, are responsible for drawing on the display and on other devices, such as printers. For print preview, the target device is a simulated printer output to the display.

Understanding your role and the framework's role in printing

Because you are using MFC wrapper classes, your responsibilities when programming MFC applications are not quite so broad as they are when you write printing code within a Windows program that does not use MFC. Specifically, it is your responsibility to ensure that your view class performs the following tasks:

- Inform the framework how many pages are in the document.
- When asked to print a specified page, draw that portion of the document.
- Allocate and deallocate any fonts or other graphics device interface (GDI) resources needed for printing.
- If necessary, send any escape codes needed to change the printer mode before printing a given page — for example, to change the printing orientation on a per-page basis.

The MFC framework, in turn, handles the following tasks that are necessary for printing:

- Display the Print dialog box.
- Create a `CDC` object for the printer.
- Call the `StartDoc()` and `EndDoc()` member functions of the `CDC` object.
- Repeatedly call the `StartPage()` member function of the `CDC` object, inform the view class which page should be printed, and call the `EndPage()` member function of the `CDC` object.
- Call overridable functions in the view at the appropriate times.

The remainder of this chapter discusses how your programs should work with the MFC framework to support printing and print preview.

Understanding the MFC printing sequence

As you will learn later in this chapter, you will find that you often override member functions in the view class(es) of your applications to correctly support printing from those classes. You will generally overload, at a minimum, three member functions to support printing within your class — `OnDraw()`, `OnBeginPrinting()`, and `OnPrepareDC()`. These functions are critically important to the printing and print previewing processes. However, other functions are also available that enable you to add even more printing power to your applications. The functions important to the printing process are listed in Table 21-1 along with a brief description.

Table 21-1
Printing Functions of a View Class

Function	*Description*
OnBeginPrinting()	Override this function to create resources, such as fonts, that you need for printing the document. You can also set the maximum page count here.
OnDraw()	This function serves triple duty, displaying data in a frame window, a print preview window, or on the printer, depending on the device context sent as the function's parameter.
OnEndPrinting()	Override this function to release resources created in OnBeginPrinting().
OnPrepareDC()	Override this function to modify the device context that is used to display or print the document. You can, for example, handle pagination here.
OnPreparePrinting()	Override this function to provide a maximum page count for the document. If you don't set the page count here, you should set it in OnBeginPrinting().
OnPrint()	Override this function to provide additional printing services, such as printing headers and footers, not provided in OnDraw().

To print a document, MFC calls the functions Table 21-1 lists in a specific order. First, it calls OnPreparePrinting(), which simply calls DoPreparePrinting(). DoPreparePrinting(), in turn, is responsible for displaying the Print dialog box and creating the printer DC. The AppWizard implements the OnPreparePrinting() function as shown here:

```
BOOL CPrint1View::OnPreparePrinting(CPrintInfo* pInfo)
 {
   // default preparation
   return DoPreparePrinting(pInfo);
 }
```

As you can see, OnPreparePrinting() receives as a parameter a pointer to a CPrintInfo object. Using this object, you can obtain information about the print job, as well as initialize attributes such as the maximum page number. Table 21-2 lists the most useful data and function members of the CPrintInfo class, along with a brief description of each.

Table 21-2
Members of the CPrintInfo Class

Member	*Description*
SetMaxPage()	Sets the document's maximum page number.
SetMinPage()	Sets the document's minimum page number.
GetFromPage()	Gets the number of the first page that the user selected for printing.
GetMaxPage()	Gets the document's maximum page number, which may be changed in OnBeginPrinting().
GetMinPage()	Gets the document's minimum page number, which may be changed in OnBeginPrinting().
GetToPage()	Gets the number of the last page the user selected for printing.
m_bContinuePrinting	Controls the printing process. Setting the flag to FALSE ends the print job.
m_bDirect	Indicates whether the document is being directly printed (as opposed to through the Windows spooler).
m_bPreview	Indicates whether the document is in print preview.
m_nCurPage	Holds the current number of the page being printed.
m_nNumPreviewPages	Holds the number of pages (1 or 2) that are being displayed in print preview.
m_pPD	Holds a pointer to the print job's CPrintDialog object.
m_rectDraw	Holds a rectangle that defines the usable area for the current page.
m_strPageDesc	Holds a page-number format string.

When the DoPreparePrinting() function displays the Print dialog box, the user can set the value of many of the data members of the CPrintInfo class. Your program then can use or set any of these values. Usually, you at least call SetMaxPage(), which sets the document's maximum page number, before DoPreparePrinting(), so that the maximum page number displays in the Print dialog box. If you cannot determine the number of pages until you calculate a page length based on the selected printer, you have to wait until you have a printer DC for the printer.

After OnPreparePrinting(), MFC calls the OnBeginPrinting() member function, which is not only another place where you can set the maximum page count, but also the function in which you should create resources, such as fonts, that you need to complete the print job. The OnPreparePrinting() member function receives, as parameters, a pointer to the printer DC and a pointer to the associated CPrintInfo object.

Next, MFC calls the OnPrepareDC() member function for the first page in the document. The call to OnPrepareDC() is the beginning of a print loop that the framework executes once for each page in the document. OnPrepareDC() is the function in which you should control what part of the whole document prints on the current page. As you will learn, you handle this task by setting the document's viewport origin.

After OnPrepareDC(), MFC calls OnPrint() to print the actual page. Normally, OnPrint() calls OnDraw() with the printer DC, which automatically directs OnDraw()'s output to the printer rather than to the screen. You can override OnPrint() to control how the application and the framework print the document. You can print headers and footers in OnPrint(), and then call the base class's version (which in turn calls OnDraw()) to print the body of the document, as shown here:

```
void CPrint1View::OnPrint(CDC* pDC, CPrintInfo* pInfo)
 {
   //TODO: Add specialized code here and call the base class

   // Call local functions to print a header and footer.
   PrintHeader();
   PrintFooter();
   CView::OnPrint(pDC, pInfo);
 }
```

To prevent the base class version from overwriting your header and footer area, restrict the printable area by setting the m_rectDraw member of the CPrintInfo object to a rectangle that does not overlap the header or footer. You will learn more about printing headers and footers later in this chapter.

Alternatively, you can remove OnDraw() from the print loop entirely by doing your own printing in OnPrint() and not calling OnDraw() at all, as shown here:

```
void CPrint1View::OnPrint(CDC* pDC, CPrintInfo* pInfo)
 {
   // TODO: Add specialized code here and call the base class

   // Call local functions to print a header and footer.
   PrintHeader();
   PrintFooter();
   // Call a local function to print the body of the document.
   PrintDocument();
 }
```

As long as there are more pages to print, MFC continues to call OnPrepareDC() and OnPrint() for each page in the document. After the last page is printed, MFC calls OnEndPrinting(), where you can destroy any resources you created in OnBeginPrinting(). Figure 21-2 summarizes the entire printing process.

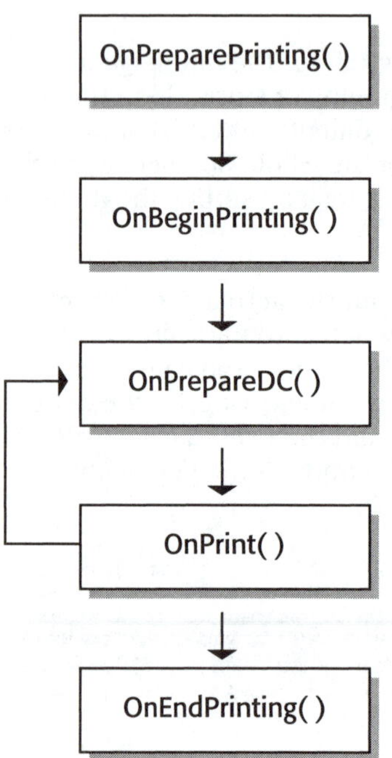

Figure 21-2: The MFC printing process uses a specific series of steps when printing any document type.

Further insight into MFC default printing

As you learned in Chapters 19 and 20, in MFC applications, the view class has a member function named OnDraw() that contains all the drawing code for that view. OnDraw() takes a pointer to a CDC object as a parameter. That CDC object represents the device context to receive the image produced by OnDraw(). When the window displaying the document receives a WM_PAINT message, the framework calls OnDraw and passes it a device context for the screen (specifically, a CPaintDC object). Accordingly, OnDraw()'s output goes to the screen.

As you have learned, sending output to the printer is very similar to sending output to the screen because the Windows graphics device interface (GDI) is hardware independent. You can use the same GDI functions for screen display or for printing simply by using the appropriate device context. If the CDC object that OnDraw() receives represents the printer, OnDraw()'s output goes to the printer.

The simplicity of passing a slightly different object into `OnDraw()` explains how MFC applications can perform simple printing without requiring extra effort on your part. The framework takes care of displaying the Print dialog box and creating a device context for the printer. When the user selects the Print command from the File menu, the view passes the default printer's device context to `OnDraw()`, which draws the document on the printer.

However, there are some significant differences between printing and screen display. When you print, you have to divide the document into distinct pages and display them one at a time, rather than display whatever portion is visible in a window. As a corollary, you have to be aware of the size of the paper (whether it's letter size, legal size, or an envelope). You may want to print in different orientations, such as landscape or portrait modes. The Microsoft Foundation Class Library cannot predict how your application will handle these issues, so it provides a protocol to add these capabilities.

The printing protocol

To print a multi-page document, the framework and view interact in the following manner. First, the framework displays the Print dialog box, creates a device context for the printer, and calls the `StartDoc()` member function of the `CDC` object. Then, for each page of the document, the framework calls the `StartPage()` member function of the `CDC` object, instructs the view object to print the page, and calls the `EndPage()` member function. If the printer mode must be changed before starting a particular page, the view object sends the appropriate escape code by calling the `Escape()` member function of the `CDC` object. When the entire document has been printed, the framework calls the `EndDoc()` member function.

Overriding view class functions and pagination

The `CView` class defines several member functions that are called by the framework during printing. By overriding these functions in your view class, you provide the connections between the framework's printing logic and your view class' printing logic. You learned about the `CView` class' overridable functions in Table 21-1. You can do printing-related processing in other functions as well, but these functions are the ones that drive the printing process.

As you learned earlier in this chapter, the framework stores much of the information about a print job in a `CPrintInfo` structure. Several of the values in `CPrintInfo` pertain to pagination, as you saw in Table 21-2. Page numbers start at 1, that is, the first page is numbered 1, not 0. For more information about other members of the `CPrintInfo` class not explained in detail within this chapter, see the Class Library Reference.

At the beginning of the printing process, the framework calls the view's OnPreparePrinting() member function, passing a pointer to a CPrintInfo structure. As you learned, AppWizard provides an implementation of OnPreparePrinting() that calls DoPreparePrinting(), another member function of CView. DoPreparePrinting() is the function that displays the Print dialog box and creates a printer device context.

At the time of the call to OnPreparePrinting(), the application does not yet know how many pages are in the document. It uses the default values 1 and 0xFFFF (32767) for the numbers of the first and last page of the document. If you know how many pages your document has, override OnPreparePrinting(), and call SetMaxPage for the CPrintInfo structure before you send it to DoPreparePrinting(). Setting the maximum page number enables you to specify the length of your document.

DoPreparePrinting() then displays the Print dialog box. When the user exits the Print dialog box, the CPrintInfo structure contains the values the user specified within the dialog box. If the user wishes to print only a selected range of pages, he or she can specify the starting and ending page numbers in the Print dialog box. The framework retrieves these values using the GetFromPage() and GetToPage() functions of the CPrintInfo class. If the user doesn't specify a page range, the framework calls GetMinPage() and GetMaxPage() and uses the values returned to print the entire document.

For each page of a document to be printed, the framework calls two member functions in your view class, OnPrepareDC() and OnPrint(). The framework passes each function two parameters, a pointer to a CDC object and one to a CPrintInfo structure. Each time the framework calls OnPrepareDC() and OnPrint(), it passes a different value in the m_nCurPage member of the CPrintInfo structure. In this way the framework tells the view which page should be printed.

The OnPrepareDC() member function is also used for screen display. It makes adjustments to the device context before drawing takes place. OnPrepareDC() serves a similar role in printing, with a couple of differences. First, the CDC object represents a printer device context instead of a screen device context, and second, the framework passes a CPrintInfo object as a second parameter. (This parameter is NULL when the framework calls OnPrepareDC() for screen display.) You must override the OnPrepareDC() member function to make adjustments to the device context based on which page is being printed. For example, you can move the viewport origin and the clipping region to ensure that the appropriate portion of the document gets printed.

The OnPrint() member function performs the actual printing of the page. As you have learned, the framework calls OnDraw() with a printer device context to perform printing. More precisely, the framework calls OnPrint() with a CPrintInfo structure and a device context, and OnPrint() passes the device context to OnDraw(). You must override OnPrint() to perform any rendering that should be done only during printing and not for screen display. For example, to print headers or footers (as you saw earlier and will see more of later), you must place the header-printing code within the OnPrint() function rather than the OnDraw() function. After you place the header and footer into the printer device context, your program should then call OnDraw() from the program's overridden OnDraw() to do the rendering common to both screen display and printing.

The fact that OnDraw() does the rendering for both screen display and printing means that your application is a "what you see is what you get" application, commonly referred to by its acronym (WYSIWYG). However, in some cases you will not use a WYSIWYG application. For example, you might create a text editor that uses a bold font for printing but displays control codes to indicate bold text on the screen. In such a situation, you should use OnDraw() strictly for screen display. When you override the OnPrint() function, you should then substitute the call to OnDraw() with a call to a separate drawing function. That function will draw the document the way it appears on paper, using the attributes that you don't display on the screen.

Understanding the CPrintInfo class

The CPrintInfo class stores information about a print or print preview job. The framework creates an object of CPrintInfo each time the Print or Print Preview command is chosen and destroys it when the command is completed. CPrintInfo contains information about both the print job as a whole (such as the range of pages to be printed) and the current status of the print job (such as the page currently being printed). Some information is stored in an associated CPrintDialog object; this object contains the values entered by the user in the Print dialog box.

A CPrintInfo object is passed between the framework and your view class during the printing process and is used to exchange information between the two. For example, the framework informs the view class which page of the document to print by assigning a value to the m_nCurPage member of CPrintInfo; the view class retrieves the value and performs the actual printing of the specified page.

Another example is the case in which the length of the document is not known until it is printed. In this situation, the view class tests for the end of the document each time a page is printed. When the end is reached, the view class sets the m_bContinuePrinting member of CPrintInfo to FALSE; this informs the framework to stop the print loop. CPrintInfo is used by the member functions of CView you learned about in Table 21-2.

Understanding printer pages versus document pages

When you refer to page numbers, it's sometimes necessary to distinguish between the printer's concept of a page and a document's concept of a page. From the point of view of the printer, a page is one sheet of paper. However, one sheet of paper doesn't necessarily equal one page of the document. For example, if you're printing a newsletter and its sheets are to be folded, one sheet of paper might contain both the first and last pages of the document, side by side. Similarly, if you're printing a spreadsheet, the document doesn't consist of pages at all. Instead, one sheet of paper might contain rows 1 through 20, columns 6 through 10.

All the page numbers in the `CPrintInfo` structure refer to printer pages. The framework calls `OnPrepareDC()` and `OnPrint()` once for each sheet of paper that will pass through the printer. When you override the `OnPreparePrinting()` function to specify the length of the document, you must use printer pages. If there is a one-to-one correspondence (that is, one printer page equals one document page), then printer pages are easy to use. If, on the other hand, document pages and printer pages do not directly correspond, you must translate between them. For example, consider printing a spreadsheet. When overriding `OnPreparePrinting()`, you must calculate how many sheets of paper will be required to print the entire spreadsheet and then use that value when calling the `SetMaxPage()` member function of `CPrintInfo`. Similarly, when overriding `OnPrepareDC()`, you must translate `m_nCurPage` into the range of rows and columns that will appear on that particular sheet and then adjust the document's viewport origin accordingly.

Implementing pagination

Many of the basic applications you will design as you get used to working with printing are likely to be fairly simple applications, which support drawings or text entries and with each one fitting a single page. To illustrate pagination, you are probably best served to add a simple extension of your program that prints each screen object as a two-page document, a title page, and the drawing or text content itself.

To add pagination to a program, perform the following steps:

1. Modify the `OnPreparePrinting()` member function.
2. Override the default `OnPrint()` member function.
3. Add two new helper functions, `PrintTitlePage()`, which prints the title page, and `PrintPageHeader()`, which prints a header on the actual page that contains content from the application.

You can try the code this section explains in any application you have created that supports the document/view architecture. For the code examples, the reference to the class name of `CSampleView` is simply to provide a context in which to review the code.

After you load your application, use the WizardBar to jump to the `OnPreparePrinting()` function definition of class `CSampleView`, and replace the existing comment and code with the code Listing 21-5 contains.

Listing 21-5: The Replacement Code You Should Place within the OnPreparePrinting() Function

```
BOOL CSampleView::OnPreparePrinting(CPrintInfo* pInfo)
 {
   BOOL bResult;
   CWinApp* pApp = AfxGetApp();

   // ask the app what the default printer is. if there
   //isn't any, punt to MFC so it will generate an error

   if (!pApp->GetPrinterDeviceDefaults(&pInfo->m_pPD->m_pd) ||
       pInfo->m_pPD->m_pd.hDevMode == NULL)
      return DoPreparePrinting(pInfo);

   HGLOBAL hDevMode = pInfo->m_pPD->m_pd.hDevMode;
   HGLOBAL hDevNames = pInfo->m_pPD->m_pd.hDevNames;
   DEVMODE* pDevMode = (DEVMODE*) ::GlobalLock(hDevMode);
   DEVNAMES* pDevNames = (DEVNAMES*) ::GlobalLock(hDevNames);

   LPCSTR pstrDriverName = ((LPCSTR) pDevNames)+
       pDevNames->wDriverOffset;
   LPCSTR pstrDeviceName = ((LPCSTR) pDevNames)+
       pDevNames->wDeviceOffset;
   LPCSTR pstrOutputPort = ((LPCSTR) pDevNames)+
       pDevNames->wOutputOffset;

   CDC dcPrinter;
   if (dcPrinter.CreateDC(pstrDriverName, pstrDeviceName,
       pstrOutputPort, NULL))
    {
      pInfo->SetMaxPage(2);  // the document is 2 pages long
      dcPrinter.DeleteDC();
      bResult = DoPreparePrinting(pInfo);
    }
   else
    {
      MessageBox("Could not create printer DC");
      bResult = FALSE;
    }

   ::GlobalUnlock(hDevMode);
   ::GlobalUnlock(hDevNames);

   return bResult;

 }
```

This function performs some pretty significant processing for your application. First, it makes sure that the user has specified a default printer. If the user has not done so, the code exits immediately by calling DoPreparePrinting() (and MFC will, therefore, handle the error). After checking that a printer exists to design around, the program code obtains the driver name, the device name, and the output port of the printer, and tries to create a device context for the printer. If successful, the program code specifies the length of the document by calling the SetMaxPage() function for the pInfo parameter. Because the program in this example is specifying that all documents are two pages long, the function uses a numeric constant rather than a variable to represent the number of the last page of the document. The title page and the content page are numbered 1 and 2, respectively. In a real application, the SetMaxPage() assignment in this function is likely to be a call to another function that computes the real number of pages in the print job based on the amount of information within the document. After performing all those steps, the program code calls the DoPreparePrinting() function to display the Print dialog box and creates another device context for the printer that only DoPreparePrinting() uses.

After you override OnPreparePrinting(), you must next override the OnPrint() function. To override the OnPrint() function, use the WizardBar to open the SampleView.cpp file in the text editor. Next, click the arrow on the action button, located on the right end of WizardBar. On the menu, click Add Virtual Function. Visual Studio will display the New Virtual Override dialog box. Within that dialog box, select OnPrint() from the New Virtual Functions list. Click the Add and Edit button. Visual Studio will display the OnPrint() function within the SampleView.cpp file. Replace the comments and existing code with the code Listing 21-6 contains.

Listing 21-6: The Replacement Code for the OnPrint() Function

```
void CHexViewView::OnPrint(CDC* pDC, CPrintInfo* pInfo)
 {
   if (pInfo->m_nCurPage == 1)     // page 1 is the title page
    {
      PrintTitlePage(pDC, pInfo);
    }
   else
    {
      CString strHeader = GetDocument()->GetTitle();

      PrintPageHeader(pDC, pInfo, strHeader);
      /* PrintPageHeader() subtracts out from the
         pInfo->m_rectDraw the
         amount of the page used for the header. */

      pDC->SetWindowOrg(pInfo->m_rectDraw.left,
          -pInfo->m_rectDraw.top);
```

```
        // Now print the rest of the page
        OnDraw(pDC);
      }
    return;
  }
```

The behavior of the OnPrint() member function depends on which of the two pages is being printed. If the title page is being printed, OnPrint() simply calls the PrintTitlePage() function and then returns. If it's the content page, OnPrint() calls PrintPageHeader() to print the header and then calls OnDraw() to do the actual drawing. Before calling OnDraw(), OnPrint() sets the window origin at the upper-left corner of the rectangle defined by m_rectDraw (which, as you will learn, was reduced in size by PrintPageHeader() to account for the size of the header). Reducing the size, as you have learned earlier in this chapter, keeps the drawing from overlapping the header.

Notice that the drawing itself isn't divided into multiple pages. Consequently, OnDraw() never has to display just a portion of the drawing (for example, it never has to display the section that fits on a particular page without displaying the surrounding sections). Either the title page is being printed and OnDraw() isn't called at all, or else the content page is being printed and OnDraw() displays the entire drawing at once.

This also explains why CSampleView doesn't override the OnPrepareDC() member function — there's no need to adjust the viewport origin or clipping region depending on which page is being printed, because you are still effectively only using a single view page for the printing.

Adding the helper functions

The next step is to add the new helper functions. By using the Add Function pop-up menu command in ClassView, you can declare and define them in one step. As you learned earlier, the PrintTitlePage() function prints a title page, and the PrintPageHeader() function prints a header on the content page. To add the PrintTitlePage() helper function, perform the following steps:

1. In the ClassView, point to CSampleView, and click the right mouse button.
2. From the pop-up menu, click the Add Member Function command.
3. In the Function Type box, type the return type of the function (in this case, void).
4. In the Function Declaration box, type the following:

```
PrintTitlePage(CDC* pDC, CPrintInfo* pInfo)
```

5. In the Access area, select Public, and click the OK button. ClassWizard adds the declaration to the `public` section of the header file and creates a starter definition in the implementation file.
6. Expand `CSampleView`, and double-click `PrintTitlePage()` to jump to the body of the definition so you can begin typing your application-specific code.
7. Fill in the starter `PrintTitlePage()` function with the code shown in Listing 21-7.

Listing 21-7: Fill-in Code for the PrintTitlePage() Function

```
void CSampleView::PrintTitlePage(CDC *pDC, CPrintInfo *pInfo)
{
   // Prepare a font size for displaying the file name
   LOGFONT logFont;
   memset(&logFont, 0, sizeof(LOGFONT));
   logFont.lfHeight = 75; //  3/4th inch high in MM_LOENGLISH

   CFont font;
   CFont* pOldFont = NULL;
   if (font.CreateFontIndirect(&logFont))
      pOldFont = pDC->SelectObject(&font);

   // Get the file name, to be displayed on title page
   CString strPageTitle = GetDocument()->GetTitle();

   // Display the file name 1 inch below top of the page,
   // centered horizontally
   pDC->SetTextAlign(TA_CENTER);
   pDC->TextOut(pInfo->m_rectDraw.right / 2, -100,
        strPageTitle);

   if (pOldFont != NULL)
      pDC->SelectObject(pOldFont);
}
```

The `PrintTitlePage()` function uses `m_rectDraw`, which stores the usable drawing area of the page as the rectangle in which the title should be centered.

Notice that `PrintTitlePage()` declares a local `CFont` object to use when printing the title page. If you needed the font for the entire printing process, you could declare a `CFont` member variable in your view class, create the font in the `OnBeginPrinting()` member function, and destroy it in `EndPrinting()`. However, because this particular application uses the font for just the title page, the font doesn't have to exist beyond the `PrintTitlePage()` function. When the function ends, the compiler automatically calls the destructor for the local `CFont` object.

Now that you have added the PrintTitlePage() function, you must add the PrintPageHeader() function to the view class. To add the PrintPageHeader() function to the CSampleView class, from within ClassView, point the mouse to CSampleView, and click the right mouse button. From the pop-up menu, click the Add Member Function command. In the Function Type box, type the return type of the function as void. In the Function Declaration box, enter the following function declaration:

```
PrintPageHeader(CDC* pDC, CPrintInfo* pInfo,
    CString& strHeader)
```

In the Access area, select Public, and click the OK button. ClassWizard adds the declaration to the public section of the header file and creates a starter definition in the implementation file. Expand CSampleView, and double-click PrintPageHeader() to jump to the body of the definition so you can begin typing your application-specific code. Fill in the starter PrintPageHeader() function with the code shown in Listing 21-8.

Listing 21-8: Fill-in Code for the Starter PrintPageHeader() Function

```
void CSampleView:: PrintPageHeader(CDC* pDC,
    CPrintInfo* pInfo, CString& strHeader)
 {
   // Specify left text alignment
   pDC->SetTextAlign(TA_LEFT);

   // Print a page header consisting of the name of
   // the document and a horizontal line
   pDC->TextOut(0, -25, strHeader);        // 1/4 inch down

   // Draw a line across the page, below the header
   TEXTMETRIC textMetric;
   pDC->GetTextMetrics(&textMetric);
   int y = -35 - textMetric.tmHeight;      // line 1/10th
                                           // in. below text
   pDC->MoveTo(0, y);                      // from left margin
   pDC->LineTo(pInfo->m_rectDraw.right, y);
   //  to right margin

   // Subtract from the drawing rectangle the space
   // the header uses from out of the rectangle.
   y -= 25;     // space 1/4 inch below (top of) line
   pInfo->m_rectDraw.top += y;
 }
```

The PrintPageHeader() member function prints the name of the document at the top of the page and then draws a horizontal line separating the header from the drawing. It adjusts the m_rectDraw member of the pInfo parameter to account for the height of the header. As you have learned, the adjustments are important because the OnPrint() function uses this value to adjust the window origin before it calls OnDraw().

Print-time pagination

In some situations, your view class may not know in advance how long the document is until it has actually been printed. For example, suppose your application isn't WYSIWYG, and so a document's length on the screen doesn't correspond to its length when printed.

Such a situation can easily cause a problem when you override OnPreparePrinting() for your view class. Because you don't know the length of a document, you can't pass a value to the SetMaxPage() function of the CPrintInfo structure. If the user doesn't specify a page number to stop in the Print dialog box, the framework doesn't know when to stop the print loop. The only way to determine when to stop the print loop is to print the document and see when it ends. Your view class must check for the end of the document while it is being printed and then inform the framework when the end is reached.

The framework relies on your view class' OnPrepareDC() function to tell it when to stop. After each call to OnPrepareDC(), the framework checks a member of the CPrintInfo structure called m_bContinuePrinting. Its default value is TRUE. As long as it remains so, the framework continues the print loop. If it is set to FALSE, the framework stops. To perform print-time pagination, override OnPrepareDC() to check whether the end of the document has been reached, and set m_bContinuePrinting to FALSE when it has.

The default implementation of OnPrepareDC() sets m_bContinuePrinting to FALSE if the current page is greater than 1. This means that if the length of the document wasn't specified, the framework assumes the document is one page long. One consequence of this is that you must be careful if you call the base class version of OnPrepareDC(). Do not assume that m_bContinuePrinting will be TRUE after calling the base class version.

Revisiting the printing of headers and footers

When you look at a document on the screen, the name of the document and your current location in the document are commonly displayed in a title bar and a status bar. When looking at a printed copy of a document, it's useful to have the name and page number shown in a header or footer. This is a common way in which even WYSIWYG programs differ in how they perform printing and screen display.

The `OnPrint()` member function is the appropriate place to print headers or footers because it is called for each page, and because it is called only for printing, not for screen display. You can define a separate function to print a header or footer and pass it the printer device context from `OnPrint()`. You might need to adjust the window origin or extent before calling `OnDraw()` to avoid having the body of the page overlap the header or footer. You might also have to modify `OnDraw()` because the amount of the document that fits on the page could be reduced.

One way to compensate for the area taken by the header or footer is to use the `m_rectDraw` member of `CPrintInfo`. Each time a page is printed, this member is initialized with the usable area of the page. If you print a header or footer before printing the body of the page, you can reduce the size of the rectangle stored in `m_rectDraw` to account for the area taken by the header or footer. Then `OnPrint()` can refer to `m_rectDraw` to find out how much area remains for printing the body of the page.

You cannot print a header, or anything else, from `OnPrepareDC()` because it is called before the program calls the `StartPage()` member function of `CDC`. At that point, the printer device context is considered to be at a page boundary. You can perform printing only from the `OnPrint()` member function.

Allocating GDI resources for printing

Suppose you need to use certain fonts, pens, or other GDI objects for printing, but not for screen display. Because of the memory such resources require, it's inefficient to allocate these objects when the application starts up. When the application isn't printing a document, that memory might be needed for other purposes. It's better to allocate them when printing begins and then delete them when printing ends.

To allocate these GDI objects, override the `OnBeginPrinting()` member function. This function is well suited to this purpose for two reasons: the framework calls this function once at the beginning of each print job, and unlike `OnPreparePrinting()`, this function has access to the `CDC` object representing the printer device driver. You can store these objects for use during the print job by defining member variables in your view class that point to GDI objects (for example, `CFont *` members, and so on).

To use the GDI objects you've created, select them into the printer device context in the `OnPrint()` member function. If you need different GDI objects for different pages of the document, you can examine the `m_nCurPage` member of the `CPrintInfo` structure and select the GDI object accordingly. If you need a GDI object for several consecutive pages, Windows requires that you select it into the device context each time `OnPrint()` is called.

To deallocate these GDI objects, override the `OnEndPrinting()` member function. The framework calls this function at the end of each print job, giving you the opportunity to deallocate printing-specific GDI objects before the application returns to other tasks. As with every other object you create within your programs, you should be sure to add the deallocation code to the project, generally at the same time as you add the allocation code.

Enlarging the printed image

As you learned in previous chapters, when you specify a position for a GDI drawing function, you use logical coordinates. You have learned how `CScrollView` moves the origin of the logical coordinate system. You can also control the scale of this coordinate system, that is, the physical size of a logical unit. By default, GDI considers logical units to be equal to device units, meaning that 1 logical unit equals 1 pixel on the screen. This one-to-one interpretation of logical units is called the `MM_TEXT` mapping mode.

When AppWizard creates an application for you, the application uses the `MM_TEXT` mapping mode by default. That is, the application considers a stroke that is 100 units long to be 100 pixels long. The physical size of the stroke depends on the device that displays it. For example, a device unit on a typical ink jet printer is 1/300 of an inch (while a laser printer is 1/600 of an inch), which is considerably smaller than a pixel on a typical screen. As a result, the images that AppWizard-created applications produce on a printer are much smaller than those it displays on the screen.

To keep your applications from producing tiny images on the printer, you need a mapping mode that ensures that a drawing remains the same size no matter what device displays it. Windows provides several such mapping modes, known as metric mapping modes. In these modes, GDI considers logical units to be equal to real-world units (or metrics), such as millimeters or inches.

When you refer to metrics and logical units when you manage printing from Windows, it is important that you recognize that you are not referring to the metric measuring system. Instead, metrics in this context refers to the measurements themselves.

✦ ✦ ✦ ✦ ✦

Understanding the Print Preview Architecture

Print preview is somewhat different from screen display and printing because, instead of directly drawing an image on a device, the application must simulate the printer using the screen. To accommodate this, the Microsoft Foundation Class Library defines a special (undocumented) class derived from `CDC`, called `CPreviewDC`. All `CDC` objects contain two device contexts, but usually they are identical. In a `CPreviewDC` object, the two device contexts are different, with the first context representing the printer being simulated and the second context representing the screen on which output is actually displayed.

The print preview process

When the user selects the Print Preview command from the File menu, the framework creates a `CPreviewDC` object. Whenever your application performs an operation that sets a characteristic of the printer device context, the framework also performs a similar operation on the screen device context. For example, if your application selects a font for printing, the framework selects a font for screen display that simulates the printer font. Whenever your application sends output to the printer, the framework instead sends the output to the screen.

Print preview also differs from printing in the order that each draws the pages of a document. During printing, the framework continues a print loop until a certain range of pages has been rendered. During print preview, one or two pages are displayed at any time, and then the application waits; no further pages are displayed until the user responds. During print preview, the application must also respond to `WM_PAINT` messages, just as it does during ordinary screen display.

The `OnPreparePrinting()` function is called when preview mode is invoked, just as it is at the beginning of a print job. The `CPrintInfo` structure passed to the function contains several members whose values you can set to adjust certain characteristics of the print preview operation. For example, you can set the `m_nNumPreviewPages` member to specify whether you want to preview the document in one-page or two-page mode.

Modifying print preview

You can easily modify the behavior and appearance of print preview in a number of ways. For example, you can, among other things:

- ✦ Cause the print preview window to display a scroll bar for easy access to any page of the document.
- ✦ Cause print preview to maintain the user's position in the document by beginning its display at the current page.
- ✦ Cause different initialization to be performed for print preview and printing.
- ✦ Cause print preview to display page numbers in your own formats.

If you know how long the document is and call `SetMaxPage()` with the appropriate value, the framework can use this information in preview mode as well as during printing. Once the framework knows the length of the document, it can provide the preview window with a scroll bar, enabling the user to page back and forth through the document in preview mode. If you haven't set the length of the document, the framework cannot position the scroll box to indicate the current position, so the framework doesn't add a scroll bar. In this case, the user must use the Next Page and Previous Page buttons on the preview window's control bar to page through the document.

For print preview, you may find it useful to assign a value to the m_nCurPage member of CPrintInfo, even though you would never do so for ordinary printing. During ordinary printing, this member carries information from the framework to your view class. This is how the framework tells the view which page should be printed.

By contrast, when print preview mode is started, the m_nCurPage member carries information in the opposite direction: from the view to the framework. The framework uses the value of this member to determine which page should be previewed first. The default value of this member is 1, so the first page of the document is displayed initially. You can override OnPreparePrinting() to set this member to the number of the page being viewed at the time the Print Preview command was invoked. This way, the application maintains the user's current position when moving from normal display mode to print preview mode.

Sometimes you may want OnPreparePrinting() to perform different initialization depending on whether it is called for a print job or for print preview. You can determine this by examining the m_bPreview member variable in the CPrintInfo structure. This member is set to TRUE when print preview is invoked.

The CPrintInfo structure also contains a member named m_strPageDesc, which is used to format the strings displayed at the bottom of the screen in single-page and multiple-page modes. By default these strings are of the form "Page n" and "Pages n - m," but you can modify m_strPageDesc from within OnPreparePrinting() and set the strings to something more elaborate. See CPrintInfo in the Class Library Reference for more information.

Enhancing an application's print preview

The default print preview capabilities are almost sufficient for most application's needs. To some extent, most of your application's print preview capabilities are enhanced when you enhance printing capabilities. Recall that in the override of OnPreparePrinting() earlier in this chapter, you called the SetMaxPages() function to specify the length of the application document. Specifying the application's pages, for example, enables the framework to automatically add a scroll bar to the preview window.

Another enhancement you can make is to change the number of pages displayed when the user invokes the preview mode. To set the number of pages displayed in preview mode, perform the following steps:

1. Use the WizardBar to jump to the OnPreparePrinting() member function in SampleView.cpp.
2. Edit the function so that it appears as shown in Listing 21-9.

Listing 21-9: Changes You Should Make to the OnPreparePrinting() Member Function

```
BOOL CSampleView::OnPreparePrinting(CPrintInfo* pInfo)
 {
   BOOL bResult;
   CWinApp* pApp = AfxGetApp();

   // ask the app what the default printer is. if there
   //isn't any, punt to MFC so it will generate an error

   if (!pApp->GetPrinterDeviceDefaults(&pInfo->m_pPD->m_pd) ||
       pInfo->m_pPD->m_pd.hDevMode == NULL)
      return DoPreparePrinting(pInfo);

   HGLOBAL hDevMode = pInfo->m_pPD->m_pd.hDevMode;
   HGLOBAL hDevNames = pInfo->m_pPD->m_pd.hDevNames;
   DEVMODE* pDevMode = (DEVMODE*) ::GlobalLock(hDevMode);
   DEVNAMES* pDevNames = (DEVNAMES*) ::GlobalLock(hDevNames);

   LPCSTR pstrDriverName = ((LPCSTR) pDevNames)+
       pDevNames->wDriverOffset;
   LPCSTR pstrDeviceName = ((LPCSTR) pDevNames)+
       pDevNames->wDeviceOffset;
   LPCSTR pstrOutputPort = ((LPCSTR) pDevNames)+
       pDevNames->wOutputOffset;

   CDC dcPrinter;
   if (dcPrinter.CreateDC(pstrDriverName, pstrDeviceName,
       pstrOutputPort, NULL))
    {
      pInfo->SetMaxPage(2);  // the document is two
                             // pages long:
      dcPrinter.DeleteDC();
      bResult = DoPreparePrinting(pInfo);

//  New Lines
      /* Preview 2 pages at a time
         Set this value after calling DoPreparePrinting to
         Override value read from registry */
      pInfo->m_nNumPreviewPages = 2;
//  End New Lines

    }
   else
    {
      MessageBox("Could not create printer DC");
      bResult = FALSE;
    }
```

(continued)

Listing 21-9 *(continued)*

```
    ::GlobalUnlock(hDevMode);
    ::GlobalUnlock(hDevNames);
    return bResult;

}
```

The new lines assign the value 2 to `m_nNumPreviewPages`. This causes the application to preview both pages of the document at once—the title page (page 1) and the drawing page (page 2). Note the value for `m_nNumPreviewPages` must be assigned after calling `DoPreparePrinting()`, because `DoPreparePrinting()` sets `m_nNumPreviewPages` to the number of preview pages used the last time the program was executed; this value is stored in the application's Registry entry.

Understanding the CPrintDialog class

The `CPrintDialog` class encapsulates the services provided by the Windows common dialog box for printing. Common print dialog boxes provide an easy way to implement Print and Print Setup dialog boxes in a manner consistent with Windows standards.

If you wish, you can rely on the framework to handle many aspects of the printing process for your application. In this case, the framework automatically displays the Windows common dialog box for printing. You can also have the framework handle printing for your application but override the common Print dialog box with your own print dialog box.

If you want your application to handle printing without the framework's involvement, you can use the `CPrintDialog` class "as is" with the constructor provided, or you can derive your own dialog class from `CPrintDialog` and write a constructor to suit your needs. In either case, these dialog boxes behave like standard MFC dialog boxes because they are derived from class `CCommonDialog`.

To use a `CPrintDialog` object, first create the object using the `CPrintDialog` constructor. Once the dialog box has been constructed, you can set or modify any values in the `m_pd` structure to initialize the values of the dialog box's controls. The `m_pd` structure is of type `PRINTDLG`. For more information on this structure, see the Win32 SDK documentation.

If you do not supply your own handles in `m_pd` for the `hDevMode` and `hDevNames` members, be sure to call the Windows function `GlobalFree()` for these handles when you are done with the dialog box. When using the framework's Print Setup implementation provided by CWinApp::OnFilePrintSetup(), you do not have to free these handles. The handles are maintained by CWinApp and are freed in CWinApp's destructor. It is only necessary to free these handles when using CPrintDialog alone.

After initializing the dialog box controls, call the DoModal() member function to display the dialog box and enable the user to select print options. DoModal() returns whether the user selected the OK (IDOK) or Cancel (IDCANCEL) button.

If DoModal() returns IDOK, you can use one of CPrintDialog's member functions to retrieve the information input by the user. The CPrintDialog::GetDefaults() member function is useful for retrieving the current printer defaults without displaying a dialog box. This member function requires no user interaction.

You can use the Windows CommDlgExtendedError() function to determine whether an error occurred during initialization of the dialog box and to learn more about the error. For more information on this function, see the Win32 SDK documentation.

CPrintDialog relies on the commdlg.dll file that ships with Windows versions 3.1 and later. To customize the dialog box, derive a class from CPrintDialog, provide a custom dialog template, and add a message map to process the notification messages from the extended controls. Any unprocessed messages should be passed on to the base class. Customizing the hook function is not required.

To process the same message differently depending on whether the dialog box is Print or Print Setup, you must derive a class for each dialog box. You must also override the Windows AttachOnSetup() function, which handles the creation of a new dialog box when the Print Setup button is selected within a Print dialog box. For more information on using CPrintDialog, see Common Dialog Classes in Visual C++ Programmer's Guide.

The HexViewMDI Program

The HexViewMDI demonstration program uses the Windows API to print pages of text files the program displays in hex mode. Highlights of the source code for HexViewMDI are given in Listing 21-10.

A demonstration program that shows how to use MFC's printing capabilities can be found on the CD-ROM in the Chap30\HexViewMDI directory. You can rebuild the program by loading the HexViewMDI.dsw project file, or just run the HexViewMDI.exe program using Explorer.

✦ ✦ ✦ ✦ ✦

Because the PortLand program uses an MDI interface, you can load as many files as you want into the program and print each file individually, so you can see how the program computes the size of the pages and how many pages to print when the user requests a print job.

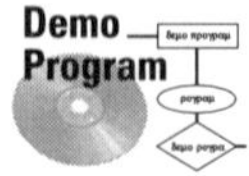

HexViewMDI

Project Name: **HexViewMDI**
CD-ROM Location: **Chap21\HexViewMDI**
Pre-Built Program: **Chap21\HexViewMDI \HexViewMDI.exe**
Source Code Highlights in Text: `HexViewMDI.cpp`

Listing 21-10: Highlights of the HexViewMDI.cpp Source Code for the HexViewMDI.exe Program

```
/////////////////////////////////////////////////////////////////////////////
// CHexViewView printing

BOOL CHexViewView::OnPreparePrinting(CPrintInfo* pInfo)
 {
   BOOL bResult;
   CWinApp* pApp = AfxGetApp();

   // ask our app what the default printer is
   // if there isn't any,  let MFC generate an error
   if (!pApp->GetPrinterDeviceDefaults(&pInfo->m_pPD->m_pd) ||
       pInfo->m_pPD->m_pd.hDevMode == NULL)
     return DoPreparePrinting(pInfo);

   HGLOBAL   hDevMode = pInfo->m_pPD->m_pd.hDevMode;
   HGLOBAL hDevNames = pInfo->m_pPD->m_pd.hDevNames;
   DEVMODE* pDevMode = (DEVMODE*) ::GlobalLock(hDevMode);
   DEVNAMES* pDevNames = (DEVNAMES*) ::GlobalLock(hDevNames);
   LPCSTR pstrDriverName = ((LPCSTR) pDevNames)+
       pDevNames->wDriverOffset;
   LPCSTR pstrDeviceName = ((LPCSTR) pDevNames)+
       pDevNames->wDeviceOffset;
   LPCSTR pstrOutputPort = ((LPCSTR) pDevNames)+
       pDevNames->wOutputOffset;

   CDC dcPrinter;
   if (dcPrinter.CreateDC(pstrDriverName, pstrDeviceName,
       pstrOutputPort, NULL))
    {
     CalcPageCount(&dcPrinter, pInfo);
     dcPrinter.DeleteDC();
     bResult = DoPreparePrinting(pInfo);
    }
```

```
   else
    {
      MessageBox("Could not create printer DC");
      bResult = FALSE;
    }
   ::GlobalUnlock(hDevMode);
   ::GlobalUnlock(hDevNames);
   return bResult;
 }

void CHexViewView::OnBeginPrinting(CDC* pDC,
  CPrintInfo* pInfo)
 {
   /* create the printer font using the user-requested font
      size  (having different printer fonts and screen fonts
      is the easiest way to make sure they both look right.)
      Since the scaling in the printer is different than the
      screen, do the  math for lfHeight again. */

   LOGFONT   lfPrintFont;
   memcpy(&lfPrintFont, &m_logfont, sizeof(lfPrintFont));

   if (m_pPrintFont != NULL)
      delete m_pPrintFont;
   m_pPrintFont = new CFont;
   lfPrintFont.lfHeight = MulDiv(m_nPointSize,
      pDC->GetDeviceCaps(LOGPIXELSX), 720);
   m_pPrintFont->CreateFontIndirect(&lfPrintFont);

   // get these again, since the user may have changed the
   // printer since you set them up
   CalcPageCount(pDC, pInfo);
 }

void CHexViewView::OnEndPrinting(CDC* pDC, CPrintInfo* pInfo)
 {
   delete m_pPrintFont;
   m_pPrintFont = NULL;
 }

void CHexViewView::OnViewFont()
 {
   // let the user change their mind about the font
   LOGFONT   lfCopy;
   memcpy(&lfCopy, &m_logfont, sizeof(lfCopy));

   // pop up the existing font in the dialog
   CFontDialog dlg(&lfCopy);
   dlg.m_cf.Flags |= CF_FORCEFONTEXIST | CF_FIXEDPITCHONLY;

   // if they say so, create the font and put it in a
```

(continued)

Listing 21-10 (continued)

```
   // member variable for use later
   if (dlg.DoModal() == IDOK)
    {
      CFont*   pFontCopy = new CFont;
      if (pFontCopy->CreateFontIndirect(&lfCopy))
       {
         m_nPointSize = dlg.GetSize();
         if (m_pFont != NULL)
            delete m_pFont;
         m_pFont = pFontCopy;
         memcpy(&m_logfont, &lfCopy, sizeof(lfCopy));
           Invalidate();
       }
      else
       {
         delete pFontCopy;
         MessageBox(_T("Could not create new font!"));
       }
    }
 }

void CHexViewView::OnPrepareDC(CDC* pDC, CPrintInfo* pInfo)
 {
   CScrollView::OnPrepareDC(pDC, pInfo);

   // remember if we're printing or not
   if (pInfo == NULL)
      m_bPrinting = FALSE;
   else
    {
      // if we're printing, figure out what line of the file
      // to start printing first
      int nHeight = MeasureFontHeight(m_pPrintFont, pDC);

      m_nPrintLine = ::MulDiv(pInfo->m_nCurPage-1,
          m_nPageHeight, nHeight);
      m_bPrinting = TRUE;
    }
 }

void CHexViewView::CalcPageCount(CDC* pDC, CPrintInfo* pInfo)
 {
   // get a pointer to the document
   CHexViewDoc* pDoc = GetDocument();
   ASSERT_VALID(pDoc);

   // figure out the page width and height
   // remember that the physical page size isn't completely
   // printable—subtract the nonprintable area from it.
   m_nPageWidth = pDC->GetDeviceCaps(PHYSICALWIDTH)
       - 2*(pDC->GetDeviceCaps(PHYSICALOFFSETX));
```

```
    m_nPageHeight = pDC->GetDeviceCaps(PHYSICALHEIGHT)
        - 2*(pDC->GetDeviceCaps(PHYSICALOFFSETY));

    // find out how high our font is
    // figure out how many lines of that font fit on a page
    int nHeight = MeasureFontHeight(m_pPrintFont, pDC);
    int nPages;
    nPages = (pDoc->m_lFileSize/16*nHeight +
        (m_nPageHeight-1)) / m_nPageHeight;

    // set up printing info structure
    pInfo->SetMinPage(1);
    pInfo->SetMaxPage(nPages);
    return;
  }

int CHexViewView::MeasureFontHeight(CFont* pFont, CDC* pDC)
  {
    // how tall is the identified font in the identified DC?
    CFont* pOldFont;
    pOldFont = pDC->SelectObject(pFont);

    CRect rectDummy;
     CString strRender = _T("1234567890ABCDEF- ");
    int nHeight = pDC->DrawText(strRender, -1, rectDummy,
       DT_TOP | DT_SINGLELINE | DT_CALCRECT);
    pDC->SelectObject(pOldFont);
    return nHeight;
  }
```

Summary

Most applications that you create, whether you use MFC or the Windows API, require some means that you can exploit to generate printed output. The Win32 API enables you to manage printers using drawing and device contexts, just as you handle screen output — though working with a physical page is different in some ways from working with a virtual (screen) page.

As you learned in this chapter, you can create printer support within your applications in two ways — through the API support functions or through the MFC wrapper classes. If you use the API to write printer support, you will typically use the Windows API functions such as `StartDoc()`, `EndDoc()`, `StartPage()`, `EndPage()`, and so on, together with functions such as `DeviceCapabilities()` and `GetDeviceCaps()` to manage your printing output.

If you use MFC to manage your printing, the task is somewhat easier. The MFC framework handles much of the underlying processing on your behalf; you can focus more on generating the output and less on placing it onto the printer page. Overriding the `OnPrint()`, `OnPreparePrinting()`, `OnDraw()`, and other functions within your view class enables you to easily add significant printing functionality to your classes. MFC also enables you to easily add headers and footers to your documents when printing.

You can also manipulate print preview from the same member functions, with slightly different implementations against member variables.

✦ ✦ ✦

CHAPTER 22

The MFC for Advanced Windows User Interfaces

This chapter expands your knowledge of the Windows and the Microsoft Foundation Classes. The Microsoft Foundation Classes and their default methods have considerable power, and it may be that you will never need to exceed that power. Still, having some knowledge of the more advanced features and of the lower-level structures on which they are built will certainly increase your knowledge and ability. Layer after layer of capability is built into these classes. Far down under the classes themselves, of course, is the original GDI API along with its defined data types and structures. You are not going to develop your own special interface objects here, but instead you will use some of these lower-level features.

✦ ✦ ✦ ✦

In This Chapter

Gaining more control over an application

Understanding the modal loop

RunModalLoop() internals

Modal windows: more than just for dialog boxes

Getting inside the modal loop

Creating and closing modal windows

Pushing the modal window further

Drawing outside the client area box

Building transparent bitmaps in device contexts

✦ ✦ ✦ ✦

Sometimes You Need More Control

In some situations it is very important to be able to organize carefully how the user may interact with your application. In fact, in some instances it is also important to limit the capability of the user to interact with the rest of the Windows system itself. There is no point in doing this just to be arbitrary. For example, modal dialog boxes, discussed in Chapter 13, give the programmer some additional control over what the user can do with the application. The modal dialog box is a way of focusing the user's activity. That is, the user must dismiss the dialog box before he or she can continue to interact with the rest of the application.

Everyone has occasionally been frustrated by a dialog box that made itself system modal when it was simply not necessary. Remember that system modal dialog boxes prevent the user from interacting with any part of the system until the dialog has been completed. So there you are, stuck with this dialog, which you would like to leave open while you go off to do something else, say copy a file. You cannot do anything else until you have closed the dialog box. So you are forced to close it, losing all the settings that you have entered, just so you can move a file from one place to another. To force a strict pattern of interaction on your users unthinkingly is not kind or a good practice. However, in some situations it is important to prevent the user from performing certain actions, or to focus the user's attention in a certain area to ensure that a task is completed.

For example, let's suppose that in a self-paced classroom environment, a tutorial were being presented about a Windows application. Suppose that the lesson were developed as a series of tutorial steps in which the user was introduced to the various parts and options of a new application. If you have done any teaching at all, you know that students don't necessarily follow along step by step with the presentation. At one end of the spectrum are students who are afraid to touch anything. Presented with so many buttons and choices, they are immediately lost because they cannot find their way among so many items on the screen. In addition to the application, before them are the Windows status bar, icons, system, tray, and so forth. Other students are very curious and independent, so they head off in their own direction to see what they can find. They begin clicking menu after menu or changing settings that they don't really understand and that they will not remember later. So the poor instructor is left trying to help them find their way back to ground zero. In situations like this, it would be good to be able to thoroughly control what a user could do.

To demonstrate some of the capability available, you are going to develop two sample programs. The sample programs will show you how to handle some of the issues previously discussed. The first sample will demonstrate how to make a modal window. That is, rather than simply generating a modal dialog box with an application wizard, you will learn how to create a window, not a dialog box, that is modal. You will also make some more advanced changes to this window that will prepare you for the second demonstration program.

This second program will build on the first by enabling you to draw on the desktop outside the client area of the application. Although this capability will be used in association with the modal window, it is not necessary that the window be modal in order to accomplish this drawing.

Understanding the Modal Loop

The modality of a window is enabled by a method inherited from CWnd. Windows, whether they are frame windows, dialog boxes, or anything else derived from the CWnd class, have the built-in capability to become modal. In other words, you do not need to derive your modal window class from some special, arcane class; rather, this capability comes along with the many other capabilities of CWnd.

CWnd has a member function named RunModalLoop(), which is very simple to call. It takes only one parameter, a flag, so it might also seem very simple to use. However, as is often the case when you start trying special things, using it requires some special handling both for the creation and destruction of the window that becomes modal. These issues will be pointed out as you develop the applications in this chapter. This member function belongs to CWnd, and its definition is:

```
int RunModalLoop( DWORD dwFlags );
```

It takes as input a single parameter that indicates which messages are to be sent to the window, which will be covered later. But first let's take a closer look at what this RunModalLoop() actually does.

RunModalLoop() Internals

The Windows documentation says little about this modal loop. Beyond a terse sentence about how RunModalLoop() is called to retrieve, translate, and dispatch messages, it says nothing about how this member function works or any of the special handling that must be given it. Fortunately, in cases like this you have access to the code in which the Microsoft Foundation Classes are defined because it is distributed as part of the development toolkit. Whenever you encounter something that you do not understand, do not be afraid to look under the hood. Sure, there will be much that you do not understand, but there will also be much that you do. Read the header files. Read the .CPP files in which the classes are defined. Doing so will expand your knowledge and ability as a programmer. This is what you will do in this chapter with RunModalLoop(). Although the following discussion directly concerns a window, it will help with your understanding of a modal dialog box as well. Remember that CDialog is derived from CWnd, so it uses this same process. Listing 22-1 is the actual code that implements RunModalLoop() taken from the Wincore.cpp file, which is distributed by Microsoft with Visual C++.

Listing 22-1: Code Clip from Microsoft's WINCORE.CPP

```
int CWnd::RunModalLoop(DWORD dwFlags)
{
// window must be created
    ASSERT(::IsWindow(m_hWnd));
// window must not already be in a modal state
    ASSERT(!(m_nFlags & WF_MODALLOOP));

    // for tracking the idle time state
    BOOL bIdle = TRUE;
    LONG lIdleCount = 0;
    BOOL bShowIdle = (dwFlags & MLF_SHOWONIDLE) &&
         !(GetStyle() & WS_VISIBLE);
    HWND hWndParent = ::GetParent(m_hWnd);
    m_nFlags |= (WF_MODALLOOP|WF_CONTINUEMODAL);
    MSG* pMsg = &AfxGetThread()->m_msgCur;

    // acquire and dispatch messages until the
    // modal state is done
    for (;;)
    {
        ASSERT(ContinueModal());

        // phase1: check to see if we can do
               //idle work
        while (bIdle &&
            !::PeekMessage(pMsg, NULL,
                             NULL, NULL, PM_NOREMOVE))
        {
            ASSERT(ContinueModal());

            // show the dialog when the
                        //message queue goes idle
            if (bShowIdle)
            {
                ShowWindow(SW_SHOWNORMAL);
                UpdateWindow();
                bShowIdle = FALSE;
            }

            // call OnIdle while in bIdle
                        //state
            if (!(dwFlags & MLF_NOIDLEMSG) &&
                              hWndParent != NULL
                              && lIdleCount == 0)
            {
// send WM_ENTERIDLE to the parent
                ::SendMessage(hWndParent,
                                    WM_ENTERIDLE,
                                    MSGF_DIALOGBOX,
                                    (LPARAM)m_hWnd);
            }
```

```
            if ((dwFlags & MLF_NOKICKIDLE) ||
                !SendMessage(WM_KICKIDLE,
                             MSGF_DIALOGBOX,
                             lIdleCount++))
            {
// stop idle processing next time
                bIdle = FALSE;
            }
        }

        // phase2: pump messages while available
        do
        {
            ASSERT(ContinueModal());

// pump message, but quit on WM_QUIT
            if (!AfxGetThread()->PumpMessage())
            {
                AfxPostQuitMessage(0);
                return -1;
            }

            // show the window when certain special
            // messages rec'd
            if (bShowIdle && (pMsg->message == 0x118  ||
                            pMsg->message ==
                            WM_SYSKEYDOWN))
            {
                ShowWindow(SW_SHOWNORMAL);
                UpdateWindow();
                bShowIdle = FALSE;
            }

            if (!ContinueModal())
                goto ExitModal;

// reset "no idle" state after pumping "normal" message
            if (AfxGetThread()->IsIdleMessage(pMsg))
            {
                bIdle = TRUE;
                lIdleCount = 0;
            }

        } while (::PeekMessage(pMsg, NULL,
                            NULL, NULL, PM_NOREMOVE));    }

ExitModal:
    m_nFlags &= ~(WF_MODALLOOP|WF_CONTINUEMODAL);
    return m_nModalResult;
}
```

Reading this code, you can see immediately that RunModalLoop() consists essentially of two loops, both of which are inside an infinite loop. The infinite loop is ended when the window receives a quit message or when the WF_CONTINUEMODAL flag is no longer set. You will see this subsequently.

The first of the inner loops makes sure that the idle messages are handled and returned to the parent. It also ensures that the window is displayed when its message queue goes idle if the MLF_SHOWONIDLE parameter was passed in the call.

The second loop is where the real work gets done. Notice first that the code checks to see whether or not ContinueModal() returns TRUE. ContinueModal() simply indicates whether or not the modal state should be ended by checking the state of a flag. This flag, WF_CONTINUEMODAL, is actually set at the bottom of this code clip. In the second loop, there are two important places to look. The first is the line that contains the call to:

```
!AfxGetThread()->PumpMessage()
```

Remember that a thread is simply a thread of execution within an application. So this line first gets the thread of the current window, or modal window, in which it is being called. Then it calls the PumpMessage() member function, which in turn does little more than call GetMessage().

The GetMessage() function simply retrieves a message from the calling thread's message queue. GetMessage() only retrieves messages that are associated with this window. PumpMessage() then calls TranslateMessage() and DispatchMessage() with each of the messages it receives so the activity of the messages is accomplished. DispatchMessage() sends the message on to the windows procedure, so the work gets done. This is how the window becomes modal, not because it inherits something from some special modal thread. RunModalLoop() does some other processing for idle messages. But basically it continues in this tight loop, pumping messages from the queue for this window.

Modal Loop Parameters

The dwFlags parameter is the single parameter for this function. It governs how certain messages are handled. It can be one of the following values:

- MLF_NOIDLEMSG
- MLF_NOKICKIDLE
- MLF_SHOWONIDLE

The explanation in the documentation is again rather cryptic. A look at the preceding code reveals how these parameters are used. MLF_SHOWONIDLE is the easiest to understand. It just checks to see whether the queue is idle. If it is, it shows the window and updates it.

MLF_NOKICKIDLE governs whether or not WM_KICKIDLE messages are sent to the window. By following the preceding code, you can see that the while loop for ShowWindow() and UpdateWindow() is no longer executed. So the line that sends the WM_KICKIDLE messages,

```
SendMessage(WM_KICKIDLE, MSGF_DIALOGBOX, lIdleCount++))
```

is no longer called.

MLF_NOIDLEMSG ensures that WM_ENTERIDLE messages are not sent to the parent window. The WM_ENTERIDLE message is sent to the parent when the window sending the message is entering an idle state. A modal window goes into an idle state when it does not have any messages in its queue and after it has just processed a previous message. So basically MLF_NOIDLEMSG makes sure that the parent is never aware that the child has gone idle.

The value that is returned from the call to RunModalLoop() is really just a value that comes back from the call to EndModalLoop(). EndModalLoop(), as you would guess, is the function that you call to break out of the modal processing loop.

Ending the Modal Loop

EndModalLoop() terminates the modal loop. EndModalLoop() is a very simple function to call. It simply takes one parameter that is the value you want returned back to from RunModalLoop(). That is, the value you pass into EndModalLoop() reappears as the value returned from RunModalLoop(). The internal process for EndModalLoop() is even simpler than that for RunModalLoop(). Inspect the following code clip from Wincore.CPP:

```
void CWnd::EndModalLoop(int nResult)
{
    ASSERT(::IsWindow(m_hWnd));

    // this result will be returned from
      //CWnd::RunModalLoop
    m_nModalResult = nResult;

    // make sure a message goes through to exit the
      //modal loop
    if (m_nFlags & WF_CONTINUEMODAL)
    {
        m_nFlags &= ~WF_CONTINUEMODAL;
        PostMessage(WM_NULL);
    }
}
```

It simply ensures that it was passed a valid window handle, turns off the `WF_CONTINUEMODAL` flag, if it is on, then posts a null message. It is the `WF_CONTINUEMODAL` flag that causes that modal loop code to exit. The value you passed in is sent back to `RunModalLoop()` by way of the `m_nModalResult` data member. Now that the basics have been covered, let's put them together with a concrete example.

Generating the Modal Application

To demonstrate the use of the modal window that will be created, you first create a simple application to which the modal window will act as a child. You won't be making many changes to this default application but will use it to set the modal window in the context of the tutorial example described previously. The most basic of document/view applications is fine for your purposes here.

Generating the Modal Code Framework

Use MFC AppWizard to generate a new workspace for a single document application. Call this application ModalWin. As you move through the AppWizard dialog boxes, follow these steps:

1. Enter the name **ModalWin** as the project name.
2. Be sure that the Win32 option is checked.
3. Click the single document radio button, and be sure that the document/view option is checked.
4. You will not need any database or compound document support, so skip over these. Be sure that the Automation and ActiveX buttons are not selected. Not that it matters so much, you just don't need the overhead for this sample.
5. For the remainder of the AppWizard dialogs, just accept the default selections for printing, status bar, 3D controls, class names, and so forth.

✦ ✦ ✦ ✦ ✦

Creating and Closing the Modal Window

Once you have generated a basic application, you can add a modal window to it. Do this by adding a class to your application using the ClassWizard. After clicking the AddClass button in the wizard dialog, enter the name of your new class. In this demonstration, you will be basing your modal window on a frame window, so enter the name **ModalFrameWnd**. For the base class, be sure to select `CFrameWnd` in the drop-down list. No automation is necessary, so you needn't select that.

Once the class has been generated, you have to add some functions to it in order to process specific messages. You might as well do that now, though you'll have to come back and make some changes to the default code that gets generated.

Adding handlers

The functions that you need to handle are pretty basic. So be sure that the class you just generated is selected in the ClassWizard, and then add handlers for these messages:

- WM_CREATE
- WM_CLOSE
- WM_LBUTTONDBLCLK

The need for handlers for the WM_CREATE and WM_CLOSE messages is obvious. The handler for ON_WM_LBUTTONDBLCLK() is useful later because it enables you to clearly demonstrate the modality of the window. You will need to make some changes to these handlers, but you can come back to that later.

Next you must create some means to cause your modal window to be created and displayed. The easiest way to do this is to simply add another menu choice to the View menu for the ModalWin application that we generated earlier:

1. In the Resource view, double-click the application menu resource for ModalWin. It should have the name IDR_MAINFRAME.
2. Click the blank menu entry under the View menu for the application.
3. Open its properties, and add a new menu ID and caption. Use ID_VIEW_GO_MODAL. Fill out the caption and prompt boxes with something appropriate.

After the new ID has been added, go back to the ClassWizard, and add a handler for this new ID. Here add the handler to the CModalWinView class:

1. Be sure that CModalWinView is selected as the class name in the ClassWizard
2. In the ObjectIDs pane, choose ID_VIEW_GO_MODAL.
3. For messages, choose Command.
4. Click Add Function.

The ClassWizard will then add a function to the CModalWinView class with the name OnViewGoModal(). This handler will be called each time the menu is selected. This menu choice is what you will use to create and display your modal window. You will add your methods to this function to create the window and to delete it when you are finished. It is also the place where you will make your call to run the modal loop.

Choosing CModalWinView ensures that the handler is associated with the view code in this application The one place that you could not put the handler for this message would be with the code for the class ModalFrameWnd, because you are using this method to instantiate the ModalFrameWnd object itself. The default code for the handler should appear like this:

```
void CModalWinView::OnViewGoModal()
{
    // TODO: Add your command handler code here

}
```

To this, you will first add a variable that will become your modal window. The code lines that you will use look like the following. Edit the code for OnViewGoModal(), and insert the following lines:

```
// Add a pointer to use for the modal window
ModalFrameWnd * pSampleModalWindow;

// Create the frame window object
pSampleModalWindow = new ModalFrameWnd();
```

But before you can use this variable, pSampleModalWindow, as you do here, you must edit the default code that was generated by the ClassWizard. It makes the constructor a protected member function. Because you are using the code here, you must make the constructor a public member function. If you do not make it a public member function, the compiler will generate an error. Remember that you will also need to include the header file for the frame window class that you generated with the ClassWizard.

At this point, the application and menu choice still do not do much. You have instantiated the object that will be the frame window, but you have not actually created the window yet. This is accomplished with the Create() member function. That line and the remaining lines for this handler look like this:

```
//Create the window
pSampleModalWindow->Create( NULL,
    _T("Modal Frame Window"),
    WS_OVERLAPPEDWINDOW,
    CFrameWnd::rectDefault,
    AfxGetApp()->m_pMainWnd );

// Turn the parent window off
::EnableWindow( AfxGetApp()->m_pMainWnd->m_hWnd, FALSE );

// Start the modal loop
pSampleModalWindow->RunModalLoop( MLF_SHOWONIDLE );

// destroy the frame
pSampleModalWindow->DestroyWindow();
```

Though you are much closer to having a working modal window, you are not there yet. If you ran the code now, there would be several problems. In fact, attempting to close the application would immediately cause an exception error. The modal loop has not been ended with the corresponding call to EndModalLoop(). In addition there is a more subtle problem with how and where the frame window object is destroyed.

First, you must choose a place to end the modal loop. This is done in the demonstration program in the handler OnClose(), which was generated earlier with the ClassWizard. In addition, because the modal window is closed by handling a double-click with the left mouse button, you need to add some code to this handler as well. This response to a double-click is not extremely useful here, but it will be in the final demonstration program where a small tutorial application is demonstrated. So find the handler for this message in the code or the class, and add to it a call to the member function OnClose().The code for this handler should look like this:

```
void ModalFrameWnd::OnLButtonDblClk(UINT nFlags, CPoint point)
{

    CFrameWnd::OnLButtonDblClk(nFlags, point);
    OnClose();
}
```

This way, when the left mouse button is double-clicked, the modal window is instructed to close. Now you need to go to this OnClose() member function and modify it somewhat. First, you must make sure to delete the default code that calls the OnClose() default member function. So delete the line

```
CFrameWnd::OnClose();
```

Next you must add the line that ends the modal loop. Because the window is not being destroyed here, you also should make a call to hide the window. Finally, you should be sure to re-enable the application window, or it will just sit there in the background. Users can click it, but it will never come to the foreground. After all these changes are made, the OnClose() member function for the modal frame window should appear something like this.

```
void ModalFrameWnd::OnClose()
{

    // Since it will not be destroyed here
    // hide the modal frame window
    ShowWindow( SW_HIDE );

    // End the modal loop, started in OnViewGoModal()
    // Return true or any other value you desire
  EndModalLoop( TRUE );

  // Do not forget to re-enable the main application window
  ::EnableWindow( AfxGetApp()->m_pMainWnd->m_hWnd, TRUE );
}
```

Notice that the code does not include a call to destroy the window. If the window is destroyed, by either an explicit call or the default processing of the frame window from which yours is derived, then it will generate an error. This happens because the member function `OnClose()` destroys the window before the return from the call to `RunModalLoop()`. Because `RunModalLoop()` is still trying to perform some processing using the message queue and other things that belong to the window, you are certain to get an exception. This is the reason that we must be careful to destroy the window after `RunModalLoop()` has returned. If you will look again at the preceding code, you can see the call to `DestroyWindow()` where you did this before.

Simple modal application

At this point you should have a working modal application like the one shown in Figure 22-1. Run the demonstration program a few times to get a feel for it. Create the modal frame window and close it a few times. With the modal frame window open, you can also try clicking the application's main window. You can see from this that the frame window is actually modal because the application's main window does not come to the foreground. However, the frame window is not system modal because you can click in other places on the desktop to start other applications and so forth. The next demonstration program will push your control over the window and the desktop even further.

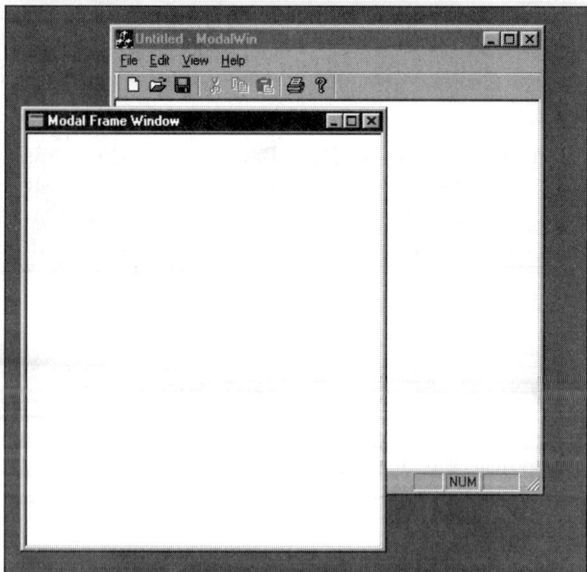

Figure 22-1: The modal window is a working application that appears on the desktop.

Once you have this sample up and running, try a couple of things to see what actually happens. Go back to the `OnClose()` method of our modal frame window, and delete the line that re-enables the parent window. Note that you cannot bring it to the foreground. Also try adding back the call to `CframeWnd::OnClose()`, as it was generated in the default code. Build a debug version and run it. Take a look at where the exception lands you.

Pushing the Modal Window Further

The previous demonstration program illustrated that, in addition to dialog boxes, regular frame windows can also be modal. Following the motivation with which this chapter began, wanting complete control over the desktop, this next demonstration program will build on the previous sample using the modal window. This second demonstration program is another step to prepare for the final demonstration in which you will draw outside the client area of your main window.

The reason for doing this is that sometimes you wish to refer directly to something on the desktop, without necessarily pasting a screen shot inside your own application. It would be useful to be able to indicate something directly on the desktop outside the client area of your application. The techniques shown here, while not as mainstream as a sample about edit controls or something similar, is more useful for getting you closer to the internals of the Windows system. You can apply this knowledge to your own projects.

What you will do here is learn how to throw a client area across the entire desktop. This means that any mouse input from the desktop will be directed through your modal window. Although certain system keys are still available to the user in this small demonstration program, considerably more control over the system has now effectively been gained by your application. Because this client area covers the desktop, it means you can draw anywhere on that desktop. The trick is to make that client area transparent, so that your drawing or animation or whatever appears to be taking place directly on the desktop. Although it hasn't been done here, you could also add code to gain more control over keyboard input.

First, change the class from which your modal window inherits. You used `CFrameWnd` in the last demonstration. Here you will change it to just `CWnd`. `CFrameWnd`, while often useful, in this situation brings a lot of capability along with it and the ensuing limitations that you do not need. You will reuse the code from the previous demonstration in this demonstration program. The chief difference will be that our modal window will not be a frame window. The name of this demonstration program is ModalArea. You can modify the names inside the Visual C++ environment, or you can simply start with a new project, making the changes to it as you did before. Just make sure that your modal window inherits from `CWnd` as it does in Listing 22-2.

Listing 22-2: The ModalArea Class Definition

```
class ModalArea : public CWnd
{
    DECLARE_DYNCREATE(ModalArea)
protected:

// Attributes
public:

// Operations
public:
// make this a public constructor
    ModalArea();used by dynamic creation
    virtual ~ModalArea();

// Overrides
    // ClassWizard generated virtual function overrides
    //{{AFX_VIRTUAL(ModalArea)
    //}}AFX_VIRTUAL

// Implementation
protected:

    // Generated message map functions
    //{{AFX_MSG(ModalArea)
    afx_msg int OnCreate(LPCREATESTRUCT lpCreateStruct);
    afx_msg void OnClose();
    afx_msg void OnLButtonDblClk(UINT nFlags, CPoint point);
    //}}AFX_MSG
    DECLARE_MESSAGE_MAP()
};
```

Now that you are not creating a frame window, you must modify the call to the member function `Create()`. The `Create()` member for the two different window classes takes slightly different parameters. You are able to specify many more options with the `CWnd Create()` member function than you can with the `CFrameWnd`. The reason for this is that `CFrameWnd` by nature has many of its characteristics defined for it already. Your call to create the modal window should have the appearance of the following:

```
pModalWinMask->Create(NULL,
    NULL,
    WS_BORDER,
    CFrameWnd::rectDefault,
    pWndDeskTop,
    CHILD_WND_ID);
```

Only a couple of the parameters in this call require comments. Perhaps the most important is the one that defines the window style. You can see here that only the flag WS_BORDER has been used. The style WS_OVERLAPPED, for example, brings along with it a frame, max and min boxes, and so forth. WS_BORDER is minimal but still useful for debugging. The one here is used only because you simply don't need anything else for your window. In fact, the border is included only to help you position the window on the screen, or to otherwise know that it is there. This window has a default client rectangle size of a frame window. Because you are soon going to make the client area even larger than the desktop, any other size could have been chosen. The window ID is arbitrary here. Just insert an integer value.

You should also notice that the parent of our modal window is the desktop. This is done by passing it the pointer pWndDeskTop. This value that was obtained above this call with the line:

```
pWndDeskTop = GetDesktopWindow();
```

Once you have instantiated and created the window, you must position it on the screen. Perform this with the code:

```
pSampleModalWindow->SetWindowPos( &wndTopMost,
        -1, -1,
        rectDeskTop.Width()+1,
        rectDeskTop.Height()+1,
        SWP_SHOWWINDOW);
```

The pointer &wndTopMost is defined by Windows. It is used here to signify that the window should appear on top of all the other windows. The coordinates that are passed position the window so that its top-left and bottom-right corners are outside the desktop area. You can also try some smaller dimensions to see the border of the window positioned on the desktop.

That's all that you need in order to get the transparent modal window to cover the desktop. The code for the OnViewGoModal() handler should now look like Listing 22-3.

Listing 22 3: Code for Going Modal

```
void CModalWinView::OnViewGoModal()
{

    // TODO: Add your command handler code here
    CRect rectDeskTop;
    CWnd * pWndDeskTop;       // Pointer to desktop

    pWndDeskTop = GetDesktopWindow();
    pWndDeskTop->GetWindowRect(&rectDeskTop);
```

(continued)

Listing 22-3 (continued)

```
      // Add a pointer to use for the modal window
      ModalArea * pSampleModalWindow;

      // Instantiate the frame window object
      pSampleModalWindow = new ModalArea();

      // Create the window
      pSampleModalWindow->Create(NULL,
              NULL,
              WS_BORDER,
              CFrameWnd::rectDefault,
              pWndDeskTop,
              CHILD_WND_ID);    //defined above

          // Turn the parent window off
     ::EnableWindow( AfxGetApp()->m_pMainWnd->m_hWnd, FALSE );

     // Position the modal window on the screen
     pSampleModalWindow->SetWindowPos( &wndTopMost,
          -1, -1,
          rectDeskTop.Width()+1,
          rectDeskTop.Height()+1,
          SWP_SHOWWINDOW);

     // Start the modal loop
     pSampleModalWindow->RunModalLoop( MLF_SHOWONIDLE );

     // destroy the frame
     pSampleModalWindow->DestroyWindow();

 }
```

Look at Figure 22-2 to see an image of the modal window. Note that it only has a border. Notice also that the main window was moved after the modal window was displayed. You could see that the modal area was not being painted by the system. It was made smaller than the desktop so you could see its extent here.

Try running this sample several times. You can still close the window by double-clicking anywhere on the desktop because that functionality was implemented in the first demonstration program. Change the position and so forth in the call to `SetWindowPos()`. Try making the main application the parent window and other operations. All of this will further your understanding.

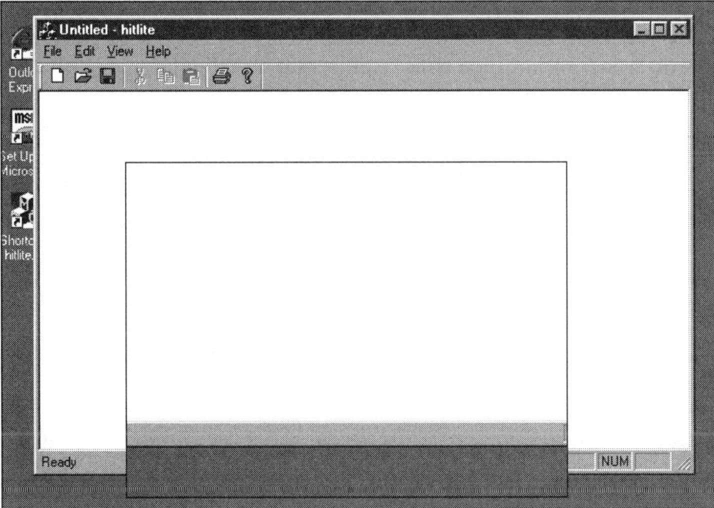

Figure 22-2: The application window was moved under the modal window.

Drawing a Transparent Bitmap on a Transparent Client Area

To continue with the description of the motivation behind our example, consider how you would highlight or point out something on the desktop to a student. You could do this in many ways. You could, for example, simply draw lines or arrows to indicate the item. You could also use `BitBlt`, a Win32 function and a member of the `CDC` class, to reverse the area. But in the example here a more sophisticated means will be used. You will circle the item to be indicated with a transparent bitmap. You could, of course, push this even further, using animation and more, but this example will get you started and demonstrate some of the techniques involved.

Once the resource editor appears on the screen, you can drag the bitmap area to make a bitmap of any size. You should use a size that is appropriate for the screen item you want to emphasize. It does not have to be an exact match, because you can use `StretchBlt()` to adjust its size when you get ready to display it on the screen. In this demonstration program you are going to use `BitBlt()` to circle the NumLock indicator that appears on the status bar of our main window. You need space for the border and enough area to draw around the indicator. The bitmap created for the demonstration program is 73 × 63 pixels, but this is not set in stone and you are welcome to create your own bitmap.

One important thing that you must decide before creating the bitmap, though, is which of the colors in the bitmap will be the color that you regard as transparent. Windows bitmaps do not have a color that is necessarily transparent; you cannot give pixels a color that is always "no color." So use a color that is unimportant for the image design of your bitmap. In the demonstration program, white was chosen as the color that would be transparent. It will not be displayed when the bitmap is drawn on the client area or desktop. The bitmap rendered for the demonstration program looks like the one shown in Figure 22-3.

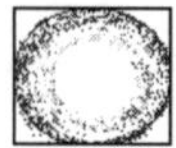

Figure 22-3: This is how the bitmap appears.

Now you start getting ready to display this bitmap. The first thing that you do is to add a member data variable to your modal window class that will keep a pointer to your main window handy. Call this data member pAppWnd. You must also add a member function to your modal window class that enables you to set its value if it is going to be a private member, which is always a good idea.

You need to capture this pointer and cast it as a frame window because the functions that you need to use later for getting pointers to the message bar class and other things are members of CFrameWnd. Your data member that is private to your modal window class and the member function used to set it must also reflect this. Here's the code used to do this:

```
void ModalArea::SetpAppWnd(CFrameWnd * pWnd)
{
    pAppWnd = pWnd;
}
```

You will get the pointer to this frame window immediately before starting the modal loop. Use the following lines in the OnViewGoModal() handler:

```
pSampleModalWindow->SetpAppWnd(
    (CFrameWnd *)AfxGetApp()->m_pMainWnd);
```

Painting the bitmap

For the sake of instructional clarity, all the work of putting the bitmap on the client area will be done in the handler for the paint message that was made a part of the modal window class earlier. When writing a similar application of your own, you might want to use the code for the transparent bitmap in a separate function or use the OnDraw() method. If you were creating a full tutorial application, of course, you would also use several different bitmaps, locations, pointers, and so forth. This is not meant to be a general example; rather, you are stepping through the process in a way that makes its operation obvious.

Because you are going to do all your drawing in the handler for the paint message, then obviously you need to add this handler. So using ClassWizard, add a handler for the WM_PAINT message to your modal window class. This handler, along with its completed code in the demonstration program, is reproduced in Listing 22-4. You can get a better sense of it if you see it in its entirety. So take a look at it first, and then the explanation for its development will be more obvious.

Listing 22-4: Blitting the Images Together

```
void ModalArea::OnPaint()
{
    // This is the device context where we will do
    // the drawing
    CPaintDC   dc(this);

    // These are various compatible device contexts
    // in which we will copy the bitmap in order to
    // mask the desired transparent bits
    CDC cdcTemp,
        cdcBackGround,
        cdcBitMask,
        cdcMemory,
        cdcScreenBits;

    // Status bar from our main application window
    CStatusBar * pMessageBar;

    // Original background color of the source
    // device context
    COLORREF   clrrefBkColor;

    // Bitmap objects for copying the masks, original,
    // and so forth back and forth
    CBitmap   cbmNewBitmap,
              cbmCopyBitMask,
              cbmCopyMemory,
              cbmCopyBackGround,
              cbmScreenBits;

    CBitmap * cbmOldBitmap;
    CBitmap * cbmBackGroundOld;
    CBitmap * cbmBitMaskOld;
    CBitmap * cbmMemoryOld;
    CBitmap * cbmScreenBitsOld;

    // bitmpap sizes and target points for the mouse
    CPoint pointBmpExtent, pointTarget, pointRange,
       pointTextOut;
```

(continued)

Listing 22-4 *(continued)*

```
// Used to put the bitmap over the NumLock pane
CRect rectNumPane, rectMessageBar, rectTarget;
BITMAP     bm;

// Get the pointer to the message bar
// of the application
pMessageBar = (CStatusBar *) pAppWnd->GetMessageBar();

//  Coordinates of the NumLock pane are relative to the
//  upper left of the status bar, so get them
//  and add them together
pMessageBar->GetItemRect(2, &rectNumPane);
pMessageBar->GetWindowRect(&rectMessageBar);
rectTarget = rectNumPane;
rectTarget.left = rectMessageBar.left
    + rectNumPane.left;
rectTarget.top = rectMessageBar.top
    + rectNumPane.top;

// Load our resource bitmap
cdcTemp.CreateCompatibleDC(&dc);
cbmNewBitmap.LoadBitmap(IDB_BITMAP1);
// Select the bitmap into the dc
cbmOldBitmap = cdcTemp.SelectObject(&cbmNewBitmap);

GetObject(HBITMAP(cbmNewBitmap),
    sizeof(BITMAP),
    (LPSTR)&bm);
pointBmpExtent.x = bm.bmWidth;
pointBmpExtent.y = bm.bmHeight;

// We need to offset our bitmap so the area of interest
// is in it center when it appears on the screen
pointRange.x =  pointBmpExtent.x / 2;
pointRange.y =  pointBmpExtent.y / 2;
pointTarget.x = (rectTarget.left - pointRange.x)
    + (rectNumPane.Width() / 2);
pointTarget.y = rectTarget.top - pointRange.y
    + (rectNumPane.Height() / 2);

// Create DCs in which to move our bitmap around
// so we can back out background
cdcBackGround.CreateCompatibleDC(&dc);
cdcMemory.CreateCompatibleDC(&dc);
cdcScreenBits.CreateCompatibleDC(&dc);
cdcBitMask.CreateCompatibleDC(&dc);

// Create the bitmaps for each of our dc's
cbmCopyBackGround.CreateBitmap(pointBmpExtent.x,
    pointBmpExtent.y, 1, 1, NULL);
cbmCopyBitMask.CreateBitmap(pointBmpExtent.x,
```

```
    pointBmpExtent.y, 1, 1, NULL);
cbmCopyMemory.CreateCompatibleBitmap(&dc,
    pointBmpExtent.x, pointBmpExtent.y);
cbmScreenBits.CreateCompatibleBitmap(&dc,
    pointBmpExtent.x, pointBmpExtent.y);

// Select the bitmaps just created into each of the dc's
cbmBackGroundOld =
    cdcBackGround.SelectObject(&cbmCopyBackGround);
cbmBitMaskOld =
    cdcBitMask.SelectObject(&cbmCopyBitMask);
cbmMemoryOld =
    cdcMemory.SelectObject(&cbmCopyMemory);
cbmScreenBitsOld =
    cdcScreenBits.SelectObject(&cbmScreenBits);

// Copy out the are of the screen that is about
// to be overwritten
BitBlt(cdcScreenBits.m_hDC, 0, 0, pointBmpExtent.x,
    pointBmpExtent.y, cdcTemp.m_hDC, 0, 0, SRCCOPY);

// Set the background color to white
// This was the color chosen to be transparent
clrrefBkColor = cdcTemp.SetBkColor(RGB( 255, 255, 255));

// Create mask for your bitmap
BitBlt(cdcBitMask.m_hDC, 0, 0, pointBmpExtent.x,
    pointBmpExtent.y, cdcTemp.m_hDC, 0, 0,
      SRCCOPY);

// Put the original background color back
cdcTemp.SetBkColor(clrrefBkColor);

// Create the reverse of the mask you just made
BitBlt(cdcBackGround.m_hDC, 0, 0, pointBmpExtent.x,
    pointBmpExtent.y, cdcBitMask.m_hDC, 0, 0,
    NOTSRCCOPY);

// Copy in the background of the paint dc first
BitBlt(cdcMemory.m_hDC, 0, 0, pointBmpExtent.x,
    pointBmpExtent.y, dc.m_hDC,  pointTarget.x,
    pointTarget.y, SRCCOPY);

// Copy in the mask for the bitmap
BitBlt(cdcMemory.m_hDC, 0, 0, pointBmpExtent.x,
    pointBmpExtent.y, cdcBitMask.m_hDC, 0, 0, SRCAND),

// Mask out the bits we have determined to be
// transparent (white ones)
BitBlt(cdcTemp.m_hDC, 0, 0, pointBmpExtent.x,
    pointBmpExtent.y, cdcBackGround.m_hDC, 0, 0, SRCAND);
```

(continued)

Listing 22-4 *(continued)*

```
    // Blend in the background
    BitBlt(cdcMemory.m_hDC, 0, 0, pointBmpExtent.x,
        pointBmpExtent.y, cdcTemp.m_hDC, 0, 0, SRCPAINT);

    // Now put it all on the display
    BitBlt(dc.m_hDC, pointTarget.x, pointTarget.y,
        pointBmpExtent.x, pointBmpExtent.y, cdcMemory.m_hDC,
        0, 0, SRCCOPY);

    // Put the instruction string for student on the screen
    LPCTSTR pInstruction =
        _T("Identify and double-click the Numlock indicator.");
    CSize sizeString = dc.GetTextExtent(pInstruction,
        lstrlen(pInstruction));
    pointTextOut.x = pointTarget.x - (sizeString.cx/2);
    pointTextOut.y = rectMessageBar.bottom + pointRange.y;
    dc.TextOut( pointTextOut.x, pointTextOut.y, pInstruction,
        lstrlen(pInstruction));
}
```

Determining where to paste the bitmap

The first line of code is the call that obtains a pointer to the message bar. The message bar, or status bar, is the window to which the panes are attached. Note that the member function `GetMessageBar()` belongs to `CFrameWnd`. This was the reason that it was necessary to cast the pointer returned for the application window to that of `CFrameWnd`. Strangely, this member function returns the pointer to the message bar as a simple pointer to a `CWnd`. This makes unavailable some of the member functions for `CStatusBar` that you will need later. For this reason, cast the pointer to `CStatusBar *`.

Next make a call to `GetItemRect()`, which is a member function of `CStatusBar`. This member puts the coordinates of the NumLock indicator into the `CRect` structure for which you pass the pointer. The NumLock indicator for a frame window has 2 for an index. So indicate that the NumLock rectangle is the pane you want by passing 2 for the `nIndex` parameter. The coordinates that it returns are measured in pixels that are relative to the upper-left corner of the status bar. Later you could try experimenting with other indexes.

Next you get the coordinates for the status bar itself. You need this because the coordinates of the NumLock pane are measured relative to that. Introduce another variable `rectTarget`, which you will use to calculate the placement of several different things. For now you can just set the target point equal to the upper-left corner of the NumLock pane.

To further determine where you will be placing your masking, transparent bitmap on the screen, you need to know the size of the bitmap. You can obtain this information with the next few lines. There are easier ways to get the size of a bitmap, but here you need to begin to prepare for all the blitting that you will be doing with the bitmap and its masks. *Blitting* is the term used to refer to when pixels are copied and combined using `BitBlt()` or `StretchBlt()`. To get ready for the blit, a compatible device context is created first.

Compatible device contexts

Use a member function of `CDC`, `CreateCompatibleDC()`, to create a memory device context that is compatible with the device for the `CPaintDC`. This function can only be used to create compatible device contexts for devices that support raster operations. But because you know that you are working with the display screen, which is definitely a raster device, it will work in this instance. Create the compatible DC by passing the pointer to the DC that was created at the top of the handler. Memory device contexts are simply a block of memory that represent a surface. They can be used to build up images before putting them on the surface of the device. Because you are going to eventually put the bitmap on the screen, use the pointer to the paint DC.

Next you must load the bitmap. The bitmap object was previously instantiated, but it does not yet have any bitmap information associated with it. So use the `LoadBitmap()` member function from `CBitmap` to load the bitmap as a resource. Pass it the ID for the bitmap that you created much earlier with the resource editor. For the demonstration program, this ID is `IDB_BITMAP1`.

The bitmap object is now filled out, but the device context is still unaware of it. When the device context was created by `CreateCompatibleDC()`, a one-by-one monochrome bitmap was selected into it by Windows. This monochrome bitmap gives the device context characteristics that are not useful here. You need color information and so forth that matches the blitting that you will be doing among these device contexts. Thus, you select the bitmap that you loaded into that context with the `CDC` member function `SelectObject()`.

The `CBitmap` class has no easy means to get the bitmap dimensions. The member function `GetBitmapDimension()` returns valid dimensions only if they have already been set with the member function `SetBitmapDimension()`. This is basically useless in the present situation because GDI does not even use these dimensions anyway. So you need to get the dimensions of the bitmaps out of the structures that are built into the bitmap itself.

The BITMAP structure

The GDI function `GetObject()` helps you prepare to get the actual bitmap dimensions. It returns information about a specified graphics object. In the present case, the graphic is the bitmap that you just loaded. To have a place to put this information, you must pass it both the size of the buffer and its location. The buffer area was created previously with the line

```
BITMAP     bm;
```

The `BITMAP` structure contains the information that defines a bitmap. Here is what it looks like:

```
typedef struct tagBITMAP {   // bm
   LONG   bmType;
   LONG   bmWidth;
   LONG   bmHeight;
   LONG   bmWidthBytes;
   WORD   bmPlanes;
   WORD   bmBitsPixel;
   LPVOID bmBits;
} BITMAP;
```

Windows documentation defines the fields within that structure as follows:

- ✦ `bmType` is always zero.
- ✦ `bmWidth` is the bitmap width.
- ✦ `bmHeight` is the bitmap height.
- ✦ `bmWidthBytes` is the number of bytes in each scan line. A scan line is a string of pixels across the displayed bitmap.
- ✦ `bmPlanes` is the count of color planes. This is interesting if you are dealing with a device driver or something low level like that, but for your purposes here it matters little.
- ✦ `bmBitsPixel` specifies the number of bits required to indicate the color of a pixel. This will usually be a value such as 24, 16, or 8. These days it is almost always 24.
- ✦ `bmBits` points to the actual bits for the bitmap.

Once `GetObject()` has returned, the structure it was given will have valid values for the bitmap. Use these to calculate where the bitmap should be placed on the screen. The corner of the pane to be surrounded with the bitmap was located. The destination of the bitmap to be displayed must be scooted back by half its height and width.

Following the calculation of this point, you must create several more device contexts. These will be similar in nature in that they will all be based on our paint DC. However, each will be used to hold a different version of pieces of the final image as you paste them up in the memory device contexts before putting the file bitmap on the display device. Four more bitmaps are created; these will serve different purposes, so they are not all created in the same manner. The first two are created with a call to the `CBitmap` member function `CreateBitmap()`. The code in the handler is:

```
cbmCopyBackGround.CreateBitmap(pointBmpExtent.x,
        pointBmpExtent.y, 1, 1, NULL);
    cbmCopyBitMask.CreateBitmap(pointBmpExtent.x,
        pointBmpExtent.y, 1, 1, NULL);
```

This `CreateBitmap()` member function initializes a device-dependent memory bitmap. It uses the height and width that is passed to it to set the new size parameters. Because you are creating two monochrome bitmaps, set the `nPlanes` and `nBitcount` parameters both to 1. The reason that these are monochrome bitmaps is that you will essentially be using these to remove the white background from your bitmap. These bitmaps cannot be selected for the display device, but they can be selected as the current bitmap for your device context, which is a memory DC.

After creating the two monochrome bitmaps, perform a similar operation for two other bitmaps. However, these will not be monochrome. They will contain pieces of the color image that you are pasting together here, so they must be able to contain color information. These bitmaps are created not with a call to `CreateBitmap()`; instead use the `CBitmap` member function `CreateCompatibleBitmap()`. The code lines that accomplish this are:

```
    cbmCopyMemory.CreateCompatibleBitmap(&dc,
        pointBmpExtent.x, pointBmpExtent.y);
    cbmScreenBits.CreateCompatibleBitmap(&dc,
        pointBmpExtent.x, pointBmpExtent.y);
```

`CreateCompatibleBitmap()` also initializes a bitmap that is compatible with the device context that you pass in. This bitmap has the same kind of color structure as the device context. Its color planes and bits-per-pixel format in this case are the same as the paint DC. The bitmap format for a nonmemory device context created with this member function is always in the format of the device. Because the color information will be added by `CreateCompatibleBitmap()`, you only need to pass in the pointer to the device context and the necessary height and width. And because these compatible bitmaps will be used to overlay the monochrome masks that were created earlier that match the file bitmap, you want to use the same height and width as that final bitmap.

Next these bitmaps will be selected into their respective device contexts. This is done with a member function that belongs to `CDC`. This member function, `SelectObject()`, has several different versions depending on the type of object that can be selected into the device context, including pens, brushes, fonts, bitmaps, and so forth. The object selected replaces the previous object in that device context. In other words, do not select several bitmaps into the same device context at the same time. In the situation here, you are selecting bitmaps into the device contexts only. The first two bitmaps, remember, are the monochrome bitmaps that were created earlier. The second two are the color bitmaps.

Blitting all the pieces together

Next a series of `BitBlts` will be performed that assemble the file bitmap in the temporary device context before displaying it on the screen. The `CDC` member function `BitBlt` copies a bitmap from the source device context to its own. Basically you can think of this as a function that takes a rectangular bitmap area and moves it from one device context to another. The last parameter in the call string, the raster operation parameter, governs how this movement of pixels appears. The pixels in the destination device context are not necessarily simply overwritten. They can be, but they can also be mixed in a variety of ways.

Common Windows raster operations

The following list is reproduced from the Windows documentation for a handy reference here.

`BLACKNESS` Turns all output black.

`DSTINVERT` Inverts the destination bitmap.

`MERGECOPY` Combines the pattern and the source bitmap using the Boolean AND operator.

`MERGEPAINT` Combines the inverted source bitmap with the destination bitmap using the Boolean OR operator.

`NOTSRCCOPY` Copies the inverted source bitmap to the destination.

`NOTSRCERASE` Inverts the result of combining the destination and source bitmaps using the Boolean OR operator.

`PATCOPY` Copies the pattern to the destination bitmap.

`PATINVERT` Combines the destination bitmap with the pattern using the Boolean XOR operator.

`PATPAINT` Combines the inverted source bitmap with the pattern using the Boolean OR operator. Combines the result of this operation with the destination bitmap using the Boolean OR operator.

`SRCAND` Combines pixels of the destination and source bitmaps using the Boolean AND operator.

`SRCCOPY` Copies the source bitmap to the destination bitmap.

`SRCERASE` Inverts the destination bitmap and combines the result with the source bitmap using the Boolean AND operator.

`SRCINVERT` Combines pixels of the destination and source bitmaps using the Boolean XOR operator.

`SRCPAINT` Combines pixels of the destination and source bitmaps using the Boolean OR operator.

`WHITENESS` Turns all output white.

In the first blit in the demonstration program:

```
cdcScreenBits.BitBlt(0, 0, pointBmpExtent.x,
    pointBmpExtent.y, &cdcTemp, 0, 0, SRCCOPY);
```

you save off the bits that were on the screen where you will eventually place the final bitmap. The reason for doing this is that these bits will first be overwritten and masked. Later you will put them back in the areas that were not masked. Notice that the bits are copied straight to a compatible color device context. This preserves the color information.

Then set the background color in the temporary device context to white. You will need to save the previous background color so you can set it back at the end of the handler. Windows uses this background color when it converts bitmaps between color and monochrome device contexts. Remember that monochrome bitmaps were selected into some of the device contexts earlier.

The code

```
cdcBitMask.BitBlt(0, 0, pointBmpExtent.x,
        pointBmpExtent.y, &cdcTemp, 0, 0,
          SRCCOPY),
```

creates a mask for the original background, in one of the monochrome device contexts, which was on the screen, relying on Windows to make the conversion. After putting the original source background color back, the inverse bitmap of the mask that was just made is then created. This is performed with the code

```
cdcBackGround.BitBlt(0, 0, pointBmpExtent.x,
        pointBmpExtent.y, &cdcBitMask, 0, 0,
        NOTSRCCOPY);
```

Notice the new raster operation. It copies the source bitmap to the destination but in an inverted form. Recall that the device context cdcBackGround was one of those into which a monochrome bitmap was selected, just as cdcBitMask was also. The blit for cdcBitMask used a raster operation of SRCCOPY, the reverse of NOTSRCCOPY. This means that you now have two monochrome copies of the same bitmap that are inversions of each other.

To begin building up the image in memory, you first copy in the background because everything else will be written on top of it. This background is copied from the original paint device context. It is copied to the device context cdcMemory where you will be putting things together. The raster operation for it is also simply a straight copy. Next the mask is blitted over the top of this using the raster operation SRCAND. This raster operation combines the pixels of the two bitmaps using the familiar AND operator. Because one of these is a monochrome bitmap, some of the pixels will be unchanged, while others will be completely masked. The ones in the bitmap will cause the pixels they overlay to be unchanged, while those pixels that overlay zeros will be zeroed. Perform a similar operation with the mask for the temporary device context. Then you are going to OR the bitmap onto the background of the destination device context. This is performed with this blit:

```
cdcMemory.BitBlt(0, 0, pointBmpExtent.x,
        pointBmpExtent.y, &cdcTemp, 0, 0, SRCPAINT);
```

Once again another different raster operation can be used. SRCPAINT mixes pixels of the destination and source bitmaps using an OR. In the final blit, the bitmap that was assembled in the cdcMemory device context is simply copied to the screen.

The final bit of code in the paint handler simply writes an instruction to the screen near the place where you pasted the bitmap around the NumLock pane. It instructs the student to double-click in the circle to signify that the student has recognized the point being made. These few lines of code rely on the same sort of calculations that were made earlier for the bitmap. The completed application is shown in Figure 22-4.

Because a lot of effort was spent blitting various pieces of the screen around and making masks for it, let's take a closer look at the image that was put together as it is displayed on the screen (see Figure 22-5).

Notice that the system highlights around the pane along with the background colors, both those of the application client area and the Windows desktop, continue to show through.

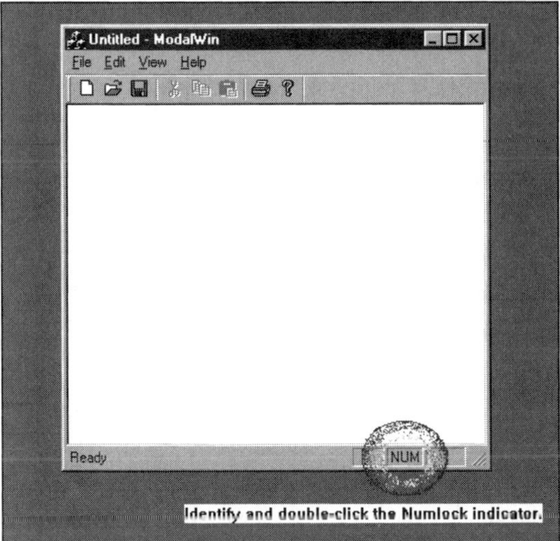

Figure 22-4: The circle is blitted with a transparent background.

Figure 22-5: A close-up of the bitmap on the screen

Making sure they noticed

To make sure that the student has recognized the item being pointed out on the screen, you must limit the area in which the double-click will be regarded as valid. You don't want to be needlessly restrictive, so calculate an area that includes any double-clicks inside the bitmapped area. The handler for our left mouse button double-clicks appears something like this:

```
void ModalArea::OnLButtonDblClk(UINT nFlags, CPoint point)
{
    // TODO: Add your message handler code here and/or
    // call default

    CWnd::OnLButtonDblClk(nFlags, point);
    if (
        ( point.x > pointTarget.x) &&
        ( point.x < (pointTarget.x + 2*pointRange.x)) &&
        ( point.y > pointTarget.y) &&
        ( point.y < (pointTarget.y + 2*pointRange.y)) )
    OnClose();
}
```

Summary

You now have the techniques to accomplish a considerable number of new tasks. These include the capability to paste up transparent bitmaps in memory device contexts. You can also now create modal windows, of `CFrameWnd` and of `CWnd`. You have also taken a much closer look at what modal really means. In addition, you have some experience now with a very important function in Windows, which is `BitBlt`. This chapter brings together a number of techniques and ideas from divergent areas of the Windows system in order to show you what more you could do with the things that are there under the hood. All you need to do is to open the hood, take a look, and start to tinker.

✦ ✦ ✦

CHAPTER 23

Status Bars and Toolbars

✦ ✦ ✦ ✦

In This Chapter

Incorporating status bars into an application

Creating your own status bars

Customizing status bars

The toolbar creation process

Customizing toolbars for your own use

Incorporating the new ReBar control into an application

✦ ✦ ✦ ✦

In this chapter, two basic parts of the Windows user interface will be examined: toolbars and status bars. A status bar is an area at the bottom of an application's main window that displays text messages, such as "CAP," which tells the user that Caps Lock is on. The status bar creation process will be examined and the default status bar settings that the Visual C++ AppWizard provides will be described. Finally, this chapter will instruct you on how to customize status bars and make them do your bidding.

After the wild and woolly world of status bars has been conquered, toolbars will be covered. Toolbars are windows with buttons or combo boxes that enable users to issue application commands with a single mouse click. The basic toolbar creation process will be examined first, and the AppWizard defaults will be described. Once you've acquired a basic grounding in toolbar creation, more advanced areas such as displaying and hiding toolbars on command, as well as creating your own toolbars, will be covered.

Creating and Using Status Bars

A status bar is the multi-field bar that appears at the bottom of a frame window. Almost all Windows applications customarily include a status bar and use the bar to display such user interface information as toolbar button help and application specifics (for example, the state of the Caps Lock key in a word processor). Because almost all Windows applications display a status bar, you should seriously consider integrating status bars into your applications. Most users expect to see a status bar, and creating and manipulating status bars is generally easy.

Creating a status bar

A status bar is represented in the MFC framework by the CStatusBar class. In most cases, a status bar is declared as a protected CStatusBar member variable of the frame window:

```
protected:
CStatusBar  m_wndStatusBar;
```

Status bar creation and initialization are also handled by the frame window, in its OnCreate() function. During the execution of this function, the status bar is created, and the status bar's display fields are defined:

```
UINT nSeparator = ID_SEPARATOR;
m_wndStatusBar.Create(this);
m_wndStatusBar.SetIndicators(&nSeparator,1);
```

After looking at the preceding code snippet, you're probably asking the question, "What is ID_SEPARATOR?" ID_SEPARATOR is a resource ID that tells MFC that no string resource is associated with this particular status bar display pane. Separators are commonly used to visually segment display panes for easier reading. In the preceding code, m_wndStatusBar.Create() creates the status bar while m_wndStatusBar.SetIndicators() creates the display panes. The preceding code creates a single blank display pane.

What if we wanted to create more than one display pane? Well, it's not that much different than what has already been done. Instead of specifying only one indicator in CStatusBar::SetIndicators(), more than one is specified:

```
UINT nIndicators[]={IDS_SBARMSG1, IDS_SBARMSG2,
  IDS_SBARMSG3};
m_wndStatusBar.Create(this);
m_wndStatusBar.SetIndicators(nIndicators,3);
```

In the preceding example, IDS_SBARMSG1, IDS_SBARMSG2, and IDS_SBARMSG3 are resource ID values for string resources that reside in the application's string table. The status bar now displays as many indicators as were specified.

What you've learned so far is great if all you wanted to do is display static text within the status bar fields. However, most status bars aren't used that way. Typically, status bars convey to the user dynamic information about the application, such as the state of the Caps Lock or Num Lock keys or toolbar help.

Rather than programmatically tracking the status of the Caps Lock or Num Lock keys and then updating the status bar, predefined constants can be used, and MFC can do the work for you. These constants are summarized in Table 23-1.

Table 23-1
Status Bar Constants

Status Bar Constant	*Status Bar Information*
ID_INDICATOR_CAPS	Displays the current state of the Caps Lock key.
ID_INDICATOR_NUM	Displays the current state of the Num Lock key.
ID_INDICATOR_SCRL	Displays the current state of the Scroll Lock key.

The following code snippet creates and displays a status bar that indicates the current states of the Caps Lock and Scroll Lock keys:

```
UINT nIndicators[]={ID_SEPARATOR, ID_INDICATOR_CAPS,
  ID_INDICATOR_SCRL};
m_wndStatusBar.Create(this);
m_wndStatusBar.SetIndicators(nIndicators,3);
```

Now the status bar has a blank first pane, a second pane that displays the status of the Caps Lock key, and a third pane that displays the status of the Scroll Lock key. Pretty simple, no?

Customizing status bars

As with most other areas of MFC, status bars and CStatusBar can be customized and extended in any number of ways. This section discusses the creation of custom status bars and explores ways to take control of the status bar's behavior.

Creating custom status bars

A status bar is generally created in the main frame window's OnCreate() member function like this:

```
m_wndStatusBar.Create(this);
```

Passing the window handle of the frame window only to CStatusBar::Create() creates a status bar that is bound to the default status bar object ID AFX_IDW_STATUS_BAR. This MFC-defined constant represents the default status bar. Status bars created in this manner also have the default attributes of a bottom-aligned, visible, child window that is linked to the main frame window. The full prototype of CStatusBar::Create() follows, and default values are indicated in bold:

```
BOOL Create( CWnd* pParentWnd, DWORD dwStyle = WS_CHILD
  | WS_VISIBLE | CBRS_BOTTOM, UINT nID =
  AFX_IDW_STATUS_BAR );
```

`CStatusBar::Create()` accepts several style flags that control the appearance and behavior of the status bar. In addition to many of the style flags accepted by all `CWnd`-derived classes, `WS_CHILD`, `Create()` also accepts six style flags that are specific to `CStatusBar`. These constants define the alignment of the status bar within the frame window. These style flags are summarized in Table 23-2.

Table 23-2
CStatusBar::Create() Constants

Style Flag	*Description*
CBRS_TOP	Status bar is at top of frame window.
CBRS_BOTTOM	Status bar is at bottom of frame window.
CBRS_NOALIGN	Status bar is not repositioned when the parent is resized.

The following function call creates a status bar that is bottom-aligned with the main frame window:

```
m_wndStatusBar.Create(this,WS_CHILD | WS_VISIBLE |
  CBRS_BOTTOM);
```

In addition to changing the alignment and appearance of the entire status bar, you can also modify the appearance of each of the status bar's display panes. `CStatusBar::SetPaneStyle()` is used to change the style, or appearance, of the individual panes. The function prototype looks like this:

```
void SetPaneStyle( int nIndex, UINT nStyle )
```

The first parameter, `nIndex`, represents an index into the array of indicators specified during the creation of the status bar. The parameter `nIndex` is an index into the array of indicators used during the status bar creation process. Remember, because the indicator array is zero-based, if you wanted to change the style of the third pane in a status bar, use `nIndex = 2` to specify the third pane. The `nStyle` parameter is used to set the style of the pane. `SetPaneStyle()` accepts the style flags listed in Table 23-3.

Using the flags listed in Table 23-3, the code to disable a status bar pane looks like this:

```
m_wndStatusBar.SetPaneStyle(2,SBS_DISABLED);
```

Table 23-3
CStatusBar::SetPaneStyle() Constants

Style Flag	*Description*
SBPS_NOBORDERS	Creates a pane that is flush with the status bar.
SBPS_POPOUT	Creates a pane that protrudes from the status bar.
SBPS_NORMAL	Creates a pane so that it is recessed on the status bar.
SBPS_DISABLED	Disables the pane. A disabled pane displays no text.
SBPS_STRETCH	Stretches the pane to take up any "slack" space on the status bar. Only one pane per status bar can have this style.
SBPS_OWNERDRAW	Creates an owner-drawn pane.

Taking control of the status bar

In some cases, you may not like the default behavior of the AppWizard when it creates the MFC skeleton of a new application. This section will look at how to take control of the AppWizard-created status bar.

When the AppWizard creates a default status bar, the status bar is created with the window ID AFX_IDW_STATUS_BAR. In some cases, you may choose not to use the default behavior of the wizard-created status bar. To disable the behavior, you must take control of the status bar and handle its updates with your own code.

First, you must change the child window ID to your own ID. Using your own window ID "disconnects" the status bar from the automatically generated functionality provided by the AppWizard. This ID should be defined in the application's resources. You can view these resources by selecting View ➪ Resource Symbols. In the examples, the constant ID_MY_STATUS_BAR is used. The status bar's window ID is assigned in the frame window's OnCreate member function. The AppWizard-generated function looks like this:

```
int CMainFrame::OnCreate(LPCREATESTRUCT lpCreateStruct)
{
...

    if (!m_wndStatusBar.Create(this) ||
        !m_wndStatusBar.SetIndicators(indicators,
          sizeof(indicators)/sizeof(UINT)))
    {
        TRACE0("Failed to create status bar\n");
        return -1;      // fail to create
...
    }

    return 0;
}
```

The line `m_wndStatusBar.Create(this)` creates the status bar with the default child window ID and binds it to the frame window. The customized version of `OnCreate()` that uses the custom window ID looks like this (changes appear in bold):

```
int CMainFrame::OnCreate(LPCREATESTRUCT lpCreateStruct)
{
...

    if (!m_wndStatusBar.Create(WS_CHILD | WS_VISIBLE |
       CBRS_BOTTOM, ID_MY_STATUS_BAR) ||
       !m_wndStatusBar.SetIndicators(indicators,
       sizeof(indicators)/sizeof(UINT)))
    {
        TRACE0("Failed to create status bar\n");
        return -1;      // fail to create
...
    }

    return 0;
}
```

Once the brand new window is created, the default status bar indicators must be replaced with ones of your own. The indicators' resource IDs are stored in a static array of unsigned integers (`UINT`s) called `indicators[]`. The array is first used in the frame window's .cpp file. The AppWizard's indicators look like this:

```
static UINT indicators[] =
{
    ID_SEPARATOR,           // status line indicator
    ID_INDICATOR_CAPS,
    ID_INDICATOR_NUM,
    ID_INDICATOR_SCRL,
};
```

These indicators create a status bar that contains a dynamic pane for help and message text along with three other panes that display the state of the Caps Lock, Num Lock, and Scroll Lock keys. The unwanted default indicators are replaced with the following:

```
static UINT indicators[] =
{
    ID_SEPARATOR,           // status line indicator
    ID_CONNECT_STATUS,
    ID_CURSOR_POSITION
};
```

Now the status bar has the same dynamic pane for help text, a pane that displays the application's current connect status (useful for database or network applications), and a pane that displays the current position of the cursor.

Here comes the fun part! Because the status bar's window ID has been modified and the indicator IDs used, the AppWizard-generated code will really have no idea how to work with the status bar. The message processing for the status bar must be programmatically handled on your own. It's generally easiest to use the ClassWizard to add the message handlers. You should add handlers for both `COMMAND` and `UPDATE_COMMAND_UI` messages.

The skeleton message handler functions have been added to the application, but the message map entries must also be added so the functions are actually called when the messages arrive. This has to be done manually because the ClassWizard won't recognize the customized message IDs. The code to do this looks like this (customized code appears in bold):

```
BEGIN_MESSAGE_MAP(CMainFrame, CFrameWnd)
    //{{AFX_MSG_MAP(CMainFrame)
    ON_WM_CREATE()
    ON_UPDATE_COMMAND_UI(ID_CONNECT_STATUS,
    OnUpdateConnect)
    //}}AFX_MSG_MAP
END_MESSAGE_MAP()
```

With the addition of the message handler functions and the message map entries, the custom function `OnUpdateConnect` is called to update the status bar. The prototype for the function looks like this:

```
void CMainFrame::OnUpdateConnect(CCmdUI* pCmdUI)
```

The code contained in this function tests the state of the database connection and updates the status bar appropriately.

As a review, these are the steps required to customize the behavior of the status bar:

1. Add a string resource for each of the custom status bar panes.
2. Add a new child window ID, and use this ID during status bar creation.
3. Replace the stock indicators with customized ones.
4. Add message handlers for the custom status bar.
5. Create message map entries to connect the messages to the custom status bar handler functions.
6. Add code to each of the message handler functions to update the status bar.

Creating and Controlling Toolbars

Toolbars provide instant access to program commands for users. Rather than digging into a menu or remembering a keystroke, users can use toolbars, which are visible on the interface. Because they occupy precious screen space, toolbars should include only the most frequently used commands. Large programs tend to have multiple toolbars for different user tasks. Even if your program has only a single toolbar, make sure you give the user the option of hiding it when it gets in the way.

From a programming perspective, a toolbar is a child window that displays a series of bitmap buttons. Once you create a toolbar and make it visible, you can all but ignore it because it generates the same message — `WM_COMMAND` — that menus and accelerators generate. However, you should synchronize toolbar command IDs with the command IDs in menus and accelerators.

The following sections cover several topics that can help you work with toolbars. Let's start with a quick look at the placement of toolbars in the MFC hierarchy. Then some of the details involved in dynamically creating and modifying toolbars will be covered.

MFC control bars

MFC's toolbar class, `CToolBar`, is one of several classes that create windows for receiving some kind of command input and displaying status information to the user. The base class for this group, known collectively as control bars, is `CControlBar`, and it's derived from `CWnd`.

This inheritance relationship has some very useful implications. For example, because all control bars are derived from `CWnd`, they are connected to a Windows API window. As a result, all of the functional capabilities of `CWnd` — creating, moving, showing, and hiding windows — are available when you're working with control bars.

`CToolBar` has several sibling classes, including `CStatusBar`, `CDialogBar`, and `COleResizeBar`. When asked, AppWizard gladly creates a status bar by spinning code that creates a `CStatusBar` object. As mentioned in the discussion of menus, status bars sit at the bottom of a frame window and can display helpful information about menu choices. A status bar can also display helpful details about different toolbar buttons as the user moves the mouse cursor over the buttons.

The `CDialogBar` class creates dialog bars, which are a cross between a toolbar and a dialog box. A dialog bar can hold controls such as a dialog box, but it stays visible in a frame window similar to a toolbar. This class is discussed further in Chapter 12, which covers dialog boxes.

✦ ✦ ✦ ✦ ✦

The final MFC control bar is `COleResizeBar`, which supports resizing of in-place OLE objects, a subject that is beyond the scope of this book.

MFC toolbars (and dialog bars) are dockable. When this feature is enabled, a user can pick up a toolbar and move it to a different edge of a frame window. It is up to the frame window, however, to indicate which edges are acceptable docking sites. As an alternative, toolbars can also be moved away from any frame edge and left in a free-floating palette.

MFC toolbars also support ToolTips, which are intended to help users understand the purpose of individual toolbar buttons. Users summon ToolTip support—when it's enabled—by moving the mouse cursor over a toolbar button (without clicking the button). After a brief interval, the ToolTip—a word or phrase—appears in a tiny text window that hovers over the toolbar buttons.

To put toolbars to work in your MFC program, you must coordinate several items, including a bitmap resource, the toolbar itself, and the frame window. To help with this effort, the following section shows how to create a toolbar of your own.

Creating and initializing a toolbar

Toolbar creation is a five-step process. First, you load a bitmap that holds the button images. Second, you build an array that maps your buttons to your program's command codes. Third, you write the code to create the toolbar and initialize it appropriately. Once the toolbar window is created, steps four and five involve connecting button images and command IDs to the toolbar. Once these minimum steps are accomplished, you can take other steps to fine-tune the behavior of your toolbar.

Creating a Toolbar

1. Load a bitmap that holds all of the button images. You'll store the bitmap as a bitmap resource, which means you'll first open your project's resource (.RC) file. You create your bitmap button images in a row, using the bitmap editor. The default size of each image is 16 pixels wide by 15 pixels high. When the AppWizard generates the default MFC project that includes a toolbar, the bitmap used for the toolbar is located in the project's `\res` subdirectory. Although you can use different sizes, a change from the default requires that you inform your toolbar object by calling `CToolBar::SetSizes()`.

2. Define an array of command codes that map button images to command IDs. As shown in the following example, this is an array of unsigned integers (`UINT`):

```
// toolbar buttons - IDs are command buttons
static UINT BASED_CODE buttons[] =
{
    // same order as in the bitmap 'bitmap1.bmp'
    ID_TOOLBAR_CREATE,
        ID_SEPARATOR,
    ID_TOOLBAR_SHOW
};
```

The two command codes are ID_TOOLBAR_CREATE and ID_TOOLBAR_SHOW. The other item, ID_SEPARATOR, adds a bit of spacing between these two buttons.

3. Create and initialize the toolbar object. As with other windows, you create a toolbar by first instantiating the object, and then calling an initialization function. Here's an example:

```
// Instantiate C++ object and create window.
m_wndToolbar = new CToolBar();
m_wndToolbar.Create(this, WS_CHILD | CBRS_TOP, 0x9100);
```

The initialization function, CToolBar::Create(), overrides the base function CWnd::Create(). As with other types of window objects, the style field—that is, the middle field—controls quite a few object attributes. This example has two style flags: WS_CHILD and CBRS_TOP. WS_CHILD is a standard windowing style that makes the toolbar a child window whose parent is pointed to by the pointer variable *this*. CBRS_TOP is a control bar–specific style that puts the toolbar at the top of the frame window. Table 23-4 lists other style flags that might be useful.

4. Load the button images into the toolbar's buttons. You accomplish this by calling CToolBar::LoadBitmap(), as in:

```
m_wndToolbar.LoadBitmap(IDR_TOOLS);
```

5. You also need to associate command IDs with buttons. As shown in the following example, you do this by calling CToolBar::SetButtons(), passing in the array of button resource IDs and the number of buttons to set:

```
m_wndToolbar.SetButtons(buttons,
  sizeof(buttons)/sizeof(UINT));
```

✦ ✦ ✦ ✦ ✦

At this point, the toolbar is complete. If you followed all the preceding steps, the toolbar should display several buttons each with a bitmap image from the application's resource file.

A demonstration program is on the CD-ROM in the Chap23\BarsDemo folder to show you how to incorporate toolbars into an MFC application. BarsDemo is a basic drawing program that enables you to draw on the screen using different geometric shapes and colors. It also demonstrates how to add bitmaps to toolbar button faces.

✦ ✦ ✦ ✦ ✦

Table 23-4
CToolBar::Create() Constants

Flag	*Description*
WS_VISIBLE	Makes the toolbar window visible initially.
CBRS_BOTTOM	Places the control bar at the bottom of the frame.
CBRS_FLYBY	Causes command descriptions to be displayed in the status window when the mouse cursor pauses over buttons.
CBRS_NOALIGN	Prevents repositioning of the control bar when its parent window is resized.
CBRS_TOOLTIPS	Displays ToolTips when the mouse cursor pauses over the toolbar's buttons.
CBRS_TOP	Places the control bar at the top of the frame.

Docking and floating

By default, a CToolBar toolbar can be moved only by program control. However, you can enable users to move the toolbar to other parts of the frame. To do so, you notify both the toolbar and the frame window. As shown in the following example, you do this by calling CToolBar::EnableDocking() and CFrameWnd::EnableDocking():

```
m_wndToolbar.EnableDocking(CBRS_ALIGN_ANY);
EnableDocking(CBRS_ALIGN_ANY);
```

Users can then dock and undock the toolbar. Or under program control, you can dock the toolbar by calling CFrameWnd::DockControlBar(), and you can undock the toolbar by calling CFrameWnd::FloatControlBar(). Once you create a toolbar, it remains attached to your frame window and works on its own. There aren't many things you'll have to do, except perhaps hide it or show it on demand. Let's see what this involves.

Showing and hiding toolbars

The key point to keep in mind when showing or hiding a toolbar is that a toolbar is a window. In practice, this means that you'll rely more on CWnd member functions than on CToolBar functions.

Before you can show or hide a toolbar, it helps to know the current visibility state of the toolbar window. The WS_VISIBLE windowing style is the key to toolbar visibility. To query all of the style bits for a window, you call CWnd::GetStyle(). To determine the visibility of a toolbar, you simply mask the style flag WS_VISIBLE against the results of GetStyle(). This code fragment sets a Boolean variable based on the visibility of a toolbar window:

```
// Query current visibility.
BOOL bVisible = (m_wndToolbar.GetStyle() &
  WS_VISIBLE);
```

A call to `CWnd::SetStyle()`enables you to change certain window styles; unfortunately, `WS_VISIBLE` is not one of them. Instead, you call `CWnd::ShowWindow()` and pass `SW_HIDE` to make the toolbar invisible, and `SW_SHOWNORMAL` to make it reappear. The following code fragment toggles the visibility flag queried in the previous example:

```
// Show or hide.
int nShow = (bVisible) ? SW_HIDE : SW_SHOWNORMAL;
m_wndToolbar.ShowWindow(nShow);
```

Whenever you programmatically change a toolbar, you must inform the frame window about the change. You do this by simply asking it to recalculate the positioning of control bars. You make this request by calling `CFrameWnd::RecalcLayout()`, which takes no parameters:

```
// Reconfigure remaining toolbar items.
RecalcLayout();
```

Adding ToolTips and flyby text

In most current applications, toolbars also provide some basic help and hints to the user in the form of ToolTips and *flyby text*. ToolTips were covered earlier in this chapter. Flyby text is a message that is displayed on the status bar, most commonly in the first "stretchy" pane. The help text provided in flyby text can be a bit longer than the ToolTips because there is more space to display the text.

When you add a toolbar button or menu selection, Visual C++ stores the resource information in the application's resource table, and a resource ID is assigned. Resource IDs cannot be duplicated within a category of resources, which means that two toolbar buttons cannot share the same resource ID, and two strings cannot share the same ID either. But it doesn't mean that a toolbar button and a string can't share the same ID. In fact, MFC takes advantage of this fact and uses it to automate display ToolTips and flyby text.

Basically, MFC takes the resource ID for a toolbar button or a menu selection and checks to see if the application has a string resource defined in its string table with the same ID. This may sound confusing at first, but just remember that resource IDs must be unique only within their category. For example, let's dissect the following resource file excerpt as shown in Listing 23-1.

Listing 23-1: Toolbar Resource File

```
IDR_TOOLBAR 16,15
BEGIN
    BUTTON ID_CUT
    BUTTON ID_COPY
    BUTTON ID_PASTE
    SEPARATOR
    BUTTON ID_PRINT_PREVIEW
    BUTTON ID_PRINT
END
STRINGTABLE
BEGIN
    ID_CUT              "Cut current selection to
                          clipboard\nCut"

    ID_COPY              "Copy current selection to
                          clipboard\nCopy"

    ID_PASTE              "Paste clipboard
                          contents\nPaste"

    ID_PRINT_PREVIEW     "Preview print output\nPrint
                          preview"

    ID_PRINT              "Print document\nPrint"
END
```

Notice how the string table entries have the same ID as the button controls on the toolbar. MFC uses this overlap to match up string table entries with each toolbar control. One string table entry contains both the flyby text and the ToolTip text. Each resource string is simply parsed: all the text before the embedded newline is displayed as flyby text while the shorter string after the newline is displayed as a ToolTip.

Adding nonbutton controls

Buttons claim the majority of toolbar real estate in comparison to the other control types. However, you can add other types of controls to a toolbar. For example, it would be convenient for a word processor to provide a combo box on a toolbar that enables users to select fonts and font styles.

The first step to adding a nonbutton control is to stake out your real estate claim on the toolbar. You can do so by editing the toolbar resource and inserting a separator as a placeholder for the control:

```
IDR_TOOLBAR 16,15
BEGIN
    BUTTON ID_CUT
    BUTTON ID_COPY
BUTTON ID_PASTE
    SEPARATOR
    SEPARATOR //Placeholder for control
END
```

The second step is to widen the area for the control by using `CToolBar::SetButtonInfo()` to increase the width of the area marked by the separator:

```
SetButtonInfo(4, IDC_FONTS, TBBS_SEPARATOR, nWidth);
```

In the preceding snippet, the first argument represents the position of the control on the toolbar, `IDC_FONTS` is the resource ID of the control, `TBBS` is an MFC constant that represents a toolbar separator, and `nWidth` holds the width of the control. After the call to `CToolBar::SetButtonInfo()` has completed, the control can be created:

```
CRect rect;
GetItemRect (4, &rect);
rect.bottom = rect.top + nHeight;
m_ctlFonts.Create(WS_CHILD | WS_VISIBLE | WS_VSCROLL
  | CBS_SORT | CBS_DROPDOWNLIST, rect, this, IDC_FONTS);
```

In practice, the preceding code as well as the call to `SetButtonInfo()` are normally included in the toolbar's `OnCreate()` handler function.

Updating nonbutton controls

A toolbar that contains only button controls uses the `CCmdUI` update mechanism to update the states of the toolbar buttons. However, this mechanism is not available for use when nonbutton controls are added to the toolbar. Don't despair though! MFC provides an answer in the form of another toolbar class, `CControlBar` and its update mechanism `CControlBar::OnUpdateCmdUI()`.

All you need do is derive the toolbar from `CControlBar` rather than `CToolBar`. Once you've changed your code, the `OnUpdateCmdUI()` function is available. You can override `OnUpdateCmdUI()` and update controls that do not have update handlers, such as combo boxes or list boxes.

Using the ReBar Control

ReBars are the latest user interface innovation from Microsoft. Before their formal introduction in Visual C++ 6.0, they were referred to as *coolbars*. In the interest of just being different, Microsoft has decided to call them *ReBars*, so we should as well.

ReBars are functionally almost exactly the same as a standard toolbar. A ReBar can host and display other controls in the same way as a toolbar. The main difference lies in their appearance. ReBars appear as a flat strip with its constituent controls drawn flush with no surrounding border. When the mouse pointer is placed over a control, the control appears to pop up from the bar and is drawn with 3D borders. Figure 23-1 displays a ReBar and its parts.

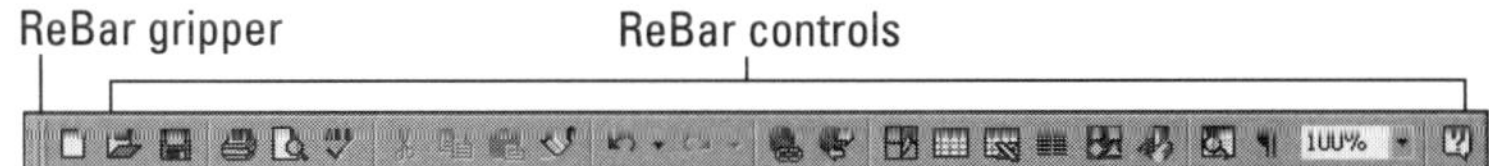

Figure 23-1: This example of a ReBar shows the gripper and the ReBar's controls.

ReBars have one advantage over toolbars. A ReBar can host multiple toolbar strips. The gripper is used to differentiate between toolbar strips on one ReBar. Each continuous line of controls, from gripper to gripper, is one toolbar strip. The user can drag the gripper to dynamically move the toolbar strips. Microsoft has made using ReBars extremely simple.

Adding ReBar Support

Follow these steps to add ReBar support to any MFC application:

1. Add a variable of type `CReBar` to the list of protected variables in `MainFrm.h`. This section of code also contains the variables for the toolbar, `m_wndToolBar`, and the status bar, `m_wndStatusBar`.
2. In `CMainFrame::OnCreate()` after the toolbar has been created and initialized, we must attach the ReBar to its parent window. This is accomplished by calling `CReBar::Create()` and passing in a pointer to the parent window:

   ```
   m_wndReBar.Create(this);
   ```

3. Once the ReBar is attached to the parent window, we need to add the toolbar to the ReBar so the toolbar's controls are displayed on the ReBar. This is conveniently accomplished using the member function `CReBar::AddBar()` and passing the function the address of the toolbar to be added:

   ```
   m_wndReBar.AddBar(&m_wndToolBar);
   ```

✦ ✦ ✦ ✦ ✦

That's it. That's all there is to adding ReBars to your application. Three lines of code and your application is now sporting new and improved toolbars. If you examine the source code for the BarsDemo program used earlier in the chapter, support for ReBars is already included but commented out. Delete the comments, and recompile to see ReBars in action.

Summary

This chapter has covered status bars and toolbars. The creation and initialization process for each object has been explored. Customizing the basic functionality for both status bars and toolbars has also been covered. Advanced topics such as custom status bar panes, docking and floating toolbars, and adding nonbutton controls to toolbars were discussed. By now, you should feel comfortable adding either of these objects to your applications.

✦ ✦ ✦

CHAPTER 24

Tree View and List View Controls

✦ ✦ ✦ ✦

In This Chapter

The basics of managing the CTreeCtrl

Editing CTreeCtrl item labels in place

Handling Enter and Esc while editing CTreeCtrl items

Adding context menus handling to the CTreeCtrl

The basics of managing the CListCtrl

Working with the CImageList

Accessing the header control of a list view control

Dynamically changing the CListCtrl view type

✦ ✦ ✦ ✦

When Windows 95 was finally released into the marketplace, it introduced several new common controls. These controls were packaged in the `COMCTL32.DLL` file and play an integral part in the document-centric interface that all the different flavors of Windows have sported since. Among these common controls are controls designed to provide an easier and more powerful means of displaying and managing lists of data. If you've ever used Windows Explorer to browse your system's namespace (the files, folders, and devices that make up your Windows system), you have seen at least two of these controls: the tree view control and the list view control. While the tree view control is used to display hierarchically structured lists of items, the list view control can display its items in one of four ways (called *views*). These different views include the Large Icon view, Small Icon view, List view, and Details or Report view. Each of these different views will be explained in detail in the section on the list view control.

The tree view control and list view control also use the functionality of other common controls to enhance their appearance and further their own functionality. For example, both the tree view control and the list view control use a common control called the *image list control*. The image list control is used to hold a list of bitmaps or icons. As you work your way through this chapter, you will see how each control uses the image list control to visually represent its respective data items. In addition to the image list control, the list view control also uses another common control: the header control. The header control is a single row of column headings used by the list control to better organize and display the data within the list control. In advanced applications, the header control enables the end user of the application to sort the list view control's data. In some applications, the header control even enables the end user to arrange the columns of data in a list view control by dragging and dropping the different columns to their desired positions.

While the tree view control and list view control have completely different capabilities, they are often used together to provide two different views of an application's data. Windows Explorer (see Figure 24-1) is an example of an application that uses the strengths of both controls to aid in the display of the same data within a single application. In fact, so many developers wanted the capability to mimic Windows Explorer look and feel that Visual C++ modified the AppWizard to contain an option for creating an application with the exact same interface as Windows Explorer. Therefore, this chapter will cover both the tree view and the list view controls and the MFC classes that encapsulate their respective functionality: `CTreeCtrl` and `CListCtrl`.

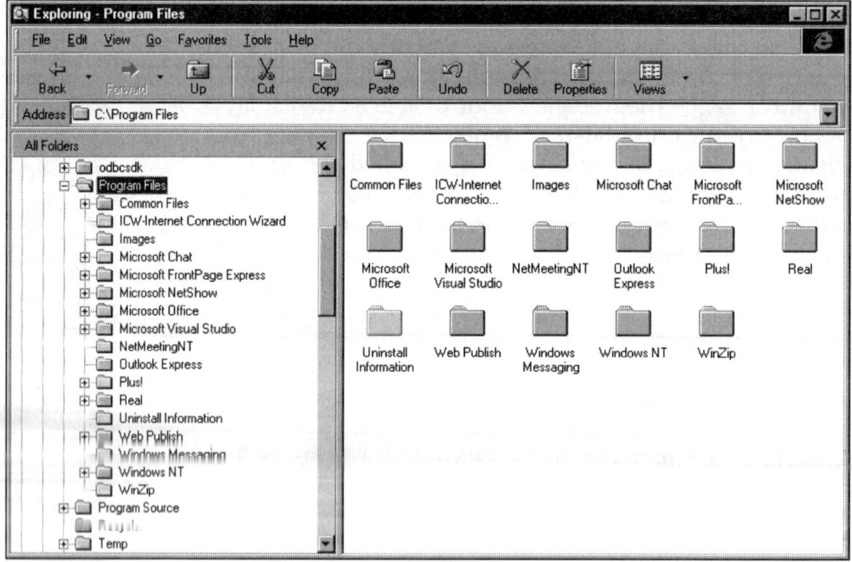

Figure 24-1: Windows Explorer is an example of an application using tree view and list view controls to display different views of the same data.

CTreeCtrl

While the MFC `CTreeCtrl` class is used to encapsulate the functionality of the tree view control, it is only a *very* thin wrapper. In fact, if you look through the MFC source for this class (located in the `winctrl2.cpp` file), you will find that the majority of the `CTreeCtrl` member functions do little above and beyond filling out data structures and sending messages to its underlying tree view control. Therefore, before getting into the `CTreeCtrl` member functions and how to use them, a full understanding of the underlying tree view control is required.

Tree view control basics

The tree view control is used to display data in a hierarchical list. Each item can optionally have a bitmap (or a pair of bitmaps) associated with it. Many applications choose to associate two images with each item. One of these images is used when the item is selected, and the other image is used when the item is not selected. Figure 24-2 shows an example of the typical images used to represent both selected items and unselected items.

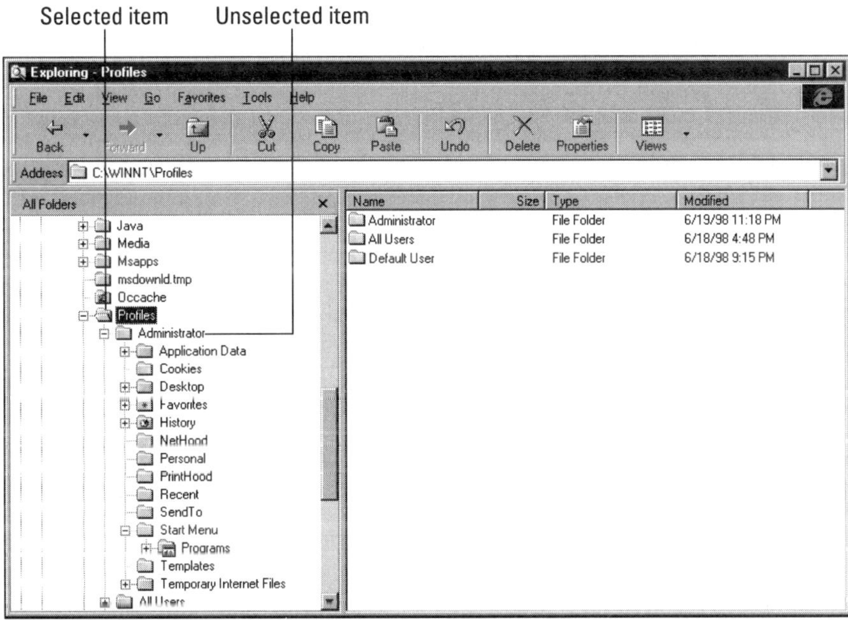

Figure 24-2: The opened folder and closed folder icons are typically used to represent selected and unselected items in a tree view.

You've seen this hierarchical representation of data in other applications besides Windows Explorer, such as Visual Studio (the project dialog bar), Outlook Express (mail and newsgroup folders), and MSDN (groupings of articles and books by subject). While each application's utilization of the tree view control is slightly different, some things are common to all tree views.

The top item in a tree view control's hierarchy is called the *root item*. It is called this because this item has no *parent item*. A parent item is an item that contains other items (called *child items*). Child items (when the parent is expanded) are always displayed indented below their parent item. While a parent item may contain any number of child items, a child item may only have one parent item. Figure 24-3 shows an example of hierarchical data being displayed in a tree view.

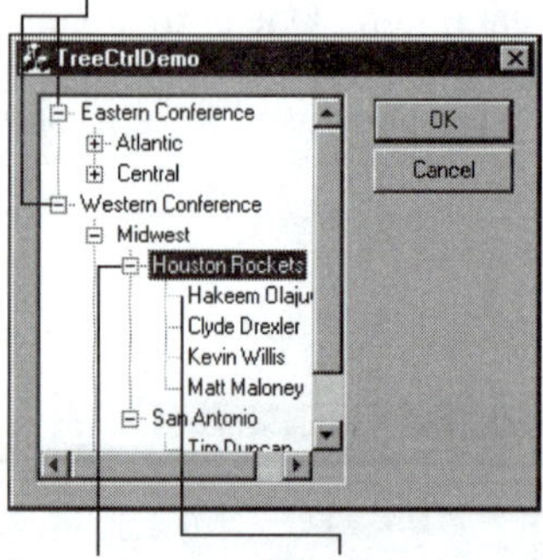

Figure 24-3: The topmost items in a tree view are called root items. Any items that have subitems are referred to as parent items with the subitems being called child items.

As you can see with the NBA team outline in Figure 24-3, the two items without a parent item (Eastern Conference and Western Conference) are root items. In addition, you should also understand that a single item can be a parent item and a child item. For example, the Midwest item is a child item of the Western Conference item. Yet it is also a parent item to the Houston Rockets and San Antonio Spurs items.

Numerous styles are associated with the tree view control. In Figure 24-3, for instance, three styles are turned on that show how the different items in the tree view control are visually related. Each of these styles was set in the resource editor via the tree control's properties dialog. However, the actual style bit constant that would be used if you were to modify these settings in code is in parentheses. These styles will be covered in more detail when the first tree view control demo is introduced.

- ✦ Has buttons (`TVS_HASBUTTONS`)—Displays plus (+) and minus (-) buttons next to parent items.
- ✦ Has lines (`TVS_HASLINES`)—Uses lines to show the hierarchy of items.

✦ Lines at root (TVS_LINESATROOT)—Uses lines to link items at the root of the tree view control.

CTreeCtrl

While the CTreeCtrl is considered to be a very lightweight wrapper for the tree view control, the CTreeCtrl does considerably lessen the amount of programming needed to manage the tree view control. It does this by hiding the idiosyncrasies of how the tree view control must be managed if it were being programmed in an SDK application and exposing much simpler member functions. For example, to simply insert an item into a tree view control, the application must first create and fill out a TV_INSERTSTRUCT structure and then send a TVM_INSERTITEM message to the tree view. In an SDK application, this looks like the following:

```
TVINSERTSTRUCT tvis;
tvis.hParent = hParent;
tvis.hInsertAfter = hInsertAfter;
tvis.item.mask = nMask;
tvis.item.pszText = (LPTSTR) lpszItem;
tvis.item.iImage = nImage;
tvis.item.iSelectedImage = nSelectedImage;
tvis.item.state = nState;
tvis.item.stateMask = nStateMask;
tvis.item.lParam = lParam;
HTREEITEM hNewItem =
 ::SendMessage(m_hWnd, TVM_INSERTITEM,
 0, (LPARAM)&tvis);
```

By contrast, using one of the CTreeCtrl member functions, the code looks like the following:

```
treeControl.InsertItem(_T("My Item"));
```

Therefore, while the CTreeCtrl doesn't add much in terms of functionality to the tree view control, it definitely makes programming the tree view control much less laborious.

Creating CTreeCtrl

Although a CTreeCtrl can be created dynamically by using its Create() member function, the most common means of creating a CTreeCtrl is via the resource editor. To create a CTreeCtrl simply do the following:

1. Drag the iconic representation of a tree view control from the Controls toolbar onto a dialog in the dialog editor.
2. From the ClassWizard Member Variables tab, click the Add Variable button.
3. Type the name of the member variable (for example, m_treeCategories).

4. From the Category combo box, select Control.
5. From the Variable type combo box, select CTreeCtrl.

Now, when you display the dialog, DDX (explained in Chapter 13) subclasses the actual tree view control with the MFC CTreeCtrl class you just added to your dialog class. This means that any calls your application makes to the CTreeCtrl member functions results in messages being sent to the class's underlying tree view control.

Inserting items into a CTreeCtrl

You saw earlier that the CTreeCtrl InsertItem() member function is used to insert items into a tree view control. However, depending on the needs of your application, there are several overloaded versions of the InsertItem() member function.

The one thing that all of the InsertItem() functions have in common is that they return an HTREEITEM. The HTREEITEM is a handle to a tree item and represents the item once it has been inserted into a tree view control. Once an item is inserted into a tree view control, it is always referred to by this HTREEITEM. For example, some of the InsertItem() functions take an HTREEITEM argument called hParent. That means that if the item being added is to be a child item of another item already in the tree view control, the hParent argument must be the HTREEITEM handle that represents that parent item in the tree view control.

```
HTREEITEM InsertItem(LPTVINSERTSTRUCT lpInsertStruct);
```

This function takes as its only argument a pointer to a TV_INSERTSTRUCT structure. This version of the InsertItem() function would normally be called only if the application needed to fill out the majority of the TV_INSERTSTRUCT members.

```
HTREEITEM InsertItem(UINT nMask, LPCTSTR lpszItem,
 int nImage, int nSelectedImage, UINT nState,
 UINT nStateMask, LPARAM lParam,
 HTREEITEM hParent, HTREEITEM hInsertAfter);
```

Like the previous InsertItem() function, this version of the InsertItem() function enables the application to specify every TV_INSERTSTRUCT structure member. The only difference is that instead of having to allocate the memory for the structure and setting each structure member's value, this function enables your application to pass each value as an argument to the function.

```
HTREEITEM InsertItem(LPCTSTR lpszItem,
 HTREEITEM hParent = TVI_ROOT,
 HTREEITEM hInsertAfter = TVI_LAST);
```

This version of the InsertItem() is by far the simplest. Using this function, your application need only supply the text of the item that will be displayed in the tree view. Even the item type defaults to a root item. However, this function does not enable you to specify the images associated with the item. The tree view control shown in Figure 24-3 was created using this version of InsertItem().

```
HTREEITEM InsertItem(LPCTSTR lpszItem, int nImage,
 int nSelectedImage, HTREEITEM hParent = TVI_ROOT,
 HTREEITEM hInsertAfter = TVI_LAST);
```

This version of the InsertItem() is the one that you probably find yourself using the most. That is because it enables you to specify the text of the item, the item's parent, where in the tree view control the item should be placed, and the images that are associated with the item. The nImage and nSelectedImage arguments represent the index. This version of the InsertItem() function will be used in the TreeCtrlDemo demo application presented at the end of this section.

Editing labels

When using Windows Explorer, you have no doubt seen that you can edit the text or label of an item in a tree view control simply by clicking the item after it is selected. Enabling this feature of the tree view control enables you to give the users of your application the capability to change an item's text without you having to provide an entire dialog that contains but a single field for the item's new text. Figure 24-4 shows an example of an item whose text is being edited.

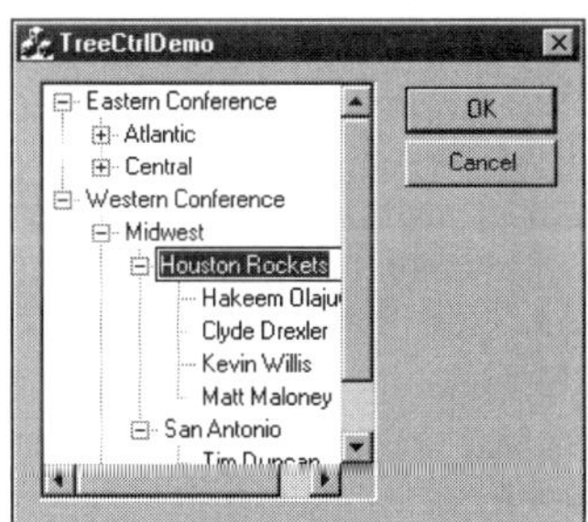

Figure 24-4: The tree view control enables the editing of item labels.

Enabling users to edit a tree view control's item text requires three simple steps:

1. Set the tree view control's TVS_EDITLABELS style.
2. Handle the TVN_BEGINLABELEDIT notification message.
3. Handle the TVN_ENDLABELEDIT notification message.

The TVS_EDITLABELS style can be set in two different ways. The first method is to modify the tree view control's settings from inside the resource editor. Simply display the dialog upon which the tree view control exists, and invoke the properties dialog for the tree view control. Once the properties dialog is displayed, select the Styles tab, and check the Edit labels check box. The second method is to set the tree view's TVS_EDITLABELS style with a call to the Win32 SDK SetWindowLong() function. Here is an example of how to that:

```
// retrieve the current tree control styles
long lStyle =
 ::GetWindowLong(m_treeCategories.GetSafeHwnd(),
 GWL_STYLE);

// turn the edit label style bit on
lStyle |= TVS_EDITLABELS;

// update the tree view styles
::SetWindowLong(m_treeCategories.GetSafeHwnd(),
 GWL_STYLE, lStyle);
```

Once you have set the TVS_EDITLABELS style, you need to handle the TVN_BEGINLABELEDIT notification message. Actually, the handling of this message is not strictly mandatory. However, many applications choose to handle this message to do such things as limit the length of the text that can be entered for the item. The ClassWizard can be used to add a handler for the TVN_BEGINLABELEDIT notification message. Here is an example of one such handler that limits the length of the text entered for the item to 15 characters:

```
void CMyTreeCtrl::OnBeginLabelEdit(NMHDR* pNMHDR,
 LRESULT* pResult)
{
 TV_DISPINFO* pTVDispInfo = (TV_DISPINFO*)pNMHDR;

 *pResult = 1;

 CEdit* pEdit = GetEditControl();
 ASSERT(pEdit);
 if (pEdit)
 {
  GetEditControl()->LimitText(15);
  *pResult = 0;
 }
}
```

The preceding code snippet is simple; however, a couple of important issues should be pointed out. First, all notification messages return void. Therefore, to indicate success or failure, the function must dereference the LRESULT pointer (pResult) and set its value to 1 for failure and 0 for success. This is why in the preceding code snippet, pResult is set to zero only if the function succeeds in setting the edit control's length. The second point to note is the call to the CTreeCtrl member function GetEditControl(). To enable the user to edit the text of an item, the tree view control dynamically creates and displays an edit control. The `GetEditControl()` function is called in order to get the pointer to a `CEdit` object that represents that edit control. That way, `CEdit` member functions can be used to do such things as limiting the text the user can enter.

While it is not necessary to handle the `TVN_BEGINLABELEDIT` notification message, it is mandatory to handle the `TVN_ENDLABELEDIT` notification message. Failing to handle this message results in the user's being able to edit the labels, but at the end of the edit, the value of the label will be set to the previous value. This message handler is where you would place code as to whether the text entered for the item is valid. For example, if your application doesn't allow items with duplicate labels, you must validate that in your handler for the `TVN_ENDLABELEDIT` message. Listing 24-1 shows an example of how a handler might verify that the new text entered by the user does not cause two sibling items to have the same text.

Listing 24-1: Validating Edited Tree View Item Labels

```
void CMyTreeCtrl::OnEndlabeledit(NMHDR* pNMHDR,
 LRESULT* pResult)
{
 TV_DISPINFO* pTVDispInfo = (TV_DISPINFO*)pNMHDR;

 BOOL bFoundDuplicate = FALSE;

 if (pTVDispInfo->item.pszText
 && strlen(pTVDispInfo->item.pszText))
 {
  HTREEITEM hParent =
   GetParentItem(pTVDispInfo->item.hItem);

  HTREEITEM hChild =
   GetChildItem(hParent ? hParent : TVI_ROOT);

  while (NULL != hChild && !bFoundDuplicate)
  {
   if (pTVDispInfo->item.hItem != hChild)
   {
    CString strText = GetItemText(hChild);
    if (0 ==
     strText.CompareNoCase(pTVDispInfo->item.pszText))
    {
     bFoundDuplicate = TRUE;
    }
    else
    {
     hChild = GetNextSiblingItem( hChild );
    }
   }
```

(continued)

Listing 24-1 (continued)

```
      else
      {
       hChild = GetNextSiblingItem( hChild );
      }
    }
  }

  *pResult = (bFoundDuplicate ? 0 : 1);
}
```

If you tried to use the preceding code snippet, you probably discovered that the only way you could finish editing the item's text was to either click somewhere else on the dialog or to switch to another application. This is because MFC was designed so that the parent window of the tree view control gets first crack at the messages through the `PreTranslateMessage` virtual function. If the parent window is a `CDialog` or `FormView` object, the Esc key and Enter key are handled by the parent, and they never reach the tree view control. Therefore, in order to enable the tree view control to process the Esc and Enter keys, you must override the `PreTranslateMessage` function.

Try This 

Handling Enter and Esc While Editing CTreeCtrl Items

These steps assume that you have created a dialog with a tree view control on it and that the dialog's class has a `CTreeCtrl` member variable (named `m_tree`) associated via DDX with that tree view control.

1. Using ClassWizard, create a new class derived from `CTreeCtrl` (for example, `CMyTreeCtrl`).
2. Place an `#include` directive in the dialog's header file before the declaration of the dialog class.
3. Change the `m_tree` type from `CTreeCtrl` to `CMyTreeCtrl`.
4. Using ClassWizard, override the `CMyTreeCtrl PreTranslateMessage` virtual member function so that it looks like the following:

```
BOOL CMyTreeCtrl::PreTranslateMessage(MSG* pMsg)
{
 BOOL bHandledMsg = FALSE;

 switch (pMsg->message)
 {
  case WM_KEYDOWN:
  {
   switch (pMsg->wParam)
   {
```

```
        case VK_ESCAPE:
        case VK_RETURN:
         if (::GetKeyState(VK_CONTROL) & 0x8000)
         {
          break;
         }

         if (GetEditControl())
         {
          ::TranslateMessage(pMsg);
          ::DispatchMessage(pMsg);
          bHandledMsg = TRUE;
         }

        break;

        default: break;
       } // switch (pMsg->wParam)
      } // WM_KEYDOWN
      break;

      default: break;
     } // switch (pMsg->message)

     // continue normal translation and dispatching
     return (bHandledMsg ?
      TRUE : CTreeCtrl::PreTranslateMessage(pMsg));
    }
```

◆ ◆ ◆ ◆ ◆

Context menus

The last thing that will be covered before the chapter's first demo is context menus and how to implement them for a tree view control and its items. With the introduction of Windows 95 and its document-centric interface came context menus. You can see an example of a context menu by clicking the right-mouse button while pointing at a file or folder in Windows Explorer.

Context menus are popular because they help to simplify the user interface. Before context menus, if an application displayed many different types of items (for example, customers, invoices, receipts, and so on), the application typically had a menu item for every action that could be invoked by the user for each of these items. Depending upon which type of item was currently selected by the user, the menu items were then enabled or disabled. However, the problem was that this caused large applications to have huge numbers of menu items that the user needed to wade through to find the desired menu items.

This user interface problem helped to bring about the idea of the context menu. Context menus enable the application to define a menu that pertains solely to the item for which it is defined. That way, only the actions that are global to the entire application need be on the application's menu, while actions that are specific to a given item can be invoked by displaying that item's context menu.

Context menus have become so popular that it's surprising when an application doesn't support context menus. In fact, the use of context menus within applications has become so prevalent that most modern keyboards even have a key that when pressed imitates a right-mouse button click by sending a message (`WM_LBUTTONCLICK`) to the current window.

For example, an application that uses context menus for items in a tree view control is Outlook Express. This popular Microsoft e-mail application has a tree view control that contains all of a user's mail and newsgroup folders. Clicking the right mouse button while pointing at the Inbox folder produces a context menu whose options are specific to the Inbox and are distinct from the context menu options for a newsgroup folder.

Adding a simple context menu entails only two steps. The first step is to create a menu resource that contains the options you want displayed in the menu. You create this menu as you would any other. For example, if you wanted to create a context menu for a customer item in an accounting application, the menu might resemble what you see in Figure 24-5.

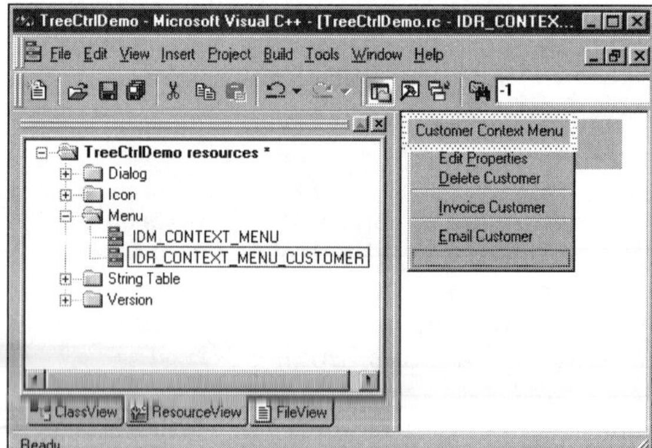

Figure 24-5: Context menus enable the programmer to display a menu that is specific to the currently selected item type.

The second step to implementing a context menu is to provide a handler for the `WM_RBUTTONDOWN` message in the `CTreeCtrl`-derived class. The code example in Listing 24-2 illustrates how to implement the display of a context menu when the right mouse button is clicked on a tree view item.

Listing 24-2: Displaying Context Menus within a Tree View

```
void CMyTreeCtrl::OnRButtonDown(UINT nFlags,
 CPoint point)
{
 // set focus to the tree control
 SetFocus();

 // map the point that is passed to the
 // function from client coordinates
 // to screen coordinates
 ClientToScreen(&point);

 // Get the currently selected item
 HTREEITEM hCurrSel = GetSelectedItem();

 // Figure out which item was right clicked
 CPoint pt(0, 0);
 ::GetCursorPos(&pt);
 ScreenToClient (&pt);
 HTREEITEM hNewSel = HitTest(pt, &nFlags);

 // Set the selection to the item that the
 // mouse was over when the user right
 // clicked
 if (NULL == hNewSel)
 {
  SelectItem(NULL);
 }
 else if (hCurrSel != hNewSel)
 {
  SelectItem(hNewSel);
  SetFocus();
 }

 // Load the context menu
 CMenu Menu;
 if (Menu.LoadMenu(IDM_CONTEXT_MENU))
 {
  CMenu* pSubMenu = Menu.GetSubMenu(0);

  if (pSubMenu!=NULL)
  {
   // Display the context menu
   pSubMenu->TrackPopupMenu(
    TPM_LEFTALIGN | TPM_RIGHTBUTTON,
    point.x, point.y, AfxGetMainWnd());
  }
 }
}
```

The code in Listing 24-2 is simple and displays the same context menu for all items in the tree view control. However, most applications will have different types of items in their tree view control. Therefore, a single context menu wouldn't be appropriate.

CTreeCtrl Demo

This chapter's first demo program will illustrate the points already covered about the tree view control and the `CTreeCtrl` class.

The source code for this demo can found on the CD in the `Chap24\TreeCtrlDemo` folder. To get started, use AppWizard to create a dialog-based application called TreeCtrlDemo.

◆ ◆ ◆ ◆ ◆

Creating the demo dialog

Once you have created the project, change the dialog so that it looks like the dialog in Figure 24-6.

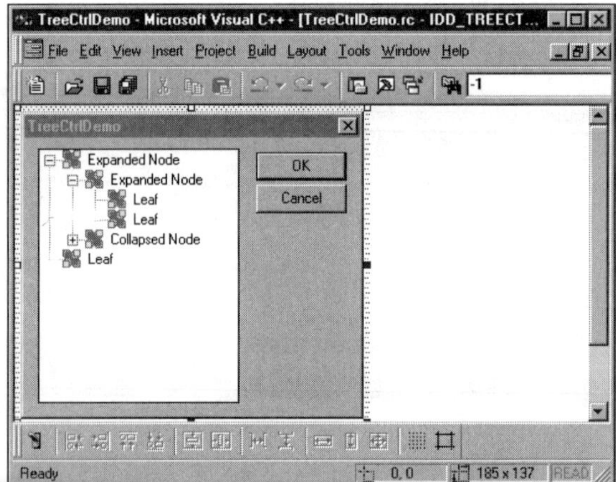

Figure 24-6: After modifying the TreeCtrlDemo dialog, it should look like this.

Once you have added the controls, change the tree view control's styles as follows:

✦ Check the Has buttons style check box.

✦ Check the Has lines style check box.

✦ Check the Lines at root check box.

✦ Check the Edit labels check box.

Using ClassWizard, create a CTreeCtrl member variable called m_tree.

Creating a CTreeCtrl-derived class

Because the user will be right-clicking the tree control view, it is a better object-oriented approach to handle the WM_RBUTTONDOWN message in the tree view control class instead of in the dialog class. Therefore, use ClassWizard to create a CTreeCtrl-derived class called CMyTreeCtrl.

Once ClassWizard has created the header file and implementation files for the CMyTreeCtrl class, place an #include directive for the header file in the dialog class' header file (TreeCtrlDemoDlg.h) before the declaration of the CTreeCtrlDemoDlg class.

```
#include "MyTreeCtrl.h"
```

Now, change the m_tree member variable type to CMyTreeCtrl so that you can start handling the tree view messages in this class.

Adding a second dialog to retrieve the item's text

Because this demo will enable the user to enter the text that will represent the item in the tree view control, you need another dialog. Create a simple dialog (IDD_ADD_ITEM) with a single edit control for the item's text. Once you have added the edit control, use ClassWizard to create a class for the dialog, and call that class CAddItemDlg.

After ClassWizard has created the files for this dialog, create a CString member variable for the edit control called m_strItem, and add an OnOK() handler for the dialog that looks like the following. This handler will ensure that the user enters a valid string when attempting to add strings to the tree view control.

```
void CAddItemDlg::OnOK()
{
 UpdateData(TRUE);
 if (1 > m_strItem.GetLength())
 {
  AfxMessageBox(_T("Sorry, but you need to "
   "specify a valid string before continuing."));
 }
 else
 {
  CDialog::OnOK();
 }
}
```

Adding the context menu

Now that you have a CTreeCtrl-derived class, let's add a menu resource, a WM_RBUTTONDOWN handler to display the context menu and a handler for the different menu options. A simple menu that will enable the user to add tree items will be added. First, create a menu resource called IDM_CONTEXT_MENU, and add an item &Add Item to the menu. Once you have added the menu resource, use ClassWizard to add a message handler to the CMyTreeCtrl class for the WM_RBUTTONDOWN message (see Listing 24-3). Modify it as follows.

Listing 24-3: Implementing the WM_RBUTTONDOWN Handler

```
void CMyTreeCtrl::OnRButtonDown(UINT nFlags,
 CPoint point)
{
 // set focus to the tree control
 SetFocus();

 // map the point that is passed to the
 // function from client coordinates
 // to screen coordinates
 ClientToScreen(&point);

 // Get the currently selected item
 HTREEITEM hCurrSel = GetSelectedItem();

 // Figure out which item was right clicked
 CPoint pt(0, 0);
 ::GetCursorPos(&pt);
 ScreenToClient (&pt);
 HTREEITEM hNewSel = HitTest(pt, &nFlags);

 // Set the selection to the item that the
 // mouse was over when the user right
 // clicked
 if (NULL == hNewSel)
 {
  SelectItem(NULL);
 }
 else if (hCurrSel != hNewSel)
 {
  SelectItem(hNewSel);
  SetFocus();
 }

 // Load the context menu
 CMenu Menu;
 if (Menu.LoadMenu(IDM_CONTEXT_MENU))
 {
  CMenu* pSubMenu = Menu.GetSubMenu(0);
```

```
    if (pSubMenu!=NULL)
    {
     // Display the context menu
     pSubMenu->TrackPopupMenu(
      TPM_LEFTALIGN | TPM_RIGHTBUTTON,
      point.x, point.y, AfxGetMainWnd());
    }
  }
}
```

At this point, clicking the right mouse button while pointing anywhere on the tree item results in the IDM_CONTEXT_MENU being displayed. Now you need to add code to the CMyTreeCtrl class so that something happens when an option is selected from that menu. To do this, use ClassWizard to add a handler to the CTreeCtrl class for the IDD_CONTEXTMENU_ADD message ID, and modify it as follows. Notice that the selected item's HTREEITEM handle is used as the parent of the newly created item. That is done so that the newly created item is always created as the child of the item that was clicked by the user. The call to the SelectItem() function ensures that the newly created item's parent will be expanded and that the new item will be visible.

```
void CMyTreeCtrl::OnContextmenuAdd()
{
 HTREEITEM hitemParent = GetSelectedItem();

 CAddItemDlg dlg;
 if (IDOK == dlg.DoModal())
 {
  HTREEITEM hitem = InsertItem(dlg.m_strItem,
   hitemParent);
  SelectItem(hitem);
 }
}
```

Avoiding duplicate siblings

Now that the user can add items, the demo must ensure that the user doesn't accidentally add duplicate sibling items. To do this, simply modify the OnContextmenuAdd() function as follows:

```
void CMyTreeCtrl::OnContextmenuAdd()
{
 HTREEITEM hitemParent = GetSelectedItem();

 CAddItemDlg dlg;
 if (IDOK == dlg.DoModal())
 {
  if (!DoesItemExist(hitemParent, dlg.m_strItem))
  {
   HTREEITEM hitem = InsertItem(dlg.m_strItem,
```

```
      hitemParent);

    SelectItem(hitem);
   }
  }
 }
```

Next, add the `DoesItemExist()` function as you see in Listing 24-4. This function simply uses the `GetChildItem()` and `GetNextSiblingItem()` `CTreeCtrl` member functions to iterate through the new item siblings to verify if a duplicate entry exists. Notice that the `GetItemText()` function is used to retrieve the text of an item identified by its `HTREEITEM` handle.

Listing 24-4: Adding the DoesItemExist Function

```
BOOL CMyTreeCtrl::DoesItemExist(HTREEITEM hitemParent,
 CString const& strItem)
{
 BOOL bDoesItemExist = FALSE;

 ASSERT(strItem.GetLength());

 HTREEITEM hChild =
 GetChildItem(hitemParent ? hitemParent : TVI_ROOT);

 while (NULL != hChild && !bDoesItemExist)
 {
  CString strText = GetItemText(hChild);
  if (0 == strText.CompareNoCase(strItem))
  {
   bDoesItemExist = TRUE;
  }
  else
  {
   hChild = GetNextSiblingItem( hChild );
  }
 }

 return bDoesItemExist;
}
```

Adding the capability to edit item labels

Now that the user can add items and duplicate items are not allowed, let's add the code necessary to enable the editing of an item's text once it has been added to the tree view control. As you saw earlier in the chapter, this is simple once you know which notification messages to handle. At this point, add a message handler for the

TVN_ENDLABELEDIT notification message to validate that the new item text is not a duplicate. When you are finished, the handler should look like Listing 24-5.

Listing 24-5: Adding a Message Handler for the TVN_ENDLABELEDIT Notification Message

```
void CMyTreeCtrl::OnEndlabeledit(NMHDR* pNMHDR,
 LRESULT* pResult)
{
 TV_DISPINFO* pTVDispInfo = (TV_DISPINFO*)pNMHDR;

 BOOL bValidItem = FALSE;

 CString strItem = pTVDispInfo->item.pszText;
 if (0 < strItem.GetLength())
 {
  HTREEITEM hParent =
   GetParentItem(pTVDispInfo->item.hItem);

  CString strItem = pTVDispInfo->item.pszText;

  bValidItem = !DoesItemExist(hParent, strItem);
 }

 *pResult = bValidItem;
}
```

The last thing you must do is to add the code while editing CTreeCtrl items. Building and testing the demo at this point should produce a simple tree view that enables the display of context menus, editing of item labels, and insertion of items (with validation that duplicate items are not added).

CListCtrl

CListCtrl encapsulates the functionality of the list view control. Like the CTreeCtrl class, CListCtrl serves as a thin wrapper for its underlying Windows common control. Therefore, before getting into the CListCtrl member functions and how to use them, a full understanding of the underlying list view control is required.

List view basics

The list view control is like the list box control in that it is used to display groups of items. However, that is where the similarity ends in terms of functionality. While the standard list box has no means of displaying a column header row, the list view control does. In fact, the column header row seen in the list view control is itself another Windows common control called the *header control*. This handy control is typically used by an application to enable users to sort the list view control's data by clicking the column that the user wants the data sorted by. Because of the header control, list view controls are perfect for displaying multiple columns of data. In addition, the list view control enables its items to be viewed in several different ways: Large Icon view, Small Icon view, List view, and Details or Report view. In the Details view (shown in Figure 24-7), detailed information about each item is displayed. This is as opposed to the other three views where the details of the items cannot be seen.

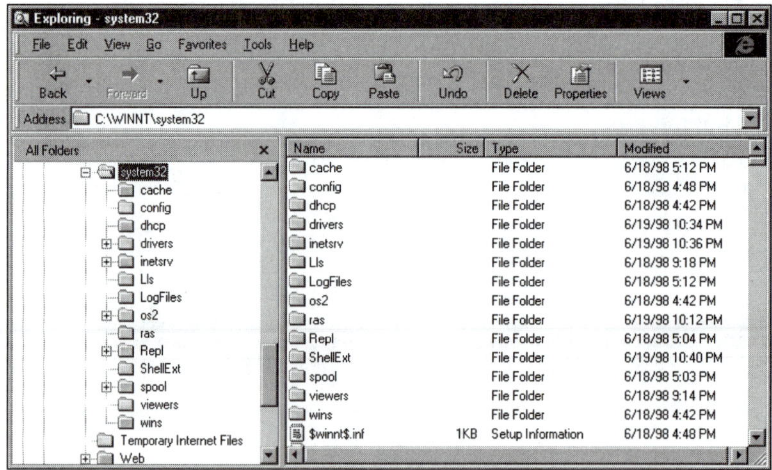

Figure 24-7: Windows Explorer uses the list view to show several different views of the files on your system.

CListCtrl

While `CListCtrl` is definitely a thin wrapper for the list view control, it does considerably lessen the amount of programming required to create and manage the list view control. Like many MFC classes, the `CListCtrl` class accomplishes this by hiding the idiosyncrasies of how the list view control must be managed if it were being programmed in an SDK application by exposing much simpler member functions. For example, to simply insert an item into a list view control, the application must first create and fill out a `LV_ITEM` structure and then send a `LVM_INSERTITEM` message to the list view control. To give you an idea of the difference, here's what inserting an item into a list view control via SDK calls looks like:

```
LV_ITEM item;
item.mask = nMask;
item.iItem = nItem;
item.iSubItem = 0;
```

```
    item.pszText = (LPTSTR)lpszItem;
    item.state = nState;
    item.stateMask = nStateMask;
    item.iImage = nImage;
    item.lParam = lParam;
    int iIndex = ::SendMessage(m_hWnd, LVM_INSERTITEM,
   0, (LPARAM)pItem);
```

Now, let's take a look at how to insert an item into a list view control using the CListCtrl class. The following line of code inserts an item with the text value of "Test" into the first row of the list view control:

```
    listCtrl.InsertItem(0, _T("Test"));
```

Therefore, while CListCtrl doesn't add much in terms of functionality to the list view control, it definitely makes programming the list view control much easier.

Create a CListCtrl

Like any CWnd-derived class, a CListCtrl can be created dynamically via its Create() member function. However, the most common method used to create a CListCtrl is with the resource editor. To create a CListCtrl on a dialog simply follow these steps:

1. Drag the iconic representation of a list view control from the Controls toolbar onto a dialog in the dialog editor.
2. Set the View style to the desired view type (Icon, Small icon, List, or Report). You can also set this style programmatically. You will see how to do this shortly.
3. From the ClassWizard Member Variables tab, click the Add Variable button.
4. Type the name of the member variable (for example, m_listCtrl).
5. From the Category combo box, select Control.
6. From the Variable type combo box, select CListCtrl.

Now, when you display the dialog, DDX (explained in Chapter 13) will subclass the actual list view control with the MFC CListCtrl class you just added to your dialog class. This means that any calls your application makes to the CListCtrl member functions result in messages being sent to the class' underlying list view control.

Setting the list view control's image list

If you want your list view control items to have images, you must create and associate an image list control with the list view control.

Creating a CImageList Object and Associating It with a CListCtrl

Follow these steps to create a `CImageList` object and associate it with a `CListCtrl`:

1. Create two bitmap resources. These bitmaps are handled much as the toolbar bitmap resources where the bitmap actually contains one to many images that are referred to in code by their index values. Of these two bitmap resources, one of these bitmaps is used for the Large Icon view, and the other is used for the Small Icon view.
2. Declare two `CImageList` member variables in the dialog's class. Once again, one image list is for the Large Icon view, and the other is for the Small Icon view.
3. After the list view control has been initialized (usually in the `OnInitDialog()` function), call the `CImageList::Create()` member function of each `CImageList` object in order create the image list controls. When calling the `Create()` member function, you simply specify the bitmap resource and the size of each image in the bitmap resource.
4. Call the `CListCtrl::SetImageList()` member function in order to associate the image list objects with the list view control. The first argument of the `SetImageList()` function enables you to specify the image list, while the second argument is used to specify which image list is being set (`LVSIL_SMALL` or `LVSIL_NORMAL`).

♦ ♦ ♦ ♦ ♦

The following code snippet assumes that you created two bitmap resources named `IDB_LARGE_IMAGES` and `IDB_SMALL_IMAGES`. It also assumes that each image is 17 dialog units wide. Obviously, in a "real" application, the images for the `IDB_LARGE_IMAGES` bitmap resource would be larger than the images in the `IDB_SMALL_IMAGE` bitmap resource. With those assumptions and information in mind, here is an example of how to create and associate the image list objects with a list view control:

```
// large icon image list
m_imageListLargeIcons.Create(IDB_LARGE_IMAGES,
 17, 1, RGB(255,255,255));
m_listCtrl.SetImageList(&m_imageListLargeIcons,
 LVSIL_NORMAL);

// small icon image list
m_imageListSmallIcons.Create(IDB_SMALL_IMAGES,
 17, 1, RGB(255,255,255));
m_listCtrl.SetImageList(&m_imageListSmallIcons,
 LVSIL_SMALL);
```

Setting and changing the view style

There are three different ways to set the View style depending on the application's needs. If the list view control is always going to have the same View style, the View style can be set in the resource editor via the list view control's property dialog. However, if the list view control's View style needs to be changed at runtime, then the CWnd::ModifyStyle() can be used as follows (where uiDesiredStyle is LVS_ICON, LVS_SMALLICON, LVS_LIST, or LVS_REPORT):

```
ModifyStyle(LVS_TYPEMASK, uiDesiredStyle);
```

Adding columns to a CListCtrl

Before you can add rows to the list view control, you must define the columns that the list view will display. This is accomplished via the InsertColumn() member function. There are two overloaded versions of the InsertColumn() function.

```
int InsertColumn(int nCol, LPCTSTR lpszColumnHeading,
 int nFormat = LVCFMT_LEFT, int nWidth = -1,
 int nSubItem =  1);
int InsertColumn(int nCol, const LV_COLUMN* pColumn);
```

To illustrate the differences between the two overloaded versions of the InsertColumn() function, let's see what it takes to insert the following columns into a list view control:

```
static struct
{
 LPTSTR szColText;
 UINT uiFormat;
} columns[] = {
 _T("Col 1"), LVCFMT_LEFT,
 _T("Col 2"), LVCFMT_CENTER,
 _T("Col 3"), LVCFMT_RIGHT
};
```

The first InsertColumn() function takes as its arguments the column number (relative to zero) and a pointer to a filled out LV_COLUMN structure. Here is an example of inserting three different columns using that function. Notice that each column's text is justified differently. Also, notice how much work is needed to simply insert a column into a list view control. That is because this version of the InsertColumn() function is almost like using the Win32 SDK to insert a column into the list view control. In fact, this version of the InsertColumn() function does nothing except send the address of the passed structure to the list view via a message.

```
for (int i = 0;
 i < sizeof columns / sizeof columns [0];
 i++)
{
 LV_COLUMN lvc;
```

```
  ::ZeroMemory(&lvc, sizeof lvc);
  lvc.pszText = (LPTSTR)columns[i].szColText;

  lvc.mask = LVCF_TEXT | LVCF_FMT;
  lvc.fmt = columns[i].uiFormat;

  CClientDC dc(this);
  CSize size = dc.GetTextExtent(lvc.pszText);
  lvc.cx = size.cx;

  m_listCtrl.InsertColumn(i, &lvc);
 }
```

The second `InsertColumn()` function is definitely much better in terms of doing more for you. With this version, most of the `LV_ITEM` structure members default to a reasonable value. Here is how this `InsertColumn()` would look with the same set of three columns:

```
for (int i = 0;
 i < sizeof columns / sizeof columns [0];
 i++)
{
 m_listCtrl.InsertColumn(i,
  columns[i].szColText, columns[i].uiFormat);
}
```

Obviously, the only reason that you would want to use the first version of the `InsertColumn()` is if the application needed to specify one of the `LV_ITEM` members that is not in the argument list of the second `InsertColumn()` function (for example, `mask`).

Sizing the columns

Once the columns have been added, they must be sized. The code snippet shown in Listing 24-6 illustrates how to size the columns so that each column's text can be viewed. Notice that the header control is retrieved via the `GetDlgItem()` function.

Listing 24-6: Resizing List View Columns

```
CHeaderCtrl* pHeader =
 (CHeaderCtrl*)m_listCtrl.GetDlgItem(0);
ASSERT(pHeader);
if (pHeader)
{
 // turn off redraw until the columns have all
 // been resized
 m_listCtrl.SetRedraw(FALSE);

 // get the nbr of columns
 int iNbrOfColumns = pHeader->GetItemCount();
```

```
int iNbrOfCols = GetColumnCount();
for (int iCurrCol = 0;
 iCurrCol < iNbrOfCols;
 iCurrCol++)
{
 m_listCtrl.SetColumnWidth(iCurrCol,
  LVSCW_AUTOSIZE);

 int nCurrWidth =
  m_listCtrl.GetColumnWidth(iCurrCol);

 m_listCtrl.SetColumnWidth(iCurrCol,
  LVSCW_AUTOSIZE_USEHEADER);

 int nColHdrWidth =
  m_listCtrl.GetColumnWidth(iCurrCol);

 m_listCtrl.SetColumnWidth(iCurrCol,
  max(nCurrWidth, nColHdrWidth));
}

// now that col sizing is finished,
// invalidate so that the control is repainted
m_listCtrl.SetRedraw(TRUE);
m_listCtrl.Invalidate();
}
```

Inserting items into a CListCtrl

As you saw earlier, the `InsertItem()` member function is used to insert items into a list view control. However, depending on the needs of your application, there are several overloaded versions of the `InsertItem()` member function:

```
int InsertItem(const LVITEM* pItem);
int InsertItem(int nItem, LPCTSTR lpszItem),
int InsertItem(int nItem, LPCTSTR lpszItem,
  int nImage);
```

The one thing that all of the functions have in common is that they return an `int` that represents the new items index (relative to zero) in the list view control. Once an item is inserted into a list view control, it is always referred to by this index.

While the `InsertItem()` inserts an item into the list view control, it only enables you to specify the first column's text. To specify the text for the other columns, you must use the `SetItemText()` member function.

```
BOOL SetItemText(int nItem, int nSubItem,
  LPCTSTR lpszText);
```

The first argument (`nItem`) in the `SetItemText()` member function represents the index of a list view control's item (returned from the `InsertItem()` function). The second and third arguments are used to specify the column number (relative to zero) and the text value to insert into that column. An example (using the three columns defined previously) of how to insert a couple of rows into a list view control can be seen in Listing 24-7.

Listing 24-7: Inserting Data into a List View Static Struct

```
{
 LPTSTR szCol1;
 LPTSTR szCol2;
 LPTSTR szCol3;
} rows [] = {
 "A1", "A2", "A3",
 "B1", "B2", "B3",
 "C1", "C2", "C3"
};

for (int iCurrRow = 0;
 iCurrRow < sizeof rows / sizeof rows[0];
 iCurrRow++)
{
 m_listCtrl.InsertItem(iCurrRow,
  rows[iCurrRow].szCol1, 0);

 m_listCtrl.SetItemText(iCurrRow, 1,
  rows[iCurrRow].szCol2);

 m_listCtrl.SetItemText(iCurrRow, 2,
  rows[iCurrRow].szCol3);
}
```

Summary

Ever since their inception, the tree view control and list view control have had a reputation as being complex and difficult to program. It is true that the developer does have to do more to make these controls work, especially when compared to working with other controls such as the edit control or combo box. However, while a list control view may be more complex to work with than a list box, the list view control also affords the developer infinitely more capabilities than a list box. Therefore, the trade-off in work required on the programmer's part to manage these controls is definitely made worthwhile in terms of the added user interface benefits these controls add to your application.

✦ ✦ ✦

CHAPTER 25

Threads

◆ ◆ ◆ ◆

In This Chapter

Threads

Understanding difficulties of programming with threads

Starting, using, and stopping threads

Sharing MFC objects among threads

Using C runtime functions in multithreaded applications

A demo program that uses threads

◆ ◆ ◆ ◆

In the Win32 environment, each running application constitutes a process and each process consists of one or more threads of execution. A *thread* is a path of execution through a process' code. One fundamental difference between 16- and 32-bit Windows is that 32-bit Windows doesn't limit its applications to just one thread each. A process in a 32-bit Windows application begins its life as a single thread, but that thread can spawn additional threads. A preemptive scheduler inside the operating system divides CPU time among active threads so that they appear to run simultaneously. Secondary threads are ideal for performing background tasks such as paginating documents and performing garbage collection. They can also play more visible roles by creating windows and processing messages to those windows, just as the primary thread processes messages sent to an application's main window.

Multithreading is not for everyone. Multithreaded applications are difficult to write and debug because the parallelism of the concurrently running threads adds an extra layer of complexity to the code. But used properly, multiple threads can dramatically improve an application's responsiveness. A word processor that does its spell checking in a dedicated thread, for example, can continue to process input in the primary thread so that the user doesn't have to wait for the spell checker to finish. What makes writing a threaded spell checker difficult is that the spell checking thread invariably has to synchronize its actions with other threads in the application.

Most programmers have been conditioned to think about their code in synchronous terms — function A calls function B, function B initializes variable C and returns to A, and so on. But threads are asynchronous by nature in a multithreaded application; you have to think about what happens if, say, two threads call function B at the same time or one thread reads a variable while another writes it. If function A launches function B in a separate thread, you also must anticipate what problems could occur if function A continues to run while function B executes. For example, it's common to pass the address of a variable created on the stack in function A to function B for processing. But if function B is in another thread, the variable may no longer exist when function B gets around to accessing it. Even the most innocent-looking code can be fatally flawed when it involves the use of multiple threads.

MFC encapsulates threads of execution in the `CWinThread` class. It also includes synchronization classes encapsulating events, mutexes, and other thread synchronization objects found in the Windows kernel. Does MFC make multithreading easier? Not exactly. Developers who have written multithreaded Windows applications in C are often surprised to learn that MFC adds complexities all its own. The key to writing multithreaded programs in MFC is having a keen understanding of what you're doing and knowing where the trouble spots are. This chapter is designed to help you do both.

Threads

As far as Windows is concerned, all threads are alike. MFC, however, distinguishes between two types of threads: user interface (UI) threads and worker threads. The difference between the two is that UI threads have message loops and worker threads do not. UI threads can create windows and process messages sent to those windows. Worker threads perform background tasks that receive no direct input from the user and therefore don't need windows and message loops.

When you open a folder in the Windows shell, the shell launches a UI thread that creates a window showing the folder's contents. If you drag-copy a group of files to the newly opened folder, that folder's thread performs the file transfers. (Sometimes the UI thread creates yet another thread — this time a worker thread — to copy the files.) The benefit of this multithreaded architecture is that once the copy operation has begun, you can switch to windows opened onto other folders and continue working while the files are copied in the background. Launching a UI thread that creates a window is conceptually similar to launching an application within an application. The most common use for UI threads is to create multiple windows serviced by separate threads of execution.

Worker threads are ideal for performing isolated tasks that can be broken off from the rest of the application and performed in the background while other processing takes place in the foreground. A classic example of a worker thread is the thread an animation control uses to play AVI clips. Basically all the thread does is draw a frame, put itself to sleep for a fraction of a second, wake up, and start again. It adds little to the processor's workload because it spends most of its life suspended between frames, and yet it also provides a valuable service. This is a great example of multithreaded design because the background thread is given a specific task to do and then allowed to perform that task over and over until the primary thread signals that it's time to end.

Creating a worker thread

There are two ways to create a thread in an MFC application. You can construct a `CWinThread` object and call that object's `CreateThread()` function to create the thread, or you can use `AfxBeginThread()` to construct a `CWinThread` object and create a thread in one step. MFC defines two different versions of `AfxBeginThread()`: one for UI threads and another for worker threads. Don't use the Win32 `::CreateThread()` function to create a thread in an MFC program unless the thread doesn't use MFC. `AfxBeginThread()` and `CWinThread::CreateThread()` aren't merely wrappers around `::CreateThread()`; in addition to launching threads of execution, they also initialize internal variables used by the framework, perform sanity checks at various points during the thread creation process, and take steps to ensure that functions in the C runtime library are accessed in a thread-safe way.

`AfxBeginThread()` makes it simple — almost trivial, in fact — to create a worker thread. The following statement starts a worker thread and passes it the address of an application-defined data structure named `ThreadInfo` that contains input to the thread:

```
CWinThread *pThread = AfxBeginThread( ThreadFunc,
  &ThreadInfo );
```

`ThreadFunc` is the thread function — the function that gets executed when the thread itself begins to execute. A very simple thread function that spins in a loop, eating CPU cycles, and then terminates looks like this:

```
UINT ThreadFunc( LPVOID pParam )
{
  UINT nIterations = (UINT) pParam;
  for( UINT i=0; i<nIterations; i++ )
    return( 0 );
}
```

We'll look at thread functions in more detail in the next section. The worker thread form of `AfxBeginThread()` accepts as many as four additional parameters that specify the thread's priority, stack size, creation flags, and security attributes. The complete function prototype follows:

```
CWinThread *AfxBeginThread( AFX_THREADPROC pfnThreadPro,
  LPVOID pParam, int nPriority = THREAD_PRIORITY_NORMAL,
  UINT nStackSize = 0, DWORD dwCreateFlags = 0,
  LPSECUTIRY_ATTRIBUTES lpSecutiryAttrs = NULL );
```

The `nPriority` parameter specifies the thread's execution priority. High priority threads are always scheduled for CPU time before low priority threads, but in practice even threads with extremely low priorities usually get all the processor time they need. The `nPriority` parameter doesn't specify an absolute priority level. It specifies a priority level relative to the priority level of the process to which the thread belongs. The default is `THREAD_PRIORITY_NORMAL`, which assigns the thread the same priority as the process that owns it. Other priority values are covered later in the chapter. A thread's priority level can be changed at any time with `CWinThread::SetThreadPriority()`.

The `nStackSize` parameter passed to `AfxBeginThread()` specifies the thread's maximum stack size. In the Win32 environment, each thread receives its own stack. The 0 default `nStackSize` value allows the stack to grow as large as 1MB. This doesn't mean that every thread receives a minimum of 1MB of memory; it means that each thread is assigned 1MB of address space in the larger 4GB address space in which 32-bit Windows applications execute. Memory isn't committed (assigned) to the stack's address space until it's needed, so most thread stacks never use more than a few kilobytes of physical memory. Placing a limit on the stack size allows the operating system to trap runaway functions that recurse endlessly and eventually consume the stack. The default limit of 1MB is fine for almost all applications.

The `dwCreateFlags` parameter can be one of two values. The default value 0 tells the system to start executing the thread immediately. If `CREATE_SUSPENDED` is specified instead, the thread starts out in a suspended state and doesn't begin running until another thread (usually the thread that created it) calls `CWinThread::ResumeThread()` on the suspended thread, as demonstrated here:

```
CWinThread *pThread = AfxBeginThread( ThreadFunc,
  &ThreadInfo, THREAD_PRIORITY_NORMAL, 0,
  CREATE_SUSPENDED );
```

Sometimes it's useful to create a thread but defer its execution until later. As you'll see later, it's also possible to create a thread that suspends itself until a specified event occurs.

The final parameter in the `AfxBeginThread()` argument list, `lpSecurityAttrs`, is a pointer to a `SECURITY_ATTRIBUTES` structure that specifies the new thread's security attributes and also tells the system whether child processes should inherit the thread handle. The `NULL` default value assigns the new thread the same properties the thread that created it has.

The thread function

A worker thread's thread function can be a static class member function or a function declared outside a class. It is prototyped this way:

```
UINT ThreadFunc ( LPVOID pParam );
```

The `pParam` argument is a 32-bit value whose value equals the `pParam` passed to `AfxBeginThread()`. Very often `pParam` is the address of an application-defined data structure containing information passed to the worker thread by the thread that created it. It can also be a scalar value, a handle, or even a pointer to an MFC object. It's perfectly legal to use the same thread function for two or more threads, but you should be sensitive to reentrancy problems caused by global and static variables. As long as the variables (and objects) a thread uses are created on the stack, no reentrancy problems occur because each thread gets its own stack.

Creating a user interface thread

Creating a UI thread is an altogether different process than creating a worker thread. A worker thread is defined by its thread function, but a UI thread's behavior is governed by a dynamically createable class derived from CWinThread that very much resembles an application class derived from CWinApp. The UI thread class shown in the following code sample creates a top-level frame window that closes itself when clicked with the left mouse button. Closing the window terminates the thread, too, because CWnd::OnNcDestroy() posts a WM_QUIT message to the thread's message queue. Posting a WM_QUIT message to a secondary thread ends the thread. Posting a WM_QUIT message to a primary thread ends the thread and ends the application, too.

```
// The CUIThread class
class CUIThread : public CWinThread
{

  DECLARE_DYNCREATE( CUIThread )

public:
  virtual BOOL InitInstance();

};

IMPLEMENT_DYNCREATE( CUIThread, CWinThread );

BOOL CUIThread::InitInstance()
{
  m_pMainWnd = new CMainWindow();
  m_pMainWnd->ShowWindow( SW_SHOW );
  m_pMainWnd->UpdateWindow();

  return( TRUE );

}

// The CmainWindow class
class CMainWindow : public CFrameWnd
{

public:
  CMainWindow();

protected:
  afx_msg void OnLButtonDown( UINT, CPoint );
  DECLARE_MESSAGE_MAP()

};

BEGIN_MESSAGE_MAP( CMainWindow, CFrameWnd )
  ON_WM_LBUTTONDOWN()
END_MESSAGE_MAP()
```

```
CMainWindow::CMainWindow()
{
  Create( NULL, "UI Thread Window" );
}

void CMainWindow::OnLButtonDown( UINT nFlags,
  CPoint Point )
{

  PostMessage( WM_CLOSE, 0, 0 );

}
```

Note the SW_SHOW parameter passed to ShowWindow() in place of the normal m_nCmdShow parameter. m_nCmdShow is a CWinApp data member, so when you create a top-level window from a UI thread, it's up to you to specify the window's initial show state.

A CUIThread is launched by calling the form of AfxBeginThread() that accepts a CRuntimeClass pointer to the thread class as follows:

```
CWinThread *pThread =
  AfxBeginThread( RUNTIME_CLASS ( CUIThread ) );
```

The UI thread version of AfxBeginThread() accepts the same four optional parameters as the worker thread version, but it doesn't accept a pParam value. Once started, a UI thread runs asynchronously with respect to the thread that created it, almost as if it belonged to another application.

Suspending and resuming threads

A running thread can be suspended with CWinThread::SuspendThread() and started again with CWinThread::ResumeThread(). A thread can call SuspendThread() on itself, or another thread can call SuspendThread() for it. However, a suspended thread can't call ResumeThread() to wake itself up; someone else must call ResumeThread() on its behalf. A suspended thread consumes next to no processor time and imposes essentially zero overhead on the system.

For each thread, Windows maintains a suspend count that's incremented by SuspendThread() and decremented by ResumeThread(). A thread is scheduled for processor time only when its suspend count is 0. If SuspendThread() is called twice in succession, ResumeThread() must be called twice also. A thread created without a CREATE_SUSPENDED flag is assigned an initial suspend count of 0. A thread created with a CREATE_SUSPENDED flag begins with a suspend count of 1. Both SuspendThread() and ResumeThread() return the thread's previous suspend count, so you can make sure a thread gets resumed no matter how high its suspend count is by calling ResumeThread() repeatedly until it returns 1. ResumeThread() returns 0 if the thread it's called on is not currently suspended.

Putting threads to sleep

A thread can put itself to sleep by calling the API function `::Sleep()`. A sleeping thread uses no processor time and is automatically awakened after a specified number of milliseconds. The following statement suspends the current thread for ten seconds:

```
::Sleep( 10000 );
```

One use for `::Sleep()` is for implementing threads whose actions are inherently time-based, such as the background thread in an animation control or a thread that moves the hands of a clock. Another use for `::Sleep()` is for relinquishing the remainder of a thread's timeslice to other threads waiting to execute. The following statement suspends the current thread and allows the scheduler to run other threads of equal priority:

```
::Sleep( 0 );
```

If no other equal priority threads are awaiting execution time, the function call returns immediately, and the scheduler resumes executing the current thread. If you write an application that uses multiple threads to draw to a display surface, a few strategically placed `::Sleep( 0 )` statements can do wonders for the quality of the output.

Terminating a thread

Once a thread begins, it can terminate in two ways. A worker thread ends when the thread function executes a return statement or calls `AfxEndThread()`. A UI thread terminates when a `WM_QUIT` message is posted to its message queue or a function within the thread calls `AfxEndThread()`. A thread can post a `WM_QUIT` message to itself with the API function `::PostQuitMessage()`. `AfxEndThread()`, `::PostQuitMessage()`, and return all accept a 32-bit exit code that can be retrieved with `::GetExitCodeThread()` after the thread has terminated. The statement that follows copies the exit code of the thread referenced by `pThread` to the `DWORD` variable `dwExitCode`:

```
DWORD dwExitCode;
::GetExitCodeThread( pThread->m_hThread, &dwExitCode );
```

If called for a thread that's still executing, `::GetExitCodeThread()` sets `dwExitCode` equal to `STILL_ACTIVE` (0x103).

Thread Handles

One complication in calling `::GetExitCode()` in an MFC application is that by default a `CWinThread` object automatically deletes itself when the corresponding thread terminates. Therefore, a `::GetExitCodeThread()` statement such as the one in the preceding code sample will probably generate an access violation if the thread has terminated because `pThread` will no longer be valid. You can avoid such problems by setting the thread object's m_bAutoDelete data member to FALSE so that the CWinThread object won't be deleted automatically upon thread termination. (Don't forget to delete the CWinThread object yourself to avoid memory leaks.)

An alternative approach is to save the thread handle stored in the CWinThread object's m_hThread data member and pass it to ::GetExitCodeThread() directly. Thread handles passed to ::GetExitCodeThread() can identify existing threads or threads that once existed but have since terminated.

✦ ✦ ✦ ✦ ✦

Terminating a thread from another thread

Generally speaking, threads can terminate only themselves. If you want thread A to terminate thread B, you must set up a signaling mechanism that allows thread A to tell thread B to terminate itself. In most cases, a simple variable can serve as a flag that signals a thread to terminate, as demonstrated here:

```
// Thread A
static BOOL bContinue = TRUE;

CWinThread *pThread =
  AfxBeginThread( ThreadFunc, bContinue );

// Do some work

// Tell thread B to terminate
bContinue = FALSE;

// Thread B
UINT ThreadFunc( LPVOID pParam )
{
  BOOL *pContinue = (BOOL*) pParam;

  while( *pContinue ){
    // Do some work
    }

  return( 0 );

}
```

Conventional wisdom says that this is a poor way for threads to communicate, but in fact it's just as effective as using a thread synchronization object. Of course, to prevent access violations, you need to ensure that bContinue doesn't go out of scope while thread B is running. That's why bContinue is declared static in the example. Even if the function that sets bContinue to FALSE in thread A returns before thread B terminates, the variable will still be valid because it's located in the application's datasegment, not on the stack.

Now suppose that you'd like to modify this example so that once it sets bContinue to FALSE, thread A stops what it's doing until thread B is no longer running. Here's the proper way to do it:

```
// Thread A
static BOOL bContinue = TRUE;
CWinThread *pThread =
  AfxBeginThread( ThreadFunc, &bContinue );

// Do some work

// Save the thread handle
HANDLE hThread = pThread->m_hThread;

// Tell thread B to terminate
bContinue = FALSE;

::WaitForSingleObject( hThread, INFINITE );


// Thread B
UINT ThreadFunc( LPVOID pParam )
{
  BOOL *pContinue = (BOOL *) pParam;
  while( *pContinue ){
    // Do some work
    }
  return( 0 );
}
```

::WaitForSingleObject() waits until the specified object — in this case, another thread — enters a signaled state. A thread object goes from nonsignaled to signaled when the thread terminates. The first parameter passed to ::WaitForSingleObject() is the handle of the object you want to wait on. (It can also be a process handle, the handle of a synchronization object, or a file-change notification handle, among other things.) The handle is retrieved from the CWinThread object before bContinue is set to FALSE because the CWinThread object may no longer exist when the call to ::WaitForSingleObject() is executed.

The second parameter is the length of time the thread that calls ::WaitForSingleObject() is willing to wait. INFINITE means wait as long as it takes. When you specify INFINITE, you take the chance that the calling thread could lock up if the object it's waiting on never becomes signaled. If you specify a number of milliseconds instead, as in

```
::WaitForSingleObject( hThread, 5000 ), WaitForSingleObject()
```

returns after the specified time — here 5 seconds — has elapsed even if the object still hasn't become signaled. You can check the return value to determine why the function returned. WAIT_OBJECT_0 means that the object became signaled, and WAIT_TIMEOUT means that it did not.

Given a thread handle or a CWinThread object wrapping a thread handle, you can quickly determine whether the thread is still running by calling ::WaitForSingleObject() and specifying 0 for the timeout period, as shown here:

```
if( ::WaitForSingleObject( hThread, 0 ) ==WAIT_OBJECT_0 )
  // The thread no longer exists
else
  // The thread still exists
```

Called this way, ::WaitForSingleObject() doesn't wait; it returns immediately. A return value equal to WAIT_OBJECT_0 means that the thread is signaled (no longer exists), and a return value equal to WAIT_TIMEOUT means that the thread is nonsignaled (still exists). Remember, because a CWinThread object is automatically deleted when a thread terminates, it doesn't make sense to call ::WaitForSingleObject() to find out whether a CWinThread is signaled or nonsignaled unless the CWinThread object's m_bAutoDelete data member is set to FALSE. Don't make the mistake of waiting for a thread to terminate by writing code like this:

```
// Thread A (don't do this!)

static BOOL bContinue = TRUE;

CWinThread *pThread =
  AfxBeginThread( ThreadFunc, bContinue );

// Do some work
HANDLE hThread = pThread->m_hThread;

// Save the thread handle
bContinue = FALSE;

// Tell thread B to terminate
DWORD dwExitCode;
do{
  ::GetExitCodeThread( hThread, &dwExitCode );
   } while( dwExitCode == STILL_ACTIVE );

// Thread B
UINT ThreadFunc( LPVOID pParam )
{
  BOOL *pContinue = (BOOL*) pParam;

  while( *pContinue ){
    // Do some work
    }

  return( 0 );

}
```

In addition to spending CPU time needlessly by forcing the primary thread to spin in a `do-while` loop, this code will probably cause the application to lock up. When a thread calls `::WaitForSingleObject()`, it waits very efficiently because it is effectively suspended until the function call returns. The thread is said "to be blocked" or "to block" until `::WaitForSingleObject()` returns.

A thread can kill another directly, but you should use this method only as a last resort. The statement `::TerminateThread( pThread->m_hThread, 0 );` terminates `pThread` and assigns it an exit code of 0. The Win32 API Reference documents some of the many problems `::TerminateThread()` can cause, which range from orphaned thread synchronization objects to DLLs that don't get a chance to execute normal thread-shutdown code.

Threads, processes, and priorities

The scheduler is the component of the operating system that decides which threads run when and for how long. Thread scheduling is a complex task whose goal is to divide CPU time among multiple threads of execution as efficiently as possible to create the illusion that all of them are running at once. On machines with multiple CPUs, Windows NT really does run two or more threads at the same time by assigning different threads to different processors. This feature is known as *symmetric multiprocessing*, or SMP. Windows 98 is not an SMP system, so it schedules all of its threads on the same CPU even if several CPUs are present.

The Windows 98 scheduler uses a variety of techniques to improve multitasking performance and to try to ensure that each thread in the system gets an ample amount of CPU time, but ultimately the decision about which thread should execute next boils down to the thread with the highest priority. At any given moment, each thread is assigned a priority level from 0 through 31, with higher numbers indicating higher priorities. If a priority-16 thread is waiting to execute and all of the other threads vying for CPU time have priority levels of 15 or less, the priority-16 thread gets scheduled next. If two priority-16 threads are waiting to execute, the scheduler executes the one that has executed the least recently. When that thread's timeslice is up, the other priority-16 thread gets executed if all of the other threads still have lower priorities. As a rule, the scheduler always gives the next timeslice to the thread waiting to execute that has the highest priority.

Does this mean that lower priority threads never get executed? Not at all. First, remember that Windows is a message-based operating system. If a thread's message queue is empty when the thread calls `::GetMessage()` to retrieve a message, the thread blocks until a message becomes available. This gives lower priority threads a chance to execute because blocked threads receive no timeslices. Most UI threads spend the major part of their time blocked on the message queue waiting for input, so as long as a high priority worker thread doesn't monopolize the CPU, even very low priority threads typically get all the CPU time they need. (A worker thread never blocks on the message queue because it doesn't process messages.)

The scheduler also plays a lot of tricks with threads' priority levels to enhance the overall responsiveness of the system and reduce the chance that any thread is starved for CPU time. A thread may have a priority level of 7, but if that thread goes for too long without receiving a timeslice, the scheduler may temporarily boost the thread's priority level to 8 or 9 or even higher to give it a chance to execute. Windows boosts the priorities of all threads that belong to the foreground process to improve the responsiveness of the application in which the user is working, and it boosts a thread's priority even further when the thread has an input message to process.

The system also uses a technique called *priority inheritance* to prevent high priority threads from blocking for too long on synchronization objects owned by low priority threads. For example, if a priority-16 thread tries to access a critical section owned by a priority-10 thread, the scheduler treats the priority-10 thread as if it had priority 16 until the thread releases the critical section. This way, the critical section comes free faster, and the priority-16 thread won't get stuck waiting on a lower priority thread.

How do thread priorities get assigned in the first place? When you call `AfxBeginThread()` or `CWinThread::SetThreadPriority()`, you specify the relative thread priority value. (The `::CreateThread()` API function that starts a thread doesn't accept a relative thread priority value. When `AfxBeginThread()` starts a thread for you, it calls `SetThreadPriority()` after it creates the thread to set the thread's relative priority.) The operating system combines the relative priority level with the priority class of the process that owns the thread to compute a base priority level for the thread. The thread's actual priority level—a number from 0 through 31—varies from moment to moment depending on whether the process that owns it is running in the foreground or the background. The actual priority level is also subject to change from the system's dynamic boosting, but most of the time it stays within 2 or 3 digits of the base priority level. You can't control boosting (and you wouldn't want to even if you could), but you can control the base priority level by setting the process priority class and the relative thread priority level.

Process priority classes

Most processes begin life with the priority class `NORMAL_PRIORITY_CLASS`. Once started, however, a process can change its priority class by calling `::SetPriorityClass()`, which accepts a process handle (obtainable with `::GetCurrentProcess()`) and one of the specifiers shown in Table 25-1.

Table 25-1
Relative Thread Priorities

Priority Class	*Description*
IDLE_PRIORITY CLASS	
NORMAL_PRIORITY_CLASS	The default process priority class. The process has no special scheduling needs.
HIGH_PRIORITY_CLASS	The process should receive priority over IDLE_PRIORITY CLASS and NORMAL_PRIORITY_CLASS processes.
REALTIME_PRIORITY_CLASS	The process must have the highest possible priority, and its threads should preempt even threads belonging to HIGH_PRIORITY_CLASS processes.

Most applications don't need to change their priority classes. HIGH_PRIORITY_CLASS and REALTIME_PRIORITY_CLASS processes can severely inhibit the responsiveness of the system and even delay critical system activities such as flushing of the disk cache. One legitimate use for HIGH_PRIORITY_CLASS is for system applications that remain hidden most of the time but pop up a window when a certain input event occurs. These applications impose little overhead on the system while they're blocked waiting for input, but once the input appears, they receive priority over normal applications. REALTIME_PRIORITY_CLASS is provided primarily for the benefit of real-time data acquisition programs that must have the lion's share of the CPU time in order to work properly. IDLE_PRIORITY_CLASS is ideal for screen savers, system monitors, and other low priority applications that operate unobtrusively in the background.

Sharing MFC objects among threads

Now for the bad news about writing multithreaded MFC applications. As long as threads are written so that they don't call member functions belonging to objects created by other threads, there are few restrictions on what they can do. However, if thread A passes a CWnd pointer to thread B and thread B calls a member function of that CWnd object, MFC is likely to halt a debug build of the application with an assertion error. A release build might work fine, but then again, it might not. There's also a possibility in this situation that a debug build won't assert but that it won't work properly, either. It all depends on what goes on inside the framework when that particular CWnd member function is called. You can avoid a potential minefield of problems by compartmentalizing your threads and having each thread create the objects it uses rather than rely on objects created by other threads. But for cases in which that's simply not practical, here are a few rules to go by.

First, many MFC member functions can be safely called on objects in other threads. Most of the inline functions defined in the .inl files in MFC's include directory can be called through object pointers passed in from other threads because they are little more than wrappers around API functions. But calling a non-inline member function is asking for trouble. For example, the following code, which passes a CWnd pointer named pWnd from thread A to thread B and has B call CWnd::GetParent() through the pointer, works without problems:

```
CwinThread *pThread =
  AfxBeginThread( ThreadFunc, (LPVOID) pWnd );

UINT ThreadFunc( LPVOID pParam )
{
  CWnd *pWnd = (CWnd *) pParam;
  CWnd *pParent = pWnd->GetParent();

  return( 0 );

}

// Simply changing GetParent() to GetParentFrame(),
// however, causes an assertion error the moment thread B
// is started:

CwinThread *pThread =
  AfxBeginThread( ThreadFunc, pWnd);

UINT ThreadFunc( LPVOID pParam )
{
  CWnd *pWnd = (CWnd *) pParam;
  // Get ready for an assertion error!
  CWnd *pParent = pWnd->GetParentFrame();

  return( ) );
}
```

Why does GetParent() work when GetParentFrame() doesn't? Because GetParent() calls through almost directly to the ::GetParent() function in the API. No problem there; m_hWnd is valid because it's part of the CWnd object that pWnd points to, and FromHandle() converts the HWND returned by GetParent() into a CWnd pointer.

But now consider what happens when you call GetParentFrame(). The line that causes the assertion error is ASSERT_VALID(this). ASSERT_VALID calls CWnd::AssertValid(), which performs a sanity check by making sure that the HWND associated with this appears in the permanent or temporary handle map the framework uses to convert HWNDs into CWnds. Going from a CWnd to an HWND is easy because the HWND is a data member of the class, but going from an HWND to a CWnd can be done only through the handle maps. And here's the problem: handle maps are local to each thread and are not visible to other threads. If the CWnd whose address is passed to ASSERT_VALID was created by another thread, the corresponding HWND won't appear in the current thread's permanent or temporary handle map and MFC will assert. Many of MFC's non-inline member functions call ASSERT_VALID, but inline functions do not — at least not in current releases.

MFC's assertions frequently protect you from calling functions that wouldn't work anyway. In a release build, GetParentFrame() returns NULL when called from a thread other than the one in which the parent frame was created. But in cases in which assertion errors are spurious — that is, in cases in which the function would work okay despite the per-thread handle tables — you can avoid assertions by passing real handles instead of object pointers. For example, it's safe to call CWnd::GetTopLevelParent() in a secondary thread if FromHandle() is called first to create an entry in the thread's temporary handle map, as shown here:

```
CwinThread *pThread =
  AfxEeginThread( ThreadFunc, (LPVOID) pWnd->m_hWnd );

UINT ThreadFunc( LPVOID pParam )
{
  CWnd *pWnd = CWnd::FromHandle( (HWND) pParam );
  CWnd *pParent = pWnd->GetTopLevelParent();

  return( ) );

}
```

That's why the MFC documentation warns that windows, GDI objects, and other objects should be passed between threads by means of handles instead of by means of pointers to MFC objects. In general, you'll have fewer problems if you pass handles instead of object pointers and then use FromHandle() to "re-create" objects in the temporary handle map of the current thread. But don't take that to mean that just any function will work. It won't.

What about calling member functions belonging to objects created from "pure" MFC classes such as CDocument and CRect — classes that don't wrap HWNDs, HDCs, or other handle types and therefore don't rely on handle maps? Just what you wanted to hear: some work and some don't. There's no problem with this code:

```
CWinThread *pThread =
  AfxBeginThread( ThreadFunc, pRect );

UINT ThreadFunc( LPVOID pParam )
{
  CRect *pRect = (CRect *) pParam;
  int nArea = pRect->Width() * pRect->Height();

  return( 0 );

}
```

But the following code will assert on you:

```
CWinThread *pThread =
  AfxBeginThread( ThreadFunc, pDoc );

UINT ThreadFunc( LPVOID pParam )
{
  CMyDocument *pDoc = (CMyDocument *) pParam;
  PDoc->UpdateAllViews( NULL );

  return( 0 );

}
```

Even seemingly innocuous functions frequently don't work when they're called from secondary threads. The bottom line is that before you go calling member functions of MFC objects created in other threads, you must understand the implications. And the only way to understand the implications is to study the MFC source code to see how a particular member function behaves. Also keep in mind that MFC isn't thread safe, a subject we'll explore later in this chapter. So even if a member function appears to be safe, ask yourself what might happen if an object created by thread A were accessed by thread B and thread A preempted thread B in the middle of the access. This is incredibly difficult stuff to sort out and only adds to the complexity of writing multithreaded applications. Avoid crossing thread boundaries with calls to MFC member functions, and you'll avoid a lot of problems, too.

Using C Runtime Functions in Multithreaded Applications

Certain functions in the standard C runtime library pose problems for multithreaded applications. `Strtok()`, `time()`, and many other C runtime functions use global variables to store intermediate data. If thread A calls one of these functions and thread B preempts thread A and calls the same function, global data stored by thread A could be overwritten by global data stored by thread B. Most modern C and C++ compilers come with two versions of the C runtime library: one that's thread safe (can be called into by multiple concurrent threads) and one that isn't. The thread-safe versions of the runtime library typically won't rely on thread synchronization objects. Instead, they store intermediate values in per-thread data structures. Visual C++ comes with six versions of the C runtime library. Which one you should choose depends on whether you're compiling a debug build or a release build, whether you want to link with the C runtime library statically or dynamically, and, of course, whether your application is single threaded or multithreaded.

ThreadDemo1 Program

This demo program, highlights of which are given in Listing 25-1, implements a multiple document framework. Each separate window is drawn by a separately instantiated thread. So if you create four child windows, four threads are at work drawing each window. The program is shown in Figure 25-1.

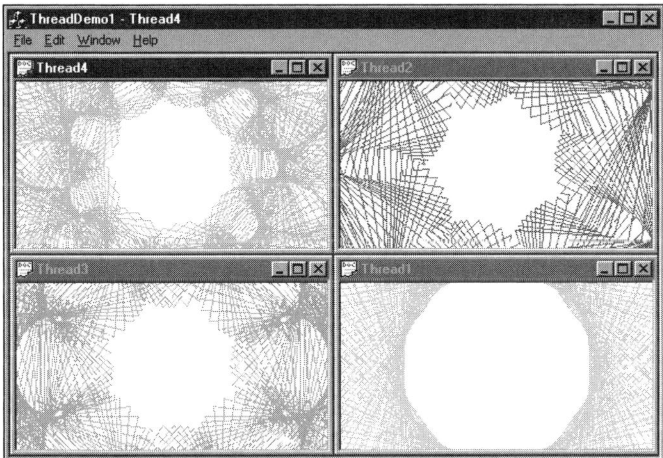

Figure 25-1: The program draws independently in different view windows.

The thread functions draw a spirograph pattern in the windows. Three values determine the shape and pattern of the spirograph pattern: the integers `nFixedRadius`, `nMovingRadius`, and `nMovingOffset`. Each time the window is drawn, these values are incremented. This makes the pattern change over time for a continuous variety of effects.

ThreadDemo1
CD-ROM Location: **Chap25\ThreadDemo1**
Program Name: `ThreadDemo1.EXE`
Source Code Modules in Text: `ThreadDemo1View.cpp`

✦ ✦ ✦ ✦ ✦

Listing 25-1: Source Code Highlights for the ThreadDemo1 Program

```
#include "stdafx.h"
#include " ThreadDemo1.h"

#include " ThreadDemo1Doc.h"
#include " ThreadDemo1View.h"

// ThreadDemo1View.cpp : implementation of
// the CThreadDemo1View class
//

UINT ThreadProc( LPVOID lpParam )
{
  // Get a THREAD_INFO pointer from the
  // parameter that was passed in.
  THREAD_INFO *lpThreadInfo =
    (THREAD_INFO *) lpParam;

  // The next six variables represent
  // values used to draw the spirograph;
  unsigned char Red, Green, Blue;
  int nFixedRadius = 80;
  int nMovingRadius = 10;
  int nMovingOffset = 70;

  // Begin colors based on the system time. This
  // makes the color somewhat random.
  Red = (unsigned char)
    ( GetTickCount() & 0x000000ff );
  Green = (unsigned char)
    ( ( GetTickCount() & 0x00000ff0 ) > 4 );
  Blue = (unsigned char)
    ( ( GetTickCount() & 0x0000ff00 ) > 8 );

  while( *lpThreadInfo->lpKillThread == FALSE ){

    // Get a DC for the window.
    HDC hDC = ::GetDC( lpThreadInfo->hWnd );

    // Get the client rect so we can
    // calculate the center point.
    RECT Rect;
    ::GetClientRect( lpThreadInfo->hWnd, &Rect );
    int nMidx = Rect.right / 2;
    int nMidy = Rect.bottom / 2;

    // Clear the window.
    ::InvalidateRect( lpThreadInfo->hWnd, NULL, TRUE );
    ::UpdateWindow( lpThreadInfo->hWnd );
```

```
// Create a pen based on the color. Select it
// into the DC and remember the old pen so
// we can select it back in later.
HPEN hPen, hOldPen;
hPen =
  ::CreatePen( PS_SOLID, 1, RGB( Red, Green, Blue ));
hOldPen = (HPEN) ::SelectObject( hdc, hPen );

// Iterate through a bunch of times and
// draw the spirograph.
int prevx, prevy, x, y;
for( int i=0; i<=500; i++ ){

  // Remember x and y.
  prevx = x;
  prevy = y;

  // Calculate the new x and y.
  x = (int) ( ( nFixedRadius + nMovingRadius ) *
    cos( (double) i ) -
    ( nMovingRadius + nMovingOffset ) *
    cos((double)(( ( nFixedRadius + nMovingRadius ) /
    nMovingRadius ) * i ) ) );
  y = (int) ( ( nFixedRadius + nMovingRadius ) *
    sin( (double) i ) -
    ( nMovingRadius + nMovingOffset ) *
    sin((double)(( ( nFixedRadius + nMovingRadius ) /
    nMovingRadius ) * i ) ) );

  // Draw the line (or move to the first
  // point if this is the first time through).
  if( i > 0 )
    ::LineTo( hdc, x + nMidx, y + nMidy );
  else
    ::MoveToEx( hdc, x + nMidx, y + nMidy, NULL );

  }

// Increment the color variables so
// that the colors move around.
Red += 6;
Green += 5;
Blue += 4;

// Increase the fixed radius and
// limit it to a max of 150.
nFixedRadius++;
if( nFixedRadius > 170 )
  nFixedRadius = 90;
// Increase the moving radius and
// limit it to a max of 120.
nMovingRadius++;
```

(continued)

Listing 25-1 (continued)

```
    if( nMovingRadius > 40 )
      nMovingRadius = 10;

    // Increase the moving offset and
    // limit it to a max of 90.
    nMovingOffset++;
    if( nMovingOffset > 100 )
      nMovingOffset = 70;

    // Select the old pen into the DC,
    // delete the pen we created, and
    // release the DC we got.
    ::SelectObject( hdc, hOldPen );
    ::DeleteObject( hPen );
    ::ReleaseDC( lpThreadInfo->hWnd, hdc );

    // Sleep so we don't chew up too
    // much CPU time.
    Sleep( 200 );
    }

  return( 0 );

}

//////////////////////////////////////////////////////////////
// CThreadDemo1View construction/destruction

CThreadDemo1View::CThreadDemo1View()
{

  // This is the flag that tells the
  // thread to quit.
  m_bKillThread = FALSE;

  // NULL the pointer to the thread so
  // we know it hasn't been created.
  m_pThread = NULL;

}

CThreadDemo1View::~CThreadDemo1View()
{
  // Get the thread handle into local space since
  // the thread will delete itself.
  HANDLE hThread = m_pThread->m_hThread;

  // Set the flag to kill the thread to TRUE;
  m_bKillThread = TRUE;

  // Wait for the thread to end.
```

```
    ::WaitForSingleObject( m_hThread, 5000 );

}

//////////////////////////////////////////////////////////
// CThreadDemo1View drawing

void CThreadDemo1View::OnDraw(CDC* pDC)
{
  CThreadDemo1Doc* pDoc = GetDocument();
  ASSERT_VALID(pDoc);

  // If the m_pThread is NULL, we need to kick
  // off the thread.
  if( m_pThread == NULL ){

    // Store the window handle and the Kill flag.
    m_ThreadInfo.hWnd = m_hWnd;
    m_ThreadInfo.lpKillThread = &m_bKillThread;

    // Start the thread.
    m_pThread =
      AfxBeginThread(ThreadProc, (LPVOID) &m_ThreadInfo);
    }

}
```

Summary

One of the things you can learn from ThreadDemo1 is that there's no such thing as a free lunch. When several threads are running, the designs are drawn much more slowly. Any thread that performs a task consumes CPU cycles. The more threads you have running, the more processor time required.

With clever planning, however, you can avoid unnecessary system slowdowns as discussed earlier. Using `::Sleep()` to yield to other threads is a polite and efficient way of making sure a thread doesn't hog CPU time. Using `::WaitForSingleObject()` to wait for threads to end was also discussed.

You'll find threads daunting at first. But once they're under control, they'll make your applications smoother and more efficient.

✦ ✦ ✦

PART

IV

Database Programming

✦ ✦ ✦ ✦

In This Part

Chapter 26:
ODBC

Chapter 27:
MFC Database Classes

Chapter 28:
DAO Database Programming

✦ ✦ ✦ ✦

You can't do much in this day and age without retrieving data from — or storing to — a database. Database types run the gamut from Access to SQL Server to Oracle; this part covers them all.

You learn how to use the MFC database classes to access databases through ODBC drivers. This connectivity standard enables your programs to meet almost every database need. Continuing from ODBC database access, you learn about DAO and other more specialized classes and functions. These advanced concepts and techniques will have your programs outperforming most others — and if you take advantage of the clear presentation found in these chapters, it won't be hard.

CHAPTER 26

ODBC

✦ ✦ ✦ ✦

In This Chapter

ODBC and database definitions

Different ODBC conformance levels

Connecting to a database using ODBC

Using the ODBC SDK to fetch data

Writing a maintenance application using ODBC

Dynamically querying a data source's schema at runtime

Writing a C++ class that can retrieve data from any data source

✦ ✦ ✦ ✦

Database development has long been thought of as one of the most difficult and time-consuming programming tasks in the field of software development. Some of the reasons for that include the fact that almost every DBMS is fundamentally different in terms of field types supported, field type attributes available, capability to access catalog or system table information, degrees of referential integrity supported, and other reasons. Adding to this problem is the fact that in order to enable programmatic access to their DBMSs, many vendors implement their own proprietary APIs. The programmer is then responsible for learning that API to access that particular database from his or her application. Therefore, if an application needs to interface to several different databases, the programmer needs to learn several different APIs, one for each DBMS.

Even databases that support the standard language for database manipulation, SQL, do so by supporting different "levels" of SQL, both in terms of SQL types and SQL syntax. These DBMS vendors also inevitably add their own "extensions" to the standard SQL they do support, further confusing the issue. Thankfully, Microsoft, like many software companies, recognized these problems and introduced a standard to aid database developers looking for a simple, yet powerful means of supporting multiple DBMSs in their applications. The solution is called ODBC (Open Database Connectivity), and it is the subject of this chapter.

In this chapter, you will begin by learning what ODBC is and how it addresses the problems previously listed. Once you have learned some basic tasks — such as how to connect to an ODBC data source, how to retrieve data, and how to execute an SQL request — two demos will be introduced. In the first demo, you will learn how to use ODBC SDK functions to connect to, fetch data from, and disconnect from a data source. After reviewing these basic ODBC functions, you will be introduced to a C++ class (`CODBCDynamic`) that can dynamically read data from any ODBC data source. This class uses the ODBC SDK to dynamically query the data source so that the data source's schema doesn't have to be known until runtime. Because the source code is encapsulated in a C++ class with a very thin interface, it can easily be "plugged" into any Visual C++ application.

Definitions of ODBC and Database Terms

Before continuing, it is necessary to clarify some terms that will be used in this chapter. In some cases, these are standard terms with universally recognized definitions (for example, DBMS and SQL). In other cases, an otherwise ambiguous term will be defined and an explanation provided of how that term will be used in this chapter's discussions.

- **DBMS (Database Management System)** — A DBMS is the software that provides access to and manipulation of structured data. Examples of some of the more popular desktop DBMSs are Microsoft Access, Microsoft SQL Server, Oracle Server, and Sybase SQL Server. Most DBMSs (including all of the aforementioned databases) provide an SQL interface.
- **SQL (Structured Query Language)** — The language used to access and manipulate data in a DBMS. SQL statements are divided into two categories: DDL (data definition language) statements that are used to do such things as create tables, indexes, and so forth and DML (data manipulation language) statements that are used to retrieve data, update data, and so on.
- **ODBC SDK** — The ODBC SDK is the API that database applications use to access ODBC services, such as interfacing to DBMSs, for which an ODBC driver exists. The ODBC SDK is also used to develop ODBC drivers; however, the development of ODBC drivers is not a simple undertaking and is outside the scope of this chapter.
- **ODBC Driver Manager** — The ODBC Driver Manager is a DLL (`ODBC32.DLL`) that is the gateway through which the application interfaces to the DBMS. The entire ODBC SDK API is exported from this DLL.
- **ODBC Cursor Library** — A DLL (`ODBCCR32.DLL`) that resides between the ODBC Driver Manager and the ODBC drivers. Once a request to a data source has returned data, this DLL is responsible for handling the scrolling through that data.
- **ODBC Driver** — As mentioned previously, the ODBC driver is the component that actually interfaces to the DBMS once the ODBC Driver Manager makes a request to it on your behalf. Any information or response is also passed back through the ODBC Driver Manager to you. For you to be able to use a particular DBMS with ODBC, you must acquire an ODBC driver for it. It should be noted that this chapter assumes that you are an application developer and are not developing an ODBC driver. Visual C++ 6.0 provides ODBC drivers for the following:

- SQL Server
- Microsoft Access
- Microsoft FoxPro
- Microsoft Excel
- dBASE
- Paradox
- Text files

✦ **Data source** — The term *data source* is used in this chapter to represent a specific instance of a DBMS that you are using. For example, suppose you are using Microsoft Access and create a database called Test. When this chapter refers to a DBMS, it is referring to Microsoft Access and its functionality, and when this chapter refers to a data source, it is referring to the Test database (`test.mdb`). For ODBC to be able to work with a data source, that data source must be "registered" with the ODBC Driver Manager. This is done by creating a DSN, or data source name. Microsoft provides a utility called the ODBC Data Source Administrator for this purpose. Figure 26-1 shows what the ODBC Driver Manager looks like.

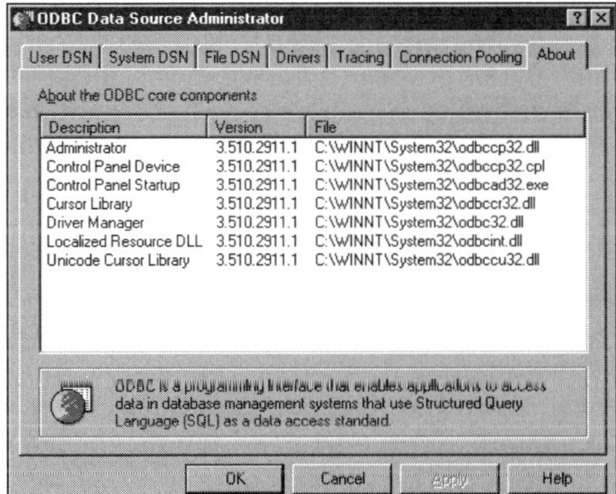

Figure 26-1: The ODBC Data Source Administrator enables the creation and modification of ODBC data source names (DSNs).

ODBC — The Need for a Standard

In the early days of the PC, database applications were developed to run on only one workstation (standalone) and support only one data source. The DBMS the application supported typically provided a proprietary API that the application used to interface to that database. Because very little PC development was being done (most applications were still being written on larger midrange or mainframe computers) and DBMSs were rarely, if ever, changed, this worked very well for many years. However, once more and more companies began accepting the PC as a viable platform on which to develop their software, the following problems arose. ODBC was designed expressly to solve these problems.

- **Scalability** — With PCs becoming more common on every employee's desk, at some point the application had to become "network" capable. In other words, the application needed to run on each desktop and interface to a DBMS running on a server. If the application had been written as a standalone application, that usually meant switching to another DBMS (one that supported multiple concurrent users), which usually incurred the cost of rewriting the application.
- **Interoperability** — If a company developed software to sell, the software was typically written to interface to a specific DBMS. If the decision was later made to interface to additional DBMSs, either the software went through massive design and coding changes, or the company developed a special version of the software for each DBMS it wished to support. Obviously, both "solutions" were extremely costly propositions. What was needed was the capability to write the software so that a single code base could interface to any DBMS.
- **Software development costs** — Because the APIs used to interface to the different DBMSs were almost always proprietary, if a company wanted to develop software to use a particular DBMS, the company had to hire developers who were proficient with that specific DBMS and its idiosyncrasies. Then if the company wanted to add support for additional DBMS systems, it had to hire additional experts for those systems as well. What was obviously needed was a standard database API — in other words, an API that would enable programmers to generically interface to a data source without regard to the specific DBMS implementation.

The ODBC standard

ODBC provides a means of communicating with a DBMS using a standard application programming interface and SQL syntax. A very important distinction must be made here. While ODBC enables access to a DBMS with an SQL-like interface, it would *not* be correct to understand that to mean ODBC is strictly a means of accessing SQL databases. While it is true that most DBMSs do indeed support SQL, ODBC does not place this restriction on any DBMS. An application using ODBC can interface to any DBMS if an ODBC driver (covered later in this chapter) exists for that DBMS. This obviously gives database developers a tremendous amount of power and flexibility in developing database applications. All that is needed to do is to write the application once and swap out the DBMS and ODBC driver when and if the decision is made to support another DBMS. ODBC offers you this flexibility by providing the following standards:

✦ SQL syntax that is based on the X/Open and SQL Access Group (SAG) SQL CAE specification

✦ A set of error codes that can be returned from an ODBC function call

✦ For configuring and maintaining the definition of your databases

✦ For connecting to your DBMS

✦ For interacting with your DBMS in terms of saving and retrieving data

✦ For interfacing with your DBMS in terms of configuring your database

✦ For disconnecting from your DBMS

The key term here is *standard*. After all, the entire reason for using ODBC is that a single code base can interface to multiple DBMSs. ODBC provides this level of abstraction through what is sometimes referred to as a *function seam*. In other words, ODBC provides a layer between your application and the DBMS.

In order to provide this layer of programmatic abstraction, the original designers of ODBC had two problems to solve. First, ODBC needed to provide database developers with a generic API that would be used to issue database requests to the underlying DBMS. Second, ODBC needed a standard means of communicating with any DBMS. This is accomplished with the ODBC Driver Manager and ODBC drivers and works as follows: when an application makes an ODBC function call, it is actually calling an exported function of the ODBC Driver Manager. The ODBC Driver Manager then calls an exported function of the ODBC driver (usually provided by the DBMS vendor). It is the responsibility of the ODBC driver's vendor to respond to the ODBC Driver Manager. Therefore, the only layer of code that has any knowledge of the inner workings of the DBMS is the ODBC driver. You can see these components at work in Figure 26-2.

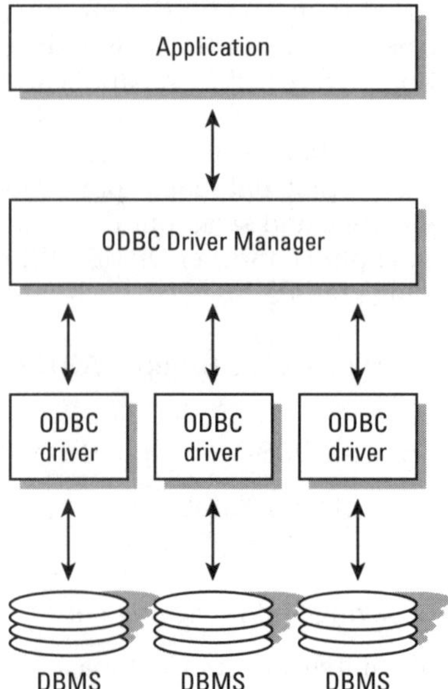

Figure 26-2: ODBC provides a layer of abstraction so that database applications can use a single code base to interface to a wide variety of DBMSs. This is accomplished because database applications that use the ODBC SDK never interface directly to any given DBMS.

ODBC API conformance levels

In order to provide an API that can work with all DBMSs, ODBC defines certain minimum requirements that every ODBC-compliant driver is required to meet. This level of conformity is called *Core Level* and it is defined by the X/Open SQL Access Group (SAG) Call Level Interface (CLI) specification. While ODBC does define a minimum conformance level, ODBC also enables more robust DBMSs the capability to make their services available by defining several levels of conformance. ODBC drivers are then defined, or categorized, by which level of conformance they adhere to.

It is important to understand that for a ODBC driver's manufacturer to claim that its driver corresponds to a given conformance level, the driver must implement *all* of the functionality defined within that level (whether or not the underlying data source does). However, drivers are not limited to only implementing functions that are defined within the level of conformance to which they adhere. An ODBC driver can, for example, be defined as a Core Level driver and still implement functionality from other levels.

Because all ODBC drivers must implement the functions defined in the Core Level, database applications do not have to check a driver's conformance level before calling a Core Level function. However, if a database application has to make an ODBC call that is not defined in the Core Level, it is the database application's responsibility to ensure that the driver supports the desired function. There are two ways to accomplish this. The simplest and least flexible way is to find out from the driver's manufacturer if the driver supports the function(s) in question. Obviously, this is not an acceptable approach if the application is being written to work in a heterogeneous manner. In order to verify whether a driver supports a specific function, ODBC provides the `SQLGetFunctions()` function.

ODBC SQL conformance levels

In addition to the different ODBC API conformance levels, ODBC also defines conformance levels for the SQL grammar and SQL data types that are supported by the ODBC driver. Actually, the definition for these conformance levels are defined in the SQL-92 specification. As with the ODBC API conformance levels, a minimum ODBC SQL conformance level is defined. This minimum level is called the *SQL minimum grammar* and can be found in the *Microsoft ODBC 3.0 Programmer's Reference*.

All ODBC-compliant drivers must support the SQL minimum grammar. If a driver purports to conform to a given SQL-92 level, then it must support all syntax that is included in that level. However, if a driver supports a given SQL-92 level, it can also support higher-level functionality. For example, let's say that a driver only supports the minimum grammar, but the driver's developers also want to support some higher-level functionality. They can do this as long as they advertise the driver as simply being compliant with the minimum grammar.

ODBC – Implementation

The best way to proceed from this point is to split the different ODBC functions into logical groups that correspond to the order in which you are most likely to use them in your application:

- ✦ Configuring ODBC
- ✦ Connecting to a data source
- ✦ Querying the data and the data source
- ✦ Preparing and executing SQL requests
- ✦ Retrieving data
- ✦ Disconnecting from a data source

Configuring ODBC

As you read earlier, ODBC provides a utility called the ODBC Data Source Administrator that is used to configure ODBC. This program, which can be accessed via the Control Panel, enables the configuration of both the ODBC drivers and the DSNs. Figure 26-3 shows an example list of configured ODBC drivers.

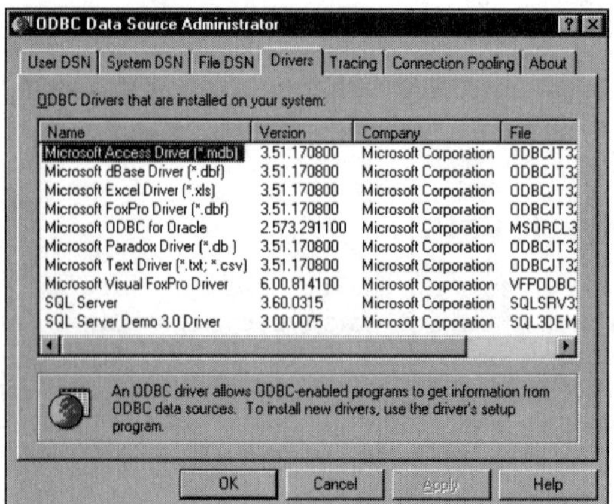

Figure 26-3: The Drivers tab of the ODBC Data Source Administrator is used to display installed ODBC drivers.

The ODBC drivers shown in Figure 26-3 are typically referred to as the *desktop drivers* because they support some of the more popular desktop DBMSs. You will sometimes hear these drivers incorrectly referred to as the *Access drivers*. This is because the majority of developers of these drivers are using them with the Microsoft Access DBMS. However, as you can see, several DBMSs are supported with these drivers.

ODBC support for a DBMS is installed by defining the ODBC driver with the ODBC Data Source Administrator. This task is usually carried out by an installation program provided by the driver's manufacturer. Once the ODBC driver has been installed and a database created, a DSN has to be created. A DSN can be defined as being any of the following three types:

- ✦ User data source — This data source is local to the computer on which it is created and can be used only by the user that creates it.
- ✦ System data source — This data source belongs to the computer on which it is created and "belongs" to that computer rather than the user who created it. Any users can access this data source as long as they have the correct privileges.
- ✦ File data source — This data source is specific to the underlying database file. In other words, the data source can be used by any user that has the appropriate driver installed.

A DSN defines a specific database to ODBC and the ODBC driver that must be used. Each ODBC driver defines what information is needed to create a DSN for a database that the driver supports. Once the ODBC driver is selected, the ODBC Data Source Administrator, when adding a DSN, instructs the driver to display its configuration dialog. At a minimum, most ODBC drivers require the database filename, whether the system is local or remote, and the folder where the database file resides. If a DSN is being created for a Microsoft Access database, the ODBC driver also enables the definition of the system database file, username, and password.

Because the information needed to create a DSN is driver specific, the documentation for that driver has to be consulted in order to create a DSN for it. Figure 26-4 shows the System DSNs on a PC under NT Server 4.0. You can see we have already added a System DSN called "Visual C++ 6 Bible" that is used for some of the demos in this chapter. Also note that the ODBC Data Source Administrator enables the creation of DSNs with very readable names (in terms of name length and imbedding spaces, dashes, and so on).

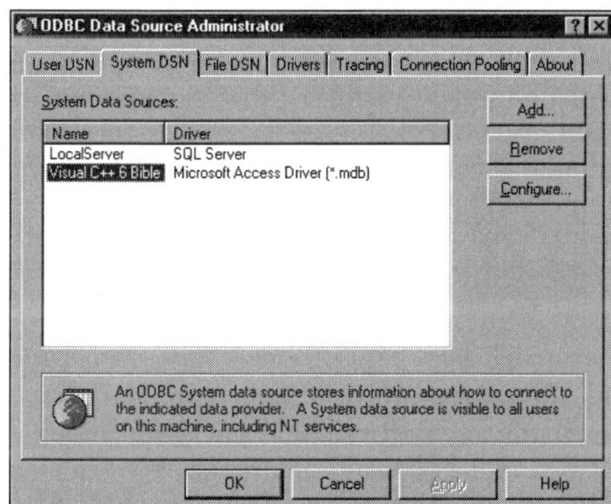

Figure 26-4: The System DSN tab of the ODBC Data Source Administrator is used to display all system-level data source names (DSNs).

Connecting to a data source

Once a DSN has been configured via the ODBC Data Source Administrator, the database that was specified when the DSN was created can be accessed via ODBC. The first programmatic step to using ODBC is to connect to the data source. This is done via a series of function calls. The general flow of connecting to a data source is as follows:

1. Initialize ODBC and acquire a unique environment handle, or henv, that uniquely represents the thread's use of ODBC. This is achieved via a call to SQLAllocHandle(). The application first declares a variable of type SQLHENV. It then calls SQLAllocHandle() specifying that an henv is desired and passes the address of the henv variable. Here is an example of how to allocate an henv:

```
SQLHENV henv;
SQLRETURN rc = SQLAllocHandle(SQL_HANDLE_ENV,
  SQL_NULL_HANDLE, &henv);
```

2. Set the version of ODBC to which the application conforms. This is done via a call to SQLSetEnvAttr(). The application calls this function and passes the SQL_ATTR_ODBC_VERSION constant to indicate the supported ODBC version. In the following example, the fact that the constant SQL_OV_ODBC3 is being passed indicates that ODBC 3.0 is the version that is supported by this application:

```
SQLSetEnvAttr(henv, SQL_ATTR_ODBC_VERSION,
  (SQLPOINTER) SQL_OV_ODBC3, SQL_IS_INTEGER);
```

3. Before an application can connect to a database, it must acquire a database connection handle, hdbc, from ODBC. This is accomplished by calling the SQLAllocHandle() function using the SQL_HANDLE_HDBC constant as its first argument. The second argument must be a valid henv that was acquired using step 1. The third and last argument must be a pointer to a variable of type SQLHDBC. Following is an example of how to acquire an hdbc:

```
SQLHDBC hdbc;
SQLRETURN  rc = SQLAllocHandle(SQL_HANDLE_ENV,
 henv, &hdbc);
```

4. Once you have an hdbc you can connect to the database. Connecting to a database can be accomplished using any of three different ODBC function calls: SQLConnect(), SQLDriverConnect(), and SQLBrowseConnect(). SQLConnect() is a straightforward and simple way of connecting to a data source. Using this function, you simply pass the DSN, user ID, and password to ODBC to connect to the data source. SQLDriverConnect() is an alternative for ODBC drivers that requires more information than can be passed using SQLConnect(). SQLBrowseConnect() is an even more advanced means of connecting to a data source. Using one or more calls to SQLBrowseConnect(), you can iteratively request the information needed to connect to a data source. The way this works is that the function returns the value SQL_NEEDS_DATA until the application has provided all of the information needed to connect to the data source, at which time the function returns SQL_SUCCESS. So that the more important topics of ODBC functionality can be concentrated on, the basic SQLConnect() function is used in the upcoming demos. Here is an example of using the SQLConnect() function to connect to a data source named "Visual C++ 6 Bible." The SQL_NTS constants simply tell ODBC that the previous argument passed was a null terminated string.

```
SQLRETURN rc = SQLConnect(hdbc,
  (SQLCHAR*)"Visual C++ 6 Bible", SQL_NTS,
  (SQLCHAR*)"", SQL_NTS, (SQLCHAR*)"", SQL_NTS);
```

Querying the data and the data source

ODBC provides a means by which database applications can interface to multiple DBMSs, each of which can have different and distinct capabilities, from a single code base by providing functions to query the ODBC driver as to its capabilities. These functions are `SQLGetFunctions`, `SQLGetInfo`, and `SQLGetTypeInfo`.

✦ `SQLGetFunctions` is used to query an ODBC driver as to the different functions, or groups of functions, the driver supports. In order to use this function, the application simply calls this function, passing it a valid `hdbc` and a numeric value (defined in the `SQLEXT.H` file that ships with the ODBC SDK) that represents either a specific ODBC function or group of ODBC functions. The application must also pass a pointer to a variable that ODBC sets to indicate if the function or group of functions is supported.

✦ `SQLGetInfo()` returns information about the ODBC driver and its capabilities — for example, to ascertain an ODBC driver's version and name as well as its level of ODBC API conformance and ODBC SQL conformance.

✦ An application calls `SQLGetTypeInfo()` when seeking information regarding what SQL data types are supported by the data source as well as certain information about the data type. The tricky part about this function is that it does not directly return a value. Instead, the driver returns the information in the form of a result set. In this way, it works in much the same way a retrieval of data from a data source would. Therefore, once the function returns, the application must retrieve the results accordingly. You will see how to retrieve data in the next section as well as in the demo applications introduced later in the chapter.

Preparing and executing SQL requests

Once you have connected to a data source, the last thing the application must do before executing SQL requests against the data source is to acquire a statement handle, or `hstmt`. To allocate the `hstmt`, simply declare a variable of type `SQLHSTMT`, and call the `SQLAllocHandle()` function specifying that an `hstmt` is desired (using the `SQL_HANDLE_STMT` constant) and passing the address of the `hstmt` variable. Following is an example of this two-step process:

```
SQLSTMT hstmt;
SQLRETURN  rc = SQLAllocHandle(SQL_HANDLE_STMT, hdbc,
 &hstmt);
```

Once the hstmt has been acquired, SQL statements can be issued against the data source. There are two different ways of executing an SQL query against a data source. One way is to call the SQLExecDirect() function specifying the SQL statement in the function's second argument. Here's an example of doing just that. This function would insert a row of data into the UserMaster table:

```
SQLRETURN rc = ::SQLExecDirect(hstmt,
  (unsigned char*)"INSERT INTO "
  "UserMaster VALUES('UserID', 'User Name', 0)",
  SQL_NTS))
```

If the statement is going to be executed multiple times, a more efficient means of issuing the SQL statement is to call the SQLPrepare function first followed by a call to the SQLExecute function, which can be seen in this example:

```
SQLRETURN rc;
LPCSTR szSQL = "INSERT INTO UserMaster "
  "values('UserID2', 'Just Another User', 0)";

if (SQL_SUCCESS == (rc = ::SQLPrepare(hstmt,
  (unsigned char*)szSQL, SQL_NTS)))
{
  if (SQL_SUCCESS == (rc = ::SQLExecute(hstmt)))
  ...
```

Retrieving data

In the previous section you saw two different methods of using an SQL statement to insert data into a table. But what do you do if the SQL statement returns data, and how do you map that data to your application's variables? That's where the next group of ODBC functions come into play. When an ODBC function is said to have returned a result set, you need to "bind" your variables to the different columns of data that are returned. ODBC provides a great deal of flexibility in retrieving the data, depending on the type of application you are developing.

If one of the application's design goals is flexibility, using the SQLNumResultCols(), SQLDescribeCol(), and SQLGetData() functions can be a tremendous benefit. These functions enable the database developer to develop the application without knowing how many columns are going to be returned or the data types involved. For example, these functions might be used in an ad-hoc query tool in which end users can define their own queries. Due to the dynamic nature of this application, the application won't know the number of columns and their respective data types until runtime.

So how does the application know what data was returned from a query that wasn't defined until runtime? Using the functions you learned in the previous section, the application would build and run the user-defined SQL statement. ODBC would then return a handle to a result set. However, the application doesn't know anything about the result set in terms of how many columns have been returned or the data type of the different columns. Therefore, the application would call the `SQLNumResultCols()` function to find out how many columns had been returned in the result set. After that, a call to `SQLDescribeCol()` for each column would yield the data type for each specified column. Once a specific column's data type is known, the `SQLGetData()` function could be used to retrieve the value for that column. Obviously, this is a simplistic description, but it provides a general overview of what is involved. These functions are illustrated in all their gory detail in the second and third demos of this chapter.

Obviously, not everyone needs the level of flexibility previously described. The majority of database developers issue SQL statements that they code in their applications and, therefore, do not need to query ODBC as to the type of data being returned in the result set. In these situations, the `SQLBindCol()` and `SQLFetch()` functions can be used to retrieve the data from an ODBC result set into your application's variables. The `SQLBindCol()` function enables you to specify the column number in the result set that you are binding, the type of data at that column position, and the address of a variable to hold the data once `SQLFetch()` is called to retrieve the data. You do not have to bind every column. You need only bind the columns whose data you wish to map into your variables. Once you have called `SQLBindCol()` for each desired column, you can call `SQLFetch()` as many times as necessary, or until you have read the entire result set. Here is an example of how to use these two functions to retrieve your data from a result set. This code segment assumes that an SQL statement has already been run to retrieve the data into a result set.

```
#define LEN_USERID 16

SDWORD cb;
char szUserID[LEN_USERID];

if (SQL_SUCCESS == (rc = SQLBindCol(hstmt, 1,
  SQL_C_CHAR, szUserID, LEN_USERID, &cb)))
{
  if (SQL_SUCESS == (rc = SQLFetch(hstmt)))
  {
    // szUserID now contains the value from
    // the first row of the returned result set
    ...
```

Disconnecting from a data source

Once you have finished using a connection to a data source, you must disconnect from the data source (via the `SQLDisconnect()` function) and release any handles that have been allocated. Here is an example of what your "cleanup" code might look like:

```
if (henv)
{
  if (hdbc)
  {
    if (bIsConnected)
    {
       if (hstmt)
       {
        ::SQLFreeHandle(SQL_HANDLE_STMT, hstmt);
       }
       ::SQLDisconnect(hdbc);
       bIsConnected = FALSE;
    }
    ::SQLFreeHandle(SQL_HANDLE_DBC, hdbc);
    hdbc = NULL;
   }
   ::SQLFreeHandle(SQL_HANDLE_ENV, henv);
   henv = NULL;
}
```

Using ODBC to Fetch Data

This demo (ODBCDemo) is a simple ODBC application that uses many of the functions that you have read about up to now. This demo demonstrates many of the basic ODBC functions of allocating the different ODBC handles, connecting to a data source, fetching data, deallocating the ODBC handles, and disconnecting from the data source. Although this application is very simple, you can use these same functions in your own application regardless of its scope or complexity.

The source code for the ODBCDemo application can be found on the companion CD in the `\Chap26\ODBCDemo` folder. If, however, you want to type in the application as you read through the explanation, simply create a Visual C++ dialog-based application called ODBCDemo, and follow the steps in the following procedure.

✦ ✦ ✦ ✦ ✦

To run the demo you must create the ODBC DSN and point it to the database provided on the companion CD in order for your application to run correctly. As mentioned earlier, this chapter assumes that you have installed the ODBC 3.0 SDK as well as the Microsoft ODBC Desktop Drivers 3.5. While you do not need the Microsoft Access product to run this demo, you will need it to open and modify the demo database. The database used in this demo is located in the same directory as the source code. The following steps are required to create the DSN.

Creating an ODBC DSN

To create an ODBC System DSN, simply do the following:

1. Open the ODBC Data Source Administrator (via the Control Panel), and select the System DSN tab.
2. Click the Add button on the right side of the dialog box.
3. Select the appropriate ODBC driver. (For the demos in this chapter, you should select the Microsoft Access Driver (*.mdb) driver.) When you have selected the desired driver, click the Finish button in the lower-right corner of the dialog box.
4. In the Data Source Name text box, type the name of the DSN. (For the demos in this chapter, set the DSN name to "Visual C++ 6 Bible".) Once you have typed the DSN, click the Select button on the left side of the dialog box.
5. Using the File dialog box, select the database that will represent the data source for the new DSN.

   (For all of the demos in this chapter, the database you will use, vc6bib.mdb, is located on the CD in the \Chap26\Database folder.) Once you have selected the database and returned to the Setup dialog box, click the OK button in the upper-right corner of the dialog box.
6. Click the OK button in the lower-left corner of the dialog box to signify that you have finished.

✦ ✦ ✦ ✦ ✦

Adding ODBC support to a Visual C++ project

The appropriate header files should be included in order to use the ODBC SDK in an application. If several modules within the same project contain calls to the ODBC SDK, it might be easier to simply include the ODBC header files in the project's `stdafx.h` file. The most common header files that an ODBC application would need are the following:

```
sql.h
sqlext.h
sqltypes.h
```

In addition to including the appropriate header file, you must also link with the ODBC Driver Manager import library (`odbc32.lib`) that is shipped with the ODBC SDK.

Modifying the ODBCDemo dialog

Because this is a dialog-based application, you already have a dialog to use for display of the customer data. At this point, locate the `IDD_ODBCDEMO_DIALOG` dialog template resource, and make the following modifications.

1. Remove the "TODO" static text control, and insert the controls as they appear in Figure 26-5. Note that the control under the "Term Codes" static text is a list box.

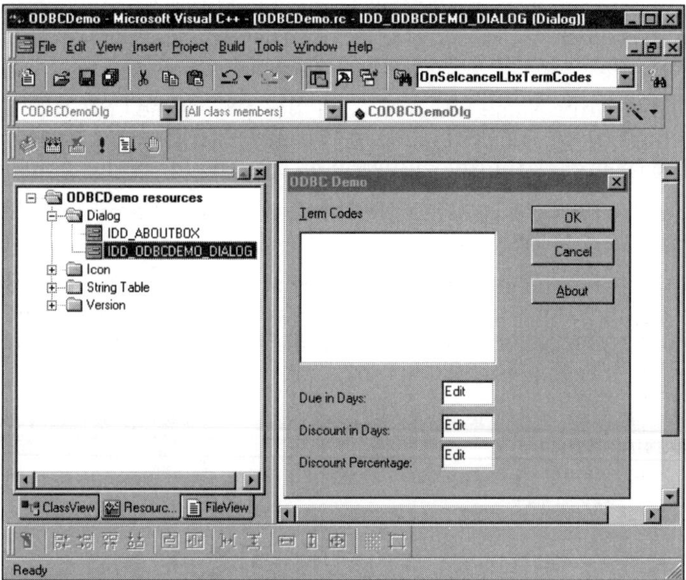

Figure 26-5: The ODBCDemo dialog box should look similar to this after the new controls have been added.

2. You should now have four input controls (a list box for the Term Code list and three Edit fields for the "Due In Days," "Discount In Days," and "Discount Percentage"). Click the list box control. Hold down the Alt key, and press the Enter key. Give this control an ID of `IDC_LBX_TERM_CODES`. Using the same key sequence, rename the remaining control IDs as follows.

Control	*Control ID*
Due in Days	`IDC_EDT_DUE_IN_DAYS`
Discount in Days	`IDC_EDT_DISCOUNT_IN_DAYS`
Discount Percentage	`IDC_EDT_DISCOUNT_PCTG`

3. Create the member variables that will be used with DDX (dynamic data exchange) for the different controls by holding down the Ctrl button and double-clicking the control. You will see an Add Member Variable dialog box that enables you to specify Member variable name, Category, and Variable Type. Do this for the following controls, filling in the appropriate information:

Control	*Category*	*Variable Type*	*Variable Name*
Term Code	Control	`CListbox`	`m_lbxTermCodes`
Due in Days	Value	`long`	`m_lDueInDays`
Discount in Days	Value	`long`	`m_lDiscountInDays`
Discount Percentage	Value	`double`	`m_dDiscountPctg`

Adding the initialization and database code

After modifying the ODBCDemo main dialog, add the following code to retrieve the data from the Access database and populate the list box:

1. Open the `ODBCDemoDlg.h` file, and find the following lines:

   ```
   // Implementation
   protected:
   ```

   Add the following function declaration. This function will be called to fill the list box with all of the Term Codes in the database:

   ```
   void FillTermCodesListbox();
   ```

2. Open the `ODBCDemoDlg.cpp` file, and add the following `#include` directive:

   ```
   #include "TermCode.h"
   ```

3. Add the following `#define` directive after the header file includes:

   ```
   #define LEN_TERM_CODE 20
   ```

4. Locate the `OnInitDialog` function, and add the following function call before the `return` statement. This call loads the list box upon initialization of the dialog box:

   ```
   FillTermCodesListbox ();
   ```

5. Add the following function at the end of the `ODBCDemoDlg.cpp` file:

   ```
   void CODBCDemoDlg:: FillTermCodesListbox ()
   {
   ```

Declare and initialize the following variables to be used in this function. The ODBC handles are set to `NULL` so that upon exiting the function, it is easier to tell which handles were successfully allocated (the ones that are not `NULL`).

```
BOOL bSuccess = FALSE;

CString strFunction;

SQLHENV henv = NULL;
SQLHDBC hdbc = NULL;
BOOL bIsConnected = FALSE;
SQLHSTMT hstmt = NULL;

SQLRETURN rc;

SWORD    sMsgNum = 0;
char     szState[7]="";
SDWORD   pfNative=0;
```

The following function calls (`::SQLAllocHandle()`, `::SQLSetEnvAttr()`, and `::SQLAllocHandle()`) initialize the ODBC and return handles to use in subsequent ODBC function calls:

```
if (SQL_SUCCESS == (rc =
::SQLAllocHandle(SQL_HANDLE_ENV, SQL_NULL_HANDLE,
&henv)))
{
 if (SQL_SUCCESS == (rc = ::SQLSetEnvAttr(henv,
 SQL_ATTR_ODBC_VERSION, (SQLPOINTER) SQL_OV_ODBC3,
 SQL_IS_INTEGER)))
 {
  if (SQL_SUCCESS == (rc =
  ::SQLAllocHandle(SQL_HANDLE_DBC, henv, &hdbc)))
  {
```

The call to `::SQLConnect()` connects this application to the DSN that was created in the Nutshell "Creating the Demo ODBC DSN" in the section "Using ODBC to Fetch Data" above.

```
rc = ::SQLConnect(hdbc,
    (SQLCHAR*)"Visual C++ 6 Bible",
    SQL_NTS,
    (SQLCHAR*)"", SQL_NTS, (SQLCHAR*)"", SQL_NTS);
   if ((SQL_SUCCESS == rc)
   || (SQL_SUCCESS_WITH_INFO == rc))
   {
    bIsConnected = TRUE;
```

Once you have connected to the DSN, allocate a statement handle to use when you submit your SQL to the data source.

```
if (SQL_SUCCESS == (rc =
::SQLAllocHandle(SQL_HANDLE_STMT, hdbc, &hstmt)))
{
```

The following code builds an SQL `SELECT` string, prepares it (via `::SQLPrepare()`), and executes it (via `::SQLExecute()`):

```
LPCSTR szSQL = "SELECT * FROM TermCodeMaster";
if (SQL_SUCCESS == (rc = ::SQLPrepare(hstmt,
(unsigned char*)szSQL, SQL_NTS)))
{
 if (SQL_SUCCESS == (rc = ::SQLExecute(hstmt)))
 {
```

After the SQL statement has been executed, bind the local variables to their corresponding columns by calling `::SQLBindCol()` for each desired column. Then call `::SQLFetch()` to retrieve the data into the bound variables.

```
SDWORD cb;
char szTermCode[LEN_TERM_CODE];
long lDueInDays;
long lDiscountInDays;
double dDiscountPctg;

SQLBindCol(hstmt, 1, SQL_C_CHAR, szTermCode,
 LEN_TERM_CODE, &cb);

SQLBindCol(hstmt, 2, SQL_C_LONG, &lDueInDays,
 0, &cb);

SQLBindCol(hstmt, 3, SQL_C_LONG,
 &lDiscountInDays, 0, &cb);

SQLBindCol(hstmt, 4, SQL_C_DOUBLE,
 &dDiscountPctg, 0, &cb);

int iIndex;

rc = SQLFetch(hstmt);
while (SQL_SUCCESS == rc)
{
```

So that the database does not have to be “hit” again each time a Term Code is selected from the list box to retrieve that Term Code’s information, create an object (`CTermCode`) that will contain all of the information for each Term Code that is read from the database. The Term Code will then be added to the list box, and its item data will be set to the `CTermCode()` object pointer so that retrieving the Term Code’s information is much more efficient.

```
            CTermCode* pTermCode = new CTermCode();
            pTermCode->m_strTermCode = szTermCode;
            pTermCode->m_lDueInDays = lDueInDays;
            pTermCode->m_lDiscountInDays=lDiscountInDays;
            pTermCode->m_dDiscountPctg = dDiscountPctg;

            iIndex=m_lbxTermCodes.AddString(szTermCode);
            m_lbxTermCodes.SetItemData(iIndex,
            (DWORD)pTermCode);

            rc = SQLFetch(hstmt);
           }
          }
         }
        }
       }
      }
     }
    }
```

Once all of the records have been read from the data source, all that is left to do is to clean up and deinitialize ODBC by disconnecting from the data source and releasing the ODBC handles.

```
 if (henv)
 {
  if (hdbc)
  {
   if (bIsConnected)
   {
    if (hstmt)
    {
     ::SQLFreeHandle(SQL_HANDLE_STMT, hstmt);
    }
    ::SQLDisconnect(hdbc);
    bIsConnected = FALSE;
   }
   ::SQLFreeHandle(SQL_HANDLE_DBC, hdbc);
   hdbc = NULL;
  }
  ::SQLFreeHandle(SQL_HANDLE_ENV, henv);
  henv = NULL;
 }
}
```

6. You now must add a function so that when a Term Code is selected from the list box, the proper information is displayed in the dialog box. To do this, bring up the ClassWizard by pressing Ctrl+W. Make sure the selected class name is `CODBCDemoDlg`. In the Object IDs list box, select the Listbox ID (`IDC_LBX_TERM_CODES`). Double-click the `LBN_SELCHANGE` entry in the Messages list box on the right. The Add Member Function dialog box displays. Press the Enter key to accept the default function name. Click the Edit button on the right-hand side of the MFC ClassWizard dialog box to edit your new function. Make sure that the function looks like the following:

```
void CODBCDemoDlg::OnSelchangeLbxTermCodes()
{
 int iIndex = m_lbxTermCodes.GetCurSel();
 if (LB_ERR != iIndex)
 {
  CTermCode* pTermCode =
   (CTermCode*)m_lbxTermCodes.GetItemData(iIndex);

  if (pTermCode)
  {
   m_lDueInDays = pTermCode->m_lDueInDays;
   m_lDiscountInDays = pTermCode->m_lDiscountInDays;
   m_dDiscountPctg = pTermCode->m_dDiscountPctg;

   UpdateData(FALSE);
  }
 }
}
```

Here's what the previous code does. When an item (a Term Code) in the list box is selected, this function will be called. The first thing that is done is to get the index of the Term Code that was selected (via the `CListbox::GetCurSel()` function). If there was not an error in getting this index, the item data is retrieved. This is the same item data that was set in the `FillTermCodesListbox()` function earlier. This item data, therefore, is a pointer to the information about this specific Term Code that was read from the data source upon initialization of the dialog. The member variables that correspond to the different dialog controls are changed to reflect the current Term Code's information. The `UpdateData` function is then called to move the data from these member variables to the controls in the dialog box.

7. You now should add a function so that when the dialog box is closed, the `CTermCode` objects that were created will be deleted, and their memory freed. To do this, bring up the ClassWizard by pressing Ctrl+W. Make sure the selected class name is `CODBCDemoDlg`. In the Object IDs list box, select the `CODBCDemoDlg` Object ID from the list box on the left side. Double-click the `DestroyWindow` entry in the Messages list box on the right. Click the Edit button on the right side of the MFC ClassWizard dialog box to edit your new function. Make sure that the function looks like the following:

```
BOOL CODBCDemoDlg::DestroyWindow()
{
 CTermCode* pTermCode;
 int nTermCodes = m_lbxTermCodes.GetCount();
 for (int i = 0; i < nTermCodes; i++)
 {
  pTermCode =
   (CTermCode*)m_lbxTermCodes.GetItemData(i);

  if (pTermCode)
  {
   delete pTermCode;
  }
 }

 return CDialog::DestroyWindow();
}
```

This code walks through every Term Code in the listbox, and after retrieving its item data, calls the C++ delete operator to free the associated memory.

8. Create a file named `TermCode.h`, and type the following lines. This object serves to hold information about each Term Code read from the data source.

```
#pragma once

class CTermCode
{
public:
  CString m_strTermCode;
  long m_lDueInDays;
  long m_lDiscountInDays;
  double m_dDiscountPctg;
};
```

9. Add the ODBC library to the project by doing the following: Click the Project menu option. From there click the Add To Project menu. You will be presented with yet another menu. On this menu, select the Files... menu options. Locate where you have installed the ODBC 3.0 SDK. Under that directory you should find a directory named `LIB32`. Change the Files of Type to list files of type "Library Files (*.lib)." Double-click the `Odbc32.lib` file.

10. Press the F7 button to build the application, and run it by pressing Ctrl+F5. Once you build and run the application, the results should be similar to what you see in Figure 26-6.

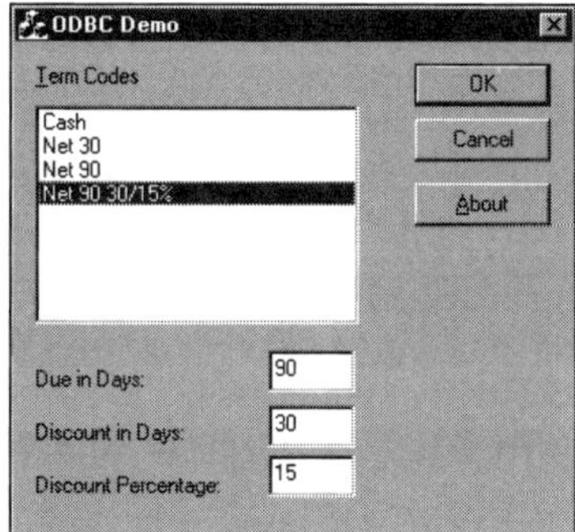

Figure 26-6: The ODBCDemo application demonstrates how to use the ODBC SDK to execute SQL queries against an ODBC data source and fetch the returned data.

Using ODBC to Dynamically Query a Data Source

As a programmer, at times you will be faced with scenarios in which you do not know the schema of a database until runtime—for example, in ad-hoc query and reporting tools. In both cases, end users can build their own SQL from a list of tables. As you saw in the previous demo, it is extremely easy to pass ODBC an SQL string, have it executed, and retrieve the resulting data. But how can you do this when you don't know the SQL string until runtime?

Luckily, ODBC provides several functions that can be used for this very purpose. After connecting to the data source, the next steps required are the following:

1. Prepare the SQL statement with the `SQLPrepare()` function.
2. Execute the SQL statement with the `SQLExecute()` function.
3. Call `SQLNumResultCols()` to find out how many columns were returned in the result set.
4. For each column, call the `SQLDescribeCol()` function to get the column type.
5. For each column, convert the SQL type returned from `SQLDescribeCol()` to a C type.
6. For each row in the result set, allocate memory for the data (depending on the C type).
7. For each row, call `SQLGetData()` to read the data into the allocated memory for that row/column.

Did I say "luckily"? Well, it may not be easy, but at least it can be done. In this demo, you will not only learn how to do everything previously mentioned, but you will also put all this code into a class called `CODBCDynamic` so that you can reduce the 400+ lines of code required to two lines of code.

Looking at the CODBCDynamic class declaration

Here is what the ODBCDynamic.h code looks like:

```
#pragma once
```

After this class' ExecuteSQL function has been called, the array (CODBCRecordArray) will contain an entry (CODBCRecord) for each record returned by the SQL statement. Each of these array elements will in turn represent the data for that record. The map is of the type CMapStringToOb, where the string is a column name and the object is a CDBVariant pointer whose value represents the database value for that record/column combination. Using a map for the record enables the programmer to either iterate through the entire map to get each column's value for that record or request a specific column's value if the column name is known.

```
typedef CTypedPtrMap<CMapStringToPtr, \
 CString /* column name */, \
 CDBVariantEx* /* value */> CODBCRecord;

typedef CTypedPtrArray<CObArray, \
 CODBCRecord*> CODBCRecordArray;

class AFX_EXT_CLASS CODBCDynamic
{
public:
```

To instantiate the class, the programmer simply passes a valid DSN to the constructor.

```
 CODBCDynamic(LPCSTR lpszDSN);
 ~CODBCDynamic();
 protected:
 void CleanOutRecordArray();

protected:
 SQLHENV m_henv;
 SQLHDBC m_hdbc;
 BOOL m_bIsConnected;

public:
 SQLHDBC GetHDBC ()
 {
  return m_hdbc;
 }

public:
 CODBCRecordArray m_ODBCRecordArray;

protected:
 short GetFieldTypeFromSQLType(short nSQLType);
```

```
void* GetDataBuffer(CDBVariantEx* pvarValue,
 short nFieldType, int* pnLen, short nSQLType,
 UDWORD nPrecision);

long GetData(SQLHSTMT hstmt, short nFieldIndex,
 short nFieldType, LPVOID pvData, int nLen,
 short nSQLType);
```

The users of your class will need only two functions. One function (`ExecuteSQL()`) enables you to pass any valid SQL string and have it executed. The resulting data is then placed in the `m_ODBCRecordArray`. The second function, `FetchData()`, is for those rare cases when you have a result set and still want to use this class' code to dynamically map the data into an easy-to-use array.

```
public:
 long ExecuteSQL(LPCTSTR lpszSQL);
 long FetchData(HSTMT hstmt);
};
```

You may have noticed that after a call to `ExecuteSQL()`the programmer has no way to initialize the class before making another call. That is because this code is in a protected function called `CleanOutRecordArray()`, and it is one of the first things the class calls when the `ExecuteSQL()` function is called.

How the CODBCDynamic class works

Because the implementation file for the `CODBCDynamic` class is over 400 lines, no trees will be killed by listing the entire file. However, it is helpful show some of the more relevant functions (in the order they are called) so that you understand just how this class dynamically retrieves data from a data source without knowing anything about the database's schema.

Connecting to the DSN

You may recall from the description of the class' header file that when a user of your class instantiates this class, they do so by passing it a DSN. The appropriate handles are then allocated, and the DSN is connected to using the basic connection functions you learned about in the first demo.

```
CODBCDynamic::CODBCDynamic(LPCSTR lpszDSN)
{
 SQLRETURN rc;

 m_henv = NULL;
 m_hdbc = NULL;
 m_bIsConnected = FALSE;

 if (SQL_SUCCESS == (rc =
 ::SQLAllocHandle(SQL_HANDLE_ENV,
  SQL_NULL_HANDLE, &m_henv)))
```

```
{
 if (SQL_SUCCESS == (rc = ::SQLSetEnvAttr(m_henv,
   SQL_ATTR_ODBC_VERSION, (SQLPOINTER) SQL_OV_ODBC3,
   SQL_IS_INTEGER)))
 {
  if (SQL_SUCCESS == (rc =
  ::SQLAllocHandle(SQL_HANDLE_DBC, m_henv, &m_hdbc)))
  {
   rc = ::SQLConnect(m_hdbc,
    (unsigned char*)lpszDSN, SQL_NTS,
    (unsigned char*)"", SQL_NTS, (unsigned char*)"",
    SQL_NTS);
   if ((SQL_SUCCESS == rc)
   || (SQL_SUCCESS_WITH_INFO == rc))
   {
    m_bIsConnected = TRUE;
   }
  }
 }
}
}
```

Executing the SQL and fetching the data

After constructing an instance of the CODBCDynamic class, the ExecuteSQL() function can be called:

```
long CODBCDynamic::ExecuteSQL(LPCTSTR lpszSQL)
{
 long lRecordsRead = 0;
```

As explained earlier, the CleanOutRecordArray() function is used to initialize the record array. This function simply uses a couple of for loops to iterate through the record array and column/value map and releases the previously allocated memory.

```
 CleanOutRecordArray();

 BOOL bSuccess = FALSE;
 SQLRETURN rc;
 SQLHSTMT hstmt = NULL;

 if (SQL_SUCCESS == (rc =
 ::SQLAllocHandle(SQL_HANDLE_STMT, m_hdbc, &hstmt)))
 {
```

The class then uses the SQLPrepare() and SQLExecute() functions to have the data source execute the SQL that was passed to this function. Remember that when you execute an SQL function, a result set is returned and is represented by an hstmt.

```
  if (SQL_SUCCESS == (rc = ::SQLPrepare(hstmt,
   (unsigned char*)lpszSQL, SQL_NTS)))
```

```
  {
   if (SQL_SUCCESS == (rc = ::SQLExecute(hstmt)))
   {
```

Once the result set has been retrieved, another member function (FetchData()) is called to retrieve the data into C variables. This function is called internally so that the same code path is used whether you are calling the ExecuteSQL() function with an SQL string or the FetchData() function with an hstmt representing a result set.

```
    lRecordsRead = FetchData(hstmt);
   }
   ::SQLFreeHandle(SQL_HANDLE_STMT, &hstmt);
  }
 }
```

When the function returns, the return value will be the total number of records that were retrieved for the SQL statement that was passed to this function.

```
 return lRecordsRead;
}
```

Now things start to get interesting. The FetchData() function is the function that really does the stuff you as an aspiring ODBC guru care about.

```
long CODBCDynamic::FetchData(HSTMT hstmt)
{
 SQLRETURN rc;

 long lRecordsRead = 0;
 CODBCRecord* pODBCRecord;

 SWORD FAR iNumResultCols = 0;
 CObArray arrODBCColumns;
```

This class is nothing more than a placeholder, if you will, for the information that defines a given column. Its use is explained in the following text.

```
 CODBCColumnInfo* pODBCColumnInfo;
```

The first record is fetched from the result set.

```
 rc = SQLFetch(hstmt);
 while (SQL_SUCCESS == rc)
 {
```

Because you wouldn't want to get the column information every time a record is fetched from the result set, some "first time" processing has to occur. First, the number of columns in this result set is ascertained via the `SQLNumResultCols()` function. A `for` loop is then used so that, for each column, the `SQLDescribeCol()` function is called to retrieve information about the column that will be needed to allocate the proper amount of memory when the data is retrieved. Next, an object of type `CODBCColumnInfo()` is created. The pointer to this object is then saved into an array where the index of the array is equal to the index of the column in the result set. That way, for example, when the function is reading the data for record *x*, column *y*, the column information can be located in this column information array at index *y*.

```
if (1 == ++lRecordsRead)
{
 if (SQL_SUCCESS == (rc = ::SQLNumResultCols(hstmt,
 &iNumResultCols)))
 {
  for (int i = 1; i <= iNumResultCols; i++)
  {
   char lpszColName[MAX_COLNAME + 1];
   SWORD nLen;
   SWORD nSQLType;
   UDWORD nPrecision;
   SWORD nScale;
   SWORD nNullability;

   if (SQL_SUCCESS == (rc = ::SQLDescribeCol(hstmt,
   i, (UCHAR*)lpszColName, MAX_COLNAME, &nLen,
   &nSQLType, &nPrecision, &nScale, &nNullability)))
   {
```

The `GetFieldTypeFromSQLType()` function simply uses a `switch` statement to determine the correct C type to be used for the column's SQL type. The C type is needed so that when the `SQLGetData()` function is called to retrieve the data into the local variables, the correct C type can be passed for the column whose data is being retrieved.

```
    // Determine the default field type and
    // get the data buffer
    short nFieldType =
      GetFieldTypeFromSQLType(nSQLType);

    pODBCColumnInfo =
      new CODBCColumnInfo(lpszColName,
      nLen, nFieldType, nSQLType, nPrecision);

    arrODBCColumns.Add((CObject*)pODBCColumnInfo);
   }
  }
 }
}
```

At this point, the column information has been retrieved. A new CODBCRecord object is created. Recall that this is simply a CObArray.

```
pODBCRecord = new CODBCRecord();
```

For each of the result set's columns, a CDBVariantEx object is created. The CDBVariant class is a simple derived class of type CDBVariant. The base class is used to hold virtually any type of data. It accomplishes this by having a member variable for a number of different types. This class is used by examining the object's m_dwType member variable. The value of that member variable tells you which member variable to retrieve the data from. For example, if m_dwType is equal to DBVT_BOOL, then the data is in the m_bVal member variable. If you want to see a complete list of all the types that this class supports, it is documented in the Visual C++ online help. The CDBVariantEx class then simply adds one member function, GetStringValue(), that enables a calling function to retrieve the object's data value into a CString regardless of the actual type.

The source code for this class is in the DBVariantEx.h file, located on the companion CD in the \Chap26\ODBCDemo folder.

✦ ✦ ✦ ✦ ✦

```
for (int j = 0; j < iNumResultCols; j++)
  {
   CDBVariantEx* pvarValue = new CDBVariantEx();
   pvarValue->Clear();

   int nGetDataBufferLen = 0;
```

The column's data type, GetDataBuffer(), is called to allocate the necessary memory. You may be wondering why there's a void pointer called pvData when there's the CDBVariantEx object that the data will be copied into. Because ODBC wouldn't know what to do with an MFC class such as CDBVariant, the GetDataBuffer() function sets the address of the pvData pointer to the appropriate member variable of the CDBVariantEx object, depending on the C type. For example, if a column's C type was a short, the pvData pointer would be set to the address of the CDBVariantEx's m_iVal member variable. That way, in effect, the data is being read directly into the CDBVariantEx object, and you don't have to go through the extra step of copying it there.

```
   void* pvData = GetDataBuffer(pvarValue,
     ((CODBCColumnInfo*)arrODBCColumns[j])->
     m_nFieldType, &nGetDataBufferLen,
     ((CODBCColumnInfo*)arrODBCColumns[j])->m_nSQLType,
     ((CODBCColumnInfo*)arrODBCColumns[j])->
     m_nPrecision);
```

You finally know the column type and have the appropriate memory allocated. Now this class' `GetData()` function is called. This function basically just calls the ODBC `SQLGetData()` function passing it the `pvData` pointer retrieved earlier. Notice the second argument (j+1). This is the column number that represents the column whose data is being retrieved. When this function returns, you will finally have the data for this record and column combination.

```
long nActualSize = GetData(hstmt, j+1,
 ((CODBCColumnInfo*)arrODBCColumns[j])->
 m_nFieldType, pvData, nGetDataBufferLen,
 ((CODBCColumnInfo*)arrODBCColumns[j])->
 m_nSQLType);

// deal with NULLs
if (-1 == nActualSize)
{
 pvarValue->Clear();
 pvarValue->m_dwType = DBVT_NULL;
}
```

Now that you have the data for this column, add the column and its `CDBVariant` to the column/value map for this record.

```
pODBCRecord->
 SetAt(((CODBCColumnInfo*)arrODBCColumns[j])->
  m_lpszColName, pvarValue);

if ((-1 != nActualSize)
&& (((CODBCColumnInfo*)arrODBCColumns[j])->
m_nFieldType == SQL_C_CHAR))
{

 // Release the string buffer
 CString strValue = (CString)*pvarValue->m_pstring;
 strValue.ReleaseBuffer(nActualSize <
  ((CODBCColumnInfo*)arrODBCColumns[j])->m_nLen
  ? nActualSize :
  ((CODBCColumnInfo*)arrODBCColumns[j])->m_nLen);
}
}
```

Once all of the columns/values have been added to the map, this record is added to the record array, and the next record is fetched.

```
 m_ODBCRecordArray.Add(pODBCRecord);
 rc = SQLFetch(hstmt);
}
```

After all of the records have been fetched from the result set, a little cleanup is necessary for the column type objects that were created when the first record was retrieved.

```
    for (int iColumn = arrODBCColumns.GetUpperBound();
    iColumn >= 0; iColumn–)
    {
     CODBCColumnInfo* pODBCColumnInfo =
      (CODBCColumnInfo*)arrODBCColumns[iColumn];

     if (pODBCColumnInfo)
     {
      delete pODBCColumnInfo;
     }
     arrODBCColumns.RemoveAt(iColumn);
    }
    ASSERT(0 == arrODBCColumns.GetSize());
```

Return the number of records read to this function's caller.

```
    return lRecordsRead;
  }
```

Using the CODBCDynamic class

Now that you have seen what's involved in writing a class like this, here's a look at what it takes to use it.

```
CODBCDynamic odbcDynamic(m_strDSN);
odbcDynamic.ExecuteSQL(CString(_T("Your SQL "
"statement goes here)));
```

That's it. Two lines of code to replace more than 400! At this point, simply iterating through the record array gives you a `CMapStringToOb` that represents all of the columns and their values for that record. You can then iterate through that map to get every column's value, or you can use the `CMapStringToOb::Lookup` function to retrieve a specific column's data (provided you know the column's name).

Figure 26-7 is an example of using the `CODBCDynamic` class. This application and its source code can be found on the CD in the `\Chap26\ODBCDynamicTest` folder.

✦ ✦ ✦ ✦ ✦

As you can see, the sample application fills a combo box with all of the DSNs in the system. Once a DSN is selected, a second combo box is filled with all of the tables that exist in the data source pointed to by the DSN. After the user selects a table, the `CODBCDynamic::ExecuteSQL()` function is called to retrieve all of the records from the table, which are then displayed in the list control.

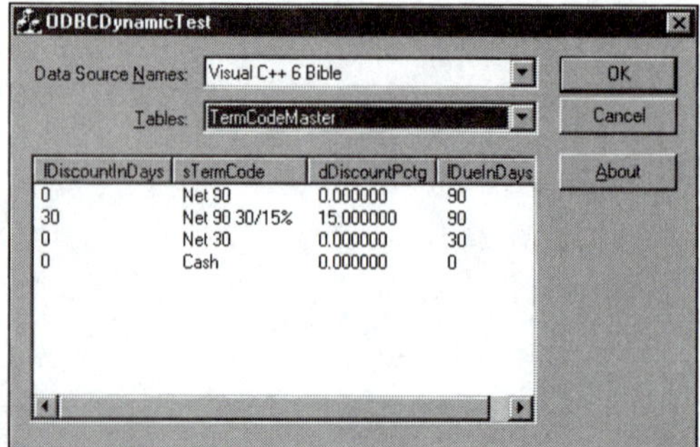

Figure 26-7: The CODBCDynamicTest application demonstrates how to use the CODBCDynamic class to query any ODBC DSN without knowing the database's schema.

Summary

In this chapter you learned about ODBC and how it provides a single API that can be used to interface to almost any DBMS from a single code base. In addition, you learned how to use the ODBC SDK to connect to, fetch data from, and disconnect from a data source. You even wrote a C++ class to encapsulate some of the more advanced ODBC SDK functions that enable you to access a data source without knowing the database's schema until runtime.

However, writing database applications using the ODBC SDK is not without its drawbacks. One trade-off to having the power and flexibility of a robust API such as the ODBC SDK is that the programming is more difficult, both in terms of what you as a programmer are responsible for and the number of lines of code necessary to carry out a given task. As you saw in the ODBCDemo application, the simple task of writing a loop to read and display all of the records in a single table required about a dozen different ODBC function calls and almost 100 lines of code! Luckily, Microsoft recognized this fact and released a set of MFC classes, collectively known as the *MFC database classes*. These classes, covered in the next chapter, give the database developer a much simpler object-oriented interface to the ODBC functionality that you have learned about throughout this chapter.

✦ ✦ ✦

MFC Database Classes

CHAPTER 27

✦ ✦ ✦ ✦

In This Chapter

Using the CDatabase object

Using the CRecordset object

Discovering the MFC database classes

Developing a simple maintenance application using the MFC database classes

Learning how to access a parameterized CRecordset

Learning how to call a parameterized Access query that returns data

✦ ✦ ✦ ✦

Chapter 26 introduced ODBC (Open Database Connectivity) and illustrated how ODBC was created to provide a means by which database applications could interface to multiple DBMSs from a single code base. While ODBC certainly has its advantages, it is not without its drawbacks. An example of one is the amount of code it takes to perform even the simplest database operations. Let's say you want your application to do something as simple as read every row from a given table. Before a database application using ODBC can even begin reading the data from the table, it must acquire an "environment handle," tell ODBC which version of ODBC the application conforms to, acquire a "database connection handle," and acquire a "statement handle." Throw in the releasing of all those handles and some error checking, and you have about 100 lines of source code—and you haven't even started reading data yet!

Therefore, no sooner had Microsoft introduced ODBC than did programmers start asking the logical question, "This is great, but when are you going to wrap this new functionality with some of the MFC classes?" Thankfully, starting with version 1.5 of MFC, Microsoft did just that by introducing a set of MFC classes that encapsulates the ODBC functionality. These classes are generally referred to as the *database classes* and are the subject of this chapter. Note that because the MFC database classes do encapsulate the rather robust ODBC SDK API, if you are not already familiar with ODBC, you might want to take a look at Chapter 26 to at least familiarize yourself with the terminology that will be used throughout this chapter.

In this chapter, you will begin by learning about the four principal database classes, `CDatabase`, `CRecordset`, `CRecordView`, and `CDatabaseException`. Once you have finished learning about these classes and their functionality, two demos will be presented. The first demo is a fully functional maintenance application using the MFC database classes. This application has all the capabilities of a traditional maintenance application (creating, reading, updating, and deleting) for maintaining a "user master" table. The second demo is actually two demos in one. In the first part, you will learn how to use parameterized recordsets to retrieve data from a Microsoft Access database, and in the second part of the demo, you will learn how to call a parameterized Microsoft Access query that returns data.

CDatabase

A `CDatabase` object represents a connection to a data source. After a `CDatabase` object is constructed, a DSN (data source name) is specified with a call to either the `Open` or the `OpenEx` member function. The connection to the DSN's underlying data source is made once one of these functions is called. A `CDatabase` object is typically used in conjunction with one or more recordsets (which are explained shortly), although a `CDatabase` object can be used by itself. An example of using a `CDatabase` object without a `CRecordset` object is when your application needs to issue an SQL statement against a data source that does not return any data. The `CDatabase::ExecuteSQL()` function exists for just this purpose. Following is an example of how easy it is to insert a record into a table using the `CDatabase` class:

```
try
{
 CDatabase db;
 if (db.Open("Visual C++ 6 Bible"))
 {
  db.ExecuteSQL("INSERT INTO UserMaster
   VALUES('TestID', 'Test User Name', 0)");

  db.Close();
 }
}
catch(CDBException* pe)
{
 AfxMessageBox(pe->m_strError);
 pe->Delete();
}
```

Compare this code segment to the more than 50 lines of ODBC SDK code that was needed to accomplish the same thing in Chapter 26! The database classes, while not as powerful as directly using the ODBC SDK, are much easier and faster to use in terms of programmer productivity than the ODBC SDK. Let's take a minute and look at the preceding code in more detail. The first thing you see in the code snippet is a `try/catch` block.

```
try
{
  ...
}
catch(CDBException* pe)
{
```

```
    AfxMessageBox(pe->m_strError);
    pe->Delete();
  }
```

Almost all of the CDatabase classes' member functions throw an exception of type CDBException if an abnormal condition occurs. The CDBException class, which is derived from CDBException, provides almost nothing above and beyond what its base class defines. In fact, except for the member variables that are inherited from the CException class, the CDBException class doesn't define any member functions at all. The three member variables that are inherited serve to tell the application what went wrong at the time the exception was thrown. Here are the three member variables and how they can be used to aid in determining the cause of the exception:

- ✦ m_nRetCode — Cause of the exception in the form of the ODBC return code (of type SQLRETURN)
- ✦ m_strError — String that describes the error that caused the exception to be thrown
- ✦ m_strStateNativeOrigin — String that describes the error that caused the exception to be thrown in terms of the ODBC error codes

Because most of the CDatabase classes' member functions can throw exceptions of type CDBException, it is wise to verify that exceptions of type CDBException (or its base class, CException) are being caught somewhere in the code path.

The next line in the preceding example constructs the CDatabase object and opens a connection to the DSN's underlying data source. As you can see, the DSN name is "Visual C++ 6 Bible." This value has been hard-coded in order to keep the example simple. In normal practice this value would be specified as a typedef, const, or string resource.

```
CDatabase db;
if (db.Open("Visual C++ 6 Bible"))
...
```

The CDatabase constructor doesn't do very much at all. As mentioned previously, a connection to the data source isn't made until either the Open() or the OpenEx() function is called. Therefore, let's concentrate on the Open() function.

```
virtual BOOL Open( LPCTSTR lpszDSN,
 BOOL bExclusive = FALSE, BOOL bReadOnly = FALSE,
 LPCTSTR lpszConnect = "ODBC;",
 BOOL bUseCursorLib = TRUE );

throw( CDBException, CMemoryException );
```

As you can see in this prototype, the application can specify several options when opening a database connection using the CDatabase::Open() function. However, only the first argument is explicitly required. In the example provided earlier, this first argument was the only argument that was passed and represented the DSN.

The bExclusive argument specifies whether to allow other connections to a data source. While this argument was not supported in past versions of Visual C++, version 6.0 finally does support a value of TRUE for this argument.

The bReadOnly argument allows the application to specify whether or not updates to the data source will be allowed once a connection is made. The default value for this argument is FALSE, meaning that updates to the data source can be made through this connection. Any CRecordset objects that are created and attached to this CDatabase automatically inherit this value.

The lpszConnect argument allows the application to specify the ODBC connect string to use when the CDatabase's underlying MFC code attempts to connect to the specified DSN via ODBC. If this argument is to be used, a value of NULL must be specified for the lpszDSN argument. The benefit of using this argument is flexibility. For example, if the application must specify a user ID and password, it can be done via the lpszConnect argument. The ODBC driver that is being used dictates the format of this argument.

Finally, the bUseCursorLib argument specifies whether the ODBC cursor library is to be used. If this value is set to TRUE (which is the default), only static snapshot or forward-only cursors are allowed for this connection. In order to use dynasets, a value of FALSE must be passed for this argument. After opening the recordset, the next line executes the SQL statement and closes the database:

```
db.ExecuteSQL("INSERT INTO UserMaster "
 "VALUES('TestID', 'Test User Name', 0)");

db.Close();
```

The CDatabase::ExecuteSQL function has a very straightforward syntax. The application need do nothing more than simply specify the SQL statement that needs to be executed by the underlying data source. Note that this function should be used only when the application does not anticipate that data will be returned as a result of executing the SQL statement.

As mentioned earlier, an alternative method of opening a database connection using the CDatabase class is via the CDatabase::OpenEx() function. Actually, according to the MFC documentation, this is now the preferred way of opening a database connection:

```
virtual BOOL OpenEx(LPCTSTR lpszConnectString,
 DWORD dwOptions = 0 );

throw( CDBException, CMemoryException );
```

The `CDatabase::OpenEx()` function takes only two arguments: a connect string and a `DWORD` that represents the connection options. The `lpszConnectString` is used to pass the ODBC connect string to the function while the `dwOptions` argument is used to set up how the connection is to be made. The following values can be used together, using the logical OR operator:

```
CDatabase::openExclusive
CDatabase::openReadOnly
CDatabase::useCursorLib
CDatabase::noODBCDialog
CDatabase::forceODBCDialog
```

These values work exactly as they do in the `CDatabase::Open()` function. The only difference is the addition of the `CDatabase::noODBCDialog` and the `CDatabase::forceODBCDialog` flags. These flags indicate whether an application wishes for the ODBC Driver Manager to present the user with the ODBC connection dialog box when the connection is attempted.

Another useful set of member functions that the `CDatabase` class supports are the functions that support transactions (sometimes called *commitment control*). Transactions give applications the capability to bracket sets of functions in logical groups. If any one of a logically grouped set of functions fails, all database changes that were made by previous function calls in the same group are undone.

As an example, let's say that an accounting application must move an amount from one account to another. What would happen if after removing the amount from one account, the attempt to update the second account's balance failed? The integrity of the database would obviously be compromised because the money was removed from one account but was not added to the second account. That is where transactions are useful. With the use of transactions, the application can specify that either both of these functions must complete successfully or neither of them should. Therefore, transactions are one means of ensuring data integrity.

Here's the way a transaction works: calling the `CDatabase::BeginTrans()` function sets a "transaction boundary." Any changes made to the data source's data after this point is subject to being "rolled back" or undone. When the `CDatabase::CommitTrans()` function is called, any changes made to the database since the last transaction boundary are committed (made permanent). If, for some reason, the application wishes to manually undo all the changes since the last transaction boundary, it can do so with a call to the `CDatabase::Rollback()` function. Note that before attempting to use transactions, the `CDatabase::CanTransact()` function should be called to verify that the ODBC driver being used supports transactions.

CRecordset

While a `CDatabase` object represents a connection to a data source, a `CRecordset` object (known as a *recordset*) represents a set of records retrieved from a data source. While the `CRecordset` class does support several types of recordsets, two types of recordsets are generally used: dynasets and snapshots. A dynaset, or keyset-driven recordset, is a dynamic set of data that supports bi-directional scrolling and stays synchronized with the updates made by other users of the data source. A snapshot, on the other hand, is a static picture of the data taken at the time the recordset was filled. This set of data is not affected by changes made by other users. In order for an application using a snapshot recordset to see changes made by other users, the recordset must be closed and reopened. The snapshot recordset also supports bi-directional scrolling.

The fastest way to illustrate using recordsets is to create one using the ClassWizard. The recordset you will use is based on the `UserMaster` table that exists in the `vc6bib.mdb` Microsoft Access database. This file is located on the companion CD in the `\Chap26\Database` folder. Figure 27-1 shows the `UserMaster` table in Microsoft Access '97.

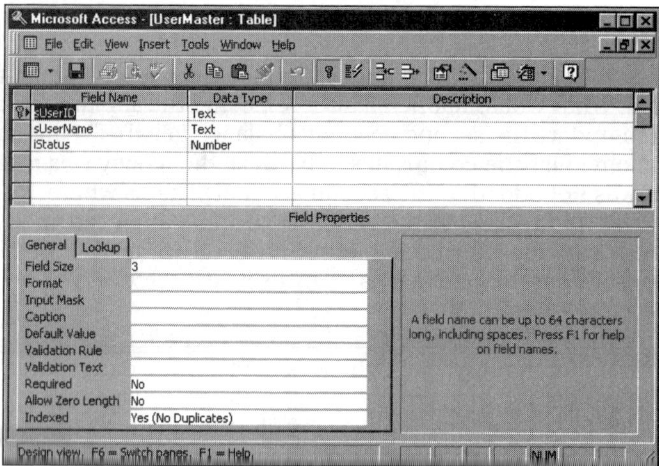

Figure 27-1: The UserMaster table (shown here in Microsoft Access 97) is used throughout this chapter and in the demo application.

Begin by opening the ClassWizard. Once the ClassWizard is displayed, click the Add Class button. From the menu that is displayed, select the New option. Figure 27-2 shows the resulting New Class dialog box.

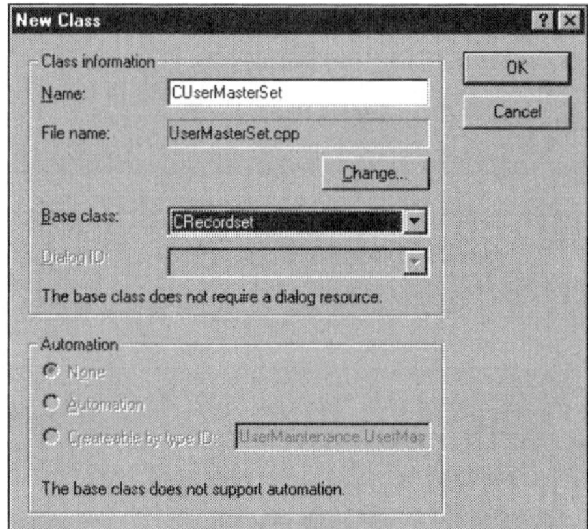

Figure 27-2: The ClassWizard New Class dialog box is used to create new MFC-derived classes.

Specify the creations of a `CRecordset`-derived class. The ClassWizard will then display a prompt to specify the type of database access used with the new recordset class. Figure 27-3 shows this dialog.

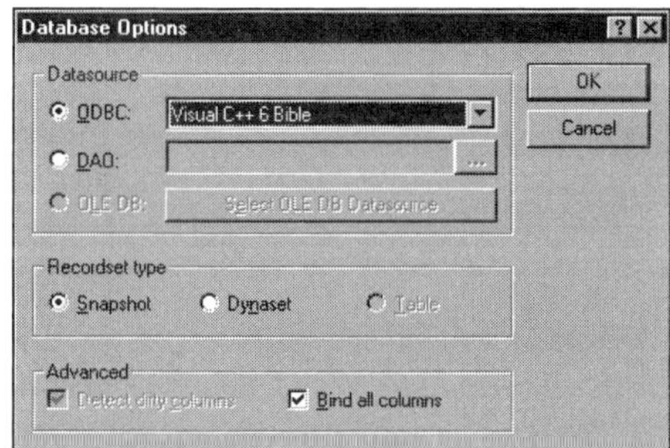

Figure 27-3: When creating a CRecordset-derived class, the Database Options dialog box enables you to specify many of the characteristics that will be used to define the new class.

After selecting the DSN, simply select the `UserMaster` table (as shown in Figure 27-4), and click the OK button. That's how easy it is to create a `CRecordset`-derived class! At this point the ClassWizard will generate about 125 lines of code automatically to make accessing data from the `UserMaster` table much easier.

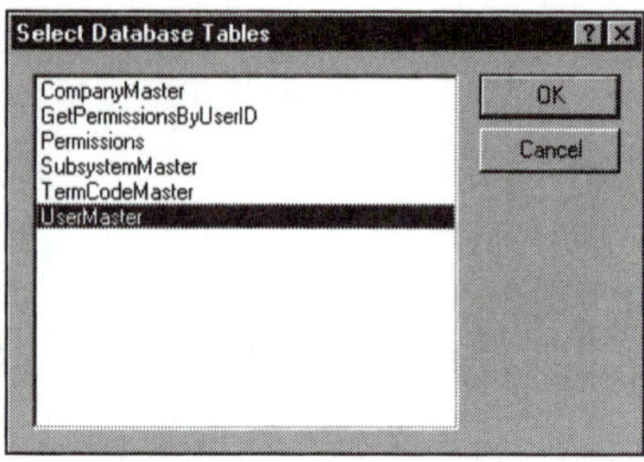

Figure 27-4: When creating a CRecordset class, the Select Database Tables dialog box is used to select the table or query that the recordset will be based on.

Listings 27-1 and 27-2 show the amount of work the ClassWizard has done. Throughout this part of the chapter you will learn what these different member variables and member functions are for and how to use them.

Listing 27-1: UserMasterSet.h

```
#pragma once

#if _MSC_VER >= 1000
#pragma once
#endif // _MSC_VER >= 1000
// UserMasterSet.h : header file
//

/////////////////////////////////////////////////////////////////
// CUserMasterSet recordset

class CUserMasterSet : public CRecordset
{
public:
 CUserMasterSet(CDatabase* pDatabase = NULL);
 DECLARE_DYNAMIC(CUserMasterSet)

 // Field/Param Data
 //{{AFX_FIELD(CUserMasterSet, CRecordset)
 CString    m_sUserID;
 CString    m_sUserName;
 int        m_iStatus;
 //}}AFX_FIELD


 // Overrides
 // ClassWizard generated virtual function overrides
 //{{AFX_VIRTUAL(CUserMasterSet)
public:
 virtual CString GetDefaultConnect();
 virtual CString GetDefaultSQL();
 virtual void DoFieldExchange(CFieldExchange* pFX);
 //}}AFX_VIRTUAL
```

```
 // Implementation
 #ifdef _DEBUG
 virtual void AssertValid() const;
 virtual void Dump(CDumpContext& dc) const;
 #endif
};

//{{AFX_INSERT_LOCATION}}
// Microsoft Developer Studio will insert additional
// declarations immediately before the previous line.
```

Listing 27-2: UserMasterSet.cpp

```
// UserMasterSet.cpp : implementation file
//

#include "stdafx.h"
#include "dbtest.h"
#include "UserMasterSet.h"

#ifdef _DEBUG
#define new DEBUG_NEW
#undef THIS_FILE
static char THIS_FILE[] = __FILE__;
#endif

/////////////////////////////////////////////////////////////////
// CUserMasterSet

IMPLEMENT_DYNAMIC(CUserMasterSet, CRecordset)

CUserMasterSet::CUserMasterSet(CDatabase* pdb)
: CRecordset(pdb)
{
 //{{AFX_FIELD_INIT(CUserMasterSet)
 m_sUserID = _T("");
 m_sUserName = _T("");
 m_iStatus = 0;
 m_nFields = 3;
 //}}AFX_FIELD_INIT
 m_nDefaultType = snapshot;
}

CString CUserMasterSet::GetDefaultConnect()
{
 return _T("ODBC;DSN=Visual C++ 6 Bible");
}
```

(continued)

Listing 27-2 *(continued)*

```
CString CUserMasterSet::GetDefaultSQL()
{
 return _T("[UserMaster]");
}

void CUserMasterSet::DoFieldExchange(
 CFieldExchange* pFX)
{
 //{{AFX_FIELD_MAP(CUserMasterSet)
 pFX->SetFieldType(CFieldExchange::outputColumn);
 RFX_Text(pFX, _T("[sUserID]"), m_sUserID);
 RFX_Text(pFX, _T("[sUserName]"), m_sUserName);
 RFX_Int(pFX, _T("[iStatus]"), m_iStatus);
 //}}AFX_FIELD_MAP
}

/////////////////////////////////////////////////////////////////
// CUserMasterSet diagnostics

#ifdef _DEBUG
void CUserMasterSet::AssertValid() const
{
 CRecordset::AssertValid();
}

void CUserMasterSet::Dump(CDumpContext& dc) const
{
 CRecordset::Dump(dc);
}
#endif //_DEBUG
```

Once you have a CRecordset-derived class, your application can use it to perform any of the following tasks:

- Construct a recordset
- Open a recordset
- Read and write data using RFX (record field exchange)
- Filter records
- Sort records returned as a result of an SQL statement
- Navigate through a result set (returned data)
- Save records
- Delete records

Constructing a recordset

The `CRecordset` constructor takes as its only argument a pointer to a `CDatabase` object. This argument has a default value of `NULL`. If the application instantiates a `CRecordset` object and specifies this value as `NULL`, MFC automatically creates a temporary `CDatabase` object using the information specified when the recordset class was created via the ClassWizard. This information can be found in the `CRecordset::GetDefaultConnect()` and `CRecordset::GetDefaultSQL()` functions. However, if the application is going to use several recordsets, it is much more efficient to create one `CDatabase` object and use that object when creating the recordsets. That way, only one `CDatabase` object is created for all of the recordsets instead of a `CDatabase` object being created for every recordset.

Opening a recordset

Once the recordset has been constructed, it is opened via the `CRecordset::Open()` function. The syntax for this function is as follows:

```
virtual BOOL Open(
 UINT nOpenType = AFX_DB_USE_DEFAULT_TYPE,
 LPCTSTR lpszSQL = NULL,
 DWORD dwOptions = none );

throw( CDBException, CMemoryException );
```

The `nOpenType` argument is used to specify the type of recordset being opened: dynaset, snapshot, forward-only, or dynamic. Each of these recordset types is represented by an `enum` value in the `CRecordset` class. The default recordset type for the `nOpenType` argument is `CRecordset::snapshot`.

```
class CRecordset : CObject
{
. . .
public:
 enum OpenType
 {
  dynaset,
  snapshot,
  forwardOnly,
  dynamic
};
. . .
```

The `lpszSQL` argument allows the application to specify the SQL statement that will be executed against the data source when the recordset is opened. If this argument is allowed to default to `NULL`, the code in the `CRecordset::GetDefaultSQL()` function will be used. In most cases, you will see only the name of a table or query being returned from this function. In this situation, the recordset retrieves all of the columns from the specified table or query without regard to filtering the data or sorting it in any way. The topic of filtering and sorting the data returned via a recordset will be covered shortly.

Reading and writing data using RFX

As mentioned earlier, to retrieve all of the records from a table without regard to order, the application can simply instantiate a CRecordset-derived class that was created via ClassWizard and call its CRecordset::Open() function. However, at this point, it's time to delve into how the data gets from the data source into the application's variables. The answer lies in something called RFX (record field exchange). When a CRecordset-derived class is created using the ClassWizard, ClassWizard enumerates all of the columns in the selected table or query and declares variables of the appropriate type in the new class' header file. ClassWizard also generates a function called DoFieldExchange() that serves to tie these member variables to their corresponding columns in the data source. This DoFieldExchange() function is then called when MFC needs to move data from the data source to your member variables or vice versa.

The underlying MFC code actually does all the nitty-gritty ODBC SDK functions (for example, binding the columns, fetching the data, and so on) that are covered in Chapter 26. However, now it all happens automatically for you! When an application opens a recordset, the CRecordset::Open() function moves to the first record. The application can then start navigating through the data using the CRecordset::MoveFirst(), CRecordset::MovePrev(), CRecordset::MoveNext(), and CRecordset::MoveLast() member functions. These functions will be explained shortly.

Filtering records

Now that you know how to use the CDatabase and CRecordset classes to open and retrieve data from a data source, the next step is to learn how to filter that data to get just the records your application needs. Actually, you can accomplish this in several ways. As you saw in the previous section entitled "Opening a recordset," an application can specify the SQL to be executed against a data source in the lpszSQL argument of the CRecordset::Open function. Following is an example of filtering records with the CRecordset::Open function. This code snippet reads only the records from the UserMaster table whose iStatus value is equal to zero:

```
try
{
 CDatabase db;
 if (db.Open("Visual C++ 6 Bible"))
 {
  CUserMasterSet* pUserMasterSet =
   new CUserMasterSet();

  pUserMasterSet->Open(CRecordset::snapshot,
   "SELECT * from usermaster where iStatus = 0");

  // use the data that was returned

  pUserMasterSet->Close();
```

```
    db.Close();
   }
  }
  catch(CDBException* pe)
  {
   AfxMessageBox(pe->m_strError);
   pe->Delete();
  }
```

A second way of filtering the data returned in a recordset is to use a parameterized recordset. Using the CUserMasterSet (see Listings 27-1 and 27-2) that was created earlier in the chapter, let's take a look at what changes would be necessary to modify the CUserMasterSet class so that when its Open function is called, only records from the UserMaster table whose iStatus value is equal to 0 will be retrieved.

1. The first step is to declare the variable(s) that will hold the "parameter data." Parameter data is data that is used in the WHERE clause of the SQL statement that MFC builds when the recordset is opened. Because this recordset will be filtered by the value of the iStatus column, a variable should be created for this column. A common naming standard when doing this is to simply add "Param" to the end of the column name that is being filtered on. Find the following block of code:

   ```
   // Field/Param Data
   //{{AFX_FIELD(CUserMasterSet, CRecordset)
   CString     m_sUserID;
   CString     m_sUserName;
   int         m_iStatus;
   //}}AFX_FIELD
   ```

   And add the following variable declaration:

   ```
   int         m_iStatusParam;
   ```

2. The next step is to initialize the variable in the recordset's constructor, and set the m_nParams value to the number of parameters that will be used. This is extremely important. If you attempt to use a parameterized recordset and do not set this value, the recordset's Open() will ASSERT during the call to DoFieldExchange(). Find the following block of code:

   ```
   //{{AFX_FIELD_INIT(CUserMasterSet)
    m_sUserID = _T("");
    m_sUserName = _T("");
    m_iStatus = 0;
    m_nFields = 3;
    //}}AFX_FIELD_INIT
   ```

When you finish it should look like the following code:

```
//{{AFX_FIELD_INIT(CUserMasterSet)
 m_sUserID = _T("");
 m_sUserName = _T("");
 m_iStatus = 0;
 m_nFields = 3;
 m_iStatusParam = 0;
 m_nParams = 1;
 //}}AFX_FIELD_INIT
```

3. Update the `DoFieldExchange()` function such that when finished, it looks like the following code. The `CFieldExchange::SetFieldType()` must be called with the `CFieldExchange::param` argument. This tells MFC that the `m_iStatusParam` variable (specified in the second argument) will hold the data that `iStatus` should be filtered on.

```
//{{AFX_FIELD_MAP(CUserMasterSet)
pFX->SetFieldType(CFieldExchange::outputColumn);
RFX_Text(pFX, _T("[sUserID]"), m_sUserID);
RFX_Text(pFX, _T("[sUserName]"), m_sUserName);
RFX_Int(pFX, _T("[iStatus]"), m_iStatus);
pFX->SetFieldType(CFieldExchange::param);
RFX_Int(pFX, _T("[iStatus]"), m_iStatusParam);
//}}AFX_FIELD_MAP
```

4. Once these changes have been made the only other changes that would have to be made are to the code that actually opens the recordset. When opening a parameterized recordset, the application needs to set the `CRecordset::m_strFilter` as follows. Once that is done, it can then set the parameter variable to the value it wants to filter on. Finally, a call to the `CRecordset::Open()` function returns only the desired records as dictated by the value of the parameter variables.

```
try
{
 CDatabase db;
 if (db.Open("Visual C++ 6 Biblo"))
 {
  CUserMasterSet* pUserMasterSet =
   new CUserMasterSet();

  pUserMasterSet->m_strFilter = "iStatus = ?";
  pUserMasterSet->m_iStatusParam = 0;
  pUserMasterSet->Open();

  // use the data that was returned

  pUserMasterSet->Close();
```

```
    db.Close();
  }
}
catch(CDBException* pe)
{
  AfxMessageBox(pe->m_strError);
  pe->Delete();
}
```

As you can see, using parameterized recordsets is not very difficult. The biggest hassle is that, unfortunately, it is a very manual process, and if you forget to do any of the steps involved you can end up losing a lot of time tracking down why your application's recordset open isn't working properly.

Sorting records returned with a recordset

As you just saw in the section "Filtering records," the CRecordset class provides a member variable (m_strFilter) that allows the filtering of records. The CRecordset class also provides another member variable to specify the order in which records are returned when the recordset is opened. This member variable is called m_strSort. To use it, your application simply needs to set it to the name of the column that the data will be sorted by. For example, in the preceding code, if you wanted the application to sort the data by sUserId, the resulting code would look like the following:

```
try
{
  CDatabase db;
  if (db.Open("Visual C++ 6 Bible"))
  {
    CUserMasterSet* pUserMasterSet =
      new CUserMasterSet();

    pUserMasterSet->m_strFilter = "iStatus = ?";
    pUserMasterSet->m_iStatusParam = 0;

    pUserMasterSet->m_strSort = "sUserID";
    pUserMasterSet->Open();

    // use the data that was returned

    pUserMasterSet->Close();
    db.Close();
  }
}
catch(CDBException* pe)
{
  AfxMessageBox(pe->m_strError);
  pe->Delete();
}
```

If your application must sort the data by more than one column, just separate each column name with a comma.

Moving through the result set

Now that you know how to retrieve a set of filtered and sorted records, let's take a look at how to navigate through the resulting records. The CRecordset class actually makes this extremely easy using the MoveFirst(), MovePrev(), MoveNext(), and MoveLast() functions. You can see from the function names what each function does. However, you should know the following when implementing these functions in your code:

✦ If the application attempts to call any of the move functions, they will throw a CDBException if the recordset did not return any records. Therefore, the application should always call the CRecordset::IsBOF() or CRecordset::IsEOF() before attempting to call one of the move functions.

✦ The MoveFirst() and MovePrev() functions are not supported for recordsets that were defined as forward-only.

✦ If an application is navigating through a recordset and the possibility exists that records in that recordset can be deleted by other users, the application should call the CRecordset::IsDeleted() function to verify that the record is still valid.

✦ If an application has moved to the last record in a recordset and calls MoveNext(), a CDBException() will be thrown. Therefore, when using MoveNext() to move sequentially through a recordset, applications should always call the IsEOF function before calling MoveNext.

Here is a simple example of moving through a recordset with a while loop. As you can see, CRecordset::IsEOF() is called after every move so that an invalid call to CRecordset::MoveNext() is not made once the end of the recordset has been reached.

```
pUserMasterSet->Open();
while (!pUserMasterSet->IsEOF())
{
 AfxMessageBox(pUserMasterSet->m_sUserID);
 pUserMasterSet->MoveNext();
}
```

Saving records

Using the CRecordset class to save records is easy. There are basically two different ways of saving data: adding new records and updating existing records.

To add a new record, an application simply needs to do the following:

1. Call the `CRecordset::AddNew()` function. This will prepare a new, blank record.
2. Move the data into the recordset's member variables.
3. Call the `CRecordset::Update()` function to create the new record in the data source.

To update an existing record, an application must do the following:

1. Call the `CRecordset::Edit()` function.
2. Move the data into the recordset's member variables.
3. Call the `CRecordset::Update()` function to update the current record in the data source.

It is very important to note the order in which you call these functions. The data must be moved into the member variables *after* calling the `Edit()` function. Otherwise, MFC will not update the data source. The reason for this is that the MFC database classes cache, or buffer, the data and do a memory compare when the `Update()` function is called. If no changes have been made to the member variables since the `Edit` function was called, the data source is not updated with the new data even though the application explicitly called the `Update()` function.

Deleting records

To delete a record from a recordset, the record must be the current record in the recordset. The application then has to call the `CRecordset::Delete()` function. After deleting the record, one of the `CRecordset` move functions must be called in order to move to a another record because the current record is no longer valid.

Using the MFC Database Classes

On the CD-ROM

The UserMaintenance demo illustrates how the MFC database classes can be used to perform the basic database operations of reading, writing, and deleting records. The source code for this application can be found on the companion CD in the `Chap27\UserMaintenance` folder. However, if you are going to either run this demo from the CD or type the code as you follow along in the book, you must create the appropriate DSN first. The DSN is called "Visual C++ 6 Bible." If you don't recall how to create a DSN, refer to the Nutshell "Creating the Demo ODBC DSN" in the section "Using ODBC to Fetch Data" in Chapter 26. Start by using ClassWizard to create a dialog-based application called UserMaintenance.

◆ ◆ ◆ ◆ ◆

Adding support for the MFC database classes

After you have created the application, you must add the include directive for the afxdb.h header file. This header file contains the declarations of the MFC database classes. While the #include directive can be placed in any file that is going to reference any of the database classes, it is usually more convenient to place it in the stdafx.h file.

Creating the UI for the demo

1. Because this demo is a dialog-based application, all of the UI is done on the dialog that was created automatically by AppWizard when the project was created. The project should have a dialog called IDD_USERMAINTENANCE_DIALOG. Locate that dialog, and edit it so that when finished it resembles the dialog shown in Figure 27-5.

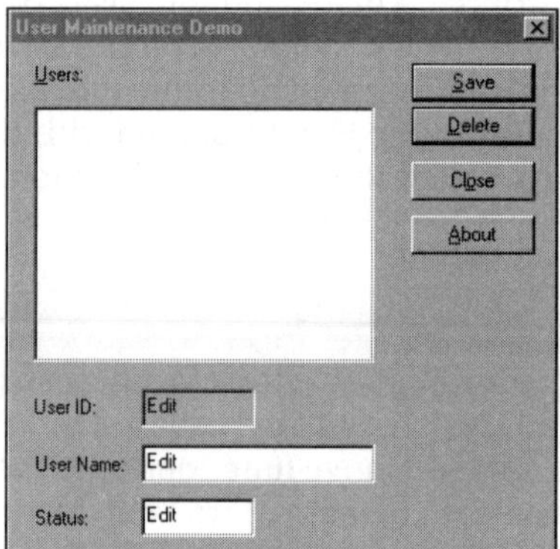

Figure 27-5: The UserMaintenance dialog box should look similar to this after the new controls have been added.

2. Once the controls have been added, make sure that their resource IDs are set as follows:

Control	*Control ID*
Users list box	IDC_LBX_USERS
User ID edit	IDC_EDT_USERID
User NName edit	IDC_EDT_USERNAME
Status edit	IDC_EDT_STATUS
Save button	IDC_BTN_SAVE
Delete button	IDC_BTN_DELETE
Close button	IDC_BTN_CLOSE

3. After the resource IDs have been set, create member variables with the following properties for each of the dialog's controls:

Control	*Category*	*Variable Type*	*Variable Name*
Users list box	Control	CListbox	m_lbxUsers
User ID edit	Value	CString	m_strUserID
User NName edit	Value	CString	m_strUserName
Status edit	Value	int	m_iStatus
Save button	Control	CButton	m_btnSave
Delete button	Control	CButton	m_btnDelete
Close button	Control	CButton	m_btnClose

Adding a utility class to encapsulate the user's data

A utility, or helper, class is needed to encapsulate each record's data. As you will see later, once a record is read, an object of type CUser is created. A string (UserID) is then inserted into the Users list box that represents that record. Each list box entry's item data, in turn, then points back to the CUser object that holds User's data. The CUser class' definition can be seen in Listing 27-3.

Listing 27-3: User.h-source code for the CUser class

```
#pragma once

class CUser
{
public:
 CString m_strUserID;
 CString m_strUserName;
 int m_iStatus;
};
```

Creating a CRecordset class for the UserMaster table

You now must create a recordset class to access the data in the `UserMaster` table. Call this class `CUserMasterSet`. Follow the directions given previously in this chapter in the section entitled "CRecordset" if you don't remember how to create a `CRecordset`-derived class.

Modifying the dialog's header file

You must make a couple of minor changes to the dialog's header file for this program:

1. Open the `UserMaintenanceDlg.h` file, and add the following include directive before the declaration of the , class:

   ```
   #include "User.h"
   ```

2. Add the following member function declarations:

   ```
   void FillListboxWithUsers();
   BOOL GetSelectedUser(int* piIndex, CUser** ppUser);
   void InitControls();
   BOOL SaveUser(CUser* pUser);
   BOOL DeleteUser(CUser* pUser);
   ```

Modifying the dialog's Implementation file

The last thing that you should do for this program is to modify the dialog's code in order to perform the database I/O.

1. Open the `UserMaintenanceDlg.cpp` file, and add the following `#include` directive:

   ```
   #include "UserMasterSet.h"
   ```

2. Locate the OnInitDialog (function, and place the following code at the end of the function before the return statement. The FillListboxWithUsers) function fills the Users list box with all of the users found in the UserMaster table. The InitControls function initializes the state of the command buttons.

```
FillListboxWithUsers();
InitControls();
```

3. At the end of the file, add the following function:

```
void CUserMaintenanceDlg::FillListboxWithUsers()
{
 int iIndex;
 CDatabase db;
 CUserMasterSet* pUserMasterSet = NULL;

 try
 {

  if (db.Open("Visual C++ 6 Bible"))
  {

   pUserMasterSet = new CUserMasterSet();
   pUserMasterSet->Open();

   while (!pUserMasterSet->IsEOF())
   {

    CUser* pUser = new CUser();
    pUser->m_strUserID = pUserMasterSet->m_sUserID;
    pUser->m_strUserName =
     pUserMasterSet->m_sUserName;
    pUser->m_iStatus = pUserMasterSet->m_iStatus;

    iIndex = m_lbxUsers.AddString(
     pUserMasterSet->m_sUserName);

    m_lbxUsers.SetItemData(iIndex, (DWORD)pUser);


    pUserMasterSet->MoveNext();
   }

   pUserMasterSet->Close();
   delete pUserMasterSet;
   db.Close();
  }
 }
```

```
 catch(CDBException* pe)
 {
  AfxMessageBox(pe->m_strError);

  if (pUserMasterSet)
  {
   if (pUserMasterSet->IsOpen())
   {
    pUserMasterSet->Close();
   }
   delete pUserMasterSet;
  }

  if (db.IsOpen())
  {
   db.Close();
  }

  pe->Delete();
 }
}
```

4. Once the `FillListboxWithUsers()` function has been defined, add the following initialization function:

```
void CUserMaintenanceDlg::InitControls()
{
 m_lbxUsers.SetCurSel(-1);

 m_strUserID = "";
 m_strUserName = "";
 m_iStatus = -1;

 m_btnSave.EnableWindow(FALSE);
 m_btnDelete.EnableWindow(FALSE);
 m_btnClose.EnableWindow(TRUE);

 m_lbxUsers.SetFocus();

 UpdateData(FALSE);
}
```

5. You must now add a function so that when a user is selected from the list box, the proper information is displayed in the dialog box. To do this, use ClassWizard to implement a message handler for the `LBN_SELCHANGE` notification message for the Users list box (`IDC_LBX_USERS`). Once you are finished, make sure the code looks as follows:

```
void CUserMaintenanceDlg::OnSelchangeLbxUsers()
{
```

```
int iIndex;
CUser* pUser;

if (GetSelectedUser(&iIndex, &pUser))
{
 m_strUserID = pUser->m_strUserID;
 m_strUserName = pUser->m_strUserName;
 m_iStatus = pUser->m_iStatus;

 m_btnSave.EnableWindow(TRUE);
 m_btnDelete.EnableWindow(TRUE);


 UpdateData(FALSE);
}
}
```

6. Add the following helper function. This function is called to retrieve the currently selected User in the list box when either the Update or Delete button is clicked.

```
BOOL CUserMaintenanceDlg::GetSelectedUser(
 int* piIndex, CUser** ppUser)
{
 BOOL bSuccess = FALSE;

 int iIndex;
 if (LB_ERR != (iIndex = m_lbxUsers.GetCurSel()))
 {
  *piIndex = iIndex;
  *ppUser = (CUser*)m_lbxUsers.GetItemData(iIndex);
   bSuccess = TRUE;
 }

 return bSuccess;
}
```

7. Add a message handler for the Close button's (`IDC_BTN_CLOSE`) `BN_CLICKED` notification message. This function simply closes the dialog.

```
void CUserMaintenanceDlg::OnBtnClose()
{
 CDialog::OnOK();
}
```

8. At this point, the application has the functions necessary to read all of the Users from the `UserMaster` table and display their respective information on the dialog. Now it's time to add "update" capability to the application. Add a message handler for the Save button's (`IDC_BTN_SAVE`) `BN_CLICKED` notification message, and implement it as follows:

```
void CUserMaintenanceDlg::OnBtnSave()
{
 int iCurrIndex;

 CUser* pUser = NULL;
 if (GetSelectedUser(&iCurrIndex, &pUser))
 {
  ASSERT(pUser);
  if (pUser)
  {
   UpdateData();

   CString strPrevUserID;
   strPrevUserID = m_strUserID;
   CString strPrevUserName;
   strPrevUserName = m_strUserName;
   int iPrevStatus = m_iStatus;

   pUser->m_strUserID = m_strUserID;
   pUser->m_strUserName = m_strUserName;
   pUser->m_iStatus = m_iStatus;

   if (SaveUser(pUser))
   {

    if (LB_ERR == m_lbxUsers.DeleteString(iCurrIndex))
    {
     AfxMessageBox("The User ID was Saved, "
      "but the previous User ID could not be "
      "removed from the listbox.");
    }
    else
    {
     int iNewIndex = m_lbxUsers.AddString(
      pUser->m_strUserName);
     if ((LB_ERR == iNewIndex) || (LB_ERRSPACE ==
      iNewIndex))
     {
      AfxMessageBox("The User ID was Saved, but "
       "the new User ID could not "
       "be added to the listbox.");
     }
     if (LB_ERR == m_lbxUsers.SetItemData(iNewIndex,
     (DWORD)pUser))
     {
      AfxMessageBox("SetItemData returned LB_ERR. "
       "This will probably cause "
       "serious problems if you attempt to update "
       "or delete this item from the listbox");
```

```
      }
     }

     InitControls();

     UpdateData(FALSE);
    }
    else
    {
     pUser->m_strUserID = strPrevUserID;
     pUser->m_strUserName = strPrevUserName;
     pUser->m_iStatus = iPrevStatus;
     AfxMessageBox("SaveUser failed");
    }
   }
  }
  else
  {
   // should never get here because of
   // enabling/disabling button on lbx selection
   AfxMessageBox("You must first select a "
   "User ID to Save");
  }
 }
```

9. Add the following help function. This function is called when the information on the dialog must be saved.

```
BOOL CUserMaintenanceDlg::SaveUser(CUser* pUser)
{
 BOOL bSuccess = FALSE;
 CDatabase db;

 try
 {
  if (db.Open("Visual C++ 6 Bible"))
  {
   CString strSQL = CString("UPDATE UserMaster SET ");
   strSQL += CString("sUserName = '") +
    pUser->m_strUserName + CString("', ");

   strSQL += CString("iStatus = ");
   char szStatus[10];
   itoa(pUser->m_iStatus, szStatus, 10);
   strSQL += szStatus;

   strSQL += CString(" WHERE sUserID = ");
   strSQL += CString("'") + pUser->m_strUserID +
    CString("'");
```

```
   db.ExecuteSQL(strSQL);

   bSuccess = TRUE;
  }
 }
 catch(CDBException* pe)
 {
  AfxMessageBox(pe->m_strError);

  if (db.IsOpen())
  {
   db.Close();
  }

  pe->Delete();
 }

 return bSuccess;
}
```

10. Add a message handler for the Delete button's (`IDC_BTN_DELETE`) `BN_CLICKED` notification message, and implement it as follows:

```
void CUserMaintenanceDlg::OnBtnDelete()
{
 int iIndex;
 CUser* pUser = NULL;
 if (GetSelectedUser(&iIndex, &pUser))
 {
  ASSERT(pUser);
  if (pUser)
  {
   UpdateData();
   CString strMsg;

   strMsg = "Are you sure that you want to delete "
    "the User ";
   strMsg += "'";
   strMsg += pUser->m_strUserName;
   strMsg += "'?";
   if (IDYES == AfxMessageBox(strMsg, MB_YESNOCANCEL))
   {
    if (DeleteUser(pUser))
    {
     if (LB_ERR == m_lbxUsers.DeleteString(iIndex))
     {
      AfxMessageBox("The User was successfully "
       "Deleted, but there was an error in "
```

```
        "removing it from the listbox.");
      }

      InitControls();

      UpdateData(FALSE);
     }
     else
     {
      AfxMessageBox("DeleteUser failed");
     }
    }
   }
  }
  else
  {
   // should never get here because of
   // enabling/disabling button on lbx selection
   AfxMessageBox("You must first select a User "
    "ID to Delete");
  }
 }
```

11. Add the following helper function at the end of `UserMaintenanceDlg.cpp` that is called when a record needs to be deleted:

```
BOOL CUserMaintenanceDlg::DeleteUser(CUser* pUser)
{
 BOOL bSuccess = FALSE;
 CDatabase db;

 try
 {
  if (db.Open("Visual C++ 6 Bible"))
  {
   CString strSQL = CString("DELETE FROM UserMaster "
    "WHERE ");

   strSQL += CString("sUserID = '") +
    pUser->m_strUserID + CString("'");

   db.ExecuteSQL(strSQL);

   bSuccess = TRUE;
  }
 }
 catch(CDBException* pe)
 {
  AfxMessageBox(pe->m_strError);
```

```
    if (db.IsOpen())
    {
     db.Close();
    }
   }

  return bSuccess;
 }
```

12. Build and test the application. Your results should be similar to what you see in Figure 27-6.

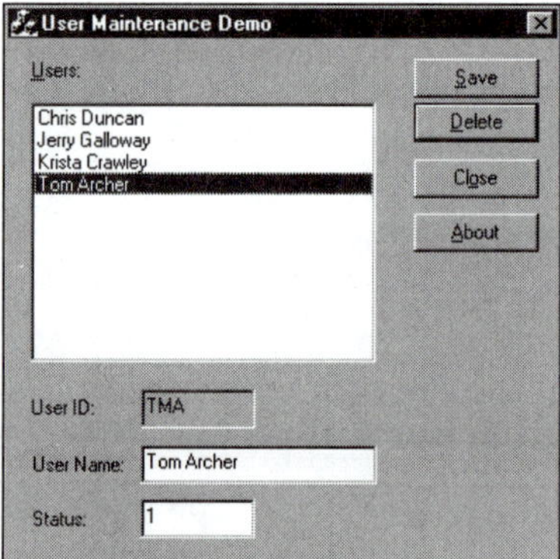

Figure 27-6: The UserMaintenance application demonstrates how to read and write data using the MFC database classes.

Parameterized Recordsets and Queries

This demo application, called Parameterized, is split into two parts. The first part illustrates the use of a parameterized recordset in a practical application. Earlier in the chapter, you learned that parameterized recordsets are recordsets that enable you to filter the records that are returned when the recordset is opened. Like this chapter's first demo application, this demo contains a dialog that will display information about Users from the `UserMaster` table. However, this demo has one very important difference. In the first demo, all of the Users were read from the `UserMaster` table upon the dialog's initialization and inserted into a list box from which the user selected one and performed various database operations (such as update, delete, and so on). In this demo, however, the dialog enables the user to enter a UserID whereupon a parameterized recordset will be used to search the `UserMaster` table for the specified User. If the UserID is located, its information will be displayed on the dialog. If the UserID cannot be located, a message box to that effect will be displayed.

The second part of the demo illustrates the use of a parameterized query that returns data. This query is based on a join of multiple tables in the demo Access database. This query takes only one argument: the UserID. If a UserID is entered into the dialog and is found in the UserMaster table, this query will be called to retrieve other information about the User. This information will then also be displayed on the dialog. To get started, create a dialog-based application called Parameterized. Once AppWizard has created the project and its files, add an #include directive for the afxdb.h file to stdafx.h.

Creating the UI for the demo

Because this demo is a dialog-based application, all of the UI is done on the dialog that was created automatically by AppWizard when the project was created. The project should have a dialog called IDD_PARAMETERIZED_DIALOG.

1. Locate the IDD_PARAMETERIZED_DIALOG dialog, and edit it so that when finished, it resembles the dialog shown in Figure 27-7.

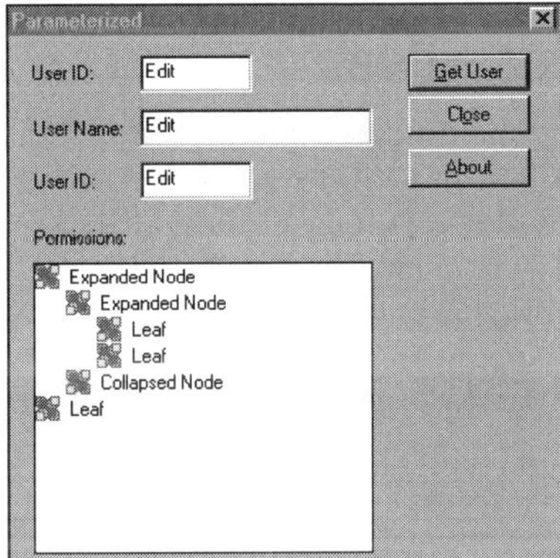

Figure 27-7: The dialog for the Parameterized CRecordset and Query demo (after the new controls have been added).

2. Once the controls have been added, make sure that their resource IDs are set as follows:

Control	*Control ID*
User ID edit	IDC_EDT_USERID
User Name edit	IDC_EDT_USERNAME
Status edit	IDC_EDT_STATUS
Permissions tree	IDC_TREE_PERMISSIONS
Get User button	IDC_BTN_GET_USER
Close button	IDCANCEL

3. Turn on the following styles for the Permissions tree:

   Has buttons
   Has lines
   Lines at root

4. After the resource IDs have been set, create member variables with the following properties for each of the dialog's controls:

Control	*Category*	*Variable Type*	*Variable Name*
User ID edit	Value	`CString`	`m_strUserID`
User Name edit	Value	`CString`	`m_strUserName`
Status edit	Value	`int`	`m_iStatus`
Permissions tree	Control	`CTreeCtrl`	`m_treePermissions`

Creating the UserMaster recordset

You now need a recordset class to access the data in the `UserMaster` table. Call this class `CUserMasterSet`. Follow the directions in the section entitled "CRecordset" presented earlier in the chapter if you don't remember how to create a `CRecordset`-derived class.

Modifying the CRecordset class to accept parameters

Once you have created the `CRecordset` derived class, you should modify it so that it can accept parameters.

1. Open the `UserMasterSet.h` file, and add the following member variable to the `CUserMasterSet` class. This variable's value will be used to filter the `UserMaster` records when the recordset is opened.

```
CString m_sUserIDParam;
```

2. Open the `UserMasterSet.cpp` file, and locate the `CUserMasterSet` constructor. Add the following at the end of the function. The first line simply initializes the parameter variable you just declared in the header file. The second line is extremely important. This line specifies how many parameters you have in this recordset. If you omit this line, you will receive an `ASSERT` when you call the `CRecordset::Open()` function.

```
m_sUserIDParam = _T("");
m_nParams = 1;
```

3. Now, locate the `CUserMasterSet::DoFieldExchange()` function, and add the following lines immediately before the end of the function. These lines

associate the parameter variable with the correct column in the UserMaster table. Take special note that the column name is the sUserID column. In the case of a parameterized recordset, you will generally have two variables pointing to the same column for each parameter defined for that recordset. One of the variables will be used to send and receive data to and from the column in your table (m_sUserID in this demo), and the other will be used only as the key to search on (m_sUserIDParam in this demo).

```
pFX->SetFieldType(CFieldExchange::param);
RFX_Text(pFX, _T("[sUserID]"), m_sUserIDParam);
```

Adding search capability to the application

Now it's time to add the functionality necessary to allow the user to search the UserMaster table for specific users.

1. Open the ParameterizedDlg.cpp file, and add the following #include directive:

   ```
   #include "UserMasterSet.h"
   ```

2. You now must add a function so that when the Get User button is clicked, the proper information is displayed in the dialog box. To do this, add a message handler for the Get User button's (IDC_BTN_GET_USER) BN_CLICKED notification message. Make sure that the function looks like the following:

   ```
   void CParameterizedDlg::OnBtnGetUser()
   {

    CUserMasterSet* pUserMasterSet = NULL;

    try
    {
     pUserMasterSet = new CUserMasterSet();
    }
    catch(CMemoryException* pe)
    {
     TRACE("CParameterizedDlg::OnOk - Memory "
      "Exception creating recordset\n");

     pUserMasterSet = NULL;

     pe->Delete();
    }

    if (pUserMasterSet)
    {
     UpdateData(TRUE);
   ```

```
     try
     {

      pUserMasterSet->m_strFilter = "sUserID = ?";
      pUserMasterSet->m_sUserIDParam = m_strUserID;
      if (pUserMasterSet->Open())
      {

       if (!pUserMasterSet->IsEOF())
       {

        m_strUserName = pUserMasterSet->m_sUserName;
        m_iStatus = pUserMasterSet->m_iStatus;

        UpdateData(FALSE);
       }
       else
       {

        CString str = m_strUserID + CString(" was not "
         "found");

        AfxMessageBox(str);
       }

       pUserMasterSet->Close();
      }

      delete pUserMasterSet;
     }

     catch(CDBException* pe)
     {
      if (pUserMasterSet->IsOpen())
      {
       pUserMasterSet->Close();
      }
      delete pUserMasterSet;

      TRACE("CParameterizedDlg::OnOk   Database "
       "Exception - %s\n", pe->m_strError);

      pe->Delete();
     }
    }
   }
```

Building the application

Now that the code has been entered to search the database for a specific record, simply build the application, and run it. Building the application at this point and running it should give results similar to what you see in Figure 27-8.

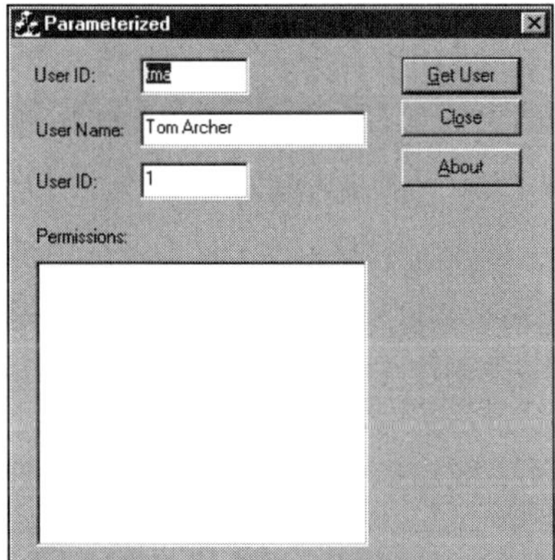

Figure 27-8: The Parameterized demo illustrates how to use parameterized recordsets.

Creating parameterized queries

Now that you have completed the first part of the demo, it is time to add the parameterized query code. You will use the `UserMaster` table that has been seen throughout this chapter, as well as some new tables. In this example, you will pretend that you are writing a large system that includes multiple subsystems — for example, a distribution system that supports subsystems such as Order Entry, Invoicing, Receiving, Purchasing, and so on. This system might also need to support multiple companies.

Many larger corporations are broken into smaller companies or divisions. Because every User would probably not have access to every subsystem for every company, the system would need to support some type of security. User Bob might have access to Order Entry and Invoicing in Company A, but he might not have any permissions in Company B. A Permissions table could be used to limit access to different parts of the system. In the example just mentioned, Bob would have two records in the Permissions table (one for each company/subsystem pair to which he has access). This scenario is the basis for the second part of this demo.

The demo database

Aside from the `UserMaster` table that has been used in the demos throughout this chapter, three new tables (already in the demo database) are required for this demo:

✦ **Company Master table** — This table lists all of the companies for the system. The only columns are for the Company ID and Company Name.

✦ **Subsystem Master table** — This table lists all of the subsystems for the system (for example, Order Entry, Receiving, and so on). The only columns are for the Subsystem ID and Subsystem Name.

✦ **Permissions table** — Because a User can have permissions for any number of companies/subsystems, an "intersection" table is required to handle this "many to many" scenario. This table only has three columns: the User ID, Company ID, and Subsystem ID. These columns represent the primary keys for their respective tables. A record exists in this table for every User/Company/Subsystem for which the User has permissions.

The demo database also includes a query (`GetPermissionsByUserID`) that is a join between all four of the tables in the database. The query takes a UserID as an argument and returns the Company Name and Subsystem Name for all of the companies and subsystems for which this User has permissions.

Using a Parameterized Query with a Recordset

Creating a `CRecordset`-derived class that is based on a parameterized query in Visual C++ is much easier in version 6.0 than it was with previous versions. The steps to follow are similar to creating any recordset with just a couple of differences. These differences are indicated in bold. As with the first part of this demo, each of these steps is described in more detail when you get to the numbered steps.

1. Use ClassWizard to create a `CRecordset`-derived class named `CPermissionsQry`.
2. **Change the recordset's `GetDefaultSQL()` member function to use the CALL syntax. Following is an example of this syntax:**

   ```
   {CALL GetPermissionsByUserID(?)}
   ```

3. Declare a parameter variable(s) in the recordset's header file.
4. Initialize the parameter variable(s) in the recordset's constructor.
5. Set the recordset's `m_nParams` member variable to the number of parameters you are going to use.
6. Update the recordset's `DoFieldExchange()`.

   When using a parameterized query, you do not need to set the `m_strFilter` variable.

7. Assign a value to the recordset's parameter variable(s).
8. Call the recordset's `Open()` function in read-only mode.

✦ ✦ ✦ ✦ ✦

Creating the permissions recordset

Now that you have seen how to create a recordset that is based on a parameterized query, let's create one for the demo application. This recordset will be based on the demo database's sole query: `GetPermissionsByUserID`.

1. Create a `CRecordset`-derived class called `CPermissionsQry`. Follow the directions in the section entitled "CRecordset" presented earlier in the chapter. Make sure to select the `GetPermissionsByUserID` query on the Select Database Tables dialog.

2. Open the `PermissionsQry.cpp` file, and locate the `GetDefaultSQL()` member function. When accessing a parameterized query through the Microsoft Desktop Drivers, you must use the `CALL` syntax. When the application calls the `CRecordset::Open()` function, MFC will check to see if the string returned by the `CRecordset::GetDefaultSQL()` starts with the string "{CALL." If it does not, MFC will attempt to build an SQL `SELECT` statement. A question mark represents the parameter that will be passed. For multiple parameters, simply add a question mark for each parameter while separating each parameter with a comma. Modify the `GetPermissionsByUserID()` function so that it looks like the following when you are done:

```
CString CPermissionsQry::GetDefaultSQL()
{
  return _T("{CALL GetPermissionsByUserID(?)}");
}
```

3. Append the following two lines of code to the `CPermissionsQry` constructor:

```
m_sUserIDParam = _T("");
m_nParams = 1;
```

4. Add the following two lines of code at the end of the `DoFieldExchange()` function:

```
pFX->SetFieldType(CFieldExchange::param);
RFX_Text(pFX, _T("[sUserID]"), m_sUserIDParam);
```

5. Open the `PermissionsQry.h` file, and declare the following member variable:

```
CString m_sUserIDParam;
```

6. Declare the following member variable in the `ParameterizedDlg.h` file. This function will be called to read all of the permissions for the User. The permissions will then be displayed in the dialog's `CTreeCtrl` control.

```
protected:
 void ShowPermissions();
```

7. Open the `ParameterizedDlg.cpp` file, and add the following include directive:

```
#include "PermissionsQry.h"
```

8. Locate the following line of code in the `OnBtnGetUser()` member function:

```
UpdateData(FALSE);
```

Add a line to show the permissions before the UpdateData() function call:

```
ShowPermissions();
```

9. Add the following function at the end of the `ParameterizedDlg.cpp` file. This function will display the permissions in the dialog's tree control. If you are new to the tree control, it (along with the list control) is covered in Chapter 24.

```
void CParameterizedDlg::ShowPermissions()
{

 m_treePermissions.DeleteAllItems();

 CPermissionsQry* pPermissionsQry = NULL;

 try
 {
  pPermissionsQry = new CPermissionsQry();
 }
 catch(CMemoryException* pe)
 {
  TRACE("CParameterizedDlg::OnOk - Memory Exception "
   "creating recordset\n");

  pPermissionsQry = NULL;

  pe->Delete();
 }

 if (pPermissionsQry)
 {
  try
  {
   pPermissionsQry->m_sUserIDParam = m_strUserID;
   if (pPermissionsQry->Open())
   {
    if (!pPermissionsQry->IsEOF())
    {
     TV_INSERTSTRUCT tvinsert;
     HTREEITEM hCompany = NULL;

     CString strPrevCompanyID;

     while (!pPermissionsQry->IsEOF())
```

```
 {
  tvinsert.hParent = NULL;
  tvinsert.hInsertAfter = TVI_LAST;
  tvinsert.item.mask = TVIF_TEXT;
  tvinsert.item.hItem = NULL;
  tvinsert.item.state = 0;
  tvinsert.item.stateMask = 0;
  tvinsert.item.cchTextMax =
   pPermissionsQry->m_sCompanyName.GetLength()
   + 1;
  tvinsert.item.iSelectedImage = 0;
  tvinsert.item.cChildren = 0;
  tvinsert.item.lParam = 0;
  tvinsert.item.pszText =
   pPermissionsQry->m_sCompanyName.GetBuffer(
   tvinsert.item.cchTextMax);

  hCompany =
   m_treePermissions.InsertItem(&tvinsert);

  strPrevCompanyID =
   pPermissionsQry->m_sCompanyID;

  while ((!pPermissionsQry->IsEOF())
  && (strPrevCompanyID ==
  pPermissionsQry->m_sCompanyID))
  {
   if (hCompany)
   {
    tvinsert.hParent = hCompany;
    tvinsert.item.cchTextMax =
     pPermissionsQry->m_sSubsystemName.GetLength()
     + 1;
    tvinsert.item.pszText =
     pPermissionsQry->m_sSubsystemName.GetBuffer(
     tvinsert.item.cchTextMax);
    m_treePermissions.InsertItem(&tvinsert);
   }

   pPermissionsQry->MoveNext();
  }
 }
}
else
{
 CString str = m_strUserID + CString(" was "
  "not found");
 AfxMessageBox(str);
}
```

```
      pPermissionsQry->Close();
     }
     delete pPermissionsQry;
    }
    catch(CDBException* pe)
    {
     if (pPermissionsQry->IsOpen())
     {
      pPermissionsQry->Close();
     }
     delete pPermissionsQry;
     TRACE("CParameterizedDlg::OnOk - Database "
      "Exception "
      "- %s\n", pe->m_strError);
    }
   }
  }
```

10. Build and run the demo application. Running the demo should produce results similar to what you see in Figure 27-9.

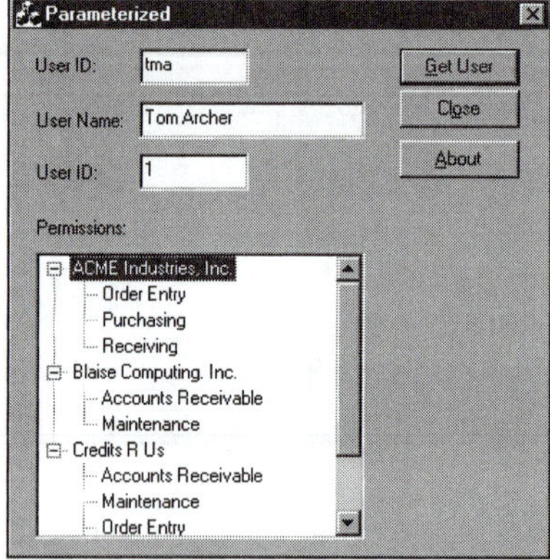

Figure 27-9: The Parameterized demo illustrates how to use parameterized Microsoft Access queries that return data.

Summary

Chapters 26 and 27 have introduced the ODBC SDK and the MFC database classes as well as describing each technology's respective strengths and weaknesses. At this point, one very important question should be addressed. Which is better—the MFC database classes or the ODBC SDK? As you have seen, having both the ODBC SDK and the MFC database classes gives the database developer two technologies with differing strengths. The advantage to using the ODBC SDK is realized in terms of power and flexibility, while the main advantage of the MFC database classes is derived from ease of use. While the ODBC SDK is a good choice for developing robust, scalable systems that interface with different DBMSs, the MFC database classes are the clear-cut winner for smaller systems that interface only to one DBMS. Therefore, choosing between these technologies comes down to a decision of priorities and, hence, is a personal choice that only the database developer can make.

✦ ✦ ✦

C H A P T E R

28

DAO Database Programming

✦ ✦ ✦ ✦

In This Chapter

Discovering the DAO object model

Learning about the MFC DAO classes

Creating a parameterized DAO recordset

Filtering and sorting records with the CDaoRecordset class

Using the MFC DAO classes to write a maintenance application

Learning about the DAO SDK

Using the DAO SDK to retrieve an Access database's reports

✦ ✦ ✦ ✦

DAO (Data Access Objects) is used by applications to interface to Microsoft Access databases. Because the Microsoft Access database engine is referred to as the *Jet* engine, the terms *DAO* and *Jet* are often used interchangeably. DAO was originally designed for Microsoft Access and later Visual Basic, and Visual Basic for Applications. For several years this meant that database programmers that needed to interface their applications to an Access database from any other language had only one option: ODBC. While ODBC (which is covered in Chapter 26) is certainly a very powerful tool for accessing heterogeneous databases, it is not the appropriate API for all database applications. This is especially true for database applications that need only to interface to Access databases.

As you learned in Chapter 26, one of the advantages of ODBC over other database technologies is its capability of enabling a single code base to interface to different databases. Unfortunately, this results in "least common denominator" code. In other words, if you are writing a single code base to work with multiple databases, you will not be able to take advantage of any specific database's capabilities without writing special case code for each database. When you start writing this special case code, you have deviated from the goal of a single code base. In addition, some of the functionality of the Access DBMS is simply not supported through the Access ODBC driver (Microsoft Desktop Drivers).

Microsoft addressed this issue with version 3.0 of DAO by exposing the full functionality of the Jet engine through Automation (formerly called *OLE Automation*). In version 3.0, DAO was released in the form of an Automation in-process server (DLL) that contains an embedded type library. As with any Automation type library, a client application can query the Automation server for descriptions of exposed objects via the OLE `IDispatch` interface. This capability opened up an entirely new paradigm to database development involving the Access DBMS. With DAO 3.0, any language that supported

Automation could have access to almost every facet of the Jet's functionality through the DAO Automation interfaces. Writing Visual C++ applications that use DAO to interface to Access databases is the subject of this chapter.

In this chapter, you will learn about the different objects that constitute the DAO object hierarchy. After that, you will be exposed to the different DAO APIs that enable you to programmatically manipulate DAO objects from your applications. Once these APIs have been covered, a demo will be introduced that uses the MFC DAO classes to write a maintenance application. While this demo is fairly simple in scope, it does teach the fundamentals necessary for writing larger, more robust database applications using the MFC DAO classes.

DAO Overview

Before jumping into the different ways to program to the DAO interface, it is important to understand a little background on DAO as well as the DAO object hierarchy.

The history of DAO

DAO was introduced in Visual Basic 2.0. At that time it didn't have an official name, though many VB programmers referred to it as the *database objects*. From that point, DAO has continued to evolve to its current incarnation as an Automation in-process server. Here is a brief outline of this evolution.

Jet 1.0

This was the initial release of Jet. It was one of the first desktop databases to include features such as updateable views, query capabilities, and seamless access to heterogeneous data.

Jet 1.1

Improvements included in this release are much improved connectivity between the Jet and ODBC databases and an increased maximum database size from 128MB to approximately 1.1GB. This upgrade of DAO also added data definition language (DDL) capabilities. These benefits were available in Visual Basic 3.0 but not in Microsoft Access 1.1.

Jet 2.0

This version was introduced with Microsoft Access 2.0. It offered major enhancements over previous versions. The major areas of improvement included the following:

✦ Enforced referential integrity and data validation at the engine level

- Optimized query performance using Rushmore technology gained in the merger with FoxPro
- Increased conformance to ANSI-standard SQL syntax rules
- Support for UNION, sub-SELECT, and data-definition queries
- A full programming interface to Jet using DAO 2.0
- Cascading update and delete support
- Capability of sending transactions via remote transaction management to servers that support them
- SQL pass-through queries
- New MSysConf settings controlling how often and how many data fetches are made against ODBC data sources
- Support for remote index joins
- New initialization settings for debugging and tuning data operations

As you can see, Jet 2.0 introduced so many new features that it was almost considered to be a totally new relational database.

Jet 2.5

Jet 2.5 was really delivered as an interim build between 2.0 and 3.0 to handle problems related to databases being incorrectly marked as corrupt. However, along with this major fix, version 2.5 also introduced support for the new ODBC Desktop Drivers shipped for the first time as a 32-bit product. And modifications were finally made to support Visual Basic for Applications (VBA) for use with the Desktop Database Drivers (VBA[32].DLL).

Jet 3.0

This was the version where DAO DLL moved to an Automation server containing an embedded type library. Jet 3.0 also introduced new features and improved performance. The most important and eagerly anticipated aspect of this upgrade was its full 32-bit implementation for use in environments such as Microsoft Windows 95 and Microsoft Windows NT.

Numerous changes were made to the database format and the way the engine handles data, with the goal of making most operations substantially faster. Among these changes was the implementation of multithreading. To deal with the fact that Jet was now being used in workplace applications, Jet 3.0 introduced replication capabilities, which enable developers to create replicable databases that can be used in different locations. Microsoft Jet can synchronize these replicas and keep data current.

Jet 3.5

One major change made in Jet 3.5 is that it enables users to replicate only specified portions of database tables, whereas previous versions of Jet enabled full replication of these tables. Jet 3.5 also introduced a new Type argument for the `OpenRecorder()` method: `dbOpenForwardOnly`. This new recordset type behaves in the same way as a DAO 3.0 snapshot-type `CdbRecordset` opened with the `dbForwardOnly()` option. In addition, a new `SetOption()` method enables you to override Microsoft Jet Registry settings at runtime. This enables you to fine-tune Microsoft Jet query performance, timeout delays, and so on.

The DAO hierarchy

As stated earlier, DAO is an API that can be used to interface to Access databases. More specifically stated, DAO is a hierarchy of objects and collections of objects packaged in a DLL. At the top of this hierarchy is the `DBEngine` object. Every other object is, in turn, a sub-object of the `DBEngine` object. Before describing some of the more important objects in detail, take a look at Figure 28-1. This figure illustrates the complete DAO object hierarchy for the Jet Workspace (workspaces are covered shortly).

The DBEngine object

The `DBEngine` is the top-level object in the DAO object hierarchy. Therefore, the `DBEngine` object contains and controls all of the other objects in the DAO object model. While many of the other DAO objects have an associated collection object, the `DBEngine` does not. That means that there is one and only one `DBEngine` object, and it is not an element of any collection.

The `DBEngine` object contains numerous methods and properties as well as two collections: the `Workspaces` collection and the `Errors` collection. The `DBEngine` object is used to do such high-level tasks as create `Workspace` objects and carry out database maintenance tasks such as compacting and repairing Access databases.

The Workspaces collection object

The `Workspaces` collection object is a nonordered collection of all active `Workspace` objects. One way to think of a `Workspace` is as a session between your application and the Jet engine. The `Workspaces` object is used to start new sessions or manage existing sessions.

As with any DAO collection object, you can retrieve any of the contained objects either by name or ordinal number. Like C/C++ arrays, DAO collection indexes are relative to zero. This means that to retrieve the first `Workspace` object from the `Workspaces` collection by ordinal number, you have to specify a value of 0.

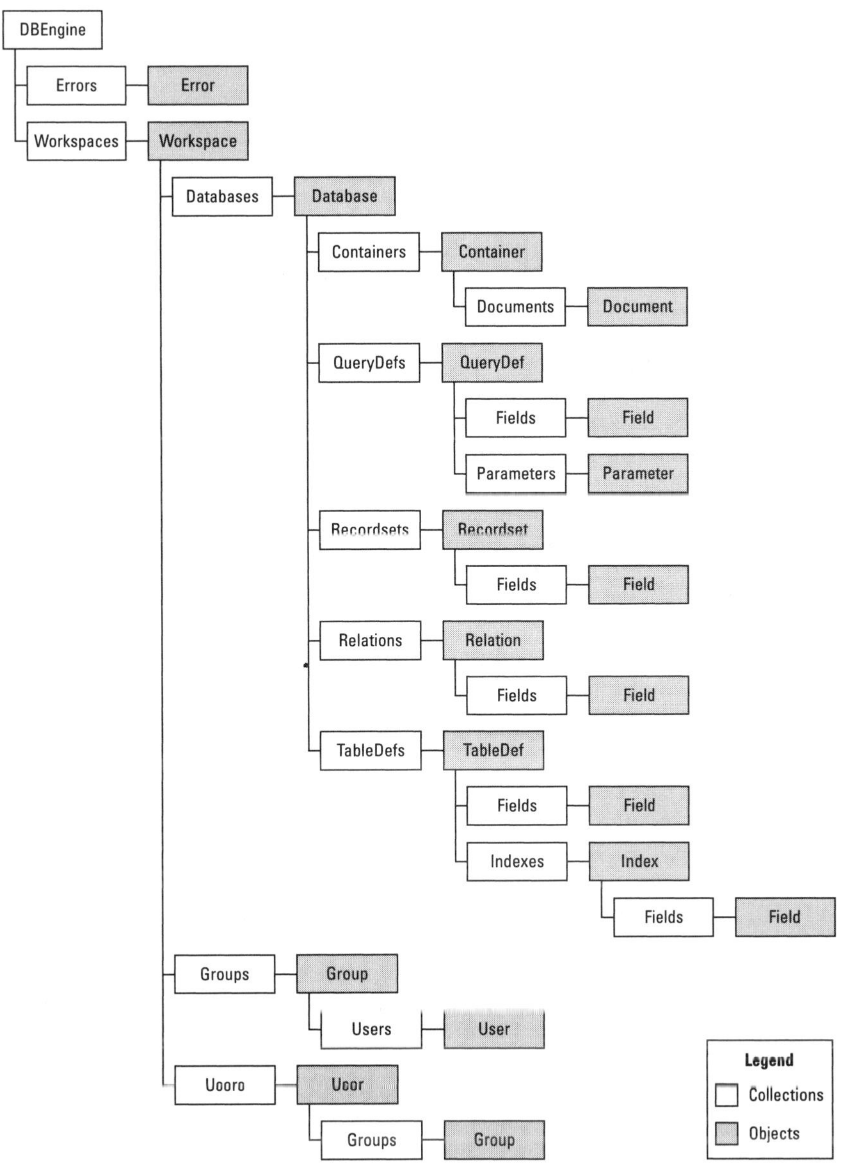

Figure 28-1: The DAO object hierarchy (Jet Workspace) is used to expose the full functionality of the Jet engine.

The Workspace object

The `Workspace` object specifies an active, named session with the Jet engine. You can use the `Workspace` object for managing transactions, creating and opening databases, and performing security-level functions such as creating users and groups.

In general, you won't have to create an object of this type because a default Workspace object is created for you. However, your application may need at times to create unique Workspace objects — for example, when using the Workspace methods to manage transactions (BeginTrans, CommitTrans, and Rollback). When multiple databases are opened within a single Workspace, *all* databases opened within the specified Workspace are affected by the transactions methods. Let's say you've opened two databases using the Workspace OpenDatabase method. If you call the BeginTrans method followed by changes to each database, and then call the Rollback method, all changes to both databases will be lost. If your application requires that these two databases manage their transactions independently, the application must create Workspace objects for each database. The CreateWorkspace method of the DBEngine object is used to create a unique, named Workspace object.

There are two types of Workspace objects: Jet and ODBCDirect. In DAO 3.5, Microsoft introduced the ODBCDirect Workspace type. This enabled programmers using DAO to also access ODBC data sources without going through the Jet engine. Figure 28-1 (shown earlier) illustrates the DAO object hierarchy for the Jet Workspace. Because this chapter concentrates solely on the Jet Workspace, refer to the *Microsoft Jet Database Engine Programmer's Guide* for more information on using ODBCDirect.

While each Workspace object is contained within the Workspaces collection, each Workspace object contains three collections of its own: Databases, Users, and Groups.

The Databases collection

The Databases collection contains all the open Database objects that were created or opened in its parent Workspace object. When a database is created or changed via the Workspace object, the associated DAO Database object is appended to that Workspace object's Databases collection.

Other than simply being a container for all of a Workspace object's open Database objects, the Databases collection doesn't provide much in terms of functionality. About the only Database collection properties and methods you might find yourself needing are the Count method (used to retrieve the total number of open Databases) and the Refresh method (used to reflect the current database schema).

The Database object

The Database object represents an open connection between an application and a database. A physical database can be managed only through DAO via an associated Database object. Once the application has created the Database object, the database can then be manipulated through the various Database object's properties and methods.

The Database object contains several collections that directly correlate to the database schema of its associated database file. For example, the QueryDefs, TableDefs, Relations, and Containers collections are all defined within the Database object and directly relate to Access entities.

It's important to realize that creating a Database object doesn't automatically establish a link with associated database's tables or queries. To do this, you must use the TableDefs collection or the Recordsets collection. However, creating a Database object is a prerequisite to accessing a database's tables or queries.

A database's schema can be changed through the Database object via its CreateQueryDef(), CreateTableDef(), CreateRelation(), and CreateProperty() methods. In addition, the MakeReplica(), Synchronize(), and PopulatePartial() methods can be used to create and synchronize full or partial replicas of the database file associated with a Database object.

The Recordsets collection

The Recordsets collection contains all of the open Recordset objects for a given Database object. The Recordset object is most often how you will deal with data using DAO. Much like the Databases collection, the Recordsets collection doesn't provide much functionality beyond the Count property and Refresh() method provided by all DAO collection objects.

The Recordset object

The Recordset object represents the data that is returned from executing a query. The major difference between the Recordset object and most of the other DAO objects is that it is not persistent. In other words, while other DAO objects such as the Database, TableDef, and QueryDef objects relate to a part of a physical database, the Recordset object represents only the set of records produced by running a query against one or more tables or queries. There are five types of supported DAO Recordsets, as follows:

✦ **Table**—An Access table that you can manipulate by adding, changing, and deleting records.

✦ **Dynaset**—A dynamic set of records that can also be manipulated by adding, changing, and deleting records.

✦ **Snapshot**—A static set of records (this type of recordset is not updateable).

✦ **Forward-Only**—Identical to the Snapshot recordset type except that you can only proceed forward through the recordset. (This newly defined recordset is ideal for a situation in which you need to traverse a recordset only once.)

✦ **Dynamic**—Similar to a Dynaset recordset, with one very important difference: after you run the query that results in a recordset of this type, if another user adds or deletes records that would have been included in this recordset, the changes are reflected in this recordset automatically.

The Recordset type is specified when the OpenRecordset() method is called. The default Recordset type is a table-type recordset. Since the Recordset object represents a set of records that were produced as a result of a query, the Recordset object also exposes methods to navigate this set of records. These methods include MoveFirst(), MoveNext(), MovePrevious(), and MoveLast(). Creating and updating records is accomplished via the AddNew(), Edit(), and Update() methods. The Move() and Seek() methods provide additional means of traversing the records.

The many (inter)faces of DAO

While the capability to communicate with the Jet engine through an industry standard mechanism like Automation was a much-heralded announcement, programming with DAO through Automation is generally thought to be a somewhat tedious task. In answer to these complaints, Microsoft released another interface to DAO called the *DAO SDK*. Actually, the DAO SDK includes a set of C++ classes called the *dbDAO classes*.

However, you will often see the terms DAO SDK and dbDAO used interchangeably. In addition to the DAO SDK, Microsoft also released a set of DAO classes specifically for use with MFC. These classes, the MFC DAO classes, are almost identical in terms of interface to the MFC database classes used for ODBC data sources.

DAO Automation interfaces

Because DAO provides a standard vtable-based implementation of Automation, the DAO SDK was released to provide C++ header files that define the DAO vtable interfaces. This, in turn, eliminated the need to use the IDispatch interface. With the DAO SDK, once an application creates an instance of the DBEngine object, instances of objects can be created through their parent objects using the DAO hierarchy previously shown in Figure 28-1. Otherwise, these objects are standard COM objects and as such, must be explicitly released when the application has finished using them. If you are familiar with COM or Automation programming, this interface may be perfect for your application. However, if you are programming in C++ and would rather use a more C++ friendly method of interfacing to the Jet engine, two other methods may be more appealing.

If you still want to try your hand at using the Automation programming method, refer to the *OLE Automation Programmer's Reference* published by Microsoft Press.

✦ ✦ ✦ ✦ ✦

dbDAO C++ classes

The dbDAO C++ classes (included as a part of the DAO SDK) were the first alternatives to directly using the DAO Automation interface. These classes not only provided C++ programmers with the convenience of encapsulating the DAO in C++ classes, but they also provided a Visual Basic-like syntax to database programming. The decision to use a Visual Basic-like syntax for the dbDAO functions was made for two reasons. First, most programmers familiar with Access databases had at least started using the Access database with Visual Basic. And second, because the ratio of Visual Basic programmers to Visual C++ programmers at the time was estimated at about 5 to 1, it only made sense to cater to the majority. Therefore, with dbDAO, Microsoft killed two birds with one stone.

Another major advantage that dbDAO has over the native DAO Automation interface is that with dbDAO, only a limited amount of COM and Automation knowledge is necessary to effectively use the classes. This is because the dbDAO classes abstract the developer from many of the underlying details of dealing directly with the DAO Automation interface. For example, dbDAO automatically handles reference counting (using the `AddRef()` and `Release()` methods), dynamic allocation and deallocation of objects, and many lower-level Automation details that the programmer would normally have to deal with.

In short, the dbDAO classes afford the database developer the same benefits as the DAO Automation interface, with the lowest possible overhead short of programming directly to the DAO Automation interfaces.

MFC DAO classes

Not to be outdone, the developers of MFC released their own DAO interface with Visual C++ 4.0. The MFC DAO classes have a hierarchy that's similar to the MFC Database classes that utilize ODBC. The advantage to this is that developers with experience with the ODBC-based MFC Database classes have a shorter learning curve with the MFC DAO classes. In addition, the MFC DAO classes are fully integrated with the MFC wizards and the MFC class hierarchy.

It should be noted that even though the syntax of the MFC DAO classes is very distinct from the dbDAO classes, both class hierarchies simply wrap the DAO Automation interface. Hence, if something can't be done using the DAO Automation interface, it's a good bet it can't be done at all with either dbDAO or MFC.

Using the MFC DAO Classes

The MFC DAO classes are comprised of eight classes: `CDaoDatabase`, `CDaoWorkspace`, `CDaoRecordset`, `CDaoTableDef`, `CDaoQueryDef`, `CDaoException`, `CDaoRecordView`, and `CDaoFieldExchange`. With the exception of the MFC doc/view-specific `CDaoRecordView` and `CDaoFieldExchange` classes and the `CdaoException` class, each of the MFC DAO classes relates to a DAO object.

In terms of class hierarchy and member function interfaces, the MFC DAO classes are designed in a very similar manner to the MFC Database classes. However, besides the fact that the MFC Database classes use the ODBC SDK internally to carry out their work (as opposed to DAO Automation), the major difference between the two sets of database access classes is that the MFC DAO classes are much more robust in terms of functionality. For example, DDL operations are supported by the MFC DAO classes while they are not supported by the MFC Database classes.

As mentioned previously, there are only eight MFC DAO classes, as opposed to almost thirty objects defined in the DAO object model (Jet Workspace). This disparity in the number of classes is due to several factors:

- ✦ The MFC DAO class hierarchy is a "flat" version of the DAO object model. In the DAO object model, if an object can contain a collection of another type of object, separate objects represent both the collection and the contained object type. For example, because a `Database` object can contain multiple `TableDef` objects, a `TableDefs` collection object and a `TableDef` object are defined in the DAO object model. However, because most DAO collection objects simply provide a method that returns the number of objects contained within the collection, the MFC DAO classes represent most DAO collections with a `CMapPtrToPtr` map.
- ✦ The MFC DAO classes do not support all of the DAO functionality. For example, the MFC DAO classes do not support any of the Jet security operations. This means that the DAO `Users` and `Groups` objects have no corollary classes in MFC. Therefore, in order to manage security for an Access database using DAO from a Visual C++ application, you have to use either the dbDAO classes or the DAO Automation interfaces.

Of the eight MFC DAO classes, this section will concentrate on the classes a "typical" database application is most likely to use: `CDaoDatabase`, `CDaoWorkspace`, `CDaoRecordset`, and `CDaoException`. The reason that the `CDaoRecordView` class is not included in this chapter is because it is nothing more than a view with an embedded `CDaoRecordset` object. Therefore, once you have learned about the `CDaoRecordset` class, using the `CDaoRecordView` class is a very straightforward proposition.

CDaoDatabase

The `CDaoDatabase` class represents a connection between an application and a database. After constructing a `CDaoDatabase` object, the application must specify the database name as the first argument in the `CDaoDatabase::Open()` member function. The `CDaoDatabase` class can be used in conjunction with one or more `CDaoRecordset` objects (the `CDaoRecordset` class will be covered shortly), or it can be used without a `CDaoRecordset`. For example, you would want to use the `CDaoDatabase` class by itself if the application needs to issue an SQL statement that does not return any data against a database. The `CDaoDatabase::Execute()` function exists for just this purpose. Following is an example of how easy it is to insert a record into a table using the `Execute` function.

The table being used in this chapter is a simple demo Access database that can be found on the accompanying CD in the `\Chap26\Database` folder.

◆ ◆ ◆ ◆ ◆

```
try
 {
  CDaoDatabase db;
  db.Open("vc6bib.mdb");

  db.Execute("INSERT INTO UserMaster "
        "VALUES('TST', 'Test User Name', 0)");

  db.Close();
 }
 catch(CDaoException* pe)
 {
  AfxMessageBox(pe->m_pErrorInfo->m_strDescription,
   MB_ICONEXCLAMATION );
  pe->Delete();
 }
```

When you use the AppWizard to create an application, one of the options provided is whether or not you will want DAO support. If you elect to use this support, the appropriate header files are included in your project. However, if you need to add DAO support to an existing project, you simply have to add the `#include` directive for the DAO header file (`afxdao.h`) to the appropriate files in your project.

◆ ◆ ◆ ◆ ◆

Let's look at the previous code in more detail. The first thing you see in the code snippet is a C++ `try/catch` block.

```
try
{
  . . .
}
CATCH(CDaoException* pe)
{
 AfxMessageBox(pe->m_pErrorInfo->m_strDescription,
  MB_ICONEXCLAMATION );
 pe->Delete();
}
```

When using the MFC DAO classes, all DAO errors are expressed as exceptions of type `CDaoException`. Because the DAO object model supports the existence of an `Errors` collection, the `CDaoException` class defines member functions to retrieve any information from multiple DAO `Error` objects stored in the `DBEngine Errors` collection. When a DAO error occurs, one or more `Error` objects are added to the `DBEngine Errors` collection. However, if a DAO operation results in one or more of the `Error` objects being created and added to the `Errors` collection, the previous `Error` objects are discarded first. If a DAO operation does not produce an error of any kind, the `Errors` collection retains its previous content. Here are a couple of the more important member functions and variables that you will use when dealing with the `CDaoException` class:

✦ `m_nAfxDaoError` — This member variable is set when a DAO component error has occurred, such as the Jet engine not being initialized.

✦ `m_pErrorInfo`—This is a pointer to a `CDaoErrorInfo` structure that includes, among other things, a member variable containing the textual representation of the error.

✦ `GetErrorCount`—This member function returns the number of `Error` objects in the database engine's `Errors` collection.

Because all of the MFC DAO classes' member functions can throw exceptions of type `CDaoException`, it is wise to wrap all code using these functions in `try/catch` blocks. The first thing the example is attempting to do in the `try` block is to a construct `CDaoDatabase` object and open it. Obviously, the name and location of the database file have been hard-coded in order to simplify the example.

```
CDaoDatabase db;
db.Open("vc6bib.mdb"))
...
```

The `CDaoDatabase` constructor doesn't do anything special. You must call the `CDaoDatabase::Open()` member function to actually connect to a database. Here is the prototype for the `CDaoDatabase::Open()` member function:

```
virtual void Open(LPCTSTR lpszName,
 BOOL bExclusive = FALSE, BOOL bReadOnly = FALSE,
 LPCTSTR lpszConnect = _T("") );
  throw( CDaoException, CMemoryException );
```

As you can see in this prototype, an application can set several options when opening a database using the `CDaoDatabase::Open` function. However, only the first argument is explicitly required for this function, and it was the only one passed in the preceding example. This first argument represents the fully qualified name of the database being opened. The remaining arguments are as follows:

✦ The `bExclusive` flag is used to specify if the database is to be opened for exclusive access. If the specified file is already opened and this flag is set to `TRUE`, an exception of type `CDaoException` is thrown by the `Open` function.

✦ The `bReadOnly` flag specifies whether or not updates to the data source are enabled. The default value is `FALSE`. Any recordsets that are created and attached to a `CDaoDatabase` object inherit this flag.

✦ The `lpszConnect` argument specifies the ODBC connect string. However, if the application is using an Access database, this argument must be an empty string.

After opening the `CDaoDatabase` object, the next lines execute the SQL statement and close the database:

```
db.Execute("INSERT INTO UserMaster "
 "VALUES('TST', 'Test User Name', 0)");

db.Close();
```

As you can see, CDaoDatabase::Execute() has a very straightforward syntax. The first (and only required) argument for this function takes a SQL statement or the name of an action query to be run. Note that this function is only used when the SQL statement or action query being run won't result in the return of data from the data source. In fact, calling an action query that returns a value results in an exception of type CDaoException being thrown by the Execute() function.

A second argument can also be specified in the Execute() function that specifies options relating to the integrity of the query. For example, this argument can be used to stipulate options such as the database performing a rollback on any updates if an error occurs during the execution of the SQL statement or action query.

CDaoWorkspace

The CDaoWorkspace class is used to manage a named database session. As mentioned previously in the section describing DAO objects, an application does not ordinarily require multiple workspaces, because when the database and its associated recordset objects are opened via the MFC DAO classes, a default DAO default workspace is used. However, the capability does exist to create additional workspaces for performing such tasks as logically grouping transactions. Remember that the transaction operations (BeginTrans, Commit, and so on) are performed at the workspace level. This means that in order to manage transactions independently across CDaoDatabase objects, the application must explicitly create additional CDaoWorkspace objects for each database that requires its transactions be handled independently.

The CDaoWorkspace object, therefore, provides access to the default workspace that is created when the DBEngine is initialized. In addition, when a workspace is opened or created (or one of its static member functions is called), the DBEngine is initialized, which then creates the default workspace for that instance of the database engine.

As alluded to earlier, another useful set of member functions that the CDaoWorkspace class supports are the functions for supporting transactions. Transactions give the application the capability to bracket a set of functions in a logical group so that if any one of those functions fail, no changes are made. For those of you not familiar with transactions, an example might be in order here. Let's say an accounting application needs to transfer an amount from one account to another. What would happen if after removing the amount from one account, the attempt to update the second account's balance failed? The integrity of the database would be compromised because the amount would not be in either account. With transactions, an application can specify that both of these financial transactions must complete successfully. If either of these transactions fails, then both accounts revert to their previous balances, and no changes are made.

Here's the way it works. An application first sets a "transaction boundary" by calling the CDaoWorkspace::BeginTrans() function. Anything done after this point is subject to being rolled back, or undone. Once the application calls the

CDaoWorkspace::CommitTrans() function, all changes made since the last transaction boundary are committed, or made permanent. If for some reason the application needs to rollback or undo any changes since the last transaction boundary, the CDaoWorkspace::Rollback() function is called. Note that before attempting to call the CommitTrans() function, an application must first call the BeginTrans() function.

CDaoRecordset

While a CDaoDatabase object represents a connection to a database, a CDaoRecordset object represents a set of records from one of those connections. As you may recall from earlier in the chapter, the DAO Recordset object supports five different types of recordsets. The MFC CDaoRecordset, however, only supports three of those: table-type, dynaset, and snapshot. A table-type recordset represents a single base table whose data can be altered by the application. A dynaset recordset is the outcome of a query whose results can also be updated by the application. Finally, a snapshot recordset is a static picture of data taken at the time the recordset was filled. This data cannot be updated.

The simplest way to get started using the CDaoRecordset class is to create one using the ClassWizard. This recordset will be based on the UserMaster table of the vc6bib.mdb file introduced earlier in the chapter. If you are following along, this file can be located on the accompanying CD in the \Chap26\Database folder. Actually, this file is a replica of the file used in the demos for Chapter 27. Therefore, the following examples and demos will, for the most part, be identical to those in Chapter 27. By using a single database for both chapters, an easier comparison between the two database technologies can be made when reading both Chapters 26 and 28. Figure 28-2 shows the UserMaster table in Microsoft Access 97 that the recordset will be based on.

To use ClassWizard, you must have an active project open in Visual Studio. Therefore, create a "dummy" project at this point. You can name this project anything you like. Once you have created the project, invoke ClassWizard, and click the Add Class button. From the menu that is displayed, select the New submenu option. Figure 28-3 shows the resulting New Class dialog box and the values you should enter for this example.

When you specify that you want to create a CDaoRecordset-derived class, ClassWizard prompts you to specify the type of database access used with your recordset class. Figure 28-4 shows this dialog with the demo database selected.

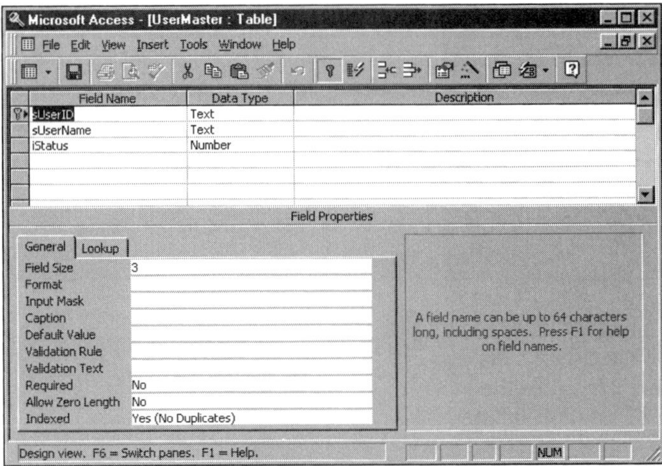

Figure 28-2: The UserMaster table (shown here in Microsoft Access 97) is used throughout this chapter and in the demo application.

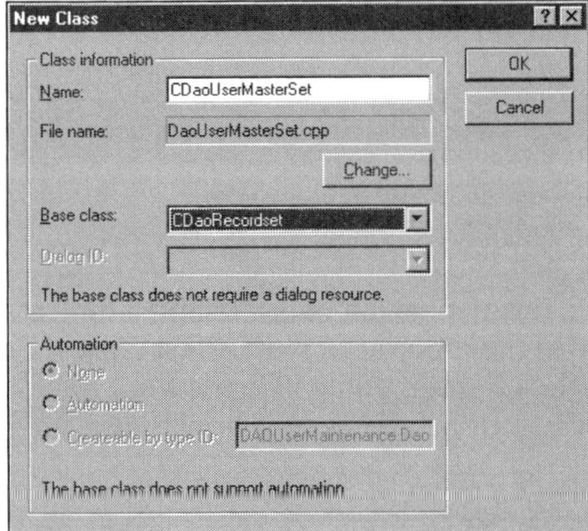

Figure 28-3: The ClassWizard's New Class dialog box is used to create new MFC-derived classes.

After selecting the Access database file, simply select the `UserMaster` table (as shown in Figure 28-5), and click OK. That's how easy it is to create a `CDaoRecordset`-derived class!

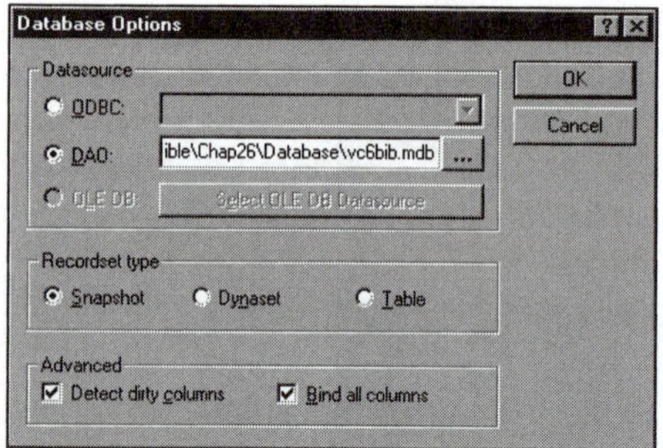

Figure 28-4: When creating a CDaoRecordset-derived class, the Database Options dialog box enables you to specify many of the characteristics that will be used to define the new class.

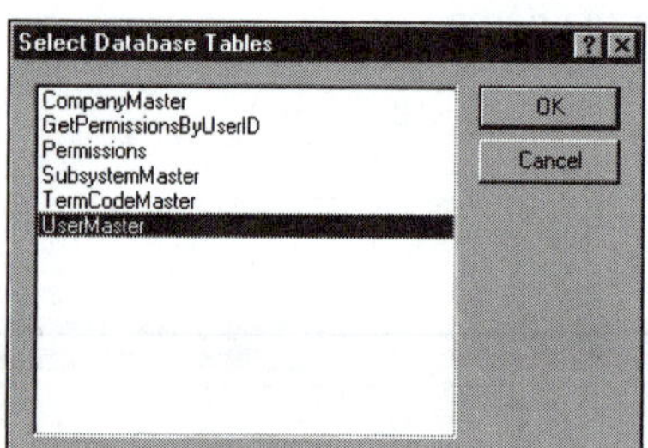

Figure 28-5: When creating a CDaoRecordset class, the Select Database Tables dialog box is used to select the table or query on which the recordset will be based.

Now that you have created the `CDaoRecordset` derived class, taking a look at Listings 28-1 and 28-2, which will show you the amount of work ClassWizard does on your behalf. Throughout this part of the chapter, you will learn what the different member variables and member functions are for and how to use them.

Listing 28-1: DaoUserMasterSet.h

```
#pragma once

#if _MSC_VER > 1000
#pragma once
#endif // _MSC_VER > 1000
// DaoUserMasterSet.h : header file
//

// CDaoUserMasterSet DAO recordset

class CDaoUserMasterSet : public CDaoRecordset
{
public:
```

```
 CDaoUserMasterSet(CDaoDatabase* pDatabase = NULL);
 DECLARE_DYNAMIC(CDaoUserMasterSet)

 // Field/Param Data
 //{{AFX_FIELD(CDaoUserMasterSet, CDaoRecordset)
 CString   m_sUserID;
 CString   m_sUserName;
 short     m_iStatus;
 //}}AFX_FIELD

 // Overrides
 // ClassWizard generated virtual function overrides
 //{{AFX_VIRTUAL(CDaoUserMasterSet)
 public:
 virtual CString GetDefaultDBName();
 virtual CString GetDefaultSQL();
 virtual void DoFieldExchange(CDaoFieldExchange* pFX);
 //}}AFX_VIRTUAL

 // Implementation
 #ifdef _DEBUG
 virtual void AssertValid() const;
 virtual void Dump(CDumpContext& dc) const;
 #endif
};

//{{AFX_INSERT_LOCATION}}
// Microsoft Visual C++ will insert additional
// declarations immediately before the previous line.

#endif // _DAO_USER_MASTER_SET_H_
```

Listing 28-2: DaoUserMasterSet.cpp

```
// DaoUserMasterSet.cpp : implementation file
//

#include "stdafx.h"
#include "DAOTestProject.h"
#include "DaoUserMasterSet.h"

#ifdef _DEBUG
#define new DEBUG_NEW
#undef THIS_FILE
static char THIS_FILE[] = __FILE__;
#endif

/////////////////
```

(continued)

Listing 28-2 *(continued)*

```
// CDaoUserMasterSet

IMPLEMENT_DYNAMIC(CDaoUserMasterSet, CDaoRecordset)

CDaoUserMasterSet::CDaoUserMasterSet(CDaoDatabase* pdb)
: CDaoRecordset(pdb)
{
 //{{AFX_FIELD_INIT(CDaoUserMasterSet)
 m_sUserID = _T("");
 m_sUserName = _T("");
 m_iStatus = 0;
 m_nFields = 3;
 //}}AFX_FIELD_INIT
 m_nDefaultType = dbOpenDynaset;
}


CString CDaoUserMasterSet::GetDefaultDBName()
{
 return _T("C:\\WINNT\\Profiles\\Administrator\\"
 "Desktop\\Books\\Visual C++ 6 Bible\\"
 "Chapter 26\\Database\\vc6bib.mdb");
}

CString CDaoUserMasterSet::GetDefaultSQL()
{
 return _T("[UserMaster]");
}

void CDaoUserMasterSet::DoFieldExchange
(CDaoFieldExchange* pFX)
{
 //{{AFX_FIELD_MAP(CDaoUserMasterSet)
 pFX->SetFieldType(CDaoFieldExchange::outputColumn);
 DFX_Text(pFX, _T("[sUserID]"), m_sUserID);
 DFX_Text(pFX, _T("[sUserName]"), m_sUserName);
 DFX_Short(pFX, _T("[iStatus]"), m_iStatus);
 //}}AFX_FIELD_MAP
}

/////////////////
// CDaoUserMasterSet diagnostics

#ifdef _DEBUG
void CDaoUserMasterSet::AssertValid() const
{
 CDaoRecordset::AssertValid();
}

void CDaoUserMasterSet::Dump(CDumpContext& dc) const
{
```

```
  CDaoRecordset::Dump(dc);
}
#endif //_DEBUG
```

Once you have a recordset to work with, you have the capability to do just about anything you want to the returned records, including the following:

- ✦ Construct a recordset.
- ✦ Open a recordset.
- ✦ Read and write data using DFX (DAO field exchange).
- ✦ Filter records.
- ✦ Sort records returned with a recordset.
- ✦ Move through the recordset.
- ✦ Save records.
- ✦ Delete records.

Constructing a CDaoRecordset object

The `CDaoRecordset` constructor takes only one argument: a pointer to a `CDaoDatabase` object. This argument has a default value of `NULL`. If the application does not specify a `CDaoDatabase` object when constructing a `CDaoRecordset`, MFC automatically creates a temporary `CDaoDatabase` object using the information specified when the recordset was created with the ClassWizard. The information that will be used can be found in the `CDaoRecordset::GetDefaultDBName` function.

However, if your application must use multiple recordsets, it is much more efficient for the application to create one `CDaoDatabase` object and use that object for subsequently created `CDaoRecordset` objects. That way, a temporary `CDaoDatabase` does not have to be created for each `CDaoRecordset` object. One way of doing this is to create a `CDaoDatabase` object when the application initializes and store the pointer in the application or document object. Then, whenever the application needs to construct a `CDaoRecordset` object, the global `CDaoDatabase` object can be used.

Opening a recordset

Once a `CDaoRecordset` object has been constructed, it can be opened using its `Open` member function. One of the arguments for this function is the recordset type. This argument is used to specify whether the recordset being opened is a dynaset, table, or snapshot recordset type. These types are represented by the `dbOpenDynaset`, `dbOpenTable`, and `dbOpenSnapshot` constants, respectively. All of these constants are defined in the `afxdao.h` header file. If the application does not specify a recordset type, the type of recordset opened is dictated by the value entered when the class was created with ClassWizard. This value is stored in the m_nDefaultType member variable and is initialized in the class constructor. If the application calls the Open() function without specifying a SQL string to be executed, the GetDefaultSQL() member function is used to determine which records end up in the recordset after the Open() function returns.

Reading and writing data using DFX

In order to retrieve all of the records from a table without regard to order, the application simply must create a CDaoRecordset-derived class (as shown previously) and call its CDaoRecordset::Open() member function. However, at this point you may be wondering how the data gets from the data source into the application's variables. The answer is DFX (DAO field exchange).

When a CDaoRecordset-derived class is created using ClassWizard, ClassWizard enumerates all of the columns in the selected table or query and declares variables of the appropriate type in the recordset's header file. ClassWizard also generates code for a function called DoFieldExchange() that serves to tie the member variables to their corresponding columns in the database. The DoFieldExchange() function is called when MFC needs to move data from the database to the class' member variables or vice versa. The underlying MFC code actually does all the low-level DAO work, such as binding the columns and fetching the data, that the application would have had to do manually if it weren't for this "helper" function.

When a CDaoRecordset object is opened with its Open member function, it moves to the first record in the recordset so that the application can immediately start using the data. The application can then start navigating through the resulting data using the CDaoRecordset::MoveFirst(), CDaoRecordset::MovePrev(), CDaoRecordset::MoveNext(), and CDaoRecordset::MoveLast() member functions. (These functions will be explained shortly.)

Filtering records

Now that you know how to open and retrieve data from a data source, you need to learn how to filter that data to get just the records you desire. Actually, there are several ways to accomplish this. As you saw in the section entitled "Opening a recordset," one way is to specify the SQL in the CDaoRecordset::Open() function. The following code is an example of using that function to filter the desired records from the UserMaster table. This code reads only the records that represent users whose status code is equal to zero.

```
CDaoDatabase db;
CDaoUserMasterSet rs;
try
{
 rs.Open(AFX_DAO_USE_DEFAULT_TYPE,
 "SELECT * from UserMaster where iStatus = 0");

 while (!rs.IsEOF())
 {
 AfxMessageBox(rs.m_sUserName);
```

```
 rs.MoveNext();
 }
}
catch(CDaoException* pe)
{
 AfxMessageBox(pe->m_pErrorInfo->m_strDescription,
  MB_ICONEXCLAMATION);
 pe->Delete();
}
```

A second way to filter the data returned in a recordset is to use a parameterized recordset. Using the `CDaoUserMasterSet` created earlier in the chapter (see Listings 28-1 and 28-2), you will change this recordset so that only records whose `iStatus` has a value of zero are retrieved. To accomplish this, follow these steps:

1. Locate the following block of variables in the `DaoUserMasterSet.h` file:

   ```
   // Field/Param Data
    //{{AFX_FIELD(CDaoUserMasterSet, CDaoRecordset)
    CString   m_sUserID;
    CString   m_sUserName;
    short     m_iStatus;
    //}}AFX_FIELD
   ```

2. Add the following variable declaration after the variable block you located in step 1:

   ```
   short m_iStatusParam;
   ```

3. Initialize the variable in the recordset's constructor (`DaoUserMasterSet.cpp`), and set the `m_nParams` value to the number of parameters that will be used, as follows (the boldface lines represent the new lines of code that you need to add):

   ```
   //{{AFX_FIELD_INIT(CDaoUserMasterSet)
   m_sUserID = _T("");
   m_sUserName = _T("");
   m_iStatus = 0;
   m_nFields = 3;
   m_iStatusParam = 0;
   m_nParams = 1;
   //}}AFX_FIELD_INIT
   m_nDefaultType = dbOpenDynaset;
   ```

   This is extremely important. If you attempt to use a parameterized recordset and do not set the `m_nParams` member variable, the recordset's `Open` will fail, and you will receive an `ASSERT` during the call to `DoFieldExchange()`.

4. Update the `DoFieldExchange()` function to look like the following:

```
void CDaoUserMasterSet::DoFieldExchange(
 CDaoFieldExchange* pFX)
{
 //{{AFX_FIELD_MAP(CDaoUserMasterSet)
 pFX->SetFieldType(
 CDaoFieldExchange::outputColumn);

 DFX_Text(pFX, _T("[sUserID]"), m_sUserID);
 DFX_Text(pFX, _T("[sUserName]"), m_sUserName);
 DFX_Short(pFX, _T("[iStatus]"), m_iStatus);
 //}}AFX_FIELD_MAP
}
```

Please note that the `CDaoFieldExchange::SetFieldType()` must be called with the `CDaoFieldExchange::param` argument, and the second argument of the `DFX_Short()` function points to the column that is being used to filter the data (`iStatus`).

5. Set the parameter's value. Here is an example of how to do this:

```
CDaoDatabase db;
CDaoUserMasterSet rs;
try
{
 rs.m_strFilter = "iStatus = ?";
 rs.m_iStatusParam = 0;
 rs.Open();

 while (!rs.IsEOF())
 {
  AfxMessageBox(rs.m_sUserName);
  rs.MoveNext();
 }
}
catch(CDaoException* pe)
{
 AfxMessageBox(pe->m_pErrorInfo->m_strDescription,
  MB_ICONEXCLAMATION );
 pe->Delete();
}
```

As you can see, using parameterized recordsets is not complex, but if you forget to do any of the steps involved, you can end up losing a lot of time tracking down why your `Open` function call is not working.

Sorting records returned with a recordset

As you just saw in the section "Filtering records," the `CDaoRecordset` class provides a member variable (`m_strFilter`) to filter the records that a recordset represents. The CDaoRecordset class also provides a member variable to specify the order in which the records are returned. This member variable is named m_strSort. To use this member variable, simply set its value to the name of the column that you want the recordset sorted by. For example, in the sample code previously used, if you wanted to sort by the iStatus column in the UserMaster table, your code would look like the following:

```
CDaoDatabase db;
CDaoUserMasterSet rs;
try
{
 rs.m_strSort = _T("iStatus");
 rs.Open();

 while (!rs.IsEOF())
 {
 AfxMessageBox(rs.m_sUserName);
 rs.MoveNext();
 }
}
catch(CDaoException* pe)
{
 AfxMessageBox(pe->m_pErrorInfo->m_strDescription,
  MB_ICONEXCLAMATION);
 pe->Delete();
}
```

If you need to sort by more than one column, simply separate each column name with a comma.

Moving through the result set

Once a recordset has been opened and the desired data has been retrieved (via the m_strFilter member variable) in the desired sequence (via the m_strSort member variable), you must know how to move through the resulting records. The CDaoRecordset class makes this easy with the MoveFirst(), MovePrev(), MoveNext(), and MoveLast() member functions. It's not difficult to figure out from the function names what each function does. However, you should know the following when attempting to navigate through a recordset:

✦ All of the move functions throw an exception if the recordset did not return any records. Therefore, the application should always call CDaoRecordset::IsBOF() or CDaoRecordset::IsEOF() before attempting to call one of the move functions.

✦ The MoveFirst() and MovePrev() functions are not supported for recordsets that were defined as forward-only. Note that this particular rule is applicable only to ODBCDirect workspaces.

✦ If the application calls one of the move functions and retrieves a record that may have been deleted by another user, the application should call the `CDaoRecordset::IsDeleted()` function to verify that the record is still valid.

Saving records

Saving data using the `CDaoRecordset` class is very easy and straightforward. There are basically two different ways to save data: by adding new records and by updating existing records. To add a new record, the application simply must do the following:

1. Call the `CDaoRecordset::AddNew()` function, which prepares a new, blank record for use.
2. Move the new data into the recordset's member variables.
3. Call the `CDaoRecordset::Update()` function.

For an application to update an existing record, do the following:

1. Call the `CDaoRecordset::Edit()` function.
2. Move the new data into the recordset's member variables.
3. Call the `CDaoRecordset::Update()` function.

It's important to note the order in which you call these functions. When updating an existing record, the data must be moved into the member variables *after* calling the `Edit()` function. Otherwise, MFC does not update the data. The reason for this is that the MFC DAO classes cache the recordset's data when the `Edit` function is called and do a memory compare when the `Update()` function is called to see if the data has changed. If no changes have been made to the member variables since the `Edit` function was called, the data will not be saved even though the `Update()` function was explicitly called.

Deleting records

To delete a record from a recordset, the current record must be the record your application needs to delete. The application then simply calls the `CDaoRecordset::Delete()` function. After deleting the record, the current record in the recordset is not a valid record, and the application must call one of the move functions until a valid record in the recordset is reached.

MFC DAO demo

This demo (DaoUserMaintenance) has all the create, update, and delete capabilities of a traditional maintenance application for maintaining users. As with all the demos in this book, you can read along, or you can perform the exercise. While this demo is fairly simple in scope, it does teach the fundamentals necessary for writing larger, more robust database applications.

In the following demo (which can be found on the companion CD in the `\Chap28\DaoUserMaintenance` folder), you will develop a fully functional maintenance application using the MFC DAO classes.

Creating the demo project

Begin by using AppWizard to create a new project with the following steps:

1. Create a project called "DaoUserMaintenance" as a dialog-based application.
2. Once the project files have been created, open the `stdafx.h` file, and add the `#include` directive for the MFC DAO header file (`afxdao.h`).

Editing the dialog for the demo application

After creating the project and adding the MFC DAO header file, you must edit the application's main dialog. Open the `IDD_DAOUSERMAINTENANCE_DIALOG` dialog template resource, and make the necessary edits so that the resulting dialog looks like the one shown in Figure 28-6. (Actually, if you use the following tip, you can save yourself some time.)

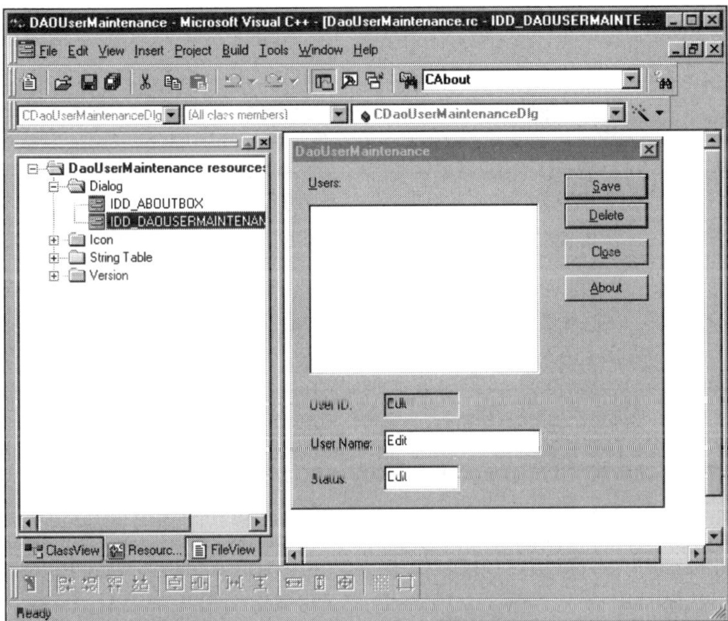

Figure 28-6: The DAOUserMaintenance dialog box should look similar to this after the new controls have been added.

Expert Tip

Using the Clipboard When Duplicating Dialogs

When duplicating the work of one dialog that exists in one resource file to another resource file, you can use the Clipboard functions. For example, because the dialog in Figure 28-6 is almost identical to the dialog used for the UserMaintenance project in Chapter 27, you can use the Clipboard so that you don't have to duplicate work you've already done. Simply open the `UserMaintenance.rc` file on the CD. Notice that it is displayed in a view instead of in the project workspace dialog bar, because only the current project's resources are displayed in the dialog bar. Once you have located the dialog from which you wish to copy the controls, select the desired controls, and copy them to the Clipboard. Make sure to note the size of the dialog. Now, return to the `IDD_DAOUSERMAINTENANCE_DIALOG`, and after resizing the dialog, paste the controls into the dialog. Not only does this save you the work of creating the controls, even the control IDs have been set correctly!

✦ ✦ ✦ ✦ ✦

Once you have copied the controls onto the dialog, create the member variables that will be used with DDX (dynamic data exchange) for the different controls. These variables are listed in Table 28-1.

Table 28-1
Member Variables for DDX

Control	*Category*	*Variable Type*	*Variable Name*
User list box	Control	`CListbox`	`m_lbxUsers`
User ID edit	Value	`CString`	`m_strUserID`
User Name edit	Value	`CString`	`m_strUserName`
Status edit	Value	`int`	`m_iStatus`
Save button	Control	`CButton`	`m_btnSave`
Delete button	Control	`CButton`	`m_btnDelete`

Adding a utility class to encapsulate the user's data

A utility class is required to encapsulate each record's data. As you will see later, when the application reads a record from the recordset, a `CUser` object is created. An entry is then made into the list box that represents that record. This list box entry's item data contains a pointer to the `CUser` object. At this point, create a file named "User.h," and edit it to look like the following;

```
#pragma once

class CUser
{
public:
```

```
 CString m_strUserID;
 CString m_strUserName;
 int m_iStatus;
};
```

Creating a CDaoRecordset class for the UserMaster table

You now need a CDaoRecordset-derived class to access the data in the UserMaster table. If necessary, follow the directions in the section entitled "CDaoRecordset," presented earlier in this chapter, in order to create this class. Name this class CDaoUserMasterSet.

Modifying the dialog's header file

You must make a couple of minor changes to the dialog's header file for this program. First, open the DaoUserMaintenanceDlg.h file, and add the following #include directive before the declaration of the dialog's class:

```
#include "User.h"
```

Now, add the following member function declarations to the CDaoUserMaintenanceDlg class:

```
void FillListboxWithUsers();
BOOL GetSelectedUser(int* piIndex, CUser** ppUser);
void InitControls();
BOOL SaveUser(CUser* pUser);
BOOL DeleteUser(CUser* pUser);
```

Modifying the dialog's implementation file

The last thing you must do is to modify the dialog's code in order to perform the database I/O. First, open the DaoUserMaintenanceDlg.cpp file, and at the top of the file, add the following #include directive (it should be listed last):

```
#include "DaoUserMasterSet.h"
```

Once you have added the #include directive for the CDaoUserMasterSet, add the following #define directive. This value will be used in scenarios in which you will use a CDaoDatabase object without a CDaoRecordset object. Obviously, the location of the database is hard-coded. Therefore, you may need to change this value if your program and database locations are different.

```
#define DEMO_DB _T("..\\..\\Chap26\\Database\\vc6bib.mdb")
```

Now locate the OnInitDialog() function, and add the following function calls right before the return statement. The FillListboxWithUsers() function fills the list box with all of the users found in the database. The InitControls() function does such things as initialize the state of the buttons (disabling the Save and Delete buttons when a user is not selected, enabling the Save and Delete buttons when a user is selected, and so on).

```
FillListboxWithUsers();
InitControls();
```

At the end of the DaoUserMaintenanceDlg.cpp file, add the following function definition:

```
void CDaoUserMaintenanceDlg::FillListboxWithUsers()
{
 int iIndex;
 CDaoDatabase db;
 CDaoUserMasterSet rs;
```

Because the MFC DAO classes throw exceptions upon encountering unexpected conditions, you must "wrap" the database code with a try/catch block.

```
 try
 {
```

Open the recordset, and start a while loop based on reaching the end-of-file.

```
  rs.Open();

  while (!rs.IsEOF())
  {
```

Note that because this code is not using any of the filtering techniques discussed in the "Filtering records" section, all of the users from the database will be retrieved.

The following code will set the list box entry's item data to the CUser pointer so that when an item is selected in the list box, the database does not have to read again in order to retrieve the user record:

```
   CUser* pUser = new CUser();
   pUser->m_strUserID = rs.m_sUserID;
   pUser->m_strUserName = rs.m_sUserName;
   pUser->m_iStatus = rs.m_iStatus;

   iIndex = m_lbxUsers.AddString(rs.m_sUserName);
   m_lbxUsers.SetItemData(iIndex, (DWORD)pUser);
```

This code creates a CUser object to contain all of the information for each user that is read from the database. The user is then added to the list box, and its item data is set to the CUser object pointer so that retrieving the user information is much more efficient. Note that by simply calling the recordset's Open() and MoveNext() functions, its member variables are set to the current record's information without any further work on your part. Now call the recordset's MoveNext() function to retrieve the next record in the recordset, as follows:

```
   rs.MoveNext();
  }
 }
```

```
  catch(CDaoException* pe)
  {
   AfxMessageBox(pe->m_pErrorInfo->m_strDescription,
    MB_ICONEXCLAMATION );
  }
}
```

Add the following initialization function to the end of the DaoUserMaintenanceDlg.cpp file:

```
void CDaoUserMaintenanceDlg::InitControls()
{
```

Initialize the controls by setting all of the Edit fields to blanks and disabling the Save and Delete buttons. These buttons will be enabled when a user is selected from the list box.

```
 m_lbxUsers.SetCurSel(-1);

 m_strUserID = "";
 m_strUserName = "";
 m_iStatus = -1;

 m_btnSave.EnableWindow(FALSE);
 m_btnDelete.EnableWindow(FALSE);

 m_lbxUsers.SetFocus();

 UpdateData(FALSE);
}
```

You now must add a function so that when a user is selected from the list box, the proper information is displayed in the dialog box. To do this, use ClassWizard to implement a message handler for the LBN_SELCHANGE notification message, as follows:

```
void CDaoUserMaintenanceDlg::OnSelchangeLbxUsers()
{
 int iIndex;
 CUser* pUser;

 if (GetSelectedUser(&iIndex, &pUser))
 {
```

Update the member variables with the currently selected user's information:

```
  m_strUserID = pUser->m_strUserID;
  m_strUserName = pUser->m_strUserName;
  m_iStatus = pUser->m_iStatus;
```

Because a user is now selected, enable both the Save and Delete buttons.

```
  m_btnSave.EnableWindow(TRUE);
```

```
      m_btnDelete.EnableWindow(TRUE);
```

Calling UpdateData() with an argument of FALSE causes DDX (dynamic data exchange) to update the dialog box controls from the member variables.

```
      UpdateData(FALSE);
    }
  }
```

Because you are going to require information about the selected user at different times (when the Update button is clicked, when the Delete button is clicked, and so on), go ahead, and write a "helper" function to perform this task.

```
BOOL CDaoUserMaintenanceDlg::GetSelectedUser(
 int* piIndex, CUser** ppUser)
{
 BOOL bSuccess = FALSE;

 int iIndex;
 if (LB_ERR != (iIndex = m_lbxUsers.GetCurSel()))
 {
  *piIndex = iIndex;
  *ppUser = (CUser*)m_lbxUsers.GetItemData(iIndex);
   bSuccess = TRUE;
 }

 return bSuccess;
}
```

At this point, the application can read all of the users from the data source and display their respective information as they are selected from the list box. Next, the capability to add records will be implemented in the application. Add a BN_CLICKED handler for the Save button, and edit it so that you have the following results when finished:

```
void CDaoUserMaintenanceDlg::OnBtnSave()
{
 int iCurrIndex;

 CUser* pUser = NULL;
 if (GetSelectedUser(&iCurrIndex, &pUser))
 {
  ASSERT(pUser);
  if (pUser)
  {
   UpdateData();
```

Add the following code to save the data the user has typed in. That way, if the SaveUser() function call fails, the data is not lost, and the Save() can be attempted again without the user having to retype the information.

```
   CString strPrevUserID;
```

```
strPrevUserID = m_strUserID;
CString strPrevUserName;
strPrevUserName = m_strUserName;
int iPrevStatus = m_iStatus;

pUser->m_strUserID = m_strUserID;
pUser->m_strUserName = m_strUserName;
pUser->m_iStatus = m_iStatus;
```

Now, call the `SaveUser()` function to save the current user.

```
if (SaveUser(pUser))
{
```

Because the User Name information is being used in the list box and it could have changed, delete it from the list box, and add the user back, as shown in Listing 28-3.

Listing 28-3: Adding the User Back

```
 if (LB_ERR == m_lbxUsers.DeleteString(iCurrIndex))
 {
  AfxMessageBox("The User ID was Saved, "
   "but the previous User ID could not be "
   "removed from the listbox.");
 }
 else
 {
  int iNewIndex = m_lbxUsers.AddString(
   pUser->m_strUserName);
  if ((LB_ERR == iNewIndex) || (LB_ERRSPACE ==
   iNewIndex))
  {
   AfxMessageBox("The User ID was Saved, but "
    "the new User ID could not "
    "be added to the listbox.");
  }
  if (LB_ERR == m_lbxUsers.SetItemData(iNewIndex,
  (DWORD)pUser))
  {
   AfxMessageBox("SetItemData returned LB_ERR. "
    "This will probably cause "
    "serious problems if you attempt to update "
    "or delete this item from the listbox");
  }
 }

 InitControls();

 UpdateData(FALSE);
}
else
{
```

Obviously, the User Name could have been checked to verify if it had been changed, but this is the "quick and dirty" way of doing it and costs nothing in terms of performance. Next, enter the following code to ensure that if the SaveUser() function fails, the dialog box values are set back to what was typed in:

```
      pUser->m_strUserID = strPrevUserID;
      pUser->m_strUserName = strPrevUserName;
      pUser->m_iStatus = iPrevStatus;
      AfxMessageBox("SaveUser failed");
     }
    }
   }
   else
   {
    // should never get here because of
    // enabling/disabling button on lbx selection
    AfxMessageBox("You must first select a "
    "User ID to Save");
   }
  }
```

Now you add the helper function that actually does the work necessary to save a given record.

```
BOOL CDaoUserMaintenanceDlg::SaveUser(CUser* pUser)
{
 BOOL bSuccess = FALSE;
 CDaoDatabase db;

 try
 {
  db.Open(DEMO_DB);
```

You can also use a CDaoDatabase object by itself (instead of with a CDaoRecordset object). In cases where you know you are going to issue a SQL statement (as in the following SQL UPDATE) against a database and you do not already have a current record, it is more efficient to use the CDaoDatabase::Execute() function. Listing 28-4 shows the SQL statement is built and passed to the Execute() function for processing.

Listing 28-4: Building and Passing the SQL Statement to the Execute Function

```
CString strSQL = CString("UPDATE UserMaster SET ");
strSQL += CString("sUserName = '") +
 pUser->m_strUserName + CString("', ");

strSQL += CString("iStatus = ");
char szStatus[10];
itoa(pUser->m_iStatus, szStatus, 10);
```

```
   strSQL += szStatus;

   strSQL += CString(" WHERE sUserID = ");
   strSQL += CString("'") + pUser->m_strUserID +
    CString("'");

   db.Execute(strSQL);

   bSuccess = TRUE;
  }
  catch(CDaoException* pe)
  {
   AfxMessageBox(pe->m_pErrorInfo->m_strDescription,
    MB_ICONEXCLAMATION );

   pe->Delete();
  }

  return bSuccess;
 }
```

Finally, it's time to see how to delete a record using DAO. To do this, add a `BN_CLICKED` handler for the Delete button, and modify it so that when finished it looks like that shown in Listing 28-5.

Listing 28-5: Adding a BN_CLICKED Handler for the Delete Button

```
void CDaoUserMaintenanceDlg::OnBtnDelete()
{
 int iIndex;
 CUser* pUser = NULL;
 if (GetSelectedUser(&iIndex, &pUser))
 {
  ASSERT(pUser);
  if (pUser)
  {
   UpdateData();
   CString strMsg;

   strMsg = "Are you sure that you want to delete "
    "the User ";
   strMsg += "'";
   strMsg += pUser->m_strUserName;
   strMsg += "'?";
   if (IDYES == AfxMessageBox(strMsg, MB_YESNOCANCEL))
   {
```

(continued)

Listing 28-5 *(continued)*

```
      if (DeleteUser(pUser))
      {
       if (LB_ERR == m_lbxUsers.DeleteString(iIndex))
       {
        AfxMessageBox("The User was successfully "
         "Deleted, but there was an error in "
         "removing it from the listbox.");
       }

                InitControls();

       UpdateData(FALSE);
      }
      else
      {
       AfxMessageBox("DeleteUser failed");
      }
    }
   }
  }
  else
  {
   // should never get here because of
   // enabling/disabling button on lbx selection
   AfxMessageBox("You must first select a User "
    "ID to Delete");
  }
 }
```

Add the following helper function at the end of the `DaoUserMaintenanceDlg.cpp` file to do the actual work of deleting a record:

```
BOOL CDaoUserMaintenanceDlg::DeleteUser(CUser* pUser)
{
 BOOL bSuccess = FALSE;
 CDaoDatabase db;

 try
 {
```

Once again, you are hard-coding the database name in the following code. Obviously, in a real application, a pointer to a database object with dialog-level scope would have been created for efficiency, or at the very least a constant would be used for the database name.

```
    db.Open(DEMO_DB);

    CString strSQL;
    strSQL.Format("DELETE FROM UserMaster WHERE "
     "sUserID = '%s'", pUser->m_strUserID);

    db.Execute(strSQL);

    bSuccess = TRUE;
   }
   catch(CDaoException* pe)
   {
    AfxMessageBox(pe->m_pErrorInfo->m_strDescription,
     MB_ICONEXCLAMATION );

    pe->Delete();
   }

   return bSuccess;
  }
```

Once you have added the support to delete records, add one last function to free up the memory allocated when the `CUser` objects were created. This can be done by adding a handler for the dialog's `WM_DESTROY` message and adding the following code:

```
  void CDaoUserMaintenanceDlg::OnDestroy()
  {
   CDialog::OnDestroy();

   CUser* pUser;

   for (int i = 0; i < m_lbxUsers.GetCount(); i++)
   {
    pUser = (CUser*)m_lbxUsers.GetItemData(i);
    if (pUser)
    {
     delete pUser;
    }
   }
  }
```

Testing the UserMaintenance application

Once you build and test the application, the results should be similar to what you see in Figure 28-7.

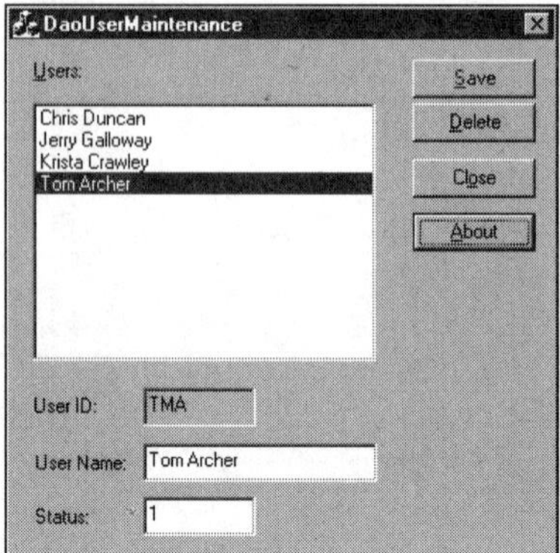

Figure 28-7: The DAOUserMaintenance application demonstrates how to read and write data using the MFC DAO classes.

Summary

In this chapter, you have learned about the basics of DAO, the different objects that constitute the DAO object hierarchy, and the different DAO APIs that enable you to programmatically manipulate the Microsoft Jet engine from your application. In addition, you learned how to use the MFC DAO classes to write a maintenance application. While no one can argue with the fact that you don't have the programmatic level of control using DAO as you do with the ODBC SDK, a simple, clean database API such as DAO is all you need at times.

✦ ✦ ✦

Extending Applications

Single developers — even teams of developers — can't do it all. There comes a time when you need to rely on third-party libraries to provide the functionality that your program needs. Some add-on libraries can cost just several hundred dollars, yet still save the development team hundreds or thousands of hours of time. This part shows you how to extend your applications with such third-party libraries.

P A R T

V

✦ ✦ ✦ ✦

In This Part

Chapter 29:
Working with DLLs

Chapter 30:
Adding Imaging to Your Programs

✦ ✦ ✦ ✦

CHAPTER 29

Working with DLLs

From the very first 16-bit version of Windows, every flavor and version of Windows has relied heavily on the functions and data stored in dynamic link libraries (DLLs). In fact, when you look at your Windows system, almost everything you see is represented in one form or another by a DLL. The fonts and icons on your display are stored in a DLL. The code necessary to display the Windows desktop and process your input is stored in a DLL. Even the Windows API is contained in DLLs. What DLLs are and how to develop them and use them with a Visual C++ application is the subject of this chapter.

Because Visual C++ defines two types of DLLs ("regular DLLs" and "extension DLLs"), this chapter is split into two sections. In the first section, you will learn the advantages of using what Visual C++ calls a *regular DLL* and how to create them with ClassWizard. You will also learn how to manage the current "module state" so that the DLL can make calls to the shared version of the MFC DLLs, and how to dynamically load a DLL and call its exported functions. In addition, you will write two demos. The first demo will illustrate Windows hooks and how to develop a Windows (keyboard) hook procedure. The second demo will teach you how to share C++ objects across multiple invocations of a DLL.

In the second section of this chapter, you will learn about MFC extension DLLs and how they are constructed. Then you will understand how to export whole classes from a DLL or even specific member functions of a given class. Once you have learned the basics of MFC extension DLLs, two demos will be presented. The first demo illustrates how to use nested MFC extension DLLs in an MFC application. The second and last demo is a DLL that encapsulates a document template, document, and view necessary to build an image-viewing application simply by linking with it and calling a single function.

✦ ✦ ✦ ✦

In This Chapter

Understanding implicit versus explicit linking

Learning about Visual C++ regular DLLs

Implementing a customized DllMain to handle multiple thread attachments

Discovering how to use the AFX_MANAGE_STATE macro

Viewing binary resources

Writing a systemwide keyboard hook

Global C++ objects across multiple invocations of a DLL

Learning about MFC Extension DLLs

Exporting entire classes and parts of classes from a DLL

Working with nested MFC extension DLLs encapsulating documents and views

✦ ✦ ✦ ✦

DLL Overview

DLLs are built on the concept of client-server communications. Functions and data are stored in a DLL (the server) and are exported for use by one or more clients. These clients can be applications or other DLLs. Therefore, when the term client is used in this chapter, it signifies any client of the DLL, whether it is an application or another DLL.

Dynamic and static libraries

A DLL is similar to a normal runtime, or static, library. In the case of a static library, the functions and data are compiled into a binary file (usually with a .LIB extension). The linker then copies these functions and data from the library and combines them with the other modules of the application to create the final executable (an .EXE file). The linker is also responsible for something called *fixup*. Fixup is the process in which calls from other modules in the executable are mapped to functions in the library. When an application links to a static library, the process is called *static linking*. Because everything the application needs from the library is copied into the executable, the library does not have to be shipped with the executable.

In the case of dynamic linking, a library's functions and data are not copied into an executable. Instead, two files are created: an import library and a DLL. The import library contains the names and locations of the functions being exported by the DLL, and the DLL contains the actual functions and data. An application that wants to use the exported functions of a given DLL then links to the import library. Actually, this is the case only if the application is implicitly linking to the DLL. The issues of implicit linking versus explicit linking are covered in the next section. Because the DLL contains the functions and data needed by clients of the DLL, the DLL must also be shipped with the executable.

The process of creating a DLL is very similar to that used in creating an executable. The library's functions are compiled into an .OBJ file (module), and a linker creates the final binary output file by linking the different modules together. However, in the case of a DLL, a special linker switch (`/DLL`) is used to tell the linker that a DLL is being created instead of an EXE. That way, the Windows loader recognizes the file as a DLL and not an application.

Loading DLLs

There are two ways to load a DLL: implicitly and explicitly. DLL clients implicitly load a DLL by either linking with the DLL's import library or by listing the DLL's exported functions in the `IMPORTS` section of the client's .DEF file. Implicit loading of a DLL is by far the most common means of loading DLLs for the simple reason that implicitly loading requires no extra work on the part of the client. The application programmer simply includes the necessary header file(s), makes the desired function calls, and links with the DLL. However, implicitly linking to a DLL has several drawbacks:

- The DLL must have an extension of .DLL.
- The client incurs the unnecessary overhead of loading the DLL if no functions in the DLL are ever called.

When a client is implicitly loading one or more DLLs, the DLLs are loaded into memory when the client is loaded. In order for Windows to load a given DLL, it must first find the actual physical file. Windows uses the following order when attempting to load a DLL:

- The current directory
- The Windows directory
- The Windows system directory
- The directory where the client resides
- The directories listed in the `PATH` environment variable (in the same order specified)
- Mapped network directories

Although implicit linking is the easiest manner for a client to link to a DLL, there are times when explicit linking has its advantages. Explicit linking involves specifically telling the Windows operating system which file to load and when to load it. Although explicitly loading a DLL requires a little more work on the application programmer's part, it has several advantages over implicit linking:

- The library can have any extension.
- The DLL is loaded only if the client loads it.
- The client has the option at runtime of choosing between loading different libraries.

A DLL is loaded explicitly as follows:

- The client calls the Win32 function `LoadLibrary`. This function returns a handle to the library. If the function fails, a `NULL` is returned, and the Win32 function `GetLastError` must be called to determine the cause of failure.
- Using the handle returned by the `LoadLibrary` function, the client calls the Win32 function `GetProcAddress`, passing to it the name of the desired function. The `GetProcAddress` function returns the address of function that can then be used to call the function.
- When the client is finished using the DLL, it should call the Win32 function `FreeLibrary` in order to unload the library from memory and free any associated resources.

Visual C++ Regular DLLs

Visual C++ defines two types of DLLs: regular DLLs and extension DLLs. Regular DLLs are used when the functions being exported are C functions, C++ classes, or C++ member functions. Note that the term *C++ classes* is not to be confused with MFC C++ classes. If your DLL needs to export an MFC class, you should look into writing and managing MFC extension DLLs, which is covered in the next section. The advantages of using a regular DLL as opposed to an MFC extension DLL include the following:

- The client does not have to be an MFC application. It simply has to be able to call C-like functions. This could be anything from an MFC application to a Delphi or Visual Basic application.
- A regular DLL can use C++ classes internally and then export only the C function wrappers. That way, any changes to these C++ classes would not affect the calling application or DLL.

Regular DLLs can be created from Visual C++ with the aid of the AppWizard. After invoking the AppWizard, simply choose the MFC AppWizard (DLL) project type. The first dialog that is displayed enables you to specify whether you want to use the MFC library and how you want the MFC libraries linked into your DLL: statically or dynamically.

Just as there are advantages to using regular DLLs over MFC extension DLLs, there are advantages and disadvantages regarding how you choose to link MFC support into your DLL:

- If a regular DLL dynamically links to the MFC libraries, its file size will be much smaller than a regular DLL that uses static linking. However, the disadvantage is that the MFC DLLs must now be shipped with the product. Obviously, this is a problem only if you are distributing your application. If the application you are developing will run on only one PC or in an environment that you control, this is not a liability.
- If you are distributing your DLL for use by another MFC application and the other application dynamically links to the MFC libraries, you will always be concerned about which version of MFC each is using. However, if your DLL is statically linking to the MFC libraries, you won't question which version your DLL is using.

As you can see, before you start working with DLLs, you must make some decisions. These decisions, by and large, are predicated on factors such as whether or not you control the environment where the DLL will be used, what language the calling application will be written in, and whether or not you want to distribute the MFC DLLs with your code. In all likelihood, you will have to go through this decision process for each application and DLL that you write.

Understanding the regular DLL internals

If you create a regular DLL with the AppWizard and take a look at the generated source code, you will find a familiar class: CWinApp. You are probably accustomed to creating MFC applications and seeing the application represented by a CWinApp object. However, when a regular DLL is created with the AppWizard, a CWinApp object also represents the DLL. In addition, if you are already familiar with creating DLLs, you may be wondering where the DllMain function went. After all, every Win32 DLL must have a DllMain entry point. Well, the answer is that AppWizard automatically creates a DllMain function, much like the WinMain function for Win32 applications. The advantage to having a CWinApp class is that you can program your DLL as you would any other CWinApp-derived class. For example, because initialization for CWinApp classes usually takes place in the InitInstance function, you can also override the CWinApp::InitInstance function for the DLL and provide global initialization there. In addition, deinitialization should be placed in the ExistInstance function derived from your DLL's CWinApp-derived class.

Implementing Your Own DllMain Function

While MFC provides a default DllMain() implementation and the MFC documentation generally advises you to do your initialization in the InitInstance function of your DLL's CWinApp-derived class, there may be times when you must implement your own DllMain() function. One potential problem with using the MFC-provided DllMain() function in conjunction with an InitInstance() function override is that the InitInstance() function is called only when a process attaches to the DLL or detaches from the DLL. This is fine in most cases, but at times your DLL may need to perform initialization and deinitialization when a thread attaches or detaches. In order to handle this scenario, it may be necessary to implement your own DllMain().

The reason you have a DllMain() function automatically compiled into your DLL is because the MFC source code links code into your DLL from the Dllmodul.cpp file. In fact, if you browse to the folder on your hard disk that contains the MFC source code, you will not only find this file, but inside it you will find the definition of the DllMain() function. In addition to the DllMain() function, the Dllmodul.cpp file contains most of the code that is used to support a regular DLL. The recommended way to override or alter this function is to copy this file into the DLL's source code folder and include it in the DLL's project. Now you can make the changes you deem necessary, and the local, modified copy of the Dllmodul.cpp file will be compiled and linked into your DLL.

◆ ◆ ◆ ◆ ◆

Another important point about regular DLLs is an issue that arises only if a regular DLL must call into the MFC. MFC keeps some internal global state information regarding the application or DLL. Therefore, if an exported function in the DLL attempts to call a function that depends on this information, the wrong data will be used. The following is a simple example to illustrate this point.

Using AppWizard, create a new MFC DLL project called "DisplayAppName." Don't forget to define this DLL as a regular DLL (it's the default AppWizard setting when creating a DLL). Once AppWizard has created the source files, declare the following function in the `DisplayAppName.h` file:

```
void DisplayAppName();
```

In the `DisplayAppName.cpp` file, define the `DisplayAppName` function as follows:

```
void DisplayAppName()
{
 CString str = AfxGetAppName();
 AfxMessageBox(str);
}
```

Now add the function to the `DisplayAppName.def` file in the `EXPORTS` section. The `EXPORTS` section should now look as follows:

```
EXPORTS
 DisplayAppName
```

Build the DLL, and copy it to a folder where Windows can load it. If you are not sure of where to place the DLL, refer back to the section entitled "Loading DLLs," earlier in the chapter. Next, create an MFC application project called "RegDllTest." After including the `DisplayAppName.h` file somewhere in your code and adding the `DisplayAppName.lib` file to the project, place a call to the `DisplayAppName` function.

Finally, build and run the application. You will see that the name that is displayed is the application name of your EXE, not the DLL. This is because MFC has placed global data on the stack that represents the current module — in this case, the application. In order to specify that you want to use the MFC global data associated with the DLL, you must use the `AFX_MANAGE_STATE` macro in your code. This macro is used to push or pop the global data associated with the module. Therefore, at the beginning of every exported function, you must set the current module state to that of the DLL. Don't worry about resetting the module state because the `AFX_MANAGE_STATE` macro actually resolves to a class whose destructor resets the previous state when the object goes out of scope. Here's how you would change the example code so that the message box reflects the name of the DLL instead of the application:

```
void DisplayAppName()
{
 AFX_MANAGE_STATE(AfxGetStaticModuleState());
 CString str = AfxGetAppName();
 AfxMessageBox(str);
}
```

Dynamically loading DLLs

As mentioned earlier, when an application is loaded, Windows automatically loads the DLLs that the application is implicitly linked to. However, you will often have to dynamically load a DLL. To load a DLL at runtime, the application simply calls the `LoadLibrary` function. As you can see in the following prototype, it takes only one argument — the name of the file:

```
HINSTANCE LoadLibrary(LPCTSTR lpLibFileName);
```

The returned `HINSTANCE` is a global handle that represents the loaded DLL. This handle is then used with the `GetProcAddress()` function to retrieve a given function's address. That address is then stored in a function pointer and can be called like any other function. When the application no longer needs the library, the `FreeLibrary()` function is called to unload the library from memory.

Examples of when to dynamically load a DLL

Now that you know the semantics of dynamically loading a DLL, here are some examples of when an application might dynamically load a DLL.

Programming function seams

A *function seam* is a layer of abstraction between a function and its caller. Its purpose is to insulate the caller from the internals of the function to be called. Let's say you have an application that supports multiple communications protocols. The application might support APPC, NetBIOS, and Named Pipes, to name a few. How can your application support all of these completely different communications APIs without your changing the main module's source code for each one?

One way would be to implement a function seam where each communications API would be placed in a separate DLL. Each DLL would then export the exact same set of functions. For example, each DLL would export a generic `Read()` function with a universally agreed-upon function definition. Using this technique, the calling function could load the appropriate DLL and call its `Read()` function and not have to worry about what the DLL is doing internally to satisfy the read request.

An example of using function seams is ODBC (which is covered in Chapter 26). After an application makes a request of the ODBC Driver Manager, that request must be passed on to the specified ODBC driver. Because the ODBC Driver Manager can't be rewritten for every ODBC driver, Microsoft accomplishes this by mandating that all ODBC drivers export a specific set of functions per a published specification. That way, the ODBC Driver Manager never has to have any understanding of how the request is being carried out and doesn't require any special coding for different ODBC drivers.

Writing multilingual applications

Another common example of when you would need to dynamically load a DLL is when programming multilingual applications. There are a couple of different ways to support more than one language, but by far the most popular technique is to use resource-only DLLs. Creating a DLL for each language that must be supported does this. Once the DLL has been created, the necessary resources (string tables, menus, and so on) are added to each DLL. It's important to note that the resources IDs must be consistent across the different DLL resource files. For example, if the resource ID for the main menu is 100 in the English DLL, then it must be 100 in the Spanish DLL.

Once you have done this, the calling program must do only two things in order to finish the process of providing multilingual capabilities. Simply load the library, and provide the `HINSTANCE` that is returned to the `AfxSetResourceHandle()` function call. Now when the application's code refers to a given resource ID, the resources in the desired resource-only DLL will be used.

When the header file or import library is not available

At times your application must call a function provided by a DLL, but the header file or import library is not available. You can place the calls to the exported functions in your application, but without the header file, you won't be able to compile your application, and without the import library, you won't be able to link your application. However, if you can dump a list of the functions the DLL exports and you know the function's prototype, you can have your application dynamically load the library and get the address of the functions you need to call. At that point, you can call the desired functions.

Retrieving resources from a binary file

Another popular reason for dynamically loading a library is to retrieve its resources. Because the resource compiler binds the resources to the application or DLL when it is built, the resources are located in the binary file itself. An example of this is the different mouse cursors that are standard with Windows. These cursors can be retrieved from the `user32.dll` by dynamically loading the DLL, calling the `LoadCursor` function, and passing the resource ID of the desired cursor.

Viewing Binary Resources

You can view the resources of a binary file from Visual Studio. Simply invoke the File Open dialog, and locate the binary file that contains the resources you want to view. After you have specified the desired binary file, change the Open As combo box to "Resources." When the file is opened, you will see all of its resources, just as if you were opening up any resource file.

✦ ✦ ✦ ✦ ✦

Windows hooks

In this section, you will learn about Windows hooks and how to write hook procedures. *Hooks* are points in the Windows messaging path where subroutines are injected, or attached, to filter certain types of messages before they reach their target destinations. Once these messages are caught, they can be modified, logged, or simply discarded. The subroutines themselves are called *filters*. These filters are classified according to the types of events they are filtering. For example, the hook that you will write in this section is known as a *keyboard hook*. When a filter function is attached to a hook, this is known as *setting a hook*. As you might imagine, there will be times when more than one hook of the same type has been set. In order to deal with this situation, Windows keeps track of the chain of filter functions. A very important point is that the most recently added filter function is the first function in that chain, and therefore, it has the first opportunity to filter any message traffic. That function can then perform its work and send the message onto the next hook procedure in the chain or discard the message completely. Table 29-1 lists the hook functions that are supported in Windows along with providing brief descriptions.

Table 29-1
Windows Hook Functions

Function	*Description*
WH_CALLWNDPROC	Monitors all Windows messages before the message is sent to its destination window procedure (see WH_CALLWNDPROCRET).
WH_CALLWNDPROCRET	Monitors messages after they have been processed by the destination window procedure.
WH_CBT	Monitors messages used by Computer-Based-Training applications.
WH_DEBUG	Aids in debugging other hook functions.
WH_GETMESSAGE	Monitors Windows messages posted to a message queue.
WH_JOURNALPLAYBACK	Posts messages previously recorded by a WH_JOURNALRECORD hook procedure.
WH_JOURNALRECORD	Records input messages posted to the system message queue.
WH_KEYBOARD	Monitors keyboard activity.
WH_KEYBOARD_LL	Monitors low-level keyboard input events (Windows NT only).

(continued)

Table 29-1 *(continued)*

Function	*Description*
WH_MOUSE	Monitors mouse messages.
WH_MOUSE_LL	Monitors low-level mouse input events (Windows NT only).
WH_MSGFILTER	Monitors messages generated as a result of an input event in a dialog box, message box, menu, or scroll bar.
WH_SHELL	Receives notification of events meaningful to shell applications.
WH_SYSMSGFILTER	Similar to the WH_MSGFILTER, monitors messages generated as a result of an input event in a dialog box, message box, menu, or scroll bar. However, WH_SYSMSGFILTER monitors these messages for all active applications.

The SetWindowsHookEx() function

In order to set a hook, the SetWindowsHookEx() function must be called. Its prototype looks like this:

```
SetWindowsHookEx(int idHook, HOOKPROC lpfn,
 HINSTANCE hMod, DWORD dwThreadId)
```

The first argument, idHook, represents a constant that identifies what type of hook is being set. Approximately 15 types of hooks can be set for Windows. The value used in the demo application is the WH_KEYBOARD constant, which specifies that a keyboard hook is being set.

The second argument, lpfn, is simply a pointer to a function of type HOOKPROC. For a keyboard hook, the function that is passed to the SetWindowsHookEx() function must have the following prototype. This function will be explained in more detail when the demo is covered.

```
LRESULT CALLBACK KeyboardProc(int code, WPARAM, LPARAM);
```

The third argument, hMod, is the HINSTANCE of the DLL that contains the filter function.

The fourth and last argument to the SetWindowsHookEx() function enables the application to specify the thread for which the hook is being set. For example, the application can set a hook for one single thread or for all threads that are currently active. For the latter, simply specify a value of NULL for this argument.

When the SetWindowsHookEx() function returns, it returns a value of type HHOOK (handle to a hook). If the hook was not successfully set, this returned value is NULL, and you would need to call the GetLastError() function in order to determine the cause of its failure.

The UnhookWindowsHookEx() function

In order to remove a hook from the hook chain, you must call the UnhookWindowsHookEx() function. This function (see the following syntax) simply takes the HHOOK value returned by successfully setting a hook via the SetWindowsHookEx() function. The UnhookWindowsHookEx() function returns a Boolean value, which can be used to test for the success or failure of this function.

```
BOOL UnhookWindowsHookEx(HHOOK hHook);
```

The CallNextHook() function

When a filter function is set for a given hook type, the filter function is placed at the head of a chain of filter functions for that hook type. Once a filter function completes its task, it can call the CallNextHook() function in order for the next filter function to perform its work. There are times, however, when you won't want processing to continue. For example, if you write a keyboard hook and want to discard the keystroke, you would not call this function. However, if you are simply logging an event and you want the message to continue along its intended messaging path, the application would need to call the CallNextHook() function once it is finished processing the message. If there are no other filter functions for this type of hook, Windows delivers the message to the appropriate message queue.

Writing the keyboard hook DLL

First, you must create the DLL that will contain the filter function for the keyboard hook. To do that, create a project named "KeybdHook" with the following settings:

- "MFC AppWizard (dll)" in the New dialog box
- "Regular DLL with MFC statically linked" as the DLL type

Open the KeybdHook.h file, and add the following lines before the CKeybdHookApp class declaration. The first #define simply provides an easy way of exporting functions that have the __stdcall calling mechanism. The second function is the actual filter function. It is the function that will be called for every single keystroke that Windows processes. Its arguments will be explained shortly.

```
#define EXPORTED_DLL_FUNCTION \
  __declspec(dllexport) __stdcall

LRESULT EXPORTED_DLL_FUNCTION KbdHookProc (int nCode,
  WPARAM  wParam, LPARAM lParam);
```

Next, open the `KeybdHook.cpp` file, and add the following lines to the top of the file. This creates a shared data segment across all uses of this DLL. That way, the values defined within it are global for all uses of this DLL. When global variables are declared, they must be initialized.

```
#pragma data_seg(".SHARDAT")
static HWND       ghWndMain  = 0;
static HHOOK      ghKeyHook = NULL ;
#pragma data_seg()

HINSTANCE ghInstance = 0;
HOOKPROC  glpfnHookProc = 0;
```

After declaring the global variables that will be used in this DLL, add the filter function shown in Listing 29-1 that will be called every time Windows processes a keystroke. As you can see, the function is simply catching the F10 keystroke. The listing is just a very simple example of catching a keystroke. Once the filter function catches the keystrokes it is filtering, you are then free to run whatever application-specific logic you require. Notice that if the keystroke is handled and you do not want Windows to continue processing the keystroke, simply return a value of `TRUE` from this function instead of calling the next filter function for this hook type.

Listing 29-1: The Filter Function Called Every Time Windows Processes a Keystroke

```
LRESULT EXPORTED_DLL_FUNCTION KbdHookProc
(int nCode, WPARAM  wParam, LPARAM lParam)
{
 BOOL bHandledKeystroke = FALSE;

 if (((DWORD)lParam & 0x40000000)
 && (HC_ACTION == nCode))
 {
  switch (wParam)
  {
   case VK_F10:
    AfxMessageBox("Caught the F10 key!");
    bHandledKeystroke = TRUE;
   break;

   default :
   break ;
  }
 }

 return (bHandledKeystroke ?
  TRUE :
  ::CallNextHookEx (ghKeyHook, nCode, wParam, lParam));
}
```

Let's do a quick run-through of the different arguments that are passed to a keyboard hook function like the one just used.

One of the values that the first argument, nCode, might contain is the HC_ACTION constant. Actually, this argument can have only one of two values: HC_ACTION and HC_NOREMOVE. In both cases, the WPARAM and LPARAM variables will contain information about the keystroke. However, in the case where nCode has a value of HC_NOREMOVE, the destination application for this keystroke has used the PeekMessage() function, specifying the PM_NOREMOVE flag. In addition, if the value of nCode is less than zero, the filter function should not attempt to process the keystroke and instead should call the CallNextHookEx() function.

The WPARAM value contains the virtual keycode of the generated keystroke, and it is used to verify which key was pressed. Finally, the LPARAM value is used to find out more information about the keystroke. For example, the repeat count and whether the key was down or up before the message was sent can be determined by examining this value.

The DLL has to export a couple of functions to enable a client to set and release the keyboard hook. First, open the KeybdHook.h file, and declare the following function that will be used to install or set the keyboard hook:

```
BOOL EXPORTED_DLL_FUNCTION InstallKeyboardHook
 (HWND hWnd);
```

Once you have declared the function, define it as follows in the KeybdHook.cpp file. If this function works successfully and the keyboard hook is set, the ghKeyHook variable will be set to the HHOOK value returned from the SetWindowsHookEx() function. Therefore, the first thing the InstallKeyboardHook() function does is to check this variable to see if it has a value. If it does, then the hook has already been set, and this function simply returns without doing anything. If the ghKeyHook variable does not have a value, this function attempts to set the keyboard hook. You already defined the glpfnHookProc variable in the previous global data segment, but what about the ghInstance variable being set? This variable will be set in the InitInstance() function for this DLL. This will be covered shortly. This function then returns success or failure based on whether or not SetWindowsHookEx() successfully set the hook.

```
BOOL EXPORTED_DLL_FUNCTION InstallKeyboardHook
 (HWND hWnd)
{
 BOOL bSuccess = FALSE;

 if (!ghKeyHook)
 {
  ghWndMain     = hWnd ;
  glpfnHookProc = (HOOKPROC) KbdHookProc ;

  bSuccess = (NULL != (ghKeyHook =
   ::SetWindowsHookEx (WH_KEYBOARD, glpfnHookProc,
```

```
    ghInstance, NULL)));
  }

 return bSuccess;
}
```

Now that you have exported a function to set the keyboard hook, you must also export a function to release the keyboard hook. Declare the following function above the `InstallKeyboardHook` function declaration in the `KeybdHook.h` file:

```
BOOL EXPORTED_DLL_FUNCTION DeInstallKeyboardHook();
```

After declaring the function to remove the keyboard hook, place the following function definition in the `KeybdHook.cpp` file. Note that the `ghKeyHook` variable is reset to `NULL` if the `UnHookWindowsHookEx()` function works successfully. That is so the user of this DLL can call `InstallKeyboardHook()` again to reset the hook if needed.

```
BOOL EXPORTED_DLL_FUNCTION DeInstallKeyboardHook()
{
 if (ghKeyHook)
 {
  if (TRUE == (0 != ::UnhookWindowsHookEx(ghKeyHook)))
  {
   ghKeyHook = NULL;
  }
 }

 return (NULL == ghKeyHook);
}
```

Now that all the code for setting and removing a keyboard hook is in place, use ClassWizard to add both an `InitInstance()` function and an `ExitInstance()` function to the `CKeybdHookApp` object. They should be defined as follows:

```
BOOL CKeybdHookApp::InitInstance()
{
  AFX_MANAGE_STATE(AfxGetStaticModuleState());
  ghInstance = AfxGetInstanceHandle();
  return TRUE;
}

int CKeybdHookApp::ExitInstance()
{
  DeInstallKeyboardHook();
  return CWinApp::ExitInstance();
}
```

After you have finished adding the `InitInstance()` and `ExitInstance()` member functions, build the DLL, and copy it to the Windows system folder.

Building a test for the keyboard hook DLL

Now that you have written the hook function, it is time to do the easy part: testing it. To test your new keyboard hook, simply use AppWizard to create a dialog-based application named "KeybdHookClient." After the project has been created, use ClassWizard to create a function for the `IDOK` button being clicked. In the handler, simply call the DLL's exported `InstallKeyboardHook()` function. Your `OnOK()` function should look like this:

```
void CKeybdHookClientDlg::OnOK()
{
 InstallKeyboardHook(GetSafeHwnd());
}
```

Next, use ClassWizard to override the dialog's `OnCancel()` function. This function simply ensures that the keyboard hook is removed before the application terminates. When finished, the `OnCancel()` function should look like the following:

```
void CKeybdHookClientDlg::OnCancel()
{
 DeInstallKeyboardHook();
 CDialog::OnCancel();
}
```

As with any DLL, now all you have to do is include the header file that contains the declarations for the functions you want to call. Add the following `#include` at the top of the `KeybdHookClientDlg.cpp` file. Obviously, you have to either fully qualify this name or place the folder where this file resides in your include folder path.

```
#include "KeybdHook.h"
```

The only thing left to do before building and running the test application is to include the keyboard hook DLL's import library, `KeybdHook.lib`.

Testing the keyboard hook DLL

As a test of the keyboard hook, simply find a product that uses the F10 key to do something. Because the F10 key is defined by CUA (Common User Access) to provide keyboard access to the menu, plenty of applications implement this keystroke. We chose the standard Notepad application that is installed with every copy of Windows. To test the keyboard hook DLL in Notepad, simply do the following:

1. Start the Notepad application. Your cursor will originally be placed in the body of the document (actually a multi-line edit control).
2. Press the F10 key, which places you on the File menu.
3. Press the Esc key to return from the menu to the document.

4. Run the KeybdHookClient application, and press the Enter key, which sets the keyboard hook.

5. Return to the Notepad application and press the F10 key.

   Instead of being placed on Notepad's File menu, you will see a message box that states that the F10 key was successfully filtered. Because the keyboard hook filter function did not call the `CallNextHook` function, this key will not be sent to the Notepad application, and you will not be able to get to the Notepad menu via this keystroke. In other words, this keystroke has been filtered and, essentially, discarded.

6. Close the KeybdHookClient application. This releases the keyboard hook.

7. Return to the Notepad application, and press the F10 key. The F10 key now works as it originally did because the keyboard hook has been released.

Figure 29-1 shows the result of this procedure having been completed. Notice that although the Notepad application was the current application when the F10 key was pressed, the filter function caught it and displayed its own message instead of enabling the Notepad application to process it.

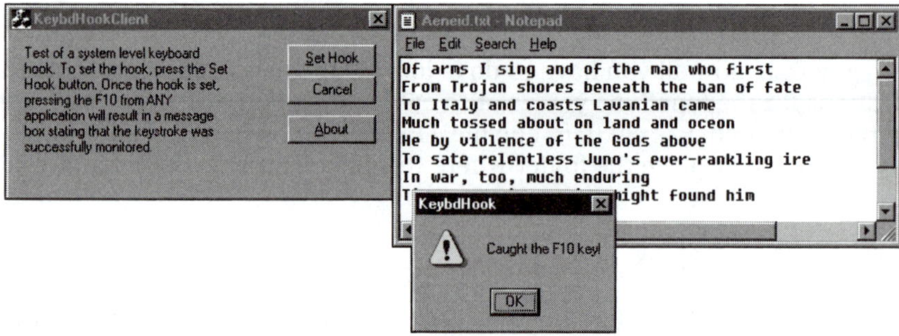

Figure 29-1: The KeybdHook DLL illustrates how easy it is to write a systemwide keyboard hook.

Global C++ objects with DLLs

Win32 DLLs are mapped into the address space of the calling process, with each invocation of the DLL getting a fresh copy of its data. However, a DLL will often want to manage data that is not specific to any one invocation, requiring the definition of global data in the DLL. As you saw in the keyboard hook demo, sharing global data across multiple invocations of a DLL is not difficult. You simply use the `#pragma` directive to name a data segment, and declare and initialize the desired global variable within that data segment. This enables the application to maintain data without regard to any one specific invocation of a DLL. Global data is useful for keeping track of things such as how many clients are attached to the DLL. Another example is a database server. The server would probably have tables and lists of currently attached clients, locked and cached records, and database handles. As you can see, declaring a global variable of a simple type (for example, `long` or `WORD`) can be used to keep track of how many clients are attached to a DLL. Unfortunately, managing more elaborate data structures such as C++ objects involves quite a bit more work on the part of the DLL.

The problem with using the previous approach to globalize C++ objects in a DLL is that each time a process attaches to the DLL, the constructor for that object is called. Here's an example of the problem:

```
#pragma  data_seg(".SHARDAT")
  _declspec(dllexport) CCounter counter;
  _declspec(dllexport) WORD wCounter = 0;
#pragma data_seg()

class CCounter
{
public:
 Ccounter() { m_wCounter = 0; }
};
```

In the preceding example code snippet, the DLL must keep track of how many clients are currently attached to it. Both lines of code attempt to do this. The first line of code uses an object that contains a member variable to keep track of the number of attached clients, while the second line uses a simple variable of type `WORD`. Assume that both counters should be incremented every time a client attaches to the DLL and decremented every time a client detaches from the DLL. Using the preceding code, the `wCounter` variable would function as expected. However, the `CCounter` object would not function correctly. This is because each time a client attaches to the DLL, the constructor for `CCounter` would be called, which would reinitialize its member variable counter back to zero.

If you scan the MSDN in search of a resolution to this problem, you will find the following advice:

> In order to share [C++ objects], you must use a memory-mapped file. For more information about memory-mapped files, see File Mapping in the Win32 SDK documentation.

If you have ever worked with memory-mapped files, this advice is not exactly the kind of answer you are looking for. While memory-mapped files can be a very powerful tool, using them to share simple objects is a little like using a shotgun to kill flies. Luckily, an alternative is available, and it involves using the `placement new` operator.

Placement new operator

Although a thorough explanation of `placement new` is outside the scope of this chapter, it will be explained sufficiently to show how and why it is used to share global objects in a DLL. Objects are normally allocated on the heap, the stack, or in static memory. These allocations are realized via dynamic allocation, automatic allocation, and static allocation, respectively. However, at times you might need to specify the exact address where an object should be created. For example, a piece of hardware may need to share data with an application. This is accomplished with the placement new operator. Here's an example where the object CRegisters is being allocated at a specific hard-coded address in memory:

```
void* pMemory = (void)0xDEADBEEF;
CRegisters* pRegisters = new (pMemory) CRegisters();
```

The storage that is allocated at the address pointed to by pMemory must be large enough to hold a CRegisters object, and it must be properly aligned to hold a CRegisters object. Note that the numeric value of pRegisters is the same as pMemory. However, the pRegisters is of type CRegisters while pMemory is a void pointer.

Obviously, you probably don't want to explicitly state at what address the object should be created. However, using placement new, you can allocate a buffer of memory and then pass the address of that buffer to the placement new operator, which would look like the following in a data_seq in your DLL:

```
#pragma data_seg(".SHARDAT")
static char lpszMemory[sizeof(CRegisters)];
CRegisters* g_pRegisters = NULL;
int g_nClients = 0;
#pragma data_seg()
```

Note that at this point, we have a buffer of memory (lpszMemory) that is the size of a CRegisters object. In addition, a CRegisters object pointer is initialized to NULL and a counter (g_nClients) is used to keep track of the number of attached clients. Now all your DLL has to do is allocate the memory and construct the CRegisters object when the first client attaches (g_pRegisters will be NULL) and delete the allocated memory when the last client detaches (g_nClients will be zero). This will be shown in more detail in a demo called GlobalDllObjects.

The GlobalDllObjects demo

Using the AppWizard, create an MFC DLL. Specify the regular DLL with MFC statically linked option. Once the project's files have been created, open the GlobalDllObjects.h file, and add the following code just before the declaration of the CGlobalDllObjectsApp class. As you learned earlier, these directives ensure that while any module can include this header file, the GLOBALDLLOBJECTS_API macro will resolve only to declspec(dllexport) if the module has defined GLOBALDLLOBJECTS_EXPORTS.

```
#ifdef GLOBALDLLOBJECTS_EXPORTS
#define GLOBALDLLOBJECTS_API __declspec(dllexport)
#else
#define GLOBALDLLOBJECTS_API __declspec(dllimport)
#endif
```

Next, add the declaration of the `CTest` class to the `GlobalDllObjects.h` file that will be instantiated and shared by the DLL (see Listing 29-2). The `new` operators have been overridden so that this class cannot be constructed using anything else but the `placement new` operator. In addition, both the class' constructor and destructor display messages when they are invoked. This is done so that when you execute this DLL's test client, you can verify that the `CTest` object's constructor and destructor are called only once regardless of how many clients attach to the DLL.

Listing 29-2: Adding the Declaration of the CTest Class

```
class GLOBALDLLOBJECTS_API CTest
{
public:
 // the only construction of the object
 // that is allowed is via the placement
 // new operator
 void* operator new(size_t) { return NULL; }
 void* operator new(size_t, void* p) { return p; }
 void operator delete(void*) {};

 // display message box during object c'tor and d'tor
 // to show that object is only being constructed
 // when first client attaches and destructed when
 // last client detaches
 CTest() {
  ::MessageBox(NULL,"CTest c'tor",
  "CTest.DLL", MB_OK);
 }

 ~CTest() {
  ::MessageBox(NULL,"CTest d'tor",
  "CTest.DLL", MB_OK);
 }

 CTest(const CTest&);
};
```

Add the following function declarations after the `CTest` class declaration. These functions enable a DLL's client to retrieve the pointer to the global `CTest` object and to inquire as to how many clients are currently attached to the DLL.

```
#define EXPORTED_DLL_FUNCTION \
 __declspec(dllexport) __stdcall

void EXPORTED_DLL_FUNCTION GetTestPtr(CTest*& rpTest);
int EXPORTED_DLL_FUNCTION GetNbrOfClients();
```

Next, open the GlobalDllObjects.cpp file, and add the following #include directive for the new.h file immediately after the #include of stdafx.h:

```
#include <new.h>
```

As mentioned previously, the DLL's main module will have to define GLOBALDLLOBJECTS_EXPORTS. Therefore, place the following #define directive before the #include directive for the GlobalDllObject.h file:

```
#define GLOBALDLLOBJECTS_EXPORTS
```

Now, add the following code to create a global mutex for the DLL. This mutex enables the DLL to synchronize the access to the global data that the DLL will have to allocate and deallocate.

```
// inter-process locking
HANDLE g_hMutex = ::CreateMutex(NULL, FALSE, "CTest");
```

Next, add the following data_seg to the GlobalDllObjects.cpp file. As you can see, the data_seg is named .SHARDAT and consists of three global variables. The first variable is a block of memory that is the size of a CTest object. The second variable is a CTest object pointer that is initialized to NULL. Finally, the third and last variable is a counter that keeps track of the number of currently attached clients.

```
#pragma data_seg(".SHARDAT")
static char lpszMemory[sizeof(CTest)];
CTest* g_pTest = NULL;
int g_nClients = 0;
#pragma data_seg()
```

Now that you have declared your global variables, you must construct the CTest object. As you learned earlier, initialization of a regular DLL can be performed in the InitInstance() member function. Therefore, use ClassWizard to implement the InitInstance() function as follows:

```
BOOL CGlobalDllObjectsApp::InitInstance()
{
```

The first thing the InitInstance() function does is to call the WaitForSingleObject() function so that multiple clients attaching to the DLL at the same time won't cause memory for CTest object to be allocated twice. In effect, access to the DLL's InitInstance() function (where the CTest object is allocated) is being serialized via this mutex.

```
::WaitForSingleObject(g_hMutex,INFINITE);
```

After the mutex has been acquired, the g_pTest pointer is tested. If it does not have a value, then the current client must be the first client to attach to the DLL.

```
if (!g_pTest)
{
 ::MessageBox(NULL,
  "CGlobalDllObjectsApp::InitInstance - "
  "constructing global CTest",
  "CTest.DLL", MB_OK);
```

In the case of the first client attaching to the DLL, the `CTest` object is constructed into the address pointed at by the `lpszMemory` global variable.

```
 g_pTest = ::new (lpszMemory) CTest;
 ASSERT(g_pTest);
}
```

The last thing the function does is increment the global variable `g_nCount` to reflect that another client has attached and released the locked `mutex` with a call to the `ReleaseMutex()` function.

```
 g_nClients++;
 ::ReleaseMutex(g_hMutex);

 return CWinApp::InitInstance();
}
```

After you have implemented the `InitInstance()` function, use ClassWizard to implement the `ExitInstance()` function as follows:

```
int CGlobalDllObjectsApp::ExitInstance()
{
```

Once again, before anything is done to alter the global variables, the global `mutex` is acquired to ensure serialized access to the variables.

```
 ::WaitForSingleObject(g_hMutex,INFINITE);
```

Once the `mutex` has been acquired, the global variable that represents the current number of attached clients (`g_nClients`) is tested. If the value of `g_nClients` is zero, the allocated memory for the `CTest` object is freed.

```
 if (0 == --g_nClients)
 {

  MSG msg;

  ::PeekMessage(&msg, NULL,
   WM_QUIT, WM_QUIT, PM_REMOVE);

  ::MessageBox(NULL,
   "CGlobalDllObjectsApp::ExitInstance - "
   "destructing global CTest",
   "CTest.DLL", MB_OK);
```

This line deletes the global CTest pointer and sets the pointer to NULL so that if another process attaches before this DLL is unloaded from memory, the pointer is reallocated.

```
  delete g_pTest;
  g_pTest = NULL;
 }
```

Release and close the handle to the global mutex used to serialize access to the global variables.

```
 ::ReleaseMutex(g_hMutex);
 ::CloseHandle(g_hMutex);

 return CWinApp::ExitInstance();
}
```

The last change you need to make to the DLL's code is to implement two functions that will be exported to the DLL's clients. The first function, GetTestPtr(), is used to retrieve the global CTest pointer. The second function, GetNbrOfClients(), retrieves the number of currently attached clients.

```
void EXPORTED_DLL_FUNCTION GetTestPtr(CTest*& rpTest)
{
 rpTest = g_pTest;
}

int EXPORTED_DLL_FUNCTION GetNbrOfClients()
{
 return g_nClients;
}
```

Now that the code has been completed for the DLL, display the Project Settings dialog for the GlobalDllObjects project by pressing the Alt+F7 keys. On the Link tab, select the Win32 Debug entry in the Settings For combo box. Then, enter the following at the *end* of the Project Options edit control at the bottom of the dialog. When you finish that, do the same thing for the Win32 Release entry in the Settings For combo box.

```
/SECTION:.SHARDAT,RWS
```

That's it. Now build the DLL, and copy it to a folder where Windows will load it. If you are not sure of where to place the DLL, refer to the section entitled "Loading DLLs," earlier in the chapter.

Next, create an MFC application project called "RegDllTest." After including the DisplayAppName.h file somewhere in your code and adding the DisplayAppName.lib file to the project, place a call to the DisplayAppName() function.

Using PeekMessage to Remove the WM_QUIT Message

In the ExitInstance() function, you might have noticed a call to the PeekMessage() function immediately before the MessageBox() function call. This is done for a couple of reasons. First, the client application (GlobalDllObjectsClient) is implicitly linking to the DLL. Therefore, if the DLL's ExitInstance() is running, it is because a client application is terminating. Second, when the main dialog of an MFC dialog-based application is closed, MFC posts a WM_QUIT message. Message boxes are not displayed if a pending WM_QUIT message is in the queue. However, calling PeekMessage() with the PM_REMOVE flag removes the message from the queue and enables the message box to be displayed. Here's an example of how to call the PeekMessage() function for this purpose:

```
MSG msg;
::PeekMessage(&msg, NULL,
 WM_QUIT, WM_QUIT, PM_REMOVE);
```

✦ ✦ ✦ ✦ ✦

The GlobalDllObjectsClient test application

Now that the DLL is built, you must build a test application to verify that it works as planned. Using AppWizard, create a dialog-based MFC application called GlobalDllObjectClient. This test application can be found on the accompanying CD in the \Chap29\GlobalDllObjectsClient folder. When AppWizard is finished creating the project's files, open the GlobalDllObjectClientDlg.cpp file, and add the following #include directive:

```
#include "GlobalDllObjects.h"
```

Add a handler for the BN_CLICKED notification message for the main dialog's IDOK button. This function calls the GlobalObjectDll's GetTestPtr() function to retrieve the DLL's global pointer to the CTest object. In addition, the GetNbrOfClients() function is called in order to retrieve the number of currently attached clients. These values are then both displayed in a message box. When you are finished the OnOK() function should look as follows:

```
void CGlobalDllObjectClientDlg::OnOK()
{
 CTest* pTest;
 GetTestPtr(pTest);
 ASSERT(pTest);
 if (pTest)
 {
  CString str;

  str.Format("CTest address = 0x%08x, "
   "Attached clients = %ld\n",
   pTest, GetNbrOfClients());

  AfxMessageBox(str);
 }
}
```

The last thing you must do is add the GlobalDllObjects import library to the GlobalDllObjectsClient project and build the application.

Testing the GlobalDllObjects DLL

Start a copy of the GlobalDllObjectsClient application. You should see two message boxes. The first message box is displayed as a result of the DLL's `InitInstance` function creating the DLL's global `CTest` object. The second message box is displayed from the constructor of the `CTest` object. You should see *only* these two message boxes when only one client is attached to the DLL. All subsequent clients should use the same `CTest` object that was created when the first client attached. In order to verify that this is working correctly, start a second copy of the application. This time you should not see any of the message boxes. However, clicking the dialog's `IDOK` button should result in a message box with the exact same data: the address of the DLL's `CTest` object and the number of currently attached clients. Figure 29-2 gives an example of two clients actively attached to the DLL.

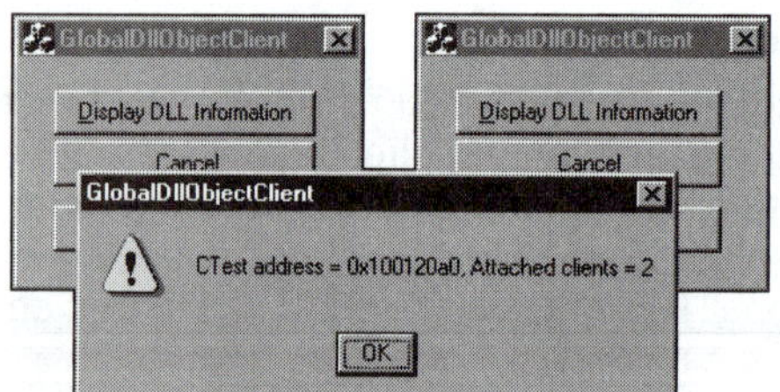

Figure 29-2: The GlobalDllObjectsClient DLL illustrates how to share C++ objects among multiple invocations of a DLL.

MFC Extension DLLs

While regular DLLs are typically used by non-MFC clients, MFC extension DLLs are used to export functions and classes that enhance MFC. For example, let's say that you have created a new toolbar that is derived from the MFC `CToolbar` class. To export this class, you must place it in an MFC extension DLL. Another example of when to use an MFC extension DLL is if your application is an MDI application, and you want to encapsulate each view or logical group of views in a separate DLL.

Understanding the internals of the MFC extension DLLs

While both MFC extension DLLs and regular DLLs can be created with the AppWizard and, therefore, can be built in a similar fashion, there are a number of fundamental differences between the two DLL types:

✦ Any client of an MFC extension DLL *must* be an MFC application.

✦ Unlike a regular DLL, an MFC extension DLL does not have a CWinApp-derived object.

✦ While regular DLLs typically do their initialization through the InitInstance() and ExitInstance() functions, an MFC extension DLL contains a DllMain() function for this purpose.

✦ MFC extension DLLs introduce a new class, CDynLinkLibrary, to enable the export of CRuntimeClasses or resources.

Exporting classes via MFC extension DLLs

MFC extension DLLs are usually implemented when a need arises to export classes that are based on MFC. Classes and their functions are exported in one of two ways, depending on whether an entire class is being exported or a subset of the class' member functions.

In the previous section covering regular DLLs, you saw that in order to export functions from a regular DLL, the .DEF file is normally used. The inconvenience this causes with C++ classes (such as the MFC classes) or member functions is that if you want to use the .DEF file to export them, you must specify the compiler-dependent mangled or decorated name. Luckily, MFC has a couple of macros that make this job much easier. When exporting entire classes from a DLL, the AFX_EXT_CLASS macro is used in the class' declaration like this:

```
class AFX_EXT_CLASS CMyFancyToolbar : public CToolbar
...
```

Exporting parts of a class is just as easy. Instead of placing the AFX_EXT_CLASS macro in front of the class name, simply place the macro in front of the function being defined that you wish to export.

```
class CMyFancyDialog : public CDialog
{
public:
 AFX_EXT_CLASS CMyFancyDialog();
 AFX_EXT_CLASS int DoModal();
public:
        BOOL Create(LPCTSTR lpszTemplateName,
   CWnd* pParentWnd = NULL);
        BOOL Create(UINT nIDTemplate, CWnd* pParentWnd = NULL);
...
```

Note that in the CMyFancyDialog class, the class constructor and DoModal() functions are exported while the two overloaded Create functions aren't. This means that a client can construct the class and call its DoModal() function. However, if calls to the two overloaded Create() functions are placed in the client's code, the client won't build due to unresolved linker errors.

More on the AFX_EXT_CLASS

As you just saw, the AFX_EXT_CLASS macro can be used to export either entire classes or parts of classes. However, when a client application includes the header file that contains the declaration of the classes that the DLL is exporting, a problem is going to arise from the fact that both modules are stating to the linker that they are responsible for exporting the class. This potential problem is resolved by the way the AFX_EXT_CLASS macro is defined, which depends on the following preprocessor definitions for the project:

- If _AFXDLL and _AFXEXT are defined for the project, the AFX_EXT_CLASS macro resolves to the following:

  ```
  __declspec(dllexport)
  ```

- If _AFXEXT is *not* defined, the AFX_EXT_CLASS macro resolves to the following for import purposes:

  ```
  __declspec(dllimport)
  ```

Therefore, when AppWizard is used to create an MFC extension DLL, both _AFXDLL and the _AFXEXT are defined. Any time the DLL's source code refers to the AFX_EXT_CLASS, the class is being exported.

Using nested MFC extension DLLs

As mentioned previously, the AFX_EXT_CLASS macro is used to export an entire class or parts of a class from a DLL. However, problems may arise if your application needs to use nested MFC extension DLLs. As an example, let's say that you have an MFC extension DLL of common routines and classes that you use on all projects. We'll call this DLL the "common" DLL. You may then have another MFC extension DLL that contains common routines and classes for a specific project, which we'll call the "project" DLL. The project DLL would almost certainly use the common DLL. This is a common example of nested MFC extension DLLs.

When you attempt to link the project DLL, you may receive linker errors because both the common and project DLLs are using the same macro and declaring the same classes, when in fact, the project DLL must import the class.

The workaround to this problem is simple. Instead of using the AFX_EXT_CLASS macro, you should use a macro that takes into consideration the project that is using it. For example, you could create a common macro called COMMON_IMPORT_EXPORT and define it as follows. The header file that is used to declare the classes and functions that the common DLL exports uses the COMMON_IMPORT_EXPORT macro instead of the AFX_EXT_CLASS macro. The advantage is that only the common DLL will be exporting its classes. Any other modules will be importing them. One way to define the _COMMON_DLL for the common DLL is to define it in the Project Setting dialog for that DLL.

```
#ifdef _COMMON_DLL
 #define COMMON_IMPORT_EXPORT  _declspec(dllexport)
#else
 #define COMMON_IMPORT_EXPORT  _declspec(dllimport)
#endif
```

Exporting resources

Each MFC application contains a linked list of `CDynLinkLibrary` objects. If your code in an MFC application requests that MFC load a resource on its behalf, MFC first attempts to load the requested resource from the current module. MFC locates this module's resources by calling the `AfxGetResourceHandle()` function. If the requested resource cannot be located, MFC "walks" the application's linked list of `CDynLinkLibrary` objects in an attempt to locate the resource. In order to set the default module that MFC uses to first locate requested resources, you must use the `AfxSetResourceHandle()` function to specify the `HINSTANCE` of the module.

Writing a demo that encapsulates documents and views in a DLL

Because this is the age of component-based reusable software, the MFC extension DLL demo will illustrate how to place document/view support into a DLL. Let's say that you have written a document and view to support the reading of .JPG files. Maybe you had to write an application that, among many other things, needed to display these files. You would normally create the document and view classes to support these files within the scope of the main application. However, what happens if tomorrow you need to provide the same JPG viewing functionality for another application? It would obviously be a much better practice to place application-independent logic (such as the viewing of JPG files) into a DLL. That way, any MFC client would be able to include that functionality simply by linking to the DLL and calling the appropriate exported functions.

Creating the MFC extension DLL for the image document and view

First, you create the MFC extension DLL. Create a project named "ImageViewer" with the following settings:

- ✦ "MFC AppWizard (dll)" in the New dialog box
- ✦ "MFC Extension DLL (using shared MFC DLL)" as the DLL type

Coding the ImageViewer's view functionality

Once you have created the project, create a form view in the resource editor called `IDD_IMAGE_VIEWER`. This form view is used to display the images. Then use ClassWizard to create a `CFormView`-derived class called `CImageViewerView` based on the `IDD_IMAGE_VIEWER` dialog template resource. Even though no changes are made to the document in this demo, use ClassWizard to create a `CDocument`-derived class called `CImageViewerDoc`.

Once you have created the DLL's document and view classes, open the ImageViewerView.h file, and add the following #include directives. This demo will use the ImageObject library to display the images. A demo of this imaging library can be found on the accompanying CD. The imageobject.h file is the main include file for that library.

```
#include "resource.h"
#include "imageobject.h"
```

After inserting the #include directives, add the following member variable to the CImageViewer class. This object is all you need to display a graphics file in the view.

```
protected:
 CImageObject* m_pImageObject;
```

Now open the ImageViewerView.cpp file, and make the following changes to the constructor and destructor:

```
CImageViewerView::CImageViewerView()
 : CFormView(CImageViewerView::IDD)
{
 m_pImageObject = NULL;
}

CImageViewerView::~CImageViewerView()
{
 delete m_pImageObject;
 m_pImageObject = NULL;
}
```

Because the purpose of this demo is placing documents and views in a DLL and not the specifics of what the document or view does, the view will simply display the requested image. To do that, use ClassWizard to create an OnDraw() function, and code it as follows:

```
void CImageViewerView::OnDraw(CDC* pDC)
{
 if (!m_pImageObject)
 {
  CDocument* pDoc = GetDocument();
  ASSERT_VALID(pDoc);

  CString strPathName = pDoc->GetPathName();
  ASSERT(0 < strPathName.GetLength());
  if (0 < strPathName.GetLength())
  {
   m_pImageObject = new CImageObject(strPathName);
  }
 }
```

```
    if (m_pImageObject)
    {
     m_pImageObject->SetPalette(pDC);
     m_pImageObject->Draw(pDC);
    }
  }
```

Encapsulating the image document and view in a class

Now that you have the document and view created and coded, let's concentrate on the important part of this demo: encapsulating the document and view in a DLL. First, create a file called "ImageViewer.h." The file will be a very simple one used to expose a `CImageViewer` class with a single function, `CImageViewer::Init`. This `Init` function is what an application calls in order to use the document and view that are coded in this DLL.

The `ImageViewer.h` file should look like the following. Once you have created and saved this file, add an `#include` to the top of the `ImageViewer.cpp` file for it.

```
#pragma once

class AFX_EXT_CLASS CImageViewer
{
public:
 BOOL Init();
};
```

Now that you already have the `ImageViewer.cpp` file open in the editor, add the following `#include` directives after the `#include` directive of the `ImageViewer.h` file:

```
#include "ImageViewerView.h"
#include "ImageViewerDoc.h"
```

Add the `Init()` function, as shown in Listing 29-3. This function simply takes as its only argument a pointer to the application object. It's required for the `AddDocTemplate()` function call. After that, this function creates a `CMultiDocTemplate` and adds it to the application object's list of document templates via the `AddDocTemplate()` function.

Listing 29-3: Adding the Init() Function

```
BOOL CImageViewer::Init()
{
 BOOL bSuccess = FALSE;

 CWinApp* pApp = AfxGetApp();
 ASSERT(pApp);
 if (pApp)
 {
  CMultiDocTemplate* pDocTemplate;

  pDocTemplate = new CMultiDocTemplate(
   IDR_IMAGEDOCTYPE,
   RUNTIME_CLASS(CImageViewerDoc),
   RUNTIME_CLASS(CMDIChildWnd),
   RUNTIME_CLASS(CImageViewerView));

  ASSERT(pDocTemplate);
  if (pDocTemplate)
  {
   pApp->AddDocTemplate(pDocTemplate);
   bSuccess = TRUE;
  }
 }

 return bSuccess;
}
```

In order for the document template to be created, you must create a string table in the DLL's resource file and add a document entry. It should have an ID of `IDR_IMAGEDOCTYPE` and a value of "\nImageV\nImageV\nImage Files (*.jpg, *.gif, *.bmp)\n.jpg;.gif;.bmp;\nImage Viewer.Document\nImageV Document".

The last step before building the DLL is to link with the ImageObject import library. Don't forget that in order to run the test application, you not only have to copy the DLL you are coding now to the appropriate folder, but you also must install the ImageObject library from the CD.

Building a test for the image document and view DLL

Now that you have written the MFC extension DLL to house the document and view for the types of files you will enable the users to open, it's time to do the easy part: create the application.

Use AppWizard to create a MDI application named "ImageViewerClient," making sure that the Document/View checkbox is checked. Then open the `ImageViewerClient.h` file, and add the following `#include` directive before the declaration of the `CImageViewerClientApp` class. This is the include file for the DLL's `CImageViewer` class; therefore, you must either point the `#include` directive to the folder where the `ImageViewer.h` file resides or set this project's Include files setting to include it.

```
#include "ImageViewer.h"
```

Add the following member variable to the application class:

```
protected:
 CImageViewer* m_pImageViewer;
```

Open the `ImageViewerClient.cpp` file, and add the following line to the application object's constructor:

```
m_pImageViewer = new CImageViewer();
```

Locate the `InitInstance()` function. Replace the entire function body with the following code:

```
BOOL CImageViewerClientApp::InitInstance()
{
 Enable3dControls();
 LoadStdProfileSettings();

 CMainFrame* pMainFrame = new CMainFrame;
 if (!pMainFrame->LoadFrame(IDR_MAINFRAME))
  return FALSE;

 pMainFrame->ShowWindow(m_nCmdShow);
 pMainFrame->UpdateWindow();
 m_pMainWnd = pMainFrame;

 ASSERT(m_pImageViewer != NULL);
 m_pImageViewer->Init();

 return TRUE;
}
```

Finally, create a destructor for `CImageViewerClient` to delete the `m_pImageViewer` object, as follows:

```
CImageViewerClientApp::~CImageViewerClientApp()
{
 delete m_pImageViewer;
}
```

The last thing you do before you can test your new application is to simply add the import library for your MFC extension DLL to this application's project.

Figure 29-3 shows the result of having run this application and opened a couple of .GIF files.

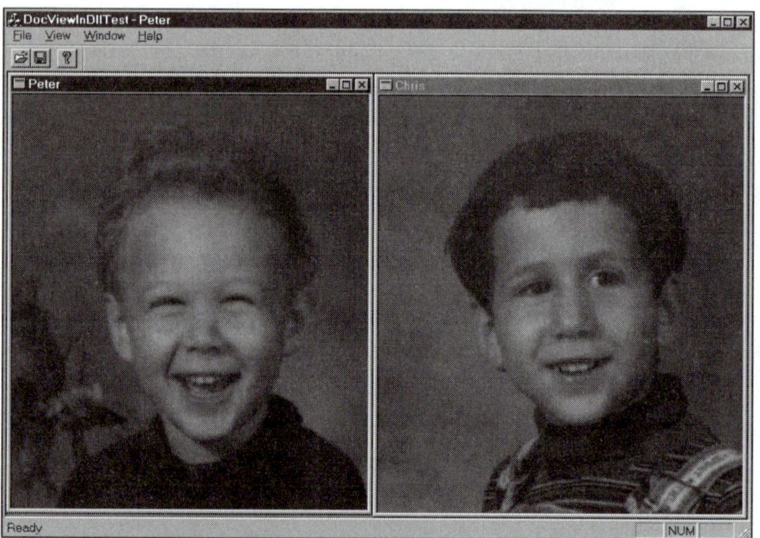

Figure 29-3: The ImageViewer DLL illustrates how to encapsulate an MFC document and view in a DLL.

Using this demo, any application can easily have image-viewing capability simply by linking with the ImageViewer import library and calling a single exported C++ function (`CImageViewer::Init`).

Summary

Throughout this chapter you've seen just how easy it is implement both regular DLLs and MFC extension DLLs to solve different programmatic problems. With regards to regular DLLs, you learned how to manage the current "module state" so that the DLL can make calls to the shared version of the MFC DLLs, and you worked through three demos. One of the demos was specific to writing regular DLLs (a system-level keyboard hook). Another demo illustrated how to share C++ objects across multiple invocations of a DLL. Insofar as MFC extension DLLs are concerned, you learned how to export whole classes or specific member functions of a class from a DLL, as well as how to place documents and views in a separate DLL from the main application. As you can see, DLLs can be used to solve a myriad every day development problems, and using Visual C++ to develop these DLLs makes this work that much easier.

✦ ✦ ✦

CHAPTER 30

Adding Imaging to Your Programs

✦ ✦ ✦ ✦

In This Chapter

Why use third-party libraries

Adding libraries to Visual C++

The ImageObject library

Image file formats

Loading images

Displaying images

The Display Image demo

Cropping, scaling, and changing color depth

Creating an image from a device context

Creating an image from the Clipboard

Saving images

Image processing

The ProcessImage program

✦ ✦ ✦ ✦

One of the things that many programmers want to do is display images in their programs. Image manipulation is often the key to making a boring, text-based program one that's professional looking. This chapter covers imaging, and how to add imaging capability to your programs.

Third-Party Libraries

When you write applications with Visual C++, you're not limited to the functionality that's built into the C language and MFC. To be more efficient, most programmers write their own functions and reuse them in other programs. This saves development time and money.

Another powerful alternative to writing your own functions is to buy third-party libraries that provide the functionality you need. With Visual C++, you can easily link in third-party, add-on libraries that provide extra functionality such as image loading, additional database functions, and telecommunications. Linking in libraries with additional functionality extends Visual C++ because it enables you to easily perform tasks that aren't built into the language or its foundation class libraries.

Another compelling, and probably more frequent, reason to buy a third-party library goes like this. Your boss comes into your office. A client has been promised application XYZ that does everything but tie shoes. This sounds like a project that'll keep you busy for a year, but your smile quickly disappears when your boss says it's due in three weeks. In this situation, the only way you can put the application together before the deadline is to eliminate every bit of development possible. This can be done using third-party libraries.

Buying third-party libraries usually costs money. These extensions are rarely free, and many times very costly. For instance, an imaging library that loads, saves, displays, and manipulates images runs between $250 and $2,000. But the cost might be inexpensive in comparison with how much it would cost to develop similar functionality on your own. Writing imaging functions to load, save, display, and manipulate images takes six months to a year. So anytime you consider buying an add-on library, you should calculate the cost of writing the code yourself and compare that with the cost of the library you're considering buying.

You can find third-party libraries advertised in practically every programming magazine. Catalogs such as *Programmer's Shop* and *Programmer's Warehouse* specialize in C++ libraries. In fact, add-on libraries for C++ are commonplace because they're cost-effective ways to add functionality to Visual C++ programs. Libraries come in a variety of ways. The most common form is a compiled .LIB file. To use the library, you simply add the library filename to the project's link section, include the .H file that also comes with the library, and make function calls to the library's API.

Adding a Library to a Visual C++ Project

Suppose you obtained a library with the filename `NewLib.LIB`. To add the library to your project, follow these steps:

1. Select Settings from the Project menu, and the Project Settings dialog box is displayed.
2. Select the Link tab.
3. Set the Category combo box to General.
4. In the Object/library modules text box, enter the library filename.

✦ ✦ ✦ ✦ ✦

Figure 30-1 illustrates the Project Settings dialog box with `NewLib.lib` added. When `NewLib.lib` is added to the Object/library modules text box, it takes effect for both the release and debug versions of your application.

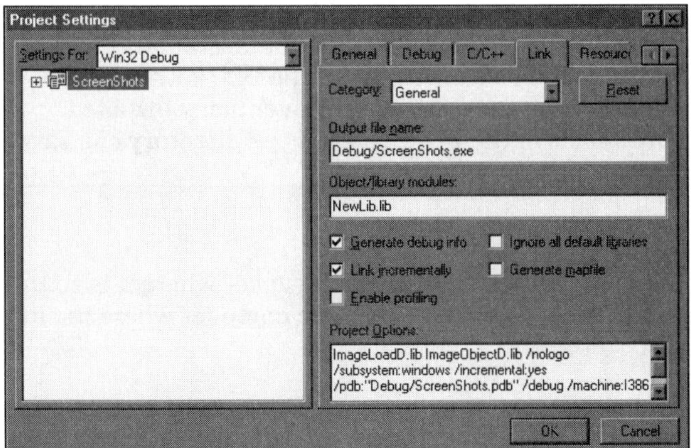

Figure 30-1: With Object/library modules set for NewLib.lib in the Project Settings dialog box, these settings take effect for both versions of your application.

The next time you compile and link, the .LIB file will be linked to your project.

Adding Both Release and Debug Libraries

Sometimes you'll get both release and debug .LIB file versions. If this is the case, you'll have to add the release and debug versions of the library separately.

1. For the release version, select Win32 Release in the Settings For combo box of the Project Settings dialog box.
2. Add the release version of the library to the Object/library modules text box.
3. For the debug version, select Win32 Debug in the Settings For combo box of the Project Settings dialog box.
4. Add the debug version of the library to the Object/library modules text box.

✦ ✦ ✦ ✦ ✦

Debug .LIB files usually have the same name as release .LIB files except that there's a "D" appended to the name. For instance, the `NewLib.LIB` file would probably be the release version of our hypothetical example, while the debug version would probably be named `NewLibD.LIB`.

Many linked libraries also come with dynamic link library (DLL) files. These must be placed in the application's directory, the `Windows` directory, or the `Windows\System` directory. It's better if you can leave the library in the application's directory. The `Windows` and `Windows\System` directories tend to collect DLLs rapidly as software is installed. Storing a DLL in the application's directory helps keep these important directories cleaner.

It's not always desirable, however, to put a DLL in the application's directory. If more than one application is to share a DLL, install it in the `Windows\System` directory. That way, you'll need only a single copy of the DLL for multiple programs. This will save the user's hard drive space. Multiplied over many installed applications, placing shared DLLs in the `Windows\System` directory can save users many megabytes of disk space.

Adding Include and Library Paths to Visual C++

When you get a third-party library, you'll must tell the linker where it is so that it can find the file at link time. You'll also want to tell the compiler where the include files are by following these steps:

1. Select Options from the Tools menu.
2. Select the Directories tab, and choose Include files in the Show directories for combo box.
3. Add the directory in which the include files for the compiler reside.
4. Then, choose Library files in the Show directories for combo box.
5. Add the directory in which the library files for the compiler reside (see Figure 30-2).

✦ ✦ ✦ ✦ ✦

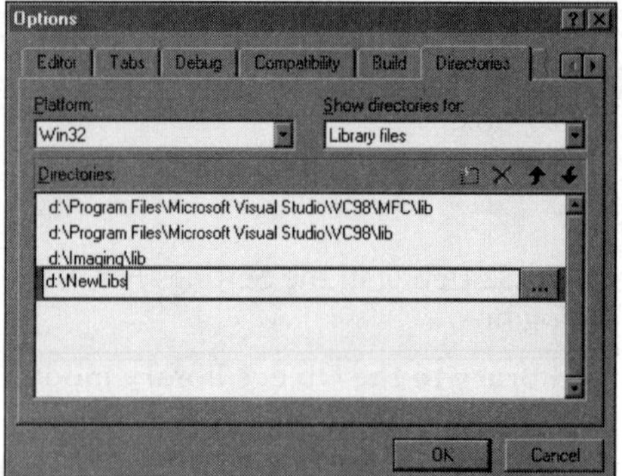

Figure 30-2: The Options dialog box shows the path for the new library files.

An alternative to adding the path of the library .LIB and .H files is to copy the .LIB and .H files into the directories that hold the compiler's include and library files. You could do this if you already have quite a few additions to the include and library file paths and you want to avoid adding any more. Adding too many paths slows things down during compile and link time.

Some libraries are available as source code modules that you must link into your project. This is rare, though, because most libraries are compiled into a .LIB file or a .LIB and .DLL combination.

The ImageObject Library in Brief

The ImageObject library enables you to easily load, save, display, manipulate, and image process pictures. It handles .BMP, .GIF, .JPG, .PCX, .TGA, and .TIF files. The version that comes with this book is fully functional except that it displays a trial version message in the upper-left corner of any image that you load. You can freely use this trial version for programs that aren't commercial in any way. If you want to sell or charge for programs that use the ImageObject library, though, you'll have to purchase a registered version. Registration and ordering information can be found in the `Ordering.TXT` file in the `Chap30` directory on the CD-ROM.

Included on the distribution CD-ROM is an imaging library that you can use in your programs. From the root of the CD-ROM, find a directory named `Chap30`. Inside of the `Chap30` directory is a self-extracting installation program named `IOSetup.exe`.

◆ ◆ ◆ ◆ ◆

Running this program, as shown in Figure 30-3, installs all of the files to your hard drive that you'll need to build applications using the ImageObject imaging library. It even sets up your compiler's include and library paths so that the compiler can find the newly installed files.

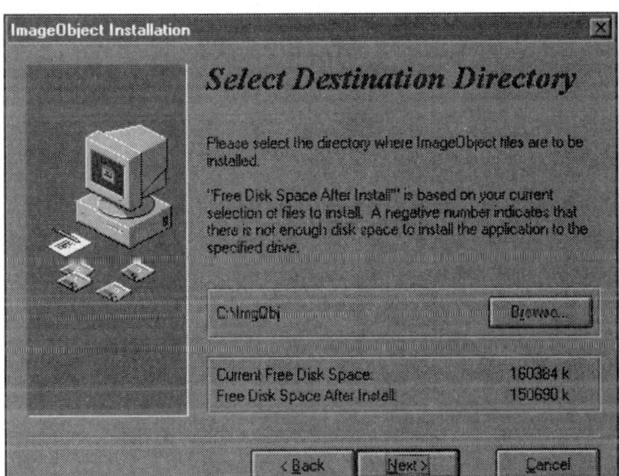

Figure 30-3: The ImageObject installation program takes care of copying files and setting the Visual C++ include and library paths.

The library combines a .LIB and a .DLL file. During installation, the `ImageLoad.DLL` file is copied to your `Windows\System` directory. That way the DLL is always available for applications because the `Windows\System` directory is always searched when the system tries to load a DLL. If you redistribute the DLL, make sure your installation program places it in the application directory, the `Windows` directory, or the `Windows\System` directory.

There's a class library that wraps the lower-level imaging function calls. The class library makes it a snap to perform the imaging functions. For instance, you can load an image with a single line of code. You can save an image with a single line of code, too. You can display an image with two lines of code from within your `OnDraw()` function.

Image manipulation functions such as cropping, stretching, and rotating are simple as well. Single lines of code perform all of these functions. Many image processing functions are available to enhance your images, filter your images, or create special imaging effects. And as with all of the other functionality of the ImageObject library, they're extremely easy to use.

A demonstration program called ImageView can be found in the `Chap30\ImageView` directory of the CD-ROM. It demonstrates the features that are available when you use this add-on library.

✦ ✦ ✦ ✦ ✦

Figure 30-4 shows the ImageView application with three image windows open. Two of the images have been partially enhanced with image processing operations.

This section explains the basics of each of the file formats supported by the ImageObject library. Because no one file format is perfect for all situations, you'll have to decide which to use based on the attributes of the image file format and your needs.

The BMP file format

The Microsoft Windows Bitmap (BMP) file format is one of several graphics file formats supported by the Microsoft Windows operating environment. BMP is the native bitmap format of Windows and is used to store virtually any type of bitmap data. Most graphics and imaging applications running under Microsoft Windows support the creation and display of BMP files.

BMP files support all of the screen resolutions and color combinations that Windows supports. For this reason, a BMP file can always be created that exactly matches a screen format.

Figure 30-4: The ImageView demonstration program is showing three images, two of which have been enhanced with the ImageObject library.

BMP files are almost always completely uncompressed. This makes them very large. A screen capture of a screen that's 800 by 600 and a color resolution of 24 bits creates a file that's 2,743,545 bytes. As you can see, if disk space is a consideration, this file format isn't a good choice.

The GIF file format

GIF stands for graphics interchange format. Its major feature is its compression, achieved by using LZW compression algorithms. The same BMP image that's 800 by 600 with a color resolution of 24 bits, after being converted to a color resolution of 8 bits, can be as small as 20K. This is the preferred image format for ordinary graphics on the Web.

One disadvantage to GIF in today's age of high color resolution is its limitation of 8 bits of color resolution. For most applications this is sufficient. For applications requiring photographic-quality images, it's not adequate.

The JPEG file format

JPEG, often referred to as JPG because of its file extension, is one of the newest file formats to become popular. Its major feature is its great compression, far greater than even GIF's compression. It achieves this great compression, though, at the expense of image integrity. Many times, losing a small amount of image quality won't be noticed. In cases such as this, JPEG is a good choice because of the fantastic image compression. The same BMP image that's 800 by 600 with a color resolution of 24 bits can be as small as 5K. JPEGs are usually used for photographic images. That's because the small amount of image degradation can rarely be detected in a photographic image. The tradeoff between file size and an unperceived loss in quality weighs in on the side of smaller file sizes.

The PCX file format

PCX was developed by Zsoft many years ago in order to provide their own paint program, PC Paint, with an image file format that offers some data compression. The compression is better than an uncompressed file, but the run-length-encoding scheme it uses can still produce large image files. The fact that the compression is not very good has PCX files fading fast from the PC scene.

The TGA file format

Targa files were developed to support hardware devices that capture video images. The Targa file format makes it easy to store many video captures to disk because very little data manipulation is required. Targa offers some compression schemes, but normally the images are stored in an uncompressed format. One big advantage of Targa files is their support for images ranging from monochrome to those of 32-bit color resolution.

The TIF file format

TIFF, or tagged image file format, was designed to be the file format that would be everything to everybody. (It's usually referred to by its file extension TIF.) As a result, the file format became difficult to maintain. Many vendors and third parties added their own tags, or modifications, making it hard to keep up with the changes in the file format. It's still used in many desktop publishing applications because it handles many photometric values that are necessary when manipulating the images. It offers several compression schemes, but TIF files are found uncompressed more often than not.

Loading Images

ImageObject was designed to be powerful but extremely easy to use. Because of this, you'll be able to load and display images in your program in minutes. The first thing you must do is create a `CImageObject` class. The constructor takes an optional filename. If you give it a filename, it loads the image file during the creation of the class. If you don't give it a filename, you'll have to use the `Load()` function at a later point to load an image file. Following are three examples of creating `CImageObject` classes and loading an image file into each one:

Example 1:

```
CImageObject m_Image( "Filename.jpg" );
```

Example 2:

```
CImageObject m_Image;
m_Image.Load( "Filename.gif" );
```

Example 3:

```
CImageObject *m_pImage;
m_pImage = new CImageObject( "Filename.tif" );
// Make sure when we're done we do the following:
// delete m_pImage;
```

Note

Remember that `ImageLoad.Dll` must be somewhere in your path before programs built with ImageObject will execute.

✦ ✦ ✦ ✦ ✦

ImageObject knows what kind of file type you're trying to load because of the extension. For example, if you try to load a .JPG file, it'll know that you're trying to load a JPEG file and use the appropriate file loading function. If the file extension isn't recognized, the file is opened, and the file type is determined from the file's header information.

If you declare a `CImageObject` class as a local variable, the class and its image are deleted as soon as it goes out of scope. If you want to keep an image in memory, make sure the class is declared in such a way that it won't go out of scope.

✦ ✦ ✦ ✦ ✦

The `Load()` function returns a `BOOL` indicating success or failure. The constructors that take a filename don't return anything. If you loaded an image file by passing a filename to the `CImageObject` constructor, there's an easy way to check whether the image has been successfully loaded. Use the `GetDib()` function to get the `CImageObject` class's internal Dib handle. If it's `NULL`, the image wasn't successfully loaded. You can then use the `CImageObject::GetLastError()` function to find out what the error was. ImageObject errors are defined in `Errors.h`. The following two examples show you how to check for errors when loading a file:

Example 1:

```
CImageObject m_Image( "Filename.tga" );
if( m_Image.GetDib() == NULL )
  AfxMessageBox( "There was a load error." );
```

Example 2:

```
CImageObject m_Image;
if( !m_Image.Load( "Filename.pcx" ) )
  AfxMessageBox( "There was a load error." );
```

Displaying Images

Just like loading images, displaying images with ImageObject is very easy. In its simplest form, all you have to do is use the `Display()` function and pass it a `CDC` pointer. From the view class' `OnDraw()` function, things couldn't be easier because a `CDC` pointer is passed in. The following example shows you how to display an image that's already been loaded into a `CImageObject` class from an application's view class `OnDraw()` function:

```
void CDevelopView::OnDraw(CDC* pDC)
{
  CDevelopDoc* pDoc = GetDocument();
  ASSERT_VALID(pDoc);

  m_Image.Draw( pDC );
}
```

The previous example works perfectly if the image has a color depth of greater than 8 bits per pixel, and the display computer is set for more than 256 simultaneous colors. That's because there's no palette to worry about. The image itself doesn't have a palette, and it displays perfectly on a high- or true-color display (displays of more than 256 colors).

A problem arises when the image has 256 colors or less, the display is set for 256 colors or less, or both. Let's say for instance, that the image has a color depth of 24 bits, and the display system is set for 256 colors. When the computer first boots, only the 20 system colors out of the 256 colors of the hardware palette are actually set. The others are all set to black. When the 24-bit image is displayed, Windows must map each of the millions of colors to the 20 system colors. The result is an ugly, 20-color rendering of the image.

If all 256 colors of the hardware palette contain values other than black, the true-color image will look much better drawn to the screen because Windows has many more colors to pick from as it maps the image pixels to the screen. For this reason, even for 24-bit images, it's a good idea to set the palette. The following example shows how to set the palette before the image is drawn, which insures the best rendering of images:

```
void CDevelopView::OnDraw(CDC* pDC)
{
  CDevelopDoc* pDoc = GetDocument();
  ASSERT_VALID(pDoc);

  m_Image.SetPalette( pDC );
  m_Image.Draw( pDC );
}
```

What if your application isn't in the foreground and another application that's in the foreground sets the palette? This spells trouble for you. A background application should yield to foreground applications as a matter of program politeness. It would be a problem if the foreground program's appearance suffered simply because you set the palette for your image without regard for its palette needs.

If you don't set the palette before ImageObject draws to the screen, it maps the image to the hardware palette as well as it can. Many times, the palette that a foreground application sets will be close enough to your image's palette that when it's drawn, it won't look horrendous. In a majority of cases, you probably won't be able to tell the difference.

You should check before you set the palette for your image to see if your window has the focus. If it does have the focus, go ahead and set the palette. If it doesn't, don't set the palette, and let ImageObject map the image to the display. The following code is the polite way to set the palette:

```
void CDevelopView::OnDraw(CDC* pDC)
{
  CDevelopDoc* pDoc = GetDocument();
  ASSERT_VALID(pDoc);

  if( GetFocus() == this )
    m_Image.SetPalette( pDC );
  m_Image.Draw( pDC );
}
```

Note

Remember that for you to use the ImageObject library in your programs, you'll have to link in the libraries. For release builds, link in `ImageLoad.lib` and `ImageObject.lib`. For debug builds, link in `ImageLoadD.lib` and `ImageObjectD.lib`.

◆ ◆ ◆ ◆ ◆

The `Draw()` function has several optional parameters that you might find useful. The second and third parameters specify the *x* and *y* coordinates to which the image will be drawn. The default values are 0, 0. This means that your image will be drawn to the upper-left corner of the window by default. If you specify different coordinates, these values will be saved internally, and until different coordinates are specified, the image will be drawn at the new *x* and *y* coordinates.

The fourth and fifth parameters specify the destination width and height. If an image is 200 by 200, but you want it to draw in a 100 by 100 rectangle, all you have to do is pass the destination width and height as the fourth and fifth parameters. One word of caution, though: not all drivers that render images to a 16-bit display do a perfect job of scaling. More than half of the Windows systems this has been tried on give unpredictable results on 16-bit displays when the `Draw()` function uses a width and height other than the width and height of the image.

Loading and Displaying Images

Here's a summary of the steps for loading and displaying images:

1. Create a `CImageObject` class. You'll usually want to make sure this isn't in local space so that it doesn't go out of scope.
2. Load an image. You can load an image by passing the filename to the `CImageObject` constructor, or you can use the `Load()` function.
3. Set the display computer's palette using the `SetPalette()` function.
4. Draw the image using the `Draw()` function.

The following code for a view class shows you the steps:

```
// MyView.h
#include "ImageObject.h"
class CMyView
{
public:
  CImageObject m_Image;
};
// MyView.cpp
CMyView()
{
  m_Image.Load( "Filename.tif" );
}
void CMyView::OnDraw( CDC *pDC )
{
  if( GetFocus() == this )
    m_Image.SetPalette( pDC );
  m_Image.Draw( pDC );
}
```

✦ ✦ ✦ ✦ ✦

The Display Program

A demonstration program can be found on the CD-ROM in the `Chap30\Display` directory. It uses the ImageObject library to load and display an image.

✦ ✦ ✦ ✦ ✦

There are a total of six lines of code that were added to an AppWizard single document program to get it to work (see Figure 30-5). Two of the lines are in the `DisplayView.h` file, and the other four are in the `DisplayView.cpp` file. You can rebuild the program by loading the `Display.dsw` project file, or just run the `Display.exe` program using Explorer.

Figure 30-5: This simple application requires only six lines of code to load and display an image.

In the `ImageView.h` file, `ImageObject.h` was included, and a `CImageObject` class named `m_Image` was declared. In the `ImageView.cpp` file, the file was loaded in the `CDisplayView` constructor with the `Load()` function. Then in the `CDisplayView::OnDraw()` function, three additional lines set the palette and draw the image. Listings 30-1 and 30-2 show highlights of a simple program that is a good illustration of how easy it is to use ImageObject.

Demo Program

Display

Project Name: **Display**
CD-ROM Location: **Chap30\Display**
Pre-built Program: **Chap30\Display\Display.exe**
Source Code Highlights in Text: `DisplayView.h` and `DisplayView.cpp`

Listing 30-1: Highlights of the DisplayView.h Source Code for the Display.exe Program

```
// DisplayView.h : interface of the CDisplayView class
//
/////////////////////////////////////////////////////////////////////

#include "ImageObject.h"

class CDisplayView : public CView
{
protected: // create from serialization only
  CDisplayView();
  DECLARE_DYNCREATE(CDisplayView)

// Attributes
public:
  CDisplayDoc* GetDocument();

  CImageObject m_Image;

// Operations
public:

// Overrides
  // ClassWizard generated virtual function overrides
  //{{AFX_VIRTUAL(CDisplayView)
  public:
  virtual void OnDraw(CDC* pDC);  // overridden to draw
                                  // this view
  virtual BOOL PreCreateWindow(CREATESTRUCT& cs);
  protected:
  //}}AFX_VIRTUAL

// Implementation
public:
  virtual ~CDisplayView();
#ifdef _DEBUG
  virtual void AssertValid() const;
  virtual void Dump(CDumpContext& dc) const;
#endif

protected:

// Generated message map functions
protected:
  //{{AFX_MSG(CDisplayView)
  //}}AFX_MSG
  DECLARE_MESSAGE_MAP()
};
```

Listing 30-2: Highlights of the DisplayView.cpp Source Code for the Display.exe Program

```
// DisplayView.cpp : implementation of the
// CDisplayView class
//

#include "stdafx.h"
#include "Display.h"

#include "DisplayDoc.h"
#include "DisplayView.h"

/////////////////////////////////////////////////////////
// CDisplayView

/////////////////////////////////////////////////////////
// CDisplayView construction/destruction

CDisplayView::CDisplayView()
{

  m_Image.Load( "File.jpg" );

}

CDisplayView::~CDisplayView()
{
}

/////////////////////////////////////////////////////////
// CDisplayView drawing

void CDisplayView::OnDraw(CDC* pDC)
{
  CDisplayDoc* pDoc = GetDocument();
  ASSERT_VALID(pDoc);

  if( GetFocus() == this )
    m_Image.SetPalette( pDC );
  m_Image.Draw( pDC );

}
```

Scaling, Cropping, and Changing Color Depth

An image library wouldn't be very useful if you couldn't perform some basic manipulations. ImageObject provides these with three functions: `Stretch()`,

Crop(), and ChangeFormat(). These three functions provide what you need to scale an image to a new size, crop it so that only a portion of the original image remains, and change the color depth.

Let's start by exploring the Stretch() function. This function should have been named Scale()because that's what it does. It takes two integer arguments, the new width and height. It then scales the image to the new width and height. If you scale an image to a size with a different aspect ratio than the original image, it'll be distorted. Avoid this unless that's the effect you want. The following code loads an image and scales it to a width and height of 150 by 125 in the CMyView constructor:

```
CMyView()
{
  m_Image.Load( "Filename.jpg" );
  m_Image.Stretch( 150, 125 );
}
```

Now let's say you want to scale an image by a certain percentage. You can do that with some simple math. You'll still need to load the image as before. You can then get the image width and height using the GetWidth() and GetHeight() functions. Based on these, you can calculate the new width and height for any percentage of scaling that you desire. The following function scales an image to a percentage:

```
void CMyView::Scale( int nPercentage )
{
  int nWidth = m_Image.GetWidth();
  int nHeight = m_Image.GetHeight();
  nWidth = ( nWidth * nPercentage ) / 100;
  nHeight = ( nHeight * nPercentage ) / 100;
  m_Image.Stretch( nWidth, nHeight );
}
```

You can scale an image to the window in which it's being drawn if you want to completely fill the window. The following code loads an image and scales a temporary image with which it draws the window client area:

```
CMyView()
{
  m_Image.Load( "Filename.gif" );
}
void CMyView::OnDraw( CDC *pDC )
{
  // We assume we're in MM_TEXT mapping mode.
  RECT Rect;
  GetClientRect( &Rect );

  // Make a copy of the image.
  CImageObject Image;
  Image = m_Image;

  // Scale the temporary image.
```

```
    Image.Stretch( Rect.right, Rect.bottom );

    // Set the palette and draw.
    if( GetFocus() == this )
      Image.SetPalette( pDC );
    Image.Draw( pDC );
}
```

As mentioned before, beware of scaling images if a greatly altered aspect ratio is undesirable. You can get very distorted pictures when scaling. A good example of this is a test program written with the previous code example. Figure 30-6 shows how distorted the airplane is when the window is resized.

There's a project on the CD-ROM that scales an image to the view window. It's named ScaleToView and can be found in the `Chap30\ScaleToView` directory.

◆ ◆ ◆ ◆ ◆

Figure 30-6: Scaling images can greatly distort them.

Cropping an image is just as easy as scaling it. The `Cropping()` function takes four parameters. The first two are the upper-left corner of the rectangle that you want to retain, and the next two are the lower-right corner of the rectangle you want to keep. For instance, if you have an image that's 200 by 250 and you want to keep a 100 by 100 rectangle whose upper-left corner is at pixel 25, 74, you'd use the following code:

```
// The original image is 200 x 250
// The new image will be 100 x 100
m_Image.Crop( 25, 74, 124, 173 );
```

As with scaling and cropping, changing the color depth of an image is easy. All you have to do is use the `ChangeFormat()` function and pass in a single integer argument. The argument tells what the new pixel depth is to be. For instance, if you wanted to change a 24-bit image to an 8-bit image, you'd use the following code:

```
m_Image.ChangeFormat( 8 );
```

Creating an Image from a Device Context

ImageObject enables you to create an image from a device context. One of the `CImageObject` overloads provides this capability. The constructor takes five arguments: a `CDC` pointer, *x* and *y* coordinates for the upper-left corner of the source rectangle, and width and height values for the width and height of the source rectangle. The following code creates an image from the `CMyView` device context:

```
void CMyView::OnDraw( CDC *pDC )
{
  RECT Rect;
  GetClientRect( &Rect );
  m_pImage = new CImageObject( pDC, 0, 0,
    Rect.right, Rect.bottom );
}
```

A sample program is on the CD-ROM in the `Chap30\CreateFromDC` directory. It draws to the view window and then saves two image files: `Test.gif` and `Test.jpg`. Figure 30-7 shows the application running and the two images that were saved. (The saved images are shown loaded with the ImageView program mentioned earlier in this chapter.)

✦ ✦ ✦ ✦ ✦

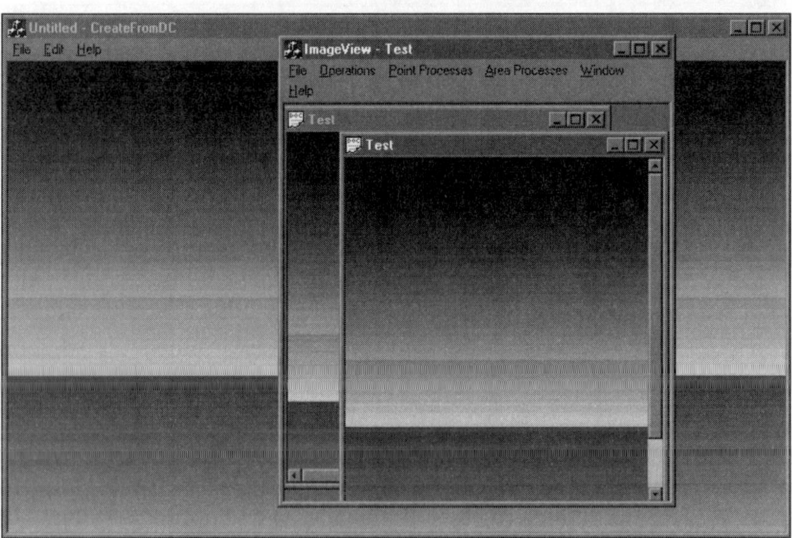

Figure 30-7: The CreateFromDC program and the two images that it saved

Creating an Image from the Clipboard

Another useful thing you can do is create a CImageObject class from the Clipboard, which is handy when you want to get images from other applications, or create an image after users have pressed the Print Scrn key. As with creating an image from a DC, one of the CImageObject constructors provides what you need to create an image from the Clipboard. It takes an HBITMAP handle as an argument. The HBITMAP is converted into native CImageObject format. The following code shows you how to create an image from the Clipboard:

```
if( OpenClipboard() ){
  HBITMAP hBitmap;
  hBitmap = (HBITMAP) ::GetClipboardData( CF_BITMAP );
  CloseClipboard();
  if( hBitmap != NULL )
    m_pImageObject = new CImageObject( hBitmap );
  }
```

A demonstration program is on the CD-ROM in the Chap30\CreateFromClipboard directory. If you run this program, you can convert any bitmaps that are on the Clipboard to an image that'll be displayed in the program's view window. Figure 30-8 shows the program with the Paint application in front of it. An image was created with Paint, copied to the Clipboard, and then acquired by the CreateFromClipboard program using the From Clipboard menu entry in the File menu.

✦ ✦ ✦ ✦ ✦

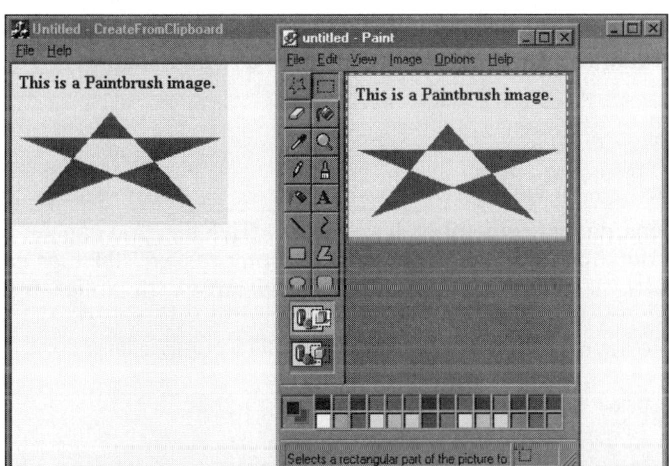

Figure 30-8: This program creates a CImageObject class from bitmaps – in this case, one produced in Paint – on the Clipboard.

Saving Images

Saving images to disk with ImageObject takes a whopping single line of code. Saving images, true to the ImageObject model, is as easy as pie. To save an image to disk, you use the `Save()` function. It takes one required parameter — the filename and one optional parameter — the destination image type. Normally, you'll let the filename's extension determine the file type that'll be saved. The following line saves an image to `ImageOne.gif`:

```
m_Image.Save( "ImageOne.gif" );
```

A warning is in order: if you save an image as a GIF file, make sure it has a color depth of 8 bits or less. The previous example is more cautiously carried out as follows:

```
CImage TempImage;
TempImage = m_Image;
if( TempImage.GetNumBits() > 8 )
  TempImage.ChangeFormat( 8 );
TempImage.Save( "ImageOne.gif" );
```

If you save an image as a JPEG file, you'll probably want to set the quality factor. It defaults to 80 percent — a reasonable value for most situations. This determines the amount of compression that you'll get when the file is saved. It also determines the corresponding amount of image degradation that the image suffers when it's saved. Values range from 1 to 99. A value of 1 provides the most image degradation and the greatest compression. A value of 99 provides the least compression and the least image degradation. The greater the value, the lower the compression ratio and lesser the image degradation. The following code saves a JPEG image with a quality factor of 80:

```
m_Image.SetQuality( 80 );
m_Image.Save( "ImageTwo.jpg" );
```

There's one last thing you must remember. If you save a TIFF file, you can set the compression type. It defaults to no compression — uncompressed TIFF files can get huge. Table 30-1 lists the compression types that are available with ImageObject.

The following example saves a TIFF image using PACKBITS compression:

```
m_Image.SetTIFCompression( TIFCOMPRESSION_PACKBITS );
m_Image.Save( "ImageThree.tif" );
```

Table 30-1
TIFF Compression Types Available with ImageObject

Compression Define	*Description*
TIFCOMPRESSION_NONE	No compression
TIFCOMPRESSION_CCITTRLE	CCITT modified Huffman RLE
TIFCOMPRESSION_CCITTFAX3	CCITT Group 3 fax encoding
TIFCOMPRESSION_CCITTFAX4	CCITT Group 4 fax encoding
TIFCOMPRESSION_LZW	Lempel-Ziv & Welch
TIFCOMPRESSION_OJPEG	6.0 JPEG
TIFCOMPRESSION_JPEG	JPEG DCT compression
TIFCOMPRESSION_NEXT	NeXT 2-bit RLE
TIFCOMPRESSION CCITTRLEW	#1 w/ word alignment
TIFCOMPRESSION_PACKBITS	Macintosh RLE
COMPRESSION_THUNDERSCAN	ThunderScan RLE
TIFCOMPRESSION_IT8CTPAD	IT8 CT w/padding
TIFCOMPRESSION_IT8LW	IT8 Linework RLE
TIFCOMPRESSION_IT8MP	IT8 Monochrome picture
TIFCOMPRESSION_IT8BL	IT8 Binary line art
TIFCOMPRESSION_PIXARFILM	Pixar companded 10bit LZW
TIFCOMPRESSION_PIXARLOG	Pixar companded 11bit ZIP
TIFCOMPRESSION_DEFLATE	Deflate compression
TIFCOMPRESSION_DCS	Kodak DCS encoding
TIFCOMPRESSION_JBIG	ISO JBIG

Image Processing

A host of image processing functions are available with two classes that reside in the ImageObject library. They are the `CImagePointProcesses` and `CImageAreaProcesses` classes. As you might guess, the `CImagePointProcesses` class performs several point process operations, while the `CImageAreaProcesses` class performs several area process operations.

The prototypes and descriptions of the functions are provided in the "Image processing" sidebar, which explains them so that you can use them in your programs.

Image processing

Following are the function prototypes and descriptions for their use:

```
CImageAreaProcesses::CImageAreaProcesses();
```

This is the CImageAreaProcesses class constructor that takes no arguments. If this constructor is used, when using any of the image processing functions, you must pass in the address of a value CImageObject class.

```
CImageAreaProcesses::CImageAreaProcesses( CImageObject * );
```

This is the CImageAreaProcesses class constructor that takes the address of a CImageObject class. Later, when you perform image processing functions, you don't need to worry about passing in the address of a CImageObject class because the CImageAreaProcesses class will already have it stored.

```
BOOL CImageAreaProcesses::MedianFilter( int nX1, int nY1,
  int nX2, int nY2, CImageObject *pImageObject );
```

This function performs a median filtering operation on an image. All the parameters are optional. If no coordinates are specified, the operation is performed on the entire image. Otherwise, you can specify a portion of the image to which the operation will be performed. You only need to pass the address of a CImageObject if one wasn't given in the CImageAreaProcesses class constructor.

```
BOOL CImageAreaProcesses::EqualizeContrast( int nX1, int nY1,
  int nX2, int nY2, int nThresholdFactor, CImageObject
  *pImageObject );
```

This function equalizes the contrast of an image. All the parameters are optional. If no coordinates are specified, the operation is performed on the entire image. Otherwise, you can specify a portion of the image to which the operation will be performed. Typical threshold values are low, in the range of about 10. You only need to pass the address of a CImageObject if one wasn't given in the CImageAreaProcesses class constructor.

```
BOOL CImageAreaProcesses::HighpassFilter( int nX1, int nY1,
  int nX2, int nY2, CImageObject *pImageObject );
```

This function performs a high pass filtering operation on an image. All the parameters are optional. If no coordinates are specified, the operation is performed on the entire image. Otherwise, you can specify a portion of the image to which the operation will be performed. You only need to pass the address of a CImageObject if one wasn't given in the CImageAreaProcesses class constructor.

```
BOOL CImageAreaProcesses::LowpassFilter( int nX1, int nY1,
  int nX2, int nY2, DWORD *dwFact, CImageObject
  *pImageObject );
```

This function performs a low pass filtering operation on an image. All the parameters are optional. If no coordinates are specified, the operation is performed on the entire image. Otherwise, you can specify a portion of the image to which the operation will be performed. The dwFact parameter should always be NULL from an application. You only need to pass the address of a CImageObject if one wasn't given in the CImageAreaProcesses class constructor.

```
BOOL CImageAreaProcesses::EdgeEnhance( int nX1, int nY1,
  int nX2, int nY2, CImageObject *pImageObject );
```

This function performs an edge enhancing operation on an image. All the parameters are optional. If no coordinates are specified, the operation is performed on the entire image. Otherwise, you can specify a portion of the image to which the operation will be performed. You only need to pass the address of a `CImageObject` if one wasn't given in the `CImageAreaProcesses` class constructor.

```
CImagePointProcesses ::CImagePointProcesses();
```

This is the `CImagePointProcesses` class constructor that takes no arguments. If this constructor is used, when using any of the image processing functions, you must pass in the address of a value `CImageObject` class.

```
CImagePointProcesses ::CImagePointProcesses( CImageObject * );
```

This is the `CImagePointProcesses` class constructor that takes the address of a `CImageObject` class. Later, when you perform image processing functions, you don't need to worry about passing in the address of a `CImageObject` class because the `CImagePointProcesses` class will already have it stored.

```
BOOL CImagePointProcesses ::ChangeBrightness( int nBrightness,
  int nX1, int nY1, int nX2, int nY2, CImageObject
  *pImageObject );
```

This function changes the brightness of an image. The first parameter specifies the percentage of the original brightness that you want the resulting image to have. All of the remaining parameters are optional. If no coordinates are specified, the operation is performed on the entire image. Otherwise, you can specify a portion of the image to which the operation will be performed. You only need to pass the address of a `CImageObject` if one wasn't given in the CImagePointProcesses class constructor.

```
BOOL CImagePointProcesses ::ReverseColors( int nX1, int nY1,
  int nX2, int nY2, CImageObject *pImageObject );
```

This function reverses the colors of an image. All the parameters are optional. If no coordinates are specified, the operation is performed on the entire image. Otherwise, you can specify a portion of the image to which the operation will be performed. You only need to pass the address of a `CImageObject` if one wasn't given in the `CImagePointProcesses` class constructor.

```
BOOL CImagePointProcesses ::MakeGray( BOOL bSetPalette,
  CImageObject *pImageObject );
```

This function changes an image into a grayscale image. All the parameters are optional. The `bSetPalette` parameter defaults to `TRUE`. You only need to pass the address of a `CImageObject` if one wasn't given in the `CImagePointProcesses` class constructor.

```
BOOL CImagePointProcesses ::Colorize( int, int, int, int,
  COLORREF, CImageObject *pImageObject );
```

This function colorizes an image. Only the last parameter is optional. You must specify the coordinates to which the operation will be performed. You also must pass the color to which the image will be colorized. You only need to pass the address of a `CImageObject` if one wasn't given in the `CImagePointProcesses` class constructor.

To use the image processing classes, you must link in `ImageAreaProcesses.lib` and `ImagePointProcesses.lib` for release builds. For debug builds, link in `ImageAreaProcessesD.lib` and `ImagePointProcessesD.lib`.

✦ ✦ ✦ ✦ ✦

Several examples that perform image processing tasks follow. The first one colorizes the rectangular region of an image bounded by the rectangular region 20, 40, 120, 140. The region will be colorized with red.

```
CImageObject ImageObject( "Filename.bmp" );
CImagePointProcesses PointProcesses( &ImageObject );
PointProcesses.Colorize( 20, 40, 120, 140,
  RGB( 255, 0, 0 ) );
```

The next example shows you how to perform a median-filtering operation on the rectangular region of an image bounded by 100, 100, 200, 200:

```
CImageObject ImageObject( "Filename.bmp" );
CImageAreaProcesses AreaProcesses( &ImageObject );
AreaProcesses( 100, 100, 200, 200 );
```

The last example shows you how to increase the brightness of an entire image to 150 percent of its original brightness:

```
CImageObject ImageObject( "Filename.bmp" );
CImagePointProcesses PointProcesses( &ImageObject );
PointProcesses.ChangeBrightness( 150 );
```

The ProcessImage Program

Because the ProcessImage program is a multiple document program, you can load in as many pictures as you have memory for. Figure 30-9 shows the ProcessImage program after it has loaded in four sample images and performed different operations on each one of the four images. The source code highlights for the program are in Listing 30-3.

ProcessImage
Project Name: **ProcessImage**
CD-ROM Location: **Chap30\ProcessImage**
Pre-built Program: **Chap30\ProcessImage\ProcessImage.exe**
Source Code Highlights in Text: `ProcessImageView.cpp`

Figure 30-9: Four sample images have been loaded and each subjected to a different process.

Listing 30-3: Highlights of the ProcessImageView.cpp Source Code for the ProcessImage.exe Program

```
// ProcessImageView.cpp : implementation of
// the CProcessImageView class
//

#include "stdafx.h"
#include "ProcessImage.h"

#include "ProcessImageDoc.h"
#include "ProcessImageView.h"
#include "MainFrm.h"
#include "ChildFrm.h"

#include "Brightness.h"

/////////////////////////////////////////////////////////////
// CProcessImageView

/////////////////////////////////////////////////////////////
```

(continued)

Listing 30-3 *(continued)*

```
// CProcessImageView construction/destruction

CProcessImageView::CProcessImageView()
{

  // Set the CImageObject class member
  // to NULL so that we won't try to
  // delete it in the destructor if an
  // image hasn't been loaded.
  m_pImageObject = NULL;

}

CProcessImageView::~CProcessImageView()
{

  // If the CImageObject class member has
  // been allocated, delete it.
  if( m_pImageObject != NULL )
    delete m_pImageObject;

}

/////////////////////////////////////////////////////////
// CProcessImageView drawing

void CProcessImageView::OnDraw(CDC* pDC)
{
  CProcessImageDoc* pDoc = GetDocument();
  ASSERT_VALID(pDoc);

  // If the CImageObject class member is NULL,
  // we'll attempt to allocate the CImageObject
  // class and load the image.
  if( m_pImageObject == NULL ){

    // Get the filename.
    CString PathName = pDoc->GetPathName();

    // Change to hourglass.
    BeginWaitCursor();

    // Allocate the CImageObject class
    // and load the image.
    m_pImageObject =
      new CImageObject( PathName.GetBuffer( 3 ),
      pDC );

    // Change from the hourglass.
    EndWaitCursor();
```

```
    // If the CImageObject class is NULL, return
    // and don't try anything else.
    if( m_pImageObject == NULL )
      return;

    // Set the scroll window size.
    CSize SizeTotal;
    SizeTotal.cx = m_pImageObject->GetWidth();
    SizeTotal.cy = m_pImageObject->GetHeight();
    SetScrollSizes (MM_TEXT, SizeTotal);

    // Get a pointer to the active child window.
    CMainFrame *pFrame =
      (CMainFrame *) AfxGetMainWnd();
    CChildFrame *pChild =
      (CChildFrame *) pFrame->MDIGetActive();

    // Set the child window width and height member
    // variables so that the child window can resize
    // correctly for the image.
    pChild->m_nWidth = m_pImageObject->GetWidth();
    pChild->m_nHeight = m_pImageObject->GetHeight();

    // Cause the child window to resize.
    pChild->SetWindowPos( NULL, 0, 0, 2500, 2500,
      SWP_NOZORDER | SWP_NOMOVE );

    }

  OnPrepareDC (pDC);

  // Set the palette and draw the image.
  if( GetFocus() == this )
    m_pImageObject->SetPalette( pDC );
  m_pImageObject->Draw( pDC );

}

void CProcessImageView::OnInitialUpdate()
{
  CScrollView::OnInitialUpdate();
  CSize sizeTotal:
  sizeTotal.cx = sizeTotal.cy = 100;
  SetScrollSizes(MM_TEXT, sizeTotal);
}

/////////////////////////////////////////////////////////////
// CProcessImageView message handlers

void CProcessImageView::OnAreaprocessesChangecontract()
{
```

(continued)

Listing 30-3 (continued)

```
  // The brightness dialog box can also be used
  // to get any other value from 0-200. All we
  // have to do is set the dialog box class members
  // to change the title and label.
  CBrightness Brightness;
  strcpy( Brightness.m_szTitle, "Set Contrast" );
  strcpy( Brightness.m_szLabel, "Contrast" );
  if( Brightness.DoModal() != IDOK ) return;

  // Create a CImageAreaProcess class and attach
  // our CImageObject class member.
  CImageAreaProcesses AreaProcesses(m_pImageObject);
  // Change to hourglass.
  BeginWaitCursor();
  // Perform the process.
  AreaProcesses.ChangeContrast(Brightness.m_nBrightness);
  // Change from the hourglass.
  EndWaitCursor();

  // Cause a window redraw.
  InvalidateRect( NULL, FALSE );
  UpdateWindow();

}

void CProcessImageView::OnAreaprocessesEdgeenhance()
{

  // Create a CImageAreaProcess class and attach
  // our CImageObject class member.
  CImageAreaProcesses AreaProcesses( m_pImageObject );
  // Change to hourglass.
  BeginWaitCursor();
  // Perform the process.
  AreaProcesses.EdgeEnhance();
  // Change from the hourglass.
  EndWaitCursor();

  // Cause a window redraw.
  InvalidateRect( NULL, FALSE );
  UpdateWindow();
}

void CProcessImageView::OnAreaprocessesEqualizecontrast()
{

  // Create a CImageAreaProcess class and attach
  // our CImageObject class member.
  CImageAreaProcesses AreaProcesses( m_pImageObject );
  // Change to hourglass.
  BeginWaitCursor();
```

```
  // Perform the process.
  AreaProcesses.EqualizeContrast();
  // Change from the hourglass.
  EndWaitCursor();

  // Cause a window redraw.
  InvalidateRect( NULL, FALSE );
  UpdateWindow();
}

void CProcessImageView::OnAreaprocessesHighpassfilter()
{

  // Create a CImageAreaProcess class and attach
  // our CImageObject class member.
  CImageAreaProcesses AreaProcesses( m_pImageObject );
  // Change to hourglass.
  BeginWaitCursor();
  // Perform the process.
  AreaProcesses.HighpassFilter();
  // Change from the hourglass.
  EndWaitCursor();

  // Cause a window redraw.
  InvalidateRect( NULL, FALSE );
  UpdateWindow();
}

void CProcessImageView::OnAreaprocessesLowpassfilter()
{

  // Create a CImageAreaProcess class and attach
  // our CImageObject class member.
  CImageAreaProcesses AreaProcesses( m_pImageObject );
  // Change to hourglass.
  BeginWaitCursor();
  // Perform the process.
  AreaProcesses.LowpassFilter();
  // Change from the hourglass.
  EndWaitCursor();

  // Cause a window redraw.
  InvalidateRect( NULL, FALSE );
  UpdateWindow();

}

void CProcessImageView::OnAreaprocessesMedianfilter()
{

  // Create a CImageAreaProcess class and attach
  // our CImageObject class member.
```

(continued)

Listing 30-3 *(continued)*

```
  CImageAreaProcesses AreaProcesses( m_pImageObject );
  // Change to hourglass.
  BeginWaitCursor();
  // Perform the process.
  AreaProcesses.MedianFilter();
  // Change from the hourglass.
  EndWaitCursor();

  // Cause a window redraw.
  InvalidateRect( NULL, FALSE );
  UpdateWindow();

}

void
CProcessImageView::OnPointprocessesChangebrightness()
{
  CBrightness Brightness;
  if( Brightness.DoModal() != IDOK ) return;

  // Create a CImagePointProcess class and attach
  // our CImageObject class member.
  CImagePointProcesses PointProcesses( m_pImageObject );
  // Change to hourglass.
  BeginWaitCursor();
  // Perform the process.
  PointProcesses.ChangeBrightness(
    Brightness.m_nBrightness );
  // Change from the hourglass.
  EndWaitCursor();

  // Cause a window redraw.
  InvalidateRect( NULL, FALSE );
  UpdateWindow();

}

void CProcessImageView::OnPointprocessesColorize()
{
  CColorDialog ColorDialog;
  if( ColorDialog.DoModal() != IDOK ) return;

  // Create a CImagePointProcess class and attach
  // our CImageObject class member.
  CImagePointProcesses PointProcesses( m_pImageObject );
  // Change to hourglass.
  BeginWaitCursor();
  // Perform the process.
  PointProcesses.Colorize( 0, 0,
    m_pImageObject->GetWidth() - 1,
    m_pImageObject->GetHeight() - 1,
```

```
    ColorDialog.GetColor() );
  // Change from the hourglass.
  EndWaitCursor();

  // Cause a window redraw.
  InvalidateRect( NULL, FALSE );
  UpdateWindow();
}

void CProcessImageView::OnPointprocessesMakegray()
{

  // Create a CImagePointProcess class and attach
  // our CImageObject class member.
  CImagePointProcesses PointProcesses( m_pImageObject );
  // Change to hourglass.
  BeginWaitCursor();
  // Perform the process.
  PointProcesses.MakeGray( TRUE );
  // Change from the hourglass.
  EndWaitCursor();

  // Cause a window redraw.
  InvalidateRect( NULL, FALSE );
  UpdateWindow();

}

void CProcessImageView::OnPointprocessesReversecolors()
{

  // Create a CImagePointProcess class and attach
  // our CImageObject class member.
  CImagePointProcesses PointProcesses( m_pImageObject );
  // Change to hourglass.
  BeginWaitCursor();
  // Perform the process.
  PointProcesses.ReverseColors();
  // Change from the hourglass.
  EndWaitCursor();

  // Cause a window redraw.
  InvalidateRect( NULL, FALSE );
  UpdateWindow();

}
```

Summary

You've seen what adding a third-party library can do for you. It extends Visual C++ and adds functionality that would take weeks, months, or years of development time. The ImageObject library provides the capability to load, save, and manipulate images easily. There are many more things it does that weren't covered in this chapter. It can acquire images from a TWAIN-compliant device. It can send images via a fax modem. It can blit one image onto another.

Look around for other add-on libraries. Imaging libraries are very popular, and database and telecommunications libraries are, too. You'll encounter many situations where third-party libraries provide a solution that's quick and relatively inexpensive.

✦ ✦ ✦

PART

VI

Component Object Modeling Programming

Microsoft says "COM is the glue that holds everything together." That might be true. Today, more and more software components are COM objects that can be reused by many applications, as long as the development language supports COM objects. With Microsoft's emphasis on COM, Visual C++, Visual Basic, Visual J++, and Visual InterDev all can use COM objects.

This part shows you how to create and use COM objects — more commonly known as ActiveX controls. You learn the basics of the topic, and can probably use the techniques in your own development immediately.

✦ ✦ ✦ ✦

In This Part

Chapter 31:
Introduction to ActiveX and ActiveX Control Design

Chapter 32:
Creating ActiveX Automation Servers Using MFC

Chapter 33:
Active Template Library

✦ ✦ ✦ ✦

CHAPTER 31

Introduction to ActiveX and ActiveX Control Design

✦ ✦ ✦ ✦

In This Chapter

Understanding the different ActiveX technologies

Deciding between ActiveX components

Basic ActiveX component design issues

Understanding the different frameworks you can use to create ActiveX components

Creating ActiveX controls with MFC

Managing registration issues

Adding methods and properties to your controls

Adding events to your controls

Understanding and using persistence in your controls

Drawing the user interface for your controls

✦ ✦ ✦ ✦

As you have learned, Visual C++ uses such built-in components as the Microsoft Foundation Classes to encapsulate various objects that you will use when you write programs. Many of the MFC classes simplify the actual writing of programs and save you from writing repetitive code to perform common tasks. As you have also learned, using MFC within your programs is consistent with the principles of object-oriented programming.

As your programs become more complex and you begin to design larger applications or applications that have distributed components over a network or the Internet, it will likely become necessary for you to take the object-oriented programming model one step further and apply it to entire programs that your application will treat as standalone objects. Within the Microsoft design structure, such objects are generally all lumped together in the category of "ActiveX objects" or "Component Object Model (COM) objects."

This chapter, and the next chapter, cover in detail the development of ActiveX automation servers, controls, and COM objects. Automation controllers, ActiveX documents, and containers entail too many interfaces and too much technology for these two chapters to effectively address in the space available.

Understanding the Origins and Uses of ActiveX

In Chapter 15, you learned about Microsoft's Dynamic Data Exchange (DDE) — a way to share information between applications. In subsequent chapters, you have used a variety of technologies that are all based on Object Linking and Embedding (OLE), the descendent and an expansion of DDE.

As data has become the major focus of interface design, the data's content is what occupies the user's attention, not the application managing the data. In such a design, applications should not limit data to its native creation and editing environment. In other words, your applications should not limit the user to creating or editing data only within its associated application window. Instead, most applications will enable the user to transfer data to other types of containers while maintaining the data's viewing and editing capability in the new container. Compound documents are a common example and illustrate the interaction between containers and their components, but they are not the only expression of this kind of object relationship that OLE can support. A *compound document* is any kind of document that contains components from multiple source locations. For example, you might create a document that includes text from a word processor, tabular data from a spreadsheet, and a sound recording and pictures that you or someone else created in other applications. Today, an ever-increasing number of documents that users create are compound documents. As Chapter 19 details, you can handle compound documents within your applications using items that you derive from the `CCmdTarget` MFC class.

From its name, you could easily guess that OLE technology supports two basic types of objects — embedded objects and linked objects. As you have learned, when a user moves or copies an object into a new location (such as within a different application container), data objects that retain their native, full-featured editing and operating capabilities are called *OLE embedded objects*. These embedded objects retain their full set of capabilities, even within their new container. Alternatively, a user can link information rather than embedding it. An *OLE linked object* provides access to another object that is in another location in the same container or in a different, separate container. Generally, containers support any level of nested OLE embedded and linked objects. For example, a user can embed a chart in a worksheet, which, in turn, can be embedded in a word processing document. The model for interaction is consistent at each level of nesting.

Now that you understand a little more clearly what OLE really means, it is time to consider ActiveX. ActiveX and OLE have become synonymous. What people once referred to as "OLE controls (OCXs)," they now refer to as "ActiveX controls." `OLE DocObjects` are now "ActiveX documents." In some cases, Microsoft has updated entire documents on how to implement OLE technologies to be ActiveX technologies, and the only material change that Microsoft made was to remove the term "OLE" and replace it with "ActiveX."

Although tremendous advances have been made and seemingly new technologies appear daily with regard to OLE and ActiveX, it is questionable whether the Internet was or is directly involved in many of these areas. The need for small, fast, reusable components (COM objects) has been around for years. Microsoft first demonstrated distributed components (DCOM objects) several years ago at the OLE 2.0 Professional Developer's Conference. The Visual Basic group played a major role in the enabling of ActiveX in its early days. In fact, the Visual Basic group developed the `BaseCtl` framework, which Microsoft included in the ActiveX Software Developer's Kit (SDK), to answer the group's need for small, lightweight controls to improve the load times of Visual Basic applications. The only contribution the Internet had was in its need for a way to implement and publish Web pages. Practically every new feature with an ActiveX label can trace its roots back to a fundamental, global need for small, fast, reusable components, all of which started with OLE and COM.

ActiveX was not meant to replace OLE but simply to broaden it to include the Internet, intranets, commercial and in-house applications development, and the tools used to develop newer, broader-in-scope applications. Microsoft has published a number of documents regarding ActiveX development. The OC 96 specification defines how you should develop controls so that your controls provide faster startup times and better drawing capabilities. The specification also describes which interfaces a control must support to qualify as an ActiveX/OLE control and which interfaces are optional. The "OLE Control and Control Container Guidelines" provide important information for Control and Container interaction. The Microsoft Web site, with its extensive knowledge base, white papers and articles, and MSDN online support, has become an extremely valuable source of information for developers who plan to create, use, or deploy ActiveX components.

In addition to the specific technologies for creating ActiveX components, Microsoft has set a standard for the use and integration of ActiveX components. Every product from Visual Basic to Microsoft Word to Microsoft's Visual J++ implementation of Java is inherently capable of using ActiveX components. Four years ago, it was almost impossible to find more than a handful of applications that were capable of integrating in such a relatively seamless fashion as is possible today.

Understanding Various ActiveX Technologies

As you have learned, ActiveX technology is a continuation and expansion of OLE technology. ActiveX technology can be, generally, divided into six basic component categories. The six basic categories are as follows:

- ✦ Automation servers
- ✦ Automation controllers
- ✦ Controls
- ✦ COM objects

- ✦ ActiveX documents
- ✦ ActiveX containers

Understanding automation servers

Automation servers are components that other applications can drive programmatically. An automation server contains at least one, and possibly more, `IDispatch`-based interfaces that other applications can create or connect to. An automation server may or may not contain a user interface (UI), depending on the nature and function of the server.

Automation servers can be *in-process* (executing in the process space of the controller), *local* (executing in its own process space), or *remote* (executing in a process space on another machine). The specific implementation of the server, in some cases, defines how and where the server will execute, but not always. A DLL can execute as either an in-process, local, or remote server; while an ActiveX EXE can execute only locally or remotely.

When designing automation servers, execution time is an important consideration. However, it is not the only consideration. For example, the fastest execution times are from servers that are in-process to the controllers using them. However, using an in-process automation server does not guarantee in-process performance. If an in-process automation server is created in one process space and then handed to a controller in another process space, the server becomes local and suffers from the same performance degradation as a local server. Especially in enterprise-based solutions, determining how gracefully a server degrades when it is not in-process, or when it degrades from local to remote, is an important design consideration.

◆ ◆ ◆ ◆ ◆

Understanding automation controllers

Automation controllers are those applications that can use and manipulate automation servers. An example of an automation controller is Visual Basic. With the Visual Basic programming language, you are able to create, use, and destroy automation servers as though they are an integral part of the language.

An automation controller can be any type of application, DLL or EXE, and can access the automation server either in-process, locally, or remotely. Typically, the Registry entries for the server and controller and how you implement the automation server determine which process space the server will execute in relation to the controller.

Defining ActiveX controls

ActiveX controls are 32-bit controls that are equivalent to what is known as OLE controls or OCXs. A typical control consists of a user interface representation both at design time and runtime, a single IDispatch interface defining all of the methods and properties of the control, and a single IConnectionPoint interface for the events that the control can fire. In addition, the control may support persistence across its execution lifetimes and support various user interface features, such as cut and paste and drag and drop. In general, a control has a large number of COM interfaces that the using container must support in order to take advantage of the control's features. However, with the release of the OLE control and ActiveX guidelines for control development, a control is no longer limited to the feature set defined in the preceding text. Rather, the developer can now choose to implement only those features that are most useful and interesting to users of the applications. The control and container guidelines published by Microsoft list all the required interfaces and their specific requirements.

ActiveX controls always execute in-process to the container in which they reside. The extension of a control is typically OCX, but in terms of execution models, a control is nothing more than a standard Windows DLL.

Understanding component object model (COM) objects

COM objects are similar in architecture to automation servers and controllers. They contain one or more COM interfaces and probably little or no user interface. These objects, however, cannot be used by the typical controller application the way automation servers can. The controller must have specific knowledge of the COM interface that it "talks" to in order to use the interface, which is not the case for automation interfaces. The Windows 95 and NT operating systems contain hundreds of COM objects and custom interfaces as extensions to the operating systems. These COM objects control everything from the appearance of the desktop to the rendering of 3D images on the screen. COM objects are an effective way to organize a related set of functions and data, while still maintaining the high-speed performance of a DLL.

Automation servers can also benefit from COM interfaces. Servers that support COM interfaces are known as dual-interface servers. The IDispatch interface of the automation server also has a companion COM interface describing the methods and properties of the object. Automation controllers such as Visual Basic can take advantage of these dual interfaces to provide even greater performance when using the server. The one drawback to dual-interface servers is that they are limited to the set of data types supported by OLE automation when defining methods and properties.

◆ ◆ ◆ ◆ ◆

Understanding ActiveX documents

ActiveX documents, or *DocObjects* as they were originally called, represent objects that are more than a simple control or automation server. A document can be anything from a spreadsheet to a complete invoice in an accounting application.

Documents, like controls, have a user interface, and you must host documents within a container application. Microsoft Word and Excel are examples of ActiveX document servers, and the Microsoft Office Binder and Microsoft Internet Explorer are examples of ActiveX document containers.

The ActiveX document architecture is an extension of the OLE linking and embedding model and gives the document more control over the container in which the user is hosting the document. The most obvious change is how the menus are presented. A standard OLE document's menu merges with the container, providing a combined feature set; whereas an ActiveX document takes over the entire menu system, thus presenting the feature set of only the document and not that of both the document and the container. The fact that the feature set of the document is exposed is the premise for all the differences between ActiveX documents and OLE documents. The container is just a hosting mechanism, and the document has all of the control.

Another difference between ActiveX documents and OLE documents is in printing and storage. An OLE document's designer intends for the document to be a part of the container's document that is hosting it. Therefore, Windows prints and stores the OLE document as a piece of the host container's document. The operating system expects ActiveX documents to support their own native printing and storage functions and therefore does not integrate them with the container's document.

You should use ActiveX documents within a uniform presentation architecture, rather than within an embedded document architecture, which is the basis for OLE documents. Microsoft Internet Explorer is a perfect example of a uniform presentation architecture (that is, an architecture that supports ActiveX documents). Internet Explorer merely presents the Web pages to the user, but the user views, prints, and stores the pages themselves as a single entity, separate from the host container. On the other hand, Microsoft Word and Microsoft Excel are examples of the OLE document architecture. If an Excel spreadsheet is embedded in a Word document, the spreadsheet is actually stored with the Word document and is an integral part of it.

ActiveX documents also have the added capability of being published as Web pages on the Internet or on a corporate intranet. Imagine an in-house tracking system for purchase orders that users can run from the same Web browsers that they use to connect to the Internet, which fully integrates with the underlying data on purchase orders and which users can interact with as if it were a program on the desktop

Understanding ActiveX containers

ActiveX containers are applications that can host automation servers, controls, and documents. Visual Basic and the ActiveX Control Pad are examples of containers that can host automation servers and controls. The Microsoft Office Binder and Microsoft Internet Explorer can host automation servers, controls, and documents.

With the decreasing requirements that the ActiveX control and document specifications define, a container must be sufficiently robust to handle the cases where a control or document lacks certain interfaces. Container applications may enable little or no interaction with the document or control they host, or they may provide significant interaction capabilities in both manipulation and presentation of the hosted component. This capability, however, is dependent upon the container hosting the component. The ActiveX control and document specifications do not indicate that such capability is required to qualify as a container.

Understanding What ActiveX Can Do for You

Understanding the power and capabilities of the different sub-types of ActiveX technologies is an important first step in determining what type of ActiveX object to create. Clearly, ActiveX components provide valuable tools that you can use to design the best possible applications — and OLE support is critical for any application that you use within the enterprise. In general, you should take into account five considerations before you design an ActiveX component:

- **Application requirements** — It is important to understand as many of the project's requirements as possible before starting your development project. Understanding the project's requirements helps to better determine whether or not to use one or more ActiveX technologies during the project's design.
- **Choosing the correct architecture and component type** — The various ways in which you can create and implement ActiveX components are crucial to a successful project. You don't want to do too much with a component (extending design times and expanding application space) or too little (resulting in bad program design or poor program implementation).
- **Choosing the correct tool** — The tool you use to develop your component also affects the project's success. Picking the right tool for the job is as important as understanding the job itself.
- **Basic ActiveX component architecture** — Each ActiveX component type has its particular architecture and construction. Understanding this architecture is important — and can save you significant headaches during the design of your application.
- **Basic ActiveX support tools** — You will find a collection of development support tools that are invaluable to your ActiveX development — not only within Visual Studio, but also on the Microsoft Web site and other ActiveX-dedicated sites.

In short, you can no longer design a set of simple standalone applications that do not interoperate with each other — or that have a very uneasy set of interoperating rules. With OLE, ActiveX, and the Internet, users expect applications to be flexible, modifiable, and extensible — all in a manner that makes the applications easy for the users to manipulate.

Spending a little extra time up front working out the design and architecture of your application, and any components that you design to use within your application, can make all the difference in the world. Very few applications whose design lacks a significant amount of forethought — regardless of whether that information is crammed into the head of one of your developers, scribbled on restaurant napkins, or written in formal documentation — ever make it to distribution or, even in the best-case scenario, distribute well. However, as a general rule, formal documentation or some other type of usable written record is probably the best policy — it makes it easier to explain to others the foundations of your great idea.

The basic principles of OLE and ActiveX are going to determine most of the specifics of the component architecture and design within your application. For example, you must develop ActiveX controls and documents within a specific set of parameters and rules so that they will correctly interact with containers. Similarly, automation servers and controllers have to conform to OLE automation rules, and COM objects must support the basic fundamentals of COM. However, you will not be able to easily address some problems based on the fundamental principles of OLE and ActiveX. For example, determining the relationships between your components and the lifetimes of the components themselves is unique to each application. Determining what containers can access what interfaces, what security the component might support, wide character support, and so on, are also all key issues to address.

Determining What Type of ActiveX Component You Need

When you begin to design one or more ActiveX components for use in your application, you must make several decisions (the broad strokes of which the previous section outlines). The first thing you must decide is what kind of component best fits your requirements. Making such a decision requires a better understanding of the benefits and limitations of the different component types, which the following sections will help you achieve.

Using automation servers and controllers

Automation servers and controllers probably have the greatest amount of flexibility of the different ActiveX technologies. Just about every major application available from Microsoft and hundreds of other manufacturers can use the servers' `IDispatch` interface. Because the interface won't suffer from the same versioning requirements placed on strict COM interfaces, the interface also lends itself well to prototyping and modeling component interactions.

A dual-interface automation server created to be an in-process server that remains in-process throughout its lifetime is the fastest type of automation server. "Dual-interface" refers to the fact that a server contains two interfaces — one based on

IDispatch and the other based on COM. The COM interface is actually the faster of the two. An "in-process server" resides in the same memory address space as the application that created it. The same-process residence of the server enables the application (through the operating system) to invoke the server's methods significantly faster than it would if the server were out-of-process because there is no burden of having to cross process boundaries every time the application calls a method. For the same reason, in-process servers load faster than a similarly sized out-of-process server because of the minimal number of steps the operating system must perform to create the server and pass its IDispatch or COM interface pointer to the calling application.

Nothing inherent in automation architecture promotes the use of a user interface, and nothing prevents you from using a user interface either. You have complete freedom and control over how calling programs implement and use your servers. Your automation servers could potentially contain a user interface in the form of a dialog, CFormView view class, or another similar dialog-based window.

Automation servers also lend themselves well to the increasingly popular multi-tiered application architectures that have become common in recent years. The separation of user interface from function is perfect for automation servers because you have complete freedom over how applications implement and use your servers. Creating servers with thin user interface layers that use other servers with no user interface to accomplish a task is at the heart of multi-tiered applications development — a technique for which Microsoft makes specific adjustments to the COM standard with the new COM+ standard. You should use automation servers just as you would any other DLL. The only difference between an automation server and a standard Windows DLL is the server uses only a restricted set of data types, while a DLL can use any type. Designing automation servers that work without the need for a user interface also makes them prime candidates for Distributed COM (DCOM) and other distributing technologies (such as COM+).

Using ActiveX controls

You should use ActiveX controls primarily as they were intended to be used. In other words, your ActiveX controls should generally be user interface–based components to enhance or support a dialog, form, or document. Controls can be expensive to load because they can potentially require a large number of interfaces, depending on the functionality the control supports. The OC 96 specification adds the QuickActivate interface to help with control load times, but the improvement was not significant. In addition, the OC 96 specification identifies a number of interfaces that are considered optional or conditional, depending on the type of control you are implementing. It is wise to review the specification to determine what you can and cannot remove from your implementation in order to improve its performance and overall size.

When creating controls, be sure to make them as lean as possible. If you do not intend to commercially distribute the control, for example, remove the "AboutBox" code. In addition, see whether you can get away with relying on the property editor of the application's development tool that will be used rather than supporting property pages. Avoid large amounts of persistence, and save the data only if you must. In other words (if you have not figured it out already), implement only those features that are truly useful and helpful for your control implementation.

Using COM objects

COM objects (custom interfaces) are far more flexible than any other component type when it comes to interface design. They are also the fastest interfaces in terms of execution times, although the fastest COM objects are those in which the COM interface is in-process to the application using it — out-of-process COM objects suffer performance degradation just as other out-of-process ActiveX components do. COM objects can use any data type within their interface definitions and do not suffer from the same restrictions as automation servers. This situation does present a problem when crossing process boundaries because the object then requires its own proxy-stub marshaling code (because the Universal Marshaler, which handles proxy-stub relationships in automation servers, only processes simple data types).

Proxy-stub marshaling is what takes place when an application resides in a process space other than the application it is communicating with. It is necessary to translate function calls and data to a context that both applications can understand. This translation process is the responsibility of the proxy-stub code and is true for all types of OLE components. Moving any component out-of-process has a profound effect on the application's performance because the operating system, the application, and the component are performing a lot more work to accomplish the specific set of operations.

Automation servers rely on built-in proxy-stub marshaling code (within the Universal Marshaler), whereas COM interfaces must create their own. While you can create your own proxy-stub marshaling code, doing so does add to the development time and effort, maintenance of the code, distribution of the object, and overall performance of the application, so you must consider those issues when you decide what type of component to develop. If you plan to develop the COM object for out-of-process execution, you should probably consider using an automation server instead, because the performance of the two will be comparable — unless you are going to come up with your own marshaling code that significantly outperforms the built-in mechanisms.

COM objects are useful in cases where the limited set of data types available to automation servers has a significant impact on the type of interface that you can create. An example of a COM object might be a simple implementation that performs calculations of a large volume of user-defined data. Instead of copying the data and passing it to the COM object, it might be more useful to pass a pointer to the data and enable the COM object to manipulate the data directly. Automation server data type restrictions would not enable the creation of this kind of interface. COM does, however. Yet, keep in mind that in this particular case the COM object can execute only in-process because it requires direct access to the data. When creating your ActiveX components with Visual C++, you have four options, which are described in the following sections.

Using Microsoft Foundation Classes to create ActiveX components

The Microsoft Foundation Class Library is the easiest choice of all the tools available for ActiveX development. The Visual C++ Integrated Development Environment (IDE) is designed specifically with MFC in mind and, as you have learned in previous chapters, provides the very useful AppWizard and ClassWizard to help you develop your applications. MFC is robust and will probably cover 90 percent of your application's needs. Unfortunately, as with most software development or other creative projects, the last 10 percent of the project is where you spend 90 percent of your time.

Going outside the bounds of what MFC defines can be difficult and, in some cases, impossible. Take, for example, the requirement to have an object that is single instance only. No matter how the object is created by the client application, you always want the same instance returned. Providing this kind of functionality is impossible with MFC without modifying the built-in Class Factory classes, which Visual Studio does not normally expose to the developer.

Supporting dual interfaces in automation servers that you design with MFC is not impossible, but it does cause enough changes in your code so that you can no longer use the ClassWizard to completely maintain your methods and properties. MFC does provide a number of features and functions when developing ActiveX components, but be prepared to live by its rules. Occasionally, you can bend the rules, but you can almost never break them. The chapters that follow this one discuss how to successfully bend the rules in MFC and implement both single instance and dual-interface servers.

A good rule of thumb when working with MFC to design ActiveX components is to avoid using the built-in classes as much as possible by utilizing the basic Windows API instead. Avoiding use of the MFC classes to solve your component application's problems has two benefits. One is that your application generally runs faster; and another is that using the Windows API prior to moving the application code to an alternative development tool such as ATL or `BaseCtl` enables you to avoid rewriting large amounts of MFC-dependent code. A large portion of the MFC classes have equivalent Windows API functions, especially in the area of GDI and drawing, and it is not that much of a departure from MFC to use the Windows API. Basic storage classes, such as lists and arrays, could be better provided by a general purpose class library, such as the Standard Template Library (STL), which can be used in combination with any and all of the ActiveX development frameworks (MFC, ATL, or `BaseCtl`).

Using the ActiveX Template Library to create ActiveX components

The ActiveX Template Library (ATL) is a newcomer to the ActiveX arena. It first appeared in the summer of 1996 and quickly became a favorite of developers. Based on the amount of development taking place by developers using ATL and the fact that, unlike the `BaseCtl` framework, ATL is actually a supported product, Microsoft and the industry have obviously seen ATL as a viable platform for creating ActiveX components. It should be around for a long time.

The initial implementation, versions 1.0 and 1.1, focused on the creation of small and fast automation servers and COM objects. With the introduction of 2.0, ATL expanded its coverage to include ActiveX controls and other ActiveX components. The level of integration with the Visual C++ IDE originally consisted only of an AppWizard that you would use to create the basic ATL project (which was, ironically, more complete than its MFC counterpart). In addition, you can use the ClassWizard to maintain the objects, methods, and properties as you do with MFC. Microsoft fully integrated ATL version 2.0 into Visual C++ 5.0 (including AppWizards, ObjectWizards, and ClassWizards) and maintains a consistent level of support for ATL within Visual C++ 6.0.

An added bonus to ATL is that you can integrate ATL components into existing MFC applications without dire consequences or enormous amounts of work. This capability gives you complete freedom to develop your component without the restrictions that MFC imposes, while still being able to use MFC classes and features (such as structures, arrays, and lists, to name a few). You will learn more about how to use the ATL in Chapter 33.

Using the BaseControl framework to create ActiveX components

BaseControl (`BaseCtl`) Framework and the ActiveX SDK is, without a doubt, the most difficult route to choose for ActiveX component development. The `BaseCtl` framework was first developed by the Visual Basic 4 development group in late 1995 and early 1996 in response to growing demands for better performance when using OCXs and Visual Basic. `BaseCtl` was intended as a bare-bones framework that knowledgeable developers could use to create lightweight OLE controls.

In an effort to quell the demand for tools to create OLE controls, the framework was put into the hands of various control developers and vendors who were in contact with Microsoft and the Visual Basic group. At the Internet Professional Developers' Conference, Microsoft packaged the `BaseCtl` framework as part of the ActiveX Software Developer's Kit (SDK), and the rest, as they say, is history.

The `BaseCtl` framework has no integration with the Visual C++ environment. In fact, the version of the `BaseCtl` framework that ships with the ActiveX SDK is little more than sample programs from which you can create new applications. The

BaseCtl framework relies on a series of object and library files that you have to build before you can use them to develop components. All of the source files that come with the SDK and those generated by the AppWizard depend on command-line compilation. With a little bit of effort, you can convert all the projects to Visual C++ projects, including the object and library files that come with the SDK—but before you start, you may want to ask yourself if such an effort is worthwhile. The documentation for the BaseCtl framework is rudimentary and somewhat cryptic.

Basic control development with the BaseCtl framework can be difficult as well. A fair number of the functions and capabilities that you are probably used to working with in MFC development are not present in BaseCtl. Worse yet, a number of the function names are different, and the architecture for persistence is completely different. BaseCtl is meant to get the job done with as little code as possible. As you probably have learned from your own development efforts, getting the job done with as little code as possible typically means a bare-bones environment at best—and BaseCtl is no different. With the BaseCtl framework, you're expected to dig into the guts of the framework and build a lot of the functions yourself.

One thing the BaseCtl framework has going for it is a fair number of samples. When installing the BaseCtl framework, you should generally install the samples as well. Chances are that if you need to do something, it's in one of the samples. Another nice feature of the BaseCtl framework is the capability to access all the source code in the BaseCtl framework directly, so if you find a bug, you can fix it yourself and move on.

In addition, using the BaseCtl framework gives you a lot more freedom in modeling your control. For example, suppose you have two controls that you want to develop. The first control is a Number control, which receives only basic numeric data input, while the second control is a Currency control, which receives only basic currency data input. Both can rely heavily on the C++ inheritance model at the code and interface levels if you create a BaseNumeric control and derive the code for the other two controls from it.

Clearly, MFC does not provide anywhere near that much freedom. However, do not let the freedom issue convince you to take the BaseCtl framework lightly—you can expect a lot of work when implementing a component with it. Even worse, the results may not justify the work. For example, converting an existing MFC control to the BaseCtl framework might, in certain cases, result in a 40 percent improvement in the average load time from the MFC version to the BaseCtl version of the control. At first blush, a 40 percent improvement sounds pretty good. Unfortunately, with the speeds of modern computers and the amount of available memory, the reduction in load time might be negligible to the user. In other words, the load times might already be so low for the MFC version of the control that you literally have to place hundreds of controls on the application's form before the load-time difference between the two versions is noticeable.

Create your own framework

The last method for control development is for you to just sit down and create the control. You can obtain code from the class libraries, samples, books, and so on, and come up with your own framework, tools, or whatever you want. But you can expect the work to be hard and time consuming. To get an idea of how much work is actually involved, stop for a minute, and take a look at some of the source files in MFC, ATL, and the `BaseCtl` framework. Literally thousands of lines of code have been implemented over the course of months and even years. Due to the constantly changing nature of OLE and ActiveX requirements, it is generally wiser to choose an existing platform rather than to try to reinvent the wheel, unless you have an extremely compelling reason to create your own framework. Remember, the key to successful control development is not in the framework that you choose to develop in, but in how you apply it.

Basic ActiveX Component Architecture

Before moving on to the actual implementation of each type of ActiveX component, you should review some of the basic concepts and architecture surrounding each component. Even though you can develop a wide variety of ActiveX components — controls, servers, documents, and so on — one thing is true for every ActiveX component you design: underlying every component is the Component Object Model or COM architecture. COM defines the standard that all ActiveX components rely on when interacting with other ActiveX components.

In addition to COM, all ActiveX components are further defined or restricted by the operating system in how they are created and used. The type of ActiveX component you create will further define or restrict your options when creating components. A wide variety of choices are available to you as a developer, and it is important to understand the importance of your choices and how a choice can affect your further development in a project.

ActiveX automation servers

Probably the easiest to implement and most flexible form of ActiveX component is the automation server. An *automation server* is an application that contains one or more `IDispatch`-based interfaces. An *interface* is a collection of related methods and properties, and an `IDispatch` interface is the name of the COM interface that the component-using application uses to generically invoke the component's methods and properties. For more information on `IDispatch` interfaces, their use, and the specifics of their implementation, you can review the Visual C++ online books available with Visual Studio. The capability to define unique methods and properties for each server and have them be accessible through a generic mechanism is the real power of automation servers.

An automation server may or may not be directly createable by other applications using the `CreateObject()` function or a similar call. It is possible to have what are referred to as *nested objects* that represent a hierarchy of objects. In such an environment, a single createable automation object is responsible for the creation and distribution of other automation objects. For example, an application may expose a document automation interface that can be created and manipulated by another application but that only exposes a `Page` interface as a method call to the document object. The lifetime of the `Page` object is less than or equal to the document object and cannot exist on its own.

In Chapter 32, you will learn how to create ActiveX automation servers using MFC. MFC is great for rapid development and ease of modification. Servers created with MFC are the largest and slowest of the three types (MFC, ATL, and `BaseCtl`). Deviating from the standard MFC implementation of automation servers can also be a limiting factor when using this tool. MFC's greatest strength is its integration with the Visual C++ IDE and the speed with which an implementation can be up and running. In only minutes, developers can create a server and implement its methods and properties, assuming that they are familiar with the tools available.

Types of automation servers

When creating an automation server, you must decide how to implement the server relative to how it is going to be used. You can create two basic types of servers: DLL-based and EXE-based. If the server does not have to run as a standalone application and performance is a critical issue, you should implement your server as a DLL. A DLL-based server is typically referred to as an *in-process server* because of how it normally executes relative to its controller. If the server application is required to run as a standalone application, you must implement it as an EXE. An EXE-based automation server is typically referred to as a local server or *out-of-process server*, and it executes in its own process space.

Automation servers also have an execution model that is independent of how the server is written. Automation servers can execute either in-process, locally, or remotely, relative to the application that has invoked or is using it.

In-process execution

An in-process server is *in-process* because it executes within the same process space as that of the application that created it. Only DLL-based automation servers can execute as in-process, but that is not a guarantee. This is very important to note when using nested objects or shared objects. If you create an object in a process space (for example, Process A) and you subsequently pass the object to another application in another process space (Process B), the server in Process A will execute as a local server relative to the application in Process B. Process B will treat the object as a local server—regardless of the fact that the server in Process A is a DLL-based server. This issue is very critical because, more times than not, in-process servers are used to improve the performance of the application using them.

Local execution

Local execution is when an automation server is executing in a process space other than the process space of the controller application. As was stated earlier, a DLL-based server may execute locally to its controller, depending on how it was created versus which application is using it. The main issue with local servers is performance because all of the method calls have to cross process boundaries. This condition requires additional code overhead to move data back and forth between the server and its controller.

Remote execution

Remote execution occurs when the server is executing on a machine other than the application that is controlling it. As with local servers, performance is an issue with this type of execution.

ActiveX controls

An ActiveX control, for all intents and purposes, is still the same OCX or OLE control that you have come to know and love over the past several years. In fact, the only change with the coming of ActiveX is a decrease in the requirements to qualify as a control.

To qualify as an ActiveX control, a component must be a COM object, implement an `IUnknown` interface, and support registration and unregistration through the exported functions, `DLLRegisterServer()` and `DLLUnregisterServer()`.

Even though your component qualifies as an ActiveX control, if all it supports is the preceding features, it will not do much more than take up space on your hard disk. If it needs a user interface, persistence, events, or any other feature common to controls, the control must implement other categories of interfaces. The exact requirements are in the *OLE Control and Control Container Guidelines, Version 1.1* published by Microsoft. All of the guidelines for ActiveX development are available on the Internet at the Microsoft Web site or on the ActiveX SDK CD.

As you have learned, you have three tools at your disposal for creating ActiveX controls: MFC, ATL, and `BaseCtl`. Similar to the situation with ActiveX automation servers, each development tool has its strengths and weaknesses. With ActiveX controls, you have only one option when creating and executing the control: as a DLL and in-process to the control's container application. Even though the extension of the control is .OCX, it is still in fact just a DLL.

Support Tools Required to Build ActiveX Components

When creating your ActiveX components, a few tools are essential to successful ActiveX development. Most of these tools are automatically installed as part of the

Visual C++ development environment. As ActiveX development matures, more and more tools will become available. Using as many tools as you can will greatly improve your understanding of how your components work, as well as improve their overall implementation.

MIDL compiler

The Microsoft MIDL compiler is a standard component of the Microsoft Visual C++ environment (added to the environment with the Visual C++ 5.0 release). The MIDL compiler compiles COM interface definitions (IDL) files into C code, which the Visual C++ compiler then compiles into the project.

The MIDL compiler also provides support for marshaling interfaces across process boundaries. Starting with Visual C++ 4.0, the MIDL compiler started shipping as a standard component of Visual C++. The MIDL compiler is also available within the Win32 SDK from Microsoft.

Mktyplib

`Mktyplib` is a type library compiler for compiling ODL files. `Mktyplib` is the predecessor to MIDL and produces the same type of output as MIDL. The use of `Mktyplib` will decrease as Microsoft moves from ODL to IDL files.

GUIDGEN

GUIDGEN is a tool that you can use to generate Globally Unique Identifiers (GUID), which you can use to create interface IDs, class IDs, or any other 128-bit Universally-Unique Identifiers (UUID), such as an RPC interface. Visual Studio installs GUIDGEN only when you select the OLE development option during the Visual C++ installation. When you run GUIDGEN, the program creates a GUID and places it onto the Windows Clipboard. After running the GUIDGEN application, the resultant GUID is pasted from the Clipboard into the code that requires a GUID.

RegEdit

RegEdit, or the registration editor, is a standard component of both the Windows 95 and Windows NT operating systems (though you are generally better served using RegEdt32 on Windows NT). The registration editor is used for browsing and altering operating system and application settings. You can also use the registration editor to install and register your COM objects.

RegEdit is a very powerful tool. You should always use it with extreme caution and should only use it at all if you are an experienced user who understands the workings of the Windows operating systems. If you use RegEdit improperly, systems can be damaged, resulting in a loss of data or a malfunctioning operating system that may, in the worst case, not even load correctly.

✦ ✦ ✦ ✦ ✦

Registration Server

The Registration Server is an application that you can use to register the settings of a COM object in the Windows Registry without the need to create a separate registration file. The application is called `regsvr32.exe` and is automatically installed if you select the OLE development option during the Visual C++ installation or if you install the ActiveX SDK.

Ole2View

Ole2View is a program that lists ActiveX components relative to their function and category. Ole2View is extremely helpful in the test and use of your components. Ole2View can be used to determine whether your component is registered properly and the type and number of interfaces your component defines. It even enables you to instantiate and access various components and interfaces within your application, and now it has expanded support for configuring components to use DCOM. When you try to determine what is the cause of problems with a troublesome component, Ole2View is an invaluable tool.

Adding the tools to the Visual C++ development environment

To maximize development productivity, the tools needed for COM programming should be integrated into the Visual C++ environment. Each of the tools needed can be added to the IDE's Tools menu. The following section illustrates how to incorporate the tools into the IDE.

Adding GUIDGEN to the Visual C++ Environment

Adding GUIDGEN to the Visual C++ environment enables you to generate a UUID from a single menu command. GUIDGEN places the generated UUID onto the Windows Clipboard, and you must then paste the UUID into the project code. Follow these steps:

1. Select the Customize command from the Tools menu. Select the Tools tab from the Customize dialog.
2. In the Menu Contents list box, scroll to the bottom of the list, select a blank line, and type **&Generate NewUUID**.
3. In the Command edit box, type **GUIDGEN.EXE**.
4. Clear all text from the Arguments edit box.
5. Clear all text from the Initial Directory edit box.
6. Click the Close button to add the entry to the Tools menu.

✦ ✦ ✦ ✦ ✦

In addition to the GUIDGEN program, you may want to consider adding to the Visual Studio Tools menu the registry editor, the capability to unregister a component, and any other tool that you find useful. You can add the other programs in a manner similar to the one that you used for GUIDGEN.

Using MFC to Create a Basic ActiveX Control

Visual C++ and MFC are powerful and flexible tools for creating ActiveX controls. In terms of rapid development and ease of use, these two tools are your best bet. In the remainder of this chapter, you will create an ActiveX control with all the basics: methods, properties, events, persistence, and drawing. In addition, you will explore some of the more advanced features and lesser known aspects of control development, such as methods with optional parameters, asynchronous properties, Clipboard support, and optimized drawing, to name just a few.

Note

MFC controls are linked dynamically to the MFC DLLs for support and implementation. Linking dynamically can impair the control's load time because the MFC DLLs are loaded in addition to the control itself. Even though the MFC DLLs may already be in memory, you still have DLL address fix-ups and memory swapping issues. When developing an ActiveX control, the developer is prudent to remove as much dependence on MFC as possible. This practice serves two purposes: this practice makes it much easier to port the control to an alternative framework such as ATL or BaseCtl, and it improves the overall performance of the control because you don't have the overhead of the MFC DLLs to contend with. As a general rule, components that are performance sensitive should avoid using DLLs of any kind. The last thing you want is a component that is disk bound.

◆ ◆ ◆ ◆ ◆

Creating the basic control project

To create an MFC ActiveX control, you should begin by taking advantage of the AppWizard that Visual C++ provides for control creation. To use the AppWizard, run the Visual C++ development environment, and from the File menu, select the New option. When Visual C++ displays the New dialog box, select the Projects tab. On the Projects tab, you can define several aspects of how the AppWizard will create the application. For example, you can define the type of application to create, the name of the application, and the location where you want the AppWizard to create the project. For the project type, select MFC ActiveX ControlWizard; enter the Project Name as MFCControl, and the Location as **C:\IDG\Chap31\MFCControl**. Figure 31-1 shows the New dialog box after you set the options to create the project.

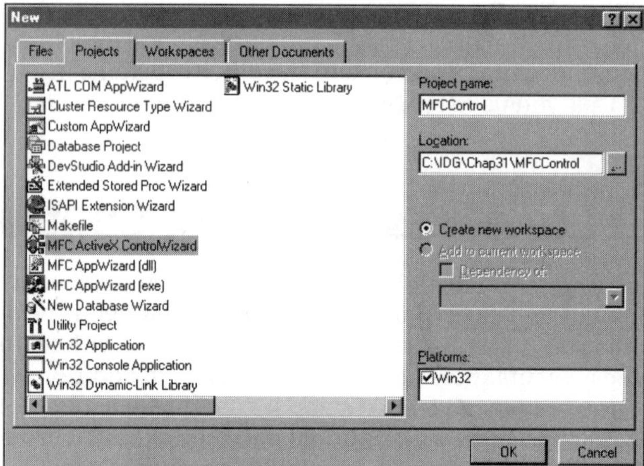

Figure 31-1: Define the new MFC control project within the New dialog box.

Click the OK button to start the ControlWizard so that you can define the properties of your control. In the first step in the ControlWizard, you define how many controls exist within your project. Using the up and down arrow buttons, select 3 for the number of controls, and leave the remainder of the properties set to their default values. Click the Next button to continue.

If you have a requirement to create more than one control and you plan to often use the controls together within the same application, you should generally be combining the controls into a single .ocx file — because of OCX load times. A single OCX always loads faster than two OCXs of comparable size. Code sharing can also be an advantage, and the end result is a control that is smaller and loads faster than the two (or more) individual controls combined would load.

◆ ◆ ◆ ◆ ◆

In Step 2 of the ControlWizard, you change the name of the control, define some of the control's features, and determine whether the control will be a subclass of an existing window's control.

Because you have instructed the ControlWizard that you want three controls for this project, the ControlWizard will create three default controls (`MFCControl1`, `MFCControl2`, and `MFCControl3`). For this project, you will rename `MFCControl1` `MFCControl2`, and `MFCControl3` to `MFCControlWin`, `MFCControlNoWin`, and `MFCControlSubWin`, respectively. To rename a class, select the name in the drop-down list box, and click the Edit Names button. Enter the new name of the control in the Short Name edit box. The names of the other files and classes change automatically to conform to the new Short Name. Click OK to close the Edit Names dialog box. Figure 31-2 shows the Edit Names dialog box after you change the `MFCControl3` control to the `MFCControlSubWin` control.

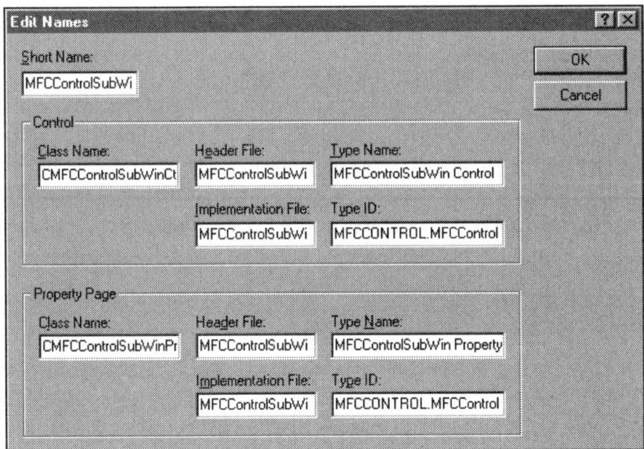

Figure 31-2: The Edit Names dialog box after you change the last control name

You use the Advanced button to display a dialog for selecting the ActiveX enhancements that you want for the control. Ensure that the `MFCControlWin` class is currently selected within the drop-down box, and click the Advanced button. All of the advanced features in the dialog are the result of the OC 96 specification that you have learned about previously. It is worthwhile, at this point in the control's development, to look at the features in detail. Table 31-1 lists the advanced features for ActiveX controls.

From the Advanced ActiveX Features dialog, select only the following options:

- ✦ Unclipped device context
- ✦ Flicker-free activation
- ✦ Mouse pointer notifications when inactive
- ✦ Optimized drawing code
- ✦ Loads properties asynchronously

Click OK to confirm the selection and close the dialog.

Select the `MFCControlNoWin` control, and click the Advanced button again. You are going to implement `MFCControlNoWin` as a windowless control just to get a feel for the difference between the windowed and windowless control implementations in MFC. From the Advanced ActiveX Features dialog, select only the following options:

- ✦ Windowless activation
- ✦ Mouse pointer notifications when inactive
- ✦ Optimized drawing code
- ✦ Loads properties asynchronously

Table 31-1
Advanced ActiveX Features

ActiveX Feature	*Description*
Windowless activation	Enables calling programs to instantiate the control without having to create a window for the control itself. In other words, the control relies on the container to create the window.
Unclipped device context	Used for controls that guarantee they will not draw outside their client area and results in disabling MFC clipping tests for the control. You cannot use this option with a windowless control.
Flicker-free activation	Used for controls that appear the same to the user whether the control is in an active or inactive state. Selecting this feature eliminates some of the flicker associated with changing states between the active and inactive states of a control. You cannot use this option with a windowless control.
Mouse pointer notifications when inactive	Enables control to receive mouse messages, even though the control is in an inactive state.
Optimized drawing code	Enables the control to draw its user interface in an optimized fashion if the container supports optimized drawing; otherwise, the control must be drawn using standard drawing techniques.
Loads properties asynchronously	Asynchronous properties are properties that load in the background and involve the transfer of a large amount of data. The properties are loaded in the background to prevent the container and the control from being disabled or inactive for too long while waiting for the data to load.

Click OK to confirm the selections and close the dialog.

For your third and final control, you will subclass an existing window's control. Be sure to select the control `MFCControlSubWin`, and in the subclassing list box, select BUTTON. Do not define any advanced ActiveX features for this control.

The MFC ActiveX ControlWizard — Step 2 of 2 dialog box also provides other features for further defining your control project. For the sample project, leave the values in their default state. For more information regarding other available options, you can review the Visual C++ documentation.

Click the Finish button on the ControlWizard dialog to complete the feature selection process. You confirm the choices you made in the New Project Information dialog box, shown in Figure 31-3.

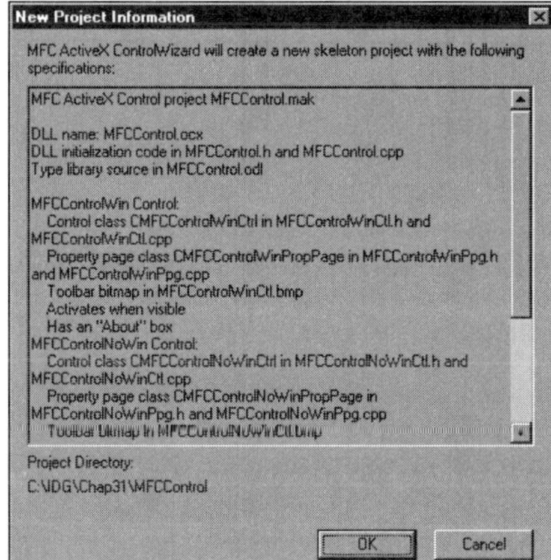

Figure 31-3: The New Project Information dialog box after you finish designing the project

After you verify that your selections are correct, click the OK button to generate the source files and the MFC control project. The first step in any control project is to ensure that it contains registration support. Without registration, no application can use the control.

Control registration

Control registration and unregistration support is provided by MFC. You are not required to make any code changes or additions to support it. Listing 31-1 shows the `UpdateRegistry()` function that the AppWizard created for the control `CMFCControlWinCtrl`. As you might expect, AppWizard created a registration function for each control.

Of special interest in the program code is the comment from Microsoft at the beginning of the code, regarding apartment model threading and how you should register your control if you know it does not conform to apartment model rules. Other than that very specific case, you will not have to make any changes to your application or this function when it comes to control registration. In fact, you can now compile and register the control you have created, but it will not be of much use because it does not contain methods, properties, or events, which are the basis of every ActiveX control.

Listing 31-1: The UpdateRegistry() Function that AppWizard Automatically Creates for the Control

```
///////////////////////////////////////////////////////////////
/* CMFCControlWinCtrl::CMFCControlWinCtrlFactory::
   UpdateRegistry - Adds or removes system registry entries
   for CMFCControlWinCtrl */

BOOL CMFCControlWinCtrl::CMFCControlWinCtrlFactory::
    UpdateRegistry(BOOLbRegister)
{

// TODO: Verify your control follows apartment-model threading
// rules.
// Refer to MFC TechNote 64 for more information.
// If your control doesn't conform to these rules, then
// you must modify the code below, changing the 6th parameter
// from afxRegApartmentThreading to 0.

   if (bRegister)
     return AfxOleRegisterControlClass(
         AfxGetInstanceHandle(),
         m_clsid, m_lpszProgID, IDS_MFCCONTROLWIN,
         IDB_MFCCONTROLWIN, afxRegApartmentThreading,
         _dwMFCControlWinOleMisc, _tlid, _wVerMajor,
         _wVerMinor);
   else
     return AfxOleUnregisterClass(m_clsid, m_lpszProgID);
 }
```

Creating methods

Now that you've successfully created your ActiveX control project, you can start off by adding a *method*, which is one of the basic requirements of component development. A method is, essentially, an encapsulated function within the control that you invoke just as you would a publicly exposed function of a class.

For the purposes of the sample control, you are going to add a method called `CaptionMethod()`. The method will accept two parameters, the second one being optional. The first parameter is a string that the control will display within its client area, and the second, optional parameter affects the alignment of the caption within the client area, either left, right, or center. To create your first method, select the View menu ClassWizard option. Visual C++ will display the MFC ClassWizard dialog box. In the MFC ClassWizard dialog box, select the Automation tab.

From the Class Name drop-down list box, select the `CMFCControlWinCtrl` class, and click the Add Method button to create a new method. Enter `CaptionMethod` in the External Name combo box as the method's name, and set the method's Return type to long. Add two parameters by clicking the appropriate column in the Parameter List control. Name the first parameter lpctstrCaption of type LPCTSTR, and name the second, as your optional parameter, varAlignment of type VARIANT. Click the OK button to add the method to the class. Next, click the OK button to close the ClassWizard dialog.

All optional parameters must be of type VARIANT, and they must fall at the end of the parameter list. Optional parameters are not managed in any way by OLE. It is the server application's responsibility to determine whether the VARIANT parameter passed to the method contains data, and to do one of the following:

- ✦ Use the data passed to the method or convert the data to a useful type, if possible.
- ✦ Ignore the parameter if invalid data was passed, and use the default value if appropriate.
- ✦ Inform the user of an error condition if one of the preceding conditions was not met.

To aid your CaptionMethod() implementation, you must add an enumeration for all the valid alignment settings and two member variables to your class definition. You must add a reference to the enumeration to the MFCCONTROLWINCTL.H class header file, as shown here:

```
/* MFCControlWinCtl.h : Declaration
     oftheCMFCControlWinCtrlActiveXControl */

#include "alignmentenums.h"

/////////////////////////////////////////////////////////////////
// CMFCControlWinCtrl: See MFCControlWinCtl.cpp for
// implementation.

class CMFCControlWinCtrl : public COleControl
 {
   // other code here
protected:
   // storage variable for the caption
   CString m_cstrCaption;
   // storage variable for the alignment
   long m_lAlignment;
 };
```

The control class uses the two member variables, m_cstrCaption and m_lAlignment, to store the caption string and the alignment setting while the container is using the control. Note the type used for the m_lAlignment member variable. The variable is declared as type long and not as the enumeration type because of the data type restrictions that are imposed upon you by ActiveX Automation. Remember that only data types that can be passed in a VARIANT can be used in methods and properties. By declaring the m_lAlignment member variable as long, you do not have to explicitly convert the value by casting to the enumerated type when it is retrieved from the VARIANT parameter in the CaptionMethod() method. On the other hand, casting the value to the enumerated type is a trivial issue and is completely up to you to implement if you desire to do so.

You add the enumeration definition as a header file so that you can also reference the enumeration from other files, which will be necessary as you continue to design the program code. You include the enumeration within the header file Alignmentenums.h, as shown here:

```
#if !defined _ALIGNMENTENUMS_H
#define _ALIGNMENTENUMS_H

// caption alignment enumeration

typedef enum tagAlignmentEnum
 {
   EALIGN_LEFT = 0,
   EALIGN_CENTER = 1,
   EALIGN_RIGHT = 2,
 } EALIGNMENT;

#endif // #if !defined _ALIGNMENTENUMS_H
```

After you finish the design of the header file, open the MFCControlWinCtl.cpp file, and in the constructor, initialize the m_Alignment member variable to the value EALIGN_LEFT as shown in the following code:

```
////////////////////////////////////////////////////////////////
// CMFCControlWinCtrl::CMFCControlWinCtrl - Constructor

CMFCControlWinCtrl::CMFCControlWinCtrl()
 {
   InitializeIIDs(&IID_DMFCControlWin,
       &IID_DMFCControlWinEvents);
   m_lReadyState = READYSTATE_LOADING;

   // TODO: Call InternalSetReadyState when the readystate
   // changes.

   // set the alignment to the default of left
   m_lAlignment = EALIGN_LEFT;
 }
```

The CaptionMethod method contains all of the code for setting the caption and the alignment style and does several things of interest that you must consider. Listing 31-2 implements the CaptionMethod() function.

Listing 31-2: Implementing the CaptionMethod() Function

```
long CMFCControlWinCtrl::CaptionMethod(LPCTSTR lpctstrCaption,
    const VARIANT FAR& varAlignment)
 {
   // return value initialized to failure result
   long lResult = FALSE;

   // if the variant is a long just use the value
   if(VT_I4 == varAlignment.vt)
    {
      // assign the value to our member variable
      m_lAlignment = varAlignment.lVal;
      // set the return value
      lResult = TRUE;
    }
   // if the user didn't supply an alignment parameter,
   // use whatever is already there

   else if(VT_ERROR == varAlignment.vt || VT_EMPTY ==
         varAlignment.vt)
      {
         // set the return value
         lResult = TRUE;
      }
     else
      {
         // get a variant to use for conversion purposes
         VARIANT varConvertedValue;

         // initialize the variant
         ::VariantInit(&varConvertedValue);

         // try to convert the data type to something useful -
         // you could also use VariantChangeTypeEx()
         if(S_OK == ::VariantChangeType(&varConvertedValue,
             (VARIANT *) &varAlignment, 0, VT_I4))
          {
            // assign the value to our member variable
            switch(varConvertedValue.lVal)
             {
               case EALIGN_CENTER:
                   m_lAlignment = EALIGN_CENTER;
                   break;

               case EALIGN_RIGHT:
                   m_lAlignment = EALIGN_RIGHT;
                   break;
               default:
                   m_lAlignment = EALIGN_LEFT;
                   break;
```

(continued)

Listing 31-2 (continued)

```
                }
                // set the return value
                lResult = TRUE;
            }
        else
            {
                /* at this point you can either throw an error
                   that indicates there was a problem converting
                   the data or change the return type of the
                   method and return the HRESULT value from the
                   the "VariantChangeType" call. */
            }
        }
    // if the alignment value is invalid
    if(m_lAlignment < EALIGN_LEFT ||
        m_lAlignment > EALIGN_RIGHT)
      // set to the default value
      m_lAlignment = EALIGN_LEFT;

    // if everything was OK
    if(TRUE == lResult)
     {
       // if we have a string
       if(lpctstrCaption != NULL)
         // assign the string to our member variable
         m_cstrCaption = lpctstrCaption;

       // did they pass us bad data?
       if(m_lAlignment < EALIGN_LEFT ||
           m_lAlignment > EALIGN_RIGHT)
         // sure did, use the default
         m_lAlignment = EALIGN_LEFT;

       // force the control to repaint itself
       this->InvalidateControl();
     }
    // return the result of the function call
    return lResult;
}
```

First, the method tries to deal with the optional parameter by looking for the data type the control really wants, VT_I4, which is a data type of long. If the VARIANT parameter does not contain a long, the method then checks to see if any data was passed at all by checking for VT_ERROR or VT_EMPTY. Checking for data is a necessary step because the parameter is optional. A VARIANT parameter can either contain data or not. It is important to check VARIANT data types not only for valid data but also for the actual existence of data. If no data was supplied, the method relies on the value already contained in the m_lAlignment class member variable.

Some automation controllers, such as Visual Basic, do not require that any or all of the optional parameters be supplied when calling a method. For example, from Visual Basic, you can call the `CaptionMethod()` method as shown here:

```
MyObject.CaptionMethod "Hello"
```

Or, alternately, as shown here:

```
MyObject.CaptionMethod "Hello", True
```

Visual Basic automatically passes in a `VARIANT` set to the type `VT_ERROR` for any parameters that the calling container omits from a method call. For automation controllers that call the standard OLE `Invoke()` method, such as C++, the calling controller *must* define all the parameters, even though the control or the container may not use the parameter. In this particular case, when he calls the method, the programmer has the option of setting the `VARIANT` type to `VT_ERROR` or `VT_EMPTY`.

When processing optional parameters, relying on the OLE `VARIANT` conversion routines in addition to looking for specific `VARIANT` data types guarantees that your control can handle any data passed to it.

◆ ◆ ◆ ◆ ◆

If the `VARIANT` is of a valid data type other than `VT_I4`, the method tries to convert it to a `VT_I4` type. This step handles cases where a user passes valid data in the form of a different data type — for example, a `short` or a string.

Note the use of the function `VariantInit()`. It is very important that your programs initialize *all* `VARIANT` variables prior to their use. This practice guarantees that the `VARIANT` does not contain invalid data type information or invalid values. Calling `VariantInit()` to initialize your `VARIANT` variables follows the basic C++ tenet of initializing all member variables to ensure that they do not contain invalid information.

If the requirements of your control demand that you deal with only specific data types, you can also add code (error messages, exceptions, and so on) to deal with the fact that the method did not receive a valid data type. In the case of the `CaptionMethod()` method, if the function `VariantChangeType()` was unable to convert the data, the method exits and returns a value of `FALSE`. A return of `FALSE` indicates to the caller of the method that the method did not succeed. Again, you can add additional error-handling code to the method to give the user more information about the error that occurred.

Before proceeding, the method ensures that the `m_lAlignment` member variable contains valid data. If the method received valid data, or converted the data to a valid value, it indicates so by setting the variable `lResult` to equal `TRUE`. The program code evaluates `lResult`. If it contains `TRUE`, the method code stores the caption and the alignment values in the class member variables, invalidates the control so it redraws its user interface based on the new information, and exits the function.

To complete your implementation of the `CaptionMethod()` function, you must modify the ODL file. When methods, properties, and events are added to a class with the ControlWizard, the ODL file is also updated with the new entries. The ODL file is compiled into a type library, which is essentially a description of the component and its interfaces that can be used by other applications to access the component. You need to add the keyword `[optional]` to the last parameter in the `CaptionMethod()` method in the ODL file. Doing so informs the container application that the last parameter is optional and should be dealt with accordingly. The following code shows how to implement the keyword change within the `MFCCONTROL.ODL` file:

```
// Other code here

 methods:
   // NOTE - ClassWizard maintains method information here.
   // Use extreme caution when editing this section.
   //{{AFX_ODL_METHOD(CMFCControlWinCtrl)
   [id(1)] long CaptionMethod(BSTR lpctstrCaption,
       [optional] VARIANT varAlignment);
   //}}AFX_ODL_METHOD

// other code here
```

You should be very careful when you modify the ODL file by hand. The ODL file must match your implementation exactly. If you change the file incorrectly, it can introduce strange bugs and/or implementation problems with your component. The ClassWizard automatically updates the ODL file when you add or remove methods, properties, and events to or from the control. Adding or removing information from the ODL could prevent the ClassWizard from correctly managing the file. Keywords such as `[optional]` do not affect the ClassWizard and its capability to automatically update the file when changes are made to a class.

✦ ✦ ✦ ✦ ✦

Properties

Properties can be categorized as user defined, stock, or ambient. *User-defined properties* are properties that are implementation specific and have meaning only to the component that contains them. User-defined properties can be further broken into those properties that are defined only as their specific data type (*normal properties*) and those with additional parameters (*parameterized properties*). *Stock properties* are a set of properties that are already defined by OLE in terms of the basic meaning. Stock properties are not implemented in the control of the container by default. They still require implementation by the control developer. They are predefined only to imply a certain level of uniformity between various control implementations. *Ambient properties,* on the other hand, are properties that are supported by the container to provide a default value to the control that uses them. In the remainder of this chapter, you will create three types of properties: normal, parameterized, and stock. You will also learn how to use ambient properties.

Creating normal user-defined properties

A *normal property* is a property that is declared as a single type, for example, long or BSTR, and has no parameters. You expose your controls' Alignment member variable through a property. Properties are added in much the same way as methods. To add a property to the control, open the ClassWizard, select the class CMFCControlWinCtrl, switch to the Automation tab, and click the Add Property button. In the Add Property dialog box, set the External name to Alignment, the Type to long, and the Implementation to Get/Set methods. Click the OK button to confirm your entries and close the dialog.

Next, double-click the Alignment property entry in the External name list box to open the source file so you can add your code to the Get/Set methods. As you can see, the code within the GetAlignment() function takes advantage of the member variable m_Alignment, which you added earlier, and uses it to get and set the property value. You will implement the GetAlignment() function as shown in the following code listing:

```
long CMFCControlWinCtrl::GetAlignment()
 {
   // return the current setting
   return m_lAlignment;
}
```

The GetAlignment() function is simple in that it returns only the value stored in the m_lAlignment member variable. The SetAlignment() function performs similar processing, except it receives an incoming long value and assigns it to the m_lAlignment member variable. You implement the SetAlignment() function as shown in the following code listing:

```
void CMFCControlWinCtrl::SetAlignment(long nNewValue)
 {
   // check incoming is in the valid range for the property
   if(nNewValue >= EALIGN_LEFT && nNewValue <= EALIGN_RIGHT)
    {
      // set the new property value
      m_lAlignment = nNewValue;

      // let the control know that the property has changed
      this->SetModifiedFlag();

      // refresh the property browser
      this->BoundPropertyChanged(dispidAlignment);

      // redraw the control
      this->InvalidateControl();
    }
 }
```

The SetAlignment() function, as you can see, does a little more than the GetAlignment() function did. First, the function checks to see if the value is within the valid ranges of values and, if so, stores the value in the m_lAlignment member variable. The function then calls the `SetModifiedFlag()` and the `BoundPropertyChanged()` functions to notify the control and the container, respectively, that the value of the property has changed. `BoundPropertyChanged()` has the effect of forcing the container to refresh its property browser to reflect the new value. Alerting the container is very important because the value of the property could change without the container's knowledge, either through the control's property sheet or, in some cases, in response to another function call. You did not add `BoundPropertyChanged()` to the `CaptionMethod` method because, while you could have, it would not do much good because the container can never execute the `CaptionMethod` member function while the control is in design mode, which is the purpose of `BoundPropertyChanged()`.

Finally, the `SetAlignment()` method invalidates the control's user interface so it will repaint using the new information.

Even though a property appears as a single member of an object, it is really a pair of related functions used to operate on a single piece of data. The ODL entries for a property will differ depending on its implementation.

For interfaces inherited from a `dispinterface` class, it is enough to have a single entry in the properties section of the class. `IDispatch` inherited interfaces will define two separate functions: one declared as `propertyget`, and the other defined as `propertyput`, both sharing the same `dispid`. You always define parameterized properties using the latter method because it is impossible to define the additional parameters without a method declaration.

The `dispinterface` keyword is a specific convention for defining `IDispatch`-based interfaces in a more C++-like fashion, as opposed to the standard `IDispatch` style, which would be entered as one variable entry versus two method entries. For more information regarding the use of `dispinterface` and other ODL keywords, see the ODL documentation Microsoft generously provides with the Visual C++ compiler.

✦ ✦ ✦ ✦ ✦

MFC and the ClassWizard provide another option when declaring properties — that is, by member variable. MFC adds a member variable of the appropriate type to the class declaration and provides a notification function if the data changes. The notification message is defined as `Onvariable_nameChanged()` and is added to the source file of the control. If you had chosen this method for the Alignment member, the function would have been called `OnAlignmentChanged()` and would have been implemented in the `MFCControlWinCtl.cpp` file. The variable style results in less code to write, but it also results in less flexibility because MFC manages all of the Get/Set property code for you. Feel free to experiment with both methods of property creation to get a feel for your best option — and remember, the more MFC-dependent your controls are, the more difficult it is to convert them to another control-creation style such as ATL.

Creating parameterized user-defined properties

A *parameterized property* is a property that, in addition to being of a specific type (for example, BSTR or long), accepts one or more additional parameters to further define the data of the property. Parameterized properties can be useful for properties that represent collections of data where the additional parameter is the index into the collection. You are going to expose the control's m_cstrCaption member variable as a parameterized property in addition to your CaptionMethod() function.

In the ClassWizard's Add Property dialog box, define the External name as CaptionProp, its Type as BSTR, and its Implementation as Get/Set methods. In addition, add a parameter called varAlignment of type VARIANT to the Parameter list box. Click the OK button to add the property to the class. Next, close the ClassWizard so you can add some code to your property. The implementation of the property CaptionProp has two methods: GetCaptionProp() and SetCaptionProp().

GetCaptionProp() is the method that the control calls to return data from the property to the calling container. In your implementation, you should ignore the varAlignment parameter because it is of no use to you in this context. Instead, you simply return the caption. You implement the GetCaptionProp() method within the MFCCONTROLWINCTL.CPP file as shown here:

```
BSTR CMFCControlWinCtrl::
     GetCaptionProp(const VARIANT FAR& varAlignment)
  {
    // return the caption as a BSTR
    return m_cstrCaption.AllocSysString();
  }
```

The GetCaptionProp() method uses the CString function AllocSysString() to create a BSTR, which is essentially a UNICODE string, that the function call returns. SetCaptionProp() simply defers to the CaptionMethod() implementation because the CaptionMethod() function already does everything that you need for SetCaptionProp() to do, as shown here:

```
void CMFCControlWinCtrl::SetCaptionProp
     (const VARIANT FAR& varAlignment, LPCTSTR lpszNewValue)
  {
    // use the "CaptionMethod" implementation
    if(TRUE == this->CaptionMethod(lpszNewValue, varAlignment))
      // let the container know that the property has changed
      this->SetModifiedFlag();
  }
```

Your final detail to set the properties is within the ODL file. You are going to make the VARIANT parameter, varAlignment, an optional parameter for the GetCaptionProp() and SetCaptionProp() implementations. You can make the varAlignment parameter optional for the SetCaptionProp() implementation because the varAlignment variable is the last in the list of actual parameters. The

BSTR lpszNewValue variable is actually the data type of the property function pairs and does not affect the parameter definition rules. You will implement the MFCCONTROL.ODL file as shown in the following code:

```
// more code here

methods:
   /* NOTE - ClassWizard will maintain method information
      here. Use extreme caution when editing this section. */
   //{{AFX_ODL_METHOD(CMFCControlWinCtrl)
   [id(2)] long CaptionMethod(BSTR lpctstrCaption,
       [optional]   VARIANT varAlignment);
   [id(3), propget] BSTR CaptionProp([optional] VARIANT
       varAlignment);
   [id(3), propput] void CaptionProp([optional] VARIANT
       varAlignment, BSTR lpszNewValue);
   //}}AFX_ODL_METHOD

//more code here
```

Because of the parameters they contain, parameterized properties are defined in the methods section of the dispinterface declaration of an object. All properties are implemented using the dual method style in IDispatch-based interfaces regardless of whether or not the property is parameterized. Only dispinterfaces contain a separate property and method section in the ODL. And only dispinterfaces enable properties to be declared as a single line entry in the ODL file.

✦ ✦ ✦ ✦ ✦

Creating stock properties

A *stock property* is a property that is understood by both a control and its container and that has a predefined meaning to both. Stock properties are intended to provide basic uniform functionality to all the controls and containers that implement them. Stock properties do not require you to implement a lot of code. Rather, you just hook the stock property into the existing property. Adding stock properties is similar to adding user-defined properties. Open the ClassWizard, and select the Automation tab. Within the Automation tab, select the class CMFCControlWinCtrl, and click the Add Property button. Instead of typing an External name this time, however, you will select one from the list the ClassWizard provides. Your stock property is the BackColor property. Select the Stock Implementation, and click OK to add the property to the class.

The BackColor property now appears in your property list and persists with all your other properties. Whenever you need the value of a stock property, you can query the container for the property with one of the stock property functions. In your case, you can use the function GetBackColor(). All of the stock properties have an associated Get/Set function pair. In addition to the default stock implementation style, you can support a member variable implementation. This option eliminates the need to query the container for the property but forces you to carry the value with you at all times, adding to your instance size.

You can also support the Get/Set implementation method and store or use the value in any way you see fit, but this option also requires additional code. The default stock implementation is obviously the easiest to implement because MFC does all the work.

Using ambient properties

Ambient properties are properties implemented in the container in which the control resides, as opposed to *stock properties,* which are implemented in the control and not the container. Ambient properties share the same set of predefined meanings and dispids as those of stock properties. A *dispid* is the unique identifier that is used to identify the property within an interface. To use an ambient property, the control need request only the property value from the container and apply it in whatever manner is appropriate for the property type. The use of ambient properties enables the control to conform to the same settings as those of the container in which it resides. This provides much better integration between the control and its container.

Take the previous example of adding the BackColor stock property to the sample control implementation. Because BackColor is defined as a stock property, the user of the control can change the background color of the control or leave it as is. If the color is different from that of the container or if the container's background color changes for some reason, the colors won't match, giving the appearance of a poorly integrated and written application. However, if the control simply used the ambient background color of its container, the control's background will always match that of the container. The specific requirements of your control implementation will decide which route you choose when implementing the properties your control supports.

To access an ambient property, you can call one of the many ambient property functions defined in the COleControl class, for example, AmbientBackColor(), or use the function GetAmbientProperty() to access the value, as shown here:

```
this->GetAmbientProperty(DISPID_BACKCOLOR, VT_COLOR,
    &varBackColor);
```

The GetAmbientProperty() function takes a dispid as its first parameter. The dispid must be one of those MFC defines. You can find a complete list of dispids within the MFC source files. The second parameter is the VARIANT data type that the program is requesting, and the third parameter is a VARIANT variable into which GetAmbientProperty() stores the data.

Creating property sheets

Property sheets are a way for a control to display its properties for review and editing and are typically implemented in a tabbed dialog format. You worked with property sheets in Chapter 14. The original intent of property sheets was for use in cases when a control container did not support property browsing facilities. While property sheets have their purpose, they are probably not necessary for all implementations. Removing the property sheets from your control implementation definitely reduces the size of your control and does not, in most cases, take away from its implementation.

Because property sheets are tabbed dialogs, most of your work will be done with the dialog editor and the ClassWizard. Select the Resource View in the Project Workspace window. From the list of dialogs, select `IDD_PROPPAGE_MFCCONTROLWIN`, and double-click the entry to open the resource editor.

Using the resource editor, remove the static text control with the caption `TODO`, and place a static text control and a combo box control on the dialog. Using the mouse, select the label control on the form, and click the right mouse button. In the menu that Visual Studio displays, select the Properties menu item. On the General tab, set the ID of the control to `IDC_ALIGNMENTLABEL`, and set the Caption to Alignment. Select the Styles tab, and set the Align Text property to Right. Close the dialog box to save the information.

Next, again using the mouse, select the combo box, use the right mouse button to click the control, and in the menu that appears, select the Properties menu item. On the General tab, set the ID of the control to `IDC_ALIGNMENTCOMBO`. On the Styles tab, set the Type to drop-down list box, and uncheck the Sort check box. Close the dialog box to save the information.

You have placed your two controls onto the property sheets and successfully modified their properties. Now you need to add some code to complete the implementation. Close the resource editor, and open the ClassWizard. Select the `CMFCControlWinPropPage` class, and select the Member Variables tab. In the Control ID's combo box, select the `IDC_ALIGNMENTCOMBO` item, and click the Add Variable button. Visual Studio will display the Add Member Variable dialog box. Within the Add Member Variable dialog box, set the Member variable name to `m_AlignmentCombo` and the Category to Control. Click the OK button to confirm the information and close the dialog box.

You've added a member variable for the control. Now you must add one for the data. Click the Add Variable button again, and set the Member variable name to `m_AlignmentValue`. Set the Category to Value and the Variable type to `int`. Click the OK button to confirm the changes and close the dialog box. Close the MFC ClassWizard dialog box to confirm the new member variables.

Within the source code, the `DoDataExchange()` function is where you are going to add the code to manage the data between the control and the property sheet. Open the source file `MFCControlWinPpg.cpp`, and locate the `DoDataExchange()` function. Notice that the ClassWizard added two lines of code to the original implementation of the `DoDataExchange()` function, as shown here:

```
void CMFCControlWinPropPage:
    :DoDataExchange(CDataExchange* pDX)
 {
   //{{AFX_DATA_MAP(CMFCControlWinPropPage)
   DDX_Control(pDX, IDC_ALIGNMENTCOMBO, m_AlignmentCombo);
```

```
    DDX_CBIndex(pDX, IDC_ALIGNMENTCOMBO, m_AlignmentValue);
    //}}AFX_DATA_MAP
    DDP_PostProcessing(pDX);
}
```

DDX_Control is the standard MFC macro for loading a control into an MFC class member. DDX_CBIndex is a standard MFC function for getting and setting the current index in a combo box using the variable supplied (in this case, m_AlignmentValue). You must change this implementation slightly to fully bind your control and property sheet, as shown in the following code:

```
void CMFCControlWinPropPage::
    DoDataExchange(CDataExchange* pDX)
{
    //{{AFX_DATA_MAP(CMFCControlWinPropPage)
    DDX_Control(pDX, IDC_ALIGNMENTCOMBO, m_AlignmentCombo);
    //}}AFX_DATA_MAP
    if(!pDX->m_bSaveAndValidate)
     {
       // make sure that we have cleared the list
       m_AlignmentCombo.ResetContent();
       m_AlignmentCombo.AddString(_T("Left"));
       m_AlignmentCombo.AddString(_T("Center"));
       m_AlignmentCombo.AddString(_T("Right"));
     }
    DDP_CBIndex(pDX, IDC_ALIGNMENTCOMBO, m_AlignmentValue,
        _T("Alignment"));
    DDX_CBIndex(pDX, IDC_ALIGNMENTCOMBO, m_AlignmentValue);
    DDP_PostProcessing(pDX);
    this->SetModifiedFlag();
```

Your modified function performs significantly more processing than the original. First, it loads the combo box with valid property data so that the property sheet matches the property values in the control and the property browser. The function next loads the combo box with only the valid choices if the DoDataExchange() function is being executed the first time by checking the m_bSaveAndValidate member variable. In other words, the code makes sure the property dialog is not saving and validating the data it contains.

To support communication between the control and the property sheet, you need to add DDP_CBIndex() before the DDX_CBIndex() line. DDP_CBIndex() instructs MFC to obtain the Alignment property value from the control and store it in the m_lAlignment member variable of the property dialog when the dialog is loading. When the property dialog is unloading, DDP_CBIndex() retrieves the current index of the combo box and sets the Alignment property of the control to the new value. DDP_CBIndex() must be before the DDX_CBIndex() function. Otherwise, the property sheet will not correctly reflect the values of the properties in the control.

It is worth noting that this property dialog box has specific implementation requirements. In other words, the class loads the list box control into the m_AlignmentCombo member variable of the class, and it is necessary to load the combo box selection list prior to setting the current selected entry in the list. Because of the property dialog box's special implementation, you had to move the DDP_CBIndex() and DDX_CBIndex() lines from between the MFC AFX_DATA_MAP macros to after the macros. Doing so enables the setting of the entries. Separating the lines in this fashion is not required in order to implement the DDX_CBIndex() and DDP_CBIndex() lines in most cases. It is, however, the only way to solve this particular problem.

When you remove the DDX_CBIndex() and DDPCBIndex() lines from between the MFC macros, they no longer appear as a member variable in the ClassWizard and are not managed automatically by Visual C++ and the ClassWizard.

◆ ◆ ◆ ◆ ◆

As you learned earlier in this chapter, you must add a BoundPropertyChanged() call to your SetAlignment() function for the property browser within the container (for example, Microsoft Visual Basic's property list window) to accurately reflect the property value after the user changes it within the property sheet. This action notifies the property browser that the value has changed and that it should be retrieved again. You will implement the SetAlignment() function as shown here:

```
void CMFCControlWinCtrl::SetAlignment(long nNewValue)
 {
   // check that the value is in the valid range
   if(nNewValue >= EALIGN_LEFT && nNewValue <= EALIGN_RIGHT)
    {
      // set the new property value
      m_lAlignment = nNewValue;

      // let the control know that the property has changed
      this->SetModifiedFlag();

      // refresh the property browser
      this->BoundPropertyChanged(dispidAlignment);

      // redraw the control
      this->InvalidateControl();
    }
 }
```

The only thing remaining is to set the default value of the member variable m_AlignmentValue to a meaningful value. First, add the include file entry to the MFCCONTROLWINPPG.CPP class file as shown here:

```
#include "MFCControlWinCtl.h"
```

Adding the include file entry enables the compiler to resolve the EALIGN_LEFT constant. Next, you must initialize the m_AlignmentValue member variable in the constructor to a value of EALIGN_LEFT, as shown here:

```
/* MFCControlWinPpg.cpp : Implementation of the
   CMFCControlWinPropPage property page class. */

#include "stdafx.h"
#include "MFCControl.h"
#include "MFCControlWinCtl.h"
#include "MFCControlWinPpg.h"

// more code here

   CMFCControlWinPropPage::CMFCControlWinPropPage() :
      COlePropertyPage(IDD, IDS_MFCCONTROLWIN_PPG_CAPTION)
    {
      //{{AFX_DATA_INIT(CMFCControlWinPropPage)
      m_AlignmentValue = EALIGN_LEFT;
      //}}AFX_DATA_INIT
    }
```

Adding events

Properties and methods are a way for a programmer to communicate with a control from within the container application. Events are a way for the control to communicate with the container. For ActiveX controls, events are nothing more than IDispatch interfaces that are implemented on the container side of the container-control relationship. The mechanism that events are based on is known as a *connection point.* A connection point is simply a description of the type of interface that is required in order to communicate with the container. Connection points are not restricted to only IDispatch interfaces, but rather they can be of any COM interface that is understood by both components. For that matter, connection points and events are not restricted only to controls, they can be used in any COM implementation. Controls were simply the first to take advantage of them. For more information regarding connection points, refer to the documentation in the OLE online help that comes with Visual Studio.

As with methods and properties, events are added and removed with the ClassWizard. To add an event, open the ClassWizard, and select the ActiveX Events tab. Within the ActiveX Events tab, select the CMFCControlWinCtrl class, and click the Add Event button. As with properties, you can choose from a list of predefined events or add your own. For the CMFCControlWinCtrl class you are going to add a Change event, and it will have two parameters. The first parameter will be a string, passed by reference (BSTR *), called cstrCaption. The second will be a long, also passed by reference (long *), called lAlignment. You are passing the parameters by reference to enable the container application the opportunity to change the values if necessary.

Click the OK button to add the event to the class. Before you use your event, you are going to create a common FireChange() function that encapsulates the code that deals with the cases where the program has changed the data passed to the event. Close the MFC ClassWizard dialog box to confirm the addition of the event to the class.

You need to add your function prototype to the class definition in the header file. In addition, you need to add the implementation to the source file. You add the prototype to the header file as shown here:

```
// more code here

protected:
   // storage variable for the caption
   CString m_cstrCaption;

   // storage variable for the alignment
   long m_lAlignment;
   void FireChange(void);
};
```

After you add the prototype to the header file, you must add the implementation to the class file. You will add the following code to the class file:

```
void CMFCControlWinCtrl::FireChange(void)
{
   // get a BSTR that can be passed via the event
   BSTR bstrCaption = m_cstrCaption.AllocSysString();

   // fire the change event
   this->FireChange(&bstrCaption, &m_lAlignment);

   // let's see what the user gave us
   m_cstrCaption = bstrCaption;

   // free the data that was passed back
   ::SysFreeString(bstrCaption);
}
```

The control is responsible for the data that is passed in to the event, so be sure to free the BSTR that was passed in when the function has returned to prevent a memory leak.

◆ ◆ ◆ ◆ ◆

The common FireChange() function enables you to hide the details surrounding the change event from the rest of the program. If you decide in the future to change the change event's implementation, it will impact only one function rather than a number of them.

The CaptionMethod() method requires that you fire a change event if the data changes, so you must add a reference to your new event there, immediately before you invoke InvalidateControl(). You will also want to add it to the SetAlignment() function. However, make sure you do not add an invocation of FireChange() to the SetCaptionProp() function because it defers to the CaptionMethod() function. In addition, do not forget to add the function to any new functions or features that you add to the control as its implementation progresses.

Persistence

Persistence refers to a component's capability to retain its state across execution lifetimes. In other words, regardless of the number of times that the control is started and stopped, it remembers that you changed its background color from white to celidon. The implementation of persistence, for MFC controls, is a no-brainer consisting of very little code. Simply add a single line to the DoPropExchange() method of your control for each one of your properties, and you are finished. You can get a little fancier and persist the properties differently, depending on whether you are saving or loading the properties, but that isn't real complicated either.

To persist the properties within your control, modify your DoPropExchange() function to persist the two member variables m_lAlignment and m_cstrCaption. You can implement the persistence in two ways. The first, and the simplest, is to add one entry for each property without regard for order or dependencies. *Dependencies* refers to the fact that as your control implementation gets more complicated or requires a larger number of properties, you may find that how or when certain properties are persisted can depend on other properties.

When you specify the default value in your persistence entries, never use the same variable as the one that is going to receive the data. The MFC persistence functions are optimized so that if the value being persisted has not changed compared to the default value, the function will not persist the value. This is to save time and space when loading or saving the persistence information. If you use the same variable, MFC thinks that the value has never changed because the MFC persistence routines perform simple address and memory comparisons. Use constants for your default persistence information, because that is what the routines expect.

◆ ◆ ◆ ◆ ◆

The simplest way to persist the properties is to call the appropriate PX_ function for the property's type. You can use the same method for each property regardless of the direction of the persistence. In other words, when you are loading or saving, MFC handles all those details for you — unlike when you are serializing data from a document. You implement the persistent DoPropExchange() function as shown here:

```
void CMFCControlWinCtrl::DoPropExchange(CPropExchange* pPX)
 {
   ExchangeVersion(pPX, MAKELONG(_wVerMinor, _wVerMajor));
   COleControl::DoPropExchange(pPX);

   // TODO: Call PX_ functions for each persistent property.

   PX_Long(pPX, _T("Alignment"), m_lAlignment, EALIGN_LEFT);
   PX_String(pPX, _T("CaptionProp"), m_cstrCaption, _T(""));
 }
```

Alternatively, if you wanted to load your properties first and then perform some implementation-specific action (and perform similar processing when saving the properties), you must implement the persistence slightly differently. The requirement to specifically order the persistence process is highly subjective and depends greatly on your implementation. In such cases, you might implement your persisting actions as shown in Listing 31-3.

Listing 31-3: Sample Code for the DoPropExchange() Function to Support Persistence within Your Controls

```
void CMFCControlWinCtrl::DoPropExchange(CPropExchange* pPX)
 {
   ExchangeVersion(pPX, MAKELONG(_wVerMinor, _wVerMajor));
   COleControl::DoPropExchange(pPX);
   // TODO: Call PX_ functions for each persistent property.
   // if loading the properties
   if(pPX->IsLoading())
    {
     PX_Long(pPX, _T("Alignment"), m_lAlignment,
         EALIGN_LEFT);
     PX_String(pPX, _T("CaptionProp"),
         m_cstrCaption, _T(""));
    }

   // if saving the properties
   if(!pPX->IsLoading())
    {
     PX_Long(pPX, _T("Alignment"), m_lAlignment,
         EALIGN_LEFT);
     PX_String(pPX, _T("CaptionProp"),
         m_cstrCaption, _T(""));
    }
 }
```

If your control contains stock properties, you must call the base class implementation `COleControl::DoPropExchange()` to support their persistence. The base class implementation does not provide much room for flexibility, though, and you may find yourself in more need of control than is allowed.

One option is to persist the stock properties yourself and ignore the base class implementation. The one major drawback to this method is that you are now required to maintain your stock property persistence code by hand and can no longer rely on the base class implementation MFC provides.

Drawing the Control

Most controls have some form of user interface. However, as you learned earlier, since the release of the OC 96 specification and ActiveX, a user interface is no longer a requirement. Drawing the user interface of a control has long been regarded as one of the most critical aspects of a control, in terms of both appearance and performance. A control that flashes or flickers a lot appears to be poorly developed regardless of its internal implementation. The same is true for how fast the control draws. With the advent of the Internet and ActiveX, it is even more crucial that containers draw a control fast and draw it well. Drawing can be broken into two major categories: standard and optimized. Optimized drawing is a highly advanced topic that you will not learn about in this book

Standard Drawing

Standard drawing is just that: standard. You have complete freedom to draw the control any way you see fit, using any method that is appropriate. You can use pens and brushes, rectangles, and circles. Remember that drawing *smart* is the goal of any application with a user interface.

Note

Probably the greatest sources of flicker and flash are overlapped painting and unnecessary drawing—drawing and redrawing areas of the control that do not need to be drawn. Try to draw only to the areas of the control that have been invalidated. Doing so saves time and prevents annoying flash. For example, if your control has a white background and a black border, draw only the white portion where it is going to be seen. Don't draw over the border because this causes the control to flash every time it gets a paint message.

✦ ✦ ✦ ✦ ✦

Before adding the `OnDraw()` implementation to your source file, add a `CBrush` member variable to the `protected` section of the `CMFCControlWinCtrl` class definition. The new member variable will hold a `CBrush` object. In the standard implementation, the control will re-create the `CBrush` every time the `OnDraw()` function executes.

The `OnDraw()` implementation is fairly straightforward. Select the font into the DC, get all of the colors that you are going to use, draw the background, draw the text, and draw the border. Then reset everything back to the way it was when you started. You can implement the `OnDraw()` function as shown in Listing 31-4.

Listing 31-4: The OnDraw() Function for the Control Handles the Control Is Redrawing

```
void CMFCControlWinCtrl::OnDraw( CDC* pdc,
    const CRect& rcBounds, const CRect& rcInvalid)
 {
   // ****** Get the text font ******
   CFont * pOldFont;

   // get the stock font
   pOldFont = this->SelectStockFont(pdc);

   // ****** Get the text font ******
   // ****** Get the colors ******
   // use the window color as the background color

   COLORREF clrTextBackgroundColor =
       this->TranslateColor(this- >GetBackColor());

   // then use the normal windows color for the text

   COLORREF clrTextForegroundColor =
       this->TranslateColor(this- >GetForeColor());

   // set to the system color
   COLORREF clrEdgeBackgroundColor =
      ::GetSysColor(COLOR_3DFACE);
   COLORREF clrEdgeForegroundColor =
      ::GetSysColor(COLOR_3DFACE);

   // ****** Get the colors ******
   // ****** Draw the background ******
   // set the text color

   COLORREF clrOldBackgroundColor =
       pdc->SetBkColor(clrTextBackgroundColor);
   COLORREF clrOldForegroundColor =
       pdc >SetTextColor(clrTextForegroundColor);

   // if we don't have a brush
   if(m_Brush m_hObject == NULL)
     // create a solid brush
     m_Brush.CreateSolidBrush(clrTextBackgroundColor);

   // select the brush and save the old one
   CBrush * pOldBrush = pdc->SelectObject(&m_Brush);

   // draw the background
   pdc->Rectangle(&rcBounds);

   // ****** Draw the background ******
   // ****** Draw the text ******
```

```
int iHor, iVer;
// get the size of the text for this DC

CSize oSize = pdc->GetTextExtent(m_cstrCaption);
switch(m_lAlignment)
 {
   case EALIGN_CENTER:
       iHor = (rcBounds.right - oSize.cx) / 2;
       iVer = rcBounds.top + 3;
       break;

   case EALIGN_RIGHT:
       iHor = rcBounds.right - oSize.cx - 3;
       iVer = rcBounds.top + 3;
       break;

   // case EALIGN_LEFT:
   default:
       iHor = rcBounds.left + 3;
       iVer = rcBounds.top + 3;
       break;
 }

// output our text
pdc->ExtTextOut(iHor, iVer, ETO_CLIPPED | ETO_OPAQUE,
    rcBounds, m_cstrCaption, m_cstrCaption.GetLength(),
    NULL);

// ****** Draw the text ******
// ****** Draw the border ******

// set the edge style and flags
UINT uiBorderStyle = EDGE_SUNKEN;
UINT uiBorderFlags = BF_RECT;

// set the edge color
pdc->SetBkColor(clrEdgeBackgroundColor);
pdc->SetTextColor(clrEdgeForegroundColor);

// draw the 3D edge
pdc->DrawEdge((LPRECT)(LPCRECT) rcBounds, uiBorderStyle,
    uiBorderFlags);

// ****** Draw the border ******
// ****** Reset the colors ******

// restore the original colors
pdc->SetBkColor(clrOldBackgroundColor);
pdc->SetTextColor(clrOldForegroundColor);

// ****** Reset the colors ******
// ****** release the text font ******
```

(continued)

Listing 31-4 *(continued)*

```
    // set the old font back
    pdc->SelectObject(pOldFont);

    // ****** Get the text font ******
    // select the old brush back
    pdc->SelectObject(pOldBrush);
}
```

Summary

All of the frameworks described in this chapter have their strengths and weaknesses. MFC enables rapid component creation and implementation, and the level of support built into the Visual C++ IDE for MFC is beyond comparison with ATL or `BaseCtl`. MFC offers a very large and robust class library for solving most, if not all, of your development problems. MFC does, however, suffer from the problem that it is everything to everyone, which results in a slower application or one that cannot easily deviate from the "norm."

ATL provides a small and deliberate framework for creating ActiveX components. ATL, however, falls very short in the area of common class and utility support, which is MFC's strength. In addition, ATL's integration with the Visual C++ IDE also leaves room for improvement.

`BaseCtl` is similar to ATL in that it is focused specifically on small, fast component development. Like ATL, it lacks the same common class and utility support that makes MFC so attractive. `BaseCtl` has an added negative of being considered only as a sample and not as a supported product by Microsoft.

The level of experience of the development team and the intended life cycle of the code and applications also affect the decision of which tool to choose to create ActiveX components. Take the time to investigate all of the options available before deciding on a platform and a direction.

After outlining the possible implementation options, the second half of this chapter focused on creating a basic MFC control implementation. Methods, properties, and events are the basis for any control implementation, and using MFC makes it truly easy to add them in a short period of time. This chapter also addressed the issues of persistence and drawing, which are necessary for a complete control implementation.

MFC was the first tool available from Microsoft for doing ActiveX development (back when it was called OLE). MFC was meant to hide all the details of implementing ActiveX/COM components from you so that you wouldn't have to learn a whole new way of developing MFC applications just to support ActiveX/COM. The fact that MFC hides all of the details is both its power and its limitation. You may be able to create ActiveX controls in a short period of time, but their size and performance may not be as desirable as a control that you create with ATL. MFC does have a distinct advantage in the area of maturity of integration with the IDE because the IDE seems to be designed around making it as easy as possible to create applications when using MFC.

Now that you have learned the basics of control creation, you should take the time to apply some of the principles that you have learned to the other two controls you created the frameworks for (the windowless control and the subclassed control). In the next chapter, you will learn how to create an automation server with MFC.

✦ ✦ ✦

Creating ActiveX Automation Servers Using MFC

◆ ◆ ◆ ◆

In This Chapter

Using the MFC ClassWizard to reduce the time required to implement your server

Generating and capturing OLE exceptions

Selecting and managing automation server interfaces

Understanding differences in exception generation

Creating automation servers

Deciding between shared and single instance servers

◆ ◆ ◆ ◆

As you learned in Chapter 31, MFC and Visual C++ provide a simple and easy-to-use framework for creating ActiveX controls. Visual C++ provides a similarly convenient framework to help you create automation servers. In fact, the Visual C++ development environment's AppWizard and ClassWizard were implemented with this in mind. Creating and manipulating automation interfaces is one of Visual C++'s primary functions.

In this chapter, you will create a simple in-process automation server using MFC for logging string data to a file. Throughout this chapter, you can use an application such as Visual Basic to test your implementation. Visual Basic is perfect for accessing automation servers because it takes so little time and code to do so. As you proceed through the chapter, you will expand on your implementation, highlighting some of the more advanced concepts of automation server creation.

Creating the Basic Project

When creating an automation server, the first step is to create a *basic project* upon which you will build your application's features and functionality. MFC provides an AppWizard that greatly simplifies this process. The AppWizard consists of a set of structured dialogs and choices that, in the end, result in a set of files representing the basic application's project.

1. To create the basic project, you start Visual C++, and select the New option from the File menu. Visual C++ will display the New dialog box.

2. Within the New dialog box, select the Projects tab. Next, select MFC AppWizard (dll) as the project type.

3. Enter the Project name as **MFCServer**, and set the Location to the `\IDG\Chap32\MFCServer` directory. Click OK to continue.

   Figure 32-1 shows the New dialog box after you set it to create the MFCServer program.

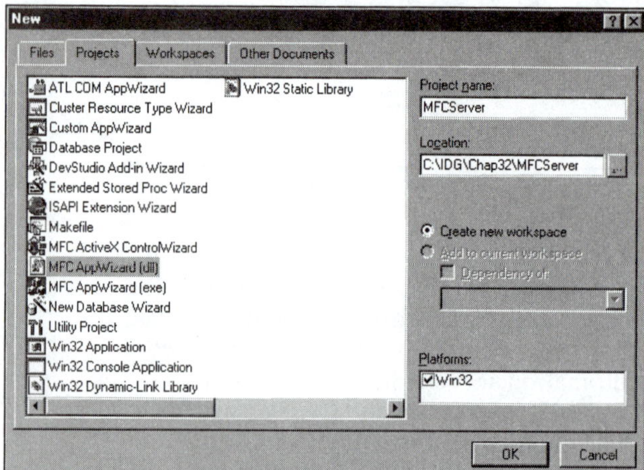

Figure 32-1: The New dialog box after setting it to create the MFCServer program

4. In the MFC AppWizard—Step 1 of 1 dialog box, you define the specifics about how the AppWizard is going to create your application. For the type of DLL to create, select Regular DLL with MFC statically linked, which results in a slightly larger application but one that should load faster because you won't have to load the MFC DLLs whenever the server is launched.

5. Select the Automation check box—because that is the reason you are creating the application in the first place. Click the Finish button within the dialog box to continue. Visual C++ will display the New Project Information dialog box.

6. The New Project Information dialog enables you to review your choices before creating the actual project. Click the OK button to complete the creation of your project. The MFC AppWizard automatically creates all the basic files that you need to create a DLL-based automation server.

Table 32-1 lists all of the files that AppWizard creates and a brief explanation of what your applications will use the files for.

Table 32-1
Basic Source Files Created by the MFC AppWizard

Filename	*Description*
`MFCServer.clw`	Visual C++ project file
`MFCServer.cpp`	Main application source file and entry point for the DLL
`MFCServer.def`	Standard application DEF file. This file contains the function export declarations needed for all in-process servers.
`MFCServer.dsp`	Visual C++ project file
`MFCServer.dsw`	Visual C++ project file
`MFCServer.h`	Main application header file
`MFCServer.ncb`	Visual C++ project file
`MFCServer.odl`	Standard Object Definition Language (ODL) file
`MFCServer.rc`	Standard resource file
`ReadMe.txt`	Text file that describes the project
`Resource.h`	Resource header file
`StdAfx.cpp`	Standard precompiled header source file
`StdAfx.h`	Standard precompiled header file. All the MFC-specific include files are added here.
`Res\MFCServer.rc2`	Standard resource 2 file. This file contains all of the resource information that you cannot edit directly from within Visual C++.

After you create the default project, you can compile it, but you can do very little with it because it does not contain interfaces, methods, or properties.

Adding an automation interface to the application

To be an automation server, an application must contain at least one or more `IDispatch`-based interfaces. In MFC, you use the `CCmdTarget` class to implement this interface (you learned about `CCmdTarget` in Chapter 19). You use the MFC ClassWizard to add automation interfaces to your application. To add the first automation interface:

1. Select the ClassWizard option from the View menu. Visual C++ will display the ClassWizard dialog box.
2. Next, click the Add Class button, and select the New menu item. Visual C++ will open the New Class dialog box.

3. Within the New Class dialog box, enter the Name **CTracker**, and select `CCmdTarget` as its base class in the Base class combo box.
4. Select the Automation radio button in the Automation radio button group. The Createable by type ID radio button and edit field are used to define the `ProgID` that you and calling applications will use to create and launch the automation server. The human readable `ProgID` is used in place of the `CLSID` because it is much easier to write and remember. Be careful not to create duplicates when defining a `ProgID`. For your application, leave the `ProgID` set to its default value.
5. Click the OK button to create your new class and add it to your application.
6. Click the OK button in the MFC ClassWizard dialog box to close the ClassWizard. Figure 32-2 shows the New Class dialog box after you enter the class information.

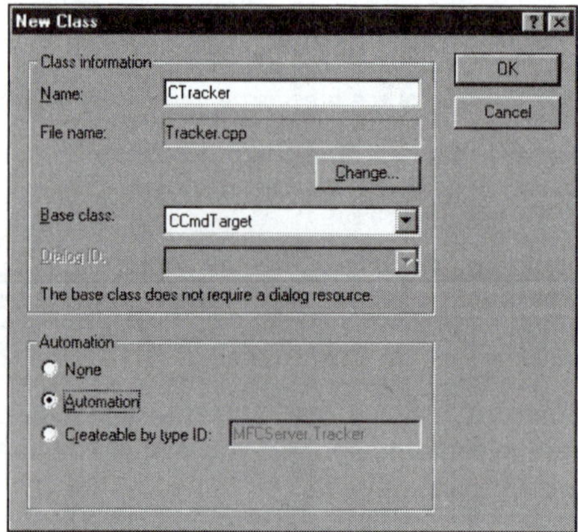

Figure 32-2: The New Class dialog box after entering the class information

When creating a new `CCmdTarget` class, MFC not only creates a header and source file with all of the appropriate information (in this case, `Tracker.h` and `Tracker.cpp`), but because you selected automation support for the class, it also updates the ODL file with the new `Dispinterface` and `CoClass` entries of your automation server, as shown in the `MFCServer.odl` file in Listing 32-1.

The `Dispinterface` is your primary `IDispatch`-based interface and is where the ClassWizard adds your new methods and properties. The `CoClass` interface identifies your class factory interface. The class factory is the part of the application that performs the actual creation of your automation server when it is necessary to do so. See the OLE and MFC documentation for more information on class factories and their role in OLE.

Listing 32-1: The MFCServer.odl File after MFC Updates It with Your Automation Server's Dispinterface and CoClass Entries

```
// MFCServer.odl : type library source for MFCServer.dll

// This file will be processed by the MIDL compiler to
// produce the type library (MFCServer.tlb).

[ uuid(2EE81064-F61D-11D1-8545-8FDA26F60349), version(1.0) ]
library MFCServer
 {
   importlib("stdole32.tlb");
   importlib("stdole2.tlb");

   //  Primary dispatch interface for CTracker

   [ uuid(2EE81071-F61D-11D1-8545-8FDA26F60349) ]
   dispinterface ITracker
    {
      properties:
         // NOTE-ClassWizard maintains property information
         // here.  Use extreme caution when editing this
         // section.
         //{{AFX_ODL_PROP(CTracker)
         //}}AFX_ODL_PROP

      methods:
         // NOTE-ClassWizard maintains method information
         // here.  Use extreme caution when editing this
         // section.
         //{{AFX_ODL_METHOD(CTracker)
         //}}AFX_ODL_METHOD

    };

   //  Class information for CTracker

   [ uuid(2EE81073-F61D-11D1-8545-8FDA26F60349) ]
   coclass Tracker
    {
      [default] dispinterface ITracker;
    };

   //{{AFX_APPEND_ODL}}
   //}}AFX_APPEND_ODL}}
 };
```

Notice from the code in the ODL file, however, that even though the MFC ClassWizard added the new interface to the server, it did not expose the interface to the outside world. Basically, what you have created thus far is an automation server that no application can create — which is, clearly, not very useful.

All ActiveX components are created through an object known as a *class factory*. MFC defines the class `COleObjectFactory` for its class factory support. However, you cannot add the `COleObjectFactory` class directly to your server implementation. Instead, MFC forces you to use two MFC-defined macros, `DECLARE_OLECREATE` and `IMPLEMENT_OLECREATE`.

To build your class factory:

1. Select the ClassView tab within the Project Workspace.
2. Expand the class list, and double-click the `CTracker` class to open the `Tracker.h` include file.
3. Add the macro `DECLARE_OLECREATE` to your class definition. The macro takes a single parameter, your class name — in this case, `CTracker`. The following code implements the changed `Tracker.h` header file:

```
// more code here

// NOTE-ClassWizard will add and remove member functions
// here.
//}}AFX_DISPATCH
   DECLARE_DISPATCH_MAP()
   DECLARE_INTERFACE_MAP()
   DECLARE_OLECREATE(CTracker)
 };
```

4. Next, again within the Project Workspace window, select the FileView tab, expand the Source Files list, and double-click the `Tracker.cpp` entry to open the file.
5. Add the macro `IMPLEMENT_OLECREATE` to your source file. The `IMPLEMENT_OLECREATE` macro takes three parameters: the class name, the `ProgID` that applications use to create the server, and the `CLSID` of the `CoClass` interface, as your ODL file defines.
6. When AppWizard created the ODL file, it also generated a `CLSID` for the type library. When the ClassWizard added the `CTracker` class, it created new `CLSID`s: one for the `Dispinterface`, and the other for the `CoClass`. You will implement the following changes (note that your `CLSID` should differ from the one used here, unless you use the files from the CD-ROM):

```
// more code here

// {11C82946-4EDD-11D0-BED8-00400538977D}
   static const IID IID_ITracker =
```

```
        { 0x11c82946, 0x4edd, 0x11d0, { 0xbe, 0xd8, 0x0,
          0x40, 0x5, 0x38, 0x97, 0x7d } };
    BEGIN_INTERFACE_MAP(CTracker, CCmdTarget)
      INTERFACE_PART(CTracker, IID_ITracker, Dispatch)
    END_INTERFACE_MAP()
    IMPLEMENT_OLECREATE(CTracker, _T("MFCServer.Tracker"),
        0x11C82947, 0x4edd, 0x11d0, 0xbe, 0xd8, 0x0, 0x40,
        0x5, 0x38, 0x97, 0x7d)

  // more code here
```

You have now enabled your server implementation with a class factory, which enables other applications to create the server. Before another application can create the server, however, OLE has to know where to find the server, which is done through the system Registry. All ActiveX components that are publicly available to other applications must support registration and must create valid Registry entries. You will learn more about server registration in the next section.

Registering the server

ActiveX components have one or more Registry entries that are used to describe various aspects of the application and how it can be used. The Registry is critical to the successful launching and using of ActiveX components. Local servers rely on command-line options for registration support. It is the responsibility of the local server developer to check for the correct command-line option and take the appropriate action. Table 32-2 lists the command-line options for local server registration.

Table 32-2
Local Server Command-Line Options for Registration Support

Command-Line Option	*Description*
R	Registers all components.
U	Unregisters all components.
S	Performs registration in silent mode, and does not display confirmation dialogs (which indicate successful registration). However, registration will still display error messages. You can combine this option with either R or U.

All in-process ActiveX components expose registration support through two functions the components export: the `DllRegisterServer()` function and the `DllUnregisterServer()` function.

The MFC AppWizard automatically adds the DllRegisterServer() function to the main application file of a project when AppWizard creates the project. You should register all of the components the application contains within this function. Further, each ActiveX component must be responsible for its own registration support.

The COleObjectFactory class automatically handles registration support. Even though you may not be aware of it, the COleObjectFactory class contains a singly linked list that it uses to keep track of all of the COleObjectFactory classes implemented in a single application. The linked list is a static member, which means that all instances of the class share the same class factory list. COleObjectFactory also contains a static function, UpdateRegistryAll(), that cycles through the list of COleObjectFactory classes, instructing each to register themselves.

Unregistering the server is slightly more complex. The MFC AppWizard does not add the exported function, DllUnregisterServer(), to a project when AppWizard creates the project. This seeming oversight is actually probably due to an inherent limitation in MFC. The MFC group apparently did not feel it was necessary to add unregistration support to the basic MFC COleObjectFactory class. This is an odd decision, because all of the Microsoft logo requirements indicate that all applications that are installed and registered must also uninstall and unregister themselves in order to qualify for the logo.

To support server unregistration, you have to add the exported function, DllUnregisterServer(), to the class and call the static function COleObjectFactory::UpdateRegistryAll(), passing FALSE as the parameter, to unregister the server. The actual unregistration code requires more work. This book does not include the unregistration code as a part of the sample code, but the implementation is straightforward. The first step is to create a new class that inherits from COleObjectFactory, and override the virtual function UpdateRegistry(). Within the overridden function, your code should check the parameter that the calling function passes to UpdateRegistry(), and based on its value, call the appropriate registration or unregistration code. MFC provides a basic registration helper function, AfxOleRegisterServerClass(), but does not define a companion helper function for unregistration. Searching the source files in MFC reveals a complete set of helper functions for the Registry, but unfortunately they are not accessible from anything but an MFC-implemented ActiveX control. Because nothing is available from MFC, you are required to implement the Registry-updating code yourself (using Windows API calls). Remember, during the unregistration process, you must remove all of the Registry entries that the server registration initially created, including the ProgID, the CLSID, and the type library.

Writing support code for the sample server

Because your sample server is used to output data to a file, you need to add some support code to your application before adding its methods and properties. The first step is to make some changes and additions to the Tracker.h header file. You must add a set of member variables for storing the file handle and timer information that you will later use throughout the server implementation. You implement the changes within the Tracker.h header file as shown here:

```
// More Code Here
   DECLARE_OLECREATE(CTracker)
protected:
   FILE * m_fileLog;
   long m_lTimeBegin;
   long m_lHiResTime;
   long m_lLastHiResTime;
 };
```

The next step is to update the source file for the class. You add the include file mmsystem.h to the Tracker.cpp file to support the functions that you are taking advantage of in the sample server implementation. You also must write a constructor and destructor for the server. You implement the changes within the Tracker.cpp file as shown in Listing 32-2.

Listing 32-2: The Tracker.cpp Source Code File After Implementing Your Constructor and Destructor

```
// more code here

#include "Tracker.h"

// needed for the high resolution timer services
#include <mmsystem.h>

#ifdef _DEBUG
  #define new DEBUG NEW
  #undef THIS FILE
  static char THIS_FILE[] = __FILE__;
#endif

/////////////////////////////////////////////////////////////////
// CTracker
IMPLEMENT_DYNCREATE(CTracker, CCmdTarget)
CTracker::CTracker()
 {
   EnableAutomation();

   // make sure that the application won't unload until the
```

(continued)

Listing 32-2 (continued)

```
    // reference count is 0
    ::AfxOleLockApp();

    // setup the timer resolution
    m_lTimeBegin = timeBeginPeriod(1);
    m_lHiResTime = m_lLastHiResTime = timeGetTime();

    // get the current date and time
    CTime oTimeStamp = CTime::GetCurrentTime();
    CString cstrFileName;

    // create a file name based on the date
    cstrFileName.Format(_T("%s.tracklog"), (LPCTSTR)
    oTimeStamp.Format("%Y%m%d"));

    // open a file
    m_fileLog = fopen(cstrFileName, _T("a"));

    // if we have a file handle
    if(m_fileLog)
     {
       // output some starting information
       fprintf(m_fileLog, _T("***********************\n"));
       fprintf(m_fileLog, _T("Start %s\n"),
          (LPCTSTR) oTimeStamp.Format("%B %#d, %Y, %I:%M %p"));
       fprintf(m_fileLog, _T("\n"));
     }
 }

CTracker::~CTracker()
 {
    // check to make sure a file handle exists
    if(m_fileLog)
     {
       // output some closing information
       CTime oTimeStamp = CTime::GetCurrentTime();
       fprintf(m_fileLog, _T("\n"));
       fprintf(m_fileLog, _T("End %s\n"), oTimeStamp.Format
          ("%B %#d, %Y, %I:%M %p"));
       fprintf(m_fileLog, _T("***********************\n"));

       // close the file
       fclose(m_fileLog);
     }

    // if has created a valid timer services
    if(m_lTimeBegin == TIMERR_NOERROR)
      // reset the timer to its original state
```

```
        timeEndPeriod(1);

      // make sure that the application can unload the component
      ::AfxOleUnlockApp();
    }

  // More code here
```

As you can see, you must also update the constructor and destructor of the server. The first function call to `EnableAutomation()` in the constructor is the result of your decisions with ClassWizard. Next, the program code must invoke the method `AfxOleLockApp()`, which ensures that the application is not unloaded from memory until the reference count (that is, the number of currently open objects of the class) reaches zero. When you use OLE in MFC applications, you must always lock the application in memory by calling the locking method. This step is critical, and you *must* include the function call in all MFC-based servers.

Next, the program code within the constructor creates a high-resolution timer and stores its current value in your member variables. The timer is useful for determining the number of milliseconds that have passed since the last method call was made. The timer output is great for tracking the performance of a particular action or set of actions.

You then get the current date, and create a filename in the format `YYYYMMDD.tracklog`. After successfully opening the file, you output some startup data to the file and exit the constructor.

The destructor does the exact opposite of the constructor. If there is a valid file handle, you write some closing information to the file and close it. Next, you terminate the timer. Remember to call the function `AfxOleUnlockApp()` to enable the operating system to remove the application from memory.

Finally, you must update the build settings for the project. Because the sample implementation is using some timer functions defined in `mmsystem.h`, you must also link your project with the appropriate library file that contains their implementation. To add the necessary linkage, select the Settings option from the Project menu. Visual C++ will display the Project Settings dialog box. From the Settings For drop-down list box in the Project Settings dialog box, select the All Configurations entry. Select the Link tab, and add the file `winmm.lib` to the Object/library modules edit field. Click the OK button to close the dialog box.

The basic support code needed for the sample implementation is now added. The server will open a file in its constructor and leave the file open during its entire lifetime. When the server is destroyed, the destructor will be called and will close the file. The next step is to make the sample more meaningful by adding methods and properties, which you will use to output data to the open file.

Booleans in Visual C++ and Visual Basic

It is important to note a fundamental difference between Visual C++ and Visual Basic when using Boolean data types. The Boolean data type is defined by C++ as being of type `integer`—that is, it is a 32-bit value. For Visual Basic, however, an `integer` is a 16-bit value. For simple MFC-based automation servers, the difference in sizes between a Visual Basic integer and Visual C++ integer is not a problem, because MFC hides the details involving the conversion of the 32-bit value to a 16-bit value, and vice versa.

For dual-interface applications, though, the size difference poses a significant problem. When accessing the custom interface of a dual-interface server, the functions are called in the same fashion as any other function in an application. Basically, the operating system pushes the parameters of the function onto a stack and then calls the function. When the function executes, the parameters are then popped off the stack. If Visual Basic calls a function in Visual C++, the stack becomes corrupt because of the different sizes that each language uses for the Boolean data type. To be safe, Visual C++ applications should define all Boolean data types as type `VARIANT_BOOL`, which is defined by OLE as a 16-bit value and is guaranteed to be the same size regardless of the language or tool being used.

The actual Boolean data value is different between Visual Basic and Visual C++ also. Visual Basic developers are used to Boolean values of 0 indicating `FALSE` and -1 indicating `TRUE`. For those of you who may be wondering why, the binary values are 00000000 and 11111111, respectively. For C++ programmers, Boolean data values are usually defined as 0 for `FALSE` and 1 or non-zero for `TRUE`.

The differences in Boolean data values can cause considerable problems when integrating Visual Basic and Visual C++ applications. In addition, Visual Basic 4 has some behavioral differences in its language, depending on the value being tested. Some Visual Basic functions do not test for zero or non-zero and test for the absolute value of 0 or -1, and vice versa, depending on the data type and function. When using Boolean data types, it is wise to also use the `VARIANT_FALSE` and `VARIANT_TRUE` constants to define the value of the variable.

Adding methods

An *automation method* consists of zero to *n* parameters and may or may not have a return value. The term *method* is synonymous with function or subroutine, depending on the particular language you are familiar with. Because your server is `IDispatch`-based, you are limited to a specific set of data types within your method calls. As you learned in the last chapter, you can pass or return only those data types that are valid `VARIANT` data types using a method.

As you learned at the beginning of this chapter, you will use the sample automation server to log strings of data to a file. The server will define the method `OutputLines()`, which is used by the user of the server to supply the string data that the server writes to the file. The method accepts an array of strings and an optional indentation parameter and will output the strings to the file. The indentation parameter is used to offset the strings by *n* number of tab characters to provide simple, yet effective, formatting to the data as it is output to the file.

To add the method, select the ClassWizard option from the View menu. Select the Automation tab, and click the Add Method button. In the Add Method dialog box, enter an External name of **OutputLines** and a Return type of `BOOL`.

You define the `OutputLines()` method to have two parameters: `varOutputArray` as a `VARIANT` passed by reference, which contains a string array of data to output to the file, and `varIndent` as a `VARIANT` passed by value, which is also an optional parameter indicating the amount of indentation the server should use when writing the string data to the file. To add the method parameters, double-click the line in the Parameter list that is directly below the Name column, and type **varOutputArray**. Click directly under the Type column to activate the Type drop-down list box. Select `VARIANT *` from the list. Repeat the same process for `varIndent`, but set the data type to `VARIANT`. Figure 32-3 shows the Add Method dialog box after you perform your entries.

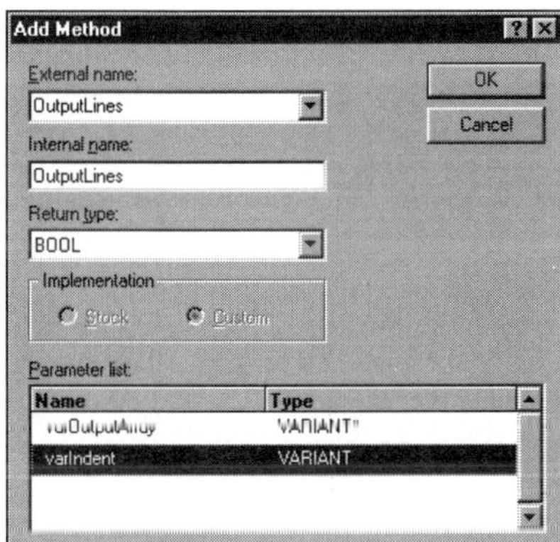

Figure 32-3: The Add Method dialog box after performing your entries

As you learned in Chapter 31, due to data type restrictions imposed by Automation, you cannot pass arrays as parameters of methods, unless you write your own marshaling code. You can, however, pass `VARIANT` data types that can contain arrays. Therefore, in the sample server, you define `varOutputArray` as a `VARIANT`. In addition, you must define `varOutputArray` as being passed by reference because the array stored in the `VARIANT` does not get copied over when you pass the parameter by value.

As you also learned, optional parameters must fall at the end of the parameter list and must be of type VARIANT. The varIndent parameter is an optional parameter that indents the text output as an added formatting feature.

Remember that the ClassWizard also added an entry to the ODL file as well as the header and source files. It is a function of the ODL file to declare a parameter of a method as being optional. To be optional, a parameter must be declared with the optional parameter attribute as you did in Chapter 31. Remember, you must add the optional attribute by hand because ClassWizard will not add it for you. You add the optional parameter attribute as shown in the following code:

```
// NOTE - ClassWizard will maintain method information here.
// Use extreme caution when editing this section.
//{{AFX_ODL_METHOD(CTracker)
   [id(1)] boolean OutputLines(VARIANT* varOutputArray,
       [optional] VARIANT varIndent);

//}}AFX_ODL_METHOD
```

Before you add the implementation of the OutputLines() method, you first must add a member variable to the class definition. The server uses the new member, m_lIndent, to store the current indentation level between calls to the method OutputLines(). You add the new member to the Tracker.h header file as shown here:

```
protected:
   FILE * m_fileLog;
   long m_lTimeBegin;
   long m_lHiResTime;
   long m_lLastHiResTime;
   long m_lIndent;

 };
```

You also must update the constructor to initialize the member to a valid starting value (such as 0). After you perform the necessary steps to add the new member variable, you can write the OutputLines() method. You implement the OutputLines() method as shown in Listing 32-3.

Listing 32-3: **Implementing the OutputLines() Method**

```
//////////////////////////////////////////////////////////////////////
// CTracker message handlers
BOOL CTracker::OutputLines(VARIANT FAR* varOutputArray,
    const VARIANT FAR& varIndent)
 {
   BOOL bResult = VARIANT_TRUE;
   // it is a file if the variant contains a string array
   if(m_fileLog && varOutputArray->vt ==
```

```
    (VT_ARRAY | VT_BSTR))
  {
    // lock the array so we can use it
    if(::SafeArrayLock(varOutputArray->parray) == S_OK)
     {
       LONG lLBound;
       // get the lower bound of the array
       if(::SafeArrayGetLBound(varOutputArray->parray, 1,
           &lLBound) == S_OK)
        {
          LONG lUBound;
          // get the number of elements in the array
          if(::SafeArrayGetUBound(varOutputArray->parray, 1,
              &lUBound) == S_OK)
           {
             CString cstrIndent;
             CTime oTimeStamp;
             BSTR bstrTemp;
             // if we have an indent parameter
             if(varIndent.vt != VT_I4)
              {
                // get a variant for conversion purposes
                VARIANT varConvertedValue;

                // initialize the variant
                ::VariantInit(&varConvertedValue);

                /* try to  convert the data type to
                   something useful; alternately, you can
                   use VariantChangeTypeEx() */
                if(S_OK ==
                    ::VariantChangeType(&varConvertedValue,
                        (VARIANT *) &varIndent, 0, VT_I4))

                // assign the value to our member variable
                m_lIndent = varConvertedValue.lVal;
              }
             else
               // assign the value to our member variable
               m_lIndent = varIndent.lVal;

          // if we have to indent the text
          for(long lIndentCount = 0;
              lIndentCount < m_lIndent;  lIndentCount++)
            // add a tab to the string
            cstrIndent += _T("\t");

          // for each of the elements in the array
          for(long lArrayCount = lLBound;
              lArrayCount < (lUBound + lLBound);
              lArrayCount++)
           {
```

(continued)

Listing 32-3 (continued)

```
                    // update the time
                    oTimeStamp = CTime::GetCurrentTime();
                    m_lHiResTime = timeGetTime();

                    // get the data from the array
                    if(::SafeArrayGetElement(varOutputArray-
                        >parray, &lArrayCount, &bstrTemp) == S_OK)
                     {
                       // output the data
                       fprintf(m_fileLog, _T("%s(%10ld)-%s%ls\n"),
                           (LPCTSTR) oTimeStamp.Format("%H:%M:%S"),
                           m_lHiResTime - m_lLastHiResTime,
                           (LPCTSTR) cstrIndent, bstrTemp);

                       // store the last timer value
                       m_lLastHiResTime = m_lHiResTime;
                       // free the bstr
                       ::SysFreeString(bstrTemp);
                     }
                  }
               }
              else
               bResult = VARIANT_FALSE;
            }
           else
             bResult = VARIANT_FALSE;
             // unlock the array we don't need it anymore
             ::SafeArrayUnlock(varOutputArray->parray);
            }
         else
           bResult = VARIANT_FALSE;
         }
        else
          bResult = VARIANT_FALSE;
        // return the result
        return bResult;
    }
```

First, the code within the method checks to see if it has a valid file handle and array of string data. The next step the code performs is to lock down the array so that you can perform operations on it. You must perform this step within all functions that you write that manipulate safe arrays. The next function call,

SafeArrayGetLBound(), determines the starting point of the array, which can be either 0 or 1. This procedure is very important to implement because programming languages such as C++ define a base of 0 for arrays, and languages such as Visual Basic can define a base of 0 or 1. Next you retrieve the number of dimensions in the array. Note that this value represents the number of dimensions and not the last dimension relative to the lower bound value.

After establishing the boundaries of the array, your code must check to see if the function also received an indentation value. You want to receive a long, VT_I4, but if you do not receive it, you try to convert the data that was given to you to a usable value. If you cannot convert the data, you simply use the value that the variable already contains. To indent the text, the function concatenates from 1 to *n* tab characters into the beginning of the string.

For each of the elements in the array of strings, the function gets the current time and the data associated with each element, and then outputs the string along with the indentation string to the open file. Then, the function frees the string element when it finishes with it. Finally, the program code unlocks the array and exits the method with the proper return value.

It is worthwhile to review the online documentation in the Visual C++ on ODL, automation, and VARIANT data types to see what kind of flexibility you have when defining methods and parameters. Now that you have added a method, you are ready to implement its counterpart, the property.

Adding properties to the server

A *property* can be thought of as an exposed variable that is defined in the automation server. Properties are useful for setting and retrieving information about the state of the server. You implement properties within your server as a pair of methods — one to get the value, and the other to set the value. The m_lIndent member variable that you added to the class definition is a perfect candidate for the server to expose as a property.

As with methods, you can add properties to your server using the ClassWizard in MFC. To add a property, select the ClassWizard option from the View menu. In the MFC ClassWizard dialog box, select the Automation tab, and click the Add Property button. In the Add Property dialog box, enter the external name of the property as **Indent**, and select the type as long. Set the Implementation to Get/Set methods, and click OK to add the property to the server. Click the Edit Code button to close the MFC ClassWizard dialog and open the source file for editing. Figure 32-4 shows the Add Property dialog box after you make your entries.

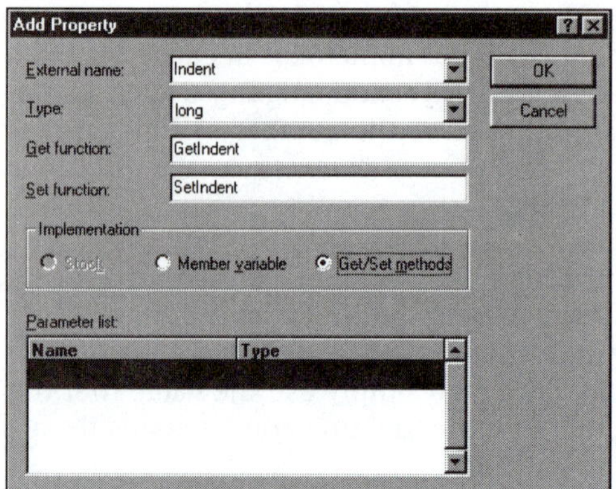

Figure 32-4: The Add Property dialog after adding the Indent property

The actual implementation of the Indent property is easy. As with the control you designed in Chapter 31, the `GetIndent()` function returns the value currently stored in the member variable, and the `SetIndent()` function stores the new value, after a little bit of error checking, in the member variable. You implement the property-management functions as shown here:

```
long CTracker::GetIndent()
 {
   // return the member variable
   return m_lIndent;
 }

void CTracker::SetIndent(long nNewValue)
 {
   // if the new value is a least 0
   if(nNewValue >= 0)
     // assign the value to our member variable
     m_lIndent = nNewValue;
 }
```

Properties, like methods, have a wide variety of implementation options, including parameterized and enumerated values. You learned about the options you have when creating properties in Chapter 31.

So far, you have added methods and properties to the server but have not really dealt with the issue of error handling in their implementation. In some cases, simply returning success or failure is not enough information for the developer to understand that an error occurred and what caused the error. You will communicate more error information through the use of OLE exceptions, which you will learn about in the next section.

Generating OLE Exceptions

While executing a method call or some other action, it is sometimes necessary to terminate the process due to some critical error that has occurred or is about to occur. For example, the controlling program calls a server method to write data to a file, but the server cannot open the file or write data to the file because there is not enough room on the hard disk. It is necessary to halt further processing until the error can be resolved. An error of this kind is known as an *exception*. Any type of error can be treated as an exception. How you treat errors depends on the requirements of your application and how you choose to deal with the errors that may result.

You must become familiar with two forms of exceptions when creating ActiveX components. The first is a C++ exception. A C++ exception is a language mechanism used to create critical errors of the type described earlier and is confined to the application in which they are defined. The second is an OLE exception. OLE exceptions are used to communicate the same kinds of errors externally to applications that are using a component. The difference between the two is that C++ exceptions are entirely internal to an application's implementation, and you can use OLE exceptions both internally and externally, though you will generally use them to communicate errors to other applications.

The `IDispatch` interface contains specific parameters in its functions for dealing with exceptions and passing them to the controller application. The MFC implementation of the `CCmdTarget` class handles the details of generating OLE exceptions. The class' default definition traps any C++ exceptions that the class receives and translates the C++ exception to the proper `IDispatch` error information. You need only create a C++ exception of type `COleDispatchException` and `throw` the exception. MFC does all of the work for you. When you create dual-interface servers, you must handle exceptions somewhat differently. You will learn how to manage dual-interface server exceptions later in this chapter.

The first step you must take to prepare to handle OLE exceptions is to add an enumeration of the types of errors that the server can generate to the ODL file. Adding the enumeration to the ODL has the effect of publishing the error constants to the applications developer that is using the server. You add the constants in the form of an include file so that you can use the same error constants file in the C++ source code implementation. You also add a `UUID` to the `typedef` so that it can be identified in the type library that is generated with the `GUIDGEN.EXE` program. You implement the enumeration within the sample server program as shown here:

```
// more code here

[ uuid(11C82947-4EDD-11D0-BED8-00400538977D) ]
coclass TRACKER
 {
   [default] dispinterface ITracker;
 };
```

```
typedef [uuid(11C82948-4EDD-11D0-BED8-00400538977D),
    helpstring("Tracker Error Constants")]
#include "trackererror.h"
//{{AFX_APPEND_ODL}}

};
```

The TrackerError.h file, in turn, contains a standard C/C++ enumeration of the errors that the application supports. The starting value of the errors falls into the range of valid user-defined errors. Be careful when you assign error numbers within your own applications because most tools first look up the system-defined error message before using the message defined in the exception file. You implement the TrackerError.h file as shown here:

```
// Error enumeration
enum tagTrackerError
  {
    MFCSERVER_E_NO_UBOUND = 46080,
    MFCSERVER_E_NO_LBOUND = 46081,
    MFCSERVER_E_NO_ARRAYLOCK = 46082,
    MFCSERVER_E_NO_FILE = 46083,
    MFCSERVER_E_BAD_ARRAY_PARAMETER = 46084,
    MFCSERVER_E_INVALID_VALUE = 46085
  }  TRACKERERROR;
```

After you define the exception values and set the ODL file to indicate the error values within the type library, the next step you must perform is to add the code that generates the exceptions to all of the appropriate locations in the server code. For the MFCServer program, you add the exception-handling code to the source files as shown in Listing 32-4 (only functions with changed code are indicated).

Listing 32-4: Functions within the Server After Adding the Exception-Handling Code

```
////////////////////////////////////////////////////////////////////
// CTracker message handlers
BOOL CTracker::OutputLines(VARIANT FAR* varOutputArray,
    const VARIANT FAR& varIndent)
  {
    BOOL bResult = VARIANT_TRUE;
    // check for a file and a string array in the variant
    if(m_fileLog && varOutputArray->vt == (VT_ARRAY | VT_BSTR))
     {
       // lock the array so we can use it
       if(::SafeArrayLock(varOutputArray->parray) == S_OK)
        {
          LONG lLBound;
          // get the lower bound of the array
          if(::SafeArrayGetLBound(varOutputArray->parray, 1,
              &lLBound) == S_OK)
```

```
{
  LONG lUBound;
  // get the number of elements in the array

  if(::SafeArrayGetUBound(varOutputArray->parray, 1,
      &lUBound) == S_OK)
   {
     CString cstrIndent;
     CTime oTimeStamp;
     BSTR bstrTemp;

     // if there is an indent parameter
     if(varIndent.vt != VT_I4)
      {
        // get a variant for conversion purposes
        VARIANT varConvertedValue;

        // initialize the variant
        ::VariantInit(&varConvertedValue);

        // see if thc program can convert the data
        // type to something useful - you could
        // also useVariantChangeTypeEx()
        if(S_OK ==
            ::VariantChangeType(&varConvertedValue,
            (VARIANT *) &varIndent, 0, VT_I4))
          // assign the value to the member variable
          m_lIndent = varConvertedValue.lVal;
      }
     else
       // assign the value to the member variable
       m_lIndent = varIndent.lVal;

     // if the program must indent the text
     for(long lIndentCount = 0;
         lIndentCount < m_lIndent; lIndentCount++)
       // add a tab to the string
       cstrIndent += _T("\t");

     // for each of the elements in the array
     for(long lArrayCount = lLBound;
         lArrayCount < (lUBound + lLBound);
         lArrayCount++)
      {
        // update the time
        oTimeStamp = CTime::GetCurrentTime();
        m_lHiResTime = timeGetTime();
        // get the data from the array
        if(::SafeArrayGetElement
            (varOutputArray->parray,
            &lArrayCount, &bstrTemp) == S_OK)
```

(continued)

Listing 32-4 *(continued)*

```
                {
                  // output the data
                  fprintf(m_fileLog,
                     _T("%s(%10ld)-%s%ls\n"),(LPCTSTR)
                       oTimeStamp.Format("%H:%M:%S"),
                       m_lHiResTime - m_lLastHiResTime,
                      (LPCTSTR) cstrIndent, bstrTemp);
                  // store the last timer value
                  m_lLastHiResTime = m_lHiResTime;

                  // free the bstr
                  ::SysFreeString(bstrTemp);
                }
             }
          }
          else
          {
            bResult = VARIANT_FALSE;

            // unable to find UBOUND for array
            COleDispatchException * pOleDispExcep = new
                COleDispatchException(_T(""), NULL, 0);

            // format the error code
            pOleDispExcep->m_scError =
                MAKE_SCODE(SEVERITY_ERROR,
                FACILITY_ITF, MFCSERVER_E_NO_UBOUND);

            // set the source file
            pOleDispExcep->m_strSource = __FILE__;

            // format the error description
            pOleDispExcep->m_strDescription = _T("Unable to
                retrieve the upper bound dimension of the
                array.");

            /* the function call failed—throw an OLE
               exception */
            throw(pOleDispExcep);
          }
       }
       else
       {
          bResult = VARIANT_FALSE;
          // unable to find LBOUND for array

          COleDispatchException * pOleDispExcep = new
              COleDispatchException(_T(""), NULL, 0);

          // format the error code
          pOleDispExcep->m_scError =
```

```
                MAKE_SCODE(SEVERITY_ERROR, FACILITY_ITF,
                MFCSERVER_E_NO_LBOUND);

            // set the source file
            pOleDispExcep->m_strSource = __FILE__;

            // format the error description
            pOleDispExcep->m_strDescription = _T("Unable to
                retrieve the lower bound dimension of the
                array.");

            // the function call failed—throw an OLE exception
            throw(pOleDispExcep);
          }
        // unlock the array - don't need it anymore
        ::SafeArrayUnlock(varOutputArray->parray);
      }
    else
      {
        bResult = VARIANT_FALSE;
        // unable to lock the array memory

        COleDispatchException * pOleDispExcep = new
            COleDispatchException(_T(""), NULL, 0);
        // format the error code
        pOleDispExcep->m_scError =
            MAKE_SCODE(SEVERITY_ERROR,
            FACILITY_ITF, MFCSERVER_E_NO_ARRAYLOCK);

        // set the source file
        pOleDispExcep->m_strSource = __FILE__;

        // format the error description
        pOleDispExcep->m_strDescription =
            _T("Unable to lock the array memory.");

        // the function call failed—throw an OLE exception
        throw(pOleDispExcep);
      }
  }
else
  {
    bResult = VARIANT_FALSE;
    /* unable to function because either no file handle or
       bad array parameter */
    COleDispatchException * pOleDispExcep = new
        COleDispatchException(_T(""), NULL, 0);

    // if no file handle
    if(!m_fileLog)
      // format the error code as NO_FILE
      pOleDispExcep->m_scError =
```

(continued)

Listing 32-4 *(continued)*

```
                MAKE_SCODE(SEVERITY_ERROR,
                FACILITY_ITF, MFCSERVER_E_NO_FILE);
        else
          // format the error code as BAD_ARRAY_PARAMETER
          pOleDispExcep->m_scError =
                MAKE_SCODE(SEVERITY_ERROR,
                FACILITY_ITF, MFCSERVER_E_BAD_ARRAY_PARAMETER);

        // set the source file
        pOleDispExcep->m_strSource = __FILE__;

        // if we didn't have a file handle
        if(!m_fileLog)
          // format the error description
          pOleDispExcep->m_strDescription =
                _T("Invalid File Handle.
                File could not be opened for output.");
        else
          // format the error description
          pOleDispExcep->m_strDescription =
                _T("The first parameter
                must be a string array passed by reference.");

        // the function call failed—throw an OLE exception
        throw(pOleDispExcep);
      }
    // return the result
    return bResult;
  }

void CTracker::SetIndent(long nNewValue)
  {
    // if the new value is a least 0
    if(nNewValue >= 0)
      // assign the value to our member variable
      m_lIndent = nNewValue;
    else
      {
        // unable to set the indent level
        COleDispatchException * pOleDispExcep = new
            COleDispatchException(_T(""), NULL, 0);

        // format the error code
        pOleDispExcep->m_scError =
            MAKE_SCODE(SEVERITY_ERROR,
            FACILITY_ITF, MFCSERVER_E_INVALID_VALUE);

        // set the source file
        pOleDispExcep->m_strSource = __FILE__;

        // format the error description
```

```
        pOleDispExcep->m_strDescription =
            _T("Invalid value. Value must be 0 or greater.");

        // the function call failed—throw an OLE exception
        throw(pOleDispExcep);
    }
}
```

As you can see, instead of returning VARIANT_FALSE (or, worse yet, ignoring an error condition), you now generate meaningful errors and messages instructing the developer as to the source of the problem. The exception-generating code is fairly straightforward. First, you create a pointer to a COleDispatchException object and set the appropriate members with the data that is necessary for the error that was generated (for information about other types of exceptions, see the Visual C++ documentation). For your implementation, you set the error code, the name of the file that generated the error, and the error message. You could also supply a help filename and a help ID to further describe the error. Note the use of the MAKE_SCODE macro to generate a valid SCODE error number for the exception.

Exceptions are useful for communicating error conditions and problems to the application and developer who are using an ActiveX component. Make use of them whenever you can to further enhance your implementation.

Understanding dual-interface servers

A dual-interface server is exactly what it sounds like: the server implementation supports two interfaces with which to talk to the server. One interface, an IDispatch interface, is what you have been working with so far. The other, a *custom interface,* is a type of interface that you have not learned about yet. The dual portion refers to the fact that no matter which interface you choose, you are always talking to the same server, and you always get the same response.

An IDispatch-based interface uses a generic mechanism for calling methods and properties in a server. When a method in a server is called, you pass the ID of the method to invoke and a structure describing its parameters and return type. This data is packaged and sent to the server, which unpackages the data and calls the appropriate method based on the ID supplied. A custom interface, on the other hand, is very different. When using a custom interface, you are talking directly to the server's functions and are not depending on a generic mechanism for invoking the methods or properties. The packaging of the parameters and return value are left to the compiler that created the applications.

Because the interfaces are written to access the same set of functions, the custom interface portion of a dual-interface server must conform to the same data type restrictions imposed by automation. This way, you are not required to create your own code to transfer data between the two applications, the controller and the server. OLE does that for you with standard marshaling.

The major advantage to dual-interface is performance. The number of steps to call a method using the custom interface is far less than the number needed to call a method when using the IDispatch interface. The main disadvantage to dual-interface support in MFC servers is that they are not supported by the ClassWizard and require manual changes for you to implement both interfaces. After you create the custom interface, the code involved with the interface is not too difficult to maintain.

The advantage of using the custom interface of a dual-interface server loses its luster when executing across process boundaries. The custom interface is still faster but not by much. The real performance benefit, a 25 to 50 percent improvement, occurs when the server is in-process to the calling application. The amount of improvement depends on the number and types of parameters that are being passed between the applications. If you are interested in seeing actual numbers regarding the amount of performance improvement, you can refer to the *Microsoft Systems Journal* archives (on Microsoft's Web site at http://www.microsoft.com/msj), which include several articles that specifically focus on performance differences between IDispatch and custom interfaces.

✦ ✦ ✦ ✦ ✦

The first step when converting an MFC-based ActiveX server to dual-interface is to change the ODL file. It is not necessary to generate new UUIDs because the functionality of the server has not changed. You must add the oleautomation and dual attributes to the interface class, though. You must also add the hidden attribute, so this second interface will not be visible within Visual Basic. This is fine because Visual Basic displays the CoClass interface and also shows all of the methods and properties for the server. As a general rule, you should always hide your interfaces and leave visible the CoClasses the controller uses to create them. This is because applications such as Visual Basic display both interfaces, and the reality is that only the CoClass name is valid in Visual Basic. In other words, if you try to reference an object by its interface name, you will get an error. The necessary changes that you must make to the ODL file to support dual-interface are shown in Listing 32-5.

Listing 32-5: Changes You Must Make to an ODL File for the Server to Support Dual Interfaces

```
 [ uuid(11C82943-4EDD-11D0-BED8-00400538977D), version(1.0) ]
library MFCServer
 {
   importlib("stdole32.tlb");

   [ uuid(11C82946-4EDD-11D0-BED8-00400538977D),
       oleautomation, dual, hidden ]
```

```
    interface ITracker: IDispatch
     {
       [id(1), propget]
           HRESULT Indent([out, retval] long * Value);
       [id(1), propput] HRESULT Indent([in] long Value);
       [id(2)] HRESULT OutputLines(
           [in] VARIANT * varOutputArray,
           [in, optional] VARIANT varIndent,
           [out, retval] boolean * RetVal);
     };

    // CoClass for CTracker
    [ uuid(11C82947-4EDD-11D0-BED8-00400538977D) ]
    coclass TRACKER
     {
       [default] interface ITracker;
     };
     typedef [uuid(11C82948-4EDD-11D0-BED8-00400538977D),
         helpstring("Tracker Error Constants")]
     #include "trackererror.h"
    //{{AFX_APPEND_ODL}}
};
```

You do not have to change the remainder of the ODL file entries to support dual-interface. However, because the server supports dual-interface, you must change your interface declaration to inherit from the IDispatch interface rather than declare the interface as type dispinterface, as in the original implementation. Dual-interface method and property declarations are different from dispinterface declarations, which are more like standard C++. Note that keywords such as method and properties are no longer within the interface declaration. Those terms are keywords related to the dispinterface keyword. As we stated earlier, properties are accessed using a pair of methods sharing the same dispid. The distinguishing factors are the method attributes propget and propput, which denote the direction of data flow. You must also change the CoClass to refer to interface and not dispinterface.

All dual-interface methods must return an HRESULT data type. If a method requires a return value, it must be specified as the last parameter of the method and must have the parameter attributes of out and retval. All parameters must have an attribute describing the direction of data flow. Table 32-3 contains a complete description of the possible attributes and combinations.

Note

The changes that you have made to the ODL file prevent the ClassWizard from updating the ODL file automatically when you add new methods and properties to the server. You are now responsible for maintaining the entries manually.

◆ ◆ ◆ ◆ ◆

Table 32-3
Parameter Flow Attributes

Attribute	*Description*
in	Parameter is passed from caller to callee.
out	Parameter is returned from callee to caller.
in, out	Parameter is passed from caller to callee, and the callee returns a parameter.
out, retval	Parameter is the return value of the method and is returned from the callee to the caller.

The ODL compiler has the capability of generating a C++ header file that describes all of the interfaces and enumerations that are contained in the type library that you have created for your server. The ODL-generated header file is useful for creating function prototypes that are required in the implementation of the server. You add the entry to the ODL file and compile it into a type library. Next, copy the new method from the header file into your class definition, and make some minor changes — and everything is finished. In addition, you now have an interface file that can be used by other applications to access the custom interface of your server as well as the enumerations that are used when accessing specific methods and properties.

To generate the header file, you must update the build settings of your project. To update the build settings, select the Settings option from the Project menu. Visual Studio will display the Project Settings dialog box. In the Settings For drop-down list box, select All Configurations. Expand the MFCServer project node and the Source Files node, and select the `MFCServer.odl` file. Select the MIDL tab, and in the Output header file name edit field, enter **TrackerInterface.h**. Whenever the type library is compiled, the compiler regenerates the `TrackerInterface.h` file to reflect the new implementation. Figure 32-5 shows the Project Settings dialog box after you make your changes.

After you make the changes to the build settings, you must include the new header file within the `Tracker.cpp` source file. You must also remove the `TrackerError.h` file because the error enumeration that you declared earlier in the chapter is also defined in the header file generated by the ODL compiler. The `TrackerInterface.h` file must be included *before* or *in* the `Tracker.h` file, because the `CTracker` class is dependent on the information in the `TrackerInterface.h` file. In other words, your include statements should appear in the following order within the `Tracker.cpp` file:

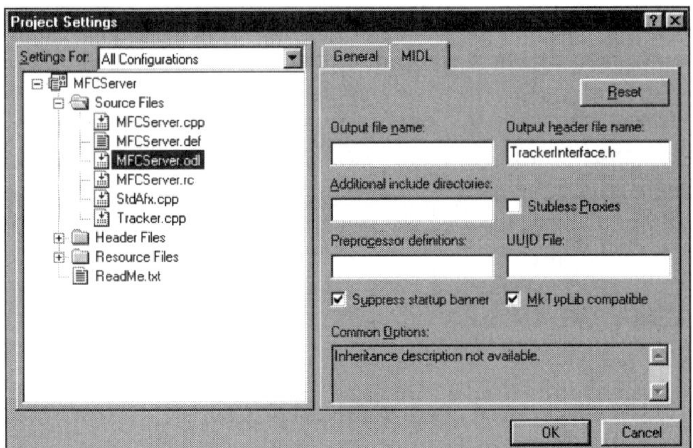

Figure 32-5: The Project Settings dialog box after updating the project settings to create the C++ header file from the ODL file

```
#include "MFCServer.h"
// ODL generated interface file
#include "trackerinterface.h"
#include "Tracker.h"
// needed for the high resolution timer services
#include <mmsystem.h>
// more code here
```

MFC defines a set of macros for describing interfaces within the context of an MFC component implementation. The interface macro defines the interface, its name, and the methods that it contains. You must add the MFC interface declaration to your class definition to describe the custom interface portion of your server. You can add the interface declaration anywhere after the `DECLARE_INTERFACE_MAP` macro. You implement the interface declaration within the `Tracker.h` file as shown in Listing 32-6.

Listing 32-6: The Tracker.h File After Implementing the Interface Declaration

```
// more code here
// needed for dual interface support
BEGIN_INTERFACE_PART(SubDispatch, ITracker)
  STDMETHOD(GetTypeInfoCount)(THIS_ UINT FAR* pctinfo);
  STDMETHOD(GetTypeInfo)(THIS_ UINT itinfo, LCID lcid,
      ITypeInfo FAR* FAR* pptinfo);
  STDMETHOD(GetIDsOfNames)(THIS_ REFIID riid,
      OLECHAR FAR* FAR* rgszNames, UINT cNames, LCID lcid,
      DISPID FAR* rgdispid);
```

(continued)

Listing 32-6 *(continued)*

```
  STDMETHOD(Invoke)(THIS_ DISPID dispidMember, REFIID riid,
      LCID lcid, WORD wFlags, DISPPARAMS FAR* pdispparams,
      VARIANT FAR* pvarResult, EXCEPINFO FAR* pexcepinfo,
      UINT FAR* puArgErr);
  virtual /* [propget][id] */ HRESULT STDMETHODCALLTYPE
      get_Indent(/* [retval][out] */ long __RPC_FAR *Value);

  virtual /* [propput][id] */ HRESULT STDMETHODCALLTYPE
      put_Indent(/* [in] */ long Value);
  virtual /* [id] */ HRESULT STDMETHODCALLTYPE
      OutputLines(
      /* [in] */ VARIANT __RPC_FAR *varOutputArray,
      /* [optional][in] */ VARIANT varIndent,
      /* [retval][out] */ VARIANT_BOOL __RPC_FAR *RetVal);

END_INTERFACE_PART(SubDispatch)
// more code here
```

The first parameter of the `BEGIN_INTERFACE_PART` macro, `SubDispatch`, is the name that is used to create a nested class within the class definition of the server. The second parameter is the name of the interface from which the nested class is inherited. The `ITracker` interface is declared in the `TrackerInterface.h` header file that was created from the ODL file. The `ITracker` declaration in the header file contains a set of pure virtual functions that need to be copied into your interface declaration. When copying the functions, remember to remove the `= 0` from the end of the function, because this is where you will implement them.

The header file contains the interface declaration, and the source file contains the interface implementation. The MFC AppWizard created a default interface implementation for the server when it was created. The original definition deferred to the default `IDispatch` interface defined in MFC. Because you have implemented an interface that inherits from `IDispatch`, it is necessary to route all `IDispatch` calls to the new interface. The interface map located in the server source file must be changed to reflect the new interface that you have declared. Change the interface from `IDispatch` to the name of the interface declared in the header file, in your case `SubDispatch`. Changing the name of the interface has the effect of routing all calls to the `IDispatch` interface to your implementation of the interface first, which you can then implement yourself or pass on to the default implementation. You implement the `ITracker` interface within the `Tracker.cpp` file as shown here:

```
// more code here
BEGIN_INTERFACE_MAP(CTracker, CCmdTarget)
  INTERFACE_PART(CTracker, IID_IDispatch, SubDispatch)
  INTERFACE_PART(CTracker, IID_ITracker, SubDispatch)
END_INTERFACE_MAP()
```

Unfortunately, MFC does not enable true C++ inheritance of the COM interfaces it contains, so it is necessary to route messages for a particular COM interface to the correct handler function in the server. Routing the messages is done through the BEGIN_INTERFACE_MAP macro. Because your implementation supports both an IDispatch interface and a custom interface, you are required to add two entries to the macro (one for each interface). In your case, you defer all IDispatch messages to the custom interface functions. The same is true of the custom interface messages.

The last step in adding dual-interface support to your server is to add the actual implementation of the functions declared in the interface. The first set of functions to implement is the base IDispatch functions that your server inherited from the IDispatch class. In all cases, you defer to the base class implementation of the method. You have the option to implement these functions yourself or rely on MFC to handle the methods for you. It's important to note the method you must use to call the basic IDispatch functions. Because the server captures all IDispatch messages and routes them to the custom interface implementation, you cannot call GetIDispatch() to retrieve the pointer to the IDispatch interface of the server (doing so would result in a recursive call because the IDispatch functions are routed to your server implementation). Instead, the implementation must call the IDispatch functions ((IDispatch*)&pThis->m_xDispatch)-> directly, bypassing the message-routing functions, which avoids the recursion problem. You implement the functions as shown in Listing 32-7.

Listing 32-7: Functions You Implement for the IDispatch Interface Handlers

```
/////////////////////////////////////////////////////////////////
// CTracker Standard IDispatch Dual Interface Handlers
ULONG FAR EXPORT CTracker::XSubDispatch::AddRef()
 {
   METHOD_PROLOGUE(CTracker, SubDispatch)
   return pThis->ExternalAddRef();
 }

ULONG FAR EXPORT CTracker::XSubDispatch::Release()
 {
   METHOD_PROLOGUE(CTracker, SubDispatch)
   return pThis->ExternalRelease();
 }

HRESULT FAR EXPORT CTracker::XSubDispatch::
    QueryInterface(REFIID riid, LPVOID FAR* ppvObj)
 {
   METHOD_PROLOGUE(CTracker, SubDispatch)
   return (HRESULT) pThis->
       ExternalQueryInterface(&riid, ppvObj);
 }
```

(continued)

Listing 32-7 *(continued)*

```
HRESULT FAR EXPORT CTracker::XSubDispatch::
    GetTypeInfoCount(UINT FAR* pctinfo)
 {
   METHOD_PROLOGUE(CTracker, SubDispatch)
   return ((IDispatch*)&pThis->m_xDispatch)->
       GetTypeInfoCount(pctinfo);
 }

HRESULT FAR EXPORT CTracker::XSubDispatch::
    GetTypeInfo(UINT itinfo, LCID lcid,
    ITypeInfo FAR* FAR* pptinfo)
 {
   METHOD_PROLOGUE(CTracker, SubDispatch)
   return ((IDispatch*)&pThis->m_xDispatch)->
       GetTypeInfo(itinfo, lcid, pptinfo);
 }

HRESULT FAR EXPORT CTracker::XSubDispatch::
    GetIDsOfNames(REFIID riid, OLECHAR FAR* FAR* rgszNames,
        UINT cNames, LCID lcid, DISPID FAR* rgdispid)
 {
   METHOD_PROLOGUE(CTracker, SubDispatch)
   return ((IDispatch*)&pThis->m_xDispatch)->
       GetIDsOfNames(riid, rgszNames, cNames, lcid, rgdispid);
 }

HRESULT FAR EXPORT CTracker::XSubDispatch::
    Invoke(DISPID dispidMember, REFIID riid, LCID lcid,
        WORD wFlags, DISPPARAMS FAR* pdispparams,
        VARIANT FAR* pvarResult,EXCEPINFO FAR* pexcepinfo,
        UINT FAR* puArgErr)
 {
   METHOD_PROLOGUE(CTracker, SubDispatch)
   return ((IDispatch*)&pThis->m_xDispatch)->
       Invoke(dispidMember, riid, lcid, wFlags, pdispparams,
       pvarResult, pexcepinfo, puArgErr);
 }
```

You should note that you must declare the nested class `SubDispatch` as `XSubDispatch` in the implementation. The `X` comes from the `BEGIN_INTERFACE_PART` macros and has no particular significance. The same is true for the member variable `m_xDispatch`.

Note the use of the macro `METHOD_PROLOGUE`, which is required in MFC-based applications to ensure that MFC is in a valid state while the function is executing.

The last step in building your dual-interface server is to implement the functions that are specific to your server. You can simplify the implementation by calling the original MFC functions from the dual-interface implementations rather than reimplementing the functions using the new style. Doing so solves several problems. First, you can still rely on the MFC message mapping functions to invoke the methods when you call them through the `IDispatch` interface, and it does not require you implement your own `IDispatch` code. Supporting the original MFC implementation also prevents having to change internal code that may rely on the already existing functions. As you will see a little later in this chapter, adding error handling to the dual-interface code is much simpler using this style. You implement the `ITracker` functions within the `Tracker.cpp` file as shown in Listing 32-8.

Listing 32-8: Implementation of the ITracker Functions within the Tracker.cpp File

```
////////////////////////////////////////////////////////////////////////
// CTracker interface handlers
HRESULT CTracker::XSubDispatch::get_Indent(LONG * Indent)
 {
   METHOD_PROLOGUE(CTracker, SubDispatch)
   HRESULT hResult = S_OK;
   *Indent = pThis->GetIndent();
   return hResult;
 }

HRESULT CTracker::XSubDispatch::put_Indent(LONG Indent)
 {
   METHOD_PROLOGUE(CTracker, SubDispatch)
   HRESULT hResult = S_OK;
   pThis->SetIndent(Indent);
   return hResult;
 }

HRESULT FAR EXPORT CTracker::XSubDispatch::
     OutputLines(VARIANT FAR* varOutputArray,
          VARIANT varIndent, VARIANT_BOOL FAR* RetVal)
 {
   METHOD_PROLOGUE(CTracker, SubDispatch)
   HRESULT hResult = S_OK;
   *RetVal = pThis->OutputLines(varOutputArray, varIndent);
   return hResult;
 }
```

After you compile the server and register it, you are ready to test its new dual-interface functionality. From C++, you can create the server as you did before, but now you may access its custom interface by using the `QueryInterface()` function and supply the correct interface IID. From Visual Basic, you need only add the type library for the server to your list of references and change the name of the variable to the name that appears in the Object References dialog box. You can also create the server using the Visual Basic `New` operator instead of the `CreateObject()` method. In other words, the following Visual Basic program code will now execute properly:

```
Dim MyTracker as TRACKER
Set MyTracker = new TRACKER
```

In C++, you call the `QueryInterface()` function and pass the `IID ITracker` interface IID. The last step in your dual-interface conversion is to handle errors correctly. As a general rule, a server cannot throw C++ exceptions from the custom interface implementation of a dual-interface server. For that matter, it can't throw them from any interface. MFC just does the job of catching the C++ exceptions and converting them to OLE exceptions that are understood by OLE. Because you are supporting a custom interface in your server, you must do the same—that is, convert the C++ exceptions into OLE exceptions that your server can pass through either interface to the controlling program.

Generating dual-interface OLE exceptions

Dual-interface rules for handling errors and exceptions are slightly different for the custom interface portion of the interface. As you learned earlier in this chapter, you must change all of the methods in the custom interface to return an `HRESULT` in place of the function's normal return value. An `HRESULT` is used to indicate that an error or exception has occurred within the context of the method that was invoked. When an automation controller invokes a method in the custom interface of a server, it should check the return value of the function to see if it returned `S_OK`. If not, the controller has the option of checking to see whether the server supports extended error information via the `ISupportErrorInfo` interface. When a server that supports the `ISupportErrorInfo` interface creates an error, it does so by creating an `IErrorInfo` object containing the error information.

MFC does not support the `ISupportErrorInfo` interface by default, so you must add it yourself. You can create a set of macros to aid in adding the `ISupportErrorInfo` interface to your automation server. The macros are based on those defined in the `ACDUAL` sample included with MFC, and you can use them to simplify the `ISupportErrorInfo` implementation. You implement the macros within the `ErrorInfoMacros.h` file as shown in Listing 32-9.

Listing 32-9: Macros within the ErrorInfoMacros.h File

```
/* this code is based on the ACDUAL MFC\OLE sample application
   provided with Visual C++  */
//////////////////////////////////////////////////////////////////
```

```
// DECLARE_DUAL_ERRORINFO expands to declare the
// ISupportErrorInfosupport class. It works together with
// DUAL_ERRORINFO_PART and IMPLEMENT_DUAL_ERRORINFO defined
// below.

#define DECLARE_DUAL_ERRORINFO() \
   BEGIN_INTERFACE_PART(SupportErrorInfo, ISupportErrorInfo) \
   STDMETHOD(InterfaceSupportsErrorInfo)(THIS_ REFIID riid); \
   END_INTERFACE_PART(SupportErrorInfo) \

/////////////////////////////////////////////////////////////
// DUAL_ERRORINFO_PART adds the appropriate entry to the
// interface map for ISupportErrorInfo, if you
// used DECLARE_DUAL_ERRORINFO.

#define DUAL_ERRORINFO_PART(objectClass) \
   INTERFACE_PART(objectClass, IID_ISupportErrorInfo,
       SupportErrorInfo) \

/////////////////////////////////////////////////////////////
// IMPLEMENT_DUAL_ERRORINFO expands to an implementation of
// ISupportErrorInfo which matches the declaration in
// DECLARE_DUAL_ERRORINFO.

#define IMPLEMENT_DUAL_ERRORINFO(objectClass, riidSource) \
   STDMETHODIMP_(ULONG) \
       objectClass::XSupportErrorInfo::AddRef() \
     { \
      METHOD_PROLOGUE(objectClass, SupportErrorInfo) \
      return pThis->ExternalAddRef(); \
     } \
   STDMETHODIMP_(ULONG) \
       objectClass::XSupportErrorInfo::Release() \
     { \
      METHOD_PROLOGUE(objectClass, SupportErrorInfo) \
      return pThis->ExternalRelease(); \
     } \
   STDMETHODIMP \
       objectClass::XSupportErrorInfo::QueryInterface( \
     REFIID iid, LPVOID* ppvObj) \
      { \
        METHOD_PROLOGUE(objectClass, SupportErrorInfo) \
        return pThis->ExternalQueryInterface(&iid, ppvObj); \
      } \
   STDMETHODIMP objectClass::XSupportErrorInfo:: \
       InterfaceSupportsErrorInfo( \
     REFIID iid) \
      { \
        METHOD_PROLOGUE(objectClass, SupportErrorInfo) \
        return (iid == riidSource) ? S_OK : S_FALSE; \
      }
```

After you create the ErrorInfoMacros.h file, make sure you add it to the Tracker.cpp file. Be sure that you include the ErrorInfoMacros.h file *before* the TrackerInterface.h file.

In addition, you must add a macro and a helper function to the class declaration of the server. The macro declares the ISupportErrorInfo interface, and the helper function is used to translate the exception into an IErrorInfo object. You implement the changes within the Tracker.h header file as shown here:

```
// more code here

   DECLARE_OLECREATE(CTracker)
     // add declaration of ISupportErrorInfo implementation
     // to indicate Server supports the OLE Automation
     // error object
     DECLARE_DUAL_ERRORINFO()
     HRESULT CreateErrorInfo(CException * pAnyException,
         REFIID riidSource);

     // needed for dual interface support
     BEGIN_INTERFACE_PART(SubDispatch, ITracker)

// more code here
```

Now that you have created your interface declaration within the header file, you must add the interface to the interface map. You must also add the implementation macro for the interface and add the implementation of the helper function. You implement the changes within the Tracker.cpp file as shown in Listing 32-10.

Listing 32-10: Changes to the Tracker.cpp File

```
BEGIN_INTERFACE_MAP(CTracker, CCmdTarget)
  INTERFACE_PART(CTracker, IID_ITracker, SubDispatch)
  DUAL_ERRORINFO_PART(CTracker)
END_INTERFACE_MAP()

IMPLEMENT_OLECREATE(CTracker, _T("MFCServer.Tracker"),
    0x11C82947, 0x4cdd, 0x11d0, 0xbe, 0xd8, 0x0, 0x40, 0x5,
    0x38, 0x97, 0x7d)

// Implement ISupportErrorInfo to indicate server supports the
// OLE Automation error handler.
IMPLEMENT_DUAL_ERRORINFO(CTracker, IID_ITracker)

/* this code is based on the ACDUAL MFC\OLE sample application
   provided with Visual C++ */
HRESULT CTracker::CreateErrorInfo(CException * pAnyException,
    REFIID riidSource)
 {
   ASSERT_VALID(pAnyException);
```

```
// create an error info object
ICreateErrorInfo * pcerrinfo;
HRESULT hr = ::CreateErrorInfo(&pcerrinfo);

// if succeessful
if(SUCCEEDED(hr))
 {
   // dispatch exception?
   if(pAnyException->
       IsKindOf(RUNTIME_CLASS(COleDispatchException)))
    {
      // specific IDispatch style exception
      COleDispatchException * e =
          (COleDispatchException *) pAnyException;

      // set the return value to the error
      hr = e->m_scError;

      // Set up ErrInfo object
      pcerrinfo->SetGUID(riidSource);
      pcerrinfo->SetDescription(e->
          m_strDescription.AllocSysString());
      pcerrinfo->SetHelpContext(e->m_dwHelpContext);
      pcerrinfo->
          SetHelpFile(e->m_strHelpFile.AllocSysString());
      pcerrinfo->
          SetSource(e->m_strSource.AllocSysString());
    }
   else if (pAnyException->
       IsKindOf(RUNTIME_CLASS(CMemoryException)))
    {
      // failed memory allocation
      hr = E_OUTOFMEMORY;

      // Set up ErrInfo object
      pcerrinfo->SetGUID(riidSource);
      CString cstrFileName(AfxGetAppName());
      pcerrinfo->SetSource(cstrFileName.AllocSysString());
    }
   else
    {
      // other unknown/unexpected error
      hr = E_UNEXPECTED;

      // Set up ErrInfo object
      pcerrinfo->SetGUID(riidSource);
      CString cstrFileName(AfxGetAppName());
      pcerrinfo->SetSource(cstrFileName.AllocSysString());
    }

   // QI for the IErrorInfo interface
   IErrorInfo * perrinfo;
```

(continued)

Listing 32-10 *(continued)*

```
        if(SUCCEEDED(pcerrinfo->
            QueryInterface(IID_IErrorInfo, (LPVOID *)
            &perrinfo)))
         {
           // set the error info object
           ::SetErrorInfo(0, perrinfo);

           // release the reference
           perrinfo->Release();
         }

        // release the reference
        pcerrinfo->Release();
      }
     // delete the exception
     pAnyException->Delete();

     // return the error value
     return hr;
   }
```

The `CreateErrorInfo()` function translates any exception into an `IErrorInfo` object. The function is based on code that is part of the ACDUAL MFC sample application included with MFC. The primary responsibility of the function is to convert `COleDispatchExceptions` into `IErrorInfo` objects. It can, however, deal with any exception that it is passed, but the level of information about the error is far less. After the exception has been translated, it is set as the error information object for the currently executing thread.

The last step is to update the custom interface methods to defer all exceptions to the helper function that you just added. The additional code that you require is straightforward and simple to implement. For each of the methods, you wrap the call to the basic implementation of the function with a `try...catch` block that translates any exception into an `IErrorInfo` object and returns the error code of the exception to the calling application. You implement the additional code within the `Tracker.cpp` file as shown in Listing 32-11.

Listing 32-11: Translating Exceptions into an IErrorInfo Object

```
/////////////////////////////////////////////////////////////////
// CTracker interface handlers
HRESULT CTracker::XSubDispatch::get_Indent(LONG * Indent)
 {
```

```
    METHOD_PROLOGUE(CTracker, SubDispatch)
    HRESULT hResult = S_OK;
    try
     {
       *Indent = pThis->GetIndent();
     }
    catch(CException * pException)
     {
       hResult = pThis->
           CreateErrorInfo(pException, IID_ITracker);
     }
    return hResult;
  }

HRESULT CTracker::XSubDispatch::put_Indent(LONG Indent)
  {
    METHOD_PROLOGUE(CTracker, SubDispatch)
    HRESULT hResult = S_OK;

    try
     {
       pThis->SetIndent(Indent);
     }
    catch(CException * pException)
     {
       hResult =
           pThis->CreateErrorInfo(pException, IID_ITracker);
     }
    return hResult;
  }

HRESULT FAR EXPORT CTracker::XSubDispatch::
    OutputLines(VARIANT FAR* varOutputArray,
        VARIANT varIndent, VARIANT_BOOL FAR* RetVal)
  {
    METHOD_PROLOGUE(CTracker, SubDispatch)
    HRESULT hResult = S_OK;
    try
     {
       *RetVal = pThis->OutputLines(varOutputArray, varIndent);
     }
    catch(CException * pException)
     {
       hResult =
           pThis->CreateErrorInfo(pException, IID_ITracker);
     }
    return hResult;
  }
```

Thus far, we have covered all of the basics of ActiveX server creation and use by applications other than your own. However, there may be situations in which you must create and use the server from within the application in which it is defined. Or your application may contain more than one server implementation, with only one server being exposed as a createable object and with the remaining servers being created only in response to a valid method call in the exposed server. These are referred to as *nested objects*. You can use many techniques to add additional power to your server objects. In the remainder of this chapter, you will consider three specific management cases for your automation servers: instantiating from C++, creating shared servers, and creating single-use servers.

Server Instantiation Using C++

While you have spent much of this chapter learning how to create and use automation servers with MFC and OLE, such design is not the only method available to you for creating and using automation servers. You can also instantiate automation servers using C++ syntax.

At times, instantiating and using automation servers is necessary from within the application that defines the server. For example, an application might contain three servers, only one of which is directly createable by outside applications using OLE. The remaining two servers can be created by the exposed server using C++ and returned via a method call to another application, which then uses the server as though it was created via OLE.

As you learned earlier in this chapter, for an application to be created by another application using OLE, the server must include the MFC macros `DECLARE_OLECREATE` and `IMPLEMENT_OLECREATE`. By removing or not including these macros, you can specify that other applications cannot instantiate the server using standard OLE server-creation mechanisms. That fact, however, does not prevent the server from being created using C++ and MFC. Note, though, that you can create any OLE server in this fashion, as opposed to just those that are not createable through standard OLE mechanisms. MFC supports a facility for creating OLE servers using a helper class known as `CRuntimeClass`.

You can use the `CRuntimeClass` object to create servers that you can use internally to the application in which you define the servers and externally as a return or parameter value supplied to another application. To support `CRuntimeClass` creation of objects, a class must define the `IMPLEMENT_DYNAMIC`, `IMPLEMENT_DYNCREATE`, or the `IMPLEMENT_SERIAL` macros within their class implementation, which is true for any MFC class inherited for `CObject`, and not just those classes that use OLE.

The following code is not included in the sample applications because of its simplicity. However, the code does use the `CTracker` server as its example server. To create a server using the `CRuntimeClass`, you use code similar to the following:

```
// create a CTracker runtime object
CRuntimeClass * pRuntimeClass = RUNTIME_CLASS(CTracker);

// create an CTracker OLE object
CTracker * opTracker =
    (CTracker *) pRuntimeClass->CreateObject();

// use the object as the application requires

// finished with the object - destroy it
delete opTracker;
```

After you create an object, you can also pass the object to another application. MFC supports two functions for retrieving OLE interfaces from a running server, the `GetIDispatch()` and `GetInterface()` functions. `GetIDispatch()` is defined and explained within the Visual C++ help file, but the `GetInterface()` function is not. `GetInterface()` accepts a single parameter—the IID of the interface that is being requested. `GetInterface()`does not increment the reference count of the pointer that is returned. The `GetIDispatch()` function gives you the options of incrementing the reference counter for the pointer or not incrementing it.

Common problems when instantiating OLE servers using C++

Two problems arise when instantiating OLE components using C++: reference counting and in-process versus out-of-process execution. For reference counting, the problems can be that too many or too few reference counts exist on the server being used. Reference counting problems can arise regardless of how the server is instantiated, with either C++ or OLE. The problem is really relative to using servers in one-to-many relationships. All of the applications that use the same server must add references and release the server properly to prevent problems. Reference counting problems manifest themselves as either the server terminating before it should or not terminating when it should. Be sure to check that all reference counts are being incremented and decremented correctly when creating and using objects in a one-to-many relationship or when a server is created and passed to another application.

The next problem that can arise is far more subtle and easier to miss, although the effects can be dramatic and obvious and involve the server's execution model. A server is not guaranteed to execute in-process to the application that is using it—only with the application that created it.

For example, Application A creates and uses an in-process server called `Server 1`. At some point, Application A creates an out-of-process server called Application B. Application A passes `Server 1` to Application B. `Server 1` executes as an out-of-process server to Application B because the `Server 1` object was created in the process space of Application A. It's important to keep this in mind when creating and using nested objects or shared objects because the performance differences between the two is so great.

So far you have looked only at how to create individual instances of objects. Next you will look at how to share objects — that is, how to enable multiple containers to access a single running instance of an object.

Creating shareable servers

OLE defines a facility for sharing objects called the *Running Object Table.* Essentially, a shareable object will publish its `CLSID` and an `IUnknown` reference to itself in the Running Object Table. Any application that so desires can ask for the running instance of the object rather than create a new instance. Using shared objects is useful for applications that may need to work with a single running instance of an application rather than create multiple copies. The `Tracker` object is a perfect candidate for this type of basic functionality. Multiple applications could use the same `Tracker` object to log information, thus saving on memory.

The first step in enabling shared object support is to add a member variable to store the ID that identifies the object in the Running Object Table. This ID must be retained because it is used later in revoking the object from the Running Object Table when the object is destroyed. For the sample implementation, you add the variable as a public member of the class. You add the variable within the `Tracker.h` header file as shown here:

```
// more code here

END_INTERFACE_PART(SubDispatch)
public:
    DWORD m_dwRegister;

protected:
    FILE * m_fileLog;

// more code here
```

When registering a server in the Running Object Table, you use the `CLSID` of the `CoClass` object to identify the object in the table. Your implementation requires that you declare the `CLSID` of the `CoClass` object in the source file. The `CLSID` is copied from the `TrackerInterface.h` header file and added to the source file. The line before the `CLSID` should be the include file `initguid.h`. The `initguid.h` file is needed to properly declare the `CLSID` and resolve it to the compiler. You implement the `CLSID` declaration within the `Tracker.cpp` file as shown here:

```
// more code here

static const IID IID_ITracker =
     { 0x11c82946, 0x4edd, 0x11d0, { 0xbe, 0xd8, 0x0, 0x40,
       0x5, 0x38, 0x97, 0x7d }
#include <initguid.h>
```

```
DEFINE_GUID(CLSID_TRACKER, 0x11C82947L, 0x4EDD, 0x11D0, 0xBE,
    0xD8, 0x00,  0x40, 0x05, 0x38, 0x97, 0x7D);
BEGIN_INTERFACE_MAP(CTracker, CCmdTarget)

// more code here
```

Next, you must add the code to the server that registers the object as running in the Running Object Table. The specifics of your server determine the exact location where you register the server as running. For your implementation, the constructor is fine. Other implementations may be dependent on a particular state being reached in the server before registering the server. The decision is completely up to you and your specific implementation. You implement the `CTracker` shared object support in the constructor of the `CTracker` class as shown in Listing 32-12.

Listing 32-12: Implementing the CTracker Shared Object Support

```
// more code here

EnableAutomation();
   // make sure that the application won't unload until the
   // reference count is 0
   ::AfxOleLockApp();

   // clear the member
   m_dwRegister = NULL;

   // QI for the IUnknown - remember no AddRef
   LPUNKNOWN pIUnknown = this->GetInterface(&IID_IUnknown);

   // if have an IUnknown
   if(pIUnknown)
    {
      // register the clsid as an active object so other
      // applications will get the same object
      if(::RegisterActiveObject(pIUnknown, CLSID_TRACKER,
          ACTIVEOBJECT_STRONG, &m_dwRegister) != S_OK)
        // make sure that the reference is clear
        m_dwRegister = NULL;
    }

   // setup the timer resolution
   m_lTimeBegin = timeBeginPeriod(1);
   m_lHiResTime = m_lLastHiResTime = timeGetTime();

   // more code here
```

In your implementation, the first step is to clear the member variable. The implementation is dependent on this member to identify whether or not the object was successfully registered as running. Next, you must retrieve the `IUnknown` reference for the object and, if successful, pass it along with an address of the member variable to the `RegisterActiveObject()` function. You specify a strong registration that results in an extra reference count on the server to keep it in memory. If you didn't register the server, make sure to clear the member variable, just to be safe.

The last step is to call `RevokeActiveObject()` to remove the server from the Running Object Table. This step is the most critical aspect of shared object support. Do not add this code to the destructor of your server, because it will never be called. The destructor is called in response to the destruction of the server, which results from the server reference count reaching 0. But because the server has an extra reference count from the `RegisterActiveObject()` call, the server never reaches this state. To ensure that you properly remove the server from the table, your best course of action is to implement the revocation in the `Release()` function of the `IUnknown` implementation of your server so that the server's reference count can be monitored. You will implement the `Release()` function as shown in Listing 32-13 to revoke the object from the Running Object Table.

Listing 32-13: **Implementing the Release() Function**

```
// more code here
ULONG FAR EXPORT CTracker::XSubDispatch::Release()
 {
   METHOD_PROLOGUE(CTracker, SubDispatch)

   // call the function and check the refcount
   long lRefCount = pThis->ExternalRelease();

   // if server running and this is the only refcount left
   if(pThis->m_dwRegister && lRefCount == 1)
    {
      // bump the refcount up so the routine doesn't destroy
      // the server until it is done
      pThis->ExternalAddRef();

      // get the registration ID
      DWORD tdwRegister = pThis->m_dwRegister;

      // clear the member variable to prevent hitting this
      // method again
      pThis->m_dwRegister = 0;

      // remove the interface from the running object table
      ::RevokeActiveObject(tdwRegister, NULL);

      // the revoke decremented the refcount by one
      // this call to Release destroys the server
      return pThis->ExternalRelease();
    }
```

```
        // exit
        return lRefCount;
    }

    // more code here
```

Each time the program calls Release(), the function begins its processing by making a call to decrement the reference count of the server, and the return value is saved. Next, the program code checks to see if the server has been registered as running, which is implied through a non-zero value in the member variable. Then, the program code checks to see if the reference count is 1. If the reference count is 1, the object is ready to be destroyed because the only application now referencing the object is the Running Object Table. Before calling RevokeActiveObject(), however, it is important to increment the reference count and clear the member variable. RevokeActiveObject()results in a recursive call to Release(), and you do not want to actually destroy the object until you are finished with the first call to Release() (otherwise, you will likely cause memory corruption and a program failure). After the RevokeActiveObject() call returns, you call the Release() function one last time to actually destroy the object and remove it from memory.

During the lifetime of the server, you can get the same instance of the server and use it from multiple applications. In Visual Basic, getting a running instance of a server is done with the GetObject() function, and in Visual C++, with the GetActiveObject() function. After the container retrieves the pointer to the server, the container can use the server as though the container created the server through normal OLE mechanisms.

This method of sharing objects is fine but requires that the application using the server take an active role in deciding to use the shared object versus an application creating its own instance of the object. Another approach can be taken: you can supply the instance of a running server to an application that calls CreateObject(), rather than relying on an application to call GetObject(). This approach is known as a *single instance server*—because the container program can never create more than that single instance.

Single instance servers

To support single instance servers, it is necessary to perform all of the steps that you learned about earlier in this chapter in the section "Creating shareable servers," from within the ClassFactory of the server and not from within the implementation of the server itself. By implementing the object-sharing code within the class factory, you are able to control the number of instances of the server without having to rely on the user of the server to program specifically for those cases.

Unfortunately, MFC does not provide simple access to the `COleObjectFactory` class, which is responsible for creating OLE servers to enable this kind of implementation. C++ inheritance, however, enables you to create a new specialized version of the `COleObjectFactory` class that can support server instance sharing.

You must add two macros to the server class declaration and implementation to enable shared server support. `DECLARE_OLECREATE_SHARED` must replace the `DECLARE_OLECREATE` macro in the class header file, and `IMPLEMENT_OLECREATE_SHARED` must replace `IMPLEMENT_OLECREATE` in the server source file. The only difference between the new macros and the originals is that a class factory of type `COleObjectFactoryShared` is added to the server implementation rather than a `COleObjectFactory` class. Creating the code to support single servers is relatively consistent with the code used to create a shared server.

The code to implement single instance servers is contained within the `sharedobject.cpp` and `sharedobject.h` files on the companion CD-ROM within the `Chap32\MFCServer` directory.

◆ ◆ ◆ ◆ ◆

Summary

In this chapter, you learned how to create a basic implementation of an MFC automation server. You also learned how to expand upon the basic framework provided by MFC to create new and interesting features within your implementation.

Other areas where your server development has room to expand are in adding a user interface to a server, possibly in the form of dialogs and event interfaces. The use of the basic MFC dialog classes can make implementation of UI an easy and rewarding part of your implementations. However, currently, no container applications recognize either of these features within an automation server. If your implementation has these requirements, you must decide how to implement them. The creation of services and remote servers also makes the prospect of implementing automation servers very enticing.

Every day more and more developers are enabling or integrating automation support as a basic feature of their applications. Any situation that calls for the transfer of data among applications can now be performed with OLE automation, whereas before data transfer would have required the exchange of data using DDE or, even worse, file import/export functions.

Automation servers provide an easy and flexible way to create lightweight ActiveX components for use by your applications. The support of both `IDispatch` interfaces and custom interfaces (a dual-interface server) also gives the user of the server a lot of flexibility in terms of implementation styles and methods.

✦ ✦ ✦

Active Template Library

✦ ✦ ✦ ✦

In This Chapter

The Active Template Library

Creating an ATL control

Adding a COM object

Adding functionality to the control

Implementing the interface functions

Using the control from C++

ATL data types

Embedding an ActiveX control in a Web page

✦ ✦ ✦ ✦

Writing Active Template Library (ATL) controls is one of the most useful techniques for sharing code. Developers often customarily share controls, full-blown ActiveX controls, and ATL controls alike.

This chapter gets you started in your ATL adventure. You learn how to create controls with Visual C++, and then how to use the control that was created in a Visual C++ program.

A Brief Look at ATL

The ATL was designed to make your job as a developer easier. ATL provides an easy and flexible way to create COM objects in C++. Its footprint is small — that is, the compiled controls are small. This means that with ATL you can create relatively small, self-contained files — most of which don't require any additional runtime DLLs.

Right now there's a movement away from monolithic, standalone applications. ATL is a good medium for developing the lightweight COM components that are needed for modern distributed applications. ATL isn't a large system of interrelated classes and libraries. It's more of a modular, time-saving library that prevents programmers from having to implement `IUnknown` and `IClassFactor` every time they write another control.

ATL does not try to be all things to all people. Version 1 provides very reasonable support for implementing `IUnknown`, `IClassFactory`, `IDispatch`, `IConnectionPointContainer`, and COM enumeration. Version 2 offers enhanced versions of the original ATL classes in addition to support for writing ActiveX controls. ATL does not provide collections and strings (ATL assumes you will use the Standard C++ Library classes for these); ODBC support (the world is moving to COM-based data access that doesn't need wrapping); WinSock wrappers (sockets are so five-minutes-ago); or a complete wrapper for the Win32 API (ATL 2.0's control implementation provides support for implementing dialogs and `WndProcs`). Also missing from ATL is MFC's document/view model. Instead, ATL assumes that you will use the more scalable and flexible COM approach of connectable outbound COM interfaces (ActiveX controls, for instance) to notify the UI-based objects.

The key idea is to use the right tool for the job. If you are building nonvisual COM components, ATL is likely to be a much better choice than MFC in terms of development effort, scalability, runtime performance, and executable size. For modern user interfaces based on ActiveX controls, ATL also produces smaller and faster code than MFC. On the other hand, ATL requires more COM knowledge than is needed to operate MFC's ClassWizard. For building double-clickable single-tier applications, ATL is currently no more helpful than the Standard Template Library (STL). For this, MFC remains the superior choice.

The design of ATL is highly inspired by STL, which has become part of the Standard C++ Library included with all ANSI/ISO-compliant C++ compilers. Like STL, ATL uses C++ templates aggressively. Templates are one of the more controversial features in C++. When abused, templates can lead to bloated executables, poor performance, and unintelligible code. Used judiciously, templates provide a degree of generality combined with type safety that is difficult to achieve otherwise. Like STL, ATL falls between these two extremes. Fortunately, compiler and linker technology is advancing at about the same pace as aggressive template usage, making STL and ATL reasonable choices for current and future development.

Despite its extensive use of templates internally, you can use ATL without ever having to type an angle bracket. This is because ATL ships with the ATL Object wizard, which generates a variety of default object implementations based on ATL's template classes. The ATL Object wizard enables anyone to get a COM object up and running in a matter of minutes without thinking about COM or ATL. Of course, to take full advantage of ATL you do need to understand C++, templates, and COM programming techniques. However, for a large class of objects, the ATL Object wizard's default implementations require only the addition of method implementations for any custom interfaces being exported, which for most developers is the whole point of implementing a COM object in the first place.

At first glance, the ATL architecture may seem quite bizarre and arcane. For mainstream component developers just getting up to speed on COM, the actual ATL architecture is irrelevant because the wizards generate perfectly reasonable skeletons that only require method definitions. For serious COM developers and systems programmers, ATL provides an elegant, extensible architecture for building COM components in C++. Once you understand the architecture and move beyond the wizards, ATL can be as expressive and powerful as raw COM programming.

Creating an ATL Control

In this section, a simple ATL control that draws a double pendulum in the view window will be created. Two functions will be added to update the double pendulum, cause it to redraw at its new position, and change the control value that determines how fast the double pendulum moves.

Start by selecting New from the File menu. When the New dialog box appears, click the Projects tab. Choose ATL COM AppWizard, and enter the project name as **DoublePendulum**. The dialog box looks like the one shown in Figure 33-1. To continue, click the OK button.

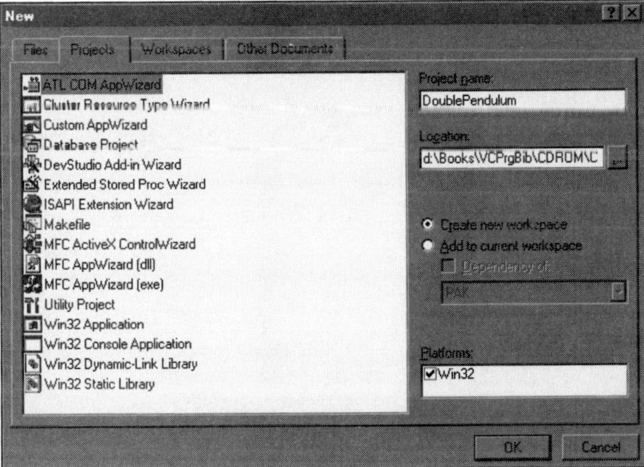

Figure 33-1: The New dialog box with ATL COM AppWizard selected and the project name DoublePendulum

The ATL COM AppWizard gives you choices for the project's options. In the first dialog box that is displayed, you can set how you want the ATL file saved. Most of the time, you'll want it saved as a DLL. Our example uses the default choice of a DLL, as shown in Figure 33-2. Click the Finish button to proceed.

The last step in the AppWizard creation process is a review of your choices. In the New Project Information dialog box, as shown in Figure 33-3, you can see the choices you've made.

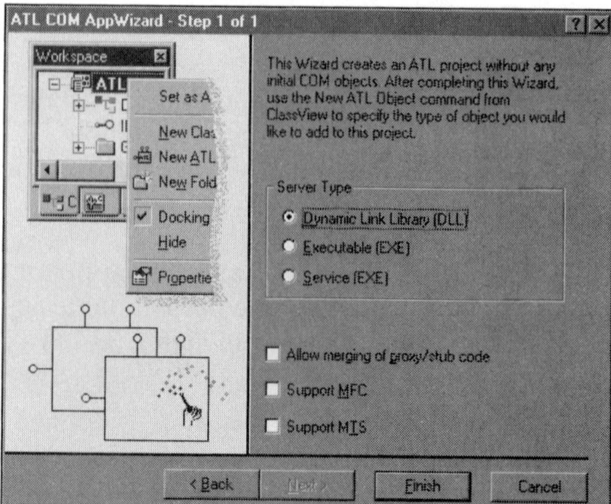

Figure 33-2: The Step 1 of 1 dialog box shows that your control will be saved as a DLL.

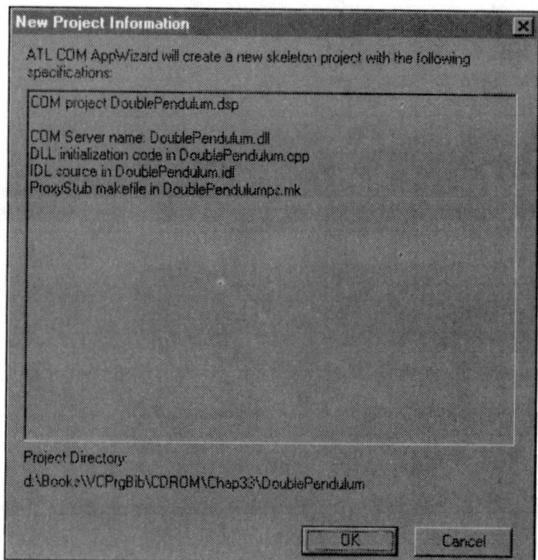

Figure 33-3: You can review all your choices in the New Project Information dialog box.

Adding a COM Object to the Project

To add a COM object to the project, you select New ATL Object from the Insert menu. A dialog box is displayed that gives you a selection of COM objects that you can add to your project, as shown in Figure 33-4.

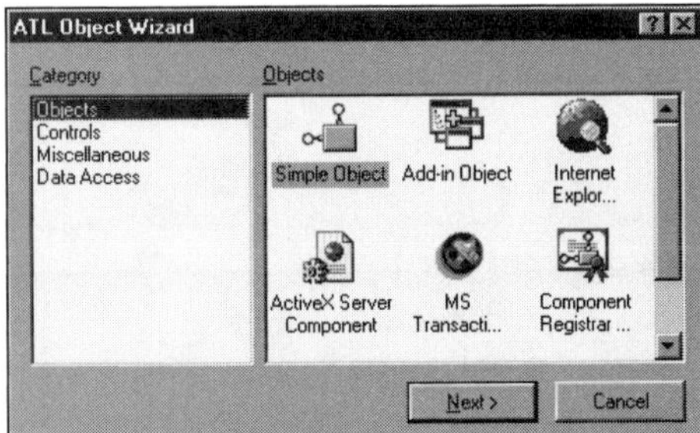

Figure 33-4: Make sure that Controls is selected in the Category list before choosing Full Control in the Objects list.

The dialog box offers four sets of COM components to choose from: Objects, Controls, Miscellaneous, and Data Access. You'll be creating a control, and you'll choose the Full Control item from the Objects.

You'll need to enter the name for the COM component in a dialog box that is displayed. For our project, you'll enter the Short Name of `DoublePend` as shown in Figure 33-5. This is used as the basis for the C++ class name that implements the component and for the names of the files containing the C++ code. It is also the basis for the name of the `CoClass`, which is the component class; the name of the interface, `IDoublePend`, that the component will support; the type name; and the Prog ID that will appear in the Registry. Note that the component class is not a C++ class — it's a COM class that identifies the interfaces that the component supports.

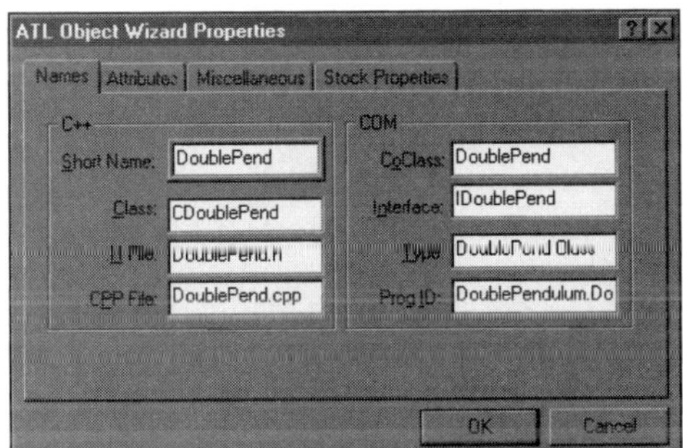

Figure 33-5: You can specify the names for the classes, files, and objects in the ATL Object Wizard Properties dialog box.

The Attributes tab in the dialog box provides options for how the component will be implemented, as shown in Figure 33-6.

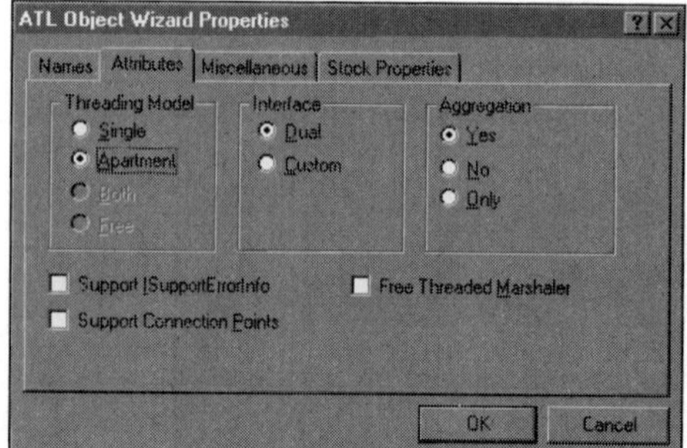

Figure 33-6: You can set the attributes for the object on the Attributes tab.

Modifying the CDoublePend Include File

After you add the ATL control, open the `DoublePend.h` file. This is the include file that was created by Visual Studio. Toward the end of the file you'll see an `OnDraw()` member function. This default `OnDraw()` function is inserted so that you can load the control from a program and verify visually that it has been loaded before you add any of your own draw code. The default `OnDraw()` function follows:

```
HRESULT OnDraw(ATL_DRAWINFO& di)
{
  RECT& rc = *(RECT*)di.prcBounds;
  Rectangle(di.hdcDraw, rc.left, rc.top, rc.right,
    rc.bottom);

  SetTextAlign(di.hdcDraw, TA_CENTER|TA_BASELINE);
  LPCTSTR pszText = _T("ATL 3.0 : Sample");
  TextOut(di.hdcDraw,
    (rc.left + rc.right) / 2,
    (rc.top + rc.bottom) / 2,
    pszText,
    lstrlen(pszText));

  return S_OK;
}
```

For our control, the code to draw the pendulum is fairly complicated. For this reason, we'll create a separate function in the `DoublePend.Cpp` file that draws the double pendulum. We'll use the `OnDraw()` function to call the `DrawPend()` function that resides in the `DoublePend.Cpp` class.

Besides the changes to the `OnDraw()` function, we'll add some initialization code to the `CDoublePend()` constructor, add several function prototypes, and add some member variables. The code in Listing 33-1 shows the changes and additions that were made to the `CDoublePend` class include file.

Listing 33-1: Changes Made in DoublePend.h

```
public:
  double m_dLength;
  double x[4], h;

  CDoublePend()
  {

    m_dLength = 100.0;
    x[0] = .7854;
    x[1] = .7854;
    x[2] = x[3] = 0.0;

    h = .1;

  }

  void Function( double *, double * );
  void FillOval( HDC, int, int, int, int, COLORREF );
  void DrawPend( HDC, RECT & );

  HRESULT OnDraw(ATL_DRAWINFO& di)
  {
    RECT& rc = *(RECT*)di.prcBounds;

    DrawPend( di.hdcDraw, rc );

    return S_OK;
  }
```

Implementing the Interface Functions

We'll need two public methods that can be called when the control is instantiated. One method, named `SetValue()`, changes the speed at which the pendulum changes. The second method updates the pendulum position and redraws it. You must add these methods so that calling applications can find them. To do this, you must implement interface methods. Start by clicking the Classes tab in the InfoViewer window. Now, right-click the `IDoublePend` interface. A pop-up menu appears with several selections. Choose Add Method. The pop-up menu is shown in Figure 33-7.

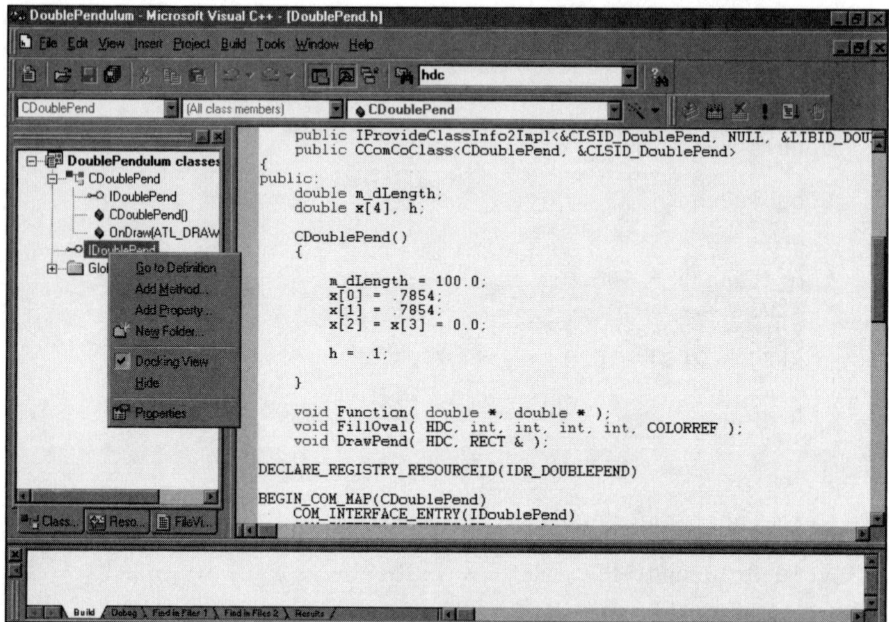

Figure 33-7: Right-click the IDoublePend interface, and choose Add Method to add a method to the class.

The Add Method to Interface dialog box is displayed, as shown in Figure 33-8. You can specify the method names and parameters for the method in this dialog box.

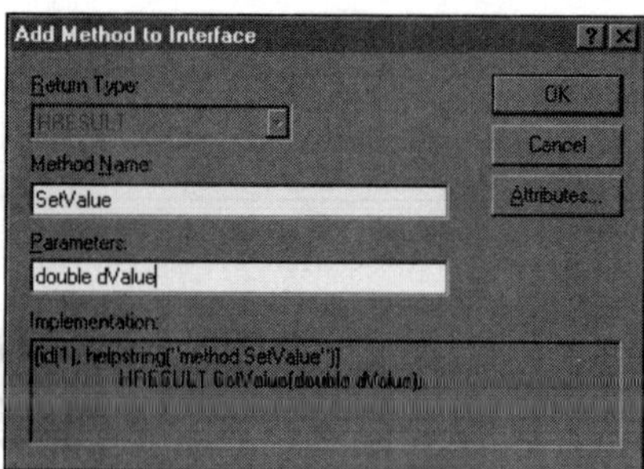

Figure 33-8: Specify the method name and parameters in the Add Method to Interface dialog box.

The last thing to do is edit the two methods we created, and add the code for the three functions that we declared in the include file. Listing 33-2 shows the source code for the `CDoublePend` class.

Listing 33-2: Source Code for the CDoublePend Class in the DoublePend.cpp File

```
// DoublePend.cpp : Implementation of CDoublePend

#include "stdafx.h"
#include "DoublePendulum.h"
#include "DoublePend.h"
#include <math.h>

/////////////////////////////////////////////////////////////
// CDoublePend

void CDoublePend::Function( double *xx, double *f )
{
  double c, c0, c1, c10, x22, x33;

  // Gravity divided by the length.
  c = 9.8 / m_dLength;

  // Calculate motion vectors.
  c0 = cos( xx[0] ) * c;
  c1 = cos( xx[1] ) * c;
  c10 = cos( xx[1] - xx[0] );
  c = sin( xx[1] - xx[0] );

  // Calculate the positions.
  x22 = xx[2] * xx[2] * c;
  x33 = xx[3] * xx[3] * c;
  c = 9.0 / ( 16.0 - 9.0 * c1 * c10 );

  // Store the values.
  f[0] = xx[2];
  f[1] = xx[3];
  f[2] = ( 2.0 * x33 / 3.0 + c10 * x22 +
    c10 * c1 - 2.0 * c0 ) * c;
  f[3] = ( -8.0 * x22 / 3.0 - c10 * x33 +
    3.0 * c10 * c0 - 8.0 * c1 / 3.0 ) * c;

}

void CDoublePend::FillOval( HDC hDC, int nX, int nY,
  int nXR, int nYR, COLORREF cColor )
{
  HBRUSH hBrush, hOldBrush;
  HPEN hPen, hOldPen;

  // Create the brush, select it into the dc,
  // and remember the old brush.
  hBrush = CreateSolidBrush( cColor );
```

(continued)

Listing 33-2 (continued)

```
  hOldBrush = (HBRUSH) SelectObject( hDC, hBrush );

  // Create the pen, select it into the dc.
  // and remember the old pen.
  hPen = CreatePen( PS_SOLID, 1, RGB( 0, 0, 0 ) );
  hOldPen = (HPEN) SelectObject( hDC, hPen );

  // Draw the ellipse.
  Ellipse( hDC, nX - ( nXR / 2 ), nY - ( nYR / 2 ),
    nX + ( nXR / 2 ), nY + ( nYR / 2 ) );

  // Select the old brush and pen back
  // into the dc.
  SelectObject( hDC, hOldBrush );
  SelectObject( hDC, hOldPen );

  // Delete the GDI objects.
  DeleteObject( hPen );
  DeleteObject( hBrush );

}

void CDoublePend::DrawPend( HDC hDC, RECT& rc )
{

  // We're going to double buffer in
  // order to reduce the redraw flicker.
  HBITMAP hOldBitmap, hBitmap;
  // Create a dc for the off-screen buffer.
  HDC hWorkDC = CreateCompatibleDC( hDC );
  // Create the off-screen buffer.
  hBitmap = CreateCompatibleBitmap( hWorkDC,
    rc.right - rc.left, rc.bottom - rc.top );
  // Select the bitmap into the newly-created
  // dc and remember the bitmap that was
  // previously selected.
  hOldBitmap =
    (HBITMAP) SelectObject( hWorkDC, hBitmap );

  // Draw a rectangle to clear the buffer.
  Rectangle( hWorkDC, rc.left, rc.top, rc.right,
    rc.bottom );

  // Calculate the width, height, and midpoint.
  int nWidth = rc.right - rc.left;
  int nHeight = rc.bottom - rc.top;
  int nMidX = rc.left + ( nWidth / 2 );
  int nMidY = rc.top + ( nHeight / 2 );

  // Calculate the endpoints of the pendulum.
  int nCx1 = nMidX + (int) ( m_dLength * cos( x[0] ) );
```

```
    int nCy1 = nMidY + (int) ( m_dLength * sin( x[0] ) );
    int nCx2 = nCx1 + (int) ( m_dLength * cos( x[1] ) );
    int nCy2 = nCy1 + (int) ( m_dLength * sin( x[1] ) );

    // Draw the three pendulum ellipses.
    FillOval( hWorkDC, nMidX,
      nMidY, 7, 7, RGB( 0, 255, 0 ) );
    FillOval( hWorkDC, nCx1,
      nCy1, 11, 11, RGB( 0, 255, 0 ) );
    FillOval( hWorkDC, nCx2,
      nCy2, 11, 11, RGB( 0, 255, 0 ) );

    // Select a black stock pen into the dc.
    SelectObject( hWorkDC, GetStockObject( BLACK_PEN ) );
    // Move to the midpoint.
    MoveToEx( hWorkDC, nMidX, nMidY, NULL );
    // Draw the first segment.
    LineTo( hWorkDC, nCx1, nCy1 );
    // Draw the second segment.
    LineTo( hWorkDC, nCx2, nCy2 );

    // Draw the off-screen buffer to the visual screen.
    BitBlt( hDC, 0, 0, nWidth, nHeight, hWorkDC, 0, 0,
      SRCCOPY );
    // Select the old bitmap into the dc, delete the
    // newly-created bitmap and dc.
    SelectObject( hWorkDC, hOldBitmap );
    DeleteObject( hBitmap );
    DeleteDC( hWorkDC );

}

STDMETHODIMP CDoublePend::Update()
{
    double x1[4], f1[4], f2[4], f3[4], f4[4], hh, hhh;

    hh = h / 2.0;
    hhh = h / 6.0;

    for( int k=0; k<16; k++ ){
      int i;

      // Update the first point.
      Function( x, f1 );
      for( i=0; i<4; i++ )
        x1[i] = x[i] + hh * f1[i];

      // Update the second point.
      Function( x1, f2 );
      for( i=0; i<4; i++ )
        x1[i] = x[i] + hh * f2[i];
```

(continued)

Listing 33-2 (continued)

```
      // Update the third point.
      Function( x1, f3 );
      for( i=0; i<4; i++ )
        x1[i] = x[i] + h * f3[i];

      // Update the fourth point.
      Function( x1, f4 );
      for( i=0; i<4; i++ )
        x[i] += hhh * ( f1[i] + 2.0 * f2[i] +
          2.0 * f3[i] + f4[i] );

      }

    // Cause a window redraw.
    InvalidateRect( NULL, FALSE );
    UpdateWindow();

    return S_OK;
  }

  STDMETHODIMP CDoublePend::SetValue(double dValue)
  {

    // Set the update rate value.
    h = dValue;

    return S_OK;
  }
```

Compile the control. Then use the ActiveX Control Test Container from the Tools menu. Select the `DoublePend` class, and you'll see the control draw as shown in Figure 33-9.

Using the Control from C++

After you create a control, you'll have to create a separate application that will use the control. Create an MFC application with an SDI interface and all other options as defaults.

From the Project menu, select Add To Project, and then choose Components and Controls. This brings up the Components and Controls Gallery dialog box. Double-click the Registered ActiveX Controls folder. Inside of this folder are all of the ActiveX controls that are registered on your computer. Find the `DoublePend` class, and double-click it. (If the DoublePendulum control hasn't been registered, the control won't show up in the list.) You'll be asked if you want to add this, to which you should reply Yes. The list of controls with the `DoublePend` class highlighted is shown in Figure 33-10.

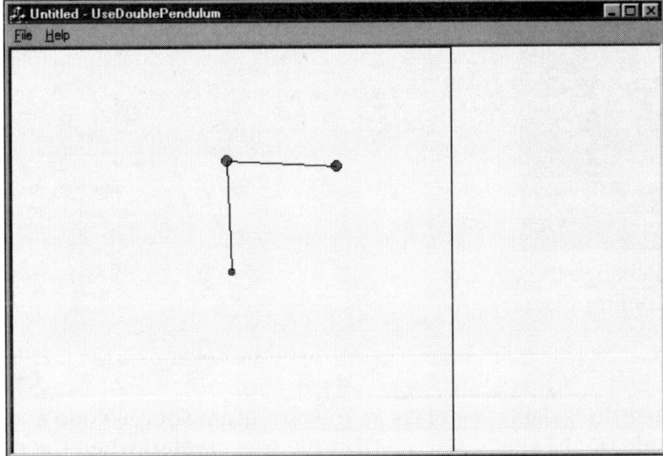

Figure 33-9: The double pendulum in the ActiveX Control Test Container window.

Once you've inserted the control class, you'll have the chance to change file and interface names from the defaults assigned by Visual Studio. Keep the defaults as shown in Figure 33-11, and click the OK button. Then click the OK button on the ClassWizard's main dialog box.

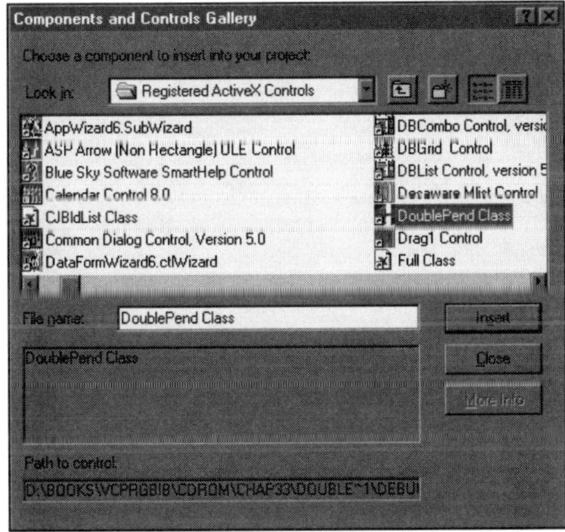

Figure 33-10: The DoublePend class appears in this list.

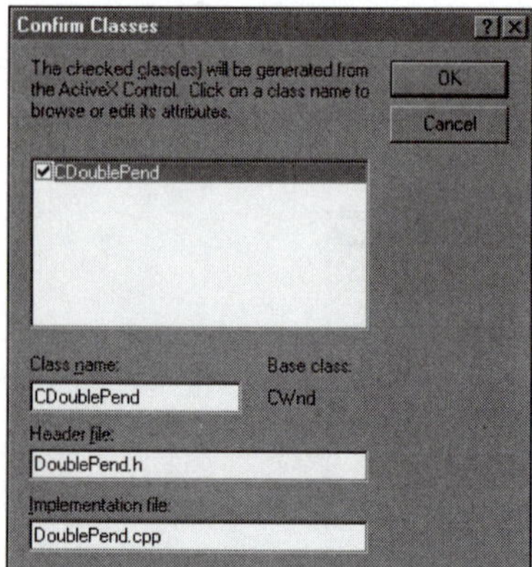

Figure 33-11: You can change the default names in the Confirm Classes dialog box.

The last thing you must do is declare a class in your program source code and initialize it. First include `DoublePendulum.h` (this file was created when the control was inserted) at the top of your application's view class `.h` file. Then add the following public declaration in the view class `.h` file:

```
DoublePend m_DoublePendulum;
BOOL m_bCreated;
```

In the view class constructor, initialize `m_bCreated` as follows:

```
m_bCreated = FALSE;
```

With the ClassWizard, create `OnCreate()` and `OnTimer()` functions in the view class. Edit the functions as follows:

```
int CUseDoublePendulumView::OnCreate(
  LPCREATESTRUCT lpCreateStruct)
{
  if (CView::OnCreate(lpCreateStruct) == -1)
    return -1;

  SetTimer( 1, 100, NULL );

  return 0;
}

void CUseDoublePendulumView::OnTimer(UINT nIDEvent)
{
```

```
  if( !m_bCreated ){
    m_bCreated = TRUE;
    RECT Rect;
    Rect.left = Rect.top = 0;
    Rect.right = Rect.bottom = 400;
    m_DoublePendulum.Create( "DoublePendulum",
      WS_VISIBLE, Rect, this, 0x5005 );
    }
  else
    m_DoublePendulum.Update();

  CView::OnTimer(nIDEvent);
}
```

A complete program, as we've described constructing, can be found in the `Chap33\UseDoublePendulum` directory on the CD-ROM. You can run the program in the project directory or rebuild the project. Make sure, though, that before you run the program that the DoublePendulum control has been registered.

✦ ✦ ✦ ✦ ✦

Data Types

If your control is written in C++ and only C++ programs use it, you'll be okay if you pass character strings back and forth. But other languages, such as BASIC, need to pass character strings as `BSTR`s. This section shows you how to perform the necessary conversions to and from `BSTR`s.

Converting to and from BSTRs

A `BSTR` is an `OLECHAR*` or a pointer to a Unicode string. The `DWORD` prior to the `OLECHAR*` indicates the actual length of the `BSTR`, and this value is set via the SysAllocString API. In other words, by referencing a `BSTR`, you have a basic Unicode string and can use the Unicode-to-ANSI macros that follow. However, if you want to free a `BSTR`, you have to use the `SysFreeString` API.

The syntax of the ATL string-conversion macros is:

```
MACRONAME( StringAddress )
```

For example:

```
A2W( lpa )
```

In the macro names, the source string type is on the left (for example, A), and the destination string type is on the right (for example, W). *A* stands for LPSTR, OLE stands for LPOLESTR, *T* stands for LPTSTR, and *W* stands for LPWSTR. Thus, A2W converts an LPSTR to an LPWSTR, OLE2T converts an LPOLESTR to an LPTSTR, and so on. The destination string is created using _alloca, except when the destination type is BSTR. Using _alloca allocates memory off the stack, so that when your function returns, it is automatically cleaned up.

If a "C" is in the macro name, the macro converts to a const string. For example, W2CA converts an LPWSTR to an LPCSTR. When using an ATL string conversion macro, specify the USES_CONVERSION macro at the beginning of your function to avoid compiler errors. For example:

```
void func( LPSTR lpsz )
{
    USES_CONVERSION;
    ...
    LPWSTR x = A2W(lpsz)
    // Do something with x
    ...
}
```

It is better to use the macros that have "T" and "OLE" in them because they resolve to the correct format when compiling for UNICODE or ANSI.

Don Box has developed some classes that help with conversions of this type. You can get them at http://www.develop.com/dbox/yacl.htm. Don also wrote an article for the August 1995 *Microsoft Systems Journal* that explains various conversion techniques.

✦ ✦ ✦ ✦ ✦

Comparing BSTRs

ATL's CComBSTR class doesn't support comparison. So other ways must be found. Following are some of your options. You can convert the BSTRs to either ANSI or Unicode strings and do the comparison from there. Something like this:

```
if( strcmp( OLE2A( bstr1 ), OLE2A( bstr2 ) ) == 0 )
```

or

```
if( _tcscmp( OLE2T( bstr1 ), OLE2T( bstr2 ) ) == 0 )
```

The Unicode version is better because BSTRs can contain embedded nulls and the ANSI conversion functions terminate when they encounter the first null. This approach also does a bitwise compare. If you want to maintain any locale-specific information, you should use the Win32 CompareString API. Looking through ATL's implementation of CComVariant, you'll find an implementation of BSTR comparison that does this:

```
return
  ( ::SysStringByteLen( bstrVal ) ==
  ::SysStringByteLen( varSrc.bstrVal ) ) &&
  ( ::memcmp( bstrVal, varSrc.bstrVal,
  ::SysStringByteLen( bstrVal ) ) == 0 );
```

Viewing the contents of a BSTR in the debugger

First, be sure to enable display of Unicode strings via `Tools/Options/Debug/Display` Unicode strings. This should enable viewing of `BSTR` types. Wrappers for `BSTR`, though, still cause problems. To display `_bstr_t` types, add this to your `\DevStudio\SharedIDE\bin\autoexp.dat` file.

```
_variant_t =vt=<vt,x> str=<bstrVal,su> short=<iVal>
long=<lVal>dbl=<dblVal,g>
_bstr_t =<m_Data->m_wstr,su>
tagVARIANT =vt=<vt,x> str=<bstrVal,su> short=<iVal>
long=<lVal>dbl=<dblVal,g>
```

Embedding an ActiveX Control in a Web Page

To get this section to work, you must have an ActiveX-aware browser installed on your PC. Internet Explorer 3.0 or later from Microsoft will do, or any other browser that supports ActiveX. If you can access the Internet but don't have an ActiveX-capable browser, you can download Internet Explorer free of charge. You'll find it at `http://www.microsoft.com`.

Web pages are defined using something called Hypertext Markup Language, commonly known as HTML. The elements of a Web page are specified by HTML tags, which usually occur in pairs and are delimited by angle brackets. Here's an example of how to add the DoublePendulum control to a Web page:

```
<HTML>
<HEAD>
<TITLE> A Page with a Double pendulum</TITLE>
</HEAD>
<BODY>
<OBJECT ID="DoublePendulum1" WIDTH=400 HEIGHT=300
  CLASSID="CLSID: B0819F01-B460-11D1-B719-0080AD17AF01">
</OBJECT>
</BODY>
</HTML>
```

In this example, the specification of the name of the object to be inserted, and the CLASSID for the object that identifies what kind of object it is, both appear in the opening `<OBJECT>` tag along with the width and height of the control. We've specified the CLASSID between quotes as the characters CLSID: followed by the hexadecimal digits for the CLSID that appeared in the arguments to the `IMPLEMENT_OLECREATE_EX` macro.

Summary

In this chapter, you've learned some background on Active Template controls. You've also learned how to create text controls from Developer Studio. Instructions for using controls in Web pages were given so that you can dive right in and bring your Web page into the leading edge of technology. Now you can begin your own experimentation and really take advantage of what you know.

Creating and using ActiveX controls can be daunting at first because you have to learn so many new things. But the power you get from them is worth the effort. Not only will your applications be able to share code written for and by other languages, but your Web applications will become much more powerful.

✦ ✦ ✦

P A R T

VII

Internet and HTML Programming

Do you need to load files from half a world away? Do you need to connect to a computer in a remote part of the hemisphere? Or do you just need to send files to your company's office on the other side of town? In any case, this part teaches you how to use the Internet to connect with other computers and share data. You learn the ins and outs of FTP, HTTP, and sockets. You'll also learn how to create simple Web browsers.

✦ ✦ ✦ ✦

In This Part

Chapter 34:
Internet Programming

Chapter 35:
The CHtmlView Class

Chapter 36:
Dynamic HTML

✦ ✦ ✦ ✦

Internet Programming

In This Chapter

The CInternetSession class

Parsing URLs

The CFtpConnection class

Sending and retrieving FTP files

An FTP demonstration program

Sockets and the CSocket class

The Sockets program

Sending e-mail with a socket connection

Retrieving an HTTP file

Automatically dialing an Internet connection

The Internet is part of just about everyone's vocabulary, and programming applications that use the Internet for data transfer should be part of every programmer's bag of tricks. Many sales people who travel around the U.S. transfer information to headquarters daily via the Internet. Some educational institutions use the Internet to share instructional materials with other institutions and students. And electronic commerce in the form of shopping and financial transactions over the Internet is commonplace.

Worldwide communications and data sharing has only just begun. The possibilities are almost endless. Application developers must be ready to meet the current challenge and prepare for future challenges. Learning to use the MFC classes to access Internet data is just the first step, and this chapter provides the foundations for doing that. The next step is to be creative and formulate additional and inventive uses for your newly found data-sharing techniques.

The main areas into which this chapter delves cover the Internet protocols specific to HTTP and FTP. Direct connections using winsock sockets will also be covered. All of these techniques are at the heart of data transfer methods for the Internet.

The CInternetSession Class

Microsoft has included some very high-level Internet classes that make your job easier. Special classes exist for FTP, HTTP, and Gopher transfers. Special functions are also available for retrieving URLs as files. All of these, though, require the creation of a `CInternetSession` class. This class is used to create and maintain the various protocol classes such as the `CFtpConnection` class. The following code shows how to create a `CInternetSession` class:

```
// Simple CInternetSession creation.
CInternetSession *pInternetSession;
pInetSession = new CInternetSession;
```

Six optional parameters can be used when creating a CInternetSession class. The prototype for the CInternetSession constructor follows, along with the descriptions of the optional parameters:

```
CInternetSession( LPCTSTR pstrAgent = NULL,
  DWORD dwContext = 1,
  DWORD dwAccessType = INTERNET_OPEN_TYPE_PRECONFIG,
  LPCTSTR pstrProxyName = NULL,
  LPCTSTR pstrProxyBypass = NULL, DWORD dwFlags = 0 );
```

The first parameter, pstrAgent, is a pointer to a string that identifies the name of the application or entity calling the Internet functions. If pstrAgent is NULL (the default), the framework calls the global function AfxGetAppName(), which returns a null-terminated string that contains an application's name. Some protocols use this string to identify your application to the server.

The second parameter, dwContext, is the context identifier for the operation. This parameter identifies the operation's status information returned by CInternetSession::OnStatusCallback. The default is set to 1; however, you can explicitly assign a specific context ID for the operation. The object and any work it does are associated with that context ID. If dwFlags includes INTERNET_FLAG_ASYNC, objects created by this object have asynchronous behavior as long as a status callback routine is registered.

The third parameter, dwAccessType, is the type of access required. You can't combine these flags as you can others with OR operators; only one value may be used. Table 34-1 provides the valid values, exactly one of which may be supplied.

Table 34-1
Valid Access Type Values

Type	*Description*
INTERNET_OPEN_TYPE_PRECONFIG	Preconfigured (in the Registry). This access type is set as the default.
INTERNET_OPEN_TYPE_DIRECT	Direct to Internet.
INTERNET_OPEN_TYPE_PROXY	Through CERN proxy.

The fourth parameter, pstrProxyName, is the name of the preferred CERN proxy if dwAccessType is set as INTERNET_OPEN_TYPE_PROXY. The default is NULL.

The fifth parameter, pstrProxyBypass, is a pointer to a string that contains an optional list of server addresses. These addresses may be bypassed when using proxy access. If a NULL value is supplied, the bypass list is read from the Registry. This parameter is meaningful only if dwAccessType is set to INTERNET_OPEN_TYPE_PROXY.

The last parameter, dwFlags, indicates various options such as caching and asynchronous behavior. The default is set to 0. The possible values are listed in Table 34-2.

Table 34-2
Possible Options Flags

Type	*Description*
INTERNET_FLAG_DONT_CACHE	Do not cache the data, either locally or in any gateway servers.
INTERNET_FLAG_ASYNC	Future operations on this object may fail with ERROR_IO_PENDING. A status callback will be made with INTERNET_STATUS_REQUEST_COMPLETE when the operation finishes. This callback is on a thread other than the one for the original request. You must call the EnableStatusCallback() function to establish a status callback routine, or the functions are completed synchronously.
INTERNET_FLAG_OFFLINE	Download operations are satisfied through the persistent cache only. If the item does not exist in the cache, an appropriate error code is returned. This flag may be combined with the bitwise OR (|) operator.

The CFtpConnection Class

You must connect to an FTP server before retrieving files from it. You must perform two simple steps to make the connection. First, you have to create a CInternetSession object. Second, you obtain an FTP connection with CInternetSession's GetFtpConnection() function.

Parsing URL strings

If you're accepting a URL address from users, they may not type it so that the MFC Internet functions such as `OpenURL()` can understand it. If your application relies on users to specify the URL, try the following code as a safety feature. It parses user-supplied URLs into a format that the Internet functions can understand. For the code to work, you must pass in the URL and the service type. Service types include `ftp://`, `http://`, and `gopher://`.

```
BOOL CClass::ConnectionFunction( CString& strURL,
  CString& strService )
{
  DWORD dwServiceType;
  CString strServer, strObject;
  int nPort;

  // Parse the URL initially. If we get a FALSE
  // return value, the parsing didn't succeed.
  if( !AfxParseURL( strURL, dwServiceType,
    strServer, strObject, nPort ) ){

    // Create a new URL string with the service
    // as a prefix. Services include ftp://
    // http:// and gopher://
    CString strNewURL = strService;
    strNewURL += strURL;

    // Make another attempt to parse the URL.
    if( !AfxParseURL( strNewURL, dwServiceType,
      strServer, strObject, nPort ) )
      return( FALSE );

    strURL = strNewURL;

    }

  return( TRUE );

}
```

The MFC class `CFtpConnection` both manages your FTP connection to an Internet server and enables direct manipulation of directories and files on that server. FTP is one of the three Internet services recognized by the MFC WinInet classes. (WinInet is the API that resides below the MFC Internet classes.) You can communicate with an FTP Internet server only after you first create an instance of `CInternetSession` and then create a `CFtpConnection` object. You never create a `CFtpConnection` object directly; instead, you call `CInternetSession::GetFtpConnection()`, which creates the CFtpConnection object and returns a pointer to it. Now for a simple example. The following code connects to ftp.microsoft.com:

```
// The internet session is created
// when the CInternetSession object
// is declared.
CInternetSession InternetSession;
CFtpConnection *m_pFtpConnection;

  try{
    // Get an FTP connection to ftp.microsoft.com.
    m_pFtpConnection =
      InternetSession.GetFtpConnection("ftp.microsoft.com");
    }

  // Catch any exceptions that are thrown as a result of
  // of attempting the FTP connection.
  catch( CInternetException *pEx ){
    TCHAR szError[1024];
    if( pEx->GetErrorMessage( szError, 1024 ) )
      AfxMessageBox( szError );
    else
      AfxMessageBox( "There was an exception." );
    pEx->Delete();
    m_pFtpConnection = NULL;
    }

  // Perform FTP operations here...

  // Close the FTP connection and delete
  // the object.
  if( m_pFtpConnection != NULL ){
    m_pFtpConnection->Close();
    delete m_pFtpConnection;
 }

  // The CInternetSession destructor will close the
  // internet session.
```

Try This

Connect to an FTP Server

Take some time now, and use what you've just talked about before moving on. Let's create a simple program that connects to an FTP server:

1. Create a single document application named FTPConnect.
2. Include afxinet.h in FTPConnectView.h.
3. Declare the following in FTPConnectView.h:

```
CInternetSession *m_pInternetSession;
CFtpConnection *m_pFtpConnection;
```

4. Add the following code to the constructor in FTPConnectView.cpp:

```
m_pInternetSession = new CInternetSession;
```

5. Add the following code to the destructor in FTPConnectView.cpp:

```
if( m_pInternetSession != NULL )
  delete m_pInternetSession;
```

6. Add WM_CREATE and WM_TIMER handlers for the CFTPConnectView class.

7. Edit the OnCreate() function as follows:

```
SetTimer( 1, 1000, NULL );
```

8. Edit the OnTimer() function as follows:

```
  KillTimer( nIDEvent );

  try{
    // Get an FTP connection to ftp.microsoft.com.
    m_pFtpConnection =
      m_pInternetSession.GetFtpConnection(
        "ftp.microsoft.com");
    }

  // Catch any exceptions that are thrown as a result of
  // of attempting the FTP connection.
  catch( CInternetException *pEx ){
    pEx->Delete();
    m_pFtpConnection = NULL;
}
```

9. Set a breakpoint in the OnTimer() function where the KillTimer() function is called.

10. Run the program in debug mode, and watch each line execute. You should connect to ftp.microsoft.com. Make sure you set a breakpoint inside the catch block so that if an exception is thrown, you'll be able to see it.

✦ ✦ ✦ ✦ ✦

Retrieving a file from an FTP server

Once an FTP connection has been established, it's a simple matter to retrieve a file from an FTP server. The CFtpConnection class has a high-level function called GetFile() that handles everything for you. A single line of code is all you need to pull a file down from a remote FTP server (as long as you're already connected). The following code gets the file from ftp.microsoft.com named disclaimer.txt with an existing CFtpConnection class and saves it to the current directory as a file named copy.txt:

```
// m_pFtpConnection was established before
// getting to this section of code.
m_pFtpConnection->GetFile("disclaimer.txt", "copy.txt" );
```

The sidebar titled "The GetFile() function" provides full details about the GetFile() function.

The GetFile() function

You call the GetFile()member function to get a file from an FTP server and store it on the local machine. GetFile() is a high-level routine that handles all of the overhead associated with reading a file from an FTP server and storing it locally. If dwFlags is FILE_TRANSFER_TYPE_ASCII, translation of file data also converts control and formatting characters to Windows equivalents. The default transfer is binary mode, in which the file is downloaded in the same format as it is stored on the server.

Prototype

```
BOOL GetFile( LPCTSTR pstrRemoteFile, LPCTSTR pstrLocalFile,
  BOOL bFailIfExists, DWORD dwAttributes, DWORD dwFlags,
  DWORD dwContext);
```

Both pstrRemoteFile and pstrLocalFile can be either partially qualified filenames relative to the current directory or fully qualified. A backslash (\) or forward slash (/) can be used as the directory separator for either name. GetFile() translates the directory name separators to the appropriate characters before they are used.

Override the dwContext default to set the context identifier to a value of your choosing. The context identifier is associated with the specific operation of the CFtpConnection object created by its CInternetSession object. The value is returned to CInternetSession::OnStatusCallback to provide status on the operation with which it is identified.

The function returns non-zero if successful; otherwise, it returns zero. If the call fails, the Win32 function GetLastError may be called to determine the cause of the error.

(continued)

(continued)

Parameters

The first parameter, pstrRemoteFile, is a pointer to a null-terminated string containing the name of a file to retrieve from the FTP server.

The next parameter, pstrLocalFile, is a pointer to a null-terminated string containing the name of the file to create on the local system.

The third parameter, bFailIfExists, indicates whether the filename may already be used by an existing file. If the local filename already exists and this parameter is TRUE, GetFile() fails. Otherwise, GetFile()erases the existing copy of the file.

The next parameter, dwAttributes, indicates the attributes of the file. This can be any combination of the following flags:

- FILE_ATTRIBUTE_ARCHIVE—Indicates that the file is an archive file. Applications use this attribute to mark files for backup or removal.
- FILE_ATTRIBUTE_COMPRESSED—Indicates that the file or directory is compressed. For a file, compression means that all of the data in the file is compressed. For a directory, compression is the default for newly created files and subdirectories.
- FILE_ATTRIBUTE_DIRECTORY—Indicates that the file is a directory.
- FILE_ATTRIBUTE_NORMAL—Indicates that the file has no other attributes set. This attribute is valid only if used alone. All other file attributes override FILE_ATTRIBUTE_NORMAL.
- FILE_ATTRIBUTE_HIDDEN—Indicates that the file is hidden. It is not to be included in an ordinary directory listing.
- FILE_ATTRIBUTE_READONLY—Indicates that the file is read-only. Applications can read the file but cannot write to it or delete it.
- FILE_ATTRIBUTE_SYSTEM—Indicates that the file is part of or is used exclusively by the operating system.
- FILE_ATTRIBUTE_TEMPORARY—Indicates that the file is being used for temporary storage. Applications should write to the file only if absolutely necessary. Most of the file's data remains in memory without being flushed to the media because the file will soon be deleted.

The fifth parameter, dwFlags, specifies the conditions under which the transfer occurs. This can be either of the following transfer type flags:

- FTP_TRANSFER_TYPE_ASCII—Transfers the file using FTP's ASCII (Type A) transfer method. Converts control and formatting information to local equivalents.
- FTP_TRANSFER_TYPE_BINARY—Transfers data using the FTP Image (Type I) transfer method. The file transfers data exactly as it exists, with no changes. This is the default transfer method.

The last parameter, dwContext, is the context identifier for the file retrieval.

The PutFile() function

You call the PutFile()member function to copy a file to an FTP server from a locally accessible drive. PutFile is a high-level routine that handles all of the overhead associated with reading a file from an FTP server and storing it locally. If dwFlags is FILE_TRANSFER_TYPE_ASCII, translation of file data also converts control and formatting characters to Windows equivalents. The default transfer is binary mode, in which the file is downloaded in the same format as it is stored on the server.

Prototype

```
BOOL PutFile( LPCTSTR pstrRemoteFile, LPCTSTR pstrLocalFile,
  BOOL bFailIfExists, DWORD dwAttributes, DWORD dwFlags,
  DWORD dwContext);
```

Both pstrRemoteFile and pstrLocalFile can be either partially qualified filenames relative to the current directory or fully qualified. A backslash (\) or forward slash (/) can be used as the directory separator for either name. PutFile() translates the directory name separators to the appropriate characters before they are used.

Override the dwContext default to set the context identifier to a value of your choosing. The context identifier is associated with the specific operation of the CFtpConnection object created by its CInternetSession object. The value is returned to CInternetSession::OnStatusCallback to provide status on the operation with which it is identified.

The function returns non-zero if successful; otherwise, it returns zero. If the call fails, the Win32 function GetLastError may be called to determine the cause of the error.

Parameters

The first parameter, pstrRemoteFile, is a pointer to a null-terminated string containing the name of a file to retrieve from the FTP server.

The next parameter, pstrLocalFile, is a pointer to a null-terminated string containing the name of the file to create on the local system.

The third parameter, bFailIfExists, indicates whether the filename may already be used by an existing file. If the local filename already exists and this parameter is TRUE, PutFile() fails. Otherwise, PutFile()erases the existing copy of the file.

The next parameter, dwAttributes, indicates the attributes of the file. These are the same values used in the GetFile() function. (See "The GetFile() function" sidebar earlier in this chapter for details.)

The fifth parameter, dwFlags, specifies the conditions under which the transfer occurs. These are the same values used in the GetFile() function. (See "The GetFile() function" sidebar earlier in this chapter for details.)

The last parameter, dwContext, is the context identifier for the file retrieval.

Sending a file to an FTP server

As with receiving a file, once an FTP connection has been established, it's a simple matter to send a file to an FTP server. The `CFtpConnection` class has a high-level function called `PutFile()` that handles everything for you. A single line of code is all you need to send a file to a remote FTP server (as long as you're already connected). The following code sends a file `mytext.txt` to `ftp.microsoft.com` with an existing `CFtpConnection` class and reads it from the current directory as a file named `text.txt`:

```
// m_pFtpConnection was established before
// getting to this section of code.
m_pFtpConnection->PutFile("text.txt", "mytext.txt" );
```

The sidebar titled "The PutFile() function" gives full details about the `PutFile()` function.

Other FTP functions

You'll find several other functions that the `CFtpConnection` class makes available extremely useful. This section describes these functions.

If you're navigating to different directories on an FTP server, you'll have to change directories. To do so, the `SetCurrentDirectory()` should be used. It takes a single argument — a character string that specifies the new directory. The following example sets the current directory to `/pub/files`:

```
if( SetCurrentDirectory( "/pub/files" ) )
  AfxMessageBox( "SetCurrentDirectory() success" );
else
  AfxMessageBox( "SetCurrentDirectory() failed." );
```

While navigating through the directories of an FTP server, it might be important to obtain the current directory. For this, the `GetCurrentDirectory()` function can be used. It takes two arguments — the first is a character buffer into which the directory is copied, and the second is the maximum size of the buffer. The following example gets the current directory and displays it in a message box:

```
char szCurDir[500];
if( GetCurrentDirectory( szCurDir, sizeof( szCurDir ) )
  AfxMessageBox( szCurrentDir );
else
  AfxMessageBox( "GetCurrentDirectory() failed." );
```

If you want to remove a directory from the server, you must use the `RemoveDirectory()` function. It takes a single argument — the directory that you want to remove. The following example removes the `temp` directory:

```
if( RemoveDirectory( "temp" ) )
```

```
    AfxMessageBox( "RemoveDirectory() success" );
  else
    AfxMessageBox( "RemoveDirectory() failed." );
```

The opposite of the RemoveDirectory() function is the CreateDirectory() function. This function creates a directory on an FTP server. It takes a single argument — a character string that specifies the new directory. The following example creates a new directory named temp1:

```
  if( CreateDirectory( "temp1" ) )
    AfxMessageBox( "CreateDirectory() success" );
  else
    AfxMessageBox( "CreateDirectory() failed." );
```

Renaming files is carried out with the Rename() function. It takes two arguments — the first is a character string with the old filename; the second is a character string with the new filename. The following example renames the file Disclaim.txt to Datclaim.txt:

```
  if( Rename( "Disclaim.txt", "Datclaim.txt" ) )
    AfxMessageBox( "Rename() success" );
  else
    AfxMessageBox( "Rename() failed." );
```

To delete a file, you use the Remove() function. It takes a single argument — a character string containing the file to remove. The following example deletes a file named Extra.doc:

```
  if( Remove( "Extra.doc" ) )
    AfxMessageBox( "Remove() success" );
  else
    AfxMessageBox( "Remove() failed." );
```

The CInternetFile class

One function that wasn't mentioned in the previous section describing other functions, but that's a member of the CFtpConnection class, is the OpenFile() function. When this function is successfully completed, a pointer to a CInternetFile class is returned. Opening a file takes from one to four parameters. The first parameter is required and is a character string containing the filename to open. The second parameter is optional and contains the flags for the access type (it defaults to GENERIC_READ). Table 34-3 shows the values for the access flags. The third parameter gives the conditions under which subsequent transfers occur (it defaults to FTP_TRANSFER_TYPE_BINARY). Table 34-4 shows the available flags. The last optional parameter specifies the context.

Table 34-3
File Open Access Flags

Flag Define	*Description*
GENERIC_READ	Open for reading
GENERIC_WRITE	Open for writing

Table 34-4
Transfer Type

Flag Define	*Description*
FTP_TRANSFER_TYPE_ASCII	The file transfers using FTP ASCII (Type A) transfer method. Converts control and formatting information to local equivalents.
FTP_TRANSFER_TYPE_BINARY	The file transfers data using FTP's Image (Type I) transfer method. The file transfers data exactly as it exists, with no changes. This is the default transfer method.

The three functions you'll use most are the `Read()`, `Write()`, and `Close()` functions. The `Read()` and `Write()` functions take two arguments — the first is a data buffer, and the second is an integer specifying the bytes to write for the `Write()` function and the maximum buffer size for the `Read()` function. The `Close()` function takes no arguments. The following example opens a file on an FTP server, reads 100 bytes, and then closes the file:

```
CInternetFile *pInternetFile;
// pFtpConnection has already been established.
pInternetFile = pFtpConnection->OpenFile( "Text.txt" );
if( pInternetFile != NULL ){
  char cbBuffer[200];
  pInternetFile->Read( cbBuffer, 100 );
  pInternetFile->Close();
  }
```

Using a `CInternetFile` class to copy files to and from an FTP server is not as convenient as using the `GetFile()` and `PutFile()` functions. It does, however, provide much greater control over the file copy operation. You can offer users a Cancel button and update a status bar during the copy operation.

The CFtpFileFind class

On occasion you'll want to find out the contents of an FTP directory. An MFC class provides this functionality. It uses the `CFtpFileFind` class. The following example creates a `CFtpFileFind` class—its constructor takes a `CFtpConnection` pointer as an argument:

```
CFtpFileFind *pFtpFind =
  new CFtpFileFind( pFtpConnection );
```

The next thing you need to do is use the two functions `FindFile()` and `FindNextFile()` to get all of the filenames in the directory. The following example gets the contents of the current directory:

```
CFtpFileFind *pFtpFind =
  new CFtpFileFind( pFtpConnection );

BOOL bContinue = lpFtpFind->FindFile( "*" );
while( bContinue )
  bContinue = lpFtpFind->FindNextFile();
```

The FTP Program

The FTP program transfers files to and from FTP servers and also obtains directory listings from FTP servers. Three menu entries call the program into action. The Get Ftp File menu entry retrieves a file from an FTP server to a local drive. The Send Ftp File menu entry sends a file from a local drive to an FTP server, and the Get Ftp Directory menu entry gets a directory listing for an FTP server.

A demonstration program can be found on the CD-ROM in the `Chap34\Ftp` directory. It's built around the `CFtpConnection` class. You can rebuild the program by loading the `Ftp.dsw` project file, or just run the `Ftp.exe` program using Explorer.

◆ ◆ ◆ ◆ ◆

Before getting and sending files and obtaining directories, a dialog box is displayed, as shown in Figure 34-1, in which you must enter necessary information. You enter the server name, username password, and local and remote files. You also enter the FTP directory to and from which you'll perform the operations.

Once the FTP program has sufficient information, it initiates a file retrieve, a file send, or a directory listing operation. There are two different thread functions. The first one is `FileThread()`, and it manages the file retrieve and file send operations. The second function is `DirectoryThread()`, and it gets the listing for the specified FTP server directory. After a file or directory operation, an alert box informs you that the operation completed. Figure 34-2 shows a completed directory listing.

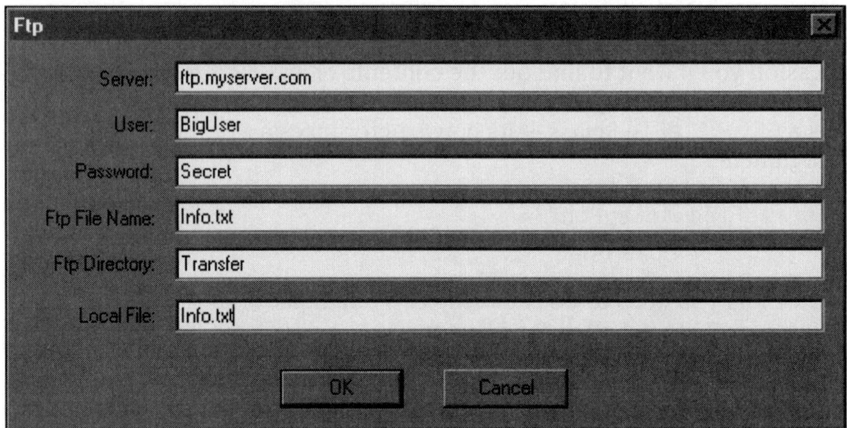

Figure 34-1: Before the program can perform any operations, it requires information about the remote server and the file you're going to transfer.

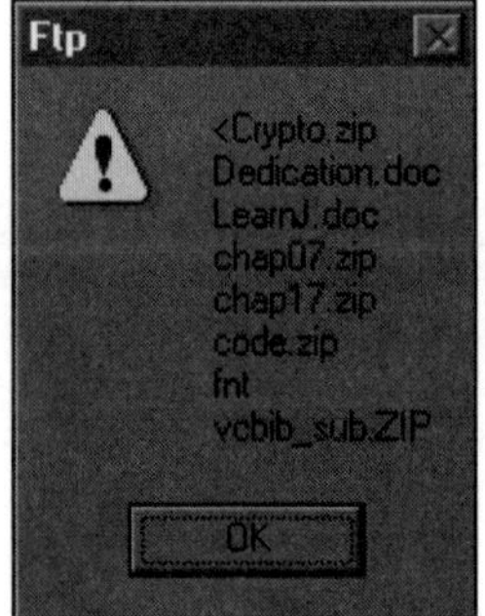

Figure 34-2: A directory listing of ten entries or less is displayed in an alert box.

The FTP program is a simple implementation of the `CFtpConnection` class. It was kept simple so that you could easily understand the basic techniques. The `FileThread()` and `DirectoryThread()` functions could have been combined. A flag indicating whether the function was to perform a file operation or a directory operation could have been used. Here again, two separate functions make the program easier to understand. The source code highlights for the FTP program are contained in Listing 34-1.

Ftp

Project Name: **Ftp**
CD-ROM Location: **Chap34\Ftp**
Prebuilt Program: **Chap34\Ftp\Ftp.exe**
Source Code Highlights in Text: `FtpView.cpp`

◆ ◆ ◆ ◆ ◆

Listing 34-1: Highlights of the FtpView.cpp Source Code for the Ftp.exe Program

```
// FtpView.cpp : implementation of the
// CFtpView class
//

#include "stdafx.h"
#include "Ftp.h"

#include "FtpDoc.h"
#include "FtpView.h"

#include "FtpFileDlg.h"

/////////////////////////////////////////////////////////
// CFtpView

/////////////////////////////////////////////////////////
// CFtpView message handlers

void CFtpView::OnFileGetftpfile()
{

  FTP_INFO *lpInfo = GetParams( FALSE, TRUE );

  if( lpInfo != NULL ){
    // Kick off the thread.
    AfxBeginThread( CFtpView::FileThread,
      (LPVOID) lpInfo );
    }

}

void CFtpView::OnFileSendftpfile()
{

  FTP_INFO *lpInfo = GetParams( TRUE, TRUE );

  if( lpInfo != NULL ){
    // Kick off the thread.
    AfxBeginThread( CFtpView::FileThread,
      (LPVOID) lpInfo );
    }

}

void CFtpView::OnFileFtpdirectory()
{
```

(continued)

Listing 34-1 *(continued)*

```
  FTP_INFO *lpInfo = GetParams( FALSE, FALSE );

  if( lpInfo != NULL ){

    // Allocate memory into which the
    // directory will be copied.
    lpInfo->hGlobal =
      GlobalAlloc( GMEM_MOVEABLE, 20000 );

    // Kick off the thread.
    AfxBeginThread( CFtpView::DirectoryThread,
      (LPVOID) lpInfo );
    }

}

FTP_INFO *CFtpView::GetParams( BOOL bSendFlag,
  BOOL bFileFlag )
{
  FTP_INFO *lpInfo = NULL;

  CFtpFileDlg FileDlg;

  // Set the dialog flag that grays
  // out the file items since we
  // don't need them specified for a
  // directory.
  FileDlg.m_bGrayOutFileItems = !bFileFlag;

  // Invoke the dialog that'll allow
  // user to enter in information for
  // the Ftp transfer.
  if( FileDlg.DoModal() == IDOK ){

    // Allocate a structure.
    lpInfo = new FTP_INFO;

    // Copy the Ftp file into
    // the structure.
    strcpy( lpInfo->szFtpFile,
      FileDlg.m_strFtpFile );

    // Copy the Ftp directory into
    // the structure.
    strcpy( lpInfo->szFtpDirectory,
      FileDlg.m_strFtpDir );

    // Copy the Local file into
    // the structure.
    strcpy( lpInfo->szLocalFile,
      FileDlg.m_strLocalFile );
```

```
    // Copy the password into
    // the structure.
    strcpy( lpInfo->szPassword,
      FileDlg.m_strPassword );

    // Copy the host name into
    // the structure.
    strcpy( lpInfo->szHost,
      FileDlg.m_strServer );

    // Copy the user name into
    // the structure.
    strcpy( lpInfo->szUser,
      FileDlg.m_strUser );

    // Copy the application name into
    // the structure.
    strcpy( lpInfo->szAppName,
      AfxGetAppName() );

    // Set our flag to indicate
    // we'll be receiving.
    lpInfo->bSendFlag = FALSE;

    // Set our flag to indicate
    // we'll be sending or receiving.
    lpInfo->bSendFlag = bSendFlag;

    }

  return( lpInfo );

}

UINT CFtpView::FileThread( LPVOID lpInf )
{
  FTP_INFO *lpInfo = (FTP_INFO *) lpInf;

  CInternetSession *lpInetSession;
  CFtpConnection *lpFtpConnection;

  // Allocate a CInternetSession object.
  lpInetSession = new CInternetSession(
    lpInfo->szAppName, 1,
    PRE_CONFIG_INTERNET_ACCESS );

  // If the CInternetSession object didn't
  // allocate, bail out.
  if( lpInetSession == NULL ){
    delete lpInfo;
    return( 0 );
```

(continued)

Listing 34-1 (continued)

```
  }

// Attempt to make the Ftp connection.
try{

  // We'll use a NULL pointer for the
  // user name since GetFtpConnection()
  // will use a default value if it
  // gets a NULL for it. If a user
  // name was given by user, go ahead and
  // point to that string.
  char *lpUser = NULL;
  if( lpInfo->szUser[0] != 0 )
    lpUser = lpInfo->szUser;

  // The same thing happens here for the
  // password. Use a NULL pointer unless
  // user gave a password.
  char *lpPassword = NULL;
  if( lpInfo->szPassword[0] != 0 )
    lpPassword = lpInfo->szPassword;

  lpFtpConnection =
    lpInetSession->GetFtpConnection(
      lpInfo->szHost, lpUser, lpPassword );
  }

// If GetFtpConnection() throws an exception,
// catch it, clean up, and return.
catch( CInternetException *lpEx ){
  lpEx->Delete();
  delete lpInetSession;
  delete lpInfo;
  return( 0 );
  }

// If user specified an Ftp directory, set to that
// directory.
if( lpInfo->szFtpDirectory[0] != 0 )
  lpFtpConnection->SetCurrentDirectory(
    lpInfo->szFtpDirectory );

if( lpInfo->bSendFlag ){
  // Attempt to send the file from
  // the local machine to the remote server.
  if( lpFtpConnection->PutFile( lpInfo->szLocalFile,
    lpInfo->szFtpFile ) )
    AfxMessageBox( "The file was sent." );
  else
    AfxMessageBox( "The file wasn't sent." );
```

```
      }
  else{
    // Attempt to retrieve the file from
    // the remote server to the local machine.
    if( lpFtpConnection->GetFile( lpInfo->szFtpFile,
      lpInfo->szLocalFile ) )
      AfxMessageBox( "The file was retrieved." );
    else
      AfxMessageBox( "The file wasn't retrieved." );

    }

  // Close the Ftp connection and delete
  // the CFtpConnection and CInternetSession
  // objects.
  lpFtpConnection->Close();
  delete lpFtpConnection;
  delete lpInetSession;
  delete lpInfo;

  return( 0 );

}

UINT CFtpView::DirectoryThread( LPVOID lpInf )
{
  FTP_INFO *lpInfo = (FTP_INFO *) lpInf;

  int nFileCount = 0;

  CInternetSession *lpInetSession;
  CFtpConnection *lpFtpConnection;

  // Allocate a CInternetSession object.
  lpInetSession = new CInternetSession(
    lpInfo->szAppName, 1,
    PRE_CONFIG_INTERNET_ACCESS );

  // If the CInternetSession object didn't
  // allocate, bail out.
  if( lpInetSession == NULL ){
    delete lpInfo;
    return( 0 );
    }

  // Attempt to make the Ftp connection.
  try{

    // We'll use a NULL pointer for the
    // user name since GetFtpConnection()
    // will use a default value if it
    // gets a NULL for it. If a user
```

(continued)

Listing 34-1 *(continued)*

```
    // name was given by user, go ahead and
    // point to that string.
    char *lpUser = NULL;
    if( lpInfo->szUser[0] != 0 )
      lpUser = lpInfo->szUser;

    // The same thing happens here for the
    // password. Use a NULL pointer unless
    // user gave a password.
    char *lpPassword = NULL;
    if( lpInfo->szPassword[0] != 0 )
      lpPassword = lpInfo->szPassword;

    lpFtpConnection =
      lpInetSession->GetFtpConnection(
        lpInfo->szHost, lpUser, lpPassword );
    }

  // If GetFtpConnection() throws an exception,
  // catch it, clean up, and return.
  catch( CInternetException *lpEx ){
    lpEx->Delete();
    delete lpInetSession;
    delete lpInfo;
    return( 0 );
    }

  // If user specified an Ftp directory, set to that
  // directory.
  if( lpInfo->szFtpDirectory[0] != 0 )
    lpFtpConnection->SetCurrentDirectory(
      lpInfo->szFtpDirectory );

  // Create a new CFtpFileFind object.
  CFtpFileFind *lpFtpFind  =
    new CFtpFileFind( lpFtpConnection );
  if( lpFtpFind == NULL )
    goto GetDirBailout;

  // Look for the first file.
  BOOL bContinue;
  bContinue = lpFtpFind->FindFile( "*" );

  // If there aren't any files,
  // bail out.
  if( !bContinue )
    goto GetDirBailout;

  // While files are found, stay in this
  // loop.
  while( bContinue ){
```

```
    // Increment the file counter.
    nFileCount++;

    // Get the next file.
    bContinue = lpFtpFind->FindNextFile();

    // Get the file name.
    CString strFilename = lpFtpFind->GetFileName();

    // Bracket the file name if it's
    // a directory and add a CR.
    if( lpFtpFind->IsDirectory() )
      strFilename = "[" + strFilename + "]";
    strFilename += "\15";

    // Lock the memory and concatenate
    // this file name to the list.
    char *pDest =
      (char *) GlobalLock( lpInfo->hGlobal );
    if( pDest != NULL ){
      strcat( pDest, strFilename );
      GlobalUnlock( lpInfo->hGlobal );
      }

    }

  if( nFileCount < 10 ){
    char *pDest =
      (char *) GlobalLock( lpInfo->hGlobal );
    if( pDest != NULL ){
      AfxMessageBox( pDest );
      GlobalUnlock( lpInfo->hGlobal );
      }
    }
  else
    AfxMessageBox( "Too many entries." );

  // Close the Ftp find object and delete it.
  lpFtpFind->Close();
  delete lpFtpFind;

GetDirBailout:
  // Close the Ftp connection and delete
  // the CFtpConnection and CInternetSession
  // objects.
  lpFtpConnection->Close();
  delete lpFtpConnection;
  delete lpInetSession;
  delete lpInfo;

  return( 0 );

}
```

Sockets and the CSocket Class

A socket is an endpoint for network communications. In other words, network communications involves two computers or two processes that pass data between each other across a network. Network professionals refer to each end of this network conversation as an *endpoint*. When your programs use a socket interface for network communications, the socket is an abstract representation of the endpoint in the network communications process.

For network communications to occur through a socket interface, your program requires a socket at each end of the network conversation. The connection between the two sockets can be connection oriented (a point-to-point connection) or connectionless.

A socket interface works similarly to a file system. When you need a socket for network communications, you define the characteristics for a socket and then use an API to ask the network software for a handle that identifies the specified socket. A socket handle, however, differs from a file handle. While a file handle points to a specific file or device, a socket handle does not represent a specific endpoint or destination address. The fact that a socket handle does not represent a specific endpoint is a departure from most file I/O systems. Socket-based programs create a socket and then as a separate step, connect the socket to a destination endpoint.

When you create TCP/IP programs, you require the capability to use connectionless and connection-oriented protocols. The socket interface enables your programs to use both types of protocols through a socket connection. Low-level socket functions are part of the WinInet API, but this chapter uses the MFC `CSocket` class that wraps these socket functions. `CSocket` is actually derived from `CAsyncSocket` and provides a more abstract wrapper for low-level sockets.

Creating sockets

You can create a socket in two steps. First, you must create a `CSocket` object. Then, the `Create()` function must then be used to create the underlying socket handle. An example of creating a socket that can communicate over port 4500 follows:

```
CSocket GenericSocket;
GenericSocket.Create( 4500 );
```

The port number is an optional parameter. If you don't specify it, MFC selects a port for you, which is usually not desired. Every time you create a socket, you require an exact port. A second optional parameter enables you to specify the socket type. The two valid socket type choices are listed in Table 34-5. The third optional parameter is a string containing the IP address of the connected socket.

Table 34-5
Possible Socket Types

Type Define	*Description*
SOCK_STREAM	Provides sequenced, reliable, two-way, connection-based byte streams. Uses Transmission Control Protocol (TCP) for the Internet address family.
SOCK_DGRAM	Supports datagrams, which are connectionless, unreliable buffers of a fixed (typically small) maximum length. Uses User Datagram Protocol (UDP) for the Internet address family. To use this option, you must not use the socket with a CArchive object.

Connecting to a socket

Once you've created a socket, you make a connection to another endpoint, or socket. To do this, you must use the Connect() function. The two arguments you pass the Connect() function are a pointer to a SOCKADDR_IN structure and the structure size in bytes. The SOCKADDR_IN structure has the following form:

```
struct sockaddr_in{
  short sin_family;
  unsigned short sin_port;
  struct in_addr sin_addr;
  char sin_zero[8];
};
```

In the Internet address family, the SOCKADDR_IN structure is used by Windows Sockets to specify a local or remote endpoint address to which to connect a socket. This is the form of the SOCKADDR structure specific to the Internet address family and can be cast to SOCKADDR. Table 34-6 describes the members of the SOCKADDR_IN structure.

Table 34-6
SOCKADDR_IN Members

Member	*Description*
sin_family	Address family (must be AF_INET).
sin_port	IP port.
sin_addr	IP address.
sin_zero	Padding to make structure the same size as SOCKADDR.

The IP address component of this structure is of type IN_ADDR. The IN_ADDR structure is defined in Windows Sockets header file WINSOCK.h as follows:

```
struct in_addr{
  union{
    struct{
       unsigned char s_b1,
                     s_b2,
                     s_b3,
                     s_b4;
     } S_un_b;

     struct{
       unsigned short s_w1,
                      s_w2;
     } S_un_w;

     struct{
       unsigned long S_addr;
     } S_un;
  }
};
```

The host, ftp.microsoft.com, has the IP address of 198.105.232.1. If you're going to connect to it using a socket, here's how you set up your SOCKADDR_IN structure (remember, ftp is on port 21):

```
SOCKADDR_IN Addr;
memset( &Addr, 0, sizeof( SOCKADDR_IN ) );
Addr.sin_family = AF_INET;
Addr.sin_port = htons( 21 );
Addr.sin_addr.s_addr = inet_addr( "198.105.232.1" );
```

The last step required to make a connection is to call the Connect() function. The following lines of code make an attempt to connect to the ftp.microsoft.com server. The code uses the SOCKADDR_IN structure that was set up in the previous code.

```
if( Socket.Connect( (SOCKADDR) &Addr, sizeof( SOCKADDR_IN) ) )
  AfxMessageBox( "The connect was successful." );
else
  AfxMessageBox( "The connect was not successful." );
```

There's one last thing you might need to do before calling another socket. Many times you'll know the name of the host but not the IP address. To get the IP address, you'll have to use the WinSock gethostbyname() and inet_ntoa() functions. The following code obtains the IP address for ftp.microsoft.com:

```
HOSTENT *lpHostEnt;
lpHostEnt = gethostbyname( "ftp.microsoft.com" );
char *lpAddr = (char *)
  inet_ntoa(*(LPIN_ADDR)*(lpHostEnt->h_addr_list) );
```

```
// lpAddr now points to the IP address (198.105.232.1)
```

One important consideration: the `Connect()` function may take time before completing its job. That means your application might hang up while trying to make the connection. Socket calls that wait for completion and run the risk of hanging up your application are called *blocking calls*. Because many `CSocket` calls such as `Read()` and `Listen()` are blocking, it's usually better to make connections from within a thread.

◆ ◆ ◆ ◆ ◆

Listening for a connection

The previous section showed you how to call out to a waiting socket in order to make a connection. To be a listening socket that's waiting for such a connection is different. You start off creating the socket in the same way. First, you create a `CSocket` object, and then you use the `Create()` function to create the underlying socket handle.

After using the `Create()` function, you need to use the `Listen()` function to listen on the port for incoming connections. This `Listen()` function doesn't return until it has answered a call or a socket error has occurred. The `Listen()` function takes an optional single argument that specifies how many pending connections can be held in a pending queue. Valid values for this are from 1 to 5. The following code listens for a connection:

```
if( Socket.Listen() )
  AfxMessageBox( "Call answered." );
else
  AfxMessageBox( "Socket error." );
```

The last thing you must do before communicating after a call has been answered is to create a second `CSocket` object. You'll use the second `CSocket` object, not the initial socket, for sending and receiving data. To create a second socket, you use the `Accept()` function. It takes as its first argument a `CSocket` object that's available for a connection. The second and third arguments are optional. The second argument, if you choose to give it, is the address of a `SOCKADDR` structure. The structure is filled in with information about the connection. The third argument is the size of the second argument and, in this case, will be the size in bytes of a `SOCKADDR` structure. The following code accepts a connection:

```
CSocket SecondSocket;
if( Socket.Accept( SecondSocket ) )
  AfxMessageBox( "Accept() function success." );
else
  AfxMessageBox( "Accept() function failed." );
```

It's very important that you remember that it's the second socket through which you'll communicate. As a matter of fact, the first socket can be reused to listen for additional connections.

◆ ◆ ◆ ◆ ◆

Reading and writing data

Once a connection has been established, reading and writing data is easy. The Receive() function reads data from the remote endpoint, and the Send() function sends data to the remote endpoint. For both the Receive() and Send() functions, the first argument is the data buffer, and the second argument is the size of the data buffer. Each function offers an optional third argument, which is described later in this section. The following two examples read and write data:

Example 1:

```
int nBytesRead;
char cbBuffer[2000];
nBytesRead =
  Socket.Receive( cbBuffer, sizeof( cbBuffer ) );
```

Example 2:

```
int nBytesWritten;
static char szMessage[] = "Hello socket world!";
nBytesWritten =
  Socket.Send( szMessage, sizeof( szMessage ) );
```

The Receive() function takes an optional third parameter. It specifies the way in which the call is made. The value can be a combination of the flags shown in Table 34-7.

Table 34-7
Optional Flags for the Receive() Function

Define	*Description*
MSG_PEEK	Peeks at the incoming data. The data is copied into the buffer but is not removed from the input queue.
MSG_OOB	Processes out-of-band data. This data may be delivered to the user independently of normal data.

The Send() function takes an optional third parameter. It specifies the way in which the call is made. The value can be a combination of the flags shown in Table 34-8.

Table 34-8 **Optional Flags for the Send() Function**	
Define	***Description***
`MSG_DONTROUTE`	Specifies that the data should not be subject to routing. A Windows Sockets supplier can choose to ignore this flag.
`MSG_OOB`	Processes out-of-band data. This is data that may be delivered to the user independently of normal ordinary data.

The Sockets Program

The Sockets program can listen for a call from a remote endpoint, or it can call to a listening endpoint. You can rebuild the program by loading the `Sockets.Dsw` project file, or just run the `Sockets.exe` program using Explorer.

A demonstration program can be found on the CD-ROM in the `Chap34\Sockets` directory. It's built around the `CSocket` class. It spawns one of two different threads, depending on the menu option that's chosen.

◆ ◆ ◆ ◆ ◆

If you choose to initiate a connection by selecting Call from the Sockets menu, a dialog box is displayed. In the dialog box, you'll have the chance to specify the destination IP address and the port over which you want to communicate. Figure 34-3 shows the dialog box for a desired connection. Highlights of the program source code can be seen in Listing 34-2.

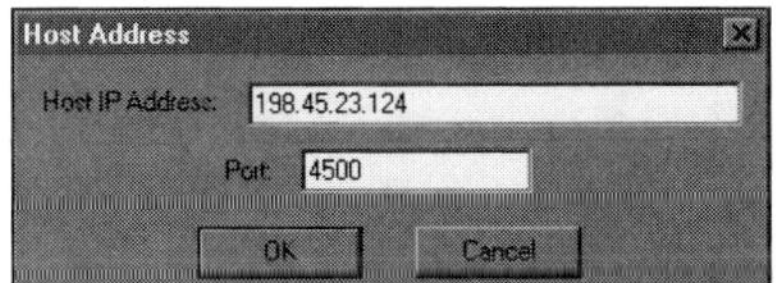

Figure 34-3: Before calling a remote endpoint, specify the IP address and the communication port.

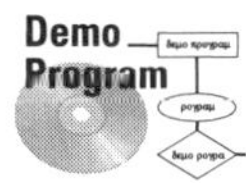

Sockets
Project Name: **Sockets**
CD-ROM Location: **Chap34\Sockets**
Prebuilt Program: **Chap34\Sockets\Sockets.exe**
Source Code Highlights in Text: `SocketsView.cpp`

◆ ◆ ◆ ◆ ◆

Listing 34-2: Highlights of the SocketsView.cpp Source Code for the Sockets.exe Program

```
 OK// SocketsView.cpp : implementation of the
// CSocketsView class
//

#include "stdafx.h"
#include "Sockets.h"

#include "SocketsDoc.h"
#include "SocketsView.h"

#include "HostAddr.h"
#include "Port.h"
#include "Message.h"

/////////////////////////////////////////////////////////////
// CSocketsView

/////////////////////////////////////////////////////////////
// CSocketsView construction/destruction

CSocketsView::CSocketsView()
{

  // Seet the thread handle to NULL.
  m_hCallAnswerThread = NULL;

  // Clear the SOCKET_INFO structure.
  memset( &m_SocketInfo, 0, sizeof( SOCKET_INFO ) );

}

CSocketsView::~CSocketsView()
{

  // Set our abort flag to TRUE.
  m_SocketInfo.bAbort = TRUE;

  // Look for the thread to end. Give it
  // ten seconds.
  if( m_hCallAnswerThread != NULL )
    WaitForSingleObject( m_hCallAnswerThread, 10000 );

}

/////////////////////////////////////////////////////////////
// CSocketsView message handlers

void CSocketsView::OnSocketAnswer()
{
```

```
  CPort Port;

  // Get the port number using the
  // dialog box.
  if( Port.DoModal() == IDOK ){

    // Set up the SOCKET_INFO fields
    // for the thread.
    m_SocketInfo.bAbort = FALSE;
    m_SocketInfo.bListening = TRUE;
    m_SocketInfo.nPort = Port.m_nPort;

    // Kick off the thread.
    CWinThread *lpThread =
      AfxBeginThread( CSocketsView::AnswerThread,
        (LPVOID) &m_SocketInfo );

    // Store the thread handle for later.
    m_hCallAnswerThread = lpThread->m_hThread;
    }

}

void CSocketsView::OnUpdateSocketAnswer(CCmdUI* pCmdUI)
{

  // Only enable if we're not calling or
  // answering or currently connected.
  pCmdUI->Enable( !m_SocketInfo.bConnected &&
    !m_SocketInfo.bCalling &&
    !m_SocketInfo.bListening );

}

void CSocketsView::OnSocketCall()
{
  CHostAddr HostAddr;

  // Get the host address and port using
  // the dialog box.
  if( HostAddr.DoModal() ){

    // Set up the SOCKET_INFO fields
    // for the thread.
    m_SocketInfo.bAbort = FALSE;
    m_SocketInfo.bCalling = TRUE;
    m_SocketInfo.nPort = HostAddr.m_nPort;
    strcpy(m_SocketInfo.szHost, HostAddr.m_strHostAddr);

    // Kick off the thread.
    CWinThread *lpThread =
      AfxBeginThread( CSocketsView::CallThread,
```

(continued)

Listing 34-2 (continued)

```
        (LPVOID) &m_SocketInfo );

    // Store the thread handle for later.
    m_hCallAnswerThread = lpThread->m_hThread;
    }

}

void CSocketsView::OnUpdateSocketCall(CCmdUI* pCmdUI)
{

  // Only enable if we're not calling or
  // answering or currently connected.
  pCmdUI->Enable( !m_SocketInfo.bConnected &&
    !m_SocketInfo.bCalling &&
    !m_SocketInfo.bListening );

}

void CSocketsView::OnSocketDisconnect()
{

  // Set the abort flag to TRUE.
  m_SocketInfo.bAbort = TRUE;

}

void CSocketsView::OnUpdateSocketDisconnect(
  CCmdUI* pCmdUI)
{

  // Only enable if we're not calling or
  // answering or currently connected.
  pCmdUI->Enable( ( !m_SocketInfo.bConnected &&
    !m_SocketInfo.bCalling &&
    !m_SocketInfo.bListening ) );

}

void CSocketsView::OnSocketSendmessage()
{
  CMessage Message;

  // Get the message text via the dialog.
  if( Message.DoModal() )

    // Copy the message text into the
    // SOCKET_INFO structure.
    strcpy( m_SocketInfo.szOutgoingMessage,
      Message.m_strMessage );
```

```
}

void CSocketsView::OnUpdateSocketSendmessage(
  CCmdUI* pCmdUI)
{

  pCmdUI->Enable( m_SocketInfo.bConnected &&
    m_SocketInfo.bCalling );

}

UINT CSocketsView::CallThread( LPVOID lpInf )
{
  SOCKET_INFO *lpInfo = (SOCKET_INFO *) lpInf;
  int nRetValue = 0;
  CSocket CallSocket;
  BOOL bDone = FALSE;

  // Create a socket.
  if( !CallSocket.Create( lpInfo->nPort ) ){
    // Record the error.
    lpInfo->dwLastError = GetLastError();
    // Set our return value.
    nRetValue = 1;
    // Bail out.
    goto CallEnd;
    }

  // Set up the SOCKADDR_IN structure.
  SOCKADDR_IN Addr;
  memset( &Addr, 0, sizeof( SOCKADDR_IN ) );
  Addr.sin_family = AF_INET;
  Addr.sin_port = htons( lpInfo->nPort );
  Addr.sin_addr.s_addr = inet_addr( lpInfo->szHost );

  // Connect to the remote socket.
  if( !CallSocket.Connect( (LPSOCKADDR) &Addr,
    sizeof( SOCKADDR_IN ) ) ){
    // Record the error.
    lpInfo->dwLastError = GetLastError();
    // Set our return value.
    nRetValue = 2;
    // Bail out.
    goto CallEnd;
    }

  // Set our connected flag to TRUE.
  lpInfo->bConnected = TRUE;
  // Give an audio signal that we're connected.
  MessageBeep( -1 );

  while( !bDone ){
```

(continued)

Listing 34-2 *(continued)*

```
      // Wait so we don't chew up processor time.
      Sleep( 200 );

      // Check the abort flag.
      if( lpInfo->bAbort )
        bDone = TRUE;

      // See if there's a message to send.
      else if( lpInfo->szOutgoingMessage[0] != 0 ){

        // Send the data.
        int nBytes =
          CallSocket.Send( lpInfo->szOutgoingMessage,
            strlen( lpInfo->szOutgoingMessage ) );

        // See if there was a problem. If so, we need
        // to bail out.
        if( nBytes == 0 || nBytes == SOCKET_ERROR )
          bDone = TRUE;

        // Zero the first character of the message
        // buffer.
        lpInfo->szOutgoingMessage[0] = 0;
        }
      }

CallEnd:
  // Reset our flags.
  lpInfo->bCalling =
    lpInfo->bListening =
    lpInfo->bConnected = FALSE;

  // Return to caller.
  return( nRetValue );

}

UINT CSocketsView::AnswerThread( LPVOID lpInf )
{
  SOCKET_INFO *lpInfo = (SOCKET_INFO *) lpInf;
  int nRetValue = 0;
  CSocket ServerSocket;
  BOOL bDone = FALSE;
  CSocket ClientSocket;

  if( !ServerSocket.Create( lpInfo->nPort ) ){
    // Record the error.
    lpInfo->dwLastError = GetLastError();
    // Set our return value.
    nRetValue = 1;
    // Bail out.
```

```
    goto AnswerEnd;
    }

  if( !ServerSocket.Listen( 1 ) ){
    // Record the error.
    lpInfo->dwLastError = GetLastError();
    // Set our return value.
    nRetValue = 2;
    // Bail out.
    goto AnswerEnd;
    }

  if( !ServerSocket.Accept( ClientSocket ) ){
    // Record the error.
    lpInfo->dwLastError = GetLastError();
    // Set our return value.
    nRetValue = 3;
    // Bail out.
    goto AnswerEnd;
    }

  // Set our connected flag to TRUE.
  lpInfo->bConnected = TRUE;
  // Give an audio signal that we're connected.
  MessageBeep( -1 );

  while( !bDone ){

    // Declare a char buffer and clear it.
    char cbBuffer[1000];
    memset( cbBuffer, 0, sizeof( cbBuffer ) );

    // Read incoming data. This function blocks. It
    // won't return until it has data or there's been
    // a socket error.
    int nBytes =
      ClientSocket.Receive( cbBuffer,
        sizeof( cbBuffer ) );

    // See if there was a problem. If so we need
    // to bail out.
    if( nBytes == 0 || nBytes == SOCKET_ERROR ||
      lpInfo->bAbort )
      bDone = TRUE;

    // Otherwise, display the message.
    else
      AfxMessageBox( cbBuffer );
    }

AnswerEnd:
```

(continued)

Listing 34-2 (continued)

```
  // Reset our flags.
  lpInfo->bCalling =
    lpInfo->bListening =
    lpInfo->bConnected = FALSE;

  // Return to caller.
  return( nRetValue );

}
```

The SendEmail Program

Let's explore how to create a program to send e-mail through the Internet.

A demonstration program can be found on the CD-ROM in the `Chap34\SendEmail` directory. It sends a text message as an e-mail message using SMTP. You can rebuild the program by loading the `SendEmail.dsw` project file, or just run the `SendEmail.exe` program using Explorer.

✦ ✦ ✦ ✦ ✦

How does the program work? It establishes a connection to a mail server on port 25, the reserved SMTP port. A conversation then follows in which the mail server is given enough information so that it can send the e-mail. The conversation is ended with a special sequence of text, and the socket connection is disconnected. Highlights of source code in the `SendEmail.exe` program are provided in Listing 34-3.

The conversation between the client and the mail server has several distinct components. The following conversation sends the message "This is a test" to a recipient on `mail.myserver.com` at e-mail address `you@yourserver.com`. These days, you must have a return e-mail address so that the mail server won't reject it as SPAM. This message contains the return e-mail address of `me@myserver.com`.

```
Sender Text Sent (includes CR/LF at end of text)
Mail Server    220 MAIL.MYSERVER.COM SMTP Service at 9 Apr 98
05:17:18 EDT
Client HELO MAIL.MYSERVER.COM
Mail Server    250 MAIL.MYSERVER.COM - Hello, MAIL.MYSERVER.COM
Client Mail From: <me@myserver.com>
Mail Server    250 MAIL accepted
Client RCPT: <you@yourserver.com>
Mail Server    250 Recipient accepted
Client DATA
Mail Server    354 Start mail input, end with .
Client From: me@myserver.com
Client To: you@yourserver.com
```

```
Client Subject: Test
Client
Client This is a test.
Client
Mail Server    250 OK
Client QUIT
Mail Server    221 MAIL.MYSERVER.COM Service closing
transmission channel
```

SendEmail

Project Name: **SendEmail**
CD-ROM Location: **Chap34\SendEmail**
Prebuilt Program: **Chap34\SendEmail\SendEmail.exe**
Source Code Highlights in Text: `Email.cpp`

◆ ◆ ◆ ◆ ◆

Listing 34-3: Highlights of the Email.cpp Source Code for the SendEmail.exe Program

```
// Email.cpp

#include "stdafx.h"
#include "Email.h"

CEmail::CEmail()
{

  // Set the thread pointer and the
  // thread to NULL.
  m_pSendEmailThread = NULL;
  m_hThread = NULL;

}

CEmail::~CEmail()
{

  // Set the abort flag to TRUE.
  m_Info.bAbort = TRUE;

  // See if the thread pointer and the
  // thread handle are NULL.
  if( m_pSendEmailThread && m_hThread != NULL )

    // Wait for the thread to end.
    ::WaitForSingleObject( m_hThread, 15000 );

}
```

(continued)

Listing 34-3 *(continued)*

```
void CEmail::Send( const char *lpszEmailAddress,
  const char *lpszMessage, const char *lpszFrom,
  const char *lpszHost, const char *lpszSubject )
{

  // If the thread pointer is not NULL,
  // a thread has already been created.
  if( m_pSendEmailThread != NULL )
    return;

  // Populate the EMAIL_INFO structure with
  // information such as the email address and
  // the message data.
  m_Info.pSendEmailThread = &m_pSendEmailThread;
  strcpy( m_Info.szEmailAddress, lpszEmailAddress );
  strcpy( m_Info.szMessage, lpszMessage );
  strcpy( m_Info.szFrom, lpszFrom );
  strcpy( m_Info.szHost, lpszHost );
  strcpy( m_Info.szSubject, lpszSubject );

  // Set the abort and completed flags to
  // FALSE, set the socket to INVALID_SOCKET
  // so we know there's no socket created yet.
  m_Info.bAbort = FALSE;
  m_Info.bCompleted = FALSE;
  m_Info.hSocket = INVALID_SOCKET;

  // Kick off the thread.
  m_pSendEmailThread =
    AfxBeginThread( CEmail::SendThread,(LPVOID)&m_Info );

  // Store the thread handle for later.
  m_hThread = m_pSendEmailThread->m_hThread;

}

BOOL CEmail::SendSocketData( EMAIL_INFO *lpInfo,
  char *cbBuffer, CSocket& MailSocket,
  const char *lpszToken )
{

  // Sleep so that the buffer will clear.
  Sleep( 100 );
  // Send the data.
  MailSocket.Send( cbBuffer, strlen( cbBuffer ) );

  // Check the last error and store it. If there's
  // an error other than WSAEWOULDBLOCK, bail out.
  lpInfo->dwLastError = GetLastError();
  if( lpInfo->dwLastError != 0 &&
    lpInfo->dwLastError != WSAEWOULDBLOCK )
```

```
    goto SendSocketDataError;
  lpInfo->dwLastError = 0;

  // Sleep so the buffer has time to empty.
  Sleep( 100 );
  // Clear the incoming buffer.
  memset( cbBuffer, 0, BUFFERSIZE );

  // Look for incoming data.
  MailSocket.Receive( cbBuffer, BUFFERSIZE );

  // Check the last error and store it. If there's
  // an error other than WSAEWOULDBLOCK, bail out.
  lpInfo->dwLastError = GetLastError();
  if( lpInfo->dwLastError != 0 &&
    lpInfo->dwLastError != WSAEWOULDBLOCK )
    goto SendSocketDataError;
  lpInfo->dwLastError = 0;

  // There are times (when lpszToken != NULL) that we
  // want to compare lpszToken to the incoming buffer.
  if( lpszToken != NULL && strnicmp( cbBuffer, lpszToken,
    strlen( lpszToken ) ) ){
    strcpy( lpInfo->szErrorMessage, cbBuffer );
    lpInfo->dwLastError = -10000;
    goto SendSocketDataError;
    }

  return( TRUE );

SendSocketDataError:
  return( FALSE );

}

UINT CEmail::SendThread( LPVOID lpInf )
{
  EMAIL_INFO *lpInfo = (EMAIL_INFO *) lpInf;

  // Declare a buffer for data transfer.
  char cbBuffer[BUFFERSIZE];

  CSocket MailSocket;
  int nBytesRead;
  BOOL bMessageTypeOK;

  // Create a socket for the transfer.
  MailSocket.Create( 25 );
  // Connect to the host.
  MailSocket.Connect( lpInfo->szHost, 25 );

  // Check for an error. If there's any other
```

(continued)

Listing 34-3 (continued)

```
// error besides WSAEWOULDBLOCK, we don't do
// the following code.
lpInfo->dwLastError = GetLastError();
if( lpInfo->dwLastError == 0 ||
  lpInfo->dwLastError == WSAEWOULDBLOCK ){

  // Set last error to 0 and store the
  // socket in the structure.
  lpInfo->dwLastError = 0;
  lpInfo->hSocket = MailSocket.m_hSocket;

  // Let the socket stabilize before we look
  // for data/
  Sleep( 100 );

  // Look for incoming data.
  nBytesRead =
    MailSocket.Receive( cbBuffer, sizeof( cbBuffer ) );

  // See if we got a '220 ' at the beginning of
  // the data we got back.
  bMessageTypeOK =
    !( strnicmp( cbBuffer, "220 ", 4 ) );

  // If we didn't get a '220 ' take the
  // appropriate action.
  if( !bMessageTypeOK ){
    strcpy( lpInfo->szErrorMessage, cbBuffer );
    lpInfo->dwLastError = -10000;
    goto EndSendThread;
    }

  // Look for an error. If we got anything
  // other than WSAAEWOULDBLOCK, bail out.
  lpInfo->dwLastError = GetLastError();
  if( lpInfo->dwLastError != 0 &&
    lpInfo->dwLastError != WSAEWOULDBLOCK )
    goto EndSendThread;

  // If we got data...
  if( nBytesRead > 0 ){

    // Format a HELO string to send to the host.
    wsprintf( cbBuffer, "HELO %s\r\n", lpInfo->szHost);
    if( !SendSocketData( lpInfo, cbBuffer, MailSocket,
      "250 " ) )
      goto EndSendThread;

    // Format a FROM string and send it to the host.
    wsprintf( cbBuffer, "MAIL FROM: <%s>\r\n",
      lpInfo->szFrom );
```

```
        if( !SendSocketData( lpInfo, cbBuffer, MailSocket,
          NULL ) )
          goto EndSendThread;

        // Format a RCPT string and send it to the host.
        wsprintf( cbBuffer, "RCPT to: <%s>\r\n",
          lpInfo->szEmailAddress );
        if( !SendSocketData( lpInfo, cbBuffer, MailSocket,
          NULL ) )
          goto EndSendThread;

        // Format a DATA string and send it to the host.
        strcpy( cbBuffer, "DATA\r\n" );
        if( !SendSocketData( lpInfo, cbBuffer, MailSocket,
          NULL ) )
          goto EndSendThread;

        // Format the email message string and send it
        // to the host.
        wsprintf( cbBuffer,
          "Subject: %s\r\nTo: %s\r\n%s\r\n\r\n.\r\n",
          lpInfo->szSubject, lpInfo->szEmailAddress,
          lpInfo->szMessage );
        if( !SendSocketData( lpInfo, cbBuffer, MailSocket,
          NULL ) )
          goto EndSendThread;

        }
      }

EndSendThread:
  // Clean up.
  lpInfo->hSocket = INVALID_SOCKET;
  lpInfo->pSendEmailThread[0] = NULL;
  lpInfo->bCompleted = TRUE;

  return( 0 );

}
```

Retrieving an HTTP File

Retrieving an HTTP file from a Web server is an often-encountered situation. This is especially true with the written Web crawler. The crawler systematically retrieves HTTP files, parses them for references to other HTTP files, and then retrieves the next file in its list.

The easiest way you retrieve an HTTP file is with the `OpenURL()` function, which is a member function of the `CInternetSession` class. The following code creates a

CInternetSession object and then retrieves the file at http://www.microsoft.com/file.txt:

```
// Create the CInternetSession object.
CInternetSession InternetSession;
try{

  // Open the Http file.
  CHttpFile *pHttpFile =
    InternetSession.OpenURL(
      "http://www.microsoft.com/file.txt" );

  // Create a CFile object and then open the file
  // for creation.
  CFile File;
  if( File.Open( "file.txt",
    CFile::modeWrite | CFile::modeCreate ) ){

    // Get the length of the Http file, allocate
    // a buffer, read the data, write the data,
    // and deallocate the buffer.
    int nLength = pHttpFile->GetLength();
    char *pBuffer = new char [pHttpFile->GetLength()];
    pHttpFile->Read( pBuffer, nLength );
    File.Write( pBuffer, nLength );
    delete [] pBuffer;
    }
  pHttpFile->Close();
  }
catch( CinternetException *e )
{
  e->Delete();
  AfxMessageBox( "An exception was thrown." );
}
```

You don't have to close the file that's wrapped by the CFile object because its destructor closes the file for you. When you delete the CHttpFile object, it cleans up everything so you don't have to explicitly call the Close() member function.

The AutoDialer Program

Let's take a look at an application to implement autodialing.

A demonstration program can be found on the CD-ROM in the Chap34\AutoDialer directory. It determines if a client machine has an Internet connection established. If it doesn't, the connection is automatically dialed and managed. You can rebuild the program by loading the AutoDialer.dsw project file, or just run the AutoDialer.exe program using Explorer.

✦ ✦ ✦ ✦ ✦

The program uses functions that are part of the Remote Access Service. The `CAutoDial` class can be reused in your program simply by copying it into your project and compiling it with the other files. The source code in Listing 34-4 shows how to use the `CAautoDial` class.

To initiate a dialup, select Send Email from the Email menu. A dialog box is displayed in which you'll enter the connection name, the username, and the user password as shown in Figure 34-4.

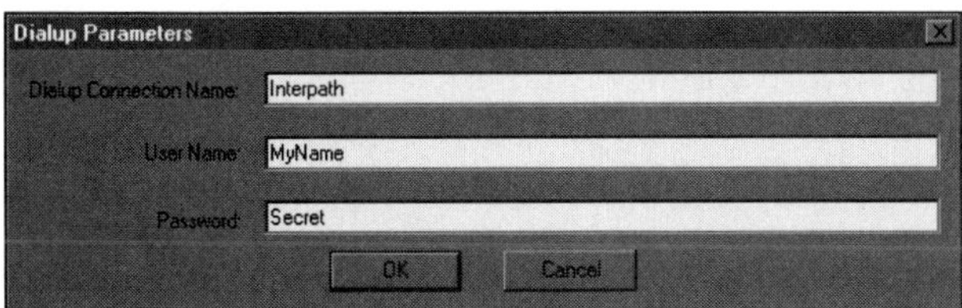

Figure 34-4: You'll have to enter this information before the program can initiate a dialup.

After entering the information, the program turns the process over to the `CAutoDial` class. The entire dialup process is maintained until either a successful connect or an error occurs. Figure 34-5 shows the `CAutoDial` class in action as it displays the dialup progress.

Figure 34-5: The CAutoDial class manages the entire process.

Project Name: **AutoDialer**
CD-ROM Location: **Chap34\AutoDialer**
Prebuilt Program: **Chap34\AutoDialer\AutoDialer.exe**
Source Code Highlights in Text: `AutoDialerView.cpp`

✦ ✦ ✦ ✦ ✦

Listing 34-4: Highlights of the AutoDialerView.cpp Source Code for the AutoDialer.exe Program

```
// AutoDialerView.cpp : implementation of the
// CAutoDialerView class
//

#include "stdafx.h"
#include "AutoDialer.h"

#include "AutoDialerDoc.h"
#include "AutoDialerView.h"

#include "DialupParams.h"

/////////////////////////////////////////////////////////
// CAutoDialerView

/////////////////////////////////////////////////////////
// CAutoDialerView construction/destruction

CAutoDialerView::CAutoDialerView()
{
}

CAutoDialerView::~CAutoDialerView()
{

  // Make sure we're disconnected.
  m_AutoDial.Disconnect();

}

/////////////////////////////////////////////////////////
// CAutoDialerView message handlers

void CAutoDialerView::OnDialerDial()
{
  CDialupParams Params;

  // Put up the dialog box to get user
  // params: Dialup name, user name, and
  // password.
  if( Params.DoModal() == IDOK ){
```

```
     // Call the connect function. Once it's
     // started, it goes in the background via
     // a callback function.
     m_AutoDial.Connect( Params.m_strUserName,
       Params.m_strPassword,
       Params.m_strDialupName );

     // Put up the dialog box that shows the
     // dialup status.
     m_AutoDial.DoModal();
     }

}

void CAutoDialerView::OnDialerHangup()
{

   // Disconnect. This can
   // be called even when user isn't
   // online without unwanted results.
   m_AutoDial.Disconnect();

}
```

Summary

This chapter has provided a lot of tools with which you can equip your programs. You can now send and receive files with the FTP protocol. You now know how to connect using the `CSocket` class and transfer data. You even know how to send e-mail. Take this chapter, and build on it. What you'll be able to do with some effort will amaze everyone.

✦ ✦ ✦

The CHtmlView Class

✦ ✦ ✦ ✦

In This Chapter

Microsoft's Web browser

Creating a CHtmlView project

Converting projects to CHtmlView projects

Navigating URLs

A demo program using CHtmlView

A URL control using CHtmlView

Writing a browser that logs navigation

Writing a browser that blocks sites

✦ ✦ ✦ ✦

In this chapter, you'll learn how to add to your programs the capability to browse the World Wide Web. It's easy to do with the tools that Microsoft provides to its developers. This chapter covers the Web Browser control and the new `CHtmlView` class that wraps the control. The Microsoft Web Browser control can be used by application developers to add the capability to browse sites on the World Wide Web, or folders and files on a local or networked file system. It's easy to create a Web application because there are relatively few steps to creating these programs compared with what it takes to develop your own browser control. The Web Browser control supports Web browsing through point-and-click hyperlinking and through direct navigation to URLs. The control even maintains a history list that lets you browse forward and backward through previously browsed sites, folders, and documents.

Applications can also use the Web Browser control as an Active Document container to host other active documents. This means that richly formatted documents, such as Microsoft Excel spreadsheets or Microsoft Word documents, can be opened and edited in place from within the Web Browser control. Web Browser is also an ActiveX control container that can host any ActiveX control.

As if the Web Browser wasn't enough, Microsoft has also provided an MFC class that encapsulates it so it's even easier to use. The `CHtmlView` class provides the functionality of the Web Browser control within the context of MFC's document/view architecture.

The Web Browser ActiveX control (and therefore `CHtmlView`) is available only to programs running under Windows 95, Windows 98, and Windows NT versions 3.51 and later, in which Internet Explorer 4.0 (or later) has been installed.

Some `CHtmlView` member functions apply to the Internet Explorer application only. These functions will succeed on the Web Browser control, but they will have no visible effect. These functions are `GetAddressBar()`, `GetFullName()`, `GetStatusBar()`, `SetAddressBar()`, `SetFullScreen()`, `SetMenuBar()`, `SetStatusBar()`, and `SetToolBar()`.

Creating a CHtmlView Project

Creating an application based on the `CHtmlView` class is a no-brainer. You start with the AppWizard. The application should be some form of a document/view program, whether it's a single document or multiple document program.

Most of the options, such as those that determine whether you have a toolbar or enable printing and print previewing, don't make any difference in the program's capability to use the `CHtmlView` class. You can set these as you wish, and the application will support the Web Browser control with no problem.

The only thing you'll have to remember during the AppWizard creation process comes toward the end. When the sixth dialog box (labeled appropriately "6 of 6") displays, you'll have the chance to change the base class of the view class to something besides the vanilla `CView` class. At this point, you'll need to select the `CHtmlView` class, as shown in Figure 35-1.

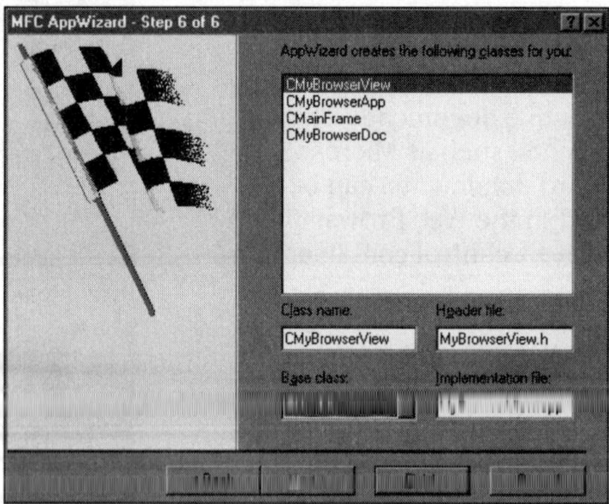

Figure 35-1: You'll have to select the CHtmlView class as your view class' base class.

Once you create the `CHtmlView`-based product, compile it, and run it. The default URL points to Microsoft's Visual C++ Web page at `www.microsoft.com/visualc`, as shown in Figure 35-2.

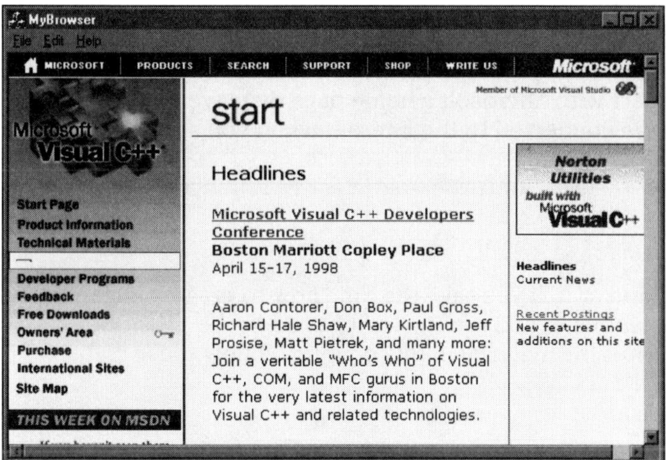

Figure 35-2: A Web page automatically comes up when the project first runs.

You can easily change the starting URL by editing the `OnInitialUpdate()` function. For instance, if you want the application to start at `www.yahoo.com`, you'd change the `OnInitialUpdate()` function as follows:

```
void CFirstCHTMLView::OnInitialUpdate()
{
  CHtmlView::OnInitialUpdate();
  Navigate2(_T("http://www.yahoo.com"),NULL,NULL);
}
```

Converting Projects to Use CHtmlView

You might have existing projects that you want to convert from a `CView`-based application to a `CHtmlView`-based application. Following is the procedure to convert an application's view class to `CHtmlView`:

1. Use the Find/Replace feature to replace all instances of your current view class (usually `CView`) in your view's .CPP file, with `CHtmlView`.
2. Repeat the same substitution in your view's .H file, replacing your current view class with `CHtmlView`.
3. In your application's `STDAFX.H` file, append the following line:

   ```
   #include <afxhtml.h>
   ```

4. Override the `OnInitialUpdate()` member function of your application's view class.

5. In the function body of `OnInitialUpdate()`, add a call to `CHtmlView::Navigate()` to cause the contained Web Browser control to load the specified HTML page. For example, the following line causes your application to start with Microsoft's home page displayed in its view (assuming you are connected to the Internet when you start the application):

```
Navigate( _T("http://www.microsoft.com"),0,0,0);
```

Try This

Create a Browser

It's time to try your hand at it. If you take the time now to create a default `CHtmlView` project, compile it, and run it, you'll have a better chance of understanding the rest of the material in this chapter. Follow these steps:

1. Run AppWizard.
2. Select an MFC EXE project and name it **FirstCHTML**.
3. Select a single document interface that supports document/view.
4. Choose all default options until dialog box 4 of 6. In that dialog box, deselect the docking toolbar, status bar, and printing options.
5. Keep the default settings for dialog box 5 of 6.
6. When dialog box 6 of 6 displays, change the `CFirstCHTMLView` class so that its base class is `CHtmlView`.
7. Compile the application.
8. Run the application.

✦ ✦ ✦ ✦ ✦

Navigating CHtmlViews

When a program that's based on the `CHtmlView` class runs, users can navigate for themselves by clicking the HTML hyperlinks. This requires absolutely no code from the application developer — the underlying Web Browser control takes care of everything. But somewhere along the way, you might have a reason for navigating to different URLs, and this section shows you how to do it.

The first obvious thing you'll want to provide users with is the capability to go backward and forward through the history list. For instance, you have to give them a way to back up to the Web page they were on just before the page they're currently on. Internet Explorer has right and left arrow icons on the toolbar that enable users to back up and go forward, but these aren't built into the Web Browser control.

The easiest user interface that enables users to go forward and backward is made up of a couple of menu selections. Later, you can add buttons to your toolbar. The following function moves to the previous Web page:

```
void CMyHtmlView::Back()
{

  GoBack();

}
```

The following function moves to the next page:

```
void CMyHtmlView::Forward()
{

  GoForward();

}
```

Three other important functions that users want are `Stop()`, `Refresh()`, `GoHome()`, and `GoSearch()`. The `Stop()` function terminates retrieval of the current Web page contents. The `Refresh()` function refreshes the current Web page by re-retrieving the data from the Web server. If users want to go to their home page, the `GoHome()` function can be used (the home page is retrieved from the Registry preferences, which are set by Internet Explorer). And the `GoSearch()` function takes users to their default search page (once again, set with Internet Explorer).

Two functions enable you to take users directly to a new URL: the `Navigate()` and `Navigate2()` functions. The only difference between them is the way in which each interprets the URL. The `Navigate()` function expects URLs to be relative, and the `Navigate2()` function expects URLs to contain a full path.

For example, a user might be viewing a Web page that's located at `www.myserver.com/first/second/test.html` and want to move to `www.myserver.com/first/second/third/othertest.html`. The new URL is simply one level deeper in the subdirectory hierarchy. The following code works perfectly to go to the new URL:

```
Navigate( "third/othertest.html" );
```

The following code, however, would not work because the `Navigate2()` function expects an absolute address:

```
Navigate2( "third/othertest.html" );
```

If you want to use the `Navigate2()` function, you'd have to do the following instead:

```
Navigate2(
 "www.myserver.com/first/second/third/othertest.html");
```

One important point: You can omit the `http://` protocol preface. The Web Browser control parses the URL and inserts it for you. For example, the previous example in which `www.myserver.com/first.second/third/othertest.html` was passed to `Navigate2()` is parsed to `http://www.myserver.com/first.second/third/othertest.html`.

The SimpleBrowser Program

The SimpleBrowser program implements six of the `CHtmlView` navigation functions. They are `GoBack()`, `GoForward()`, `GoHome()`, `Navigate2()`, `Stop()`, and `GoSearch()`.

A demonstration program can be found on the CD-ROM in the `Chap35\SimpleBrowser` directory. It's built around `CHtmlView`, and it provides a simple browser without many extras. You can rebuild the program by loading the `SimpleBrowser.dsw` project file, or just run the `SimpleBrowser.exe` program using Explorer.

✦ ✦ ✦ ✦ ✦

We've already mentioned the `Navigate2()` function. The `GoBack()` function navigates back to the previous URL. The `GoForward()` function navigates to the next URL. The `GoHome()` function finds the home page that the browser is set to and navigates to that page. The `Stop()` function terminates any data retrieval and data requests for the current page. The `GoSearch()` function finds the search page that the browser is set to and navigates to that page. Besides menu choices for invoking the six functions, a toolbar has been implemented to enable users to make these choices with a single mouse click.

The code for the `SimpleBrowserView.cpp` file is trivial. And that's a tribute to how easy Microsoft has made it to use the `CHtmlView` class. When the program first runs, it goes to `http://www.microsoft.com/visualc/` as shown in Figure 35-3. This is the default URL that's inserted in the startup code by the AppWizard. Users can easily navigate by clicking the HTML hyperlinks. They can also use the navigation buttons in the toolbar. The source code highlights are shown in Listing 35-1.

SimpleBrowser

Project Name: **SimpleBrowser**

CD-ROM Location: **Chap35\SimpleBrowser**

Prebuilt Program: `Chap35\SimpleBrowser\SimpleBrowser.exe`

Source Code Highlights in Text: `SimpleBrowserView.cpp`

✦ ✦ ✦ ✦ ✦

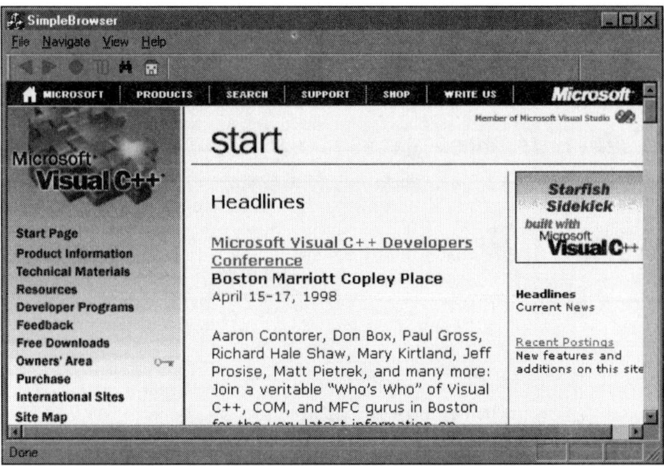

Figure 35-3: The SimpleBrowser program starts by loading Microsoft's Visual C++ Web page.

Listing 35-1: **Highlights of the SimpleBrowserView.cpp Source Code for the SimpleBrowser.exe Program**

```
// SimpleBrowserView.cpp : implementation of the
// CSimpleBrowserView class
//

#include "stdafx.h"
#include "SimpleBrowser.h"

#include "SimpleBrowserDoc.h"
#include "SimpleBrowserView.h"

#include "NewURL.h"

/////////////////////////////////////////////////////////
// CSimpleBrowserView

void CSimpleBrowserView::OnInitialUpdate()
{
  CHtmlView::OnInitialUpdate();

  Navigate2(_T("http://www.microsoft.com/visualc/"),
    NULL,NULL);
}

/////////////////////////////////////////////////////////
```

(continued)

Listing 35-1 *(continued)*

```
// CSimpleBrowserView message handlers

void CSimpleBrowserView::OnNavigateBack()
{

  // Call the CHtmlView function
  // that goes to the previous
  // URL.
  GoBack();

}

void CSimpleBrowserView::OnNavigateForward()
{

  // Call the CHtmlView function
  // that goes to the next URL.
  GoForward();

}

void CSimpleBrowserView::OnNavigateGoto()
{
  CNewURL NewURL;

  // Put up a dialog box that asks
  // user for a URL.
  if( NewURL.DoModal() == IDOK )

    // If the click on the OK button,
    // go to the new URL.
    Navigate2( NewURL.m_strNewURL,
      0, 0, 0 );

}

void CSimpleBrowserView::OnNavigateHome()
{

  // Call the CHtmlView function
  // that goes to the home page.
  GoHome();

}

void CSimpleBrowserView::OnNavigateSearch()
{
```

```
    // Call the CHtmlView function
    // that goes to the search page.
    GoSearch();

}

void CSimpleBrowserView::OnNavigateStop()
{

    // Call the CHtmlView function
    // that stops the transfer.
    Stop();

}
```

The MultiBrowser Program

The MultiBrowser program doesn't offer the same navigation functions that the SimpleBrowser program offers. That's because it serves a special purpose. It's intended to help you look through search results from a search engine.

A demonstration program can be found on the CD-ROM in the `Chap35\MultiBrowser` directory. As with the SimpleBrowser program, it's built around the `CHtmlView` class. You can rebuild the program by loading the `MultiBrowser.dsw` project file, or just run the `MultiBrowser.exe` program using Explorer.

◆ ◆ ◆ ◆ ◆

When the program first runs, you'll see four child windows. The child windows are tiled so that users can see the contents of all of them equally well. The lower right window loads the Excite search engine found at `www.excite.com`. The other windows are blank when the program first runs, as shown in Figure 35-4.

Each link in the Excite window that you click causes the requested URL to be displayed in one of the other windows. For instance, if you search for Teddy Bears, get a list of 10,000 results, and click the first one, one of the blank windows loads the requested URL, as shown in Figure 35-5. In the figure, a search for Teddy Bears was performed, and the first result was selected. Notice that one of the blank windows loads the Teddy Bear URL.

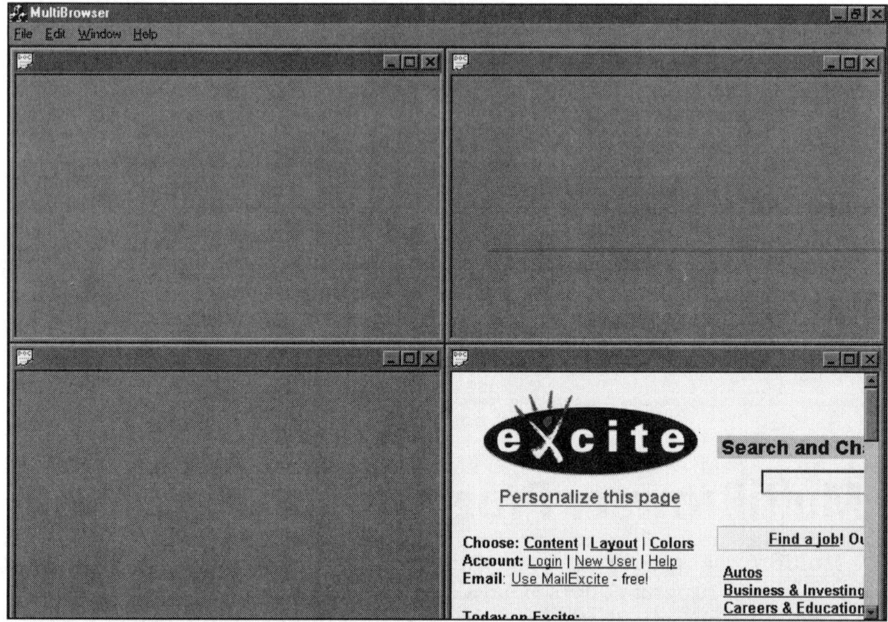

Figure 35-4: Only one window loads a URL at first, and the other three are empty.

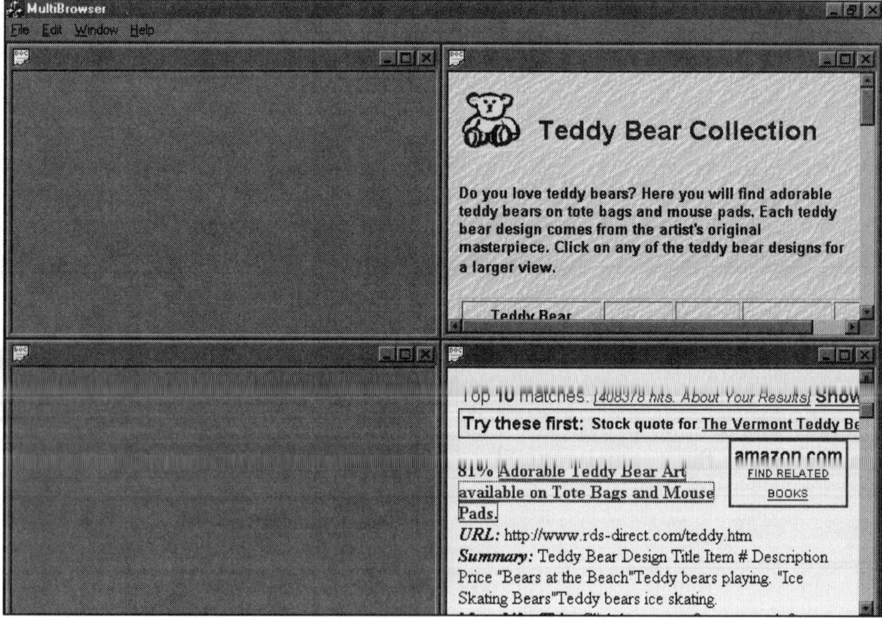

Figure 35-5: Clicking a search result causes the program to load the requested URL in one of the empty windows.

The way the program works is to override the `CHtmlView::OnBeforeNavigate2()` member function. This function looks at the request and then forwards the request to one of the other three windows. The selected window then loads the URL and displays its contents.

Search engines request URLs to display their results. But these URLs always have HTML arguments. An HTML argument list always follows the URL. But the key is that the URL and the argument list are separated by a question mark (?). That's how the overridden `OnBeforeNavigate2()` function knows the difference between a search result request that should be displayed in a window and a URL request that displays search results. Highlights of the source code are shown in Listing 35-2.

MultiBrowser

Project Name: **MultiBrowser**
CD-ROM Location: **Chap35\MultiBrowser**
Prebuilt Program: `Chap35\MultiBrowser\MultiBrowser.exe`
Source Code Highlights in Text: `MultiBrowserView.cpp`

◆ ◆ ◆ ◆ ◆

Listing 35-2: Highlights of the MultiBrowserView.cpp Source Code for the MultiBrowser.exe Program

```
// MultiBrowserView.cpp : implementation of the
// CMultiBrowserView class
//

#include "stdafx.h"
#include "MultiBrowser.h"

#include "MultiBrowserDoc.h"
#include "MultiBrowserView.h"

static int nCounter = 0;
static CMultiBrowserView *pView[4] =
  { NULL, NULL, NULL, NULL };

/////////////////////////////////////////////////////////////
// CMultiBrowserView

/////////////////////////////////////////////////////////////
// CMultiBrowserView construction/destruction

CMultiBrowserView::CMultiBrowserView()
{
```

(continued)

Listing 35-2 *(continued)*

```
  m_nMyCount = nCounter;
  m_nLastUpdated = 1;
  m_bInitialUpdate = TRUE;

  if( nCounter < 4 )
    pView[nCounter++] = this;

}

void CMultiBrowserView::OnInitialUpdate()
{
  CHtmlView::OnInitialUpdate();

  // We'll only go the the search
  // engine if this is the first view window.
  if( m_nMyCount == 0 )
    Navigate2(_T("http://www.excite.com/"),
      NULL,NULL);

}

////////////////////////////////////////////////////////////////
// CMultiBrowserView message handlers

void CMultiBrowserView::OnBeforeNavigate2(
  LPCTSTR lpszURL,
  DWORD nFlags, LPCTSTR lpszTargetFrameName,
  CByteArray& baPostedData, LPCTSTR lpszHeaders,
  BOOL* pbCancel )
{

  // Skip this is this is the initial update.
  // Make sure we only do this code if this
  // is the first view window. Also, make sure
  // the URL doesn't have a '?' character. The
  // '?' indicates a parameter and shows that
  // the user is navigating the search engine.
  if( !m_bInitialUpdate &&
    m_nMyCount == 0 &&
    strstr( lpszURL, "?" ) == NULL ){

    // If the view class pointer isn't NULL,
    // make it navigate to the URL.
    if( pView[m_nLastUpdated] != NULL )
      pView[m_nLastUpdated]->Navigate2( lpszURL );

    // Increment our counter index so that we'll
    // update the remaining three windows in
    // sequential order.
    m_nLastUpdated++;
```

```
        if( m_nLastUpdated > 3 )
          m_nLastUpdated = 1;

        // Cancel the navigation of the
        // search window.
        *pbCancel = TRUE;

        }

      // Set our flag so we know this isn't the
      // initial update.
      m_bInitialUpdate = FALSE;

    }
```

Direct Use of the Web Browser Control

Although this chapter is about the `CHtmlView` class, by now you may be wondering if you can add a browser to your program that's not in a view window. The answer is yes. You can use the Microsoft Web Browser control very easily. The following steps show you how.

Using the Microsoft Web Browser Control

If you need to use HTML or DHTML in your C++ programs, the Microsoft Web Browser is your best bet for easily loading, displaying, and enabling users to interact with HTML files. Here are the steps you need to follow:

1. From the Project menu, select the Add To Project item and the Components and Controls submenu.
2. From the Components and Controls Gallery dialog, select Registered ActiveX Controls.
3. In the list, select Microsoft Web Browser. Answer yes when it asks if you want to insert this component.
4. You'll get a dialog box in which a default name for the derived class and its files are displayed. You can change the names, or accept them. Once you click the OK button, the class is created. Close the Components and Controls Gallery dialog.
5. You must create the Web Browser control and attach it to a window. For example, this procedure creates a dialog to which the Web Browser control is attached. Create a dialog box with no controls. Make sure you leave the System Menu property selected so that users can kill the dialog. Also make sure the dialog is big enough for a reasonably sized browser.
6. Create a class for the dialog; in this example it's `CWebDialog`.

7. In the WebDialog.h file, include the header file for the Web Browser control. If you kept the default filenames when you inserted the Web Browser component, the include file is named webbrowser2.h.

```
#include "webbrowser2.h"
```

8. Declare a CWebBrowser2 class named m_WebBrowser in the WebDialog.h file. Once again, the CWebBrowser2 class is the default name that was created when the component was inserted into your program.

```
CWebBrowser2 m_WebBrowser;
```

9. Use the ClassWizard to create an OnInitDialog() function (select the WM_INITDIALOG message).

10. In the OnInitDialog() function, add the following code:

```
RECT Rect;
GetClientRect( &Rect );
m_WebBrowser.Create( "Test", WS_VISIBLE, Rect,
  this, 2000 );
m_WebBrowser.ShowWindow( SW_SHOWNORMAL );
m_WebBrowser.Navigate( "http://www.yahoo.com",
  NULL, NULL, NULL, NULL );
```

11. Add a menu item to the Help menu named "Show Web Browser."

12. Use the ClassWizard to add a command function, and add the following code:

```
CWebDialog WebDialog;
WebDialog.DoModal();
```

13. To the top of the source code module in which the menu command function was added, include your dialog class .h file (in this case, WebDialog.h).

```
#include "WebDialog.h"
```

14. Compile and run the program. Figure 35-6 shows what the program looks like after it has run and Show Web Browser is selected from the Help menu.

Figure 35-6: In the UseBrowser program, a Microsoft Web control has been placed in a dialog box.

A sample program is included on the CD-ROM in the `Chap35\UseBrowser` directory.

Writing a Browser That Logs Navigation

At times, especially in some business settings, there's a need to log all URLs that have been navigated to. It's pretty easy to do if you override the `OnBeforeComplete2()` function. Following is code to log all URLs to a log file:

```
void CCHtmlDemo2View::OnNavigateComplete2(LPCTSTR strURL)
{
  CFile cf;

  // Attempt to open an existing file.
  if( !cf.Open( "URLHist.dat",
    CFile::modeRead | CFile::modeWrite ) ){

    // If the file didn't exist, attempt to create it.
    if( !cf.Open( "URLHist.dat",
      CFile::modeCreate | CFile::modeWrite ) )
        return;
    }

  // Seek to the end of the file so we'll append.
  cf.SeekToEnd();
  // Write the URL.
  cf.Write( strURL, strlen( strURL ) );
  // Write a carriage return/line feed pair.
  cf.Write( "\15\12", 2 );
```

```
  // Get a pointer to the frame window.
  CMainFrame *pFrame = (CMainFrame *) AfxGetMainWnd();
  // Set the frame window's caption text to contain
  // the URL.
  pFrame->SetWindowText( strURL );

}
```

Writing a Browser That Blocks Sites

Dozens of packages are available to protect children from undesirable Internet sites or keep employees from wasting company time visiting sites that have no relationship to the business. You can write your own custom browser very easily by overriding the `OnBeforeNavigate2()` function. Using the overridden function, you can examine the requested URL and determine if it's okay to navigate to it. An overridden `OnBeforeNavigate2()` function follows that validates all URLs that are requested. It assumes that all URLs to be blocked are in a `CStringArray` named `m_strBlockList`.

```
void CCHtmlDemo2View::OnBeforeNavigate2( LPCTSTR lpszURL,
  DWORD nFlags, LPCTSTR lpszTargetFrameName,
  CByteArray& baPostedData, LPCTSTR lpszHeaders,
  BOOL* pbCancel )
{

  // Look through the list.
  for( int i=0; i<m_strBlockList.GetSize(); i++ ){

    // Pull out the string at this index. It's
    // easier to work with a single CString than
    // messing with the CStringArray.
    CString strTemp;
    strTemp = m_strBlockList.GetAt( i );

    // Use strnicmp to compare the string in the list
    // with the string that's passed in.
    if( !strnicmp( lpszURL, strTemp,
      strTemp.GetLength() ) ){

      // If we find a match, we'll block.
      *pbCancel = TRUE;

      // Alert user to the block.
      AfxMessageBox( "The site is blocked." );
      break;
      }
    }

}
```

Summary

Well, there you have it. Writing applications that browse the World Wide Web has never been easier. Within about ten minutes, you can create an application that's surfing the Web.

The uses for custom browsers is almost endless. You can build applications for businesses that restrict access to certain sites, or you can make it easier to access certain sites. You can write special educational applications that protect children from undesirable sites, or you can make it easier for them to get to the educational content that's out there.

✦ ✦ ✦

CHAPTER 36

Dynamic HTML

✦ ✦ ✦ ✦

In This Chapter

HTML fundamentals

DHTML basics

Cascading Style Sheets (CSS)

Building a simple DHTML file viewer

The DHTML object model

Scripting elements

Changing things other than text elements

Running a script

Scripting dialogs

✦ ✦ ✦ ✦

Using the new classes and controls for Web technologies in Visual C++ 6.0 along with the new capabilities that have evolved with Dynamic HMTL and JavaScript, you have more power than ever to present interactive information to the users of your C++ applications. You also have more capacity to create and modify both the presentation and the interface for this on the fly.

With the `CHtmlView` class and browser control, you are able to load and present HTML documents, which is a fine thing in of itself, but the new powers located in DHTML make this even more exciting and useful. These HTML documents can simply be files on your machine; they do not require that the machine have an active connection to a network or the Internet.

Once HTML was simply a page layout language to facilitate creating and displaying Web pages, but now all sorts of information is distributed as HTML files. The real power recently available to you comes with the new event and object models that are parts of DHTML. The new object models and scripting, both with JavaScript and VBScript, enable you to embed active code in your documents.

HTML, DHMTL, and JavaScript deserve entire books of their own. The purpose of this chapter is to give background information on the programming models and sufficient experience with working DHMTL samples so that you can evaluate how these might work in your own development efforts. Despite the hype, not every person on the planet already knows HTML; so in case you have been busy just keeping up with C++, let's first cover the basics of HTML.

HTML Fundamentals

You can think of every document as composed of three parts. The most obvious is its content, which includes titles, the main body of text, images, page numbers, lists, and so forth. What is not so obvious is that this document also often has a structure. For example, if the document is a book, it may be simple text from end to end, but the text in the table of contents has a different purpose and organization than the text in the index, or the text in the chapters. In addition to this structure, the document often is formatted. This format, if it is done well, helps the reader understand the structure of the document. Centered chapter titles in bold, for example, are set off from the text in the body of the chapter, so the reader does not start reading the chapter title, thinking it is the first sentence of the first paragraph.

Formatting helps reveal structure, but it is not structure, nor is it content, at least for the structural definitions used in this chapter. HyperText Markup Language (HTML) is defined with the Standard Generalized Markup Language (SGML). SGML is a formal structure for creating text markup languages. Markup languages, such as HTML, are tag languages. That is, each distinct element of the document is associated with a tag in some manner to define the type, or quality, of the element. HTML is simply one of many possible definitions that could be generated with the larger SGML structure.

SGML defines a document as a hierarchy of nested elements. This is seen in practice as a formal definition contained within a Document Type Definition (DTD). HTML is defined by a DTD; HTML is not simply a bunch of formatting tags all stuck together the way a person might throw together a bunch of style tags in a word processor. HTML is a formal definition with a defined set of elements and attributes. The HTML DTD also defines which elements in HTML contain other elements. Ideally the HTML language defines the structure of the document only, without reference to how it would be formatted or displayed. This issue will be covered later.

Some years back, HTML documents were created by hand, using a text editor. Of course, since then, many versatile tools for generating HTML documents have been developed. Many people who use HTML documents may not even be aware of the underlying formal language that makes the fancy display of their documents possible. Following is the HTML text for a simple document that will be develop further as the chapter progresses.

This code is included on the CD-ROM that accompanies this book in the Chap36 folder as `html1.htm`.

✦ ✦ ✦ ✦ ✦

```
<HTML>
<HEAD>
<TITLE>HTML1</TITLE>
</HEAD>

<BODY>
<H1>
The Text on This Page is Alive</H1>
<H1>
```

```
The Text on This Page is Alive</H1>
<H1>
The Text on This Page is Alive</H1>
</BODY>
</HTML>
```

Looking at this HTML sample as a programmer, several things are obvious, even if you have never seen HTML before. First, the text is composed of ASCII character strings that begin and end with special tags that are set off from the text with angle brackets. Next, you probably notice that these tagged strings, or elements, are nested. That is, the <HTML> </HTML> pair of tags surround two other elements, <BODY> and <HEAD>. Inside the body element are three elements marked <H1>. You will also notice that no font or display information of any sort is embedded in this document. Nor is there an associated file in which any secret formatting information is kept. This issue will be covered later. One thing that is not obvious is that the line breaks and spaces as they exist in the text file itself largely do not matter. Formatting is accomplished with tags, not the layout of the text in the file.

You can see how this HTML file is displayed by opening it with the first demonstration program that you will build in this chapter or by using your browser. Figure 36-1shows how the HTML file is displayed.

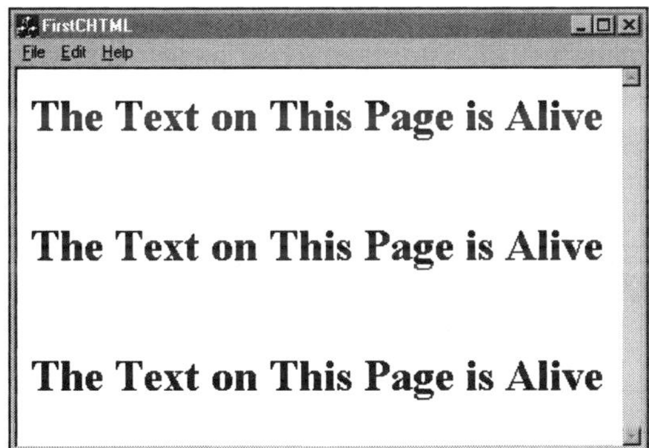

Figure 36-1: A simple HTML file when it is displayed

HTML, in its pure form, does not determine the font, color, or weight that will be used to display the text of the document. Nor does HTML determine what the background screen color is. The appearance of the document when it is displayed is determined by the software that interprets the HTML tagged document. This has generally been some form of browser software. However, with the addition of the `CHtmlView` class and the browser control in VC++, HTML documents can easily be interpreted and displayed in your applications. Mercifully, you will not need to interpret and position all the text and image elements on the page; you will simply open the file in the view. All the interpretation and flow of the document is provided by the code behind these objects.

It is certainly not the purpose of this chapter to teach all of HTML, but a basic familiarity with the common tags is helpful for understanding the simple scripts developed later in the chapter. The following is the minimal framework for an HTML document:

```
<HTML>
<HEAD>
</HEAD>
<BODY>
</BODY>
</HTML>
```

The document may have a title, which is just a character string between the beginning and ending title tags, `<TITLE>` and `</TITLE>`. Tags that are generally global in scope go between the beginning and ending tags for the header, `<HEAD>` and `</HEAD>`. Most of the tags and content of the document are located between the two body tags, `<BODY>` and `</BODY>`. These tags generally are text, formatting tags, images, links, applets, or scripts.

Table 36-1 provides a simple list of some basic tags for HTML documents. Each of these tags has a matching tag that begins with a slash to indicate the tag's end, except <HR>, `<IMG>`, and `<LINK>`. This list is by no means exhaustive, and many of these tags take additional parameters that modify their behavior. There are many good sources for learning about HTML, both on the Web and in your local bookstore. Another good way is to simply open up the cached pages from your browser in a text editor and look at how others used HTML tags.

Table 36-1
Common HTML Tags

Tag	*Description*
<BLOCKQUOTE>	Causes text to be displayed indented from the left margin.
 	Forces a new line break.
<CITE>	Causes text to be displayed in italic, as if for a quotation.
<DL>	This is a definition list. Each definition will be is indented beneath the item that it references.
<EM>	Adds emphasis to the text, usually italic.
<HR>	Creates a horizontal rule in the display.
<H*n*>	Marks a heading level, where *n* is replaced with one of 1, 2, 3, 4, 5, or 6.
<IMG>	Causes an image to be displayed in the document.
<LI>	This is an item in a list.
<LINK>	Marks a link to another URL.

Tag	*Description*
<OL>	Displays as an ordered list. Each item will begins with a number. The items will are marked with <LI>.
<P>	HTML ignores carriage returns in the ASCII text of its document. This tag signifies a new tag.
<STRONG>	Generally causes the text to be displayed as bold.
<SUB>	Displays as subscript.
<SUP>	Displays as superscript.
<U>	Underlines text.
<UL>	Displays as an unordered list. Each item will begins with a bullet.

Cascading Style Sheets

HTML was not intended to contain any information about the presentation of the document. However, for convenience, tags were incorporated in it that enabled document designers to mark text as bold or to change the font. This practice ignored the wisdom of keeping the structure separate from the presentation. This meant it was not possible for the interpreter of the document to completely determine its appearance because instructions for its display were embedded in the document. To separate style completely from both content and structure, the concept of Cascading Style Sheets (CSS) was developed.

If you have ever worked in the publications department of a corporation, you have no doubt had experience with corporate guidelines for publishing. These are generally specifications for the kinds of fonts, colors, paper, and so forth that are used for company publications. These guidelines do not say much about what should be in a business letter or on a package end-flap, but they are usually pretty specific about how things should look. Style sheets are similar. Style sheets govern how a document appears, without governing its content.

CSS enables you to define properties for appearance and associate those with the elements of a document. Essentially, this means that you can set the style and appearance for specific tags within your HTML documents, enabling you to attach formatting to the structuring information of the document. The *cascade* in the name comes from the idea that an ordered sequence of style sheets may be used in which declarations in later sheets have precedence over those that came before. Simultaneously with giving more control, they also reduce the amount of information embedded in a document. If all the information for styles is kept in a separate file, which is possible with CSS, this file needs to be transmitted only once, rather than sending the font information, for example, with every single tag in the document. With scripting, which is another part of the document that we will cover later, you also have the capability to make this appearance dynamic because you may modify these properties on the fly.

If you want to make all your <H1>, first-level heading, tags display in an 18-point Courier typeface, you can accomplish this with the line:

```
H1  {font-size: 18pt;  font-family: "Courier" }
```

Styles can be kept in three places. They can be embedded in the document as inline instructions that change the style for a single instance of a tag. They can be located in the header of the document, which causes the style to be applied to all the tags in that document. Styles can be defined and kept in separate files, generally with the extension .CSS; styles are then associated with the document using a <LINK> tag embedded in the document. Each of these three cases uses the tag <STYLE> to designate the style attribute.

Inline styles that apply to only single instances of a tag, of course, have limited use. Basically the inline style is associated directly with the tag in the document.

For example, Listing 36-1 shows HTML with a simple inline style definition for the third list item.

Listing 36-1: A List of Items in HTML

```
<HTML>
<HEAD>
<TITLE>DHTML2</TITLE>
</HEAD>
<BODY>

<H1>
Blue Things Outside Today</H1>

<UL>
<LI>
Blue river</LI>

<LI>
Blue sky</LI>

<LI STYLE="font-size:100%; text-align:right">
Blue flowers in the flower bed</LI>
<LI>
Well OK, they are actually kind of purple</LI>
</UL>
</BODY>
</HTML>
```

One of the list items is instructed to be displayed at the right margin and in a larger font. Notice, while you are looking at Listing 36-1, that the list item tags <LI> are nested inside another container. The unordered list pair of tags, <UL> and </UL>, contain the list items. When this HTML document is opened in the small HTML viewer, which you will create later in this chapter as a demonstration, it appears as it does in Figure 36-2.

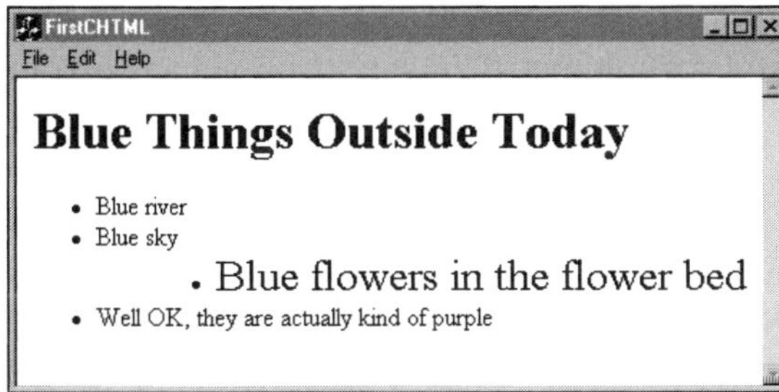

Figure 36-2: The inline style changes the display of one of the lines.

Global style sheets

The next more general level of style sheet is one that is included in the header of the HTML document. This is called a *global style sheet.* Putting the style sheet in the header makes modifying the appearance of the document relatively easy. The styles that are indicated for particular tags apply to those tags throughout the document. The beginning of a style sheet in the header is indicated by the tag:

```
<STYLE TYPE="text/css">
```

Its end is marked with the tag </STYLE>.

The literals "text/css" indicate that the language for the style sheet is CSS. It need not necessarily be CSS for all browsers, but that is the language, or code, used by Microsoft's and Netscape's browsers.

Between the beginning and ending style sheet tags are a series of selectors with an associated style. For example, to return to our previous example, if you wanted all the list items to appear right justified, you would include the following lines in the header of your HTML document:

```
<STYLE TYPE="text/css">
LI {text-align:right}
</STYLE>
```

Before describing the format of these declarations of selectors and styles, let's consider the final and most powerful means for defining style sheets. This is done with a mechanism called a *linked style sheet*. A linked style sheet is one in which the style information is kept in a separate file.

To link a style sheet with your HTML document, you use the link tag in the header to indicate that an associated style sheet exists and what its URL is. The URL points to an external style sheet file. If this HTML document is being downloaded across a network, it is cached locally. The file that is pointed to by this URL must specify information pertaining only to style definitions. It must not contain any extraneous HTML markup. The line for linking a style sheet has a form like:

```
<LINK  REL="stylesheet" TYPE="text/css" HREF="afile.css">
```

where `afile.css` is replaced by the appropriate URL. The `REL` attribute is used to indicate that the file for this link is a style sheet. The `TYPE` attribute is the same as in the example. The `HREF` attribute is the URL for the file `afile.css`.

Style sheet syntax

A style sheet that is kept as a separate file has the same form as that which is embedded in the header of an HTML document. This section covers the basics of style sheet form. Each rule in a style sheet has two parts. The first is the selector, which may be a simple selector or a contextual selector. The simple selector indicates what the style of a tag should be without regard to its context. It is the easiest to use. The contextual selector determines the appearance of an HTML element based on its context.

Simple selectors consist of the HTML tag followed by its presentation rule. Contextual selectors have a space-delimited string, such as `H2 LI`, which means, in this case, that the selector applies to all list items that are contained within the second-level heading element. Obviously, this is a simplified description; the sidebar "Style Sheet Properties" provides a more complete list of style sheet declaration syntax.

Following the selector in the rule is the declaration. The declaration is also made of two parts: a property and a value. The rule has the form `{font-family:courier}` or `{ margin: 6em }`. The rule begins and ends with a curly brace. Enclosed within it are the property and its associated value separated by a colon. The full syntax for CSS is involved necessarily because it must define the appearance of the myriad possible elements that make up a page. Following is a list of some of the possible properties. The value list for each of these is even more varied. If you are going to design a complete CSS style sheet, you should refer to the Web site of the W3C (World Wide Web Consortium) at `www.w3.org`. This Web site has reference documents that thoroughly define all the properties and values.

Style sheet properties

Here is a list of some of the more useful object properties for style sheets:

Font Properties

`font`	`font-style`
`font-family`	`font-variant`
`font-size`	`font-weight`

Background Properties

`background`	`background-position`
`background-attachment`	`background-repeat`
`background-color`	`color`
`background-image`	

Text Properties

`letter-spacing`	`text-indent`
`line-height`	`text-transform`
`text-align`	`vertical-align`
`text-decoration`	`word-spacing`

Box Properties

`border`	`height`
`border-bottom`	`margin`
`border-bottom-width`	`margin-bottom`
`border-color`	`margin-left`

(continued)

(continued)

`border-left`	`margin-right`
`border-left-width`	`margin-top`
`border-right`	`padding`
`border-right-width`	`padding-bottom`
`border-style`	`padding-left`
`border-top`	`padding-right`
`border-top-width`	`padding-top`
`border-width`	`width`

Simple File Viewer

To create a simple application to explore the things that you have learned about HTML and CSS, you can build a small file viewer based on the `CHTMLView` class. This application will be similar to the application that you created in Chapter 35. However, rather than navigating back and forth among URLs on a network, you will add the facility to open HTML files by using a filename returned from a common file dialog as the URL. This means that the machine on which you use this application does not need an active connection to the Internet or some other network. The file, if it is a valid HTML file, will be opened and displayed in the main window of the application. Begin as you did in Chapter 35, creating a default `CHtmlView` project. The chief difference is that rather than naming the application FirstCHTML, name it HTMViewer, as follows:

1. Run AppWizard.
2. Select an MFC.EXE project and name it HTMViewer.
3. Select a single-document interface that supports document/view.
4. Choose all default options until dialog box 4. In that dialog box, deselect the docking toolbar, status bar, and printing options.
5. Keep the default settings for dialog box 5.
6. When dialog box 6 appears, change the `HTMViewer` base class so that its base class is `CHtmlView`.
7. In the `OnInitialUpdate` method of the `CHTMViewerView` class, comment out or delete the line:

```
Navigate2(_T("http://www.microsoft.com/visualc/"),
NULL,NULL);
```

8. Use the ClassWizard to add a handler for the `ID_FILE_OPEN` object ID for the `CHTMViewerView` class.

9. In the `HTMViewerView.CPP` file, add these lines to the `OnFileOpen` handler that was generated by the ClassWizard:

```
CFileDialog dlgFile(TRUE);
dlgFile.m_ofn.lpstrFilter =
_T("HTM files\0*.htm;*.html\0");
dlgFile.m_ofn.nFilterIndex = 1;
dlgFile.m_ofn.hwndOwner =
AfxGetMainWnd()->GetSafeHwnd();
if ( dlgFile.DoModal() == IDOK)
Navigate2(dlgFile.GetPathName(),
NULL,NULL);
```

10. Compile and run this application. You can now open and view the small samples developed in this chapter.

Event and Object Models

To place scripting in its proper context, you must first have a general sense for the architecture of the window and document object model. Do not confuse this with Windows, although the concepts are similar, and your familiarity with Windows will facilitate your understanding.

In DHMTL, the window object occupies the most general level. It is the container for the document, events, frame windows, and so on. Do not confuse the window object with the browser window itself, although they are closely related. The window object of DHMTL provides a means to use the information about the browser, its frames, and dialogs. It also enables you to modify the browser's appearance. Its chief role though is architectural. It is the container for several other things with which your code and the user will interact. These include:

- Document
- Event
- Frames
- History
- Location
- Screen

The details of interacting with the window are covered more thoroughly later, but let's first introduce some of the other objects that the window contains.

The most important is the document object. The document object is a property of the window. So are the other items listed previously. You can think of a property as similar to a C++ member, either function or data. All the pieces of an HTML document are accessible through the document property of the window. The tagged bits of text, links, and images are objects in the document. These elements become available as collections of items contained by the document object. This enables you to access and change items within the document. The global style of the document, for example, can be changed by modifying an element in the style sheet collection. The document object contains the following collections:

- Anchors
- Applets
- Elements
- Forms
- Frames
- Images
- Links
- Scripts
- Style sheets

Of similar importance to the document object, the event object is also contained by the window object. The event object makes things happen. Events are signals sent due to the activity of a user or because of changes of state in a document or window. Changes in a document that cause events include:

- The change of focus from one element to another
- The document or other objects being loaded
- Errors

Two characteristics of this new model greatly increase its power. One is event bubbling; the other is the concept of default actions. Every element in the hierarchy that contains the element in which the event originally occurred has the chance to respond to that event. You can think of this as an event bubbling up through the hierarchy. You could also think of it as a ripple that flows out from the most interior element to those that surround it. This progress of the event continues until the top level is reached, unless the bubbling is canceled by an element. Default actions are simply those supplied by the browser, but these can be overridden by custom actions. This makes your coding overhead easier, in that you need to respond only to events for which you want to add some special handling.

Some events

Here are a few events to which objects may respond:

onabort	onerror	onmouseover
onafterupdate	onerrorupdate	onmouseup
onbeforeunload	onfilterchange	onreadystatechange
onbeforeupdate	onfinish	onreset
onblur	onfocus	onresize
onbounce	onhelp	onrowenter
onchange	onkeydown	onrowexit
onclick	onkeypress	onscroll
ondataavailable	onkeyup	onselect
ondatasetchanged	onload	onselectstart
ondatasetcomplete	onmousedown	onstart
ondblclick	onmousemove	onsubmit
ondragstart	onmouseout	onunload

In the past, if an HTML element signaled an event but no handler was present for it, the event would simply be ignored and lost. With event bubbling these unhandled events are forwarded to the parent element. The event travels the element hierarchy until it is handled and canceled. This bubbling reduces the amount of code you must create and maintain because you are able to handle many events with code in one place at a higher level. It also facilitates making changes because code need not be changed all over the document.

DHTML has a language-independent means for using the event. It also enables you to cancel the event so it does not travel further up the hierarchy. This capability is part of the event object, which is one of the properties of the window object.

Scripting

The last subject that must be covered in this survey of DHMTL is scripting. With the basic knowledge that you have gained in the previous sections along with what you will learn here, you can begin experimenting with some active DHMTL documents.

The DHMTL object model is used by scripts that are associated with an HTML document. Scripts can be either embedded in the document or referenced in an external library using the script element tag. Scripts can be written in either VBScript or JavaScript. In this section, you will be experimenting with JavaScript. The general syntax for a script element is:

```
<SCRIPT LANGUAGE="language"
[TYPE="MIMEtype"]
[SRC="optionalfilename"]
[DEFER]>
Script statements and functions
</SCRIPT>
```

The `language` placeholder is replaced with one of JScript, JavaScript, or VBScript, depending on the language in which the script is written. If present, the `TYPE` overrides the `LANGUAGE` attribute. For JavaScript, use a type of `"text/JavaScript"`. For VBScript, use `"text/VBScript"`. `SRC` is used to specify that the script's statements are located in an external file. `DEFER` does not exactly defer the execution of the script. Rather, it indicates to the browser that the script does not contain anything except function declarations. This way, the browser can go on loading and displaying the page, rather than fully parsing and interpreting the script before continuing. `DEFER` is used to improve the appearance of performance.

A document may contain many different scripts. These scripts can be located either in the head or the body of the document. In a way, the activity of a script is like that of an interpreted language. That is, scripts can be executed as the document is parsed. So it is important, as you are writing scripts, to consider whether or not the properties and objects that you reference in the script are available. It is not like C++ where everything must be defined up front and the executable is built in two or more passes of a compiler. You can throw in not only variables, but members inside already defined variables, at any time.

In addition to scripts that appear as separate functions, you may associate a script directly with a specific element as an inline event attribute. This has the form:

```
<element eventName="script statements">
```

The element can be any of the HTML identifiers such as `<H1>` or `<HREF>`. The event name is something like `onselect` or `onmouseover`. The script consists of statements in either VBScript or JavaScript. You will see examples of this later.

JavaScript and the DHTML object model deserve whole books of their own. Rather than attempting to exhaustively define the subject here, this survey was designed to give you enough knowledge to try a few things out. The remainder of this chapter will present several scripts in the context of the issues covered in this chapter to give you a feel for the subject.

Scripting for Elements

First let's return to our simple HTML document and add the capability to change the font when the mouse moves over a list item. Let's make the text stretch over the page when the mouse passes over it. You can do this by adding an inline script that modifies one of the properties of the <H1> object in response to an event. In the example presented here, you increase the letter spacing in response to a mouse over event. Following is the HTML that accomplishes this:

```
<HTML>
<HEAD>
<TITLE>script1</TITLE>
</HEAD>

<BODY>
<H1>
The Text on This Page is Alive</H1>
<H1  onmouseover="this.style.letterSpacing = '1.0em' ;" >
Well, at least this line is</H1>
<H1>
The Text on This Page is Alive</H1>
</BODY>
</HTML>
```

This HTML document can be opened in the demonstration HTML viewer you created earlier in the chapter. When the mouse pointer is moved over the center heading, notice that its text stretches across the window (see Figure 36-3). Notice also that when the mouse pointer is moved off the heading, the text does not return to its previous appearance, because the mouse pointer moving off the text is another event, onmouseout, for which code has not been included in this HTML document.

Figure 36-3: The text changes when the mouse pointer moves over it.

You can modify an almost unimaginable number of properties, each of which may have several different associated values specific to its use. For a partial list of properties, refer to Table 36-2. For a complete list of object properties and their possible associated values, refer to Microsoft's Internet Client SDK.

Table 36-2
Some Properties Modifyable in Scripts

AccessKey	background PositionX	border RightColor	checked	colSpan
action	background PositionY	border RightStyle	classid	compact
active Element	Background Repeat	border RightWidth	className	complete
align	balance	borderStyle	clear	connection Speed
aLink	behavior	borderTop	clientHeight	content
alinkColor	bgColor	borderTopColor	client Information	cookie
Alt	agProperties	borderTopStyle	clientLeft	cookieEnabled
AltHTML	borderBottom	borderTopWidth	clientTop	coords
altKey	border BottomColor	borderWidth	clientWidth	cpuClass
appCodeName	border BottomStyle	bottomMargin	clientX	cssText
AppMinor Version	borderBottom Width	browser Language	clientY	ctrlKey
appName	borderColor	bufferDepth	clip	cursor
appVersion	borderColorDark	button	closed	data
availHeight	borderColorLight	cancelBubble	code	dataFld
availWidth	borderLeft	caption	codeBase	dataFormatAs
background Attachment	borderLeft Color	cellIndex	codeType	dataPageSize
background Color	borderLeft Style	cellPadding	color	dataSrc
background Image	borderLeft Width	cellSpacing	colorDepth	default Charset
background Position	borderRight	charset	cols	default Checked

default Selected	fontSmoothing Enabled	id	listStyle Image	multiple
default Status	fontStyle	indeterminate	listStyle Position	name
default Value	fontVariant	index	listStyle Type	name
defer	fontWeight	innerHTML	location	noHref
dialog Arguments	form	innerText	loop	noResize
dialog Height	frame	isMap	lowsrc	noShade
dialogLeft	frameBorder	isTextEdit	map	noWrap
dialogTop	frameSpacing	keyCode	margin	object
dialogWidth	fromElement	lang	margin Bottom	offscreen Buffering
face	hash	language	margin Height	offsetHeight
fgColor	height	lastModified	marginLeft	offsetLeft
file Created Date	Hidden	left	marginRight	offsetParent
file Modified Date	host	leftMargin	marginTop	offsetTop
fileSize	hostname	length	marginWidth	offsetWidth
file Updated Date	href	letter Spacing	maxLength	offsetX
filter	hspace	lineHeight	media	offsetY
font	htmlFor	link	method	onLine
fontFamily	htmlText	linkColor	Methods	opener
fontSize	httpEquiv	listStyle	mimeTypes	outerHTML

(continued)

Table 36-2 *(continued)*

outerText	pixelTop	returnValue	selected	text
overflow	pixelWidth	rev	selected Index	textAlign
owning Element	platform	rightMargin	self	textDecoration
padding	plugins	rowIndex	shape	textDecoration Blink
padding Bottom	pluginspage	rows	shiftKey	textDecoration LineThrough
paddingLeft	port	rowSpan	size	textDecoration None
padding Right	posHeight	rules	source Index	textDecoration Overline
paddingTop	position	screenX	span	textDecoration Underline
pageBreak After	posLeft	screenY	src	textIndent
pageBreak Before	posTop	scroll	src Element	textTransform
palette	posWidth	scrollAmount	srcFilter	thead
parent	protocol	scrollDelay	start	tfoot
parent Element	readOnly	scrollHeight	status	title
parentStyle Sheet	readyState	scrolling	style	toElement
parentText Edit	reason	scrollLeft	style Float	top
parent Window	recordNumber	scrollTop	system Language	topMargin
pathname	recordset	scrollWidth	tabIndex	trueSpeed
pixelHeight	referrer	search	tagName	type
pixelLeft	rel	sectionRow Index	target	updateInterval

units	userAgent	verticalAlign	volume	x
url	userLanguage	visibility	vspace	y
urn	vAlign	vLink	width	zIndex
useMap	value	vlinkColor	wrap	

Changing Things Other Than Text Elements

You can change other properties besides text properties. For example, you can change the file from which an image element is loaded in response to mouse events.

To do this, you can use the same sort of construction that was used in the previous HTML document. In this case, the `SRC` property is modified in response to mouse events. This time add an additional handler for the event generated when the mouse pointer moves off the element. Following is the HTML document that accomplishes this:

```
<HTML>
<HEAD>
<TITLE>script2</TITLE>
</HEAD>

<BODY>
<P>
<IMG SRC="out.JPG" HEIGHT=141 WIDTH=308
onmouseover="this.src = 'over.jpg';""
onmouseout="this.src = 'out.jpg';">
</BODY>
</HTML>
```

Figures 36-4 and 36-5 illustrate the changes in the actual image as the mouse pointer is moved back and forth across the image element. Use the HTMViewer that you created to open the `script2.htm` file and try this yourself.

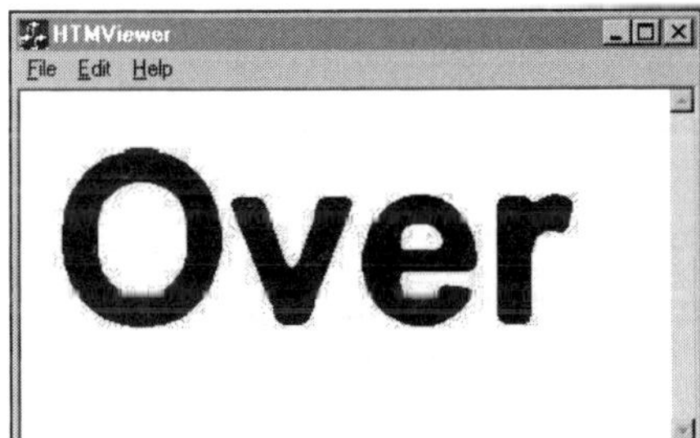

Figure 36-4: The image changes in response to the mouse pointer moving over events.

Figure 36-5: The image changes again in response to the mouse pointer moving off the graphic.

Running a Script As the Document Is Loaded

Let's take a look at a more advanced demonstration of JavaScript, events, and HTML elements. In this script, you will see how to define and call functions that are not necessarily associated only with individual elements. You will learn how to call a function as the HTML document is being loaded and how to obtain information about elements on the page that you will later use to modify the position of the element. To give this discussion some context, take a look at Figure 36-6 to see the appearance of the HTML document in our demonstration HTML viewer.

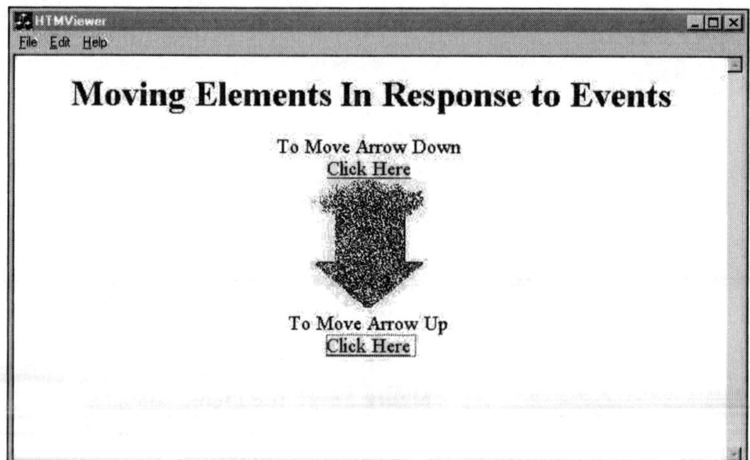

Figure 36-6: The graphic on this page can move.

The HTML document that becomes this image includes JavaScript that responds to two events. One is a mouse button click with the mouse pointer on text near the top of the document; the other is a mouse button click with the mouse pointer near the bottom. The script also includes code that initializes some variables as the document is loaded. Refer to the HTML code in Listing 36-2. This HTML has been formatted to make its structure more obvious.

Listing 36-2: HTML That Displays a Moving Graphic

```
<HTML>
<HEAD>
<TITLE>script3</TITLE>

<SCRIPT language="javascript">
   <!—
function doSomeSetup() {
aPosition = arrowPosition.style
aPosition.yPlace = parseInt(aPosition.top)
aPosition.temp = 0
   }

function moveDown() {
aPosition.temp = aPosition.top
aPosition.top = 160
aPosition.yPlace = aPosition.temp
   }

function moveUp() {
aPosition.top = aPosition.yPlace
   }
   //—>
</SCRIPT>
</HEAD>
<BODY onload="doSomeSetup()">
<CENTER>
<H1>
Moving Elements In Response to Events
</H1>
</CENTER>

<CENTER>
<FONT SIZE=+1>
To Move Arrow Down
</FONT>
</CENTER>

<CENTER>
<FONT SIZE=+1>
<A HREF="javascript:moveDown()">
Click Here
</a>
</FONT>
</CENTER>

<CENTER>
<FONT SIZE=+1>
</FONT>
</CENTER>
```

(continued)

Listing 36-2 *(continued)*

```
<DIV ID="arrowPosition" STYLE="position:relative; ">
<CENTER>
<IMG SRC="arrow.jpg" HEIGHT=114 WIDTH=107>
</CENTER>
</DIV>

<CENTER></CENTER>
<CENTER></CENTER>
<CENTER></CENTER>
<CENTER></CENTER>
<CENTER></CENTER>
<CENTER></CENTER>
<CENTER></CENTER>
<CENTER></CENTER>
<CENTER></CENTER>

<CENTER>
<FONT SIZE=+1>
To Move Arrow Up
</FONT>
</CENTER>


<CENTER>
<FONT SIZE=+1>
<A HREF="javascript:moveUp()">
Click Here
</A>
</FONT>
</CENTER>

</BODY>
</HTML>
```

Before taking up the JavaScript itself in the header of the document, look at the body of the document. The heading followed by several lines of centered text makes up most of the document. The most interesting lines for our purposes here are the two anchor tags surrounding the text instructions "Click Here" at the top and bottom of the body. These two are:

```
<A HREF="javascript:moveDown()">
Click Here
</a>
<AHREF="javascript:moveUp()">
Click Here
</a>
```

Notice how the beginning and ending tags of the anchors are surrounding the text.

This causes each of the text lines to send notification of an event to their respective associated functions. This event includes the mouse pointer moving over the text and the mouse pointer moving off the text Take a look at the functions defined previously in the header to see that they are coded to respond to mouse button clicks.

Next inspect the code from which the initial position of the image is saved for later use, when you want to return the image to its starting position. The code that notes this initial position is the following:

```
<div id="arrowPosition" style="position:relative; ">
<CENTER>
<IMG SRC="arrow.jpg" HEIGHT=114 WIDTH=107>
</CENTER>
</div>
```

The `<DIV>` tag is a container tag. It is used to mark chapters, sections, and so forth. Here you use it as a means to apply an ID to itself so you have a means to refer to it and the things that it contains. You also use it to give the object an inline CSS style for the position; `relative` is used here. Other choices are `absolute` and `static`. `absolute` would take the element out of the flow of the document. When things are changed, the browser automatically reorders the appearance of the document. `absolute` sets a definite position for the element without respect for the other elements in the document. Again you can research this topic in the Internet Client SDK.

The last item in the body to look at is the line that calls the JavaScript function that is used to initialize the variables to be called. That line is the following:

```
<BODY onload="doSomeSetup()">
```

In this line the event handler for a loading event is bound to the `<BODY>` tag. This event is fired immediately when the object is loaded. In the case in which the `onload` handler is associated with the body tag, it will be fired for the window.

Turn your attention now to the JavaScript. Look at the initialization function `doSomeSetup()` first. Notice that both variables and properties for those variables are simply summarily inserted into the script, without regard for explicit definition or typing. This takes some getting used to if you have been programming in C and C++ for some time. For example, you add a property, `yPlace`, to the variable `aPosition`, simply by using the name. This can be disconcerting, and it can also make things difficult to debug. But this is the nature of JavaScript. If you are going to do much programming in JavaScript, you should certainly refer to a thorough book on the language.

The functions `moveUp()` and `moveDown()` simply swap coordinates around in response to the button click events. They are simple to understand. Notice, however, that the image is not explicitly instructed to move or update itself; this update occurs because the browser window reflows the document in response to events. Because the position has changed, the image is drawn in its new place as a result of the document flow.

Let's take a look at one more thing before leaving this example. The line

```
aPosition.yPlace = parseInt(aPosition.top)
```

takes the `aPosition` variable, which you made equal to the style property of the ID `arrowposition`, and uses it in a call to the method `parseInt()`. This is a method supplied by JavaScript. It takes as input a string and returns an integer variable that is used here to position the container, `arrowposition`, for the image graphic.

Scripting Dialogs

With JavaScript and the new object model of DHMTL, you can manipulate far more than the contents of the HTML document. You can also manipulate multiple windows, create new instances of the browser, create collections of frames, and display a variety of dialog boxes. The next demonstration document illustrates some of these manipulations. For this simple example, you are going to create some of the predefined window types that are supplied by DHMTL. Your windows will all be modal dialog boxes, but DHMTL also supplies the functionality to use modeless windows. Listing 36-3 contains the script that creates the document and modal dialog shown in Figure 36-7.

Listing 36-3: HTML That Creates a Window

```
<HTML>
<HEAD>
<TITLE>Script 4</TITLE>

<SCRIPT LANGUAGE="JavaScript">
function anAlertDialog() {
window.alert
   ("Pressing the button\ncalls this function!")
   }

function aConfirmDialog() {
if( window.confirm("Confirm button change") )
        {
buttonText = buttonID.style
buttonText.color = "red"
        }
   }

function aModalDialog() {
window.showModalDialog("script2.htm", "",
"dialogWidth:22em; dialogHeight:12em")
   }

</SCRIPT>
</HEAD>
```

```
<BODY>
<INPUT TYPE=BUTTON VALUE="Alert Dialog"
ONCLICK="anAlertDialog();">
<INPUT TYPE=BUTTON VALUE="Confirm Dialog"
ID="buttonID"
ONCLICK="aConfirmDialog();">
<INPUT TYPE=BUTTON VALUE="Modal Dialog"
ONCLICK="aModalDialog();">
</BODY>
</HTML>
```

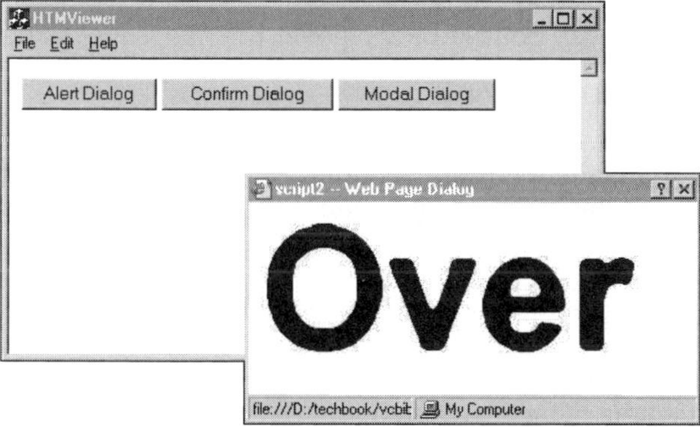

Figure 36-7: The modal dialog is displayed over the viewer window.

Once again, before you turn your attention to the JavaScript in the header, take a look at the contents of the body. It consists of three similar elements. Each of these begins with the INPUT tag. The `TYPE` of the input control is set to `BUTTON`, so a button is what appears in the displayed document. Several other types are possible, including those to create check boxes and radio buttons. In the case of a button control, the value becomes the text that is written on the face of the button. A button can respond to a number of different events. These events are listed in Table 36-3.

Table 36-3
Button events

onblur	onkeydown	onmouseout
onclick	onkeypress	onmouseover
ondblclick	onkeyup	onmouseup
onfocus	onmousedown	onresize
onhelp	onmousemove	onselect

Notice that, although the button responds to many events, it does not respond to all the possible events listed in Table 36-3. This is true for many elements, so you must be aware of which events an element can respond to.

In the example here, the button responds to the `onclick` event by executing the JavaScript function assigned to the event. Each of the buttons in this sample has been given a different task to perform in response to the event. Notice that the second element, for the confirmation dialog has been given an additional property. This ID should be familiar to you from the previous demonstration JavaScript. In this case, rather than using it to change the position of an element, you use it to give the button text a different color.

One of the previous scripts was used as the document for the dialog window. Notice that it responds to the mouse pointer moving over the image just as it did in the browser window earlier.

Take a look now at the JavaScript. Each of the functions refers to a window object. Remember this window object is the highest-level object in the DHMTL hierarchy. Therefore, the HTML document has access to it because the document exists as an object within the window object.

The window object exposes many more properties and methods than those that we have used here. You may insert messages in the status bar. You may modify the location of the browser window itself. You may even gather information about the screen on which the document is being displayed.

Summary

DHMTL and JavaScript are important technologies to which more capability is being added all the time. With the demonstration samples here, you have gained enough experience to see the kind of capability they make available. You have learned how to modify formatting, move images, respond to events, and display dialogs using JavaScript and DHTML. Using these capabilities is made even easier by the `CHtmlView` and browser controls that are included in Visual C++.

✦ ✦ ✦

P A R T

VIII

Advanced Visual Studio Use

✦ ✦ ✦ ✦

In This Part

Chapter 37:
Visual Studio Scripting

Chapter 38:
Writing a Custom AppWizard

✦ ✦ ✦ ✦

This part covers two tools that make Visual Studio more powerful: scripting and custom AppWizards. Visual Studio's scripting tools enable you to automate common tasks and perform powerful operations in just a keystroke. Custom AppWizards give you flexibility in developing your own tools for application development: for instance, there are going to be cases when your company needs to standardize a Visual C++ project that's not exactly like those that the AppWizard churns out. You can write your own Wizard that guides users through the creation of custom projects.

CHAPTER 37

Visual Studio Scripting

✦ ✦ ✦ ✦

In This Chapter

Quick Macros

Recording macros

Editing macros

Using macros

Understanding VBScript

Visual Studio object model

Sample macros

✦ ✦ ✦ ✦

As a programmer, you are familiar with the idea that computers are here to make our lives simpler by automating much of the work you do. This is what you are doing for others or yourself by creating programs with Visual C++. With the latest version of this product, you can also automate the way you use Visual C++.

Visual Studio scripting enables you to take control of your work and automate all those tasks you are constantly repeating. In order to get the most out of this chapter, take a look at the way you work with Visual C++, and notice anything you are repeatedly doing, and wish a toolbar button or other command could do that task. For example, do you get source code that just isn't formatted the way you want and spend a lot of time reformatting the code? Do you find your function declarations are self-documenting, but you still have to add comments for them?

These are some of the things that can be handled with Visual Studio scripting. Visual Studio includes two types of macros for automating work. One type is macros that can be edited using VBScript, and another is Quick Macros that can be used when you need a macro in a hurry. This chapter explains how to use macros and scripting to get the most out of Visual Studio.

Visual Studio Macros

Visual Studio has two types of macros that can be used to automate your work. One is the Quick Macro. The Quick Macro can be quite helpful, although you can only have one Quick Macro. As soon as you record a new Quick Macro, the old one is forgotten. If you find that you require a couple of Quick Macros, or you want a little more control over the macros, you can create editable macros, which are stored in macro files for later use.

Standard macros can either be recorded, similar to the way Quick Macros are recorded, or written from scratch using VBScript. Recorded macros are automatically translated into VBScript commands when they are stored in the macro file.

Quick Macros

Before recording any macro, think about the steps you want to record. You may even want to practice the macro before recording it or write down the steps. At first this seems a bit odd because a macro is generally a repeat of commonly performed tasks, but practicing the macro or writing down its steps is really a good idea. By writing down the steps, you can eliminate mistakes and think of ways to streamline the macro.

One of the best reasons for thinking out or practicing a macro is that you cannot record context-menu commands. You must find another way of accessing the command. There should be a standard menu option that will work in its place.

◆ ◆ ◆ ◆ ◆

Recording a Quick Macro

One commonly repeated task is to add new files to a project. This is really a simple task and wouldn't usually be considered for automation, unless you commonly add a standard comment header to all your files. This sample macro automates the steps used in creating a new file with a simple comment header.

Adding Files to a Project

Follow these steps to record a macro for adding files to a project.

1. Select Record Quick macro from the Tools menu. The Record toolbar will be displayed as shown in Figure 37-1, and Visual Studio will begin recording all of your keystrokes and menu command selections.
2. In the Project menu, select New from the Add to Project submenu. The familiar New dialog box opens.
3. Assign a type of file and name to your new file as you normally would.
4. Select OK to close the dialog box and open up your new file.
5. Add any generic comments to the top of your new file, just as you normally would. These may include your name, the date, or other fairly generic information used in all your files for this project.
6. Save the file.
7. Click the Stop button on the Record toolbar, and the toolbar disappears. You have successfully recorded a macro.

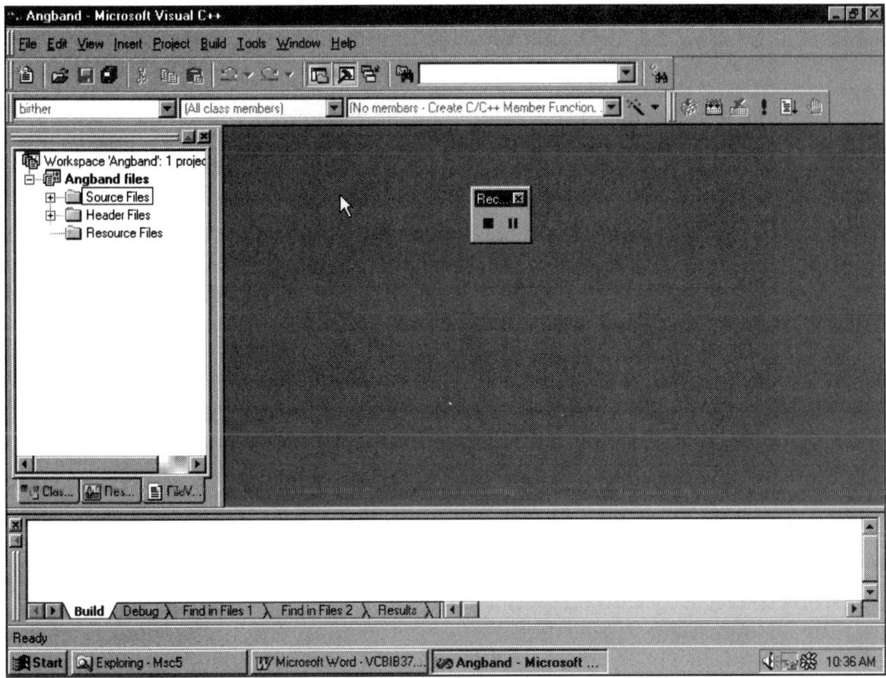

Figure 37-1: The Record toolbar enables you to pause or stop recording your macros.

✦ ✦ ✦ ✦ ✦

Using Quick Macros

Now a Quick Macro is available for you to work with. Do not use it yet, because the macro has a minor problem. If you select Play Quick Macro from the Tools menu to run the macro, the macro will run and create a new file with the same name. Essentially, this deletes any changes you may have made in the previous file.

Be extremely careful when using macros. Macros exist to automate your work and are quite useful. However, they have the capability to edit your files and settings and can really mess things up if they are not working properly.

✦ ✦ ✦ ✦ ✦

Your first thought would normally be to debug the code. However, Quick Macro code is not available for debugging or editing. If a Quick Macro doesn't work properly, simply record a new one. In the case of the demo Quick Macro, you could record a macro that adds comments to the top of a file. Simply eliminate steps 2 through 4 in the "Recording a Quick Macro" section.

Another option is to create a macro that can be edited. This can be done by recording a standard macro that is described later in this chapter. A standard macro contains code that can be edited and debugged.

Creating VBScript Macros

There are three main differences between VBScript macros and Quick Macros. VBScript macros may be edited, debugged, and saved in a file. These additional features provide greater flexibility in using these macros as opposed to Quick Macros.

To use the VBScript macros, you can create them either using the macro recorder or writing VBScript code. The quickest way to create a macro is often to use the recorder and then edit your code by hand. Another way to get access to a macro is to load a file someone else created for you.

Before creating a macro, it is often a good idea to do a practice run beforehand. This makes it easier to remember what keystrokes and menu options you wish to record. It also prevents your adding unnecessary undo steps to your macro. You will also find the new macro code easier to follow when editing it later.

◆ ◆ ◆ ◆ ◆

Recording a VBScript Macro

The steps to creating a VBScript macro are quite similar to the steps used in creating a Quick Macro described earlier in the chapter. This procedure even uses the same example. One of the big differences is that you have to provide a name for the macro.

1. Select Macro from the Tools menu. The first time you do this, a dialog box is displayed that tells you that a macro icon will be displayed on the taskbar while you are running a macro.
2. Deselect the Show this next time option so the dialog box isn't displayed again, and select OK. The dialog box is closed, and the Macro dialog box is displayed as shown in Figure 37-2.

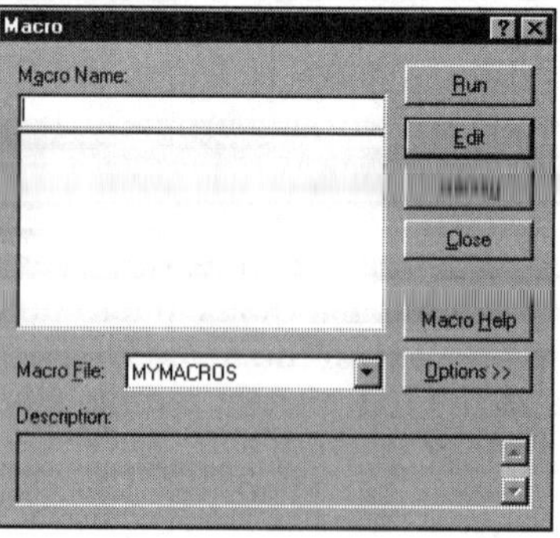

Figure 37-2: The Macro dialog box is used to control macros.

3. Enter a name for the macro, such as AddNewFileToProject, in the Macro Name field. This macro will be stored in the files specified in the Macro File combo box.
4. Click the Record button. This opens the Add Macro dialog box shown in Figure 37-3.

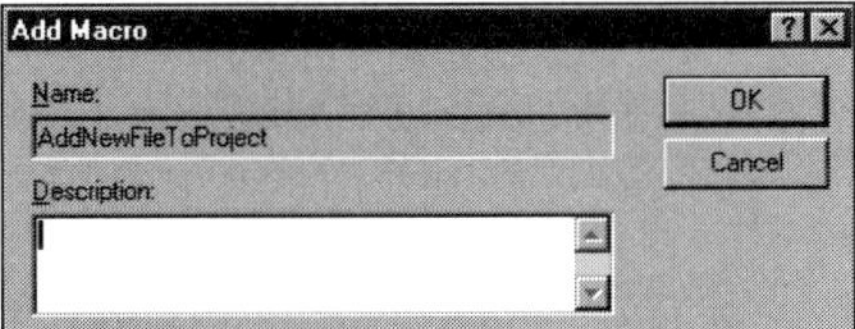

Figure 37-3: The Add Macro dialog box is useful for describing your macro.

5. Describe your new macro in the Description field. This description will be included in the macro file with your macro.
6. Click OK to close the Add Macro dialog box. The Record toolbar is displayed, and Visual Studio will begin recording all of your keystrokes and selected menu commands into a macro.
7. On the Project menu, select New from the Add to Project submenu.
8. Assign a type of file and name to your new file as you normally would.
9. Click OK to create the new file. The file will automatically open for editing.
10. Add any generic comments to the top of your new file, as you normally would. These may be your name or other information generic to all your files.
11. Save the file.
12. Click the Stop button on the Record toolbar. The toolbar closes, and your macro will open for editing, as shown in Figure 37-4.

This macro has the same problem that the Quick Macro version did. However, this version of the macro can be edited so that it prompts the user for a filename and is thereby a lot more useful.

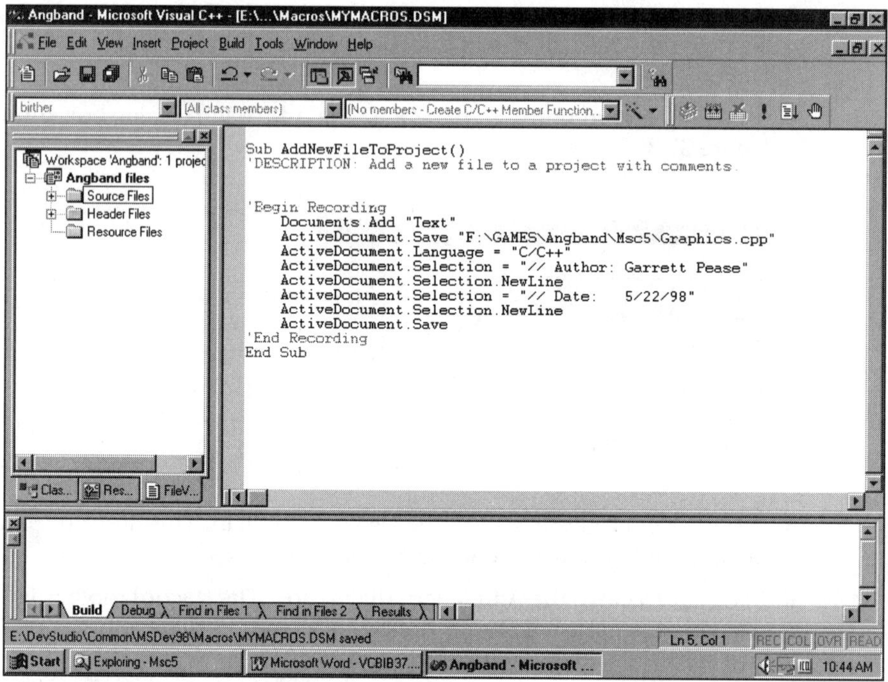

Figure 37-4: Your new macro is ready to be edited.

Tip

When you create your own macros, you may want to use the Options button in the Macro dialog box (see Figure 37-2). This button expands the dialog box so that you can assign your new macro to a toolbar, keystroke, or a new file when you first start working with the macro.

Understanding a VBScript macro

The following is the code created from the recorded macro:

```
Sub AddNewFileToProject()
'DESCRIPTION: Add a new file to a project with comments.


'Begin Recording
  Documents.Add "Text"
  ActiveDocument.Save "F:\GAMES\Angband\Msc5\Graphics.cpp"
  ActiveDocument.Language = "C/C++"
  ActiveDocument.Selection = "// Author: Garrett Pease"
  ActiveDocument.Selection.NewLine
  ActiveDocument.Selection = "// Date:   5/22/98"
  ActiveDocument.Selection.NewLine
```

```
    ActiveDocument.Save
  'End Recording
  End Sub
```

The macro is written in VBScript, and if you are not familiar with VBScript, you'll find a small tutorial included later in this chapter.

The first line of code adds a new text document. This new document is accessed through the `ActiveDocument` object. It is assigned a language type of C/C++. Then the comments are added to the text. This is done using the `ActiveDocument`'s `Selection` property. The file is then saved with all of these changes.

The sample code contains a few things that must be changed to make the code more useful. First of all, the code should ask for a new name for the file. Second, the code would be more useful if it automatically put the name of the file in the comments as well as putting in the current date and time. Finally, the macro doesn't add the file to the project even though that was the first menu command selected. The following section describes how to edit the code so that it fulfills the original requirements.

Editing a VBScript macro

Editing macros is necessary when you want to change a recorded macro or create a macro from scratch. This example edits the previously created AddNewProjectToFile macro into a more general purpose macro.

Editing the AddNewProjectToFile Macro

Follow these steps to edit the AddNewProjectToFile macro into a more general purpose macro.

1. Select Macro from the Tools menu. An informational dialog box may be displayed if you haven't disabled it by deselecting the Show this next time option.
2. In the Macro dialog box, select the macro you wish to edit from the list, and the name is displayed in the Macro Name field.
3. Select the Edit button. An edit window appears with your macro's code.
4. Edit the old macro code to match the following:

```
ExecuteCommand "FileNewInProject"
 ActiveDocument.Selection = "// File:   " & _
   ActiveDocument.Name
 ActiveDocument.Selection.NewLine
 ActiveDocument.Selection = "// Author: Garrett Pease"
 ActiveDocument.Selection.NewLine
 ActiveDocument.Selection = "// Date:   " & Now
 ActiveDocument.Selection.NewLine
 ActiveDocument.Save
```

5. Save your changes.
6. Right-click the file, and select Reload Macro File from the menu. Before you can use the new macro, you must reload it.

♦ ♦ ♦ ♦ ♦

The first change in the new code is to use the `ExecuteCommand` command. This command enables you to call menu commands, such as FileNewInProject. FileNewInProject is the name of the menu command originally recorded but was translated into VBScript commands.

After creating the new file, the macro adds a comment line to the top of the file that states the name of the file. This is done by retrieving the new file's name with the `ActiveDocument.Name` property. The final change was in the date comment. This line of code now retrieves the date and time using the VBScript `Now` function.

After editing, the macro finally meets the original requirements. Instead of simply opening a new text file, the macro calls the menu command that opens up the New dialog box and enables the user to enter a filename and type of file. When the file is saved, the macro adds a few comments to the top of the file including the filename, the author, and the date.

Creating an empty macro

Another way to create a macro is by entering VBScript code by hand. This process generally requires more knowledge on the part of the programmer, because you must know all the VBScript commands you are going to use. It is generally easier to record a macro, which converts commands into VBScript for you. Of course, in the preceding example of the AddNewFileToProject macro, it could be seen that the commands are not always converted in the best fashion.

Creating a Macro by Hand

1. Select Macro from the Tools menu. This opens the Macro dialog box shown in Figure 37-5.
2. Enter a name in the Macro Name field.
3. Select the Edit button. This opens the Add Macro dialog box
4. Enter a description of your new macro in the dialog box.
5. Click OK. The dialog box is closed, and your macro file is opened so that you can edit the new macro as shown in Figure 37-6.
6. Enter the code for your macro.
7. Save the macro file.

Figure 37-5: The Macro dialog box is used to create new macros.

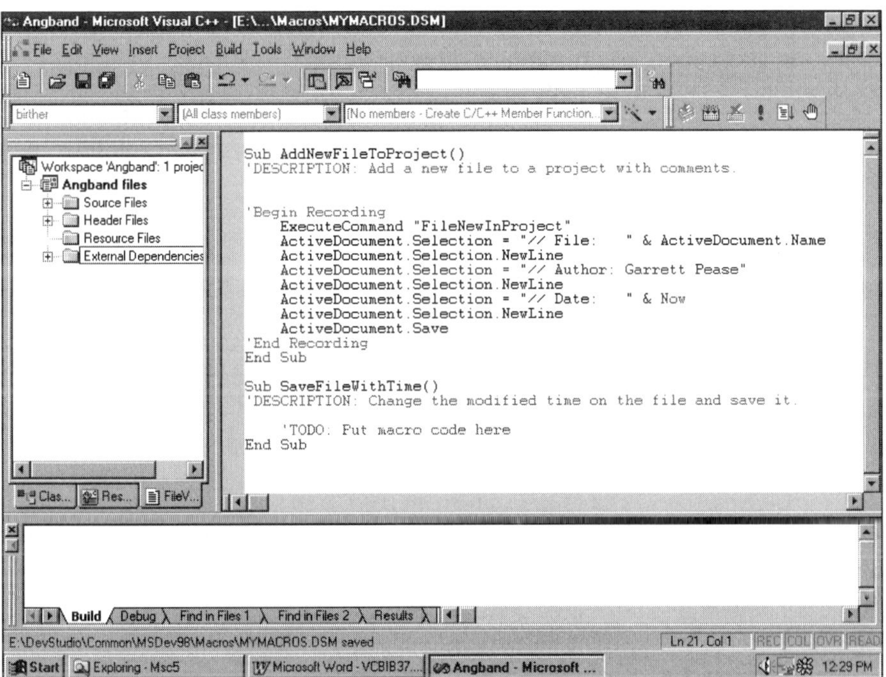

Figure 37-6: New macros are displayed in an edit window ready for changes.

✦ ✦ ✦ ✦ ✦

You now have a new macro that you have created with VBScript. Remember that before using the macro, you have to reload the macro file.

Using VBScript Macros

Macros are stored in plain text files with the .DSM extension. The default location where the Developer Studio looks for macro files is `devstudio/common/MSDev98/Macros/`. There may already be three files in that directory. You will want to keep all of your macro files in this directory, including the sample macro file included on the book's CD-ROM. This will make it easier to access your macros.

The three files you may find in this directory are the `TemporaryQuickMacro.DSM`, `MyMacros.DSM`, and `Sample.DSM` files. The `TemporaryQuickMacro.DSM` and `MyMacros.DSM` are created by the Developer Studio when they are required and will not be in the directory unless you have begun creating your own macros. The `TemporaryQuickMacro.DSM` should be left alone because this file is where the Developer Studio temporarily stores the information about your current Quick Macro. The `MyMacros.DSM` file is the default file for new macros. The `Sample.DSM` file includes several sample macros provided by Microsoft.

The `Sample.DSM` file includes several sample macros you can look at, use, and learn from. One of the more useful aspects of these macros is the fact that most of them are designed to work with several types of files, while the samples in this chapter are designed with the C++ programmer in mind. If you develop HTML files as well, you may want to take a look at these sample macros for examples on how to make your macros work on different types of files.

✦ ✦ ✦ ✦ ✦

Loading macro files

To use any of the macros included in the macro files, you must load the macro file. When you record or edit a macro, its file is automatically loaded. Other files, such as the `VCBible.DSM` or the `Sample.DSM` file, must be loaded manually.

Loading Macro Files

1. Copy the `VCBible.DSM` file from the CD to the `devstudio/common/MSDev98/Macros/` directory.
2. Select Customize from the Tools menu. This opens up the Customize dialog box.
3. Select the Add-ins and Macro Files tab. The Customize dialog box is displayed as shown in Figure 37-7.
4. Select the macro files you wish to use from the Add-ins and macro files list by clicking the square next to the filenames. If you have forgotten what a particular file is, select the file, and a description is displayed.
5. You can optionally use the Browse button to locate macro files not in the default directory.

6. Click the Close button. If two of the selected files have macros with the same name, a dialog box warns you about this conflict, and one of the files will not be loaded.

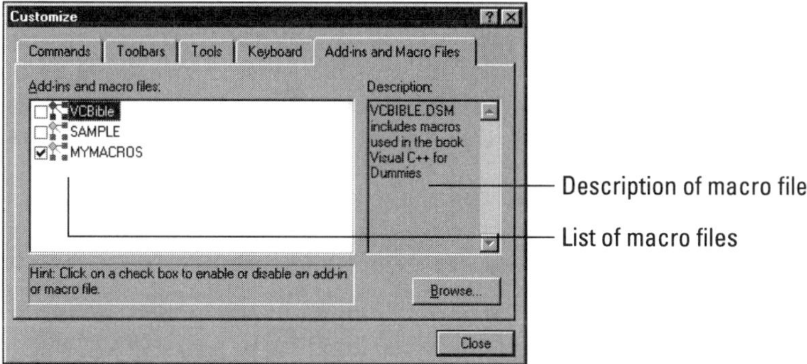

Figure 37-7: The Customize dialog box controls which macro files are loaded.

✦ ✦ ✦ ✦ ✦

Make sure that you have loaded the most recent copy of a macro file. This can be important when editing macros. If you try to run a modified macro or even access your macros through the Macro dialog box when a file has been modified, a dialog box prompts you to reload the macro file.

The Macro dialog box provides the simplest interface for controlling your macros. It enables you to run and edit them. Another way to access macros is to assign them to keystroke combinations and toolbar buttons.

Macro files include descriptions that are placed in a comment that begins "FILE DESCRIPTION:", located toward the top of the file. This label is case insensitive as can be seen from the following sample description:

```
'File Description: Code Formatting Macros
```

Running VBScript macros

Once you have loaded a macro file, you will want to run the macro. To do this, you can assign the macro to a toolbar button, a keystroke combination, or use the Macro dialog box to run the macro.

Running a Macro from the Macro Dialog Box

1. Select Macro from the Tools menu, and the Macro dialog box is displayed.
2. Select a loaded macro file from the Macro File drop-down list.
3. Select a macro from the list below the Macro Name field. A description of the macro is displayed at the bottom of the dialog box.
4. Select the Run button, and Visual Studio will run the macro. A small icon is displayed on the taskbar while the macro is running.

✦ ✦ ✦ ✦ ✦

Assigning macros to toolbars

The toolbar is a good place to put commonly used macros. This is especially true if you have a macro that is similar in function to an existing toolbar button. For example, the AddNewFileToProject macro used in this chapter would be an excellent choice to place near the New button, or to replace it completely.

To assign a macro to a toolbar, first make certain the macro file containing the macro you wish to use is loaded. Then select Customize from the Tools menu. This opens up the Customize dialog box. Select the Commands tab. The Customize dialog box is displayed as shown in Figure 37-8.

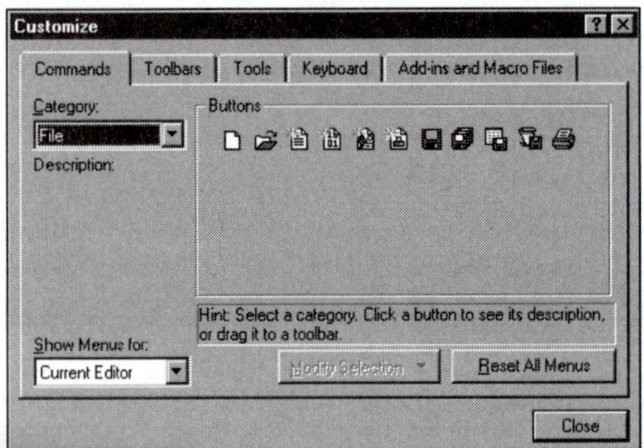

Figure 37-8: The Customize dialog box enables you to assign macros to the toolbar.

Next, select Macros from the Category drop-down list. A list of the loaded macros is displayed in the Commands list. Select a macro from the Commands list, and a description of the macro is displayed below the Category drop-down list. Drag the macro's name to where you want the button on the toolbar. The Button Appearance dialog box, shown in Figure 37-9, is displayed when you let go of the mouse button.

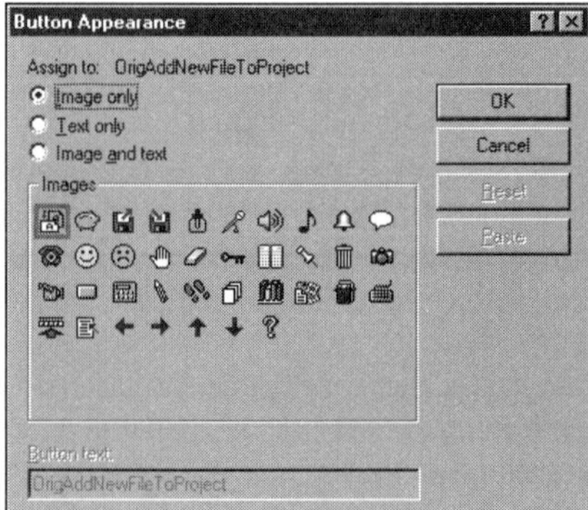

Figure 37-9: The Button Appearance dialog box enables you to determine the appearance of your macro's button on the toolbar.

Select an appropriate option that describes the appearance of your macro's button, and then select an icon or enter text describing the macro as appropriate for your selection of the button's appearance. Select OK, and your new button is displayed on the toolbar. If the button isn't displayed where you expected it, you still can reposition it. Continue assigning macros to toolbar buttons in the same way until you are done. Then select Close to close the Customize dialog box.

Assigning macros to keystrokes

Another way to run a macro is to assign it to a keystroke, which is good for frequently used macros. One such macro could be the CommentOut sample macro included with Visual Studio. This macro comments out the selected text and even works with different file types such as C++ files or HTML files.

Make certain the macro file containing the macro you wish to use is loaded, and then select Customize from the Tools menu. This opens up the Customize dialog box. Select the Keyboard tab, which is shown in Figure 37-10.

Select Macros from the Category drop-down list. A list of the loaded macros is displayed in the Commands list. Select a macro from the Commands list, and a description of the macro is displayed below at the bottom of the dialog box. Then click the Press new shortcut key field. If the keystroke you pressed is already assigned, a message is displayed below the field describing the command already using that keystroke. Finally, press the keystroke you wish to use.

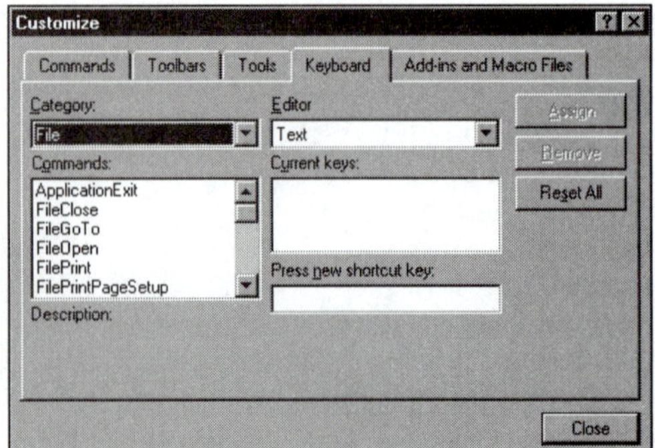

Figure 37-10: The Keyboard tab on the Customize dialog box enables you to assign macros to keystrokes.

Understanding VBScript

VBScript is the latest addition to Microsoft's Visual Basic family of programming languages. If you are familiar with either Visual Basic or Visual Basic for Applications, VBScript is easy to use. In fact, VBScript is simply a subset of Visual Basic for Applications, or VBA.

VBScript differs somewhat from the other Visual Basic languages. For one thing, VBScript is a hosted language; it requires a host application. VBScript derives a large part of its functionality from the host. In this case, the host is the Developer Studio. Other VBScript hosts you may be familiar with include the Internet Explorer and the Windows Scripting Host. You can even add VBScript hosting to your own programs.

As part of its hosted nature, VBScript is designed as a platform-independent language and is missing a few features common to the other versions of Visual Basic. For one thing, VBScript doesn't include the same file I/O support found in the other languages. This doesn't mean that you don't have file I/O. It simply means that you have to handle file I/O in a roundabout fashion. The Developer Studio includes several objects that can be used to provide file I/O, which are discussed later in this chapter.

This section describes a few of the basic aspects of VBScript programming for those who are not familiar with VB scripting. Because this discussion is limited, you may want to look elsewhere for more detailed information. One source is the VBScript online documentation that includes a description of all of its built-in functions. Another source is a book about VBScripting. Most of the VBScript books are designed for Internet programming, such as Steve Holzner's *Web Scripting with VBScript*, but a lot of that information can be used with the Developer Studio as well.

Programming VBScript

VBScript is an interpreted language, unlike C or C++. This makes for a few differences when writing VBScript code. The code is taken one line at a time, interpreted, and run. This means that a line of code must be complete. As a general rule, you can't spread an instruction over several lines the way you can with Visual C++. In order to split a line of code, place an underscore at the end of the line of code. The following is an example of a long piece of code spread across many lines:

```
ActiveDocument.Selection = "<TABLE>" + vbLF + _
    "<TH COLSPAN=2><BIG>" + Description + _
    "</BIG></TH>" + vbLF & Descr & "</TABLE><BR>" + vbLF
```

Another consequence of VBasic being interpreted is that you cannot use the compile option to test your code. The code is only checked at runtime, which is the only time you can check for syntactical errors. Often you can run a bit of code and get an error that asks whether you wish to debug the code. When you select yes, a debugger opens, and you will be able to look at your code. Often the error is simply a syntax error that is caught only when you run the macro.

When an error occurs in a macro, Visual Studio asks if you want to debug the macro. This is a great idea because it's the easiest way to discover where the error is located. A debugging screen is displayed with a highlighted error. Because you cannot edit code in this window, you must write down a note or remember where the error is located. When you close the debug window, Developer Studio also closes.

Using variables

VBScript only has one data type. This is the variant data type that can represent Booleans, strings, dates, or numbers. Because of the lack of data types, you may want to use Hungarian notation, which is used by Microsoft in their sample code and header files, or some other naming convention to keep track of what types of information you are storing in your variables.

Variables do not have to be declared before they are used. However, they can be declared using the `Dim`, `Public`, or `Private` keywords. For example, you could create a variable to store today's date with the statement `Dim TodaysDate`. By placing the statement `Option Explicit` at the top of a macro file, you can require that a variable be declared before using it.

Using constants

Constants can also be used in VBScript. These are defined using the `Const` keyword. Some of the sample macro code in this chapter uses constants. For example, `Const Author = "John A. Programmer"` is a constant that is displayed at the top of a file and is used to insert the programmer's name into comments created by different macros.

VBScript also uses intrinsic constants. These constants are defined by the VBScript language. Such intrinsic constants as vbOKOnly and vbYesNo can be used to define the type of message box VBScript displays. Other intrinsic constants are defined by the Developer Studio for use with its objects. As a general rule, intrinsic constants begin with the letters "vb."

Using functions and procedures

VBScript enables you to create functions similar to C++ functions. There are two types: VBScript procedures that do not return values, and functions, which do return values. VBScript macros are all procedures. Procedures begin with a Sub and end with End Sub as follows:

```
Sub AGenericProcedure
'code goes here.
  MsgBox "This procedure is running."
End Sub
```

Functions are similar in design, but they can return a value. In order to return a value, simply assign the value to the function as follows:

```
Function GetAuthor () As String
'code goes here
GetAuthor = InputBox ("What is your name?")
End Function
```

Using the Developer Studio Object Model

The Developer Studio includes several objects that can be used by VBScript macros and Developer Studio add-ins to automate your work. These objects are described in Table 37-1.

Accessing the object model

The relationships between the various objects is depicted in Figure 37-11. Notice two Application objects in this figure. This is because the application, the Developer Studio, has an Application object for a parent. Two Window objects are also listed. One is for text windows, and the other covers other types of windows.

Table 37-1
Developer Studio Objects

Object	*Description*
`Application`	This object represents the Developer Studio application, and may be used to access all other objects.
`Breakpoint`	An object used during debugging.
`Breakpoints`	A collection of all set breakpoints.
`BuildProject`	A project along with all of the configuration information needed to build it.
`Configuration`	Settings used when building a project.
`Configurations`	A collection of all configuration objects for a project.
`Debugger`	An object tied to the debugging process that enables you to inspect a program's execution.
`Document`	An open document such as a resource file.
`Documents`	A collection of all open documents that may include `Document` and `TextDocument` objects.
`Project`	A collection of related files.
`Projects`	A collection of one or more projects in the active workspace.
`TextDocument`	Any open text file such as a source code file.
`TextEditor`	The Developer Studio text editor.
`TextSelection`	Selected text in an open text file, or `TextDocument`.
`TextWindow`	A window, or view, containing an open text file.
`Window`	A Developer Studio child window containing a document.
`Windows`	A collection of all open `Window` objects.

Using the Application object

As you can see in Figure 37-11, the `Application` object is the top object in the Developer Studio object hierarchy. You can use the `Application` object's methods and properties to access all of the other objects.

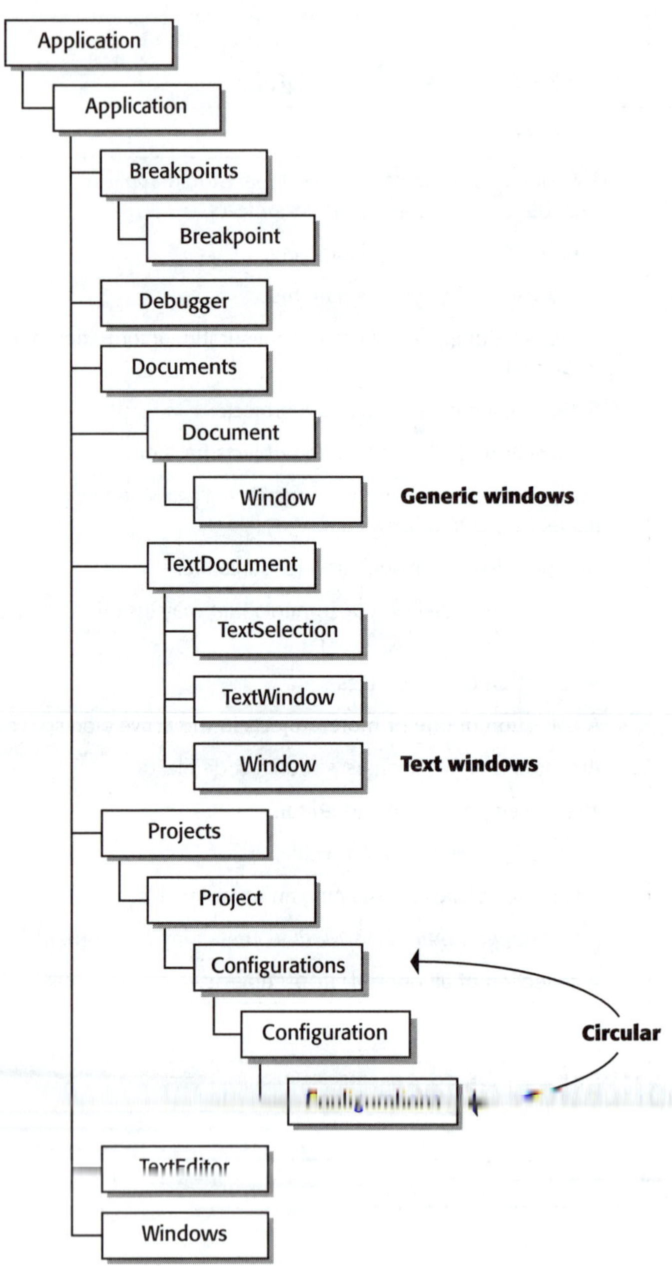

Figure 37-11: The Developer Studio object model illustrates the relationships between the different objects.

The `Application` object is also the default object, which means you can access all of its properties and methods without referring to the object. To call the `RebuildAll` method, you can simply use the command `RebuildAll` instead of `Application.RebuildAll`. Effectively, this makes these properties and methods extensions to the VBScript language. These properties are listed in Table 37-2, and the methods are listed in Table 37-3 for your convenience.

Table 37-2
Useful Application Object Methods

Object	*Description*
`AddKeyBinding`	Binds a keystroke to a command. When doing this you should be careful not to create a conflict with existing bindings.
`AddProject`	Creates and adds a new project to the workspace.
`Build`	Builds a project using the active configuration, unless you specify a configuration. Only changed files are processed.
`Clean`	Deletes all intermediate and output files of the active configuration, unless a different configuration is specified.
`EnableModeless`	Enables or disables existing modeless windows in Developer Studio. This is typically done before displaying a modal dialog box ensuring that the user cannot click the windows while the dialog box is displayed.
`ExecuteCommand`	Executes a VBScript macro or other command, such as a menu command.
`ExecuteConfiguration`	Executes the program in the current workspace.
`GetPackageExtension`	Enables access of third-party extensions to the Developer Studio object model.
`PrintToOutputWindow`	Sends output from a macro to the Macro tab of the Output window, and is generally used with data that wouldn't be placed in a message box.
`Quit`	Prompts the user to save any changes that may have been made to documents, and then closes the documents and exits the Developer Studio.
`RebuildAll`	Builds a project using the active configuration, unless you specify a configuration. This method processes all files.

Table 37-3
Useful Application Object Properties

Object	*Description*
`ActiveConfiguration`	Enables you to access the active configuration for the current project.
`ActiveDocument`	Enables you to access the active document. This is either a `Document` or `TextDocument`.
`ActiveProject`	Enables you to access the active project.
`ActiveWindow`	Controls the active window.
`Application`	An object that may be used to access all of the objects in the Developer Studio object model.
`CurrentDirectory`	Sets or returns the directory path used by the `Open` command.
`Debugger`	Accesses the `Debugger` object.
`Documents`	Accesses a collection of open documents.
`Errors`	Returns a value corresponding to the number of errors in the last build. A value of -1 signifies that no build has occurred, 0 signifies no errors, and a value of 1 signifies errors occurred.
`FullName`	Returns the full path and filename of the Developer Studio executable.
`Height`	Returns or sets the distance from the top to the bottom of the main Developer Studio window.
`Left`	Returns or sets the distance from the screen to the left of the Developer Studio window.
`Path`	Returns the path of the Developer Studio executable.
`Projects`	Accesses a collection of projects in the loaded workspace.
`TextEditor`	Accesses the `TextEditor` object.
`Top`	Returns or sets the distance from the top of the screen to the top of the Developer Studio window.
`Version`	Returns a string representing the version number of the Developer Studio.
`Visible`	Returns or sets whether the main Developer Studio window is visible.
`Warnings`	Returns a value corresponding to the number of warnings in the last build. A value of -1 signifies that no build has occurred, 0 signifies no warnings, and a value of 1 signifies warnings occurred.

Object	Description
`Width`	Returns or sets the distance from the left to the right of the main Developer Studio window.
`Windows`	Accesses a collection of all open windows.
`WindowState`	Returns or sets the Developer Studio window to one of three values. `DsWindowStateMaximized` maximizes the window, while `dsWindowStateMinimized` minimizes the window, and `dsWindowStateNormal` sets the window to a normal, non-maximized state.

Using Sample Applications

The `VCBible.DSM file` included with this book contains sample macros that can be used with your programs and as learning aides on how to program VBScript macros. This section describes the CreateFunctionDescriptionFile sample macro.

Running the sample macro

The CreateFunctionDescriptionFile macro is a macro that is useful for creating documentation for your source code. The macro goes through a source code file gathering function headers and creates a basic description of the functions in an HTML file.

To take a look at what the function does, open up a C++ source code file in the Developer Studio. Make sure that the `VCBible.DSM` macro file is loaded into the Developer Studio so that the macro can be used. Loading macro files was covered earlier in the chapter. Use the Macro command from the Tools menu to load the Macro dialog box, select the CreateFunctionDescriptionFile macro from the list, and select the Run button. If the macro isn't available, check the Macro File field, and make sure that VCBible is selected in the list of macro files.

The macro creates a new HTML file that will include information about the functions used in your source code file. You can then load the file into your Web browser. Figure 37-12 shows an HTML description file.

You should be aware of a couple of things when using this macro. The macro expects that all function declarations are located on one line right before the opening brace of the function, similar to the following:

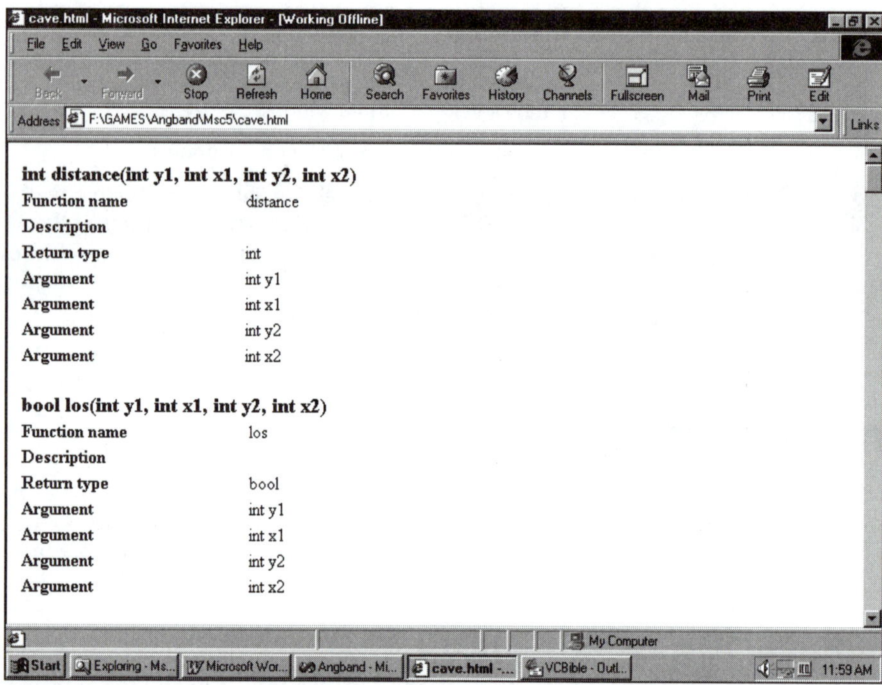

Figure 37-12: This Internet Explorer window displays an HTML documentation file.

```
int Stat::setCurrentStat(int newCurrentValue)
{
   int oldValue = currentStat;
   currentStat = newCurrentValue;
   return oldValue;
}
```

It is easy to change the macro by using a different system of coding. Of course, if you don't change the macro before running it, you will see warnings. The macro displays a warning dialog box if it thinks the function declaration has an error in it. A multi-line function declaration results in this type of warning. In case of a warning, the macro simply continues on to the next function.

Understanding the sample macro

The CreateFunctionDescriptionFile macro found in Listing 37-1 uses an `OutputDescription` function to create the description of the function. This is based on the `AddFunctionDescription` provided with Visual Studio. The only real changes have been to change the output so that it will put a description of the function in an HTML table.

The HTML table describing the function includes a row for a description of a function. This description currently has to be entered by hand. However, if you have a standard commenting style that includes a function description, the macro can be changed to include the comments from your code into the HTML file.

Listing 37-1: Code for Creating an HTML Description File from a Source File

```
Sub CreateFunctionDescriptionFile()
'DESCRIPTION: This function copies the function declarations
'from a C/C++ file to an HTML file and creates a
'description of the function.

'Create the HTML file for the source description
  CurrentSourceFileName = ActiveDocument.FullName
  TempString = CurrentSourceFileName
  Position = InStrRev(TempString,".")
  CurrentHTMLFileName = Left(TempString, Position) + "html"

  Documents.Add "Text"
  ActiveDocument.Save CurrentHTMLFileName
  ActiveDocument.Language = "HTML - IE 3.0"

'Create header for HTML File
  ActiveDocument.Selection = "<HTML>"
  ActiveDocument.Selection.NewLine
  ActiveDocument.Selection = "<HEAD>"
  ActiveDocument.Selection.NewLine
  ActiveDocument.Selection = _
   "<TITLE>" & ActiveDocument.Name &"</TITLE>"
  ActiveDocument.Selection.NewLine
  ActiveDocument.Selection = "</HEAD>"
  ActiveDocument.Selection.NewLine
  ActiveDocument.Selection = "<BODY>"
  ActiveDocument.Selection.NewLine

'Document the first function and get its line number
  Documents(CurrentSourceFileName).Active = True
  ActiveDocument.Selection.StartOfDocument
  ActiveDocument.Selection.FindText "{"
  'Copy the function declaration
  LineNumber = ActiveDocument.Selection.CurrentLine
  ActiveDocument.Selection.LineUp
  ActiveDocument.Selection.EndOfLine dsExtend
  FunctionText = ActiveDocument.Selection.Text

  'Copy the function declaration to the HTML file
  ' and create a description of the function
  Documents(CurrentHTMLFileName).Active = True
```

(continued)

Listing 37-1 *(continued)*

```
    ActiveDocument.Selection.NewLine
    OutputDescription FunctionText
    ActiveDocument.Selection.NewLine

  'Move to the end of the first function and search the
  ' rest of the source document for functions making sure
  ' not to document the first function again.
    Documents(CurrentSourceFileName).Active = True
    ActiveDocument.Selection.LineDown
    ExecuteCommand "GoToMatchBrace"
    ActiveDocument.Selection.LineDown
    While (ActiveDocument.Selection.FindText("{") = True _
       And ActiveDocument.Selection.CurrentLine > LineNumber)
      'Copy the function declaration
      ActiveDocument.Selection.LineUp
      ActiveDocument.Selection.EndOfLine dsExtend
      FunctionText = ActiveDocument.Selection.Text

      'Copy the function declaration to the HTML file
      ' and create a description of the function
      Documents(CurrentHTMLFileName).Active = True
      OutputDescription FunctionText
      ActiveDocument.Selection.NewLine

      'return to the source file and move to the end
      ' of the function.
      Documents(CurrentSourceFileName).Active = True
      ActiveDocument.Selection.LineDown
      ExecuteCommand "GoToMatchBrace"
      ActiveDocument.Selection.LineDown
      Wend

  'Create end of HTML File and close
    Documents(CurrentHTMLFileName).Active = True
    ActiveDocument.Selection = "</BODY></HTML>"
    ActiveDocument.Selection.NewLine
    ActiveDocument.Save

  'Return
  End Sub
```

The first step in creating the description file is to create a new HTML file, which is done by getting the name of the source file using the `FullName` property. The name is changed so it has an .HTML extension, and then a new file is created with the `New` and `Save` methods.

After creating a new HTML file, a header is created. This is a standard header that is needed by any HTML file. If you have comments located at the top of your source code files, you can change the macro to include the comments at the top of the HTML file in this part of the macro.

After creating the HTML file, the macro switches back to the source code file. As you watch the macro run, you will see that the macro switches back and forth quite frequently. This is done by changing the active state of a document using the following code:

```
Documents(CurrentSourceFileName).Active = True
```

`CurrentSourceFileName` is the full name of the document to be made active. Instead of using the full name, you could use a filename, but doing so can be confusing if you have more than one file with the same name. Using the full name including the path is the best option.

The macro moves to the first of the file using the `StartOfDocument` method and then looks for the opening brace of a function. Because this is the first opening brace, the macro stores its line number. This is important when it comes to determining when the macro should quit.

The `FindText` method doesn't include an easy way to test for an end of the file. It simply searches from the current location in a file for a string of text, and if it doesn't find the string, the method returns to the top of the file and begins the search again. While a message is displayed on the Visual Studio status bar stating that the search has gone beyond the end of the file, this message is not passed on to the macro. It is up to you to find another way to test for passing beyond the end of a file.

◆ ◆ ◆ ◆ ◆

After setting the `LineNumber` variable so that it remembers where the first function is located, the macro moves to the line before the function body where its declaration can be found using the `LineUp` method. Then that line of text is selected by moving to the end of the code with the `EndOfLine` method. The `dsExtend` option tells VBScript to select the text and not to simply move the cursor. The selected text is saved in the `FunctionText` variable as follows:

```
ActiveDocument.Selection.LineUp
ActiveDocument.Selection.EndOfLine dsExtend
FunctionText = ActiveDocument.Selection.Text
```

The macro then switches to the HTML file so that it can add the function's declaration and description. The actual description is created by the `OutputDescription` function that is described in Listing 37-2. The following code shows how this is done:

```
Documents(CurrentHTMLFileName).Active = True
ActiveDocument.Selection.NewLine
OutputDescription FunctionText
```

After creating a description for the first function, the macro returns to the source code file and must find its way to the next function. Because the macro looks for an opening brace and it's possible to have many sets of braces in a function, it is necessary to jump to the end of the current function. This is done by returning to the brace of the function and then using the `GoToMatchBrace` function to jump to the matching brace that marks the end of the function.

After finishing going through the first function, a `while` loop is used to go through the rest of the source code and to pull out the functions so they can be described in the HTML file. As part of the condition to see when the macro is finished, the current location is tested against the location of the first function. When the macro gets to the first function it exits.

Listing 37-2: Code for Creating a Function's Description Based on Its Header

```
Sub OutputDescription(ByVal Description)

  Header = StripTabs(Trim(Description))

  'Get the function return type.
  if Header <> "" then
    Reti = InStr(Header, " ")
    Loc = InStr(Header, "(")
    if Reti < Loc Then
      RetTp = Left(Header, Reti)
      Header = Right(Header, Len(Header) - Reti)
    End If

    'Get the function name.
    Loc = InStr(Header, "(") - 1
    Loc2 = InStr(Header, ")")
    'make sure there is a '(' and a ')'
    If Loc > 0 And Loc2 > 0 then
      fcName = Left(Header, Loc)
      Header = Right(Header, Len(Header) - Len(fcName))

      'Do we have storage type on the return type?
      Trim (fcName)
      If InStr(fcName," ") <> 0 Then
        retTp = retTp + Left(fcName,InStr (fcName," "))
        fcName = Right(fcName, Len(fcName) - _
                 InStr(fcName," "))
      End If

      'Get the function parameters.
```

```
iPrm = 0
iPrmA = 0
prms = Header

'Count the number of parameters.
Do While InStr(prms, ",") <> 0
  iPrm = iPrm + 1
  prms = Right(prms, Len(prms) - InStr(prms, ","))
Loop

'Store the parameter list in the array.
If iPrm > 0 Then  ' If multiple params.
  iPrm = iPrm + 1
  iPrmA = iPrm
  Redim ParamArr(iPrm)
  Do While InStr(header, ",") <> 0
    ParamArr(iPrm) = Left(Header, _
        InStr (Header, ",") - 1)
    'Remove brace from first parameter.
    If InStr(ParamArr(iPrm), " (") <> 0 Then
      ParamArr(iPrm) = Right(ParamArr(iPrm), _
          Len(ParamArr(iPrm)) - _
             InStr(ParamArr(iPrm)," ("))
      Trim(ParamArr(iPrm))
    End If
    Header = Right(Header, Len(Header) - _
             InStr(Header,","))
    iPrm = iPrm - 1
    Loop
  ParamArr(iPrm) = Header
  'Remove trailing brace from last parameter.
  If InStr(ParamArr(iPrm), ")") <> 0 Then
    ParamArr(iPrm) = Left(ParamArr(iPrm), _
        InStr(ParamArr(iPrm), ")") - 1)
    Trim(ParamArr(iPrm))
  End If
Else 'Possibly one param.
  Redim ParamArr(1)
  ' Strip the first brace.
  Header = Right(Header, Len(Header) - 1)
  Trim(Header)
  ParamArr(1) = StripTabs(Header)
  If InStr(ParamArr(1), ")") <> 1 Then
    ParamArr(1) = Left(ParamArr(1), _
         InStr(ParamArr(1), ")") - 1)
    Trim(ParamArr(1))
    iPrmA = 1
  End If
End If

'Position the cursor one line above the selected text.
ActiveDocument.Selection.LineUp
```

(continued)

Listing 37-2 *(continued)*

```
      ActiveDocument.Selection.LineDown
      ActiveDocument.Selection.StartOfLine
      ActiveDocument.Selection = vbLf

      Descr = "<TR><TD><B>Function name</B></TD><TD>" + _
        fcName +  "</TD></TR><TR><TD><B>Description</B>" + _
        "</TD></TR><TR><TD><B>Return type</B>" + _
        "</TD><TD>" + RetTp + "</TD></TR>"

      'Print the parameter list.
      Last = iPrmA
      Do While iPrmA <> 0
        'Remove a line feed from any of the arguments.
        If InStr(ParamArr(iPrmA), vbLf) <> 0 Then
          ParamArr(iPrmA) = Right(ParamArr(iPrmA), _
              (Len(ParamArr(iPrmA)) - _
              InStr(ParamArr(iPrmA), vbLf)))
          Trim(ParamArr(iPrmA))
        End If
        ParamArr(iPrmA) = StripTabs(ParamArr(iPrmA))
        'If there are 2+ parameters, the first parameter will
        'have a '(' prepended to it, remove it here:
        if iPrmA = Last AND Last <> 1 then
          ParamArr(iPrmA) = Right(ParamArr(iPrmA), _
            Len(ParamArr(iPrmA)) - 1)
        End If
        Descr = Descr + "<TR><TD><B>Argument</B></TD>" + _
            "<TD>" + ParamArr(iPrmA) + "</TD></TR>"
        iPrmA = iPrmA - 1
      Loop
      ActiveDocument.Selection = "<TABLE>" + vbLF + _
          "<TH COLSPAN=2><BIG>" + Description + _
          "</BIG></TH>" + vbLF & Descr & _
          "</TABLE><BR>" + vbLF
    Else
      MsgBox("It is possible that the function you are _

          " trying to"+ work with has a syntax error.")
    End If
  End If
End Sub
```

The `OutputDescription` function begins by taking a look at the function header received in the `Description` variable to determine its name and return type and to create a separate list of parameters. This is done using a couple of VBScript's string manipulation functions. The `Trim` function removes white space from the beginning and end of a string. `InStr` searches for a string inside of another string, and the `Left` function returns a number of characters from a string.

After finding the basic information about the function being documented, an array is used to store the parameters. Before this can be done, the macro counts the number of parameters used by counting the number of commas in the declaration using the following code:

```
Do While InStr(prms, ",") <> 0
  iPrm = iPrm + 1
  prms = Right(prms, Len(prms) - InStr(prms, ","))
Loop
```

In the code, iPrm is the number of parameters. Prms is a temporary string holding all of the parameters. After finding a comma, the string is shortened by removing it from the string. The Right function returns a number of characters from the string beginning at the right end. The number of characters is determined by subtracting the location of the comma from the total length of the string.

Once the number of strings is determined, the array is set up to store the parameter information. This generally requires correcting the size of the array using the ReDim function. This sizes the array to hold enough elements for all of the parameters.

After storing all of the information about the function in variables, the function name and return value are placed into a string that stores the HTML table that will be sent to the HTML description file. The following code illustrates this:

```
Descr = "<TR><TD><B>Function name</B></TD><TD>" + fcName + _
        "</TD></TR><TR><TD><B>Description</B>" + _
        "</TD></TR><TR><TD><B>Return type</B>" + _
        "</TD><TD>" + RetTp + "</TD></TR>"
```

If you are not familiar with HTML, it is worth pointing out that HTML uses tags to describe how to format information. All the tags have a beginning tag and an ending tag. For example, <TR> starts a table row, and </TR> tells the browser where to end a row. HTML can be quite useful, especially for documentation that may have to be shared with others working on a project.

The description field does not have any information next to it. This is because there are many ways to comment a function and if you have a standard style, the macro can be edited to automatically add comments into the description field of the table.

The parameters are the last piece of information placed in the table. This is done with a while loop that counts through the number of parameters being used and stores the information into the array using a bit more string manipulation.

After creating the Descr variable, the HTML file is prepared for the description, by beginning an HTML table with the <TABLE> element and then adding a table header that is the full declaration of the function, using the following statement:

```
ActiveDocument.Selection = "<TABLE>" + vbLF + _
   "<TH COLSPAN=2><BIG>" + Description + _
```

```
        "</BIG></TH>" + vbLF & Descr & "</TABLE><BR>" + vbLF
```

One additional function was used by the macro. The `StripTabs` is included with the sample functions provided with the Developer Studio and is listed in the following code:

```
Function StripTabs (ByVal MyStr)
  Do While InStr(MyStr, vbTab) <> 0
    MyStr = Right(MyStr, Len(MyStr) - InStr(MyStr, vbTab))
  Loop
  StripTabs = Trim(MyStr)
End Function
```

This function makes use of VBScript's string manipulating functions to remove any tabs from the left of a string. This function also uses the built-in constant `vbTab` that represents the Tab character.

Summary

As you have seen, Visual Studio is a programmable environment. Macros can be used to simplify editing tasks and to automate frequently used commands. This can be done by recording Quick Macros or by creating macro files with a collection of macros. These macros may even be shared with other people to make life easier for others on your project as well.

Because VBScript is the language chosen for the macros, it may require learning a bit of the Basic language. However, Basic is a simple language to learn and is similar to the macro language used in other Microsoft products, as well as being a popular language on the Internet.

✦ ✦ ✦

Writing a Custom AppWizard

✦ ✦ ✦ ✦

In This Chapter

How the AppWizard works

Multitrack wizards

The AppWizard dictionary

Creating a custom AppWizard to preset a project's default settings

Creating a custom AppWizard to include personal information on every About box

Adding custom dialogs to AppWizard

Modifying templates to customize the skeleton

AppWizard directives

Changing the AppWizard's confirmation dialog

Using the Registry to store Custom AppWizard information

✦ ✦ ✦ ✦

One of the most powerful tools that Visual Studio provides is a wizard, AppWizard, for creating new projects. In Windows terminology, a wizard is an application that presents a series of dialogs that leads the user through the options necessary to perform a given task. Likewise, the AppWizard gives programmers the capability to define a new project by displaying a series of dialogs for a specific project type. Each dialog displays options that are specific to the new project's type. For example, when creating a Windows DLL with the AppWizard, the first dialog presented enables the programmer to specify options such as what type of DLL is being created (regular or MFC extension), whether automation support should be included, and whether to include source code comments.

Once the different dialogs have been filled out, AppWizard creates the starter files necessary to build the project. These starter files include the project file, workspace file, source files, header files, resource files, and so on. Although it is probably the most frequently used Visual Studio tool, AppWizard suffered from only one drawback, which was that it could be used only to create projects from a static list of predefined projects. This all changed when version 4.0 of Visual C++ introduced custom AppWizards.

Custom AppWizards are used when multiple projects with similar options are created, and like the AppWizards that are shipped with Visual C++, custom AppWizards are used to create generic project types that can repetitively generate common functionality. For example, if you find that you are always creating MFC SDI applications with automation, you could create a custom AppWizard with these options preset. This reduces the time required to create each new project of this type and eliminates the possibility of forgetting to set the necessary options.

Custom AppWizards can also be used to modify the code that the AppWizard produces. Let's say that you want all projects that you create to contain an About box containing your company's logo as well as contact and sales information. This can easily be accomplished via a custom AppWizard. You can even define and display your own customized dialogs that will be displayed when the custom AppWizard is run. These customized dialogs could then be used to retrieve options that are specific to your project type. How the AppWizards work and developing new Custom AppWizards is the subject of this chapter.

After you learn about the internals of how the AppWizard works, demo custom AppWizards will be presented. This first demo will illustrate how to preset a project's default settings. A second demo will be used to show how to create a custom AppWizard that displays a customized dialog to retrieve information. This information will then be used to create the definition of an About box that will contain the application's description and contact information about you or your company. The About box will even have a command button that transfers the user to the Web page of your choosing.

The Internal Workings of the AppWizard

Before you can create a Custom AppWizard, you must understand how the AppWizard works. Let's take a moment and look at exactly how the AppWizard goes about creating a project from the options you choose.

The AppWizard manager

When you create a custom AppWizard, it does not run as a standalone application. Custom AppWizards run within the framework of Visual Studio. Actually, an AppWizard "manager" (MFCAPWZ.DLL) controls the execution of the different AppWizards. When the New file dialog is displayed and the Projects tab is selected, a preset list of project types is presented in a list box. In addition, any custom AppWizards that you have created are also listed. For a custom AppWizard to be listed, it must have an extension of .awx and be located in a specific folder.

If the default folder locations are accepted when Visual C++ 6.0 is installed, any custom AppWizard files that are created will be located in the \Program Files\Microsoft Visual Studio\Common\msdev98\Template folder. Figure 38-1 shows an example of the Visual Studio New dialog. Notice the two entries "MFC

AppWizard (exe) — About box" and "MFC AppWizard (exe) — SDI/Automation." These are two custom AppWizards that were developed for use with this chapter. As you can see, these custom AppWizards are automatically displayed along with the standard Visual C++ AppWizards.

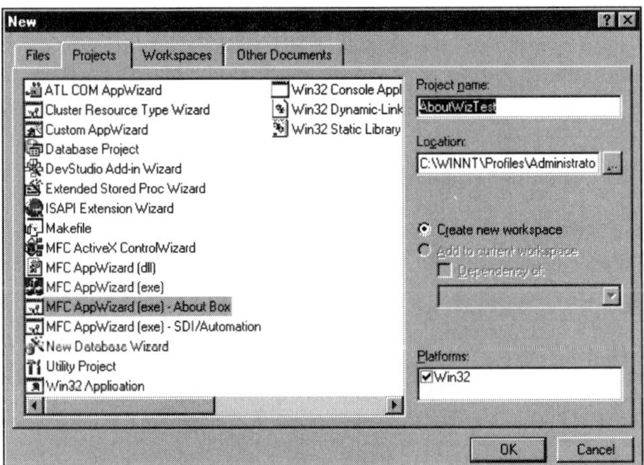

Figure 38-1: Once you have written a custom AppWizard, it is automatically displayed with the standard Visual C++ AppWizards.

The CCustomAppWiz class and the Dictionary

The `CCustomAppWiz` base class provides communications services between the `MFCAPWZ.DLL` and the Custom AppWizard. The implementations of the `CCustomAppWiz()` member functions reside in `MFCAPWZ.DLL`. To implement application-specific behavior, you only have to derive a class from the `CCustomAppWiz` class, override the desired virtual member functions, and register the derived class with the `MFCAPWZ.DLL` at runtime via a call to the `SetCustomAppWizClass()` function.

As mentioned earlier, the AppWizard presents a series of dialogs to retrieve the settings necessary to create new projects. As each dialog is presented and the different options are selected, AppWizard is storing these values in a string map. This string map is referred to as the *Dictionary*. The Dictionary is actually a `CMapStringToString` member variable (`m_Dictionary`) of the `CCustomAppWiz` class. The Dictionary maps AppWizard's macros and their associated values. A *macro* is the name of a project option or setting. For example, when creating an MFC application, you have the option of defining the application as an SDI application. Therefore, the Dictionary has a macro called `PROJTYPE_SDI`. If the project is an MFC SDI application, the value for this entry in the Dictionary will be 1. Otherwise, the macro's associated value will be a 0.

The m_Dictionary member variable can be used to create macros, remove macros, or update the value of macros. Because the m_Dictionary member variable is a CMapStringToString object, familiar member functions can be used to retrieve the values of the different macros. The following code returns the value of the PROJTYPE_SDI macro that could then be used to determine if the project has been defined as being an SDI application:

```
m_Dictionary.Lookup("PROJTYPE_SDI", m_strProjType);
if (_T("1") == m_strProjType)
{
 // sdi app
}
else // some other type
{
}
```

While the standard macros are supplied by MFCAPWZ.DLL, any additional macros that are required by a custom AppWizard are added to the Dictionary with the SetAt member function. A complete list of the more than 60 standard macros can be found in the online documentation. The second demo of this chapter illustrates how to create new macros to display information on a customized dialog.

Once the programmer has clicked the Finish button on a Custom AppWizard, MFCAPWZ.DLL uses the Dictionary to create the new project's files. Each AppWizard (standard or custom) has a set of template files that are used to create the project that AppWizard was designed to create. The values in the Dictionary are used in conjunction with the template files to create the final output (the new project's files). Following is an example. The template resource file for the English-language version of a dialog-based application's resource file is named DlgLoc_enu.rc. Following is an excerpt from that file:

```
...
IDD_ABOUTBOX DIALOGEX 0, 0, 160, 129
STYLE DS_MODALFRAME | WS_POPUP | WS_CAPTION | WS_SYSMENU
CAPTION "About $$ROOT$$"
...
```

Take special notice of the $$ROOT$$ string in the preceding example. When MFCAPWZ.DLL creates the new project's files, it first scans each template file looking for strings that begin with the "$$" prefix and end in the "$$" suffix. The textual string between the prefix and suffix is referred to as a *placeholder*. Each placeholder is used as the name of a macro to retrieve from the Dictionary. The MFCAPWZ.DLL looks up the value for the placeholder in the Dictionary and uses that value to replace the placeholder. Once all of the placeholders have been replaced with the corresponding Dictionary values, the file is created. Figure 38-2 gives an overview of how MFCAPWZ.DLL uses the Dictionary to create a new project.

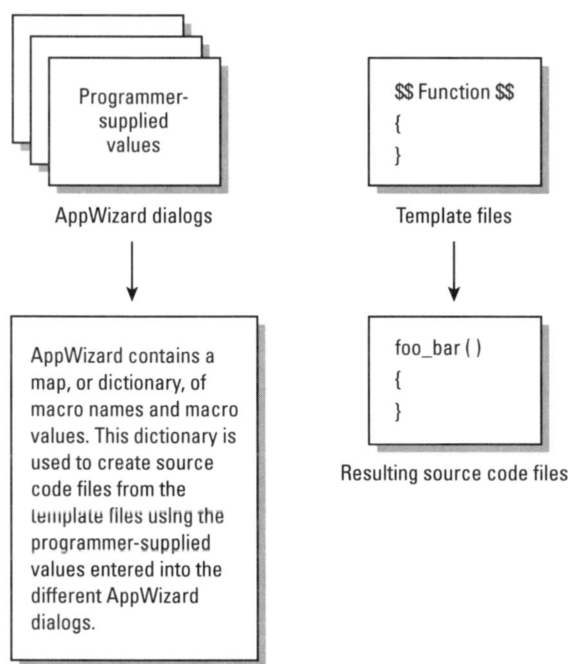

Figure 38-2: MFCAPWZ.DLL uses the Dictionary's values to replace the placeholders in the template files in order to create the new project's files.

Try This

Using MFCAPWZ.DLL to Replace Placeholders

To see an example of the `MFCAPWZ.DLL` using Dictionary values to replace template file placeholders:

1. Use AppWizard to create a dialog-based application. Call this project MyTestDlgApp.
2. Once AppWizard has created the project's files, open the `MyTestDlgApp.rc` file as a text file (select the Text entry in the Open As combo box).
3. Locate the dialog template resource with the id of `IDD_ABOUT`.
4. You should see that the `$$ROOT$$` placeholder that was in the original template file has been replaced with the name of the project (MyTestDlgApp). This is because the Dictionary has a macro called ROOT and by default its value is set to the name of the project.

◆ ◆ ◆ ◆ ◆

While some macros are used to define replacement values for placeholders defined in the template files, other times AppWizard uses macros to aid it in the process of presenting the dialogs or deciding which template files will be used in order to create the new project's files. For example, if the `PROJTYPE_SDI` macro has a value of 1 in the Dictionary, then an SDI application is being created. However, if the `PROJTYPE_DLG` macro has a value of 1, then a dialog-based application is being created. Depending on which of these values is set to 1, `MFCAPWZ.DLL` uses different template files to create the project's files.

Most wizards present a fixed series of dialogs. However, some wizards need to present different dialogs depending on options selected in previous dialogs. These multiple series of dialogs are referred to as *tracks*. An example of a *multi-track* AppWizard would be the AppWizard used to create an MFC application.

Multitrack AppWizards in Action

Multitrack AppWizrards provide a more sophisticated setup of applications. To see a multitrack AppWizard, follow these steps:

1. Press Ctrl+N to create a new file.
2. Click the Projects tab, and then select the "MFC AppWizard (exe)" entry in the Projects list.
3. Notice that the dialog's title bar reads "MFC AppWizard - Step 1" and doesn't state the total number of steps. This is because the total number of steps (and track) won't be known until you decide which type of MFC project you want to create.
4. Take a look at the different types of project options available: single document (SDI), multiple document (MDI), and dialog-based. Select a project type of multiple document, and click the Next button.
5. Notice the title bar now has the total number of steps. It should read "MFC AppWizard—Step 2 of 6." The total number of steps is now known because you have selected the "MDI track" and that track contains six dialogs, each of which contain options specific to document-based MFC applications.
6. Now, click the Back button, select the "Dialog based" project type, and then click the Next button. The title bar should now read "MFC AppWizard—Step 2 of 4." This is because the dialog track contains only four dialogs that present options specific to creating a dialog-based application.

✦ ✦ ✦ ✦ ✦

Enough talking about AppWizards and custom AppWizards. It's time to put some of this knowledge to use and see how this works firsthand.

Creating a Custom AppWizard

AppWizard is used to create the framework for a custom AppWizard. At this point, press Ctrl+N to display the New dialog. From the Projects tab, select the Custom AppWizard. Once the project name has been entered and the OK button clicked, the first of two dialogs used to create the Custom AppWizard will be displayed.

The first dialog contains only three fields. The first field is the *starting point* for the new Custom AppWizard. There are three options available for this field:

- **Existing project**—This option should be selected when an existing project will be used as the template for new projects. There are two caveats to this option. First, AppWizard must have been used to create the existing project. Second, the existing project's files and classes must have the same names that were created by AppWizard. Remember the code snippet earlier with the `$$ROOT$$` placeholder?
- **Standard MFC AppWizard steps**—This is the most commonly used option when creating custom AppWizards. By selecting this option, you are basically telling AppWizard, "Create for me every single template that could be used for every project type supported." At this point, you have the most flexibility in terms of being able to modify any header file, implementation file, resource file, and so on that is used to create an MFC project. Because this is the most common custom AppWizard type, and the most difficult to implement, the examples and demos in this chapter will use this starting point.
- **Your own customized steps**—Use this option to display an entirely new set of dialogs and options. For example, let's say that you are creating a custom AppWizard to automate the creation of a non-MFC application. The programmer would still have to select some of the options; however, none of the MFC dialogs would make any sense to a non-MFC application. You would therefore select this option and create all of your own customized dialogs.

The second field on this dialog enables you to name the new custom AppWizard. This name will be used in the New dialog's Project list.

The last field on this dialog is used to specify the number of custom steps, or dialogs, that will be added to the new custom AppWizard. There are some cases in which no additional steps are required for a custom AppWizard. Therefore, the first demo (coming up shortly) will not have any custom steps, while the second demo will incorporate a custom step.

Once the options for this dialog have been selected, press the Next button to proceed to the second (and last) dialog required to create a custom AppWizard. This dialog contains only two fields, both of which are self-explanatory. The first field defines whether or not the new custom AppWizard will be used to create an MFC application or an MFC DLL. The second field stipulates which languages will be supported.

A Demo to Preset a Project's Default Settings

As mentioned earlier, there are a number of instances in which you might want to change the default settings of a project. In this section, you will create a custom AppWizard demo project called SDIAutomationWiz. Once the Custom AppWizard has been created, you will modify it so that any project created with this custom AppWizard has a default project type of SDI as well as automation support.

Creating the SDIAutomationWiz demo project

The instructions in this section will illustrate how to write a custom AppWizard.

The source code for this demo can be found on the companion CD in the `\Chap38\SDIAutomationWiz` folder.

✦ ✦ ✦ ✦ ✦

To begin, create a new Custom AppWizard project called SDIAutomationWiz. On the first dialog, specify the "Standard MFC AppWizard steps" as the starting point. Set the Project list name to anything you want to appear in the AppWizard list when a new project is created. It is standard practice to name the custom AppWizards so that they are grouped according to functionality. For example, because this custom AppWizard will be an MFC AppWizard with changes to some minor default settings, the demo project name is "MFC AppWizard (exe) — SDI/Automation." Because no customized dialogs will be used for this demo, set the number of custom steps to 0, and click the Next button. On the next dialog, select "MFC AppWizard Executable," and click the Finish button. When the confirmation dialog is displayed, click the OK button to create the project for your new custom AppWizard.

Defining the CCustomAppWiz class

Even though custom AppWizards have a special suffix (.AWX), they are still the same run-of-the-mill DLLs you are accustomed to using. If you open the `SDIAutomationWiz.cpp` file that you created in this project, you will see the `DLLMain()` function defined as shown in Listing 38-1.

Listing 38-1: Defining the DLLMain() Function

```
extern "C" int APIENTRY
DllMain(HINSTANCE hInstance, DWORD dwReason,
LPVOID lpReserved)
{
 if (dwReason == DLL_PROCESS_ATTACH)
 {
  TRACE0("SDIAUTOMATIONWIZ.AWX Initializing!\n");

  // Extension DLL one-time initialization
  AfxInitExtensionModule(SDIAutomationWizDLL, hInstance);
```

```
    // Insert this DLL into the resource chain
    new CDynLinkLibrary(SDIAutomationWizDLL);

    // Register this Custom AppWizard with MFCAPWZ.DLL
    SetCustomAppWizClass(&SDIAutomationWizaw);
  }
  else if (dwReason == DLL_PROCESS_DETACH)
  {
    TRACE0("SDIAUTOMATIONWIZ.AWX Terminating!\n");

    // Terminate the library before destructors are called
    AfxTermExtensionModule(SDIAutomationWizDLL);
  }
  return 1;   // ok
}
```

In addition to the usual tasks such as the creation of a CDynLinkLibrary, which is always created for an MFC extension DLL, a call to the SetCustomAppWizClass() function is also made. This function is exported from the MFCAPWZ.DLL and is used to pass the address of the custom AppWizard's CCustomAppWiz-derived class. Because the MFCAPWZ.DLL manages the execution of all AppWizards through the calling of CCustomAppWiz member functions, it requires this pointer so that it can call your overridden versions of these functions.

An important point to always remember is that even though you have created a custom AppWizard, MFCAPWZ.DLL is still in control. In other words, your custom AppWizard is simply used to do things such as displaying customized dialogs, deciding the order in which the dialogs are displayed, and setting default options for the new project. It is still MFCAPWZ.DLL that does the lion's share of the work such as parsing the template files, merging the Dictionary's macros and the placeholders in the template files, and creating the project's files.

As mentioned earlier, the CCustomAppWiz class servers as a means of communicating with the MFCAPWZ.DLL. Actually, the communications is usually one-sided. The MFCAPWZ.DLL tells your CCustomAppWiz object when it needs something by calling the appropriate virtual member functions.

While the CCustomAppWiz class contains about ten functions, only about five are routinely seen and used. The purpose of most of these functions can be deduced by their names. For example, the InitCustomAppWiz() function is called after the custom AppWizard is loaded to give it the opportunity to perform any necessary initialization. This is where the custom AppWizard would do things such as initializing macros. Besides the InitCustomAppWiz() function, the ExitCustomAppWiz() function is called when the custom AppWizard is about to be unloaded.

In addition, two functions that are used to control the ordering of the dialogs are the Next() and Back() functions. As you probably guessed, these functions directly correlate to the Next and Back buttons on the AppWizard's dialogs.

The last function of importance here is the `CustomizeProject()` function. Once the programmer has finished setting the project's options, AppWizard creates the project's make file and defines the default debug and release configurations for the project. The AppWizard then calls `CustomizeProject()` function so that the custom AppWizard has an opportunity to change any make file settings before the project is saved.

Working with macro dictionaries

Now that you know about the `CCustomAppWiz` class and the fact that you normally set a macro's initial value in the `InitCustomAppWiz()` function of this class, it's time to actually work with the different macros. As mentioned earlier, the `CCustomAppWiz` class contains a member variable, `m_Dictionary`, that stores the macro names and their values. Because this member variable is a `CMapStringToString`, you can simply use the standard MFC map functions to get and set the different macros, as the following code snippet indicates:

```
// retrieve value for Automation
CString strValue;
m_Dictionary.Lookup(_T("AUTOMATION"), strValue);

// Include support for context sensitive help
m_Dictionary.SetAt(_T("HELP"), strValue.Compare("1"));
```

At this point, open the `SDIAutomationWizAW.cpp` file, and type the following code at the end of the `InitCustomAppWiz()` function:

```
m_Dictionary.SetAt(_T("PROJTYPE_SDI"), _T("1"));
m_Dictionary.SetAt(_T("PROJTYPE_MDI"), _T("0"));
m_Dictionary.SetAt(_T("AUTOMATION"), _T("1"));
```

Now you can build the custom AppWizard project. You may recall from earlier in the chapter that custom AppWizard files must reside in a specific folder so that the `MFCAPWZ.DLL` can find them. When you build a custom AppWizard the resulting file is automatically copied to that folder. Once you have successfully built the custom AppWizard, a quick look at the Output window confirms where the file was copied.

At this point, the new custom AppWizard should appear as an entry in the Project list of the New dialog. If you invoke your new custom AppWizard, you will see that the default options are for an SDI application that automatically has automation support enabled. While this was obviously a very simple demo, it does illustrate how easy it is to initialize whatever project defaults your particular application may require.

If you create custom AppWizards for distribution, the only file that has to be distributed is the .AWX file. Simply copy this file to the Visual Studio templates file on the destination PC. If for some reason the custom AppWizard is not located in the correct folder, it will not be included on the New dialog's Project list when the programmer attempts to create a new project.

✦ ✦ ✦ ✦ ✦

A More Advanced Custom AppWizard

In this demo, called AboutWiz, you will create a custom AppWizard that produces an About box that contains your (or your company's) contact information and a button that when clicked transfers your application's end users to the Web site specified when the project was created. While the first demo was a very simple, and not very practical, custom AppWizard, it was meant to get your feet wet creating custom AppWizards. This demo, however, will illustrate several advanced topics needed to develop practical custom AppWizards more along the lines of what you might have to create in the real world.

First, you will learn how to define a customized dialog for use with a custom AppWizard. After that, you will learn how to add your own custom AppWizard-specific macros to the Dictionary. Finally, you will learn how to modify the template files that will be used by your custom AppWizard to create the new project's starter files.

The source code for the AboutWiz demo can be found on the companion CD in the `Chap38\AboutWiz` folder. If you are performing the procedures in this chapter as you go along, create a new custom AppWizard project, and call it AboutWiz. On the first dialog, specify the "Standard MFC AppWizard steps" as the starting point. Set the Project list name to anything you would want to see in your Project list.

◆ ◆ ◆ ◆ ◆

In keeping with the naming convention discussed in the first demo, the demo custom AppWizard's is named "MFC AppWizard (exe) — About Box." Because an extra dialog is going to be used in this custom AppWizard, set the number of custom steps to 1, and click the Next button. On the next dialog, select "MFC AppWizard Executable," and click the Finish button to dismiss this dialog. Click the OK button to dismiss the confirmation dialog.

Adding a customized dialog

The first thing you need to do is to create a customized dialog template resource. This dialog will be used to gather information that will later appear on the About box of any application created with this Custom AppWizard.

Select the Resource tab on the AboutWiz's workspace dialog bar. Under the entry for Dialog resources, you should find a dialog with a resource ID of IDD_CUSTOM1. Figure 38-3 shows how this dialog should appear after you finish adding the necessary controls. Once you have added the different edit controls, set their resource IDs as shown in Table 38-1. Also set the General Information edit control's `Multiline` style property.

Table 38-1
Resource IDs for Controls

Control	*Control ID*
Programmer edit	IDC_EDT_PROGRAMMER
Web Page edit	IDC_EDT_WEB_PAGE
General Information edit	IDC_EDT_GENERAL_INFO

Once you have added the new controls to the dialog resource, use ClassWizard to create member variables of type CString for the Programmer, Web Page, and General Information edit controls. These member variables should be called m_strProgrammer, m_strWebPage, and m_strGeneralInfo, respectively.

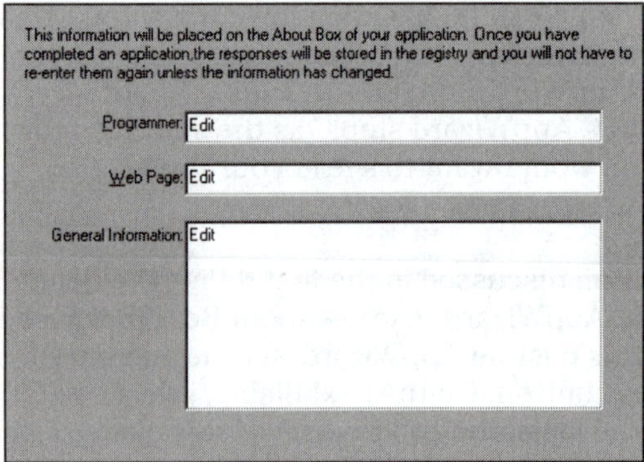

Figure 38-3: The AboutWiz dialog box after adding the new controls

Use ClassWizard to implement the OnInitDialog() member function for the CCustom1Dlg class. Once the OnInitDialog() function has been added, insert the following lines of code just before the return statement. This code retrieves the values of the custom AppWizard's macros from the Dictionary. The AboutWizAW object is a global object of type CAboutWizAppWiz (derived from CCustomAppWiz) and is defined in the AboutWizAW.h file.

```
AboutWizaw.m_Dictionary.Lookup("PROGRAMMER",
 m_strProgrammer);
AboutWizaw.m_Dictionary.Lookup("GENERAL_INFO",
 m_strGeneralInfo);
AboutWizaw.m_Dictionary.Lookup("WEB_PAGE",
 m_strWebPage);

UpdateData(FALSE);
```

Once you've changed the CCustom1Dlg::OnInitDialog() function, delete the three initialization lines from the CCustom1Dlg's constructor. Their values will be initialized in the CAboutWizAppWiz::InitCustomAppWiz() function.

Now there's only one thing left to do: save the data by changing the CCustom1Dlg::OnDismiss() function to look like the following. This code simply updates the Dictionary with the information the programmer creating the new project has entered.

By the way, you have now seen the same literals hard-coded into two different sections of the same module. Normally these literals would be defined via #defines directives or string resources. However, these values have been hard-coded for this demo in an effort to make the reading of the chapter and the source code easier.

```
BOOL CCustom1Dlg::OnDismiss()
{
 if (!UpdateData(TRUE)) return FALSE;

 AboutWizaw.m_Dictionary.SetAt("PROGRAMMER",
  m_strProgrammer);
 AboutWizaw.m_Dictionary.SetAt("GENERAL_INFO",
  m_strGeneralInfo);
 AboutWizaw.m_Dictionary.SetAt("WEB_PAGE",
  m_strWebPage);

 return TRUE;
}
```

If you were to build the custom AppWizard and use it to create a new project, you would see your new dialog. But the question now is "how do the values that are entered into the customized dialog and then saved as macros in the AppWizard's Dictionary get used in the new project?" The answer is that placeholders in template files that the custom AppWizard uses to build the new project's files reference them. In the next section, you will see how to create a new file template that will be copied to every project created with your new custom AppWizard.

Creating your own templates

When a default MFC application is created via the AppWizard, the same file is used to define both the About box dialog object and the application object. However, this demo will illustrate how to create a brand new template file that is then created by the custom AppWizard when the rest of the new project's files are created. Therefore, create a new file named About.h in the project's Template folder that looks like Listing 38-2.

Listing 38-2: Create This About.h File in the Project's Template Folder

```
#pragma once

/////////////////////////////////////////////
// CAboutDlg dialog used for App $$Root$$

class CAboutDlg : public CDialog
{
 public:
 CAboutDlg();

 // Dialog Data
 //{{AFX_DATA(CAboutDlg)
 enum { IDD = IDD_ABOUTBOX };
 //}}AFX_DATA

 // ClassWizard generated virtual function overrides
 //{{AFX_VIRTUAL(CAboutDlg)
 protected:
 virtual void DoDataExchange(CDataExchange* pDX);
 //}}AFX_VIRTUAL

 // Implementation
 protected:
 //{{AFX_MSG(CAboutDlg)
  afx_msg void OnOk();
 //}}AFX_MSG
 DECLARE_MESSAGE_MAP()
 };

CAboutDlg::CAboutDlg() : CDialog(CAboutDlg::IDD)
{
//{{AFX_DATA_INIT(CAboutDlg)
//}}AFX_DATA_INIT
}

void CAboutDlg::DoDataExchange(CDataExchange* pDX)
{
 CDialog::DoDataExchange(pDX);
 //{{AFX_DATA_MAP(CAboutDlg)
 //}}AFX_DATA_MAP
}

BEGIN_MESSAGE_MAP(CAboutDlg, CDialog)
 //{{AFX_MSG_MAP(CAboutDlg)
 ON_BN_CLICKED(IDOK, OnOk)
 //}}AFX_MSG_MAP
END_MESSAGE_MAP()

void CAboutDlg::OnOk()
```

```
{
 CString strURL;
 GetDlgItem(IDOK)->GetWindowText(strURL);
 if (!strURL.IsEmpty())
 {
  if (32 >= (int)ShellExecute(NULL, "open", strURL,
   NULL, NULL, SW_SHOWNORMAL))
  {
   AfxMessageBox("::ShellExecute failed to open "
    "this link!");
  }
 }
 else
 {
  AfxMessageBox("No URL defined on button!");
 }
}
```

As you can see, the only major thing added is the `OnOk()` handler. When this message handler is called, the `IDOK` button's text is retrieved and used in a call to the Win32 SDK `ShellExecute()` function.

Where does the button get its text value? This question will be answered in the "Changing the AppWizard templates" section later in this chapter. But before we get to that, you must do one more thing to add a template to a project.

As mentioned earlier, when a project is created using a custom AppWizard, it is `MFCAPWZ.DLL` that is responsible for creating the new project's files using the custom AppWizard's template files. So how do you tell AppWizard that you have a new template file that needs to be used when the other files of the new project are created? Actually, this is a two-step process. First, you must update the resource file by inserting a user-defined resource for each file you want the custom AppWizard to create when a new project is created. To see how this is done, open the `AboutWiz.rc` file in "text mode," and locate the following comment:

```
// TEMPLATE
```

What you should see after that is all the template files that are used to create new projects with this custom AppWizard. Because we want to add the `about.h` file to the template files, add an entry for it as follows:

```
ABOUT.H TEMPLATE DISCARDABLE "template\\about.h"
```

Next, you need to update the `newproj.inf` file.

Changing the newproj.Inf file

This file is sort of like a "bill of materials" for a custom AppWizard. MFCAPWZ.DLL uses this file when creating a new project's files. At this point, open the newproj.inf file. It is located in the custom AppWizard's Template folder.

As you will recall from earlier, placeholders are delimited by a "$$" prefix and suffix and relate to macro names whose values are stored in the Dictionary. However, the "$$" is also used to denote certain commands. These commands are called AppWizard *directives* and are used to process template files.

The first directive in this file is a comment and is denoted by the fact that the "$$" is followed by "//" characters. Any text after this four-letter combination is ignored by MFCAPWZ.DLL during its parsing. Here is an example of a comment using the AppWizard directives:

```
$$// newproj.inf = template for list of template files
```

Normally when you see a template file that is to be copied as one of the new project's files, a macro is used to help name the destination file. However, some standard files will always have the same name regardless of the project type. The standard include file, stdafx.h, is an example.

The following lines simply instruct MFCAPWZ.DLL to copy the stdafx.h and stdafx.cpp files to the new project folder, while keeping the same filenames. One very important point to note here is that the two filenames (source template file and destination file) are separated by a Tab character. Therefore, if you manually insert a line of code similar to the following, make sure you place a Tab character between the two files and not a space or series of spaces:

```
stdafx.h	StdAfx.h
stdafx.cpp	StdAfx.cpp
```

The next directive to take note of in the newproj.inf file is $$IF. This directive simply tests the Boolean state of the macro enclosed in parentheses. Note that it is the $$IF directive that requires the parentheses, not the use of the macro itself. In other words, if you want to refer to the macro in other places in your code, do so by encasing the macro name with $$ (for example, $$PROGRAMMER$$).

As you can see in the following code, the first two lines of code simply state that if the project type is not a DLL and it is not a dialog-based application, copy the Frame.h and Frame.cpp templates to files whose filenames are dictated by the frame_hfile and frame_ifile macros. You may recall from using AppWizard to create an MDI application that the last dialog is one that enables you to name the files that will house the different classes. Because the programmer can change these class names, the values are stored in macros. That particular dialog, just like the custom dialog you saw in the previous section, used the filenames entered into the dialog and updated these macros in the Dictionary. Here they are being used to actually name the destination files:

```
$$IF(!PROJTYPE_DLL)
$$IF(!PROJTYPE_DLG)
frame.h     $$frame_hfile$$.h
frame.cpp   $$frame_ifile$$.cpp
```

This $$IF line works just like the two previous $$IF lines. The only differences are the macro being tested and the resulting template-to-file copy.

```
$$IF(MDICHILD)
childfrm.h    $$child_frame_hfile$$.h
childfrm.cpp    $$child_frame_ifile$$.cpp
```

And, finally, as you might expect, each $$IF directive must have a matching $$ENDIF directive. Also notice that like C++, you can add a comment to the end of a line with the // character sequence:

```
$$ENDIF //MDICHILD
$$ENDIF //!PROJTYPE_DLG
```

Now that you see how easy it is to read the newproj.inf file, insert the following lines at the top of the file (after the comments explaining how to read and use the directives). Remember to tab between the source template file and the destination file.

```
$$IF(PROJTYPE_DLG)
$$IF(ABOUT)
about.h    about.h
$$ENDIF //ABOUT
$$ELIF(PROJTYPE_MDI)
about.h    about.h
$$ELIF(PROJTYPE_SDI)
about.h    about.h
$$ENDIF //PROJTYPE_DLG
```

What you're basically doing with this code is making sure that the about.h file is copied in each of three scenarios: when the project type is dialog-based and the programmer did not uncheck the About box, when the project type is SDI, or when the project type is MDI.

Changing the ClassWizard files

Something else you should do when adding new classes or moving standard classes is to update the ClassWizard file (.CLW). This is done by editing the root.clw and dlgroot.clw files. At this point, open the root.clw file, and search for the line that contains the text "[CLS:CAboutDlg]." Once you have located it, change the HeaderFile and ImplementationFile lines to look like the following:

```
HeaderFile=about.h
ImplementationFile=about.h
```

When you have finished editing the root.clw file, open the dlgroot.clw file, and make the same modification to it.

Changing the AppWizard templates

In the previous section, you learned how to create a new template file and have it added to the new project (via the newproj.inf file). Now you will learn how to alter some of the generic templates created for you by the AppWizard when you created your custom AppWizard.

Changing the template resource files

Because this custom AppWizard will contain a new dialog, you have to insert a dialog template resource in the resource template file. When you created the custom AppWizard, you specified that you wanted your starting point to be "Standard MFC AppWizard steps." If you are following along by typing the demo, take a look in your project's Template folder. All of the template files necessary for creating every type of MFC executable have been copied there. This means that you can change anything you want. The first problem, however, is figuring out what to change! A resource file must be changed, but which one? The beta version of Visual C++ 6.0 used by the authors has created 17 different resource files (your mileage may vary). However, with a little investigation, it is easy to see which resource files should be changed.

The majority of these resource files end in a three-letter suffix that indicates the language support (English=enu, German=deu, and so on). There are also localized Macintosh versions of each resource file. Therefore, for an English-language application that is targeting an Intel PC running Windows, the number of resource files to contend with can be pared down to four: all.rc, dlgall.rc, dlgloc_enu.rc, and loc_enu.rc.

Opening the all.rc and dlgall.rc files and looking at the directives and macros indicates that these files are used as base resource files for all languages and platforms. These files, in turn, include the necessary language-specific and platform-specific resource files for things such as string tables and dialog resources. By process of elimination, the two files that must be updated with the new dialog resource are the loc_enu.rc and dlgloc_enu.rc files. The reason that two resource files exist for each language is because one file (loc_enu.rc) is used for document-based applications (SDI or MDI), and the other file (dlgloc_enu.rc) is used for dialog-based applications.

Now that which resource files to alter is known, you can add your dialog. Unfortunately, you cannot use the resource editor to create your dialog template resource as you normally would. This is because when you attempt to open the template resource file, the resource editor attempts to compile the file's resources.

Because these template files contain the AppWizard directives you've learned about, the file won't compile, and, hence, Visual Studio won't enable you to open it in the normal manner. You can, however, open a template resource file by setting the Open As option to Text in the File Open dialog.

However, because you certainly don't want to manually type the code required to define the dialog template resource, there has to be a better way. One common method is to create a dummy project solely for the purpose of creating the custom AppWizard dialog(s). Once the dialog is created in the dummy project, the code for the dialog template resource can be copied to the Clipboard. The custom AppWizard project can then be reopened, and the dialog template resource code pasted from the Clipboard into the desired resource file.

At this point, open the `loc_enu.rc` file, and replace its `IDD_ABOUT` dialog template resource definition with the following code:

```
IDD_ABOUTBOX DIALOGEX 0, 0, 160, 129
STYLE DS_MODALFRAME | WS_POPUP | WS_CAPTION
 | WS_SYSMENU
CAPTION "About $$ROOT$$"
FONT 8, "MS Sans Serif"
BEGIN
 CTEXT             "Written by"
  " $$PROGRAMMER$$",99998,7,64,143,12,NOT WS_GROUP,
 WS_EX_CLIENTEDGE | WS_EX_STATICEDGE
 LTEXT             "$$GENERAL_INFO$$",99999,7,7,144,40
 DEFPUSHBUTTON     "$$WEB_PAGE$$",
  IDOK,7,89,143,14,WS_GROUP
 PUSHBUTTON        "Cl&ose",IDCANCEL,7,107,143,14
END
```

Once you have finished with that `loc_enu.rc` file, open the `dlgloc_enu.rc` file, and make the same modification. Notice how the macros are being used in the dialog's definition. This is how the information the user entered in your custom AppWizard's dialog finally ends up in a resource file.

At this point, if you were to build the custom AppWizard, the user of your new custom AppWizard would be able to choose a dialog-based application, fill out the programmer and Web page information, and build a new project containing a spiffy About box. However, what if the end user of this application never looks at the system menu? This About box is meant to be seen! After all, you're creating this About box to get the application's end user to your Web site. Therefore, the last change that must be made to the template resource file is to add an About button to the main dialog defined in the `dlgloc_enu.rc` file. This means that every dialog-based application that is built with your new custom AppWizard will automatically contain an About button. To add an About button to the main dialog, simply open the `dlgloc_enu.rc` file, and replace the main dialog with the code in Listing 38-3. Notice that the Help button's position is based on whether or not an About button will be created.

Listing 38-3: Creating an About Button

```
IDD_$$SAFE_ROOT$$_DIALOG DIALOGEX  0, 0, 185, 92
STYLE DS_MODALFRAME | WS_POPUP | WS_VISIBLE |
WS_CAPTION | WS_SYSMENU
EXSTYLE WS_EX_APPWINDOW
CAPTION "$$TITLE$$"
FONT @@8@@, "@@MS Sans Serif@@"
BEGIN
 DEFPUSHBUTTON   "@@OK@@",IDOK,128,7,50,14
 PUSHBUTTON      "@@Cancel@@",IDCANCEL,128,23,50,14
 $$IF(ABOUT)
  PUSHBUTTON "@@&About@@",
   ID_APP_ABOUT,128,45,50,14
  $$IF(HELP)
   PUSHBUTTON      "@@&Help@@",IDHELP,128,62,50,14
  $$ENDIF // HELP
 $$ELIF(HELP)
  PUSHBUTTON      "@@&Help@@",IDHELP,128,45,50,14
 $$ENDIF
 LTEXT "@@TODO: Place dialog controls here.@@",
  IDC_STATIC,5,34,113,8
END
```

Changing the view and dialog template files

The very last code change that must be made involves changes to the view and dialog class implementation and header files. The reason that you have to change these is because the default view and dialog implementation files are used to declare the CAboutDlg class, which isn't what you want, however, because the about.h file created earlier already contains the CAboutDlg class declaration.

If you use the AppWizard to create an SDI or an MDI application called MyApp, the main application class will be declared in a file named MyApp.h and implemented in a file named MyApp.cpp. This is because a macro named $$ROOT$$ is set to the value project name and is used to name the file that contains the application class' definition and declaration. Here is a snippet from the NewProj.inf file that shows this. As you can see, the template header and implementation files for a document-based application class are named root.h and root.cpp, respectively.

```
root.h    $$root$$.h
root.cpp  $$root$$.cpp
```

Open the root.cpp file (located in the Template folder), and make the following changes:

1. Remove the CAboutDlg class declaration at the top of the file.
2. Remove all of the CAboutDlg member functions.

3. Include the about .h file at the top of the file after the include of $$root$$.h.

Now that the document-based template files are complete, it's time to modify the dialog-based template files. Because root.h and root.cpp are the template files used to define the application class for all dialog-based applications, the dlgroot.h and dlgroot.cpp files are used for the same purpose for dialog-based applications. However, unlike a document-based application, the CAboutDlg dialog for a dialog-based application is not defined in the same files as the application class. Instead, it is defined in the main dialog's implementation file, which is named dialog.cpp. Open the dialog.h file (located in the Template folder), and locate the following line of code:

```
afx_msg void OnSysCommand(UINT nID, LPARAM lParam);
```

Insert the following function declaration:

```
afx_msg void OnAbout();
```

Open the dialog.cpp file, and make the following changes:

1. Remove everything from the line containing the text $$IF(ABOUT) to the $$ENDIF, inclusive.
2. After the inclusion of the header file needed for automation support, add the following lines:

   ```
   $$IF(ABOUT)
   #include "about.h"
   $$ENDIF //ABOUT
   ```

3. Locate the ON_WM_SYSCOMMAND() entry in the MESSAGE_MAP section, and add the following line:

   ```
   ON_BN_CLICKED(ID_APP_ABOUT, OnAbout)
   ```

4. Add the following function definition to the end of the file.

   ```
   $$IF(ABOUT)
   void $$DLG_CLASS$$::OnAbout()
   {
    CAboutDlg().DoModal();
   }
   $$ENDIF //ABOUT
   ```

You are finished with the main code necessary to make your custom AppWizard work. However, let's add a couple of niceties to the application before building and testing it. Every time you use AppWizard to generate a project, the last dialog is a confirmation dialog that displays the options you have selected throughout the sequence of dialogs that were displayed. In the next section, you will learn how incredibly easy it is to modify this file to also display the options that were selected from your custom dialog(s).

Changing the CONFIRM.INF file

If you open the `confirm.inf` file (located in the Template folder), you will see that it looks a great deal like the `newproj.inf` file in terms of making heavy use of the AppWizard directives and macros. All you have to do to add your text to this file is simply enter it using the macros that you defined. Here is an example of how you might want to display the information entered for the About box. You can simply place this code at the top of the `confirm.h` file:

```
$$IF(PROJTYPE_DLG)
$$IF(ABOUT)
About Box Information
     Programmer:      $$PROGRAMMER$$
     Web Page:    $$WEB_PAGE$$
     App Desc:    $$GENERAL_INFO$$
$$ENDIF //ABOUT
$$ELIF(PROJTYPE_MDI)
About Box Information
     Programmer:      $$PROGRAMMER$$
     Web Page:    $$WEB_PAGE$$
     App Desc:    $$GENERAL_INFO$$
$$ELIF(PROJTYPE_SDI)
About Box Information
     Programmer:      $$PROGRAMMER$$
     Web Page:    $$WEB_PAGE$$
     App Desc:    $$GENERAL_INFO$$
$$ENDIF //PROJTYPE_DLG
```

As you may recall, the `$$IF/$$ELIF/$$ENDIF` structure mimics exactly what's in the `newproj.inf` to determine whether or not the `about.h` file is to be copied for the new project. The lines between these directives are simply lines of text to be displayed, verbatim, on the AppWizard's Confirmation dialog.

Using the Registry for persistent macros

Now let's think about this demo in terms of usability. You have a custom AppWizard that enables a programmer to create an MFC application that always contains an About box that displays the programmer's contact information. However, the way the code stands at this point, this information must be entered every time the programmer creates a new project. Even if the programmer is going to place an application description in the General Information field, two out of the three fields would have to be re-entered every time a new project is created with this custom AppWizard. Adding to that is the possibility that the same generic description may be used for every project.

For example, the description can be something as generic as "Please check out my Web page by clicking the button below to see other really cool applications I've done." or "Click the button below to view an up-to-date catalog of our products online." To solve this usability problem, you are simply going to modify the custom

AppWizard to save these values in the Registry so that they do not have to be re-entered for every project unless they are being changed.

Modifying the CAboutWizAppWiz class to use the Registry

Using the CRegistry class introduced earlier in the book makes this part quite simple. As a matter of fact, only one class must be modified (CAboutWizAppWiz). When you have completed the steps outlined in this section, you will be ready to build and test your new custom AppWizard.

1. Copy the registry.h and registry.cpp files from the companion CD (\Chap38\AboutWiz folder) into your custom AppWizard's folder, and add the registry.cpp file to the AboutWiz project.

2. Open the AboutWizAw.cpp file, and add the following #include directive to the top the file after the include of the chooser.h include file:

```
#include "Registry.h"
```

3. Add the following Registry key value #define before the InitCustomAppWiz member function definition:

```
#define ABOUTWIZ_KEY \
 "Software\\Visual C++ 6 Bible\\AboutWiz"
```

4. After the #define directive of the ABOUTWIZ_KEY, define the following static structure to contain the macro names, default macro values, Registry value names, and macro default values. The Registry value names are used to search the Registry in the key specified by ABOUTWIZ_KEY. If a value cannot be found (for example, the first time the application is run), the value contained in the macro default value is used to populate the custom dialog.

```
static struct
{
  char szMacroName[50];
  char szRegValName[50];
  char szMacroDefaultValue[50];
} macros[] = {
 "PROGRAMMER", "Programmer", "Programmer Name",
 "GENERAL_INFO", "General Info", "App Desc",
 "WEB_PAGE", "Web Page", "Web Page"
};
```

5. Place the following code at the end of the CAboutWizAppWiz::InitCustomAppWiz() function. As you can see, this code simply creates a CRegistry object on the stack and then iterates through the static macro's structure defined in step 4. For each entry in the macro's structure, the code attempts to locate the macro's value in the

Registry. If a value cannot be located, a default value is used. In either case, once a macro value has been established, the Dictionary is updated to reflect the macro's value.

```
CRegistry reg(HKEY_LOCAL_MACHINE, ABOUTWIZ_KEY);
CString strValue;
for (int i = 0;
 i < sizeof macros / sizeof macros[0];
 i++)
{
 if (reg.ReadString(macros[i].szRegValName,
  strValue.GetBuffer(strValue.GetLength())))
 {
  m_Dictionary.SetAt(
   macros[i].szMacroName, strValue);
 }
 else
 {
  m_Dictionary.SetAt(macros[i].szMacroName,
   macros[i].szMacroDefaultValue);
  if (m_Dictionary.Lookup(macros[i].szMacroName,
   strValue))
  {
   reg.WriteString(macros[i].szRegValName,
    strValue.GetBuffer(strValue.GetLength()));
  }
 }
}
```

6. Place the following code at the end of the `CAboutWizAppWiz::ExitCustomAppWiz()` function. The AppWizard DLL calls this function when the custom AppWizard DLL is being unloaded. You will use this function to save the values entered by the user.

```
CRegistry reg(HKEY_LOCAL_MACHINE, ABOUTWIZ_KEY);
CString strValue;
for (int i = 0;
 i < sizeof macros / sizeof macros[0];
 i++)
{
 if (reg.ReadString(macros[i].szRegValName,
  strValue.GetBuffer(strValue.GetLength())))
 {
  m_Dictionary.SetAt(
   macros[i].szMacroName, strValue);
 }
 else
 {
  m_Dictionary.SetAt(macros[i].szMacroName,
```

```
        macros[i].szMacroDefaultValue);
      if (m_Dictionary.Lookup(macros[i].szMacroName,
        strValue))
      {
        reg.WriteString(macros[i].szRegValName,
          strValue.GetBuffer(strValue.GetLength()));
      }
    }
  }
```

Now it's finally time to build and test the custom AppWizard. First, specify the active configuration as a release build. Then, build the project. As mentioned earlier, the custom AppWizard DLL filename will be the name of the project with an extension of AWX. When successfully built, this file will be copied into Visual Studio's Template folder.

Once you have built the project, you can test it by simply creating a new project and selecting the Wizard that you just created. For example, create a dialog-based application called `AboutWizTest`. The custom dialog will be the last dialog displayed. Figure 38-4 shows your customized dialog at work. Once you have entered the information for this dialog and clicked the Finish button, the Confirmation dialog is displayed. Verify that the information entered on the custom dialog is also displayed on this dialog. Click the OK button to create the `AboutWizTest` project.

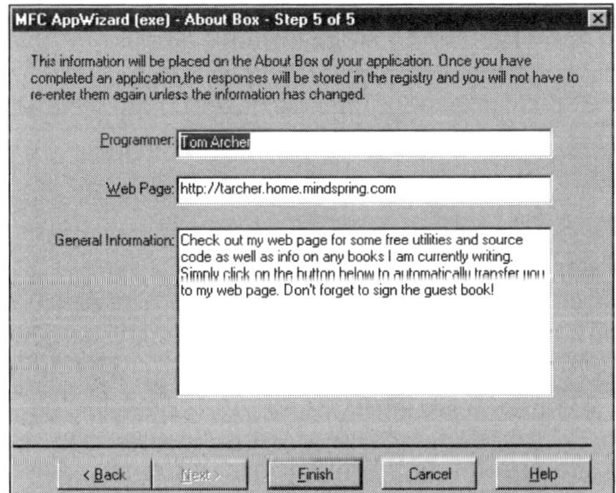

Figure 38-4: The AboutWiz custom AppWizard automatically creates an About box that can contain any contact information your application requires.

Once the `AboutWizTest` project has been created, build it, and run it. It should appear with an OK button, a Cancel button, and an About button. Clicking the About button should produce results similar to those shown in Figure 38-5.

That's it! You now have a custom AppWizard that will place an About box displaying your name, general information, and Web page in every application you create with your new custom AppWizard.

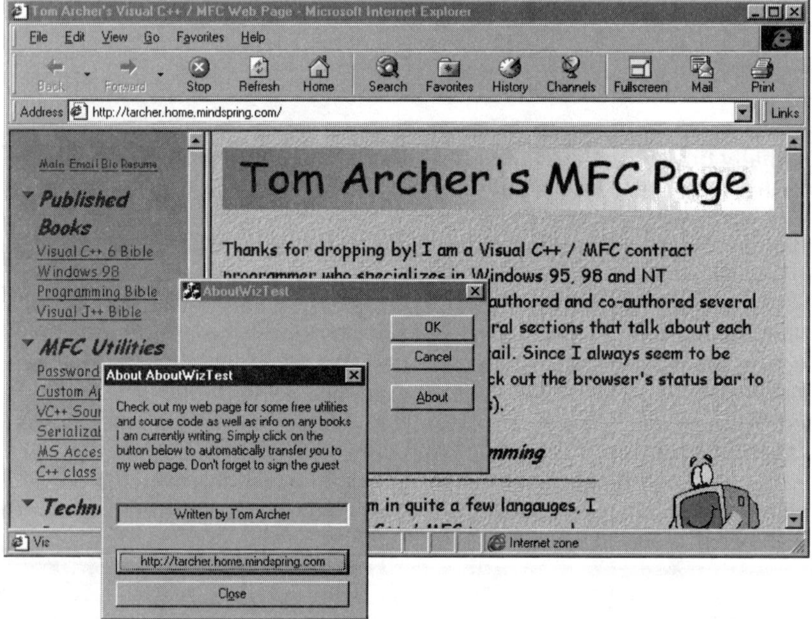

Figure 38-5: The AboutWiz custom AppWizard's About box includes a button that when pressed will automatically open the Web page of your choosing.

Summary

As you have seen throughout this chapter, the ability to create custom AppWizards is a great tool for increasing productivity because it enables you to define generic functionality in a given class of projects. While the steps involved are not difficult, they are time consuming until you get used to them.

The first custom AppWizard I programmed was the AboutWiz DLL that was used as the main demo in this chapter. Due to the learning curve involved as well as a lack of documentation on developing custom AppWizards, it took approximately 10 hours to finish. However, my second custom AppWizard took only 45 minutes. Hopefully, this chapter will enable you to traverse that learning curve a little quicker and enable you to create your first custom AppWizard in much less time.

✦ ✦ ✦

APPENDIX

What's on the CD-ROM

✦ ✦ ✦ ✦

The CD-ROM accompanying this book is organized into two sections. The first section contains the chapter-related content: all of the demonstration programs and supporting files can be found here. Each chapter except Chapters 3–7 and Chapter 18, has a corresponding folder. For instance, the folder for Chapter 2 is named Chap2, the folder for Chapter 29 is named Chap29, and so on. Within each of the chapter folders are subfolders for each of the demonstration programs noted in the chapter. For a guide to this section of the CD-ROM, see the section "Chapter Content," later in this appendix.

Note that throughout the text of the book, when a demonstration program is mentioned, the folder in which it resides is listed. For instance, in Chapter 10, the text for the first demo program is preceded by a line that reads as follows:

CD-ROM Location: **Chap10\BlitDemo**

Note also, if you use Explorer to copy the demonstration program folders to your hard drive, all the files have the read-only attribute set. You can change this from DOS: while you are in any of the folders on your hard drive, type **ATTRIB *.* /s –r**. This removes the read-only attribute for all files in the folder and their child folders.

You can also copy the files with the DOS XCOPY command. When you do this, the attribute bits won't be set.

There's one additional alternative. All the chapter content folders have been collected into a self-extracting file named `InstallContents.EXE`. If you run this program, the chapter content folders will be installed to your hard drive with none of the read-only attribute bits set.

The second section on the CD-ROM is for programming tools. For descriptions of these tools, see the section "Programming Tools," later in this appendix. The files can all be found on the CD-ROM in the Programming Tools folder.

Chapter Content

This section describes the CD-ROM contents that directly relate to the chapter content.

Chap1

This chapter is an introduction to Windows 98 and the Visual Studio set of tools. Included are C++ programs, an ATL-created ActiveX control, a J++ applet, a J++ application, and a Visual Basic Program.

HelloWorld1

The first program created for this chapter is a variation of the traditional "Hello World" program with which all C and C++ programmers start. The program was created with the MFC AppWizard. The only one of the default settings throughout the AppWizard process that was changed was to make the application a single document interface program.

It's important to note that you can now create programs with AppWizard that don't have document/view architecture support. This is a tremendously valuable option. Many times I created document/view programs that simply displayed graphics or images and totally ignored all the document features. Every time this happened, I'd look at the files in the project and long to delete the document source code files. (Good thing I never did; the project wouldn't have compiled if I had.)

HelloWorld2

I never thought there was a place for Win32 console applications until two things happened. First, I began teaching C++ at Rockingham Community College. I started my classes by creating AppWizard-based Windows applications. It only took about 15 minutes before I realized how lost everyone was. I then quickly learned about Win32 console applications. With these gems, I was able to teach C++ concepts without students getting lost in the myriad project and MFC classes.

Once I made this startling revelation, I began to realize the Win32 console [illegible] effort, I can create programs that do useful things, such as move and rename files, convert binary files to source code, and other tasks software developers need. I don't yearn for the old days when I could whip up a DOS application in five minutes to automate some programming tasks. And I (usually) don't even have to worry about segmented pointers or running out of memory.

This second program is a Win32 console application that displays "Hello Visual C++ Console World!" When you create a Win32 console application, one of the choices, believe it or not, is a "Hello World" application.

HelloWorld3

It won't be long into your programming career, especially with the direction in which Microsoft is pushing, that you'll need to create ActiveX controls. For most situations, the best way to do this is with the Active Template Library (ATL) Wizard. This creates the startup code for an ATL project and saves you the time and drudgery of doing it yourself.

Despite the ease with which you can create an ATL control, the control's footprint turns out to be relatively small. A full control with minimal code that's added (such as the HelloWorld3 control) ends up at about 37K. ATL controls have many options; one is the capability to use MFC. If you want to use MFC, be prepared for another 80–100K that'll be added to the footprint.

Chap2: Learnide

This chapter covers the Visual Studio IDE. In it, you learn how to use the features and tools to increase your productivity.

The Learnide program helps you get used to the Visual Studio IDE, and it teaches you how to use its features so that you maximize your performance as a developer.

CD-ROM Location: **Chap2\Learnide**

Program Name: **Learnide**

This is a completed version of the project.

Chap8

This chapter shows you how to respond to mouse and keyboard events. Three demo programs teach you how to create ClassWizard handlers and then use the command functions to respond.

MouseDemo1

This is a simple demo program that shows you how to respond to the main mouse events. It handles mouse movement events, mouse button down events, and mouse button up events. It does not handle middle mouse button events.

MouseDemo2

A special program named MouseDemo2 demonstrates how to change mouse cursors within an application. The program loads in 16 cursors and sets the cursor depending on the mouse position.

The application locates the current position of the mouse in the view window. Dividing the view window into 16 rectangular regions enables the program to decide which of 16 mouse cursors to use. When you run the program and move the mouse around inside the view window, you see the mouse cursor change. The name of the mouse cursor is also displayed.

Chap9

Chapter9 covers the topic of graphics. The three demo programs that accompany this chapter show readers how to perform basic draw operations.

PenBrushDemo

The first demo program in this chapter shows you how to use `CPen` and `CBrush` objects. Because these MFC classes encapsulate GDI pens and brushes, they make it easier for programmers to draw with pens and brushes.

With a menu selection, you can alternate between drawing lines and rectangles to the window. Another menu selection enables you to set the line width with which the lines and rectangle border will be drawn.

When lines are drawn to the window, you'll see the defined line patterns such as `PS_DASH` and `PS_DOT`. When rectangles are drawn to the window, you'll see the defined fill patterns such as `HS_BDIAGONAL` and `HS_CROSS`.

GraphicsDemo1

The GraphicsDemo1 program illustrates the basic techniques of drawing to a window. When the program runs, you can draw lines, rectangles, and ellipses. You can select the color with which the program will draw with the color selector common dialog. In addition, you can set the ROP code so draw operations are performed with different results.

To draw in the window, click the left mouse in the window. To change the draw operation, draw color, and ROP code, use the menu selections.

GraphicsDemo2

This program shows you how to create a clipping rectangle and use it to limit the window area in which draw operations occur. The program enables you to move the clipping rectangle around on the screen so you can experiment. To change the clipping rectangle to a different location, click the left mouse button in the window.

To draw the star-shaped figure, move the mouse around in the window. It'll draw in the window, centered around the mouse coordinates. You will, however, only see part of the figure because a rectangular clipping region is selected.

Chap10

Chapter 10 covers bitmaps and palettes. The subfolders in the Chap10 folder all contain programs and files related to the material in this chapter.

BlitDemo

This demo program shows you how to load and display bitmaps. The bitmaps are stored as resource objects, and the program loads them with the `LoadBitmap()` function. Four different `BitBlt()` rasters operations are shown: `SRCCOPY`, `SRCINVERT`, `SRCAND`, and `SRCPAINT`.

ShowDIB

This program contains a specially written class named `CDib`. The `CDib` class makes it easy to load, display, and save DIBs. You can use the `CDib` class in any of your programs by using the `DIB.cpp` and `DIB.h` files from this program.

Miscellaneous

In the Chap10 folder are two files. The `HSV.c` file contains a single function that converts RGB values to HSV values. The `Transparent.c` file contains a single function that draws a `CBitmap` object to the screen but masks it with a transparent color.

Chap11: FileExceptionTest

This chapter teaches the basics of implementing exception handling in your Win32 Visual C++ applications. The FileExceptionTest dialog-based application illustrates how to throw and catch exceptions (of type `CFileException`) in your C++/MFC code. The different `CFileException` causes are loaded into a combo box in `OnInitDialog()`. When an entry in the combo box is selected, an exception of that type is thrown and caught. The resulting exception description is then displayed on the dialog. The purpose of this demo is to illustrate how to throw and catch exceptions across function boundaries.

Chap12: MiniEdit

This chapter covers how to use the basic controls that are a part of the Windows operating system. The control creation process is examined, and you learn the differences between placing controls in a dialog box and placing them on a window. The different types of controls and how each of them are used is also covered.

The MiniEdit program is a minimal text file editor. It only understands files with the extension .mne. Using this application you can search directories for files. You can open, display, edit, and save these files as well as creating new ones. MiniEdit was implemented using Visual Studio's AppWizard to create a dialog-based application.

Chap13: AddressBook

This chapter teaches you how to create and use modal and modeless dialog boxes in your applications. Creating and using derived custom controls as well as serializing data from a dialog-based application are also illustrated.

The AddressBook dialog-based application is built up throughout this chapter and demonstrates many techniques useful in designing and programming dialogs. The demo teaches you the concepts of how to use DDX and DDV to facilitate moving data from the dialog's controls to the application's variables (and vice versa). In addition, a derived custom control (`CAutoCompleteComboBox`) is introduced and used with the demo. Finally, how to serialize data from dialog-based application is illustrated.

Chap14: ModalPropertySheetDemo

This chapter covers many aspects of the property sheet and property page controls that aren't covered elsewhere.

The ModalPropertSheetDemo shows how to programmatically create and control a modal property sheet and its property pages. In addition, techniques for doing things not inherently supported with property sheets and property pages, such as disabling tabs, enabling mnemonics, changing a tab's font, and so on, are illustrated.

Chap15

MFC provides plenty of tools to deal with data. This chapter covers the `CString` and `CFile` classes and the `CWnd` Clipboard support. It also provides some non-MFC classes that make it easier to deal with other types of data. One class is intended to give you easy access to the serial port: with the `CSerial` class you can communicate with other computers through your modem. Another thing that MFC left out was easy access to the Registry. This is the accepted way of storing configuration information for applications, and as an application developer you'll have to go to the Registry often.

The StringDemo Program

A demo program named `StringDemo` shows you how to use the basic `CString` functions. The application loads a file named `AESOP.txt` when it first runs. This text file contains many fables from *Aesop's Fables*.

You can search the text for any string. You can choose to do a case-sensitive search or a case-insensitive search. You can also perform a search and replace operation on the file. Once the search and replace operation is done, you'll be able to view the altered text inside of WordPad. (When you view it in WordPad, make sure WordPad's set for text wrapping.)

The FileDemo Program

You'll often use the `CFile` class to load and save buffers of data. For that reason, a program named FileDemo was written that does just that. It enables you to create a list of files and then saves all of the files to one large file.

You can also copy a single file from one source to a destination. To do this, just select Copy First File. The program then copies the first file in the list to a destination file you select.

CompressFile

This directory contains all of the files for the compression class library. You can build the .lib files by compiling this project.

CompressDemo

This is a simple demonstration program that shows what the class library can do. Using File Manager or Program Manager, run the program named `CompressDemo.exe`. It's a multiple document program. When it first runs, all you'll see is an empty application window.

CopyFile

One of the most common things that programs require with regard to file operations is a function that copies a file. A function that copies a file is called `CopyFile()`, and it takes three arguments. The first is the source filename, and the second is the destination filename. The third argument is the size of the buffer that the copy operation will use. The larger the buffer, the faster the copy operation. If the buffer specified is too large, the allocation may fail. Approximately 50K is recommended. The function returns a Boolean value indicating whether or not it was successful.

The `CopyFile()` function catches all file exceptions and displays an error message if an exception is caught. It's also part of the FileDemo program that is described later in the chapter.

Registry

To make it easier to access the Registry, a special class named `CRegistry` is included on this directory. To use it, just copy the two files into your project's directory, and add them to your project. Descriptions of the class functions along with examples follow.

Serial

A special class named `CSerial` is in the `Serial` directory. It enables you to easily add serial communications to your programs.

Chap16

This chapter covers the topics of sound and music. Playing wave files, MIDI files, and CD audio tracks is taught.

WaveDemo

The first demo program in this chapter plays six different prerecorded sounds. Three of the sounds are saved to disk as .wav files. The other three are part of the program's resource file. Users can select any of the six sounds and play them. The sounds can be played directly from disk or the resource file, or they can be loaded and then played at a later time.

MIDIDemo

The MIDIDemo program shows you how to play and manage MIDI files. Four MIDI files are in the MIDIDemo folder, and any one of them can be loaded and played. The program uses the `CMidi` class for performing MIDI operations. It makes playing MIDI files easy.

CDPlayer

Few programs play CD audio music. Most programs load and play MIDI files. This program plays the high-quality sound data found on audio CDs. It does so with the `CCDAudio` class.

Because the CD that comes with the book doesn't have any CD audio tracks, you'll have to put one of your own in the CD drive. After you do this, you can play any of the tracks on the CD. This program also enables you to pause playback and move around inside of each track.

Library

For convenience, use the `Sound.lib` and `Sound.h` files found in the Library folder of the CD-ROM. This makes adding sounds to any of your applications easier because you won't have to link in any source code.

Chap17

This chapter covers the topic of timers and idle processing. Both these techniques can make your program work smoother by letting things happen on a periodic basis.

Clock

The first demo program shows you how to create a clock application using a timer. The `SetTimer()` function passes a `NULL` as its third parameter and, therefore, causes a `WM_TIMER` message to be posted to the window.

This program enables you to view either an analog clock or a digital clock. To change the display, simply change the setting in the Type menu.

OnIdleDemo

The OnIdleDemo program shows you how to override and use the `OnIdle()` function. It shows numeric values for the `OnIdle lCount` value and the elapsed time since `lCount` was reset.

The OnIdleDemo program shows you a bar graph with the relative amount of time given to the program's `OnIdle()` function.

The program also draws a bar graph to provide a graphical indication of the relative amount of idle processing the application has made available to the `OnIdle()` function. If you move the mouse or perform window operations, such as resizing, the graph decreases. That's because all the messages Windows services reduce the amount of processing time available to the `OnIdle()` function.

Chap19: HexView

Chapter 19 covers single document interface (SDI) applications, documents, and views. The subdirectory in the `Chap19` directory contains the program and files related to the material in Chapter 19.

The HexView demo program loads text and other files and displays them as hexadecimal output, with the original text output compressed along the window's right side. It implements the `CScrollView` class and shows the user how to adjust the size of the scroll bars based on the current contents of the view itself.

Chap20

Chapter 20 covers multiple document interface (MDI) applications and splitter windows. The subdirectories in the `Chap20` directory contain programs and files related to the material in Chapter 20.

PaintObj

This demo program enables you to draw simple graphics (lines, circles, and boxes) onto multiple document windows (and then save those windows). The program teaches you to create and implement multiple documents from a single document/view pair.

DynSplit

This program shows you how to use the `CSplitterWnd` class to create and allocate dynamic splitter windows in a single document interface. The program performs no significant processing beyond displaying the splitter windows and implementing the code to split the windows. You can, however, use the code as a starting point for applications that do implement splitter window functionality.

Chap21

Chapter 21 covers printing routines. The subdirectories in the `Chap21` directory contain programs and files related to the material in Chapter 21.

HexViewMDI

This demo program loads text and other files and displays them as hexadecimal output. The program then teaches you how to print the contents of the screen display, including changing font pitches. The program uses MFC functions for all its processing.

PortLand

This program uses a simple set of Windows API function calls to print two pages, one in portrait mode and one in landscape mode, to the default Windows printer. The program uses no MFC functions and shows how to use the API for printing.

Chap22: MFCControl

This chapter covers advanced MFC topics. You learn how to use MFC's features to give your programs advanced capabilities.

The `MFCControl` control can be used in other programs. You can use it from Visual Basic, Visual J++, or Visual C++.

Chap23: BarsDemo

This chapters covers status and toolbars. A demonstration program is on the CD to show you how to incorporate toolbars into a MFC application.

BarsDemo is a basic drawing program that enables you to draw on the screen using different geometric shapes and colors. It also serves as a demonstration of how to add bitmaps to toolbar button faces.

Chap24

This chapter covers many aspects of the tree view and list view common controls that are not covered anywhere else.

ListCtrlDemo

This demo illustrates the basics of the list view control such as creating the control, adding columns and rows, setting the view type, and associating images with each row of data. In addition, this demo teaches how to dynamically size columns so that all columns are viewable without wasting valuable screen real estate, how to sort a column based on its content, and how to update the header control to show which column the data is being sorted by.

TreeCtrlDemo

This demo illustrates the basics of the tree view control such as creating the control, adding data to the control, and setting the different styles. In addition, this demo teaches how to edit tree view item labels in place and how to present and process context menus specific to each tree view item.

Chap25: ThreadDemo

This chapter covers the difficult topic of threads: how to use them and how to avoid the pitfalls.

The ThreadDemo program implements a multiple document framework. Each separate window is drawn by a separately instantiated thread. So if you create four child windows, four threads are at work drawing each window.

The thread functions draw a spirograph pattern in the windows. Three values determine the shape and pattern of the spirograph pattern, the integers `nFixedRadius`, `nMovingRadius`, and `nMovingOffset`. Each time the window is drawn, these values are incremented. This changes the pattern over time for a continuous variety of effects.

Chap26

This chapter teaches the concepts of the ODBC SDK and how to use it.

Database

This folder contains the sample database (`vc6bib.mdb`) that is used in the database chapters on ODBC (Chapter 26), MFC database classes (Chapter 27), and DAO (Chapter 28).

ODBCDemo

This is the first demo of the ODBC chapter and shows the basics of using the ODBC SDK. Boilerplate code is presented to allocate the different environment handles, connect to a data source, disconnect from a data source, and free the environment handles. In addition, this demo dynamically prepares SQL statements, executes the prepared SQL statements, binds program variables to result set columns, and fetches data from a result set using numerous ODBC SDK functions. It's important to note that you will need to create a DSN for the sample database for these demos to work. The steps for creating the DSN are outlined in Chapter 26.

ODBCClasses

This DLL presents a powerful class (`CODBCDynamic`) that shows off some of the more powerful capabilities of ODBC. This class enables the retrieval of data from any ODBC data source without your application having to know anything about the database schema until runtime. The only thing your application has to do in order to use this class is simply pass it the DSN and the SQL string to execute. The class accomplishes the rest by executing the specified SQL and using the `SQLNumResultCols()` and `SQLDescribeCol()` functions to dynamically query the data type that was returned for each column in the result set. Then, each column's SQL type is converted into its corresponding C data type so that the correct amount of memory can be allocated for each column of data. Once the memory has been allocated, the SQLGetData() function is used to actually retrieve the data. Based on the type of data being read in, this memory is mapped into the appropriate CDbVariant member variable and inserted into an MFC collection for your application's retrieval either by column name or by iterating through the collection.

ODBCDynamicTest

This application provides a boilerplate example of how to use the CODBCDynamic class. A dialog-based application, ODBCDynamicTest displays a combo box that lists every DSN in the system. When you select one of the DSNs, every table and query is then loaded into another combo box. Selecting one of these tables or queries results in the demo using the CODBCDynamic class to load every record and display it in a tree view control on the dialog. Note that all of this is done dynamically without the ODBCDynamicTest application having any knowledge of the database schemas of any of the data sources.

Chap27

This chapter covers the topic of programming with the MFC database classes.

UserMaintenance

This demo uses the MFC database classes to present a fully functional "user" maintenance application. The MFC database classes CDatabase and CRecordset are used to provide all the basic database operations (add/delete/update) for a sample Microsoft Access database (provided on the CD). Both sequential and random access I/O are used in this application to illustrate how each type of I/O is accomplished with the MFC database classes. When the application initializes, all of the Users in the UserMaster table are read and loaded into a list box, illustrating the manner in which a CRecordset object can be used to sequentially navigate a set of records. When a user is selected from the list box, its data (User Name, User Status, and so on) is displayed on the dialog. Once the user's data is displayed on the dialog, it can be changed and updated via a command button. Updates and deletes are performed via the CDatabase class' ExecuteSQL() function. Note that the demos in this chapter use the database (vc6bib.mdb) located in the Chap26/Database directory. In addition, you must create a DSN for that database, as outlined in Chapter 26, for this chapter's demos to work properly.

Parameterized

This demo shows how to use both parameterized recordsets and parameterized queries to retrieve data. This parameterized application works by displaying a dialog that enables the search and retrieval of users from a sample database (vc6.bib.mdb). This search is done via a parameterized CRecordset. The different steps necessary to create and use parameterized CRecordset are outlined in the chapter. In addition, once a record is retrieved, another CRecordset-derived class is used to retrieve other data concerning the user. This second recordset is based on a multi-table Microsoft Access query that returns data.

Chap28

This chapter covers the topic of DAO programming from a Visual C++ application.

DaoUserMaintenance

This demo application uses the MFC DAO classes to present a fully functional "user" maintenance application. The MFC DAO classes CDaoDatabase and CDaoRecordset are used to provide all the basic database operations (add/delete/update) for a sample Microsoft Access database (vc6bib.mdb) that is located in the Chap26\Database directory. Upon initialization, all of the users in the UserMaster table are read and loaded into a list box, illustrating the manner in which a CDaoRecordset object can be used to sequentially navigate a set of records. When a user is selected from this list box, its data (User Name, User Status, and so on) is then displayed on the dialog. Once the user's data is displayed on the dialog, it can be changed and updated. Updates and deletes are performed via the CDaoDatabase class' Execute function.

Chap29

This chapter teaches the programming of Windows DLLs. Both regular DLLs and extension DLLs are covered.

ImageViewer

This DLL demonstrates how to implement MFC document/view support for a given file type in a DLL. Basically it works by defining the document, view, frame, and resources required for the document template and exporting an initialization function for any application that requires support for the file type. Once you've placed your doc/view code into a DLL, any time an application requires implement support for the file type being supported, the application need only link with an import library and call the DLL's initialization function. The DLL automatically takes care of creating the document template and adding it to the application object's document template list.

ImageViewerClient

This is the client application for the ImageViewer DLL. Using this application, you can open any graphics files supported by the ImageObject imaging library. The document template used for opening and displaying the files is actually contained in the ImageViwer DLL. This application simply calls a single exported function, and the application automatically has support for any files that the document template supports.

KeybdHook

The DLL exports several functions for the purpose of illustrating how to install, control, and de-install a Windows hook function for monitoring keyboard activity. While the demo application was written specifically for the purpose of a keyboard hook function, the chapter and the majority of the source code can be used for almost any type of Windows hook function.

GlobalDllObjects

This DLL illustrates the not so simple task of sharing C++ objects across multiple invocations of a DLL. While sharing simple data is trivial via the `#pragma data_seg` directive, doing the same with C++ objects is not quite so simple. When a DLL declares a global C++ object, each time a client attaches to the DLL, the object's constructor is called. Obviously, this causes a problem when the DLL needs one C++ object that contains data for all attached clients. The GlobalDllObjects DLL utilizes the C++ *placement new* operator so that only one C++ object is created regardless of how many clients are attached to the DLL.

GlobalDllObjectsClient

This demo is the test application for the GlobalDllObjects DLL. This application simply attaches to the DLL and requests a global C++ object that the DLL creates when the first client attaches. This dialog-based application has a button that when pushed, displays (in a message box) the different information about the DLL's global C++ object (including its address in memory). By running multiple instances of this application, you can verify that only one instance of the C++ object is created and that once all clients of the DLL have "detached," the C++ object is destroyed.

Chap31: MFCControl

Chapter 31 covers the fundamental concepts of ActiveX, the different types of ActiveX components, and ActiveX control design with the Microsoft Foundation Classes. The subdirectory in the `Chap31` directory contains the compiled ActiveX control (OCX) and the source code files related to the material in Chapter 31.

The MFCControl demo program implements a simple, ActiveX control. The ActiveX control displays simple information and includes implementation of properties, methods, and events, as well as code to most efficiently redraw the control. The ActiveX control uses MFC functions to create and implement the interfaces that it exposes to calling programs.

Chap32: MFCServer

Chapter 32 expands on the knowledge that you acquired in Chapter 31 about creating a simple ActiveX control by applying it to using MFC to create ActiveX automation servers. The ActiveX in-process DLL that you create in Chapter 32 uses MFC to create a simple server program to log string entries to a file. The subdirectory in the `Chap32` directory contains the compiled ActiveX in-process server (DLL) and the source code files related to the material in Chapter 32.

The MFCServer demo program implements a simple, ActiveX in-process automation server. The ActiveX automation server outputs simple text logging information to a file. The ActiveX automation server uses MFC functions to create and implement the interfaces that it exposes to calling programs.

Chap33

This chapter covers the topic of the Active Template Library (ATL). In this chapter, you learn how to create ATL controls and use them in C++ programs.

DoublePendulum

This directory contains a project, a simple ATL control, that draws a double pendulum in the view window. Two functions are added that enable the radius and color of the design drawn to be altered. Code is added to the control's `OnDraw()` function to draw the double pendulum.

UseDoublePendulum

Once the ATL DoublePendulum control has been created, you need a separate application that uses the control. This program is a simple, single document program. Visual C++ has the capability to easily load and create a wrapper class for ActiveX components, and that's how this program was created.

Chap34

This chapter covers Internet programming. Topics such as FTP and sockets are among the valuable subjects taught.

AutoDialer

A demonstration program can be found on the CD-ROM in the `Chap34\AutoDialer` directory. It determines if a client machine has an Internet connection established. If it doesn't, the connection is automatically dialed and managed. You can rebuild the program by loading the `AutoDialer.dsw` project file, or just run the `AutoDialer.exe` program using Explorer.

The program uses functions that are part of the Remote Access Service. The `CAutoDial` class can be reused in your program simply by copying it into your project and compiling it with the other files.

Ftp

The Ftp program transfers files to and from FTP servers, and also obtains directory listings from FTP servers. Three menu entries call the program into action. The Get FTP File menu entry retrieves a file from an FTP server to a local drive. The Send

FTP File menu entry sends a file from a local drive to an FTP server. And the Get FTP Directory menu entry gets a directory listing for an FTP server.

A demonstration program can be found on the CD-ROM in the `Chap34\Ftp` directory. It's built around the `CFtpConnection` class. You can rebuild the program by loading the `Ftp.dsw` project file or just run the `Ftp.exe` program using Explorer.

SendEmail

A demonstration program can be found on the CD-ROM in the `Chap34\SendEmail` directory that sends a text message as an email message using SMTP. You can rebuild the program by loading the `SendEmail.dsw` project file or just run the `SendEmail.Exe` program using Explorer.

The program establishes a connection to a mail server on port 25, the reserved SMTP port. A conversation then follows in which the mail server is given enough information so that it can send the email. The conversation is ended with a special sequence of text, and the socket connection is disconnected.

Sockets

The Sockets program can either listen for a call from a remote endpoint or call to a listening endpoint. You can rebuild the program by loading the `Sockets.Dsw` project file or just run the `Sockets.Exe` program using Explorer.

A demonstration program can be found on the CD-ROM in the `Chap34\Sockets` directory that's built around the `CSocket` class. It spawns one of two different threads, depending on the menu option that's chosen.

Chap35

This chapter covers the `CHtmlView` class. This all powerful class enables you to easily create applications that can browse the Internet.

The MultiBrowser Program

The MultiBrowser program doesn't offer the same navigation functions that the SimpleBrowser program offers. That's because it serves a special purpose. It's intended to help you look through search results from a search engine.

A demonstration program can be found on the CD-ROM in the `Chap35\MultiBrowser` directory. As with the SimpleBrowser program, it's built around the `CHtmlView` class. You can rebuild the program by loading the `MultiBrowser.dsw` project file or just run the `MultiBrowser.exe` program using Explorer.

The SimpleBrowser Program

The SimpleBrowser program implements six of the `CHtmlView` navigation functions: `GoBack()`, `GoForward()`, `GoHome()`, `Navigate2()`, `Stop()`, and `GoSearch()`.

A demonstration program can be found on the CD-ROM in the `Chap36\SimpleBrowser` directory. It's built around `CHtmlView` and it gives you a simple browser without many extras. You can rebuild the program by loading the SimpleBrowser.dsw project file, or just run the SimpleBrowser.exe program using Explorer.

The UseBrowser Program

A sample program is included on the CD-ROM in the `Chap36\UseBrowser` directory.

Chap37

Macros are stored in plain text files with the .dsm extension. The default location where the Developer Studio looks for macro files is `devstudio/common/MSDev98/Macros/`. Three files may already be there. You may want to copy the `VCBible.DSM` file included on the CD accompanying this book in the `Chap37` directory.

The three files you may find in this directory are the `TemporaryQuickMacro.DSM`, `MyMacros.DSM`, and `Sample.DSM` files. The `TemporaryQuickMacro.DSM` file should be left alone because this is where the Developer Studio temporarily stores the information about your current Quick Macro. The `MyMacros.DSM` file is the default file for new macros. The `Sample.DSM` file includes several sample macros provided by Microsoft.

Chap38

This chapter covers the advanced topic of creating custom AppWizards for use with your own project types.

SDIAutomationWiz

This is a custom AppWizard that shows how to set default options for new projects. This particular application sets the project type to SDI and turns on automation for every new project created with this custom AppWizard. Custom AppWizards are great for situations where you must have the same default settings for multiple projects. Using this application's source code as a template, you can easily personalize it to preset almost any setting for your own custom AppWizard. In order to use the custom AppWizard without building it, you must copy the `SDIAutomationWiz.AWX` file into the Visual Studio template folder. By default, this folder is located on `C:\Program Files\Microsoft Visual Studio\Common\MSDev98\Template`.

AboutWiz

A much more advanced custom AppWizard, this application illustrates how to create and display customized dialogs, how to retrieve and set user-defined variables, and how to control which dialogs appear and in what order based on user interaction with the AppWizard. The end result is a custom AppWizard that automatically adds an About box into every new project created with this custom AppWizard. The About box provided contains contact information and a command button that brings up your Web page in a browser for the end users of the application that was built with this custom AppWizard. The custom AppWizard even saves this information in the system Registry so that the reader doesn't have to type it every time a new project is created. In order to use the custom AppWizard without building it, you copy the `AboutWiz.AWX` file into the Visual Studio template folder. By default, this folder is located on `C:\Program Files\ Microsoft Visual Studio\Common\MSDev98\Template`.

Programming Tools

The ProgrammingTools folder on the CD-ROM contains programs that'll help you when you need extensions to MFC. A few of the programs are full-blown applications based on a programming library. Some of the programs are demonstrations of programming tools. The libraries will make your job easier by adding functionality you need.

Three companies are represented in the collection of programming tools: Stingray Software, Dundas Software, and Lead Technologies. This section organizes these tools by company.

Most of the programs on the CD-ROM are self-extracting programs that automatically install when you run them. If the files have .exe extensions, run the program, and it will install. If a file has a .zip extension, you must use a program similar to WinZip or PKUNZIP to uncompress the file. Instructions for installing files that are compressed into a .zip file can be found after the archive has been uncompressed.

Stingray Software

Stingray software specializes in MFC extensions. These tools give your programs what they need to compete with the best software on the market.

Objective Grid Samples

Filename: `OG60DB.exe`

This file illustrates the various features of the objective grid. This tool gives your MFC applications a great grid control. With this grid control, you can create spreadsheet-type applications or many other things requiring a grid.

Objective Grid Demobrowser

Filename: `og60dbx.exe`

This demo shows off a DAO bound grid, with a dynamic splitter and a status bar record counter. It performs data access using the MFC DAO classes.

Objective Grid Designer

Filename: OGDesign.exe

This is the Objective Grid designer that ships with Objective Grid 6.0. This tool enables you to specify the layout of the grid with no programming. You can load the sample .OGL files provided.

Objective Grid CCE Evaluation Version

Filename: ogcceeval.exe

This is the evaluation version of Objective Grid CCE. This advanced version of the Objective Grid control enables you to experiment with creating your own grid-based programs.

Objective Toolkit

Filename: OT_Demo.exe

Now, for the first time, see all the Objective Toolkit features in one easy-to-use Explorer-style demobrowser. You'll be amazed at how many features exist when they are all put in an easily navigable tree. This toolkit sports MFC extension features such as extended tree controls and enhanced toolbars.

Objective Toolkit/X

Filename: OTX_Eval.exe

Objective Toolkit/X, or OT/X, makes the power of Objective Toolkit Pro available as an ActiveX control. With the strength of OT Pro and the flexibility of ActiveX, OT/X creates a unique, untapped market for a modern, Win32 GUI, with the ease of VB.

Objective Toolkit Demos

Filename: otpdemos.exe

This file contains the additional features you can use in the Objective Toolkit. By running these demos, you'll see how flexible and full-featured Objective Toolkit is.

Objective Chart Demobrowser

Filename: OC_Demo.exe

This is the new Objective Chart demo. It shows you how to use the Objective Chart library. With it, you can add charts and graphs to your MFC programs.

Diagram Demobrowser

Filename: od10demo.zip

This file includes Circuit, Logger, and white paper all in one package. These programs show you how to use the diagram controls. All demos include full source.

Objective Edit Demobrowser

Filename:`oe10demo.exe`

This file contains the Objective Edit Demobrowser. It's a tool that enables you to perform editing functions far more versatile and useful than the edit controls that come with MFC.

Dundas Software

Dundas Software specializes in grid controls and wizard-creation tools. Their libraries and tools are intended for use in MFC-based programs.

Ultimate Grid 97 for MFC Demo

Filename: `ug97demo.exe`

This demonstration program shows most of the grid's main features. Over 30 demonstrations are included, with each one covering a separate function group. Features include text style, cell types, scrolling, highlighting, column swapping, graphics, ballistics, finding, sorting, column and row locking, excel style, access style, charting, real-time data, calendar, hints.

Ultimate Wizard Factory

Filename: `uwfdemo.exe`

This program demonstrates the use of the wizards you can create with the Ultimate Wizard Factory. A program that executes a wizard to create class skeleton files is a nice utility to have around, especially if most of your customers are C++ developers. Until, of course, you can make your own using the Ultimate Wizard Factory.

Compuware NuMega Labs

NuMega Labs is the leading vendor of smart debugging tools for Windows programming. Its products include BoundsChecker, SoftICE, CodeReview, Smart Check, and TrueTime, among others.

BoundsChecker

Filename: `setup.exe`

NuMega's BoundsChecker, version 5.03, is the leading run-time error detection and debugging tool for Visual C++. BoundsChecker automates debugging within Visual C++ to improve development speed and efficiency. Its clear, detailed analyses of errors unique to C++ provide a special value to the programmer. BoundsChecker debugs errors in static, stack and heap memory, memory and resource leaks. It also validates over 5000 APIs at run time, including the latest Windows APIs, ODBC, ActiveX, COM, and Internet APIs.

✦ ✦ ✦

Index

& (ampersand), 109, 113
* (asterisk), 67, 68, 413, 530
\ (backslash), 413, 1027
, (comma), 823
- (dash), 63
/ (forward slash), 63, 1027, 1084
() (parentheses), 21
. (period), 413, 530
+ (plus sign), 21
? (question mark), 57, 413
_ (underscore), 498
#define directive, 368, 498, 849, 1161
#include directive, 356, 688, 693, 778, 780, 791, 825, 827, 853, 866–868, 1161
#pragma directive, 854
3D graphics, 280, 284–287, 423

A

abort procedure, 599
AbortDoc() function, 599–601
About button, 1157–1158
About.h, 1151–1153, 1159
AboutWiz project, 1150, 1161, 1181–1182
AboutWizAw.cpp, 1161
AboutWizAW.h, 1150
AboutWizTest project, 1163–1164
Accept() function, 1043
accelerator keys
  accelerator tables for, 113, 114–115, 118–121
  assigning macros to, 1121–1122
  adding, 24–26
  basic description of, 107, 113–121
  context menus and, 128
  defining, 114–115
  deleting, 23, 24–26
  editing, 24–26
  selecting appropriate, 116–118
  for single-stepping commands, 42
  standard Windows, 116–117
  viewing current, 23–24
  the Windows logical keyboard and, 151
Access (Microsoft), 97, 103–105, 731, 766, 801–802, 809, 814–815
access type values, 1020–1021
Active Desktop, 4
ActiveConfiguration() method, 1128
ActiveDocument property, 1128
ActiveProject property, 1128
ActiveWindow property, 1128
ActiveX, 4, 34–35. *See also* ActiveX controls
  basic description of, 905–952
  components, 74–76, 918–923
  SDK (Software Developer's Kit), 907, 916–917, 920, 922
ActiveX Control Test Container command, 14
ActiveX controls, 4, 905–909. *See also* ActiveX
  basic description of, 908–909
  creating, 11–14, 923–946
  drawing, 947–949
  embedding, 1015–1016
  MFC support for, 97, 105
  profiling, 74–76
  registering, 927–928
  using, 913–914
Add button, 743
Add Macro dialog box, 1113, 1116–1117
Add Member Variable dialog, 323, 333, 336
Add Property dialog box, 969
Add Variable button, 699
Add Windows Message Handler option, 133, 134
AddAtom() function, 471
AddBar() function, 677
AddDocTemplate member function, 527, 528, 535, 537, 558, 594, 867
AddFunctionDescription macro, 1130
AddItem() function, 525
AddKeyBinding() method, 1127
AddNew() function, 777, 824
AddNewObj() member function, 522, 523
AddNewProjectToFile macro, 1115–1116, 1118–1121
AddObject() function, 523
AddPage() function, 356
AddProject() method, 1127
AddRef() method, 809
Address field, 38
address space
  reserving, 482–484
  Windows 98 per-process, 474–475
AddressBook project, 312–319, 326–332, 337–348, 1169–1170
AddressBookDlg.h, 328, 339, 341–348
addressing mode, Intel-86 32-bit paged, 472–474
AddString() member function, 285
Advanced button, 925
Advanced Breakpoint dialog box, 40–41
Advanced Options dialog box, 532
AESOP.txt, 381–382
afile.css, 1088

AfxBeginThread() function, 98, 707–708, 710, 716
_afxBreakAlloc counter, 490–491
AfxCheckMemory() function, 491, 492
afxdao.h, 811, 819
afxDump object, 45
AfxDumpMemoryLeaks() function, 492
AfxEndThread() function, 711
AFX_EXT_CLASS macro, 863, 864
AfxGetApp() function, 536
AfxGetMainWnd() function, 453, 544
AfxGetResourceHandle() function, 120, 865
AFX.H, 490
afxinet.h, 1023
AFXMEM.CPP, 487, 489–491
AfxMessageBox() function, 45
AfxOleLockApp() function, 963
AfxOleRegisterServerClass() function, 959
AfxRegisterWndClass() function, 561, 562
afxres.h, 108, 114
AfxSetAllocHook() function, 491
AfxThreadData object, 43
Align Bottom button, 317–318
Align Left button, 317–318
Align Right button, 317–318
Align Top button, 317–318
AlignButtons() function, 359
Alignment property, 941
all.rc, 1156
allocMemDF flag, 491
Alpha processors (Digital), 472
AmbientBackColor() function, 939
ampersand (&), 109, 113
analog clocks, 454–461
AND operation, 216
ANSI (American National Standards Institute), 183, 498, 1000
ANSI_CHARSET constant, 183
Appcore.cpp, 462
AppendMenu() function, 124
applications
- AboutWiz application, 1150, 1161, 1181–1182
- AboutWizTest application, 1163–1164
- AddressBook application, 312–319, 326–332, 337–348, 1169–1170
- AutoDialer application, 1058–1061, 1179
- BarsDemo application, 1174
- BlitDemo application, 215–222, 1169
- CDAudio application, 438–441
- CDPlayer application, 440–447, 1172
- Clock application, 454–461, 1172
- CODBCDynamicTest application, 759–760
- CompressDemo application, 400–402, 407–410, 1171
- CompressFile application, 1171
- CopyFile application, 1171
- CreateFromClipboard application, 889
- DaoUserMaintenance application, 824–836, 1177
- Database application, 1175
- DisplayView application, 882–885
- DoublePendulum application, 1004–1005, 1007–1012, 1179
- Dynsplit application, 586–590, 1173
- FileDemo application, 392–400, 1170
- FileExceptionTest application, 261–272, 1169
- FirstCHTML application, 1090–1091
- GlobalDllObjects application, 856–861, 1178
- GlobalDllObjectsClient application, 861–862, 1178
- GraphicsDemo1 application, 1168
- GraphicsDemo2 application, 1168
- HelloWorld1 application, 5–9, 1166
- HelloWorld2 application, 9–11, 1166
- HelloWorld3 application, 11–14, 1167
- HexView application, 531, 545, 1173
- HexViewMDI application, 627–631, 1174
- HTMLViewer application, 1090–1091, 1099, 1100–1104
- ImageViewer application, 865–870, 1177
- ImageViewerClient application, 868–869, 1177
- KeybdHook application, 849–852, 1178
- KeybdHookClient application, 853–854
- Learnide application, 21–22, 1167
- Library application, 1172
- ListCtrlDemo application, 1174
- MFCControl application, 923–927, 1174, 1178
- MFCServer application, 1178–1179
- MFCTracer application, 48
- MIDIDemo application, 432–437, 1172
- Mini Editor application, 302, 1169
- ModalDemo application, 354–357
- ModalWin application, 640–661
- MouseDemo1 application, 136–142, 1167
- MouseDemo2 application, 144–149, 1167
- MultiBrowser application, 1071–1075, 1180
- ODBCClasses application, 1175–1176
- ODBCDemo application, 742–757, 1175
- ODBCDynamicTest application, 1176
- OnIdleDemo application, 463–466, 1172–1173
- PaintObj application, 566–571, 1170
- Parameterized application, 791, 795–798, 1176
- PenBrumDemo application, 1168
- PortLand application, 603–605, 628, 1174
- ProcessImage application, 894–901
- Registry application, 1171
- SendEmail application, 1052–1057, 1180
- Serial application, 1171
- ShowDIB application, 238–231, 1169
- SimpleBrowser application, 1068–1071, 1180–1181
- Sockets application, 1045–1052, 1180
- StringDemo application, 381–388, 1170
- ThreadDemo application, 1175

ThreadDemo1 application, 721–725
TreeCtrlDemo application, 692–697, 1174–1175
UseBrowser application, 1181
UseDoublePendulum application, 1179
UserMaintenance application, 780–788, 1176
WaveDemo application, 428–431, 1172
Apply button, 359–360
AppWizard
control registration and, 927–928
creating the Address Book project with, 312–319
creating a basic single document project with, 19–21
creating DLLs with, 862
creating FileExceptionTest with, 261
creating HelloWorld1 with, 5–9
creating HelloWorld2 with, 9–11
creating ModalWin with, 640
debugging with, 21–22, 31
document/view designs and, 513–516, 526–537, 555
manager (MFCAPWZ.DLL), 1140–1144, 1147, 1153–1155
MDI and, 557–558, 583–584
menu resources and, 108
multi-track, 1144
splitter windows and, 583–584
status bars and, 544
writing a custom, 1139–1164
ascent, 603
ASCII (American Standard Code for Information Interchange), 37, 413
keyboard input and, 115, 119, 150
Profiler data and, 69
records and, 71–72, 73
strings, null-terminated, 232
Asert Failed error message, 532
assembly language code, viewing, during debugging, 39
ASSERT macro, 46–47
ASSERT_VALID macro, 46–47
assertion(s)
basic description of, 46–47
errors, 718
Assign button, 25, 26
Assume No Aliasing option, 55
AssumeAliasing Across Function Calls option, 56
asterisk (*), 67, 68, 413, 530
/AT option, 64
ATL (Active Template Library), 5, 916, 920
basic description of, 105, 999–1016
controls, creating, 1000–1002
controls, using, 1010–1013
HelloWorld3 control, 11–14
atoms, 471
Attach() function, 127
AttachOnSetup() function, 627
Attributes tab, 1003–1004
audio. *See also* CD audio
basic description of, 423–448
playing recorded, 423–428
recording, 427–428
WAV files, 401, 423–428
Auto tab, 36
AutoCompleteComboBox.h, 337–339
AutoDialer project, 1058–1061, 1179
AutoDialer.dsw, 1058–1061
AutoDialer.exe, 1058–1061
AutoDialerView.cpp, 1060–1061
Automatic tab, 928
automation controllers (ActiveX), 905–908
basic description of, 908
using, 912–913
Automation interfaces, 808, 809
automation methods, 964–969
automation servers (ActiveX)
adding properties to, 969–970
basic description of, 905–908, 918–920, 953–998
instantiation of, 992–998
proxy-stub marshaling and, 914
registering, 959–960
types of, 919
using, 912–913
AVI clips, 706

B

Back() function, 1147
BackColor property, 938, 939
background
color, 166, 175, 938, 939, 1089
properties, in style sheets, 1089
Background color attribute, 166
Background mode attribute, 166, 175
backslash (\), 413, 1027
backward compatibility, 476
BarsDemo project, 1174
BaseCtl (BaseControl) framework, 907, 916–918, 920
_based keyword, 510
based pointers, 509–510
BASEMENU, 120
batch files, 61, 67–68
BCSMAKE, 87–89
beFailIfExists property, 1026, 1027
BeginPath() function, 187
_beginthread() function, 496
BeginTrans() function, 765, 813–814
BeginTrans() method, 806
behaviors, for the OnIdleDemo project, 464–466
bExclusive argument, 764
bExclusive flag, 811
bFileMappingObject parameter, 506

binary file(s)
  resources, viewing, 260, 846
  resources, retrieving, 846
Binder (Microsoft Office), 910
bit planes, 204–205
BitBlt() function, 209–212, 241–243, 649, 655, 658
BITMAP structure, 206–207, 210, 656–658
BITMAPFILEHEADER structure, 230–231
BITMAPINFOHEADER structure, 230–231
bitmap(s). *See also* graphics; images
  basic description of, 162
  buttons, 304–306
  compressing, 401
  device-dependent, 204
  displaying, 211–212, 293–294
  handling, in the ImageObject library, 875–877
  memory, 203–206, 209, 242–243
  objects, creating, 206–207
  objects, drawing, to the screen, 209–212
  painting, 650–654
  pasting, 654–655
  as pseudodevices, 164–165
  transparent, 649–650
bits per pixel, 204–205
BITSPIXEL constant, 205
bitwise operations, 524
BLACKNESS raster operation, 658
BlitDemo project, 215–222, 1169
BlitDemo.exe, 216–222
BlitDemoView.cpp, 216–222
blocking calls, 1043
<BLOCKQUOTE> tag, 1084
bmBits field, 656
bmBitsPixel field, 656
bmHeight field, 656
bmPlanes field, 656
bmType field, 656
bmWidth field, 656
bmWidthBytes field, 656
BN_CLICKED message, 346–348, 786, 830, 833–834
<BODY> tag, 1084
Boolean data type, 158, 182–183, 378–379, 964
Border property, [illegible]
BoundPropertyChanged() function, 936
Bounds Checker (Nu-Mega), 480
Bounds rectangle attribute, 166
box properties, 1089–1090

 tag, 1084
Break option, 42
Breakpoint object, 1125–1126
breakpoint(s)
  basic description of, 30–31, 35
  inactive, 41
  inserting, 39–42
  location, 40
  using, 39–43
Breakpoints dialog box, 31
Breakpoints object, 1125–1126
Breakpoints option, 40
brightness values, 224
Browse dialog box, 87
browse files
  creating, 87
  using, 87–89
Browse toolbar, 88
browsers
  Internet Explorer browser, 910, 1122, 1130, 1063, 1066–1068
  MFC, 89–90
  writing, 1078
Brush attribute, 166
Brush origin attribute, 166
brushes, 185, 187–189
BS_3STATE style flag, 281
BS_AUTO3STATE style flag, 281
BS_AUTOCHECKBOX style flag, 281
BS_AUTORADIOBUTTON style flag, 281, 282
BS_BITMAP button style, 305–306
BS_CHECKBOX style flag, 281
BSCMAKE.EXE, 87
BS_DEFPUSHBUTTON style flag, 281
BS_GROUPBOX style flag, 281
BS_ICON button style, 305–306
BS_PUSHBUTTON style flag, 281
BS_RADIOBUTTON style flag, 281
BSTRs, 1013–1015
buffers, 241–243, 255, 489
Build button, 21
Build Configurations dialog box, 26
Build learnide.exe command, 21–22
Build menu
  Build learnide.exe command, 21–22
  Build projectname.exe command. 62
  Execute learnide.exe command, 22
Build() method, 1127
Build projectname.exe command. 62
Build toolbar, 21
BuildProject object, 1125–1126
bUseCursorLib argument, 764
button(s)
  bitmap, 304–306
  captions, changing, 360–361
  messages, handling, 281–282, 286
  notifications, 332
  removing standard, 359–361
  repositioning standard, 359–360
  resource IDs for, 258
bytes per line, 231

C

CAboutDlg class, 1158
CAboutWizAppWiz class, 1161–1164
CAccelerators class, 119
CAccessDb class, 249–251
cache hit rates, 474
CAddItemDlg class, 693
CAddressBookDlg class, 345–346
call graphs, displaying, 89
Call Graph window, 89
CALL instructions, 76
Call Stack window, 38–39
callback procedures, setting timers with, 452–454
CALL.DPP, 77
CallNextHook() function, 849, 854
CallNextHookEX() function, 851
CallWindowProc() function, 591
Cancel button, 359–360, 599–601
CanSerialize() function, 344
CanTransact() function, 765
cap.ini, 77–78
cap.txt, 77
CAPDUMP.EXE, 78
Caption field, 108, 109
Caption property, 351
CaptionMethod() method, 928–934, 936, 937, 944
CArchive class, 340, 341, 345
Cartesian coordinate system, 170
case-sensitivity, 117, 381
catch blocks, 247–248, 254, 256–257, 267–271
CATCH macro, 254
catching exceptions
    basic description of, 246–248
    catching multiple exception types, 256–257
    selecting functions for, 267–269
CAutoCompleteComboBox class, 337–339
CAutoDial class, 1059
/CB option, 64
CBitmap class, 104, 204–207, 209–212, 215–222, 241–243, 480, 655, 657
CBitmapButton class, 102, 304–306
CBRS_BOTTOM constant, 673
CBRS_BOTTOM style flag, 666
CBRS_FLYBY constant, 673
CBRS_NOALIGN constant, 673
CBRS_NOALIGN style flag, 666
CBRS_TOOLTIPS constant, 673
CBRS_TOP constant, 673
CBRS_TOP style flag, 666
CBrush class, 103–104, 187–189, 480, 947
CBS_AUTOHSCROLL style flag, 299
CBS_DISABLENOSCROLL style flag, 299
CBS_DROPDOWN style flag, 299
CBS_DROPDOWNLIST style flag, 299
CBS_HASSTRINGS style flag, 299
cbSize parameter, 297
CBS_LOWERCASE style flag, 299
CBS_OEMCONVER style flag, 299
CBS_OWNERDRAWFIXED style flag, 299
CBS_OWNERDRAWVARIABLE style flag, 299
CBS_SIMPLE style flag, 299
CBS_SORT style flag, 299
CBS_UPPERCASE style flag, 299
CButton class, 98, 102, 278, 281–283, 826
CCachedDataPathProperty class, 99
CCDAudio class, 431, 438–447
CCheckListBox class, 102
CClientDC class, 104, 172–173
CClockView class, 454–461
CCmdTarget class, 524–526, 906, 955–956, 972
CColorDialog class, 101
CComboBox class, 102, 278
CCommaDelimitedFile class, 248–249
CCommonDialog class, 101
CCompressDemoView class, 408
CCompressedFile class, 399–400
CContact class, 327–328, 330–332, 341–342, 346
CControlBar class, 676
CCtrlView class, 100, 542
CCustomAppWiz class, 1141–1144, 1146–1147, 1148
CCustomer class, 266
CCustomerException class, 264–265
CCustomerException exception, 264–265
CD audio. *See also* sound
    advantages/disadvantages of, 437–438
    basic description of, 437–441
    CDAudio project and, 438–441
    CDPlayer project and, 440–447, 1172
    MIDI and, comparison of, 431–432, 437
CDaoDatabase class, 104, 809–813, 819, 827, 832
CDaoException class, 809–810, 811–813
CDaoQueryDef class, 104
CDaoRecordset class, 104, 809–810, 814–824, 827
CDaoRecordView class, 101, 542, 809–810
CDaoTableDef class, 104
CDaoWorkspace class, 104, 809–810, 813–814
CDatabase class, 104, 762–765
CDataPathProperty class, 99
CDAudio project, 438–441
CDBException class, 763
CDBVariant class, 757, 758
CDBVariantEX class, 757
CDC class, 104, 166, 168–169, 172–173, 176–177, 226, 242–243, 606, 610, 622
_cdecl keyword, 498
CDialog class, 101, 311, 319–322, 331, 350, 351, 635, 688
CDialogBar class, 670
CDib class, 229, 232–238
CDocItem class, 524–526
CDocManager class, 535–536

CDocTemplate class, 531–532, 535, 555, 556
CDocument class, 47, 111, 112, 515–527, 536, 554, 555, 556–558, 564–565
CDoublePend class, 1004–1010
CDPlayer project, 440–447, 1172
CDPlayer.exe, 440
CDPlayerDlg.cpp, 440–447
CDragListBox class, 102
CD-ROMs, detecting, 502
CDumpContext class, 45
CDynLinkLibrary class, 863, 865, 1147
CDynsplitDoc class, 586
CEdit class, 102, 277, 278, 287–290, 322–323, 333, 335, 687
CEditView class, 100, 542
CException class, 98, 247, 253–267, 271
CFile class, 99, 245, 388–400, 408, 409, 1058
CFileDialog class, 101
CFileException class, 258–263
CFileException exception, 245, 255–256
CFindReplaceDialog class, 101
CFindSheet class, 361–363
CFirstCHTMLView class, 1066
CFont class, 104, 179–180, 270–280
CFontDialog class, 101
CFormView class, 101, 542, 543
CFrameWnd class, 109, 111–113, 122, 126, 129, 514, 543–544, 640, 645–646, 650, 654
CFrameWnd() function, 561
CFtpConnection class, 1021–1032
CFtpFileFind class, 1031
CGA video, 204–205
CGlobalDllObjectsApp class, 856
CGopherFile class, 99
CHANGECBCHAIN message, 41
ChangeFormat() function, 886, 887
CHeaderCtrl class, 102
check boxes
  creating, 283
  setting/interrogating, 283
checkAlwaysMemDF flag, 491
CheckMenuItem() function, 124
Checkpoint() function, 47, 48
child windows, subclassing, 391–394
CHotKeyCtrl class, 102
chroma, 224
CHTMLView class, 4, 542, 1063–1106
CImageAreaProcesses class, 891–894
CImageObject class, 878, 879, 880, 882–883, 889
CImagePointProcesses class, 891–894
CImageViewer class, 867
CImageViewerClientApp class, 869
CImageViewerDoc class, 865
CInternetFile class, 1029–1030
CInternetSession class, 1019–1020, 1057
<CITE> tag, 1084
CKeybdHoopApp class, 849, 852
class factories, 958, 997
Class View, 18–19, 21
classes (listed by name)
  CAboutDlg class, 1158
  CAboutWizAppWiz class, 1161–1164
  CAccelerators class, 119
  CAccessDb class, 249–251
  CAddItemDlg class, 693
  CAddressBookDlg class, 345–346
  CArchive class, 340, 341, 345
  CAutoCompleteComboBox class, 337–339
  CBitmap class, 104, 204–207, 209–212, 215–222, 241–243, 480, 655, 657
  CBitmapButton class, 102, 304–306
  CBrush class, 103–104, 187–189, 480, 947
  CButton class, 98, 102, 278, 281–283, 826
  CCachedDataPathProperty class, 99
  CCDAudio class, 431, 438–447
  CCheckListBox class, 102
  CClientDC class, 104, 172–173
  CClockView class, 454–461
  CCmdTarget class, 524–526, 906, 955–956, 972
  CColorDialog class, 101
  CComboBox class, 102, 278
  CCommaDelimitedFile class, 248–249
  CCommonDialog class, 101
  CCompressDemoView class, 408
  CCompressedFile class, 399–400
  CContact class, 327–328, 330–332, 341–342, 346
  CControlBar class, 676
  CCtrlView class, 100, 542
  CCustomAppWiz class, 1141–1144, 1146–1147, 1148
  CCustomer class, 266
  CCustomerException class, 264–265
  CDaoDatabase class, 104, 809–813, 819, 827, 832
  CDaoException class, 809–810, 811–813
  CDaoQueryDef class, 104
  CDaoRecordset class, 104, 809–810, 814–824, 827
  CDaoRecordView class, 101, 542, 809–810
  CDaoTableDef class, 104
  [illegible]
  CDatabase class, 104, 762–765
  CDataPathProperty class, 99
  CDBException class, 763
  CDBVariant class, 757, 758
  CDBVariantEX class, 757
  CDC class, 104, 166, 168–169, 172–173, 176–177, 226, 242–243, 606, 610, 622
  CDialog class, 101, 311, 319–322, 331, 350, 351, 635, 688
  CDialogBar class, 670
  CDib class, 229, 232–238
  CDocItem class, 524–526

CDocManager class, 535–536
CDocTemplate class, 531–532, 535, 555, 556
CDocument class, 47, 111, 112, 515–527, 536, 554, 555, 556–558, 564–565
CDoublePend class, 1004–1010
CDragListBox class, 102
CDumpContext class, 45
CDynLinkLibrary class, 863, 865, 1147
CDynsplitDoc class, 586
CEdit class, 102, 277, 278, 287–290, 322–323, 333, 335, 687
CEditView class, 100, 542
CException class, 98, 247, 253–267, 271
CFile class, 99, 245, 388–400, 408, 409, 1058
CFileDialog class, 101
CFileException class, 258–263
CFindReplaceDialog class, 101
CFindSheet class, 361–363
CFirstCHTMLView class, 1066
CFont class, 104, 179–180, 270–280
CFontDialog class, 101
CFormView class, 101, 542, 543
CFrameWnd class, 109, 111–113, 122, 126, 129, 514, 543–544, 640, 645–646, 650, 654
CFtpConnection class, 1021–1032
CFtpFileFind class, 1031
CGlobalDllObjectsApp class, 856
CGopherFile class, 99
CHeaderCtrl class, 102
CHotKeyCtrl class, 102
CHTMLView class, 4, 542, 1063–1106
CImageAreaProcesses class, 891–894
CImageObject class, 878, 879, 880, 882–883, 889
CImagePointProcesses class, 891–894
CImageViewer class, 867
CImageViewerClientApp class, 869
CImageViewerDoc class, 865
CInternetFile class, 1029–1030
CInternetSession class, 1019–1020, 1057
CKeybdHoopApp class, 849, 852
Clearnide class, 21
CLearnideView class, 21
CList class, 540
CListBox class, 102, 277, 278, 283–286, 826
CListCtrl class, 102, 607–704, 680
CListView class, 100, 542
CLongBinary class, 104
CMainFrame class, 514, 527, 356
CMainWindow class, 97, 453
CMDIChildFrame class, 112
CMDIChildWnd class, 100, 554, 555, 562–563, 566, 576, 577, 582
CMDIFrameWnd class, 100, 111, 112, 116, 543, 560–562
CMemFile class, 99
CMemoryState class, 47–48
CMenu class, 122–123, 125–130
CMetaFileDC class, 104
CMFCControlWinCtrl class, 927, 928–929, 935, 938, 947
CMFCControlWinPropPage class, 940
CMFControlWinCtrl class, 943
CMidi class, 432–437, 438
CModalWinView class, 641, 642
CMonikerFile class, 99
CMouseHandlerView class, 134
CMultiDocTemplate class, 112, 531, 554, 556, 564, 566, 867
CMyDoc class, 527
CMyTreeCtrl class, 695
CMyView class, 527
CNumericEdit class, 334, 336
CObject class, 46–47, 98, 99, 103–104, 127, 521, 524
CODBCDynamic class, 729, 751–759
CODBCRecord class, 757
COleClientItem class, 524–525
COleControl class, 102, 939
COleDBRecordView class, 542
COleDocument class, 524, 538, 557
COleIPFrameWnd class, 100
COleObjectFactory class, 958, 960, 998
COleResizeBar class, 670
COleServerItem class, 524–525
COleStreamFile class, 99
COMBOBOX class, 278
CPaintDC class, 104
CPaintobjDoc class, 566
CPalette class, 104, 204, 226, 228–229
CPen class, 103–104, 185–187, 480
CPoint class, 135
CPreviewDC class, 622–623
CPrintDialog class, 101, 626–627
CPrintInfo class, 607–608, 613, 621
CProgressCtrl class, 1029
CPropertyPage class, 350–357, 367–372
CPropertyPageDialog class, 101
CPropertySheet class, 350–358, 365, 370, 372
CReBar class, 677
CRecentFileList class, 99
CRecordset class, 104, 766–777, 780, 790–791, 794, 795
CRecordView class, 101, 542
CRect class, 278, 280
CRegistry class, 413–417, 1161
CRgn class, 104, 200–201
CRichEditCtrl class, 102
CRichEditView class, 100, 542

(continued)

classes (listed by name) *(continued)*
- CRuntimeClass class, 580–581, 863, 992
- CSampleDocument class, 536
- CSampleView class, 614, 617, 618, 619
- CScrollBar class, 102, 278, 294–298
- CScrollView class, 101, 542, 545, 622
- CSerial class, 410–417
- CSharedFile class, 99
- CSimpleException class, 265–266
- CSimpleTermDoc class, 516–517
- CSingleDocTemplate class, 112, 527, 528, 529–531, 533–534, 556, 586
- CSliderCtrl class, 102
- CSocket class, 1040–1052
- CSocketFile class, 99
- CSpinButtonCtrl class, 102
- CSplitterWnd class, 94, 95, 98, 100, 559–560, 574–586
- CStatic class, 102, 278, 290–294
- CStatusBar class, 544, 664, 665–669, 670
- CStatusBarCtrl class, 102
- CStdioFile class, 99
- CString class, 98, 375–388, 531, 693, 826, 1150
- CSubbedEdit class, 593–594
- CSupplier class, 266
- CTabCtrl class, 103
- CTest class, 272–275, 858–862
- CTestException class, 271–273
- CToolBar class, 533, 544, 670–671, 673, 862
- CToolBarCtrl class, 103
- CToolTipCtrl class, 103
- CTracker class, 958, 992
- CTreeCtrl class, 103, 680–697, 795
- CTreeView class, 100, 542
- CUser class, 828
- CUserException class, 266
- CUserMasterSet class, 773
- CValidatePtr class, 256–257
- CView class, 21, 100, 111, 112, 537–544, 554, 555, 556, 611–613, 1064
- CWave class, 424, 428–431, 430
- CWebDialog class, 1075
- CWinApp class, 112, 119, 461–463, 528, 534, 535, [illegible]
- CWinThread class, 95, 119, 705, 707, 709, 711–714
- CWnd class, 21, 94, 95, 97, 98, 100, 120, 171, 277, 280, 420, 453, 645–646, 717–718
- DoublePend class, 1010–1012
- EDIT class, 278
- FrameWnd class, 100
- GetScrollInfo class, 297
- HIGH_PRORITY_CLASS class, 717
- IDLE_PRIORITY_CLASS class, 717
- LISTBOX class, 278
- LoadAccelerators class, 119
- ModalFrameWnd class, 642
- NORMAL_PRORITY_CLASS class, 716, 717
- REALTIME_PRORITY_CLASS class, 717
- SetScrollInfo class, 297
- TranslateAccelerator class, 119
- VWnd class, 541
- WindApp class, 112

ClassWizard
- adding handlers with, 651
- creating classes with, 321–322, 351
- creating dialogs with, 321–322, 326, 334, 336
- creating functions with, 539, 866
- creating menus with, 110, 121–122
- creating recordsets with, 814–815
- creating variables with, 261
- files, changing, 1155–1156

ClassWizard dialog box, 929
Clean() method, 1127
CleanOutRecordArray() function, 754
Clearnide class, 21
CLearnideView class, 21
CLI (Call Level Interface) specification, 734
client areas, 170, 649–661
ClientToScreen() function, 129, 135
Clipboard, 538, 889
- commands, keystroke combinations for, 117
- duplicating dialogs with, 826
- formats, predefined, 418–420
- memory management and, 480
- pasting the UUID from, 922
- using, 417–421

ClipCursor() function, 149
clipping
- basic description of, 164
- modes, 201
- regions, 166, 200–201

Clipping region attribute, 166
CList class, 540
CListBox class, 102, 277, 278, 283–286, 826
CListCtrl class, 102, 607–704, 680
CListView class, 100, 542
Clock project, 454–461, 1172
Clock.exe, 454
ClockView.cpp, 454–461
CLongBinary class, 104
Close button, 783
Close() function, 405, 409–411, 416, 427, 433, 440, 1030, 1058
CMainFrame class, 514, 527, 356
CMainFrame() function, 130
CMainWindow class, 97, 453
CMDIChildFrame class, 112
CMDIChildWnd class, 100, 554, 555, 562–563, 566, 576, 577, 582

CMDIFrameWnd class, 100, 111, 112, 116, 543, 560–562
CMDIMsg() function, 111
CMemFile class, 99
CMemoryState() function, 48
CMemoryState class, 47–48
CMenu class, 122–123, 125–130
CMetaFileDC class, 104
CMFCControlWinCtrl class, 927, 928–929, 935, 938, 947
CMFCControlWinPropPage class, 940
CMFControlWinCtrl class, 943
CMidi class, 432–437, 438
CModalWinView class, 641, 642
CMonikerFile class, 99
CMouseHandlerView class, 134
CMultiDocTemplate class, 112, 531, 554, 556, 564, 566, 867
CMY color, 223. *See also* color
CMyDoc class, 527
CMYK color, 223
CMyTreeCtrl class, 695
CMyView class, 527
CN_UPDATE_COMMAND_UI message, 110–111
CNumericEdit class, 334, 336
CObject class, 46–47, 98, 99, 103–104, 127, 521, 524
CoClass interface, 956–958, 978, 994, 1003
CODBCColumnInfo() function, 756
CODBCDynamic class, 729, 751–759
CODBCDynamicTest project, 759–760
CODBCRecord class, 757
Code Generation option, 33
COleClientItem class, 524–525
COleControl class, 102, 939
COleDBRecordView class, 542
COleDispatchException exception, 972
COleDocument class, 524, 538, 557
COleIPFrameWnd class, 100
COleObjectFactory class, 958, 960, 998
COleResizeBar class, 670
COleServerItem class, 524–525
COleStreamFile class, 99
color
  background, 166, 175, 938, 939, 1089
  in bitmaps, 657, 659–660
  brushes and, 188–189
  CMY color, 223
  CMYK color, 223
  for common shades, 173–174
  for controls, 307–308
  converting, between color systems, 224–225
  depth, 204–205, 885–887
  GDI support for, 173–176
  palettes, 205, 222–229, 880–882
  pens and, 186
  raster operations and, 212
  selection states and, 159
  static, 225
  text, 180
  of values during debugging, 37
COLORREF data type, 173–174
columns
  adding, to list views, 701–703
  sizing, 702–703
COM objects, 905, 907, 909, 912, 914–915, 918, 1000, 1002–1003
COM ports, 411
COMBOBOX class, 278
comctl32.dll, 277, 679
command IDs, 121–122
command line, 32–34, 959–960
Command list box, 25
Command tab, 27
commands. *See also* commands (listed by name)
  adding, to the Tools menu, 85–86
  editing, 86
commands (listed by name). *See also* commands
  ActiveX Control Test Container command, 14
  Build learnide.exe command, 21–22
  Copy command, 519
  Customize command, 24, 26, 922
  Cut command, 541
  Execute learnide.exe command, 22
  Exit command, 23
  Go To command, 87
  Macro command, 1129
  MCI_CLOSE command, 426, 439–440
  MCI_OPEN command, 426, 439–440
  MCI_PAUSE command, 439
  MCI_PLAY command, 426
  MCI_PLAY command, 426, 439–440
  MCI_RECORD command, 426
  MCI_SAVE command, 426
  MCI_SEEK command, 426, 439–440
  MCI_SET command, 439
  MCI_STATUS command, 439
  MCI_STOP command, 426, 439–440
  Open command, 401
  Option command, 51
  Paste command, 115, 107, 520, 541
  Print command, 613
  Profile command, 60
  Record Quick Macro command, 1110
  Remote Connection command, 50, 60
  Run to Cursor command, 42
  Set Next Statement command, 43
  Source Browser command, 87, 89
  Step Into command, 42
  Step Out command, 42
  Step Over command, 42
  Threads command, 44
  TRACE command, 21, 23
  XCOPY command, 1164

commdlg.dll, 627
CommDlgExtendedError() function, 627
CommentOut macro, 1121–1122
comments, in the Add Member Variable dialog box, 336
Commit() function, 271
commitment controls, 765
CommitTrans() function, 765, 814
COMMON_IMPORT_EXPORT macro, 864–865
Company Master table, 794
Compare() function, 378
CompareNoCase() function, 378
CompareString API, 1014
comparisons, of CString objects, 378–379
compatibility, backward, 476
compiler(s)
  ActiveX controls and, 921
  ATL and, 1000
  extensions, 498
  ISO-compliant compilers, 1000
  keywords, 498–499
  memory, 488–492
  multithreading and, 720
  options, for debugging, 32
  project performance and, 54–56
compound documents, 906
CompressDemo project, 400–402, 407–410, 1171
CompressDemo.exe, 400
CompressFile project, 1171
compression
  with the CompressDemo project, 400–402, 407–410, 1171
  with the CompressFile project, 1171
  Huffman compression, 402, 403, 409
  LZSS compression, 402, 404, 409
  LZW compression, 402, 404–405, 409, 877
  opening files after, 409
  PACKBITS compression, 890–891
  methods, overview of, 402–410
comSpec environment variable, 79
Configuration object, 1125–1126
Configurations object, 1125–1126
confirm.h, 1160
CONFIRM.INF, 1160
Connect button, 50
Connect() function, 1041, 1042, 1043
connection points, 943
constants. *See also* constants (listed by name)
  bitmap positioning, 306
  CScrollbar attribute, 297
  text alignment, 177
  VBScript, 1123–1124
constants (listed by name). *See also* constants
  ANSI_CHARSET constant, 183
  BITSPIXEL constant, 205
  CBRS_BOTTOM constant, 673
  CBRS_FLYBY constant, 673
  CBRS_NOALIGN constant, 673
  CBRS_TOOLTIPS constant, 673
  CBRS_TOP constant, 673
  dbOpenDynaset constant, 819
  dbOpenSnapshot constant, 819
  dbOpenTable constant, 819
  DEFAULT_CHARSET constant, 183
  FW_BLACK constant, 182
  FW_BOLD constant, 182
  FW_DEMIBOLD constant, 182
  FW_DONTCARE constant, 182
  FW_EXTRABOLD constant, 182
  FW_EXTRALIGHT constant, 182
  FW_HEAVY constant, 182
  FW_LIGHT constant, 182
  FW_MEDIUM constant, 182
  FW_NORMAL constant, 182
  FW_REGULAR constant, 182
  FW_SEMIBOLD constant, 182
  FW_THIN constant, 182
  FW_ULTRABOLD constant, 182
  FW_ULTRALIGHT constant, 182
  HC_ACTION constant, 851
  HC_NOREMOVE constant, 851
  ID_FILE_SEND_MAIL constant, 521
  ID_INDICATOR_CAPS constant, 665
  ID_INDICATOR_NUMS constant, 665
  ID_INDICATOR_SCRL constant, 665
  ID_MY_STATUS_BAR constant, 667–668
  OEM_CHARSET constant, 183
  SBPS_DISABLED constant, 667
  SBPS_NOBORDERS constant, 667
  SBPS_NORMAL constant, 667
  SBPS_OWNERDRAW constant, 667
  SBPS_POPOUT constant, 667
  SBPS_STRETCH constant, 667
  SHIFTJIS_CHARSET constant, 183
  SYMBOL_CHARSET constant, 183
  UPDATE_OBJECT constant, [illegible]
  WS_VISIBLE constant, 673
Contact.cpp, 342–343
contact.h, 327–328, 341
containers (ActiveX), 905–908, 910–911
Containers collection, 807
context (pop-up) menus, 123–126, 128–130, 689–692, 694
Control Panel, 79
control(s). *See also* ActiveX controls
  adding, to dialog templates, 315–316
  advanced programming for, 302–308
  arranging, 317–318
  basic description of, 277–310, 920

classes for, 101–103, 333–336
color of, 307–308
dominant, 316
loading, into container projects, 14
modifying the behavior of, 303–304
positioning, 279
registering, 14
selecting groups of, 316–317
setting properties for, 316
sizing, 317–318
controls toolbar, 315, 699
ControlWizard, 924, 926–927
converting projects, 1065–1066
coolbars, 677
coordinates, 170
copy action, 289–290
Copy command, 519
Copy() function, 289
CopyFile() function, 392
CopyFile project, 1171
CopyFile.cpp, 392
CorelDRAW! (Corel), 179
Count() method, 806
CPaintDC class, 104
CPaintobjDoc class, 566
CPalette class, 104, 204, 226, 228–229
CPen class, 103–104, 185–187, 480
CPoint class, 135
CPreviewDC class, 622–623
CPrintDialog class, 101, 626–627
CPrintInfo class, 607–608, 613, 621
CPrintInfo structure, 611, 612, 613–614, 621, 623–624
CProgressCtrl class, 1029
CPropertyPage class, 350–357, 367–372
CPropertyPageDialog class, 101
CPropertySheet class, 350–358, 365, 370, 372
CPUs (central processing units), 77, 163, 462
compression and, 405
memory management and, 472–474, 499, 500
threads and, 705, 715, 716
Create member function, 126, 280, 291, 296, 299–300, 321, 350, 352, 561–563, 576, 578–579, 583, 642, 646, 665–666, 672, 677, 683, 699–700, 863, 1040, 1043
CreateBitmap() function, 208, 657
CreateBitmapIndirect() function, 206–207
CreateColumnChart macro, 74
CreateCompatibleBitmap() function, 207, 242, 657
CreateCompatibleDC() function, 242, 655
CreateDC() function, 597
CreateDirectory() function, 1029
CreateErrorInfo() function, 990
CreateEx() function, 280
CreateFile() function, 502, 504
CreateFileMapping() function, 504–505, 508, 509
CreateFont() function, 181
CreateFontIndirect() function, 180
CreateFromClipboard project, 889
CreateFunctionDescriptionFile macro, 1129–1138
CreateGrayCaret() member function, 154
CreateHalfTonePalette() function, 228
CreateHashBrushIndirect() function, 188
CreateIndexes() function, 251
CreateObject() function, 919
CreatePen() function, 185
CreatePenIndirect() function, 185
CreateProperty() method, 807
CreateQueryDef() method, 807
CreateRelation() method, 807
CreateSolidCaret() member function, 154
CreateStockObject() function, 186
CreateTableDef() method, 807
CreateThread() function, 79, 707
CreateView() function, 580–583
CReBar class, 677
CRecentFileList class, 99
CRecordset class, 104, 766–777, 780, 790–791, 794, 795
CRecordView class, 101, 542
CRect class, 278, 280
CRegistry class, 413–417, 1161
CRgn class, 104, 200–201
CRichEditCtrl class, 102
CRichEditView class, 100, 542
Crop() function, 886
Cropping() function, 887
cropping images, 885–887
CRuntimeClass class, 580–581, 863, 992
CSampleDocument class, 536
CSampleView class, 614, 617, 618, 619
CScrollBar class, 102, 278, 294–298
CScrollView class, 101, 542, 545, 622
CSerial class, 410–417
CSharedFile class, 99
CSimpleException class, 265–266
CSimpleTermDoc class, 516–517
CSingleDocTemplate class, 112, 527, 528, 529–531, 533–534, 556, 586
CSize() function, 579
CSliderCtrl class, 102
CSocket class, 1040–1052
CSocketFile class, 99
CSpinButtonCtrl class, 102
CSplitterWnd class, 94, 95, 98, 100, 559–560, 574–586
CSS (Cascading Style Sheets), 1085–1090, 1103
CStatic class, 102, 278, 290–294
CStatusBar class, 544, 664, 665–669, 670
CStatusBarCtrl class, 102
CStdioFile class, 99
CString class, 98, 375–388, 531, 693, 826, 1150
CSubbedEdit class, 593–594
CSupplier class, 266
CTabCtrl class, 103
CTermCode() function, 747

CTest class, 272–275, 858–862
CTestException class, 271–273
ctlRect parameter, 278
CToolBar class, 533, 544, 670–671, 673, 862
CToolBarCtrl class, 103
CToolTipCtrl class, 103
CTracker class, 958, 992
CTreeCtrl class, 103, 680–697, 795
CTreeView class, 100, 542
CUA (Common User Access), 853
Current position attribute, 166
current selection, 538
CurrentDirectory property, 1128
cursors, changing, 143–149
CUser class, 828
CUserException class, 266
CUserMasterSet class, 773
Custom Button dialog box, 27
Customize command, 24, 26, 922
Customize dialog box, 24–28
Customize option, 55
CustomizeProject() function, 1148
cut action, 289–290
Cut command, 541
Cut() function, 289
CValidatePtr class, 256–257
CView class, 21, 100, 111, 112, 537–544, 554, 555, 556, 611–613, 1064
CWave class, 424, 428–431, 438
CWebDialog class, 1075
CWinApp class, 112, 119, 461–463, 528, 534, 535, 536, 537, 554, 843, 863
CWinThread class, 95, 119, 705, 707, 709, 711–714
CWnd class, 21, 94, 95, 97, 98, 100, 120, 171, 277, 280, 420, 453, 645–646, 717–718
CWndCreate() function, 646

D

DAC (Digital Adapter Color), 225
DAO (Data Access Objects), 103–104
  basic description of, 801–836
  history of, 802–804
  interfaces, [illegible]
  object hierarchy, 804–808
  SDK, 808–809
  versions of, 802–804
DaoUserMaintenance dialog box, 825
DaoUserMaintenance project, 824–836, 1177
DaoUserMaintenanceDlg.cpp, 827–836
DaoUserMaintenance.h, 827
DaoUserMasterSet.cpp, 817–819, 821
DaoUserMasterSet.h, 816–817, 821
dash (-), 63
data I/O, 375–422, 500–507
Data Source Administrator, 731, 735–737, 743
data sources
  basic description of, 731
  configuring, 735–737
  connecting to, 737–739
  disconnecting from, 742
  querying, 739, 751–756
data types, 1013–1016. *See also* Boolean data type
Database object, 806–807, 810
Database Options dialog box, 816
Database project, 1175
Databases collection, 806, 807
DataTips, 43–44
Date Picker, 4
dBASE, 731
DBEngine object, 804
DBEngineErrors collection, 811
dbForwardOnly() function, 804
DBMSs (database management systems), 729–731, 732–734, 801
dbOpenDynaset constant, 819
dbOpenSnapshot constant, 819
dbOpenTable constant, 819
DCs (device contexts), 103–104, 165–173, 655, 888
DDE (dynamic data exchange), 481, 532, 543, 906
DDEML (DDE-Management Library), 481
DDL (data definition language), 802
DDLMain() function, 1146
DDX (Dialog Data Exchange), 280, 323, 331–336, 699, 826, 941–942
DDX_CBIndex() function, 941–942
DDX_Control() function, 324
DDX_Control macro, 941–942
Debug button, 31
Debug DLL option, 33
Debug menu
  Step Out command, 42
  Step Over command, 42
  Step Into command, 42
  Threads command, 44
debug mode, 31, 34–35
Debug Monitor, 49–50
debug session field, 34
[illegible]
Debug tab, 34–35, 48, 51
Debugger object, 1125–1126
Debugger property, 1128
debugging, 62, 803, 1015. *See also* errors
  basic description of, 21–22, 29–52
  with the integrated debugger, 31–45
  Just-In-Time, 30, 51–52
  memory management and, 490–491
  profiling and, 57
  project performance and, 54–57, 60, 62
  remote, 48–50, 60
  threads and, 717
DECLARE_DYNAMIC macro, 526

DECLARE_DYNCREATE macro, 563
DECLARE_OLECREATE macro, 998
DECLARE_OLECREATE_SHARED macro, 998
DECLARE_SERIAL macro, 526
_declspec keyword, 498
DEF (module definition) files, 510–512, 840–841, 863
DEFAULT_CHARSET constant, 183
#define directive, 368, 498, 849, 1161
delayFreeMemDF flag, 491
Delete button, 86, 786, 826–834
Delete() member function, 253–254, 470, 777, 824
delete operator, 47–48, 561
DeleteAtom() function, 471
DeleteContents() function, 520, 521
DeleteString() member function, 285
deleting
  CException objects, 254–255
  items from list boxes, 285
  keyboard shortcuts, 23, 24–26
  records, 777, 824
  tools from the Tools menu, 86
demo programs
  AboutWiz program, 1150, 1161, 1181–1182
  AboutWizTest program, 1163–1164
  AddressBook program, 312–319, 326–332, 337–348, 1169–1170
  AutoDialer program, 1058–1061, 1179
  BarsDemo program, 1174
  BlitDemo program, 215–222, 1169
  CDAudio program, 438–441
  CDPlayer program, 440–447, 1172
  Clock program, 454–461, 1172
  CODBCDynamicTest program, 759–760
  CompressDemo program, 400–402, 407–410, 1171
  CompressFile program, 1171
  CopyFile program, 1171
  CreateFromClipboard program, 889
  DaoUserMaintenance program, 824–836, 1177
  Database program, 1175
  DisplayView program, 882–885
  DoublePendulum program, 1004–1005, 1007–1012, 1179
  Dynsplit program, 586–590, 1173
  FileDemo program, 392–400, 1170
  FileExceptionTest program, 261–272, 1169
  FirstCHTML program, 1090–1091
  GlobalDllObjects program, 856–861, 1178
  GlobalDllObjectsClient program, 861–862, 1178
  GraphicsDemo1 program, 1168
  GraphicsDemo2 program, 1168
  HelloWorld1 program, 5–9, 1166
  HelloWorld2 program, 9–11, 1166
  HelloWorld3 program, 11–14, 1167
  HexView program, 531, 545, 1173
  HexViewMDI program, 627–631, 1174
  HTMLViewer program, 1090–1091, 1099, 1100–1104
  ImageViewer program, 865–870, 1177
  ImageViewerClient program, 868–869, 1177
  KeybdHook program, 849–852, 1178
  KeybdHookClient program, 853–854
  Learnide program, 21–22, 1167
  Library program, 1172
  ListCtrlDemo program, 1174
  MFCControl program, 923–927, 1174, 1178
  MFCServer program, 1178–1179
  MFCTracer program, 48
  MIDIDemo program, 432–437, 1172
  Mini Editor program, 302, 1169
  ModalDemo program, 354–357
  ModalWin program, 640–661
  MouseDemo1 program, 136–142, 1167
  MouseDemo2 program, 144–149, 1167
  MultiBrowser program, 1071–1075, 1180
  ODBCClasses program, 1175–1176
  ODBCDemo program, 742–757, 1175
  ODBCDynamicTest program, 1176
  OnIdleDemo program, 463–466, 1172–1173
  PaintObj program, 566–574, 1173
  Parameterized program, 791, 795–798, 1176
  PenBrumDemo program, 1168
  PortLand program, 603–605, 628, 1174
  ProcessImage program, 894–901
  Registry program, 1171
  SendEmail program, 1052–1057, 1180
  Serial program, 1171
  ShowDIB program, 238–231, 1169
  SimpleBrowser program, 1068–1071, 1180–1181
  Sockets program, 1045–1052, 1180
  StringDemo program, 381–388, 1170
  ThreadDemo program, 1175
  ThreadDemo1 program, 721–725
  TreeCtrlDemo program, 692–697, 1174–1175
  UseBrowser program, 1181
  UseDoublePendulum program, 1179
  UserMaintenance program, 780–788, 1176
  WaveDemo program, 428–431, 1172
descent, 603
DestroyCaret() member function, 154
DestroyWindow() member function, 561–562, 644
Detach() function, 126, 127
Developer Studio
  object model, 1124–1129
  online help, information on classes in, 98
development cycles, 57
DeviceCapabilities() function, 601
DeviceCount() function, 433
DFX, 820, 822

DHTML (Dynamic HTML), 4, 1075
dialog box(es)
  adding, 693
  AddressBook project and, 312–319, 326–332, 337–339, 340, 1169–1170
  basic description of, 311–348
  CHTMLView class and, 1104–1106
  creating/displaying property sheets within, 354
  custom AppWizards and, 1149–1151
  derived control classes and, 333–332
  duplicating, 826
  header files, 780, 827
  implementation files, 780–788, 827–835
  serialization and, 339–347
  templates, 312–319
  testing, 319
dialog editor, 312–319
dialog toolbar, 317–318
DialogBox() function, 319
dialog.cpp, 1159
DIBs, 229–231
Difference() function, 48
digital clocks, 454–461
Dim keyword, 1123
directives
  #define directive, 368, 498, 849, 1161
  #include directive, 356, 688, 693, 778, 780, 791, 825, 827, 853, 866–868, 1161
  #pragma directive, 854
DirectoryThread() function, 1031, 1032
DirectSound, 423–424
DirectX gaming API, 423
Disable (Debug) option, 56
Disabled check box, 351
DisablePage() function, 363
Disassembly window, 35, 39–40, 42–43
disks, saving data to, 341, 388–392
DispatchMessage() function, 303, 452, 453, 638
dispid, 939
dispinterface keyword, 936
Dispinterface interface, 936, 937, 956–958
Display() function, 880
Display.exe, 882, 883
DisplayAppName() function, 860
DisplayAppName.def, 844
DisplayAppName.h, 844, 860
DisplayAppName.lib, 844, 860
DisplayFileException() function, 262
DisplayView project, 882–885
DisplayView.cpp, 882–885
DisplayView.h, 882, 883, 884
DISs (device-independent bitmaps), 204–206
<DL> tag, 1084
dlgall.rc, 1156
dlgloc_enu.rc, 1156, 1157
dlgroot.clw, 1155–1156
dlgroot.cpp, 1159
DllMain() function, 843–844, 863
DllRegisterServer() function, 920, 959–960
DLLs (Dynamic Link Libraries), 801, 1139–1140, 1162
  ActiveX controls and, 913, 919, 923
  basic description of, 839–870
  debugging, 34–35, 49
  global C++ objects with, 854–862
  maximizing the speed of, 56
  memory management and, 472, 475–477, 483, 487, 497–500
  MFC extension, 839, 842, 862–870
  minimizing the size of, 56
  profiling, 74
  project performance and, 56, 70, 74–76, 78
  regular, 839, 842–862
DLLUnregisterServer() function, 920, 959–960
DM.dll, 49
DOCINFO structure, 597
document(s)
  ActiveX, 905–908, 909
  classes, declaring, 515–517
  complex combinations of, 557–565
  data, complex, 521–524
  importance of the InitInstance() function to, 526–537
  managing, 527–528, 557–565
  message processing and, 519–520
  pages, printer pages versus, 613–614
  /view model, 6, 94, 97, 99–103, 119–120, 513–515, 554–555, 594
Document object, 1125–1126
Documents property, 1128
Documents object, 1125–1126
DoDataExchange() function, 323–325, 334, 940–941
DoesItemExist() function, 696
DoFieldExchange() function, 772, 773, 774, 790, 794–795, 820–821
DoModal member function, 320, 321, 325, 350, 352, 356, 627, 863
DoPreparePrinting() function, 599, 607, 612, 616, 626
DoPropExchange() method, 945–946
DOS (Disk Operating System), 10, 149–150, 473, 476, 477, 503, 1164
DosAllocSeg() function, 481
doSomeSetup() function, 1103
DoSomething() function, 271–272
DoublePend class, 1010–1012
DoublePend.cpp, 1004–1005
DoublePend.h, 1004–1005, 1007–1010
DoublePendulum project, 1004–1005, 1007–1012, 1179
DoublePendulum.h, 1012
Draw() function, 236–238, 881, 882
DrawBitmap() function, 210

DrawFocusRect() function, 156–157
Drawing mode attribute, 167
DrawText() function, 193
DrawTransparent() function, 214
Driver Manager, 730–731, 733, 743, 845
dsExtend option, 1133
DSNs (data source names), 731, 735–737, 742–743, 746, 752–754, 763, 777
DSTINVERT raster operation, 658
DT_WORDBREAK flag, 193
DTDs (Document Type Definitions), 1082
Dump() function, 47
DumpAllObjectsSince() function, 47
DumpStatistics() function, 48
Dundas Software, 1184
DuplicateHandle() function, 505, 506
dwAccess property, 1020
dwAction parameter, 484
dwAttributes property, 1026
dwContext property, 1020, 1026, 1027
dwCreateFlags property, 708
dwDesiredAccess argument, 506
dwExitCode variable, 711
dwFileOffsetHigh parameter, 506
dwFileOffsetLow parameter, 506
dwFlags property, 1020, 1021, 1026, 1027
dwMaxSizeHight argument, 505
dwMaxSizeLow parameter, 505
dwNumberOfBytesToMap parameter, 506
dwOptions argument, 765
DWORDs, 496, 497, 1013–1014
dwProtect parameter, 505
dwROP parameter, 209
dwSize argument, 484
Dynamic recordset, 807
DYNAMIC_DOWNCAST macro, 536
Dynaset recordset, 807
Dynsplit project, 586–590, 1173
Dynsplit.cpp, 586–590
Dynsplit.exe, 586–590
dynspvw.cpp, 586–590

E

echoing keyboard focus, 153–159
EDIT class, 278
edit controls, 287–290
Edit() function, 777, 824
Edit menu
  Go To command, 87
  Paste command, 115, 107
Editor combo box, 25
Ellipse() function, 186
<EM> tag, 1084
Empty() function, 376
empty macros, 1116–1117
EmptyClipboard() function, 421
Enable Profiling option, 57, 61
EnableAutomation() function, 963
EnableMenuItem() function, 124
EnableModeless() method, 1127
EnablePage() function, 365–367
EnableTab() function, 366–367
encapsulating data, 826, 867
EndDoc() function, 597, 598, 606, 611
EndModalLoop() function, 639–640, 643
EndOfLine() method, 1133
EndPath() function, 187, 597, 606, 611
endpoints, 1040
EndWaitCursor() function, 143–144
Enterprise Edition (Visual C++), 61
enum structure, 258–259, 265, 266
EnumFontFamilies() function, 184
ErrFunc() function, 45
error(s). *See also* debugging
  assertion errors, 718
  CHTMLView class and, 1092
  codes, dealing with, 248–249
  handling, in the correct context, 249–251
  when loading images, 879
  ODBC and, 733
Error object, 811
ErrorInfoMacros.h, 986–988
Errors property, 1128
ES_AUTOHSCROLL style flag, 287
ES_AUTOVSCROLL style flag, 287
escape sequences, 597, 611
ES_CENTER style flag, 287
ES_HSCROLL style flag, 287
ES_LEFT style flag, 287
ES_LOWERCASE style flag, 287
ES_NOHIDESEL style flag, 287
ES_OEMCONVERT style flag, 287
ES_RIGHT style flag, 287
ES_UPPERCASE style flag, 287
ES_VSCROLL style flag, 287
ES_WANTRETURN style flag, 287
event(s)
  adding, 943–944
  buttons, 1105–1106
  models, 1091–1093
/EXC option, 63–64, 76
/EXCALL option, 62–66
Excel (Microsoft)
  DocObject Containment and, 4
  importing Profiler data into, 70
  macro files, 70, 74
  ODBC and, 731
  processing Profiler output with, 74
  splitter windows and, 574

exception handling, 971–977, 986–992.
    See also errors
  basic description of, 245–276
  catching exceptions, 246–248, 256–257, 267–269
  SEH (structured exception handling), 246
  selecting functions for, 267–269
Excite Web site, 1071–1073
Execute() function, 810, 813, 832–833
Execute learnide.exe command, 22
ExecuteCommand() method, 1127
ExecuteConfiguration() method, 1127
ExecuteSQL() function, 754, 755, 759, 762, 764
Exit command, 23
ExitCustomAppWiz() function, 1147, 1162
ExitInstance() function, 852, 859, 861, 863
ExitTextOut() function, 193
Explorer (Windows), 531, 680, 689, 882
exporting data, 69, 863, 865
Extended Combo Box control, 4
extensible architecture, 98
extraction, of substrings, 380
ExtraDDX entries, 334–336
ExtTextOut() function, 178

F

_far keyword, 469, 498
Favor Fast Code option, 55–56
Favor Small Code option, 56
/FC option, 64
fcover.bat, 61
FetchData() function, 753, 755
fFixedDisk field, 503
FIFO (first-in first-out) order, 557
file(s)
  commands, keystroke combinations for, 117
  extensions, 75, 76, 530
  loading, 408
  objects, creating, 502–506
  open access flags, 1030
  services, 99
  use of the term, 99
File menu
  Exit command, 23
  Open command, 401
File Open dialog box, 846
File View, 18–19
file1.obj, 62
file2.obj, 62
FileDemo project, 392–400, 1170
FileDemo.exe, 392
FileDemoView.cpp, 392–400
FileExceptionTest project, 261–272, 1169
FileExceptionTestDlg.cpp, 261–272
FileOpen dialog box, 147
FileText() method, 1133
FileThread() function, 1031, 1032
FillTermCodesListbox() function, 749
filters, 820–822, 847–854
Find() function, 381
FindAtom() function, 471
Finder tool, 83
FindFileInArchive() function, 406
FindOneOf() function, 381
FindString() member function, 286, 337, 338
FindStringExact() function, 286
FireChange() function 943–944
FirstCHTML project, 1090–1091
fixups, 840
flags. *See also* flags
  debug memory flags, 491
  file open flags, 389–391
  Internet programming flags, 1021
  MCI command flags, 440
  menu flags, 125
  palette entry flags, 226
  sound flags, 425
flags (listed by name).
    See also flags (listed by name)
  allocMemDF flag, 491
  bExclusive flag, 811
  BS_3STATE flag, 281
  BS_AUTO3STATE flag, 281
  BS_AUTOCHECKBOX flag, 281
  BS_AUTORADIOBUTTON flag, 281, 282
  BS_BITMAP button style, 305–306
  BS_CHECKBOX flag, 281
  BS_DEFPUSHBUTTON flag, 281
  BS_GROUPBOX flag, 281
  BS_PUSHBUTTON flag, 281
  BS_RADIOBUTTON flag, 281
  CBRS_BOTTOM flag, 666
  CBRS_NOALIGN flag, 666
  CBRS_TOP flag, 666
  CBS_AUTOHSCROLL flag, 299
  CBS_DISABLENOSCROLL flag, 299
  CBS_DROPDOWN flag, 299
  [illegible]
  CBS_HASSTRINGS flag, 299
  CBS_LOWERCASE flag, 299
  CBS_OEMCONVER flag, 299
  CBS_OWNERDRAWFIXED flag, 299
  CBS_OWNERDRAWVARIABLE flag, 299
  CBS_SIMPLE flag, 299
  CBS_SORT flag, 299
  CBS_UPPERCASE flag, 299
  checkAlwaysMemDF flag, 491
  delayFreeMemDF flag, 491
  DT_WORDBREAK flag, 193
  ES_AUTOHSCROLL flag, 287

ES_AUTOVSCROLL flag, 287
ES_CENTER flag, 287
ES_HSCROLL flag, 287
ES_LEFT flag, 287
ES_LOWERCASE flag, 287
ES_NOHIDESEL flag, 287
ES_OEMCONVERT flag, 287
ES_RIGHT flag, 287
ES_UPPERCASE flag, 287
ES_VSCROLL flag, 287
ES_WANTRETURN flag, 287
GENERIC_READ flag, 1030
GENERIC_WRITE flag, 1030
GMEM_DDESHARE flag, 507
GMEM_SHARE flag, 507
HEAP_NO_SERIALIZE, flag, 494
LBS_DISABLENOSCROLL flag, 284
LBS_EXTENDEDSEL flag, 284
LBS_HASSTRINGS flag, 284
LBS_MULTICOLUMN flag, 284
LBS_MULTIPLESEL flag, 284
LBS_NOINTEGRALHEIGHT flag, 284
LBS_NOREDRAW flag, 284
LBS_NOSEL flag, 284
LBS_NOTIFY flag, 284
LBS_SORT flag, 284
LBS_STANDARD flag, 284
LBS_USETABSTOPS flag, 284
LBS_WANTKEYBOARDINPUT flag, 284
MF_BITMAP flag, 125
MF_BYCOMMAND flag, 125
MF_BYPOSITION flag, 125
MF_CHECKED flag, 125
MF_ENABLED flag, 125
MF_GRAYED flag, 125
MF_MENUBARBREAK flag, 125
MF_MENUBREAK flag, 125
MF_OWNERDRAW flag, 125
MF_POP-UP flag, 125
MF_SEPARATOR flag, 125
MF_STRING flag, 125
MF_UNCHECKED flag, 125
MEM_COMMIT flag, 484, 485
MEM_DECOMMIT flag, 485
MEM_RESERVE flag, 471, 484
MSG_DONTROUTE flag, 1045
MSG_OOB flag, 1044, 1045
MSG_PEEK flag, 1044
PAGE_NOACCESS flag, 484
PAGE_READONLY flag, 505
PAGE_READWRITE flag, 505
PAGE_REWRITE flag, 484
PAGE_WRITECOPY flag, 505
PC_EXPLICIT flag, 226
PC_NOCOLLAPSE flag, 226
PC_RESERVED flag, 226
PM_REMOVE flag, 861
SBS_BOTTOMALIGN flag, 295
SBS_HORZ flag, 295
SBS_LEFTALIGN flag, 295
SBS_RIGHTALIGN flag, 295
SBS_SIZEBOX flag, 295
SBS_SIZEBOXBOTTONLEFTALIGN flag, 296
SBS_SIZEBOXBOTTONRIGHTALIGN flag, 295
SBS_TOPALIGN flag, 296
SBS_VERT flag, 296
SND_ASYNC flag, 425
SND_LOOP flag, 425
SND_MEMORY flag, 425
SND_NODEFAULT flag, 425
SND_NOSTOP flag, 425
SND_SYNC flag, 425
SS_BITMAP flag, 283
SS_BLACKFRAME flag, 292
SS_BLACKRECT flag, 292
SS_CENTER flag, 292
SS_CENTERIMAGE flag, 292
SS_CENTERNOWORDWRAP flag, 292
SS_ENHMETAFILE flag, 283
SS_ETCHEDFRAME flag, 292
SS_ETCHEDHORZ flag, 292
SS_ETCHEDVERT flag, 283
SS_GRAYFRAME flag, 292
SS_GRAYRECT flag, 292
SS_ICON flag, 283
SS_LEFT flag, 292
SS_LEFTNOWORDWRAP flag, 292
SS_NOPREFIX flag, 292
SS_NOTIFY flag, 283, 294
SS_REALSIZEIMAGE flag, 283
SS_RIGHT flag, 292
SS_RIGHTNOWORDWRAP flag, 292
SS_SIMPLE flag, 292
SS_SUNKEN flag, 292
SS_WHITEFRAME flag, 292
SS_WHITERECT flag, 292
WS_BORDER flag, 647
WS_EX_CLIENTEDGE flag, 280
WS_OVERLAPPED flag, 647
flicker, 241–242, 925–926
Flicker-free activation option, 925–926
floating-point registers, 37
FlushFileBuffers() function, 502
flyby test, 674–675

font(s), 279–280, 601–603, 1085–1090
  basic description of, 178–184
  point size for, 195–196
  substitution support, 601–602
  for tabs, 370
footers, 620–621
for loops, 756
forward slash (/), 63, 1027, 1084
Forward-Only recordset, 807
FoxPro (Microsoft), 731, 803
frame windows, 100, 529, 543–544, 557–565
frame.cpp, 1154
Frame.h, 1154
Frame-Pointer Omission option, 55, 57
FrameWnd class, 100
free() function, 470
FreeLibrary() function, 841
FromHandle() function, 127, 128, 719
/FT option, 64
ftime.bat, 61
FTP (File Transfer Protocol), 1019, 1028–1029, 1030
  FTP project and, 1031–1039, 1179–1180
  servers, 1023–1028, 1031–1039
Ftp.dsw, 1031
Ftp.exe, 1031, 1032–1039
FTPConnectView.cpp, 1024
FTPConnectView.h, 1023
FtpView.cpp, 1032–1039
Full Optimization option, 56
Full Screen option, 27
FullName property, 1128, 1132
FullSrvr.exe, 75
function(s). *See also* functions (listed by name)
  call hierarchy, listing, during debugging, 38–39
  counting, 60, 76
  coverage, 60, 67, 76
  descriptions, 1134–1137
  helper functions, 617–620, 783, 820, 832, 834
  IntelliSense and, 6
  names, 63, 66
  seams, 845–846
  [illegible]
  in VBScript, 1124
functions (listed by name). *See also* functions
  AbortDoc() function, 599–601
  Accept() function, 1043
  AddAtom() function, 471
  AddBar() function, 677
  AddDocTemplate function, 527, 528, 535, 537, 558, 594, 867
  AddItem() function, 525
  AddNew() function, 777, 824
  AddNewObj() function, 522, 523
  AddObject() function, 523
  AddPage() function, 356
  AddString() function, 285
  AfxBeginThread() function, 98, 707–708, 710, 716
  AfxCheckMemory() function, 491, 492
  AfxDumpMemoryLeaks() function, 492
  AfxEndThread() function, 711
  AfxGetApp() function, 536
  AfxGetMainWnd() function, 453, 544
  AfxGetResourceHandle() function, 120, 865
  AfxMessageBox() function, 45
  AfxOleLockApp() function, 963
  AfxOleRegisterServerClass() function, 959
  AfxRegisterWndClass() function, 561, 562
  AfxSetAllocHook() function, 491
  AlignButtons() function, 359
  AmbientBackColor() function, 939
  AppendMenu() function, 124
  Attach() function, 127
  AttachOnSetup() function, 627
  Back() function, 1147
  BeginPath() function, 187
  _beginthread() function, 496
  BeginTrans() function, 765, 813–814
  BitBlt() function, 209–212, 241–243, 649, 655, 658
  BoundPropertyChanged() function, 936
  CallNextHook() function, 849, 854
  CallNextHookEX() function, 851
  CallWindowProc() function, 591
  CanSerialize() function, 344
  CanTransact() function, 765
  CFrameWnd() function, 561
  ChangeFormat() function, 886, 887
  CheckMenuItem() function, 124
  Checkpoint() function, 47–48
  CleanOutRecordArray() function, 754
  ClientToScreen() function, 129, 135
  ClipCursor() function, 149
  Close() function, 405, 409–411, 416, 427, 433, 440, 1030, 1058
  CMainFrame() function, 130
  CMDIMsg() function, 111
  [illegible]
  CODBCColumnInfo() function, 756
  CommDlgExtendedError() function, 627
  Commit() function, 271
  CommitTrans() function, 765, 814
  Compare() function, 378
  CompareNoCase() function, 378
  Connect() function, 1041, 1042, 1043
  Copy() function, 289
  CopyFile() function, 392
  Create function, 126, 280, 291, 296, 299–300, 321, 350, 352, 561–563, 576, 578–579, 583, 642, 646, 665–666, 672, 677, 683, 699–700, 863, 1040, 1043
  CreateBitmap() function, 208, 657

CreateBitmapIndirect() function, 206–207
CreateCompatibleBitmap() function, 207, 242, 657
CreateCompatibleDC() function, 242, 655
CreateDC() function, 597
CreateDirectory() function, 1029
CreateErrorInfo() function, 990
CreateEx() function, 280
CreateFile() function, 502, 504
CreateFileMapping() function, 504–505, 508, 509
CreateFont() function, 181
CreateFontIndirect() function, 180
CreateGrayCaret() function, 154
CreateHalfTonePalette() function, 228
CreateHashBrushIndirect() function, 188
CreateIndexes() function, 251
CreateObject() function, 919
CreatePen() function, 185
CreatePenIndirect() function, 185
CreateSolidCaret() function, 154
CreateStockObject() function, 186
CreateThread() function, 79, 707
CreateView() function, 580–583
Crop() function, 886
Cropping() function, 887
CSize() function, 579
CTermCode() function, 747
CustomizeProject() function, 1148
Cut() function, 289
CWndCreate() function, 646
dbForwardOnly() function, 804
DDLMain() function, 1146
DDX_CBIndex() function, 941–942
DDX_Control() function, 324
Delete() function, 253–254, 470, 777, 824
DeleteAtom() function, 471
DeleteContents() function, 520, 521
DeleteString() function, 285
DestroyCaret() function, 154
DestroyWindow() function, 561–562, 644
Detach() function, 126, 127
DeviceCapabilities() function, 601
DeviceCount() function, 433
DialogBox() function, 319
Difference() function, 48
DirectoryThread() function, 1031, 1032
DisablePage() function, 363
DispatchMessage() function, 303, 452, 453, 638
Display() function, 880
DisplayAppName() function, 860
DisplayFileException() function, 262
DllMain() function, 843–844, 863
DllRegisterServer() function, 920, 959–960
DLLUnregisterServer() function, 920, 959–960
DoDataExchange() function, 323–325, 334, 940–941
DoesItemExist() function, 696
DoFieldExchange() function, 772, 773, 774, 790, 794–795, 820–821
DoModal function, 320, 321, 325, 350, 352, 356, 627, 863
DoPreparePrinting() function, 539, 607, 612, 616, 626
DosAllocSeg() function, 481
doSomeSetup() function, 1103
DoSomething() function, 271–272
Draw() function, 236–238, 881, 882
DrawBitmap() function, 210
DrawFocusRect() function, 156–157
DrawText() function, 193
DrawTransparent() function, 214
Dump() function, 47
DuplicateHandle() function, 505, 506
Edit() function, 777, 824
Ellipse() function, 186
Empty() function, 376
EmptyClipboard() function, 421
EnableAutomation() function, 963
EnableMenuItem() function, 124
EnablePage() function, 365–367
EnableTab() function, 366–367
EndDoc() function, 597, 598, 606, 611
EndModalLoop() function, 639–640, 643
EndPath() function, 187, 597, 606, 611
EndWaitCursor() function, 143–144
EnumFontFamilies() function, 184
ErrFunc() function, 45
Execute() function, 810, 813, 832–833
ExecuteSQL() function, 754, 755, 759, 762, 764
ExitCustomAppWiz() function, 1147, 1162
ExitInstance() function, 852, 859, 861, 863
ExitTextOut() function, 193
ExtTextOut() function, 178
FetchData() function, 753, 755
FileThread() function, 1031, 1032
FillTermCodesListbox() function, 749
Find() function, 381
FindAtom() function, 471
FindFileInArchive() function, 406
FindOneOf() function, 381
FindString() function, 286, 337, 338
FindStringExact() function, 286
FireChange() function 943 944
FlushFileBuffers() function, 502
free() function, 470
FreeLibrary() function, 841
FromHandle() function, 127, 128, 719
GenerateDB() function, 249–250, 251
GetActiveObject() function, 997

(continued)

functions (listed by name) *(continued)*
GetAddressBar() function, 1064
GetAlignment() function, 935
GetAmbientProperty() function, 939
GetAt() function, 377
GetBackColor() function, 938
GetBitmapDimension() function, 655
GetBuffer() function, 247, 377
GetCaretPos() function, 154
GetCharWidth() function, 195
GetCheck() function, 283
GetChildItem() function, 696
GetClientRect() function, 191
GetCurrentProcess() function, 716
GetCurSel() function, 285, 749
GetCursorPos() function, 135
GetData() function, 758
GetDataBuffer() function, 757
getDefaultConnect() function, 771
GetDefaultDBName() function, 819
GetDefaultSQL() function, 771, 794, 795, 820
GetDeviceCaps() function, 173, 195, 196, 205, 601
GetDevices() function, 427
GetDib() function, 879
GetDlgItem() function, 702
GetDocString() function, 531
GetDocTemplate() function, 519
GetDocument() function, 46–47, 523, 539
GetEditControl() function, 686–687
GetErrorMessage() function, 253–255, 259, 263, 265–266
GetExitCodeThread() function, 711, 712
GetFieldTypeFromSQLType() function, 756
GetFile() function, 1024–1027
GetFirstDocTemplatePosition() function, 536
GetFirstViewPosition() function, 517–518, 536
GetFromPage() function, 608
GetFtpConnection() function, 1021
GetFullName() function, 1064
GetHeight() function, 886
[illegible]
GetIDispatch() function, 993
GetIndent() function, 969
GetInterface() function, 993
GetItem() function, 368
GetItemRect() function, 654
GetItemText() function, 696
GetKerningPairs() function, 602
GetLastError() function, 505, 841, 879
GetLength() function, 376, 392, 406
GetLine() function, 288
GetLineCount() function, 288–289
GetMaxPage() function, 608, 612
GetMenu() function, 123, 128
GetMenuItemID() function, 124
GetMenuString() function, 124
GetMessage() function, 453, 638, 715
GetMessageBar() function, 654
GetMessageString() function, 125
GetMinPage() function, 608, 612
GetNbrOfClients() function, 860, 861
GetNextDocTemplate() function, 536
GetNextItem() function, 525
GetNextSiblingItem() function, 696
GetNextView() function, 536
GetObject() function, 210, 656, 997
GetOutlineTextMetrics() function, 602
GetParent() function, 718
GetParentFrame() function, 718, 719
GetPathName() function, 519
GetPermissionsByUSerID() function, 795
GetPosition() function, 406
GetProcAddress() function, 841
GetProcessHeap() function, 471, 494, 495
GetProp() function, 471
GetStartPosition() function, 525
GetStatus() function, 392
GetStatusBar() function, 1064
GetStyle() function, 673
GetSubMenu() function, 123
GetSysColor() function, 159
GetTabbedTextExtent() function, 195
GetTestPtr() function, 860, 861
GetTextExtent() function, 195, 196–198
GetTextMetrics() function, 195, 198, 602
GetToPage() function, 608
GetTopLevelParent() function, 719
GetWidth() function, 886
GetWindowText() function, 288, 293
GlobalAddAtom() function, 471
GlobalAlloc() function, 470, 482, 507
GlobalFindAtom() function, 471
GoBack() function, 1068
GoForward() function, 1068
[illegible]
GoSearch() function, 1067, 1068
GoToMatchBrace() function, 1133
GrayString() function, 193
HeapAlloc() function, 487, 495
HeapCompact() function, 495
HeapCreate() function, 471, 494, 495
HeapDestroy() function, 495
HeapFree() function, 495
HeapLock() function, 495
HeapReAlloc() function, 495
HeapSize() function, 495
HeapUnlock() function, 495
HeapValidate() function, 495, 496

HeapWalk() function, 495, 496
HideCaret() function, 154
inet_ntoa() function, 1042
Init() function, 868
InitControls() function, 781, 827
InitCustomAppWiz() function, 1147, 1148, 1150, 1161
InitInstance() function, 526–537, 556, 558, 594, 843, 851–852, 858–859, 862–863, 869
InsertColumn() function, 701
InsertItem() function, 684, 685, 703–704
InsertMenu() function, 124
InsertString() function, 285
InstallKeyboardHook() function, 851, 852, 853
Invalidate() function, 171
InvalidateControl() function, 944
InvalidateRect() function, 171
IsBOF() function, 776, 823
IsDeleted() function, 776, 824
IsDialogMessage() function, 303
IsEmpty() function, 376
IsEOF() function, 776, 823
IsKindOf() function, 257, 273, 536
IsModified() function, 518
IsOpen() function, 416
IsPlaying() function, 433
IsSelected() function, 539–540
KillTimer() function, 450, 454, 1024
Left() function, 380
LineTo() function, 189
Listen() function, 1043
Load() function, 232–235, 878, 879, 882, 883
LoadBitmap() function, 208–209, 215, 672
LoadCursor() function, 846
LoadFrame() function, 109, 113, 126, 561, 562–563
LoadFromDisk() function, 427
LoadFromRes() function, 427
LoadLibrary() function, 496, 499, 841
LoadMappedBitmap() function, 209
LoadMenu() function, 129
LoadRecords() function, 344, 345
LocalAlloc() function, 470, 482
LogException() function, 271–272
Lookup() function, 759
main() function, 268
MakeNewFile() function, 405, 408, 409
malloc() function, 48, 470, 487–488, 490
MapViewOfFile() function, 472, 499, 506, 508
mciSendCommand() function, 425, 426, 439, 440
mciSendString() function, 425
MessageBox() function, 861
moveDown() function, 1103
MoveFirst() function, 772, 776
MoveLast() function, 772, 776
MoveNext() function, 772, 776, 828–829
MovePrev() function, 772, 776
MoveTo() function, 177, 189
moveUp() function, 1103
MoveWindow() function, 359
MulDiv() function, 195
Navigate() function, 1066, 1067
Navigate2() function, 1067, 1068
new() function, 470
Next() function, 1147
OnAlignmentChanged() function, 936
OnBeforeComplete2() function, 1077
OnBeforeNavigate2() function, 1078
OnBeforeNavigate2() function, 1073
OnBeginPrinting() function, 606, 607, 608, 609, 610, 618, 621
OnBtnFind() function, 369
OnBtnGetUser() function, 796
OnCancel() function, 853
OnChar() function, 304, 334
OnClose() function, 454, 562, 643–644, 645
OnCloseDocument() function, 520
OnCmdMsg() function, 111
OnContextmenuAdd() function, 695
OnCreate() function, 452, 454, 544, 665, 668, 677, 1012
OnDestroy() function, 454
OnDraw() function, 6, 21, 168–169, 180–181, 207, 209, 211, 226, 242, 408, 538, 539, 540, 605, 609, 610–611, 612–613, 617, 621, 650, 866, 880, 883, 947, 948–950, 1004–1005
OnEditUpdate() function, 337, 338
OnEndPrinting() function, 607, 610, 622
OnFileNew() function, 527, 535
OnFilePrintSetup() function, 627
OnFileSaveAs() function, 408
OnFileSendMail() function, 521
OnIdle() function, 461, 462, 463, 464, 492
OnInitDialog() function, 261, 325, 328–330, 341, 345, 354, 358–360, 365, 368, 369, 781, 1150–1151, 1076
OnInitialUpdate() function, 1065–1066, 1090
OnLButtonDown() function, 541
OnMouseMove() function, 134–135
OnNCDestroy() function, 709
OnNewDocument() function, 516–517, 520
OnNotify() function, 363–364
OnOK() function, 266–267, 271, 325, 676, 853, 1153
OnOpenDocument() function, 520
OnPaint() function, 94
OnPaletteChanged() function, 229
OnPrepareDC() function, 540, 606, 607, 609, 610, 612–614, 620, 621, 623–626

(continued)

functions (listed by name) *(continued)*
OnPreparePrinting() function, 607, 609, 612, 614, 615–616
OnPrint() function, 607, 609, 610, 612, 613, 614, 616–617, 621
OnRButtonDown() function, 129
OnSaveAs() function, 408
OnSaveDocument() function, 520, 521
OnTimer() function, 450, 452, 1012, 1024
OnUpdate() function, 518, 523, 540
OnUpdateCmdUI() function, 676
OnUpdateConnect() function, 669
OnUpdateFileSendMail() function, 521
OnViewGoModal() function, 641, 642, 647
Open() function, 245, 249, 388, 405, 406, 408, 411, 416, 433, 440, 763, 765, 771–774, 790, 794, 810, 812, 819–820, 822, 828
OpenClipboard() function, 420–421
OpenEx() function, 763, 764, 765
OpenFile() function, 502, 504, 1029
OpenFileMapping() function, 505
OpenRecorder() function, 804
OpenURL() function, 1022–1023, 1057
OutputDescription() function, 1133, 1136
parseInt() function, 1104
Paste() function, 290
Pause() function, 433, 441
PeekMessage() function, 851, 861
PerformWork() function, 268
Play() function, 427, 433, 441
PlayFromDisk() function, 428
PlayFromRes() function, 428
PlaySound() function, 424–425
PostNcDestroy() function, 561
PostQuitMessage() function, 711
PreCreateWindow() function, 120
PreTranslateMessage() function, 119, 120, 303, 338, 371–372
Print2Page() function, 598
PrintPageHeader() function, 614, 617, 619–620
[illegible]
PumpMessage() function, 119, 462, 638
PutFile() function, 1027
QueryInterface() function, 986
Read() function, 249, 390, 407, 408, 409, 845, 1030, 1043
ReadByte() function, 406
ReadData() function, 412
ReadDataWaiting() function, 412
ReadDWORD() function, 416
Receive() function, 1044
Record() function, 427–428
Refresh() function, 1067
RegisterActiveObject() function, 996
Release() function, 996–997
ReleaseBuffer() function, 377
ReleaseCapture() function, 148
ReleaseMutex() function, 859
RemoveDirectory() function, 1028–1029
RemoveItem() function, 525
RemoveMenu() function, 124
RemoveProp() function, 471
ReportError() function, 253–255
ResetContent() function, 285
ResumeThread() function, 708, 710
ReverseFind() function, 381
RevokeActiveObject() function, 996–997
Right() function, 380, 1137
Rollback() function, 271, 765, 814
RunModalLoop() function, 635–640, 644
SafeArrayGetLBound() function, 969
Save() function, 235–236, 263, 271, 428, 890
SaveInvoice() function, 271
SaveRecords() function, 345–346
SaveUser() function, 830–832
Scale() function, 886
Seek() function, 391
SeekToEnd() function, 391
SelectClipRgn() function, 200
SelectItem() function, 695
SelectObject() function, 179, 655, 658
SelectString() function, 285–286
SelItemRange() function, 286
Send() function, 1044–1045
SendData() function, 412
Serialize() function, 340–345, 516–517, 520, 523–524, 557, 565
SerializeElements() function, 524
SetAbortProc() function, 599
SetActivePage() function, 371
SetAddressBar() function, 1064
SetAlignment() function, 935–936, 944
SetBitmap() function, 208
SetBitmapDimension() function, 655
[illegible]
SetBkMode() function, 176, 189
SetButtonInfo() function, 676
SetCaptionProp() function, 944
SetCapture() function, 148
SetCaretPos() function, 154
SetColor() function, 307
SetCurrentDirectory() function, 1028
SetCurSel() function, 285, 338
SetDisabledTab() function, 362, 363
SetDocString() function, 532
SetEditSel() function, 338
SetEnabledText() function, 366
SetExtendedUI() function, 300

SetFieldType() function, 774, 822
SetFont() function, 307, 370
SetFullScreen() function, 1064
SetImageList() function, 700
SetIndent() function, 969
SetIndicators() function, 664
SetItem() function, 367–369
SetItemText() function, 703–704
SetMapMode() function, 190
SetMaxPage() function, 608, 614, 616, 623
SetMenuBar() function, 1064
SetMinPage() function, 608, 620
SetModifiedFlag function, 518, 523, 936
SetOption() function, 804
SetPalette() function, 238, 882
SetPaneStyle() function, 666–667
SetPathName() function, 519
SetPriorityClass() function, 716
SetProp() function, 471
SetRect() function, 280
SetResults() function, 368, 369
SetScrollPos() function, 296
SetSel() function, 286
SetSizes() function, 671
SetStatus() function, 392
SetStatusBar() function, 1064
SetStyle() function, 674
SetSystemPaletteUse() function, 229
SetTabStops() function, 288
SetTextAlign() function, 176–177
SetTextCharacterExtra() function, 178
SetTextColor() function, 175, 307
SetTextJustification() function, 178
SetThreadPriority() function, 708, 716
SetTimer() function, 450, 451–452, 454
SetTitle() function, 518
SetToolbar() function, 1064
SetViewportOrg() function, 190, 191
SetWindowLong() function, 591, 592, 686
SetWindowOrg() function, 190, 191
SetWindowPos() function, 354, 648
SetWindowsHookEx() function, 848–849, 851
SetWindowText() function, 288, 293
ShowCaret() function, 154
ShowPermissions() function, 796
ShowWindow() function, 321, 710
Sleep() function, 711
SloppyFunc() function, 47
SomeFunction() function, 269–270, 273
SQLAllocHandle() function, 738, 739
SQLBindCol() function, 741, 747
SQLConnect() function, 738, 746
SQLDescribeCol() function, 740–741, 751, 756
SQLDisconnect() function, 742
SQLDriverConnect() function, 738
SQLExecDirect() function, 740
SQLExecute() function, 751, 754
SQLFetch() function, 741, 747
SQLGetData() function, 740–741, 756, 758
SQLGetFunctions() function, 735, 739
SQLGetInfo() function, 739
SQLGetTypeInfo() function, 739
SQLNumResultCols() function, 740–741, 751, 756
SQLPrepare() function, 751, 754
SQLSetEnvAttr() function, 738
StartDoc() function, 597, 606, 611
StartPage() function, 597, 606, 611, 621
Stop() function, 427, 428, 433, 441, 1067, 1068
strcmp() function, 375
strcpy() function, 375
Stretch() function, 885
StretchBlt() function, 649, 655
StrokePath() function, 187
SubclassWindow() function, 592–594
SuspendThread() function, 710
TerminateThread() function, 715
TextOut() function, 177, 193–194, 196–197
ThreadFunc() function, 707
time() function, 720
TimerProc() function, 453
TlsAlloc() function, 471, 497
TlsFree() function, 497
TlsGetValue() function, 497
TlsSetValue() function, 497
TrackPopupMenu() function, 127, 129
TranslateMessage() function, 119, 152, 303, 638
Trim() function, 1136
Undo() function, 290
UnhookWindowsHookEx() function, 849, 852
UnsubclassWindow() function, 594
Update() function, 777, 824
UpdateAllViews() function, 518, 523, 540, 550, 558, 585
UpdateData() function, 323–325, 331, 585, 796, 830
UpdateRegistry() function, 927–928
UpdateRegistryAll() function, 959
UpdateWindow() function, 171, 172, 639
VariantChangeType() function, 933
VariantInit() function, 933
VirtualAlloc() function, 471, 482, 484–486, 487, 494, 495, 499, 502
VirtualFree() function, 485
VirtualLock() function, 486
VirtualProtect() function, 486
VirtualProtectEx() function, 486
VirtualQuery() function, 486, 494, 500
VirtualQueryEx() function, 486

(continued)

functions (listed by name) *(continued)*
VirtualUnlock() function, 486
WaitForSingleObject() function, 713, 714, 715, 858
WH_CALLWNDPROC function, 847
WH_CALLWNDPROCRET function, 847
WH_CBT function, 847
WH_DEBUG function, 847
WH_GETMESSAGE function, 847
WH_JOURNALPLAYBACK function, 847
WH_JOURNALRECORD function, 847
WH_KEYBOARD function, 847, 848
WH_KEYBOARD_LL function, 847
WH_MOUSE function, 848
WH_MOUSE_LL function, 848
WH_MSGFILTER function, 848
WH_SHELL function, 848
WH_SYSMSGFILTER function, 848
WinMain() function, 120
Write() function, 391, 407, 409, 1030
WriteByte() function, 407
WriteDWORD() function, 417
WriteString() function, 417
/FV option, 64
FW_BLACK constant, 182
FW_BOLD constant, 182
FW_DEMIBOLD constant, 182
FW_DONTCARE constant, 182
FW_EXTRABOLD constant, 182
FW_EXTRALIGHT constant, 182
FW_HEAVY constant, 182
FW_LIGHT constant, 182
FW_MEDIUM constant, 182
FW_NORMAL constant, 182
FW_REGULAR constant, 182
FW_SEMIBOLD constant, 182
FW_THIN constant, 182
FW_ULTRABOLD constant, 182
FW_ULTRALIGHT constant, 182

G

GDI (graphics device interface)
[illegible]
devices, 163–165
memory management and, 479–480, 504, 506
printing and, 597, 606, 610, 621–622
gdi32.lib, 61
General category, 32
GenerateDB() function, 249–250, 251
GENERIC_READ flag, 1030
GENERIC_WRITE flag, 1030
Get User button, 791
GetActiveObject() function, 997
GetAddressBar() function, 1064
GetAlignment() function, 935
GetAmbientProperty() function, 939
GetAt() function, 377
GetBackColor() function, 938
GetBitmapDimension() function, 655
GetBuffer() function, 247, 377
GetCaptionProp() method, 937–938
GetCaretPos() member function, 154
GetCharWidth() function, 195
GetCheck() function, 283
GetChildItem() function, 696
GetClientRect() function, 191
GetCurrentProcess() function, 716
GetCurSel() function, 285, 749
GetCursorPos() function, 135
GetData() function, 758
GetDataBuffer() function, 757
getDefaultConnect() function, 771
GetDefaultDBName() function, 819
GetDefaultSQL() function, 771, 794, 795, 820
GetDeviceCaps() function, 173, 195, 196, 205, 601
GetDevices() function, 427
GetDib() function, 879
GetDlgItem() function, 702
GetDocString() member function, 531
GetDocTemplate() function, 519
GetDocument() member function, 46–47, 523, 539
GetEditControl() function, 686–687
GetErrorMessage() function, 253–255, 259, 263, 265 266
GetExitCodeThread() function, 711, 712
GetFieldTypeFromSQLType() function, 756
GetFile() function, 1024–1027
GetFirstDocTemplatePosition() function, 536
GetFirstViewPosition() function, 517–518, 536
GetFromPage() function, 608
GetFtpConnection() function, 1021
GetFullName() function, 1064
GetHeight() function, 886
gethostbyname() function, 1042
GetIDispatch() function, 993
GetIndent() function, 969
GetInterface() function, 993
GetItem() function, 368
GetItemRect() function, 654
GetItemText() function, 696
GetKerningPairs() function, 602
GetLastError() function, 505, 841, 879
GetLength() function, 376, 392, 406
GetLine() function, 288
GetLineCount() function, 288–289
GetMaxPage() function, 608, 612
GetMenu() function, 123, 128
GetMenuItemID() function, 124
GetMenuString() function, 124
GetMessage() function, 453, 638, 715
GetMessageBar() function, 654
GetMessageString() function, 125

GetMinPage() function, 608, 612
GetNbrOfClients() function, 860, 861
GetNextDocTemplate() function, 536
GetNextItem() function, 525
GetNextSiblingItem() function, 696
GetNextView() function, 536
GetObject() function, 210, 656, 997
GetOutlineTextMetrics() function, 602
GetPackageExtension() method, 1127
GetParent() function, 718
GetParentFrame() function, 718, 719
GetPathName() function, 519
GetPermissionsByUSerID() function, 795
GetPosition() function, 406
GetProcAddress() function, 841
GetProcessHeap() function, 471, 494, 495
GetProp() function, 471
GetScrollInfo class, 297
GetStartPosition() function, 525
GetStatus() function, 392
GetStatusBar() function, 1064
GetStyle() function, 673
GetSubMenu() function, 123
GetSysColor() function, 159
GetTabbedTextExtent() function, 195
GetTestPtr() function, 860, 861
GetTextExtent() function, 195, 196–198
GetTextMetrics() function, 195, 198, 602
GetToPage() function, 608
GetTopLevelParent() function, 719
GetWidth() function, 886
GetWindowText() function, 288, 293
GIF (Graphics Interchange Format) images, 875, 877, 888, 890. *See also* images
global
  C++ objects, 854–862
  heaps, 470
  information records, 71–72, 73
  style sheets, 1087–1088
Global Optimizations option, 55, 56
GlobalAddAtom() function, 471
GlobalAlloc() function, 470, 482, 507
GlobalDllObjects project, 856–861, 1178
GlobalDllObjects.cpp, 858
GlobalDllObjects.h, 856, 857
GlobalDllObjectsClientDlg.cpp, 861
GlobalDllObjectsClient project, 861–862, 1178
GlobalFindAtom() function, 471
GMEM_DDESHARE flag, 507
GMEM_SHARE flag, 507
Go To command, 87
Go To dialog box, 87–88
GoBack() function, 1068
GoForward() function, 1068
GoHome() function, 1067, 1068
GoSearch() function, 1067, 1068
GoToMatchBrace() function, 1133
granularity, memory allocation, 487–488, 493
graphic(s). *See also* GDI (graphics device interface); images
  devices, 103–104
  displaying a moving, with HTML, 1100–1104
  family of MFC classes, 103–104
  raster graphics, 162–163
  types of, 162–164
  vector graphics, 163
Graphics mode attribute, 167
GraphicsDemo1 project, 1168
GraphicsDemo2 project, 1168
graphs, 89
GrayString() function, 193
Groups object, 809
GUIDGEN (Globally Unique Identifiers), 921–923, 972
GUIDGEN.EXE, 922, 972

H

<H1...H6> tag, 1083, 1084, 1094, 1095
halftone palettes, 227
handle maps (look-up tables), 126–128
handlers
  adding, 641–644
  creating, 330
  mouse event, 133–134, 136–142
hatch styles, 188–189
HC_ACTION constant, 851
HC_NOREMOVE constant, 851
header(s). *See also* header files
  controls, 698
  printing, 620–621
header files. *See also* headers
  modifying, 780, 827
  unavailable, 846
HEAP_NO_SERIALIZE, flag, 494
HeapAlloc() function, 487, 495
HeapCompact() function, 495
HeapCreate() function, 471, 494, 495
HeapDestroy() function, 495
HeapFree() function, 495
HeapLock() function, 495
HeapReAlloc() function, 495
heaps, 481, 487–488, 492–499
HeapSize() function, 495
HeapUnlock() function, 495
HeapValidate() function, 495, 496
HeapWalk() function, 495, 496
height, of text, 603
Height property, 1128
"Hello Windows 98" message, 172–173
HelloWorld1 project, 5–9, 1166
HelloWorld1.exe, 7–9
HelloWorld2 project, 9–11, 1166
HelloWorld2.exe, 10–11

HelloWorld3 project, 11–14, 1167
HelloWorld3.dll, 11–14
Help button, 360
helper functions, 617–620, 783, 820, 832, 834
HexView project, 531, 545, 1173
HexView.cpp, 70, 545–551
HexViewDoc.cpp, 545–551
HexView.dsw, 545
HExView.exe, 545
HexViewMDI project, 627–631, 1174
HexViewMDI.cpp, 628–631
HexViewMDI.dsw, 627
HexViewMDI.exe, 627–631
HexView.rc, 529–530
HexViewView.cpp, 545–551
hFile parameter, 504
HideCaret() member function, 154
hiding/displaying toolbars, 26–28, 673–674
HIGH_PRORITY_CLASS priority class, 717
hImage handler, 293–294
hInstance variable, 37
hit counts, 67–68
HKEY_CLASSES_ROOT Registry key, 414, 415
HKEY_CLASSES_USER Registry key, 414
HKEY_CURRENT_CONFIG Registry key, 414
HKEY_CURRENT_USER Registry key, 415
HKEY_DYN_DATA Registry key, 414
HKEY_LOCAL_MACHINE Registry key, 414–415, 416
HKEY_USERS Registry key, 414, 415
hooks, 847–854
<HREF> tag, 1094
HSV color, 224–225
HSV.c, 224–225
HTML (HyperText Markup Language), 1015–1016, 1085–1090
  CHTMLView class, 4, 542, 1063–1106
  HTMLViewer project and, 1090–1091, 1099, 1100–1104
  macro documentation in, 1130–1132
  tags, list of common, 1084–1085
<HTML> tag, 1083, 1084
html1.htm, 1082
HTMLViewer project, 1090–1091, 1099, 1100–1104
HTMLViewerView.cpp, 1091
HTTP (HyperText Transfer Protocol), 1019, 1057–1058
Huffman compression, [illegible]
hWnd parameter, 453

I

IConnectionPoint interface, 909
ID field, 108
ID_FILE_SEND_MAIL constant, 521
ID_INDICATOR_CAPS constant, 665
ID_INDICATOR_NUMS constant, 665
ID_INDICATOR_SCRL constant, 665
ID_MY_STATUS_BAR constant, 667–668
IDB_LARGE_IMAGES resource, 700
IDB_SMALL_IMAGES resource, 700
IDC_CUSTS parameter, 278
IDD_IMAGE_VIEWER resource editor, 865–866
IDE (Integrated Development Environment), 915, 919, 922
  basic description of, 17–28
  debugging and, 35, 36
  context menus and, 128
  creating your first project with, 19–23
  customizing, 23–26
  four main areas of, 17–19
  Profiler and, 57, 59
  toolbars, using, 26–28
idHook argument, 848
IDispatch interface, 801, 808, 908, 909, 912–913, 918–920, 936, 937, 943, 955–959, 964, 972, 977–986, 999
IDLE_PRIORITY_CLASS priority class, 717
IDoublePend interface, 1003, 1005–1006
IDR_MAINFRAME menu resource, 108, 529–521, 533, 558, 561, 641
IErrorInfo object, 990–991
Illegal Operation dialog box, 31
image(s). *See also* graphics
  adding, 871–902
  creating, from the Clipboard, 889
  creating, from device contexts, 888
  documents, 865–870
  cropping, 885–887
  displaying, 293–294, 880–882
  libraries, 871–878, 881
  list controls, 679–680
  loading, 878–882
  processing, 891–894
  saving, 890–891
  scaling, 885–887
ImageLoad.lib, 881
imageobject.h, 866
ImageObject.lib, 875–878, 881
ImageViewer project, 865–870, 1177
ImageViewerClient project, 868–869, 1177
ImageViewerClient.h, 868
ImageViewer.cpp, 867
ImageViewer.h, 867, 869, 883
ImageViewerView.h, 866
ImageViewerView.cpp, 866
<IMG> tag, 1084
IMPLEMENT_DYNAMIC macro, 526, 992
IMPLEMENT_DYNCREATE macro, 992
IMPLEMENT_SERIAL macro, 526
import libraries, unavailable, 846
importing Profiler data, 69–70
Improve Float Consistency option, 56
/INC option, 62–64, 66

#include directive, 356, 688, 693, 778, 780, 791, 825, 827, 853, 866–868, 1161
include paths, 874
index property, 531–532
inet_ntoa() function, 1042
Informix, 103
InfoViewer, 1005
INIT environment variable, 61
Init() function, 868
InitControls() function, 781, 827
InitCustomAppWiz() function, 1147, 1148, 1150, 1161
initialization code, 745–751
InitInstance() function, 526–537, 556, 558, 594, 843, 851–852, 858–859, 862–863, 869
Inline Function Expansion option, 56
inlined code, profiling, 76
InProc.dll, 75–76
Insert Resource dialog box, 313, 351
InsertColumn() function, 701
InsertItem() function, 684, 685, 703–704
InsertMenu() function, 124
InsertString() member function, 285
InstallContents.EXE, 1164
InstallKeyboardHook() function, 851, 852, 853
instantiation, of automation servers, 992–998
integrated debugger. *See also* debugging
  basic description of, 31–45
  using, when you run an project, 34–35
Intel
  iRMX operating system, 473
  processors, 475
IntelliSense, 6, 21
interfaces. *See also* interfaces (listed by name)
  basic description of, 808–809, 918
  custom, 977
  dual-interface servers, 977–986
interfaces (listed by name). *See also* interfaces
  CoClass interface, 956–958, 978, 994, 1003
  Dispinterface interface, 936, 937, 956–958
  IConnectionPoint interface, 909
  IDispatch interface, 801, 808, 908, 909, 912–913, 918–920, 936, 937, 943, 955–959, 964, 972, 977–986, 999
  IDoublePend interface, 1003, 1005–1006
  ISupportErrorInfo interface, 986–988
  ITracker interface, 982
  MCI (Media Control Interface), 424–426, 439–441
  Page interface, 919
  QuickActivate interface, 913
  RPC interface, 921
Internet
  access control for, 1078
  programming, 1019–1062
Internet Explorer browser (Microsoft), 910, 1122, 1130, 1063, 1066–1068
Internet Professional Developers' Conference, 916
interoperability, 732
INVALID_HANDLE_VALUE preprocessor symbol, 503
Invalidate() function, 171
InvalidateControl() function, 944
InvalidateRect() function, 171
Invoke() method, 933
IO filename option, 65
iRMX operating system (Intel), 473
IsBOF() function, 776, 823
IsDeleted() function, 776, 824
IsDialogMessage() function, 303
IsEmpty() function, 376
IsEOF() function, 776, 823
IsKindOf() function, 257, 273, 536
IsModified() member function, 518
ISO-compliant compilers, 1000
IsOpen() function, 416
IsPlaying() function, 433
IsSelected() function, 539–540
ISupportErrorInfo interface, 986–988
IT filename option, 65
ITracker interface, 982
IUnknown, 999

J

JavaScript, 1100, 1102–1103, 1106, 1081, 1094
JPEG images, 865, 875, 877–878, 888, 890. *See also* images

K

kernel, 78, 503, 504, 506, 706
KERNEL objects, 503, 504, 506
KERNEL32.DBG, 78
KERNEL32.DLL, 78
kerning pairs, 602
KeybdHook project, 849–852, 1178
KeybdHookClient project, 853–854
KeybdHookClientDlg.cpp, 853
KeybdHook.cpp, 850–852
KeybdHook.h, 849
keyboard(s). *See also* keyboard shortcuts
  cursors, creating/maintaining, 153–156
  focus, echoing, 153–159
  input, handling, 131–132, 149–161
  interfaces, adding, 302–303
  Microsoft Natural keyboard, 128
  scan codes, 149–150
Keyboard Map, 23–24
keyboard shortcut(s)
  accelerator tables for, 113, 114–115, 118–121
  assigning macros to, 1121–1122
  adding, 24–26
  basic description of, 107, 113–121
  context menus and, 128

(continued)

keyboard shortcut(s) *(continued)*
    defining, 114–115
    deleting, 23, 24–26
    editing, 24–26
    selecting appropriate, 116–118
    for single-stepping commands, 42
    standard Windows, 116–117
    viewing current, 23–24
    the Windows logical keyboard and, 151
Keyboard tab, 24–26
KillTimer() function, 450, 454, 1024

L

labels
    adding the capability to edit, 696–697
    editing, 685–689
LBN_SELCHANGE message, 829
LBS_DISABLENOSCROLL style flag, 284
LBS_EXTENDEDSEL style flag, 284
LBS_HASSTRINGS style flag, 284
LBS_MULTICOLUMN style flag, 284
LBS_MULTIPLESEL style flag, 284
LBS_NOINTEGRALHEIGHT style flag, 284
LBS_NOREDRAW style flag, 284
LBS_NOSEL style flag, 284
LBS_NOTIFY style flag, 284
LBS_SORT style flag, 284
LBS_STANDARD style flag, 284
LBS_USETABSTOPS style flag, 284
LBS_WANTKEYBOARDINPUT style flag, 284
/LC option, 65
lCount parameter, 461, 462, 463
lcount.bat, 61
lcover.bat, 61
leading, external/internal, 198–199, 603
Learnide project, 21–22, 1167
learnide.exe, 21–22
Left() function, 380
Left property, 1128
<LI> tag, 1084, 1085
Library project, 1172
life cycles, for templates, 533–534
line coverage option, 60, 61, 76
line counting option, 60, 67–69, 76
line profiling option, 59–61, 67–68, 76
LineTo() function, 189
LineUp() method, 1133
Link tab, 33–34, 57, 61, 872
<LINK> tag, 1084, 1086
linked style sheets, 1088
linker options, for debugging, 32
list(s)
    boxes, 278, 283–286
    HTML for, 1084, 1085–1087
    views, 679–680, 697–704
LISTBOX class, 278
ListCtrlDemo project, 1174
Listen() function, 1043
Load() function, 232–235, 878, 879, 882, 883
LoadAccelerators class, 119
LoadBitmap() function, 208–209, 215, 672
LoadCursor() function, 846
LoadFrame() member function, 109, 113, 126, 561, 562–563
LoadFromDisk() function, 427
LoadFromRes() function, 427
LoadLibrary() function, 496, 499, 841
LoadMappedBitmap() function, 209
LoadMenu() function, 129
LoadRecords() function, 344, 345
Loads properties asynchronously option, 925–926
loc_enu.rc, 1156–1157
local information records, 72, 73, 74
local heaps, 470. *See also* heaps
LocalAlloc() function, 470, 482
Locals tab, 36
Location box, 20
LOGBRUSH structure, 188
LogException() function, 271–272
logic errors, 29–30. *See also* errors
logical inches, 279
LOGPALETTE structure, 225–226
Lookup() function, 759
loops
    for loops, 756
    modal loops, 635–661
    OnIdle loops, 449, 461–466, 1172–1173
    while loops, 776, 1133
lpctstrCaption property, 929
lpszConnect argument, 764, 811
lpszMapName argument, 505
lpszNewItem parameter, 124
lpszSQL argument, 771, 772
lpvAddress parameter, 484
/LV option, 65
LVM_INSERTITEM message, 698
LZSS compression, 402, 404, 409
LZW compression, 402, 404–405, 409, 877

M

/M compiler switch, 33
/M filename option, 65
macro(s)
    basic description of, 1109–1110
    creating, 1112–1117
    custom AppWizards and, 1141–1142
    dictionaries, 1148
    for handling button messages, 286
    for handling CEdit messages, 290, 291
    keystroke combinations and, 120
    persistent, 1160–1161
Macro command, 1129

Macro dialog box, 1112, 1119–1120, 1129
main() function, 268
MainFrm.cpp, 228–229, 356–357, 514
MainFrm.h, 677
makefiles, 32, 52
MAKEINTRESOURCE() macro, 120
MakeNewFile() function, 405, 408, 409
MakeReplica() method, 807
malloc() function, 48, 470, 487–488, 490
MAP files, 63, 67–68, 74, 76, 79
MAPI (Messaging API), 52, 521, 543
Mapping mode attribute, 167
mapping modes, 167, 189–191
MapViewOfFile() function, 472, 499, 506, 508
Maximize Speed option, 55
MCGA video, 205
MCI (Media Control Interface), 424–426, 439–441
MCI_CLOSE command, 426, 439–440
MCI_OPEN command, 426, 439–440
MCI_OPEN message, 426
MCI_PAUSE command, 439
MCI_PLAY command, 426
MCI_PLAY command, 426, 439–440
MCI_RECORD command, 426
MCI_SAVE command, 426
MCI_SEEK command, 426, 439–440
mciSendCommand() function, 425, 426, 439, 440
mciSendString() function, 425
MCI_SET command, 439
MCI_STATUS command, 439
MCI_STOP command, 426, 439–440
MDI (Multiple Document Interface), 97, 513–515, 518, 1144–1145
  projects, layout of, 553–596
  document/view designs and, 533
  frame windows and, 543
  keystroke combinations, 117
  message processing sequences, 112
MEM_COMMIT flag, 484, 485
MEM_DECOMMIT flag, 485
MEM_RESERVE flag, 471, 484
member functions (listed by name). *See also* functions
  AddDocTemplate member function, 527, 528, 535, 537, 558, 594, 867
  AddNewObj() member function, 522, 523
  AddString() member function, 285
  CreateGrayCaret() member function, 154
  CreateSolidCaret() member function, 154
  Delete() member function, 253–254, 470, 777, 824
  DeleteString() member function, 285
  DestroyCaret() member function, 154
  DestroyWindow() member function, 561–562, 644
  DoModal member function, 320, 321, 325, 350, 352, 356, 627, 863
  FindString() member function, 286, 337, 338
  GetCaretPos() member function, 154
  GetDocString() member function, 531
  GetDocument() member function, 46–47, 523, 539
  HideCaret() member function, 154
  InsertString() member function, 285
  IsModified() member function, 518
  LoadFrame() member function, 109, 113, 126, 561, 562–563
  OnBtnGetUser() member function, 796
  OnClose() member function, 454, 562, 643–644, 645
  OnCreate() member function, 452, 454, 544, 665, 668, 677, 1012
  OnDraw() member function, 6, 21, 168–169, 180–181, 207, 209, 211, 226, 242, 408, 538, 539, 540, 605, 609, 610–611, 612–613, 617, 621, 650, 866, 880, 883, 947, 948–950, 1004–1005
  OnFileNew() member function, 527, 535
  OnLButtonDown() member function, 541
  OnNewDocument() member function, 516–517, 520
  OnPaint() member function, 94
  OnPrepareDC() member function, 540, 606, 607, 609, 610, 612–614, 620, 621, 623–626
  OnUpdate() member function, 518, 523, 540
  OnUpdateFileSendMail() member function, 521
  PostNcDestroy() member function, 561
  ResetContent() member function, 285
  Serialize() member function, 340–345, 516–517, 520, 523–524, 557, 565
  SetCaretPos() member function, 154
  SetDocString() member function, 532
  SetModifiedFlag member function, 518, 523, 936
  SetTitle() member function, 518
  ShowCaret() member function, 154
  UpdateAllViews() member function, 518, 523, 540, 556, 558, 585
Member Variables tab, 940, 699
memory. *See also* memory page(s); RAM (random-access memory)
  bitmap, 203–206, 209, 242–243
  cleanup, 478–481
  contents, viewing, during debugging, 37–38
  contexts, 474–475
  GDI and, 169–170
  heaps, 481, 487–488, 492–499
  leaks, 47–48
  loading files into, 408
  management, 469–481, 507–512
  -mapped file I/O, 500–507
  private process, 481–499
  process, 477–478, 481–499
  sound and, 427, 428
  stack space, allocating, 486
  threads and, 708
  types of, available to MFC/Win32 programs running on Windows 98, 470–472

memory page(s)
  allocating, 482–486
  protection flags for, 505
  shared, allocating, 507–512
  tables, 473, 474–475, 499–500
menu(s)
  changing, at runtime, 122–123
  creating, 108–112
  dynamically changed, 121–128
  modification flags, 125
  pop-up (context), 123–126, 128–130, 689–692, 694
menu flags
  MF_BITMAP menu flag, 125
  MF_BYCOMMAND menu flag, 125
  MF_BYPOSITION menu flag, 125
  MF_CHECKED menu flag, 125
  MF_ENABLED menu flag, 125
  MF_GRAYED menu flag, 125
  MF_MENUBARBREAK menu flag, 125
  MF_MENUBREAK menu flag, 125
  MF_OWNERDRAW menu flag, 125
  MF_POP-UP menu flag, 125
  MF_SEPARATOR menu flag, 125
  MF_STRING menu flag, 125
  MF_UNCHECKED menu flag, 125
Merge option, 60
MERGECOPY raster operation, 658
MERGEPAINT raster operation, 658
message(s). *See also* messages (listed by name)
  basic description of, 131–132
  boxes, speeding up debugging with, 45
  handlers, 131–134
  pumps, 302
  viewing, with Spy++, 81–90
MessageBox() function, 861
messages (listed by name). *See also* messages
  BN_CLICKED message, 346–348, 786, 830, 833–834
  CHANGECBCHAIN message, 41
  CN_UPDATE_COMMAND_UI message, 110–111
  LBN_SELCHANGE message, 829
  LVM_INSERTITEM message, 698
  [illegible]
  TVN_BEGINLABELEDIT message, 685, 686, 687
  TVN_ENDLABELEDIT message, 685–686, 687, 697
  WM_CHAR message, 149, 151–152, 155, 281–282, 334
  WM_CLOSE message, 641
  WM_CREATE message, 111, 129, 452, 641
  WM_CTLCOLOR message, 307–308
  WM_DDE_DATA message, 481
  WM_DESTROY message, 85, 330–331, 835
  WM_GETFOCUS message, 228
  WM_HSCROLL message, 298
  WM_KEYDOWN message, 149, 151, 152
  WM_KEYUP message, 149, 151, 152
  WM_KILLFOCUS message, 154–155, 157–158
  WM_LBUTTONDOWN message, 132, 133, 147, 148, 157
  WM_LBUTTONUP message, 132, 147, 148
  WM_MBUTTONUP message, 132
  WM_MOUSEMOVE message, 132, 133, 134, 148
  WM_MOVE message, 111
  WM_NCDESTROY message, 85
  WM_NCHITTEST message, 143, 148
  WM_NCLBUTTONDOWN message, 142, 143
  WM_NCLBUTTONUP message, 143
  WM_NCMBUTTONWDOWN message, 143
  WM_NCMOUSEMOVE message, 143
  WM_NCRBUTTONDOWN message, 143
  WM_NCRBUTTONUP message, 143
  WM_PAINT message, 104, 155, 158–159, 168–173, 193, 461, 610, 623, 651
  WM_PALETTECHANGED message, 229
  WM_QUERYNEWPALETTE message, 228–229
  WM_QUIT message, 709, 711, 861
  WM_RBUTTONDOWN message, 129, 132, 690, 693, 694–695
  WM_RBUTTONUP message, 132
  WM_SETCURSOR message, 143, 148
  WM_SETFOCUS message, 154, 157–158
  WM_SIZE message, 111
  WM_SYSCOMMAND message, 85
  WM_SYSTIMER message, 461
  WM_TIMER message, 450–454
  WM_VSCROLL message, 298
Messages window, 83–85
metafiles, 164–165, 293–294
Method field, 73
methods. *See also* methods (listed by name)
  adding, 964–969
  creating, 928–934
methods (listed by name). *See also* methods
  ActiveConfiguration() method, 1128
  AddKeyBinding() method, 1127
  AddProject() method, 1127
  AddRef() method, 805
  BeginTrans() method, 806
  Build() method, 1127
  CaptionMethod() method, 928–934, 936, 937, 944
  Clean() method, 1127
  Count() method, 806
  CreateProperty() method, 807
  CreateQueryDef() method, 807
  CreateRelation() method, 807
  CreateTableDef() method, 807
  DoPropExchange() method, 945–946
  EnableModeless() method, 1127
  EndOfLine() method, 1133

ExecuteCommand() method, 1127
ExecuteConfiguration() method, 1127
FileText() method, 1133
GetCaptionProp() method, 937–938
GetPackageExtension() method, 1127
Invoke() method, 933
LineUp() method, 1133
MakeReplica() method, 807
Move() method, 808
MoveFirst() method, 808, 820, 823
MoveLast() method, 808
MoveNext() method, 808, 820, 823
MovePrevious() method, 808, 820, 823
New() method, 1132
OpenRecordSet() method, 808
OutputLines() method, 965, 966–969
PopulatePartial() method, 807
PrintToOutputWindow() method, 1127
Quit() method, 1127
RebuildAll() method, 1127
Refresh() method, 806, 807
Release() method, 809
Rollback() method, 806
Save() method, 1132
Seek() method, 808
SetCaptionProp() method, 937–938
SetValue() method, 1005
StartOfDocument() method, 1133
Synchronize() method, 807
Update() method, 808
MFC (Microsoft Foundation Classes)
for advanced Windows user interfaces, 633–662
advantages of using, 95–97
basic description of, 23, 94–95
control bars, 670–671
DAO classes, 809–810
DAO demo, 824–836
database classes, 761–800
debugging and, 45–46, 48
design philosophy, 95
diagnostic allocator, 488–492
extension DLLs, 839, 842, 862–870
features, 97–98
hierarchy design, 98–105
power of, 94
printing with, 605–622
programming, overview of, 93–106
source code, browsing, 89–90
MFC.Bsc, 89–90
MFCAPWZ.DLL (AppWizard manager), 1140–1144, 1147, 1153–1155
MFCControl project, 923–927, 1174, 1178
MFCControlNoWin control, 924, 925
MFCControl.odl, 934
MFCControlSubWin control, 924, 926
MFCControlWin control, 924–925
MFCControlWinCtl.cpp, 937–938
MFCControlWinCtl.h, 929, 930–932
MFCControlWinPpg.cpp, 940–942
MFCServer project, 1178–1179
MFCServer.clw, 955
MFCServer.cpp, 955
MFCServer.def, 955
MFCServer.dsp, 955
MFCServer.dsw, 955
MFCServer.h, 955
MFCServer.ncb, 955
MFCServer.odl, 955–958, 980
MFCServer.rc, 955
MFCTracer project, 48
Microsoft Exchange, 77–79
Microsoft Jet, 103. *See also* Microsoft Access
Microsoft Natural keyboard, 128
Microsoft Web site, 907, 978, 1015, 1058, 1064
microprocessors, 77, 163, 462
compression and, 405
memory management and, 472–474, 499, 500
threads and, 705, 715, 716
MIDI (Musical Instrument Digital Interface), 431–437, 1172
MIDIDemo project, 432–437, 1172
MIDIDemo.exe, 434
MIDIDemoView.cpp, 434–437
Mini Editor project, 302, 1169
Minimize Size option, 55
Mktyplib compiler, 921
MLF_NOIDLEMSG parameter, 638–639
MLF_NOKICKIDLE parameter, 638–639
MLF_SHOWONIDLE parameter, 638–639
MM_ANSIOTROPIC mapping mode, 190–191
MM_HIENGLISH mapping mode, 190–191
MM_HIMETRIC mapping mode, 190–191
MM_ISOTROPIC mapping mode, 190–191
MM_LOENGLISH mapping mode, 190–191
MM_LOMETRIC mapping mode, 190–191
mmsystem.h, 426, 439, 961, 963
MM_TEXT mapping mode, 135, 170, 190–191, 622
MM_TWIPS mapping mode, 190–191
mnemonics, 109, 113, 370–372
modal
dialogs, 319, 320–321
loops, 635–661
property sheets, 352, 354–357
windows, creating/closing, 640–645
ModalDemo project, 354–357
ModalFrameWnd class, 642
ModalPropertySheetDemo project, 1170
ModalWin project, 640–661

modeless
  dialogs, 321
  property sheets, 352–353
modems, 105, 411
modifier keys, 114
module, use of the term, 487
monolithic projects, 105
Month Calendar controls, 4
mouse
  capture, 147–148
  cursor, changing, 143–149
  event handlers, 133–134, 136–142
  events, nonclient, 142–143
  input, 131–149
  message handlers, 131–134
  movement, limiting, 148–149
Mouse pointer notifications when inactive option, 925–926
MouseDemo1 project, 136–142, 1167
MouseDemo1.EXE, 136–142
MouseDemo1View.cpp, 136–142
MouseDemo2 project, 144–149, 1167
MouseDemo2.exe, 144–149
MouseDemo2View.cpp, 144–149
Move Down button, 86
Move() method, 808
Move Up button, 86
moveDown() function, 1103
MoveFirst() function, 772, 776
MoveFirst() method, 808, 820, 823
MoveLast() method, 808
MoveLast() function, 772, 776
MoveNext() function, 772, 776, 828–829
MoveNext() method, 808, 820, 823
MovePrev() function, 772, 776
MovePrevious() method, 808, 820, 823
MoveTo() function, 177, 189
moveUp() function, 1103
MoveWindow() function, 359
MS-DOS, 10, 149–150, 473, 476–477, 503, 1164
MSG_DONTROUTE flag, 1045
MSG_OOB flag, 1044, 1045
MSG_PEEK flag, 1044
Msvcom.exe, 49
Msvcp60.dll, 49
Msvcrt.dll, 49
MSysConf settings, 803
MulDiv() function, 195
multi-track AppWizards, 1144
MultiBrowser project, 1071–1075, 1180
MultiBrowser.dsw, 1071–1075
MultiBrowser.exe, 1071–1075
multilingual projects, 846
multimedia timers, 451–452
Multiple Select Properties dialog box, 316
multithreading, 76–77, 98, 705–706, 720
MyApp.cpp, 1158
MyApp.h, 1158
MyMacros.DSM, 1118
MYPROG.PBT, 69
MYPROG.TXT, 69
MyTestDlgApp.rc, 1143

N

Name field, 36
Named Pipes, 845
Navigate() function, 1066, 1067
Navigate2() function, 1067, 1068
nBitcount property, 657
_near keyword, 469, 498
nested
  MFC extension DLLs, 864–865
  objects, 919, 992
NetBIOS, 845
New button, 27
New Class dialog box, 321–322, 334, 766–767, 956
New dialog box, 530, 954, 1001
new() function, 470
New() method, 1132
new operator, 47–48, 481, 487, 488, 857
New Project Information dialog box, 927, 954
New Projects dialog box, 19–20
New Virtual Overide dialog box, 616
newline (/n) character, 109, 530
newproj.inf, 1154–1155, 1158, 1160
Next() function, 1147
nFlags parameter, 124
nHeight parameter, 181, 206, 209
nIDNewItem parameter, 124
nMovingOffset parameter, 721
nMovingRadius parameter, 721
"no-man's-land" areas, 489
/NOLOGO option, 65
nOpenType argument, 771
NORMAL_PRORITY_CLASS priority class, 716, 717
Notepad, 85, 853–854
Notepad.exe, 85
NOTSRCCOPY raster operation, 658, 660
NOTSRCERASE raster operation, 658
nPlanes property, 657
nPos parameter, 123
nPriority property, 707
NULL values, 476, 500, 503–505, 771, 841, 858, 860, 879
nWeight parameter, 182
nWidth parameter, 206, 209

O

object(s)
  dumping, 47
  models, 1091–1093
  nested, 919, 992
<OBJECT> tag, 1016

OC 96 specification, 913, 947
OCXs (OLE controls), 906, 924
/Od compiler option, 32
ODBC (Open Database Connectivity)
advantages/disadvantages of, 801
API conformance levels, 734–735
basic description of, 729–760
configuring, 735–737
DAO and, 801, 809, 811
fetching data with, 742–757
implementation, 735–742
MFC support for, 97, 103–105
SDK, 729, 730, 733, 739, 742, 743, 762
SQL conformance levels, 735
standard, 732–734
support, adding, 743
terminology, 730–731
odbc32.lib, 743, 750
ODBCClasses project, 1175–1176
ODBCDemo project, 742–757, 1175
ODBCDemoDlg.h, 745
ODBCDirect object, 806
ODBCDynamic.h, 752
ODBCDynamicTest project, 1176
OEM character set, 183
OEM_CHARSET constant, 183
OFSTRUCT structure, 502–503
/OI filename option, 65
<OL> tag, 1085
OLE (Object Linking and Embedding), 906–907, 910–912, 963
automation, 524–526, 801
CFormView class and, 543
Consumer and Provider templates, 4–5
CView class and, 538, 539
document/view designs and, 532
embedded objects, 906
exceptions, 971–977, 986–992
frame windows and, 543
guidelines, 920
linked objects, 906
the Registry and, 413, 415
string resources and, 531
toolbars and, 670
Ole2View, 922
/OM option, 65
ON_CBN_CLOSEUP macro, 301
ON_CBN_DBLCLK macro, 301
ON_CBN_DROPDOWN macro, 301
ON_CBN_EDITCHANGE macro, 301
ON_CBN_EDITUPDATE macro, 301
ON_CBN_ERRSPACE macro, 301
ON_CBN_KILLFOCUS macro, 301
ON_CBN_SELCHANGE macro, 301
ON_CBN_SELENDCANCEL macro, 301
ON_CBN_SELENDOK macro, 301
ON_CBN_SETFOCUS macro, 301
ON_COMMAND_RANGE macro, 122
ON_EN macros, 291–292
ON_LBN_DBLCLK macro, 286
ON_LBN_ERRSPACE macro, 286
ON_LBN_KILLFOCUS macro, 286
ON_LBN_SELCANCEL macro, 286
ON_LBN_SELCHANGE macro, 286
ON_LBN_SETFOCUS macro, 286
ON_STN_CLICKED macro, 294
ON_STN_DBLCLK macro, 294
ON_STN_DISABLE macro, 294
ON_STN_ENABLE macro, 294
ON_WM_CTLCOLOR_REFLECT macro, 308
OnAlignmentChanged() function, 936
OnBeforeComplete2() function, 1077
OnBeforeNavigate2() function, 1078
OnBeforeNavigate2() function, 1073
OnBeginPrinting() function, 606, 607, 608, 609, 610, 618, 621
OnBtnFind() function, 369
OnBtnGetUser() member function, 796
OnCancel() function, 853
OnChar() function, 304, 334
OnClose() member function, 454, 562, 643–644, 645
OnCloseDocument() function, 520
OnCmdMsg() function, 111
OnContextmenuAdd() function, 695
OnCreate() member function, 452, 454, 544, 665, 668, 677, 1012
OnDestroy() function, 454
OnDraw() member function, 6, 21, 168–169, 180–181, 207, 209, 211, 226, 242, 408, 538, 539, 540, 605, 609, 610–611, 612–613, 617, 621, 650, 866, 880, 883, 947, 948–950, 1004–1005
OnEditUpdate() function, 337, 338
OnEndPrinting() function, 607, 610, 622
OnFileNew() member function, 527, 535
OnFilePrintSetup() function, 627
OnFileSaveAs() function, 408
OnFileSendMail() function, 521
OnIdle() function, 161, 162, 163, 164, 492
OnIdle loops, 449, 461–466, 1172–1173
OnIdleDemo project, 463–466, 1172–1173
OnIdleDemo.cpp, 464
OnIdleDemo.exe, 464
OnInitDialog() function, 261, 325, 328–330, 341, 345, 354, 358–360, 365, 368, 369, 781, 1150–1151, 1076
OnInitialUpdate() function, 1065–1066, 1090
OnLButtonDown() member function, 541
OnMouseMove() function, 134–135
OnNCDestroy() function, 709
OnNewDocument() member function, 516–517, 520
OnNotify() function, 363–364

OnOK() function, 266–267, 271, 325, 676, 853, 1153
OnOpenDocument() function, 520
OnPaint() member function, 94
OnPaletteChanged() function, 229
OnPrepareDC() member function, 540, 606, 607, 609, 610, 612–614, 620, 621, 623–626
OnPreparePrinting() function, 607, 609, 612, 614, 615–616
OnPrint() function, 607, 609, 610, 612, 613, 614, 616–617, 621
OnRButtonDown() function, 129
OnSaveAs() function, 408
OnSaveDocument() function, 520, 521
OnTimer() function, 450, 452, 1012, 1024
OnUpdate() member function, 518, 523, 540
OnUpdateCmdUI() function, 676
OnUpdateConnect() function, 669
OnUpdateFileSendMail() member function, 521
OnViewGoModal() function, 641, 642, 647
Open command, 401
Open() function, 245, 249, 388, 405, 406, 408, 411, 416, 433, 440, 763, 765, 771–774, 790, 794, 810, 812, 819–820, 822, 828
OpenClipboard() function, 420–421
OpenEx() function, 763, 764, 765
OpenFile() function, 502, 504, 1029
OpenFileMapping() function, 505
OpenRecorder() function, 804
OpenRecordSet() method, 808
OpenURL() function, 1022–1023, 1057
optimizations, 32, 54–56, 925–926
Optimized drawing code option, 925–926
Option command, 51
Options dialog box, 874
OR operation, 216
Oracle, 103
Ordering.TXT, 875
OS/2 operating system, 481, 473
/OT filename option, 65
Output window, 48
OutputDescription() function, 1133, 1136
OutputLines() method, 965, 966–969
OWL (Object Window Library), 93

P

<P> tag, 1085
PACKBITS compression, 890–891
page(s)
  allocating, 482–486
  protection flags for, 505
  shared, 472, 499–500, 507–512
  tables, 473, 474–475, 499–500
Page interface, 919
PAGE_NOACCESS flag, 484
PAGE_READONLY flag, 505
PAGE_READWRITE flag, 505
PAGE_REWRITE flag, 484
PAGE_WRITECOPY flag, 505
pagination, when printing, 614–617, 620
PaintObj project, 566–574, 1173
Paintobj.cpp, 566–474
Paintobj.exe, 566–474
Paintobjvw.cpp, 566–474
Paintvw.cpp, 566, 586–590
Palette attribute, 167
palette manager, 225–226
palettes, color, 205, 222–229, 880–882
PALETTEENTRY structure, 225–226
palettized devices, 225
palettized images, 225
panes, using different views in, 579–580
Paradox, 731
parameterized queries, 793, 794
Parameterized project, 791, 795–798, 1176
ParameterizedDlg.cpp, 791, 795–798
parameters
  bFileMappingObject parameter, 506
  cbSize parameter, 297
  ctlRect parameter, 278
  dwAction parameter, 484
  dwFileOffsetHigh parameter, 506
  dwFileOffsetLow parameter, 506
  dwMaxSizeLow parameter, 505
  dwNumberOfBytesToMap parameter, 506
  dwProtect parameter, 505
  dwROP parameter, 209
  hFile parameter, 504
  hWnd parameter, 453
  IDC_CUSTS parameter, 278
  lCount parameter, 461, 462, 463
  lpszNewItem parameter, 124
  lpvAddress parameter, 484
  MLF_NOIDLEMSG parameter, 638–639
  MLF_NOKICKIDLE parameter, 638–639
  MLF_SHOWONIDLE parameter, 638–639
  nFlags parameter, 124
  nHeight parameter, 181, 206, 209
  nIDNewItem parameter, 124
  nMovingOffset parameter, 721
  nMovingRadius parameter, 721
  nPos parameter, 123
  nWeight parameter, 182
  nWidth parameter, 206, 209
  pSrcDC parameter, 209
  this parameter, 278
  uStyle parameter, 503
  WS_VISIBLE parameter, 278
  WS_VSCROLL parameter, 278
parent items, 682
parentheses, 21
parseInt() function, 1104

_pascal keyword, 498
passwords, for remote debugging, 50
paste action, 289–290. *See also* Paste command
Paste command, 115, 107, 520, 541
Paste() function, 290
PATCOPY raster operation, 658
PATH environment variable, 79, 841
Path property, 1128
pathnames, setting fully qualified, 519
PATINVERT raster operation, 658
PATPAINT raster operation, 658
Pause() function, 433, 441
PBI files, 59, 63, 69
PBO files, 63, 69
PBT files, 59, 63, 69, 70
PC_EXPLICIT flag, 226
PC_NOCOLLAPSE flag, 226
pContext property, 579, 582
PC_RESERVED flag, 226
PCX images, 875, 878
PeekMessage() function, 851, 861
Pen attribute, 167
PenBrumDemo project, 1168
pens, 185–187
PerformWork() function, 268
period (.), 413, 530
permissions recordset, 795–799
Permissions table, 794
PermissionsQry.h, 795
persistence, 945–946
physical devices, 164
pixels, 162–163
placement new operator, 855–856, 857
Play() function, 427, 433, 441
PlayFromDisk() function, 428
PlayFromRes() function, 428
PlaySound() function, 424–425
PLIST tool, 59, 69–70, 71–72
plus sign (+), 21
PM_REMOVE flag, 861
pointer(s)
  movement modes, for the Seek() function, 391–392
  sharing, between processes, 509–510
  verifying, 46–47
points, 195–196
Polygon filling mode attribute, 167
pop-up (context) menus, 123–126, 128–130, 689–692, 694. *See also* menus
PopulatePartial() method, 807
portable executable format, 475–476
PortLand project, 603–605, 628, 1174
PortLand.cpp, 603–605
PortLand.dsw, 603
PortLand.exe, 603
POSITION type, 536
PostNcDestroy() member function, 561
PostQuitMessage() function, 711
pParam argument, 708
PreCreateWindow() function, 120
PREP tool, 59, 61–66, 69, 72, 79
PreTranslateMessage() function, 119, 120, 303, 338, 371–372
Print command, 613
Print dialog box, 606, 611
print preview, 605, 613, 622–627
Print2Page() function, 598
printable character messages, 151–152
printer(s). *See also* printing
  font substitution support, 601–602
  GDI and, 164
  information, 601–602
  pages, versus document pages, 613–614
  support, Windows API, 597–603
printing. *See also* printers
  basic description of, 597–632
  enlarging printed images, 622
  headers/footers, 620–621
  helper functions for, 617–620
  MFC support for, 97
  pagination when, 614–617
  protocol, 611
PrintPageHeader() function, 614, 617, 619–620
PrintTitlePage() function, 614, 617, 618, 619
PrintToOutputWindow() method, 1127
priority
  inheritance, 716
  values for threads, 707–708, 715–716
private heaps, 471, 492–499
Private keyword, 1123
private memory, 471, 481–500
private pages, 471, 500
procedures, in VBScript, 1124
process list, 82–83
Process window, 83
processes, 715–717
ProcessImage project, 894–901
ProcessImage.exe, 894–901
ProcessImageView.cpp, 894–901
Professional Edition (Visual C++), 61
processors, 77, 163, 462
  compression and, 405
  memory management and, 472–474, 499, 500
  threads and, 705, 715, 716
Profile command, 60
Profile dialog box, 58, 60, 61, 66, 67
PROFILE tool, 59
PROFILE.DLL, 75, 79
Profiler, 57–61, 69–74
profiler.ini, 61
profiler.xlm, 70
profiler.xml, 74

profiling
  basic description of, 57–61
  from the development environment, controlling, 62–63
  enabling, 61–77
  inlined code, 76
  multithreaded projects, 76–77
  project performance, 77
  Windows NT services, 79
Project Database for Edit and Continue option, 32
Project object, 1125–1126
Project Settings dialog box, 32–35, 61, 864, 872, 873, 963
Project Settings property sheet, 54, 57
Project View, 18, 21
Project object, 1124, 1125–1129
project performance. *See also* profiling
  improving, 53–80
  optimizing code, 54–56
Project property, 1128
projects
  AboutWiz project, 1150, 1161, 1181–1182
  AboutWizTest project, 1163–1164
  AddressBook project, 312–319, 326–332, 337–348, 1169–1170
  AutoDialer project, 1058–1061, 1179
  BarsDemo project, 1174
  BlitDemo project, 215–222, 1169
  CDAudio project, 438–441
  CDPlayer project, 440–447, 1172
  Clock project, 454–461, 1172
  CODBCDynamicTest project, 759–760
  CompressDemo project, 400–402, 407–410, 1171
  CompressFile project, 1171
  CopyFile project, 1171
  CreateFromClipboard project, 889
  DaoUserMaintenance project, 824–836, 1177
  Database project, 1175
  DisplayView project, 882–885
  DoublePendulum project, 1004–1005, 1007–1012, 1179
  Dynsplit project, 586–590, 1173
  FileDemo project, 392–400, 1170
  FileExceptionTest project, 261–272, 1169
  FirstCHTML project, 1090–1091
  GlobalDllObjects project, 856–861, 1178
  GlobalDllObjectsClient project, 861–862, 1178
  GraphicsDemo1 project, 1168
  GraphicsDemo2 project, 1168
  HelloWorld1 project, 5–9, 1166
  HelloWorld2 project, 9–11, 1166
  HelloWorld3 project, 11–14, 1167
  HexView project, 531, 545, 1173
  HexViewMDI project, 627–631, 1174
  HTMLViewer project, 1090–1091, 1099, 1100–1104
  ImageViewer project, 865–870, 1177
  ImageViewerClient project, 868–869, 1177
  KeybdHook project, 849–852, 1178
  KeybdHookClient project, 853–854
  Learnide project, 21–22, 1167
  Library project, 1172
  ListCtrlDemo project, 1174
  MFCControl project, 923–927, 1174, 1178
  MFCServer project, 1178–1179
  MFCTracer project, 48
  MIDIDemo project, 432–437, 1172
  Mini Editor project, 302, 1169
  ModalDemo project, 354–357
  ModalWin project, 640–661
  MouseDemo1 project, 136–142, 1167
  MouseDemo2 project, 144–149, 1167
  MultiBrowser project, 1071–1075, 1180
  ODBCClasses project, 1175–1176
  ODBCDemo project, 742–757, 1175
  ODBCDynamicTest project, 1176
  OnIdleDemo project, 463–466, 1172–1173
  PaintObj project, 566–574, 1173
  Parameterized project, 791, 795–798, 1176
  PenBrumDemo project, 1168
  PortLand project, 603–605, 628, 1174
  ProcessImage project, 894–901
  Registry project, 1171
  SendEmail project, 1052–1057, 1180
  Serial project, 1171
  ShowDIB project, 238–231, 1169
  SimpleBrowser project, 1068–1071, 1180–1181
  Sockets project, 1045–1052, 1180
  StringDemo project, 381–388, 1170
  ThreadDemo project, 1175
  ThreadDemo1 project, 721–725
  TreeCtrlDemo project, 692–697, 1174–1175
  UseBrowser project, 1181
  UseDoublePendulum project, 1179
  UserMaintenance project, 790–799, 1174
  WaveDemo project, 428–431, 1172
Projects object, 1125–1126
Projects property, 1128
Projects tab, 954
PROJTYPE_SDI macro, 1141, 1144
Prompt field, 108, 109
properties. *See also* properties (listed by name)
  ActiveX controls and, 934–939
  ambient, 934, 939
  basic description of, 969–970
  normal, 934, 935
  parameterized, 934, 937–938
  stock, 934, 938–939

in style sheets, 1089
user-defined, 934, 935–936
properties (listed by name). *See also* properties
ActiveDocument property, 1128
ActiveProject property, 1128
ActiveWindow property, 1128
Alignment property, 941
Project property, 1128
BackColor property, 938, 939
beFailIfExists property, 1026, 1027
Border property, 351
Caption property, 351
CurrentDirectory property, 1128
Debugger property, 1128
Documents property, 1128
dwAccess property, 1020
dwAttributes property, 1026
dwContext property, 1020, 1026, 1027
dwCreateFlags property, 708
dwFlags property, 1020, 1021, 1026, 1027
Errors property, 1128
FullName property, 1128, 1132
Height property, 1128
index property, 531–532
Left property, 1128
lpctstrCaption property, 929
nBitcount property, 657
nPlanes property, 657
nPriority property, 707
Path property, 1128
pContext property, 579, 582
Projects property, 1128
pstrLocalFile property, 1026, 1027
pstrProxyBypass property, 1021
pstrProxyName property, 1021
pstrRemoteFile property, 1026, 1027
Selection property, 1115
Style property, 351
SW_SHOW property, 710
TextEditor property, 1128
Top property, 1128
varAlignment property, 929
Version property, 1128
Visible property, 1128
Warnings property, 1128
Width property, 1129
Windows property, 1129
WindowState property, 1129
property pages, 349–374
property sheets, 349–374, 939–943
prototype page table entries, 500
proxy-stub marshaling, 914
pseudodevices, 164–165
pSrcDC parameter, 209
pstrLocalFile property, 1026, 1027
pstrProxyBypass property, 1021
pstrProxyName property, 1021
pstrRemoteFile property, 1026, 1027
Public keyword, 1123
PumpMessage() function, 119, 462, 638
push buttons, creating, 281
PutFile() function, 1027

Q

QueryDefs collection, 807
QueryInterface() function, 986
question mark (?), 57, 413
Quick Macros, 1109–1111, 1113
QuickActivate interface, 913
QuickWatch dialog box, 35
QuickWatch window, 43–44
Quit() method, 1127

R

RAD (Rapid Project Development) tools, 51
radio buttons, 282–283
RAM (random-access memory). *See also* memory
allocating, 474
GDI and, 164
requirements, 477
raster graphics, 162–163. *See also* graphics
raster operation(s), 158, 658–661
basic description of, 191–201, 212–215
codes, 213–214
Read() function, 249, 390, 407, 408, 409, 845, 1030, 1043
readability, of code, improving, 251–252
ReadByte() function, 406
ReadData() function, 412
ReadDataWaiting() function, 412
ReadDWORD() function, 416
ReadMe.txt, 955
read-only accesss, 506
read-write access, 506
REALTIME_PRORITY_CLASS priority class, 717
ReBar control, 677
RebuildAll() method, 1127
Receive() function, 1044
record(s). *See also* recordsets
deleting, 777, 824
filtering, 772–775, 820–822
formats, 71–72
global information, 71–72
local information, 72
saving, 776–777
sorting, 775–776, 822–823
Record() function, 427–428
Record Quick Macro command, 1110
Recordset object, 807–808

recordsets, 766–777.
See also records
constructing, 771
DAO, 807–808
opening, 771
parameterized, 788–790
permissions, 795–799
sorting records returned with, 775–776, 822–823
Recordsets collection, 807
rectangles
drawing, with the OnDraw() function, 168–169
keyboard focus, 156–159
reference, locality of, 474
Refresh() function, 1067
Refresh() method, 806, 807
RegEdit, 921
RegisterActiveObject() function, 996
Registers window, 37
Registration Server, 922
Registry. *See also* CRegistry class; Registry keys
keys, commonly used, 414–415
keys, predefined, 414
registering automation servers in, 959–960
string resources and, 531
using, for persistent macros, 1160–1161
Registry keys. *See also* Registry
HKEY_CLASSES_ROOT key, 414, 415
HKEY_CLASSES_USER key, 414
HKEY_CURRENT_CONFIG key, 414
HKEY_CURRENT_USER key, 415
HKEY_DYN_DATA key, 414
HKEY_LOCAL_MACHINE key, 414–415, 416
HKEY_USERS key, 414, 415
Registry project, 1171
registry.cpp, 1161
registry.h, 1161
Regsvr32, 14. 75, 922
regsvr32.exe, 922
Relations collection, 807
Release build settings, 25
Release() function, 996–997
[illegible]
ReleaseBuffer() function, 377
ReleaseCapture() function, 148
ReleaseMutex() function, [illegible]
Remote Access Service, 1059
Remote Connection command, 50, 60
Remote Connection dialog box, 50
RemoveDirectory() function, 1028–1029
RemoveItem() function, 525
RemoveMenu() function, 124
RemoveProp() function, 471
ReportError() function, 253–255
ResetContent() member function, 285
Resource Editor, 4
resource IDs, 529–530, 532–533
for buttons, 258
for controls, 1150
for menus, 108, 109–110
Resource View tab, 312–314
resource.h, 114, 955
resources. *See also* resource IDs
exporting, 865
memory management and, 470
retrieving, from binary files, 846
viewing, 846
result sets, moving through, 776, 823–824
ResumeThread() function, 708, 710
return statement, 246–247, 261, 328, 781
ReverseFind() function, 381
RevokeActiveObject() function, 996–997
RFX (record field exchange), 772
RG_AND clipping mode, 201
RG_COPY clipping mode, 201
RG_DIFF clipping mode, 201
RG_OR clipping mode, 201
RG_XOR clipping mode, 201
RGB color, 173–176, 186, 205, 207, 222–229
RGB macro, 222–229
RGB() macro, 173
RGBQUAD structure, 231
Right() function, 380, 1137
Rollback() function, 271, 765, 814
Rollback() method, 806
root items, 682
root.clw, 1155–1156
root.cpp, 1158
root.h, 1158
ROP codes, 158
rotation factor, 541
RPC interface, 921
RS-232 standard, 411
RTTI (runtime type information), 248
rubber banding, 316
Run to Cursor command, 42
RunModalLoop() function, 635–640, 644
Running Object Table, 994–997
[illegible]
runtime library linking, 33–34
RUNTIME_CLASS macro, 528

S

SafeArrayGetLBound() function, 969
SAG (SQL Access Group), 733, 734
Sample.DSM, 1118
SampleApp.cpp, 61
SampleView.cpp, 616, 624–625
saturation, 224
Save button, 348, 826, 829–830
Save() function, 235–236, 263, 271, 428, 890
Save() method, 1132

SaveInvoice() function, 271
SaveRecords() function, 345–346
SaveUser() function, 830–832
saving
buffers of data, 392–400, 408–409
compressed files, 409–410
to disk files, 388–392, 428
images, 890–891
records, 776–777
SBPS_DISABLED constant, 667
SBPS_NOBORDERS constant, 667
SBPS_NORMAL constant, 667
SBPS_OWNERDRAW constant, 667
SBPS_POPOUT constant, 667
SBPS_STRETCH constant, 667
SBR files, 87
SBS_BOTTOMALIGN style flag, 295
SBS_HORZ style flag, 295
SBS_LEFTALIGN style flag, 295
SBS_RIGHTALIGN style flag, 295
SBS_SIZEBOX style flag, 295
SBS_SIZEBOXBOTTONLEFTALIGN style flag, 296
SBS_SIZEBOXBOTTONRIGHTALIGN style flag, 295
SBS_TOPALIGN style flag, 296
SBS_VERT style flag, 296
scalability, 732
Scale() function, 886
scaling images, 885–887
scan codes, 149–150
script2.htm, 1099
scripting, 1100–1106, 1109–1138, 1093–1099
scroll bars, 147, 278, 298, 584–585
SDI (Single Document Interface), 9, 112, 127, 518, 533, 557–558
CFormView class and, 543
custom AppWizards and, 1144, 1148
document/view designs and, 513–515
frame windows and, 329, 543
HexView project and, 545–551
InitInstance() function and, 527
SDIAutomationWiz project and, 1146–1148, 1181
search and replace operations, 381–388
SECTIONS keyword, 511–512
Seek() function, 391
Seek() method, 808
SeekToEnd() function, 391
SEH (structured exception handling), 246
Select Database Tables dialog box, 816
SELECT statement, 795
SelectClipRgn() function, 200
Selection property, 1115
selection states, 159–160
SelectItem() function, 695
SelectObject() function, 179, 655, 658
SelectString() function, 285–286
SelItemRange() function, 286
Send() function, 1044–1045
SendData() function, 412
SendEmail project, 1052–1057, 1180
SendEmail.dsw, 1052–1057
SendEmail.exe, 1052–1057
sentinels (no-man's-land areas), 489
serial communications, 410–417
Serial project, 1171
serialization, 339–347, 494
Serialize() member function, 340–345, 516–517, 520, 523–524, 557, 565
SerializeElements() function, 524
Set Next Statement command, 43
SetAbortProc() function, 599
SetActivePage() function, 371
SetAddressBar() function, 1064
SetAlignment() function, 935–936, 944
SetBitmap() function, 208
SetBitmapDimension() function, 655
SetBkColor() function, 175, 189, 307
SetBkMode() function, 176, 189
SetButtonInfo() function, 676
SetCaptionProp() function, 944
SetCaptionProp() method, 937–938
SetCapture() function, 148
SetCaretPos() member function, 154
SetColor() function, 307
SetCurrentDirectory() function, 1028
SetCurSel() function, 285, 338
SetDisabledTab() function, 362, 363
SetDocString() member function, 532
SetEditSel() function, 338
SetEnabledText() function, 366
SetExtendedUI() function, 300
SetFieldType() function, 774, 822
SetFont() function, 307, 370
SetFullScreen() function, 1064
SetImageList() function, 700
SetIndent() function, 969
SetIndicators() function, 664
SetItem() function, 367–369
SetItemText() function, 703–704
SetMapMode() function, 190
SetMaxPage() function, 608, 614, 616, 623
SetMenuBar() function, 1064
SetMinPage() function, 608, 620
SetModifiedFlag member function, 518, 523, 936
SetOption() function, 804
SetPalette() function, 238, 882
SetPaneStyle() function, 666–667
SetPathName() function, 519
SetPriorityClass() function, 716
SetProp() function, 471
SetRect() function, 280
SetResults() function, 368, 369
SetScrollInfo class, 297
SetScrollPos() function, 296

SetSel() function, 286
SetSizes() function, 671
SetStatus() function, 392
SetStatusBar() function, 1064
SetStyle() function, 674
SetSystemPaletteUse() function, 229
SetTabStops() function, 288
SetTextAlign() function, 176–177
SetTextCharacterExtra() function, 178
SetTextColor() function, 175, 307
SetTextJustification() function, 178
SetThreadPriority() function, 708, 716
SetTimer() function, 450, 451–452, 454
Settings option, 32, 54
SetTitle() member function, 518
SetToolbar() function, 1064
SetValue() method, 1005
SetViewportOrg() function, 190, 191
SetWindowLong() function, 591, 592, 686
SetWindowOrg() function, 190, 191
SetWindowPos() function, 354, 648
SetWindowsHookEx() function, 848–849, 851
SetWindowText() function, 288, 293
SGML (Standard Generalized Markup Language), 1082
shared memory, 482, 499–500
shared pages, 472, 499–500, 507–512
sharedobject.cpp, 998
sharedobject.h, 998
SHIFTJIS_CHARSET constant, 183
shortcuts, keyboard
    accelerator tables for, 113, 114–115, 118–121
    assigning macros to, 1121–1122
    adding, 24–26
    basic description of, 107, 113–121
    context menus and, 128
    defining, 114–115
    deleting, 23, 24–26
    editing, 24–26
    selecting appropriate, 116–118
    for single-stepping commands, 42
    standard Windows, 116–117
    viewing current, 23–24
    the Windows logical keyboard and, 151
Show Messages button, 83
ShowCaret() member function, 154
ShowDIB project, 238–231, 1169
ShowDIBView.cpp, 238–231
ShowDIBView.exe, 238
ShowPermissions() function, 796
ShowWindow() function, 321, 710
shut down information, accessing, 83
siblings, avoiding duplicate, 695–696
SIMPLE.EXE, 79
SimpleBrowser project, 1068–1071, 1180–1181
SimpleBrowser.exe, 1068–1071
SimpleBrowserView.cpp, 1068–1071
Single document option, 20
single instance servers, 997–998
sizing handles, 316
Sleep() function, 711
SloppyFunc() function, 47
SMP (symmetric multiprocessing), 715–716
Snapshot recordset, 807
SND_ASYNC flag, 425
SND_LOOP flag, 425
SND_MEMORY flag, 425
SND_NODEFAULT flag, 425
SND_NOSTOP flag, 425
SND_SYNC flag, 425
SOCKADDR structure, 1043
SOCKADDR_IN structure, 1041–1043
sockets, 1040–1052, 1180
Sockets project, 1045–1052, 1180
Sockets.Dsw, 1045
Sockets.exe, 1045–1052
SocketsView.cpp, 1045–1052
SomeFunction() function, 269–270, 273
sorting records, 775–776, 822–823
sound. *See also* CD audio
    basic description of, 423–448
    playing recorded, 423–428
    recording, 427–428
    WAV files, 401, 423–428
Sound.h, 438, 447
Sound.lib, 438, 447
Source Browser, 32, 87, 89
Source Browser command, 87, 89
spell checkers, 705
splitter windows, 574–585
Spy++, 81–90, 143–144
SQL (Structured Query Language), 729–735
    basic description of, 730
    DAO and, 803, 812–813, 820, 832–833
    executing, 739–740, 754–759
SQL Server (Microsoft), 103–104, 730, 731
SQLAllocHandle() function, 738, 739
SQLBindCol() function, 741, 747
SQLConnect() function, 738, 746
SQLDescribeCol() function, 740–741, 751, 756
SQLDisconnect() function, 742
SQLDriverConnect() function, 738
SQLEXT.H, 739
SQLExecDirect() function, 740
SQLExecute() function, 751, 754
SQLFetch() function, 741, 747
SQLGetData() function, 740–741, 756, 758
SQLGetFunctions() function, 735, 739
SQLGetInfo() function, 739
SQLGetTypeInfo() function, 739
SQLNumResultCols() function, 740–741, 751, 756
SQLPrepare() function, 751, 754
SQLSetEnvAttr() function, 738

SRCAND raster operation, 658, 660
SRCCOPY raster operation, 659, 660
SRCERASE raster operation, 659
SRCINVERT raster operation, 659
SRCPAINT raster operation, 659
SS_BITMAP style flag, 283
SS_BLACKFRAME style flag, 292
SS_BLACKRECT style flag, 292
SS_CENTER style flag, 292
SS_CENTERIMAGE style flag, 292
SS_CENTERNOWORDWRAP style flag, 292
SS_ENHMETAFILE style flag, 283
SS_ETCHEDFRAME style flag, 292
SS_ETCHEDHORZ style flag, 292
SS_ETCHEDVERT style flag, 283
SS_GRAYFRAME style flag, 292
SS_GRAYRECT style flag, 292
SS_ICON style flag, 283
SS_LEFT style flag, 292
SS_LEFTNOWORDWRAP style flag, 292
SS_NOPREFIX style flag, 292
SS_NOTIFY style flag, 283, 294
SS_REALSIZEIMAGE style flag, 283
SS_RIGHT style flag, 292
SS_RIGHTNOWORDWRAP style flag, 292
SS_SIMPLE style flag, 292
SS_SUNKEN style flag, 292
SS_WHITEFRAME style flag, 292
SS_WHITERECT style flag, 292
stadafx.h, 743
StartDoc() function, 597, 606, 611
StartOfDocument() method, 1133
StartPage() function, 597, 606, 611, 621
static colors, 225
static splitters, 582
static string arrays, 258–259
status bars, 544, 663–669
stdafx.cpp, 955, 1154
stdafx.h, 825, 858, 955, 1065, 1154
_stdcall keyword, 490
Step Into command, 42
Step Out command, 42
Step Over command, 42
Stingray Software, 1182–1184
STL (Standard Template Library), 915, 1000
stock properties, 934, 938–939
stock view, 532–533
Stop() function, 427, 428, 433, 441, 1067, 1068
strcmp() function, 375
strcpy() function, 375
Stretch() function, 885
StretchBlt() function, 649, 655
strings. *See also* CString class
  creating, 376
  data, accessing, 377–378
  resources, 530–532
  searching for, 380–381
  sub-, extraction of, 380
StringDemo project, 381–388, 1170
StringDemo.exe, 382–388
StringDemoView.cpp, 382–388
StrokePath() function, 187
<STRONG> tag, 1085
structures
  BITMAP structure, 206–207, 210, 656–658
  BITMAPFILEHEADER structure, 230–231
  BITMAPINFOHEADER structure, 230–231
  CPrintInfo structure, 611, 612, 613–614, 621, 623–624
  DOCINFO structure, 597
  enum structure, 258–259, 265, 266
  LOGBRUSH structure, 188
  LOGPALETTE structure, 225–226
  OFSTRUCT structure, 502–503
  PALETTEENTRY structure, 225–226
  RGBQUAD structure, 231
  SOCKADDR structure, 1043
  SOCKADDR_IN structure, 1041–1043
  TEXTMETRIC structure, 198, 280
  TV_INSERTSTRUCT structure, 685
style flags. *See also* style flags (listed by name)
  for the CButton class, 281
  for the CComboBox class, 299–300
  for the CEdit class, 287
  for the CListBox class, 284
  for the CScrollBar class, 295–296
  for the CStatic class, 292–293
  for status bars, 666
style flags (listed by name). *See also* style flags
  BS_3STATE style flag, 281
  BS_AUTO3STATE style flag, 281
  BS_AUTOCHECKBOX style flag, 281
  BS_AUTORADIOBUTTON style flag, 281, 282
  BS_BITMAP button style, 305–306
  BS_CHECKBOX style flag, 281
  BS_DEFPUSHBUTTON style flag, 281
  BS_GROUPBOX style flag, 281
  BS_PUSHBUTTON style flag, 281
  BS_RADIOBUTTON style flag, 281
  CBRS_BOTTOM style flag, 666
  CBRS_NOALIGN style flag, 666
  CBRS_TOP style flag, 666
  CBS_AUTOHSCROLL style flag, 299
  CBS_DISABLENOSCROLL style flag, 299
  CBS_DROPDOWN style flag, 299
  CBS_DROPDOWNLIST style flag, 299
  CBS_HASSTRINGS style flag, 299
  CBS_LOWERCASE style flag, 299
  CBS_OEMCONVER style flag, 299

(continued)

style flags (listed by name) *(continued)*
- CBS_OWNERDRAWFIXED style flag, 299
- CBS_OWNERDRAWVARIABLE style flag, 299
- CBS_SIMPLE style flag, 299
- CBS_SORT style flag, 299
- CBS_UPPERCASE style flag, 299
- ES_AUTOHSCROLL style flag, 287
- ES_AUTOVSCROLL style flag, 287
- ES_CENTER style flag, 287
- ES_HSCROLL style flag, 287
- ES_LEFT style flag, 287
- ES_LOWERCASE style flag, 287
- ES_NOHIDESEL style flag, 287
- ES_OEMCONVERT style flag, 287
- ES_RIGHT style flag, 287
- ES_UPPERCASE style flag, 287
- ES_VSCROLL style flag, 287
- ES_WANTRETURN style flag, 287
- LBS_DISABLENOSCROLL style flag, 284
- LBS_EXTENDEDSEL style flag, 284
- LBS_HASSTRINGS style flag, 284
- LBS_MULTICOLUMN style flag, 284
- LBS_MULTIPLESEL style flag, 284
- LBS_NOINTEGRALHEIGHT style flag, 284
- LBS_NOREDRAW style flag, 284
- LBS_NOSEL style flag, 284
- LBS_NOTIFY style flag, 284
- LBS_SORT style flag, 284
- LBS_STANDARD style flag, 284
- LBS_USETABSTOPS style flag, 284
- LBS_WANTKEYBOARDINPUT style flag, 284
- SBS_BOTTOMALIGN style flag, 295
- SBS_HORZ style flag, 295
- SBS_LEFTALIGN style flag, 295
- SBS_RIGHTALIGN style flag, 295
- SBS_SIZEBOX style flag, 295
- SBS_SIZEBOXBOTTONLEFTALIGN style flag, 296
- SBS_SIZEBOXBOTTONRIGHTALIGN style flag, 295
- SBS_TOPALIGN style flag, 296
- SBS_VERT style flag, 296
- SS_BITMAP style flag, 283
- SS_BLACKFRAME style flag, 292
- SS_BLACKRECT style flag, 292
- SS_CENTER style flag, 292
- SS_CENTERIMAGE style flag, 292
- SS_CENTERNOWORDWRAP style flag, 292
- SS_ENHMETAFILE style flag, 283
- SS_ETCHEDFRAME style flag, 292
- SS_ETCHEDHORZ style flag, 292
- SS_ETCHEDVERT style flag, 283
- SS_GRAYFRAME style flag, 292
- SS_GRAYRECT style flag, 292
- SS_ICON style flag, 283
- SS_LEFT style flag, 292
- SS_LEFTNOWORDWRAP style flag, 292
- SS_NOPREFIX style flag, 292
- SS_NOTIFY style flag, 283, 294
- SS_REALSIZEIMAGE style flag, 283
- SS_RIGHT style flag, 292
- SS_RIGHTNOWORDWRAP style flag, 292
- SS_SIMPLE style flag, 292
- SS_SUNKEN style flag, 292
- SS_WHITEFRAME style flag, 292
- SS_WHITERECT style flag, 292
- WS_EX_CLIENTEDGE style flag, 280

Style property, 351
style sheets, 1085–1090
<STYLE> tag, 1086, 1087–1088
Styles tab, 314–315
<SUB> tag, 1085
SubclassWindow() function, 592–594
Subsystem Master table, 794
<SUP> tag, 1085
SuspendThread() function, 710
SW_SHOW property, 710
switch statements, 756
Sybase, 103
symbol
- definitions, 87, 88
- references, 88

SYMBOL_CHARSET constant, 183
Synchronize() method, 807
syntax errors, 29, 51. *See also* errors
SysFreeString API, 1013
system path, 49

T

tab(s)
- adding functions to disable, 362–363
- captions, setting, 367–369
- -delimited format, 69–70, 72–74
- dialogs, 349–350
- disabled, creating variables to hold, 362
- disabling, in property sheets, 361–365
- font for, 370
- indexes, creating variables to store, 361–362
- order, setting, 318–319

tab character, 115
TableDef object, 809
TableDefs collection, 807, 809
TaskManager, 156
TCP/IP (Transmission Control Protocol/Internet Protocol), 49, 50, 98
TEB (thread environment block), 496
TEMP environment variable, 521
template(s), 515, 529–536, 557–558, 1156–1159
- adding, to template collections, 527
- for the AddressBook project, 326–332
- creating, 313, 1151–1153

dialog box, 312–319
STL (Standard Template Library) for, 915, 1000
temporary handle maps, 127
TemporaryQuickMacro.DSM, 1118
TermCode.h, 750
TerminateThread() function, 715
TEST.CMP, 402, 410
test.cpp, 64–66
Test.gif, 888
testing
the AddressBook project, 332
the capability to disable tabs, 365
cursor-creation code, 156
image documents, 868–869
keyboard hook DLLs, 853–854
the UserMaintenance project, 835–836
text. *See also* fonts
aligning, 176–177
centering, 199
characteristics, importance of, 602–603
characters, measurements/metrics that apply to, 603
color, 173–176
coordinate calculations, 194–199
drawing functions, 192–194
justifying, 178
keys, 113
manipulating, 173–178
properties, in style sheets, 1089
Text alignment attribute, 167
Text color attribute, 168, 175
Text extraspacing attribute, 168
Text justification attribute, 168
textboxes, 199
TextDocument object, 1125–1126
TextEditor object, 1125–1126
TextEditor property, 1128
TEXTMETRIC structure, 198, 280
TextOut() function, 177, 193–194, 196–197
TextSelection object, 1125–1126
TextWindow object, 1125–1126
TGA images, 875, 878
THCBs (thread control blocks), 496
this parameter, 278
THRDCODE.CPP, 492
thread(s)
basic description of, 83, 494, 705–726
control blocks (THCBs), 496
functions, 708
local storage, 471, 496–499
memory management and, 503
putting to sleep, 711
sharing MFC objects among, 717–720
suspending/resuming, 710
terminating, 711–715
viewing, with Spy++, 81–83
worker threads, 79, 707–708
thread keyword, 498
thread list, 82–83
ThreadDemo project, 1175
ThreadDemo1 project, 721–725
ThreadDemo1.cpp, 721–725
ThreadDemo1.exe, 721
ThreadFunc() function, 707
Threads command, 44
Threads dialog box, 44–45
throw statement, 246–247
TIF images, 875, 878, 890–891
time() function, 720
TimerProc() function, 453
timers, 449–461
<TITLE> tag, 1084
TLBs (translation lookaside buffers), 474
TlsAlloc() function, 471, 497
TlsFree() function, 497
TlsGetValue() function, 497
TlsSetValue() function, 497
toggle keys, 113–114
toolbar(s)
creating, 27–28, 663, 669–678
displaying/hiding, 26–28, 673–674
docking/floating, 673
dragging and dropping items to, 28
initializing, 671–672
naming, 544
resource file, 675
using, 26–28
Toolbars tab, 26, 27
Tools menu
ActiveX Control Test Container command, 14
Customize command, 24, 26, 922
customizing, 85–86
deleting tools from, 86
Macro command, 1129
Options command, 51
Profile command, 60
Record Quick Macro command, 1110
Remote Connection command, 50, 60
Source Browser command, 87, 89
Tools tab, 85, 86
tools.ini, 61
ToolTips, 109, 671, 674–675
Top property, 1128
<TR> tag, 1137
TRACE command, 21, 23
TRACE macro, 21, 23, 45
trace utilities, 30
TRACE0 macro, 45
TRACE1 macro, 45
TRACE2 macro, 45
TRACE3 macro, 45

tracer.exe, 48
tracing, 30, 48
Tracker.cpp, 956, 961–964, 980–983, 985–991, 994–995
TrackerError.h, 980
Tracker.h, 956, 961, 966, 981–982, 988
TrackerInterface.h, 980, 982
TrackError.h, 972
TrackPopupMenu() function, 127, 129
transaction boundaries, 813–814
transfer type flags, 1030
TranslateAccelerator class, 119
TranslateMessage() function, 119, 152, 303, 638
Transparent.c, 214–215
tree views, 679–697
TreeCtrlDemo project, 692–697, 1174–1175
Trim() function, 1136
TrueType fonts, 183
try blocks, 247, 249, 254, 267–270
TRY macro, 254
try/catch blocks, 762, 811, 828, 990
tstcon32.exe, 34
TV_INSERTSTRUCT structure, 685
TVN_BEGINLABELEDIT message, 685, 686, 687
TVN_ENDLABELEDIT message, 685–686, 687, 697
TVS_EDITLABELS style, 685

U

<U> tag, 1085
<UL> tag, 1085, 1087
Unclipped device context option, 925–926
underscore (_), 498
undo action, 289–290
Undo() function, 290
UnhookWindowsHookEx() function, 849, 852
Unicode, 45
Universal Data Acces, 4
UNIX, 473
UnsubclassWindow() function, 594
Update() function, 777, 824
Update() method, 808
UpdateAllViews() member function, 518, 523, 540, 556, 558, 585
UpdateData() function, 323–325, 331, 585, 796, 830
UPDATE_OBJECT constant, 323
UpdateRegistry() function, 927–928
UpdateRegistryAll() function, 959
UpdateWindow() function, 171, 172, 639
URLs (Uniform Resource Locators), 1019, 1022–1023
  CHTMLView class and, 1066–1075
  logging, to log files, 1077–1078
  validating, 1078
UseBrowser project, 1181
UseDoublePendulum project, 1179
user32.dll, 846
user32.lib, 61
user-defined properties, 934, 935–936
user.exe, 277
UserMaintenance project, 780–788, 1176
UserMaintenanceDlg.h, 780
UserMaintenanceDlg.cpp, 780–788
UserMaintenance.rc, 826
UserMaster recordset, 790
UserMaster table, 766, 767–768, 780, 781, 783, 788–789, 791, 793, 814–824, 827
UserMasterSet.cpp, 769–770, 790
UserMasterSet.h, 768–769, 790
Users object, 809
uStyle parameter, 503
utility classes, 779–780, 826
UUIDs (Universally-Unique Identifiers), 921

V

valid access type values, 1020–1021
validation, of dialog data, 322–325
varAlignment property, 929
variables
  creating, 261, 323, 336, 361–362
  in VBScript, 1123
  watching, 30
VariantChangeType() function, 933
VariantInit() function, 933
VBA (Visual Basic for Applications), 801, 803
VBScript, 1122–1123, 1081, 1094
VCBible.DSM, 1118, 1129
vector graphics, 163. *See also* graphics
Version property, 1128
VGA monitors, 205
video memory, 203–207, 209
view(s)
  basic description of, 679
  classes, declaring, 537–539
  complex combinations of, managing, 557–565
  encapsulating, in a class, 867
  managing, 527–528
  objects, creating, 506–507
  [illegible]
  splitter windows and, 581–582
  window classes, 100–101
  working with, 541
Viewport extent attribute, 168
Viewport origin attribute, 168
VirtKey, 115
virtual addresses, 473–474
virtual document functions, 520–521
virtual functions, 271–275
virtual key codes, 150–153
virtual memory, 483

VirtualAlloc() function, 471, 482, 484–486, 487, 494, 495, 499, 502
VirtualFree() function, 485
VirtualLock() function, 486
VirtualProtect() function, 486
VirtualProtectEx() function, 486
VirtualQuery() function, 486, 494, 500
VirtualQueryEx() function, 486
VirtualUnlock() function, 486
Visible property, 1128
Visual Basic (Microsoft), 51, 801, 808, 907
Visual C++ Insiders Summit, 3
Visual J++ (Microsoft), 51, 907
VK_ prefix, 115, 151–152
VK_APPS key code, 152
VK_CONTROL key code, 152
VK_DELETE key code, 152
VK_DOWN key code, 152
VK_END key code, 152
VK_F1 through VK_F12 key code, 152
VK_MENU key code, 152
VWnd class, 541

W

W3C (World Wide Web Consortium) Web site, 1088
WaitForSingleObject() function, 713, 714, 715, 858
Warnings property, 1128
Watch window, 36–37
watching variables, 30
WAV files, 401, 423–431, 1172
WaveDemo project, 428–431, 1172
WaveDemo.exe, 428
WaveDemoView.cpp, 428
wCounter variable, 854
Web browser(s)
  ActiveX controls, 1063, 1066–1068, 1075–1077
  Internet Explorer browser, 910, 1122, 1130, 1063, 1066–1068
  MFC, 89–90
  writing, 1070
Web pages, embedding ActiveX controls in, 1015–1016
Web sites
  Excite Web site, 1071–1073
  Microsoft Web site, 907, 978, 1015, 1058, 1064
  W3C (World Wide Web Consortium) Web site, 1088
  Yahoo! Web site, 1065
WebDialog.h, 1076
WH_CALLWNDPROC function, 847
WH_CALLWNDPROCRET function, 847
WH_CBT function, 847
WH_DEBUG function, 847
WH_GETMESSAGE function, 847
WH_JOURNALPLAYBACK function, 847
WH_JOURNALRECORD function, 847
WH_KEYBOARD function, 847, 848
WH_KEYBOARD_LL function, 847
WH_MOUSE function, 848
WH_MOUSE_LL function, 848
WH_MSGFILTER function, 848
WH_SHELL function, 848
WH_SYSMSGFILTER function, 848
while loops, 776, 1133
WHITENESS raster operation, 659
Width property, 1129
wildcard characters, 413
Wincore.cpp, 635–637, 639–640
winctrl2.cpp, 681
WindApp class, 112
Windows logical keyboard, 150–151
Windows property, 1129
WindowState property, 1129
WinMain() function, 120
winmm.lib, 424, 963
Winwrap.Lib, 52
WizardBar, 616, 624
WM_CHAR message, 149, 151–152, 155, 281–282, 334
WM_CLOSE message, 641
WM_CREATE message, 111, 129, 452, 641
WM_CTLCOLOR message, 307–308
WM_DDE_DATA message, 481
WM_DESTROY message, 85, 330–331, 835
WM_GETFOCUS message, 228
WM_HSCROLL message, 298
WM_KEYDOWN message, 149, 151, 152
WM_KEYUP message, 149, 151, 152
WM_KILLFOCUS message, 154–155, 157–158
WM_LBUTTONDOWN message, 132, 133, 147, 148, 157
WM_LBUTTONUP message, 132, 147, 148
WM_MBUTTONUP message, 132
WM_MOUSEMOVE message, 132, 133, 134, 148
WM_MOVE message, 111
WM_NCDESTROY message, 85
WM_NCHITTEST message, 143, 148
WM_NCLBUTTONDOWN message, 142, 143
WM_NCLBUTTONUP message, 143
WM_NCMBUTTONWDOWN message, 143
WM_NCMOUSEMOVE message, 143
WM_NCRBUTTONDOWN message, 143
WM_NCRBUTTONUP message, 143
WM_PAINT message, 104, 155, 158–159, 168–173, 193, 461, 610, 623, 651
WM_PALETTECHANGED message, 229
WM_QUERYNEWPALETTE message, 228–229
WM_QUIT message, 709, 711, 861
WM_RBUTTONDOWN message, 129, 132, 690, 693, 694–695
WM_RBUTTONUP message, 132
WM_SETCURSOR message, 143, 148
WM_SETFOCUS message, 154, 157–158

WM_SIZE message, 111
WM_SYSCOMMAND message, 85
WM_SYSTIMER message, 461
WM_TIMER message, 450–454
WM_VSCROLL message, 298
Word (Microsoft), 4, 907
WordPad (Microsoft), 381
worker threads, 79, 707–708
Workspace object, 804–806
Workspaces collection object, 804–805
wrapper classes, 514, 605–606
Write() function, 391, 407, 409, 1030
WriteByte() function, 407
WriteDWORD() function, 417
WriteString() function, 417
WS_BORDER flag, 647
WS_EX prefix, 280
WS_EX_CLIENTEDGE style flag, 280
WS_OVERLAPPED flag, 647
WS_VISIBLE constant, 673
WS_VISIBLE parameter, 278
WS_VSCROLL parameter, 278

X

XCOPY command, 1164
XOR operations, 191–201, 213

Y

Yahoo! Web site, 1065

Z

zoom factor, 537–538, 541

IDG BOOKS WORLDWIDE, INC.
END-USER LICENSE AGREEMENT

READ THIS. You should carefully read these terms and conditions before opening the software packet included with this book ("Book"). This is a license agreement ("Agreement") between you and IDG Books Worldwide, Inc. ("IDGB"). By opening the accompanying software packet, you acknowledge that you have read and accept the following terms and conditions. If you do not agree and do not want to be bound by such terms and conditions, promptly return the Book and the unopened software packet to the place you obtained them for a full refund.

1. **License Grant**. IDGB grants to you (either an individual or entity) a nonexclusive license to use one copy of the enclosed software programs (collectively, the "Software") solely for your own personal or business purposes on a single computer (whether a standard computer or a workstation component of a multiuser network). The Software is in use on a computer when it is loaded into temporary memory (RAM) or installed into permanent memory (hard disk, CD-ROM, or other storage device). IDGB reserves all rights not expressly granted herein.

2. **Ownership**. IDGB is the owner of all right, title, and interest, including copyright, in and to the compilation of the Software recorded on the disk(s) or CD-ROM ("Software Media"). Copyright to the individual programs recorded on the Software Media is owned by the author or other authorized copyright owner of each program. Ownership of the Software and all proprietary rights relating thereto remain with IDGB and its licensers.

3. **Restrictions on Use and Transfer**.

   (a) You may only (i) make one copy of the Software for backup or archival purposes, or (ii) transfer the Software to a single hard disk, provided that you keep the original for backup or archival purposes. You may not (i) rent or lease the Software, (ii) copy or reproduce the Software through a LAN or other network system or through any computer subscriber system or bulletin-board system, or (iii) modify, adapt, or create derivative works based on the Software.

   (b) You may not reverse engineer, decompile, or disassemble the Software. You may transfer the Software and user documentation on a permanent basis, provided that the transferee agrees to accept the terms and conditions of this Agreement and you retain no copies. If the Software is an update or has been updated, any transfer must include the most recent update and all prior versions.

4. **Restrictions on Use of Individual Programs**. You must follow the individual requirements and restrictions detailed for each individual program in the Appendix of this Book. These limitations are also contained in the individual license agreements recorded on the Software Media. These limitations may include a requirement that after using the program for a specified period of time, the user must pay a registration fee or discontinue use. By opening the Software packet(s), you will be agreeing to abide by the licenses and restrictions for these individual programs that are detailed in the Appendix and on the Software Media. None of the material on this Software Media or listed in this Book may ever be redistributed, in original or modified form, for commercial purposes.

5. **Limited Warranty**.

   (a) IDGB warrants that the Software and Software Media are free from defects in materials and workmanship under normal use for a period of sixty (60) days from the date of purchase of this Book. If IDGB receives notification within the warranty period of defects in materials or workmanship, IDGB will replace the defective Software Media.

   (b) **IDGB AND THE AUTHORS OF THE BOOK DISCLAIM ALL OTHER WARRANTIES, EXPRESS OR IMPLIED, INCLUDING WITHOUT LIMITATION IMPLIED WARRANTIES OF MERCHANTABILITY AND FITNESS FOR A PARTICULAR PURPOSE, WITH RESPECT TO THE SOFTWARE, THE PROGRAMS, THE SOURCE CODE CONTAINED THEREIN, AND/OR THE TECHNIQUES DESCRIBED IN THIS BOOK. IDGB DOES NOT WARRANT THAT THE FUNCTIONS CONTAINED IN THE SOFTWARE WILL MEET YOUR REQUIREMENTS OR THAT THE OPERATION OF THE SOFTWARE WILL BE ERROR FREE.**

   (c) This limited warranty gives you specific legal rights, and you may have other rights that vary from jurisdiction to jurisdiction.

6. **Remedies**.

   (a) IDGB's entire liability and your exclusive remedy for defects in materials and workmanship shall be limited to replacement of the Software Media, which may be returned to IDGB with a copy of your receipt at the following address: Software Media Fulfillment Department, Attn.: *Visual C++ 6 Bible*, IDG Books Worldwide, Inc., 7260 Shadeland Station, Ste. 100, Indianapolis, IN 46256, or call 1-800-762-2974. Please allow three to four weeks for delivery. This Limited Warranty is void if failure of the Software Media has resulted from accident, abuse, or misapplication. Any replacement Software Media will be warranted for the remainder of the original warranty period or thirty (30) days, whichever is longer.

   (b) In no event shall IDGB or the authors be liable for any damages whatsoever (including without limitation damages for loss of business profits, business interruption, loss of business information, or any other pecuniary loss) arising from the use of or inability to use the Book or the Software, even if IDGB has been advised of the possibility of such damages.

(c) Because some jurisdictions do not allow the exclusion or limitation of liability for consequential or incidental damages, the above limitation or exclusion may not apply to you.

7. **U.S. Government Restricted Rights.** Use, duplication, or disclosure of the Software by the U.S. Government is subject to restrictions stated in paragraph (c)(1)(ii) of the Rights in Technical Data and Computer Software clause of DFARS 252.227-7013, and in subparagraphs (a) through (d) of the Commercial Computer-Restricted Rights clause at FAR 52.227-19, and in similar clauses in the NASA FAR supplement, when applicable.

8. **General.** This Agreement constitutes the entire understanding of the parties and revokes and supersedes all prior agreements, oral or written, between them and may not be modified or amended except in a writing signed by both parties hereto that specifically refers to this Agreement. This Agreement shall take precedence over any other documents that may be in conflict herewith. If any one or more provisions contained in this Agreement are held by any court or tribunal to be invalid, illegal, or otherwise unenforceable, each and every other provision shall remain in full force and effect.

CD-ROM Installation Instructions

The CD-ROM that accompanies this book contains a complete set of demonstration programs developed in the text, plus a selection of programming tools from several vendors. For the demo programs from the text, simply copy the files into a new folder on your hard disk (see the Appendix for notes on dealing with read-only attributes to files copied from the CD) or run the `InstallContents.EXE` file to install all the demo programs at once. For the programming tools, simply double-click each self-extracting installer to install the files. For more details on the content of the CD-ROM and how to use it, see the Appendix.